LET'S GO

■ THE RESOURCE FOR THE INDEPENDENT TRAVELER

"The guides are aimed not only at young budget travelers but at the indepe-
dent traveler; a sort of streetwise cookbook for traveling alone."

—The New York Times

"Unbeatable; good sight-seeing advice; up-to-date info on restaurants, hotels,
and inns; a commitment to money-saving travel; and a wry style that brightens
nearly every page."

—The Washington Post

"Lighthearted and sophisticated, informative and fun to read. [Let's Go] helps
the novice traveler navigate like a knowledgeable old hand."

—Atlanta Journal-Constitution

"A world-wise traveling companion—always ready with friendly advice and
helpful hints, all sprinkled with a bit of wit."

—The Philadelphia Inquirer

■ THE BEST TRAVEL BARGAINS IN YOUR PRICE RANGE

"All the dirt, dirt cheap."

—People

"Anything you need to know about budget traveling is detailed in this book."

—The Chicago Sun-Times

"Let's Go follows the creed that you don't have to toss your life's savings to
the wind to travel—unless you want to."

—The Salt Lake Tribune

■ REAL ADVICE FOR REAL EXPERIENCES

"The writers seem to have experienced every rooster-packed bus and lunar-
surfaced mattress about which they write."

—The New York Times

"A guide should tell you what to expect from a destination. Here Let's Go
shines."

—The Chicago Tribune

LET'S GO PUBLICATIONS

TRAVEL GUIDES

Alaska & the Pacific Northwest 2003
Australia 2003
Austria & Switzerland 2003
Britain & Ireland 2003
California 2003
Central America 8th edition
Chile 1st edition **NEW TITLE**
China 4th edition
Costa Rica 1st edition **NEW TITLE**
Eastern Europe 2003
Egypt 2nd edition
Europe 2003
France 2003
Germany 2003
Greece 2003
Hawaii 2003 **NEW TITLE**
India & Nepal 7th edition
Ireland 2003
Israel 4th edition
Italy 2003
Mexico 19th edition
Middle East 4th edition
New Zealand 6th edition
Peru, Ecuador & Bolivia 3rd edition
South Africa 5th edition
Southeast Asia 8th edition
Southwest USA 2003
Spain & Portugal 2003
Thailand 1st edition **NEW TITLE**
Turkey 5th edition
USA 2003
Western Europe 2003

CITY GUIDES

Amsterdam 2003
Barcelona 2003
Boston 2003
London 2003
New York City 2003
Paris 2003
Rome 2003
San Francisco 2003
Washington, D.C. 2003

MAP GUIDES

Amsterdam
Berlin
Boston
Chicago
Dublin
Florence
Hong Kong
London
Los Angeles
Madrid
New Orleans
New York City
Paris
Prague
Rome
San Francisco
Seattle
Sydney
Venice
Washington, D.C.

BRITAIN & IRELAND

2003

SONJA NIKKILA EDITOR
TERESA ELSEY ASSOCIATE EDITOR

RESEARCHER-WRITERS
JENNY PEGG
ANGIE SUN
SARAH A. TUCKER
JOHN T. WITHERSPOON
DANIEL ZWEIFACH

MATTHEW HARTZELL MAP EDITOR
ABIGAIL BURGER MANAGING EDITOR
KEVIN H. YIP & DAN BARNES TYPESETTERS

ST. MARTIN'S PRESS ✖ NEW YORK

HELPING LET'S GO

If you want to share your discoveries, suggestions, or corrections, please drop us a line. We read every piece of correspondence, whether a postcard, a 10-page email, or a coconut. Please note that mail received after May 2003 may be too late for the 2004 book, but will be kept for future editions. **Address mail to:**

Let's Go: Britain & Ireland
67 Mount Auburn Street
Cambridge, MA 02138
USA

Visit Let's Go at **http://www.letsgo.com,** or send email to:

feedback@letsgo.com
Subject: "Let's Go: Britain & Ireland"

In addition to the invaluable travel advice our readers share with us, many are kind enough to offer their services as researchers or editors. Unfortunately, our charter enables us to employ only currently enrolled Harvard students.

WHO WE ARE

A NEW LET'S GO FOR 2003

With a sleeker look and innovative new content, we have revamped the entire series to reflect more than ever the needs and interests of the independent traveler. Here are just some of the improvements you will notice when traveling with the new *Let's Go*.

MORE PRICE OPTIONS

Still the best resource for budget travelers, *Let's Go* recognizes that everyone needs the occassional indulgence. Our "Big Splurges" indicate establishments that are actually worth those extra pennies (pulas, pesos, or pounds), and price-level symbols (❶ ❷ ❸ ❹ ❺) allow you to quickly determine whether an accommodation or restaurant will break the bank. We may have diversified, but we'll never lose our budget focus—"Hidden Deals" reveal the best-kept travel secrets.

BEYOND THE TOURIST EXPERIENCE

Our Alternatives to Tourism chapter offers ideas on immersing yourself in a new community through study, work, or volunteering.

AN INSIDER'S PERSPECTIVE

As always, every item is written and researched by our on-site writers. This year we have highlighted more viewpoints to help you gain an even more thorough understanding of the places you are visiting.

IN RECENT NEWS. *Let's Go* correspondents around the globe report back on current regional issues that may affect you as a traveler.

CONTRIBUTING WRITERS. Respected scholars and former *Let's Go* writers discuss topics on society and culture, going into greater depth than the usual guidebook summary.

THE LOCAL STORY. From the Parisian monk toting a cell phone to the Russian *babushka* confronting capitalism, *Let's Go* shares its revealing conversations with local personalities—a unique glimpse of what matters to real people.

FROM THE ROAD. Always helpful and sometimes downright hilarious, our researchers share useful insights on the typical (and atypical) travel experience.

SLIMMER SIZE

Don't be fooled by our new, smaller size. *Let's Go* is still packed with invaluable travel advice, but now it's easier to carry with a more compact design.

FORTY-THREE YEARS OF WISDOM

For over four decades *Let's Go* has provided the most up-to-date information on the hippest cafes, the most pristine beaches, and the best routes from border to border. It all started in 1960 when a few well-traveled students at Harvard University handed out a 20-page mimeographed pamphlet of their tips on budget travel to passengers on student charter flights to Europe. From humble beginnings, *Let's Go* has grown to cover six continents and *Let's Go: Europe* still reigns as the world's best-selling travel guide. This year we've beefed up our coverage of Latin America with *Let's Go: Costa Rica* and *Let's Go: Chile;* on the other side of the globe, we've added *Let's Go: Thailand* and *Let's Go: Hawaii.* Our new guides bring the total number of titles to 61, each infused with the spirit of adventure that travelers around the world have come to count on.

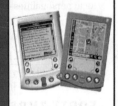

CONTENTS

TO SHETLANDS
& ORKNEYS
(SEE INSET)

SHETLAND
ISLANDS

ORKNEY
ISLANDS

Thurso

HEBRIDES

Ullapool

OUTER

Skye

Inverness

**Highlands& Islands
pp. 625-691**

Aberdeen

Fort
William

**Central
Scotland
pp. 594-624**

St. Andrews

Mull

HEBRIDES

Oban

INNER

Arran

Glasgow   Edinburgh

**Southern
Scotland
pp. 546-593**

Dumfries

Newcastle-upon-Tyne

Derry

Larne

**Northern
Ireland
pp. 692-716**

Belfast

Stranraer

Carlisle

Durham

Sligo

Isle of
Man

**Northwest
England
pp. 352-402**

**Northeast
England
pp. 403-456**

York

Galway

Dublin

**Republic
of Ireland
pp. 717-810**

Holyhead

Liverpool

Manchester

Leeds

Sheffield

Lincoln

Bangor

Limerick

**North Wales
pp. 499-534**

Shrewsbury

**The Midlands
pp. 304-324**

Aberystwyth

Birmingham

Norwich

**East
Anglia
pp. 325-351**

Cork

Rosslare
Harbour

Stratford-
upon-Avon

Cambridge

Fishguard

**South Wales
pp. 465-498**

**The Heart of England
pp. 267-303**

Oxford

Swansea

Cardiff

**London
pp. 90-149**

Bristol

Bath

Salisbury

**South England
pp. 150-196**

Canterbury

**Southwest England
pp. 197-266**

Portsmouth

Brighton

Dover

FRANCE

Plymouth

Isle of Wight

Penzance

N
LG

0   100 miles

0   100 kilometers

Britain & Ireland

MAP LEGEND

⊞	Hospital	✈	Airport	⌂	Hotel/Hostel	⋔	Stone Monument
⛨	Police	⛌	Bus Station	⛺	Camping	⌒	Cave
✉	Post Office	⛟	Train Station	⏚	Food & Drink	∫	Waterfall
ⓘ	Tourist Office	⊖	London Tube Station	★	Nightlife/Clubs	▲	Park Ranger Station
$	Bank	M	Subway Station	⛉	Pubs	▲ ▲	Mountain Peaks
℞	Pharmacy	⚓	Ferry Terminal	🎭	Theatre		Mountains
•	Service	TAXI	Taxi Stand	🏛	Museum		Countour Lines
■	Site or Point of Interest	⚲	Beach	⛰	Mountain Pass		Tunnel
⚑	Embassy or Consulate	✝	Church/Cathedral	⛪	Observatory		Ferry Route
▣	Library	P	Parking	⛫	Castle		Pedestrian Zone
▤	Internet Café	⋂	Gate or Entrance	🗼	Lighthouse		Stairs
							Footpaths/Trails
							Railroads

RESEARCHER-WRITERS

Jenny Pegg *Wales, Isle of Man, Midlands, Northwest England*

Like a latter-day Owain Glyndŵr, Welsh-speaking Jenny oozed enthusiasm, spreading her love for Wales and polishing copy everywhere she went. Next, England, where she countered imperialism with humor and verve. Buses, ATMs, and trials by fire couldn't stop this hardcore RW from freeing toys and hunting hobbits. An astrophysics student when she's not country-hopping, our Jenny proved herself a star.

Angie Sun *Midlands, Southwest, Heart of, and Northern England*

With the flair of a restaurant critic, this California native scoured the English cities for the poshest shops and chicest clubs, racking up new listings like so many impassive sheep. Then she traded football and castles for fish'n'chips, leaving stunning new coverage and boundless thoroughness in her wake. By air, by land, or by sea, this *Let's Go* office vet exceeded expectations—and three full days ahead, to boot.

Sarah A. Tucker *South and Heart of England, Midlands, East Anglia, Yorkshire*

A fresh face at *Let's Go* but already a globetrotter *par excellance*, Sarah added the macabre museums and countless castles and cathedrals of England to a travel repertoire including Kenya, Cambodia, China, Romania, Spain, Amsterdam, Portugal, and her own Little Rock, AR. Her academic interest in all things French hardly hampered, but rather made for a discriminating palate and a taste for fine dining.

John T. Witherspoon *Glasgow, Central Scotland, Highlands & Islands*

While John's knowledge of Russian history may not have helped him much, Eagle Scout honors and a lifetime rambling the wilderness of the Pacific Northwest were an ideal dress rehearsal for the hell-bat drivers, mercenary birds, and belligerent sheep of the Scottish Highlands. Baffling Spoon and his trusty little Peugeot were the perfect team—as his editors and countless lovelorn TIC lasses will surely attest.

Daniel Zweifach *Northern England, Southern and Central Scotland*

As a former RW and many-times-over editor, Dan came in with more *Let's Go* experience than the rest of us combined. This San Diego native has tackled five continents, and—despite *two* finicky laptops and food poisoning in the land of haggis and fried haggis—it came as no surprise to us that he re-evaluated, re-wrote, re-organized, and generally toned North England and lower Scotland into Works of Art.

CONTRIBUTING WRITERS

Chris Gregg *Dublin, Southeast Ireland*

International man of mystery and soon-to-be high-school teacher, Chris used his seven-year stint with the US Navy to help him find Ireland's best aquatic activities, running covert operations while engaging with the friendlies often.

Sarah Jessop *County Cork, Limerick City*

A former associate editor for *Let's Go: South Africa* and RW in Italy, Sarah traversed the southern coast and explored Limerick's music scene, off-season and on-the-spot.

Jack Pettibone Riccobono *Southwest Ireland*

Jack, a former RW for *Let's Go: Eastern Europe*, took his experience and dedication all the way to the far reaches of rural Ireland.

Abigail E. Shafroth *Belfast, Derry, Sligo, Galway*

Abby adapted quickly to the mixed blessing of visiting almost every major city in Ireland. This fearless, rugby-playing Virginian churned out consistently great work—sacrificing sleep, dryness, and, at times, her sanity.

Kira Whelan *Northwest Ireland*

Confident, determined, and full of energy, Kira conquered the northwest with unrivaled enthusiasm; not even a car-eating ditch or bumper-trailing *garda* could slow her down.

John Mazza *London*

An avid rugby player and soccer fan, as well as an RW veteran, John was more than willing and able to tackle London's exhaustive nightlife and score some stellar interviews.

Nathaniel Popper *London*

Nathaniel—former *Let's Go* RW, editor, and Personnel Manager—is as overqualified as they come. We'd love to have him back, but next year he'll be on fellowship in Germany.

Andrew Sodroski *London*

A medieval religious, cultural, and social historian, Andrew found his niche among Wren's churches, Bloomsbury's academia, and Kensington's Albertopolis.

David James Bright *Editor, Let's Go: Ireland*

Kathleen Marie Rey *Associate Editor, Let's Go: Ireland*

Eustace Santa-Barbara *Editor, Let's Go: London*

Brian Algra, who is pursuing a doctoral degree at the University of Edinburgh, gave us the scoop on the Glaswegian football rivalry (see "Pitched Battle," p. 593).

Sarah Kerman, a literature student, wrote on the Channel Tunnel and immigration issues (see "Crossing Over," p. 160).

HOW TO USE THIS BOOK

Are you ready, Dear Reader? Take a deep breath, and remember to keep your hands and arms inside at all times. Off we go. The first chapter, **Discover Britain & Ireland**, contains highlights of the British Isles, complete with **Suggested Itineraries** (p. 7). The **Essentials** (p. 10) section contains practical information on planning a budget, making reservations, and renewing your passport, and has other useful tips about traveling in both Britain and Ireland. Take some time to peruse the **Life and Times** sections, which begin the coverage of each separate country (England, p. 70; Wales, p. 457; Scotland, p. 535; Northern Ireland, p. 692; Republic of Ireland, p. 717). The **Appendix** (p. 811) has climate information, a list of bank holidays, measurement conversions, and a glossary. Lastly, the **Index** is full of treasures.

Let's Go: Britain & Ireland launches out of **London,** and we begin a whirling tour through **England**—from the idyllic **South** down into the **Southwest,** through the **Heart** of it all, to **East Anglia** and the misunderstood **Midlands,** then across the cities, lakes, and peaks of the **Northwest** (with a quick hop out to the Isle of Man) and finally the moors and dales of the **Northeast.** We begin anew in **Wales,** sweeping from Cardiff up through **South Wales** into mountainous **North Wales.** Rinse and repeat with **Scotland.** From Edinburgh we wheel around **Southern Scotland** to Glasgow, then trek north into **Central Scotland** and embark on a tour of the rugged and remote **Highlands & Islands.** Next, it's across the Irish Sea to the Emerald Isle. Beginning in Belfast we tour the people and places of **Northern Ireland,** then, bidding farewell to the UK, we career through the **Republic of Ireland.** We leave you, Dear Reader, in the lovely hinterlands of the Donegal *gaeltacht.* It's been a wild ride, watch your step on the way out, and thank you for flying *Let's Go.*

PRICE RANGES AND RANKINGS. Our researchers list establishments in order of value from best to worst. Our absolute favorites are denoted by the *Let's Go* thumbs-up (🖑). Since the best value does not always mean the cheapest price, we have incorporated a system of price ranges for food and accommodations covered in the guide. The table below lists how prices fall within each bracket.

GREAT BRITAIN & N. IRELAND	❶	❷	❸	❹	❺
ACCOMM.	Under £10	£10-19	£20-30	£31-59	£60 and up
FOOD	Under £5	£5-9	£10-14	£15-20	£21 and up
REPUBLIC OF IRELAND	❶	❷	❸	❹	❺
ACCOMM.	Under €15	€15-24	€25-39	€40-54	€55 and up
FOOD	Under €5	€5-9	€10-14	€15-19	€20 and up

PHONE CODES AND TELEPHONE NUMBERS. Area codes for each region appear opposite the name of the region and are denoted by the ☎ icon. Phone numbers in text are also preceded by the ☎ icon.

A NOTE TO OUR READERS The information for this book was gathered by *Let's Go* researchers from May through August of 2002. Each listing is based on one researcher's opinion, formed during his or her visit at a particular time. Those traveling at other times may have different experiences since prices, dates, hours, and conditions are always subject to change. You are urged to check the facts presented in this book beforehand to avoid inconvenience and surprises.

ACKNOWLEDGMENTS

TEAM B&I THANKS. Dan, John, Sarah, Angie, and **Jenny,** the best thing to happen to Britain. Ever. **Abi,** for her struggles amid our "for" constructions and semi-colon abuse. Mad, mad **Mapper Matt** and his icon wizardry. Fellow members of the award-winning Commonwealth Pod: **Dave** and **Kathleen,** for 109 brilliant pages of IRE, **Rebecca** and **Mark** for NZ "farmers" and Fijian half-nekkidness. **Eustace,** for the Wacky World of LON. **Hannah**—you mean the W/EURld to us. The **Prod Boys,** our compu-saviors—especially Kevin for typesetting our baby. Office Gurus **Anne** and **Alex. Cain** and **Clayton** for the ferries. **Noah** the $$$Man. Proofers all. Google.com, who knows all and sees all. Line edits. And of course **The Hobgoblins.**

SONJA THANKS. Teresa. Champion of the Leek, willing accomplice and keeper-in-check, fellow hobgoblin-slayer and bad-ass woman, *il miglior fabbro.* The **Hiring Gods,** for a bookteam that every day amazes anew. The whole office, for a second, far superior year—especially EUR & West B for letting me bother. **The Calvin Crew:** Kyle, Louise, Owen, Dave, and above all, Megan. My **blockmates**—four years and counting. Graeme—"Tttmuh, muw." Theme Movie Thursdays. George the Lamb. Rollerblades. Mangos. The Red Wings—#10! **CB**—boo! Scotland—ready or not... And my **families:** Antoinette, VK, and EG; the Nikkila/Sinko clan; the mafficking of Macunovii; Kerry; **Mom, Dad, and Cory.** For teaching me who to be and loving me even when I'm not.

TERESA THANKS. Sonja, for infectious enthusiasm, unimpeachable editorial judgment, ceaseless cheerfulness, and misunderstood genius. When I grow up, I want to be like her. The best team of **researchers** anyone could ask for and their brilliant copy. **Amber,** for Harvard lore, repression, Star Trek, knot magic, the Mari Lwyd, and not believing anything I say emphatically. **Chris,** who washes dishes, recognizes the color pink when he sees it, and is a good sport about everything. Wales, which has weathered more oppression than any country deserves. Sheep. Alt-0151. **Gina** and **Christine,** who remember when, and **Jenny,** who was there all along the way. **Jeff,** with *amore.* The collective **Elsey** and **Yee** families, for lots of love and lots of laughs. **Matt,** who's going to be one heckuva Wolverine. **Dad,** who made the bet that got me here, and **Mom,** for love always.

MATT THANKS. Sonja and Teresa, the most thorough editors I know. My **mapmaking comrades,** whose antics lightened the burden of renumbering icons. **Britain** herself, land of convoluted streets. And finally, **my family.**

Editor Sonja Nikkila
Associate Editor Teresa Elsey
Managing Editor Abigail Burger
Map Editor Matthew Hartzell

Publishing Director
Matthew Gibson
Editor-in-Chief
Brian R. Walsh
Production Manager
C. Winslow Clayton
Cartography Manager
Julie Stephens
Design Manager
Amy Cain
Editorial Managers
Christopher Blazejewski,
Abigail Burger, D. Cody Dydek,
Harriett Green, Angela Mi Young Hur,
Marla Kaplan, Celeste Ng
Financial Manager
Noah Askin
Marketing & Publicity Managers
Michelle Bowman, Adam M. Grant
New Media Managers
Jesse Tov, Kevin Yip
Online Manager
Amélie Cherlin
Personnel Managers
Alex Leichtman, Owen Robinson
Production Associates
Caleb Epps, David Muehlke
Network Administrators
Steven Aponte, Eduardo Montoya
Design Associate
Juice Fong
Financial Assistant
Suzanne Siu
Office Coordinators
Alex Ewing, Adam Kline,
Efrat Kussell

Director of Advertising Sales
Erik Patton
Senior Advertising Associates
Patrick Donovan, Barbara Eghan,
Fernanda Winthrop
Advertising Artwork Editor
Leif Holtzman
Cover Photo Research
Laura Wyss
President
Bradley J. Olson
General Manager
Robert B. Rombauer
Assistant General Manager
Anne E. Chisholm

Britain & Ireland

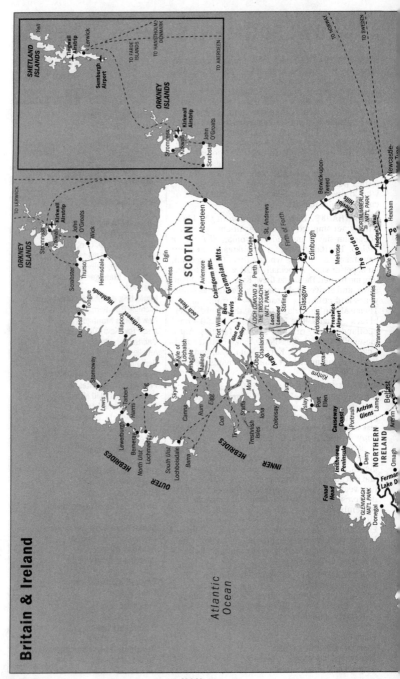

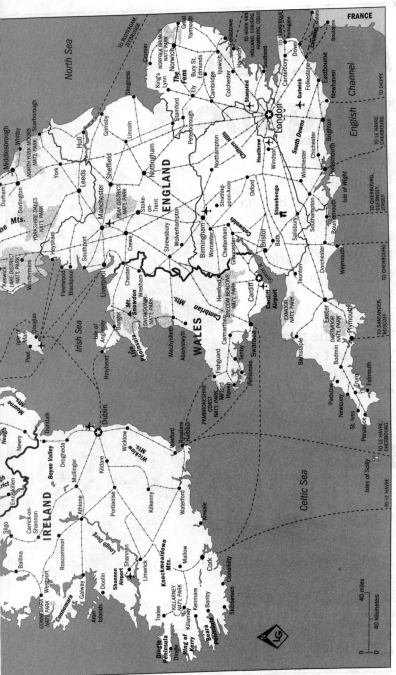

DISCOVER BRITAIN AND IRELAND

Having spearheaded the Industrial Revolution, colonized two-fifths of the globe, and won just about every foreign war in its long and quarrelsome history, Britain seems intent on making the world forget its tiny size. But this small island nation is just that: small. The rolling farms of the south and the rugged peaks of the north are only a day apart by train, and peoples as diverse as London clubbers, Cornish miners, Welsh students, and Gaelic monks all occupy a land area half the size of Spain. Perhaps it's because its residents keep such close quarters that Britain has been rocked by a political history bloodier and more thrilling than most, a past whose defiant fortresses, subterranean dungeons, imposing castles, and expansive battlefields still account for much of the island's appeal. But beyond the stereotypical snapshots of Merry Olde England—gabled cottages with blooming borders, tweed-clad farmers shepherding their flocks—Britain today is a cosmopolitan destination driven by international energy. Though the Empire may have gone out with a whimper, its legacy survives in multicultural urban centers and a dynamic arts and theater scene—the most accessible in the world, as long as English remains the planet's most widespread language. Brits eat kebab as often as they do lemon curd and scones, and five-storey dance clubs in post-industrial settings draw as much attention as fairytale country homes with picturesque views.

Travelers who come to Ireland with images from poetry or film in mind will not be disappointed: spectacular, windswept scenery wraps the coast, mist cloaks dramatic mountain peaks, and the dazzling greens of Ireland's hills and vales prove the moniker "Emerald Isle" no mere marketing slogan. Traditional music and pub culture thrive in village and city alike, and despite the pervasive influences of globalization on one of Europe's fastest-growing economies, the voices—literary, mythical, wise-cracking—of an older Ireland still sound out loud and strong.

FACTS AND FIGURES

POPULATIONS England: 50 million, Wales: 2.9 million, Scotland: 5.1 million, Northern Ireland: 1.7 million, Republic of Ireland: 3.8 million.

PATRON SAINTS George (England), David (Wales), Andrew (Scotland), Patrick (Ireland).

MONARCHS Kings: 35. Queens: 7. Longest reign: 64 years (Victoria). Shortest reign: 9 days (Lady Jane Grey).

SUN STATS Average hours of sunshine per day in South England: 4.65, in Wales: 4, in Ireland: 3.5, in the Scottish Highlands: 3. Hours of total darkness, midsummer, Shetland Islands: 0.

MOST COMMON NAMES Jack (it's a boy!), Chloe (it's a girl!), The Red Lion (it's a pub!).

BEVERAGES Tea (per person per year): 10 lb. Beer: 178 pints.

WELSH VOWELS 7

WHEN TO GO

Britain and Ireland's popularity as tourist destinations makes it wise to plan around the multitudes smothering the Isles in high season (June-Aug.). Spring or autumn (Apr.-May and Sept.-Oct.) are more appealing times to visit; the weather is still reasonable and flights are cheaper, though there may be fewer high-season services in the far reaches of the Isles. If you intend to visit the large cities and linger indoors at museums and theaters, the off season (Nov.-Mar.), is most economical. Keep in mind, however, that sights and accommodations often close or run reduced hours, especially in rural regions.

WEATHER. "Rain, Rain, Go Away" is less a hopeful plea than an exercise in futility. Regardless of when you go, **it will rain;** have warm, waterproof clothing on hand at all times. Eliot thought it the cruellest, but, relatively speaking, April is the driest month. Aside from the heavenly drool, the mild weather of the Isles is subject to frequent changes but few extremes. Excluding high altitudes and northern Scotland, temperatures average in the mid-60°s F (15-20°C) in summer and the low 40°s F (5-7°C) in winter. Another factor to consider is hours of **daylight**—the Isles are more northerly than you may suspect. In Scotland, the midsummer sun lasts almost to the witching hour, but in winter may set as early as 3:45pm.

THINGS TO DO

With Manchester's clubs only an hour from the Lake District fells, Britain and Ireland provide unparalleled opportunities in an amazingly compact space. For more specific regional attractions, see the **Highlights** box at the start of each chapter.

AU NATURAL

Forget satanic mills and madding crowds: the diversity of Britain and Ireland's natural landscapes is worthy of a small continent. Discover your inner romantic (or Romantic) among the gnarled crags and crystalline waters of the peaceful **Lake District** (p. 382). The **South Downs Way** (p. 166) ambles through some perfectly picturesque countryside. With seasprayed bravura, Wales meets the Atlantic Ocean at **Pembrokeshire Coast National Park** (p. 491), where sandy beaches are fringed with lofty cliffs and idyllic harbors. **The Trossachs and Loch Lomond** (p. 610) recently became Scotland's first national park—a trip on the West Highland Railway slices through the Highlands north from Glasgow, steps away from those bonnie, bonnie banks, and passes big guy **Ben Nevis** (p. 644). Farther up, the amethyst sea and misty peaks of the **Northwest Highlands** (p. 670) look as though they jumped off your postcard home. In Northern Ireland, the honeycomb columns of the **Giant's Causeway** (p. 712) are a geological freak-out in the middle of Antrim's rocky outcrops and pristine white beaches. Southwest in the Republic, the **Ring of Kerry** (p. 776) encircles a peninsula rippled with mountains, waterfalls, and cliffs.

HISTORY, PRE-1066

Britain and Ireland had been one of Europe's hotspots long before the arrival of Conquerin' Will and his Stormin' Normans. **Stonehenge** (p. 204) is the most famous of the Stone Age sites, though next-door neighbor **Avebury** (p. 205) is bigger and less touristed. In Ireland's Co. Meath, the underground passages and 5000-year-old designs of the **Boyne Valley** (p. 756) still stump engineers. On Scotland's Isle of Lewis, the **Callanish Stones** (p. 662) reveal ancient knowledge of astronomy and math, while the burial tomb of Wales's **Bryn Celli Ddu** (p. 522) pops up in the middle of a modern farm. Before they declined and fell, the Romans had themselves an orgiastic time in old Britannia. Fabulous mosaics and a theater have been excavated at **St. Albans** (p. 267), once a raging capital second only to London, and **Bath** (p. 205) was the place to, well, take a dip. On the then-border with Scotland, **Hadrian's Wall** (p. 447) marks an emperor's frustration with his pesky neighbors to the north. Finding the light in the Dark Ages, early Christianity got its start in Canterbury, where the **Church of St. Martin** (p. 155) is Britain's oldest house of worship. But a new era of British history was soon to be inaugurated in that fateful year when William trounced the Saxons at **Hastings** (p. 164).

CHURCH AND STATE

The abundance of defensive and religious sites throughout Britain and Ireland makes for a wild game of connect-the-dots. Wherever a castle or cathedral could be imposingly built (or defiantly razed), it was. Edward I of England had a rough time containing the Welsh; his massive fortresses in Wales—**Beaumaris** (p. 523), **Caernarfon** (p. 513), **Conwy** (p. 525), and **Harlech** (p. 507)—are lined like spectacular soldiers along the northwestern coast. Two castles, equally grand, top extinct volcanoes in Scotland, one ringed with gargoyles, in **Stirling** (p. 607), the other perched high above **Edinburgh** (p. 546). Cross the Irish Sea to kiss a rock at **Blarney Castle** (p. 772), or visit opulent, medieval **Kilkenny** (p. 757). Explore the "secret" tunnels of **Dover's** clifftop fortress (p. 161), or join the camera-toters at **Eilean Donan Castle** (p. 671). In the Heart of England, **Warwick Castle** (p. 305) impresses with its castellated gatehouses and stately apartments; but plays serious second-fiddle to glorious **Windsor Castle** (p. 271), the largest inhabited castle in the world. You can play the lord or lady at hilltop **Durham Castle** (p. 438), which lets out its rooms to travelers, as does 15th-century **St. Briavel's Castle** (p. 474), now a hostel near Tintern. Not strictly castles at all, the sumptuous **Castle Howard** (p. 426) and **Blenheim Palace** (p. 283) give a heady taste of how the other 0.001% still lives.

In northeast England, **York Minster** (p. 424), the country's largest Gothic house o' worship, jockeys with **Durham Cathedral** (p. 438) to chalk up the most awe-inspired pilgrims, while **Salisbury Cathedral** (p. 202) sets a record of its own with England's tallest spire. In London, thousands flock to **Westminster Abbey** (p. 111) and **St. Paul's Cathedral** (p. 113), where Poets' Corner and the Whispering Gallery take their breath away. Across the Irish Sea, Dublin's **Christ Church Cathedral** (p. 741) is a medieval masterpiece; the quiet interior belies its contested history.

LITERARY LANDMARKS

Even if you've never been to Britain or Ireland, their landscapes may look familiar from the pages of your English Lit notes. **Jane Austen** grew up in Winchester (p. 191), wrote in Bath (p. 205), took the odd trip to Lyme Regis (p. 225), and immortalized each in her writing. Farther north, the **Brontës**—Charlotte, Emily, and Anne—lived in the parsonage in Haworth (p. 410), and captured the wildness of Yorkshire's moors (p. 426) in their novels. **Thomas Hardy** was a Dorchester (p. 223) man, whose fictional county of Wessex mirrored southwest England perfectly. **Sir Arthur Conan Doyle** set Sherlock Holmes's house on 221b Baker St. in London (p. 129), but sent the sleuth to Dartmoor (p. 234) to find the Hound of the Baskervilles. **Virginia Woolf** drew inspiration for her novel *To the Lighthouse* from St. Ives (p. 263) and the Isle of Skye (p. 652). Long after shuffling off his mortal coil, **William Shakespeare** lives on in Stratford-upon-Avon (p. 284). **Wordsworth** grew up in the Lake District (p. 382), and his buddy **Coleridge** envied him deeply for it—much of their poetry was inspired by walks near its waters and along its mountain ridges. Welshman **Dylan Thomas** was born in Swansea (p. 484), moved to Laugharne (p. 490), and today enjoys a fanatical following. Scotland's national poet is **Robbie Burns**, and every town in Dumfries and Galloway (p. 572) pays tribute to him, while Edinburgh cherishes its favorite **Scott, Sir Walter.** Irishman **W.B. Yeats** scattered his poetic settings throughout the island, but chose Co. Sligo (p. 801) for his gravesite. **James Joyce** is the most famous of the dear, dirty Dubliners (p. 744). Oh, and **Salman Rushdie** has come out of hiding, but we're not sure where he is. London, probably.

A SPORTS FAN'S PARADISE

Football (soccer, if you must) fanaticism is unavoidable: the Queen Mum was an Arsenal fan, and the police run a National Hooligan Hotline. At the **football grounds** of London, become a gunner for a day at Highbury, chant for the Spurs at White Hart Lane, or don the Chelsea blue. Then head up to **Old Trafford** (p. 369), Manchester United's hallowed turf on Sir Matt Busby Way, or move west to the stadia of bitter rivals **Everton** and **Liverpool** (p. 363). **Rugby** scrums are held in gaping **Millennium Stadium,** Cardiff (p. 471). Discouraged by the terrace yobs and the mud? Throwers of tree-trunks and other wearers of kilts reach their own rowdy heights annually at the **highland games** in **Braemar** (p. 631) and elsewhere. **Cricket** is altogether more refined, darling; watch the men in white at London's **Lords** grounds. **Tennis**, too, demands genteel conduct, and the strawberries and cream at **Wimbledon** are a perfect accompaniment. **Golf** draws its driven followers to the revered coastal courses of **St. Andrews** (p. 595). The surf is up along the Atlantic coast at alternative **Newquay** (p. 252), artsy **St. Ives** (p. 263), and hardcore **Lewis** (p. 663). Go canyoning or whitewater rafting at **Fort William** (p. 644), or try the more tranquil punting at **Oxford** (p. 272) or **Cambridge** (p. 326). **Snowdonia National Park** (p. 515) challenges hikers, while every park has plenty of cycling trails. And, of course, any town worth its boots will offer spontaneous kickabouts: go forth and seek your game.

FEELING FESTIVE?

It's difficult to travel in Britain without bumping into some kind of festival. Every town seems to celebrate its right to, well, celebrate. The **Edinburgh International Festival** and its **Fringe** (p. 562) take over Scotland's capital with a head-spinning program of performances. The whole of Scotland turns to the streets to welcome the New Year for **Hogmanay**, while a month later in London, things turn fiery during the **Chinese New Year Festival**. In Manchester's Gay Village, **Mardi Gras** (p. 370) is the wildest of street parties, while the **Glastonbury Festival** (p. 219) is Britain's biggest homage to rock. The **International Musical Eisteddfod** is Wales's version of the mega-fest, annually swelling modest Llangollen (p. 532). For a celebration of all things Welsh and wonderful, check out the **National Eisteddfod** (p. 464).

In the warmer months, virtually all of Ireland's villages find reason to tune their fiddles and gather their sheep (or goats or bachelors) for show. Joycean scholars join an 18hr. ramble through Dublin's streets on June 16, **Bloomsday** (p. 746). Around August, every set in Ireland tunes in to the nationally televised **Rose of Tralee Festival and Pageant** (p. 783), a personality contest of epic proportions.

ADDITIONAL RESOURCES

Britain and Ireland are among the most literarily prolific of nations, with kazillions of books from, about, and concerning each. For a taste of the many places and faces covered in the pages to follow, we've listed some favorites. However, a brief browse in any library or bookstore will turn up hundreds more.

NON-FICTION

The Isles: A History, by Norman Davies

The Rise and Fall of the British Empire, by Lawrence James

A History of the English-Speaking Peoples, by Winston Churchill

The English: A Social History 1066-1945, by Christopher Hibbert

London: The Biography, by Peter Ackroyd

A History of Wales, by John Davies

How the Scots Invented the Modern World, by Arthur Herman

The Troubles: Ireland's Ordeal and the Search for Peace, by Tim Pat Coogan

How the Irish Saved Civilization, by Thomas Cahill

FICTION AND POETRY

The Adventures of Sherlock Holmes, Arthur Conan Doyle

Alice in Wonderland, Lewis Carroll

Carry On, Jeeves, by P.G. Wodehouse

Charlie and the Chocolate Factory, by Roald Dahl

England, England, by Julian Barnes

How Green Was My Valley, by Richard Llewellyn

Trainspotting, by Irvine Welsh

Poems, Chiefly in the Scottish Dialect, by Robert Burns

Dubliners, by James Joyce

North, by Seamus Heaney

TRAVEL BOOKS

Let's Go: Ireland and Let's Go: London

In Search of England, by H.V. Morton.

The Kingdom by the Sea, by Paul Theroux

A Writer's House in Wales, by Jan Morris

Journal of a Tour to the Hebrides, by James Boswell

Round Ireland with a Fridge, by Tony Hawks

The Worst-Case Scenario Survival Handbook: Travel, by J. Piven and D. Borgenicht

The Hitchhiker's Guide to the Galaxy, by Douglas Adams

⚃ LET'S GO PICKS

BEST PUB CRAWLS Tradition mandates a pub crawl in **Edinburgh** (p. 546); funkier folks try Oldham St. in **Manchester** (p. 364). If the blonde in the black skirt is your drink of choice, the pubs of **Dublin's** Grafton St. (p. 726)—not to mention the rest of Ireland—serve up copious pints of Guinness.

BEST NIGHTLIFE The Beatles' hometown, **Liverpool** (p. 357), comes together every night, while **Brighton** (p. 170) does native son Fatboy Slim proud. Students command most of **Newcastle** (p. 441)—must be something in the ale. Oh, and **London** (p. 147) is rumored to have the odd club, here and there.

BEST PLACE TO CATCH A WAVE Hang ten at **Newquay** (p. 252) on the dazzling Cornwall coast, or brave the 20 ft. rollers at **Lewis** (p. 663). Britain's pebbly shores got you down? Unspoiled sands stretch near **Tenby** (p. 488) and on the colorful **Isle of Wight** (p. 188).

BEST EXCUSE FOR BAD TEETH Sets of antique dentures glint at **Old Bridge House Museum,** Dumfries (p. 572), where unwieldy old appliances give new credence to dentophobes. 4 out of 5 dentists believe **Cadbury World,** in Birmingham (p. 309), promotes tooth decay.

BEST NECKWEAR 5,000 neckties wallpaper **The Bear** pub in Oxford (p. 272), est. 1242. The **Dog Collar Museum** in Leeds Castle (p. 157) boasts a collection of medieval pooch-attire. The morbid set can sample the gallows at the **Galleries of Justice** in Nottingham (p. 318).

BEST SUNSETS The walled Welsh city of **Caernarfon** (p. 513) sits on the water, facing the western horizon full on. In Ireland, Yeats still can't get enough of the views from **Drumcliff** (p. 803) toward Benbulben. The extreme northern location of **Shetland** (p. 686) makes for breathtaking skies, while **Arthur's Seat** (p. 559) grants 360° views of shimmering Edinburgh.

BEST FLIPPERS Swim with the sleek at the **Blakeney Point Nature Reserve** (p. 341), the only permanent seal colony in Britain. Otherwise, zip up your wetsuit and take a dip with Fungi the dolphin in **Dingle Bay** (p. 781).

BEST LIVESTOCK Don't pet Northumberland's psychotic **Wild White Cattle,** inbred for seven centuries (p. 452). The Highlands have the harrowing **Bealach-na-ba ("Cattle") Pass** (p. 672), featuring plunging cliffs, hairpin turns, and daredevil cows. The fine goats on Ireland's **Cape Clear Island** (p. 773) produce fine goat-milk ice cream.

BEST PLACE FOR A SNOOZE Join King Arthur, asleep (supposedly) on **Glastonbury Tor** (p. 219). Legend holds that nappers on Snowdonia's **Cader Idris** (p. 507) will awake either poets or madmen. Travelers who don't like those odds can dine on a bed at Manchester's sultry **Tribeca** (p. 369).

SUGGESTED ITINERARIES

THE BEST OF BRITAIN AND IRELAND

THE BEST OF BRITAIN AND IRELAND (6 WEEKS)

Start in swinging **London** (4 days; p. 90) for the world's best museums, shopping, theater, and nightlife. Head down to **Salisbury** (1 day; p. 200), close enough for a visit to **Stonehenge**, the giants on the plain (p. 204). Zoom through Cornwall to **Penzance** (1 day; p. 259) and the breathtaking inlets of the **Lizard Peninsula** (p. 258). Explore **Exmoor National Park** (1 day; p. 230), then plunge into spa town **Bath** (1 day; p. 205), to take the waters and picture-perfect vistas. In **Oxford** (2 days; p. 272), stroll the university quads, then head to **Stratford-upon-Avon** (1 day; p. 284), a perpetual celebration of Shakespeare. Cross into Wales through the quaint villages of the **Cotswolds** (1 day; p. 296), then head west for a stopover in **St. David's** (1 day; p. 495) or a trek into **Pembrokeshire Coast National Park** (p. 491). Head north past fantastic coastal fortresses like **Harlech** (1 day; p. 507). Take on steadfast **Caernarfon** (1 day; p. 513), with its world-famous castle and proximity to towering **Mt. Snowdon** (1 day; p. 515). From Holyhead (p. 524), ferry over to **Dublin** (2 days; p. 726), home to Joyce and Guinness. Run along the coast to trendy **Cork** (1 day; p. 766), and inland to **Killarney** (1 day; p. 776), where you can follow the tourists around the **Ring of Kerry** (p. 776), then relax on the stunning **Dingle Peninsula** (1 day; p. 780). Next, hit **Galway** (2 days; p. 790), an Irish cultural capital, and brave the plunging **Cliffs of Moher** (p. 786). Slip into the traditional *gaeltacht* culture in County **Donegal** (1 day; p. 808), and head for politically-divided **Belfast** (2 days; p. 697), with a daytrip to see the **Antrim Coast** (p. 710). Cross the Irish Sea to Stranraer (p. 576), where a train leads to hip **Glasgow** (2 days; p. 581) and verdant **Loch Lomond** (p. 611). Take the West Highland Railway through **Fort William** (p. 644) to **Mallaig** (1 day; p. 649), where you can catch a boat out to the **Isle of Skye** for a taste of the glorious Hebrides (2 days; p. 652). Search for Nessie as you pass through **Inverness** (p. 637) on your way to exuberant **Edinburgh** (3 days; p. 546), where castles and *ceilidhs* meet cosmopolitan life. Cross back into England for the picturesque **Lake District** (2 days; p. 382), and on to historic **York** (1 day; p. 420). After **Liverpool** (2 days; p. 357), where the Beatles still top the charts, let loose in happening **Manchester** (1 day; p. 364), the capital of urban nightlife. Swing southward to **Cambridge** (1 day; p. 326) for college-spotting and culture, then wash it all away in debauched **Brighton** (1 day; p. 170). Finish your trip with a hike along part of the **South Downs Way**, ambling through the gentle Sussex landscape (1 day; p. 166).

ENGLAND (1 MONTH)

All-encompassing England offers highlights from pastoral plains to cutting-edge clubs. Start in **London** (5 days; p. 90), the cosmopolitan center of everything English. Then head southeast, to gaze at the Continent from the white cliffs of **Dover** (1 day; p. 157). For an infamously "dirty weekend," trace the coast to **Brighton** (2 days; p. 170). Catch a piece of the idyllic **South Downs Way** (1 day; p. 166), stopping to admire the fairytale castle at **Arundel** (p. 178). Use **Salisbury** (2 days; p. 200), famous for steak and stakes (its cathedral has Britain's tallest spire), as a base to explore the stone circles at **Stonehenge** (p. 204) and **Avebury** (p. 205). Then

DISCOVER

THE BEST OF ENGLAND

young, international capital, boasts a newly developed waterfront and a flourishing arts scene. From picturesque **Chepstow** (1 day; p. 473), it's just a quick jaunt to haunting **Tintern Abbey** (p. 474), which still inspires Wordsworthian paeans. Creep north into the gorgeous **Wye Valley** (2 days; p. 472), then to **Brecon** (p. 478) in the rugged **Brecon Beacons** (1 day; p. 479). Head west to soak up some rays at **Tenby**, beach resort town with flair (1 day; p. 488). Magical, mystical **St. David's** (1 day; p. 495) is crowned with a disproportionately majestic cathedral; nearby **Pembrokeshire Coast National Park** (p. 491) beckons with scenic coastal hikes. Then jump to lush, mountainous North Wales—start with a dip into **Snowdonia**, stopping over in **Machynlleth**

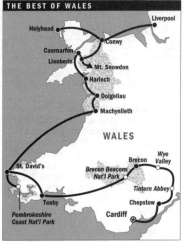

THE BEST OF WALES

head southwest to **Penzance** (p. 259) and **St. Ives** (2 days; p. 263) on the tip of the striking Cornish coast, and up to **Newquay** (1 day; p. 252) for an incongruous slice of surfer culture. Devon's **Exmoor National Park** is perfect for a day of rambling (1 day; p. 230). After stunning **Bath** (1 day; p. 205), Georgian England's most fashionable watering hole, you can unwind by hiking between rustic **Cotswold villages** (2 days; p. 296). Next, snatch a pint and a punt in the medieval university city of **Oxford** (2 days; p. 272) and catch a play in **Stratford-upon-Avon** (1 day; p. 284), Shakespeare's hometown. Live it up in the northwestern cities—the post-industrial clubbing mecca of **Manchester** (1 day; p. 364), Beatles-mad **Liverpool** (1 day; p. 357), and terrifically gaudy **Blackpool** (1 day; p. 371). Partied too hard? Wander north to the peaceful, Wordsworthian **Lake District** (2 days; p. 382). Scuttle along **Hadrian's Wall** (p. 447) to **Newcastle,** home of the famous brown ale and great nightlife (1 day; p. 441), then make your way south to age-old **York** (1 day; p. 420). Finish your trip in elegant **Cambridge** (1 day; p. 326), topped off with a quick train back to London.

WALES (2 WEEKS) With vast expanses of untouristed country punctuated by ancient and dramatic towns, Wales may be Britain's last undiscovered realm. **Cardiff** (2 days; p. 465), the resurgent nation's

(1 day; p. 503) and tiny, stony **Dolgellau** (1 day; p. 506). Coastal **Harlech** (1 day; p. 507) boasts panoramas of sea, sand, and summits—not to mention Wales's most dramatic fortress. A Byzantine castle and Roman ruins draw visitors to ancient, walled **Caernarfon** (1 day; p. 513). From idyllic **Llanberis** (1 day; p. 518), ascend lofty **Mt. Snowdon** (p. 519) then head to eclectic **Conwy** (1 day; p. 525), where curious attractions flank a turquoise harbor. From here, let your wanderlust be your guide: east to **Liverpool** (p. 357), in England, or west to **Holyhead** (p. 524), to hop a ferry to Dublin.

SCOTLAND (2 WEEKS) Home to more than just men in kilts, Scotland balances remote, unspoiled islands with lively cities. Start off in **Glasgow** (2 days; p. 581), a city of art, culture, and nightlife, and base for a daytrip to the bonnie banks of **Loch Lomond** (p. 611). The scenery only gets better as you trek to **Fort William** and scale Scotland's highest peak, **Ben Nevis** (1 day; p. 644). From Mallaig (p. 649), make the quick crossing to the **Isle of Skye** (2 days; p. 652) for enviable hiking and dramatic views of the **Cuillin Mountains.** Cross back to the mainland at Kyle of Lochalsh (p. 653), and into the beautiful Highlands. Pass through spectacularly scenic **Durness** (p. 676) on your way to John O'Groats, ferryport for timeless **Orkney** (2 days; p. 678). Head back south to **Inverness** (1 day; p. 637)—more transport hub than destination, but a good base for seeing **Loch Ness** (p. 642) and perhaps its infamous resident. Next, hit up **Aberdeen** (1 day; p. 626) for city life and sea breezes, then drop by medieval and musical **Dunkeld** and **Birnam** (1 day; p. 603). Hit the homestretch with a stop in golf-mad **St. Andrews** (p. 595) and **Stirling** (1 day; p. 607), home of Scottish heroes and a stunning castle. Finish your tour in **Edinburgh** (4 days; p. 546), fantastic during festival time in August, but sparkling year-round with the historic Royal Mile and unbeatable pubs.

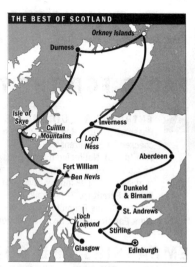

THE BEST OF SCOTLAND

Orkney Islands
Durness
Isle of Skye
Cuillin Mountains
Inverness
Loch Ness
Aberdeen
Fort William
Ben Nevis
Dunkeld & Birnam
St. Andrews
Loch Lomond
Stirling
Glasgow
Edinburgh

ESSENTIALS

FACTS FOR THE TRAVELER

ENTRANCE REQUIREMENTS
Passport (p. 12). Required for all foreign nationals, though they may not be checked for EU citizens.
Visa (p. 13). Not required for citizens of Australia, Canada, New Zealand, South Africa, the US, and many other Western countries. Call your local embassy or complete an online inquiry (www.ukvisas.gov.uk) if you are unsure.
Driving Permit (p. 38). A valid foreign driver's license is required and an International Driving Permit is recommended for those planning to drive.
Work Permit (p. 64). Required for non-EU citizens for work in Britain or Ireland.

EMBASSIES AND CONSULATES

UK CONSULAR SERVICES ABROAD

For addresses of British embassies in countries not listed here, consult the **Foreign and Commonwealth Office** (☎020 7270 1500; www.fco.gov.uk) or your local telephone directory. Some large cities have a local British consulate that can handle most of the same functions as an embassy.

Australia: British High Commission, Commonwealth Ave., Yarralumla, Canberra, ACT 2606 (☎02 6270 6666; www.uk.emb.gov.au). Consulate-General, Level 10, SAP House, Canberra, ACT 2601 (☎19 0294 1555). Consulates-General in Brisbane, Melbourne, Perth, and Sydney; Consulate in Adelaide.

Canada: British High Commission, 80 Elgin St., Ottawa, ON K1P 5K7 (☎613-237-1530; www.britain-in-canada.org). British Consulate-General, College Park, 777 Bay St., Suite 2800, Toronto, ON M5G 2G2 (☎416-593-1290). Consulates-General also in Montreal and Vancouver; Consulates in Calgary, St. John's, Quebec City, Dartmouth, Winnipeg.

Ireland: British Embassy, 29 Merrion Rd., Ballsbridge, Dublin 4 (☎01 205 3700; www.britishembassy.ie).

New Zealand: British High Commission, 44 Hill St., Thorndon, Wellington 1 (☎04 924 2888; www.britain.org.nz); mail to P.O. Box 1812, Wellington. Consulate-General, 17th Fl., NZI House, 151 Queen St., Auckland 1 (☎09 303 2973); mail to Private Bag 92014, Auckland 1.

South Africa: British High Commission, 91 Parliament St., Cape Town 8001 (☎021 405 2400); also at 255 Hill St., Pretoria 0002 (☎012 483 1200; www.britain.org.za). Consulate-General in Durban; Consulate in Port Elizabeth.

US: British Embassy, 3100 Massachusetts Ave. NW, Washington, D.C. 20008 (☎202-588-6500; www.britainusa.com). Consulate-General, 845 3rd Ave., New York, NY 10022 (☎212-745-0200). Other Consulates-General in Atlanta, Boston, Chicago, Houston, Los Angeles, San Francisco. Consulates in Dallas, Denver, Miami, Seattle.

IRISH CONSULAR SERVICES ABROAD

Australia: Irish Embassy, Arkana St., Yarralumla, Canberra ACT 2600 (☎062 73 30 22).

Canada: Irish Embassy, Ste. 1105, 130 Albert St., Ottawa, K1P 5G4, Ontario (☎613-233-6281; emb.ireland@sympatico.ca).

New Zealand: Honorary Consul General, 6th Fl., 18 Shortland St. 1001, Auckland 1 (☎09 997 2252, www.ireland.co.nz).

South Africa: Irish Embassy, 1st Fl., Southern Life Plaza, 1059 Schoeman St., Arcadia 0083, Pretoria (☎012 342 5062).

UK: Irish Embassy, 17 Grosvenor Pl., London SW1X 7HR (☎020 7235 2171). Consulates: 16 Randolph Cres., Edinburgh EH3 7TT (☎0131 226 7711); Brunel House, 2 Fitzalan Rd., Cardiff CF24 0EB (☎0207 225 7700).

US: Irish Embassy, 2234 Massachusetts Ave. NW, Washington, D.C. 20008 (☎202-462-3939). Consulates: 345 Park Ave., 17th Fl., New York, NY 10154-0037 (☎212-319-3552); 400 N. Michigan Ave., Chicago, IL 60611 (☎312-337-1868); 44 Montgomery St., #3830, San Francisco, CA 94104 (☎415-392-4214); 535 Boylston St., Boston, MA 02116 (☎617-267-9330).

CONSULAR SERVICES IN THE UK

Australia: Australian High Commission, Australia House, The Strand, London WC2B 4LA (☎020 7379 4334; www.australia.org.uk).

Canada: Canadian High Commission, 38 Grosvenor St., London W1K 4AA (☎020 7258 6600; www.dfait-maeci.gc.ca/london).

Ireland: See **Irish Consular Services Abroad,** above.

New Zealand: New Zealand High Commission (consular section), New Zealand House, 80 Haymarket, London SW1Y 4TQ (☎020 7930 8422; www.nzembassy.com).

South Africa: South African High Commission (consular section), 15 Whitehall, London SW1A 2DD (☎020 7925 8910; www.southafricahouse.com); mail to Trafalgar Sq., London WC2N 5DP.

US: American Embassy, 24 Grosvenor Sq., London W1A 1AE (☎020 7499 9000; www.usembassy.org.uk). Consulate in Scotland at 3 Regent Terr., Edinburgh EH7 5BW (☎0131 556 8315).

CONSULAR SERVICES IN IRELAND

Australia: 2nd Fl., Fitzwilton House, Wilton Terr., Dublin 2 (☎01 676 1517).

Canada: The Republic, Canadian Embassy, 65/68 St. Stephen's Green, Dublin 2 (☎01 478 1988). **Northern Ireland,** Consulate of Canada, 378 Stranmills Rd., Belfast, BT9 5 ED (☎028 660 212).

South Africa: The Republic, South Africa Embassy, Alexandra House, Earlsfort Terr., 2nd Fl., Dublin 2 (☎01 661 5553).

UK: See **UK Consular Services,** above.

US: The Republic, Embassy of the United States of America, 42 Elgin Rd., Dublin 4 (☎01 668 8777/7122). **Northern Ireland,** Consulate-General, Queen's House, 14 Queen St., Belfast BT1 6EQ (☎028 9032 8239).

TOURIST OFFICES

BRITISH TOURIST AUTHORITY. The BTA is an umbrella organization for the four separate UK tourist boards. (☎020 8563 3000; www.visitbritain.com.)

Australia: Level 16, Gateway, 1 Macquarie Pl., Circular Quay, Sydney NSW 2000 (☎02 9377 4400; www.visitbritain.com/au).

ESSENTIALS

ESSENTIALS

Canada: 5915 Airport Rd., Suite 120, Mississauga, Ontario L4V 1T1 (☎888-847-4885 or 905-405-1720; www.visitbritain.com/ca).

Ireland: 18-19 College Green, Dublin 2 (☎01 670 8000; www.visitbritain.com/ie).

New Zealand: 151 Queen St., NZI House, 17th Fl., Auckland 1 (☎09 303 1446; www.visitbritain.com/nz).

South Africa: Lancaster Gate, Hyde Park Ln., Hyde Park 2196 (☎011 325 0343; www.visitbritain.com/za); mail to P.O. Box 41896, Craighall 2024.

US: 551 Fifth Ave., 7th Fl., New York, NY 10176 (☎800-462-2748 or 212-986-2266; www.travelbritain.org).

WITHIN THE UK AND IRELAND. The **Britain Visitor Centre** (see below) coordinates the activities of the BTA and the national tourist boards and can provide tourism information for all of Britain and Ireland.

English Tourist Board, Britain Visitor Centre, 1 Lower Regent St., London SW1Y 4XT (www.visitbritain.com). Open M 9:30am-6:30pm, Tu-F 9am-6:30pm, Sa-Su 10am-4pm; June-Sept. extended hours Sa 9am-5pm.

Welsh Tourist Board, Brunel House, 2 Fitzalan Rd., Cardiff CF24 0UY (☎029 2049 9909; www.visitwales.com).

Scottish Tourist Board (☎0131 332 2433; www.visitscotland.com).

Northern Ireland Tourist Board, 59 North St., Belfast BT1 1NB (☎028 9023 1221; www.discovernorthernireland.com).

Irish Tourist Board (Bord Fáilte): Baggot St. Bridge, Dublin 2 (☎01 850 230 330 or 602 4000; www.ireland.travel.ie).

DOCUMENTS AND FORMALITIES

PASSPORTS

REQUIREMENTS. Citizens of all countries need valid passports to enter Britain and Ireland and to re-enter their home countries. EU citizens (including Irish visitors to Britain and vice versa) should carry their passports, though they might not be checked. Depending on your nationality, you may be prevented from entering either country if you have less than six months left before your passport expires; check with your local consulate or embassy. Arriving home with an expired passport is always illegal and may result in a fine.

NEW PASSPORTS. Citizens of Australia, Canada, Ireland, New Zealand, the UK, and the US can apply for a passport at post offices, passport offices, and courts of law. Citizens of South Africa can apply for a passport at any office of Home Affairs. New passport or renewal applications must be filed well in advance of the departure date, although most passport offices offer rush services for a steep fee. As of 2002, American passports can no longer be issued abroad. In the case of "emergency travel" consulates can only issue temporary papers. More detailed information is available at http://www.usembassy.it/cons/acs/passport-lost.htm.

PASSPORT MAINTENANCE. Photocopy the page of your passport with your photo, as well as your visas, traveler's check serial numbers, and any other important documents. Carry one set of copies in a safe place, apart from the originals, and leave another set at home. Carrying an expired passport or an official copy of your birth certificate (separate from your other documents) is advisable as well.

ONE EUROPE. The idea of European unity has come a long way since the birth of the European Economic Community (EEC) in 1958. The EEC has since become the European Union (EU), with political, legal, and economic institutions spanning 15 member states: Austria, Belgium, Denmark, Finland, France, Germany, Greece, Ireland, Italy, Luxembourg, the Netherlands, Portugal, Spain, Sweden, and the UK. What does this have to do with the average non-EU tourist? In 1999, the EU established **freedom of movement** across 15 European countries—the entire EU minus Ireland and the UK, but plus Iceland and Norway. This means that border controls between participating countries have been abolished, and visa policies harmonized. While you're still required to carry a passport (or government-issued ID card for EU citizens) when crossing an internal border, once you've been admitted to one country, you're free to travel to all participating states. The British Isles have also formed a **common travel area,** abolishing passport controls between the UK and the Republic of Ireland.

For more important consequences of the EU for travelers, see **Customs in the EU** (p. 14) and **The Euro** (p. 15).

ESSENTIALS

If you lose your passport, immediately notify the local police and the nearest embassy or consulate of your home government. To expedite its replacement, you will need to know all information previously recorded and show ID and proof of citizenship. In some cases, a replacement may take weeks to process, and it may be valid only for a limited time. Any visas stamped in your old passport will be irretrievably lost. In an emergency, ask for immediate temporary traveling papers that will permit you to re-enter your home country.

VISAS AND WORK PERMITS

VISAS. EU citizens do not need a visa to enter Britain. For visits shorter than six months, citizens of Australia, Canada, New Zealand, South Africa, and the US do not need a visa; neither do citizens of Iceland, Israel, Japan, Malaysia, Mexico, Norway, Singapore, Switzerland, and some Eastern European, Caribbean, and Pacific countries. Citizens of most other countries need a visa to enter Britain. If you are uncertain, contact your embassy or complete an online inquiry at www.ukvisas.gov.uk. Tourist visas cost £33 for a one-time pass and allow you to spend up to six months in the UK. Visas can be purchased from your nearest British consulate (listed under **Embassies & Consulates,** on p. 10). If you need a **visa extension** while in the UK, contact the Home Office, Immigration and Nationality Directorate (☎ 0870 606 7766; www.ind.homeoffice.gov.uk).

WORK AND STUDY PERMITS. The right to work legally in Britain and Ireland is authorized only by a work permit, obtained on your behalf by your prospective employer. Entering Britain or Ireland to study does not require a special visa. For more information, read the following **Alternatives to Tourism** chapter (p. 61).

IDENTIFICATION

When you travel, always carry two or more forms of identification on your person, including at least one photo ID. Never carry all your forms of ID together. Split them up in case of theft or loss and keep photocopies in your luggage and at home.

STUDENT, YOUTH, AND TEACHER IDENTIFICATION. The **International Student Identity Card (ISIC),** the most widely accepted student ID, provides discounts on sights, accommodations, and transport; access to a 24hr. emergency helpline (in North America call ☎ 877-370-ISIC; elsewhere call US collect ☎ 715-345-0505);

and insurance benefits for US cardholders (see **Insurance,** p. 23). The ISIC is preferable to an institution-specific card (such as a university ID) because it is more likely to be recognized abroad. Applicants must be degree-seeking students of a secondary or post-secondary school and at least 12 years of age. For non-students under 26 years old, the **International Youth Travel Card (IYTC)** offers similar benefits. The **International Teacher Identity Card (ITIC)** offers teachers the same insurance coverage and similar, but limited, discounts. Each of these cards costs about US$22. ISIC and ITIC cards are valid for roughly one and a half academic years; IYTC cards are valid for one year from the date of issue. Many student travel agencies issue these cards; for more information or a list of issuing agencies, contact the **International Student Travel Confederation (ISTC),** Herengracht 479, 1017 BS Amsterdam, Netherlands (☎20 421 28 00; fax 421 28 10; istcinfo@istc.org; www.istc.org).

CUSTOMS

Upon entering Britain or Ireland, you must declare certain items from abroad and pay a duty on the value of those articles that exceed the allowance established by Her Majesty's Customs or by the Irish authorities. It is wise to make a list, including serial numbers, of any valuables that you carry with you from home; if you register this list with customs before your departure and have an official stamp it, you will avoid import duty charges and ensure an easy passage upon your return.

Do not bring dogs, cats, or other pets into the United Kingdom or Ireland. Strict anti-rabies laws mean that Fido will be kept in quarantine for six months. If you and your pet arrive in Britain from a Western European nation or by air from certain countries (Australia and New Zealand; the US and Canada may soon be added), you can avoid the quarantine by participating in the **PETS** "pet passport" scheme. Provisions include having your pooch or feline friend microchipped, vaccinated, bloodtested, and certified against tapeworm and ticks six months before entering the UK. Call the PETS helpline (☎087 0241 1710) or consult www.defra.gov.uk/animalh/quarantine for a thorough list of requirements.

 CUSTOMS IN THE EU. As well as freedom of movement of people within the EU (see p. 13), travelers in EU member countries can also take advantage of the freedom of movement of goods. This means that there are no customs controls at internal borders (i.e., you can take the blue customs channel at the airport), and travelers are free to transport whatever legal substances they like as long as it is for their personal (non-commercial) use—up to 800 cigarettes, 10L of spirits, 90L of wine (60L of sparkling wine), and 110L of beer. You should also be aware that duty-free was abolished on June 30, 1999 for travel between EU member states; however, travelers between the EU and the rest of the world still get a duty-free allowance when passing through customs.

If you're leaving for a non-EU country, you can claim back any **Value Added Tax** paid (see p. 18). Keeping receipts will help establish values when you return. Upon returning home, you must declare all articles acquired abroad and pay a **duty** on the value of articles that exceed the allowance established by your country's customs service. Goods and gifts purchased at **duty-free** shops are not exempt at your point of return; you must declare these items as well. "Duty-free" merely means that you need not pay a tax in the country of purchase.

MONEY

CURRENCY AND EXCHANGE

The **pound sterling** is the main unit of currency in the **United Kingdom,** which includes Northern Ireland. Residents may refer to pounds as "bob" or "quid," as in "ten quid." The pound is divided into 100 pence, issued in standard denominations of 1p, 2p, 5p, 10p, 20p, 50p, £1, and £2 in coins, and £5, £10, £20, and £50 in notes. Northern Ireland and Scotland have their own bank notes (including Scottish £1 and £100 notes), which can be used interchangeably with English currency, though they may not be accepted outside of Northern Ireland and Scotland. The **Republic of Ireland** recently made the changeover from the Irish pound to the **euro.**

The currency chart below is based on August 2002 exchange rates between the pound and the Australian dollar (AUS$), Canadian dollar (CDN$), New Zealand dollar (NZ$), South African rand (ZAR), US dollar (US$), and euro (€). Check the currency converter on financial websites such as www.bloomberg.com and www.xe.com, or a large newspaper for the latest exchange rates.

BRITISH POUND		
AUS$1 = £0.35		£1 = AUS$2.84
CDN$1 = £0.42		£1 = CDN$2.40
NZ$1 = £0.30		£1 = NZ$3.32
ZAR1 = £0.06		£1 = ZAR16.19
US$1 = £0.65		£1 = US$1.53
€1 = £0.67		£1 = €1.56

As a rule, it's cheaper to convert money in Britain or Ireland than at home. However, you should bring enough foreign currency to last the first 24 to 72 hours of a trip to avoid being penniless should you arrive after bank hours or on a holiday. When changing money abroad, try to go only to banks or bureaux de change that have at most a 5% margin between their buy and sell prices. Since you lose money with every transaction, convert as much as you think prudence allows.

Carrying cash is risky but necessary; foreign personal checks are never accepted, and even traveler's checks may not be accepted in some locations—it's a good idea to have the equivalent of US$50 on your person in small bills. Store your money in a variety of forms; ideally, you will at any given time be carrying cash, traveler's checks, and a cash and/or credit card.

 THE EURO. The official currency of 12 EU members—Austria, Belgium, Finland, France, Germany, Greece, Ireland, Italy, Luxembourg, the Netherlands, Portugal, and Spain—is now the euro. Although the UK sticks by the pound, the euro has some important—and positive—consequences for travelers hitting more than one euro-zone country. For one thing, money-changers across the euro-zone are obliged to exchange money at the official, fixed rate (see below) and at no commission (though they may still charge a small service fee). Second, euro-denominated traveler's checks allow you to pay for goods and services across the euro-zone, again at the official rate and commission-free. At the time of printing, €1=£0.67=US$0.98=CDN$1.53=AUS$1.82=NZ$2.11=ZAR10.35.

TRAVELER'S CHECKS

Traveler's checks are one of the safest and least troublesome means of carrying funds. American Express, Travelex/Thomas Cook, and Visa are the most widely recognized brands in the UK. Many banks and agencies sell them for a small commission. Check issuers provide refunds if the checks are lost or stolen, and many provide additional services, such as toll-free refund hotlines abroad, emergency message services, and stolen credit card assistance.

American Express: At AmEx offices and select banks (US and Canada ☎ 800-221-7282; UK ☎ 0800 521 313; Australia ☎ 800 25 19 02; New Zealand ☎ 0800 441 068). US residents can purchase by phone (☎ 888-887-8986) or online (www.aexp.com). **AAA** (see p. 40) offers members commission-free checks.

Visa: At banks worldwide. Call for the location of the nearest office (US ☎ 800-227-6811; UK ☎ 0800 895 078; elsewhere call UK collect ☎ 020 7937 8091).

Travelex/Thomas Cook: US and Canada ☎ 800-287-7362; UK ☎ 0800 622 101; elsewhere call UK collect ☎ 01733 318 950.

CREDIT, CASH, AND DEBIT CARDS

Credit cards are accepted by many businesses in Britain and Ireland. However, small establishments—including many B&Bs—either do not take them or add a surcharge. Where they are accepted, credit cards offer superior exchange rates. Particular cards may also offer services such as insurance or emergency help, and card numbers are sometimes required to reserve accommodations or rental cars. **MasterCard** (a.k.a. **Access** in Britain) and **Visa** (a.k.a. **Barclaycard**) are widely accepted. **American Express** cards work at some ATMs and at AmEx offices and major airports, but their surcharges annoy B&B proprietors. Credit cards can also get you **cash advances** from associated banks and ATMs (if you have a four-digit PIN), but hefty transaction fees (up to US$10, plus 2-3% extra) make this a technique best reserved for emergencies.

Cash cards (or **ATM cards**) are widespread in both Britain and Ireland, and you can assume that most have 24hr. ATMs (sometimes called "cashpoints") unless otherwise stated. Depending on the system that your home bank uses, you can probably access your personal bank account from abroad. ATMs get the same wholesale exchange rate as credit cards, but there is often a limit on the amount of money you can withdraw per day (around US$500), and computer networks sometimes fail. There is typically also a surcharge of US$1-5 per withdrawal. **European ATMs require four-digit PINs;** if yours is longer, ask your bank if you can simply use the first four numbers or whether you'll need a new PIN. Be sure to **memorize your PIN in numeric form** since machines abroad often don't have letters on their keys.

Debit cards are as convenient as credit cards but have a more immediate impact on your funds—the money is withdrawn directly from your account (either checking or savings; many British ATMs will not give you an option). A debit card can be used wherever its associated credit card company (usually Mastercard or Visa) is accepted. Debit cards often also function as ATM cards and can be used to withdraw cash from associated banks and ATMs throughout Britain and Ireland.

The two major international money networks are **Cirrus** (to locate ATMs, US ☎ 800-424-7787 or www.mastercard.com) and **PLUS** (US ☎ 800-843-7587 or www.visa.com). The ATMs of major British and Irish banks (including Barclays, HSBC, Lloyds TSB, National Westminster, Royal Bank of Scotland, Bank of Scotland, Allied Ireland Bank, and Ulster Bank) usually accept both networks.

GETTING MONEY FROM HOME

If you run out of money while traveling, the easiest and cheapest solution is to have someone back home make a deposit to your credit card or cash (ATM) card. Failing that, consider one of the following options.

WIRING MONEY. It is possible to arrange a bank money transfer, which means asking a bank back home to wire funds to a bank in Britain or Ireland. This is the cheapest way to transfer cash, but also the slowest, usually taking several days. Note that some banks may release your funds in local currency, potentially sticking you with a poor exchange rate. Transfer services like **Western Union** are faster, more convenient, and much pricier. To find a worldwide office, visit www.western-nunion.com or call US ☎800-325-6000, Canada ☎800-235-0000, the UK ☎0800 833 833, Ireland ☎800 395 395, Australia ☎800 501 500, New Zealand ☎800 27 0000, or South Africa ☎0860 100 031. Thomas Cook offices also offer money transfer.

US STATE DEPARTMENT (US CITIZENS ONLY). In dire emergencies, the US State Department will forward money within hours to the nearest consular office, which will then disburse it according to instructions for a US$15 fee. If you wish to use this service, contact the Overseas Citizens Service division of the US State Department (☎202-647-5225; nights, Sundays, and holidays ☎202-647-4000).

COSTS

The cost of your trip will vary considerably, depending on where you go, how you travel, and where you stay. The most significant expenses will probably be your **airfare** to Britain or Ireland (see **By Plane**, p. 24) and a **railpass** or **bus pass** (see **By Train**, p. 30 and **By Bus**, p. 37). Before you go, calculate a reasonable daily **budget.**

PRICE RANGES. Price ranges, marked by the numbered **icons** below, are now included in food and accommodation descriptions. They are based on the lowest cost for one person, excluding special deals or prices. The table below is a guide to how prices and icons match up.

GREAT BRITAIN & N. IRELAND	❶	❷	❸	❹	❺
ACCOMM.	Under £10	£10-19	£20-30	£31-59	£60 and up
FOOD	Under £5	£5-9	£10-14	£15-20	£21 and up
REPUBLIC OF IRELAND	❶	❷	❸	❹	❺
ACCOMM.	Under €15	€15-24	€25-39	€40-54	€55 and up
FOOD	Under €5	€5-9	€10-14	€15-19	€20 and up

STAYING ON A BUDGET. Britain is expensive. To give you a general idea, a bare-bones day in **Britain** (camping or sleeping in hostels, buying food at supermarkets) would cost about £25 (US$37); a slightly more comfortable day (sleeping in B&Bs and the occasional budget hotel, eating one meal a day at a restaurant, going out at night) would run £50 (US$73); and for a luxurious day, the sky's the limit. In **Ireland,** expect to spend €24-35 (US$23-34) per bare-bones day. Don't forget to factor in emergency reserve funds (at least US$200) when planning how much money you'll need.

TIPS FOR SAVING MONEY. Some simple ways include searching out opportunities for free entertainment, splitting accommodation and food costs with other trustworthy fellow travelers, and buying food in supermarkets rather than eating out. Bring a **sleepsack** (see p. 24) to save on sheet charges in some hostels, and do your **laundry** in the sink. That said, don't go overboard with your budget obsession. Staying within your budget is important, but shouldn't come at the expense of your health or a great travel experience.

TIPPING AND BARGAINING

Tips in restaurants are often included in the bill (sometimes as a "service charge"); if gratuity is not included, you should tip your server about 15%. Tipping the barman in pubs is almost never done. Taxi drivers should receive a 10-15% tip, and bellhops and chambermaids usually expect somewhere between £1-3. If you're at an outdoor market, bargaining is sometimes acceptable (don't expect to bargain anywhere else). A general rule is not to haggle if there's a price tag.

TAXES

Both Britain and Ireland have a 17.5% **Value Added Tax (VAT)**, a sales tax applied to everything but food, books, medicine, and children's clothing. The tax is **included** in the amount indicated on the price tag—no extra expenses should be added at the register. The prices stated in *Let's Go* include VAT.

Upon exiting Britain, non-EU citizens can reclaim VAT (minus an administrative fee) through the **Retail Export Scheme**, though the complex procedure is probably only worthwhile for large purchases. Refunds can only be obtained for goods you take out of the country (i.e., not accommodations or meals). Participating shops display a "Tax Free Shopping" sign and may have a purchase minimum of £50-100 before they offer refunds. To claim a refund, fill out the form you are given in the shop and present it with the goods and receipts at customs upon departure (look for the Tax Free Refund desk at the airport). At peak times, this process can take as long as an hour. You can receive your refund directly at most airports. To obtain the refund by check or credit card, send the form (stamped by customs) back in the envelope provided. You must leave the country within three months of your purchase in order to claim a refund, and you must apply before leaving the UK.

SAFETY AND SECURITY

PERSONAL SAFETY

The **national emergency number** in both Britain and Ireland for police, ambulance, fire, and (in appropriate areas) coast guard and mountain rescue services is ☎ **999**. The ☎ **112** EU-wide number will also work.

EXPLORING. Traveling in Britain and Ireland is relatively safe. Be alert about your belongings, surroundings, and companions, and exercise caution in larger cities. To avoid unwanted attention, try to blend in as much as possible; avoid looking like the gawking camera-toter. Familiarize yourself with your surroundings before setting out, and carry yourself with confidence; if you must check a map, duck into a shop rather than stopping in the middle of the sidewalk. If you are traveling alone, be sure someone at home knows your itinerary, and never admit that you're on your own. When walking at night, stick to busy, well-lit streets. If you ever feel uncomfortable, leave the area as quickly and directly as you can.

SELF DEFENSE. There is no sure-fire way to avoid all the threatening situations you might encounter when you travel, but a good self-defense course will give you concrete ways to react. **Impact, Prepare, and Model Mugging** can refer you to local self-defense courses in the US (☎ 800-345-5425). Visit www.impactsafety.org for a list of nearby chapters. Workshops start at US$50; full courses run US$350-500.

DRIVING. Driving in Britain and Ireland is relatively safe, and the roads and motorways are generally in excellent condition. Britons and the Irish drive on the left—if you come from a country that drives on the right, expect to spend a few hours becoming acclimated. Learn local driving signals and wear a seatbelt. Children under 40 lb. should ride in a carseat, available for a small fee from most car rental agencies. Study route maps before you hit the road, especially in Northern Scotland, where shoulders, motorways, and gas stations are rare. If your car breaks down on a motorway, call ☎999 and wait for the police to assist you. For long drives in desolate areas, invest in a cellular phone and a **roadside assistance program** such as the RAC or the AA (see p. 39). Sleeping in your car is one of the most dangerous (and often illegal) ways to get your rest. (See also **By Car,** p. 38.)

Let's Go does not recommend **hitchhiking** under any circumstances, particularly for women traveling alone—see **By Thumb** (p. 42) for more information.

CYCLING. Cyclists should wear reflective clothing and ride on the same side as the traffic. Learn and use the international signals for turns. Know how to fix your bike and change a tire; a few simple tools and a good bike manual are invaluable. Cycling on motorways is illegal and dangerous.

PUBLIC TRANSPORT. Britain's system of public transport is well developed and reasonably safe. Avoid getting into train or subway cars by yourself late at night, and stick to populated parts of the platform when waiting for a train. **Night buses** are a reliable if unsavory way of traveling around big cities. Taxis fall into two groups—government-licensed **taxis** and freelance **minicabs.** The former is usually the safer option: while *Let's Go* lists some reputable minicab firms, others are less reliable and may compromise your safety.

TERRORISM. Terrorism has become a serious international concern, and it is enormously difficult to predict where or when attacks will occur, even in a stable and developed country like Britain. The UK instituted the **Anti-Terrorism, Crime and Security Act 2001** following the September 11 attacks in the United States. The Act strengthens earlier legislation against terrorism and demonstrates the UK's commitment to fight terrorist activity at home and abroad. The UK has also dealt with attacks from terrorist groups in Northern Ireland over the past several decades, though most Irish terrorist organizations set out to cause maximum monetary damage but minimum casualties. Stay alert—if you see **unattended packages** or notice any **suspicious behavior,** notify an authority immediately. More information on international and domestic terrorism and the UK's response is available from the Foreign and Commonwealth Office (☎020 7270 1500; www.fco.gov.uk), the Prime Minister's office website (www.pm.gov.uk), and the Metropolitan Police (☎020 7230 1212; www.met.police.uk).

The most important thing for travelers is to gather as much information as possible before leaving and to **keep in contact** while overseas. The US Department of State website (www.state.gov) is a good place to research the current situation anywhere you may be planning to travel. Depending on the circumstances at the time of your trip, you may want to register with your home embassy or consulate when you arrive in Britain. The **travel advisories** box (below) lists offices to contact and websites to visit to get the most updated list of advisories for travelers.

FINANCIAL SECURITY

PROTECTING YOUR VALUABLES. There are a few steps you can take to minimize the financial risk associated with traveling. First, **bring as little with you as possible.** Leave expensive watches, jewelry, cameras, and electronic equipment at home. Second, buy a few combination **padlocks** to secure your belongings either in your pack or in a hostel or train station locker. Third, **carry as little cash as possible;** instead carry traveler's checks and cash/credit cards, keeping them in a money belt—not a "fanny pack"—along with your passport and ID cards. Don't put a wallet in your back pocket or in the back of your backpack, and never count your money in public.

ESSENTIALS

TRAVEL ADVISORIES. The following government offices provide travel information and advisories by telephone, by fax, or via the web:

Australian Department of Foreign Affairs and Trade: ☎ 1300 555 135; faxback service 02 6261 1299; www.dfat.gov.au.

Canadian Department of Foreign Affairs and International Trade (DFAIT): In Canada and the US call ☎ 800-267-6788, elsewhere ☎ 613-944-6788; www.dfait-maeci.gc.ca. Ask for their free booklet, *Bon Voyage...But.*

New Zealand Ministry of Foreign Affairs: ☎ 04 494 8500; fax 494 8506; www.mft.govt.nz/trav.html.

United Kingdom Foreign and Commonwealth Office: ☎ 020 7008 0232; fax 7008 0155; www.fco.gov.uk.

US Department of State: ☎ 202-647-5225 or 202-647-4000, toll-free 888-407-4747; faxback service 202-647-3000; http://travel.state.gov. For *A Safe Trip Abroad,* call ☎ 202-512-1800.

Fourth, keep a **small cash reserve** separate from your primary stash. This should be about US$50 sewn into or stored in the depths of your pack, along with your traveler's check numbers and important photocopies.

CON ARTISTS AND PICKPOCKETS. In large cities **con artists** (including children) often work in groups. Beware of certain classics: sob stories that require money, rolls of bills "found" on the street, something spilled onto your shoulder to distract you. **Don't ever let your passport or your bags out of your sight.** Watch out for **pickpockets** in city crowds, especially on public transportation. Take care between 8-10am and 4-6pm—rush hour is no excuse for strangers to press up against you on the Tube or on buses—and be alert in public telephone booths.

ACCOMMODATIONS AND TRANSPORTATION. Never leave your belongings unattended; crime can occur in even the most demure-looking hostel or hotel. Bring your own padlock for hostel lockers, and don't ever store valuables in a locker. Be particularly careful on **buses** and **trains.** Carry your backpack in front of you where you can see it, and keep important documents and other valuables on your person. When traveling with others, sleep in alternate shifts. When alone, try to stay awake, and use good judgement in selecting a train compartment: never stay in an empty one, and use a lock to secure your pack to the luggage rack. If traveling by **car,** don't leave valuables in it while you are away.

DRUGS AND ALCOHOL

A meek "I didn't know it was illegal" will not suffice. Remember that you are subject to the laws of the country in which you travel, and it's your responsibility to familiarize yourself with these laws before you go. If you carry insulin, syringes, or any other **prescription drugs** while you travel, it is vital to have a copy of the prescriptions themselves and a note from your doctor. The Brits and the Irish certainly love their drink, and the pub scene is one of unavoidable vibrance. **Public drunkenness,** on the other hand, *is* to be avoided; it can jeopardize your safety. The drinking age in Britain and Ireland is 18.

Needless to say, **illegal drugs** are best avoided altogether; the average sentence for possession in the United Kingdom is around two years. One of the worst things you can do is carry drugs across an international border: not only could you end up in prison, you could be blessed with a "Drug Trafficker" stamp on your passport for the rest of your life. If arrested, call your country's consulate. Refuse to carry anyone's excess luggage onto a plane; it's not chivalrous, we know, but neither will you risk winding up in jail for possession of a controlled substance.

HEALTH

BEFORE YOU GO

In your **passport,** write the names of any people you wish to be contacted in case of a medical emergency, and list any allergies or medical conditions. Matching a prescription to its British or Irish equivalent is not always easy, safe, or possible, so carry up-to-date, legible prescriptions or a statement from your doctor stating the medication's trade name, manufacturer, chemical name, and dosage. While traveling, be sure to keep all medication with you in your carry-on luggage. Experienced travelers will tell you that a basic **first-aid kit** is a great idea (see **Packing,** p. 24).

No injections are specifically required for entry into the UK, though protection against hepatitis B and tetanus is highly recommended. Travelers should be sure that their standard vaccinations are up to date and check that their home country does not require further vaccinations for re-entry.

USEFUL ORGANIZATIONS AND PUBLICATIONS

The US **Centers for Disease Control and Prevention (CDC;** ☎877-FYI-TRIP (394-8747); toll-free fax 888-232-3299; www.cdc.gov/travel) maintains an international travelers' hotline and an informative website. The CDC's comprehensive booklet *Health Information for International Travel,* an annual rundown of disease, immunization, and general health advice, is free online or US$25 via the Public Health Foundation (☎877-252-1200). Consult the appropriate government agency of your home country for consular information sheets on health, entry requirements, and other issues for various countries (see the box on **Travel Advisories,** p. 20). For quick information on health and other travel warnings, call the **Overseas Citizens Services** (☎202-647-5225 or 888-407-4747; after 10pm and on weekends ☎202-647-1512), or contact a passport agency, embassy, or consulate abroad. For information on medical evacuation services and travel insurance firms, see the US government's website at http://travel.state.gov/medical.html or the **British Foreign and Commonwealth Office** (www.fco.gov.uk). For detailed information on travel health, including a country-by-country overview of diseases, try the **International Travel Health Guide,** by Stuart Rose, MD (US$19.95; www.travmed.com). For general health info, contact the **American Red Cross** (☎800-564-1234; www.redcross.org).

MEDICAL ASSISTANCE ON THE ROAD

In both Britain and Ireland, medical aid is readily available and of the quality you would expect in major Western countries. For minor ailments, **chemists** (drugstores) are plentiful. Individual chemists often hang green, symmetrical crosses outside their stores, whereas the **Boots** chain has a blue logo and can be found in almost every town. **Late night pharmacies** are rare, even in big cities. If you are in need of more serious attention, most major hospitals have a **24hr. emergency room** (called a "casualty department" or "A&E," short for Accident and Emergency). Call the numbers listed in the box below for assistance.

Call the local police station for the nearest doctor or hospital casualty department. In England and Wales you can also call **NHS Direct,** a 24hr. advice service staffed by nurses (☎0845 4647). In Scotland, the **NHS Helpline** (☎0800 224 488) offers information on health services. In more serious emergencies, the emergency number for ambulance assistance is ☎**999** in both Britain and Ireland, and the EU-wide ☎**112** works as well.

In Britain, the state-run **National Health Service (NHS)** encompasses the majority of healthcare centers (☎ 020 7210 5025; www.doh.gov.uk/nhs). Larger cities may have private hospitals, but these cater to the wealthy and are not often equipped with full surgical staff or complete casualty units. Citizens of EU countries and other countries with which the UK has reciprocal agreements are entitled to free medical care at any NHS hospital or clinic. Access to free care is based on residence, not British nationality or payment of taxes; those working legally or undertaking long-term study in the UK may also be eligible. **Health insurance** is a must for all other visitors, who will be charged for medical services. Most travel insurance covers health care, while most American health insurance plans (except Medicare) cover medical emergencies during trips abroad; check with your insurance carrier to be sure. For more information, see **Insurance,** p. 23.

If you are concerned about obtaining medical assistance while traveling, you may wish to employ special support services like the *MedPass* from **Global-Care, Inc.,** 6875 Shiloh Rd. E, Alpharetta, GA 30005, USA (☎ 800-860-1111; fax 678-341-1800; www.globalems.com) or the **International Association for Medical Assistance to Travelers (IAMAT;** US ☎ 716-754-4883, Canada ☎ 416-652-0137; www.iamat.org). If your regular **insurance** policy does not cover travel, you may wish to purchase additional coverage (see p. 23). Those with medical conditions (such as diabetes, allergies to antibiotics, epilepsy, heart conditions) may want to obtain a **Medic Alert** membership (first year US$35, annually thereafter US$20), which includes a stainless steel ID tag and a 24hr. collect-call number. Contact the Medic Alert Foundation, 2323 Colorado Ave, Turlock, CA 95382, USA (☎ 888-633-4298; outside US ☎ 209-668-3333; www.medicalert.org).

ONCE IN BRITAIN AND IRELAND

LIVESTOCK- AND WATER-BORNE DISEASES

Two recent diseases originating in British livestock have made international headlines. **Bovine spongiform encephalopathy (BSE),** better known as **mad cow disease,** is a chronic degenerative disease affecting the central nervous system of cattle. The human variety is called new variant Cruetzfeldt-Jakob disease (nvCJD), and both forms involve invariably fatal brain damage. Information on nvCJD is not conclusive, but the disease is thought to be caused by consuming infected beef. The risk is extremely small (around 1 case per 10 billion meat servings); regardless, travelers might consider avoiding beef and beef products while in the UK. Milk and milk products are not believed to pose a risk.

The UK and Western Europe experienced a serious outbreak of **Foot and Mouth Disease (FMD)** in 2001. FMD is easily transmissible between cloven-hoofed animals (cows, pigs, sheep, goats, and deer); but does not pose a threat to humans, causing mild symptoms, if any. In January 2002, the UK regained **international FMD free status.** Nearly all restrictions on rural travel have been removed. Further information on these diseases is available through the CDC (www.cdc.gov/travel) and the British Department for Environment, Food & Rural Affairs (www.defra.gov.uk).

Parasites like microbes and tapeworms hide in unsafe water and food. **Giardiasis,** for example, is acquired by drinking untreated water from streams or lakes. When **camping,** boil your water or treat it with **iodine tablets** (available at any camping store), and eat only cooked food. Tap water throughout Britain and Ireland is safe.

AIDS, HIV, AND STDS

For detailed information on **Acquired Immune Deficiency Syndrome (AIDS)** in Britain, call the **US Centers for Disease Control** 24hr. hotline at ☎ 800-342-2437, or contact the **Joint United Nations Programme on HIV/AIDS (UNAIDS)**, 20, Ave. Appia, CH-1211 Geneva 27, Switzerland (☎ 22 791 3666; fax 22 791 4187). **Sexually transmitted diseases** (STDs) such as gonorrhea, chlamydia, genital warts, syphilis, and herpes are easier to catch than HIV and can be just as deadly. **Hepatitis B** and **C** can also be transmitted sexually. Though condoms may protect you from some STDs, oral or even tactile contact can lead to transmission. If you think you may have contracted an STD, see a doctor immediately.

INSURANCE

Travel insurance generally covers four basic areas: medical/health problems, property loss, trip cancellation/interruption, and emergency evacuation. Although your regular insurance policies may well extend to travel-related accidents, you might consider purchasing travel insurance if the cost of potential trip cancellation or interruption is greater than you can absorb. Prices for travel insurance run about US$50 per week for full coverage, while trip cancellation/interruption may be purchased separately at about US$5.50 per US$100 of coverage.

Medical insurance (especially university policies) often covers costs incurred abroad; check with your provider. **US Medicare** does not cover foreign travel. **Canadians** are protected by their home province's health insurance plan for up to 90 days after leaving the country; check with the provincial Ministry of Health or Health Plan Headquarters for details. **Australians** traveling in the UK are entitled to many of the services that they would receive at home as part of the Reciprocal Health Care Agreement. **Homeowners' insurance** often covers theft during travel and loss of travel documents (passport, plane ticket, railpass, etc.) up to US$500.

ISIC and **ITIC** (see p. 13) provide basic insurance benefits, including US$100 per day of in-hospital sickness for up to 60 days, US$3000 of accident-related medical reimbursement, and US$25,000 for emergency medical transport. Cardholders can access a toll-free 24hr. helpline (run by the insurance provider **TravelGuard**) for medical, legal, and financial emergencies overseas (US and Canada ☎ 877-370-4742, elsewhere call US collect ☎ 715-345-0505). **American Express** (US ☎ 800-528-4800) grants most cardholders automatic car rental insurance (collision and theft, but not liability) and ground travel accident coverage of US$100,000 on flight purchases made with the card.

INSURANCE PROVIDERS. Council and **STA** (see p. 25) offer a range of plans that can supplement your basic coverage. Other private insurance providers in the US and Canada include: **Access America** (☎ 800-284-8300); **Berkely Group/Carefree Travel Insurance** (☎ 800-323-3149; www.berkely.com); **Globalcare Travel Insurance** (☎ 800-821-2488; www.globalcare-cocco.com); and **Travel Assistance International** (☎ 800-821-2828; www.travelassistance.com). Providers in the **UK** include **Columbus Direct** (☎ 020 7375 0011). In **Australia,** try **AFTA** (☎ 02 9375 4955).

PACKING

Pack lightly. Lay out what you absolutely need, then take half the clothes and twice the money. If you intend to do a lot of hiking, see **Camping and the Outdoors,** p. 47.

LUGGAGE. If you plan to cover most of your itinerary by foot, a sturdy **frame backpack** is unbeatable. (For the basics on buying a pack, see p. 50.) Toting a **suitcase** or **trunk** is fine if you plan to live in one or two cities and explore from there, but a very bad idea if you're going to be moving around a lot. In addition to your main piece of luggage, a **daypack** (a small backpack or courier bag) is a must.

ESSENTIALS

CLOTHING. Even summers can be chilly in Britain and Ireland, so it's always a good idea to bring a **warm jacket** or wool sweater. No matter when you're traveling, pack a **rain jacket,** sturdy shoes or **hiking boots,** and **thick socks. Flip-flops** or waterproof sandals are must-haves for grubby hostel showers. Those intending to go out at night will want a dressier outfit (and a nicer pair of shoes, if space permits); everyone should remember respectful, modest dress for religious and cultural sites.

SLEEPSACK. Some hostels require that you either provide your own linen or rent sheets from them. Save cash by making your own sleepsack: fold a full-size sheet in half the long way, then sew it closed along the long side and one of the short sides.

CONVERTERS AND ADAPTERS. In Britain and Ireland, electricity is 230 volts AC, enough to fry any 110V North American appliance; most European 220V appliances are fine. **Americans** and **Canadians** should buy an **adapter** (which changes the shape of the plug to the three-square-pin kind used in the UK) and a **converter** (which changes the voltage; US$20). Don't make the mistake of using only an adapter (unless appliance instructions explicitly state otherwise). **New Zealanders, South Africans,** and **Australians** won't need converters, but will need adapters.

TOILETRIES. Toothbrushes, towels, cold-water soap, talcum powder (to keep feet dry), deodorant, razors, tampons, and condoms are widely available. **Contact lenses,** however, may be expensive and difficult to find, so bring enough extra pairs and solution for your entire trip, as well as a pair of backup glasses.

FILM. Film in Britain generally costs £4 for a roll of 24 color exposures; film in Ireland costs around €5. Pack film in your carry-on luggage, since higher-intensity X-rays are used on checked luggage; if you are particularly concerned, buy a lead-lined pouch or ask security to hand-inspect your film.

OTHER USEFUL ITEMS. For safety purposes, bring a money belt and small padlock. Basic **outdoors equipment** (water bottle, compass, waterproof matches, pocketknife, sunglasses, sunscreen, hat) may also be useful. Don't forget a **first aid kit** with essential medical supplies like bandages and antiseptic. A needle and thread allow quick repairs of torn garments; also consider bringing electrical tape to patch tears. **Other things** you're liable to forget: an umbrella, sealable plastic bags (for damp clothes, food, shampoo, and other spillables), an alarm clock, safety pins, rubber bands, a flashlight, earplugs, garbage bags, and a small calculator.

IMPORTANT DOCUMENTS. Don't forget your passport, traveler's checks, ATM and/or credit cards, and adequate ID (see p. 12). Also check that you have any of the following that might apply: hosteling membership card (see p. 43), driver's license (see p. 38), travel insurance forms, and rail or bus passes (see p. 30).

GETTING THERE

BY PLANE

When it comes to airfares, a little effort can save you a bundle. If your plans are flexible enough to deal with the restrictions, courier fares are the cheapest. Tickets bought from consolidators and standby seating are also good deals, but last-minute specials, airfare wars, and charter flights often beat these fares. The key is to hunt around, to be flexible, and to ask persistently about discounts. Students, seniors, and those under 26 should never pay full price for a ticket.

AIRFARES

Airfares to Britain and Ireland peak between June and September; holidays (such as Christmas and Easter) are also expensive. The cheapest flights tend to arrive very early in the morning, local time. Midweek (M-Th morning) round-trip flights run US$40-50 cheaper than weekend flights. Traveling with an "open return" ticket can be pricier than fixing a return date when buying the ticket. Round-trip flights are by far the cheapest; "open-jaw" (arriving in and departing from different cities) tickets tend to be pricier. Patching one-way flights together is the most expensive way to travel. Most long-haul flights into Britain land at one of the two major London airports, **Heathrow** or **Gatwick**. Some fly directly to regional airports such as **Manchester** or **Edinburgh**. Flights to Ireland usually land in **Dublin** or **Shannon**.

If Britain or Ireland is only one stop on a more extensive globe-hop, consider a round-the-world (RTW) ticket. Tickets usually include at least five stops and are valid for about a year; prices range US$1200-5000. Try **Northwest Airlines/KLM** (US ☎800-447-4747; www.nwa.com) or **Star Alliance**, a consortium of 22 airlines including United Airlines (US ☎800-241-6522; www.star-alliance.com).

Fares for round-trip flights to London from the US or Canadian east coast cost US$600-800, US$400-600 in the off season (mid-September through early June); from the US or Canadian west coast US$800-1000, US$600-800 off season; from Australia AUS$3500 and up; from New Zealand NZ$3000 and up. Fares increase the later you buy your tickets.

BUDGET AND STUDENT TRAVEL AGENCIES

Travelers holding **ISIC and IYTC cards** (see p. 13) qualify for big discounts from student travel agencies. Most flights from budget agencies are on major airlines, but in peak season some may sell seats on less reliable chartered aircraft.

usit world (www.usitworld.com). Over 50 **usit campus** branches in the UK, including 52 Grosvenor Gardens, **London** SW1W 0AG (☎0870 240 10 10); **Manchester** (☎0161 273 1880); and **Edinburgh** (☎0131 668 3303). Nearly 20 **usit NOW** offices in Ireland, including 19-21 Aston Quay, O'Connell Bridge, **Dublin** 2 (☎01 602 1600; www.usit-now.ie); and **Belfast** (☎02 890 327 111; www.usitnow.com). Offices also in Athens, Auckland, Brussels, Frankfurt, Johannesburg, Madrid, Paris, Sofia, and Warsaw.

Council Travel (www.counciltravel.com). Countless US offices, including branches in most major US cities. Check the website or call ☎800-2-COUNCIL (2-268-6245) for the office nearest you. Also an office at 28A Poland St. (Oxford Circus), **London,** W1V 3DB (☎0207 437 77 67). As of May 2002, Council was subsumed under STA (see below). However, their offices are still in existence and transacting business.

CTS Travel, 44 Goodge St., **London** W1T 2AD, UK (☎0207 636 0031; fax 0207 637 5328; ctsinfo@ctstravel.co.uk).

STA Travel, 7890 S. Hardy Dr., Ste. 110, Tempe, AZ 85284, USA (24hr. reservations and info ☎800-781-4040; www.sta-travel.com). A student and youth travel organization with over 150 offices worldwide (check their website for a listing of all their offices), including **US** offices in most major cities. In the **UK,** 11 Goodge St., London W1T 2PF (☎0207 436 7779). In **New Zealand,** Shop 2B, 182 Queen St., Auckland (☎09 309 0458). In **Australia,** 366 Lygon St., Carlton Vic 3053 (☎03 9349 4344).

Travel CUTS (Canadian Universities Travel Services Limited), 187 College St., **Toronto,** ON M5T 1P7 (☎416-979-2406; fax 979-8167; www.travelcuts.com). 60 offices across Canada. Also in the UK, 295-A Regent St., **London** W1R 7YA (☎0207 255 1944).

Wasteels, Skoubogade 6, 1158 Copenhagen K. (☎3314 4633; fax 7630 0865; www.wasteels.dk/uk). A huge chain—165 locations across Europe.

FLIGHT PLANNING ON THE INTERNET. ▧ **StudentUniverse** (www.studentuniverse.com), **STA** (www.sta-travel.com), and **Orbitz.com** provide quotes on student tickets, while **Expedia** (www.expedia.com) and **Travelocity** (www.travelocity.com) offer full travel services. **Priceline** (www.priceline.com) lets you name a price and obligates you to buy any ticket that meets or beats it; be prepared for antisocial hours and odd routes. **Skyauction** (www.skyauction.com) allows you to bid on last-minute and advance-purchase tickets.

An indispensable resource on the Internet is the *Air Traveler's Handbook* (www.cs.cmu.edu/afs/cs/user/mkant/Public/Travel/airfare.html), a comprehensive listing of links to everything you need to know before you board a plane.

COMMERCIAL AIRLINES

The commercial airlines' lowest regular offer is the **APEX** (Advance Purchase Excursion) fare, which provides confirmed reservations and allows "open-jaw" tickets. Generally, reservations must be made seven to 21 days ahead of departure, with seven- to 14-day minimum-stay and up to 90-day maximum-stay restrictions. These fares carry hefty cancellation and change penalties (fees rise in summer). Book peak-season APEX fares early; by May you will have a hard time getting your desired departure date. Use **Microsoft Expedia** (http://msn.expedia.com) or **Travelocity** (www.travelocity.com) to get an idea of the lowest published fares, then use the resources outlined here to try and beat them. Low-season fares should be appreciably cheaper than the high-season (mid-June to Sept.) ones listed here.

TRAVELING FROM NORTH AMERICA

Basic round-trip fares to London range US$200-600. Standard commercial carriers like American (☎800-433-7300; www.aa.com) and United (☎800-241-6522; www.ual.com) will probably offer the most convenient flights, but they may not be the cheapest. Foreign carriers may offer better deals, if any of their limited departure points is convenient for you. **Icelandair** (☎800-223-5500; www.icelandair.com) flies from the eastern US to London and offers free stopovers in Iceland. **Finnair** (☎800-950-5000; www.us.finnair.com) flies from New York, San Francisco, and Toronto to Helsinki connecting in London.

TRAVELING FROM AUSTRALIA AND NEW ZEALAND

Air New Zealand: New Zealand ☎0800 737 000; www.airnz.co.nz. Auckland to London.

Qantas Air: Australia ☎13 13 13, New Zealand ☎0800 808 767; www.qantas.com.au. Flights from Australia and New Zealand to London.

Singapore Air: Australia ☎13 10 11, New Zealand ☎0800 808 909; www.singaporeair.com. Flies from Auckland, Sydney, Melbourne, and Perth to London.

Thai Airways: Australia ☎1300 65 19 60, New Zealand ☎09 377 02 68; www.thaiair.com. Auckland, Sydney, and Melbourne to London.

TRAVELING FROM SOUTH AFRICA

Air France: ☎011 770 16 01; www.airfrance.com/za. Johannesburg to Paris; connections to London.

British Airways: ☎0860 011 747; www.british-airways.com/regional/sa. Cape Town and Johannesburg to the UK.

Lufthansa: ☎0861 842 538; www.lufthansa.co.za. From Cape Town, Durban, and Johannesburg to London with connections through Germany.

Virgin Atlantic: ☎011 340 34 00; www.virgin-atlantic.co.za. Flies to London from both Cape Town and Johannesburg.

AIR COURIER AND CHARTER FLIGHTS

Those who travel light should consider **courier flights.** Couriers help transport cargo on international flights by using their checked luggage space for freight. Generally, couriers must travel with carry-ons only and deal with complex flight restrictions. Most flights are round-trip only, with short fixed-length stays (usually one week) and a limit of one ticket per issue. Many operate only out of major gateway cities, mostly in North America. Most flights leave from New York, Los Angeles, San Francisco, or Miami in the US and from Montreal, Toronto, or Vancouver in Canada. Generally, you must be over 21 (in some cases 18). In summer, the most popular destinations usually require an advance reservation of about two weeks (you can usually book up to two months ahead). Super-discounted fares are common for "last-minute" flights (three to 14 days ahead). The organizations below provide members with lists of opportunities and courier brokers for an annual fee. Round-trip courier fares from the US to Britain and Ireland run about US$300-700.

Air Courier Association, 350 Indiana St. #300, Golden, CO 80401, USA (☎800-282-1202; www.aircourier.org). 10 departure cities throughout the US and Canada to London ($200-600). One-year membership US$49.

International Association of Air Travel Couriers (IAATC), PO Box 980, Keystone Heights, FL 32656, USA (☎352-475-1584; fax 475-5326; www.courier.org). From 9 North American cities to London. One-year membership US$45.

Global Courier Travel, PO Box 3051, Nederland, CO 80466, USA (www.globalcourier-travel.com). Searchable online database. 6 departure points in the US and Canada to London. Departures from Sydney and Auckland are also often available. Lifetime membership US$40, 2 people US$55.

Charters are flights a tour operator contracts with an airline to fly extra loads of passengers during peak season. Charter flights fly less frequently than major airlines, make refunds particularly difficult, and are almost always fully booked. Schedules and itineraries may also change or be cancelled at the last moment (as late as 48hr. before the trip and without a full refund), and check-in, boarding, and baggage claim are often much slower. However, they can also be cheaper. **Discount clubs** and **fare brokers** offer members savings on last-minute charter and tour deals. Study contracts closely; you don't want to end up with an unwanted overnight layover. **Travelers Advantage** specializes in European travel and tour packages (☎203-365-2000; www.travelersadvantage.com; US$60 annual fee includes discounts and cheap flight directories).

STANDBY AND TICKET CONSOLIDATORS

Traveling **standby** requires considerable flexibility in arrival and departure dates and cities. Companies dealing in standby flights sell vouchers rather than tickets, along with the promise to get to your destination (or near your destination) within a certain window of time (typically 1-5 days). Call in before your specific window of time to hear flight options. You can then decide which flights you want to try to make, show up at the airport, present your voucher, and board if space is available. You may receive a monetary refund only if every available flight within your date range is full; if you opt not to take an available (but perhaps less convenient) flight, you can only get credit toward future travel. Carefully read agreements with any company offering standby flights as tricky fine print can leave you in a lurch. To check on a company's service record in the US, call the Better Business Bureau (☎212-533-6200). It is difficult to receive refunds, and clients' vouchers will not be honored if an airline fails to receive payment in time.

ESSENTIALS

Ticket consolidators, or **"bucket shops,"** buy unsold tickets in bulk from commercial airlines and sell them at discounted rates. The best place to look is in the Sunday travel section of any major newspaper, where many bucket shops place tiny ads. Call quickly, as availability is typically extremely limited. Not all bucket shops are reliable, so insist on a receipt that gives full details of restrictions, refunds, and tickets, and pay by credit card so you can stop payment if you never receive your tickets. For more info, see www.travel-library.com/air-travel/consolidators.html. Numerous ticket consolidators are based in North America. **Travel Avenue** (☎800-333-3335; www.travelavenue.com) searches for best available published fares and then uses several consolidators to attempt to beat that fare. Other consolidators worth trying are **Interworld** (☎305-443-4929; fax 443-0351); **Pennsylvania Travel** (☎800-331-0947); **Rebel** (☎800-227-3235; www.rebeltours.com); **Cheap Tickets** (☎800-377-1000; www.cheaptickets.com); and **Travac** (☎800-872-8800; fax 212-714-9063; www.travac.com). Yet more consolidators on the web include the **Internet Travel Network** (www.itn.com); **Travel Information Services** (www.tiss.com); **TravelHUB** (www.travelhub.com); and **The Travel Site** (www.thetravelsite.com). Keep in mind that these are just suggestions to get you started in your research; *Let's Go* does not endorse any of these agencies. As always, be cautious, and research companies before you hand over your credit card number.

BY CHANNEL TUNNEL

In 1994, the **Channel Tunnel** (Chunnel) was completed, connecting England and France. The primary British terminus of the **Eurostar** cross-channel train is London's **Waterloo Station.** (Napoleon is not amused.) Traversing 27 mi. under the sea, the Chunnel is undoubtedly the fastest, most convenient, and least scenic route between England and France.

BY TRAIN. Eurostar, Eurostar House, Waterloo Station, London SE1 8SE (UK ☎08705 186 186; US ☎800-387-6782; elsewhere call UK 020 7928 5163; www.eurostar.com; www.raileurope.com) runs frequent trains between London and the continent. Ten to 28 trains per day run to Paris (3hr., US$75-159, 2nd class) and Brussels (3hr., 50min., US$75-159, 2nd class). Routes include stops at Ashford International in Kent, England, and Calais and Lille in France. Book at major rail stations in the UK, at the office above, by phone or on the web.

BY BUS. Both **Eurolines** and **Eurobus** provide bus-ferry combinations (see p. 37).

BY CAR. Eurotunnel shuttles cars between Kent and Nord-Pas-de-Calais. Return fares range from £219-317 with car, £259-636 with caravan. Same-day return costs £110-150, five-day return £139-195. Book by phone or online. (UK ☎0800 969 992; Customer Relations, P.O. Box 2000, Folkestone, Kent CT18 8XY; www.eurotunnel.co.uk.) Travelers with cars can also look into crossings by ferry (see below).

BY FERRY

Ferry travel is dependable, inexpensive, and slow. Most European ferries are comfortable and well equipped; the cheapest fare class often includes a reclining chair or couchette where you can sleep. Almost all sailings in summer are **controlled sailings,** which means that you must book the crossing at least a day in advance. If you're traveling with a **car** in July or August, reserve through a ferry office or travel agency. Advance planning and reserved ticket purchases through a travel agency can spare you days of waiting in dreary ports. Ask ahead where to board, arrive at the port an hour in advance, and remember your passport. Unlike train or air travel, ferries lack the convenience of location: you often land in odd parts of the country and must then arrange connections to larger cities.

Prices vary greatly by ports, season, and length of stay. In the summer expect to pay at least £25 per person to cross from France and £60 from Belgium and the Netherlands. Limited-day returns (usually 5-10 nights including travel) are generally not much more expensive than the single fare. Ask for **discounts;** ISIC holders can sometimes get student fares, and Eurail pass-holders can get many reductions and free trips (check the brochure that comes with your railpass). Children under four years often travel free, and bicycles can be carried for a small fee, if any. Some travelers ask car drivers to let them travel as one of the four or five free passengers allotted to a car. This can reduce costs considerably, but consider the risks before getting into a stranger's car. The main ferry companies operating between Britain and France or Northern Europe are listed below; call or write for brochures with complete listings of routes and fares.

The fares listed below are **one-way** for adult foot passengers unless otherwise noted. Though return fares are usually twice the one-way fare, **fixed-period returns** (usually within five days) are frequently cheaper. Ferries run **year-round** unless otherwise noted. For a **camper/trailer,** add anywhere from £20-140 to the "with car" fare. A directory of ferries can be found at www.seaview.co.uk/ferries.html.

Brittany Ferries: UK ☎08703 665 333; France ☎08 25 82 88 28; www.brittany-ferries.com. **Plymouth** from **Roscoff, France** (6hr.; in summer 1-3 per day, off-season 1 per week; £20-58 or €21-46) and **Santander, Spain** (24-30hr., 1-2 per week, return £80-145). **Portsmouth** from **St-Malo, France** (8¾hr., 1-2 per day, €23-49) and **Caen, France** (6hr., 1-3 per day, €21-44). **Poole** from **Cherbourg, France** (4¼hr., 1-2 per day, €21-44). **Cork** from **Roscoff** (13½hr., Apr.-Sept. 1 per week, €52-99).

DFDS Seaways: UK ☎08705 33 30 00; www.dfdsseaways.co.uk. **Harwich** from **Hamburg** (20hr.) and **Esbjerg** (19hr.). **Newcastle** from **Amsterdam** (14hr.); **Kristiansand, Norway** (19hr.); and **Gothenburg, Sweden** (22hr.).

Fjord Line: www.fjordline.no. Norway ☎55 54 88 00; UK ☎0191 296 1313; booking@fjordline.com. **Newcastle, England** from **Stavanger** (19hr.) and **Bergen, Norway** (26 hr., £50-110, students £25-110). Also between **Bergen** and **Egersund, Norway,** and **Hanstholm, Denmark.**

Hoverspeed: UK ☎0870 240 8070; France ☎00800 1211 1211; www.hover-speed.co.uk. **Dover** from **Calais** (35-55min., every hr., £24) and **Ostend, Belgium** (2hr., 5-7 per day, £28). **Newhaven** from **Dieppe, France** (2-4hr., 1-3 per day, £28).

Irish Ferries: France ☎01 44 88 54 50; Ireland ☎1890 313 131; UK ☎08705 171 717; www.irishferries.ie. **Rosslare** from **Cherbourg** and **Roscoff** (17-18hr.; Apr.-Sept. 1-9 per week; €60-120, students €48); and **Pembroke, UK** (3¾hr.; €25-39, students €19). **Dublin** from **Holyhead, UK** (2-3hr.; return £20-31, students £15).

P&O North Sea Ferries: UK ☎0870 129 6002; www.ponsf.com. Daily ferries to **Hull** from **Rotterdam, Netherlands** (13½hr.) and **Zeebrugge, Belgium** (14hr.). Both £38-48, students £24-31, cars £63-78. Online bookings.

P&O Stena Line: UK ☎087 0600 0611; from Europe ☎01304 864 003; www.posl.com. **Dover** from **Calais** (1¼hr., every 30-60min., 30 per day, £24).

SeaFrance: UK ☎08705 711 711; France ☎08 03 04 40 45; www.seafrance.co.uk. **Dover** from **Calais** (1½hr., 15 per day, £15).

Stena Line: UK ☎01233 646 826; www.stenaline.co.uk. **Harwich** from **Hook of Holland** (5hr., £26). **Fishguard** from **Rosslare** (1-3½hr.; £18-21, students £14-17). **Holyhead** from **Dublin** (4hr.; £23-27, students £19-23) and **Dún Laoghaire** (1-3½hr.; £23-27, students £19-23). **Stranraer** from **Belfast** (1¾-3¼hr.; £14-36, students £10).

ESSENTIALS

GETTING AROUND

Fares on all modes of transportation are either **single** (one-way) or **return** (round-trip). "Period returns" require you to return within a specific number of days; "day return" means you must return on the same day. Unless stated otherwise, *Let's Go* always lists single fares. Return fares on trains and buses in Britain and Ireland are often less than double the one-way fare.

BY PLANE

Though flying is almost invariably more expensive than traveling by train or ferry, it works for those short on time (or flush with cash). Student travel agencies sell cheap tickets, and budget fares are frequently available in the spring and summer on high-volume routes. The Irish and British national carriers, **Aer Lingus** (Ireland ☎ 0818 365 000; UK ☎ 0845 084 4444; www.aerlingus.ie) and **British Airways** (☎ 0845 722 2111; www.british-airways.com), fly regularly between London and Dublin (Aer Lingus 1¼hr., every hr.; BA 1¼hr., 3 flights per day) and other major cities. If you can manage multiple restrictions, Aer Lingus return fares can be as low as £60. Travelers to the **Shetland Islands** (see p. 686) or the **Isle of Man** (see p. 396) may find that the time saved is worth the extra cost of flying.

If you can book in advance and/or travel at odd hours, the newly popular discount airlines (see listings below) may be another high-speed option for travel within the British Isles, as well as a way of making cheap, quick jaunts from Britain and Ireland to the continent. A good source of offers are the travel supplements of newspapers or the classifieds in *Time Out*; many of the airlines also advertise fares (and sell tickets) online.

British Midland (UK ☎ 0870 607 0555; from abroad ☎ 01332 854 854; www.british-midland.com). Service between Aberdeen, Belfast, Dublin, Edinburgh, Glasgow, Leeds, Heathrow, Manchester, Teesside (Newcastle); also to Europe and North America.

easyJet (☎ 0870 600 0000; www.easyjet.com). London Luton to Aberdeen, Belfast, Edinburgh, Glasgow, and Inverness; Belfast to Edinburgh, Glasgow, and Liverpool; and to Britain from many European cities.

Go (UK ☎ 0870 607 6543; from abroad ☎ 01279 666 388; www.go-fly.com). From London Stansted, Bristol, East Midlands, Edinburgh, and Glasgow; around the UK and to the continent.

Ryanair (Ireland ☎ 0818 303 030; UK ☎ 0871 246 0000; www.ryanair.ie). Flies throughout Ireland and the UK, as well as to European destinations.

Virgin Express (UK ☎ 020 7744 0004; www.virgin-express.com). Flies from London Heathrow to Europe.

BY TRAIN

TRAINS IN BRITAIN

Britain's train network is extremely well-developed, criss-crossing the length and breadth of the island. In cities with more than one train station, the city name is given first, followed by the station name (for example, "Manchester Piccadilly" and "Manchester Victoria" are Manchester's two major stations). In general, traveling by train costs more than by coach or bus. *Let's Go* quotes one-way prices for standard (2nd-class) seats, unless specified otherwise. Railpasses covering specific regions are sometimes available from local train stations; these may include travel on bus and ferry routes. *Let's Go* lists available passes where appropriate.

Prices and schedules often change; find up-to-date information from **National Rail Inquiries** (☎ 08457 484 950) or online at **Railtrack** (www.railtrack.co.uk; schedules only). For information on using the **London Underground,** see p. 94.

TICKET TYPES. The array of available tickets on British trains is bewildering, and prices aren't always set logically—it's entirely possible that buying an unlimited day pass to the region will cost you less than buying a one-way ticket. Instead of just stating a destination, which will get you a single, you might ask what the cheapest ticket to the destination is. **Single** tickets are valid for just one trip. There are two types of return tickets: **day return** tickets, which allow a return trip only on the same day and usually cost only slightly more than a single, and more expensive **open return** (or **period return**) tickets, which allow a return within 30 days. Prices rise on Friday and Saturday and are often higher before 9:30am. Always keep your ticket with you, as it will sometimes be inspected on the journey or collected at the station when you arrive. Purchase tickets before boarding, except at unstaffed train stations, in which case tickets are bought on the train.

Several types of **discount tickets** are available. **APEX** (Advance Purchase Excursion) tickets must be bought at least seven days in advance; **SuperAdvance** tickets must be purchased before 6pm the day before you travel. **Saver** tickets are valid any time, but may be restricted to certain trains at peak times; **SuperSaver** tickets are similar, but are only valid at off-peak times (usually Su-Th).

BRITRAIL PASSES. If you plan to travel a great deal on trains within Britain, the **BritRail Pass** can be a good buy. Eurail passes are *not* valid in Britain, but there is often a discount on BritRail passes if you purchase the two simultaneously. BritRail passes are only available outside Britain; **you must buy them before traveling to Britain.** They allow unlimited train travel in England, Wales, and Scotland, regardless of which company is operating the trains, but they do not work in Northern Ireland or on Eurostar. Pass prices are listed below. **Youth** passes are for travelers under 26, while **senior** passes are for travelers over 60. One child aged 5-15 can travel free with each adult pass, as long as you ask for the **Family Pass** (free). Additional children pay half-fare, while all children under five travel free. Groups can ask for the **Party Pass,** which gets the third and fourth travelers in a party a 50% discount on their railpasses. Other varieties of passes (e.g., passes for rail travel including Eurostar) are also available. Check with BritRail (US ☎ 877-677-1066; www.britrail.net) or one of the distributors listed below for details.

Classic: Consecutive days travel: 4 days (1st-class US$279, standard-class US$185), 8 days (US$399/$265), 15 days (US$599/$499), 22 days (US$759/$499), 1 month (US$899/$599).

> **Youth Classic**: Standard-class only; consecutive days travel: 4 days US$149, 8 days US$215, 15 days US$279, 22 days US$355, 1 month US$419.

> **Senior Classic**: 1st-class only; consecutive days travel: 4 days US$239, 8 days US$339, 15 days US$509, 22 days US$639, 1 month US$759.

Flexipass: Travel within a 2-month period: any 4 days (1st-class US$349, standard-class US$235), any 8 days (US$509/$339), any 15 days (US$769/$515).

> **Youth Flexipasses:** Standard-class only; travel within a 2-month period: 4 days US$185, 8 days US$239, 15 days US$359.

> **Senior Flexipasses:** 1st-class only; travel within a 2-month period: 4 days US$299, 8 days US$435, 15 days US$655.

Britrail Pass Plus Ireland: Travel for a limited number of days within 1 month on all British and Irish (both Northern Ireland and the Republic of Ireland) trains, plus a round-trip crossing on Stena Ferries: any 5 days (1st-class US$529, standard-class US$399), any 10 days (US$749/$569).

Freedom of Scotland Travelpass: Standard-class travel on all trains within Scotland, the Glasgow Underground, and selected ferry routes to the islands. 4 out of 8 days US$134, 8 out of 15 days US$168.

Freedom of Wales Flexipass: Standard-class only pass, valid for travel on any 4 days out of 8 by rail with daily bus travel (adult US$85, child US$56), or any 8 days out of 15 by rail with daily bus travel (adult US$159, child US$105). Includes discounts on sights, YHA hostels, and the Welsh system of historic private railways.

BRITRAIL DISTRIBUTORS. Passes and additional details on discounts are available from most travel agents (see p. 25). The distributors listed below will either sell you passes directly or tell you the nearest place to buy passes; the BritRail website (www.britrail.net) can direct you to other distributors worldwide.

Australia: Rail Plus, Level 3, 459 Little Collins St., Melbourne, Victoria 3000 (☎09 9642 8644; www.railplus.com.au). **Concorde International Travel** (Rail Tickets), Level 9, 310 King St., Melbourne Victoria 3000 (☎03 9920 3833; www.concorde.com.au).

Canada and US: Rail Europe, 226 Westchester Ave., White Plains, NY 10604 (Canada ☎800-361-7245, US ☎800-456-7245; www.raileurope.com), is the North American distributor for BritRail. Or try **Rail Pass Express** (☎800-722-7151; www.railpass.com).

Ireland: BritRail Ireland, 123 Lower Baggot St., Dublin 2 (☎01 661 2866).

New Zealand: Holiday Shoppe (☎0800 729 435, www.holidayshoppe.co.nz).

South Africa: World Travel Agency, Liberty Life Centre, 7th Fl., 22 Long St., P.O. Box 2889, Cape Town 8000 (☎021 425 2470; www.world-travel.co.za).

RAIL DISCOUNT CARDS. Unlike the passes above, these can be purchased in Britain, at staffed rail stations and through travel agents. Passes are valid for one year and generally offer 30% off standard fares. They are available for young people (£18, must be 16-25 or full-time student, requires passport-sized photo), seniors (£18, must be over 60), families (£20), and people with disabilities (£14, application form required). Visit the **Railcards** website (www.railcard.co.uk) for details.

TRAINS IN IRELAND

Iarnród Éireann (Irish Rail) is useful only for travel between urban areas. For schedule information, pick up an *InterCity Rail Travelers Guide* (€0.60), available at most train stations. A **Faircard** (€10) gets anyone age 16 to 26 up to 50% off any InterCity trip. Those over 26 can get the less potent **Weekender** card (€6.35; up to 33% off, valid F-Tu only). Both are valid through the end of the year. The **Rambler** ticket allows unlimited train travel on five days within a 15-day period (€122). Information is available from the Irish Rail information office, 35 Lower Abbey St., Dublin (☎01 836 3333; www.irishrail.ie). Train tickets sometimes allow travelers to break a journey into stages while paying the price of a single-phase trip. Bikes can be carried on most trains for a small fee; check at the station for restrictions.

While the **Eurailpass** is not accepted in Northern Ireland, it *is* accepted on trains in the Republic. The month-long **BritRail+Ireland** works in both the North and the Republic with rail options and round-trip ferry service between Britain and Ireland (5 days US$399, 10 days US$569). Travelers under 26 can reap the benefits of a youth pass. It's easiest to buy a Eurailpass before you arrive in Europe; contact Council Travel, Travel CUTS, or another travel agent (see p. 25). **Rail Europe** (see above) also sells point-to-point tickets.

ESSENTIALS

BY BUS AND COACH

The British and the Irish distinguish between **buses** (covering short local routes) and **coaches** (covering long distances). *Let's Go* uses the term "buses" for both. Regional **passes** offer unlimited travel within a given area for a certain number of days; these are often called **Rovers, Ramblers,** or **Explorers.**

BUSES IN BRITAIN

Long-distance coach travel is more extensive in Britain than most of Europe, and is the cheapest option. **National Express** (☎08705 808 080; www.gobycoach.co.uk) is the principal operator of long-distance coach services in Britain, although **Scottish Citylink** (☎08705 505 050; www.citylink.co.uk) has extensive coverage in Scotland. National Express tickets can usually be purchased at the bus station; otherwise, *Let's Go* lists a ticket agent in the town. **Discount Coachcards** are available for seniors (over 50), students, and young persons (ages 16-25) for £9 (valid for 1 year) and reduce fares on National Express by about 30%; other discount cards are available for families and repeated travel. For those planning a lot of coach travel, the **Tourist Trail Pass** offers unlimited travel for a number of days within a given period. (2 days out of 3 £49, concessions £39; 5 of 30 £85/£69; 8 of 30 £135/£99; 15 of 30 £190/£145; 15 of 60 £205/£160.) Tourist information centres carry timetables for regional buses and will help befuddled travelers decipher them. Most National Express buses from **London** leave from **Victoria Station** (p. 94).

BUSES IN IRELAND

Buses in the Republic reach many more destinations and are less expensive than trains. The national bus company, **Bus Éireann** (Dublin general helpline ☎01 836 6111; www.buseireann.ie), operates both long-distance Expressway buses, which link larger cities, and local buses, which serve the countryside and smaller towns. The invaluable bus timetable book (€3) is hugely difficult to obtain, though you may find one at Busáras Central Bus Station in Dublin as well as in the occasional tourist office. **Private bus services** can be faster and cheaper than Bus Éireann; *Let's Go* lists these private companies in areas they cover. In Donegal, private bus providers take the place of Bus Éireann's nearly nonexistent local service. Return (round-trip) tickets are always a great value. Bus Éireann's **Rambler** ticket offers unlimited bus travel within Ireland for three of eight consecutive days (€45; under 16 €25), 8 of 15 consecutive days (€100/€55), or 15 of 30 consecutive days (€145/€80), but is generally less cost-effective than individual tickets. A combined **Irish Explorer Rail/Bus** ticket allows unlimited travel on trains and buses for 8 of 15 consecutive days (€145; under 16 €72). Purchase tickets from Bus Éireann at their main station on Store St. in Dublin (☎01 836 6111) or at their Travel Centres in Cork (☎021 450 8188), Galway (☎091 562 000), and other major cities.

Ulsterbus (☎028 9033 3000, Belfast office 028 9032 0011; www.ulsterbus.co.uk), the North's version of Bus Éireann, runs extensive and reliable routes throughout Northern Ireland, where there are no private bus services. Pick up a free regional timetable at any station. The **Irish Rover** pass covers Bus Éireann and Ulsterbus services. Unless you're planning to spend lots of time on the bus, its true value is debatable (unlimited travel for 3 of 8 days €60, child €33; 8 of 15 days €135/€75; 15 of 30 €195/€110). The **Emerald Card** offers unlimited travel on: Ulsterbus; Northern Ireland Railways; Bus Éireann Expressway, Local, and City services in Cork, Dublin, Galway, Limerick, and Waterford; and intercity, DART, and suburban rail Iarnród Éireann services. The card works for 8 of 15 consecutive days (€168/£108, under 16 €84/£54) or 15 of 30 consecutive days (€290/£186, under 16 €145/£93).

BUS TOURS

Staffed by young and energetic guides, these tours cater to backpackers, with minibuses stopping right at the doors of hostels. They are a good way to meet other people traveling independently and to get to places that public transport doesn't reach. Some tours are "hop-on/hop-off," which means you can stay for as long as you like at any of the stops. Accommodations are not included in the prices, although the companies will usually book beds in hostels.

Celtic Connection, 7/6 Cadiz St., Edinburgh EH6 7BJ (☎0131 225 3330; www.thecelt-icconnection.co.uk). 3- to 7-day tours combining Scotland and Ireland (£85-149).

Contiki Holidays (888-CONTIKI; www.contiki.com) offers a variety of European vacation packages designed for 18- to 35-year-olds. For an average cost of $60 per day, tours include accommodations, transportation, guided sightseeing and some meals.

HAGGiS, 60 High St., Edinburgh EH1 1TB (☎0131 557 9393; www.haggisadven-tures.com). Hop-on/hop-off flexitours through Scotland (£69). Day trips and 3- to 6-day tours also available. Sister tours **HAGGiS Britain** (same contact) and **The Shamrocker Ireland** (☎01 672 7651) run 3-7 days through England, Wales, and Ireland.

Karibuni (☎01788 522 850; www.karibuni.co.uk) runs weekend adventure tours in England and Wales from London, with activities including biking, kayaking, surfing, horseback riding, and camping (£50-185). Longer tours also available.

MacBackpackers, 105 High St., Edinburgh EH1 1SG (☎0131 558 9900; www.mac-backpackers.com). Hop-on/hop-off flexitour (£55) of Scotland and 1- to 7-day tours.

Stray Travel, 171 Earl's Court Rd., London SW5 9RF (☎020 7373 7737; www.stray-travel.com). Hop-on/hop-off, ticket good for 4 months. Circuit through England, Wales, and Scotland (£159) or Ireland (£149). Also shorter routes.

BY CAR

Cars offer speed, freedom, access to the countryside, and an escape from the town-to-town mentality of trains; unfortunately, they introduce the hassle of driving and parking in large cities and the high cost of petrol (gasoline). If you can't decide between train and car travel, you may benefit from a combination of the two; BritRail pass distributors (p. 33) sell combination rail-and-drive packages.

Remember you may not be used to **driving on the left,** or driving **manual transmission** ("stick-shift"; far more common than automatic in cheap rental cars). Be particularly cautious at **roundabouts** (rotary interchanges), and remember to give way to traffic from the right. The **Association for Safe International Road Travel (ASIRT),** 11769 Gainsborough Rd., Potomac, MD 20854, USA (☎301-983-5252; www.asirt.org), will send travelers country-specific Road Travel Reports. Road atlases for the UK are available in travel bookshops and from many tourist information centres. Petrol is sold by the liter; there are about four liters to the gallon.

Most credit cards cover standard **insurance.** If you rent, lease, or borrow a car, you will need a **Green Card,** or **International Insurance Certificate,** to certify that you have liability insurance that applies abroad. Green Cards can be obtained at rental agencies, car dealers, some travel agents, and some border crossings.

DRIVING PERMITS. If you plan to drive in Britain or Ireland, you *must* have **a valid foreign driver's license.** An **International Driving Permit** (IDP) is also advisable. Valid for one year, an IDP must be issued in your own country before you depart. An application requires two passport-sized photos, a current local license, an additional form of identification, and a fee. You must be 18. EU license-holders do not need an IDP to drive in Britain or Ireland. Purchase an IDP through one of the automobile associations listed below—those sold by irreputable online dealers may be overpriced, invalid, or illegal.

Australia: Royal Automobile Club (☎ 08 9421 4400; www.rac.com.au/travel) or National Royal Motorist Association (www.nrma.com.au). AUS$15.

Canada: Canadian Automobile Association, 1145 Hunt Club Rd., Suite 200, Ottawa K1V 0Y3 (☎ 613-247-0117; www.caa.ca). CDN$13.

New Zealand: Automobile Association, 99 Albert St., Auckland City (☎ 09 377 4660; www.nzaa.co.nz). NZ$12.

South Africa: Automobile Association of South Africa, P.O. Box 596, Johannesburg 2000 (☎ 011 799 1000; www.aasa.co.za).

US: American Automobile Association (AAA) (☎ 800-222-7448; www.aaa.com). US$10.

DRIVING IN BRITAIN AND IRELAND

You must be 17 to drive in Britain. The country is covered by a high-speed system of **motorways** ("M-roads") that connect London with major cities around the country. These are supplemented by a tight web of "A-roads" and "B-roads" that connect towns: A-roads are the main routes, while B-roads are narrower but often more scenic. **Distances** on road signs are in miles (1mi.=1.6km). **Speed limits** are 70mph (113km/h) on motorways (highways) and dual carriageways (divided highways), 60mph (97km/h) on single carriageways (non-divided highways), and usually 30mph (48km/h) in urban areas. Speed limits are always marked at the beginning of town areas; upon leaving, you'll see a circular sign with a slash through it, signaling the end of the restriction. Drivers and all passengers are required to wear **seat belts.** Driving in **London** is a nightmare superseded only by parking in London—to maintain sanity, stick to public transport. The **Highway Code,** which details Britain's driving regulations, is accessible online (www.roads.detr.gov.uk/roadsafety/hc/index.shtml) or can be purchased at most large bookstores or newsagents. For a primer on British road signs and conventions, check out the "Signs and Markings" section.

In the event of a breakdown in Britain, try contacting the **Automobile Association** (☎ 0800 028 9018) or the **Royal Automobile Club** (☎ 0800 828 282). Membership may be required for breakdown assistance, but is sometimes available on the spot. Call ☎ **999** in an emergency.

RENTING OR LEASING A CAR

You can rent a car from a US-based firm with European offices, from a Europe-based company with local representatives, or from a tour operator that arranges rentals from a European company at its own rates. Multinationals offer greater flexibility, but tour operators often strike better deals. Some airlines offer special fly-and-drive packages. Rental prices vary by company, season, and pickup point; expect to pay at least £130 per week for a small car. Automatics are generally more expensive than manuals (stick-shifts). If possible, reserve well before leaving for Britain or Ireland and pay in advance; it's less expensive to reserve a car from the US than from Europe. The following agencies rent cars in Britain and Ireland:

Auto Europe (US and Canada ☎ 888-223-5555; www.autoeurope.com).

Avis (US ☎ 800-230-4898; Canada ☎ 800-272-5871; UK ☎ 0870 606 0100; Australia ☎ 136 333; New Zealand ☎ 0800 65 51 11; www.avis.com).

Budget (US and Canada ☎ 800-527-0700; Quebec ☎ 800-268-8900; UK ☎ 01442 280181; www.budgetrentacar.com).

Europe by Car (US ☎ 800-223-1516 or 212-581-3040; www.europebycar.com).

Europcar International (US ☎ 877-940-6900; UK ☎ 0870 607 5000; www.europcar.com).

Hertz (US ☎ 800-654-3001; Canada ☎ 800-263-0600; UK ☎ 08705 996 699; Australia ☎ 9698 2555; www.hertz.com).

Kemwel (US ☎ 877-820-0668; www.kemwel.com).

At most agencies, all you need to rent a car is a driver's license; some will ask for an additional ID confirming your home address. Renters in Britain must be over 21; those under 23 (or even 25) may have to pay hefty additional fees. In Ireland, those under 23 generally cannot rent.

For trips longer than 17 days, leasing can be a cheaper option; it's often the only option for those ages 18-21. The cheapest leases are agreements to buy the car and then sell it back to the manufacturer at a prearranged price; as far as you're concerned, though, it's a lease and doesn't entail enormous financial transactions. Leases generally include insurance coverage and are not taxed. Expect to pay around US$1100-1800 (depending on size of car) for 60 days. **Auto Europe, Europe by Car,** and **Kemwel** (above) handle leases as well as rentals; **Renault Eurodrive** (US ☎800-221-1052; www.renaultusa.com) only leases.

BY FERRY

Ferry services connecting ports in England, Scotland, Wales, and Ireland are inexpensive and usually the cheapest way of crossing the Irish Sea. Ferry companies advertise special low rates for day returns in local papers; otherwise, expect to pay £20-30 depending on route, season, and length of stay. Ferry companies often offer special discounts in conjunction with bus or train companies. A little advance research can save you and your wallet much angst.

Caledonian MacBrayne, The Ferry Terminal, Gourock PA19 1QP (☎01475 650 100; www.calmac.co.uk). CalMac's the daddy of Scottish ferries, with routes in the Hebrides and along the west coast of Scotland.

Irish Ferries, 2-4 Merrion Row, Dublin 2 (Republic of Ireland ☎1890 313 131; Northern Ireland ☎0800 018 2211; www.irishferries.ie) and Corn Exchange Building, Brunswick St., Liverpool L2 7TP (☎08705 171 717). Dublin to Holyhead (2-3hr., €25-39); Rosslare to Pembroke (4hr., €25-31).

Isle of Man Steam Packet Company serves the Isle of Man; see p. 396 for details.

P&O Irish Sea, Terminal 3, Dublin Port, Dublin 1 (☎1800 409 049) and Larne Harbour, Larne, BT40 1AQ (☎0870 242 4777; www.poirishsea.com). Dublin to Liverpool and Mostyn (near Chester); Larne to points in Scotland and England.

Northlink Ferries, Stromness, Orkney, KW16 3BH (☎01856 851 144, reservations 0845 600 0449). Sails between Aberdeen, Lerwick, Stromness, and Scrabster.

SeaCat, SeaCat Terminal, Donegall Quay, Belfast BT1 3AL (Belfast ☎08705 523 523; Dublin ☎01 836 4019; www.seacat.co.uk). Belfast to Heysham, England and Troon, Scotland; Dublin to Liverpool.

Stena Line, Park St., Ashford, Kent TN24 8EX (UK ☎08705 707 070; Ireland ☎01 204 7777; worldwide ☎1232 647022; www.stenaline.co.uk) Dún Laoghaire (near Dublin) to Holyhead (£23-29); Belfast to Stranraer (£14-24); Rosslare to Fishguard (£18-23).

Swansea-Cork Ferries: (UK ☎01792 456 116; Ireland ☎021 427 1166); www.swansea-cork.ie. Swansea to Ringaskiddy, Co. Cork (10hr., £24-34).

BY BICYCLE

Biking is a key element of the classic budget voyage. Much of the British and Irish countryside is well-suited for cycling, as many roads are not heavily traveled. Consult tourist offices for local touring routes, and always bring along the appropriate **Ordnance Survey maps.** Keep safety in mind—even well-traveled routes often cover highly uneven terrain.

GETTING OR TRANSPORTING A BIKE. Many airlines will count a bike as part of your luggage, although a few charge an extra US$60-110 each way. If you plan to explore several widely separated regions, you can combine cycling with train travel. In addition, bikes often ride free on ferries leaving Britain and Ireland. A better option for some is to buy a bike in Britain and Ireland and sell it before leaving. A bike bought new overseas is subject to customs duties if brought home; used bikes, however, are not taxed. **Renting** ("hiring") a bike is preferable to bringing your own if your touring will be confined to a few regions. *Let's Go* lists bike rental stores in many towns.

BICYCLE EQUIPMENT. Riding a bike with a frame pack strapped to it or your back is about as safe as pedaling blindfolded over a sheet of ice; **panniers** are essential. You'll also need a suitable **bike helmet** (US$25-50) and a U-shaped **Citadel** or **Kryptonite lock** (from US$30). British law requires a white light at the front of your bike and a red light and red reflector at the back.

INFORMATION AND ORGANIZATIONS. The **National Cycle Network** encompasses 6000 mi. of biking and walking trails in the UK; it will be extended to 10,000 by 2005. Information and route maps are available through **Sustrans,** the sustainable transport charity. (☎0117 929 0888; www.sustrans.org.uk.) The **Big Bike Site** (www.cyclists.org.uk) maintains an encyclopedic collection of British bicycling news and links. The **Cyclists Touring Club,** 69 Meadrow, Godalming, Surrey GU7 3HS (☎0870 873 0060; www.ctc.org.uk), provides route maps and books. Membership costs £27 (under 26 £10, over 65 £16.50) and includes free touring advice and a bimonthly magazine. To purchase *England by Bike* or *Ireland by Bike* (each US$15) or general bicycling guides, try **Mountaineers Books** (☎800-553-4453; www.mountaineersbooks.org).

TOURS. Commercial tours are an alternative if you're nervous about striking out on your own. **CBT Tours** (☎800-736-2453; www.cbttours.com) offers 9- to 13-day biking, mountain-biking, and hiking trips through Europe, including Britain and Ireland. **Bicycle Beano** (UK ☎01982 560 471; www.bicycle-beano.co.uk) offers vegetarian tours in Wales; **Cycle Scotland** (☎0131 556 5560; www.cyclescotland.co.uk) operates "Scottish Cycle Safaris"; and **Irish Cycle Tours** (☎028 9064 2222; www.irishcycletours.com) runs trips through Ireland.

BY FOOT

BRITAIN. An extensive system of well-marked and well-maintained long-distance paths cover Britain, ranging from the gently rolling paths of the **South Downs Way** (p. 166) to the rugged mountain trails of the **Pennine Way** (p. 407). Ordnance Survey 1:25,000 maps mark almost every house, barn, standing stone, graveyard, and pub; less ambitious hikers will want the 1:50,000 scale maps. Tourist information centres, hostel owners, and fellow travelers are all fine sources of footpath recommendations. The **Ramblers' Association,** Camelford House, 2nd Fl., 87-90 Arnold Embankment, London SE1 7TW (☎020 7339 8500; www.ramblers.org.uk), publishes a *Yearbook* on walking and places to stay, as well as free newsletters and magazines. Their website abounds with information. (Membership £20, concessions £11.) The **National Cycle Network** (see above) includes walking trails.

IRELAND. Ireland's mountains, fields, and heather-covered hills make walking and hiking an arduous joy. The **Wicklow Way,** a popular trail through mountainous Co. Wicklow, features hostels within a day's walk of each other. The best hillwalking maps are the *Ordnance Survey Discovery Series* (€6.60). Other remarkable trails include the **Kerry Way** and the **Burren Way.** There are a multitude of other trails all over the island; consult Bord Fáilte (see p. 12) for more information. The 560 mi. Ulster Way of Northern Ireland no longer exists, but is being split into new regional **Waymarked ways.** Contact any tourist office in Northern Ireland for more information. For those looking to avoid some of the pitfalls of hiking, **guided tours** may be the solution. Though expensive (upwards of €80 per day), the package includes an area expert guide, a bus for luggage transports, accommodations, and meals. Less expensive and more independent, **self-guided tours** include luggage transport and accommodations but usually do away with meals (and, of course, the guide). For a list of tours, see www.walking.travel.ie. **Tír na nÓg Tours,** 57 Lower Gardiner St., Dublin 1 (☎01 836 684), is a reputable and acclaimed choice.

BY THUMB

 Let's Go strongly urges you to consider seriously the risks before you choose to hitch. We do not recommend hitching as a safe means of transportation, and none of the information presented here is intended to do so.

No one should hitchhike without careful consideration of the risks involved. Hitching means entrusting your life to a random person who happens to stop and risking theft, assault, sexual harassment, and unsafe driving. Nonetheless, hitching can allow you to meet local people and get where you're going, especially in rural parts of Scotland, Wales, and Ireland (lower Scotland and England are tougher for prospective hitchers), where public transportation is sketchy. The choice remains yours. Depending on the circumstances, men and women traveling in groups and men traveling alone might consider hitching. If you're a woman traveling alone, don't hitch—it's just too dangerous. A man and a woman are a safer combination, two men will have a hard time, and three will go nowhere.

Where one stands is vital. Experienced hitchers pick a spot outside built-up areas, where drivers can stop, return to the road without causing an accident, and have time to look over potential passengers as they approach. Hitching or even standing on motorways (any road labelled "M") is illegal. Success also depends on appearance. Smart hitchers travel light and stack their belongings in a compact but visible cluster. Drivers prefer hitchers who are neat and wholesome.

Safety precautions are always necessary, even for those not hitching alone. Safety-minded hitchers will not get into a car that they can't get out of again in a hurry (especially the back seat of a two-door car) and never let go of their backpacks. If they feel threatened, they insist on being let off, regardless of where they are. Acting as if they are going to open the car door or vomit on the upholstery usually gets a driver to stop. Hitching at night can be particularly dangerous and difficult; experienced hitchers stand in well-lit places and expect drivers to be leery.

ACCOMMODATIONS

HOSTELS

Hostels are generally laid out dorm-style, often with large single-sex rooms and bunk beds, although some offer private rooms for families and couples. They sometimes have kitchens and utensils for your use, bike or moped rentals, storage areas, and laundry facilities. There can be drawbacks: some hostels (particularly

YHA hostels in rural areas) close during certain daytime "lockout" hours, have a curfew, don't accept reservations, impose a maximum stay, or, less frequently, require that you do chores. In Britain, a hostel bed will cost about £9 in rural areas, £13 in larger cities, and £15-20 in London; in Ireland, €12.

HOSTELLING INTERNATIONAL

Youth hostels in the UK and Ireland are run by the **Youth Hostels Association** (YHA; England and Wales), the **Scottish Youth Hostels Association** (SYHA), **Hostelling International Northern Ireland** (HINI), and **An Óige** (an-OYJ) in the Republic of Ireland. Joining the youth hostel association in your own country (listed below) automatically grants you membership privileges in **Hostelling International** (HI), a federation of national hosteling associations.

Many hostels accept reservations via the **International Booking Network** (Australia ☎02 9261 1111; Canada ☎800-663-5777; England and Wales ☎01629 581 418; Northern Ireland ☎028 3232 4733; Republic of Ireland ☎01 830 1766; NZ ☎03 379 9808; Scotland ☎8701 55 32 55; US ☎800-909-4776; www.hostelbooking.com). HI's umbrella organization's web page (www.iyhf.org) lists the web addresses and phone numbers of all national associations.

Unless noted as "self-catering," the YHA hostels listed in *Let's Go* offer cooked meals at roughly standard rates—breakfast £3.20, small/standard packed lunch £2.80/£3.65, evening meal £4.15, and children's meals (£1.75-2.70).

Most HI hostels also honor **guest memberships**—you'll get a blank card with space for six validation stamps. Each night you'll pay a non-member supplement (one-sixth the membership fee) and earn one guest stamp; get six stamps, and you're a member. Most student travel agencies (see p. 25) sell HI cards, as do all of the national hosteling organizations listed below. All prices listed below are valid for one-year memberships unless otherwise noted.

Australian Youth Hostels Association (AYHA), Level 3, 10 Mallett St., Camperdown NSW 2050 (☎02 9565 1699; www.yha.org.au). AUS$52, under 18 AUS$16.

Hostelling International-Canada (HI-C), 400-205 Catherine St., Ottawa, ON K2P 1C3 (☎800-663-5777 or 613-237-7884; www.hihostels.ca). CDN$35, under 18 free.

An Óige (Irish Youth Hostel Association), 61 Mountjoy St., Dublin 7 (☎830 4555; fax 830 5808; www.irelandyha.org). €15, under 18 €7.50.

Youth Hostels Association of New Zealand (YHANZ), P.O. Box 436, 193 Cashel St., Union House, Christchurch 1 (☎03 379 9970; www.yha.org.nz). NZ$40, under 17 free.

Hostels Association of South Africa, 73 St. George's St. Mall, P.O. Box 4402, Cape Town 8000 (☎021 424 2511; fax 424 4119; www.hisa.org.za). ZAR45.

Scottish Youth Hostels Association (SYHA), 7 Glebe Cres., Stirling FK8 2JA (☎01786 891 400; fax 891 333; www.syha.org.uk). £6.

Youth Hostels Association, Trevelyan House, Dimple Rd., Matlock, Devonshire DE4 3YH (☎01629 592 600; www.yha.org.uk). For England and Wales. £13, under 18 £6.50.

Hostelling International Northern Ireland (HINI), 22-32 Donegall Rd., Belfast BT12 5JN (☎02890 315 435; fax 439 699; www.hini.org.uk). £10, under 18 £6.

Hostelling International-American Youth Hostels (HI-AYH), 733 15th St. NW, #840, Washington, D.C. 20005 (☎202-783-6161; www.hiayh.org). US$25, under 18 free.

Independent hostels tend to attract younger crowds, be located closer to city centers, and have a much more relaxed attitude about lockouts or curfews than their YHA or An Óige counterparts. On the other hand, they may not have single-sex rooms, nor be as family-oriented. A number of Irish hostels belong to the **IHH (Independent Holiday Hostels)** organization. IHH hostels require no membership card, accept all ages, and usually have no lockout or curfew; all are Bord Fáilte-approved. For a free booklet with complete descriptions of IHH hostels, contact the IHH office at 57 Lower Gardiner St., Dublin 1 (☎ 01 836 4700; www.hostels-ireland.com). A useful website for hostel listings throughout the UK is **Backpackers UK** (www.backpackers.co.uk). **Hostels.com** (www.hostels.com) and **Eurotrip** (www.eurotrip.com/hostels) are other comprehensive websites. For an extensive list of independent hostels in Britain and Ireland, see *The Independent Hostel Guide: Britain & Europe* (The Backpackers Press, £4.95).

BED AND BREAKFASTS (B&BS)

For a cozier alternative to impersonal hotel rooms, B&Bs and guest houses (often private homes with rooms available to travelers) range from the acceptable to the sublime. B&B owners sometimes go out of their way to be accommodating, giving personalized tours or offering home-cooked meals. Some B&Bs, however, do not provide private bathrooms (rooms with private baths are referred to as **ensuite**) and most do not provide phones. A **double** room has one large bed for two people; a **twin** has two separate beds. The cheapest rooms in British B&Bs cost £12-20 for a single—not always easy to find—and £20-40 for a double. London, as always, boasts a stratospheric price range all its own. In Ireland, expect to pay €12-18 for a single. *Let's Go* lists B&B prices by room type unless otherwise stated.

You can book B&Bs by calling directly or by asking the local **tourist information centre** (TIC) to help you find accommodations; most can also book B&Bs in other towns. TICs usually charge a 10% deposit on the first night's or the entire stay's price, deductible from the amount you pay the B&B proprietor. Often a flat fee of £1-3 is added on. In Wales, a £1 fee is always added to the 10%.

The British tourist boards operate a B&B **rating system**, using a scale of one to five diamonds (in England) or stars (in Scotland and Wales). Rated accommodations get to be part of the tourist board's booking system, but don't treat these ratings as the final word. It costs money to be rated; some perfectly good small B&Bs choose not to participate. Approval by the Tourist Board is legally

ESSENTIALS

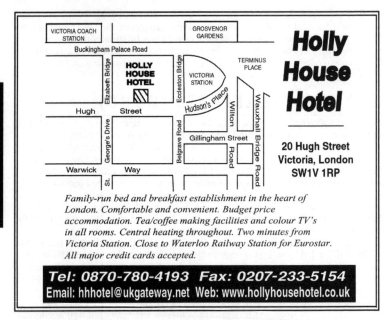

Holly House Hotel

20 Hugh Street
Victoria, London
SW1V 1RP

Family-run bed and breakfast establishment in the heart of London. Comfortable and convenient. Budget price accommodation. Tea/coffee making facilities and colour TV's in all rooms. Central heating throughout. Two minutes from Victoria Station. Close to Waterloo Railway Station for Eurostar. All major credit cards accepted.

Tel: 0870-780-4193 Fax: 0207-233-5154
Email: hhhotel@ukgateway.net Web: www.hollyhousehotel.co.uk

required of all Northern Ireland accommodations. Bord Fáilte's standards are very specific and, in some cases, far higher than budget travelers expect—approved accommodations in the Republic are marked with a green shamrock. Most TICs in Ireland will refer only to approved accommodations; some may not tell you how to get to an unapproved hostel, B&B, or campground. For more info on B&Bs, see **InnFinder** (US ☎608-285-6600; fax 285-6601; www.innfinder.com) or **InnSite** (www.innsite.com).

OTHER TYPES OF ACCOMMODATIONS

HOTELS, GUEST HOUSES, AND PENSIONS

Basic **hotel singles** in Britain cost about £70 per night, doubles £95. You'll typically share a hall bathroom; a private bathroom may cost extra. Some hotels offer "full pension" (all meals) and "half pension" (no lunch). Smaller **guest houses** and **pensions** are often cheaper than hotels. If you make **reservations** in writing, indicate your night of arrival and the number of nights you plan to stay. The hotel will send you a confirmation and may request payment for the first night. Not all hotels take reservations, and few accept checks in foreign currency.

UNIVERSITY DORMS

Many universities open their residence halls to travelers when school is not in session (mid-June to mid-October, and sometimes for the Christmas and Easter holidays); some do so even during term-time. These dorms offer the privacy of personal space, are often close to student areas, and are usually clean, though many do not offer private bathrooms. Getting a room may take a couple of phone calls and require advanced planning, but rates tend to be low. *Let's Go* lists dorm rooms where available, and **Venuemasters,** The Workstation, Paternoster Row, Sheffield S1 2BX (☎0114 249 3090; www.venuemasters.co.uk), has a list of rates and schedules on their website.

HOME EXCHANGES

Home exchange offers the traveler various types of homes (houses, apartments, condominiums, villas, even castles in some cases), plus the opportunity to live like a native and to cut down on accommodation costs. For more information, contact **HomeExchange.Com** (US ☎800-877-9723; www.homeexchange.com), **Intervac International Home Exchange** (UK ☎01225 892 011, Ireland ☎041 983 0930; www.intervac.com), or **The Invented City: International Home Exchange,** 41 Sutter St., San Francisco, CA 94404, USA (☎800-788-CITY (2489), elsewhere US collect ☎415-252-1141; www.invented-city.com). Home exchange services generally charge a fee to list your home, though you may be able to browse listings for free.

CAMPING AND THE OUTDOORS

Britain and Ireland have quite a number of campsites, which sadly tend to be a hike away from many of the popular sights and cities. Campsites are often privately owned, with basic sites costing £3 per person, and posh ones costing up to £10 per person. Since much of the land in national parks is privately owned, never pitch your tent in a park without permission.

USEFUL PUBLICATIONS AND RESOURCES

An excellent general resource for travelers planning on camping or spending significant time in the outdoors is the **Great Outdoor Recreation Pages** (www.gorp.com). Contact the publishers and organizations listed below for further information on camping, hiking, and biking.

GET CARD.

TRAVEL HARD.

SCENIC DRIVE

FOOD + GAS

LOOKOUT

There's only one way to max out your travel experience and make the most of your time on the road: The International Student Identity Card.

 Packed with travel discounts, benefits and services, this card will keep your travel days and your wallet full. Get it before you hit it!

Visit **ISICUS.com** to get the full story on the benefits of carrying the ISIC.

90 minutes, wash & dry (one sock missing).
5 minutes to book online (Detroit to Mom's)

Save money & time on student and faculty
travel at **StudentUniverse.com**

 StudentUniverse.com   Real Travel Deals

Automobile Association, Contact Centre, Car Ellison House, William Armstrong Drive, Newcastle-upon-Tyne NE4 7YA, UK. (General info ☎0870 600 0371; fax 0191 235 5111; www.theaa.co.uk). Publishes *Caravan and Camping Britain & Ireland* (£10) as well as road atlases and numerous outdoors guides.

The Caravan Club, East Grinstead House, East Grinstead, West Sussex, RH19 1UA, UK (☎01342 326 944; fax 410 258; www.caravanclub.co.uk). For £27.50, members receive equipment discounts, a directory and handbook, and a monthly magazine.

Ordnance Survey (☎08456 050 505; worldwide helpline ☎023 8079 2912; www.ordsvy.gov.uk). Britain's national mapping agency (also known as OS) publishes topographical maps, available at TICs and National Park Information Centres (NPICs) and many bookstores. Their excellent *Explorer* (£7) and *Pathfinder* (£4.50) map series cover the whole of Britain in detailed 1:25,000 scale.

Sierra Club Books, 85 Second St., 2nd Fl., San Francisco, CA 94105, USA (☎415-977-5500; www.sierraclub.org/books). Publishes general resource books on hiking and camping, and for women traveling in the outdoors.

The Mountaineers Books, 1001 SW Klickitat Way, #201, Seattle, WA 98134, USA (☎800-553-4453 or 206-223-6303; fax 223-6306; www.mountaineersbooks.org). Over 400 titles on hiking, biking, mountaineering, natural history, and conservation.

NATIONAL PARKS

Seeing the national parks of Britain, including the well-known Lake District, Peak District, and Snowdonia, is well worth the journey from London. The parks are in large part privately owned, but generally provide expansive areas for public use. There are 12 national parks in England and Wales (a number always growing). Scotland has traditionally designated National Scenic Areas; however the Trossachs and Loch Lomond and the Cairngorms were named its first national parks in July 2002. Each park is administrated by its own National Park Authority.

Association of National Park Authorities, 126 Bute Street, Cardiff, CF10 5LE (☎029 2049 9966; fax 029 2049 9980; www.anpa.gov.uk). The overarching organization for the National Park Authorities.

Council for National Parks, 246 Lavender Hill, London, SW11 1LJ (☎020 7924 4077; fax 020 7924 5761; www.cnp.org.uk). Umbrella organization for more than 40 groups working to promote and protect Britain's national parks.

National Trust, 36 Queen Anne's Gate, London, SW1H 9AS (☎020 7222 9251; fax 020 7222 5097; www.nationaltrust.org.uk). Private charity that owns and protects much of Britain's countryside and coastline, including parts of the national parks, as well as numerous historic sites. One-year membership £32.50.

National Trust for Scotland, Wemyss House, 28 Charlotte Square, Edinburgh EH2 4ET (☎0131 243 9300; fax 0131 243 9301; www.nts.org.uk). Charitable organization that promotes the preservation of Scotland's natural and cultural sites. Membership £30.

WILDERNESS SAFETY

Stay warm, stay dry, and stay hydrated to avoid the vast majority of life-threatening wilderness situations. Pack raingear, hat and mittens, first-aid kit, reflector, high energy food, and extra water for any hike. Dress in wool or layers of synthetic materials designed for the outdoors; never rely on cotton in wet weather.

To avoid **hypothermia,** keep dry, wear layers, and stay out of the wind. *Do not let hypothermia victims fall asleep.* When the temperature is below freezing, watch out for **frostbite.** If skin turns white, waxy, and cold, do not rub the area. Drink warm beverages and slowly warm the area with dry fabric or steady body contact until a doctor can be found. **Heat exhaustion** can lead to fatigue, headaches, and wooziness. Avoid it by drinking plenty of fluids, eating salty foods (e.g. crackers), and avoiding dehydrating beverages (e.g. alcohol and caffeinated beverages). Continuous heat stress can eventually lead to **heatstroke,** characterized by a rising temperature, severe headache, and cessation of sweating. Victims should be cooled off with wet towels and taken to a doctor. Be aware of insects—particularly fleas and lice—in wet or forested areas. Tick bites may cause **Lyme disease,** a bacterial infection marked by a circular bull's-eye rash.

Check **weather forecasts** and pay attention to the skies when hiking, since conditions can change suddenly. Let someone know when and where you are going hiking—either a friend, your hostel, a park ranger, or a local hiking organization. Do not attempt a hike beyond your ability. Remember also that you'll have to carry everything you pack, and carrying an excessive amount of equipment or supplies may hurt more than it will help—be smart about what you bring with you.

If you do get in trouble in the wilderness and can reach a phone, **call ☎999.** If not, six blasts on a **whistle** are standard to summon help (three are the reply); a constant long blast also indicates distress.

CAMPING AND HIKING EQUIPMENT

WHAT TO BUY...

Good camping equipment is both sturdy and light. Camping equipment is generally more expensive in Britain and Ireland than in North America.

Sleeping Bag: Most sleeping bags are rated by season. They are made of **down** (warmer and lighter, but more expensive and miserable when wet) or of **synthetic** material (heavier, more durable, and warmer when wet). Prices range US$80-210 for a summer synthetic to US$250-300 for a good down winter bag. **Sleeping bag pads** include foam pads (US$10-20), air mattresses (US$15-50), and self-inflating pads (US$45-80).

Tent: The best tents are free-standing (with their own frames and suspension systems), set up quickly, and only require staking in high winds. Low-profile dome tents are the best all-around. Good 2-person tents start at US$90, 4-person tents at US$300. Seal your tent seams with waterproofer, and make sure it has a rain fly. Other tent accessories include a **battery-operated lantern,** a **plastic groundcloth,** and a **nylon tarp.**

Backpack: Internal-frame packs mold better to your back, lower your center of gravity, and flex adequately to allow you to hike difficult trails. **External-frame packs** are more comfortable for long hikes over even terrain, as they keep weight higher and distribute it more evenly. Make sure your pack has a strong, padded hip-belt to transfer weight to your legs. Sturdy backpacks cost anywhere from US$125-420—this is one area in which it doesn't pay to economize. Buy a **waterproof backpack cover** or store all of your belongings in plastic bags inside your pack.

Boots: Wear hiking boots with good **ankle support.** They should fit snugly and comfortably over 1-2 pairs of wool socks and thin liner socks. Break them in over several weeks before you leave to spare yourself painful blisters.

Other Necessities: Synthetic layers, like those made of polypropylene, and a **pile jacket** will keep you warm even when wet. A **"space blanket"** helps retain body heat and doubles as a groundcloth (US$5-15). Plastic **water bottles** are virtually shatter- and leak-proof. Bring **water-purification tablets** for when you can't boil water. Most British and Irish campsites forbid fires or the gathering of firewood, so you'll need a **camp stove** and a propane-filled **fuel bottle.** For campgrounds with campfire sites, you may want a small **metal grate** or grill. Don't forget a **first-aid kit, pocketknife, insect repellent, calamine lotion,** and **waterproof matches** or a **lighter.**

...AND WHERE TO BUY IT

The mail-order/online companies listed below offer lower prices than many retail stores, but a visit to a local camping or outdoors store will give you a good sense of the look and weight of certain items.

Campmor, 28 Parkway, P.O. Box 700, Upper Saddle River, NJ 07458, USA (US ☎888-226-7667; elsewhere call US ☎201-825-8300; www.campmor.com).

Discount Camping, 880 Main North Rd., Pooraka, South Australia 5095, Australia (☎08 8262 3399; fax 8260 6240; www.discountcamping.com.au).

Eastern Mountain Sports (EMS), 1 Vose Farm Rd., Peterborough, NH 03458, USA (☎888-463-6367 or 603-924-7231; www.shopems.com).

Mountain Designs, 51 Bishop St., Kelvin Grove, Queensland 4059, Australia (☎07 3856 2344; fax 3856 0366; www.mountaindesigns.com).

Recreational Equipment, Inc. (REI), Sumner, WA 98352, USA (☎800-426-4840 or 253-891-2500; www.rei.com).

YHA Adventure Shop, 152-160 Wardour St., London, W1F 8YA, UK (☎020 7025 1900; www.yhaadventure.com). Main branch of one of Britain's largest outdoors suppliers.

CAMPERS, RVS, AND CARAVANS

Renting a camper van (RV in the US) is always more expensive than tenting or hosteling, but it's cheaper than staying in hotels and renting a car (see **Renting or Leasing a Car,** p. 38), and the convenience of bringing along your own bedroom, bathroom, and kitchen makes it an attractive option, especially for older travelers and families with children. Rates vary widely by region, season (July and August are the most expensive months), and type of van; contact several companies to compare vehicles and prices. **Auto Europe** (US ☎800-223-5555; UK ☎0800 169 6414; www.autoeurope.com) rents caravans in London.

ORGANIZED ADVENTURE TRIPS

Organized adventure tours offer another way of exploring the wild. Activities include hiking, biking, skiing, canoeing, kayaking, rafting, climbing, photo safaris, and archaeological digs. **Specialty Travel Index** (US ☎800-442-4922 or 415-459-4900; info@specialtytravel.com; www.specialtytravel.com) lists more than 500 adventure and specialty tour operators worldwide; tourist bureaus and outdoors organizations are also good sources of information.

KEEPING IN TOUCH

BY MAIL

SENDING MAIL FROM BRITAIN AND IRELAND

Airmail is the best way to send mail home from Britain and Ireland—mark the envelope "air mail" or "par avion." From Britain, postcards cost 37p to send within Europe and 40p to the rest of the world; airmail letters (up to 20g) are 37p within Europe and 65p to the rest of the world. **Aerogrammes,** printed sheets that fold into envelopes and travel via airmail (40p), are available at post offices. **Surface mail** is by far the cheapest and slowest way to send mail. It takes one to three months to cross the Atlantic and two to four to cross the Pacific—good for items like souvenirs that you won't need to see for a while.

ENVIRONMENTALLY RESPONSIBLE TOURISM. The idea behind responsible tourism is to leave no trace of human presence. A campstove is a safer (and more efficient) way to cook than using vegetation, but if you must make a fire, keep it small and use only dead branches or brush. Make sure your campsite is at least 150 ft. from water supplies or bodies of water. If there are no toilet facilities, bury human waste (but not paper) at least 4 in. deep and above the high-water line, 150 ft. or more from water sources and campsites. Pack your trash in a plastic bag and carry it with you until you reach a trash receptacle. For more information, contact one of the organizations listed below.

Earthwatch, 3 Clock Tower Place #100, Box 75, Maynard, MA 01754, USA (☎800-776-0188 or 978-461-0081; www.earthwatch.org).

International Ecotourism Society, 28 Pine St., Burlington, VT 05402, USA (☎802-651-9818; fax 651-9819; www.ecotourism.org).

National Audubon Society, Nature Odysseys, 700 Broadway, New York, NY 10003, USA (☎212-979-3000; fax 979-3188; www.audubon.org).

Tourism Concern, Stapleton House, 277-281 Holloway Rd., London N7 8HN, UK (☎020 7753 3330; fax 7753 3331; www.tourismconcern.org.uk).

SENDING MAIL TO BRITAIN AND IRELAND

Sending postcards and letters to Britain and Ireland via airmail costs approximately $0.70-0.80 from the US, $1.25-1.75 from Canada, $1-1.50 from Australia, and $1.50-3 from New Zealand (prices in local currency). Airmail from overseas should reach Britain or Ireland in 7-10 days. In addition to the standard postage system, **Federal Express** (www.fedex.com; Australia ☎13 26 10; US and Canada ☎800-247-4747; New Zealand ☎0800 73 33 39; UK ☎0800 123 800) handles express mail services from most countries to Britain and Ireland; for example, they can get a letter from New York to London in two days for US$28.50.

RECEIVING MAIL IN BRITAIN AND IRELAND

There are several ways to arrange pick-up of letters sent to you by friends and relatives while you are abroad. Mail can be sent via **Poste Restante** (General Delivery) to almost any city or town in Britain and Ireland with a post office. Address Poste Restante letters like so: William SHAKESPEARE, Poste Restante, 2/3 Henley St., Stratford-upon-Avon CV37 6PU, UK. The mail will go to a special desk in the central post office, unless you specify a post office by street address or post code, as in the example above. It's best to use the largest post office, since mail may be sent there regardless. It is usually safer and quicker, though more expensive, to send mail express or registered. Bring your passport (or other photo ID) for pick-up. The UK national inquiries number for post offices is ☎08457 223 344. *Let's Go* lists post offices in the **Practical Information** section for each city and most towns.

   American Express travel offices throughout the world offer a free **Client Letter Service** (mail held up to 30 days and forwarded upon request) for cardholders who contact them in advance. Some offices will offer these services to non-cardholders (especially AmEx Traveler's Cheque holders), but call ahead to make sure. *Let's Go* lists AmEx office locations for most large cities in **Practical Information** sections; for a complete, free list, call ☎800-528-4800.

BY TELEPHONE

INTERNATIONAL CALLING

A **calling card** is probably your cheapest bet. You can frequently call collect even if you don't own a company's calling card just by calling their access number (often posted in phone booths) and following the instructions. To **call home with a calling card,** contact the operator for your service provider in Britain or Ireland by dialing their toll-free access number. Many newsagents in the UK sell **prepaid international phonecards,** such as those offered by Swiftcall. These cards are usually the cheapest way to make long international phone calls, but sometimes carry a minimum charge per call, which make quick calls less cost-effective. Stores such as **Call Shop** offer cheap international calls from their booths, and can be found in parts of cities with large numbers of tourists or immigrants.

You can make direct international calls from **payphones,** but if you aren't using a calling card you may need to drop your coins as quickly as your words. **BT phonecards** and occasionally major credit cards can also be used for direct international calls, but are less cost-efficient. In-room **hotel calls** invariably include an arbitrary, sky-high surcharge (as much as £6); the rare B&B that has in-room phones tends to be less expensive, but still more costly than using calling cards. See the box (below) for directions on how to place a direct international call. Placing a **collect call** through an international operator is even more expensive, but may be necessary in an emergency. The number for the **international operator** in Britain is ☎ 155.

PLACING INTERNATIONAL CALLS. To call Britain and Ireland from home or to call home from Britain and Ireland, dial:

1. The **international dialing prefix.** To dial *out of* Australia, dial 0011; Canada or the US, 011; the Republic of Ireland, New Zealand, or the UK, 00; South Africa, 09.
2. The **country code** of the country you want to call. To *place a call to* Australia, dial 61; Canada or the US, 1; the Republic of Ireland, 353; New Zealand, 64; South Africa, 27; the UK, 44.
3. The **city/area code.** *Let's Go* lists the city/area codes for cities and towns in Britain and Ireland opposite the city or town name, next to a ☎. If the first digit is a zero (e.g., 020 for London), omit the zero when calling from abroad (e.g., dial 20 from Canada to reach London).
4. The **local number.**
5. **Examples:** To call the US embassy in London from New York, dial 011 44 20 7499 9000. To call the British embassy in New York from London, dial 00 1 202 588 6500.

Let's Go has recently partnered with **ekit.com** to provide a calling card that offers a number of services, including e-mail and voice messaging. Before purchasing any calling card, always be sure to compare rates with other cards, and to make sure it serves your need. For more information, visit www.letsgo.ekit.com.

CALLING WITHIN BRITAIN AND IRELAND

To make a call within a city or town, just dial the number; from outside the region, dial the phone code and the number. For **directory inquiries,** which are free from payphones, call ☎ 192 in the UK or ☎ 1190 in Ireland. *Let's Go* lists phone codes opposite the city or town name next to the ☎ symbol; all phone numbers in that town use that phone code unless specified otherwise. To call Britain from the

ESSENTIALS

Republic of Ireland, or vice versa, you will have to make an international call. Northern Ireland is part of the UK phone network, and calls there should be treated like calls to any other part of the UK.

PHONE CODES. Recent changes to British phone codes have produced a system in which the first three numbers of the phone code identify the type of number being called. **Premium rate calls,** costing about 50p per minute, can be identified by their 090x phone code, while **freephone** (toll-free) numbers have a 080x code. Numbers with the 084x code incur the **local call rate,** while calling the 087x code incurs the **national call rate** (the two aren't significantly different for short calls). Your British friends might give you their **mobile phone** (cell phone) number; note that calling a mobile is more expensive than a regular phone call. All mobile phone numbers carry 077, 078, or 079 codes, and pager numbers begin with 076.

Note that several regions underwent recent phone code changes. London (020), Cardiff (029), Coventry (024), Portsmouth and Southampton (023), and Northern Ireland (028) began using their new codes in April 2000. *Let's Go* lists all new area codes, but you might see old codes listed in brochures and advertising.

PUBLIC PHONES IN BRITAIN. Public payphones in Britain are mostly run by **British Telecom (BT),** recognizable by the ubiquitous piper logo, although in larger cities you may find some run by upstart competitors such as Mercury. Many public phones in the UK now only accept **phonecards** or credit cards. The BT phonecard, available in denominations from £3 to £20, is a useful purchase, since BT phones tend to be omnipresent. Still, it's a good idea to carry some change in addition to a BT phonecard, since non-BT phones will not accept the phonecards.

Public phones charge a minimum of 10p for calls and don't accept 1p, 2p, or 5p coins. The dial tone is a continuous purring sound; a repeated double-tone means the line is ringing. A series of harsh beeps will warn you to insert more money when your time is up. For the rest of the call, the digital display ticks off your credit in suspenseful 1p increments. You may use remaining credit on a second call by pressing the "follow on call" button (often marked "FC"). Otherwise, once you hang up, your remaining phonecard credit is rounded down to the nearest 10p, or unused coins are returned. Pay phones do *not* give change—if you use 22p out of a 50p coin, the remaining 28p is gone once you put the receiver down.

PUBLIC PHONES IN IRELAND. Using Irish pay phones can be tricky. Public coin phones will give you back unused coins (but not fractions of coins; don't insert a €1 coin for a 20 cent call), but private pay phones (called "one-armed bandits") in hostels and restaurants do not. Do not insert money into any pay phone until asked to or until the call goes through. The frightening pip-pip noise the phone makes as you wait for it to start ringing is normal. Local calls cost 20 cents on public phones; "one-armed bandits" can charge 30 cents, or whatever they please. Local calls are not unlimited—one unit pays for four minutes.

The smart option for non-local calls is buying a **prepaid phone card,** which carries a certain amount of phone time depending on the card's denomination. The time is measured in minutes or talk units (e.g. one unit/one minute), and the card usually has a toll-free access telephone number and a personal identification number (PIN). Newsagents sell phone cards in denominations of €2, €5, €10, or €20. Card phones have a digital display that ticks off the perilous plunge your units are taking. When the unit number starts flashing, you may push the eject button on the card phone; you can then pull out your expired calling card and replace it with a fresh one. If you try to wait until your card's units fall to zero, you'll be disconnected. Eject your card early and use the remaining unit or two for a local call.

TIME DIFFERENCES

Britain and Ireland are on **Greenwich Mean Time (GMT)**. GMT is five hours ahead of New York, eight hours ahead of Vancouver and San Francisco, two hours behind Johannesburg, ten hours behind Sydney, and 12 hours behind Auckland, although the actual time differences depend on local time observances, such as daylight savings time. Both Britain and Ireland observe **daylight savings time** between the last Sunday of March and the last Sunday of October.

BY E-MAIL AND INTERNET

ESSENTIALS

Britain is one of the world's most connected countries, and cyber cafes or public terminals can be found in all larger cities (*Let's Go* lists them under **Internet Access** in the **Practical Information** section of cities and towns). They tend to cost £4-6 an hour, but often you pay only for time used, not for the whole hour. Cyber cafes can also be found in the larger cities of Ireland and cost €4-6 per hour. Many hostels are also starting to offer Internet service to their residents, charging about the same rates. **Libraries** usually have Internet access, often at lower rates than cyber cafes; the downside is that you might have to wait, or even make an advance reservation, to use their computers.

Although in some places it's possible to forge a remote link with your home server, in most cases this is a much slower (and thus more expensive) option than taking advantage of free **web-based e-mail accounts** (e.g., www.hotmail.com and www.yahoo.com). Two online guides to cyber cafes in Britain and Ireland—updated daily—are **The Cybercafe Search Engine** (www.cybercaptive.com) and **Cybercafes.com** (www.cybercafes.com).

SPECIFIC CONCERNS

If you need to talk confidentially about emotional problems, the **Samaritans** number in the UK is ☎ 08457 909 090; in Ireland ☎ 1850 609 090. Both are open 24hr., and can also refer you to appropriate resources.

WOMEN TRAVELERS

Britain and Ireland are among the world's best destinations for women travelers. Women exploring on their own, however, inevitably face some additional safety concerns, particularly in larger cities such as London, Cardiff, Glasgow, Belfast, and Dublin. The following suggestions shouldn't discourage women from traveling alone—it's easy to keep your sense of adventure without taking undue risks.

Stick to **centrally located accommodations** and avoid solitary late-night treks or metro/Tube rides. You might consider staying in places that offer single rooms that lock from the inside. Some hostels offer safer communal showers than others; check them before settling in. Always carry extra money for a phone call, bus, or taxi. If catching a bus at night, wait at a well-populated stop. Choose train or Tube compartments occupied by other women or couples. **Hitchhiking** is never safe for a lone woman, or even for two women traveling together.

Carry a **whistle** on your keychain or a **rape alarm** (about £10), and don't hesitate to use it in an emergency. Mace and pepper sprays are illegal in Britain. The national **emergency** number is ☎ 999. The **Rape Crisis Federation Wales and England** (☎ 0115 934 8474, www.rapecrisis.co.uk) provides referrals to local rape crisis and sexual abuse counseling services throughout the UK; the **Dublin Rape Crisis Centre** helpline is ☎1800 778 888. *Let's Go* lists other hotlines in the **Practical Information** section of our city write-ups. An **IMPACT Model Mugging** self-defense course can prepare you for a potential attack, as well as raise your confidence and your level of awareness of your surroundings (see **Self Defense**, p. 18).

WOMEN'S HEALTH. Women traveling are vulnerable to **urinary tract** and **bladder infections,** common and very uncomfortable bacterial conditions that cause a burning sensation and painful (sometimes frequent) urination. Over-the-counter medicines can sometimes alleviate symptoms, but if they persist, see a doctor. Women who need an **abortion** or **emergency contraception** while in the UK should call the **fpa** (formerly the Family Planning Association) helpline (☎0845 310 1334, M-F 9am-7pm), visit the website (www.fpa.org.uk), or contact the London office, 2-12 Pentonville Rd., N1 9PF (☎020 7837 5432), for more information. Abortions are illegal in Ireland; call the London office if you need help.

TRAVELING ALONE

There are many benefits to traveling alone, including independence and greater interaction with locals. On the other hand, any solo traveler is a more vulnerable target of harassment and street theft. As a lone traveler, look confident, be especially careful in deserted or very crowded areas, and try not to stand out as a tourist. Never admit that you are traveling alone. Maintain regular contact with someone at home who knows your itinerary.

For the socially-inclined, backpacker bus tours (see p. 38) are a good way to meet people. For more tips, get any of the numerous books written on traveling alone, or subscribe to **Connecting: Solo Travel Network,** 689 Park Road, Unit 6, Gibsons, BC V0N 1V7, Canada (☎604-886-9099; www.cstn.org; membership US$35). **Travel Companion Exchange,** P.O. Box 833, Amityville, NY 11701, USA (☎631-454-0880, or in the US ☎800-392-1256; www.whytravelalone.com; US$48), will link solo travelers with companions with similar travel habits and interests.

OLDER TRAVELERS

Senior citizens are often eligible for a wide range of discounts on transportation, sights, restaurants, and accommodations. Discount prices are sometimes listed under "concessions" or "OAPs" (Old Age Pensioners). If you don't see a senior-citizen price listed, ask, and you may be delightfully surprised. The British Tourist Authority devotes a portion of its American site (www.travelbritain.org) to mature travelers. A useful resource while traveling in Britain is the information line of the national pressure group **Age Concern** (☎0800 009 966). Two British magazines targeted to the growing older population are *Yours*, a nostalgic, middle-of-the-road publication, and Richard Ingrams's hilariously dour *The Oldie*.

Agencies for senior group travel are growing in enrollment and popularity. These are only a few:

Elderhostel, 11 Ave. de Lafayette, Boston, MA 02111, USA (☎877-426-8056; www.elderhostel.org). Organizes 1- to 4-week "educational adventures" in Britain and Ireland on varied subjects for those 55+.

The Mature Traveler, P.O. Box 15791, Sacramento, CA 95852, USA (☎800-460-6676). Deals, discounts, and travel packages for the 50+ traveler. Subscription US$30.

Walking the World, P.O. Box 1186, Fort Collins, CO 80522, USA (☎800-340-9255; www.walkingtheworld.com), organizes outdoors trips for 50+ travelers to Ireland and other destinations.

ESSENTIALS

BISEXUAL, GAY, & LESBIAN TRAVELERS

Britain has long had an open and accepting gay scene, but even this is far from perfect. As is true elsewhere, people in rural areas of Britain and Ireland may not be as accepting of gay travelers as those in big cities. Public displays of affection in Ireland and most of Britain may bring you verbal harassment. The legal age of consent for homosexual and heterosexual sex is 16 in the UK.

Large cities, notably London, Dublin, Edinburgh, Manchester, and Brighton, are far more open to gay culture than rural Britain, though evidence of bigotry and violence remains. The events magazine *Time Out* has a Gay Listings section, and numerous bisexual-, gay-, and lesbian-specific periodicals make it easy to learn about the current concerns of Britain's gay community. The *Pink Paper* (free) is available from newsagents in larger cities, covering stories of interest to the pink community. *Gay Times* (£3) covers political issues; *Diva* (£2.25) is a monthly lesbian lifestyle magazine with an excellent mix of features and good listings. **Out and About** (www.outandabout.com) offers a bi-weekly newsletter for gay and lesbian travelers and a comprehensive website. Listed below are organizations and mail-order bookstores which offer materials addressing specific concerns.

British Tourist Authority (US ☎800-462-2748, see p. 11) devotes a portion of its American site (www.travelbritain.org) to gay and lesbian travel information and publishes the guide *Britain: Inside & Out*. Visit www.gaybritain.org.

Gay's the Word, 66 Marchmont St., London WC1N 1AB, UK (☎020 7278 7654; www.gaystheword.co.uk). The largest gay and lesbian bookshop in the UK, with both fiction and non-fiction titles. Mail-order service available.

Giovanni's Room, 1145 Pine St., Philadelphia, PA 19107, USA (☎215-923-2960; www.queerbooks.com). An international gay and lesbian bookstore, mail-order service.

International Gay and Lesbian Travel Association, (US ☎954-776-2626 or 800-448-8550; www.iglta.com). An organization of over 1350 companies serving gay and lesbian travelers worldwide. Call for lists of travel agents, accommodations, and events.

Ireland's Pink Pages (www.pink-pages.org). Ireland's web-based bisexual, gay, and lesbian directory. Extensive urban and regional info for both the Republic and the North.

London Lesbian and Gay Switchboard (☎020 7837 7324; www.llgs.org.uk). Confidential advice, information, and referrals. Open 24hr.

International Lesbian and Gay Association (ILGA), 81 rue Marché-au-Charbon, B-1000 Brussels, Belgium (☎+32 2 502 2471; www.ilga.org). Provides political information, such as homosexuality laws of individual countries.

TRAVELERS WITH DISABILITIES

With a little advance planning, Britain and Ireland can be quite accessible to travelers with disabilities. **Rail** may be the most convenient form of travel: many stations have ramps, and some trains have wheelchair lifts, special seating areas, and specially equipped toilets. Large stations in Britain are equipped with wheelchair facilities, and selected routes are designated accessible; call ahead to check and make reservations. The National Rail website (www.nationalrail.co.uk) provides general information for travelers with disabilities as well as assistance phone numbers for individual rail companies; it also describes the Disabled Persons Railcard (£14), which allows the bearer and a companion one-third off most fares. Most major trains in the Republic of Ireland are accessible. **Bus** travel is also an option—most transportation companies are conscientious about providing facilities and services to meet the needs of travelers with disabilities and will provide assistance if notified ahead of time. National Express is conducting accessibility trials in preparation for regulations going into effect in 2005; call the Additional Needs Help Line (☎0121 423 8479) for information and bookings. The London **Underground** is slowly improving accessibility; Transport for London Access & Mobility (☎020 7941 4600) can provide information on public transportation within the city. Some major **car rental** agencies (Hertz, Avis, and National), as well as local agencies, such as Wheelchair Travel in Surrey (☎01483 233 640), can provide and deliver hand-controlled cars.

The British Tourist Boards have begun rating accommodations and attractions using the **National Accessible Scheme** (NAS), which designates three categories of accessibility. Look for the NAS symbols in Tourist Board guidebooks, or ask a site directly for their ranking. Many **theaters** and performance venues have space for wheelchairs; some larger theatrical performances include special facilities for the hearing-impaired. Guide dogs fall under the new PETS regulations (see p. 14) concerning bringing animals to the UK.

USEFUL ORGANIZATIONS & TOUR AGENCIES

dial UK, St. Catherine's, Tickhill Road, South Yorkshire DN4 8QN, UK (☎01302 310 123; www.dialuk.org.uk). Network of local disability information and advice services in the UK.

Holiday Care Service, Imperial Bldg., Victoria Rd., Horley RH6 7PZ, UK (☎01293 774 535; reservation service 773 716; fax 784 647.) Provides information on site accessibility and books accommodations around the UK for travelers with disabilities.

Mobility International USA (MIUSA), P.O. Box 10767, Eugene, OR 97440, USA (☎541-343-1284, voice and TDD; www.miusa.org). Sells *A World of Options: A Guide to International Educational Exchange, Community Service, and Travel for Persons with Disabilities* (US$35).

Society for Accessible Travel & Hospitality (SATH), 347 Fifth Ave., #610, New York, NY 10016, USA (☎212-447-7284; www.sath.org). Advocacy group that publishes free online travel information and the travel magazine *Open World* (US$18, free for members). Annual membership US$45, students and seniors US$30.

Tripscope, The Vassall Centre, Gill Avenue, Bristol BS16 2QQ, UK (☎08457 585 641; outside UK ☎0117 939 7782; www.tripscope.org.uk). Provides transportation information for the elderly and disabled in the UK. Helpline available M-F 9am-5pm.

Directions Unlimited, 123 Green Ln., Bedford Hills, NY 10507, USA (☎800-533-5343). Books individual and group vacations for the physically disabled. Not an info service.

The Guided Tour Inc., 7900 Old York Rd., #114B, Elkins Park, PA 19027, USA (☎800-783-5841; www.guidedtour.com). Organizes travel programs for persons with developmental and physical challenges; destinations include London and Ireland.

MINORITY TRAVELERS

Minorities make up about 10% of Britain's population. The majority of Britain's ethnic communities are centered around London or other English cities. Ireland is only beginning to experience racial diversity, while rural Scotland and Wales remain predominantly white. Minority travelers should expect reduced anonymity in the latter regions, but onlookers are usually motivated by curiosity rather than ill will and should not cause you to alter your travel plans. Minorities will feel less conspicuous in London, Manchester, the university towns of Oxford and Cambridge, and other large English cities, though this is not to say that these cities do not have problems with racism. The **Commission for Racial Equality (CRE),** Elliot House, 10-12 Allington St., London SW1E 5EH (☎020 7828 7022; www.cre.gov.uk) offers a wide variety of publications on diversity and race relations and can provide advice to minority travelers who encounter harassment or discrimination.

TRAVELERS WITH CHILDREN

Family vacations usually require that you slow your pace and always require that you plan ahead. If you pick a B&B or a small hotel, call to make sure it allows children; if you rent a car, make sure the company provides a car seat. Your child should carry some sort of ID in case of an emergency or in case he or she gets lost. Many restaurants in Britain and Ireland have children's menus, and almost all tourist attractions have a children's rate. Children under two years generally fly for 10% of the adult fare, though this does not necessarily include a seat. International fares can be discounted 25% for children aged 2-11.

DIETARY CONCERNS

Vegetarians should have no problem finding meals in Britain and Ireland. Virtually all restaurants have vegetarian selections on their menus, and many cater specifically to vegetarians. *Let's Go* notes restaurants with good vegetarian selections. For more information about vegetarian travel, contact **The Vegetarian Society of the UK** (☎0161 925 2000; www.vegsoc.org) or the **North American Vegetarian Society** (☎518-568-7970; www.navs-online.org).

Travelers who keep **kosher** should contact synagogues in larger cities for information; your own synagogue or college Hillel should have access to lists of Jewish institutions across Britain and Ireland. The significant Orthodox communities in North London (in neighborhoods such as **Golders Green** or **Stamford Hill**), Leeds, and Manchester provide a market for kosher restaurants and grocers. Kosher options decrease in rural areas, but most restaurants and B&Bs will try to accommodate your dietary restrictions. The *Jewish Travel Guide* lists synagogues, kosher restaurants, and Jewish institutions in over 100 countries including Britain and Ireland (Vallentine-Mitchell Publishers, US$17).

WEB RESOURCES

Let's Go tries to cover all aspects of budget travel, but we can't put *everything* in our guides. Listed below are websites that can serve as jumping off points for your own research. Almost every aspect of budget travel (the most notable exception, of course, being experience) is accessible via the web. Listed here are some sites to start off your surfing; other relevant websites are listed throughout the book. Because website turnover is high, use search engines (such as **www.google.com**) to strike out on your own. You might also check our recommended reading lists (p. 5) for information of the printed variety.

 WWW.LETSGO.COM Our newly designed website now features the full online content of all of our guides. In addition, trial versions of all nine City Guides are available for download on Palm OS™ PDAs. Our website also contains our newsletter, links for photos and streaming video, online ordering of our titles, info about our books, and a travel forum buzzing with stories and tips.

INFORMATION ON BRITAIN AND IRELAND

The British and Irish Tourist Authorities as well as the tourist boards of England, Scotland, Wales, and Northern Ireland all have excellent websites (see p. 12).

British Information Services (BIS): www.usabritain.com. An encyclopedic living-and-traveling in Britain website maintained through the British Embassy in the US.

The British Council: www.britishcouncil.org. An indispensable resource on education, arts, and science in the UK. International branch sites include www.britain-usa.org.

Department for Culture, Media, and Sport (DCMS): www.culture.gov.uk. What to see and do in Britain, from movie filming locations to rugby matches to heritage libraries.

The National Trust: www.nationaltrust.org.uk. From the fine people who care for Britain's castles, gardens, museums, and natural wonders.

24 Hour Museum: www.24hourmuseum.org.uk. A database of more than 2500 museums and galleries throughout the UK.

Contours Walking Holidays: www.contours.co.uk. Walking holidays in England, Scotland, and Wales.

British Broadcasting Corporation: www.bbc.co.uk. What *don't* they do?

The London Times: www.timesonline.co.uk. For the worst of and best of.

The Irish Times: www.ireland.com. The Republic's major daily newspaper online.

CIA World Factbook: www.odci.gov/cia/publications/factbook. Tons of vital statistics on Britain and Ireland's geography, government, economy, and people.

Prickly Ball Farm: www.hedgehog.org.uk. Because they're so darned cute.

ALTERNATIVES TO TOURISM

Traveling may be a memorable experience, but *Let's Go* devotes this chapter to what may be even more rewarding ways to see the world. Working, volunteering, or studying for an extended period of time can be an opportunity to gain a deeper understanding of life in Britain and Ireland. Alternatives to Tourism outlines some of the different ways to get to know a place, whether you want to pay your way through, or just get the personal satisfaction that comes from studying and volunteering. In many cases, you will feel a part of something more meaningful and educational—something that the average budget traveler often misses out on.

The British Isles are an ideal place to cool your wanderlust and settle down for a time. The lack of a language barrier and the solid infrastructure make volunteering and working in Britain relatively painless. The academic reputations of universities like Oxford, Cambridge, and Trinity College Dublin are a draw to students from around the world and tend to foster large international populations.

> **VISA AND PERMIT INFORMATION**
> Citizens of the EU and of most Western countries do not need a **visa** to study in Britain and Ireland; you can check if a visa is required from your home country by visiting www.ukvisas.gov.uk. To work legally in Britain, most non-EU citizens must have a **work permit** (see p. 64). EU citizens may work without a permit in Britain. You should contact the British embassy or consulate in your home country for further information (see **Embassies and Consulates,** p. 10).

STUDYING ABROAD

Study abroad programs range from basic language and culture courses to college-level classes, often for credit. In order to choose a program that best fits your needs, you will want to research all you can before making your decision—determine costs and duration, as well as what kind of students participate in the program and what sort of accommodations are provided.

Fluent English-speakers should find it fairly easy to enroll directly in a British university, although getting college credit may be more difficult. Some American schools have strict requirements for credits obtained elsewhere; you should check with your school about specific conditions. A good resource for finding programs that cater to your particular interests is **www.studyabroad.com,** which has links to various semester abroad programs based on a variety of criteria, including desired location and focus of study. The **British Council** is an invaluable source of information for people wishing to study in the UK. (10 Spring Gardens, London SW1A 2BN; ☎0161 957 7755; www.britishcouncil.org.)

Students can be placed in a British university through an American program or university, or may choose to apply directly to a British school. The following is a list of organizations that can help arrange study abroad opportunities.

AMERICAN PROGRAMS

American Institute for Foreign Study, College Division, River Plaza, 9 West Broad St., Stamford, CT 06902, USA (☎800-727-2437, ext. 5163; www.aifsabroad.com). Organizes programs for high school and college study in universities abroad.

Arcadia University for Education Abroad, 450 S. Easton Rd., Glenside, PA 19038, USA (☎866-927-2234; www.arcadia.edu/cea). Costs range from US$2200 (summer) to US$29,000 (full-year).

Association of Commonwealth Universities (ACU), John Foster House, 36 Gordon Sq., London WC1H OPF (☎020 7380 6700; www.acu.ac.uk). Publishes information about Commonwealth universities, including those in the UK.

Central College Abroad, Office of International Education, 812 University, Pella, IA, 50219, USA (☎800-831-3629 or 641-628-5284; www.central.edu/abroad). Offers internships, as well as summer-, semester-, and year-long programs in England and Wales. US$25 application fee.

School for International Training, College Semester Abroad, Admissions, Kipling Rd., P.O. Box 676, Brattleboro, VT 05302, USA (☎800-336-1616 or 802-257-7751; www.sit.edu). Runs the **Experiment in International Living** (☎800-345-2929; fax 802-258-3428; www.usexperiment.org), 3- to 5-week summer programs that offer high-school students cross-cultural homestays, community service, ecological adventure, and language training in Britain and Ireland. US$1900-5000.

Council on International Educational Exchange (CIEE), 633 3rd Ave., 20th Fl., New York, NY 10017-6706 (☎800-407-8839; www.ciee.org/study) sponsors work, volunteer, academic, and internship programs.

International Association for the Exchange of Students for Technical Experience (IAESTE), 10400 Little Patuxent Pkwy. Suite 250, Columbia, MD 21044-3519, USA (☎410-997-2200; www.aipt.org). 8- to 12-week programs for college students who have completed 2 years of technical study. US$25 application fee.

PROGRAMS IN BRITAIN

Tens of thousands of international students study abroad in Britain every year, drawn by the prestige of some of the world's oldest and most renowned universities. **Oxford** and **Cambridge** are flooded year-round with students from all over the globe, participating in any number of programs. **London** has a bevy of universities, including the London School of Economics and University College London. Scotland offers its own share of ancient seats of learning, including **Edinburgh, St. Andrews,** and **Glasgow Universities.** Major Welsh universities include **Cardiff** and **Swansea.** Almost every other city in Britain has its own university, from **Nottingham** (recently voted the most popular school in the country) to **Bath** to **Newcastle.** Your best strategy is to contact the university which interests you—typically you'll want to get in touch with the school's International Office. The **British Council** (see p. 61) publishes numerous reports and pamphlets, including the e-Zine **Education UKOnline,** which is directed at US students interested in studying in Britain. The Council's US website, **www.britishcouncil-usa.org,** is another good place to look for advice, program openings, and contact information.

PROGRAMS IN IRELAND

Most American undergraduates enroll in Irish programs sponsored by US universities, though good local universities can be much cheaper. Some schools that offer study abroad programs to international students are listed below.

Irish Studies Summer School, at usit NOW, 19-21 Aston Quay, O'Connell Bridge, Dublin (☎01 602 1600). 7-week program offering courses in Irish culture and history.

National University of Ireland, Galway, University Rd., Galway (☎091 524 411; www.nuigalway.ie). Offers half- and full-year opportunities for junior-year students who meet the college's entry requirements. **Summer school** courses offered July-Aug. include Irish studies, education, and creative writing.

Queen's University Belfast, University Rd., Belfast BT7 1NN (International Office ☎028 9033 5415; www.qub.ac.uk). Study abroad in Belfast for a semester or year. A 4-week **Introduction to Northern Ireland** program in January covers the political, social, and economic questions unique to the North.

Trinity College Dublin, Office of International Student Affairs (☎01 608 2011/2683; www.tcd.ie/isa). Offers a 1-year program of undergraduate courses for visiting students.

University College Cork. Students from around the world are encouraged to enroll through **Cultural Experiences Abroad** (☎800-266-4441; www.gowithcea.com) for semester- or year-long programs in various disciplines

University College Dublin, International Summer School, Newman House, 86 St. Stephen's Green, Dublin (☎01 475 2004; www.ucd.ie/summerschool). Offers a 2-week international summer course examining Irish culture and tradition.

University of Ulster, Shore Rd., Newtownabbey, Antrim, BT37 0QB, Northern Ireland (☎028 9036 6151; www.ulst.ac.uk). Offers semester- or year-long programs for visiting international students.

LANGUAGE STUDY

Many come to Britain and Ireland to improve their English; others to study the various Celtic languages—Irish, Welsh, and Scottish Gaelic—of the Isles. The British Council has a special web site dedicated to English language education: **www.englishinbritain.co.uk.** Colleges and universities are excellent places to begin looking for language courses, but you'll also find many independently-run international or local organizations, which rarely offer college credit. Some language program organizations and schools include:

Eurocentres, 101 N. Union St., Ste. 300, Alexandria, VA 22314, USA (☎703-684-1494; www.eurocentres.com) or in Europe, Head Office, Seestr. 247, CH-8038 Zurich, Switzerland (☎+41 1 485 50 40; fax 481 61 24). Language programs for beginning to advanced students with homestays and work opportunities in Bournemouth, Brighton, Cambridge, London, and Oxford.

Clì—The New Gaels, North Tower, The Castle, Inverness IV2 3EU (☎01463 226 710; www.cli.org.uk). Organization for the promotion of Scottish Gaelic culture. Language courses offered; searchable database of Gaelic centers and classes on their website.

Sabhal Mór Ostaig, Teangue, Isle of Skye, IV44 8RQ (☎01471 888 000; fax 01471 888 001; www.smo.uhi.ac.uk). College on the Isle of Skye, offering long- and short-term courses in Gaelic language and culture. Fees for short-term Gaelic classes £120-200.

The University of Edinburgh, Office of Lifelong Learning, 11 Buccleuch Pl., Edinburgh EH8 9LW (☎0131 650 4400 or 0131 662 0783; www.cce.ed.ac.uk). Has a wide range of short-term classes including language courses.

School of Welsh, Trinity College Carmarthen, Wales SA31 3EP (☎0126 676 746; www.trinity-cm.ac.uk). Offers Welsh language courses of varying intensity from 1 day to 30 weeks. Contact Dr. Lowri Lloyd for an application.

Acen, Ivor House, Bridge St., Cardiff, Wales CF10 2EE (☎029 2030 0808; www.acen.co.uk). Promotes the Welsh language through classes and publications; has contacts with organizations and schools throughout Wales.

ALTERNATIVES TO TOURISM

Daltaí na Gaeilge (www.daltai.com). Gaelic for "Students of the Irish Language," this non-profit corporation runs language programs throughout the US, Europe, and Australia. Website includes an extensive list of course offerings (check for individual contacts and fees), as well as online grammar and language games and exercises.

Donegal Gaeltacht Cultural Centre, Loughanure, Annagry, Co. Donegal, Ireland (☎/fax 075 48081; www.lochgael.com). Offers accommodations and cultural weekends of dance, song, and literature; week-long Irish language courses for adults in Oct. and Apr. (summer US$425 per week, winter $280; cultural weekends $40; Irish courses $120).

Oideas Gael, Glencolmcille, Co. Donegal, Ireland (☎073 30248; fax 30348; www.oideas-gael.com). Offers week-long Irish language and culture courses from April to late August (US$150).

WORKING

There are two main schools of thought. Some travelers want long-term jobs that allow them to get to know another part of the world in depth. Other travelers seek short-term work to finance their travel. They usually seek employment in the service sector or in agriculture, working for a few weeks at a time to finance the next leg of their journey. This section discusses both short-term and long-term opportunities for working in Britain and Ireland. Make sure you contact the British or Irish embassy or consulate in your home country about **entry requirements** for working abroad. Most non-EU citizens will need a **work permit** to work legally in Britain and Ireland. An individual cannot apply for a work permit; the action must be taken by your prospective employer. For further information, consult **Work Permits (UK),** Department of Education and Employment, W5 Moorfoot, Sheffield, S1 4PQ (☎0114 259 4074; www.workpermits.gov.uk). Those wishing to work in the Republic of Ireland should also get in touch with the **Department of Employment,** Davitt House, 65a Adelaide Rd., Dublin (☎01 631 2121; www.entemp.ie). American citizens who are full-time students and are older than 18 can apply for a special permit from the **British Universities North America Club (BUNAC),** which allows them to work for up to six months. Contact BUNAC at: P.O. Box 430, Southbury, CT 06488 (US ☎203-264-0901, UK ☎020 7251 3472; www.bunac.org.uk).

If you live in a Commonwealth country (including Australia, Canada, New Zealand, and South Africa) and if your parents or grandparents were born in the UK, you can apply for **UK Ancestry-Employment,** which allows you to work without a permit. Commonwealth citizens between the ages of 17-27 can work permit-free under a **working holiday visa.** Contact your British embassy for further information.

LONG-TERM WORK

There are many job opportunities in Britain, a country whose average unemployment rate is only about 3%. Most jobs are available in service and tourist industries, particularly in the Heart of England, along the South and Southwest coasts, and in the Lakes District. Northern England and Scotland have more heavy industries, like steel and petroleum products. You'll find that agricultural opportunities begin far from the city-sprawl around the capital. London itself has all the offerings you'd expect of a major metropolitan center, as well as a particularly thriving job market for banking and finance.

If you're planning on spending a substantial amount of time (more than three months) working in Britain, search for a job well in advance. International placement agencies are often the easiest way to find employment abroad. **Internships,** usually for college students, are a good way to segue into working abroad and gain worthwhile experience (some university-run programs offer college credit), although they are often unpaid or poorly paid. Be wary of companies that claim the ability to get you a job abroad for a fee—often the same listings are available online or in newspapers. Some reputable agencies include:

Council Exchanges, 52 Poland St., London W1F 7AB (☎020 7478 2000, US ☎888-268-6245; www.councilexchanges.org). Arranges short-term working authorizations (US$300-475 fee); offers information on different job and volunteering opportunities in Britain and Ireland.

University of North London, Office of International Programs, 228 Miller Bldg., Box 2000, SUNY Cortland, Cortland, NY 13045 (☎697-753-2209; www.cortland.edu/html/ipgms.html). Offers fall and spring internship openings in London. Students pay SUNY tuition costs plus program fees (US$4500-5500).

Hansard Scholar Programme, St. Philips, Building North, Sheffield St., London WC2 2EX (☎020 7955 7459; fax 7955 7492; www.hansard-society.org.uk). Combines classes at the London School of Economics with internships in British government.

IAESTE—US, 10400 Little Patuxent Pkwy., Ste. 250L, Columbia, MD 21044 (☎410 997 3068; www.aipt.org/iaeste.html). Arranges internships, in technical fields.

Anders Glaser Wills, 4 Maddison Ct., Southampton, SO1 0BU (☎0703 223 511; fax 227 911). An international job placement agency with 5 offices in Britain.

Working Ireland, 26 Eustace St., Dublin 2, Ireland (☎01 677 0300; www.workingireland.ie). Multi-tasking agency arranges accommodations and job placement throughout the country. They also help you collect tax refunds and arrange travel home.

TEACHING IN BRITAIN AND IRELAND

Teaching jobs abroad are rarely well-paid, although some elite private schools can pay somewhat competitive salaries. In almost all cases, you must have at least a bachelor's degree to be a full-fledged teacher, although college undergraduates can often get summer positions teaching or tutoring. The British school system is comprised of **state** (public, government-funded), **public** (independent, privately funded), and **international** (often for children of expatriates in the UK) schools, as well as **universities.** Applications to teach at state schools must be made through the local government; independent and international schools must be applied to individually. University positions are typically only available through fellowship or exchange programs. Non-UK citizens wishing to teach in Britain may need a work permit (see **Working,** p. 64). The **British Council** has extensive information for people wishing to teach abroad (see **Studying Abroad,** p. 61). A good website for information on student teaching in Ireland, complete with a tutorial on the Irish education system and first-hand accounts from student teachers, is **Americans in Ireland** (www.geocities.com/teachingirish). Placement agencies are often a good way to find teaching jobs in Britain, although vacancies are also listed in major newspapers. The following organizations may be of help in your search:

Independent Schools Information Service, 56 Buckingham Gate, London SW1E 6AG (☎020 7630 8793; fax 020 7630 5013; www.iscis.uk.net). A list of British independent schools and further information on teaching opportunities.

International Schools Services (ISS), 15 Roszel Rd., Box 5910, Princeton, NJ 08543-5910, USA (☎609-452-0990; fax 609-452-2690; www.iss.edu). Hires teachers for more than 200 overseas schools; candidates should have experience teaching or with international affairs, 2-year commitment expected.

European Council of International Schools, 21B Lavant St., Petersfield, Hampshire GU32 3EL, UK (☎0730 268 244; fax 0730 267 914; www.ecis.org). Contact details for British international schools, as well as placement opportunities.

Fulbright Teaching Assistantship, U.S. Student Programs Division, Institute of International Education, 809 United Nations Plaza, New York, NY 10017 (☎212-984-5330; www.iie.org). Competitive program sends college grads to teach all over the world.

Council for International Exchange of Scholars, 3007 Tilden St. NW, Ste. 5M, Washington DC 20008, USA (☎202-686-4000; www.iie.org/cies).

AU-PAIR WORK

Au-pairs are typically women (aged 18-27) who work as live-in nannies, caring for children and doing light housework in exchange for room, board, and a small stipend. Typically au-pairs work about 30 hours per week plus a few nights of babysitting. The average weekly pocket money allowance is between £50-70. Citizens of certain countries may not be eligible for au-pair work in the UK, but may find placement instead as a **mother's helper.** Mother's helpers work 40-50 hours per week caring for children under the supervision of a parent. They are also responsible for light housework and a few nights of babysitting. Both au-pairs and mother's helpers may need work permits—contact your embassy for further information. The placement agencies below are a good starting point for finding au-pair work.

Au Pair in Europe, P.O. Box 68056, Blakely Postal Outlet, Hamilton, Ontario, Canada L8M 3M7 (☎905-545-6305; fax 905-544-4121; www.princeent.com).

Childcare International, Ltd., Trafalgar House, Grenville Pl., London NW7 3SA (☎020 8906 3116; fax 8906 3461; www.childint.co.uk).

Douglas Au Pair Agency Ltd., 28 Frankfield, Douglas, Cork, Ireland (☎/fax 21 489 1489; www.aupairhere.com).

Dublin Childcare Recruitment Agency, Newcourt House, Strandville Ave., Clontarf, Dublin 3, Ireland (☎01 833 2281; www.childcare-recruitment.com).

Shamrock Au Pair Agency, Magheree, Kilmorony, Athy, Co. Kildare, Ireland (☎507 25533; www.aupairireland.com).

SHORT-TERM WORK

Roaming the globe for long periods of time can be expensive; many travelers try their hand at odd jobs for a few weeks at a time to make some extra cash. Britain does not issue work permits for short-term manual or domestic labor, such as work on farms or in private residences. Another popular option is to work several hours a day at a hostel in exchange for free or discounted room and/or board. Pub work is widely available and may not require a permit, depending on the attitude of your employer. As always, check with the British embassy in your country to be sure of specific requirements.

Most often, short-term jobs are found by word of mouth, either by asking around or talking to the owner of a hostel or restaurant. BUNAC (see p. 64) has listings for establishments that have employed short-term workers in the past. *Let's Go* lists temporary jobs whenever possible; check the practical information sections in large or popular cities.

ENGLAND. Most English cities and larger towns have job spaces to fill, especially during the **high tourist season;** most opportunities are in pubs or restaurants. Your job hunt may be harder in the northern cities, where unemployment is higher than around London and the South. TICs can often be a good place to start your search (many post listings on their bulletin boards), though you will frequently be advised simply to check newspapers or individual establishments. **Job placement organizations** arrange temporary jobs in service or office industries. They can be found in most cities, including the Manpower office in **Manchester** (see p. 365), Blue Arrow in **Cambridge** (p. 327), and JobCentres throughout the southwest; try **Bristol** (p. 214), **Wells** (p. 216), **Bournemouth** (p. 221), or **Newquay** (p. 252). **Hostel work** is another good option. The YHA website (www.yha.org.uk) lists current openings for "general assistants"; you can also inquire personally at independent hostels.

WALES. Many areas of Wales are economically depressed and suffer unemployment rates higher than the British average. Picking up short-term work as a traveler may be more of a challenge here than in England. **Cardiff,** a large, well-touristed city, is perhaps the most feasible option (see p. 467); smaller towns may have listings posted at TICs or outside markets. Opportunities for YHA **hostel work** extend to Wales as well as England (see above).

SCOTLAND. **Edinburgh** (see p. 546) is an excellent place to look for short-term work, especially during Festival in August. The backpacker culture fosters plenty of opportunities, and most of the larger hostels post their own lists of job openings throughout the city. **Glasgow** (p. 581) experiences a similar boom during the summer season. In both cities, domestic and food service jobs are easy to procure and low-paying; computer skills may net you higher-paying office work. **Inverness** has a JobCentre (p. 639) that can help you find temp placements. Archaeological digs are commonplace in both Orkney and Shetland, but the application to spend a summer digging through the dirt is competitive. A better option is the **fish-processing industry** in **Shetland** (p. 686). The work is hard, the pay is good, the scenery is better, and they are usually hiring. Like its southern counterpart, the **SYHA hostel network** has openings listed on its website (www.syha.org.uk); independent hostels also hire many of their short-term workers from a pool of globetrotters.

IRELAND. Some of the most common forms of short-term employment in Ireland include **food service, domestic,** and **farm work.** Another popular option is working several hours a day at a **hostel** in exchange for free or discounted room and/or board. Most often, these jobs are found by word of mouth, or by talking to the owners of hostels and restaurants. Due to the turnover in the tourism industry, many establishments are eager for high-season temporary help. As with all capital cities, **Dublin** and **Belfast** are good places to look for work: Dublin's Community and Youth Information Centre posts job listings (see p. 726), while Belfast has several placement agencies (p. 697). **Galway** is another excellent city for short-term work; try FAS or the People's Resource Centre for guidance and advice (p. 790). Tourist towns in the Southwest—like **Kenmare** (p. 780), **Killarney** (p. 776), and **Dingle** (p. 781)—usually have openings during high season.

FARMING IN BRITAIN AND IRELAND

Agricultural work may be one of the most interesting and rewarding experiences you can have on the British Isles—working on a farm offers you a chance to get away from the urban sprawl of London and the big cities, and to wander for a time among sheep rather than tourist hordes. There are a few organizations that can help set up short-term work and exchange programs in the farming industry:

Fruitful Ltd., Unit 3 Ind. Est., Honeybourne, Evesham, Worcester, WR117QF (☎01386 83255; www.fruitfuljobs.com). Sets up farm work for backpackers and students all over the UK; online application available.

Future Farmers of America (FFA) Global, P.O. Box 68960, 6060 FFA Drive, Indianapolis, IN 46268 (☎317-802-4220; www.ffa.org/international/). Sponsors international exchange and work experience programs, including Agricultural Ambassadors to the UK.

Global Outreach, P.O. Box 25883, Alexandria, VA 22313, USA (☎703-299-9551; fax 703-299-9557; www.globaloutreach.net). Arranges short- and long-term international exchange programs. Program fees US$800-2500.

World Wide Opportunities on Organic Farms (WWOOF), UK Main Office, P.O. Box 2675, Lewes, East Sussex BN7 1RB (www.wwoof.org). Arranges volunteer work with independent host farms across Britain and Ireland.

VOLUNTEERING

Volunteering can be one of the most fulfilling experiences you have in life, especially if you combine it with the thrill of traveling in a new place. Many volunteer services charge you a fee to participate. These costs can be surprisingly hefty (although they frequently cover airfare and most, if not all, living expenses). Try to do research on a program before committing—talk to people who have previously participated and find out exactly what you're getting into, as living and working conditions can vary greatly. Remember also that different programs are geared toward different ages and levels of experience. The more informed you are and the more realistic your expectations, the more enjoyable the program will be.

Most people choose to go through a parent organization that takes care of logistical details and frequently provides a group environment and support system. There are two main types of organizations—religious and non-sectarian—although there are rarely restrictions on participation for either. The largest volunteer organization in Britain is the **British Trust for Conservation Volunteers (BTCV)**, 36 St. Mary's St., Wallingford, Oxfordshire OX10 0EU (☎01491 821 600; www. btcv.org). They offer volunteering opportunities for environmental conservation. Their counterpart in Scotland is the **Scottish Conservation Projects Trust**, Ballahan House, 24 Allan Park, Stirling FK8 2QG (☎01786 479 697). Many of Britain's national parks have volunteer programs— the **Association of National Park Authorities** can get you in touch with the individual park offices (see **National Parks**, p. 49). Northern Ireland's Volunteering **Freephone** connects callers to local volunteer bureaus listing services sites (☎0800 052 2212). Some other British, Irish, and international volunteer organizations are:

Archaeological Institute of America, Boston University, 656 Beacon St., Boston, MA 02215-2006, USA (☎617-353-9361; www.archaeological.org). The *Archaeological Fieldwork Opportunities Bulletin*, available on the organization's website, lists field sites throughout Europe, including parts of Ireland.

Christian Aid: The Republic: 17 Clanwilliam Terr., Grand Canal Dock, Dublin 2 (☎01 611 0801). **Northern Ireland:** 30 Wellington Park, Belfast, BT9 6DL (☎028 9038 1204; www.christian-aid.org.uk). Individuals or groups of volunteers may work in various fundraising and administrative roles, occasionally for a small stipend.

Earthwatch, 3 Clocktower Pl., Suite 100, Box 75, Maynard, MA 01754, USA (☎800-776-0188 or 978-461-0081; www.earthwatch.org). Arranges 1- to 3-week programs to promote conservation of natural resources. Fees vary based on program location and duration, costs average $1700 plus airfare.

Elderhostel, Inc., 11 Avenue de Lafayette, Boston, MA 92111-1746, USA (☎877-426-8056; fax 877-426-2166; www.elderhostel.org). Sends volunteers age 55 and over around the world to work in construction, research, teaching, and many other projects. Costs average $100 per day plus airfare.

Habitat for Humanity International, 121 Habitat St., Americus, GA 31709, USA (☎229-924-6935; www.habitat.org). Volunteers build houses in over 83 countries for anywhere from 2 weeks to 3 years. Short-term program fees US$1200-4000.

Mental Health Ireland, Mensana House, 6 Adelaide House, Dún Laoghaire, Co. Dublin, Ireland (☎01 284 1186; www.mentalhealthireland.ie). Volunteer activities include fundraising, housing, "befriending," and promoting mental health in various regions of Ireland. Opportunities listed in their newsletter, *Mensana News*, available online.

Northern Ireland Volunteer Development Agency, Annsgate House, 70-74 Anne St., Belfast, BT1 4EH (☎0232 236 100; info.nivda@cinni.org). Helps arrange individual and group volunteer efforts in Northern Ireland. IAVE membership fees for individuals US$30 per year; groups US$100.

The National Trust, Volunteering and Community Involvement Office, 33 Sheep St., Cirencester GL7 1RQ, UK (☎01285 651 818; www.nationaltrust.org.uk/volunteers). Arranges numerous volunteer opportunities, including Working Holidays.

Royal Society for the Protection of Birds (RSPB), UK Headquarters, The Lodge, Sandy, Bedfordshire SG19 2DL (☎01767 680 551; www.rspb.org.uk). Hundreds of volunteer opportunities at sites throughout the UK—ranging from a day constructing nestboxes in East Anglia to week-long bird surveys off the Pembrokeshire coast to several months monitoring invertebrates in the Highlands. Work available for all levels of experience.

Service Civil International (SCI), SCI USA, 3213 W. Wheeler St., Seattle, WA 98199, USA (☎/fax 206-350-6585; www.sciint.org). Arranges placement in work camps for those 18+. Registration fee US$65-125.

Volunteering Ireland, Carmichael Centre for Voluntary Groups, Coleraine House, Coleraine St., Dublin 7, Ireland (☎01 872 2622; www.volunteeringireland.com). Offers opportunities for individuals or groups in various volunteering and advocacy settings.

Volunteers for Peace, 1034 Tiffany Rd., Belmont, VT 05730, USA (☎802-259-2759; www.vfp.org). Arranges 2- to 3-week placement in work camps. Membership required for registration. Programs average US$200-500.

FOR FURTHER READING ON ALTERNATIVES TO TOURISM

Alternative Travel Directory: The complete guide to traveling, studying, and living overseas, by Hubbs.

How to Get a Job in Europe, by Sanborn and Matherly.

How to Live Your Dream of Volunteering Overseas, by Collins, DeZerega, and Heckscher.

International Directory of Voluntary Work, by Whetter and Pybus.

International Jobs, by Kocher and Segal.

Jobs for People Who Love to Travel, by Krannich, Krannich, and Krannich.

Overseas Summer Jobs 2002, by Collier and Woodworth.

Work Abroad: The Complete Guide to Finding a Job Overseas, by Hubbs, Griffith, and Nolting.

Work Your Way Around the World, by Griffith.

ENGLAND

While the terms "Great Britain" and "England" may seem interchangeable, England is in fact only one part—along with Scotland and Wales—of the island of Great Britain, the largest of the British Isles, which together with Northern Ireland forms Her Majesty's United Kingdom of Great Britain and Northern Ireland (more concisely known as the UK). Never refer to the Scots or the Welsh as "English" or to the Irish as "British"; besides betraying your sorry ignorance, you may make some blood enemies. United itself by the end of the first millennium AD, England had conquered Wales and Ireland by the 17th century, and Scotland in 1707. The Republic of Ireland won its independence in 1921, and while Wales and Scotland have long been a part of a nation administrated primarily from London, they are, like Ireland, separate and distinct lands with their own languages, culture, and customs. This chapter focuses on the history, literature, and culture of England; **Wales** (p. 457) and **Scotland** (p. 535) are treated separately, as are **Northern Ireland** (p. 692) and the **Republic of Ireland** (p. 717).

LIFE AND TIMES

ENGLAND OF OLDE

History will be kind to me, for I intend to write it.
—Winston Churchill

AN ISLAND TO CALL THEIR OWN. Once connected to the European continent by a land bridge, Britain has been inhabited for nearly half a million years. While little may be known about the island's prehistoric residents, the megalithic, astronomically precise, and utterly mysterious stone circles left behind at **Stonehenge** (p. 204) and **Avebury** (p. 205) prove they were anything but Neanderthals. Seeking shelter on Britain's isolated shores, **Celts** and nature-loving **Druids** emigrated from the continent in the first millennium BC, only to submit to the carnage-loving armies of Emperor Claudius in AD 43. Despite agitation by Celtic warrior-queen **Boudicca**, by the end of the first century, the **Romans** held all of "Britannia" (England and Wales), their northernmost colony, and had established major cities at **Londinium** (London) and **Verulamium** (St. Albans, p. 267), as well as a resort spa (**Bath**, p. 205). Expansion north was to prove more difficult. Scared spearless by the fiercely resistant Picts, the Romans constructed **Hadrian's Wall** (p. 447) to keep out unfriendly neighbors. The 4th century saw the decline of the Roman Empire, leaving Britannia vulnerable to raids. The Angles and Saxons—Germanic tribes from Denmark and northern Germany—were particularly successful invaders, and established their own settlements and kingdoms in the south. The name "England" derives from "Anglaland," land of the Angles.

CHRISTIANS AND VIKINGS AND NORMANS, OH MY! Christianity caught on in AD 597 when hotshot missionary **Augustine** converted King Æthelbert and founded England's first papal church at **Canterbury** (p. 150). From the 8th to the 10th century, Norsemen sacked Scotland, Ireland, and the north, while Danish Vikings raided England's east coast. In 878, the legendary **Alfred the Great** defeated the Danes, English power grew, and by the mid-11th century, looting and pillaging was a thing of the past. Better known for his piety, Edward the Confessor was the last Anglo-Saxon king, having promised the throne to an up-and-coming Norman named Will. Better known as **The Conqueror,** William I invaded in 1066, won the pivotal **Battle of Hastings** (p. 164), slaughtered his rival Harold II—and for good measure, his two brothers—and promptly set about cataloguing his new English acquisitions—down to each peasant, cow, and bale of hay—in the epic **Domesday Book** (p. 191). Painfully remembered as the "Norman Yoke," William introduced **feudalism** to Britain, doling out vast tracts of land to the king's cronies and subjugating English tenants to French lords. Norman French became the language of the educated and elite, and English was marginalized; Henry IV (crowned 1399) was the next king whose mother tongue was English.

WAR AND MORE WAR; ALSO, WAR. The Middle Ages in England were a time of bloody conquest and infighting. Henry Plantagenet ascended the throne as Henry II in 1154 and initiated the conquest of Ireland, proclaiming himself its overlord in 1171. His son **Richard the Lionheart** was more interested in the Crusades than in the well-being of his subjects, and spent only six months of his ten-year reign on the island. Tired of such royal pains, noblemen forced his hapless brother and successor, King John, to sign the **Magna Carta** in 1215. The document, often seen as a battle cry against oppression, also started the rise of modern English democracy—the first **Parliament** convened 50 years later. In 1284, **Edward I** (who wasn't such a fan of this whole "democracy" thing) absorbed Wales under the English crown. But while English kings expanded the nation's boundaries, the **Black Death** ravaged its population, killing more than one-third of all Britons between 1348 and 1361. Many more fell in the **Hundred Years' War** (or the 116 Years' War, to be precise), a costly squabble over the French throne.

In 1399, Henry Bolingbroke invaded Britain and usurped the throne from his cousin Richard II (on holiday in Ireland), putting his own House of Lancaster in control and giving Shakespeare something decent to write about. Bolingbroke's son **Henry V** defeated the French in the **Battle of Agincourt** (1415), a legendary victory for the British underdogs that rendered the young prince heir to the French throne. But the next Henry blew it when, failing to stave off French resistance under Joan of Arc, he lost almost all English land in France. Things got worse before they got better; the **Wars of the Roses** (1455-85)—a lengthy crisis of royal succession between the houses of Lancaster and York (whose respective emblems were a red and a white rose)—culminated when Richard of York put his nephew, boy-king Edward V, in the Tower of London for safe-keeping. When Edward disappeared, Uncle Dick was there, conveniently, to be crowned Richard III.

THE 3 R'S: REFORMATION, RENAISSANCE, AND REVOLUTION. When the last of the Lancasters, Henry VII, won the throne in 1485, he inaugurated the rule of the **House of Tudor.** The following **Henry (VIII,** for those of you keeping score) reinforced England's control over the Irish and had some much-celebrated trouble producing a male heir. In his equally infamous battle with the Pope over divorce, the King converted Britain from Roman Catholicism to Protestantism, establishing the **Anglican Church** and placing himself at its head—ironic, considering how many of his wives lost theirs. Protestantism's birth was long and painful—Henry's first successor, nine-year-old Edward VI, was quickly overshadowed by the fiery personality of his second successor and staunch Catholic **Bloody Mary,** who earned her gory nickname for mass burnings of Protestants. In a nice spate of sibling rivalry, **Elizabeth I** reversed the religious convictions imposed by her sister and cemented the success of the **Reformation.** Under her reign the English defeated the **Spanish Armada** in 1588, **Sir Francis Drake** circumnavigated the globe, and Britain became the leading Protestant power in Europe. Henry VII's great-granddaughter, the Catholic **Mary, Queen of Scots,** briefly threatened the stability of the throne in this age of unparalleled splendor. Her implication in a plot on the Queen's life led to 20 years in prison and a comparably swift execution (see p. 539).

The first union of England, Wales, and Scotland effectively took place in 1603, when **James VI** of Scotland, Mary's son, ascended to the throne as **James I** of England. But James and his successor, **Charles I,** began to irk a largely Puritan parliament with their Catholic sympathies, extravagant spending, and insistence upon the "divine right" of kings. Charles ruled without Parliament for 11 years, after which erupted the **English Civil Wars** (1642-51). The monarchy was abolished when Parliament saw to it that Charles I and his head parted ways, and the first British Commonwealth was founded in 1649.

TWO MORE R'S: REPUBLICANISM AND RESTORATION. liver Cromwell emerged as the charismatic but hopelessly despotic military leader of the new Commonwealth. His conquest of Ireland led to the death of nearly half its population, while his oppressive measures at home (swearing and the theater were outlawed) betrayed a deep religious fanaticism. Much to the relief of the masses, the Republic collapsed under the lackluster leadership of Cromwell's son Richard. As **Thomas Hobbes** observed in his 1651 treatise **Leviathan,** life was "poor, nasty, brutish, and short" in the absence of an absolute sovereign: **Charles II** returned to power unconditionally in 1660. Yet even the Restoration did not end England's troubles; debate raged over whether to exclude Charles's fervently Catholic brother **James II** from the succession. Side-taking established England's first political parties: the **Whigs,** who insisted on exclusion, and the **Tories,** who supported hereditary succession.

ENLIGHTEN ME. James II took the throne in 1685, but lost it three years later to his son-in-law, Dutch Protestant **William of Orange.** William marched on London in 1688 in a bloodless military coup called the **Glorious Revolution.** After James fled to France, William and his wife Mary wrote the **Bill of Rights** to ensure the Protestantism of future kings. Supporters of James II (called **Jacobites**) remained a threat until 1745, when James II's grandson, **Bonnie Prince Charlie,** failed in his attempt to invade and recapture the throne (see p. 540). The ascension of William and Mary marked the end of a century of upheaval and the debut of a more liberal age in which Britain rose to economic and political superstardom. By the end of the **Seven Years' War** (1756-1763), Britain controlled Canada and 13 unremarkable colonies to the south, as well as much of the Caribbean. Meanwhile, **Sir Isaac Newton** theorized the laws of gravity and invented calculus on the side, while **John Locke** cleared the philosophical slate by developing **empiricism.** Increased secularism was countered mid-century by a wave of religious fervor, with bible-thumping **Methodists** (think early televangelists) preaching to outdoor crowds. Parliament prospered thanks to the ineffectual leadership of the Hanoverian kings, **Georges I, II,** and **III.** The office of Prime Minister eclipsed the monarchy as the seat of power, held by superstars like master negotiator **Robert Walpole,** fiery orator **William Pitt the Elder,** and first income-taxer **Pitt the Younger.**

EMPIRE AND INDUSTRY. During the 18th and 19th centuries, Britain came to rule more than one quarter of the world's population and two-fifths of its land. Originally, such domination stemmed from private companies working in overseas trade—control of the Cape of Good Hope secured shipping routes to the Far East, while plantations in the New World produced lucrative staples like sugar and rum. The **Napoleonic Wars** (1800-15) were high-times for renewing the Anglo-French rivalry and for racking up the colonies; by 1858 India—jewel of the imperial crown—was headlining a list that included Ceylon (Sri Lanka), South Africa, Hong Kong, the Falkland Islands, Australia, New Zealand, and the Western Pacific islands. **Imperialism** topped the economic and moral agenda, as Englishmen considered it their duty to "civilize" the non-Christian world. Despite the loss of the American colonies in 1776, by the mid-1800s it could be (and was) said that "the sun never set on the British Empire." (Although, as modern wits and postcolonialists would remind us, perhaps it was that the sun never rose.) The **Industrial Revolution** gave Britain the economic fuel needed for a long day's work colonizing. With the perfection of the steam engine by **James Watt** in 1765 and the mechanization of the textile industry, England soared ahead in machine-driven production. Massive portions of the rural populace, pushed off the land and lured by rapidly growing opportunities in industrial employment, migrated to towns like **Manchester** (p. 364) and **Leeds** (p. 411). The age-old gulf between landowners and farmers was replaced by a wider gap between factory owners and their laborers. The **Gold Standard,** which Britain adopted in 1821, ensured the pound's value with gold and became an international financial system, securing Britain's economic supremacy.

VICTORIAN ERA. The long and stable rule of **Queen Victoria** (1837-1901) dominated the 19th century in foreign and domestic politics and even stylistic mores. A series of **Factory** and **Reform Acts** throughout the century limited child labor, capped the average workday, and made sweeping changes in (male) voting rights. Prime Minister **Robert** "Bobbie" **Peel** restored order by establishing the London police force in 1829. The high point of the era was unquestionably Prince Albert's 1851 **Great Exhibition,** in which over 10,000 consumer goods from Britain's far-flung realms were assembled in London's **Crystal Palace,** a prototype shopping mall. Yet while commercial self-interest defined middle-class conservatism, not everyone approved. In *Utilitarianism* (1863), **John Stuart Mill** claimed citizens must do the greatest good for the greatest number of people. Similar crowd-pleasing jingles were taken up by the socialist **Fabian Society** in 1884, which had, if nothing else, the literary weight of George Bernard Shaw and H.G. Wells.

By the end of the century, trade unionism strengthened, and found a political voice in the **Labour Party** in 1906. Yet pressures to alter the position of other marginalized groups proved ineffectual, as the rich and bohemian embraced fin-de-siecle decadence. Increasing troubles with Ireland had plagued the nation for half a century, but Prime Minister **William Gladstone's** attempts in 1886 and 1892 to introduce a Home Rule Bill splintered the Liberal Party and ended in defeat (see p. 721). Meanwhile, the **Suffragettes,** led by **Emmeline Pankhurst,** fought for voting rights by disrupting Parliament and staging hunger strikes; women, however, would have to wait for the vote until after the trauma of **World War I.**

HAVE WE MENTIONED WAR? The **Great War,** as WWI was known until 1939, brought British military action back to the European stage, scarred the British spirit with the loss of a generation of young men, and dashed Victorian dreams of a peaceful, progressive society. The technological explosion of the 19th century was manifested in horrific new weaponry and unprecedented casualties on all sides. The war demoralized the nation: by the end of four years of fighting, almost a million British men were dead and twice as many were wounded.

A sense of aimlessness overtook the nation's politics after WWI. The 1930s brought **depression** and mass unemployment; in a 1936 publication, social economist **John Maynard Keynes** argued presciently that German war reparations would come to no good. That same year, King Edward VIII shocked the world and shamed the Windsor family with the announcement of his **abdication** for the sake of twice-divorced Baltimore socialite Wallis Simpson. Meanwhile, tensions in Europe were once again escalating with the German reoccupation of the Rhineland. Prime Minister **Neville** "Peace in Our Time" **Chamberlain** pushed through a controversial (and, as it turns out, disastrous) appeasement agreement with Hitler. Germany invaded Poland, Britain declared war on September 3, 1939, and for the second time in 25 years the world went up in flames. The previous, devastating Great War yet failed to prepare the British Isles for the utter devastation of **World War II.** German air raids started the prolonged **Battle of Britain** in the summer of 1940.

London, Coventry, and other English cities were further demolished by the thunderous **"Blitzkriegs,"** which destroyed military factories and left scores of Britons orphaned or homeless or both. The near-immediate fall of France in 1940 precipitated the creation of a war cabinet, led by the determined and eloquent **Winston Churchill**. British invasion of Europe commenced only with the 1944 **D-Day Invasion** of Normandy, augmented by American forces; the move swung the tide of the war and eventually produced peace in Europe in May 1945.

THE POST-WAR YEARS. With increasing immigration from former colonies and a growing rift between the rich and poor, post-war Britain faced economic and cultural problems that still rankle today. Left-wing politics enjoyed a boost when the 1946 institution of the **National Health Service** guaranteed free medical care to all Brits, a radical socialist experiment. In keeping with the spirit of the 60s, the Labour government relaxed divorce and homosexuality laws and abolished capital punishment. Britain joined the **European Economic Community (EEC)** in 1971, a move that received a rocky welcome from many Britons and continues to inflame passions today. Britain's new economic liberalism, however, was unable to counter losses incurred by the decline of its colonial empire, which began in earnest after WWII. Unemployment and economic unrest culminated in a series of public service strikes in 1979's **"Winter of Discontent."**

It was against this backdrop that Britain grasped for change, electing "Iron Lady" **Margaret Thatcher** as Prime Minister, putting faith in her nationalism, Victorian values, and world-famous helmet-hair. Thatcher turned from the dispute over the **Falkland Islands** to the state of the British Isles, denationalizing and dismantling the welfare state with quips like "there is no such thing as society." Her policies brought dramatic prosperity to many but sharpened the divide between the haves and have-nots. Aggravated by her stubborn clinging to the unpopular **poll tax** and resistance to the EEC, the Conservative Party conducted a vote of no confidence that led to Thatcher's 1990 resignation and the election of **John Major.** In 1993, the Major government suffered its first embarrassment when the British pound toppled out of the EC's monetary regulation system. In August of the same year, Britain ratified (barely) the Maastricht Treaty on a closer **European Union (EU).** Major remained unpopular, and by 1995 his ratings were so low that he resigned as Party leader to force a leadership election. He won the election, but the Conservatives lost parliamentary seats and continued to languish in the polls.

ENGLAND TODAY

HOW BRITANNIA IS RULED. Britain managed to become one of the world's most stable constitutional monarchies without the aid of a written constitution. A combination of parliamentary legislation, common law, and convention creates the flexible system of British government. Although the kings of yore ruled with fists of varying degrees of iron, since the 1700s the monarch been a purely symbolic role, leaving real political power to **Parliament.** Consisting of the **House of Commons,** with its elected Members of Parliament (MPs), and the **House of Lords,** most of whom are government-appointed Life Peers, Parliament holds supreme legislative power and may change and even directly contradict its previous laws. Of Parliament's two houses, power has shifted from the Lords to the Commons over the course of the centuries, and the latest move to abolish hereditary peerage is just one step in this process. All members of the executive branch, which includes the **Prime Minister** and the **Cabinet,** are also MPs; this fusing of legislative and executive functions, called the "efficient secret" of the British government, ensures the quick passage of the majority party's programs into bills. The Prime Minister, who rules from his roost on **10 Downing Street** (or, in the case of Tony Blair and his large brood, No. 11; see p. 122), is generally the head of the majority party and chooses the members of the Cabinet, who serve as heads of the government's departments. British politics is a group effort; the Cabinet may bicker over policy in private, but their sense of collective responsibility ensures that they present a cohesive platform to the public. Political parties also keep their MPs in line on most votes in Parliament and provide a pool of talent and support for the smooth functioning of the executive. The two main parties in UK politics are **Labour** and the **Conservatives,** representing roughly the left and the right respectively; a smaller third party, the **Liberal Democrats,** tries its best to be the fulcrum on which power balances shift.

CURRENT EVENTS. The Labour Party, under the leadership of charismatic **Tony Blair,** reduced ties with the labor unions, refashioned itself into the alternative for discontented voters, and finally began to rise in popularity. The "new" Labour Party won a clear victory under Blair in 1997, earning the biggest Labour majority to date, and garnered a second landslide victory in June 2001. Blair spent 1998 nurturing closer relations with the EU, maintained a moderate economic and social position, and got himself named one of *People*'s "50 Most Beautiful People." All in all, not a bad year for Tony. 1999 was more turbulent, with Britain's stance on the **Kosovo** crisis gaining Blair the title of "little Clinton" for what critics called his blind conformity to American foreign policy, a loyalty demonstrated again in the wake of the September 11 attacks. Britain was the United States' staunchest ally in the **war on terrorism,** lending military support in actions like **Operation Snipe,** which sent Royal Marines to Afghanistan to search for Taliban and al-Qaeda members. The UK also implemented further **anti-terrorism measures** at home, including the identification of possible terrorist targets in Britain, and the passage of a new Anti-Terrorism, Crime and Security Act. The Act has provisions for tracking terrorist groups—like asset-freezing and sharing of information—and amends the rubric of racially motivated hate crimes (now carrying a stricter penalty) to include religious hatred.

Blair's detractors believe that Britain's refusal to adopt the new EU currency, the **euro,** is another sign that his sympathies with the US are greater than those with Europe. But as the euro received a generally warm welcome throughout the EU and the value of the pound slipped, Blair came out in support of the shiny new currency and re-iterated his commitment to European solidarity—a move the anti-Blair camp calls political rather than economic, and one which could leave him on the Downing St. doorstep come the next election. Throughout 2002 the British government prepared for the perhaps-inevitable switchover, conducting five "tests" for the home economy to see if Britain and the euro are compatible. If it turns out that country and coin are a match made in heaven, the issue will go before the voters in a **referendum** sometime in 2003. The fate of the pound remains a heated issue, and the referendum forecasts change depending on which newspaper you read. Mogul-of-the-Moment Rupert Murdoch, for one, has vowed to use his media might to stave off any possibility of a euro threat.

Blair's Labour government has also tackled various constitutional reforms promised in its platform, beginning with domestic **devolution** in Scotland and Wales. The Scots voted in a 1997 referendum to have their own Parliament, which opened in 1999, paving the way for greater independence (p. 541), and the Welsh opened the first session of their National Assembly in 1999 (p. 461). Progress has been more halting in the latest attempts at **Northern Irish autonomy;** the British government suspended Belfast's **Stormont Assembly** in 2000, hoping to instigate the decommissioning of arms by the IRA and their Unionist counterparts. A lack of progress satisfactory to either side led to a year of violence throughout 2001 (including another suspension and reinstatement of the Assembly) and into 2002.

The Good Friday Agreement continues a precarious existence between cease-fires, election outcomes, and disarmament promises (see p. 696).

A ROYAL MESS? The royal family has had its share of troubles in recent years. In 1992, over a hundred rooms in Windsor Castle burned on Queen Elizabeth II's wedding anniversary, and in 1993 she started paying (gasp!) income tax. The spectacle of royal life took a tragic turn in 1997, when **Princess Diana** and **Dodi Al-Fayed** died in a car crash in a Paris tunnel. The subsequent outpouring of grief has now calmed, but tourists still mourn at the Diana memorial at Althorp, in Northamptonshire. The immediate fate of the royals will depend on whether the monarchy embraces Diana's fervent populism or retreats with traditional aloofness to the private realm. **Charles** and his long-time paramour **Camilla Parker-Bowles** are making tentative steps toward public acceptance, if not a fully legitimized union—royal-watchers were tittering over Camilla's seat in the Queen's box (though several prudent rows distant from Liz herself) during the opening ceremonies for 2002's **Golden Jubilee** (a year-long bash celebrating the monarch's 50 fine years on the throne). Said royal-watchers still have their eyes on Charles's baby brother, **Edward,** whose 1999 marriage to **Sophie Rhys-Jones** could offset the divorce record of the other royal siblings (3-for-3 so far). A quick stop at a drug rehab clinic in 2002 heralded the onset of adult celebrity (and tabloid notoriety) for **Harry,** the younger of Charles and Diana's sons. However, it is the young **Prince William** on whom the spotlight shines. After Wills finished his studies at Eton, speculation on his university of choice (he studies at St. Andrews in Scotland) and revelations of a correspondence with pop princess Britney Spears consumed his adoring, often pre-pubescent, public. Whether "His Royal Sighness" will gracefully survive his trip to adulthood under the paparazzi's unforgiving lens remains to be seen.

CULTURE AND CUSTOMS

Great Britain, roughly the size of the state of Oregon, has more people than the combined populations of California and New York; five-sixths of the 60 million Britons live in England. Such close quarters make the people around you far more important to your trip than the moldy old castle next on your itinerary. The English culture and character is as impossible to summarize as any on earth—Jane Austen, Sid Vicious, and Winston Churchill are each quintessentially "English," yet share almost nothing in common. Stiff upper lips sit next to football hooligans on the Tube, the local who stares at you as though you were mad because you tried to strike up conversation at a bus stop would likely talk your ear off over a pint "down the local," and the crusader of the Royal Society for the Prevention of Cruelty to Animals shares a hedgerow with a dedicated huntsman.

In a country full of such idiosyncrasies, there is very little a traveler can do that will inadvertently cause offense. That said, *Let's Go* would like to share a few cultural quirks we believe could make your dealings with the natives easier. The English do indeed place some weight on proper decorum, including **politeness** ("thanks" comes in many varieties, including "ta" and "cheers," and you should use it), **queueing** (that is, lining up—never, ever line jump or otherwise disrupt the queue...never), keeping a certain **respectful distance** (personal space is cherished; cheek-kissing and vigorous hand-shaking is a Continental trend that did not catch on in the Isles), and being **punctual** (though this is valued less and less the farther from London you get). You'll find, however, that the British **sense of humor**—fantastically wry, explicit, even raunchy (witness the daily topless girl on page three of *The Sun*)—is somewhat at odds with any notion of coldness and reserve.

THE ARTS

LANGUAGE AND LITERATURE

Outdone worldwide only by Mandarin Chinese in sheer number of speakers, the English language reflects in its history the diversity of the hundreds of millions who use it today. Originally a minor Germanic dialect, English was enriched by words and phrases from Danish, French, and Latin, thus giving even its earliest speakers, poets, and wordsmiths a supple and vast vocabulary rivalled by few world languages. In the last few centuries, with English spread to the corners of the world by British colonialism, the language has endlessly borrowed from other tongues and serves as the voice literary and popular of people far removed from the British Isles. A well-chosen novel or collection of poems will illuminate any sojourn in Britain, and the following survey hopes to give an idea of the range of choices available. Welsh (p. 462), Scottish (p. 542), and Irish (p. 723) languages and literatures are treated separately.

BARDS AND BIBLES. Most of the earliest poetry in English was part of an oral tradition of which little survives. The finest piece of Anglo-Saxon (Old English) poetry for which record does exist is *Beowulf*, the 7th-century account of a prince, a monster, and the monster's mommy. **Geoffrey Chaucer** tapped into the spirited side of Middle English; his *Canterbury Tales* (c. 1387) remain some of the funniest, sauciest, most incisive stories in the English canon. The anonymously authored *Sir Gawain and the Green Knight* (c. 1375) is a romance of Arthurian chivalry in a mysterious, magical landscape. **John Wycliffe** made the Bible accessible to the masses by translating it into English in the 1380s. The hoity-toity, French-speaking, Catholic authorities did not approve; a later, persecuted Biblical translator **William Tyndale** was martyred in 1524, and his work became the model for the **King James Version** (completed in 1611 under James I).

THE ENGLISH RENAISSANCE. English literature flourished under the reign of Elizabeth I. **Sir Philip Sidney's** glittering sonnet sequences and **Edmund Spenser's** moral allegories (like *The Faerie Queene*) earned both of them favor at court,

SHAKESPEARE MADE EASY

I love you.	"For where thou art, there is the world itself...and where thou art not, desolation." (*Henry VI, Part II*)
I hate you.	"Thou art a boil, a plague-sore, or embossed carbuncle, in my corrupted blood." (*King Lear*)
I totally kicked his butt.	"I took by the throat the circumcised dog, and smote him, thus." (*Othello*)
Dude, you suck.	"Methink'st thou art a general offense and every man should beat thee." (*All's Well That Ends Well*)
Hey, can I get a pint over here?	"I would give all my fame for a pot of ale." (*Henry V*)

ENGLAND

while **John Donne** wrote metaphysical poetry and penned erotic verse on the side. The era's greatest contributions were dramatic, with the appearance of the first professional playwrights. **Christopher Marlowe** lost his life to a dagger in a pub brawl, but fortunately not before he guided *Tamburlaine* (c. 1587) and *Dr. Faustus* (c. 1588) into the world of English letters. Meanwhile, **Ben Jonson,** when he wasn't languishing in jail (for acts as varied as insulting Scotland and killing an actor in a sword-fight), redefined satiric comedy in works like *Volpone* (1606). And then we come to the son of a glove-maker from Stratford-upon-Avon (p. 284). **William Shakespeare** is not only the giant looming over all of English literature and the inventor of any number of words (try "scuffle," "whizzing," or "arouse"), but also held one of the filthiest feathers ever to scrawl a page. Long live the Bard.

HOW NOVEL! The British Puritans of the late 16th and early 17th centuries produced a huge volume of obsessive and beautiful literature, like **John Milton's** epic *Paradise Lost* (1667) and **John Bunyan's** allegorical *Pilgrim's Progress* (1678). The 18th century saw the poetry of **John Dryden's** neoclassical revival, **Alexander Pope's** satires, and **Dr. Samuel Johnson's** lovably idiosyncratic English dictionary, the first in the English language. The 18th century also marked the humble birth of a new literary form. In 1719, **Daniel Defoe** inaugurated the era of the English **novel** with his popular island-bound *Robinson Crusoe* (a work proving that traveling was far more dangerous in pre-*Let's Go* times). Authors like **Samuel Richardson** (*Clarissa*, 1749) and **Fanny Burney** (*Evelina*, 1778) helped the novel develop along more traditional lines, while **Henry Fielding's** wacky *Tom Jones* (1749) and **Laurence Sterne's** experimental *Tristram Shandy* (1759-67) invigorated the art form. By the end of the century, **Jane Austen** had perfected the narrative technique; most of her great novels were written in a cottage near Winchester (p. 191). In the Victorian period, poverty and social change spawned the classic, sentimental novels of **Charles Dickens;** *Oliver Twist* (1838) and *David Copperfield* (1849) draw on the bleakness of his childhood in Portsmouth (p. 183) and portray the harsh living conditions of working class Londoners. Secluded in the wild Yorkshire moors (see Haworth, p. 410), the **Brontë sisters** staved off tuberculosis long enough to give *Wuthering Heights* (Emily; 1847) and *Jane Eyre* (Charlotte; also 1847) to adolescent girls everywhere. Weighing in at over 800 pages, *Middlemarch* (1871) is **George Eliot's** (Mary Ann Evans's) "Study of Provincial Life" in a mid-century Midlands town. **Thomas Hardy** brought the Victorian age to a somber end in the fate-ridden Wessex (that is, southwest England) landscapes of *Tess of the d'Urbervilles* (1891) and *Jude the Obscure* (1895).

ROMANTICISM AND WHAT CAME AFTER. Partly in reaction to the rationalism of the preceding century, the Romantic movement of the early 1800s found its greatest expression in verse. Painter-poet **William Blake's** *Songs of Innocence and Experience* (1794) was a precursor to the movement, but the watershed event launching **Romanticism** was the 1798 *Lyrical Ballads* by **William Wordsworth** and **Samuel Taylor Coleridge,** which included such classics as "Lines Composed a Few Miles above Tintern Abbey" (p. 474) and "The Rime of the Ancient Mariner." The Romantic poets celebrated the transcendent beauty of nature, the power of the imagination, and the profound influence of childhood experiences. Wordsworth's poetry reflects on a long, full life—he drew inspiration from the Lakes (p. 382) and Snowdonia (p. 515), Cambridge, and London—but many of his younger colleagues died tragically young. **John Keats** succumbed to tuberculosis at 26, with just time enough to have penned the maxim "beauty is truth, truth beauty" in one of his astonishingly beautiful odes. **Percy Bysshe Shelley** drowned off the Tuscan coast at

29, and **Lord Byron's** *Don Juan* (1819-24) established him as the heartthrob of the age before he was killed in the Greek War of Independence.

The poetry of the Victorian age struggled with the impact of societal changes and religious skepticism. **Lord Alfred Tennyson** spun verse about faith and doubt for over a half-century and inspired a medievalist revival with Arthurian idylls like "The Lady of Shalott" (1842). Combining skepticism and the grotesque, **Robert Browning** composed piercing dramatic monologues, and his wife **Elizabeth Barrett** counted the ways she loved him. **Matthew Arnold** abandoned poetry in 1867 to become the greatest cultural critic of the day. Jesuit priest **Gerard Manley Hopkins** penned tortuous verse with verbal technopyrics and unique "sprung rhythm" that make him the chief forerunner of poetic modernism.

THE MODERN AGE. "On or about December 1910," wrote **Virginia Woolf,** "human nature changed." Woolf, a key member of London's bohemian intellectual **Bloomsbury Group,** tried to capture the spirit of the time and the real life of the mind in her novels; she and Irish expatriate James Joyce (see p. 724) were among the most groundbreaking practitioners of **Modernism** (1910-1930). One of Modernism's poetic champions was **T.S. Eliot,** who grew up a Missouri boy but became the "Pope of Russell Square" (p. 137). *The Waste Land* (1922), among the last century's most important works, portrays London as a fragmented and barren desert awaiting redemption. **D.H. Lawrence** explored tensions in the British working-class family in *Sons and Lovers* (1913). Although he spoke only a few words of English when he arrived in the country at 21, **Joseph Conrad** demonstrated his mastery of the language in *Heart of Darkness* (1902). Disillusionment also pervades **E.M. Forster's** half-Modernist, half-Romantic novels, such as *A Passage to India* (1924). Authors in the 1930s captured the tumult and depression of the decade: **Evelyn Waugh** turned a ruthlessly satirical eye on society, while **Graham Greene** studied moral ambiguity. More optimistic poets such as **W.H. Auden** saw in Freud and socialism hope for a better future.

LATER 20TH-CENTURY. Fascism and the horrors of WWII led to writer's musings on the nature of evil, while the ravenous totalitarian state of **George Orwell's** *1984* (1949) strove to strip the world of memory and words of meaning. Violence, anarchy, and speculations on the possible futures are themes recurring in works like *A Clockwork Orange,* by **Anthony Burgess** (1962). Later, the end of Empire, rising affluence, and the growing gap between the classes splintered British literature in a thousand directions. Nostalgia pervades the poems of **Philip Larkin** and **John Betjeman,** an angry working class found mouthpieces in **Allan Sillitoe** and **Kingsley Amis,** and postcolonial voices like **Salman Rushdie** and 2002 Nobel laureate **V.S. Naipaul** have become an important literary force. Although some believe that the weight of fiction in English has shifted west across the Atlantic or out to the former colonies since WWII, the home island continues to produce acclaimed works from writers like **A.S. Byatt** and **Martin Amis.** British playwrights continue to innovate: **Harold Pinter** infused living rooms with horrifying silences and **Tom Stoppard** challenged everything you thought you knew about theater in plays like *Rosencrantz and Guildenstern are Dead* (1967).

OUTSIDE THE CLASSROOM. English literature holds its own away from the ivory tower as well. The elegant mysteries of **Dorothy L. Sayers** and **Agatha Christie** are known the world over. The espionage novels of **John le Carré** and Fleming, **Ian Fleming,** provide thrills of another sort. **P.G. Wodehouse** (featuring Jeeves, the consummate butler) hilariously satirizes the idle aristocrat. **James Herriot** (Alf Wight), beloved author of *All Creatures Great and Small* (1972), faced a backlash when a flock of steadfastly unanthropomorphized sheep broke his leg. **Douglas Adams** parodied sci-fi in his hilarious series *Hitchhiker's Guide to the Galaxy,* and

ENGLAND

Helen Fielding's hapless *Bridget Jones* speaks for singletons everywhere. Britain has also produced volumes of children's literature. **Lewis Carroll's** *Alice's Adventures in Wonderland* (1865) and **C.S. Lewis's** *Chronicles of Narnia* (1950-56) continue to enchant generations. A linguist named **J.R.R. Tolkien,** Lewis's companion in letters and Oxford pub-readings (see p. 272), wrote fanciful tales of elves, wizards, short folk, and rings (*The Hobbit*, 1934; *Lord of the Rings*, 1954-56). **Roald Dahl** spun tales of chocolate fantasy for children (and tales of other types of fantasy for adults). Recently, **J.K. Rowling** has swept the world with her tale of juvenile wizardry in the blockbuster *Harry Potter* series.

ART AND ARCHITECTURE

HOUSES OF GODS AND MEN. British art has long been bolstered by patronage and dominated by influences from abroad, and the many cathedrals and castles of England's skyline trace a history of foreign conquests and invasions. Houses of worship began as sturdy stone **churches** like **St. Martin's Chapel** in Canterbury (p. 150), but gave way to the sculptured towers of cathedrals like **Winchester** (p. 191). The Normans introduced **Romanesque** architecture (round arches and thick walls), evident in Durham cathedral (p. 438), and the **Gothic** period ushered in a new world of intricate, elegant, and deceptively delicate buildings like the Wells (p. 216) and Salisbury (p. 200) cathedrals and King's College Chapel in Cambridge (p. 326). After the **Renaissance,** architects had near-magical engineering capabilities—attested to by **Christopher Wren's** fantastic dome on St. Paul's Cathedral (p. 113), which he built after the Great Fire of London (1666).

GET THEE TO A NUNNERY Residents of early England may have kept their glossary of cathedral terminology up-to-date, but we modern types are not always so capable. Read on for a demystification of common terms.

Buttress: a spidery, external support that absorbs stress and weight

Clerestory: the uppermost part of a cathedral wall whose windows welcome light and lessen the weight of the structure's soaring heights

Cruciform: the cross-shaped floor-plan of many Norman churches

Nave: the central aisle of a church leading from its entrance to the altar

Quire: where the choir sings, to the east of the nave

Tracery: carved stonework such as lacy Gothic windows

Transept: the transverse part of a church with a cruciform floor plan

Vaulting: a lofty, arched structure supported by columns or a wall that serves as a roof or as further support for upper storeys

...and, because we're looking out for you,

Reredorter: a monastic toilet

Early domestic architecture in Britain progressed from the **stone dwellings** of sensible pre-Christian folk (see Skara Brae, p. 683) to the Romans' **forts and villas** (see Hadrian's Wall, p. 447) to the squat, square **Norman castles** like the Tower of London (p. 114). Warmongering Edward I constructed a string of superbly **fortified cliff castles** along the Welsh coast (see Harlech, p. 508; Caernarfon, p. 513; Beaumaris, p. 523), setting the tone for the military residences of the turbulent Middle Ages. The Renaissance was ushered in with sumptuous **Tudor homes** like Henry VIII's Hampton Court (p. 132), which transitioned into an 18th-century competition between the heady **Baroque** style of Castle Howard (p. 426) and the severe symmetry of the **Palladian** Houghton Hall (p. 341). **Stately homes** like Howard and Houghton (all the rage until well into the 20th century) were furnished with **Chippendale** furniture, stocked with **Wedgwood** crockery, and surrounded by equally stately **gardens** (the most famous designed by prolific green thumb **Capability Brown;** see Blenheim Palace, p. 283). The **Arts and Crafts** movement, which gave us the traditional English **cottage garden** (see Sissinghurst, p. 156), was part of a backwards-looking **revival craze** during the Victorian period; thus we have the **neo-Gothic** Houses of Parliament (p. 112) and the **neo-Classical** British Museum (p. 133). Today, hotshot, high-profile types **Richard Rogers** and **Norman Foster** vie for bragging rights as England's most influential architect, littering London with wonderful, wacky new additions like the Lloyd's Building (p. 117), City Hall, and all the **Millennium madness** (Dome, p. 98; Tower; and Bridge, p. 118).

ON THE CANVAS. Britain's early, religion-oriented art, like **illuminated manuscripts** gave way to secular patronage and the institution of court painters: portraitists like **Hans Holbein the Younger** (1497-1543) and **Nicholas Hilliard** (1547-1619), and general Renaissance men **Peter Paul Reubens** (1577-1640) and his pupil **Anthony Van Dyck** (1599-1641). Vanity, and thus portraiture, continued to flourish into the 18th century, with **Joshua Reynolds** and **Thomas Gainsborough.** Along with the English drive to better their homes and gardens came an interest in **landscape painting,** which was propagated by Gainsborough and peaked in the 19th century with close contemporaries **J.M.W. Turner** and **John Constable.** The Victorian fascination for reviving old art forms sparked movements like **Dante Gabriel Rossetti's** (1828-82) Italian-inspired, damosel-laden Pre-Raphaelite school. Victorians also dabbled in new art forms like photography, and took advantage of early mass media with engravings and cartoons. Modernist trends from the Continent, like Cubism and Expressionism, were picked up by **Wyndham Lewis** (1882-1957) and **Henry Moore** (1898-1986). WWII broke art wide open (as it did most things), giving us experimental, edgy works by **Francis Bacon** and **Lucian Freud** (whose portrait of the Queen was unveiled in 2002... and received almost as much critical debate as an artist could hope for). **David Hockney** (b. 1937) gave American pop art a dose of British wit. The precocious **Young British Artists (YBAs)** of the 1990s include sculptor **Rachel Whitbread** and multi-media artist **Damien Hirst.** The new, fabulous, and factory-like Tate Modern (p. 118) is the place for contemporary art, while galleries in London (Tate Britain, p. 134; the British Museum, p. 133; the National Gallery p. 133) continue to hold their reputation among the world's greatest collections.

FASHION. Inspired by the hip street energy of London in the 1960s along with movements like Op and Pop Art, England's fashion designers have achieved international fame. A revolution was sparked when **Mary Quant** (b. 1934) invented the miniskirt. **Vivienne Westwood** (b. 1941) is credited with originating punk fashion in the early 1970s, and her label is still known for its references to costume history. The most recent string of young British designers have been making their marks at prestigious fashion houses—**John Galliano** (b. 1960) at Dior, **Alexander McQueen** (b. 1970), named British Designer of the Year in 2001, at Givenchy, and Sir Paul's daughter **Stella McCartney** (b. 1972) at Chloe.

MUSIC

CLASSICAL. In the middle ages, traveling, Pete Seeger-like **minstrels** sang narrative folk **ballads** in the courts of the rich. During the Renaissance, English ears were tuned to cathedral anthems, psalms, madrigals, and the odd lute performance. **Henry Purcell** (1659-1695) rang in the baroque with instrumental music for Shakespeare's plays as well as England's first great opera, *Dido and Aeneas.* The 18th century, regarded as England's musical Dark Age, welcomed the visits of the foreign geniuses Mozart, Haydn, and the nationally-challenged **George Frideric Handel,** a German composer who wrote operas in the Italian style but spent most of his life in Britain. Thanks to Handel's influence, England experienced a wave of **opera-**

mania in the early 1700s, but enthusiasm waned when listeners realized they couldn't understand what the performers were saying. The turning point occurred when **John Gay** satirized the opera house in *The Beggar's Opera* (1727), a low-brow comedy in which Italianate arias were set to English folk tunes. Today's audiences are probably familiar with the operettas of **W.S. Gilbert** (1836-1911) and **Arthur Sullivan** (1842-1900); the pair were rumored to hate each other, but managed to produce gems such as *The Mikado* and *The Pirates of Penzance*. A second renaissance of more serious music began under **Edward** "Pomp 'n' Circumstance" **Elgar** (1857-1934), today most often appreciated at graduation ceremonies. **Gustav Holst** (1874-1934), in contrast to his suites for military band, adapted Neoclassical methods and folk materials to Romantic moods in *The Planets*.

Also borrowing elements from folk melodies, **Ralph Vaughan Williams** (1872-1958) and **John Ireland** (1879-1962) brought musical modernism to the island. The world wars provided adequate fodder for this continued musical resurgence, provoking **Benjamin Britten's** (1913-76) heartbreaking *War Requiem* and **Michael Tippett's** (1905-98) humanitarian oratorio, *A Child of Our Time*. Although the popular **Proms** at Royal Albert Hall (p. 145) afford a rousing evening surrounded by Brits waving flags, blowing whistles, and singing along to their favorite traditional national songs, later 20th-century trends—**Oliver Knussen's** one-act opera of Maurice Sendak's *Where the Wild Things Are* and **Andrew Lloyd Webber's** blend of opera, popular music, and falling chandeliers—demonstrate the lowbrow but commercially lucrative shift of British musical influence.

THE BRITISH ARE COMING. England's tag as "a land without music" (coined for the island's lack of an original classical composer since the Renaissance) can be disproved by a glance at any Billboard chart from the past forty years. Invaded by American blues and rock 'n' roll following WWII, Britain staged an offensive unprecedented anywhere in history: the **British Invasion** groups of the 60s infiltrated the colonies with a more daring, controversial sound. Native Liverpudlians (p. 357), the **Beatles** were the ultimate trendsetters, still influential more than three decades after their break-up. The edgier lyrics and grittier sound of the **Rolling Stones** shifted teens' thoughts from "I Wanna Hold Your Hand" to "Let's Spend the Night Together." Over the next 20 years, England imported the hard-driving **Kinks**, the Urban "mod" sound of **The Who**, the psychedelia-meets-Motown **Yardbirds**, and guitar gurus Eric Clapton of **Cream** and Jimmy Page of **Led Zeppelin**.

ANARCHY IN THE UK. Despite (or perhaps because of) England's conservative national character, homosexuality became central to the mid-70s flamboyant scene. British rock schismed, as the theatrical excesses of **glam rock** performers like **Queen, Elton John,** and **David Bowie** contrasted with the conceptual, album-oriented **art rock** emanating from **Pink Floyd** and Phil Collins's **Genesis**. With civil unrest on the rise due to high unemployment and an energy crisis, dissonant **punk rock** bands like **Stiff Little Fingers** and the **Clash** emerged from Britain's industrial centers as a counter to self-indulgence. Meanwhile, the **Sex Pistols** stormed the scene with profane and wildly successful antics—their angry 1977 single "God Save the Queen" topped the charts despite being banned in the UK. Sharing punk's anti-establishment impulses, the metal of **Ozzy Osbourne** and **Iron Maiden** was much less acclaimed but still attracted a cult following. Sheffield's **Def Leppard** carried the hard-rock-big-hair ethic through the 80s, while punk offshoots like **The Cure** and **goth** bands played against the backdrop of conservative Thatcherism.

I WANT MY MTV. Buoyed by a booming economy, British bands continued to achieve popular success on both sides of the Atlantic thanks to the 1980s advent of America's Music Television. **Dire Straits** introduced the first computer-animated music video, while **Duran Duran,** the **Eurythmics, Boy George, Tears for Fears,** and the

Police enjoyed many top-10 hits. England is also responsible for some of the giants of the lipstick-and-synthesizer age, including **George Michael** and **Bananarama.** At the end of the decade, a crop of guitar-noise bands from Manchester galvanized the early **rave** movement. Any clubber worth her tube-top can tell you about England's influence on dance music, from the **Chemical Brothers** and Brighton-bred **Fatboy Slim** (see p. 170) to the house, trip-hop, and ska sounds of **Basement Jaxx, Massive Attack,** and **Jamiroquai.** Home to the original boy band, England produced Robbie Williams (survivor of the bubblegummy **Take That**) and, in a moment of inspired equality of the sexes, gave us the **Spice Girls** and their astonishingly clever lyrics ("What I really really really want is zig-a-zig-ah!"). Beatles-esque bands the **Verve** and **Oasis** cherish dreams of rock 'n' roll stardom, leaving trashed hotel rooms in their wake, while the tremendous popularity of American **grunge rock** inspired a host of poseurs in the UK, beginning with **Bush** but reaching maturity with Oxford's conceptual innovators, **Radiohead.**

> **GET YER ROCKS OFF** If you're looking for road tunes, you could do worse than to pick something from this selection of albums.
>
> **British Invasion:** The Beatles, *Sergeant Pepper's Lonely Hearts Club Band;* The Rolling Stones, *Beggar's Banquet;* and *Something Else by the Kinks.*
> **Punk/post-punk:** The Clash, *London Calling;* Joy Division, *Permanent;* and The Sex Pistols, *Never Mind the Bollocks, Here's the Sex Pistols.*
> **Synth-pop:** Duran Duran, *Decade;* Pet Shop Boys, *Discography;* The Police, *Every Breath You Take: The Singles;* and *(The Best of) New Order.*
> **Indie:** The Smiths, *The Queen is Dead;* Blur, *Parklife;* Oasis, *What's the Story (Morning Glory);* Pulp, *Different Class;* and Radiohead, *OK Computer.*
> **Dance:** Fatboy Slim, *On the Floor at the Boutique;* Massive Attack, *Blue Lines;* Portishead, *Dummy;* and Roni Size and Reprazent, *New Forms.*

FILM
British film has endured an uneven history, marked by cycles of relative independence from Hollywood followed by increasing drains of talent to America. **Charles Chaplin** and Archibald Alec Leach (a.k.a. **Cary Grant**) were both Briton-born but made their names in US films. The **Royal Shakespeare Company** has produced a heavyweight set of alumni (like **Dame Judi Dench, Sir Ian McKellen,** and **Jeremy Irons**) who made the transition to celluloid. Earlier Shakespeare impresario **Laurence Olivier** worked both sides of the camera in *Henry V* (the 1944 brainchild of government-sponsored WWII propaganda), and his *Hamlet* (1948) is still the hallmark Dane. Master of suspense **Alfred Hitchcock** snared audiences with films produced on both sides of the Atlantic, scaring the bejeebies out of motel-goers and shower-takers. The 60s phenomenon of "swingin' London" created new momentum for the film industry and jump-started international interest in British culture. American Richard Lester made the **Beatles'** *A Hard Day's Night* in 1963, and a year later Scot **Sean Connery** downed the first of many martinis as **James Bond** in *Dr. No.*

Elaborate costume drama and offbeat independent films have come to represent contemporary British film. The sagas *Chariots of Fire* (1981) and *Gandhi* (1982) swept the Oscars in successive years. Director-producer team **Merchant-Ivory** have led the way in adaptations of British novels like Forster's *A Room with a View* (1986). **Kenneth Branagh** has focused his talents on adapting Shakespeare for the screen, with glossy, acclaimed works such as *Hamlet* (1996) and even glossier, not-so-acclaimed attempts like a musical version of *Love's Labour's Lost* (2000). The dashing **Guy** "Mr. Madonna" **Ritchie** has tapped into earlier cinematic conventions with his dizzying *Lock, Stock and Two Smoking Barrels* (1998). **Nick Park** took claymation and British quirk to a new level with the *Wallace and Gromit* shorts. Recent British films have

garnered a fair number of international awards; the working-class feel-goods *The*
Monty (1997) and *Billy Elliot* (2000), and **Mike Leigh's** affecting *Secrets and L*
(1995) and costume extravaganza *Topsy-Turvy* (1999) all took home some hardw
from sources like the Academy, the Screen Actors' Guild, and MTV. New entries
the world of blockbusterdom are the *Harry Potter* (filmed at gorgeous Alnwick (
tle, p. 453) and *Lord of the Rings* franchises, both of which kicked off in 2001.

MEDIA

ALL THAT'S FIT TO PRINT. In a culture with a rich print-media history, the in
ence of newspapers remains enormous. The UK's plethora of national newspap
yields a range of political viewpoints. **The Times,** long a model of thoughtful disc
tion and mild infallibility, has turned Tory under the ownership of Rupert "Buy
Murdoch. **The Daily Telegraph,** dubbed "Torygraph," is fairly conservative and
fashioned. **The Guardian** leans left, while **The Independent** answers for its name
the infamous tabloids, **The Sun,** Murdoch-owned and better known for its pa
three topless pin-up than for its reporting, is among the most influential. Am
the others, **The Daily Mail, The Daily Express,** and **The London Evening Standard** (
only evening paper) make serious attempts at popular journalism, although
first two tend to position themselves as the conservative voice of Middle Engla
The Daily Mirror, The News of the World, and **The Star** are as shrill and lewd as
Sun. **The Financial Times,** on pleasing pink paper, does more elegantly for the (
what *The Wall Street Journal* does for Wall Street. Although closely associa
with their sister dailies, Sunday newspapers are actually separate entities. **The**
day Times, The Sunday Telegraph, The Independent on Sunday, and the highly polis
Observer, the world's oldest paper and sister to *The Guardian,* offer detailed a
sports, and news coverage, together with more "soft bits" than the dailies.

A quick glance around any High St. newsagent will prove Britain has no short
of magazines. World affairs are covered with refreshing candor and wit by
Economist. The New Statesman on the left and **The Spectator** on the right cover p
tics and the arts with verve. The satirical **Private Eye** is subversive, hilarious,
overtly political. Some of the best music mags in the world—**Melody Maker,** I
Musical Express (NME), Q, and Gramophone—are UK-based. Movie and other en
tainment news comes in the over-sized **Empire.** The indispensable London jou
Time Out is the most comprehensive listings guide to the city and features fasci
ing pieces on British culture; its website (www.timeout.co.uk) also keeps tabs
events in Dublin, Edinburgh, and Glasgow. Recent years have seen the explos
of "lad's magazines" such as **FHM** and **Loaded,** which feature scantily-clad wor
and articles on beer, "shagging," and "pulling."

ON THE AIRWAVES. The **BBC** (British Broadcasting Corporation, sometin
known as the Beeb) established its reputation for cleverly styled fairness with
radio services, and its World Service continues to provide citizens of count
around the world with a glimpse into British life. Within the UK, the BBC
Radios 1-5, covering news (4; 93.5FM), sports (5; 693MW/AM), and the whole sp
trum of music from rock (1; 98.8FM) to classical (3; 91.3FM) to catch-all
89.1FM). Each region also has a variety of local commercial broadcasting servi
British radio is responsible for the introduction of the **soap opera** (*The Archer*
still broadcast weekdays on Radio 4), a form now dominated by television incar
tions *Eastenders* and *Coronation Street.*

Aside from the daytime suds, British television has brought to the world s
mighty comic wonders as *Monty Python's Flying Circus* and *Mr. Bean.*
BBC has made some stellar literary adaptations into **miniseries**—1996's *Pride*
Prejudice is widely considered one of the best film versions of Austen's w

(and sparked an international "Darcy-fever" for Colin Firth). At the other end of things is Britain's current obsession with do-it-yourself home-improvement shows, cooking programs, and (like the rest of the *Survivor*-crazed world) voyeur TV. A commercial-free repository of wit and innovation, the BBC broadcasts on two national channels. **BBC1** carries news as well as various Britcoms. Telecast on **BBC2** are cultural programs and fledgling sitcoms (*Absolutely Fabulous* and the marvelous *Blackadder* both started here). **ITV,** Britain's first and most established commercial network, carries drama, comedy, and news. **Channel 4** has the hilarious *Big Breakfast* morning show, highly respected arts programming, and imported American shows. **Channel 5,** the newest channel, features late-night sports shows and action movies. Rupert Murdoch's satellite **Sky TV** shows football, futbol, soccer, and other incarnations of the global game on its Sky Sports channel, while its Sky One channel features mostly American shows.

FOOD AND TEA

English cooking, like the English climate, is a training for life's unavoidable hardships.
—R.P. Lister

British cuisine has a deservedly modest reputation, but redeems itself in the few specialties without which the world's palate would be sadly incomplete. Britons like to start their day off heartily with the famous, cholesterol-filled, meat-anchored **English breakfast,** served in most B&Bs across the country. The best native dishes for lunch or dinner are **roasts**—beef, lamb, and Wiltshire hams—and **puddings**—including the standard Yorkshire. **Bangers and mash** and **bubble and squeak,** despite their stunning names, are basically left-overs (of sausages and potatoes, and cabbage and potatoes, respectively). Vegetables, often boiled into a flavorless, textureless mush, are typically the weakest part of the meal. Beware the British salad—often a few limp lettuce leaves mixed with an abundance of sweetened mayonnaise called "salad cream."

The British like their **desserts** exceedingly sweet and gloopy. Fools, sponges, trifles, tarts, the celebrated **spotted dick** (spongy raisin cake), and puddings of endless variety will satiate even the severest of sweet teeth. Most desserts are served with large dollops of thick, yellow **custard** or whipped **cream.**

FLAKES AND FRUITS
British food has character (of one sort or another), and the traditional snack menu is a unique hodgepodge of sweets, crisps, and squashes. **Cadbury's chocolate** bars to die for include Flake, the honeycombed Crunchie, and the classic Dairy Milk. **Sweets** come in many forms—the fizzy Refreshers, the chewy Wine Gums, or frosted Fruit Pastilles. Potato chips, or **crisps** as they are known in England, are not just salted, but take on a range of flavors, from Prawn Cocktail to Cheese 'n' Onion. All this sugar and salt washes down with a bottle of Ribena, a blackcurrant manna from heaven. This beverage belongs to a family of drinks known as **squash,** fruit-based syrups watered down to drink. And you wonder how Roald Dahl managed to dream up Willy Wonka...

Pub grub is fast, filling, and a fine option for budget travelers. Hot meals could be meat pies like **Cornish pasties** (PAH-stees), meat pies like **shepherd's pie,** or meat pies like **steak and kidney pie.** The inexpensive **ploughman's lunch,** a staple in country pubs, is simply bread, cheese, and pickles. More cheap culinary options abound at the perennial chippy—deep fried **fish and chips** are served in a cone of paper, dripping with grease, salt, and vinegar. In recent years, restaurant chains have sprung up in the larger cities. **Outdoor markets** and **supermarkets** provide another source of cheap food, especially for picnics—try Stilton cheese with digestive biscuits and find a suitably picturesque view. Britain's history of imperialism has resulted in an abundance of excellent **ethnic restaurants** throughout the country. For a welcome alternative to traditional Isles fare, try Chinese, Greek, and especially Indian cuisines—Britain offers some of the best **tandoori** and **curry** outside of India, particularly in London and the larger northern cities.

British **"tea"** refers both to a drink and a social ceremony. The ritual refreshment, accompanying almost every meal, is served strongly steeped and milky. The standard tea, colloquially known as a nice **cuppa,** is mass produced by PG Tips or Tetleys; more refined cups specify particular blends such as **Earl Grey, Darjeeling,** or **Lapsang Souchong.** The oft-stereotyped British ritual of afternoon **high tea,** served around 2-4pm, includes cooked meats, salad, sandwiches, and pastries. Fans of Victorianism will appreciate the dainty **cucumber sandwiches** served at classy tea joints like Fortnum and Mason's or the Savoy Hotel in London. **Cream tea,** a specialty of Cornwall and Devon, includes toast, shortbread, crumpets, scones, and jam, accompanied by clotted cream (a cross between whipped cream and butter). The summer teatime potion called **Pimms** is a sangria-esque punch of fruit juices and gin (the precise recipe is claimed to be a well-guarded secret). Many Britons take short tea breaks each day, including mornings ("elevenses"), but Sunday takes the cake for teatime decadence.

PUBS AND BEER

> O Beer! O Hodgson, Guinness, Allsopp, Bass! Names that should be on every infant's tongue!
> —S.C.L. Calverley

Sir William Harcourt believed that English history was made in the pubs as much as in the Houses of Parliament. You may not witness history in the making, but you will certainly absorb the spirit of the region if you pause within the wood-panelled walls of a local tavern. The routine inspired by the pub is considerable; to stop in for a sharpener at lunchtime and then again after work is not uncommon. Brits rapidly develop affinities for neighborhood establishments, becoming loyal to their **locals,** and pubs in turn tend to cater to their regulars and develop a particular character. Pubs have a Starbucks-like (but far superior) ubiquity; even the smallest village can support a decent **pub crawl.** The drinking age is a skimpily-enforced 18, and you need only be 14 to enter a pub.

Bitter, named for its sharp, hoppy aftertaste, is the standard pub drink and should be hand-pumped or pulled from the tap at cellar temperature into government-stamped pint glasses (20oz.) or the more modest but socially scorned half-pints. **Real ale** retains a die-hard cult of connoisseurs in the shadow of giant corporate breweries (check out St. Albans' Campaign for Real Ale, p. 269). **Brown, pale,** and **India pale ales**—less common varieties—all have a relatively heavy flavor with noticeable hop. **Stout,** the distinctive subspecies of ale, is rich, dark, and creamy; try the Irish Guinness (p. 725) with its silky foam head, rumored to be a recipe stolen from the older Beamish. Most draught ales and stouts are served at room temperature; if you can't stand the heat, try a **lager,** the tasty precursor of American beer. **Cider,** a fermented apple juice served sweet or dry, is one potent, cold, and tasty alternative to beer. Variations on the standard pint include the **shandy,** a combination of beer and fizzy lemonade that no respectable drinker would go near; **black velvet,** stout and champagne; **black and tan,** layers of stout and ale; and **snakebite,** a murky mix of lager and cider with a dash of blackcurrant Ribena.

Visitors will learn to their dismay that government-imposed **closing times** force revels to end early. Drinking hours enforced to prevent WWI munitions workers from arriving drunk to work are still in place; generally, drinks are served 11am-11pm Monday to Saturday, and noon-3pm Sunday and 7-10:30pm Sunday. A bell ten or so minutes before closing time signifies "last orders." (Many a barstool jockey has argued that the most painful words in all of Eliot's *The Waste Land* are the publican-god's cry, "HURRY UP PLEASE IT'S TIME.") More recently, the government has been making noise about **extending hours,** or doing away with restrictions altogether. Many establishments, particularly in larger towns and cities, find ways around closing times anyway—serving food or having an entertainment license allows an establishment to serve alcohol later, so late-night wine bars are popular, and around pub-closing time people pack into clubs.

SPORTS

Many evils may arise which God forbid.
—King Edward II, banning football in London, 1314

FOOTBALL. The game of **football** (soccer), whose rules were formalized by the English Football Association (FA; www.the-fa.org) in 1863, remains the island's—and the world's—most popular sport. In the highest echelon are the 20 **clubs** (teams) of the **Premier League,** which are populated with world-class players from Britain and abroad. Below the Premiership lie the three divisions of the Nationwide League. At the end of the season, the three clubs with the worst records in the Premiership face relegation to the First Division, whose top three clubs are promoted. The **F.A. Cup,** held every May on the hallowed turf of **Wembley** (soon to be replaced by the new **National Stadium** currently on the drawing board) is the top knockout competition, and the ultimate achievement for an English football club is to "do the Double"—win the Premier League and the F.A. Cup in one season.

The English Premier League is dominated by teams like London Arsenal, Liverpool, Leeds, and Chelsea, but **Manchester United** ("Man U"; p. 369), now owned by Rupert "Mine All Mine" Murdoch, is the red victory machine that every Brit loves to hate. Unfortunately, the four British international teams (England, Scotland, Wales, and Northern Ireland compete as separate countries) have not performed well in **World Cups** and **European Championships**—England's 1966 World Cup victory being the glorious exception. The next round of mania is slated for Germany, in 2006; qualifiers for the 2004 **Euro Cup** (in Portugal) will be running throughout 2003.

Over half a million fans attend professional matches in Britain every weekend from mid-August to May, and they spend the few barren weeks of summer waiting for the publication of the coming season's **fixtures** (match schedules). If you can get tickets, a match is well worth attending for a glimpse of British **football culture.** Worship at postmodern cathedrals—grand, storied stadia full of painted faces and team colors, resounding with a rowdy chorus of uncannily synchronized (usually rude) songs and chants. Intracity rivalries (London's Arsenal-Tottenham or Liverpool's Everton-Liverpool) have been known to divide families. Violence and vandalism used to dog the game, causing tension between fans and the police who tried to control huge crowds in old stadia. **Hooligans** are usually on their worst behavior when the England national team plays abroad; things are a bit better at home, though far from perfect. The atmosphere in stadia has become safer (albeit pricier) now that clubs have been forced to convert to seating-only, rather than standing spaces in the once-infamous terraces.

LESSER GAMES. According to legend, **rugby** was born one glorious day in 1823 when William Webb Ellis, an inspired (or perhaps slightly confused) Rugby School student, picked up a soccer ball and ran it into the goal. Since then, rugby has evolved into a complex, subtle, and thoroughly lunatic game. The amateur **Rugby Union** and professional **Rugby League**, both 19th-century creations, have slightly different rules and

different numbers of players (15 and 13); in Britain, the former is associated w
Scotland, Wales, and the Midlands, and the latter with northwest England. With li
stoppage of play, no non-injury substitutions, and not much protective gear to sp
of, rugby is a *melée* of blood, mud, and drinking songs. An oval-shaped ball is carr
or passed backward until the team is able to touch the ball down past the goal line
"try" and worth five points) or kick it through the uprights (three points). The club s
son runs from September to May, while the culmination of international rugby is
Rugby World Cup, which will happen Down Under in October of 2003.

While fanatically followed within the Commonwealth, **cricket** remains a p
nomenally confusing spectacle to the uninitiated. The game is played by two
player teams on a 22-yard green, marked at each end by two **wickets** (made of th
stumps and two bails; www.cricket.org has explanations and diagrams of the
mysterious contraptions). In an innings, one team acts as **batsmen** and the other
fielders. The batting team sends up two batsmen, and a **bowler** from the field
side throws the ball so that it bounces toward the wickets. The goal of the field
is to try to get the batsmen out by **taking** the wickets (hitting the wickets so t
the bails fall) or by catching the ball. The batsmen's goal is to make as many r
as they can while protecting their wickets, scoring every time they switch plac
The teams switch positions once ten batsmen are out; usually both sides bat twi
Matches last one to five days. (No, Alice, we aren't in Wonderland any mor
International games are known as **Test** matches; the **Ashes,** named for the rema
of a cricket bail, are the prize in England's Test series with Australia. Cricket I
its own **World Cup,** of course, set for February and March of 2003 in South Afri
London's **Lords** cricket grounds is regarded as the spiritual home of the game.

Tennis, a sport with a long history, was becoming the game of the upper class
the end of the 15th century, when Henry VII played in slimming black velvet.
the game developed, cooler white became the traditional color, while today alm
any high-tech garb goes. For two weeks in late June and early July, tennis buffs
over the world focus their attention on **Wimbledon,** a bastion of strawberries-a
cream lovers and home to the only Grand Slam event played on grass.

HORSES AND COURSES. The Brits have a special affinity for their horses, de
onstrated in the tallyhooing of fox-killing excursions and Princess Anne's com
tition in **equestrian** during the 1976 Olympics. In late June, **polo** devotees flock
the **Royal Windsor Cup.** Horse-racing also pretends to noble status. An import
society event, the Royal Gold Cup Meeting at **Ascot** has occurred in the seco
half of June for every summer since 1711, though some see it as an excuse for B
of all strata to indulge in drinking and gambling while wearing over-the-top ha
Top hats also distinguish the famed **Derby** (DAR-bee), which has been run sir
1780 on Epsom Racecourse, Surrey, on the first Saturday of June.

Britain remains a force in rowing, and the annual **Henley Royal Regatta,** on
Thames in Oxfordshire, is the most famous series of rowing races in the wor
The five-day regatta ends on the first Sunday in July; Saturday is the most popu
day, but some of the best races are the Sunday finals. The **Boat Race** (also on
Thames, but in London), between Oxford and Cambridge, enacts the traditio
rivalry between the schools. Britain is the center of Formula One racecar desi
and the **British Grand Prix** is held every July at Silverstone racecourse in Northar
tonshire. Meanwhile, the **T.T. races** bring hordes of screeching motorcycles to
Isle of Man during the first two weeks of June (p. 398).

ENGLAND

HOLIDAYS AND FESTIVALS

It's difficult to travel anywhere in the British Isles without bumping into some kind of festival. Every town seems to celebrate its right to, well, celebrate. And that's *before* the World Cup games begin. Below is a not-at-all-comprehensive list of festivals in England; the local tourist information centre for any town can point you toward the nearest scene of revelry and merry-making, and *Let's Go* tries to list individual events in the appropriate towns. The chart below also includes the UK-wide **public** and **bank holidays;** see the corresponding sections of Scotland (p. 545), Wales (p. 464), and Ireland (p. 720) for more country-specific festivals.

2003 HOLIDAYS AND FESTIVALS

DATE	NAME & LOCATION	DESCRIPTION
January 1	New Year's Day	UK holiday for champagne recovery purposes
February 1	Chinese New Year, London	Fireworks! Lots of fireworks!
April 18	Good Friday	UK holiday
April 21	Easter Monday	UK holiday
April 23	St. George's Day	Honoring England's dragon-slaying patron saint
May 5	May Day Bank Holiday	UK holiday, just because
May 3-25	Brighton Festival	Largest mixed-arts festival in England
May 20-23	Chelsea Flower Show	London owns the world's premier garden event
May 24-June 6	TT Races, Isle of Man	The big event in the Road Racing Capital of the World
May 26	Spring Bank Holiday	UK holiday, just because
June 6-7	The Derby, Surrey	Horses and Hats!
June 27-29	Glastonbury Festival	Britain's biggest homage to rock
June 17-20	Royal Ascot, London	Hats and Horses!
June 23-July 6	Wimbledon	A lot of racquets and a BIG silver dish
July 2-6	Henley Royal Regatta	The world's premier boat race
August 22-25	Mardi Gras, Manchester	A wild street party in Manchester's Gay Village
August 24-25	Notting Hill Carnival	Mad London street party
August 25	Summer Bank Holiday	UK holiday, just because
December 25	Christmas Day	UK holiday for worship of commercialization
December 26	Boxing Day	UK holiday for continued consumerism

ENGLAND

LONDON

 London's phone code is **020**.

A man who is tired of London is tired of life; for there is in London all that life can afford.
—Samuel Johnson

Ever an assault on the senses, London defies easy categorization. Those expecting tea-drinking, Royal-loving, Kensington-bred green-thumbs will quickly find equal numbers of slinky, black-clad young things lounging in Soho bars, Indian take-away owners in the East End, and pinstriped bankers in the City. While London abounds with remnants of Britain's long history, a trip to one of many futuristic boutiques will eclipse any impression (culled from bobbies, Beefeaters, and Big Ben) that this city is chained to bygone days. Many pubs may close early, but London roars on, full throttle, around the clock. One of the world's greatest centers for the arts, London dazzles with concert halls, theaters, museums, and bookshops. This is a world where trends bloom and die—buy it here and six months later you'll see it on the catwalks—and despite the dismal reputation of British food, London has steadily gained status as a culinary center. This is in no small measure due to a large and diverse multinational population, ever-growing and ever renewing the metropolis with energy and optimism. For more detailed coverage of this great and good city, get thee to a bookstore for a copy of *Let's Go: London 2003.*

HIGHLIGHTS OF LONDON

THE POSTCARD STUFF To catch the Unmissables, start at stately **Westminster Abbey** (p. 111), gaze up at **St. Paul's Cathedral** (p. 113), watch your head at the imposing **Tower of London** (p. 114), do a spot of shopping and grab a bite in **Covent Garden** (p. 120), and finish off with a night of **clubbing** (p. 147).

IN THE GALLERIES Revel in magnificent museums—some of the finest in the world—from the revered **British Museum** (p. 133) and **National Gallery** (p. 133) to quirky **Sir John Soane's Museum** (p. 137) and the sleek new **Tate Modern** (p. 134).

ON THE STAGE Forget the West End—turn your theatrical attention to **Shakespeare's Globe Theatre** (p. 118), where you can jostle with the other "groundlings" or cram onto hard wooden benches while seeing the Bard as he was meant to be seen.

✈ INTERCITY TRANSPORTATION

BY PLANE

For information on international flights to London, see p. 24.

HEATHROW

Ugly, sprawling, crowded, and chaotic, Heathrow (☎(0870) 000 0123) feels more like a shopping mall with a runway than the world's busiest international airport.

Underground: ☎7222 1234. Heathrow's 2 Tube stations form a loop on the end of the **Piccadilly Line.** Trains stop first at Terminal 4 and then at Terminals 1,2,3 (50-70min. from central London; every 4-5min.; £3.60, under 16 £1.50).

Heathrow Express: ☎ (0845) 600 1515. A speedy link to **Paddington Station.** Buy tickets at Heathrow Express counters, on board, or at self-service machines; railpasses not valid (15min.; every 15min.; £11, return £20, £3 extra if bought on board).

Bus: National Express (☎ (08705) 808 080) sends **Airbus A2** to **King's Cross**, stopping at various points on the way (1¼-1¾hr.; about 2 per hr. 5:30am-9:45pm; £7, return £10). Also operates coaches to **Victoria Coach Station** (40-80min., 2 per hr.).

Taxis: Licensed (black) cabs cost at least £40 and take 50min.-1½hr.

GATWICK

Thirty miles south of the city, Gatwick (☎ (0870) 000 2468) may look distant, but three train services to London make transport a breeze. The **train station** is in the **South Terminal.** The **Gatwick Express** (☎ (08705) 301 530) service to **Victoria Station** would like you to think it's the only train to London (30min.; every 15min. 6am-8pm, every 30min. through the night; £11, return £21). In fact, cheaper **Connex** (☎ (0870) 603 0405) trains run the same route almost as frequently and take only 10min. longer (£8.20, return £16.40). Additionally, **Thameslink** (☎ (0845) 330 6333) trains head regularly to **King's Cross Station,** stopping at **London Bridge** and **Blackfriars** (50min.; every 15-30min.; £9.80, return £19.60). Gatwick's distance from London makes **road services** slow and unpredictable. National Express's **Airbus A5** travels to **Victoria Coach Station** (1½hr; about 2 per hr. 5:30am-9:45pm; £7, return £10). A licensed **taxi** will take at least 1hr. and cost at least £90.

STANSTED AND LUTON

Many charters and discount airlines operate from London's secondary airports. **Stansted** (☎ (0870) 000 0303) is halfway between London and Cambridge. **Stansted Express** (☎ (08705) 301 530) trains run to **Liverpool St. Station** (42min.; every 15-30min.; £13, return £23). National Express's **Airbus A6/A7** runs to **Victoria Station;** A6 via the West End, A7 via the City (1¼-1¾hr.; about 2 per hr. 5:30am-9:45pm; £7, return £10). From **Luton Airport, Thameslink** trains head to **King's Cross, Blackfriars,** and **London Bridge** (30-50min.; every 15-30min.; £9.50, return £18), while **Green Line 757** (☎ (0870) 608 7261) buses serve the **West End** and **Victoria Station** (1-1¾hr.; every 30min. 8am-8pm, every hr. 8pm-midnight and 3am-8am; £8, return £13).

BY TRAIN

London's array of mainline stations dates from the Victorian era, when each railway company had its own city terminus; see the box below for service information. All London termini are well served by bus and Tube; major stations sell various **Railcards,** which offer regular discounts on train travel (see **By Train,** p. 30); they do *not* sell BritRail passes, which must be purchased abroad.

LONDON TRAIN STATIONS

Charing Cross: Kent (Canterbury, Dover)

Euston: Northwest (Birmingham, Glasgow, Holyhead, Liverpool, Manchester)

King's Cross: Northeast (Cambridge, Edinburgh, Leeds, Newcastle, York)

Liverpool St.: East Anglia (Cambridge, Colchester, Ipswich, Norwich), Stansted

Paddington: West (Oxford), Southwest (Bristol, Cornwall), South Wales (Cardiff)

St. Pancras: Midlands (Nottingham), Northwest (Sheffield)

Victoria: South (Brighton, Canterbury, Dover, Hastings), Gatwick

Waterloo: South and Southwest (Portsmouth, Salisbury), Paris, Brussels

L O N D O N

Central London

● SIGHTS

Albert Memorial, 10	B4	Chelsea Physic Garden, 21	C5	Lincoln's Inn, 74	E3
All Souls Langham Place, 33	C3	Chinatown, 46	D3	London Eye, 70	D4
Apsley House, 26	C4	Design Museum, 99	F4	London Planetarium, 23	C3
Bank of England, 94	F3	The Gilbert Collection, 67	D3	Madame Tussaud's, 24	C3
Banqueting House, 53	D4	Gray's Inn, 72	E3	Millennium Bridge, 91	E4
The Barbican, 87	E3	Guildhall, 89	E3	Museum of London, 88	E3
British Library, 42	D2	Hayward Gallery, 69	D4	National Gallery, 48	D4
British Museum, 44	D3	HMS Belfast, 96	F4	National Portrait Gallery, 47	D4
Buckingham Palace, 32	C4	The Houses of Parliament, 56	D4	Natural History Museum, 12	B5
Cabinet War Rooms, 54	D4	ICA, 51	D4	Old Bailey, 83	E3
		Imperial War Museum, 78	E5	Queen's Gallery, 31	C4
		Jewel Tower, 58	D4	Royal Academy, 35	D4
		Kensington Palace, 7	B4	Royal Albert Hall, 11	B4

Royal Courts of Justice, **75**	E3	Southwark Cathedral, **95**	E4	The Temple, **76**	E3
The Royal Hospital, **22**	C5	St. Bartholomew the Great, **82**	E3	Theatre Royal, Dury Lane, **63**	D3
The Royal Mews, **30**	C4	St. Bride's, **79**	E3	Tower Bridge , **97**	F4
Royal Opera House, **62**	D3	St. James's Church, **39**	D4	The Tower of London, **98**	F4
Samuel Johnson's		St. James's Palace, **40**	D4	Trafalgar Sq. , **49**	D4
House, **77**	E3	St. John's Square, **81**	E3	Transport Museum, **65**	D3
Savile Row, **34**	D3	St. Margaret's Westminster, **55**	D4	University College London, **43**	D3
Science Museum, **13**	B5	St. Martin-ince-Fields, **50**	D4	Victoria and Albert Museum, **14**	B5
Serpentine Gallery, **9**	B4	St. Mary-le-Bow, **90**	E3	The Wallace Collection, **25**	C3
Shakespeare's Globe Theatre, **92**	E4	St. Mary-le-Strand, **66**	D3	The Wellington Arch, **27**	C4
Sherlock Holmes Museum, **19**	C3	St. Paul's Cathedral, **86**	E3	Westminster Abbey, **57**	D4
Sir John Soane's Museum, **73**	E3	St. Paul's Church, **64**	D3	Westminster Cathedral, **36**	D5
Smithfield Market, **80**	E3	Tate Britain, **59**	D5	Whitehall, **52**	D4
South Bank Centre, **68**	D4	Tate Modern, **85**	E4		

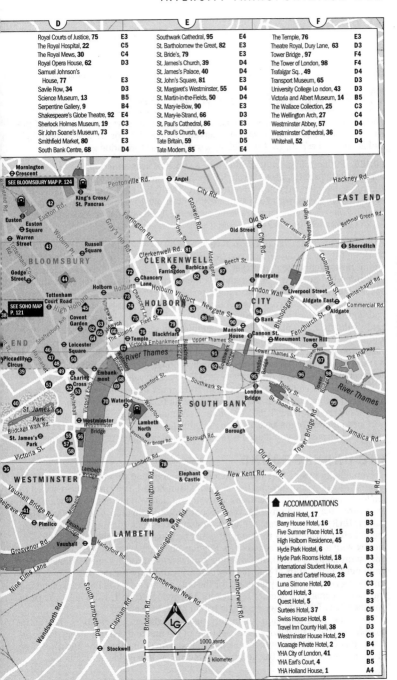

ACCOMMODATIONS

Admiral Hotel, **17**	B3
Barry House Hotel, **16**	B3
Five Sumner Place Hotel, **15**	B5
High Holborn Residence, **45**	D3
Hyde Park Hostel, **6**	B3
Hyde Park Rooms Hotel, **18**	B3
International Student House, **A**	C3
James and Cartref House, **28**	C5
Luna Simone Hotel, **20**	C3
Oxford Hotel, **3**	B5
Quest Hotel, **5**	B3
Surtees Hotel, **37**	C5
Swiss House Hotel, **8**	B5
Travel Inn County Hall, **38**	D3
Westminster House Hotel, **29**	C5
Vicarage Private Hotel, **2**	B4
YHA City of London, **41**	D5
YHA Earl's Court, **4**	B5
YHA Holland House, **1**	A4

BY BUS

Most long-distance buses trundle into **Victoria Coach Station** (Tube: Victoria), on Buckingham Palace Rd. **Green Line** (☎ (0870) 608 7261), which serves much of the area around London, leaves from **Eccleston Bridge Station**, behind Victoria. **National Express** (☎ (08705) 808 080) is the major intercity operator. (See **By Bus,** p. 37.)

☰ LOCAL TRANSPORTATION

Though locals are convinced otherwise, London's transport system is one of the world's best: there's nary a spot not served by Tube, bus, or train. For 24hr. info and advice call ☎ 7222 1234 or click to www.transportforlondon.gov.uk.

ZONES. Public transport is divided into a series of **concentric zones;** ticket prices depend on the zones passed through during your journey. To confuse matters, the zoning system depends on type of transport. The Tube, DLR, and rail operate on a system of six zones, with **Zone 1** the most central. Buses reduce this to four zones, though Zones 1, 2, and 3 are the same as for the Tube. Almost everything of interest to visitors is found in Zones 1 and 2.

PASSES. You're almost certain to save money by investing in a travel pass. Passes work on the zone system, and can be purchased at Tube, DLR, and rail stations, and at newsagents. Beware **ticket touts** hawking secondhand passes—there's no guarantee the ticket will work, and it's illegal (penalties are stiff). Note that **all passes expire** at 4:30am the morning after the printed expiry date. If you travel beyond the validity of your pass, you must purchase an **excess fare** at the start of your journey; failure to do so counts as fare evasion. Passes include **One Day Travelcards,** valid for bus, Tube, DLR, and commuter rail services from 9:30am weekdays and all day weekends; **LT Cards,** which differ only in being valid before 9:30am; **Family Travelcards,** for 1-2 adults and 1-4 children traveling together; **Weekend** and **Weekly Travelcards,** valid two consecutive days on weekends and public holidays or seven consecutive days, respectively; and **Bus Passes,** valid only on buses.

To qualify for child fares, teens **aged 14-15** must display a **child-rate Photocard** when purchasing tickets and traveling on public transport. These can be obtained free of charge from any Tube station on presentation of proof of age and a passport-sized photo. Teens **aged 16-17** are eligible for 30% discounts on period Travelcard and bus passes: you'll need a **16-17 Photocard,** available at Tube stations.

THE UNDERGROUND

Universally known as **"the Tube,"** London's Underground provides a fast and convenient way of getting around the capital. Within Zone 1, the Tube is best suited to longer journeys: adjacent stations are so close that you might as well walk, and buses are cheaper and often get you closer to your destination. The **Docklands Light Railway (DLR)** is a driverless, overland version of the Tube running in East London; the ticketing structure is the same. If you'll be traveling by Tube a lot, you'll save money with a **Travelcard** (see above). Regular ticket prices depend on two factors: how many zones traveled, and whether you traveled through Zone 1. Tickets must be bought at the **start of your journey** and are valid only for the day of purchase (including returns). **Keep your ticket** for the entire journey; it will be checked on the way out. A **carnet** is a pack of ten tickets for travel in Zone 1, valid one year from purchase (£11.50); otherwise a single trip in Zone 1 costs £1.60.

The Tube runs daily approximately **6am-midnight,** giving clubbers that extra incentive to party till dawn. The exact time of the first and last train from each station is posted in the ticket hall: check if you plan on taking the Tube any time after 11:30pm. Trains run less frequently early mornings, late nights, and Sundays.

BUSES

Excellent signposting makes the bus system easy to use even for those with no local knowledge; most stops display a map of local routes and nearby stops, together with a key to help you find the bus and stop you need. Officially, bus stops are either **regular** or **request:** buses are supposed to stop at regular stops (red logo on white background), but only pull up at request stops (white on red) if someone on board rings the bell or someone at the stop indicates with an outstretched arm. In reality, it's safest to ring/indicate for all stops. On the older open-platform "Routemaster" buses, you're free to hop on or off as you like. Normal buses run approximately 5:30am-midnight; a reduced network of **Night Buses** (see below) fills in the gap. Double-deckers generally run every 10-15min., while single-decker hoppers should come every 5-8min. (These are averages—it's not uncommon to wait 30min. only for three buses to show up in a row.)

On newer buses, show your pass or buy a ticket from the driver as you board: state your destination or just say the price. Older buses still use conductors, who make the rounds between stops to collect fares. Despite the "exact change" warnings posted on buses, drivers and conductors will give change, though a £5 note will elicit grumbles and anything larger risks refusal. **Keep your ticket** until you get off the bus, or you face a £5 on-the-spot fine. Trips including Zone 1 cost £1; journeys wholly outside Zone 1 cost 70p. Before 10pm, children aged 5-15 pay 40p regardless of zones traveled; after 10pm they pay adult fares.

NIGHT BUSES. When honest folk are in bed, London's Night Buses come out to chauffeur clubbers and other creatures of the twilight. Night Bus route numbers are prefixed with an **"N";** they typically operate on more or less the same routes as their daytime equivalents and cost the same. Many start from **Trafalgar Square.** Most Night Buses run 1-2 per hr. midnight-5:30am, then revert to pumpkins.

SUBURBAN RAILWAYS

Almost nonexistent in the city center, in the suburbs London's **commuter rail network** is nearly as extensive as the Tube—and in much of South and East London it's the only option. Though trains run less frequently than the Tube (generally every 20-30min.), they can dramatically reduce transit time thanks to direct cross-town links, and service often continues later into the night. For journeys combining rail travel with Tube and DLR, you can buy a single ticket valid for the entire trip. Travelcards are also valid on most suburban rail services, though not on inter-city lines that happen to make a few local stops.

TAXIS

Taxis in London come in two forms: licensed taxis, known as **black cabs,** and **minicabs,** essentially private cars that offer pre-arranged pickups. As symbolic of London as gondolas are of Venice, black cabs are also almost as expensive. That's because driving a London taxi is skilled work: your driver has studied for years to pass a rigorous exam called "The Knowledge" to prove she knows the name of every street in central London and how to get there by the shortest possible route. These cabs are specially designed for London's narrow streets and can turn on a sixpence—don't be afraid to hail one from the other side of the road. Available cabs are indicated by the blue "for hire" light by the driver and the orange "taxi" sign on the roof. **Pickups** attach a minimum £2 fee; dispatchers include **Computer Cabs** (☎ 7286 0286), **Dial-a-Cab** (☎ 7253 5000), and **Radio Taxis** (☎ 7272 0272).

Anyone with a car and a driver's license can set themselves up as a "minicab" company; while only licensed cabs can ply the streets for hire, there are no regulations concerning pre-arranged pickups. As a result, competition is fierce and prices are lower than licensed cabs. Unless you know a reliable company, ordering a minicab is something of a crapshoot, though there's rarely any danger involved (aside from a few hair-raising moments). Be especially careful with the dodgy drivers who turn up outside clubs at closing—jot down a phone number and call from the club, or arrange a pickup in advance. Always agree on a price with the driver before getting in; some firms have standardized price lists. One good choice is **Teksi** (☎ 7267 9999), offering 24hr. pickup anywhere in London.

■ ORIENTATION

CENTRAL LONDON NEIGHBORHOODS: THE BIG FOUR

THE CITY OF LONDON. "The City" is where London began, yet to most Londoners, Europe's most important financial center is now an outlying irrelevance. A quarter of a million people may work here during the day, but by night the City's population shrinks to a measly 8000, not even close to the number of tourists who daily storm St. Paul's Cathedral and the Tower of London.

THE SOUTH BANK. Close to the City, but long exempt from its party-pooping laws, the South Bank was for centuries London's entertainment center, renowned for theaters, cock-fighting, bull-baiting, and other less reputable diversions. The **"Millennium Mile"** stretches from the London Eye in the west to the swank restaurants of Butler's Wharf in the east, passing by the cultural powerhouses Festival Hall, Hayward Gallery, National Theatre, Tate Modern, and Shakespeare's Globe.

THE WEST END. Whether shopping, eating, theatergoing, or clubbing, you'll find the West End is London's heartland, with a wider variety of activities than anywhere else in the city. The well-heeled live in **Mayfair** and socialize in the gentlemen's clubs of neighboring **St. James's.** On the other side of Piccadilly Circus, **Soho** is London's nightlife nexus—and, around Old Compton St., its gay nexus. **Oxford St.** has been London's premier shopping drag for over 150 years. The fashion-conscious head to the boutiques of **Covent Garden,** southwest of Soho. To the south, the **Strand** leads to Westminster's majestic, pigeon-infested Trafalgar Square.

WESTMINSTER. Home to **Parliament,** the Prime Minister, and the Queen herself, Westminster exudes privilege. But away from the bustle of **Trafalgar Square,** the bureaucracy of **Whitehall,** and the gothic grandeur of the **Abbey,** Westminster is surprisingly down-to-earth. **Pimlico,** south of Victoria, is a quiet residential district with some of London's best B&Bs. Don't come here for food, shopping, or nightlife; but with some of London's top sights and trendier neighborhoods nearby, whatever you don't find in Westminster can't be far away.

OTHER CENTRAL LONDON NEIGHBORHOODS

BAYSWATER. Once London's most stylish neighborhood, Bayswater's downfall arrived with the Paddington canal and then the railway and their attendant slums. Today, the area graciously accommodates thousands of travelers in the B&Bs lining the streets around **Queensway** and **Paddington.** Bayswater has always been one of the most ethnically diverse neighborhoods in the city; it can rightly claim to be the original London home of those two English staples, curries and kebabs.

BLOOMSBURY. Home to dozens of universities, colleges, and specialist hospitals, not to mention both the **British Museum** and the **British Library,** Bloomsbury is London's undisputed intellectual powerhouse. In the early 20th century, the quiet squares and Georgian terraces resounded to the intellectual musings of the Bloomsbury Group, including T.S. Eliot, E.M. Forster, Virginia Woolf, Bertrand Russell, Vanessa Bell, and John Maynard Keynes; today, they house student halls and dozens of affordable accommodations, with lots of good restaurants nearby.

CHELSEA. In the 1960s and 70s, Chelsea was the epitome of swinging London—the **King's Road** gave the world miniskirts and punk rock. A century earlier, Chelsea buzzed with the discussions of Edgar Allen Poe, George Eliot, Dante Gabriel Rossetti, Oscar Wilde, J.M.W. Turner, John Singer Sargent, and James MacNeill Whistler. Stifled by a surfeit of wealth, Chelsea of late has little stomach for radicalism—these days, local luminaries include Hugh Grant, Liz Hurley, and a string of B-list celebrities, models, and trust-fund kids known as "Sloane Rangers."

HOLBORN AND CLERKENWELL. London's second-oldest area, **Holborn** was the first part of the city settled by Saxons, and is today associated with two unholy professions: law and journalism. After seeing the sights, there's little to do here but sit in one of the many pubs once frequented by Dr. Johnson. North and east of Holborn, **Clerkenwell's** heady combination of nightlife and restaurants, fueled by a growing media presence, makes comparison with Soho hard to avoid.

KENSINGTON AND EARL'S COURT. Until recently the stomping ground of Princess Diana, **Kensington** divides more or less equally between the label-obsessed consumer mecca of **Kensington High St.** in the west and the incredible array of museums and colleges of **South Kensington's** "Albertopolis" in the east. Both High St. and South Ken have a smattering of budget accommodations, but neither can compare with **Earl's Court** to the southwest, which combines cheap lodgings and food with good transport links to central London.

KNIGHTSBRIDGE AND BELGRAVIA. **Knightsbridge** has been one of London's most desired addresses for centuries—Apsley House, the Duke of Wellington's former abode, revels in the address "No. 1, London." Like the locals, famed department stores Harrods and Harvey Nichols are secure in their sense of superiority. The boutiques of **Sloane St.,** meanwhile, have no need to envy their Bond St. cousins—if anything, they're glitzier and more exclusive. **Belgravia,** east of Sloane St., is a cultural desert of 19th-century mansions and millionaires' apartments.

MARYLEBONE AND REGENT'S PARK. Marylebone is an elusive district; easy to find on a map, it nonetheless lacks cohesion and a sense of identity. Largely residential and respectable, its best parts are the edges. Forming the northern border of Marylebone, **Regent's Park** is a giant and popular expanse of greenery surrounded by elegant Regency terraces. Nearby, **Marylebone Rd.** and **Baker St.** provide several of the most shameful tourist thrills in London.

NOTTING HILL. For decades one of London's most vibrant, ethnically mixed areas, in the past few years (helped on by a certain movie) Notting Hill has become victim to its own trendiness. Only on the edges can you catch glimpses of the old Notting Hill. Still, once a year, the whole neighborhood explodes with Caribbean color and sound during its **Carnival,** attended by over 2 million people.

GREATER LONDON NEIGHBORHOODS

NORTH LONDON. Green and prosperous, North London's inner suburbs are some of London's older outlying communities: **Hampstead** and **Highgate** were pleasant country retreats for centuries before the urban sprawl engulfed them, and they still retain their village feel. Closer to the center, **Camden Town** and **Islington** were grimy working-class areas for most of the 19th and 20th centuries, but in the 1980s their stock shot up and both are now solidly populated with wealthy liberals. In recent years, Islington's **Upper St.** has become one of London's top dining destinations, with over 100 eateries within walking distance of Angel Tube station. **Maida Vale** and **St. John's Wood** are wealthy extensions of Marylebone and Bayswater.

LONDON

EAST LONDON. At Aldgate, the wealth of the city gives way to the historically impoverished **East End.** Older residents still remember when this was a predominantly Jewish neighborhood, but today it's solidly Bangladeshi. East of **Whitechapel,** the East End remains poor and working-class until you hit **Docklands.** Since the late 1980s, this vast manmade archipelago has become a city-within-a-city: the skyscrapers of **Canary Wharf** are establishing it as London's second financial center. Steeped in history, **Greenwich** is a beautiful district with a wealth of sights, though the **Millennium Dome**—while still visible—is closed to visitors.

SOUTH LONDON. Only developing in the last two centuries, South London contains some of London's most dynamic neighborhoods in its Victorian railway muddle. **Brixton** is a vibrant melting pot where African, Caribbean, and English traditions collide and fuse—with London's highest concentration of under-40s, this is home to some thumping nightlife. Neighboring **Dulwich** couldn't be more different: this prosperous hilly village is the south's answer to Hampstead.

WEST LONDON. The garden of London, the area along the western riverbank stretches for miles before petering out in the hills and vales of the Thames valley. Historically, these reaches were fashionable spots for country retreats, and by the time you reach affluent **Richmond,** the river winds carelessly through the grounds of stately homes and former royal palaces on its way to **Hampton Court.**

◨ PRACTICAL INFORMATION

TOURIST INFORMATION CENTRES AND LOCAL SERVICES

Britain Visitor Centre, 1 Lower Regent St. (www.visitbritain.com). Tube: Oxford Circus. Open M 9:30am-6:30pm, Tu-F 9am-6:30pm, Sa-Su 10am-4pm; June-Sept. extended hours Sa 9am-5pm.

London Visitor Centres (www.londontouristboard.com). Tube branches at: **Heathrow Terminals 1,2,3** (open Oct.-Aug. daily 8am-6pm; Sept. M-Sa 9am-7pm and Su 8am-6pm); **Liverpool St.** (open June-Sept. M-Sa 8am-7pm, Su 8am-6pm; Oct.-May daily 8am-6pm); **Victoria** (open Easter-Sept. M-Sa 8am-8pm, Su 8am-6pm; Oct.-Easter daily 8am-6pm); **Waterloo** (open daily 8:30am-10:30pm). There are also **TICs** in **the City** (St. Paul's Churchyard; ☎7332 1456; Tube: St. Paul's; open Apr.-Sept. daily 9:30am-5pm; Oct.-Mar. M-F 9:30am-5pm, Sa 9:30am-12:30pm) and **Greenwich** (Pepys House, 2 Cutty Sark Gdns.; ☎(0870) 608 2000; open daily 10am-5pm).

Gay and Lesbian Resources: London Lesbian & Gay Switchboard (☎7837 7324; www.queery.org.uk). 24hr. helpline and information. **GAY to Z** (www.gaytoz.com). Online and printed directory of gay resources and gay-friendly businesses in Britain.

EMERGENCY AND MEDICAL CARE

Emergency: ☎999

Dental Care: Dental Emergency Care Service (☎7955 2186) refers callers to the nearest open dental surgery. Open M-F 8:45am-3:30pm.

Samaritans: ☎(08457) 909 090. 24hr. emotional support for depression and suicide.

Hospitals: Charing Cross, Fulham Palace Rd. (☎8846 1234), entrance on St. Dunstan's Rd., Tube: Baron's Ct. or Hammersmith. **Royal Free,** Pond St. (☎7794 0500), Tube: Belsize Park. **St. Thomas's,** Lambeth Palace Rd. (☎7928 9292), Tube: Waterloo. **University College Hospital,** Grafton Way (☎7387 9300), Tube: Warren St.

Pharmacies: Most chemists keep standard hours (usually M-Sa 9:30am-5:30pm); a "duty" chemist in each neighborhood opens Su, though hours may be limited. Late-night and 24hr. chemists are rare; one 24hr. option is **Zafash Pharmacy,** 233 Old Brompton Rd. (☎7373 2798). Tube: Earl's Ct.

Police: London is covered by 2 police forces: the **City of London Police** (☎ 7601 2222) for the City and the **Metropolitan Police** (☎ 7230 1212) for the rest. At least 1 station in each of the 32 boroughs is open 24hr. (☎ 7230 1212 to find the nearest station).

COMMUNICATIONS

Internet Access: Most B&Bs and hostels now offer Internet access; however rates are lower at the scores of cyber cafes. Try the ubiquitous **easyInternet Cafe** (☎ 7241 9000). Locations include 9-16 Tottenham Court Rd. (Tube: Tottenham Court Rd.); 456/459 The Strand (Tube: Charing Cross); 358 Oxford St. (Tube: Bond St.); 9-13 Wilson Rd. (Tube: Victoria); 160-166 Kensington High St. (Tube: High St. Kensington). Prices vary with demand, from £1 per hr.; minimum charge £2. All open 24hr.

Post Office: Post offices are found on almost every major road. When sending mail to London, be sure to include the full post code, since London has 7 King's Rds., 8 Queen's Rds., and many other opportunities for misdirected mailings. The largest office is the **Trafalgar Square Post Office,** 24-28 William IV St. (☎ 7484 9304). Tube: Charing Cross. All mail sent Poste Restante or general delivery to unspecified post offices ends up here. Open M-Th and Sa 8am-8pm, F 8:30am-8pm. **Post Code:** WC2N 4DL.

⌐ ACCOMMODATIONS

CENTRAL LONDON

THE CITY OF LONDON

YHA City of London, 36 Carter Ln. (☎ 7236 4965). Tube: St. Paul's. In the frescoed former buildings of St. Paul's Choir School, in spitting distance of the cathedral. Secure luggage storage, currency exchange, laundry, and Internet. English breakfast included. Single-sex dorms have sinks and lockers. Reception 7am-11pm. 10- to 15-bed dorms £23, under 18 £20; 5- to 8-bed £24/£20; 3- to 4-bed £25/£21.50. Private rooms: singles £30, under 18 £24; doubles £52, £44 with 1 child under 16; triples £74/£63; quads £96/£84; quints £120/£105; sextuples £140/£125. AmEx/MC/V. ❸

THE SOUTH BANK

▨ **Travel Inn County Hall,** Belvedere Rd. (☎ (0870) 238 3300; www.travelinn.co.uk). Tube: Westminster or Waterloo. Don't expect grand views—the riverfront is hogged by a Marriott—but it's seconds from the South Bank and Westminster. Clean, modern rooms with bath, kettle, and color TV. Facilities include elevator, restaurant, and bar. Prices by the room are a deal for families. Reserve at least 1 month ahead. Breakfast £5-6, children £3.50. Singles, doubles, and family rooms £75 F-Su, £80 M-Th. AmEx/MC/V. ❺

THE WEST END

▨ **High Holborn Residence,** 178 High Holborn (☎ 7379 5589; fax 7379 5640; www.lse.ac.uk/vacations). Tube: Holborn or Tottenham Court Rd. Comfortable modern student residence near Covent Garden. "Flats" of 4-5 rooms, each with phone; shared kitchen and bathroom. Laundry, bar, and TV/game room. Continental breakfast included. Open mid-June to late Sept. Singles £29-36; twins £48-58, with bath £58-68; triples with bath £68-78. Rates highest in July, lowest mid-Aug. to Sept. MC/V. ❸

YHA Oxford Street, 14-18 Noel St. (☎ 7734 1618; fax 7734 1657). Tube: Oxford Circus. Small and sparse, but unbeatable location for nightlife. TV lounge with Internet. Well-equipped kitchen. Towels £3.50. Prepackaged continental breakfast £3.40. Reserve at least 1 month ahead. 3- to 4-bed dorms £22, under 18 £17.75; 2-bed dorms £24. ❸

WESTMINSTER

▨ **Westminster House Hotel,** 96 Ebury St. (☎ 7730 7850; www.westminsterhousehotel.co.uk). Tube: Victoria. The extremely welcoming Joneses run this small B&B as if it were their home, which it is. 10 spotless rooms each have TV and hot drinks; almost all with private bath. Full English breakfast included. Singles £50, with bath £55; doubles £70/£80; triples with bath £90; quad with bath £100. ❹

▨ **Luna Simone Hotel,** 47/49 Belgrave Rd. (☎ 7834 5897; www.lunasimonehotel.com). Tube: Victoria or Pimlico. Victorian facade conceals ultra-modern yellow rooms with TV, phone, kettle, safety deposit box, and hair dryer. Internet access. Some singles are cramped. English breakfast included. Reserve 2 weeks ahead. Singles £40, with bath £60; doubles £60/£80; triples £80/£110. ❹

▨ **Surtees Hotel,** 94 Warwick Way, (☎ 7834 7163; www.surtees-hotel.co.uk). Tube: Victoria. A flurry of flowers welcomes guests to this hospitable B&B. Rooms range from singles to small, bright doubles and triples to a bunk-bed quad to the giant 6-bed, 2-room basement suite. English breakfast included. Singles £30, with bath £50; doubles £55/ £70; triples £70/£80; quad £80/£90; family suite with bath £100. ❸

BAYSWATER

▨ **Hyde Park Rooms Hotel,** 137 Sussex Gdns. (☎ 7723 0225). Tube: Paddington. Run by jovial Londoners who take pride in every detail of the airy, spotless rooms. English breakfast in the beautiful dining room included. Reserve ahead in summer. Singles £30, with bath £40; doubles £40-45/£50-55; triples £60/£72; quads £80/£96. ❸

Barry House Hotel, 12 Sussex Pl. (☎ 7723 7340; www.barryhouse.co.uk). Tube: Paddington. Very bright if slightly tight rooms with phone, TV, kettle, and hair dryer; almost all have private bath. Singles £38, with bath £52; doubles £75; triples £90; quads £105; quints £120. AmEx/DC/MC/V. ❹

Admiral Hotel, 143 Sussex Gdns. (☎ 7723 7309; www.admiral143.demon.co.uk). Tube: Paddington. Beautifully kept family-run B&B. 19 non-smoking rooms with bath, TV, and kettle, decorated in summer colors. Ask for one of the tiled baths. English breakfast included. Reserve 2 weeks ahead in summer. Singles £40-50; doubles £58-75; triples £75-90; quads £88-110; quints £100-130. MC/V. ❹

Hyde Park Hostel, 2-6 Inverness Terr. (☎ 7229 5101; www.astorhostels.com). Tube: Queensway. Backpacker spirit pervades this Astor chain hostel—flimsy foam mattresses and cramped quarters, but making up in fun what it lacks in comfort. Residents-only bar with dance space, DJs, and theme parties. Kitchen, laundry, TV lounge, Internet, secure luggage room. Continental breakfast and linen included. Ages 16-35. Reserve 2 weeks ahead. Online booking with 10% deposit. 10- to 18-bed dorms £11-13.50; 8-bed £14.50-15.50; 6-bed £15.50-16.50; 4-bed £16.50-17.50; doubles £42-45. ❷

Quest Hotel, 45 Queensborough Terr. (☎ 7229 7782; www.astorhostels.com). Tube: Bayswater or Queensway. Another in the Astor chain, but with better beds and a more personal feel. Dorms are mostly co-ed, and many have baths; those that don't could be 2 floors from a shower. Laundry, kitchen. Continental breakfast and linen included. No lockers; leave valuables at reception. Book 2 weeks ahead for the 2 twins, 2-3 weeks for dorms in summer. 4- to 8-bed dorms £13-16; twins £36 per person. MC/V. ❷

BLOOMSBURY

▨ **Jenkins Hotel,** 45 Cartwright Gdns., entrance on Barton Pl. (☎ 7387 2067; www.jenkinshotel.demon.co.uk). Tube: Euston or King's Cross/St. Pancras. Non-smoking rooms with large windows and antique-style furniture have TV, kettle, phone, fridge, hair dryer, and safe. Tennis courts in Cartwright Gardens. Tiny prefab baths in some rooms. English breakfast included. Reserve 1-2 months ahead. Singles £52, with bath £72; doubles with bath £85; triples with bath £105. ❺

■ **Crescent Hotel,** 49-50 Cartwright Gdns. (☎7387 1515; fax 7383 2054; www.crescenthoteloflondon.com). Tube: Russell Sq. A real family-run feel; well-decorated rooms have TV, kettle, and phone. Tennis courts in front of the hotel (racquets and balls available). Reserve 3 weeks ahead for weekends. Singles £45, with shower £50, with bath £72; doubles with bath £87; triples with bath £97; quads with bath £106. More for single-night stays; less for over a week. MC/V. ❹

■ **Langland Hotel,** 29-31 Gower St. (☎7636 5801; www.langlandhotel.com). Tube: Goodge St. Family atmosphere, wood-framed beds, and plenty of spacious, sparkling bathrooms (cleaned twice daily) help this B&B stand out from its neighbors. Comfy satellite-TV lounge. English breakfast included. Singles £40, with bath £55; doubles £50/£75; triples £70/£90; quint £100. AmEx/MC/V. ❹

■ **Arosfa Hotel,** 83 Gower St. (☎/fax 7636 2115). Tube: Warren St. or Goodge St. The Iberian owners ensure that this small, non-smoking B&B lives up to its Welsh name ("place to rest"). Room sizes vary—prefab baths make for some unusual shapes—but all have TV and sinks. Lovely garden. English breakfast included. Reserve 1-2 months ahead. Singles £37; doubles £50, with bath £66; triples £68/£79; quad with bath £92. MC/V. ❹

■ **The Generator,** Compton Pl., off 37 Tavistock Pl. (☎7388 7655; www.the-generator.co.uk). Tube: Russell Sq. or King's Cross/St. Pancras. Less hostel than dystopian vision of the future: metal bunks in cell-like sleep units; a "Turbine" with video games and pool tables; Internet in the "Talking Head" area. Bar with big-screen TV. Staff strict about rules, but with 800 beds, can you blame them? Reserve 1 week ahead. 8-bed dorms £15; 6-bed £16; 4-bed £17. Mar.-Oct. singles £42; doubles £53; triples £67.50; quads £90; quints £112.50. Nov.-Feb. £40/£47/£60/£80/£100. MC/V. ❷

■ **Ashlee House,** 261-265 Gray's Inn Rd. (☎7833 9400; www.ashleehouse.co.uk). Tube: King's Cross/St. Pancras. Location may not be the most pleasant, but it's massively convenient. Quiet, friendly, "backpackers only." Blue steel bunks crammed in clean, bright rooms. Sightseeing tour Th-Sa. TV room, Internet, laundry, kitchen; continental breakfast included. Towels £1. May-Sept. 16-bed dorms £15; 8- to 10-bed £17; 4- to 6-bed £19. Singles £36; doubles £48. Oct.-Apr. £13/£15/£17/£34/£44. ❷

YHA St. Pancras International, 79-81 Euston Rd. (☎7388 9998). Tube: King's Cross/St. Pancras. Opposite the British Library. Triple glazing and comfortable wooden bunks for a sound night's sleep. Most dorms have private bath; all have lockers. Lounge with video games. Laundry, kitchen, Internet, English breakfast, and linen included. Reserve 2 weeks ahead in summer, 1 month ahead for doubles. Dorms £24, under 18 £20; doubles £52, with bath £57.50; quads with bath £104. AmEx/MC/ V. ❸

Pickwick Hall International Backpackers, 7 Bedford Pl. (☎7323 4958). Tube: Russell Sq. or Holborn. Besides an 8-bed room, mostly 2- to 3-bed single-sex dorms. Clean if a bit shabby; friendly owner makes a concerted effort to keep things pleasant and safe. No smoking, no food in the dorms, and no guests. Continental breakfast and linen included. Laundry, kitchen, TV lounge. Reception 8-10am. Book 2-3 days ahead, 6 weeks for July-Aug. Dorms £15; singles £25; doubles £40; triples £54. AmEx/MC/V. ❷

KENSINGTON AND EARL'S COURT

■ **Five Sumner Place Hotel,** 5 Sumner Pl. (☎7584 7586; www.sumnerplace.com). Tube: South Kensington. The amenities of a luxury hotel with the charm of the small, independent converted Victorians in the area. Surprisingly spacious rooms with large windows have private bath, TV, fridge, phone, and hair dryer. Unbeatable location and warm staff—no surprise it's won the award for the best small hotel in London. Full English breakfast. Book 1 month ahead in summer. Singles £85; doubles £130. ❺

■ **Vicarage Private Hotel,** 10 Vicarage Gate (☎7229 4030; fax 7792 5989; www.londonvicaragehotel.com). Tube: High St. Kensington. Beautifully kept Victorian house with ornate hallways, TV lounge, and superb rooms: cast-iron beds, solid wood furnishings, and luxuriant drapes. English breakfast included. Reserve months ahead. Singles £46; doubles £76, with bath £100; triples £93; quads £100. ❹

■ **Swiss House Hotel,** 171 Old Brompton Rd. (☎ 7373 2769; fax 7373 4983; www.swiss-hh.demon.co.uk). Tube: Gloucester Rd. or South Kensington. Charming B&B, from the plant-filled hall to large wood-floored rooms with TV, phone, fan, and bath. Continental breakfast included; English breakfast £6.50. Book 1 month ahead in summer. Singles £71, with shower only £51; doubles £89-104; triples £120; quads £134. Discount for stays over 1 week and cash payments. AmEx/MC/V. ❺

■ **Oxford Hotel,** 24 Penywern Rd. (☎ 7370 1161; www.the-oxford-hotel.com). 3min. from the Connex train to Heathrow or Gatwick. Large rooms with enormous windows afford grand views of the gardens. Sparkling-clean baths. Minimal, high-quality furnishings. Continental breakfast included. Reserve 2-3 weeks ahead for June, 3-4 weeks ahead for singles. Singles with shower £36, with bath £50; doubles £57/£67; triples £69/£79; quads £87/£93; quints £105/£115. Discount on stays over 1 week. AmEx/MC/V. ❹

YHA Holland House, Holland Walk (☎ 7937 0748), on the edge of Holland Park. Tube: High St. Kensington or Holland Park. Split between a 17th-century mansion and a less attractive 1970s unit; dorms in both are similar, with 12-20 interlocking bunks. Caters mostly to groups. Lockers, laundry, TV room, luggage storage, and kitchen. Breakfast included. Book 1 month ahead in summer. £20.50, under 18 £18.50. AmEx/MC/V. ❸

YHA Earl's Court, 38 Bolton Gdns. (☎ 7373 7083). Rambling Victorian townhouse more casual and better appointed than most YHAs. 4- and 16-bed dorms are single sex. Garden, kitchen, laundry, 2 TV lounges, Internet, luggage storage. Linen included, breakfast included only for private rooms and 12- and 16-bed dorms. Book 6 weeks ahead for private rooms; 2 weeks for dorms. 12- and 16-bed dorms £16.70; 4- and 8-bed £19. Private rooms (only bookable online): doubles £52; quads £76. AmEx/MC/V. ❷

KNIGHTSBRIDGE AND BELGRAVIA

James and Cartref House, 108 and 129 Ebury St. (☎ 7730 7338 or 7730 6176; www.jamesandcartref.co.uk). Tube: Victoria. 2 separate, well-kept B&Bs under the same family's ownership. The James has a bright breakfast room overlooking the garden; the Cartref feels older, with more private baths and ornate dining room. All rooms have TV, kettle, hair dryer, and fan. English breakfast included. Singles £52, with bath £62; doubles £70/£85; triples £95/£110; family room with bath £135. MC/V. ❹

MARYLEBONE AND REGENT'S PARK

International Student House, 229 Great Portland St. (☎ 7631 8300; www.ish.org.uk). Tube: Great Portland St. International metropolis in a great location near Regent's Park. Most rooms similar in size, varying primarily in the number of beds, and have desk, sink, phone, and fridge. Spartan 8- to 10-bed dorms have sink and lockers. 3 bars, nightclub, cafeteria, fitness center (£3 per day), and cinema (Su only); guests get 15min. free Internet, then £2 per hr. Continental breakfast included except for dorms (£2); English breakfast £3. Laundry facilities. £10 key deposit. Book 1 month ahead in summer; singles and doubles mostly booked through the school year. 3-week max. stay. Dorms £10. Singles £31, with bath £33; doubles £50/£52; triples £60; quads £72. MC/V. ❷

GREATER LONDON

NORTH LONDON

■ **YHA Hampstead Heath,** 4 Wellgarth Rd. (☎ 8458 9054; fax 8209 0546). From Tube: Golders Green (Zone 3), turn left on North End Rd.; Wellgarth Rd. is 10min. up on the left. Out-of-the-way location is main disadvantage of this manorial hostel. Large garden, Internet, laundry, lockers, and self-service restaurant. Breakfast included. Reception 24hr. 4- to 6-bed dorms £20.40; doubles £47; triples £67; quads £84; quints £103; sextuples £124. Families get significant discounts on larger rooms. AmEx/MC/V. ❸

■ **Kandara Guesthouse,** 68 Ockendon Rd. (☎ 7226 5721; www.kandara.co.uk). From Tube: Angel, take bus #38, 56, 73, or 341 to Essex and Ockendon—be alert, it's a small stop. Far from the Tube, but many buses to the West End (including 2 night buses). Classically decorated family-run B&B, with new beds and sparkling clean rooms. Breakfast included. Book 2 weeks ahead. Singles £41-49; doubles £51-62; triples £64-72; inquire about quad. MC/V. ❹

WEST LONDON

■ **Star Hotel,** 97-99 Shepherd's Bush Rd. (☎ 7603 2755; www.star-hotel.net). Tube: Goldhawk Rd. or Hammersmith. Friendly owner throws heart and soul into his B&B. Rooms are relatively spacious; all with TV, large bath, wood furniture, and new carpeting. English breakfast in skylit dining area. Book 2 months ahead for July-Aug.; most singles are already booked M-F through 2003, but will be available F night to Su. Singles £42; doubles £62; triples £75; quads £95. Discount for stays over 2 nights. MC/V. ❹

◗ FOOD AND PUBS

Forget stale stereotypes: London's restaurants offer a gastronomic experience as diverse, stylish, and satisfying as you'll find anywhere on the planet. Any restaurant charging under £10 for a main course is regarded as "cheap"; add drinks and service and you're nudging £15. That said, it *is* possible to eat cheaply—and well— in London. Lunchtime and early-evening **special offers** save cash, and there's always good old **pub grub.** Many of the best budget meals are found in the amazing variety of **ethnic restaurants.** For the best and cheapest ethnic food, head to the source: Whitechapel for Bengali baltis, Islington for Turkish *meze*, Marylebone for Lebanese *shwarma*, and for Cantonese *dim sum*. Often the cheapest places to get the ingredients for your own meal in London are local **street markets;** there's generally at least one in each neighborhood. Branches of **Hart's** supermarkets are open 24hr. If you're willing to splurge, the food halls of **Harrods, Harvey Nichols, Selfridges,** and **Fortnum and Mason** are attractions in their own right.

AFTERNOON TEA

Social ritual as much as meal, this apex of English cuisine involves a long afternoon of sandwiches, scones, pastries, tinkling china, and restrained conversation. Perhaps the main attraction of afternoon tea is the chance to lounge in sumptuous surroundings that at any other time would be beyond all but a sultan's budget. Following The Ritz, London's premier tea spot, most other **major hotels** have gotten in on the act. Hoity-toity **department stores** (see p. 138), such as Fortnum and Mason and Harrods, are also popular choices. However, a less-ritualized tea can be had at (dress-codeless) eateries across the city.

■ **The Lanesborough,** Hyde Park Corner (☎ 7259 5599). Tube: Hyde Park Corner. For sheer opulence, the Regency interior out-ritzes The Ritz. Tea is served in the Oriental-fantasy conservatory, with heavy silk furnishings, palm fronds, painted vases, and mannequin mandarins. Dress smart casual. Set tea £23, champagne tea £27; scones with jam and clotted cream £6.50. Minimum charge £9.50 per person. ❸

Brown's, Albemarle St. (☎ 7493 6020). Tube: Green Park. Opened by Lord Byron's butler in 1837, this was London's first luxury hotel and still reeks with old-fashioned charm. Tea is taken in the cozy drawing room, with dark paneling and comfy settees. M-F sittings 3 and 4:45pm (book 1 week ahead for Th-F); Sa-Su tea served 3-4:45pm (no reservations). Dress smart casual. Set tea £23, champagne tea £33. AmEx/MC/V. ❺

CENTRAL LONDON

THE CITY OF LONDON

■ **Futures,** 8 Botolph Alley (☎ 7623 4529), between Botolph Ln. and Lovat Ln. Tube: Monument. Suits besiege this tiny takeaway, which dishes out a daily-changing variety of vegetarian soups, salads, and hot dishes (£2-4); breakfast on a wide variety of pastries (80p) or porridges and cereals (£1). Open M-F 7:30-10am and 11:30am-3pm. ❶

■ **Cafe Spice Namaste,** 16 Prescot St. (☎ 7488 9242). Tube: Tower Hill or DLR: Tower Gateway. The standard-bearer for a new breed of Indian restaurants. Bright, carnivalesque decor brings an exotic feel to this old Victorian warehouse. Meat dishes are on the pricey side (£11-13), but vegetarian meals are a bargain (£7-8). Open M-F noon-3pm and 6:15-10:30pm, Sa 6:30-10pm. AmEx/MC/V. ❷

Simpson's, Ball Ct. (☎ 7626 9985), off 38½ Cornhill. Tube: Bank. Est. 1757, this pub remains so traditional that a man stands in the door to greet you. Different rooms divide the classes, from the basement wine bar (sandwiches £2-4) to the upstairs restaurants (entrees £6-7). Open M-F 11:30am-3pm. ❶

THE SOUTH BANK

■ **Cantina del Ponte,** 36c Shad Thames, Butler's Wharf (☎ 7403 5403). Tube: Tower Hill or London Bridge. Amazing riverside location by Tower Bridge. Given the quality of the Italian-style food (especially the desserts), the set menu is a bargain at £10 for 2 courses, £12.50 for 3 (available M-F noon-3pm and 6-7:30pm). Live Italian music Tu and Th. Open M-Sa noon-3pm and 6-10:45pm, Su noon-3pm and 6-9:45pm. MC/V. ❸

■ **Tas,** 72 Borough High St. (☎ 7403 7200), Tube: London Bridge and 33 The Cut (☎ 7928 2111), Tube: Waterloo. Dynamic duo of stylish and affordable Turkish restaurants. Tasty stews and baked dishes—many vegetarian—outshine the respectable kebabs. Entrees £6-8; set menus include 2 courses for £7 and *mezes* (selection of starters) £7-10. Live music daily from 7:30pm. Evening reservations essential. Open M-Sa noon-11:30pm, Su noon-10:30pm. AmEx/MC/V. ❷

THE WEST END

■ **busaba eathai,** 106-110 Wardour St. (☎ 7255 8686). Wildly popular Thai eatery. Get in line for great food (£5-8) at shared tables in a cozy, wood-paneled room. Open M-Th noon-11pm, F-Sa noon-11:30pm, Su noon-10pm. AmEx/MC/V. ❷

■ **Mô,** 23 Heddon St. (☎ 7434 4040). Tube: Piccadilly Circus or Oxford Circus. A "salad bar, tearoom, and bazaar," Mô transports you to Marrakesh. The interior is hung with lanterns and festooned with Moroccan crafts, all for sale. Wash down traditional salads, dips, and meats (£6-7.50) with sweet mint tea (£2). Popular, but no reservations—arrive early or late. Open M-W 11am-11pm, Th-Sa noon-midnight. ❷

■ **Mr. Kong,** 21 Lisle St. (☎ 7437 7341). Do people really eat "goose web with fish lips and sea cucumber," or is it just there to convince Westerners of this small restaurant's authenticity? £7 minimum for dinner. Open daily noon-3am. AmEx/MC/V. ❷

■ **Pâtisserie Valerie,** 44 Old Compton St. (☎ 7437 3466). Frills are saved for the renowned cakes in this continental *pâtisserie*. The upstairs restaurant is more luxurious, but the sweet-smelling bakery will keep you on the ground floor. Croissants 90p, sandwiches £3.50-6. Open M-F 7:30am-8pm, Sa 8am-8pm, Su 9:30am-7pm. AmEx/MC/V. **Branches:** 8 Russell St. and 105 Marylebone High St. ❶

Bar Italia, 22 Frith St. (☎ 7437 4520). A fixture of the late-night Soho scene, immortalized by *Pulp,* and still *the* place for a post-club panini (£4-6), though no alcohol is served. The large, loud TV is never off—appropriate, since John Logie Baird gave the first-ever demonstration of television upstairs in 1922. Open 24hr. except M 3-7am. ❷

Lamb and Flag, 33 Rose St. (☎ 7497 9504). Once called the "Bucket of Blood" for the violence of the bare-knuckle fights held upstairs. The traditional dark-wood interior and no-music policy make it a great place for a quiet pint, though the 2 floors (and courtyard) fill with local workers after 6pm. Live jazz Su from 7:30pm. Open M-Th 11am-11pm, F-Sa 11am-10:45pm, Su noon-10:30pm; food served daily noon-3pm. ❷

Tinseltown 24-Hour Diner, 44-46 St. John St. (☎ 7689 2424). Tube: Farringdon. Cavernous underground haven for pre- and post-clubbers. The hours are more commendable than the burgers (£5.50). Excellent shakes (£3.50). Internet access. Open 24hr. ❷

WESTMINSTER

▨ **Jenny Lo's Teahouse,** 14 Eccleston St. (☎ 7259 0399). Tube: Victoria. Long before noodle bars hit the big time, Jenny Lo was offering stripped-down Chinese fare at communal tables. Teas (from 85p) blended in-house and served in hand-turned stoneware. Open M-F 11:30am-3pm and 6-10pm; Sa opens at noon. £5 minimum. Cash only. ❷

Red Lion, 48 Parliament St. (☎ 7930 5826). Tube: Westminster. The MPs' hangout. TVs carrying the Parliament cable channel allow them to listen to the debates, while a "division bell" alerts them to drink up when a vote is about to be called. Despite the distinguished clientele, the food (sandwiches £3, hot dishes £6) is decidedly ordinary. Open M-Sa 11am-11pm, Su noon-7pm; food served daily noon-3pm. MC/V. ❶

BAYSWATER

▨ **Royal China,** 13 Queensway (☎ 7221 2535). Tube: Bayswater or Queensway. The glitzy, swan-themed decor isn't mirrored in the prices. London's best *dim sum* (£2-3 per dish; count on 3-4 dishes each). Set meals £7-10. *Dim sum* served M-Sa noon-5pm, Su 11am-5pm; on weekends, arrive early or expect to wait 30-45min. Open M-Th noon-11pm, F-Sa noon-11:30pm, Su 11am-10pm. AmEx/MC/V. ❸

▨ **La Bottega del Gelato,** 127 Bayswater Rd. (☎ 7243 2443). Tube: Queensway. Now in his 70s, Quinto Barbieri still gets up at 4:30am to make the best *gelati* this side of the Rubicon. Perfect to take on a stroll in the Kensington Gardens. Scoops from £1.30. Open daily 10am-7pm, later in summer. Cash only. ❶

▨ **Aphrodite Taverna,** 15 Hereford Rd. (☎ 7229 2206). Tube: Bayswater. Pantelis and Rosanna's 20 years of experience are everywhere apparent in this warm Greek restaurant. Entrees from £7, chef specials £10-17. The cafe next door has some of the specialties at cheaper prices and a full sandwich menu. Restaurant open M-Sa noon-midnight; cafe open daily 8:30am-5pm. AmEx/DC/MC/V. ❸

BLOOMSBURY

▨ **Diwana Bhel Poori House,** 121-123 Drummond St. (☎ 7387 5556). Tube: Euston or Euston Sq. No frippery—just great, cheap South Indian vegetarian food. Pass on the £5.95 lunch buffet (daily noon-2:30pm), as £4.85 will get you a *paneer dosa* (rice pancake filled with potato and cheese) that's more than enough. *Thali* set meals offer great value (£4-6). Open daily noon-11:30pm. AmEx/MC/V. ❷

▨ **ICCo (Italiano Coffee Company),** 46 Goodge St. (☎ 7580 9250). Gleaming, brushed-steel interior filled with lounging and lunching students. Delicious 11" pizzas, made to order, are an eye-popping £3.50. Sandwiches and baguettes on new-baked bread from £1.50. Buy any hot drink before noon and get a free fresh-baked croissant; sandwiches half-off after 4pm. Open M-Sa 7am-11pm, Su 9am-11pm. Cash only. ❶

▨ **Vats,** 51 Lamb's Conduit St. (☎ 7242 8963). Tube: Russell Sq. Small front conceals a long romantic space. Food is pricey (starters £5-6, entrees £9-16) but delicious. Long wine list leans towards Bordeaux, with "good ordinary claret" £3.50 per glass, £14.50 per bottle. Open M-Sa noon-11:30pm; food served 6-9:30pm. AmEx/MC/V. ❸

THE BIG SPLURGE

BY GORDON!

Gordon Ramsay—celebrity star chef, former footballer, student of Joel Robuchon. Rumor has him abrasive in the kitchen, but as London's best chef, he is allowed to be and make whatever he wants.

His style is "Modern European," meaning French—refreshingly free of the modern British influence (£50 fish and chips) or fusion (soy-sauce-makes-it-trendy). It's also light, avoiding the butter and heavy creams that characterize much French cooking, and seeking instead brighter, livelier flavors. The £35 set lunch menu features such delights as pot-roasted pigeon on a bed of cabbage and truffle consommé. Dinner is more expensive, with a 7-course menu for £80 or 3 courses for £65, with numerous and tempting options including lobster ravioli poached in lobster bisque on a bed of crushed garden peas.

The extensive wine list has slightly pricey wines, like the 1947 Pétrus (£12,300). Decor is traditional, elegant, relaxed; service is impeccable, attentive, unobtrusive. Jacket and tie certainly, suit and tie better.

You can't reserve more than a month ahead, but getting a dinner reservation is still difficult (nearly impossible on Sa). Lunch is easier—book two weeks ahead and you should have no problems. *(Gordon Ramsay. 68 Royal Hospital Rd., Chelsea. Tube: Sloane Sq. ☎ 7352 4441. Open M-F noon-2:20pm and 6:45-11pm.)*

The Lamb, 94 Lamb's Conduit St. (☎ 7405 0713). Tube: Russell Sq. Popular with doctors from the nearby hospitals, regulars also include Peter O'Toole. Fading photos of past thespian tipplers line the walls. The "snob screens" around the bar originally provided privacy for "respectable" men meeting with ladies of illrepute. Open M-Sa 11am-11pm, Su noon-10:30pm; food served M-Sa noon-2:30pm and daily 6-9pm. MC/V. ❶

CHELSEA

▨ **Bluebird,** 350 King's Rd. (☎ 7559 1222). Designer food emporium includes flashy, date-worthy restaurant, sprawling outdoor cafe, and gourmet supermarket with cheap sandwich and smoothie bars. Cafe food (£4.25-10) includes creative salads, sandwiches, and steaks; more expensive restaurant fare starts at £16.25 (try roast rabbit with proscuitto and spinach). Cafe open M-Sa 8am-11pm, Su 10am-6pm; restaurant M-F noon-3pm and 6-11pm, Sa 11am-3:30pm and 6-11pm, Su 11am-3:30pm and 6-10pm; store M-W 9am-8pm, Th-Sa 9am-9pm, Su 11am-5pm. AmEx/MC/V. ❷

▨ **Chelsea Kitchen,** 98 King's Rd. (☎ 7589 1330). Dimly lit diner booths provide intimacy and quiet decadence. Entrees, like the roast chicken and mozzarella salad, hover around £4; wine is £1.50 per glass and £5.80 per bottle. Open daily 7am-midnight; breakfast served until 11:30am. MC/V. ❶

▨ **New Culture Revolution,** 305 King's Rd. (☎ 7352 9281). Prophetically named—when it opened in 1994, serving simple steaming bowls of noodles in a modern, functional setting, East Asian food in London was associated with greasy takeaways or stodgy Chinatown eateries. Cantonese noodles and dumplings plus lots of fish and vegetables make up the bulk of the menu, all under £6. Open M-Th noon-3:30pm and 5:30-11pm, F noon-11pm, Sa-Su 1-11pm. AmEx/MC/V. ❷

HOLBORN AND CLERKENWELL

▨ **Bleeding Heart Tavern** (☎ 7404 0333), corner of Greville St. and Bleeding Heart Yard. This 2-level establishment is split between a laid-back upstairs pub and a cozy restaurant below, where fresh roses and candles make a romantic backdrop to hearty Olde English fare (spit-roasted pork £8). Open M-F 11am-11pm. AmEx/MC/V. ❸

▨ **Ye Olde Cheshire Cheese,** Wine Office Ct., Fleet St. (☎ 7353 6170). Tube: Blackfriars or St. Paul's. 3-floor labyrinth of oak-panelled rooms, dating from 1667. Former haunt of Johnson, Dickens, Twain, and Teddy Roosevelt. Bars and restaurants in every price range; sandwiches (£4-5) in the Cheshire bar; meaty traditional dishes (entrees £7-10) in the Chophouse; daily hot specials (£4.75) in the cellar bar; fancier cuisine (£7-13) in the Johnson Room. Open M-F 11:30am-11pm, Sa 11:30am-3pm and 5:30-11pm, Su noon-3pm; food served M-F noon-9:30pm, Sa noon-2:30pm and 6-9:30pm, Su noon-2:30pm. AmEx/MC/V. ❷

▨ **St. John,** 26 St. John St. (☎ 7251 0848). Tube: Farringdon. It's stormed the London restaurant scene, winning countless prizes for its eccentric English cuisine—they call it "nose to tail eating," and certainly few body parts are wasted. Prices in the posh restaurant are high (entrees £14), but you can enjoy similar bounty (in smaller quantities) in the airy bar: lamb sandwich £5, roast bone-marrow salad £6, brawn (pig's feet and cow's head stew... yum) £5.50. Bar open M-F 11am-11pm, Sa 6-11pm. MC/V. ❷

KENSINGTON AND EARL'S COURT

▨ **La Brasserie,** 272 Brompton Rd. (☎ 7584 1668). Tube: South Kensington. Bustling brasserie serves large portions, including fresh pastas and gorgeous meats. The oyster bar is deservedly famous. Fairly pricey (entrees £12-17), but dinner set menus (£14-17) are a great value. Open M-Sa 8am-11:30pm, Su 9am-11:30pm. MC/V. ❹

▨ **Zaika,** 1 Kensington High St. (☎ 7795 6533; www.zaika-restaurant.co.uk). Tube: High St. Kensington. One of London's best Indian restaurants. Elegant decor, attentive service, and food both original and tremendously sophisticated. Neither cheap nor casual, but when the food's this good, who's complaining? Starters £6-8, entrees £13-18, desserts £4-5 (2-course minimum for dinner). Lunch £12 for 2 courses, £14 for 3; dinner £33.50 for 5, £40 with wine. Reservations recommended. Lunch M-F noon-2:30pm, Su noon-2:45pm; dinner M-Sa 6:30-10:45pm, Su 6:30-9:45pm. MC/V. ❹

KNIGHTSBRIDGE AND BELGRAVIA

▨ **Stockpot,** 6 Basil St. (☎ 7589 8627). Tube: Knightsbridge. A den of cheap food and intimate charm in a forest of luxury. Plebeian park-goers eat among lords and ladies. Traditional menu focuses on roasted meats (£3.50-4) and pasta, but includes plenty of vegetarian options and big salads. Open M-Sa 7:30am-11pm, Su noon-10:30pm. **Branch** in Chelsea, at 273 King's Rd. ❶

Gloriette, 128 Brompton Rd. (☎ 7589 4750). Tube: Knightsbridge. Venerable *pâtisserie* serves hot meals in a bright cafe atmosphere. Leaf teas £2 per pot, delicious cakes and pastries £2.60-3.30, sandwiches £5-7. More substantial fare includes 3-course set meals (£10). Open M-F 7am-8pm, Sa 7am-7pm, Su 9am-5pm. MC/V. ❷

MARYLEBONE AND REGENT'S PARK

▨ **Mandalay,** 444 Edgware Rd. (☎ 7258 3696). About 7min. north from Tube: Edgware Rd. Looks ordinary, tastes extraordinary; the walls of this down-to-earth Burmese restaurant are plastered with awards. Great value lunch specials (curry and rice £3.70; 3 courses £6). Most dishes aren't too spicy, but ask the charming owner and he'll gladly turn up the heat. No smoking. Open M-Sa noon-2:30pm and 6-10:30pm. AmEx/MC/V. ❶

Giraffe, 6-8 Blandford St. (☎ 7935 2333). Tube: Bond St. or Baker St. Branch of the popular world-food micro-chain. Winning combination of delicious eats (around £8), modern decor, and great music, though communal tables leave little room for romance. Open M-F 8am-11:30pm, Sa 9am-11:30pm, Su 9am-11pm. AmEx/MC/V. ❷

NOTTING HILL

▨ **George's Portobello Fish Bar,** 329 Portobello Rd. (☎ 8969 7895). Tube: Ladbroke Grove. George opened here in 1961, and the fish and chips are still as good as ever. Choose from the fillets on display or ask the bustling Greek servers to rustle up another (£4-5), add a generous helping of chips (£1), and wolf it down outside (no inside seating). Open M-F 11am-midnight, Sa 11am-9pm, Su noon-9pm. Cash only. ❷

■ **The Grain Shop,** 269a Portobello Rd. (☎ 7229 5571). Tube: Ladbroke Grove. It's hard for passers-by to ignore the aromatic invitation of this sweet-smelling mini-bakery. The main attractions are the homemade takeaway bakes and salads; mix as many dishes as you like to make up a small (£2.25), medium (£3.45), or gut-bustingly large (£4.60) box. Organic breads baked on-site (£1-2). Even on non-market days, the fast-moving line stretches out onto Portobello Rd. Open M-Sa 9:30am-6pm. MC/V. ❶

GREATER LONDON

NORTH LONDON

■ **Tartuf,** 88 Upper St. (☎ 7288 0954). Tube: Angel. Have a fantastic cutlery-free experience with an Alsatian *tarte flambée* (£5-6), a cross between a crepe and a pizza, only much tastier. Before 3pm get 1 savory and 1 sweet *tarte* for £4.90. Open M-F noon-3pm and 5-11:30pm, Sa-Su noon-11:30pm. MC/V. ❶

■ **Gallipoli,** 102 Upper St., and **Gallipoli Again,** 120 Upper St. (☎ 7359 0630). Tube: Angel. Hanging lamps and Anatolian pop complement Turkish delights like "Iskender Kebab": grilled lamb with yogurt and marinated pita bread (£7). Make reservations F-Sa. Open M-Th 10am-11pm, F-Sa 10am-midnight, Su 10am-10:30pm. MC/V. ❷

■ **Odette's Wine Bar,** 130 Regent's Park Rd. (☎ 7586 5486). Tube: Chalk Farm. Odette's Restaurant, upstairs, is one of London's best, with a modern British menu £14.50-20. The basement wine bar offers slightly simpler dishes from the same kitchen at far lower prices. Romantic alcove tables; the infernally slow service will give you plenty of time to gaze into your lover's eyes. Most starters £5-7, entrees £8-10. House wine from £12 per bottle. Open M-Sa 12:30-2:30pm and 5:30-10:30pm. MC/V. ❸

■ **Le Crêperie de Hampstead,** 77 Hampstead High St. Tube: Hampstead. Watch as delicacies like Mushroom Garlic Cream (£3) and Banana Butterscotch Cream Dream (£2.40) are prepared before your eyes. 35p gets you gooey Belgian chocolate instead of sticky syrup. Open M-Th 11:45am-11pm, F-Su 11:45am-11:30pm. Cash only. ❶

■ **Carmelli Bakery,** 128 Golders Green Rd. (☎ 8455 2074). Tube: Golders Green. The golden, egg-glazed challah (£0.72-1.80) is considered the best in London; the bagels and sinfully good pastries (£1.50) aren't far behind. Packed F afternoons; popular enough at other times to warrant frequent 24hr. opening. Open M-W 6am-1am (summer until 3am), then continuously from 6am Th to about 1hr. before sunset or 6pm (whichever comes first) on F, and again from nightfall Sa to 1am M morning. ❶

Mango Room, 10-12 Kentish Rd. (☎ 7482 5065). Tube: Camden Town. Small Caribbean menu uses plenty of mango, avocado, and coconut (£4-6) and has an array of potent tropical drinks. Reserve for weekends. Open Tu-Sa noon-3pm and 6pm-midnight, Su noon-11pm, M 6pm-midnight. MC/V. ❷

EAST LONDON

Grand Central, 93 Great Eastern St. (☎ 7613 4228). Tube: Old St. You could spend all day here: waffles and maple syrup for breakfast (£3.40; until noon), an open-faced, hot salt-beef sandwich (£5.25) for lunch, wild salmon hash (£6.50) for dinner. Nighttime crowds pile in to hear DJs play the latest electronica, soul, hip-hop, house, and R&B. Su Plasma Sessions are replete with music, brunch, and Bloody Marys. Open M-F 7:30am-midnight, Sa 10am-midnight, Su noon-10:30pm. MC/V. ❶

Aladin, 132 Brick Ln. (☎ 7247 8210). One of Brick Ln.'s more popular balti joints—even the Prince of Wales has been here. You may not get the royal treatment, but you will get an authentic meal. The *shahi moglai* (£5.50) is the perfect blend of chicken and beef. Open daily 11:30am-11:30pm. Cash only. ❷

Arkansas Café, Old Spitalfields Market (☎ 7377 6999). Arkansan Bubba tends his oak-fired pits at this indoor-outdoor BBQ shack. The beef is all hormone-free US meat, the chickens are free-range from France. Salad and sweetcorn rather than fries with your burger (£4.50) or wild boar sausage (£6.50). Keep it Yankee with a New York-style cheesecake (£2.50). Open M-F noon-2:30pm, Su noon-4pm. £5 minimum. MC/V. ❷

The Grapes, 76 Narrow St. (☎ 7987 4396). DLR: Westferry. Cast as "The Six Jolly Porters" in Dickens's *Our Mutual Friend.* Known for seafood, served at the bar (pint of prawns £4.75, dressed crab £7) and in the upstairs restaurant (entrees from £11). Open M-F noon-3pm and 5:30-11pm, Sa 7-11pm, Su noon-3pm and 7-10pm. Food served M-Sa noon-3pm and 7-9pm, Su noon-3pm. MC/V. ❸

Cafe Dos Amigos, 33 Greenwich Church St. (☎ 8853 4880). DLR: Cutty Sark. Spices up Greenwich with tapas (£3-5) and mouthwatering desserts—try *capriccio* chocolate (£3). Live Spanish music. Open Tu-F 8:30pm until late. MC/V. ❷

SOUTH LONDON

▨ **Café Bar and Juice Bar,** 407 Coldharbour Ln. (☎ 7738 4141). Tube: Brixton (Zone 2). Plop into a deep leather chair or perch atop a (surprisingly ergonomic) upended bucket in this quirky and immensely cozy cafe. Laid-back staff; amazing smoothies (£4); made-to-order Caribbean-influenced soups (£4.50), quiches (£4.50), and open sandwiches (£4.50). Open daily 10am-midnight. MC/V. ❶

WEST LONDON

▨ **Café Zagora,** 38 Devonshire Rd. (☎ 8742 7922). Tube: Turnham Green (Zone 2). From the Tube, walk south to Chiswick High St.; turn right, then left onto Devonshire Rd. Oozes elegance, from the attentive, discreet service to the warm North African interior. Very reasonably priced Lebanese-Moroccan cuisine (entrees £6.50-13; small dishes £2.50-4). Desserts are £3.50 and worth every penny—heavenly mint tea comes with pillowy baklava. Open M-Sa 11am-3pm and 5-11pm. MC/V. ❷

◐ SIGHTS

ORGANIZED TOURS. The classic London tour is on an open-top **double-decker bus**—and in fine weather, it's undoubtedly the best way to get a good overview of the city. **The Big Bus Company,** 48 Buckingham Palace Rd. (☎ 7233 9533; Tube: Victoria), runs hop-on/hop-off tours every 15min., including 1hr. walking tours and a mini Thames cruise. (Tickets valid 24hr. from first use. £16, children £6.) **London Frog Tours,** County Hall (☎ 7928 3132; Tube: Waterloo or Westminster), operates a fleet of amphibious vehicles that follow a 60-70min. road tour with a 30min. splash into the Thames (£15, concessions £13, children £10). **Original London Walks** (☎ 7624 3978) is the city's oldest and biggest walking-tour company, running 12-16 walks per day, from "Magical Mystery Tour" to nighttime "Jack the Ripper's Haunts," and guided visits to larger museums. (Most walks 2hr. £5, concessions £4, children free.) The **London Bicycle Tour Company** runs leisurely tours designed to keep contact with traffic to a minimum; prices include bike, helmet, and comprehensive insurance. (From the LBTC store, Gabriel's Wharf. ☎ 7928 6838. Tube: Waterloo or Southwark. East Tour Sa 2pm, Royal West Su 2pm; both 9 mi., 3½hr. Middle London M-F 2pm; 6mi., 3hr. Book ahead. £15.) **Catamaran Cruises** operates a nonstop sightseeing Thames cruise with recorded commentary. (☎ 7987 1185. Leaves year-round from Waterloo Pier, Apr.-May from Embankment Pier. July-Aug. £7, seniors £6.30, children £5; Sept.-June £6.70/£6/£4.70. 33% discount with Travelcard.)

THE LOCAL STORY

QUEEN'S GUARD

Let's Go got the scoop on a London emblem, interviewing Corporal of Horse Simon Knowles, an 18 year veteran of The Queen's Guard.

LG: What sort of training did you undergo?
SK: In addition to a year of basic military camp, which involves mainly training on tanks and armored cars, I was also trained as a gunner and radio operator. Then I joined the service regiment at 18 years of age.

LG: So it's not all glamor?
SK: Not at all, that's a common misconception. After armored training, we go through mounted training on horseback in Windsor for 6 months where we learn the tools of horseback riding, beginning with bareback training. The final month is spent in London training in full state uniform.

LG: Do the horses ever act up?
SK: Yes, but it's natural. During the Queen's Jubilee Parade, with 3 million people lining the Mall, to expect any animal to be fully relaxed is absurd. The horses rely on the rider to give them confidence. If the guard is riding the horses confidently and strongly, the horse will settle down.

LG: Your uniforms look pretty heavy. Are they comfortable?
SK: They're not comfortable at all. They were designed way back in Queen Victoria's time, and the leather trousers and boots are very solid. The uniform weighs about 3 stone [about 45 lb.] in all.

MAJOR ATTRACTIONS
See these: you might choose to skip the admission prices, but you'll want the snapshots in your photograph album.

BUCKINGHAM PALACE

At the end of the Mall, between Westminster, Belgravia, and Mayfair. Tube: St. James's Park, Victoria, Green Park, or Hyde Park Corner. ☎ 7839 1377; www.royal.gov.uk.

Originally built for the Dukes of Buckingham, Buckingham House was acquired by George III in 1762, converted into a full-scale palace by George IV, and found to be too small for Victoria's brood. The solution was to close off the three-sided courtyard, concealing the best architecture with Edward Blore's uninspiring facade.

THE STATE ROOMS. The Palace opens to visitors for two months every summer while the royals are off sunning themselves. Don't look for any insights into the Queen's personal life—the State Rooms are used only for formal occasions; as such, they are also the most sumptuous in the Palace, if not all of Britain. The **Galleries** display many of the finest pieces in the outstanding Royal Collection. Since 2001, Liz has also graciously allowed commoners into the **gardens**—keep off the grass! *(Entrance on Buckingham Palace Rd. Tickets available at ☎ 7321 2233 or (from late July) the Ticket Office, Green Park. Book ahead. Open early Aug. to Sept. daily 9:30am-4:30pm. £11, seniors £9, children £5.50, under 5 free, families £27.50.)*

CHANGING OF THE GUARD. The Palace is protected by a detachment of **Foot Guards** in full dress uniform, including (fake) bearskin hats. Accompanied by a band, the "New Guard" starts marching down Birdcage Walk from Wellington Barracks around 10:30am, while the "Old Guard" leaves St. James's Palace around 11:10am. When they meet at the central gates of the palace, the officers of the regiments then touch hands, symbolically exchanging keys, *et voilà*, the guard is officially changed. Show up well before 11:30am and stand directly in front of the palace; for a less-crowded close-up of the guards (but not the ceremony), watch along the routes of the troops between the Victoria Memorial and St. James's Palace or along Birdcage Walk. *(Apr.-Oct. daily; Nov.-Mar. every other day, provided the Queen is in residence, it's not raining too hard, and there are no pressing state functions.)*

WESTMINSTER ABBEY

Parliament Sq., Westminster; access Old Monastery, Cloister, and Garden from Dean's Yard, behind the Abbey. Tube: Westminster or St. James's Park. Abbey ☎7222 7110, Chapter House ☎7222 5897; www.westminster-abbey.org. Abbey open M-Tu, Th-F 9:30am-3:45pm; W 9:30am-7pm; Sa 9:30am-1:45pm; Su for services only. Museum daily 10:30am-4pm. Chapter house Apr.-Oct. daily 9:30am-4:45pm; Nov.-Mar. 10am-4pm. Cloisters daily 8am-6pm. Garden Apr.-Sept. Tu-Th 10am-6pm; Oct.-Mar. 10am-4pm. Audioguides available M-F 9:30am-3pm, Sa 9:30am-1pm; £2. 90min. guided tours M-F 10, 11am, 2, 3pm; Sa 10, 11am; Apr.-Oct. also M-F 10:30am and 2:30pm; £3. Abbey and museum £6, concessions £3, under 11 free, families £12. Entry to services free. Chapter House £1, concessions 80p. Cloisters and garden free. No photography.

On December 28, 1065, Edward the Confessor, last Saxon King of England, was buried in his still-unfinished abbey church of the West Monastery; almost exactly a year later, the abbey saw the coronation of William the Conqueror. Thus even before it was completed, the abbey's twin traditions as figurative birthplace and literal resting place of royalty had been established. Later monarchs continued to add to the abbey, but the biggest change was constitutional rather than physical: in 1540 Henry VIII dissolved the monasteries, expelling the monks and stripping their wealth. Fortunately, the king's respect for his royal forebears outweighed his vindictiveness against the Pope, and so uniquely among England's great monastic centers, Westminster escaped desecration.

INSIDE THE ABBEY. Visitors enter through the **Great North Door** into **Statesman's Aisle**, littered with monuments to 18th- and 19th-century politicians. From here, the **ambulatory** leads past a string of chapels to the left and the **Shrine of St. Edward** to the right. Around the Confessor's shrine, the **House of Kings** displays the tombs of monarchs from Henry III (d. 1272) to Henry V (d. 1422). At the far end of the Shrine stands the **Coronation Chair,** built for Edward I; the shelf below the seat was made to house the Scottish Stone of Scone, which the sticky-fingered Edward yoinked in 1296 (see **Stoned,** below). Stairs lead from the chair to the **Lady Chapel,** now a Tudor mausoleum; side aisles hold **Elizabeth I,** in the north, and **Mary, Queen of Scots,** in the south. Returning to the central part of the Lady Chapel, the nave is dominated by the carved stalls of the **Order of the Bath;** at its end, **Henry VII** lies within a wrought-iron screen.

The south transept holds the abbey's most famous and popular attraction: **Poets Corner.** Its founding member was buried here for reasons nothing to do

LG: How do you overcome the itches, sneezes, and bees?
SK: Inherent discipline is instilled in every British soldier during training. We know not to move a muscle while on parade no matter what the provocation or distraction—unless, of course, it is a security matter. But our helmets are akin to wearing a boiling kettle on your head; to relieve the pressure, sometimes we use the back of our sword blade to ease the back of the helmet forward.

LG: How do you make the time pass while on duty?
SK: The days are long. At Whitehall the shift system is derived upon inspection in Barracks. Smarter men work on horseback in the boxes in shifts from 10am-4pm; less smart men work on foot from 7am-8pm. Some guys count the number of buses that drive past. Unofficially, there are lots of pretty girls around here, and we are allowed to move our eyeballs.

LG: What has been your funniest distraction attempt?
SK: One day a taxi pulled up, and out hopped 4 Playboy bunnies, who then posed for a photo shoot right in front of us. You could call that a distraction if you like.

with literary repute—**Chaucer** had a job in the abbey administration. Plaques at his feet commemorate both poets and prose writers, as does the stained-glass window above. At the very center of the abbey, a short flight of steps leads up to the **Sanctuary,** where coronations take place; the stall to the left of the altar is used by the royal family. Cordons prevent you from climbing up to admire the 13th-century Cosmati mosaic floor. After a detour through the cloisters, including optional visits to the Old Monastery and gardens (see below), visitors return to the **nave.** At the western end is the **Tomb of the Unknown Warrior,** bearing the remains of an unidentified WWI soldier, with an oration poured from molten bullets; just beyond is **Winston Churchill's** simple grave. Stretching eastward, the North Aisle starts with memorials to 20th-century prime ministers before transmuting into **Scientists Corner,** even less of a corner than its poetic equivalent. **Isaac Newton's** massive monument, set into the left-hand quire screen, presides over a tide of physicists around his grave in the nave itself, while in the aisle biologists cluster around **Charles Darwin.**

STONED

On Christmas Day, 1950, daring Scottish patriot Ian Hamilton—posing as a visitor—hid himself in Westminster Abbey until it closed. He meant to steal the 200kg Stone of Scone ("Stone of Destiny") and return it to its rightful home in Scotland, but as he approached the door near Poets Corner to let in his three accomplices, he was detected by a watchman. Hamilton (later a prominent Scottish MP) talked fast enough to convince the watchman that he had been locked in involuntarily.

That same night, the foursome forcibly entered the abbey and pulled the stone out of its wooden container, in the process inadvertently breaking the famed rock into two uneven pieces. The stone was repaired in a Glasgow workyard, but the patriots were frustrated that they could not display it in a public place. On April 11, 1951, Hamilton and Co. carried the stone to the altar at Arbroath Abbey where it was discovered and returned to England. The final chapter of the story is that Glasgow councilor Bertie Gray revealed, before he died, that the stone was copied and the one in the abbey was a fake. The real deal resides at Edinburgh Castle (see p. 555).

OLD MONASTERY, CLOISTERS, AND GARDENS. The abbey complex stretches far beyond the church itself. All these sights are accessible through Dean's Yard without going through the abbey. The **Great Cloisters** hold yet more tombs and commemorative plaques; a passageway running off the southeastern corner leads to the idyllic **Little Cloister** and 900-year-old **College Gardens.** A door off the east cloister leads to the octagonal **Chapter House,** the original meeting place of the House of Commons, whose 13th-century tiled floor is the best-preserved in Europe. Dark and windowless, the **Pyx Chamber** is one of the few surviving parts of the original 11th-century monastic complex. Originally a chapel, it was converted into a treasury in the 13th century. Next door, the **Abbey Museum** is housed in the Norman undercroft. The self-proclaimed highlight of the collection is the array of **funeral effigies,** from the unhealthy-looking wooden models of the 14th century to fully-dressed 17th-century wax versions.

THE HOUSES OF PARLIAMENT

*Parliament Sq., Westminster. Enter at St. Stephen's Gate, between Old and New Palace Yards. Tube: Westminster. Commons Info Office ☎ 7219 4272; www.parliament.uk. Lords ☎ 7219 3107; www.lords.uk. **Prime Minister's Question Time** W 3-3:30pm; tickets required; UK residents write your MP, non-residents contact your embassy. **Commons** in session M-W 2:30-10:30pm, Th 11:30am-7:30pm, F 9:30am-3pm. **Lords** usually sits M-W from 2:30pm, Th 3pm, occasionally F 11:30am; closing times vary. **Tours:** UK residents (year-round M-W 9:30am-noon and F 2:30-5:30pm) contact your MP. Non-residents (Oct.-July F 3:30-5:30pm) apply in writing 4 weeks ahead to: Parliamentary Education Unit, Norman Shaw Building, SW1A 2TT (☎ 7219 4600). Summer tours open* *to all Aug.-Sept. M-Sa 9:15am-4:30pm. Reserve through Firstcall ☎(0870) 906 3773. £7, concessions £3.50.*

The **Palace of Westminster,** as the building in which Parliament sits is officially known, has been at the heart of English governance since the 11th century, when Edward the Confessor established his court here. William I found the site to his liking, and under the Normans the palace was greatly extended. Westminster Hall aside, what little remained of the Norman palace was entirely destroyed in the massive conflagration of 1834; the rebuilding started a year later under the command of Charles Barry and Augustus Pugin. Access has been restricted since a bomb killed an MP in 1979. If you can't land a spot on a tour, don't despair: everyone is allowed in to see debates while the Houses are in session (Oct.-July).

OUTSIDE THE HOUSES. Facing the statue of Cromwell at about the midpoint of the complex, **Old Palace Yard** is the triangular area to the right. On the site of past executions (including those of Walter Raleigh and Guy Fawkes), a statuesque Richard I lords it over parked cars. On the left, **New Palace Yard** is a good place to spy your favorite MPs entering the complex through the Members' entrance. Behind Cromwell squats **Westminster Hall,** sole survivor of the 1834 fire. Unremarkable from the outside, its chief feature is a magnificent 14th-century hammerbeam roof, considered the finest timber roof ever made. Famous defendants during its centuries as a law court include Thomas More and Charles I. These days, it's used for public ceremonies and occasional exhibitions. The **Clock Tower** is universally mis-known as **Big Ben,** a moniker referring only to the bell within, cast in 1858 under the supervision of rotund Commissioner of Works Benjamin Hall.

DEBATING CHAMBERS. Visitors to the debating chambers must first pass through **St. Stephen's Hall,** which stands on the site of St. Stephen's Chapel. Formerly the king's private chapel, in 1550 St. Stephen's became the meeting place of the House of Commons. The Commons have since moved on, but four brass markers point out where the Speaker's Chair used to stand. At the end of the hall, the **Central Lobby** marks the separation of the two houses, with the Lords to the south and the Commons to the north. The ostentatious **House of Lords** is dominated by the sovereign's Throne of State under a gilt canopy. The Lord Chancellor presides over the Peers from the **Woolsack,** a red behemoth the size of a VW Beetle. Next to him rests the man-sized **Mace,** brought in to open the House each morning. In contrast is the restrained **House of Commons,** with simple green-backed benches under a plain wooden roof. This is not entirely due to the difference in class—the Commons was destroyed by bombs in 1941, and rebuilding took place during an era of post-war austerity. The Speaker sits at the center-rear of the chamber, with government MPs to his right and the opposition to his left. The front benches are reserved for government ministers and their opposition "shadows"; the Prime Minister and the Leader of the Opposition face off across their dispatch boxes. With room for only 437 out of 635 MPs, things can get hectic when all are present.

ST. PAUL'S CATHEDRAL

St. Paul's Churchyard, the City. Tube: St. Paul's or Mansion House. ☎7246 8348; www.stpauls.co.uk. Open M-Sa 8:30am-4:30pm, last admission 4pm; open for worship daily 7:15am-6pm; dome open M-Sa 9:30am-4pm. Audioguide available 8:45am-3:30pm; £3.50, concessions £3. 90min. tours M-F 11, 11:30am, 1:30, 2pm; £2.50, concessions £2, children £1. Evensong M-Sa 5pm (45min., free); arrive at 4:50pm for seats in the quire. Cathedral £6, concessions £5, children £3; worshipers free.

Sir Christopher Wren's masterpiece is the fifth cathedral to occupy this site; the original was built in AD 604. Wren's succeeded **"Old St. Paul's,"** begun in 1087 and topped by a steeple one-third the height of the current 364 ft. dome. By 1666, when the Great Fire swept it away, Old St. Paul's was ripe for replacement, having been used as a marketplace and barracks during the Civil War. Even so, only in 1668 did the authorities invite Wren to design a new cathedral. When the bishops rejected his third design, Wren, with Charles II's support, just started building—sneakily, he persuaded the king to let him make "necessary alterations" as work progressed, and the building that emerged from the scaffolding in 1708 bore little resemblance to the "Warrant Model" Charles had approved.

INTERIOR. The entrance leads to the north aisle of the **nave,** the largest space in the cathedral, with seats for 2500 worshipers. Unlike Westminster Abbey, no one is actually buried in the cathedral floor—the graves are all downstairs in the crypt. The second-tallest freestanding **dome** in Europe (after St. Peter's in the Vatican) seems even larger from inside, exaggerated by the false perspective of the paintings on the inner surface. The stalls in the **quire** escaped a bomb, but the altar did not. It was replaced with the current marble **High Altar,** above which looms the mosaic of *Christ Seated in Majesty.* The north quire aisle holds Henry Moore's *Mother and Child.* One month after the sculpture's arrival, guides insisted a plaque be affixed because no one knew what it was. The **statue of John Donne** in the south quire aisle is one of the few monuments to survive from Old St. Paul's.

SCALING THE HEIGHTS. The dome is built in three parts: an inner brick dome, visible from the inside of the cathedral; an outer timber structure; and, between the two, a brick cone that carries the weight of the lantern on top. A network of stairs pierces the structure, carrying brave visitors up, up, and away. First stop is the narrow **Whispering Gallery,** reached by 259 shallow steps or (for those in need only) a small, non-wheelchair-accessible elevator. Encircling the base of the inner dome, the gallery is a perfect resounding chamber: whisper into the wall, and your friends on the other side should be able to hear you. Well, they could if everyone else wasn't trying the same thing. From here, climb another 119 steps (this time steep and winding) to the **Stone Gallery,** outside the cathedral at the base of the outer dome. The heavy stone balustrade, not to mention taller modern buildings, results in an underwhelming view, so take a deep breath and persevere up the final 152 vertiginous steps to the **Golden Gallery** at the base of the lantern.

PLUMBING THE DEPTHS. St. Paul's crypt is riddled with tombs of great Britons. **Admiral Nelson** commands pride of place, amid radiating galleries festooned with monuments to other heroes, including **Florence Nightingale** and Epstein's bust of **T.E. Lawrence** (of Arabia). The neighboring chamber holds the **Duke of Wellington's** massive tomb. The rear of the crypt bears the graves of artists, including **William Blake, J.M.W. Turner,** and **Henry Moore,** crowded around the black slab concealing **Wren** himself. Inscribed on the wall above is his epitaph: *Lector, si monumentum requiris circumspice* ("Reader, if you seek his monument, look around").

THE TOWER OF LONDON

Tower Hill, next to Tower Bridge, in the City, within easy reach of the South Bank and the East End. Tube: Tower Hill or DLR: Tower Gateway. ☎ 7709 0765; www.hrp.org.uk. Open Mar.-Oct. M-Sa 9am-6pm, Su 10am-6pm; buildings close at 5:45pm, last ticket sold 5pm, last entry 5:30pm; Nov.-Feb. all closing times 1hr. earlier, M opens 10am. Audioguide £3. Admission £11.50, concessions £8.75, children £7.50, under 5 free, families £34. Tickets also sold at Tube stations; buy ahead as queues can be horrendous.

The Tower of London, palace and prison of English monarchs for over 900 years, is steeped in blood and history. Conceived by William the Conqueror more to provide protection from than for his new subjects, the wooden palisade of 1067 was replaced in 1078 by a stone structure that grew into the White Tower. **Yeomen Warders,** or "Beefeaters" (a reference to their daily allowance of meat in former times), still guard the fortress, dressed in their blue everyday or red ceremonial uniforms.

The fortress has been divided into seven self-contained areas, which can be visited in any order. A **Yeoman Warders' Tour** will fill you in on the Tower's history and legends. *(Meet near entrance. 1hr.; every 90min. M-Sa 9:30am-2:30pm, Su 10am-2:30pm.)*

WESTERN ENTRANCE AND WATERLANE. From **Middle Tower**, where today tickets are collected and bags searched, you pass over the moat (now a garden) and enter the **Outer Ward** though **Byward Tower**. Just beyond Byward is the massive **Bell Tower**, dating from 1190; the curfew bell has been rung here nightly for over 500 years. The stretch of the Outer Ward along the Thames is **Water Lane**, which until the 16th century was adjacent to the river. **Traitor's Gate** was built by Edward I for his personal use, but is now associated with the prisoners who passed through it.

MEDIEVAL PALACE. In this sequence of rooms, archaeologists have attempted to recreate the look and feel of the Tower during the reign of Edward I (1275-1279). The tour starts at **St. Thomas's Tower**, a half-timbered set of rooms above Traitor's Gate. In other rooms, costumed guides greet visitors. The tour also takes in **Wakefield Tower**, presented as a putative throne room. Tower lore claims that Henry VI was murdered while imprisoned here in 1471 by Edward IV, though recent evidence suggests he was kept in the adjacent **Lanthorn Tower**.

WALL WALK. The walk runs along the eastern wall constructed by Henry III in the mid-13th century. The wall is entered via **Salt Tower**, long used as a prison and said to be haunted—apparently dogs refuse to enter it. At the end of the walk is **Martin Tower**, home to a fascinating collection of retired crowns, *sans* gemstones, along with paste models of some of the more famous jewels, including the **Cullinan diamond,** the largest ever found at 3106 carats. The stone was mailed third class from the Transvaal in an unmarked parcel, a scheme Scotland Yard believed was the safest way of getting it to London.

CROWN JEWELS. The queue at the **Jewel House** is a miracle of crowd management. After passing through room after room of video projections of the jewels in action, the crowd is finally ushered into the vault and onto moving walkways that whisk them past the crowns. Most of the items come from the Coronation regalia. The eye is naturally drawn to the **Imperial State Crown,** home to the Stuart Sapphire and a cocktail party of 16 other sapphires, 2876 diamonds, 273 pearls, 11 emeralds, and a mere five rubies, but don't miss the **Sceptre with the Cross,** topped with First Star of Africa, the largest cut diamond in the world. The **Queen Mother's Crown** is set with the Koh-I-Noor diamond, which legend claims will only bring luck to women.

WHITE TOWER. The Conqueror's original castle has served as royal residence, wardrobe, storehouse, records office, mint, armory, and prison. Visitors are given the option of long or short routes. The long version starts with the first-floor **Chapel of St. John the Evangelist.** The spacious hall next door was most likely the royal **bedchamber,** adjacent to the larger **Great Hall.** Today it houses a collection of armor and weapons. The visit then passes through more displays of weaponry before meeting up with the start of the short route. This trails through a set of historic misrepresentations, starting with the **Spanish Armory**—torture instruments displayed in the 17th century as being captured from the Spanish Armada (1588), but actually from the Tower's own repertoire o' weapons.

TOWER GREEN. The grassy western side of the Inner Ward marks the site of the Tower's most famous executions, surrounded by residential buildings. The Tudor **Queen's House** (which will become the King's House when Charles ascends the throne) is occupied by the Governor of the Tower. Nearby, the **Beauchamp Tower** was usually reserved for high-class "guests," many of whom carved intricate inscriptions into the walls during their detention. On the north of Tower Green is the **Chapel Royal of St. Peter ad Vinculum.** Three queens—Anne Boleyn (Henry VIII Wife #2), Catherine Howard (#5), and Lady Jane Grey—are buried here, as well as Catholic martyrs Sir

Thomas More and John Fisher. *(Open only by Yeoman tours or after 4:30pm.)* Across the green, **Bloody Tower** is named for the probability that here Richard III imprisoned and murdered his nephews, the rightful Edward V (aged 12) and his brother, before usurping the throne in 1483. In 1674, the bones of two children were unearthed nearby and subsequently reinterred in Westminster Abbey.

CENTRAL LONDON

THE CITY OF LONDON

The City of London (**"the City"**) is the oldest part of the capital—for most of its 2000 years, this *was* London, the rest being outlying villages. Yet its appearance is much newer: following the Great Fire of 1666 and the Blitz of 1940-43, the financial area underwent a cosmetic rearrangement that left little of its history behind.

LUDGATE HILL AND AROUND

Legend holds that London takes its name from the mythical King Lud, supposedly buried beneath Lud Gate, one of the original Roman entryways into the City. As the City's highest spot, Ludgate Hill was the obvious spot to build **St. Paul's Cathedral** (see p. 113), which still towers above its surroundings.

OLD BAILEY. Technically the **Central Criminal Courts,** Old Bailey crouches under a copper dome and a wide-eyed figure of Justice. The current building is the third courthouse on the site; the previous two were incorporated into notorious Newgate Prison, demolished in 1902. William Penn, founder of Pennsylvania, was tried here for evangelizing in 1670. After declaring him "not guilty," the jury was imprisoned. This led to the establishment of the "rights of juries to give their verdict according to their convictions." *(Old Bailey and Newgate St.; public entry via Warwick Passage. Tube: St. Paul's. ☎ 7248 3277. Open M-F 10am-1pm and from 2pm until the courts rise, around 5pm. No cameras, drinks, food, electronics, or large bags; no cloakroom facilities.)*

ST. MARY-LE-BOW. Another Wren creation, St. Mary's is most famous for its **Great Bell**—true-blue cockneys are born within its range. The church had to be almost completely rebuilt after the Blitz, but the 11th-century **crypt,** whose bows (arches) gave the church its epithet, survived. Since the 12th century, it has hosted the **Court of Arches,** in which the Archbishop of Canterbury swears in bishops. *(Cheapside, by Bow Ln. Tube: St. Paul's or Mansion House. ☎ 7246 5139. Open M-F 6:30am-6pm. Free.)*

OTHER SIGHTS. Dwelling incongruously in the shadow of the Temple Court building are the remains of the 3rd-century Roman **Temple of Mithras,** discovered during construction work in 1954 and shifted up 18 ft. to street level. *(Queen Victoria St. Tube: Mansion House or Bank.)* Built in 1450, **St. Sepulchre-without-Newgate** (i.e., outside) was gutted in the Great Fire; the interior dates from 1670. Also in the church is the bell of Newgate Prison, rung outside the cells of the condemned on the eves of their executions. *(Holborn Viaduct, opposite the Old Bailey. ☎ 7248 3826. Open W 11am-3pm and Th noon-2pm. Concerts most W at 1pm. Free.)*

GUILDHALL AND LONDON WALL

GUILDHALL. This vast Gothic hall, dating from 1440, is where the representatives of the City's 102 guilds, from the Fletchers (arrow-makers) to the Information Technologists, meet at the **Court of Common Council,** presided over by the Lord Mayor bedecked in traditional robes and followed by a sword-wielding entourage. The Court is held in public every third Thursday of the month. *(Enter the Guildhall through the modern annex. ☎ 7606 3030 for info. Occasional tours. Open May-Sept. daily 10am-5pm; Oct.-Apr. closed Su. Last admission 4:30pm. Free.)*

THE BARBICAN. In the aftermath of WWII, the Corporation of London decided to develop this bomb-flattened 35-acre plot into a textbook piece of reintegration. At the middle of the resulting concrete labyrinth is the **Barbican Centre** cultural complex. Described at its 1982 opening as "the City's gift to the nation," it incorporates a concert hall, two theaters, a cinema, three art galleries, and cafeterias, bars, and restaurants—if you can find any of them. *(Main entrance on Silk St. From Tube: Moorgate or Barbican, follow the yellow painted lines. ☎ 7638 8891. Open M-Sa 9am-11pm, Su 10:30am-11pm.)* For more on Barbican events, see p. 132 and p. 141.

BANK TO THE TOWER

"Bank" refers to *the* Bank—that is, the **Bank of England.** Around this convergence of six streets stand hallowed institutions: the **Stock Exchange,** on Throgmorton St.; the neoclassical **Royal Exchange,** between Cornhill and Threadneedle St., founded in 1566 as Britain's first mercantile exchange; and the 18th-century **Mansion House,** on Walbrook, official residence of the Lord Mayor.

BANK OF ENGLAND. Government financial difficulties led to the 1694 founding of the "Old Lady of Threadneedle St." as a way to raise money without raising taxes—the bank's creditors supplied £1.2 million, and the national debt was born. The windowless outer wall, 8 ft. thick, is the only remnant of Sir John Soane's 1788 building; above it rises the current 1925 edifice. *(Threadneedle St. Tube: Bank.)* Top-hatted guards in pink tailsuits re-direct those who wander into the main entrance to the **Bank of England Museum** around the corner. *(Bartholomew Ln. ☎ 7601 554; www.bankofengland.co.uk. Open M-F 10am-5pm. Free.)*

MONUMENT. The only non-ecclesiastical Wren building in the City, this Doric pillar topped with a gilded flaming urn is a lasting reminder of the Great Fire. Erected in 1677, the 202 ft. column stands exactly that distance from the bakery on Pudding Lane where flames first broke out. The column offers an expansive view of London; bring stern resolution to climb its 311 steps. *(Monument St. Tube: Monument. ☎ 7626 2717. Open 9:30am-5pm, last admission 4:40pm. £1.50, children 50p.)*

TOWER BRIDGE. Perhaps the most iconic symbol of London—which helps explain why tourists often mistake it for its plainer upriver sibling, London Bridge. Folklore claims that when London Bridge was sold and moved to Arizona, the Yanks thought they were getting Tower Bridge. For a deeper understanding of the history and technology behind the bridge, try the **Tower Bridge Experience,** with its tour of the Engine Room and its cheesy animation. Don't expect too much of the view—iron latticework gets in the way. *(Enter Tower Bridge Experience through the west side (upriver) of the North Tower. Tube: Tower Hill or London Bridge. ☎ 7940 3985, lifting schedule 7378 7700. Open daily 9:30am-6pm, last entry 5pm. £4.50, concessions £3.)*

OTHER SIGHTS. St. Stephen Walbrook (built 1672-79) is arguably Wren's finest church. The plain exterior gives no inkling of the wide dome that floats above Henry Moore's 1985 freeform altar. *(39 Walbrook. Tube: Bank or Cannon St. ☎ 7283 4444. Open M-Th 9am-4pm, F 12:30pm for 1hr. organ concert. Free.)* The most famous modern structure in the City is **Lloyd's of London,** built by Richard Rogers in 1986. With metal ducts, lifts, and chutes on the outside, it wears its heart (or at least its internal organs) on its sleeve. *(Leadenhall. Tube: Bank.)* **All Hallows-by-the-Tower** bears its longevity proudly, incorporating a Saxon arch from AD 675 and a Roman pavement in the undercroft "museum." *(Byward St. Tube: Tower Hill. ☎ 7481 2928. Church open M-F 9am-5:45pm, Sa-Su 10am-5pm; crypt M-Sa 10:30am-4pm, Su 1-4pm. Free.)*

THE SOUTH BANK

LONDON EYE. Also known as the **Millennium Wheel,** the 443 ft. London Eye is the biggest observational wheel in the world. Ellipsoid glass "pods" give uninterrupted views from the top of each 30min. revolution; on clear days you can see as far as

Windsor. *(Jubilee Gardens. Tube: Waterloo or Westminster. ☎ (0870) 500 0600. Open late May to early Sept. daily 9:30am-10pm; Apr. to late May and rest of Sept. 10:30am-8pm; Jan.-Mar. and Oct.-Dec. 10:30am-7pm. Ticket office in corner of County Hall; advance booking recommended. May-Sept. £10.50, seniors £8.50, children £5; Oct.-June £9.50/£7.50/£5.)*

SOUTH BANK CENTRE. Sprawling on either side of Waterloo Bridge along the Thames, this symphony in concrete is Britain's cultural center. Its nucleus is the **Royal Festival Hall,** a classic piece of 1950s architecture. Close by, the **Purcell Room** and **Queen Elizabeth Hall** host smaller concerts; just behind it, the spiky ceiling of the **Hayward Gallery** shelters modern art exhibitions. On the embankment beneath Waterloo Bridge, the **National Film Theatre** offers London's most varied cinematic fare, while past the bridge looms the **National Theatre.** To find out how one of the world's largest, most modern theaters operates, join a 1hr. backstage tour. *(On the riverbank between Hungerford and Waterloo Bridges. Tube: Waterloo or Embankment. National Theatre ☎ 7452 3000. Tours M-Sa 10:15am, 12:15 or 12:30pm, 5:15 or 5:30pm, depending on performances. £5, concessions £4.25.)* For events, see p. 142.

TATE MODERN AND THE MILLENNIUM BRIDGE. Squarely opposite each other on Bankside are the biggest success and most abject failure of London's millennial celebrations. **Tate Modern** (see p. 134), created from the shell of the former Bankside power station, is as visually arresting as its contents are thought-provoking. Built to link the Tate to the City, the striking **Millennium Bridge** was not only completed six months too late for the Y2K festivities, but, following a (literally) shaky debut, closed down within days. Engineers promised to fix it in weeks, but a year later no progress had been made; it has now been successfully stabilized. *(Queen's Walk, Bankside. Tube: Southwark, Blackfriars, or St. Paul's.)*

SHAKESPEARE'S GLOBE AND THE ROSE. In the shadow of Tate Modern, the half-timbered Globe (opened 1997) rises just 700 yd. from where the original burned down in 1613. Arrive in time for a tour, given mornings only during the performance season. *(Bankside. Tube: Southwark or London Bridge. ☎ 7902 1500. Open May-Sept. daily 9am-noon and 1-4pm (exhibition only); Oct.-Apr. 10am-5pm. £8, concessions £6.50, children £5.50, families £24; 50p reduction when no tour operates.)* For Globe events, see p. 143. Nearby lie the ruins of the **Rose Theatre,** Bankside's first, where both Shakespeare and Marlowe performed. The site was rediscovered in 1989; not much besides the outline is left. *(56 Park St. ☎ 7593 0026. Open daily 11am-5pm. £4, concessions £3, children £2, families £10; £1 off with same-day Globe exhibition ticket.)*

SOUTHWARK CATHEDRAL. Though Christians have worshiped here since AD 606, the church of St. Saviour only made cathedral status in 1905. The oldest complete part of the building is the **retrochoir,** separated from the main quire by a 16th-century altar screen. The **north aisle** holds the tomb of John Gower (d. 1408), the "first English poet," while across the 19th-century nave, the **south aisle** bears a window and monument to Shakespeare, whose brother Ed is buried here. The new **Visitor Centre** houses a high-tech exhibition on the area. *(Montague Close. Tube: London Bridge. ☎ 7367 6700. Open daily 8am-6pm; exhibition 10am-6pm. Cathedral £2.50 donation; exhibition £3, concessions £2.50, children £1.50, families £12. Camera permit £1.50.)*

HMS BELFAST. This enormous battleship led the bombardment of Normandy during D-Day and supported UN forces in Korea before graciously retiring in 1965. Kids will love clambering over the decks and aiming the anti-aircraft guns at dive-bombing seagulls. Dozens of narrow passages, steep staircases, and ladders make exploring the boat a physical challenge in itself. *(At the end of Morgan's Ln. off Tooley St. Tube: London Bridge. ☎ 7940 6300. Open Mar.-Oct. daily 10am-6pm; Nov.-Feb. 10am-5pm; last admission 45min. before close. £5.80, concessions £4.40, children free.)*

OTHER SIGHTS. County Hall, almost directly opposite the Houses of Parliament, houses two of London's most advertised and least impressive sights, the **London Aquarium** and **Dalí Universe.** *(Westminster Bridge Rd. Tube: Westminster or Waterloo. Aquarium* ☎ *7967 8000. Open daily 10am-6pm, last admission 5pm. £8.75, concessions £6.50, children £5.25, families £25. Dalí* ☎ *7620 2720. Open daily 10am-5:30pm. £8.50, concessions £7.50, children £5, under 10 free, families £22.)* **Vinopolis** is a Dionysian Disneyland offering patrons an interactive (yes, that means samples) tour of the world's wine regions. *(1 Bank End. Tube: London Bridge.* ☎ *(0870) 444 4777. Open M 11am-9pm, Tu-F and Su 11am-6pm, Sa 11am-9pm. Last admission 2hr. before close. £11.50, seniors £10.50, children £5.)* The ▧**Old Operating Theatre and Herb Garret** is bizarrely located in the loft of an 18th-century church. The oldest operating theater in the world is accompanied by a fearsome array of saws, knives, and primitive surgical instruments. *(9a St. Thomas's St. Tube: London Bridge.* ☎ *7955 4791. Open daily 10:30am-4:45pm. Closed Dec. 12-Jan. 5. £3.50, concessions £2.50, children £1.75, families £8.)* Full of less authentic horrors, the **London Dungeon** is always mobbed with kids reveling in tasteful displays about Jack the Ripper, the Great Fire, and anything else remotely connected to the macabre and Britain. *(28-34 Tooley St. Tube: London Bridge.* ☎ *7403 7224. Open mid-July to Sept. daily 10:30am-8pm; Apr. to mid-July and Sept.-Oct. 10:30am-5:30pm; Nov.-Mar. 10:30am-5pm. £11, students £9.50, seniors and children £7; advance tickets £1 extra.)*

THE WEST END

OXFORD AND REGENT STREETS

Oscar Wilde famously quipped that London's famous shopping strip, **Oxford St.,** is "all street and no Oxford." **Regent St.** is more imposing, though none of John Nash's original Regency arcades have survived. To the north, near Oxford Circus, **Carnaby St.** was at the heart of Swinging London in the 1960s. After that psychedelic high followed 30 years as a lurid tourist trap; now Carnaby swings again for the naughty noughties with an influx of trendy boutiques. *(Tube: Oxford Circus.)*

ALL SOULS LANGHAM PLACE. Forced to make an ungainly kink by linking Regent St. to Portland Place, Nash designed All Souls to soften the bend. Unlike any other church in London, the main building barely brushes against its circular entrance hall, whose central spire pierces a double wedding-cake tier of columns. A bust of Nash adorns the outside of the hall. *(Tube: Oxford Circus.)*

MARBLE ARCH. Designed by Nash in 1828 as the front entrance to Buckingham Palace, but rendered useless by a spate of palatial extensions, the Marble Arch was moved to the present site as an entrance into Hyde Park. Then new roads cut the arch off, leaving it stranded forlornly on a traffic roundabout. *(Tube: Marble Arch.)*

MAYFAIR AND ST. JAMES'S

Many would-be sights of London's aristocratic quarter, such as St. James's Palace and the gentlemen's clubs, are out-of-bounds to all but the bluest of bloods.

PICCADILLY, BOND STREET, AND SAVILE ROW. Frilly ruffs were big business in the 16th century—one local tailor named his house after these "piccadills," and the name stuck. Clogged with traffic, **Piccadilly** is no longer the preferred address of gentlemen, as it was in the late 18th century, but it's still posh with a capital P. *(Tube: Piccadilly Circus or Green Park.)* Running into Piccadilly is **Old Bond St.,** London's swankiest shopping street; this end is dominated by art and jewelry dealers, while most of the designer boutiques are on **New Bond St.,** nearer Oxford St. *(Tube: Bond St. or Green Park.)* **Savile Row,** running parallel to Bond St., is synonymous with elegant and expensive tailoring; less well-known is that the **Beatles** performed their last ever live gig on the roof of No. 3 while filming *Let It Be*. *(Tube: Piccadilly Circus.)*

ST. JAMES'S CHURCH. William Blake was baptized in this Wren church, whose exterior is darkened by the soot of London's satanic mills. The current structure is largely a post-war reconstruction; the flowers, garlands, and cherubs by master carver Grinling Gibbons fortunately escaped the Blitz. *(Enter at 197 Piccadilly or off Jermyn St. ☎ 7734 4511. Open daily 8am-7pm.)*

ST. JAMES'S PALACE. St. James's, constructed in 1536, is London's only remaining purpose-built palace. (Buckingham was a rough-and-ready conversion job). The massive gateway is one of the few original parts of the palace remaining. Unless your name starts with HRH, the only part you're likely to get into is the **Chapel Royal.** *(Services Oct.-Easter Su 8:30 and 11am.)* From Easter to September, services are held in the Inigo Jones-designed **Queen's Chapel,** across Marlborough Rd.

SOHO

Soho has a history of welcoming all colors and creeds to its streets. Early settlers were led by 17th-century French Huguenots fleeing religious persecution, but these days Soho is less gay Paris, more just gay: a concentration of gay-owned restaurants and bars has turned **Old Compton St.** into the heart of gay London. A blue plaque at 28 Dean St. marks the two-room flat where **Karl Marx** lived with his wife, maid, and five children while writing *Das Kapital*.

PICCADILLY CIRCUS. Five of the West End's arteries merge and swirl around Piccadilly Circus, and the entire tourist population of London seems to bask under its lurid neon signs. The **statue of Eros** was dedicated to the Victorian philanthropist Lord Shaftesbury: the god originally pointed his arrow down Shaftesbury Ave., but recent restoration has put his aim significantly off. *(Tube: Piccadilly Circus.)*

LEICESTER SQUARE. Amusements here range from London's largest cinemas to the **Swiss Centre** glockenspiel, whose atonal renditions of Beethoven's *Moonlight Sonata* are enough to make even the tone-deaf weep. *(Rings M-F at noon, 6, 7, 8pm; Sa-Su noon, 2, 4, 5, 6, 7, 8pm.)* Be true to your inner tourist and buy violets from a flower-seller or sit for a caricature. *(Tube: Leicester Sq. or Piccadilly Circus.)*

CHINATOWN. Pedestrianized, tourist-ridden **Gerrard St.,** with scroll-worked dragon gates and pagoda-capped phone booths, is the self-proclaimed heart of this tiny slice of Canton, but gritty **Lisle St.,** one block south, has a more authentic feel. Chinatown is most vibrant during the year's two major festivals: the raucous **Chinese New Year Festival** in February and the **Mid-Autumn Festival** at the end of September. *(Between Leicester Sq., Shaftesbury Ave., and Charing Cross Rd.)*

COVENT GARDEN

On the very spot where, 350 years ago, Samuel Pepys saw the first Punch and Judy show in England, street performers entertain the thousands who flock here summer and winter, rain and shine, Londoner and tourist alike. *(Tube: Covent Garden.)*

ST. PAUL'S. Not to be confused with the famous cathedral, this simple Inigo Jones church is the sole remnant of the original square. Known as "the actor's church," the interior is festooned with plaques commemorating of thespians from Vivien Leigh to Tony Simpson. The **churchyard's** leafy gardens belie its status as a bubonic burial ground—Margaret Ponteous, the first victim of the Great Plague, was interred here on April 12, 1665. *(On Covent Garden Piazza; enter via King St., Henrietta St., or Bedford St. ☎ 7836 5221. Open M-F 8:30am-4:30pm and Su for morning services.)*

THE ROYAL OPERA HOUSE. The Royal Opera House reopened in 2000 after a major expansion. During the day, the public is free to wander the ornate lobby of

Soho and Covent Garden

ACCOMMODATIONS
High Holborn Residence, 6
YHA Oxford Street, 8

★ **NIGHTLIFE**
The Box, 10
Comptons of Soho, 12
First Out, 4
Freud, 5
G-A-Y, 2
Heaven, 18
Ku Bar, 13
Sound, 15
Vespa Lounge, 3

ENTERTAINMENT
Comedy Store, 16
Donmar Warehouse, 11
English National Opera, 17
London Astoria (LA1), 1
Pizza Express Jazz Club, 7
The Prince Charles, 14
Ronnie Scott's, 9

LONDON

HOLBORN

COVENT GARDEN

SOHO

MAYFAIR

STRAND

Theatre Royal, Drury Lane
Russell St.
Catherine St.
Wellington St.
Bow St.
Royal Opera House
Covent Garden Piazza
Transport Museum
Theatre Museum
St. Paul's Church
Covent Garden
Savoy St.
Carting Ln.
Burleigh St.
Tavistock St.
Southampton St.
Exeter St.
Strand
Maiden Ln.
Bedford St.
Bedfordbury
New Row
Rose St.
Garrick St.
King St.
Floral St.
Long Acre
Langley St.
Mercer St.
Shelton St.
Earlham St.
Neal St.
Endell St.
Shorts Gdns.
Drury Ln.
High Holborn Rd.
St. Giles High St.
St. Giles
Seven Dials
Monmouth St.
The Photographer's Gallery
Charing Cross Rd.
CAMBRIDGE CIRCUS
Cambridge Tower St.
Greek St.
Bateman St.
Frith St.
Dean St.
Old Compton St.
Romilly St.
St. Anne's
Shaftesbury Ave.
Soho Sq.
SOHO SQ.
Sutton Row
Charles II Statue
Great Chapel St.
Carlisle St.
Wardour St.
Berwick St.
Broadwick St.
Poland St.
D'Arblay St.
Lexington St.
Marshall St.
Carnaby St.
Beak St.
Kingly St.
Great Pulteney St.
Bridle Ln.
Brewer St.
Great Windmill St.
Glasshouse St.
Sherwood St.
GOLDEN SQ.
Regent St.
Oxford St.
New Oxford St.
Noel St.
Great Marlborough St.
Savile Row
Old Bond St.
Albemarle St.
Dover St.
Berkeley St.
Jermyn St.
Duke of York St.
Charles St.
Haymarket
Whitcomb St.
Panton St.
Coventry St.
Rupert St.
Wardour St.
Lisle St.
Gerrard St.
Newport St.
Little Newport St.
Leicester Sq.
LEICESTER SQ.
Leicester Pl.
Irving St.
Cranbourn St.
Orange St.
National Gallery
TRAFALGAR SQ.
St. Martin's Ln.
St. Martin's Pl.
St. Martin's St.
St. Martin-in-the-Fields
Chandos Pl.
William IV St.
Charing Cross
Craven St.
Victoria Embankment
Victoria Embankment Gardens
Embankment
PICCADILLY CIRCUS
Piccadilly
Regent St.
Piccadilly
Museum of Mankind
Royal Academy
Burlington Arcade
Marlborough Fine Arts
St. James's Church
Mercer St.
Odeon
BERKELEY SQ.

100 yards
100 meters

TO Tottenham Ct. Rd., 1 & 2 (100m)
TO Oxford Circus (100m)

the original 1858 theater, as well as the enormous glass-roofed space of **Floral Hall.** From there, take the escalator to reach the **terrace** overlooking the Piazza, with great views of London. *(Enter on Bow St. or through "the Link" in the northeast of the Piazza. 1¼hr. backstage tours M-Sa 10:30am, 12:30, 2:30pm; reservations essential. Open daily 10am-3:30pm. £8, concessions £7.)* For performances at the Opera House, see p. 145.

THEATRE ROYAL, DRURY LANE. Founded in 1663, this is the oldest of London's surviving theaters. Charles II met Nell Gwynn here in 1655 and David Garrick ruled the roost in the 18th century. There's even a ghost—in the 19th century, a corpse and dagger were found bricked up in the wall. This and other bits of Drury Lane lore are resurrected in actor-led tours. *(Entrance on Catherine St. ☎ 7240 5357. Tours M-Tu and Th-F 2:15 and 4:45pm; W and Sa 10:15am and noon. £8.50, children £6.50.)*

WESTMINSTER

TRAFALGAR SQUARE AND THE STRAND

John Nash suggested laying out **Trafalgar Square** in 1820, but it took almost 50 years for London's largest traffic roundabout to take on its current appearance: Nelson arrived in 1843, and the bronze lions in 1867. The long-empty **fourth plinth** now holds specially commissioned modern sculpture. Every December the square hosts a giant **Christmas tree,** donated by Norway as thanks for British assistance against the Nazis. *(Tube: Charing Cross or Leicester Sq.)*

ST. MARTIN-IN-THE-FIELDS. James Gibbs's 1720s creation is instantly recognizable as the model for countless Georgian churches in Britain and America. It's still the Queen's parish church; look for the royal box left of the altar. Handel and Mozart performed here, and St. Martin's still hosts frequent concerts. Downstairs the **crypt** has a life of its own, home to a cafe, bookshop, art gallery, and the **London Brass Rubbing Centre.** *(St. Martin's Ln., northeast corner of Trafalgar Sq.; crypt on Duncannon St. Tube: Charing Cross or Leicester Sq. ☎ 7766 1100. Brass rubbing daily 10am-7pm.)*

ST. MARY-LE-STRAND. The slender steeple and elegant portico of this 1724 church rise above a sea of traffic. Designed by Gibbs, the church overlooks the site of the original **Maypole,** claimed by Isaac Newton for a telescope stand. Inside, the Baroque decoration reflects not only the glory of God but also Gibbs's Romanesque architectural training. *(☎ 7836 3205. Open M-F 11am-4pm.)*

WHITEHALL

A long stretch of imposing facades housing government ministries, "Whitehall" is synonymous with the British civil service. From 1532 until a devastating fire in 1698, however, it was the home of the monarchy and one of the greatest palaces in Europe. Today all that remains are Henry VIII's wine cellars, hidden under the monolithic **Ministry of Defence** and viewable only on written application, and Inigo Jones's **Banqueting House.** Opposite Banqueting House, the burnished hussars of the Household Cavalry stand at attention at **Horseguards.** *(Guard changed M-F 11am, Sa 10am, dismount for inspection daily 4pm.)* Where Whitehall becomes Parliament St., gates mark the entrance to **Downing St.;** No. 10 is the official residence of the Prime Minister, but Tony Blair's family is too big, so he's swapped with Chancellor Gordon Brown, at No. 11. *(Between Trafalgar Sq. and Parliament Sq. Tube: Westminster, Embankment, or Charing Cross.)*

BANQUETING HOUSE. All that remains of the Palace of Whitehall, Banqueting House was built in 1622 by Inigo Jones for James I. Essentially a one-up, one-down affair—the vaulted undercroft below and the great hall above—it's still used for state dinners. Charles I commissioned Rubens to paint the great ceiling panels with scenes extolling the monarchy; unfortunately for him, Parliament wasn't impressed, and on January 27, 1649, Charles stepped out of the window onto the scaffold where he was beheaded. *(Whitehall, opposite Horseguards. ☎ 7930 4179. Open M-Sa 10am-5pm, last admission 4:30pm. £4, concessions £3, children £2.60.)*

PARLIAMENT SQUARE

Laid out in 1750, Parliament Square rapidly became the focal point for opposition to the government. Today, demonstrators are dissuaded by a continuous stream of heavy traffic, with no pedestrian crossings. Standing opposite the **Houses of Parliament** (see p. 112), a bronze Winston Churchill was famously given a turf mohican during the May 2000 anti-capitalist demonstrations. South of the square rises **Westminster Abbey** (see p. 111) while to the west looms the great dome of **Methodist Central Hall,** where the United Nations first met in 1946. *(Tube: Westminster.)*

ST. MARGARET'S WESTMINSTER. Literally in Westminster Abbey's shadow, St. Margaret's has been the official church of the House of Commons since 1614. The **Milton Window** (1888), to the right of the main entrance above the North Aisle, shows the poet dictating *Paradise Lost* to his daughters. The **East Window** celebrates the wedding of Henry VIII to Catherine of Aragon (Wife #1). Opposite, the **West Window** commemorates Sir Walter Raleigh, now lying in the chancel. *(Tube: Westminster. ☎ 7222 6382. Open M-F 9:30am-3:45pm, Sa 9:30am-1:45pm, Su 2-5pm. Free.)*

JEWEL TOWER. Cut off from the Houses of Parliament by Millbank, Jewel Tower is a lone survivor of the medieval Palace of Westminster. Built by Edward III in the 14th century, from 1621 to 1869 it was used to store the parliamentary archives (now in Victoria Tower, across the street). These days it houses the **Parliament Past and Present** exhibition, which explains that body's history and workings. *(Tube: Westminster. ☎ 7222 2219. Open Apr.-Sept. daily 10am-6pm; Oct. 10am-5pm; Nov.-Mar. 10am-4pm. £1.60, concessions £1.20, children 80p, under 5 free.)*

OTHER WESTMINSTER SIGHTS

WESTMINSTER CATHEDRAL. Following Henry VIII's break with Rome, London's Catholic community remained without a cathedral for over three centuries—until 1887, when the Church purchased a derelict prison as the site from which the neo-Byzantine church was to rise. The architect's plan outran available funds; in 1903, when work stopped, the interior remained unfinished. The three blackened brick domes contrast dramatically with the swirling marble of the lower walls and the magnificence of the side chapels. A lift carries visitors up the striped 273 ft. **bell tower** for a view of Westminster, the river, and Kensington. *(Cathedral Piazza, off Victoria St. Tube: Victoria. ☎ 7798 9055. Cathedral open daily 7am-7pm. Suggested donation £2. Bell Tower open Apr.-Nov. daily 9am-5pm; Dec.-Mar. Th-Su. £2, concessions £1, families £5.)*

THE ROYAL MEWS. A working carriage house doubling as a museum, the Mews' main attraction is the Queen's collection of conveyances, from the "glass coach" used to carry Diana to her wedding to the four-ton Gold State Coach. Kids will enjoy a chance to get up close to the horses, each named personally by the Queen. *(Buckingham Palace Rd. Tube: St. James's Park or Victoria. ☎ 7839 1377. Open Apr.-Oct. daily 11am-4pm, last admission 3:15pm. Horses and carriages liable to be absent without notice; opening hours subject to change. £4, seniors £3.60, children £2.60, families £11.80.)*

ST. JAMES'S PARK AND GREEN PARK

The run-up to Buckingham Palace is flanked by two expanses of greenery. **St. James's Park,** acquired along with St. James's Palace by Henry VIII in 1531, owes its informal appearance to a re-landscaping by Nash in 1827. Across the Mall, **Green Park** is the creation of Charles II; "Constitution Hill" refers not to the king's interest in political theory, but to his daily exercises. *(The Mall. Open daily 5am-midnight.)*

LONDON

LONDON

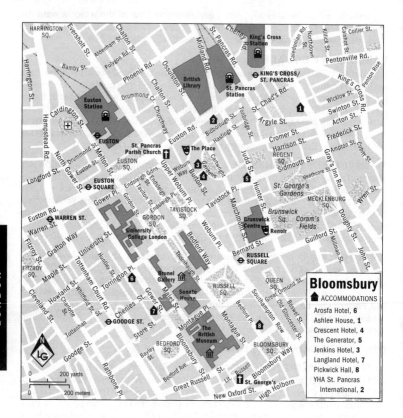

Bloomsbury

⛺ ACCOMMODATIONS

Arosfa Hotel, **6**
Ashlee House, **1**
Crescent Hotel, **4**
The Generator, **5**
Jenkins Hotel, **3**
Langland Hotel, **7**
Pickwick Hall, **8**
YHA St. Pancras
International, **2**

BLOOMSBURY

ACADEMIA. The strip of land along **Gower St.** and immediately to its west is London's academic heartland. The stunning 🏛**British Library** (p. 137) is on Euston Rd. Established in 1828 to educate those excluded from Oxford and Cambridge, **University College London** was the first institution of higher learning in Britain to admit Catholics, Jews, and women. The embalmed body of founder **Jeremy Bentham** occupies the South Cloister. *(Main entrance on Gower St. South Cloister entrance through the courtyard. Tube: Warren St. or Euston Sq.)* Now the administrative HQ of the University of London, **Senate House** was the model for the Ministry of Truth in *1984*—George Orwell worked there as part of the BBC's propaganda unit in WWII. *(At the southern end of Malet St. Tube: Goodge St. or Russell Sq.)*

OTHER BLOOMSBURY SIGHTS. Next to the British Library are the soaring Gothic spires of **St. Pancras Station.** Formerly housing the Midland Grand Hotel, today Sir George Gilbert Scott's facade is a hollow shell awaiting redevelopment as a Marriott. *(Euston Rd. Tube: King's Cross/St. Pancras.)* Started in 1816, **St. Pancras Parish Church** is a replica of the 2500-year-old Erectheon in Athens, with an octagonal tower based on the Acropolis's Tower of the Winds. *(Euston Rd. and Upper Woburn Pl. Tube:*

Euston.) The shrapnel-scarred Corinthian portico of Nicholas Hawksmoor's **St. George's Bloomsbury** is in desperate need of repair, but the interior is in perfect condition. *(Bloomsbury Way. Tube: Russell Sq. Open M-Sa 9:30am-5:30pm.)*

CHELSEA

The stomping ground of the Sloane Rangers—well-bred, dim-witted aristocratic scions—Chelsea nevertheless retains a unique vibrancy. Henry VIII's right-hand man (and later victim) Sir Thomas More was the first big-name resident, but it was in the 19th century that the neighborhood became an artistic hothouse: **Cheyne Walk** was home to J.M.W. Turner, George Eliot, Dante Gabriel Rossetti, and more recently Mick Jagger (at No. 48); Oscar Wilde, James Singer Sargent, James McNeill Whistler, and Bertrand Russell lived on **Tite St.**; while Mark Twain, Henry James, T.S. Eliot, and William Morris were also Chelsea residents. *(Tube: Sloane Sq. From there, buses #11, 19, 22, 211, and 319 run down the King's Rd.)*

THE ROYAL HOSPITAL. Charles II established the Hospital—designed by Christopher Wren—as a retirement community for army veterans in 1692. It remains a military institution, with the uniformed "Chelsea Pensioners" arranged in companies under the command of a retired officer. French cannons from Waterloo guard the open south side of **Figure Court,** named for Grinling Gibbons's statue of Charles II, while the north is divided between the **chapel** and the **Great Hall.** The outhouses harbor a small **museum,** detailing the hospital's history and a displaying a slew of medals. *(Royal Hospital Rd. ☎ 7881 5204. Open M-Sa 10am-noon and 2-4pm; Su 2-4pm. Free.)*

CHELSEA PHYSIC GARDEN. Founded in 1673 to provide medicinal herbs, the Physic Garden was the staging post from which tea was introduced to India and cotton to America. Today it remains a living repository of all manner of plants, from opium poppies to carrots. *(66 Royal Hospital Rd., entrance on Swan Walk. ☎ 7352 5646. Open early Apr. to late Oct. W noon-5pm, Su 2-6pm; M-F noon-5pm during Chelsea Flower Show (late May) and Chelsea Festival (mid-June). £4, concessions £2.)*

OTHER CHELSEA SIGHTS. Sloane Square serves as the eastern end of the **King's Road,** until 1829 a private royal route from Hampton Court to Whitehall. The 60s were launched here in 1955 when Mary Quant dropped the miniskirt on an unsuspecting world. In **Carlyle's House,** which remains much as it was during Thomas's lifetime, the historian, writer, and "Sage of Chelsea" entertained Dickens, Tennyson, Eliot, and Ruskin. *(24 Cheyne Row. ☎ 7352 7087. Open Apr.-Oct. W-F 2-5pm, Sa-Su 11am-5pm; last admission 4:30pm. £3.60, children £1.80.)* Where Cheyne Walk spills onto Chelsea Embankment stands **Chelsea Old Church,** looking remarkably new following post-WWII restoration. Fortunately, the bombs spared the southern chapel, designed by Thomas More in the 16th century. Henry VIII is reported to have married Jane Seymour (Wife #3) here before the official wedding. *(Old Church St. Open Tu-F 2-5pm; services Su 8, 11am, 12:15, 6pm.)*

HOLBORN AND CLERKENWELL

Squeezed between the City and the West End, **Holborn's** crush of streets hides many a marvel, chiefly the four **Inns of Court,** venerable institutions providing apprenticeships to law students and housing the chambers of practising barristers. Most were founded in the 13th century when a royal decree barred the clergy from the courts, giving rise to a class of professionals. Northeast of Holborn, **Clerkenwell** may be tagged the new Soho, but it's actually far older. From the 12th century until Henry VIII's break with Rome, Clerkenwell was dominated by the great monastic foundations—traces of which can still be found.

INNS OF COURT

THE TEMPLE. South of Fleet St., this labyrinthine compound encompasses the inns of the **Middle Temple** to the west and the **Inner Temple** neighboring it on the east—there was once an Outer Temple, but it's long gone. *(Between Fleet St., Essex St., Victoria Embankment, and Temple Ave./Bouvier St.; numerous passages lead to the Temple. Tube: Temple or Blackfriars.)* From 1185 until the order was dissolved in 1312, this land belonged to the crusading Knights Templar; sole remnant of this time is the **Temple Church.** Adjoining the round church is a Gothic nave, built in 1240, with an altar screen by Wren. *(☎7353 3470. Open W-Th 11am-4pm, Sa 10am-2:30pm, Su 12:45-4pm. Free.)* While the Inner Temple was leveled during the Blitz—with the exception of the Tudor **Inner Temple Gateway,** 16-17 Fleet St., all is reconstruction—the Middle Temple was hardly touched. **Middle Temple Hall,** closed to the public, still has its 1574 hammerbeam ceiling as well as a dining table made from the hatch of Sir Francis Drake's *Golden Hinde.* According to Shakespeare's *Henry VI,* the red and white flowers that served as emblems in the Wars of the Roses were plucked in **Middle Temple Garden,** south of the hall. *(Garden open May-Sept. M-F noon-3pm. Free.)*

LINCOLN'S INN. Just east of **Lincoln's Inn Fields,** London's largest square, sprawl the grounds of Lincoln's Inn. Donne, More, Walpole, Pitt, Gladstone, and Disraeli are a few former Inn-mates. The main gates deposit you in **New Square,** appearing much as it did when built in the 1690s. Next to New Square are the **Old Buildings,** including the 15th-century **Old Hall** (closed to the public). The **chapel,** whose foundation stone was laid in 1620 by John Donne, sits above an open undercroft. *(Between Lincoln's Inn Fields and Chancery Ln. Tube: Chancery Ln. or Holborn. Chapel and gardens open M-F noon-2:30pm. Free.)*

GRAY'S INN. The exterior of Gray's Inn does not inspire joy—Dickens dubbed it "that stronghold of melancholy." Entering through the 1688 **gatehouse** on High Holborn, you pass the 16th-century **hall** to your right; its screen was carved from the timbers of a Spanish galleon. Francis Bacon maintained chambers here and is the purported designer of the expansive **gardens.** *(Between Theobald's Rd., Jockey's Fields, High Holborn, and Gray's Inn Rd. Tube: Chancery Ln. Gardens open M-F noon-2:30pm.)*

FLEET STREET

Named for the river (now underground) that flows from Hampstead to the Thames, Fleet St.'s association with publishing goes back more than 450 years. Times—and *The Times*—have changed, however: Rupert Murdoch's 1986 move to Docklands initiated a mass exodus. Though "Fleet Street" is still synonymous with the British press, the famous facades, such as the Greek and Egyptian Revival *Daily Telegraph* building and the Art Deco *Daily Express* manse, now house corporate offices. *(Tube: Temple.)*

■ **ROYAL COURTS OF JUSTICE.** Straddling the official division between the City of Westminster and the City of London, this sprawling neo-Gothic structure encloses courtrooms (open to the public during trials) and the Great Hall (home to Europe's largest mosaic floor) amid labyrinthine passageways. At the top of the stairs at the rear of the hall are a few glass boxes dedicated to the history of legal costume. *(Where the Strand becomes Fleet St. Tube: Temple or Chancery Ln. ☎7936 6000. Open M-F 9am-6pm, last admission 4:30pm; trials start around 10am, with a 1-2pm break. Free.)*

ST. BRIDE'S. The unusual spire of Wren's 1675 church is the world's most imitated piece of architecture. Dubbed "the printers' cathedral" in 1531, when Wyken de Worde set up his press, St. Bride's literary associations include Samuel Pepys and John Milton. The **crypt,** closed in 1853 after a cholera epidemic, was reopened for post-Blitz restoration. *(St. Bride's Ave., off Fleet St. Open daily 8am-4:45pm. Free.)*

SAMUEL JOHNSON'S HOUSE. Dr. Johnson, a self-described "shrine to the English language," lived here from 1748 to 1759, completing the first definitive English dictionary, though rumor falsely insists that he omitted "sausage." He compiled the landmark lexicon by reading the great books of the age and marking the words he wanted to include. *(17 Gough Sq.; follow the signs down the alley opposite 54 Fleet St. ☎ 7353 3745. Tube: Blackfriars or Chancery Ln. Open May-Sept. M-Sa 11am-5:30pm, Oct.-Apr. M-Sa 11am-5pm. £4, concessions £3, children £1, families £9.)*

CLERKENWELL

ST. JOHN'S SQUARE. Bisected by busy Clerkenwell Rd., St. John's Square occupies the site of the 12th-century **Priory of St. John,** formerly the English seat of the crusading Knights Hospitallers. Arching grandly over the square's entrance is 16th-century **St. John's Gate,** home to an odd mixture of artifacts relating to the original priory and Hospitallers and high-tech displays detailing the exploits of the modern-day Order of St. John. Join a tour to see the upstairs council chamber and the **priory church,** complete with 12th-century crypt and the 1480 *Weston Triptych. (St. John's Ln. ☎ 7324 4405. Tours Tu and F-Sa 11am and 2:30pm; £5, seniors £3.50. Gate open M-F 10am-5pm, Sa 10am-4pm; free. Church open only for tours.)*

ST. BARTHOLOMEW THE GREAT. Visitors must enter through a 13th-century arch, disguised as a Tudor house, to reach this Norman gem. William Hogarth was baptized in the 15th-century font, and Ben Franklin worked for a printer in the Lady's Chapel. The tomb near the altar belongs to **Rahere,** who founded both the church and **St. Bartholomew's Hospital** across the street in 1123. *(Little Britain, off West Smithfield. Tube: Barbican or Farringdon. ☎ 7606 5171. Open Tu-F 8:30am-5pm, Sa 10:30am-1:30pm, Su 8:30am-1pm and 2:30-8pm. Free.)*

SMITHFIELD MARKET. On the site of medieval St. Bartholomew's Fair, Smithfield has been London's main **meat market** since the 19th century. The association with butchery predates the Victorians: Wat Tyler, leader of the 1381 Peasants' Revolt, and William "Braveheart" Wallace were among those executed here. *(Charterhouse St. Tube: Barbican or Farringdon. Open M-F 4-10am.)*

KENSINGTON AND EARL'S COURT

Nobody took much notice of Kensington before 1689, when the newly crowned William and Mary moved into Kensington Palace and high society tagged along. The next significant date in Kensington's history was 1851, when the Great Exhibition brought in enough money to finance a slew of museums and colleges. In Kensington's southwestern corner, Earl's Court is a grimier district, dubbed "Kangaroo Valley" in the 1960s and 1970s for its popularity with Australian expats.

KENSINGTON PALACE. In 1689, William and Mary commissioned Wren to remodel Nottingham House into a proper palace. Parts are still in use as a royal residence—Princess Diana was the most famous recent inhabitant. Inside, the **Royal Ceremonial Dress Collection** displays intricate courtier costumes, together with a number of the Queen's demure evening gowns and Di's racier numbers. In the **State Apartments,** Hanoverian economy is evident in the *trompe l'oeil* decoration throughout. *(Eastern edge of Kensington Gardens; enter through the park. Tube: High St. Kensington or Queensway. ☎ 7937 9561. Open Mar.-Oct. daily 10am-6pm; Nov.-Feb. 10am-5pm; last admission 30min. before close. £10, concessions £7.50, children £6.50, families £30.)*

HYDE PARK AND KENSINGTON GARDENS. Surrounded by London's wealthiest neighborhoods, giant **Hyde Park** has served as the model for city parks around the world, including New York's Central Park and Paris's Bois de Boulogne. The contiguous **Kensington Gardens** were created in the late 17th century when Kensington Palace became the new royal residence. Officially known as the **Long Water** west of the Serpentine Bridge, the 41-acre **Serpentine** was created in 1730. South of Long Water, some way from the lake itself, basks the **Serpentine Gallery**, the unlikely venue for contemporary art shows. Running through the southern section of the park, the dirt track of **Rotten Row** stretches west from Hyde Park Corner. Originally *Route du Roi* or "King's Road," it was the first English thoroughfare lit at night to deter crime. At the northeastern corner of the park, near Marble Arch, proselytizers, politicos, and flat-out crazies dispense their knowledge to bemused tourists at **Speaker's Corner** on Sundays. *(Framed by Kensington Rd., Knightsbridge, Park Ln., and Bayswater Rd. Tube: Queensway, Lancaster Gate, Marble Arch, Hyde Park Corner, or High St. Kensington. ☎ 7298 2100. Park open daily 5am-midnight. Gardens open dawn-dusk. Both free.)*

ALBERTOPOLIS. The Great Exhibition of 1851 was the brainchild of Prince Albert, Queen Vic's husband. By the time the exhibition closed a year later, six million people had passed through, and the organizers were left with a £200,000 profit. (Take that, Millennium Dome.) Again at Albert's suggestion, the cash was used to buy 86 acres to be dedicated to institutions promoting British arts and sciences. The most famous of these are the trio of the **Victoria and Albert Museum** (p. 134), **Science Museum** (p. 137), and **Natural History Museum** (p. 137), and the **Royal Albert Hall,** an all-purpose venue that has hosted a full-length marathon and the first public display of electric lighting, as well as the annual **Proms** (see p. 145). The discs hanging from the ceiling are an attempt to muffle the hall's booming echo. *(Kensington Gore. Tube: South Kensington or High St. Kensington. Box office ☎ 7589 8212.)* Opposite the hall, His Highness is commemorated by Gilbert Scott's **Albert Memorial,** either nightmarish or fairytale, depending on your opinion of Victorian High Gothic. *(Kensington Gore. ☎ 7495 0916. 45min. tours Su 2 and 3pm; £3.50, concessions £3.)*

KNIGHTSBRIDGE AND BELGRAVIA

It's hard to imagine that **Knightsbridge,** now home to London's most expensive stores, was once a racy district known for taverns and highwaymen. Neighboring **Belgravia** was catapulted to respectability by the presence of royalty at nearby Buckingham Palace in the 1820s. **Belgrave Square,** the setting for *My Fair Lady,* is the most impressive of the set-pieces, now so expensive that the aristocracy has had to sell out to foreign governments—this is embassyland.

APSLEY HOUSE. "No. 1, London" was bought in 1817 by the **Duke of Wellington,** whose heirs still occupy the top floor. On display is Wellington's outstanding collection of art, much of it given in gratitude by the crowned heads of Europe following the battle of Waterloo. The majority of the paintings hang in the **Waterloo Gallery,** where the Duke held his annual Waterloo banquet. In the basement, one cabinet is filled with Wellington's medals, while another holds newspaper caricatures from his later political career. *(Hyde Park Corner. Tube: Hyde Park Corner. ☎ 7499 5676. Open Tu-Su 11am-5pm. £4.50, students £3, children and seniors free.)*

WELLINGTON ARCH. At the center of London's most infamous intersection, Wellington Arch was built in 1825 as the "Green Park Arch." In 1838 it was dedicated to the good duke, and—much to the horror of architect Decimus Burton—eight years later was encumbered by a gigantic statue of the man. Wellington's statue was finally replaced in 1910 by the *Quadriga and Peace,* designed by army vet Adrian Jones. Inside the arch, exhibitions on the building's history and the changing nature of war memorials play second fiddle to the viewing platforms. *(Hyde Park Corner. Tube: Hyde Park Corner. ☎ 7930 2726. Open Apr.-Sept. W-Su 10am-6pm; Oct. 10am-5pm; Nov.-Mar. 10am-4pm. £2.50, concessions £1.90, children £1.30.)*

MARYLEBONE AND REGENT'S PARK

Marylebone's most famous resident (and address) never existed. Armchair sleuths come searching for 221b Baker St., fictional home of the fictional Holmes, but find instead the headquarters of the Abbey National bank. The **Sherlock Holmes Museum** gives its address out as 221b, although a quick bit of deducing reveals that it actually stands at No. 239. *(Tube: Baker St. ☎ 7935 8866; www.sherlock-holmes.co.uk. Open daily 9:30am-6:30pm. £6, children £4.)*

MADAME TUSSAUD'S AND THE PLANETARIUM. Back in the 18th century, Mrs. T got her big break with a string of commissions for death masks of guillotined aristos, including a freshly beheaded Marie Antoinette. Despite its revolutionary beginnings, the display of waxworks positively fawns over royalty and other more and less worthy celebrities. Giant, green, and eerily reminiscent of a silicone-filled breast, the **London Planetarium** rises alluringly next to Madame Tussaud's masculine bulk. As cinematic spectacle, it's tough to beat, but entertainment value has completely swamped any educational ideals the Planetarium formerly aspired to. *(Marylebone Rd. Tube: Baker St. ☎(0870) 400 3000. Open M-F 10am-5:30pm, Sa-Su 9:30am-5:30pm. Planetarium shows 2 per hr. Tickets sold at both Madame Tussaud's and Planetarium and valid for both. £15, seniors £11.70, children £10.50; July-Aug. 9am-2pm, all tickets £2 more. Advance booking highly recommended; £1 extra.)*

REGENT'S PARK. Perhaps London's most attractive and most popular park, with landscapes ranging from football-scarred fields to Italian-style formal plantings. It's all very different from John Nash's vision of wealthy villas hidden among exclusive gardens; fortunately for us common folk, in 1811 Parliament intervened and guaranteed the space would remain open to all. *(Tube: Baker St., Regent's Park, Great Portland St., or Camden Town. ☎7486 7905. Open daily from 6am. Closes between 4:30 and 9pm, depending on season. Free.)*

THE LONDON ZOO. With a long and often pioneering history, many of the zoo's buildings are as interesting as the critters they contain (or don't, as the earliest are now considered too small to house anything except a menagerie of stuffed toys)—pick up the free *Animal Architecture* leaflet. *(Main gate on Outer Circle, Regent's Park. Bus #274 or 12min. signposted walk from Tube: Camden Town; 15min. walk from Tube: Regent's Park. ☎7449 6576; www.londonzoo.com. Open Apr.-Oct. daily 10am-5:30pm, last admission 4:30pm; Nov.-Mar. 10am-4:30pm. £11, concessions £9.30, children £8, families £34.)*

GREATER LONDON

NORTH LONDON

CAMDEN TOWN

An island of honest tawdriness in an increasingly affluent sea, Camden Town has thrown off attempts at gentrification thanks to the ever-growing **Camden Market** (see p. 141), London's fourth most popular tourist attraction, centered in **Camden Lock.** For a display of life nearly as diverse as the market on a weekend, take a leisurely jaunt up the Regent's Canal to the **London Zoo,** in Regent's Park (see above).

HAMPSTEAD

Hampstead caught the attention of well-heeled Londoners in the 17th century, when it became fashionable to take the waters at Hampstead Wells, on the site of today's **Well Walk.** In the 1930s, Hampstead found itself at the forefront of a European avant-garde in flight from fascism: residents Aldous Huxley, Piet Mon-

THE INSIDER'S CITY

THE JUBILEE LINE EXTENSION

Begun in 1977 to honor Queen Elizabeth's first 25 years on the throne, the Jubilee Line of the London Underground was recently extended—just in time for Liz's 50th anniversary. The designers of the four stations listed below were specially commended for their innovative work. Their phenomenal underground architecture combines with proximity to London's most intriguing above-ground sights for a fascinating tour.

1 Westminster Underground: An abundance of glass and massive pillars, pipes, and escalators. **Overground:** State-of-the-art gives way to the stately British brilliance of Big Ben and Parliament.

2 Southwark Underground: Steep walls, high skylit ceilings, and an ominous elevator lead to daylight at the rotunda-like exit. **Overground:** Gleaming beams (the now sturdy Millennium Bridge) and the chic brick Tate Modern.

3 Canary Wharf Underground: Precipitous escalator, arching transparent overhang, and a sloping concrete ceiling. **Overground:** A financial mecca of glass skyscrapers and thriving urbanity.

4 North Greenwich Underground: Bold purple floods the walls, then yields to a cool, airy breezeway. **Overground:** The vast Millennium Dome rests as an eye-catching, albeit hollow, testament to modern architecture.

drian, Barbara Hepworth, and Sigmund Freud have lent the area an enduring cachet.

HAMPSTEAD HEATH. Hampstead Heath is one of the last remaining traditional commons in England, open to all since at least 1312. **Parliament Hill** is the highest open space in London, with excellent views across the city. Farther north, ■**Kenwood** is a picture-perfect 18th-century country estate, designed by Robert Adams and home to the impressive **Iveagh Bequest** (see p. 137) of Old Masters. *(Train to Hampstead Heath or Tube: Hampstead. Heath open 24hr.; be extremely careful after dark. Kenwood open Apr.-Sept. daily 8am-8pm; Oct.-Mar. 8am-4pm.)*

KEATS HOUSE. While living here (1818-20), John Keats produced some of his finest work, including *Ode to a Nightingale*, and fell in love with and married Fanny Brawne. Inside, poems lie scattered about the reconstructed rooms. *(Keats Grove. Train to Hampstead Heath or Tube: Hampstead. ☎ 7435 2062. Tours Sa-Su 3pm. Open Jan.-Oct. Tu-Su noon-5pm; Nov.-Dec. noon-4pm. £3, concessions £1.50, children free.)*

EAST LONDON

WHITECHAPEL AND THE EAST END

The boundary between the East End and the City of London is as sharp today as it was when Aldgate and Bishopsgate were real gateways in the wall separating the rich and powerful City from the poorer quarters to the east. The best reasons to visit are the vibrant **markets** (see p. 141), which draw shoppers from all over.

CHRIST CHURCH. A splotch of Anglicanism amid a spectrum of other traditions, this is Nicholas Hawksmoor's largest church, considered by many his masterpiece. Alas, the 1714 building is in a sorry state: derelict since 1957, only now is it slowly being restored to its former glory. *(Commercial St., opposite Spitalfields market. Tube: Liverpool St. ☎ 7247 0165.)*

BRICK LANE. Even the street signs are in Bengali in this epicenter of Bangladeshi Britain. Most famous for its **Sunday market** and scores of **curry houses**, Brick Ln. has recently become the unlikely focus of the East End's creative renaissance: the former **Truman Brewery**, at No. 91 and 150, is now occupied by design and media consultants, sleek stores, and a cafe-bar-club trio—one of London's hottest nightspots. *(Tube: Shoreditch, Aldgate East, or Liverpool St.)*

DOCKLANDS

Countering heritage-obsessed Greenwich across the Thames, brash young Docklands is the largest commercial development in Europe. Until the 1960s, this man-made archipelago was the heart of British commerce, with an endless stream of cargoes from across the empire being loaded and unloaded. In 1981, the London Docklands Development Corporation (LDDC) was founded to redevelop the area. The showpiece is **Canary Wharf,** with Britain's highest skyscraper, the 800 ft., pyramid-topped **One Canada Square.** Under the tower, vast **Canada Place** and **Cabot Square** malls suck in shoppers, while the dockside plaza is lined with pricey corporate feeding troughs. *(Tube/DLR: Canary Wharf.)*

GREENWICH

Seat of the Royal Navy until 1998, Greenwich's position as the "home of time" is intimately connected to its maritime heritage—the Royal Observatory, site of the **Prime Meridian,** was originally founded to produce the accurate star-charts essential to navigation. *(All sights are closest to DLR: Cutty Sark.)*

RIVER TRIPS. Enhance your Greenwich experience with a 1hr. **boat trip** from Westminster. (Travelcard holders get 33% off riverboat fares.) **City Cruises** operates from Westminster Pier to Greenwich via the Tower of London. *(☎ 7930 9033. Apr.-Oct. daily every 40min. 10am-5:40pm. £7, all-day ticket £8; children £3/4; family all-day £20.)* **Westminster Passenger Association** boats also head for Greenwich from Westminster Pier. Their "Sail&Rail" deal combines a one-way trip with unlimited all-day travel on the DLR. *(☎ 7930 4097. Apr. to early Oct. daily every 3min. 10:30am-5pm, last departure from Greenwich 6pm, from Thames Barrier 3:30pm. £6, return £7.50, Sail&Rail £8.75; seniors £5/£6/£7; children £3/£3.75/£4.20; families £16/£20/£23.)*

ROYAL OBSERVATORY GREENWICH. Charles II founded the Royal Observatory in 1675 to find a way of calculating longitude at sea. Though the problem was eventually solved without reference to the sky, the connection lives on—the **Prime Meridian** (marking 0° longitude) started out as the axis along which astronomers' telescopes swung. Next to the meridian, Wren's **Flamstead House** retains its original interior in **Octagon Room.** Climb the **Observatory Dome** to see the 28" scope, constructed in 1893. It hasn't been used since 1954, but you can see the stars at the **Planetarium** in the South Building. *(At the top of Greenwich Park, a steep climb from the National Maritime Museum; or take The Avenue from the top of King William Walk. ☎ 8312 6565. Open daily 10am-5pm, last admission 4:30pm. Free.)*

ROYAL NAVAL COLLEGE. On the site of Henry VIII's Palace of Placentia, the Naval College was founded by William III in 1694 as the Royal Hospital for Seamen. In 1873 it became the Royal Naval College, but the nautical association ended in 1998 when the University of Greenwich blew in. Mary II had insisted that the new buildings not restrict the view from the Queen's House; Wren responded with two symmetrical wings separated by a colonnaded walkway. Buy a ticket to the **Painted Hall,** which took 19 years to complete, and the simple **chapel.** *(King William Walk. ☎8269 4741. Open daily 12:30-5pm. £3, concessions £2, children free.)*

OTHER GREENWICH SIGHTS. Now part of the National Maritime Museum (see p. 138), Inigo Jones's **Queen's House** was commissioned in 1616 by Anne of Denmark, James I's queen, but only completed 22 years later for Charles I's wife, Henrietta Maria. *(At the foot of Greenwich Park, on Trafalgar Rd.)* Last of the great tea clippers, the **Cutty Sark** has thoroughbred lines even landlubbers will appreciate—she was the fastest ship of her time, making the round-trip to China in only 120 days. The deck and cabins have been restored to their 19th-century prime, while the hold holds an exhibition on the ship's history and a collection of figureheads. *(King William Walk, by Greenwich Pier. ☎8858 2698. Open daily 10am-5pm, last admission 4:30pm. £3.90, concessions £2.90, families £9.10.)* Close by the *Cutty Sark,* **Gypsy Moth** is a 54 ft. craft in which 64-year-old Francis Chichester sailed nearly 30,000 solo miles in 1966.

WEST LONDON

▨ KEW GARDENS. Founded in 1759 by Princess Augusta as an addendum to Kew Palace, the Royal Botanical Gardens have since expanded to swallow the palace grounds entirely, now extending in a 300-acre swath along the Thames. Kew is a leading research center, thanks in no small part to its living collection of thousands of flowers, fruits, trees, and vegetables from across the globe. The three great **conservatories** and their smaller offshoots, housing a staggering variety of plants ill-suited to the English climate, are the highlight of the gardens. Most famous is the steamy **Palm House,** home to "The Oldest Pot Plant In The World"—not at all what it sounds like, but interesting nonetheless. The **Temperate House** is the world's largest ornamental greenhouse, although the snazzy **Princess of Wales Conservatory** has a larger area, thanks to its innovative structure. The interior is divided into ten different climate zones, including one entirely devoted to orchids. *(Main entrance and visitors center at Victoria Gate. Tube: Kew Gardens (Zone 3). ☎ 8832 5000. Hop-on/hop-off shuttle makes 35min. rounds of the gardens; first departs Victoria Gate 11am, last 3:35pm. £3, children £1. Gardens open Apr.-Aug. M-F 9:30am-6:30pm, Sa-Su 9:30am-7:30pm; Sept.-Oct. daily 9:30am-6pm; Nov.-Jan. daily 9:30am-4:15pm; Feb.-Mar. 9:30am-5:30pm. Greenhouses close Apr.-Oct. 5:30pm; Nov.-Mar. 3:45pm; last admission 30min. before close. £6.50, "late entry" (45min. before close) £4.50; concessions £4.50; children free.)*

HAMPTON COURT PALACE. Although a monarch hasn't lived here for 250 years, Hampton Court still exudes regal charm. Cardinal Wolsey built the first palace here in 1514, showing the young Henry VIII how to act the part of a powerful ruler—a lesson Henry learned all too well, confiscating Hampton in 1528, and embarking on a massive building program. In 1689, William and Mary employed Wren to bring the Court up to date, but less than 50 years later George II abandoned it for good. The **palace** is divided into six 45min.-1hr. tour routes, all starting at **Clock Court,** where you can pick up a program of the day's events and an audioguide. In **Henry VIII's State Apartments,** only the massive Great Hall and exquisite Chapel Royal hint at past magnificence. Below, the **Tudor Kitchens** offer insight into how Henry ate himself to a 54" waist. Predating Henry's additions, the 16th-century **Wolsey Rooms** are complemented by Renaissance masterpieces. Most impressive are Wren's **King's Apartments,** restored after a 1986 fire to their original appearance under William of Orange. The **Queen's Apartments** weren't completed until 1734, postponed by Mary II's death. The **Georgian Rooms** were created by William Kent for George II's family. Scarcely less impressive are the **gardens,** with Mantegna's *Triumphs of Caesar* secreted away in the Lower Orangery. North of the palace, the **Wilderness,** a pseudo-natural area earmarked for picnickers, holds the ever-popular **maze,** planted in 1714. Its small size belies its devilish design. *(Take the train from Waterloo (32min., 2 per hr., day return £4) or a boat from Westminster Pier (☎ 7930 2062; 4hr.; 4 per day; £10, return £14). To leave time to see the palace, take the boat one way and return by train. ☎ 8781 9500. Open mid-Mar. to late Oct. M 10:15am-6pm, Tu-Su 9:30am-6pm; late Oct. to mid-Mar. M 10:15am-4:30pm, Tu-Su 9:30am-4:30pm; last admission 45min. before close. Palace and gardens £11, concessions £8.25, children £7.20, families £33. Maze or South Gardens only £3, children £2. Other gardens free.)*

▥ MUSEUMS AND GALLERIES

Centuries as the capital of an empire upon which the sun never set, together with a decidedly English penchant for "collecting," have endowed London with a spectacular set of museums. Even better, after a decade of rising museum prices, admission to all major collections is now free indefinitely, in celebration of the Queen's Golden Jubilee.

MAJOR COLLECTIONS

BRITISH MUSEUM

Great Russell St., Bloomsbury. Rear entrance on Montague St. Tube: Tottenham Court Rd., Russell Sq., or Holborn. ☎ 7323 8000; www.thebritishmuseum.ac.uk. Audioguides £2.50. Tours start at Great Court info desk. Highlights Tour (1½hr.): M-Sa 10:30am and 1pm; Su 11am, 12:30, 1:30, 2:30, 4pm. Book ahead. £7, concessions £4. Focus tour (1hr.): M-W and Sa 3:15pm; Th-F 3:15, 5:30, 7pm; Su 4:30pm. £5/£3. Great Court open M 9am-6pm, Tu-W and Su 9am-9pm, Th-Sa 9am-11pm. Galleries open Sa-W 10am-5:30pm, Th-F 10am-8:30pm. £2 suggested donation. Special exhibits about £7/£3.50.

The funny thing about the British Museum is that there's almost nothing British in it. In 1753, the "BM" was founded as the personal collection of Sir Hans Sloane; in 1824 work began on the current Neoclassical building, which took 30 years more to finish. The December 2000 opening of the **Great Court**—Europe's largest covered square—finally restored the museum's focal point, the enormous rotunda of the **Reading Room.** These desks have shouldered the weight of research by Marx, Lenin, and Trotsky, plus most major British writers and intellectuals.

The most famous items in the collection are found in the **Western Galleries.** Room 4 harbors an unrivaled collection of Egyptian sculpture, including the **Rosetta Stone,** and Room 18 is entirely devoted to the **Elgin Marbles.** Other highlights include giant Assyrian and Babylonian reliefs, the Roman Portland Vase, and bits and bobs from two Wonders of the Ancient World, the **Temple of Artemis** at Ephesus and the **Mausoleum of Halikarnassos.** Just when you thought you'd nailed antiquity, the **Northern Galleries** strike back with eight rooms of mummies and sarcophagi and nine of artifacts from the ancient Near East, including the **Oxus Treasure** from Iran. Also in the northern wing are the excellent African and Islamic galleries, the giant Asian collections, and the frankly weak Americas collection. The upper level of the **South** and **East Galleries** is dedicated to ancient and medieval Europe, some of which is actually British. The preserved body of **Lindow Man,** an Iron Age Celt sacrificed in a gruesome ritual, and treasures excavated from the **Sutton Hoo Burial Ship** fill Room 41. Next door, Room 42 is home to the enigmatic **Lewis Chessmen,** an 800-year-old chess set abandoned in the Outer Hebrides (see p. 662).

NATIONAL GALLERY

Main entrance on north side of Trafalgar Sq., Westminster. Tube: Charing Cross or Leicester Sq. ☎ 7747 2885; www.nationalgallery.org.uk. Audioguides free; £4 suggested donation. Tours start at Sainsbury Wing info desk. Free 1hr. gallery tours daily 11:30am and 2:30pm, W also 6:30pm. Open daily 10am-6pm, W until 9pm; special Sainsbury Wing exhibitions occasionally until 10pm. Admission free; some temporary exhibitions £5-7, seniors £4-5, students and children £2-3.

The National Gallery was founded by an Act of Parliament in 1824, and began as 38 pictures displayed in a townhouse. It grew so rapidly in size and popularity that it was decided to construct a purpose-built gallery in 1838. The most recent extension is the massive **Sainsbury Wing,** which Prince Charles described as "a monstrous carbuncle on the face of a much-loved and elegant friend." Its climate-controlled rooms house the oldest, most fragile paintings, including the 14th-century English *Wilton Diptych*, Botticelli's *Venus and Mars*, and the *Leonardo Cartoon*, a detailed preparatory drawing by da Vinci for a never-executed painting. The **West Wing** is dominated by the Italian **High Renaissance** and **early Flemish** art. In room 8, Rome and Florence duke it out, with versions of the *Madonna and Child* by Raphael and Michelangelo. The **North Wing** spans the **17th century,** with exceptional Flemish works spread over ten rooms. Room 23 boasts 17 Rembrandts; the famous *Self Portrait at 63* gazes knowingly at his *Self Portrait at 34.* The **East Wing,** home to paintings from **1700-1900,** is the gallery's most popular, thanks to a stippling of Impressionists, including Van Gogh's *Sunflowers* and two of Monet's *Waterlilies.* A reminder that there was art on this side of the Channel too, Room 34 flies the flag with six luminescent Turners.

TATE BRITAIN

Millbank, near Vauxhall Bridge, in Westminster. Tube: Pimlico. ☎ 7887 8008; www.tate.org.uk. Audioguides £1. Free 1hr. tours: Highlights M-F 11:30am, Sa 3pm; Turner M-F 2:30pm. Open daily 10am-5pm. Free; special exhibitions £3-9.

The original Tate opened in 1897 as a showcase for "modern" British art—modern being extended back to 1790 to allow the inclusion of the **Turner Bequest** of 282 oils and 19,000 watercolors. Before long, the repertoire had expanded to include contemporary art from all over the world, as well as British works from the Middle Ages on. Despite numerous expansions, it was clear that the dual role was too much for one building; the problem was resolved in 1999 with the relocation of almost all the contemporary art to the Tate Modern at Bankside (see below). At the same time, the original Tate was rechristened Tate Britain, and rededicated to British art—a tag that includes foreign artists working on the island and Brits working abroad. The **Clore Gallery** displays the Turner Bequest; other painters to feature heavily are William Blake, John Constable, Joshua Reynolds, Dante Gabriel Rossetti, John Hodgkin, Lucien Freud, and David Hockney. Sculptors are less well represented, though Jacob Epstein's *Jacob and the Angel* (1940-41), in the **Sackler Octagon,** is a crowd favorite. The annual **Turner Prize** for contemporary art is awarded here; shortlisted works are on the walls from November to mid-January.

TATE MODERN

Bankside, on the South Bank; main entrance on Holland St., secondary entrance on Queen's Walk. Tube: Southwark or Blackfriars. ☎ 7887 8888; www.tate.org.uk. Audioguides £1. Free themed tours meet on the gallery concourses daily; Level 3 11am and noon, Level 5 2 and 3pm. Open Su-Th 10am-6pm, F-Sa 10am-10pm. Free; special exhibitions £5-7, concessions £4-6.

Since opening in May 2000, Tate Modern has been credited with single-handedly reversing the long-term decline in British museum-going. The largest modern art museum in the world, its most striking aspect is the building itself, formerly Bankside Power Station. The conversion to gallery added a seventh floor with wraparound views of north and south London, and turned the old **Turbine Hall** into an immense atrium that often overpowers the installations commissioned for it. For all its popularity, the Tate has been criticized for its controversial curatorial method, which groups works according to themes rather than period or artist—the four overarching divisions are **Still Life/Object/Real Life** and **Landscape/Matter/ Environment** on Level 3, and **Nude/Action/Body** and **History/Memory/Society** on Level 5—but even skeptics admit that this arrangement throws up some interesting contrasts. The thematic display forces visitors into contact with an exceptionally wide range of art. It's now impossible to see the more famous pieces, which include Marcel Duchamp's *Large Glass* and Picasso's *Weeping Woman*, without also stumbling on challenging and invigorating works by lesser-known artists.

VICTORIA AND ALBERT MUSEUM

Main entrance on Cromwell Rd., in Kensington. Tube: South Kensington. ☎ 7942 2000; www.vam.ac.uk. Free tours meet at rear of main entrance. Introductory tours daily 10:30, 11:30am, 1:30, 2:30pm; W also 4:30pm. Focus tours daily 12:30 and 1:30pm. Free 45min.-1hr. gallery talks daily 1pm. Talks, tours, and live music W from 6:30pm; last F of month also fashion shows, debates, and DJs. Open daily 10am-5:45pm, W and last F of month until 10pm. Free, except some special exhibitions.

Founded in 1852 to encourage excellence in art and design, the V&A is the largest museum of the decorative arts in the world—as befits an institution dedicated to displaying "the fine and applied arts of all countries, all styles, all periods." The subject of a £31 million refit, the vast **British Galleries** hold a series of recreated rooms from every period between 1500 and 1900, mirrored by the vast **Dress Collection,** a dazzling array of the finest *haute couture* through the ages. The ground-floor **European** collections range from 4th-century Byzantine tapestry to Alfonse Mucha posters; if you only see one thing, make it the **Raphael Gallery,** hung with six massive paintings commissioned by Pope Leo X in 1515. The **Sculpture Gallery,** home to Canova's *Three Graces* (1814-17), is not to be confused with the **Cast Courts,** a plaster-replica collection of the world's sculptural greatest hits, from Trajan's Column to Michelangelo's *David.* The V&A's **Asian** collections are particularly formidable—if the choice of objects occasionally relies on national cliches, it says more about how the V&A has formed opinion than followed it.

In contrast to the geographically laid-out ground floor, the **upper levels** are mostly arranged by material; here you'll find specialist galleries devoted to everything from jewelry to musical instruments to stained glass. An exception to the themed arrangements is the large **20th-century** collection, featuring design classics from Salvador Dali's 1936 "Mae West" sofa lips to a pair of 1990s rubber hotpants. The six-level **Henry Cole wing** is home to **British** paintings, including some 350 works by Constable and numerous Turners. Also here is a display of Rodin bronzes, donated by the artist in 1914, and the "world's greatest collection" of miniature portraits. The **Frank Lloyd Wright gallery** contains a full-size recreation of the office commissioned by Edgar J. Kauffmann for his Pittsburgh department store in 1935.

OTHER COLLECTIONS

THE CITY OF LONDON

■ **MUSEUM OF LONDON.** In the corner of the **Barbican** complex (see p. 116), this engrossing collection traces London's history from foundation to present day, with a strong selection of Roman objects and the gold-plated **Lord Mayor's State Coach,** built in 1757. *(London Wall; enter through the Barbican or from Aldersgate. Tube: St. Paul's or Barbican.* ☎ *7600 3699; www.museumoflondon.org.uk. Free 30min. tours Tu 2:30pm. Open M-Sa 10am-6pm, Su noon-6pm; last admission 5:30pm. Free.)*

THE SOUTH BANK

DESIGN MUSEUM. Housed in a classic Art Deco riverfront building, this thoroughly contemporary museum explores the development of mass-market design with a constantly changing selection of objects; most fun are the dozens of funky chairs that patrons are encouraged to try out. *(28 Shad Thames, Butler's Wharf. Tube: Tower Hill or London Bridge.* ☎ *7403 6933; www.designmuseum.org. Open daily 10am-5:45pm, last entry 5:15pm. £6, concessions £4, families £16.)*

THE WEST END

■ **THE COURTAULD INSTITUTE GALLERIES.** The Courtauld's outstanding small collection ranges from 14th-century Italian to 20th-century abstraction, focusing on Impressionism; masterpieces include Manet's *A Bar at the Follies Bergères,* van Gogh's *Self Portrait with Bandaged Ear,* and Cézanne's *The Card Players.* *(Somerset House, the Strand. Tube: Charing Cross or Temple.* ☎ *7848 2526; www.courtauld.ac.uk. Open daily 10am-6pm. £5, concessions £4, children free; M 10am-2pm free to all.)*

■ **LONDON'S TRANSPORT MUSEUM.** Kids and adults will find themselves engrossed in this informative and fun history of London's public transportation.

Clamber over dozens of buses to try your hand at a Tube simulator. *(Southeast corner of Covent Garden Piazza. Tube: Covent Garden. ☎ 7565 7299; www.ltmuseum.co.uk. Open Sa-Th 10am-6pm, F 11am-6pm; last admission 5:15pm. £6, concessions £4, children free.)*

■ INSTITUTE OF CONTEMPORARY ARTS (ICA). A grand Neoclassical pediment in London's most conservative neighborhood is the last place you'd expect to find Britain's national center for the contemporary arts—at least it's conveniently located for attacking the establishment. *(Nash House, the Mall. Tube: Charing Cross or Piccadilly Circus. ☎ 7930 3647; www.ica.org.uk. Open M noon-11pm, Tu-Sa noon-1am, Su noon-10:30pm; galleries close 7:30pm. Galleries M-F £1.50, Sa-Su £2.50, concessions £1/£1.50. Cinema £6.50, M-F before 5pm £5.50; concessions £5.50/£4.50.)*

■ ROYAL ACADEMY. Founded in 1768 as both art school and meeting place for Britain's foremost artists and housed in spectacular **Burlington House** (built 1665, the only survivor of Piccadilly's aristocratic mansions), the Academy holds outstanding exhibitions of all manner of art. Anyone can submit a piece for inclusion in the Summer Exhibition (June-Aug.), held every year since 1769. *(Tube: Piccadilly Circus or Green Park. ☎ 7300 8000; www.royalacademy.org.uk. Open Sa-Th 10am-6pm, F 10am-10pm. Around £7, concessions £3-6.)*

NATIONAL PORTRAIT GALLERY. This artistic *Who's Who* in Britain began in 1856 as "the fulfillment of a patriotic and moral ideal." To see the paintings in historical order, take the long escalator to the top floor Tudor gallery and work your way around and down to the contemporary works on the ground floor. The size of the collection, however, makes such a tour a long and exhausting prospect, not helped by endless galleries of bewhiskered Victorians. "Britain Today" is represented by Posh Spice and Fatboy Slim; whether they'll still be on show in 50 years is debatable. *(St. Martin's Pl., at the start of Charing Cross Rd. Tube: Leicester Sq. or Charing Cross. ☎ 7312 2463; www.npg.org.uk. Audioguides free; £4 suggested donation. Open M-W and Sa-Su 10am-6pm, Th-F 10am-9pm. Free; exhibitions free-£6.)*

THE GILBERT COLLECTION. On the lower level of **Somerset House,** the Gilbert Collection of Decorative Arts opened in 2000 to widespread acclaim. Pick up a free audioguide and magnifying glass as you enter—the latter is invaluable for studying the displays of micromosaics and ornate bejewelled snuffboxes. *(Somerset House, the Strand. Tube: Charing Cross or Temple. ☎ 7420 9400; www.gilbert-collection.org.uk. 1hr. tours Sa 2:30pm, £6.50, concessions £6, includes admission. Open daily 10am-6pm. £5, concessions £4, children free; free to all after 4:30pm.)*

WESTMINSTER

■ CABINET WAR ROOMS. For six tense years, Churchill, his cabinet and generals, and dozens of support staff haunted these underground quarters; the day after the war ended, the rooms were shut up and left undisturbed until their 1981 reopening. Highlights include the room containing the top-secret transatlantic hotline—official word was that it was Churchill's personal loo. *(Clive Steps, King Charles St. Tube: Westminster. ☎ 7930 6961; www.iwm.org.uk/cabinet. Open Apr.-Sept. daily 9:30am-6pm; Oct.-Mar. 10am-6pm; last admission 5:15pm. £5.80, concessions £4.20, children free.)*

QUEEN'S GALLERY. "God Save the Queen" is the rallying cry at this recently opened exhibit of items from the Royal Collection. Five exquisite rooms extol the glory of Her Majesty. Whatever the medium—painting, furniture, or jewelry—you can count on it being gaudy. *(Buckingham Palace Rd. Tube: St. James's Park. ☎ 7839 1377. Open daily 10am-5:30pm, last admission 4:30pm. £6.50, seniors £5.)*

BLOOMSBURY

■ **BRITISH LIBRARY GALLERIES.** The British Library presents an appropriately stunning display of books and manuscripts, from the 2nd-century *Unknown Gospel* to the Beatles' hand-scrawled lyrics to *Paperback Writer*. Other highlights include a Gutenberg Bible, Joyce's handwritten draft of *Finnegan's Wake*, and pages from da Vinci s notebooks. *(96 Euston Rd. Tube: King's Cross.* ☎ *7412 7332. Tours M, W, F 3pm, Sa 10:30am and 3pm; £5, concessions £3.50. Tours including reading rooms Tu 6:30pm, Su 11:30am and 3pm; £6/£4.50. Reservations recommended. Open M and W-F 9:30am-6pm, Tu 9:30am-8pm, Sa 9:30am-5pm, Su 11am-5pm. Free.)*

HOLBORN AND CLERKENWELL

SIR JOHN SOANE'S MUSEUM. Eccentric architect John Soane gave his imagination free rein when designing this intriguing museum for his personal collection of art and antiquities. Idiosyncratic cupolas cast light on a bewildering panoply of ancient carvings; in the **Picture Room,** multiple Hogarths hang from fold-out panels. *(13 Lincoln's Inn Fields. Tube: Holborn. Tours Sa 2:30pm, tickets sold from 2pm; £3. Open Tu-Sa 10am-5pm, first Tu of month also 6-9pm. Free; £1 donation requested.)*

KENSINGTON AND EARL'S COURT

■ **NATURAL HISTORY MUSEUM.** Architecturally the most impressive of the South Kensington museums, this cathedral-like building is home to an outstanding collection of critters, rocks, and other wonders. Highlights include the remarkably realistic T-Rex (complete with bad breath) in the **Dinosaur** exhibit, the engrossing interactive **Human Biology** gallery, and the giant **Mammals** hall. *(Cromwell Rd. Tube: South Kensington.* ☎ *7942 5000; www.nhm.ac.uk. Free 45min. highlight tours noon, 1, 2, 3pm; reserve at the main info desk. Open M-Sa 10am-5:50pm, Su 11am-5:50pm; last admission 5:30pm. Free; special exhibits £5, concessions £3.)*

SCIENCE MUSEUM. Dedicated to the Victorian ideal of Progress (with a capital P), the Science Museum focuses on the transformative power of technology. You'll find a mix of state-of-the-art interactive displays, priceless historical artifacts, and some mind-numbing galleries (standard weights and measures? light bulbs?). Most impressive is the gigantic **Making of the Modern World** hall, a collection of pioneering contraptions from 1815 "Puffing Billy," the oldest surviving steam locomotive, to the Apollo 10 command module. The high-tech exhibits of the blue-lit **Wellcome Wing** are literally overshadowed by the overhead curve of the vast **IMAX cinema.** *(Exhibition Rd. Tube: South Kensington.* ☎ *(0870) 870 4868, IMAX (0870) 870 4771. IMAX shows every 75min. 10:45am-5pm; £7, concessions £6. Museum open daily 10am-6pm. Free.)*

MARYLEBONE AND REGENT'S PARK

■ **THE WALLACE COLLECTION.** Housed in palatial Hertford House, this is a stunning array of paintings, porcelain, and medieval armor. The **first floor** is home to a world-renowned collection of 18th-century French art as well as the **Great Gallery,** housing 17th-century works. *(Hertford House, Manchester Sq. Tube: Bond St. or Marble Arch.* ☎ *7563 9500; www.wallace-collection.com. Free 1hr. tours W and Sa 11:30am and Su 3pm. Free talks M-F 1pm, occasionally Sa 11:30am. Open M-Sa 10am-5pm, Su noon-5pm.)*

NORTH LONDON

■ **THE IVEAGH BEQUEST.** A stout collection bequeathed by Edward Guinness, Earl of Iveagh, the Kenwood setting and the magnificent pictures make it one of London's finest small galleries. Highlights include works by Rembrandt, Vermeer, Turner, and Botticelli. *(Kenwood House. Tube: Hampstead.* ☎ *8348 1286. Open Apr.-Sept. Sa-Tu and Th 10am-6pm, W and F 10:30am-6pm; Oct. closes 5pm; Nov.-Mar. closes 4pm. Free.)*

■ **ROYAL AIR FORCE MUSEUM.** Exhibitions detail every aspect of RAF life, but the real stars are the planes—scores of 'em, from 1914 wood-and-cloth biplanes to the Harriers of the 1980s. *(Grahame Park Way. From Tube: Colindale (Zone 4), it's a 10-15min. walk. ☎8205 2266. Open daily 10am-6pm; last admission 5:30pm. Free.)*

EAST LONDON

■ **NATIONAL MARITIME MUSEUM.** The NMM's broad-ranging displays cover almost every aspect of seafaring history. Its galleries resemble a nautical theme park—once the kiddies get into the **All Hands** interactive gallery, it'll be hard to get them out. Pride of the naval displays is the **Nelson Room**, which tells the stirring tale of a 12-year-old midshipman's rise through the ranks. *(Trafalgar Rd., between Royal Naval College and Greenwich Park. DLR: Cutty Sark. ☎8858 4422; www.nmm.ac.uk. Open June to early Sept. daily 10am-6pm; mid-Sept. to May 10am-5pm; last admission 30min. before close. Free.)* The collection of the NMM resides in the **Queen's House** (see p. 131), where the galleries of past admirals take second place to Inigo Jones's architecture.

WHITECHAPEL ART GALLERY. Long the sole artistic beacon in a culturally and materially impoverished area and now at the forefront of the East End's buzzing art scene, Whitechapel hosts excellent, often controversial, shows of contemporary art. *(Whitechapel High St. Tube: Aldgate East. ☎7377 7888; www.whitechapel.org. Open Tu and Th-Su 11am-5pm, W 11am-8pm. Free.)*

SOUTH LONDON

■ **IMPERIAL WAR MUSEUM.** A pair of massive 15-inch naval guns guard the entrance to the Imperial War Museum; formerly the infamous lunatic asylum known as Bedlam, today it illustrates another type of human madness. The commendably un-jingoistic exhibits follow every aspect of war since 1914, covering conflicts both large and small. The largest and most publicized display, the **Holocaust Exhibition,** graphically documents Nazi atrocities and provides recorded testimonies from survivors. *(Lambeth Rd., Lambeth. Tube: Lambeth North or Elephant & Castle. ☎7416 5320, recorded info 7416 5000; www.iwm.org.uk. Holocaust exhibition not recommended for children under 14. Open daily 10am-6pm. Free.)*

■ **DULWICH PICTURE GALLERY.** Designed by Sir John Soane, this marvelous array of Old Masters was England's first public art gallery. Rubens and van Dyck feature prominently, as does Rembrandt's *Portrait of a Young Man. (Gallery Rd., Dulwich. 10min. from North or West Dulwich rail station, or bus P4 from Tube: Brixton. ☎8693 5254; www.dulwichpicturegallery.org.uk. Free tours Sa-Su 3pm. Open Tu-F 10am-5pm, Sa-Su 11am-5pm. £4, seniors £3, students and children free; free for all F.)*

◻ SHOPPING

From its earliest days, this has been a trading city, and today (even more so than at the Empire's height), London's economy is truly international. Thanks to the eclectic taste of Londoners, the range of goods is unmatched anywhere.

DEPARTMENT STORES

Liberty, 210-220 Regent St. (☎7734 1234). Tube: Oxford Circus. Focus on top-quality design and handicrafts. Enormous hat department and a whole hall of scarves. Open M-W 10am-6:30pm, Th 10am-8pm, F-Sa 10am-7pm, Su noon-6pm. AmEx/MC/V.

Fortnum and Mason, 181 Piccadilly (☎7734 8040). Tube: Green Park or Piccadilly Circus. London's smallest, snootiest department store, est. 1707. Famed for its sumptuous food hall. Few make it to the upper floors. Open M-Sa 10am-6:30pm. AmEx/MC/V.

Hamley's, 188-189 Regent St. (☎ 7734 3161). Tube: Oxford Circus. 7 floors filled with every conceivable toy and game; dozens of strategically placed product demonstrations are guaranteed to turn any mummy's darling into a snarling, toy-demanding menace. Open M-F 10am-8pm, Sa 9:30am-8pm, Su noon-6pm. AmEx/MC/V.

Harrods, 87-135 Old Brompton Rd. (☎ 7730 1234). Tube: Knightsbridge. The only thing bigger than the bewildering store is the mark-up on the goods— no wonder only tourists and oil sheikhs actually shop here. Open M-Sa 10am-7pm. AmEx/MC/V/your soul.

Harvey Nichols, 109-125 Knightsbridge (☎ 7235 5000). Tube: Knightsbridge. Bond St., Rue St-Honoré, and Fifth Avenue all rolled up into 5 floors of fashion, from the biggest names to the hippest contemporary unknowns. Open M-Tu and Sa 10am-7pm, W-F 10am-8pm, Su noon-6pm. AmEx/MC/V.

Selfridges, 400 Oxford St. (☎ (0870) 837 7377). Tube: Bond St. The total department store. Covers the gamut from traditional tweeds to space-age clubwear. 14 eateries, hair salon, bureau de change, and hotel. Open M-W 10am-7pm, Th-F 10am-8pm, Sa 9:30am-7pm, Su noon-6pm. AmEx/MC/V.

MAJOR CHAINS

As with any large city, London retailing is dominated by chains. Fortunately, local shoppers are picky enough that buying from a chain doesn't mean abandoning the flair and quirky stylishness for which Londoners are famed. Most chains have a flagship on or near Oxford St. Different branches have slightly different hours, but almost all the stores listed below are open daily 10am-7pm, starting later (noon) on Su and staying open an hour later one night of the week (usually Th).

▨ Karen Millen (☎ (01622) 664 032). 8 locations including 262-264 Regents St. (Tube: Oxford Circus); and 22-23 James St. (Tube: Covent Garden). Best known for embroidered brocade suits and evening gowns, but edging towards a more casual line.

▨ Lush (☎ (01202) 668 545). 6 locations, including Garden Piazza (Tube: Covent Garden) and 40 Carnaby St. (Tube: Oxford Circus). All-natural cosmetics that look good enough to eat; soap is hand-cut from blocks masquerading as cakes and cheeses (£3-5) and guacamole-like facial masks are scooped from tubs.

FCUK (☎ 7529 7766). Flagship at 396 Oxford St. (Tube: Bond St.) Home of the advertising coup of the 90s, FCUK offers an extensive collection of items with their vaguely offensive, mildly subversive moniker. AmEx/MC/V.

Jigsaw (☎ 8392 5678). Flagship at 126 New Bond St. (Tube: Bond St.). The essence of Britishness, distilled into quality mid-priced womenswear. AmEx/MC/V.

Muji (☎ 7287 7323). Flagship at 41 Carnaby St. (Tube: Oxford Circus.) Minimalist lifestyle stores, with a Zen take on everything from clothes to kitchenware. AmEx/MC/V.

Topshop/Top Man/Miss Selfridge (☎ 7927 0000). Flagship at 214 Oxford St. (Tube: Oxford Circus.) Cheap fashions—over-25s will feel middle-aged. Topshop sells strappy shoes and skimpy clubwear on 3 floors. Miss Selfridge has an even younger, girlier feel; Top Man is all shiny Ts and cargo pants. 10% student discount. AmEx/MC/V.

SHOPPING BY NEIGHBORHOOD

CENTRAL LONDON

OXFORD AND REGENT STREETS. Beyond the unprecedented atmosphere in the department stores and mainstream chains of Oxford St. and Regent St., fashionable boutiques line pedestrian **South Molton St.,** stretching south into Mayfair from Bond St. Tube, and **Foubert's Place,** near youth-oriented Carnaby St. Also in the area are a couple of choice sale shops.

MAYFAIR. Mayfair's aristocratic pedigree is evident in the scores of high-priced shops, many bearing Royal Warrants to indicate their status as official palace suppliers. **Bond St.** is the location of choice for the biggest names. Less mainstream designers set up shop on **Conduit St.,** where Old Bond St. meets New Bond St.; here you'll find Vivienne Westwood, Alexander McQueen, and Yohji Yamamoto. Cheap (relatively speaking) duds abound at **Paul Smith Sale Shop,** 23 Avery Row (Tube: Bond St.); find a smallish range of last-season and clearance items from the acknowledged master of modern British menswear. Exclusive **Sotheran's of Sackville Street,** 2-5 Sackville St. (☎ 7439 6151; Tube: Piccadilly Circus), founded in 1761, has a charming staff and plenty of affordable books, while **Waterstone's,** 203-206 Piccadilly (☎ 7851 2400; Tube: Piccadilly Circus), is Europe's largest bookshop.

SOHO. Despite its eternal trendiness, Soho has never been much of a shopping destination. The main exception is the record stores of **D'Arblay St.** and **Berwick St.** including **Reckless Records,** 26 and 30 Berwick St. (☎ 7437 3362 and 7437 4271); **Sister Ray,** 94 Berwick St. (☎ 7287 8385); and top DJ hangout **Uptown Records,** 3 D'Arblay St. (☎ 7434 3639; all Tube: Oxford Circus). Keeping up the musical theme are the excellent instrument and equipment shops of **Denmark St.**

COVENT GARDEN. Covent Garden is increasingly mainstream, though there are enough quirky shops left to make it worth a wander. North of the piazza, **Floral St.** is firmly established as the area's smartest. Ever-popular **Neal St.** is a top destination for funky footwear and mid-priced club clobber, though the fashion focus has shifted to nearby **Shorts Gardens, Earlham St.,** and **Monmouth St.** A best bet for women's clothing is **Miss Sixty,** 39 Neal St. (☎ 7836 3789), feeding the Italian clothing craze with laid-back and sexy style. Their new men's equivalent, **Energie,** 47-49 Neal St., is nearby. Treat your feet at **Office,** 57 Neal St. (☎ 7379 1896), the largest outlet of London's foremost fashion footwear retailer. Alternatively, the **Dr. Marten's Dept. Store,** 1-4 King St. (☎ 7497 1460), is a tourist-packed megalith.

BLOOMSBURY. Besides intellectuals, Bloomsbury's main commodity is **books.** The streets around the British Museum in particular are crammed with specialist (**Gay's the Word;** 66 Marchmont St.; ☎ 7278 7654; Tube: Russell Sq.) and cut-price booksellers (**Unsworths;** 12 Bloomsbury St.; ☎ 7436 9836; Tube: Tottenham Court Rd.). For a blast from the past, the small selection of vintage clothes in ▧**Delta of Venus,**

151 Drummond St. (☎7387 3037; Tube: Warren St. or Euston), is unbeatable and spans the 1960s to the early 80s. For a blast into the future, head to **Tottenham Court Rd.** for electronics.

CHELSEA AND KNIGHTSBRIDGE. No serious shopper can ignore Chelsea. If **Sloane Square** is too, well, sloaney ("preppy," to Americans), the **King's Road,** with one-off boutiques at all price ranges, is all things to all shoppers. The main shopping arteries of **Knightsbridge** are the **Old Brompton Road,** with upmarket chains, and **Sloane St.,** full of exclusive boutiques. **World's End,** 430 King's Rd. (☎7352 6551), is the fountain of cool. This boutique's past incarnations include SEX, the proto-punk store that gave birth to the Sex Pistols. Vivienne Westwood still runs it, though the clothes are now as unaffordable as they are unwearable.

NOTTING HILL. The best reason to visit Notting Hill is **Portobello Market,** which brings an influx of color and vivacity to an otherwise gentrified area. The "Market" is actually several distinct markets occupying different parts of the street and operating on different days; Saturdays, when all come together in a mile-long row, is the best day to visit. The **antiques market,** north along Portobello from Chepstow Villas to Elgin Cres. (Tube: Notting Hill Gate; Sa 7am-5pm) sells cheapish bric-a-brac, little of it truly rare or very old; the **general market,** from Elgin Cres. to Lancaster Rd. (Tube: Westbourne Park or Ladbroke Grove; M-W 8am-6pm, Th 9am-1pm, F-Sa 7am-7pm) sells food, flowers, and household essentials; and the **clothes market,** north of Lancaster Rd. (Tube: Ladbroke Grove; F-Sa 8am-3pm) has a wide selection of secondhand clothes, New Age bangles, and cheap clubwear. Also in the area is **The Travel Bookshop,** 13-15 Blenheim Cres. (☎7229 5260), the specialist bookshop featured in *Notting Hill,* today besieged by Grantophiles. **Dolly Diamond,** 51 Pembridge Rd. (☎7792 2479; Tube: Notting Hill Gate), allows you to choose "your" look—Jackie O. or Audrey Hepburn?—from a great selection of classic 50s-70s clothes and elegant 20s-40s evening gowns.

NORTH LONDON

In **Camden Town,** you'll find hundreds of identical stores flogging the same chunky shoes and leather trousers they've been selling for years. Arrive early and have a game plan—amid the dross there are genuine bargains and incredible finds. The **Camden markets** are located off Camden High St. and Chalk Farm Rd. (Tube: Camden Town). The **Stables Market** (most shops open daily) is nearest Chalk Farm and the best of the bunch, offering good vintage clothes plus some of the most outrageous club- and fetish-wear ever made. **Camden Canal Market** (open F-Su) is down the tunnel opposite Camden Lock, and starts out promisingly with jewelry and watches, but degenerates rapidly into sub-par clubbing duds and tourist trinkets. **Camden Lock Market** (most stalls open F or Sa-Su), located between the railway bridge and the canal, is arranged around a food-filled courtyard on the Regent's Canal. **The Camden Market** (open F-Su), nearest to Camden Tube and correspondingly the most crowded and least innovative, offers jeans, sweaters, and designer fakes. Our fave Camden shop is ⬛**Cyberdog/Cybercity,** arch 14 of the Stables Market (☎7482 2842), with unbelievable club clothes for superior life forms. Alien gods and goddesses will want to try on the fluorescent body-armor or steel corsets with rubber breast hoses. Even if it's not your thing, a quick peek will give great insight into London's fanatic clubbing psyche.

Meanwhile in **Islington,** the **Camden Passage,** Islington High St., behind "The Mall" antiques gallery on Upper St., is *the* place for antiques, especially prints and drawings. Shops outnumber stalls. (Tube: Angel. Most open W and Sa 8:30am-6pm.)

EAST LONDON

In East London, the street-market tradition is alive and well, helped along by large immigrant communities. The **Brick Lane Market** (open Su 8am-2pm; Tube: Shoreditch or Aldgate East) has a South Asian flair, with food, rugs, spices, bolts of fabric, and strains of sitar, while the **Petticoat Lane Market** (open Su 9am-2pm, starts shutting down around noon; Tube: Liverpool St., Aldgate, or Aldgate East) has block after block of cheap clothing. **Spitalfields Market** (Tube: Shoreditch or Liverpool St.) was formerly one of London's main wholesale vegetable markets, but is now a new-agey crafts klatsch, with a wide range of foods (crafts market M-F 11am-3:30pm, Su 10am-5pm; organic market F and Su 10am-5pm).

SOUTH LONDON

If you're looking for the fruits of West Indian cultures, **Brixton Market,** along Electric Ave., Pope's Rd., and Brixton Station Rd., as well as indoors in Granville Arcade and Market Row, is the place to be. (Tube: Brixton. Open M-Tu and Th-Sa 8:30am-5pm, W 8:30am-1pm.)

🎭 ENTERTAINMENT

On any given day, you can choose from a range of entertainment as wide as any city can offer. The West End is perhaps the world's theater capital, supplemented by an adventurous "Fringe" and a justly famous National Theatre, while new bands spring eternal from the fountain of London's many music venues. Whatever you're planning to do, the listings in *Time Out* (£2.20, every W) are indispensable.

THEATER

The stage for a dramatic tradition over 500 years old, London theaters maintain unrivaled breadth of choice. At a **West End** theater (a term referring to all the major stages, whether or not they're actually in the West End), you can expect a professional (if mainstream) production and top-quality performers. **Off-West End** theaters tend to present more challenging works, while remaining as professional as their West End brethren. The **Fringe** refers to scores of smaller, less commercial theaters, often just rooms in pub basements with a few benches and a team of dedicated amateurs. **tkts,** formerly the **Leicester Square Half-Price Ticket Booth,** on the south side of Leicester Square, is run jointly by London theaters and is the only place where you can be sure your discount tickets are genuine. You can only buy on the day of the performance, in person and in cash, on a strict first-come, first-served basis, and with no choice in seating. There's no way of knowing in advance which shows will have tickets, but you can expect a wide range. Noticeboards display what's available; there's a £2.50 booking fee per ticket but no limit on the number you can buy. (Open M-Sa 10am-7pm, Su noon-3pm. Most tickets £15-25.)

WEST END AND REPERTORY COMPANIES

Barbican Theatre, main entrance on Silk St. (☎ 7638 8891). A huge, futuristic auditorium with steeply raked, forward-leaning balconies. Hosts touring companies and short-run shows, as well as frequent contemporary dance performances. **The Pit** is largely experimental, while **Barbican Hall** houses the London Symphony Orchestra (see p. 145). Tickets £6-30. Student and senior standbys from 9am day of performance.

National Theatre, just downriver of Waterloo bridge (info ☎ 7452 3400, box office ☎ 7452 3000; www.nationaltheatre.org.uk). Tube: Waterloo or Embankment. At the forefront of British theater since opening under the direction of Laurence Olivier in

1976. Popular musicals and hit plays, which often transfer to the West End, subsidize experimental works. The **Olivier** stage seats 1080, the **Lyttelton** is a proscenium theater, and the **Cottesloe** offers flexible staging for experimental dramas. Box office open M-Sa 10am-8pm. Tickets £10-30; from 10am day of performance £10; standby (2hr. before curtain) £15; standing places, only if all seats sold, £6. Concessions available.

Open-Air Theatre, Inner Circle, Regents Park (☎ 7486 2431; www.open-air-theatre.org.uk). Tube: Baker St. Bring blankets and waterproofs—performances take place rain or shine. Program runs early June to early Sept., and includes 2 Shakespeare works, a musical, and a children's production. Barbecue before evening shows. Performances M-Sa 8pm (matinees most Th and every Sa 2:30pm). Children's performances M-W, F, and occasionally Th 2:30pm; Sa 11am. £8.50-25; children half-price with adult ticket; student and senior standbys from 1hr. before curtain £8.

Royal Court Theatre, Sloane Sq. (☎ 7565 5000). Called "the most important theater in Europe," dedicated to new writing and innovative interpretations of classics. Main stage £7.50-26; concessions £9; standing room 1hr. before curtain 10p. Upstairs £12.50-15, concessions £9. M all seats £7.50.

Sadler's Wells, Rosebery Ave. (☎ 7863 8000). Tube: Angel. London's premier dance space, with everything from classical ballet to contemporary tap, plus occasional operas. £10-45; student, senior, and child standbys 1hr. before curtain £10-18.50 (cash only). Box office open M-Sa 9am-8:30pm.

■ **Shakespeare's Globe Theatre,** 21 New Globe Walk (☎ 7401 9919). Tube: Southwark or London Bridge. A faithful reproduction of the original 16th-century playhouse. Opt for backless wooden benches or stand as a "groundling." For tours, see p. 118. Performances mid-May to late Sept. Tu-Sa 7:30pm, Su 6:30pm; from June also Tu-Sa 2pm, Su 1pm. Box office open M-Sa 10am-6pm, and at 8pm on performance days. Seats £12-27, concessions £10-24; standing £5.

MAJOR FRINGE THEATERS

The Almeida, Almeida St. (☎ 7359 4404). Tube: Angel or Highbury & Islington. Top fringe in London, if not the world. Hollywood stars, including Kevin Spacey and Nicole Kidman, queue up to prove their acting cred here. Will open in spring 2003 following renovations. Show times and prices to be announced.

Donmar Warehouse, 41 Earlham St. (☎ 7369 1732). Tube: Covent Garden. Serious contemporary theater. £14-35; concessions standby £12, 30min. before curtain.

Young Vic, 66 The Cut (☎ 7928 6363). Tube: Waterloo. With only 8 rows of seats surrounding the flat stage, Vic can be unnervingly intimate. Box office open M-Sa 10am-8pm. £19, seniors £12.50, students and children £4-9.50.

CINEMA

The heart of the celluloid monster is **Leicester Square** (p. 120), where the latest releases premiere a day before hitting the city's chains. The dominant mainstream cinema chain is **Odeon** (☎ (0870) 5050 007). Tickets to West End cinemas cost £8-10+; weekday matinees before 5pm are usually cheaper. For less mainstream offerings, try the **Electric Cinema,** 191 Portobello Rd. (Tube: Ladbroke Grove), for the combination of baroque stage splendor and the buzzing effects of a big screen. For that extra special experience, choose a luxury armchair or 2-seat sofa. (☎ 7908 9696, tickets 7229 8688. Late-night reruns Sa 11pm; classics, recent raves, and double bills Su 2pm. M £7.50, Tu-Su £12.50; 2-seat sofa M £20, Tu-Su £30; Su double bills £7.50.) The **ICA Cinema,** Nash House, is also fairly indie (see p. 136); the **National Film Theatre (NFT),** on the South Bank, underneath Waterloo Bridge (Tube: Waterloo, Embankment, or Temple), promises a mind-boggling array of films—six different movies hit the three screens every evening, starting around 6pm (☎7928 3232; £7.20, concessions £5.50). **The Prince Charles,** Leicester Pl. (Tube: Leicester Sq.), will let you *Sing-a-long-a-Sound-of-Music*, with Von Trappists dressed as everything from nuns to "Ray, a drop of golden sun." (☎7957 4009 or 7420 0000. F 7:30pm, Su 2pm; £12.50, children £8.)

COMEDY

Capital of a nation famed for its sense of humor, London takes comedy seriously. On any given night, you'll find at least ten comedy clubs in operation: check listings in *Time Out* or a newspaper to get up to speed. Summertime giggle-seekers should note that London empties of comedians in **August,** when most head to Edinburgh to take part in the annual festival, but that means **July** provides plenty of comedians trying out their material. Robin Williams once did frequent impromptu acts at the ◪**Comedy Store,** 1a Oxenden St. (Tube: Piccadilly Circus), the UK's top comedy club and sower of the seeds that gave rise to *Ab Fab, Whose Line is it Anyway?,* and *Blackadder.* Tuesday is contemporary satire, Wednesday and Sunday improv, Thursday through Saturday standup. (TicketMaster ☎7344 0234. Shows Tu-Su 8pm, F-Sa also midnight. Book ahead. 18+. £12-15, concessions £8.) East London's ◪**Comedy Cafe,** 66 Rivington St., merits a health warning: prolonged exposure may lead to uncontrollable laughter. (☎7739 5706. Reserve F-Sa. Doors 7pm, show 9pm, dancing until 2am. W free try-out night, Th £5, F £10, Sa £14.)

MUSIC

ROCK AND POP

Birthplace of the Stones, the Sex Pistols, Madness, and the Chemical Brothers, home to Madonna (sort of) and McCartney, London is a town steeped in rock.

Brixton Academy, 211 Stockwell Rd. (Ticketweb ☎7771 2000). Tube: Brixton. 1929 ex-theater; sloping floor ensures everyone can see the band. Covers all bases, from the Pogues to Senegalese stars. 4300 capacity. Box office open only on performance evenings. £15-30. Cash only at the door.

Dublin Castle, 94 Parkway (☎8806 2668). It's Madness in the back room every Tu, with a Blur of record execs and talent scouts on the lookout for the next big thing at *Club Fandango.* 3 bands nightly 8:45-11pm; doors open 8:30pm. £5, students £4.

Forum, 9-11 Highgate Rd. (☎7284 1001, box office 7344 0044). Tube: Kentish Town. Turn right and cross the road. Lavish Art Deco theater with great sound and views. Van Morrison, Bjork, Oasis, Jamiroquai, and others have played this 2000-capacity space. When no gigs are on, a cheesy 60s-80s disco takes over (Sa 10pm-2am; £8).

London Astoria (LA1), 157 Charing Cross Rd. (☎7344 0044). Tube: Tottenham Court Rd. Originally a pickle factory, then a strip club and music hall before turning to full-time rock in the late 1980s. Su-W sees not-quite-big acts; Th-Sa hosts the popular G-A-Y club night (see p. 149). £5-20.

The Water Rats, 328 Grays Inn Rd. (☎7837 7269). Tube: King's Cross/St. Pancras. Pub-cafe by day, stomping ground for top new talent by night. Oasis was signed here after their first London gig. Open for coffee M-F 8am-noon, surprisingly good lunches (£5-6) M-F noon-3pm, and music M-Sa 8pm-11pm (cover £5, with band flyer £4).

CLASSICAL

Home to four world-class orchestras, three major concert halls, two opera houses, two ballet companies, and more chamber ensembles than you could Simon Rattle your baton at, London is ground zero for serious music—and there's no need to break the bank. To hear some of the world's top choirs for free, head to Westminster Abbey (p. 111) or St. Paul's Cathedral (p. 113) for **Evensong.**

Barbican Hall (see **Barbican Theatre,** p. 142). Tube: Barbican or Moorgate. One of Europe's leading concert halls. The resident **London Symphony Orchestra** plays over 80 concerts a year. Tickets £6-33.

English National Opera, at the Coliseum, St. Martin's Ln. (☎ 7632 8300). Tube: Charing Cross or Leicester Sq. All the classics, plus contemporary and avant-garde work. Sung in English. £6-60; children half-price. Same-day seats (balcony £3, dress circle £31) released M-F 10am (12:30pm by phone); max. 2 per person. Standbys from 3hr. before curtain; students £12.50, seniors £18, Sa also available to general public for £28. Standing room for sold-out shows £3.

The Proms, at the Royal Albert Hall (see p. 128). This summer season of classical music has been held since 1895, with concerts every night from mid-July to mid-Sept. "Promenade" refers to the tradition of selling dirt-cheap standing tickets, but it's the presence of up to 1000 dedicated prommers that gives the concerts their unique atmosphere. Lines for standing places often start mid-afternoon. Tickets (£5-30) go on sale in mid-May; standing room (£4) from 1½hr. before the concert.

Royal Opera House, Bow St. (☎ 7304 4000). Tube: Covent Garden. Known as "Covent Garden" to the aficionado, the Opera House is also home to the **Royal Ballet.** Box office open daily 10am-8pm. Best seats £100+, but standing room and restricted-view upper balcony can be under £5. Concessions standby 4hr. before curtain £12.50-15. 67 seats from 10am day of performance £10-40.

South Bank Centre, on the South Bank (☎ 7960 4201). Tube: Waterloo or Embankment. All manner of "serious" music is on the program here; the **London Philharmonic** is the orchestra-in-residence for the **Royal Festival Hall.** Tickets for all events at the Festival Hall box office (open daily 10am-9pm); **Queen Elizabeth Hall** and **Purcell Room** box offices open 45min. before curtain. Some concessions; standbys may also be released 2hr. before performance (check ☎ 7921 0973).

Wigmore Hall, 36 Wigmore St. (☎ 7935 2141; www.wigmore-hall.org.uk). Tube: Oxford Circus. London's premier chamber music venue, in a beautiful setting with excellent acoustics. Occasional jazz. £1 fee for box office phone bookings. Concerts most nights 7:30pm, no concerts July-Aug. £8-20, student and senior standbys 1hr. before curtain £8-10 (cash only). Daytime concerts Su 11:30am (£10) and M 1pm (£8, seniors £6).

JAZZ, FOLK, AND WORLD

This ain't Chicago when it comes to **jazz,** but top clubs still pull in big-name performers. **Folk** (which in London usually means Irish) and **world** music keep an even lower profile, mostly restricted to pubs and community centers. International performers occasionally make appearances at major concert halls such as the **South Bank Centre,** the **Barbican,** and the **Wigmore Hall** (see above).

Jazz Cafe, 5 Parkway (tickets ☎ 7344 0044). Tube: Camden Town. With a crowded front bar and balcony restaurant, this would be a popular nightspot even without the top jazz, soul, funk, and Latin performers (£10-16). Jazzy club nights follow the show F-Sa (£8-9). Toot your own horn at the Su jam session (noon-4pm; £1). Open M-Th 7pm-1am, F-Sa 7pm-2am, Su 7pm-midnight. MC/V.

Pizza Express Jazz Club, 10 Dean St. (☎ 7439 8722). Tube: Tottenham Court Rd. Underneath a branch of the popular chain, diners tuck into pizza while feasting their ears on the music. Atmospheric lighting and a laid-back ambience make a great date spot. Cover added to the bill (£12-20). Doors normally open 7:45pm, with music 9-11:30pm; 2 shows some F-Sa, doors open at 6 and 10pm. MC/V.

Ronnie Scott's, 47 Frith St. (☎ 7439 0747). Tube: Tottenham Court Rd. or Piccadilly Circus. London's oldest and most famous jazz club. 2 bands alternate 4 sets M-Sa, opener at 9:30pm and headline around 11pm; Su brings lesser-known bands (from 7:30pm). Reservations often essential. Food £5-12, cocktails £7-8. Cover M-Th £15, F-Sa £25, Su £8-12; students M-W £10. Box office open M-Sa 11am-6pm. Club open M-Sa 8:30pm-3am, Su 7:30-11pm. AmEx/MC/V.

◪ NIGHTLIFE

The West End, and in particular **Soho,** is the scene of most of London's after-dark action. Hundreds of bars and clubs range from the glitzy (and best avoided) Leicester Square tourist traps like the Hippodrome and Equinox to semi-secret underground hotspots. Soho is also the center of London's **gay** and **lesbian** scene—you'll find more gay bars in the few streets around Old Compton St. than in the rest of the city put together. The other major nightlife axis is **Shoreditch** and **Hoxton** (collectively known as **Shoho**) in East London; dead until a few years ago, it's now the city's most cutting-edge area, though parts are still pretty deprived. Style and attitude are essential; most bars and clubs here are for posing as much as for getting on down. Outside these two areas, **Notting Hill, Brixton** (in South London), and **Camden Town** and **Islington** (both in North London) have a sprinkling of nightspots.

BARS

In London these days, drinking is the new dancing, and bars are the new nightclubs. An explosion of **club-bars** has invaded the previously forgotten gap between pubs and clubs, offering seriously stylish surroundings and top-flight DJs together with plentiful lounging space. Club-bars are usually open from noon or early evening, allowing you to skip the cover charge (if there is one) by arriving early and staying put as the scene shifts around you. On the other hand, they tend to close earlier than "real" clubs, usually between midnight and 2am.

▨ **Filthy MacNasty's Whisky Café,** 68 Amwell St. (☎ 7837 6067). Tube: Angel. This Irish pub is frequented by a galaxy of stars—the drop-in list includes Shane MacGowan, U2, Johnny Depp, Kate Moss, and Ewan McGregor. 2 spaces with separate entrances, linked by the passage marked "toilets." Live music most Th (usually rock) and Su (usually Irish). Occasional readings fulfill the erudite bad-boy atmosphere. 32 different whiskies (around £2). Thai dishes mostly £5. Open M-Sa 11am-11pm, Su noon-10:30pm.

▨ **Freud,** 198 Shaftesbury Ave. (☎ 7240 9933). Invigorate your psyche in this underground hipster hangout. Sand-blasted walls occasionally echo with live music (including didgeridoo-playing waiters). Cheap cocktails (from £3.40), bottled beer under £3. Light meals noon-4:30pm (£3.50-6). Open M-Sa 11am-11pm, Su noon-10:30pm. MC/V.

▨ **Soshomatch,** 2 Tabernacle St. (☎ 7920 0701; www.matchbar.com). Tube: Moorgate or Old St. A 2-floor bar/restaurant that converts into a stylish club Th-Sa. Perfect for those seeking to combine a DJ-driven atmosphere with acres of comfy leather couches. The young, relaxed crowd is stylish but without that Hoxton pretension. Th rare groove to jazz, disco, and house (10pm-2am; free); F world-influenced house (10pm-2am; cover £5, free before 10pm); Sa nu-jazz to tribal voices to house (6pm-2am; £5, free before 9pm). Open M-W 11am-midnight, Th-Sa 11am-2pm. AmEx/MC/V.

The Social, 5 Little Portland St. (☎ 7636 4992). Tube: Oxford Circus. DJ-driven bar (voted best by *Time Out*) in the narrow space under Little Portland St. Glass tiles let in moonlight. Upstairs resembles a low-key fluorescent-lit diner with eccentric pub food. Cocktails £4.80, shooters £3. DJs from 7pm. Open M-Sa noon-midnight. No cover.

NIGHTCLUBS

Every major DJ in the world either lives in London or makes frequent visits. While the US may have introduced house music to the world, the UK has taken the lead in developing and experimenting with new types of dance music. Club culture in London is all-pervasive. Even weekly publications have trouble keeping up—*Time Out*, the Londoner's clubbing bible, only lists about half the happenings any given night. The scene revolves around promoters and the nights they organize rather than the bricks-and-mortar clubs themselves, creating both the incredible range and the infuriating ephemerality; top nights come, go, and move around unpredictably. To stay on top of things, comb through *Time Out*, which also prints the "TOP" pass, giving you discounts on many of the week's shenanigans.

Working out how to get home afterwards is crucial; remember that the Tube and regular buses stop shortly after **midnight**, and after **1am** black cabs are like gold dust. If there's no convenient **Night Bus** home, ask the club in advance if they can order a **minicab** (unlicensed taxi) for you; otherwise, order your own before you leave. Although it's technically illegal for minicabs to ply for hire, whispered calls of "taxi" or honking horns signal their presence—unfortunately, you've no guarantee that the driver is reputable or even insured. If you have no other option, agree on a price before you get in, and never ride alone.

DRESS. Clubs tend to fall into one of two categories: those for dancing, and those for posing. In the former, dress codes are generally relaxed; it's not uncommon to find nothing fancier than jeans, stylish t-shirts, and trainers, though women are usually expected to make more of an effort. At posers' clubs, however, dress is crucial, and what's expected depends very much on the scene. If you're not sure what to wear, call the club beforehand (although answers like "New York super-funk glam" aren't always that helpful); otherwise, **black and slinky** is usually safe. **Retro** and **theme** nights mean you have to work a bit harder.

Fabric, 77a Charterhouse St. (☎ 7336 8898). Tube: Farringdon. Bigger than a B-52 and 100 times as loud. When they power up the underfoot subwoofer, lights dim across London. 3 dance floors, chill-out beds, multiple bars, and unisex toilets, crammed with up to 1900 crazed creatures. F hip-hop and breakbeat (9:30pm-5am), Sa house and techno (10pm-7am), Su polysexual night, house (10pm-5am). Cover £10-15.

Bug Bar, Crypt, St. Matthew's Church (☎ 7738 3184). Tube: Brixton (Zone 2). The super laid-back crowd gives this former church crypt genuine vibe. You'll be groovin' in the aisles—the dance floor is nowhere near big enough for the movers and shakers. W live acts; Th funk, jazz, and R&B; F rare beats and breaks; Sa various one-offs, from hip-hop to jazz; Su garage, R&B, funk, hip-hop, and "boogie classics." Cover £4-6, often free or discounted before 8 or 9pm. Open W-Th 7pm-1am, F-Sa 8pm-3am, Su 7pm-2am.

Notting Hill Arts Club, 21 Notting Hill Gate (☎ 7460 4459). Tube: Notting Hill Gate. No-frills basement—turntables on folding tables and no decoration beyond projections and leftover art—is consistently one of the city's coolest hotspots. A chill, friendly crowd sips absinthe (£5.50) and grooves to eclectic music. Acts vary; W rock, F deep house, and Sa eclectic band showcase are staples.

Scala, 275 Pentonville Rd. (☎ 7833 2022, tickets 08700 600 100). Tube: Kings Cross. Brilliant nights in a seedy area. Main floor DJs spin from the projectionist's box of this former cinema; ramped balconies provide a multi-level experience. Room 2 is larger than many whole clubs, while the tiny floor by the entrance provides intimate sweaty relief. Dress up. F gay/mixed eclectica; Sa garage and R&B; every other Su salsa with a free dance workshop 8:30-9:30pm (8pm-2am; £8). Occasionally open other nights.

Ministry of Sound, 103 Gaunt St. (☎ 7378 6528; www.ministryofsound.co.uk). Tube: Elephant & Castle. Take the exit for South Bank University. Mecca for serious clubbers

—arrive early or queue all night. Massive main room, smaller 2nd dance floor, and overhead balcony bar (often VIP only). Emphasis on dancing rather than decor; dress generally casual, but err on the side of smartness (no trainers). F garage and R&B (10:30pm-5am; £12); Sa US and vocal house (11pm-8am; £15).

The Dogstar, 389 Coldharbour Ln. (☎ 7733 7515). Tube: Brixton (Zone 2). One of the first to cash in on Brixton's popularity as a bohemian hang-out for aspiring media-types. At 9pm, tables are cleared from the dance floor and the projectors above the bar are switched on. Open Su-Th noon-2am, F-Sa noon-4am. M ambient chill-out session; Tu world music; W dirty digital funk; Th drum'n'bass; F-Sa varied house-oriented; Su 60s-80s pop. Su-Th no cover; F cover £5, £4 10-11pm, free before 10pm; Sa £7/£5/free.

AKA, 18 West Central St. (☎ 7419 9199), next to The End. Tube: Holborn. Going west on High Holborn, turn right at Museum St.; look for the lavender building. Laid-back, innovative, and leaning toward the bar side of club-bar. Candlelit island lounge, high above the dance floor, is perfect people-watching. Cocktails £5-9.50. Casual dress. M free movies; admission until 6:30pm, film 7pm. M hip-hop and R&B; Tu board games; W house; Th tech-house; F soul. M-F cover free-£7. Sa joins The End for **As One** (£15, after 9pm £10 for AKA only). Su house, rotating themes (cover varies). Open Su-F 6pm-3am, Sa 7pm-7am. Restaurant open daily 6:30-11pm; bar food served daily 6:30pm-1am.

93 Feet East, 150 Brick Ln. (☎ 7247 3293). Tube: Aldgate East or Liverpool St. In a former brewery. Benefits from East London's danger-cool image while far enough from Shoho to be off the wannabe radar. The stark main floor is a dance space; the sofa-strewn upstairs combines dancing and lounging; and the hard-to-find 3rd room is candlelit for chill-out time. Music changes every night; call for details.

333, 333 Old St. (☎ 7739 5949). Tube: Old St. Once the definitive Shoho hangout, a victim of its own hipness. Nevertheless, the crowds happily line up to cram into this large, 3-floor venue. The main room, complete with airline seating, literally bounces to the beat; the basement feels like a sweaty student venue; the heaving upstairs is visibly a former pub. F monthlies include *Menage à Trois,* with 3 promoters taking you from techno-trance to funkadelia (10pm-5am; cover £10, £5 before 11pm); Sa is eclectic funky on the main floor; upstairs is BYO music (10pm-5am; £10, £5 before 11pm).

Cargo, Kingsland Viaduct, 83 Rivington St. (☎ 7739 3440). Tube: Old St. Superclub trimmings—enormous arched rooms, fab acoustics, and an intimate candlelit lounge—but crippled by a 1am license. Feels more like a pre-club hangout; on the plus side, it's kicking by 9:30pm. Strong Latin line-up. Restaurant serves world food (£2-5). Cover £3-7. Open M-F noon-1am, Sa 6pm-1am, Su noon-midnight; sets M-Sa from 8pm, Su 6pm.

The Fridge, Town Hall Parade, Brixton Hill (☎ 7326 5100). Tube: Brixton (Zone 2). Turn left from the station and bear right at the fork onto Brixton Hill; it's opposite the church. Giant split-level dance floor and stepped wraparound balcony bar give it away as a former cinema. Though hard benches in the "restaurant" dissuade loungers, there's plenty of seating upstairs. F total trance; Sa usually gay night.

The End, 16A West Central St. (☎ 7419 9199). Tube: Tottenham Court Rd. or Holborn. With 2 huge dance floors and speaker walls capable of earth-shattering bass, The End is best known as a house-and-garage hotspot. M glam rock to cutting edge (10pm-3am; cover £4). Th "laid-back mixed-gay clubbing" (10pm-4am; cover £7, £5 before midnight). F one-offs and monthlies. Sa joins up with AKA (see above); Su all-day hard house (3pm-midnight; cover £7, £5 before 5pm).

Herbal, 12-14 Kingsland Rd. (☎ 7613 4462). Tube: Old St. Slightly away from the main Shoho drag, retains a relaxed, friendly feel. Appeals more to loungers than serious booty-shakers, though there's plenty of motion on the dance floor. Wide range of varying one-offs and monthlies, cover never over £5. Open daily 7:30pm-2am.

Sound, 10 Wardour St. (☎ 7287 1010). Tube: Leicester Sq. or Piccadilly Circus. Commercial location can't keep this swinger down. A real maze of a club, with the large, loud main room and balcony bar on the 1st and 2nd floor, the (sometimes separate) Sound Bar on the ground floor, and a basement restaurant and semi-detached club. Periodically attracts some of the biggest names in Europe. Th open mic and talent show (10pm-3am; cover £8; £6 before 11pm).

GAY AND LESBIAN

The Box, 32-34 Monmouth St. (☎ 7240 5828). Recently renovated, this spacious gay/ mixed bar-brasserie is popular with a stylish media/fashion crowd. Food specials change daily (entrees about £9). Open M-Sa 11am-11pm, Su noon-10:30pm. Food served until 5pm. MC/V.

Comptons of Soho, 53 Old Compton St. (☎ 7479 7461). Tube: Leicester Sq. or Piccadilly Circus. Soho's "official" gay pub. Crowds early and is always busy with a no-nonsense male crowd of all ages. Horseshoe bar encourages the exchange of meaningful glances; upstairs (opens 6pm) offers a more mellow scene. Open M-Sa 11am-11pm, Su noon-10:30pm. MC/V.

First Out, 52 St. Giles High St. (☎ 7240 8042). Tube: Tottenham Court Rd. Skip the cafe serving so-so veggie standards (£5) and head to the funky-but-friendly basement bar. Predominantly lesbian, but plenty of gay men except F, when *Girl Friday* takes over. Open M-Sa 10am-11pm, Su 11am-10:30pm. Cash only.

G-A-Y (☎ 7434 9592; www.g-a-y.co.uk). M and Th at the Mean Fiddler, 165 Charing Cross Rd., F-Sa at the Astoria. Tube: Tottenham Court Rd. London's biggest gay/lesbian night. Frequently besieged by teenage girls on weekends—the Spice Girls and Boyzone both played here—but the majority-gay door policy keeps the atmosphere camp. M 90s classics with 70s-80s faves in the bar; Th house, dance, and a little pop; F 70s and 80s cheese; Sa commercial-dance DJs and live pop performances (£10). Cover usually £1-3. Open M 12:30pm-4am, Th-F 11pm-4am, Sa 10:30pm-5am.

Heaven, The Arches, Craven Terr. (☎ 7930 2020). Tube: Charing Cross or Embankment. "The world's most famous gay disco," though runs regular mixed nights. Intricate interior rewards explorers—fantastically lit main floor, upstairs 2nd room, 3rd bar-cum-dance floor, coffeebar, and elusive red chill-out room. M chart-toppers, 70s-80s disco hits, commercial house (mixed; 10:30pm-3am; cover £4); W house, garage, soul, and swing (gay; 10:30pm-3am; £6, £4 before 11:30pm); F hard house and trance (mixed); Sa dance, trance, house, and disco (gay/lesbian; 10pm-5:30am; £12).

Ku Bar, 75 Charing Cross Rd. (☎ 7437 4303). Tube: Leicester Sq. Don't be fooled by the naked-lady mosaic; this fashionable hangout is definitely gay, attracting well-dressed men in "suits and boots." Cocktail pitchers £7 before 9pm, Carlsberg £1 per bottle all day M-F. Bottled beer from £2.90. Open M-Sa 1-11pm, Su 1-10:30pm.

Vespa Lounge, St. Giles Circus (☎ 7836 8956). Tube: Tottenham Court Rd. Above the Conservatory restaurant, at the foot of Centrepoint tower. Relaxed lesbian lounge bar with blue walls, comfy seats, and pool table. Thai food supplied by downstairs restaurant. "Laughing Cows" comedy night first Su of month (£4-6), plus occasional theme nights. Gay men welcome as guests. Open M-Sa 6-11pm.

SOUTH ENGLAND

South England's sprawling pastures unfold with a history that asserts Britain's island heritage and expresses a continental link deeper than the Channel Tunnel. Early Britons crossed the Channel the hard way, and settled the counties of Kent, Sussex, and Hampshire. The later, modestly titled European tourist William the Conqueror left his mark in the form of intimidating castles and inspiring cathedrals, many built around settlements begun by Romans. More recently, German bombings during WWII uncovered long-buried evidence of Caesar's invasion. Victorian mansions balance atop seaside cliffs and the masts of restored ships spike the skyline, summoning a chorus of voices from England's naval and literary past. Geoffrey Chaucer's pilgrims colored the way to Canterbury with their bawdy tales. Jane Austen's acerbic pen scratched in an archipelago of houses near the southern downs and borders. Charles Dickens drew mammoth novels from his early experiences in Portsmouth, while E.M. Forster, Virginia Woolf, and other Bloomsbury-ites vacationed and lived near the South Downs.

HIGHLIGHTS OF SOUTH ENGLAND

BRIGHTON Wander the tacky paradise by day and shimmy at the nightclubs 'til the break of dawn (p. 170).

DOVER Don't miss the famous chalk-white cliffs, either from the commanding headland or aboard the ferry bringing you to port or whisking you away (p. 157).

SOUTH DOWNS WAY Hike through landscape which inspired the "Idea of England," and sleep among Bronze Age burial mounds (p. 166).

KENT

CANTERBURY   ☎ 01227

And specially from every shires ende
Of Engelond to Caunterbury they wende.
—Geoffrey Chaucer, *General Prologue to The Canterbury Tales*

Archbishop Thomas à Becket met his demise in Canterbury Cathedral in 1170 after an irate Henry II asked, "Will no one rid me of this troublesome priest?" A few footloose knights took his question a bit too literally, and what began as a routine clash between church and state became the making of a saint. The site of Britain's most gruesome execution became the focus for countless pilgrims first bent on acquiring the (seemingly infinite) drops of Becket's purportedly miracle-inducing blood, and later merely hoping to take a holy moment at his tomb. Chaucer ensured Canterbury's literary immortality with his ribald *Canterbury Tales*, creating a reference point for present-day "pilgrims" from all over the world.

South England

SOUTH ENGLAND

▟ THE SHIPMAN'S TALE

Trains: East Station, Station Rd. East, off Castle St., southwest of town. Open M-Sa 6:10am-8:20pm, Su 6:10am-9:20pm. **Connex South trains** from **London Victoria** (1½hr.; 2 per hr.; £15.90, day return £16.20). **West Station,** Station Rd. West, off St. Dunstan's St. Open M-F 6:15am-8pm, Sa 6:30am-8pm, Su 7:15am-9:30pm. Connex South from **London Charing Cross** and **London Waterloo** (1½hr.; every hr.; £15.90, day return £16.20). Ask everyone in your compartment to tell a story.

Buses: Bus station, St. George's Ln. (☎ 472 082). Open M-Sa 8:15am-5:15pm. **National Express** from **London** (2hr., every hr., £9.50). Book tickets by 5pm. **Explorer** tickets allow 1 day's unlimited bus travel in Kent (£6.50, concessions £4.50, families £13.60). Canterbury, on the rail and bus lines from **Dover** and **Folkestone,** is often a stop for travelers from the Continent (see p. 157).

Taxis: Longport (☎ 458 885). Available daily 7am-2am.

Bike Rental: Downland Cycle Hire, West Station (☎ 479 543). Reserve in advance. £10 per day, childrden £7. Bike trailers £6 per day. £25 deposit.

▟ ▟ THE REEVE'S TALE

Canterbury center is roughly circular, defined by the eroding city wall. An unbroken street crosses the city from northwest to southeast, changing names from **St. Peter's St.** to **High St.** to **The Parade** to **St. George's St.** Butchery Ln. and Mercery Ln., each only a block long, run north to the **Cathedral Gates.**

Tourist Information Centre: The Buttermarket, 12/13 Sun St. (☎ 378 100; fax 378 101; canterburyinformation@canterbury.gov.uk). Bursting with maps and guides. Books beds for £2.50 and 10% deposit. Open M-Sa 9:30am-5:30pm, Su 10am-4pm.

Tours: 1½hr. **guided tours** of the city from the TIC. Apr.-Oct. daily 2pm; July-Aug. also M-Sa 11:30am. £3.50, concessions £3, under 14 free, families £8.50. **Kent and Canterbury Ballooning** (☎ (01303) 230 250). £130 for 1 person, £240 for couples.

Financial Services: Banks mingle near the big-name department stores. **Thomas Cook,** 14 Mercery Ln. (☎ 767 656). Open Th-Tu 9am-5:30pm, W 10am-5:30pm.

Launderette: 20 Dover St. (☎ 765 473). Open M-Sa 8:30am-8:30pm.

Police: Old Dover Rd. (☎ 762 055), outside the eastern city wall.

Hospital: Kent and Canterbury Hospital (☎ 766 877), off Ethelbert Rd.

Internet Access: Chai Data Ltd., corner of St. Dunstan's St. and Station Rd. West (☎ 478 778). Fast and cheap at £3 per hr. Open M-Sa 10am-10pm, Su 11am-7pm.

Post Office: 28 High St. (☎ 473 811), across from Best Ln. Open M-Sa 8:30am-5:30pm. **Post Code:** CT1 2BA.

▟ THE INNKEEPER'S TALE

Canterbury is busy and singles are scarce; reserve ahead or arrive by mid-morning. **B&Bs** cluster around High St. and near West Station. The cheaper ones (£18-20) on **New Dover Rd.,** ½ mi. from East Station, fill fast. Turn right from the station and continue up the main artery, which becomes Upper Bridge St. At the second roundabout, turn right onto St. George's Pl., which becomes New Dover Rd.

▨ **Kipps, A Place to Sleep,** 40 Nunnery Fields (☎ 786 121; info@kipps-hostel.com), 5-10min. from city center. Comfy place for a kip; self-catering kitchen, friendly management, and an atmosphere that's social without being overbearing. Internet £1 per 15min. Laundry £3. Key deposit £10. Dorms £11-13; singles £17.50; doubles £30. ❷

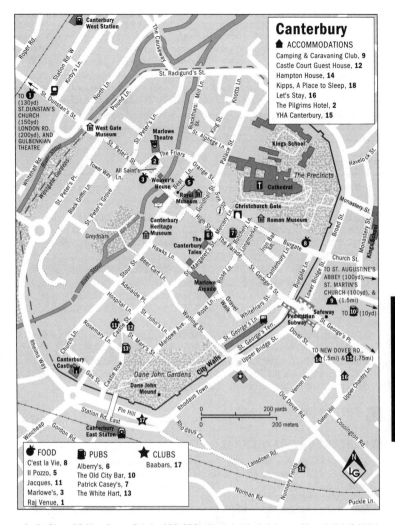

Canterbury

♠ ACCOMMODATIONS
Camping & Caravaning Club, 9
Castle Court Guest House, 12
Hampton House, 14
Kipps, A Place to Sleep, 18
Let's Stay, 16
The Pilgrims Hotel, 2
YHA Canterbury, 15

🍴 FOOD
C'est la Vie, 8
Il Pozzo, 5
Jacques, 11
Marlowe's, 3
Raj Venue, 1

🍺 PUBS
Alberry's, 6
The Old City Bar, 10
Patrick Casey's, 7
The White Hart, 13

★ CLUBS
Baabars, 17

SOUTH ENGLAND

Let's Stay, 26 New Dover Rd. (☎463 628). Hostel-style lodgings with a delightful Irish hostess. Vegetarian breakfast available; engaging conversation included. Ask about the origin of the name! Call before arrival. £11 per person. ❷

Hampton House, 40 New Dover Rd. (☎464 912). Luxurious house with quiet rooms and heavenly mattresses. Tea and coffee room service and English breakfast. Summer £20-25 per person, winter about £17; family room £35-45. ❸

Castle Court Guest House, 8 Castle St. (☎/fax 463 441). Quiet B&B a few minutes from Eastgate in the old town. Vegetarian breakfast available. £20 per person, with bath £22. 5% discount for *Let's Go* users. ❸

YHA Canterbury, 54 New Dover Rd. (☎462 911; canterbury@yha.org.uk), in a lovely big house ¾ mi. from East Station and ½ mi. southeast of the bus station. Laundry facilities. Lockers £1 plus deposit. Kitchen; meals available. Relaxing lounge with Internet access (£2.50 per 30min.) and games. **Bureau de change.** Reception 7:30-10am and 1-11pm. Book at least 2 weeks ahead in summer. Dorms £11.25, under 18 £8. ❷

The Pilgrims Hotel, 18 The Friars (☎464 531). Spacious rooms and soft beds for weary pilgrims, as well as a restaurant/bar for hungry ones. The city-center location is a veritable Canterbury miracle. Singles £45; doubles £65-75; family rooms £85. ❹

Camping: The Camping and Caravaning Club Site, Bekesbourne Ln. (☎463 216), off the A257, 1½ mi. east of the city center. Take Longport Rd. from the city wall. Laundry facilities. £5 per pitch; £3.90-5.50 per person. Electricity and showers. ❶

▢ THE COOK'S TALE

The **Safeway** supermarket, St. George's Pl., is 4min. from the town center. (☎769 335. Open M-Sa 8am-8pm, Su 10am-4pm.)

▨ **Marlowe's,** 55 St. Peter's St. (☎462 194). English food with Mexican improvisations. Choose from 8 toppings for 8 oz. burgers (£6.60) or select a veggie dish (£6.35-9). Try the Steak and Strawberry special for £6. Open daily 11:30am-10:30pm. ❷

C'est la Vie, 17b Burgate (☎457 525). Fresh, inventive takeaway sandwiches (£1.90-2.20). 10% student discount before noon and after 2pm. Open daily 9am-6pm. ❶

Jacques, 71 Castle St. (☎781 000). "Fresh ingredients cooked with imagination," served with live music in candlelit, intimate surroundings. Friendly owner Peter is on hand to attend to every need. Entrees £10-16. Open M-F 11am-2:30pm and 6-9:30pm, Sa 10am-10pm. AmEx/MC/V. ❸

Il Pozzo, 15 Best Ln. (☎450 154). Rich, aromatic food distinguishes it from the scads of Italian joints. Entrees around £11. Open M-Sa noon-2pm and 7-10pm. MC/V. ❸

Raj Venue, 92 St. Dunstan's St. (☎462 653). Fairly portioned Indian food (many dishes £4.50-7) will please the gourmet, and the 10% student discount will please the cash-strapped traveler. Open daily noon-2:30pm and 6-11:30pm. ❷

▢ THE TOURIST'S TALE

▨ CANTERBURY CATHEDRAL

Central and conspicuous. ☎762 862. Cathedral open M-Sa 9am-5pm, Su 12:30-2:30pm and 4:30-5:30pm. Evensong M-F 5:30pm, Sa 3:15pm, Su 6:30pm. Precincts open daily 7am-9pm. £3.50, concessions £2.50. Tickets at the gate; wander the precincts for free after hours. 75min. tours 4 per day; £3, concessions £2, children £1.20; check nave or welcome center for times. Self-guided tour £1.25. 25min. audio tour £2.50. Photography permit £2.

Pilgrim contributions funded most of Canterbury Cathedral's wonders, including the early Gothic **nave,** constructed mostly between the 13th and 15th centuries on a site allegedly consecrated by St. Augustine 700 years earlier. Among the nave's entombed residents are Henry IV, his wife Joan of Navarre, and the Black Prince. A taste for the macabre has drawn the curious since 1170, when Archbishop **Thomas à Becket** was beheaded at the cathedral with a strike so forceful it broke the axe-blade. The murder site is closed off by a rail—a kind of permanent police line—around the Altar of the Sword's Point, while a 14min. audiovisual re-creation of the homicide plays just off the cloisters (shown continuously 10am-4pm; £1, concessions 70p, children 50p). In the adjacent **Trinity Chapel,** a solitary candle marks where Becket's body lay until 1538, when Henry VIII burned his remains and destroyed the shrine to show how he dealt with unruly bishops. The eerily silent **crypt,** billed as a site for quiet reflection, hosts both tourists and funerals. Keep alert for an orange-striped cat, known as Tom, padding across a tomb or napping in a pew. The mysterious kitty comes and goes as he pleases, and is most famous for trailing the Archbishop during a televised high mass.

In a structure plagued by fire and rebuilt time and again, the **Norman crypt,** a huge 12th-century chapel, remains intact. The **Corona Tower,** 105 steps above the eastern-most apse, recently reopened after renovations (60p, children 30p). Under the **Bell Harry Tower**—at the crossing of the nave and western transepts—perpendicular arches support intricate 15th-century fan vaulting.

OTHER SIGHTS

THE CANTERBURY TALES. Let the gap-toothed Wife of Bath and her waxen companions entertain you in an abbreviated version of the Tales, complete with smells of sweat, hay, and general grime. The museum reenacts the journey of Chaucer's pilgrims, only this time with headsets and in several languages. *(St. Margaret's St. ☎479 227. Open July-Aug. daily 9am-5:30pm; Mar.-June and Sept.-Oct. 9:30am-5:30pm; Nov.-Feb. Su-F 10am-4:30pm, Sa 9:30am-5:30pm. £6, concessions £5.50, families £19.)*

ST. AUGUSTINE'S ABBEY. Soaring arches and crumbling walls are all that remain of what was once among the greatest abbeys in Europe, built in AD 598. Exhibits and a free audio tour reveal the abbey's history as burial place, royal palace, pleasure garden, and World Heritage Site. Don't miss St. Augustine's humble tomb under a pile of rocks. *(Outside the city wall near the cathedral. ☎767 345. Open Apr.-Oct. daily 10am-6pm; Nov.-Mar. 10am-4pm. £3, concessions £2.30, children £1.50.)*

CHURCH OF ST. MARTIN. In this parish church, the oldest in Britain, Pagan King Æthelbert was married to the Christian French Princess Bertha in AD 562, paving the way for England's conversion to Christianity. Here, too, Joseph Conrad slumbers in darkness. *(North Holmes St. ☎459 482. Open M-Su 9am-5pm. Free.)*

CANTERBURY HERITAGE MUSEUM. Housed in the medieval Poor Priests' Hospital, the museum spans Canterbury's history, from St. Thomas to WWII bombings to beloved children's-book character Rupert Bear. An animated and rather tongue-in-cheek video account of Becket and Henry II's relationship gives the oft-ignored background to their final grisly encounter. *(Stour St. ☎452 747. Open June-Oct. M-Sa 10:30am-5pm, Su 1:30-5pm; Nov.-May M-Sa 10:30am-5pm. £2.60, concessions £1.65.)*

WEST GATE MUSEUM. The remainder of medieval Canterbury bunches near the West Gate (one of the few medieval fortifications to survive wartime blitzing), through which pilgrims traditionally entered the city. Just within, the museum—a former prison surrounded by well-tended gardens—keeps armor, old weapons, a faux prisoner, and commanding views of the city. *(☎452 747. Open M-Sa 11am-12:30pm and 1:30-3:30pm. £1, concessions 65p, children 50p, families £2.30.)*

GREYFRIARS. England's first Franciscan friary, Greyfriars was built over the River Stour in 1267 by Franciscan monks. A small museum devoted to the local order and a chapel are found inside the simple building. For a quiet break, walk through Greyfriars's **riverside gardens.** *(Stour St. Open in summer M-F 2-4pm. Free.)*

BEST OF THE REST. A 15th-century Huguenot home on the river, the **Weaver's House,** 1 St. Peter's St., features an authentic witch-dunking stool. **Weaver's River Tours** runs 30min. cruises leaving several times a day. *(☎464 660. £4, concessions £3.50, children £3.)* The **Royal Museum and Art Gallery** showcases local talent and recounts the history of the "Buffs," one of the oldest regiments of the British Army. *(In the library, 18 High St. ☎452 747. Open M-Sa 10am-6pm. Free.)* Near the city walls to the southwest lie the massive, solemn remnants of the Conqueror's **Canterbury Castle.** Outside the walls to the northwest, the vaults of **St. Dunstan's Church** contain a relic said to be the head of Thomas More; legend has it that his daughter bribed the executioner at the Tower of London for it.

THE TAVERNKEEPER'S TALE

The Old City Bar, Oaten Hill Pl. (☎766 882). Students and twentysomethings pack into the pub and beer garden. BBQ and live music on weekends. Open daily noon-11pm; food served noon-2:30pm.

Patrick Casey's, Butchery Ln. (☎463 252). With a vast menu of traditional Irish foods and amply flowing beverages, Casey's warms a traveler's stomach. Live folk music Th and F at 9pm, Su 8:30pm. Open M-Sa 11am-11pm, Su noon-10:30pm.

The White Hart, Worthgate Pl. (☎765 091), near East Station. Congenial pub with homemade lunch specials and sweets (£4.50-6), plus some of Canterbury's best bitters (£2). Enjoy both in the city's largest beer garden. Open daily 10am-11pm.

Alberry's, 38 St. Margaret's St. (☎452 378). A stylish wine bar that pours late into the evening. Happy hour 5:30-7pm. Open M-W noon-11pm, Th noon-1am, F-Sa noon-2am.

Baabars, 15 Station Rd. East (☎761 233). 3-way split personality on weekends: Baabars, the charty/party 1st floor; the Bizz, the all-dance 3rd floor; and the Works, musically and architecturally in between. No jeans or trainers F-Su. Cover £3-6. Open M-Th 7pm-2am, F-Sa 7pm-3am (bar closes at 2am), Su 7pm-11:30pm.

THE PLAY-ACTOR'S TALE

For up-to-date entertainment listings, pick up *What, Where, When,* free at the TIC. **Buskers,** especially along St. Peter's St. and High St., play streetside Vivaldi while bands of impromptu players ramble from corner to corner, acting out the more absurd of Chaucer's scenes. The task of regaling today's pilgrims with stories falls to the **Marlowe Theatre,** The Friars, which receives touring London productions. (☎787 787. Box office open M-Sa 10am-9pm. Tickets £6.50-22. Concessions available.) The **Gulbenkian Theatre,** at the University of Kent, University Rd., west of town on St. Dunstan's St., stages a range of shows. (☎769 075. Box office open M-F 11am-5:30pm. Tickets £5-21, £5 rush available from 7pm performance nights.)

For information on summer arts events and the **Canterbury Festival**—two full weeks (Oct. 11-25 in 2003) of drama, opera, cabaret, chamber music, dance, and exhibitions inspired by French culture—call ☎452 853. The April **Chaucer Festival Spring Pilgrimage** (☎470 379) brings a medieval fair and period-costumed performers. In Ashford, 5 mi. southwest of Canterbury, the **Stour Music Festival,** a popular celebration of Renaissance and Baroque music, lasts for ten days at the end of June. The festival takes place in and around All Saint's Boughton Aluph Church, on the A28 and accessible by rail from West Station. Call the Canterbury bookings office a month in advance for tickets (☎455 600; £5-14).

DAYTRIPS FROM CANTERBURY

SISSINGHURST CASTLE GARDEN

Catch a train from Canterbury West to Staplehurst, where buses #4 and 5 run to Sissinghurst. ☎(01580) 710 700; infoline 710 701. Admission by timed ticket. Open Apr. to mid-Oct. Tu-F 1-6:30pm, Sa-Su 10am-6:30pm; last admission 1hr. before close. £6.50, children £3.

A masterpiece of floral design and execution by Vita Sackville-West and her husband, Harold Nicholson, both of Bloomsbury Group fame, Sissinghurst is Britain's most popular garden. The flowers that spill onto narrow paths in an overwhelming mosaic of color may seem like the chaotic victory of Mother Nature, but the garden is organized according to the best-laid of human plans, profoundly influenced by Gertrude Jekyll's cottage-style landscape design and the Arts and Crafts movement of the early 20th century. After savoring the serenity of the White Garden or fiery Cottage Garden, stroll along the moat to forested, tranquil lakes.

LEEDS CASTLE

23 mi. southwest of Canterbury on the A20, near Maidstone. Trains run from Canterbury West to Bearsted (every hr., return £9.40); a shuttle goes from station to castle (return £3.40). ☎(01622) 765 400 or (0870) 600 8880. Castle open Mar.-Oct. daily 11am-7:30pm; Nov.-Feb. 10:15am-5:30pm. Grounds open Mar.-Oct. daily 10am-7pm; Nov.-Feb. 10am-5pm. Last admission 2hr. before close. Castle and grounds £11, concessions £9.50, children £7.50, families £32. Grounds only £9.50/£8/£6.20/£27.

Billed as "the Loveliest Castle in the World," Leeds was built immediately after the Norman Conquest and remained a favorite royal playground until Edward VI, Henry VIII's long-sought son, sold it for a song. The 500 acres of woodlands and gardens host unusual waterfowl, including black swans. The ground floor is a quintessential royal Tudor residence, in sharp contrast to the more modern second floor, impeccably outfitted according to the tastes of 20th-century owner Olive, Lady Baillie, by the same interior decorator responsible for Jackie Kennedy's White House overhaul. One wing displays an alarming collection of **medieval dog collars**. Outdoors, lose yourself in a **maze** of 2400 yew trees, though the sculpted grounds are practically a maze in themselves.

DOVER ☎01304

And thence to France shall we convey you safe,
And bring you back, charming the narrow seas.
  —William Shakespeare, *Henry V*

From the days of Celtic invaders to the age of the Chunnel, the white chalk cliffs of Dover have been the first impression made upon many a traveler to England. Any hope of tranquility has been disrupted by the puttering of ferries and the hum of hovercraft—urban Dover has sacrificed whatever charm it once had to the business of getting travelers in and out fast. On the other hand, a few minutes' walk along the cliffs or an exploration of the magnificent castle will restore any visitor's childhood imaginings of crashing waves and lordly Normans.

GETTING THERE AND CROSSING THE CHANNEL

Trains: Priory Station, Station Approach Rd. Ticket office open M-Sa 4:15am-11:20pm, Su 6:15am-11:20pm. Trains (☎(08457) 484 950) from **Canterbury** (20min., 2 per hr., £4.90) and several **London** stations (2hr., 2 per hr., £21). Check schedules to see which trains branch off en route.

Buses: Pencester Rd., between York St. and Maison Dieu Rd. (☎(01304) 240 024). Office open M-Tu and Th-F 8:45am-5:15pm, W 8:45am-4pm, Sa 8:30am-noon. The TIC also sells tickets. **National Express** (☎(08705) 808 080) from **London,** continuing to the **Eastern Docks** (2¾hr., 23 per day, £10). **Stagecoach** (☎(01227) 472 082) from **Canterbury** (45min., £4.70) and **Deal** (40min., £3.40). A bus runs from **Folkestone,** the terminus for Channel Tunnel trains (30min., 2 per hr., £3).

SOUTH ENGLAND

Ferries: Major companies operate ships from the **Eastern Docks** to **Calais, France** and **Oostend, Belgium;** the TIC offers a ferry booking service. **P&O Stena** lines (☎(08706) 000 600; www.posl.com) to Calais for £26 (35 per day); **SeaFrance** (☎(08705) 711 711; www.seafrance.com) for £17 (15 per day). Special deals common in summer. **Hovercraft** leave the Hoverport at **Prince of Wales Pier** for **Calais** (£27). Free bus service leaves Priory Station for the docks 45min. to 1hr. before sailing. (See **By Ferry,** p. 28.) The **Channel Tunnel** offers passenger service on **Eurostar** and car transport on **Le Shuttle** to and from the continent. (See **By Train,** p. 28.)

Taxis: Central Taxi Service (☎240 0441). 24hr.

🛈 PRACTICAL INFORMATION

Tourist Information Centre: Townwall St. (☎205 108; fax 245 409), a block from shore. Multilingual staff sells ferry, bus, and hovercraft tickets; after hours call for accommodations list. Open daily 9am-6pm.

Tours: Guide Friday (☎205 108) operates 1hr. hop-on/hop-off tours with stops at Priory Station, TIC, Market Sq., and Dover Castle. Daily 10am-4pm. £6.50, concessions £5.50, children £2.50, families £15.50. **White Cliffs Boat Tour** (☎/fax 271 388) sails every hr. from the Marina. £5, children £3, families £12.

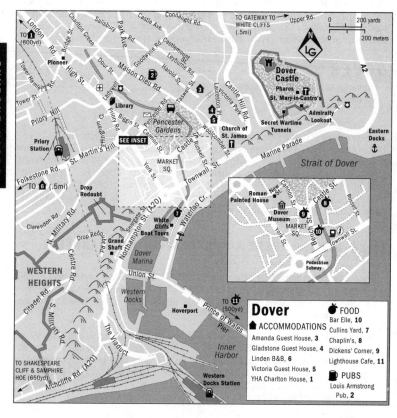

Dover

🍎 **FOOD**

🏠 **ACCOMMODATIONS**

Amanda Guest House, **3**
Gladstone Guest House, **4**
Linden B&B, **6**
Victoria Guest House, **5**
YHA Charlton House, **1**

Bar Elle, **10**
Cullins Yard, **7**
Chaplin's, **8**
Dickens' Corner, **9**
Lighthouse Cafe, **11**

🍺 **PUBS**

Louis Armstrong
Pub, **2**

Financial Services: Several **banks** bump elbows in Market Sq. **Thomas Cook,** 3 Cannon St. (☎204 215). Open M-Tu and Th-Sa 9am-5:30pm, W 10am-5:30pm.

Launderette: Cherry Tree Ave. (☎242 822), off London Rd., past the hostel. Full service available. Open daily 8am-8pm, last wash 7:15pm.

Police: Ladywell St. (☎218 183), off High St.

Hospital: Buckland Hospital, Coomb Valley Rd. (☎201 624), northwest of town. Take bus D9 or D5 from outside the post office.

Internet Access: Library, Biggin St. (☎204 241). Free, max. 1hr.; book ahead. Open M-Tu and Th 9:30am-6pm, W 9:30am-1pm, F 9:30am-7pm, Sa 9:30am-5pm. **En-Route 66 CyberCafe,** 8 Bench Street (☎206 633). £4 per hr. Open daily 9am-7pm.

Post Office: 68 Pencester Rd. (☎241 747), inside Alldays. Open M-F 8:30am-5:30pm, Sa 8:30am-noon. **Post Code:** CT16 1PW.

🛏 ACCOMMODATIONS

Plan ahead—rooms are scarce in high season and the ferry terminal makes an ugly and unsafe campground. Cheaper B&Bs congregate on **Folkestone Rd.,** a hike past the train station. Some stay open all night; if the lights are on, ring the bell. Find pricier B&Bs near the city center on **Castle St.** A "White Cliffs Association" plaque signals good, moderately priced rooms. Most B&Bs ask for a deposit.

YHA Charlton House, 306 London Rd. (☎201 314). ½ mi. from Priory station; turn left on Folkestone Rd., then left again at the roundabout on High St. 69 beds, lounge, game room with pool table, kitchen, forceful showers, and lockers. Discounts on sights. Overflow at **14 Goodwyne Rd.** (closer to town). 60 beds, kitchen, and lounge. Bring exact change. Lockout 10am-1pm. Curfew 11pm. Dorms £11, under 18 £7.80. ❷

Gladstone Guest House, 3 Laureston Pl. (☎208 457; kud3gladstone@aol.com). Tasteful furniture with the owner's handmade cherry finish. Some views of rolling hills and fish ponds. Singles £25-30; doubles £38-54; families £18 per person, under 10 free. ❸

Victoria Guest House, 1 Laureston Pl. (☎/fax 205 140). Well-traveled hosts extend a friendly welcome. Think twice about complaining of sore muscles; your neighbor may have just swum the Channel. Singles £15-19; doubles £30-46; family room £50-56. ❷

Linden Bed & Breakfast, 231 Folkestone Rd. (☎205 449; lindenrog@aol.com). A ways off, but this plush B&B makes every effort to accommodate—ask about pickup from the train station or docks. Discount vouchers for Dover sights. £20-27.50 per person. ❸

Amanda Guest House, 4 Harold St. (☎201 711; pageant@port-of-dover.com). Hall bathrooms are a small price to pay for elegant Victorian light fixtures and marble fireplaces in a house built by the former mayor. Jul.-Aug. twins £40-42, Sept.-June £34-38. ❹

Camping: Harthorn Farm (☎852 658), at Martin Mill Station off the A258 between Dover and Deal. Near the railway; follow the signs from the train station. Open Mar.-Oct. £13 per 2 people with car and tent. Without car £4 per person. Electricity £2.❶

🍴 FOOD AND PUBS

Despite (or perhaps because of) the proximity of the Continent, Dover's cuisine remains staunchly English—grease fires rage in the chippers on London Rd. and Biggin St. Get groceries at **Pioneer,** on the corner of Bridge St. and High St. (Open M-F 8:30am-10pm, Sa 7:30am-10pm, Su 10am-4pm.) Health nuts can swing by **Holland & Barrett,** 35 Biggin St. (☎241 426. Open M-Sa 9am-5:30pm.)

CROSSING OVER
Refugee Immigration and the Channel Tunnel

When the $15 billion Channel Tunnel ("Chunnel") was completed in 1994, it was hailed as a tremendous advance in Europe's infrastructure. No longer would ferries or airplanes be needed to cross between England and France—the English Channel could be traversed in a mere 20 minutes. However, it turns out that the Chunnel serves as the most convenient route not only for cargo, but also for refugees who are desperate to find a way onto British soil.

Soon after its completion, refugees from Eastern Europe, the Middle East, and Central Asia began to mass on the French side of the Chunnel, hoping for passage to England. Britain has a well-deserved reputation for being the most hospitable nation in Europe to those fleeing their homes, providing shelter and food vouchers while considering applications for asylum. English is also the only foreign language many refugees know.

For many refugees, the journey begins by paying smugglers to secure passage to the tiny French town of Sangatte, unofficial waiting site for the men hoping to make the hazardous journey to England. (Those who attempt the crossing are almost entirely young males.) Often, they have forfeited their life savings to ride in the backs of trucks—or, if they are lucky, in private cars—across Europe to Sangatte. There they are greeted by Red Cross workers who supervise the camp, providing food and, more often than not, encouragement. Marc Gentilini, president of the French Red Cross, defends his organization's complicity: "These people have traveled thousands of miles to get here, and it is impossible to make them believe they can't go the last 32 miles."

Refugees pay smugglers for tips on the best ways of getting through the Chunnel—either by hitching rides on freight trains or, more dangerously, on the outside of the Eurostar, which can reach speeds up to 180 mph. They must sneak over fences and past security guards, then onto the trains by sprinting after them or leaping from an overpass. Hidden in the trucks carried on freight trains, on metal ledges under the body of the carriage, or on the sloping roofs of passenger cars, they wait for the train to arrive in England, where they can turn themselves over to the police and ask for asylum. Those who make it must face the British social services, waiting in limbo while they apply for asylum. If they are approved, they commonly face xenophobia during the search for positions for which they are overqualified. (Those who can afford a smugglers' passage are often successful professionals or students who end up working in restaurants or as manual labor.)

In November 2001, in an effort to stem the tide of refugees, the French rail service reduced by two-thirds the number of freight trains it sent through the Chunnel. A $9 million investment to improve security, including electric fences and more security personnel, has had some effect—50,000 would-be immigrants were apprehended in 2001. Nevertheless, there is still enough chance of success that people keep trying, occasionally planning mass invasions of the trainyards to overwhelm security forces. As long as the Chunnel affords some hope for a new life, refugees will continue to make their way across by whatever means possible. Despite all the difficulties, England provides a safe haven, far from the wars, political repression, and persecution many of them are fleeing. As Shewan, a migrant from northern Iraq who arrived in England a few years ago, plainly stated, "I feel safe in England. Here I am sure of my life. I know I'm going to stay alive."

Sarah Kerman holds a degree in Literature from Harvard University. She has done some freelance writing and has worked as a writing tutor at the Johns Hopkins Center for Talented Youth.

Bar Elle, Market Sq. (☎204 541). Check the score on Bar Elle's snazzy flat-screen TV, or just chat at the bar over livelier-than-usual pub grub, including Thai Green Curry (£5.50) and a variety of panini (£4). Open M-Sa noon-11pm, Su noon-10pm. ❷

Cullins Yard, 11 Cambridge Rd. (☎211 666). Primarily a seafood restaurant, this water-side venue also offers traditional English food. Don't mistake it for a pub, however—everything is exquisitely prepared and priced to match (entrees £10-20). ❹

Dickens' Corner, 7 Market Sq. (☎206 692). The ground floor bustles with channelers wolfing baguettes and sandwiches (£3-4); the upstairs tearoom moves at a more refined pace. People-watch from the outdoor tables. Open M-Sa 9am-5:30pm. ❶

Louis Armstrong Pub, 59 Maison Dieu Rd. It's easy to overlook the Louis, its presence indicated only by a tiny, weather-beaten picture of Satchmo himself. Live music and a continual crowd make it more than worth the search. Just pub, no grub. Open M-Sa 11am-11pm, Su noon-2pm and 7pm-11pm. ❶

The Lighthouse Cafe and Tea Room (☎242 028), at the end of Prince of Wales Pier. Basic chipper fare, not a basic location: gaze at castle, beaches, and white cliffs as you sip tea from ½ mi. offshore. Worth the visit for the vista alone. Open summer daily 10am-5:30pm (check the sign at the start of the pier). ❶

Chaplin's, 2 Church St. (☎204 870). Classic diner with pictures of Charlie. Shoe leather sadly not on the menu, but you won't miss it with specials like kidney pie (£5). Stroooong coffee. Open daily 8:30am-9pm, off season closes 8:30pm. ❶

SIGHTS

▨DOVER CASTLE. The view from Castle Hill Rd., on the east side of town, reveals why Dover Castle is famed both for its magnificent setting and for its impregnability. It seems every power in Europe has tried to take such a for-tress at one point or another, from the French in 1216 to the Germans during both World Wars. Boulogne, 22 mi. across the Channel, can (barely) be seen on clear days from the castle's top. Hitler's "doodle-bug" missiles destroyed the **Church of St. James,** the ruins crumbling at the base of the hill. Beside **St. Mary-in-Castro's,** a tiled Saxon church, towers the **Pharos lighthouse**—the only extant Roman lighthouse and the tallest remaining Roman edifice in Britain. Climb to the platform of the **Admiralty Lookout** for unsurpassable views of the cliffs and harbor; 50p gets you a binocular look at France. The (no longer) ▨**Secret War-time Tunnels** constitute an impressive 3½ mi. labyrinth only recently declassi-fied. Built in the late 18th century under the threat of attack by Napoleon, the vast underground burrows reach five storeys down and served as the base for the WWII evacuation of Allied troops from Dunkirk. The lowest level, not yet open to the public, was intended to house the government should the Cuban Missile Crisis have gone sour. Tours fill quickly, and there is usually a long wait; check in at the tunnels first. *(Buses from the town center run Apr.-Sept. daily every hr. (55p); otherwise, scale Castle Hill. There's a pedestrian ramp and stairs by the first castle sign. Open daily Apr.-Sept. 10am-6pm; Oct. 10am-5pm; Nov.-Mar. 10am-4pm. £7.50, concessions £5.60, children £3.80, families £18.80. Prices include tunnels tour.)*

DOVER MUSEUM. This engaging museum renders even the Bronze Age exciting. The first floor depicts Dover's Roman days as Dubras, an important colonial out-post, while the third floor's high-tech gallery (mind the polar bear) features the oldest seafaring vessel yet discovered—at 3600 years, it's older than Moses. *(Market Sq. ☎201 066; fax 241 186. Open Apr.-Oct. daily 10am-6pm; Nov.-Mar. 10am-5:30pm. £1.75, concessions 95p, families £4.50. 50% YHA discount.)*

THE WHITE CLIFFS. Covering most of the surrounding coastline, the white cliffs make a beautiful backdrop for a stroll along the pebbly beach. A few miles west of Dover, the whitest, steepest, and most famous of them all is known as **Shakespeare Cliff** because it is traditionally identified as the site of blind Gloucester's battle with the brink in *King Lear*. *(25min. by foot along Snargate St.)* To the east of Dover, past Dover Castle, the **Gateway to the White Cliffs** overlooks the Straits of Dover and serves as an informative starting point for exploration. *(Buses and Guide Friday go to Langdon Cliff at least 1 per hr. ☎202 746. Open Mar.-Oct. 10am-5pm; Nov.-Feb. 11am-4pm.)* Dozens of **cliff walks** lie a short distance from Dover; consult the TIC for trail info.

THE GRAND SHAFT. This 140 ft. triple spiral staircase was shot through the rock in Napoleonic times to link the army on the Western Heights with the city center. The first stairwell was for "officers and their ladies," the second for "sergeants and their wives," the last for "soldiers and their women." *(Snargate St. ☎201 200. Ascend July-Aug. W-Su 2-5pm; summer bank holidays 10am-5pm. £1.50, concessions £1.)*

OTHER SIGHTS. Recent excavations have unearthed a remarkably well-preserved **Roman painted house** off Cannon St. near Market Sq. It's the oldest Roman house in Britain, complete with underground central heating and indoor plumbing. *(New St. ☎203 279. Open Apr.-Sept. Tu-Su 10am-5pm. £2, concessions 80p.)* For striking views, take the A20 toward Folkestone to **Samphire Hoe,** a well-groomed park planted in the summer of 1997 with material dug from the Channel Tunnel. The D2 **bus** to Aycliffe (£1) stops about a 10min. walk from the park.

▣ DAYTRIP FROM DOVER

DEAL

Trains from Dover Priory arrive in Deal Station (15min., at least 1 per hr., £3.10). The TIC, Town Hall, High St., books beds for a 10% deposit and provides the free Deal Historic Town Trails, *which details 10 walks in the area. (☎(01304) 369 576. Open Oct.-May M-F 9am-12:30pm and 1:30-5pm; June-Sept. also Sa 10am-2pm.)*

Julius Caesar came ashore here with an invasion force in 55 BC, and Deal's castles represent Henry VIII's 16th-century attempt to prevent similar occurrences. Quiet and serene today, the close proximity to castles and beaches *sans* ferry traffic makes for a pleasant daytrip. **Deal Castle,** south of town at the corner of Victoria Rd. and Deal Castle Rd., is one of Henry's largest Cinque Ports fortifications (anti-pirate establishments in Kent and Sussex). A symmetrical maze of corridors and cells is guaranteed to entangle visitors. Note the subliminal advertising: the castle's six buttresses form the distinctive shape of Henry's Tudor Rose. (☎(01304) 372 762. Open Apr.-Sept. daily 10am-6pm; Oct.-Mar. W-Su 10am-4pm. £3.20, concessions £2.40, children £1.60.)

Walmer Castle, ½ mi. south of Deal via the beachfront pedestrian path or the A258, is the best-preserved and most elegant of Henry VIII's citadels. Walmer has been transformed into a country estate which, since the 1700s, has been the official residence of the Lords Warden of the Cinque Ports. Notable Wardens past include the Duke of Wellington (whose famed boots are on display), William Pitt, and Winston Churchill. The most recent warden was the Queen Mother; the beautiful gardens are planted with her favorite flowers. (☎(01304) 364 288. Free and worthwhile 30min. audio tour. Open Apr.-Sept. daily 10am-6pm; Oct. 10am-5pm; Nov.-Dec. and Mar. W-Su 10am-4pm; Jan.-Feb. Sa-Su 10am-4pm; call ahead in July, when the castle is often closed. £5, concessions £3.80, children £2.75.) Perhaps the most famous restaurant in Kent, **Dunkerley's Bistro ❹,** 19 Beach St., overlooks the sea. Residents from all over the region flood in to dine on local fish for around £12. (☎375 016. Open Tu-Sa noon-2:30pm and 6-10pm, Su noon-9:30pm.)

PLAYING WITH YOUR FOOD The northernmost of the Cinque Ports, **Sandwich** first tasted fame 250 years ago, when the 4th Earl of Sandwich popularized the culinary masterpiece of same name. A hardcore gambler, the Earl was usually too busy playing cards to bother himself with such superfluities as knives or forks; instead, he'd ask for meals between two slices of bread so he could eat from one hand and play rummy with the other. It's unlikely that the Earl was the first to hit upon the idea, but no one else was lucky enough to get his name attached. Since this gastronomical revolution, however, not much has happened to the tiny town.

SUSSEX

RYE
☎ 01797

Settled before the Roman invasion, Rye's status soared with its admission to the elite membership of the Cinque Ports, a defensive organization initiated by Edward the Confessor and still in operation today. As though Rye were getting too big for its boots, nature interfered and choked the waterways with silt. Hence, the name Rye, from the French *la rie*—the waste spot. 18th-century Rye saw some excitement in the form of ruffian smugglers, but today's town has no such shady side. Its sleepy cobblestone streets and half-timbered houses are beautiful to look at, but they don't hold much excitement.

⧉⧉ TRANSPORTATION AND PRACTICAL INFORMATION. Trains (☎ (08457) 484 950) puff into the station off Cinque Port St. from: **Brighton** (1¾hr., £12); **Dover** (1¾hr., £9.80); **Eastbourne** (1hr., £6.90); **London Bridge** (1½hr., £17.60). **National Express** (☎ (08705) 808 080) runs from **London** (£12). **Buses** (☎ 223 343) covering south England stop in the train station's carpark.

Rye sits at the mouth of the **River Rother.** To get to the TIC from the station, steer yourself to Cinque Port St. proper and turn right onto Wish St.; turn left onto the **Strand Quay** and the TIC is on the left. To reach the oldest part of town, hike 5min. up Market Rd. to **High St., Lion St.,** and **Mermaid St.** The **tourist information centre,** in the Heritage Centre, distributes the free *Rye: 1066 Country* guide. (☎ 226 696; www.rye.org.uk. Open mid-Mar. to Oct. M-Sa 9am-5:30pm, Su 9am-5pm; Nov.-Feb. daily 10am-4pm.) The TIC also shows a "laser and light film" ("movie," in normal-speak) about Rye's smuggling past and hands out self-guided audio tours (£2.50, concessions £1.50). Other services include: **banks** on High St.; a **launderette,** in Ropewalk Arcade (open daily 8:30am-6pm); the **police,** Cinque Port St. (☎ (08457) 607 0999); **Internet access** at the **library** (☎ 223 355; free, max. 1hr.; open M 9:30am-5:30pm, W 10am-5:30pm, Th 9:30am-12:30pm, F 9:30am-6pm, Sa 9:30am-5pm) and the **post office,** 22-24 Cinque Port St. (☎ 222 163; open M-Tu and Th-F 8:30am-5:30pm, W and Sa 9am-5:30pm). **Post Code:** TN31 7AA.

⧉⧉ ACCOMMODATIONS AND FOOD. The area's only **YHA hostel ❶,** on Rye Rd., is 7 mi. south of Rye and 5 mi. north of Hastings. From Rye, head down the A259 past Winchelsea and Icklesham (look for the sign on the right). Alternatively, take bus #711 from Rye to the White Hart in Guestling (M-Sa roughly 2 per hr. until 7:45pm; £1.85); from there, the hostel is downhill to the left. You can also take the train to Three Oaks (£1.90) and follow the signs 1½ mi. (☎ 812 373; book through YHA (0870) 770 5850. Open July-Aug. daily; May-June and Sept.-Oct. 6 days per week, schedule varies; Nov.-Dec. F-Sa. Dorms £10.25, under 18 £7. **Camping** £5.)

Many of Rye's inexpensive **B&Bs** are outside the town proper, either on the roads past the train station or on **Winchelsea Rd.,** across the river from the TIC (10min. walk); call ahead and you may get a lift. To reach the B&B at beautiful **Glencoe Farm ❸,** West Undercliff, exit right from the train station and turn right on Ferry Rd. across the tracks; after Ferry Rd. becomes Udimore Rd., West Undercliff comes up on the left; follow the signs (10-15min.). The farm has friendly owners, livestock to pet, and two airy rooms with bath—book well ahead. (☎224 347. £20 per person.) **Vine Cottage Bed and Breakfast ❸,** 25a Udimore Rd., offers privacy and comfort, and attends to guests in English, Spanish, or German. (☎222 822. Singles £25; twins £36.) **Aviemore Guest House ❸,** 28 Fishmarket Rd., lets eight rooms at the midway point between train station and town center. (☎223 052. £25 per person.)

For groceries, visit **Budgens,** across from the train station. (☎226 044. Open M-Sa 8am-10pm, Su 10am-4pm.) At the bend of one of Rye's most charming streets, **Ye Olde Bell Inn ❶,** 33 The Mint, serves toasted sandwiches (£2-2.50) and other dainties in a cottage garden. (☎223 323. Open M-Th 11am-11pm, F-Sa 11am-midnight, Su 11am-10:30pm.) In deference to thy sweete toothe, climb to **Ye Olde Tuck Shoppe ❶,** 89 High St., to sample homemade fudge and heavenly cakes. (☎222 230. Open M 9:30am-12:30pm, W 12:15pm-4pm, Th 10am-3pm, F-Sa 10am-5pm, and Su 11am-5pm.) More substantial meals (£5-10) are served in colorful surroundings at **Simply Italian ❷,** The Strand (☎226 024. Open daily noon-3pm and from 6pm.)

◑ 〥 SIGHTS AND ENTERTAINMENT. Well-preserved half-timbered homes justify Rye's frequent role as picturesque backdrop in English cinema. Henry James, a perennial costume-drama favorite, wrote his later novels while living in **Lamb House,** perched on the top of the hill at the corner of West St. and Mermaid St. Ponder James's rather gloomy feeling of being "doomed to live here" while kicking-back in the sweetly-scented garden. (Open Apr.-Oct. W and Sa 2-6pm. £2.60, children £1.30.) Before descending the hill, check out **St. Mary's Church,** at the top of Lion St., a huge 12th-century parish church that houses one of the oldest functioning clocks in the country. A climb up the tower steps reveals a terrific view of the river valley, but avoid the ascent when the bell is about to chime—your ears may never forgive you. (☎222 430. Open M-W and F 9am-6pm, Th 10:40am-6pm, Sa 9am-5:30pm, Su 11:40am-5:30pm. Suggested donation £2.50.)

Around the corner from the church, **Ypres Tower,** built in 1350, was intended to fortify the town against invaders from the sea. After a stint as a jail, the tower now contains the **Rye Museum.** (☎226 728. Open Apr.-Oct. M and Th-F 10am-5pm, Sa-Su 10:30am-5pm, closed 1-2pm; Nov.-Mar. Sa-Su 10:30am-3:30pm. Tower and museum £3, concessions £2, children £1.50, families £5.) A walk down Mermaid St. leads to the famed **Mermaid Inn,** where smugglers once cavorted until dawn before vanishing into the secret tunnels underneath the Inn. (☎223 065. Open M-Sa 11am-11pm, Su noon-10:30pm.) You can watch potters mold the famous Rye pottery at many shops sprinkled through the town. Rye's **festival** during the first two weeks of September celebrates art, theater, and music. (☎224 442. Tickets £4-14.)

 DAYTRIPS FROM RYE

HASTINGS

Trains arrive from Rye (20min., every 45min., £3). The TIC, at Queens Sq. and The Stade, signposted from the station, books accommodations. (☎(01424) 781 111; www.hastings.gov.uk. Open Apr.-Oct. M-F 8:30am-6:15pm, Sa 9am-5pm, Su 10am-4:30pm; Nov.-Mar. M and F 8:30am-6:15pm, Tu-Th 8:30am-5pm, Sa 9am-5pm, Su 10am-4:30pm.)

SOUTH ENGLAND

Having surrendered its name and identity to a decis... still revels in its thousand-year-old claim to fame. Loo... mentary remains of **Hastings Castle,** built by William the C... where the French duke's troops camped before trouncing h... ons. The castle met its demise in the 13th century, when part of... and took half the fortifications with it; during WWII, homeward-b... finished the job by dropping excess explosives on Hastings. Catch the... an interactive display on the famous spat between Conquerin' Will and Ha... visit the castle's underground "dungeons." (Take the East or West Hill Cl... from George St. to the top of the hill. Return 80p, concessions 40p. ☎ (01424) ... 111. Open daily 10am-5pm. £3.20, concessions £2.60, children £2.10.) Before heading back to sea level, duck into St. Clements Caves for the **Smuggler's Adventure.** Historical-site-cum-theme-park, these miles of caves and tunnels were once the nerve center of the Sussex smuggling ring. A ghostly apparition of Hairy Jack is your guide through this spooky lair. (☎ (01424) 422 964. Open Easter-Sept. daily 10am-5:30pm, last admission 5pm; Oct-Easter 11am-4:30pm, last admission 4pm. £5.50, concessions £4.75, children £3.50, families £15.) Hastings is also famous for its unique **Net Shops,** clusters of slim black buildings used by fishermen for storage. More information on the area's nautical past can be found in a variety of museums, most notably the **Shipwreck Heritage Centre.** (☎ (01424) 437 452. Open Apr.-Oct. daily 10am-5pm; Feb.-Mar. 10am-4pm. Free.) Present-day Hastings is packed with tourists and all the amenities that come with them—the town center boasts mainstream shops, and offshooting streets are speckled both with traditional pubs and Starbucks-style coffee houses.

BATTLE

Bus #5 runs to the Battle Abbey from Hastings, near the bank buildings (20min.; M-Sa every hr., Su every 2hr.; £4.90). The TIC, 88 High St., opposite Battle Abbey, books accommodations. (☎ (01424) 773 721; battletic@rother.gov.uk. Open Apr.-Sept. daily 10am-6pm; Oct.-Mar. M-Sa 10am-4pm.)

Appropriately renamed after the 1066 tiff between Norman and Anglo-Saxon, the town of Battle makes a fine expedition from Rye. To commemorate his victory in the Battle of Hastings, William built **Battle Abbey** in 1094, spitefully positioning its high altar upon the very spot where Harold was felled by an arrow in the eye (see p. 70). Little now remains apart from the gate and a handsome series of 13th-century common quarters. (☎ (01424) 773 792. Open Apr.-Sept. daily 10am-6pm; Oct. 10am-5pm; Nov.-Mar. 10am-4pm. £4.50, concessions £3.50, children £2.50, families £11.50.) The battlefield where Harold's troops were taken by surprise is now a pasture marched across by sheep. In summer, you can take a free audio tour of the abbey and walk the **battlefield trail,** a 1 mi. jaunt up and down the green hillside.

PEVENSEY

Trains run hourly from Rye and Hastings to Pevensey (£5.60).

William I's march to Battle began from **Pevensey Castle,** a Roman fortress that was already 800 years old when the Norman forces landed. Considered one of the best examples of Roman building in England, the original walls—12 ft. thick and 30 ft. high—are all that's left. (☎ (01323) 762 604. Open Apr.-Sept. daily 10am-6pm; Oct. 10am-5pm; Nov.-Mar. W-Su 10am-4pm. £3, concessions £2.30, children £1.80.) The best part of Pevensey, however, owes its origins to commerce rather than conquest. The **Mint House,** on High St., originally a Norman mint, was transformed by Henry VIII's physician into a country retreat, and eventually became a smugglers' den, complete with sliding ceiling panels. It now teems with stuffed birds and other fascinating Victorian miscellany. (☎ (01323) 762 337. Open M-F 9am-5pm, Sa 10:30am-4:30pm. £1.50, children 50p.)

UTH DOWNS WAY

The South Downs Way, perhaps Britain's most famous hiking trail, stretches 99 mi. from Eastbourne west toward Portsmouth and Winchester. It meanders through the rolling hills and livestock-laden greens that typify pastoral England, never far from coastal towns yet rarely crossing into civilization's domain. The Downs once provided land that prehistoric tribes could cultivate, but the air raids of WWII robbed much of their bucolic innocence. Forts and settlements dot the former paths of Bronze and Iron Age tribes, who were followed by Romans, Saxons, and Normans. Fertile ground for legend, the windswept slopes and salt-sprayed cliffs of the Downs have borne words as prodigiously as flowers, from William I's *Domesday Book* to A.A. Milne's Pooh Bear stories. The Way is well marked from start to finish, and the walking is moderate enough even for novice hikers, making the South Downs—only recently designated a national park—one of the most accessible and rewarding outdoors experiences England has to offer.

⌐ TRANSPORTATION

Trains (☎(08457) 484 950) run to **Eastbourne** from **London Victoria** (1½hr., 2 per hr., £20) and to **Petersfield** from **London Waterloo** (1hr., 3 per hr., £20). From the west, take a train to **Amberley** (via **Horsham**), where the Way greets the River Arun. Eastbourne's helpful **Bus Stop Shop,** Arndale Centre, dispenses info on local buses. From the train station, turn left onto Terminus Rd.; Arndale Centre is on the left. (☎(01323) 416 416. Open M-Sa 9am-5pm.)

Walking the entire path takes about ten days, but public transportation makes it possible to traipse segments. **Trains** connect **Lewes** to **Southease** (3 per hr., £3); **County Bus** #1232 heads from **Lewes** to **Kingston** (20min., 6 per day, £2.10) and **Rodmell** (15min., 1 per day, £1.70). Bus #126 runs 5 times per day from **Eastbourne** to **Alfriston** (40min., £2.80) and **Wilmington** (30min., £3.10). For schedules, call **Eastbourne Buses** (☎(01323) 416 416) or **East Sussex County Busline** (☎(01273) 474 747).

Cycling has long been a popular means of seeing the downlands: D.H. Lawrence cycled the Way in 1909, on a visit to his friend Rudyard Kipling. Cyclists and **horses** have access to most of the trail, but in a number of places their routes diverge

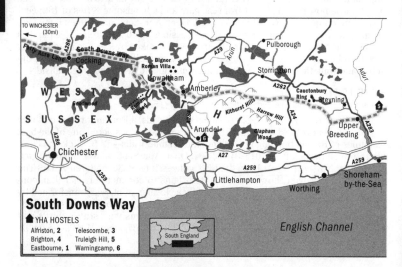

South Downs Way

⛺ YHA HOSTELS

Alfriston, **2**	Telescombe, **3**
Brighton, **4**	Truleigh Hill, **5**
Eastbourne, **1**	Warningcamp, **6**

from those of the walkers. The **Harvey** map shows these in detail—purchase it at any of the South Downs TICs for £9. **Cuckmere Cycle Company** rents bikes from four locations along the Way. (☎(01323) 870 310. £3.50 per hr., £20 per day.) If you're starting from Eastbourne, **Les Smith Cycles,** 134 Terminus Road (☎(01323) 639 056) and **Nevada Bikes,** 324 Seaside (☎(01323) 411 549) are also good options. At the other end of the trail, in Winchester, **Halford's,** Moorside Rd. (☎(01962) 853 549), is another to try. The **Cyclists Touring Club** (☎(01483) 417 217) gives thorough answers to cycling questions. Information for equestrians is available from the **British Horse Society** (☎(01926) 707 700). **Audiburn Riding Stables,** Ashcombe Ln., Kingston, conducts guided 1hr. horseback tours. (☎(01273) 474 398. £15 per person.)

ORIENTATION: FINDING YOUR WAY TO THE WAY

Serious hikers will want to begin their exploration in **Eastbourne,** the official start of the Way. Eastbourne's **Beachy Head** (see p. 169) is accessed by bus and well signposted from the train station. From the **Winchester** town center (see p. 191), at the far other end of the Way, head east on Bridge St., turn right on Chesil St., then left on East Hill. When East Hill splits, take the right fork onto Petersfield Rd. and head for the carpark—signs broadcasting "South Downs Way" should be appearing by this point. From the midpoint village of **Amberley,** just north of Arundel (see p. 178), the Way runs north, parallel to the main road (B2139).

PRACTICAL INFORMATION

Eastbourne is the best place to arrange accommodations and find local services.

Tourist Information Centres

Brighton: Bartholomew Sq., see p. 171.

Eastbourne: Cornfield Rd. (☎(01323) 411 400). Provides vague maps (free) and detailed 1:50,000 Ordnance Survey Landranger maps (#185 and 197-99 are the most useful; around £5). Also sells a number of guides (see below). Open M-Sa 9am-6pm, Su 10am-1pm.

Lewes: 187 High St. (☎(01273) 483 448). Books rooms and sells Ordnance Survey maps and guides (see below). Open M-F 9am-5pm, Sa 10am-5pm; summer also Su 10am-2pm.

Winchester: The Guildhall, see p. 192.

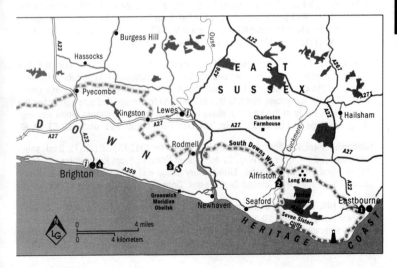

Guidebooks: In Print: Paul Millmore's ▨ *South Downs Way* (£13) is the Bible of the Downs. The Eastbourne and Lewes TICs sell *On Foot in East Sussex* (£3.20) and *Along the South Downs Way* (£6), useful for trekkers. *Exploring East Sussex* (£2) lists various guided walks and cycle rides; *The South Downs Way* photocopied edition (£2) has info on accommodations. **Online:** The Way also crops up on the Internet—2 websites to try are the **South Downs Way Virtual Information Centre** (www.vic.org.uk) and the **Southeast Walks** site (www.southeastwalks.com).

Outdoors Supplies: Millets Leisure, 146 Terminus Rd., Eastbourne (☎(01323) 723 840), stocks camping supplies and Ordnance Survey maps. Open M-Sa 9am-5:30pm, Su 10:30am-4pm. Those commencing from the middle of the Way will have more trouble avoiding than finding outdoor shops in hiker-friendly **Brighton.**

Financial Services: All major **banks** are located in the **Eastbourne** town center. Be sure to pick up your sterling before hitting the trail. **Thomas Cook,** 101 Terminus Rd. (☎(1323) 725 431). Open M-Tu and Th-Sa 9am-5:30pm, W 10am-5:30pm.

◤ ACCOMMODATIONS

There are few towns along the Way, and **B&Bs** fill quickly. Consider making daytrips; **Brighton** (p. 170) makes a good base, as do **Lewes** (see p. 177), **Arundel** (see p. 178), and Southcliff Ave. in **Eastbourne.** For a final night of comfort (ensuite bathrooms and a cocktail bar) before hitting the trail, take a seafront room at **Alexandra Hotel ❸,** King Edward's Parade, in Eastbourne. (☎(01323) 720 131. Singles £24; doubles £32.) **Camping** on the Way is permitted with the landowner's permission. The following four **YHA hostels** lie along or near the Way, each within a day's walk of the next, and each with a 10am-5pm lockout and 11pm curfew. Be sure to call at least 2-3 weeks ahead; the hostels are often full at the same time. For other hostels, check the **Accommodations** sections in Brighton (p. 172) or Arundel (p. 178).

Eastbourne: East Dean Rd., Eastbourne (☎/fax 721 081). Converted golf clubhouse on the A259, about 3 mi. from Beachy Head. From Eastbourne Station, turn right and follow the A259 (Seaford/Brighton) for 1½ mi.; gasp at the steep hill leading to the hostel. Buses #711-712 depart from Shelter H on Terminus Rd., left of the station (80p). Spare, clean rooms with bunks. Breakfast £3.75. Open July-Sept. daily; Apr.-June Th-M; closed Oct.-Mar. Dorms £11, under 18 £7.40. ❷

Alfriston: Frog Firle, Alfriston (☎870 423; alfriston@yha.org.uk). 1½ mi. from the Way and from Alfriston, 8 mi. from Eastbourne. Bus #126 passes the front door of the hostel; by foot from Alfriston, turn left from the market cross and pass the village green, then follow the overgrown riverside trail to Litlington footbridge and turn right along the path; the hostel is at the end in a stone house with bovine neighbors. Open July-Aug. daily; Feb.-June and Sept.-Oct. M-Sa; Nov.-Dec. F-Sa. Dorms £11, under 18 £7.40. ❷

Telscombe: Bank Cottages, Telscombe Village (☎/fax (01273) 301 357). 2 mi. south of Rodmell, 2 mi. from the Way, 12 mi. west of Alfriston. From Rodmell (see p. 169), follow signs directly to hostel. 18th-century house and cheery staff. Open July-Aug. daily; Easter-June W-M; closed Sept.-Easter. Dorms £10.80, under 18 £7. ❷

Truleigh Hill: Tottington Barn, Truleigh Hill, Shoreham-by-Sea (☎(01903) 813 419). Halfway along the Way, 10 mi. from Brighton, 4 mi. from Shoreham station. A converted 1930s summer house with panoramic views and ultra-modern facilities. Meals £3.75-5. Open June-Sept. daily; Apr.-May and Sept.-Oct. Tu-Sa. Dorms £11, under 18 £8. ❷

HIKING

EASTBOURNE TO ALFRISTON

The best place to begin walking the Way is the Victorian seaside city of **Eastbourne,** which lives in the shelter of **Beachy Head,** the path's official starting point. (No sand and surf here: *beau chef* means "fine headland.") The open-topped **bus** #3, from Terminus Rd. in Eastbourne, brings you to the top of Beachy Head (Su-F 9 per day, £2), though you can save money and gain scenic vistas by asking to be let off at the bottom and climbing it yourself. Make the strenuous ascent and follow the fields upward past some inquisitively bent trees. Mountaineers claim that Beachy Head, 543 ft. above the sea, has the same vertiginous effects as Alpine ridges. Whatever breath you have left after the climb will be taken away by the view of the **Seven Sisters,** a series of chalk ridges carved by centuries of receding waters and surpassing the Head in majesty. The queenly sisters hold court about 4½ mi. away, over a windswept series of hills. Far below, 19th-century lighthouse **Belle Tout** threatens to fall into the sea.

From Beachy Head, the path winds past a number of *tumuli*—Bronze Age burial mounds dating to 1500 BC—but the overgrown brush makes them impossible to distinguish. The Way continues westward along the cliff-line to **Birling Gap,** the last undeveloped stretch of coast in south England. To reach **Alfriston,** a sleepy one-road village called "the last of the old towns," follow the Way 4 mi. over a path reputedly used by smugglers who once docked among the cliffs. You can also take bus #711 or 712 from Terminus Rd. in Eastbourne (35min., M-Sa 6 per day, £1.60).

Another option is the shorter **bridleway path** to Alfriston (8 mi.). The bridleway can be joined from a trail just below the **YHA Eastbourne** (see p. 168) and passes through the village of **Wilmington** and by its famous **Long Man,** a 260 ft. earth sculpture of mysterious origins. Varyingly attributed to prehistoric peoples, Romans, 14th-century monks, and aliens, the Long Man is best viewed from a distance and is almost invisible when you first come over his hillside on the Way. It is rumored that Victorian prudes robbed the fellow of male attributes that might have shed some light on his name. Food for thought, to be sure, but the real thing can be found at the **Giant's Rest ❶** pub, on The Street in Wilmington (☎(01323) 870 207). Proceeding back through the Long Man's gate and onto the South Downs Way path over Windover Hill will lead you to Alfriston.

ALFRISTON TO FORTY ACRE LANE

From Alfriston town center, join the Way behind the Star Inn, on High St. (the *only* street), and continue 7 mi. to **Southease** among hills so green and vast that one might fear Julie Andrews is lurking tunefully over the next ridge. The slopes here are fairly gentle and not terribly strenuous. The Way directly crosses **Firle Beacon,** with a mound at the top said to contain a giant's silver coffin. Reaching Southease, proceed north ¾ mi. to **Rodmell.** More Merchant-Ivory film set than town, Rodmell's single street contains **Monk's House,** home of Leonard and Virginia Woolf from 1919 until their deaths. The house retains its intimacy and most of the original furnishings. The faithful can retrace the writer's last steps to the River Ouse (1 mi. away), where she committed "the one experience I shall never describe"; her ashes nourish a fig tree in the garden. (Call the **National Trust** office for more info ☎(01892) 890 651. Open Apr.-Oct. W and Sa 2-5:30pm. £3, children £1.50, families £16.) The **Abergavenny Arms ❶** (☎(01273) 472 416) is a good place to fuel up for the 2 mi. between Rodmell and the **YHA Telscombe** (see p. 168).

The closest that the Way actually comes to **Lewes** (LEW-is) is at the village of **Kingston** to the southwest—here is where hikers from **Brighton** should pick up the trail, perhaps after tucking in to some pub grub at **Juggs Inn ❶** (☎ (01273) 472 523). A stone at the parish boundary, called **Nan Kemp's Corner,** feeds one of the more macabre Downs legends: townspeople whisper that Nan, jealous of her husband's affection for their newborn, roasted it for him to eat, then killed herself at the site of the present stone. After shaking off the willies, continue from Kingston on an 8 mi. stretch to **Pyecombe,** which brings you to **Ditchling Beacon,** the highest point in East Sussex's Downs. The hill was one in a series that relayed the message of the defeat of the Spanish Armada to Elizabeth I. If you've come all the way from Telscombe, **YHA Brighton** (see p. 172), 2 mi. from Pyecombe, offers a night's respite.

Ambling out from Pyecombe to **Upper Beeding** (8 mi.) takes you to **Devil's Dyke,** a dramatic chalk cliff that looks like a hillside cross section. Local legend says that the Dyke was built by Lucifer himself in a diabolical, but ultimately unsuccessful, attempt to let the sea into the Weald and float away all the churches. Climb through fields overrun with crimson poppies to reach the **YHA Truleigh Hill** (p. 168), just 1½ mi. east of Upper Beeding. On the path from Upper Beeding to **Washington** (6¾ mi.) lies the grove of **Chanctonbury Ring**—trees planted in the 18th century around a 3rd-century Roman template, built on a previous Celtic layout.

Completing the 6½ mi. trek from Washington to **Amberley** brings you to a path leading to **Burpham,** from which the **YHA Warningcamp** (in Arundel, see p. 178) is 3 mi. away. Find a quick Burpham dinner at the **George and Dragon ❶** (☎ (01903) 883 131). The 19 mi. of orchids and spiked rampion fields from Amberley to **Buriton,** passing through **Cocking,** complete the Way to the northwest. Southward, across the River Arun to **Littleton Down,** are views of the Weald and the North Downs. The spire of Chichester Cathedral marks the beginning of **Forty Acre Lane,** the Way's final arm, which touches the West Sussex-Hampshire border.

BRIGHTON   ☎ 01273

In Lydia's imagination, a visit to Brighton comprised every possibility of earthly happiness.
    —Jane Austen, *Pride and Prejudice*

The undisputed home of the dirty weekend, Brighton (pop. 180,000) relishes its reputation for the risqué. According to legend, the future King George IV sidled into Brighton around 1784 for some hanky-panky. Having staged a fake wedding with a certain "Mrs. Jones" (Maria Fitzherbert), he headed off to the farmhouse known today as the Royal Pavilion, and the regal rumpus began. Since then, Brighton has turned a blind eye to some of the more scandalous activities that occur along its shores, as holiday-goers and locals alike peel it off—all off—at England's first bathing beach. Kemp Town (jokingly known as Camp Town), among other areas, has a thriving gay and lesbian population, while the immense student crowd, augmented by flocks of foreign youth purportedly learning English, feeds the notorious clubbing scene of this "London-by-the-Sea."

▐▛ TRANSPORTATION

Trains: Brighton Station, uphill at the northern end of Queen's Rd. Ticket office open 24hr. Travel center open M-Sa 8:15am-6pm. **Trains** (☎ (08457) 484 950) from: **Arun-**

del (50min., 3 per hr., £6.50); **London** (1¼hr., 6 per hr., £11.90); **Portsmouth** (1½hr., every hr., £11.70); **Rye** (1½hr., every hr., £11.30).

Buses: Pool Valley, at the southern edge of Old Steine. Tickets and info at **One Stop Travel,** 16 Old Steine (☎700 406). Open M-F 8:30am-5:45pm, Sa 9am-5pm; June-Sept. also Su 11am-4:30pm. **National Express** (☎(08705) 808 080) from **London** (2hr., 15 per day, £8 return).

Public Transportation: Local buses operated by **Brighton and Hove** (☎886 200) congregate around Old Steine. The TIC can give route and price information for most buses; all carriers charge £1 in the central area.

Taxis: Brighton Taxis (☎202 020). 24hr.

Bike Rental: Freedom Bikes, 45 George St. (☎681 698). £10 per day, £50 per week. £50 deposit. Open M-Sa 9:30am-5:30pm. Waterfront vendors also rent small watercraft, bikes, and in-line skates, but prices are higher and quality somewhat lower.

■ ORIENTATION

Queen's Rd. connects the train station to the English Channel, becoming **West St.** at the intersection with **Western St.** halfway down the slope. Funky stores and alternative restaurants cluster around **Trafalgar St.**, which runs east from the train station. The narrow streets of **the Lanes**, a pedestrian shopping area, provide an anarchic setting for Brighton's nighttime carousing; head east onto **North St.** from **Queen's Rd.** to reach them. **Old Steine,** a road and a square, runs in front of the **Royal Pavilion,** while **King's Rd.** parallels the waterfront.

■ PRACTICAL INFORMATION

Tourist Information Centre: 10 Bartholomew Sq. (☎(0906) 711 2255; fax 292 595; www.visitbrighton.com). Enthusiastic staff vends materials on practically every subject, books National Express tickets, and reserves rooms for £1 plus a 10% deposit. Open M-F 9am-5pm, Sa 10am-5pm; Mar.-Oct. also Su 10am-4pm.

Tours: Walking tours leave from the TIC June-Aug. £3. **Guide Friday** (☎746 205) gives 1hr. bus tours departing from Palace Pier, the train station, and a few other sites. 2 per hr. £7, concessions £5.50, children £3, families £16.50.

Financial Services: Banks line North St., near Old Steine. **Thomas Cook,** 58 North St. (☎325 711). Open M-Tu and Th-Sa 9am-5:30pm, W 10am-5:30pm. **American Express,** 82 North St. (☎321 242). Open M-Tu and Th-Sa 9am-5pm, W 9:30am-5pm.

Disabled Information: Snowdon House, 3 Rutland Gdns., Hove (☎203 016). Open M-F 10am-4pm. The **TIC** has a phenomenal printout detailing local services.

Gay/Lesbian Information & Services: Lesbian and Gay Switchboard, 6 Bartholomews, Brighton (☎204 050). Open daily 5pm-11pm. The **TIC** also offers an extensive list of gay-friendly accommodations, clubs, and shops.

Launderette: 5 Palace Rd. (☎327 972). Open daily 8am-8pm.

Police: John St. (☎(0845) 607 0999).

Hospital: Royal Sussex County, Eastern Rd. (☎696 955), parallel to Marine Parade.

Internet Access: SprachCaffe, 5 Preston St. (☎ 323 161 ext. 424). 50p per 15min., £1 per 30min, £2.40 per hr. Students £1.20 per hr. Open daily 10am-10pm. **Pursuit Internet,** Preston St. (☎823 282). Before noon and 5-10pm 4p per min., noon-5pm 5p.; students 3p/4p. Open daily 10am-10pm. **Library,** Church St. (☎296 971), across from the Brighton Museum. Free. 1hr. max. Book ahead. Open M and Th-F 9:30am-5pm, Tu 9:30am-7pm, Sa 9:30am-4pm.

Post Office: 51 Ship St. (☎573 209), off Prince Albert St. **Bureau de change.** Open M-Sa 9am-5:30pm. **Post Code:** BN1 1BA.

ACCOMMODATIONS

Brighton's best budget beds are in its four **hostels.** The city's **B&Bs** and cheaper **hotels** begin at £18-20 and skyrocket from there. Many mid-range B&Bs line **Madeira Pl.;** the shabbier establishments collect west of **West Pier** and east of **Palace Pier.** To the east and running perpendicular to the sea, **Kemp Town** boasts a huge number of B&Bs. Rooms may be cheaper in the **Hove** area, just west of Brighton. Frequent conventions make rooms scarce—book early or consult the TIC. The TIC also keeps a list of guest houses owned and operated by gays or lesbians.

Baggies Backpackers, 33 Oriental Pl. (☎733 740; guest phone 203 611). Go past West Pier along King's Rd.; Oriental Pl. is on the right. Live music, spontaneous parties/potlucks, and exquisite murals set the tone for this mellow hostel. Talking, singing, and drinking in the candlelit lounge beats a seedy club-hop. 50 beds in spacious dorms; some doubles. Kitchen and laundry. Key deposit £5. Dorms £11; doubles £27. ❷

Hotel Pelirocco, 10 Regency Sq. (☎327 055). Rock-star longings fulfilled at over-the-top, hip-to-be-camp Pelirocco. Each of 19 individually themed swanky rooms (try leopard-print "Betty's Boudoir") houses a PlayStation2 and private bath. Downstairs bar open until 4am on weekends. 4 different breakfast options, including cinnamon french toast with fresh fruit. Singles £50-55; twins £85-100; doubles £85-125. ❹

Cavalaire Guest House, 34 Upper Rock Gdns. (☎696 899; fax 600 504). Comfortable rooms, all with TV and CD player, are ideal for a lazy weekend. Wonderful breakfasts, from tropical to vegetarian. Internet £5 per hr. Singles £29; doubles £65-70. ❸

Brighton Backpackers Hostel, 75-76 Middle St. (☎777 717; stay@brightonbackpackers.com). Lively, international flavor and great location. Surround-speakers and pool table make the downstairs lounge an all-night party, Internet access and satellite TV upstairs further the social atmosphere. The quieter **annex** faces the ocean. Inexpensive meals. Kitchen and laundry. Dorms £11-12, weekly £60-65; doubles £25-30. ❷

YHA Brighton, Patcham Pl. (☎556 196). 4 mi. north on the London Rd; take Patcham bus #5 or 5A from Old Steine (stop E) to the Black Lion Hotel (£1.40). Georgian country house filled with friendly staff. Good jumping-off point for the South Downs Way (see p. 166), but not the place if you want to party late. Laundry. Lockout 10am-1pm. Curfew 11pm. Book ahead July-Aug. Closed Jan. Dorms £11, under 18 £7. ❷

Court Craven Hotel, 2 Atlingworth St. (☎607 710), off Marine Parade. A well-decorated guest house in Kemp Town for gay and lesbian travelers. Clean and elegant, with a bar and deluxe kitchen. Reserve well ahead. Singles £25; doubles £50; prices vary. ❸

The Langham, 16-17 Charlotte St. (☎682 123; www.langhambrighton.co.uk), off Marine Parade. 20 rooms connected by ultra-pink hallways just steps from the Channel. Hotel quality for B&B prices. Singles Su-Th £25, F-Sa £35; doubles £48/£60; triples £66/£80; quads £80/£100. ❸

Nineteen, 19 Broad Street (☎675 529; www.hotelnineteen.co.uk). Stylish Kemp Town B&B. Enormous beds on glass platforms and a continuously rotating selection of artwork pose in 7 uber-modern doubles. Champagne breakfasts complete the picture. £50-£75 per person, depending on season. ❹

Friese Greene, 20 Middle St. (☎747 551). Bohemian, family-run hostel in the heart of Brighton's nightlife attracts seasoned travelers, many of whom stay on. And on. £5 deposit for key and linen. Laundry, kitchen, pool, and TV. Dorms £11, weekly £55. ❷

Brighton

▲ **ACCOMMODATIONS**
Baggies Backpackers, **3**
Brighton Backpackers, **18**
Cavalaire Guest House, **25**
Court Craven Hotel, **26**
Friese Greene, **14**
Hotel Pelirocco, **6**
The Langham, **27**
Nineteen, **23**
YHA Brighton, **1**

◆ **FOOD**
The Blue Nile, **4**
Bombay Aloo, **10**
Crepe Dentelle, **5**
Nia Cafe, **2**
One Paston Place, **28**

📖 **PUBS**
Font and Firkin, **12**
Fortune of War, **20**
Mash Tun, **9**
Queen's Arms, **22**
Smugglers, **19**
Squid, **16**
Ye Olde King and Queen, **8**

★ **CLUBS**
The Beach, **21**
Casablanca, **13**
Club New York, **7**
Event II, **17**
Paradox, **15**
Zanzibar, **24**

SOUTH ENGLAND

Bristol Rd.
Charlotte St.
Ashlingworth St.
Marine Parade
Upper Rock Gdns.
St. James's Ave.
St. James's St.
New Steine
Margaret
Wentworth
Devonshire Pl.
Chapel St.
High St.
Camelford
Broad St.
Madeira Pl.
Charles St.
Manchester St.
Sea Life Centre
One Stop
Travel Safeway
St. James's St.
Old Steine
Dorset Gdns.
George St.
Edward St.
Prince's St.
Black St.
White St.
Mighell St.
Carlton Hill
John St.
Tarner Rd.
Elmore Rd.
Sussex St.
John St.
Ashton Rise
Richmond St.
Albion Hill
Grove St.
Belgrave St.
Lewes St.
Newark St.
Southover St.
Richmond Ter.
Albion St.
Richmond Pl.
St. Peter's
Ditchling Rd.
York Pl.
St. George's Pl.
Gloucester St.
Grand Parade
VICTORIA GARDENS
Morley St.
Ivory Pl.
Circus St.
William St.
John St.
Marlborough Pl.
North Pl.
Cheltenham Pl.
London Rd.
Cheapside
Pelham St.
Whitecross S
Blackman St.
Trafalgar St.
Sydney St.
Vine St.
Kensington Gardens
Gloucester Rd.
Kensington Pl.
Upper Gardner St.
Gardner St.
Regent St.
Tichborne St.
Brighton Museum & Art Gallery
The Dome
Royal Pavilion
Theatre Royal
Komedia
New Rd.
CASTLE SQ.
East St.
Bond St.
Castle St.
Brighton Toy & Model Museum
Brighton Railway Station
Station St.
Terminus Rd.
Railway St.
Guildford Rd.
Surrey St.
Frederick Pl.
Gloucester Pl.
Frederick St.
Over St.
Kemp St.
Trafalgar Ln.
Foundry St.
Bread St.
Spring Gdns.
North Rd.
Portland St.
Windsor St.
Church St.
Kew St.
New Dorset St.
North Gdns.
Queen's Rd.
Clifton St.
Buckingham Rd.
Centurion Rd.
North St.
Ship St.
Meeting House Ln.
THE LANES
Prince Albert St.
Black Lion St.
Market St.
BARTHOLOMEW SQ.
King's Rd.
Grand Junction Rd.
Beachfront
Fishing Museum
King's Rd. / Arches
West St.
South St.
Middle St.
Boyce St.
Dukes Ln.
Ship St.
Duke St.
West Hill St.
West Hill Rd.
Compton Ave.
Buckingham Rd.
St. Nicholas Rd.
Alfred Rd.
Albert Rd.
Dyke Rd.
Regent Hill
Upper North St.
Clifton Terr.
Clifton Rd.
Clifton Hill
Powis Grove
Vine Pl.
St. Nicholas
Regency Row
QUEEN SQ.
Clock Tower
CHURCHILL SQ.
Brighton Centre
Russell Rd.
Cannon Pl.
Russell Pl.
CLARENCE SQ.
RUSSELL SQ.
Western Rd.
Crown St.
Dean St.
Spring St.
Marlborough St.
Stone St.
Castle St.
Preston St.
REGENCY SQ.
Grand Hotel
King's Rd.
Powis Rd.
POWIS SQ.
St. Michael's Pl.
Victoria St.
Montpelier St.
Montpelier Ter.
Montpelier Villas
Montpelier Pl.
Montpelier Rd.
Denmark Terr.
Clifton Hill
Vernon Terr.
Victoria Rd.
Windlesham Rd.
Windlesham Ave.
York Ave.
Temple Gardens
Norfolk Terr.
Montpelier Pl.
Temple St.
Borough St.
Norfolk Rd.
Bedford St.
BEDFORD SQ.
Oriental Pl.
Sillwood Pl.
Sillwood Rd.
Little Preston St.
Sillwood St.
West Pier

English Channel

Community Base

0 500 yards
0 500 meters

N

LG

TO (3mi)
TO (28)

THE HIDDEN DEAL

FOOD FOR FRIENDS

Meal deals are the word at this continually packed vegetarian joint, where the portions are large and the flavors intense. Arteries hardened by weeks of traditional English breakfasts will be ready for a second wind if you treat them to a "Greek breakfast" of yogurt and honey (£1.75), muesli with yogurt and fruit (£2.25), or the whole-grain- and fruit-oriented Breakfast Taster (£4.75).

Come lunchtime, fish and chips are out, and tarts and veggie risottos are definitely in. The Taster Max entitles you to a heaping plate of all the hot food they've got on display, for the amicable price of £6.95. Or pare it down to a truly friendly £5 for the Taster Trio.

And should you start to feel a little TOO responsible in your eating habits, not to worry—there are plenty of desserts to finish off, most dolloped with soy cream on request. You and your stomach will be best buddies again after a meal at Brighton's Food for Friends. (*17a-18a Prince Albert St. ☎ 202 310. Open M-Sa 8am-10pm, Su 9:15am-10pm.*)

☐ FOOD

Except for the picks below, the Lanes area is full of suspiciously trendy places waiting to gobble tourist cash. The chippers along the beach or north of the Lanes offer better value. Get groceries at **Safeway**, 6 St. James's St. (☎570 363. Open M-Sa 8am-9pm, Su 11am-5pm.) Sate sugar cravings with **Brighton Rock Candy**, available at any of the multitude of shops claiming to have invented it.

◪ **Crepe Dentelle,** 65 Preston St. (☎323 224). Sweet or savory crepes (£3-5) and galettes (meal crepes, £5.50-9); non-crepe entrees and extensive wine and (French) beer list. Takeaway 20% less. Open M-F 10am-3pm and 6-10pm, Sa-Su noon-10pm. ❷

Nia Cafe, 87 Trafalgar St. (☎671 371). Generous helpings (£4-8) are the norm in this hip cafe near the Laine. Open daily 10am-8pm. MC/V. ❷

Bombay Aloo, 39 Ship St. (☎776 038). Pure buffet and purely vegetarian at this inventive Indian restaurant. £5 all-you-can-eat from 18 steaming vats (£3.50 from 3:15-5:15pm). Entrees £3-7. Open noon-midnight. ❶

The Blue Nile, 17 Preston St. (☎326 003). Gently spiced Sudanese meats and stews with names more outlandish than their flavors. Entrees £5-7; wash it all down with a huge glass of mango juice (£1.50). Open daily 6pm-10pm. ❷

One Paston Place, 1 Paston Place (☎606 933). Exquisitely prepared French dishes for holiday-goers more interested in pampering than partying. Adventurous eaters can start with veal sweetbreads (£11); entrees are generally meat-centered and hover around £22. Open noon-3pm and from 6pm. ❺

☉ ☐ SIGHTS AND BEACHES

In 1750, Dr. Richard Russell wrote a treatise on the merits of drinking seawater and bathing in brine to treat glandular disease; before then, sea-swimming was thought nearly suicidal. Thus began the transformation of the sleepy village of Brighthelmstone into a fashionable town with a decidedly hedonistic bent.

ROYAL PAVILION. Perhaps it's wrong to reduce an entire city to one of its parts, but the proudly extravagant Royal Pavilion may be credited with much of Brighton's present gaudiness. George IV enlisted architect John Nash to turn an ordinary farm villa into an Oriental/Indian/Gothic/Georgian wunderhouse. Rumor has it that George wept tears of joy upon entering it, proving that wealth does not give one taste. After living there for a month, Queen Victoria decided to have it demolished—proving that wealth does not deny one taste—until the town offered to buy the royal playground. Enjoy the pavilion from the surrounding parks by renting a deck chair (£1), or take in the view and a sandwich at **Queen Adelaide's Tea Room.** (☎ 290 900. Open June-Sept. daily 10am-6pm; Oct.-May 10am-5pm. Tours 11:30am and 2:30pm, £1.25. Audio tour £1. Admission £5.20, concessions £3.75, children £3.20.)

BRIGHTON PIER AND OTHER PIERS. The gaudiness permeates to the beachfront, where the relatively new Brighton Pier, England's fourth largest tourist attraction, has slot machines, video games, and condom dispensers galore, with a roller coaster thrown in for good measure. **Volk's Railway,** Britain's first 3 ft. gauge electric train, shuttles along the waterfront. (☎ 681 061. Open Apr.-Sept. daily 11am-6pm. £1.50, children £1.) The **Grand Hotel,** King's Rd., home to many political conventions, has been rebuilt since a 1984 IRA bombing that killed five but left Margaret Thatcher unscathed. Farther along, the once lavish, now decrepit **West Pier** lies abandoned out in the sea. Full-scale renovation was set to begin in the spring of 1999, but the abrupt collapse of part of the pier put a wrinkle in the plans. (☎ 207 610. West Pier tour M-F 1:30pm; Sa-Su noon, 1:30, 3pm. £10, concessions £7.50.) A short walk along the coast past West Pier leads to the smaller community of **Hove.**

DOWN BY THE SEA. Brighton's main attraction is, of course, the beach, but those who associate the word "beach" with sand and sun may be sorely disappointed. The weather can be quite nippy even in June and July, and the closest thing to sand here are fist-sized brown rocks. Fortunately, turquoise waters, hordes of bikini-clad beachgoers, and umbrella-adorned drinks aplenty allow delusions of the tropics to persist. To visit **Telescombe Beach,** 4½ mi. east of Palace Pier, follow the sign for "Telescombe Cliffs" at the Telescombe Tavern.

BRIGHTON MUSEUM AND ART GALLERY. More edifying than most of the town's attractions, this recently renovated gallery features paintings, pottery, and Art Deco and Art Nouveau collections, as well as an extensive Brighton historical exhibit that fully explicates the phrase "dirty weekend." In the fine **Willett Collection of Pottery,** postmodern porcelains and neolithic relics simultaneously reflect the varied faces of this seaside escape. (Church St., around the corner from the Pavilion. ☎ 290 900. Open Tu 10am-7pm, W-Sa 10am-5pm, Su 2pm-5pm. Free.)

LANES AND LAINES. Small fishermen's cottages once thrived in the Lanes, a jumble of 17th-century streets (some no wider than 3 ft.) south of North St. in the heart of Old Brighton. Now filled with overpriced antique jewelry shops, the Lanes have lost some of their charm. Those looking for fresher shopping opportunities—as well as a more of-the-moment atmosphere—should head to **North Laines,** off Trafalgar St., where alternative merchandise and colorful cafes dominate. On Saturdays, the area is closed to traffic and cafe tables and street performers take over.

OTHER SIGHTS. Although England's largest aquarium has freed its dolphins, many other creatures remain at the **Sea Life Centre,** trapped in glass tanks for your viewing pleasure. (Marine Parade, near Palace Pier. ☎ 604 234. Open daily 9am-5pm, last admission 4pm. £7, seniors £5, children £4.50.) If you'd like to change gaudy for godly, head to **St. Nicholas's Church,** on Dyke Rd., which dates from 1370. Its baptismal font is thought to be the most beautiful Norman carving in Sussex. **St. Bartholomew's Church,** on Ann St., was originally called "The Barn" or "Noah's Ark"—one look at it and you'll see why. This obscure hiccup of Victorian genius rises to 134 ft., higher than Westminster Abbey. (Take bus #5, 5A, or 5B from Old Steine.)

SOUTH ENGLAND

� 🎵 NIGHTLIFE & ENTERTAINMENT

For info on hot-and-happening scenes, check *The Punter*, a monthly found at pubs, newsagents, and record stores, which details evening events, or *What's On*, a poster-sized flyer found at record stores and pubs. **Gay and lesbian** venues can be found in the latest issues of *Gay Times* (£2.75), available at newsstands; *What's On* also highlights gay-friendly events.

The City Council spent £5 million installing surveillance equipment along the seafront and major streets to ensure safety during late-night partying, but still try to avoid walking alone late at night through Brighton's spaghetti-style streets. **The Lanes,** in particular, can be a bit too deserted for comfort. **Night buses** N97-99 run infrequently but reliably in the early morning, picking up passengers at Old Steine and in front of many clubs, usually hitting each spot twice between 1 and 2:30am (£2.50). 24hr. **cabs** are a more expensive option.

PUBS

J.B. Priestley once noted that Brighton was "a fine place either to restore your health, or… to ruin it again"; the city's sea of alcohol presents ample opportunity to demonstrate the latter. The waterfront between West Pier and Brighton Pier is particularly good for reveling. This is a student town, and where there are students there are cheap drinks. Many pubs offer fantastic specials during the week—some budget-minded travelers find no reason to go out into the crowds on weekends.

🔲 **Mash Tun,** 1 Church St. (☎ 684 951). Alternative pub attracts an eclectic student crowd with "friendly food, tasty barstaff; real music, groovy ales." Sample their hot chocolate and dark rum concoction (£2.90). Open M-Sa noon-11pm, Su noon-10:30pm. MC/V.

Fortune of War, 157 King's Road Arches (☎ 205 065), beneath King's Rd. by the beach. Grab a Guinness and relax on the sand—the spot to be at sunset. Open M-Sa 10:30am-11pm, Su 11am-10:30pm.

Font and Firkin, Union St., the Lanes (☎ 747 727). The altar in this former parish house now honors the gods of rock. Worshipers libate many a pint of ale and are rewarded for their devotion by a monthly **Elvis appearance.** Live entertainment W and F-Sa. Food served until 8:30pm. Open M-Sa noon-11pm, Su noon-10:30pm. MC/V.

Squid, 78 Middle St. (☎ 727 114). Next door to Brighton Backpackers hostel and linked to Zap Club. Packed with pre-clubbers. Open M-Sa 5-11pm, Su 5-10:30pm.

Queen's Arms, 8 George St. (☎ 696 873). Draws an enthusiastic gay and lesbian crowd with Sa night cabaret. Fairly inexpensive pints (£2.30). Entertainment nightly; check the board outside. Open M-Sa 1-11pm, Su 2-10:30pm.

Ye Olde King and Queen, Marlborough Pl. (☎ 607 207). TV football, groovy dance floor, beautiful beer garden, and multiple bars. Open M-Sa 11am-11pm, Su noon-10:30pm.

Smugglers, 10 Ship St. A pirate's den with a techno beat. Bedsteads, 2 dance floors, velvet couches, and vodka-bottle chandeliers make this pub raucous, to say the least. Pints £1.60. Happy hour M-F noon-8pm. Open M-Sa noon-11pm, Su 7:30-10:30pm.

CLUBS

Brighton is the hometown of Norman Cook, better known as Fatboy Slim, and major dance record label Skint Records—it should come as no surprise that these Brightonians know a thing or two about dance music. Most clubs are open M-Sa 9pm-2am; after 2am the party moves to the waterfront. Like pubs, many clubs have student discounts on weeknights and higher covers ($4-10) on weekends.

The Beach, 171-181 King's Rd. Arches (☎ 722 272). Adds monstrous big beat to the music on the shore. Fatboy Slim still mixes here some F nights, when queues begin at 8-9pm. Also open for daytime drinks and snacks (noon-2pm). Cover £4-10, Th free before 11pm. A student ID will pare down weeknight cover.

Casablanca, Middle St. (☎ 321 817). Plays live jazz, funk, and Latin tunes to a mix of students and late-twentysomethings. Get ready to sweat it again, Sam.

Event II, West St. (☎ 732 627). Among the most technically armed (over £1 million spent on dance-floor trimmings) and massively populated (crammed with a down-from-London crowd looking for thrills). Experienced Brighton clubbers tend to go for less conventional venues, but all agree it's great for a no-surprises good time.

Zanzibar, 129 St. James's St. (☎ 622 100). Gay clubbers flock to zany Zanzibar for fun nightly entertainment and a constant flow of brew. Check the billing outside for the week's special events.

Club New York, 11 Dyke Rd. (☎ 208 678). A bit off the beaten track—offers a refreshing change of pace from more mainstream, techno-oriented clubs. Upstairs, it's salsa night every night, downstairs plays everything from rock and indie to traditional African beats.

Paradox, West St. (☎ 321 628). Perhaps the paradox is that, despite its commercialism, this remains one of Brighton's mainstays. Monthly "Wild Fruit" gay night is popular among people of all persuasions.

MUSIC, THEATER, AND FESTIVALS

Brighton Centre, King's Rd. (☎ 290 131), and **The Dome,** 29 New Rd. (☎ 709 709), host Brighton's biggest events, from Chippendales shows to music concerts. (Both offices open M-Sa 10am-5:30pm. TIC also sells tickets.) Local plays and touring London productions take the stage at the **Theatre Royal** on New Rd., a Victorian beauty with a plush interior. (☎ 328 488. Tickets £6-20. Open M-Sa 10am-8pm.) **Komedia,** on Gardner St., houses a cafe, bar, theater, comedy club, and cabaret. (☎ 647 100; tickets@komedia.co.uk. Tickets £5-8; discounts available. Standby tickets 15min. before curtain. Box office open daily 10am until start of last show.)

The **Brighton Festival** (☎ 292 950, box office 709 709), held each May, is one of the largest festivals in England, celebrating music, film, and other art forms. Gays and lesbians celebrate the concurrent **Brighton Pride Festival** (☎ 730 562). For more info or a program of events, contact the TIC.

◤ DAYTRIPS FROM BRIGHTON

LEWES. The historic town of Lewes, second home to Thomas Paine, has an appealing location in the Sussex chalklands and makes a perfect jumping-off point for **South Downs Way** trails (see p. 166). The views from the flower-strewn ruins of the Norman **Lewes Castle,** High St., 5min. northwest of the train station, merit a visit. (☎ (01273) 486 290. Open M-Sa 10am-5:30pm or dusk, Su 11am-5:30pm or dusk. £4.20, concessions £3.70, children £2.10.) The 15th-century **Anne of Cleves House Museum,** Southover High St., 15min. from the castle, celebrates Henry VIII Wife #4, the clever woman who not only managed to leave Henry with her head on her shoulders, but got to keep the house as well. (Trains from Brighton's Queen's Rd. station (return £3) leave for Lewes every 10min. ☎ (01273) 474 610. Open Feb.-Oct. M-Sa 10am-5pm, Su noon-5pm; Nov.-Feb. Tu, Th and Sa 10am-5pm. £2.80, children £1.40. Castle and Museum combination ticket £5.80, concessions £5, children £2.80, families £14.)

THE CHARLESTON FARMHOUSE. The country retreat of the Bloomsbury Group originally lacked amenities such as electricity and a telephone, but nevertheless became a center for literary, artistic, and intellectual life in Britain. Frequent guests included art theorist Clive Bell, novelist Virginia Woolf, and economist John Maynard Keynes, who terrorized the help with his "time experiments," setting all the clocks off an hour. On Fridays, visitors may sneak a peak at Vanessa Bell's studio and take longer guided tours. *(East of Lewes, off the A27. Take bus #125 from the Lewes station (6 per day).* ☎ *(01323) 811 265. Open July-Aug. W-Sa 11:30am-6pm, Su 2-6pm; Apr.-June and Sept.-Oct. W-Su 2-6pm. Last admission 5pm. £6, concessions £4.50 (W and Th only); Connoisseur Fridays £7. Garden only £2.50, children £1.)*

ARUNDEL ☎ 01903

Adorable Arundel sits in the shadow of towers and spires, but the town refuses to let them dim its character. Most visitors do come drawn by the fairytale castle, wearisome antique shops do clutter the winding streets, and yet travelers will find that the town's storybook beauty stems less from souvenir shops than from the rippling River Arun and the idyllic hillside location—a perfect place from which to explore the surrounding countryside and the **South Downs Way** (see p. 166).

🖅 📍 TRANSPORTATION AND PRACTICAL INFORMATION

Trains (☎ (08457) 484 950) arrive from: **Brighton** (1hr., 3 per hr., £6.10); **Chichester** (20min., 2 per hr., £3.40); **London Victoria** (1½hr.; 2 per hr.; £12, day return £16.10); **Portsmouth** (50min., every hr., £7.40). Many routes require connections at **Littlehampton** to the south or **Barnham** to the west. **Buses** stop across from the Norfolk Arms on High St., and come from **Littlehampton** (#702, 1-2 per hr.). **South Downs Cycle Hire** is 3 mi. east of Arundel on Blakehurst Farm. (☎ 889 562. £7 per half-day, £10 per day.) Call **Castle Cars** (☎ 884 444) for a **taxi.**

The friendly **tourist information centre**, 61 High St., dispenses the free *Town Guide* and information on the South Downs Way. (☎ 882 268. Open Easter-Oct. M 9:30am-5pm, Tu-Su 9am-5pm; Oct.-Easter daily 10am-3pm.) Other services include: **Lloyds TSB**, 14 High St. (☎ 717 221; open M-F 9:30am-4:30pm); **police** (☎ (0845) 607 0999), on the Causeway; **post office**, 2-4 High St. (☎ 882 113; open M-F 9am-5:30pm, Sa 9am-12:30pm). **Post Code:** BN18 9AA.

🏠 ACCOMMODATIONS AND CAMPING

B&Bs are consistent with Arundel's elegance, and priced accordingly (singles £25-30). Reserve ahead in summer to avoid anxiety and a severe wallet-gouging. The TIC posts an up-to-date list of vacancies.

Arundel House, 11 High St. (☎ 882 136; arundelhouse@btinternet.com). Moderately priced with immoderate luxuries, including 400-year-old architecture and an incredible location. Singles, doubles, and twins all have bathrooms and TVs. £20 per person. ❸

Arden House, 4 Queens Ln. (☎ 882 544). 8 rosy rooms, some with wood-beamed ceilings, in a convenient location. Singles £25-30; doubles £40, with bath £44. ❸

YHA Warningcamp (☎ 882 204; fax 870 615), ½ mi. out of town. Turn left from the train station and right on the public footpath (signposted). Follow the River Arun, cross the railroad tracks, then go through the gate and make a left. Family- and group-oriented accommodations in a Georgian house with aqua-green interior. Huge kitchen and laundry facilities. Lockout 10am-5pm. Curfew 11pm. Open July-Aug. daily; Sept.-Oct. Tu-Sa;

Nov.-Dec. F-Sa; Apr.-June M-Sa. Dorms £9.50, under 18 £6.50. Camping £4. ❶

Camping: Ship and Anchor Site (☎(01243) 551 262), 2 mi. from Arundel on Ford Rd. along the River Arun. Inglorious field with pub and shops nearby. Open Apr.-Sept. £3.50 per person, children £1.75. £1.50 per vehicle. Showers free. ❶

🏷 FOOD

Arundel's pubs and tea shops are generally expensive and unremarkable. A few fruit and bread peddlers line High St. and Tarrant St. **Alldays,** 17 Queen St., sells groceries practically... all day. (Open M-Sa 6:30am-11pm, Su 7:30am-11pm.)

Country Life Cafe, Tarrant Sq. (☎883 456). A pubbish atmosphere with quality vegetarian, vegan, and traditional English (read: none of the above) options for around £4. Open M-W and F-Sa 10:30am-5pm, Su 11am-5pm. ❶

White Hart, 12 Queen St. (☎882 374). Serves pub grub and local ales (pints £2.20). Entrees, though slightly pricey (£7-8), are good; seek out homemade specials and vegetarian selections. Open M-F 11am-3pm and 5:30-11pm, Sa-Su 11am-11pm. Food served M-Sa noon-2:30pm and 6:30pm-9pm, Su noon-2:20pm and 7pm-8:30pm. ❷

Belinda's, 13 Tarrant St. (☎882 977). Locals frequent this 16th-century tearoom for its large selection of traditional English fare. Linger over cream teas (£2) and Belinda's famous homemade jam. Open Tu-Sa 9am-5pm, Su 11am-5:30pm. ❶

Castle Tandoori, 3 Mill Ln. (☎884 224). Dishes out standard, spicy Indian cuisine for about £10 per entree. Open daily noon-2:30pm and 6pm-midnight. ❸

📷 🌸 SIGHTS AND FESTIVALS

Poised above town like the backdrop of a Disney flick, **Arundel Castle** is lord of the skyline. The castle, hereditary seat of the Dukes of Norfolk, was built in the 11th century, restored piecemeal in the 18th and 19th centuries, and may be the best-preserved castle in the land. Winding passages and 131 steps lead to the keep, with breathtaking vistas of the town below and the emerald countryside beyond. The long, lovely library, meticulously carved in the late 18th century, along with the family chapel, will make you want to marry nobility (the Earl of Arundel, current resident, is taken, so don't ask). Note the graphically termed death warrant served against one of the Norfolk Dukes by agreeable Elizabeth I, and be sure to take a cream tea (£4) among the flowers in the cas-

THE BIG SPLURGE

FIT FOR A KING: A NIGHT AT THE NORFOLK ARMS

Attention latter-day knights and ladies: if the grandeur of Arundel Castle leaves you feeling that your own furnishings are somewhat less than your inner princess demands, you might want to treat yourself to an evening wandering the red carpets at the Norfolk Arms Hotel.

Each enormous room includes all the practical trimmings (like TV and tea and coffee), then goes the extra mile with four-poster beds, luxurious private bathrooms, and an electric trouser press. Amid the gentle ticking of a grandfather clock, guests relax in brocade chairs beneath chandeliers in the elaborate tearoom. Later they take their three-course dinner (£18.50) on bright white tablecloths in the hotel restaurant.

Unique to the hotel is its pet-friendly policy: not only are cats and dogs welcome, but the hotel stocks vittles for them. (High St. ☎882 101; norfolkarms@forestdale.com. 34 ensuite rooms. Check-in after 2pm. Check-out noon. Singles £70; doubles £110.)

tle's Tea Garden, on the grounds near the carpark. (☎882 173. Open Apr.-Oct. Su-F noon-5pm, last entry 4pm. £7.50, seniors £6.50, children £5, families £21. Grounds only £3.)

Along the river across from the castle, a placard recounts the troubled past of the monks of **Blackfriars,** the Dominican priory whose remains are nearby. Atop the same hill as Arundel Castle, the **Cathedral of Our Lady and St. Philip Howard** is more impressive for its French Gothic exterior than its fairly standard interior. During the May holiday of **Corpus Christi,** thousands of flowers are laid in a pattern stretching 93 ft. down the center aisle, a tradition dating to 1873. (☎882 297. Open summer daily 9am-6pm; winter 9am-dusk. Free.) Concealed observation blinds at the **Wildfowl and Wetlands Trust Centre,** less than a mile past the castle on Mill Rd., permit visitors to "come nose to beak with nature." Over 12,000 birds roost on 60 acres. (☎883 355. Open summer daily 9:30am-5pm; winter 9:30am-4:30pm. Last entry 1hr. before closing. £4.75, concessions £3.75, children £2.75.)

TREADING THE LINE Many can define the word "schism"—a division within a church—but few can describe what one looks like. Those few must have visited Arundel's **Parish Church of St. Nicholas** (☎882 262; open dawn-dusk), across from the cathedral. The church, built in 1380, straddles a property line such that when the Anglicans broke from the Roman Catholics, the western portion of the building fell under the Church of England's control, while the eastern portion remained property of the Catholic Duke of Norfolk. Hence, though the one side operates as a Protestant place of worship, the other, called the Fitzalan Chapel (accessible from castle grounds), remains a Catholic burial chamber. Today, a glass wall separates the halves, making St. Nicholas's England's only example of two faiths operating under one roof.

Right around the August bank holiday, the castle is the centerpiece of the **Arundel Festival,** ten days of musical, Shakespearean, and artistic shows. The **Festival Fringe** simultaneously offers free or inexpensive events. Tickets for both go on sale six to eight weeks ahead of time. (☎883 690; box office 883 474. Tickets up to £20.)

◆ DAYTRIP FROM ARUNDEL: PETWORTH HOUSE

Take the train to Pulborough (10min.) and walk the remaining 2 mi. to the house or catch bus #1. ☎(01798) 342 207. House open Apr.-Oct. M-W and Sa-Su 1-5:30pm, last admission 4:30pm; extra rooms shown M-W. Grounds open daily 8am-dusk. House and grounds £6, children £3. Grounds only £1.50, children free.

Situated among acres of sculpted lawns and gardens designed by Capability Brown, Petworth House has one of the UK's finest art collections. J.M.W. Turner often painted the house and landscape, and many of his works hang alongside canvases by Van Dyck, Bosch, Dahl, Reynolds, and a bevy of other paint-slingers. Petworth is also famous for the Petworth Chaucer, an early 15th-century manuscript of *Canterbury Tales,* and the intricate carvings in the legendary **Carving Room.**

CHICHESTER ☎ 01243

Confined for centuries within eroding Roman walls, the citizens of well-preserved Chichester take pride in their town's position as a center of English culture. The settlement still thrives on its markets (cattle, corn, and others), and all roads still lead to the ornate 16th-century Market Cross, but Chichester's chief attractions include one of the country's best theaters, an arts festival, a host of gallery exhibits, and a nearby summer motor-racing spectacular. The quirky cathedral provides more permanent delight, while the nearby Fishbourne Roman Palace is one of the better ancient attractions in the region.

TRANSPORTATION. Chichester is 45 mi. southwest of London and 15 mi. east of Portsmouth. **Trains** (☎(08457) 484 950) serve **Southgate station** from: **Brighton** (50min.; 2-3 per hr.; £7.80); **London Victoria** (1½hr.; 3 per hr.; £16.90, day return £17.20); **Portsmouth** (40min.; 2-3 per hr.; £4.80). The **bus station** (☎(01903) 237 661) is also on Southgate. **National Express** (☎(08705) 808 080) buses come from **London** (1 per day, return £9). **Stagecoach Coastline** buses connect Chichester with **Brighton** (#702, 3hr., 2 per hr., £4.60) and **Portsmouth** (#700-701, 1hr., 2 per hr., £4). An **Explorer** ticket grants a day's unlimited travel on bus service in southern England from Kent to Salisbury. (£5.25, seniors £3.85, children £2.60, families £10.50). For **taxis,** call **Central Cars of Chichester** (☎(0800) 789 432).

ORIENTATION AND PRACTICAL INFORMATION. Four Roman streets named for their compass directions divide Chichester into quadrants that converge at **Market Cross,** the main plaza. The **tourist information centre** is at 29a South St.; from the train station, exit left onto Southgate (which becomes South St.). Check the 24hr. computer terminal in the front window for accommodations or use the booking service inside. (☎775 888; www.chichester-web.co.uk. Open M-Sa 9:15am-5:15pm, July-Aug. also Su 10am-4pm.) **Guided tours** depart from the TIC. (May-Sept. Tu 11am, Sa 2:30pm. £2.) Other services include: **banks** on East St.; **Thomas Cook,** 40 East St. (☎536 733; 2% commission; open M and W-Sa 9am-5:30pm, Tu 10am-5:30pm); **launderette,** 11 Eastgate (open daily 8am-8pm, last wash 7pm); the **police,** Kingsham Rd. (☎(0845) 607 0999); **Internet access** at **Junction Club,** 2 Southgate (☎776 644; £1.50 per 30min.; open M-F 10am-10pm, Sa 10am-8pm, Su 11am-4pm); and the **post office,** 10 West St., with a **bureau de change** (☎(08457) 223 344; open M 8:45am-5:30pm, Tu-Sa 9am-5:30pm). **Post Code:** PO19 1AB.

ACCOMMODATIONS AND FOOD. B&Bs abound, but cheap rooms are rare, especially on big racecourse weekends; plan on paying at least £20, and expect a 15min. walk from the town center. **Bayleaf ❸,** 16 Whyke Rd., welcomes guests with colorful geraniums, freshly squeezed orange juice, and sugared grape-fruits. (☎774 330. No smoking. £23 per person.) **University College Chichester ❸,** College Ln., rents out single rooms as B&Bs between June and August. (☎816 070. £24-32, many with bath.) Pitch your tent at **Southern Leisure Centre ❶,** Vinnetrow Rd., a 15min. walk southeast of town. (☎787 715. Clean facilities with showers and laundry. Open Apr.-Oct. £3 per person; £8-10 per pitch.)

A **market** convenes (W and Sa) in the parking lot off Market Ave., which crosses over East Street. Bakeries line North St., while groceries chill at **Iceland,** 55 South St. (Open M-Th and Sa 8:30am-6pm, F 8:30am-8pm, Su 10am-4pm.) The town's best eateries congregate around the cathedral and tend to be expensive. The **Pasta Factory ❷,** 6 South St., rolls out fresh pasta daily; its cannelloni inspire sweet, sweet dreams (☎785 764. Average entree £7-10.) The Francophiles at **Maison Blanc Boulangerie and Patisserie ❶,** 56 South St., fill pastries from eclairs to passionata (pain au chocolat £1.25) and build sandwiches on organic bread for £4. (☎539 292. Open M-F 8:45am-5:30pm, Sa 8:45am-6pm; June-Sept. also Su 9am-5pm.) Upscale **Platters ❹,** 15 Southgate, serves meticulously prepared cuisine in an elegant setting. (☎530 430. Open Tu-Sa noon-1:45pm and from 7pm.) Mingle with twentysomethings and the pre-theater set at **Woodies Wine Bar and Brasserie ❸,** 10 St. Pancras, the oldest wine bar in Sussex. (☎779 895. Open M-Sa noon-2:30pm and 6-11pm, Su 6-11pm.)

Patrons gulp ale beneath soaring ceilings and stained glass at the **Slurping Toad** ❶, West St., set in the parish church across from the cathedral. (☎539 637. Drinks £1.50 Tu-F 5:30-8:30pm. Cover £1. Open M-Sa 11am-11pm.)

◙ **SIGHTS.** Begun in 1091, **Chichester Cathedral,** west of the Market Cross, is a millennium-spanning architectural grab-bag. Norman arches frame Reformation stained glass, a floor cutaway reveals a Roman mosaic, and Queen Elizabeth II and Prince Philip peer from the newly renovated West Front. Chagall's stained-glass depiction of Psalm 150 celebrates music and the arts in vibrant colors, while in the South Transept one of Cromwell's soldiers plucks out the eye of Edward IV. Also in the cathedral is an incredibly rare depiction of medieval hand-holding in the 14th-century effigy of Earl Fitzalan, which inspired Larkin's poem "An Arundel Tomb," displayed on a nearby pillar. (☎782 595. Open summer daily 7:30am-7pm; winter 7:30am-5pm. Tours Apr.-Oct. M-Sa 11am and 2:15pm. Evensong M-Sa 5:30pm, Su 3:30pm. Free lunchtime concerts Tu. £2 requested donation.)

Chichester's other attractions include the **Pallants,** a quiet area with elegant 18th- and 19th-century houses in the quadrant between South St. and East St. **The Pallant House,** 9 North Pallant, is an impeccably restored Queen Anne building, attributed to Christopher Wren, that draws visitors for its collection of 20th-century art. A vigorous schedule of temporary exhibitions, concerts, and gallery talks ensures that something interesting happens daily, and a quaint self-serve kitchen offers cocoa and tea. (Open Tu-Sa 10am-5pm, last admission 4pm. Free tours Sa 3pm. £4, students £2.50, seniors £3, children free.)

◪ ▧ **ENTERTAINMENT AND FESTIVALS.** Unexpectedly located in a residential neighborhood north of town, the **Chichester Festival Theatre,** Oaklands Park (☎781 312), is the cultural center of Chichester. Founded by Sir Laurence Olivier, the internationally renowned venue has attracted such artists as Maggie Smith, Peter Ustinov, and Julie Christie. The newer **Minerva Studio Theatre** is a smaller space for more intimate productions. The **Theatre Restaurant and Cafe** caters to theater-goers from 12:30pm on matinee days, 5:30pm for evening shows. (Box office open M-Sa 9am-8pm; until 6pm non-performance days. Tickets £15-20, 60 rush seats (£6-8) available at 10am on day of show.) During the first two weeks in July, artists and musicians collaborate to produce one of the finest spells of concentrated creativity in England: the **Chichester Festivities.** (☎780 192. Tickets £2. Box office, 45 East St., open mid-May until festival's end M-Sa 10am-5:30pm.)

▶ DAYTRIPS FROM CHICHESTER

FISHBOURNE ROMAN PALACE. Built around AD 80, possibly as the home of a local king, the palace is the largest domestic Roman building found in Britain; archaeologists believe the original residents possessed wealth of Pompeian proportions. The remains include the country's oldest mosaic floors and a formal garden replanted according to the original excavated layout. *(About 2 mi. west of the town center; follow the signs from the end of Westgate Street. ☎(01243) 785 859. Open Aug. daily 10am-6pm; Mar.-July and Sept.-Oct. 10am-5pm; Feb. and Nov.-Dec. 10am-4pm; Jan. Su 10am-4pm. £4.70, concessions £4, children £2.50, families £12.20.)*

GOODWOOD. Three miles northeast of Chichester, splendid Canalettos, Reynoldses, and Stubbses, as well as a world-famous sculpture collection, vie for attention in the 18th-century home of the Duke of Richmond. *(Take bus #268 from Chichester, and follow the signs 1 mi. ☎(01243) 755 040. Open Aug. Su-Th 1-5pm; Apr.-July and Sept. Su-M 1-5pm. £6.50, seniors £6, children £3, under 12 free.)* The rich and famous prefer **Racing at Goodwood,** an equestrian tradition that just celebrated its 200th birthday. (☎ *755 022.*) The plebeian set, on the other hand, look forward to the rumble of motorcars in July's **Festival of Speed** and September's **Motorcar Revival Race.** (☎ *755 055.*)

WEALD AND DOWNLAND OPEN AIR MUSEUM. For a leisurely stroll through English architectural memory, head to this 50-acre museum in Singleton. Over the past 25 years, 40 buildings representing different eras have been uprooted from their original sites and reconstructed here. Visitors can time-travel from a medieval farm to a Tudor market to a Victorian school. *(7 mi. north of Chichester off the A286; take bus #56 to Singleton Horse and Groom.* ☎ *(01243) 811 348. Open Mar.-Oct. daily 10:30am-6pm, last admission 5pm; Nov.-Feb. W and Sa-Su 10:30am-4pm. £7, children £4.)*

HAMPSHIRE

PORTSMOUTH   ☎ 023

Don't talk to me about naval tradition. It's nothing but rum, sodomy, and the lash.
   —Winston Churchill

Set Victorian seaside holidays against prostitutes, drunkards, and a bloody lot of cursing sailors, and the 900-year history of Portsmouth (pop. 190,500) will emerge. Henry VIII's *Mary Rose*, which sank in 1545 and was raised 437 years later, epitomizes an incomparable naval heritage in a city that will appeal most to those fascinated by the saga of the Royal Navy. On the seafront, older visitors relive D-Day while fresh faces learn of the days when Britannia ruled the waves.

▣ SHIP AHOY!

Trains: Portsmouth and Southsea Station, Commercial Rd., in the city center. Ticket office open M-Sa 5:40am-8:30pm, Su 6:40am-8:40pm. Travel center open M-F 8:40am-6pm, Sa 8:40am-4:30pm. **Portsmouth Harbour Station,** The Hard, ¾ mi. away at the end of the line sends ferries to the Isle of Wight. Office open M-F 5:50am-7:30pm, Sa 6am-7:30pm, Su 6:40am-8:10pm. **Trains** (☎(08457) 484 950) go to both stations from **Chichester** (40min.; 2 per hr.; £4, day return £4.90) and **London Waterloo** (1½hr.; 3 per hr.; £20, day return £21).

Buses: The Hard Interchange, The Hard, next to Harbour Station. **National Express** (☎(08705) 808 080) rumbles from **London** (2½hr., every hr., £10.50) and **Salisbury** (2hr., every hr., £8.25). Office open M-F 7:45am-5pm, Sa 7:45am-4pm.

Ferries: Wight Link (☎(0870) 582 7744) chugs to the Isle of Wight from the harbor (15min.; 1-2 per hr.; return £11.70, children £5.60). **Hovertravel** (☎9281 1000) departs from Clarence Esplanade for Ryde, Isle of Wight (9min.; 2 per hr.; return £10.90, children £5.60). For services to the Continent, consult **By Ferry,** p. 28.

Public Transportation: A reliable and comprehensive bus system connects the city. **Local bus** companies **First Provincial** (☎9286 2412) and **Stagecoach** (☎(01903) 237 661) run throughout. Daily pass £2, weekly pass £10.

Taxis: Aqua Cars (☎9281 8123) or **Streamline Taxis** (☎9281 1111).

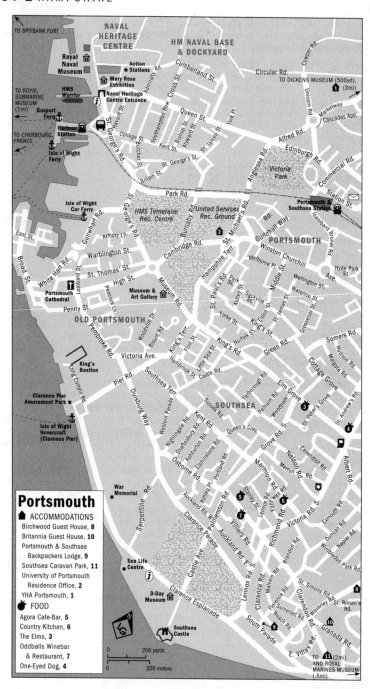

TO SPITBANK FORT

NAVAL HERITAGE CENTRE

HM NAVAL BASE & DOCKYARD

Royal Naval Museum

Action Stations

Cumberland St.

Circular Rd.

TO DICKENS MUSEUM (500yd), (3mi)

Mary Rose Exhibition

TO ROYAL SUBMARINE MUSEUM (1mi)

HMS Warrior

Naval Heritage Centre Entrance

Gosport Ferry

Harbour Station

Admiralty Rd.

Cross St.

Southampton Row

Queen St.

Bishop St.

Alward St.

York Pl.

St. James St.

Alfred Rd.

Edinburgh Rd.

Cowper Rd.

Unicorn Rd.

Marketway

Cascades App.

Commercial Rd.

Isle of Wight Ferry

TO CHERBOURG, FRANCE

St. George's Rd.

Havant St.

Butcher St.

College St.

Kent St.

Britain St.

St. George's St.

Anglesea Rd.

Victoria Park

Station St.

Isle of Wight Car Ferry

Park Rd.

Portsmouth & Southsea Station

HMS Temeraire Rec. Centre

United Services Rec. Ground

Isambard Brunel Rd.

East St.

Broad St.

Gunwharf Rd.

Lombard St.

Armory Ln.

Warblington St.

St. Thomas' St.

High St.

Burnaby Rd.

Cambridge Rd.

St. Michaels Rd.

Guildhall Way

PORTSMOUTH

Winston Churchill

Hampshire Terr.

St. Paul's Rd.

Park St.

Melbome Pl. St.

Middle St.

Wellington St.

Waterloo St.

Hyde Park St.

Ave.

White Hart Rd.

Portsmouth Cathedral

Penny St.

Peacock Ln.

Museum & Art Gallery

Museum Rd.

Astley St.

Sackville St.

Eldon St.

St. James St.

Groveland Rd.

Somers Rd.

Hudson Rd.

Margate Rd.

OLD PORTSMOUTH

Pembroke Rd.

Woodville Dr.

Blount Rd.

King's Terr.

Flint St.

Yorke St.

King's St.

Norfolk St.

Green Rd.

Cottage Grove

Victoria Ave.

Little Sea St.

Castle Rd.

St. Andrew's Rd.

King's Bastion

Long Curtain Rd.

Pier Rd.

Southsea Terr.

Hambrook St.

Sussex Rd.

Elm Grove

St. Peter's Grove

Clarence Pier Amusement Park

Duisburg Way

Western Parade

Kent Rd.

SOUTHSEA

Yarborough Rd.

Pelham Rd.

Woodpath

Nelson Rd.

Cavendish Rd.

Albert Rd.

Isle of Wight Hovercraft (Clarence Pier)

Nightingale Rd.

Shaftesbury Rd.

Ashburton Rd.

Grove Rd. S.

Merton Rd.

Exmouth Rd.

Duncan Rd.

Napier Rd.

Wimbledon Park Rd.

Serpentine Rd.

Osborne Rd.

Elphinstone Rd.

Queen's Cres.

Marmion Rd.

Richmond Rd.

Victoria Rd. S.

War Memorial

Auckland Rd.

Ashley Pl.

Portland Rd.

Ashley St.

Stanley St.

Foot well Rd.

Lennox Rd.

Auckland Rd. E. S.

Clarence Parade

Villiers Rd.

Palmerston Rd.

Brandon Rd.

Castle Ave.

Sea Life Centre

D-Day Museum

Clarence Esplanade

Lennox Rd.

Clarence Parade

Malvern Rd.

Florence Rd.

Somerset Rd.

Beach Rd.

Clarendon Rd.

St. Simons Rd.

Waverley Rd.

St. Ronan's Rd.

Granada Rd.

South Parade

Southsea Castle

E. Villas Rd.

TO (2mi) AND ROYAL MARINES MUSEUM (.5mi)

0   200 yards

0   200 meters

Portsmouth

ACCOMMODATIONS

Birchwood Guest House, **8**
Britannia Guest House, **10**
Portsmouth & Southsea
    Backpackers Lodge, **9**
Southsea Caravan Park, **11**
University of Portsmouth
    Residence Office, **2**
YHA Portsmouth, **1**

FOOD

Agora Cafe-Bar, **5**
Country Kitchen, **6**
The Elms, **3**
Oddballs Winebar
    & Restaurant, **7**
One-Eyed Dog, **4**

◄▶ ☒ SET YOUR COURSE

Portsmouth sprawls along the coast for miles—**Portsmouth, Old Portsmouth** (near the Portsmouth and Southsea train station and Commercial Rd.), and the resort community of **Southsea** (stretching to the east) can seem like altogether different cities. Major sights cluster at Old Portsmouth, **The Hard,** and Southsea's **Esplanade.**

Tourist Information Centre: The Hard (☎9282 6722; www.visitportsmouth.co.uk), by the historic ships. Bursting with brochures; the library map is worth the 20p. Free accommodations booking. Open daily 9:30am-5:45pm. **Seasonal offices** (☎832 464) near the Sea Life Centre and Clarence Esplanade.

Tours: Guide Friday (☎(01273) 540 893) hop-on/hop-off buses stop at major points of interest. 2 per hr.; 10am-6pm; £7, concessions £5.50, children £3. **Waterbus** (☎9282 2584) offers 1hr. guided rides in Portsmouth Harbour, leaving from The Hard. 9:30am-4:30pm; £3.50, concessions £3, children £2.

Financial Services: Banks hover around the Commercial Rd. shopping precinct, north of Portsmouth and Southsea Station. **American Express,** 110 Commercial Rd. (☎9286 5865). Open M-Tu and Th-F 9am-5:30pm, W 9:30am-7:30pm, Sa 9am-5pm.

Launderette: Laundrycare, 121 Elm Grove. Open M-Su 8am-6pm, last wash 4:45pm.

Police: Winston Churchill Ave. Hampshire hotline ☎(0845) 454 545.

Hospital: QA Hospital (☎9228 6000) handles emergencies. Also **St. Mary's Hospital,** Milton Rd. (☎9282 2331).

Internet: The Cyber Cafe (☎9266 4158), at Victoria Rd. South and Albert Rd. 4p per min., free membership gets 2p per min. Open M-Tu and Th-Sa 11am-9pm, W 1:30-9pm, Su noon-6pm. **The Online Cafe** has 2 locations in Southsea: 163 Elm Grove (☎9283 2206) and 23 Highland Rd. (☎9286 1221). £3 per hr. Open daily 10am-9pm.

Post Office: Slindon St. (☎(08457) 223 344), near the train station. Open M and Th 8:45am-5:30pm, Tu-W and F-Sa 9am-5:30pm. **Post Code:** PO1 1AA.

⌐ BERTHS AND BUNKS

Moderately priced B&Bs (around £20) clutter **Southsea.** Many are located along Waverly Rd., Clarendon Rd., and South Parade. If you're arriving via the Portsmouth and Southsea Station, catch one of the frequent buses on Commercial Rd. (#16 and 5 are good choices). From Portsmouth Harbor, hop aboard any of several buses (#5 will work) that make the trek from The Hard to South Parade.

▨ **Portsmouth and Southsea Backpackers Lodge,** 4 Florence Rd. (☎/fax 9283 2495). Take any Southsea bus to The Strand. Immaculate rooms in a 4-storey home. Pan-European crowd and energetic owners; 'packers have been known to come for 2 days and stay for 2 months. Comfy lounge, satellite TV, kitchen, grocery counter, laundry (£2), and Internet access (£1 per 15min.). Dorms £10; doubles £22, with bath £25. ❶

Birchwood Guest House, 44 Waverly Rd. (☎9281 1337). A touch of quiet elegance in a city of carnivals and sailors. Bright, spacious rooms recently refurbished with aboriginal art. Incredibly personable hosts provide ample breakfasts. Singles and quads £18-20 per person; doubles, triples, and quads with bath £20-30 per person. ❷

Britannia Guest House, 48 Granada Rd. (☎814 234). Colorful rooms, oriental carpets, and the owners' maritime interests make this B&B a good diving-in point for Portsmouth. Full English breakfast included. Singles £20; doubles £40-£45. ❸

University of Portsmouth Halls of Residence, Nuffield Centre, St. Michael's Rd. (☎9284 3178), overlooking Southsea Common. 15min. from The Hard. Small, modern rooms in **Rees Hall** are reasonably convenient and available mid-July to Sept. Booking ahead is recommended, but last-minute arrivals should head over to Rees Hall directly (bus #5). Singles £29; doubles £49 with full English breakfast (cheaper self-catering). ❸

YHA Portsmouth, Old Wymering Ln., Cosham (☎9237 5661). From Portsmouth, take a bus to Cosham and follow the signs. From Cosham train station, walk up High St., take Wayte St left., and cross the roundabout to Medina Rd.; Old Wymering Ln. is on the right after 6 blocks. Though far from town, this former home of Catherine Parr (Henry VIII Wife #6) features exquisitely detailed woodwork. Lockout 10am-5pm. Curfew 11pm. Open Feb.-Aug. daily; Sept.-Nov. F-Sa. Dorms £9.50, under 18 £6.50. ❶

Camping: Southsea Caravan Park, Melville Rd., Southsea (☎9273 5070). At the eastern end of the seafront, 5-6 mi. from The Hard. Pretty site with toilets, showers, laundry facilities, shop, restaurant-bar, and pool. No reservations, but call ahead for availability. 2-person tent £9-10 per night. ❶

GRUB AND GROG

Good restaurants reside along the waterfront, Palmerston Rd., Clarendon Rd., and between the shopping districts in Southsea and on Commercial Rd. There is no drought of pubs in Portsmouth; the weary sailor can easily find galley fare and a pint, especially near The Hard or along Palmerston. Ethnic foods add spice to the scene on Albert Rd. The **Tesco** supermarket is on Craswell St., just outside the town center, and tends to cut prices ridiculously low just before closing. (☎839 222. Open continuously from M 7am to Sa 10pm, Su 10am-4pm.)

Country Kitchen, 59a Marmion Rd. (☎9232 1148). Savory vegetarian and vegan dishes (around £4.50) and un-decadent desserts please the taste buds and the wallet. Genial service pleases the well-mannered. Open daily 9:30am-5pm. ❶

Oddballs Winebar and Restaurant, 12 Clarendon Rd. (☎9275 5291). Sophisticated wine list and complex dishes made unintimidating by friendly staff and simple surroundings. The menu changes, but entrees—like confit of crispy duck and Jamaican spiced chicken breast—are consistently £8-12. Open M-Sa noon-11pm, Su noon-10:30pm. ❸

The Elms, 128 Elm Grove (☎9282 4295). The proud, rainbow-bedecked center of the Portsmouth gay and lesbian community—and one of the busiest spots in town to boot. DJ or live music F-Sa. 18+. Open M-Sa 11am-11pm, Su noon-10:30pm. ❶

One Eyed Dog (☎9282 7188), corner of Elm Grove and Victoria Rd. South. This bright blue cross between a pub and a trendy bar draws a steady flow of twentysomethings afternoon and night. The place to sate your thirst but not your hunger pains (bar snacks only). Open M-F 4-11pm, Sa 1-11pm, Su 4-10:30pm. ❶

Agora Cafe-Bar and Restaurant, 9 Clarendon Rd. (☎9282 2617). Traditional English breakfasts (£3-5 all day) and steaming cups of coffee draw a relaxed crowd. Entrees (£4-9) include omelettes, falafels, and sirloin steak. Open daily 9:20am-5pm. ❶

👁 SPLENDID, SALTY SIGHTS

Portsmouth overflows with magnificent ships and seafaring relics. The bulk of sights worth seeing anchor near The Hard, delighting war buffs, intriguing historians, and looking like some pretty big boats to the rest of the world. In summer, the colorful boardwalk attracts the attention of landlubbers.

▧ PORTSMOUTH HISTORIC DOCKYARD

In the Naval Yard. Entrance next to the TIC; follow the signs. ☎9286 1512 or 9286 1533. Ships open Mar.-Oct. daily 10am-5:30pm; Nov.-Feb. 10am-5pm. Last entry 4:45pm. Each *sight £6-6.50, seniors £5.30-5.80, children £4.50-4.80. The **Passport ticket** allows one-time entrance to every site and is valid for a year. £18, concessions £14.50.*

Historians and armchair admirals will want to plunge head-first into the unparalleled Historic Dockyard, which brings together a virtual armada of Britain's most storied ships and nautical artifacts. Resurrect the past with these floating monuments to Britannia's mastery of the seas—even the staunchest army man can't help but be awed by the history within these hulls. The five galleries of the **Royal Naval Museum** fill in the temporal gaps between the three ships.

MARY ROSE. Henry VIII's *Mary Rose*, holding court in the harbor, is one of England's earliest warships. Henry was particularly fond of her, but, like many of his women, she died before her time, sinking just after setting sail from Portsmouth in July 1545. Not until 1982 was Henry's flagship raised from her watery grave. The eerie, skeletal hulk was sprayed with a preservative mixture, a 20-year process that should make *Mary* live forever. Thousands of artifacts discovered with the ship are on display in the **Mary Rose Exhibition** gallery.

HMS VICTORY. Napoleon must be rolling in his tiny grave to know that the HMS *Victory* is still afloat. Cinching Britain's reputation as monarch of the waves with its defeat of Boney's forces at Trafalgar in 1805, the *Victory* embodies the strict order and invincible regimentation of Nelson's navy. It vividly portrays the dismal, cramped conditions for press-ganged recruits, and the spot where **Admiral Nelson** expired has become a veritable shrine. *Victory* is only on view via a guided tour—check your admission ticket for your time slot.

HMS WARRIOR. The HMS *Warrior* provides an intriguing companion to its neighbor the *Victory*. The pride of Queen Victoria's navy and the first iron-clad battleship in the world, *Warrior* never saw battle. Nonetheless, a metaphor-challenged Napoleon III called it "The Black Snake among the Rabbits in the Channel."

ACTION STATIONS. Scale walls, navigate enemy seas, pilot a helicopter, and experience other simulated trials of naval fire in this high-tech new addition to the dockyards. The short Omni film *Command Approved*, played continuously, reveals a "typical" day aboard a Type 23 frigate: missiles and bravado fly as the ship engages in an all-out war with evil modern-day island pirates.

OTHER NAVAL SIGHTS

Not surprisingly, Portsmouth's museums rarely deal with more than the sea and its inhabitants. **Spitbank Fort** has protected Portsmouth through two World Wars and remains relatively unscathed. *(☎9250 4207. 25min. crossing from the Dockyard, Easter-Oct. W and Su 2:45pm. £6.95, children £5.)* The **Royal Navy Submarine Museum** surfaces in Britain's only walk-on submarine, the HMS *Alliance*. The Gosport ferry continuously crosses from the Harbour train station (£1.80); then follow the signs or take bus #9 to Haslar Hospital. *(☎9252 9217. £4, concessions £2.75, families £11.)* The **Royal Marines Museum** chronicles the 400 years in which the British Empire was established, teetered, and was lost. It includes a prodigious display of medals, a jungle tour (beware the scorpions), and an animated marine in drag. *(☎9281 9385. Open June-Aug. daily 10am-5pm, Sept.-May 10am-4:30pm. £4, children £2.25.)*

THE BEST OF THE REST

SOUTHSEA. The ■**D-Day Museum,** on Clarence Esplanade, leads visitors through life-size dioramas of the June 6, 1944 invasion, sharing perspectives from soldiers as well as the families they left behind. It also houses the Overlord Embroidery, an abstract and emotional tapestry, commissioned in 1968 to recount the Allied victory. *(☎9282 7261. Open Apr.-Sept. daily 10am-5:30pm; Oct.-Mar. 10am-5pm. £5, conces-*

sions £3-3.75, families £13. Admission and special events during the D-Day anniversary week £2.50. Audioguide to embroidery 50p.) **Southsea Castle,** built by Henry VIII at the point of the Esplanade, was an active fortress into the 20th century. Don't miss the secret underground tunnels. *(Open Apr.-Sept. daily 10am-5:30pm. £2.50, concessions £1.50-1.80, families £2.50.)* The **Sea Life Centre** retains a squad of squid and such. (☎ 9287 5222. *Open summer daily 10am-7pm; winter 10am-5pm. £6, concessions £5-5.50, children £4.50.)*

CHARLES DICKENS BIRTHPLACE MUSEUM. Charles Dickens was born in Portsmouth in 1812; today his birthplace is an uninspired museum. The only authentic Dickensiana are the couch on which he died (transplanted from Kent) and a lock of his precious hair. *(393 Old Commercial Rd., ¾ mi. north of Portsmouth and Southsea station. ☎ 9282 7261. Open Apr.-Oct. daily 10am-5:30pm; Nov.-Dec. and Feb. 7, Dickens's Birthday, 10am-5pm. £2.50, seniors £1.80, students and children £1.50, families £6.50.)*

ISLE OF WIGHT ☎ 01983

She thinks of nothing but the Isle of Wight and she calls it the Island, as if there were no other island in the world.
    —Jane Austen, *Mansfield Park*

Far more tranquil and sun-splashed than its mother island to the north, the Isle of Wight offers travelers stunning scenery, bright sandy beaches, and peaceful family breaks. The life of the Isle has softened the hardest of hearts through the centuries, from Queen Victoria, who reportedly found much amusement here (and little elsewhere), to Karl Marx, who proclaimed the island "a little paradise!"

◀ TRANSPORTATION

Ferries: Wight Link (☎ (0870) 582 7744) services include: **Lymington** to **Yarmouth** (return £9, children £4.80); **Portsmouth Harbour** to **Fishbourne** (return £9/£4.80); **Portsmouth Harbour** to **Ryde** (15min., return £11.70/£5.60). **Red Funnel** ferries (☎ (023) 8033 4010) steam from **Southampton** to **East Cowes** (every hr., return £8.20/£4.30). **Hovertravel** (☎ 811 000; www.hovertravel.co.uk) sails from **Southsea** to **Ryde** (9min., 34 per day, return £11.30/£5.70).

Public Transportation: Train service on the **Island Line** (☎ 562 492) is limited to the eastern end of the island, including Ryde, Brading, Sandown, Shanklin, and a few points between. **Buses** by **Southern Vectis** (☎ 532 373; www.svoc.co.uk) cover the entire island; TICs and Travel Centres (☎ 827 005) in Cowes, Shanklin, Ryde, and Newport sell the complete timetable (50p). Buy tickets on board. The **Island Rover** ticket gives you unlimited bus travel (1-day £7, children £3.50; 2-day £12/£6).

Car Rental: South Wight Rentals, 10 Osborne Rd. (☎ 864 263), in Shanklin, offers free pickup and drop-off. From £25 per day. Open daily 8:30am-5:30pm. **Solent Self Drive** (☎ 282 050 or (0800) 724 734), at Marghams Garage, Crocker St., Newport, and Red Funnel Terminal, West Cowes. £28-£41 per day, £165-£270 per week.

Bike Rental: Offshore Sport, 19 Orchardleigh Rd. (☎ 866 269), in Shanklin. £5 per half-day, £9 per day, £35 per week; deposit £30 plus ID. Open Apr.-Sept. daily 9am-6pm; Oct.-Mar. 9am-5:30pm.

◀ ❼ ORIENTATION AND PRACTICAL INFORMATION

The Isle of Wight is 23 mi. by 13 mi. and shaped like a squat diamond, with towns clustered along the coasts. **Ryde** and **Cowes** are to the north, **Sandown, Shanklin,** and **Ventnor** lie along the east coast heading south, and **Yarmouth** is on the west coast. The capital, **Newport,** sits in the center, at the origin of the **River Medina.**

Tourist Information Centres: Each supplies an individual town map as well as the free *Isle of Wight Official Pocket Guide*. A **general inquiry service** (☎813 818; fax 863 047; www.islandbreaks.co.uk) directs questions to one of the seven regional offices listed below—call this number first. In the winter, TICs tend to close earlier than their posted hours. For accommodations, call the central booking line (☎813 813).

Cowes: Fountain Quay (☎291 914), in the alley next to the ferry terminal for RedJet. Open M-Sa 9am-5pm, Su 10am-4pm; during Cowes week (1st week in Aug.) daily 8am-8pm.

Newport: The Guildhall, High St. (☎823 366), signposted from the bus station. Open M-Sa 9:30am-5:30pm, Su 10am-4pm.

Ryde: Western Esplanade (☎562 905), at the corner with Union St., opposite Ryde Pier and the bus station. Open M-Sa 9:30am-5:30pm, Su 10am-4pm.

Sandown: 8 High St. (☎403 886), across from Boots Pharmacy. Open Apr.-Oct. M-Sa 9:30am-5:30pm, Su 10am-4pm. Call the central line for winter hours.

Shanklin: 67 High St. (☎862 942). Open Apr.-Oct. M-Sa 9:30am-5:30pm, Su 10am-4pm. Call the central line for winter hours.

Ventnor: 34 High St. (☎853 625). Open Apr.-Oct. M-Tu and Th-Sa 9:30am-5:30pm, Su 10am-3pm. Open W in July and Aug. Call the central line for winter hours.

Yarmouth: The Quay (☎813 818), signposted from ferry. Open M-Sa 9am-5:30pm, Su 9am-5pm.

Financial Services: Banks can be found in all major town centers. Fill your pockets in the bigger cities, as ATMs are rare in the smaller towns.

Police: Hampshire hotline ☎(0845) 454 545.

Medical Assistance: St. Mary's Hospital (☎524 081), in Newport. Disabled travelers can seek assistance from **Dial Office** (☎522 823).

Internet Access: The idea of peddling Internet access is beginning to catch on; ask the local TIC for the nearest location. **Internet Cafe,** 16-18 Melville St. (☎408 294), off High St. by the pier in Sandown, is your best bet for fast service. £1.75 per 30min. Open Tu-Sa 11am-6pm. **Inpress,** 19 Union St., Ryde (☎616 261). £3 per 30min., £5 per hr. Open M-F 9am-5pm. **Lord Louis Library** (☎823 800) in Newport and the **Ryde Library** (☎562 170) both offer access. £3 per 30min., £5 per hr.; book ahead.

Post Office: Post offices are in every town center. **Post Code:** PO30 1AB (Newport).

▚ ACCOMMODATIONS AND CAMPING

Accommodations on Wight tend to require a two-night minimum stay. Prices range from decent to absurd, often depending on proximity to the shore. Budget travelers should try one of the YHA hostels at either end of the island, look into less-visited areas, or try their luck with the **Accommodation Booking Service** (☎813 813).

▨ **Claverton House,** 12 The Strand, Ryde (☎613 015). Lavishly appointed bedrooms and flower-scented private bathrooms with puffy lavender towels could tempt even the most ardent sightseer to spend the day afloat in the tub... but the ocean view from the dining room will tempt you out again. £40 for 2 nights. ❷

YHA Sandown, The Firs, Fitzroy St., Sandown (☎402 651). Signposted from town center; from the train station, take Station Ave. to Fitzroy St. on the right. Ultra-clean dorms, kitchen, and lounge on one of the more popular beaches—a pleasant respite from a hard day's sunbathing. Meals £2.20-5. Luggage storage and wet-weather shelter available during lockout (10am-5pm). Curfew 11pm, key for late access. Open late Mar. to mid-Sept. daily; mid-Sept. to Dec. and Mar. W-Su. Dorms £11.25, under 18 £8. ❷

YHA Totland Bay, Hurst Hill, Totland Bay (☎752 165; fax 756 443), on the west end of the island. Take Southern Vectis bus #7 or 7A to Totland War Memorial; turn left up Weston Rd., and take the 2nd left onto Hurst Hill. Comfortable lodgings in a fantastic location—a lucky few get sea-vistas from their windows. Cliffs, walking trails, and Alum Bay are all nearby. Lockout 10am-5pm. Curfew 11pm. Open July-Aug. daily; Sept.-Oct. F-Sa; Mar.-June M-Sa. Dorms £11.25, under 18 £8. ❷

Seaward Guest House, 14-16 George St., Ryde (☎563 168; seaward@FSBDial.co.uk). Near the hovercraft, bus, and train stations. Friendly proprietor and dog offer airy, pastel rooms and hearty breakfasts. Singles £18-20; doubles £30-36, with bath £36-44. ❷

Camping: Sites are plentiful; check the free Isle of Wight *Camping and Touring Guide*, available from all TICs. **Beaper Farm Camping Site** (☎615 210), between Ryde and Sandown, accessible by bus #7. Sheltered by a grove of trees, with 150 pitches, 24 electricity hookups, showers, and laundry facilities. 2-person tent £7. ❶

FOOD

Hungry wanderers on Wight can begin their hunt for food on the local High St. or Esplanade; these commonly named roads often feature uncommonly excellent restaurants. Locally caught fish is a specialty. *The Official Guide to Eating Out*, free and distributed by TICs, offers additional dining options. Most larger cities have supermarkets, and thirsty vacationers need not look far for a pub—the island harbors nearly one public house per square mile. When using Ryde as a center for island exploration, feast on exquisite gourmet baguettes and pastries (£1.30-3.30) from the **Baguette Factory ❶**, 24 Cross St. (☎611 115. Open M-Sa 8:30am-4pm.) A night out in Sandown calls for a sampling of the decadent Italian dishes (£7.50-17) served at **La Scala ❹**, 26 High St., in a downstairs alcove that goes unnoticed by those who don't know to look for it. (☎403 778. Open daily 6:15pm-11:30pm.) **S. Fowler & Co. ❷**, 41-43 Union St., Ryde, buzzes with tourists and locals alike—and no wonder, with plenty of meals under £5, including several vegetarian options. (☎613 937. Open daily 10am-midnight, food served until 10pm. AmEx/MC/V.)

◎ SIGHTS

Wight's natural treasures are especially prominent in the west, with rolling hillsides, multicolored beaches, and the famous Needles; bus #7, 7A, and 7B to Alum Bay catch breathtaking views while whizzing along cliff roads. Zoos specialize in everything from butterflies to dinosaurs to tigers, and one museum is dedicated to the fine art of smuggling. All these sights are listed in the *Official Pocket Guide* and are bound to delight, but don't miss the following must-sees.

OSBORNE HOUSE. The image of Queen Victoria as an austere monarch in perpetual mourning is shattered by the spacious splendor of Osborne House, backdrop to the 1997 film *Mrs. Brown*. Completed in 1846, the house was meant to serve as a "modest" country home and refuge from affairs of state. Victoria used it as a long-term retreat after Albert's death in 1861 and died here herself 40 years later. Mementos and family pictures give the home an unusual personal touch (Vic was proud of her nine kids, who she married into almost every royal house in Europe), while the India Exhibit in the resplendent **Durbar Room** speaks to the Queen's public persona. A **horse-and-carriage ride** (£1) through the manicured grounds passes the children's Swiss Cottage; free minibuses follow the same route with less grandeur. *(Take Southern Vectis bus #4 or 5 from Ryde or Newport. ☎200 022. Open Apr.-Sept. daily 10am-6pm; Oct. 10am-5pm; Nov. to mid-Dec. and Feb.-Mar. by tour only. House and grounds £7.50, concessions £5.60, under 16 £3.80. Grounds only £4/£3/£2.)*

CARISBROOKE CASTLE. If whoever controls the castle controls the island, then the six Carisbrooke **donkeys** who wander the ruins are the rightful rulers of Wight. The Norman castle's most famous resident, however, was here not in command but in chains: Charles I fled to Carisbrooke in 1647, where he was captured and imprisoned until his execution. Chaz didn't accept his fate lying down—visitors climbing through the ruins can still see the window in which the deposed king got stuck while trying to escape. A museum details the structure's history, and includes the **Tennyson Room,** with the poet's hat, desk, cloak, and funeral pall. William the Conqueror's **Chapel of St. Nicholas** has been restored as a WWII memorial, and still holds regular services. *(From Newport, with the bus station on your left, follow Upper St. James St., turn right on Trafalgar St., and bear left onto Castle Rd., which becomes Castle Hill. ☎ 522 107. Open Apr.-Sept. daily 10am-6pm; Oct. 10am-5pm; Nov.-Mar. 10am-4pm. £4.60, concessions £3.50, children £2.30, families £11.50. Tour £1, children 50p.)*

ALUM BAY AND THE NEEDLES. Some of Wight's most charmed sights predate both Victorians and Normans. On the western tip of the island, the white chalk **Needles** jut into a dark sea; local cruises in **Alum Bay** afford a good view. *(Tickets at the Ryde bus station. £12, seniors £11, children £6.50; includes transport from Ryde).* Alum's pleasure park may distract you from the natural beauty of the bay, but a **chairlift** runs down the mosaic-like cliffs to the famous colored beaches—used by those resourceful Victorians for their paint pigments—and back (return £3, children £2).

WALKING AND CYCLING. Walkers and cyclists enjoy the coastal path stretching from **Totland,** past lighthouses both modern and medieval at **St. Catherine's Point,** to **St. Lawrence** at the southern end of the island. Explore the island's 500 mi. of well-maintained footpaths during the annual **Walking Festival** (mid-May) and **Cycling Festival** (late September), when participants pace along scenic routes or race over strenuous courses. Racing ships speed past the coastline in the regatta that takes place during **Cowes Week,** held August 2-9 in 2003. Visit a TIC for more details.

WINCHESTER ☎ 01962

Best known for its dramatic cathedral and as home to wordsmiths Jane Austen and John Keats, Winchester has a strain of notability dating back to Roman times. Both Alfred the Great and William the Conqueror deemed it the center of their kingdoms, monks painstakingly prepared the *Domesday Book* for William here (see p. 70), and the town was also temporary court for Charles II during the Great Plague of 1665. While its grandest days have passed, Winchester has managed to polish some luster into its old walls. Locals amble through quiet gardens along the River Itchen, and the pedestrian area bustles with students and shoppers.

▐ TRANSPORTATION

Just north of Southampton, Winchester makes an excellent daytrip from **Salisbury,** 25 mi. west, or **Portsmouth,** 27 mi. south.

Trains: Winchester Station, Station Hill, northwest of the city center. Tourist center open M-F 9am-6pm, Sa 9am-5pm, Su 9am-4:30pm. Ticket counter open M-F 6am-8:30pm, Sa 6am-7:30pm, Su 7am-8:30pm. Trains (☎ (08457) 484 950) from: **Brighton** (1½hr., every hr., £16.10); **London Waterloo** (1hr., 2 per hr., £16.60); **Portsmouth** (1hr., every hr., £7). Be prepared to change trains at Basingstoke or Fareham.

Buses: Buses stop outside on Broadway near Alfred's statue, or inside the **bus station.** (Open M 7:30am-5:30pm, Tu-F 8:30am-5:30pm, Sa 8:30am-12:30pm.) **National Express** (☎ (08705) 808 080) runs from **London** via **Heathrow** (1½hr., 7 per day, £12) and **Oxford** (2½hr., 2 per day, £6.75). **Hampshire Stagecoach** (☎ (01256) 464 501) heads to: **Portsmouth** (#69, 1½hr., 12 per day, return £4.45); **Salisbury** (#68/87, 45min., 7 per day, return £4.45); **Southampton** (#47, 50min., 2 per hr., return £2.90). **Explorer** tickets are available for buses in Hampshire and Wiltshire (£5.25, seniors £3.85, children £2.60, families £10.50). **Local buses** (☎ (01256) 464 501) stop by the bus and train stations. Ask for a timetable of Winchester buses at the TIC.

Taxis: Francis Taxis (☎ 884 343) by the market. Handicap-accessible cabs available.

✦ 🛈 ORIENTATION AND PRACTICAL INFORMATION

Winchester's major (and commercial) axis, **High St.**, stretches from the statue of Alfred the Great at the east end to the arch of **West Gate** opposite. The city's bigger roads stem off High St., which transforms into **Broadway** as you approach Alfred.

Tourist Information Centre: The Guildhall, Broadway (☎ 840 500; fax 850 348; www.winchester.gov.uk), across from the bus station. Stocks free maps, seasonal

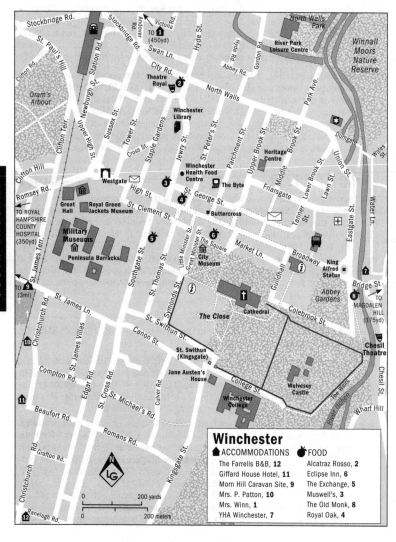

Winchester

⬆ ACCOMMODATIONS
- The Farrells B&B, **12**
- Giffard House Hotel, **11**
- Morn Hill Caravan Site, **9**
- Mrs. P. Patton, **10**
- Mrs. Winn, **1**
- YHA Winchester, **7**

🍴 FOOD
- Alcatraz Rosso, **2**
- Eclipse Inn, **6**
- The Exchange, **5**
- Muswell's, **3**
- The Old Monk, **8**
- Royal Oak, **4**

What's On guides, and city guides (£1). **Walking tours** £3, children free. Helpful multilingual staff books accommodations for £3 plus a 10% deposit. Open May-Sept. M-Sa 9:30am-5:30pm, Su 11am-4pm; Oct.-Apr. M-Sa 10am-5pm.

Financial Services: Major **banks** cluster at the junction of Jewry St. and High St. **Thomas Cook,** 30 High St. (☎841 661). Open M-Tu and Th-Sa 9am-5:30pm, W 10am-5:30pm.

Launderette: 27 Garbett Rd., Winnall (☎840 658). Climb Magdalen Hill, turn left on Winnall Manor Rd., and follow until Garbett Rd. on your left. Soap 25p. £2 per load. Open M-F 8am-8pm, Sa 8am-6pm, Su 10am-4pm. Last wash 1hr. before close.

Police: North Walls (☎(08450) 454 545), near the intersection with Middle Brook St.

Hospital: Royal Hampshire County, Romsey Rd. (☎863 535), at St. James Ln.

Internet Access: The Byte Internet Cafe and Training Centre, 10 Parchment Street (☎863 235). 18 terminals; £1.50 per 30min. Open M-Th 9am-9pm, F 9am-5pm, Sa 10am-5pm. The **Winchester Library,** Jewry St. (☎853 909). 1 terminal; from £1 per 15min. Open M-Tu and F 9:30am-7pm, W-Th 9:30am-5pm, Sa 9:30am-4pm.

Post Office: Middle Brook St. (☎(08457) 223 344). Turn off High St. at Marks and Spencer. **Bureau de change.** Open M-Sa 9am-5:30pm. **Post Code:** SO23 8WA.

▟ ACCOMMODATIONS AND CAMPING

Winchester's B&Bs cluster half a mile southwest of the TIC, near Ranelagh Rd., on the corner of Christchurch Rd. and St. Cross Rd. Buses #29 and 47 make the journey from the town center twice an hour; #69 runs the same route each hour. Many pubs also offer accommodations, but try to book early. A steady stream of Londoners drives up prices, making Winchester's hostel particularly attractive.

YHA Winchester, 1 Water Ln. (☎853 723). Located in an 18th-century watermill perched atop the rush of the River Itchen. A "simple" hostel, which means creative bed arrangements between the mill's roofbeams. Kitchen available. Breakfast £1.70-£3.40. Lockout 10am-5pm. Stringent 11pm curfew. Open daily late Mar. to early Nov., weekends only Nov.-Mar. Dorms £9.50, students £8.25, under 18 £7. ❶

Mrs. Winn, 2 North Hill Close (☎864 926). Comfortable, cheap rooms just up the road from the train station. The price of proximity is the dull rumble of coaches. Still, it's tended by warm hosts with an affection for backpackers and other budget travelers. Mind the teddy bears as you climb the stairs. £16 per person. ❷

Mrs. P. Patton, 12 Christchurch Rd. (☎854 272), between St. James Ln. and Beaufort Rd., 5min. from the cathedral on a silent street of stately houses. Graceful double rooms, recently repainted and refurbished. Look for the partridge-in-a-pear-tree curtains in the bedroom on the right. Singles £25-28; doubles £33-40. ❸

The Farrells B&B, 5 Ranelagh Rd. (☎/fax 869 555), off Christchurch Rd., a 10min. walk from town. Furniture a mother would rave about in a well-kept home. Feels instantly welcoming, with decades of family photos on the wall. £20 per person, with bath £22. ❸

Giffard House Hotel, 50 Christchurch Rd. (☎852 628). Pinch yourself as you make your way past the sitting room's tasteful artwork and leather couches; ascend the red-carpeted stairs to luxurious rooms, complete with TVs, private bathrooms, and a chocolate on your pillow. Singles £57; doubles £37.50-£47.50 per person. ❺

Camping: Morn Hill Caravan Club Site, Morn Hill (☎869 877), 3 mi. east of Winchester off A31, toward New Forest. Mainly for caravans, so extra facilities are limited. Open Apr.-Oct. Campers £6.20-13.80 per night, tents at warden's discretion; call ahead. ❶

📋 🔲 FOOD AND PUBS

High St. and St. George's St. are home to several food markets, fast-food venues, and tea houses. Restaurants dish out more substantial fare on Jewry St., where you'll find the **Winchester Health Food Centre,** 41 Jewry St. (☎851 113. Open M-F 9:15am-5:45pm, Sa 9am-5:30pm.) **Sainsbury's,** at Middle Brook St. off High St., hawks groceries. (☎861 792. Open M-Sa 7am-8pm, Su 11am-5pm.) If you're looking for a **market,** vendors sell fruits and vegetables (W-Sa 8am-6pm) on Middle Brook St., behind Marks and Spencer and across from the town library.

Muswell's, 8-9 Jewry St. (☎842 414). Zany bartenders, toe-tapping dance tunes, deals on meals, and rotating student nights draw a youthful pub crowd. Snag an open-air table to people-watch by day or take a drink at night. Su all-day happy hour. Open M-W 11am-midnight, Th-Sa 11am-1am, Su noon-10:30pm. ❶

The Eclipse Inn, The Square (☎865 676). Winchester's smallest pub is in a 16th-century rectory the claustrophobic should avoid. Pub grub (from £4) attracts regulars and, according to tales passed over pints, a ghost or two. Open M-Sa 11am-11pm, Su noon-11pm. Food served daily noon-3pm. ❶

The Old Monk, 1 High St. (☎855 111), on the river. Enjoy a meal or a drink on the patio or lounge inside on leather chairs. Hundreds of students flock here after class and stay into the night. Open Su-Th noon-11pm, F-Sa noon-1am. Food served until 7pm. ❶

Royal Oak, Royal Oak Passage (☎842 701), next to the Godbegot House off High St. Despite its refurbished gleam, this is yet another pub that claims to be the kingdom's oldest. Descend into the 900-year-old subterranean foundations and enjoy the locally brewed hogshead cask ale (£1.75) and English cuisine (£3-6). Open daily 11am-11pm; food served Su-Th noon-9pm, F-Sa noon-6pm. AmEx/MC/V. ❶

The Exchange, 9 Southgate St. (☎854 718). A wild menu, with crocodile, vegan nut, and (for the truly adventurous) beef burgers, as well as more traditional grub like sandwiches and jacket potatoes (£2-7). Discounts for students and seniors. Open M-Sa 10am-11pm, Su noon-11pm; last call for food orders 2pm. ❷

Alcatraz Rosso, 24-26 Jewry St. (☎860 047), next door to the Theatre Royal. Offers familiar Italian pastas and pizzas (£7-8), as well as innovative salads and meat dishes (£7.50-12). Marble floors, white tablecloths, and fresh flowers in a quiet setting, perfect for a pre-show dinner. Open daily noon-3pm and 6-10:30pm. ❷

🔄 SIGHTS

WINCHESTER CATHEDRAL. Duck through the archway (note the stones from William the Conqueror's palace), pass through the square, and behold the 900-year-old cathedral. Its whopping 556 feet make it the longest medieval building in Europe. Magnificent tiles, roped off for preservation, cover much of the floor near the chancel. While gazing at Jane Austen's memorial plaque in the northern aisle of the nave, don't walk past (or over) Jane herself, buried in the floor. Near the front of the cathedral is a glimmering icon screen, complete with a "How to Pray to Icons" guide. The oddly Cubist stained glass window in the rear is compliments of Cromwell's soldiers: the pattern was lost after they smashed the original. *(5 The Close. ☎857 225 or 857 208. Open daily 7:15am-5:30pm; visiting encouraged after 8:30am. East End closes at 5pm. Free 50min. tours depart from the west end of the nave daily 10am-3pm. 1¼hr. tower tours also available. Suggested donation £3.50, concessions £2.30, children 50p, families £7. Photography permit £2.)*

The **Norman crypt,** allegedly the oldest and definitely one of the finest in England, can only be viewed in the summer by guided tour. The crypt contains the statues of two of Winchester's most famous figures: Bishop William of Wykeham, founder of Winchester College (England's first public school), and St. Swithun, patron saint of weather. St. Swithun was interred at the cathedral against his will; in retaliation, the saint brought torrents down on the culprits for 40 days. Legend holds that if it rains on July 15 (St. Swithun's Day), it will rain for the next 40 days. Considering this is England, it might anyway. The **Triforium Gallery** at the south transept contains several relics. The 12th-century Winchester Bible resides in the **Library.** Outside to the south of the cathedral is tiny **St. Swithun's Chapel,** rebuilt in the 16th century, nestled above **King's Gate.** *(Free 20min. crypt tours depart from crypt door. Gallery and Library open M-Sa 11am-4:30pm. £1, students 50p, families £2.)*

GREAT HALL. Henry III built his castle on the remains of a previous fortress of William the Conqueror, and it became a favorite haunt for early royals. What remains is the Great Hall, a gloriously intact medieval structure containing a Round Table modeled after King Arthur's. Henry VIII tried to pass the table off as authentic to Holy Roman Emperor Charles V, but the repainted "Arthur," resembling Henry himself, fooled no one. *(At the end of High St. atop Castle Hill. Open Mar.-Oct. daily 10am-5pm; Nov.-Feb. M-F 10am-5pm, Sa-Su 10am-4pm. Free.)*

MILITARY MUSEUMS. Just through **Queen Eleanor's Garden,** in the Peninsula Barracks, five military museums detail the story of the city and the country's military power. The **Royal Greenjackets Museum** is the must-see of the bunch. Explore 400 years of British imperial history while going head-to-head with a French guillotine, testing your marksmanship (10p), and ducking German artillery fire. The heart of the museum is the 276 sq. ft. diorama of the Battle of Waterloo containing 21,500 tiny soldiers and their 9600 tiny steeds. *(☎828 549. Open M-Sa 10am-1pm and 2-5pm, Su noon-4pm. £2, concessions £1, families £6. Hours for the other 4 museums vary.)*

WOLVESEY CASTLE. Some may find the walk along the river to Wolvesey Castle more enjoyable than the site itself, as it is ruined, ruined, ruined. The Norman bishop used to live here, exerting bishoply influence over the surrounding area. The current bishop resides in the newer mansion next door. *(☎252 000. Open Apr.-Oct. daily 10am-6pm. £2, concessions £1.80, children £1.)*

CITY MUSEUM. Pristine, interactive galleries explore Winchester's past, from its days as the Roman Venta Belgarum through the Anglo-Saxon invasion and Middle Ages to the present. The Roman gallery is the most impressive, crammed with dazzling artifacts including a rare complete floor mosaic from the local ruins of a Roman villa. *(☎848 269. Open Apr.-Oct. M-Sa 10am-5pm, Su noon-5pm; Nov.-Mar. Tu-Sa 10am-4pm, Su noon-4pm. Free.)*

WALKS. The Buttercross, standing at 12 High St., is a good starting point for any of several walking routes through town. The statue, portraying St. John, William of Wykeham, and King Alfred, derives its name from the shadow it cast over the 15th-century market to keep butter cool. An ideal walk is along the **River Itchen,** the same taken by poet John Keats; directions and his "Ode To Autumn" are available at the TIC (50p). For a lovely view of the city, including the Wolvesey ruins, climb to **St. Giles's Hill Viewpoint** at sunset. Pass the Mill and take Bridge St. to the gate marked Magdalen Hill; follow the paths up from there. *The Winchester Walk*, detailing the various possible walking tours of Winchester, is free at the TIC.

🎵 🌿 ENTERTAINMENT AND FESTIVALS

Weekend nights attract hordes of revelers to bars along **Broadway** and **High St.** For a different type of fun, and since the weather won't let you stay dry anyway, go aquatic at **River Park Leisure Centre.** The park contains a huge pool, as well as Twister the Water Slide, included in the price of a swim. (☎848 700. Open daily 6:30am-11pm. £2, concessions £1.) In all its Edwardian glory, **Theatre Royal,** Jewry St. (☎840 440), hosts regional dramatic companies and concerts. Late May features the **Homelands Music Festival,** and though smaller than Glastonbury's summer music orgy, bands still play to sell-out crowds. Acquire tickets from the TIC. In early July, the **Hat Fair** (☎849 841), the longest running street festival in Britain, fills a weekend with free theater, street performances, and peculiar headgear.

🔳 DAYTRIPS FROM WINCHESTER

AUSTEN'S COTTAGE. Jane Austen lived in the meek village of **Chawton,** 15 mi. northeast of Winchester, from 1809-17. Visitors have come in droves since the recent cinematic fad for adaptations of her novels. It was here, at a tiny wooden table in the dining room of an ivy covered "cottage," that Lizzie Bennett, Emma Woodhouse, and their respective suitors were born. A now-famous creak was deliberately left in the door to warn Austen so she could hide her writing amid her needlework. Personal letters and belongings, first editions of her books, and period displays adorn the walls and fill the bookcases. *(Take Hampshire bus X64 (M-Sa 11 per day, return £5.30), or London and Country bus #65 on Su, from Winchester. Ask to be let off at the Chawton roundabout and follow the brown signs. ☎/fax (01420) 83262. Open Mar.-Dec. daily 11am-4:30pm; Jan.-Feb. Sa-Su 11am-4:30pm. £4, concessions £3, under 18 50p.)*

THE NEW FOREST. The New Forest, 20 mi. southwest of Winchester in **Lyndhurst,** was William the Conqueror's 145 sq. mi. personal hunting ground and remains, 1000 years later, an idyllic example of rural England. The **Rufus Stone** (near Brook and Cadnam) marks the spot where William's son was accidentally slain. Today, wild ponies, donkeys, and deer wander freely alongside winding roads. The **Museum and Visitor Centre** has a list of campsites. *(Take bus #66 to Romsey (every hr.) and transfer to a Lyndhurst bus; summer Su bus X66 (3 per day, return £4.10). Or catch a train to Southampton and then a bus to Lyndhurst. ☎(023) 8028 2269; www.thenewforest.co.uk. Open daily 10am-5pm. £2.50, seniors £2, children £1.50, families £6.50.)*

SOUTHWEST ENGLAND

The rolling hills and salty sea air of the chiefly agricultural southwest provide a refreshing change from city rhythms. In England's West Country, mists of legend shroud the counties of Dorset, Devon, and Cornwall almost as densely as the fog drifting in from the Atlantic. King Arthur was allegedly born at Tintagel on Cornwall's northern coast and is said to have battled Mordred on Bodmin Moor. One hamlet purports to be the site of Camelot, another claims to be the resting place of the Holy Grail, and no fewer than three small lakes are identified as the grave of Arthur's sword, Excalibur. In a more modern myth, the ghost of Sherlock Holmes still pursues the Hound of the Baskervilles across Dartmoor. Legends aside, the southwest has been a place of refuge for several distinct peoples, all of whom left their mark on the land and culture. Cornwall was the last stronghold of the Celts in England, while stone circles and excavated remnants of even older Neolithic communities leave volumes to the imagination. Farther east, the landmarks define other eras, from Salisbury's medieval cathedral and Bath's Roman baths to enigmatic Stonehenge and the fossils of Dorset's Jurassic Coast.

HIGHLIGHTS OF SOUTHWEST ENGLAND

STONEHENGE Puzzle over one of history's most astounding engineering feats and one of the world's great mysteries (p. 204).

BATH Dally in the world of 18th-century pleasure-seekers who repaved this Roman spa town with their elegant buildings and improper behavior (p. 205).

CLOVELLY Travel back in time to a tiny fishing village which, save for the tourist trappings, has weathered the last 50 years unchanged (p. 246).

ST. IVES Ride the surf or wander the art galleries in Cornwall's sophisticated coastal crossroads (p. 263).

⊏ TRANSPORTATION IN SOUTHWEST ENGLAND

It tends to be easier to get to Somerset, Avon, and Wiltshire than to regions farther southwest. **Trains** (☎ (08457) 484 950) offer fast and frequent service from London and the north. The region's primary east-west line from **London Paddington** passes through **Taunton, Exeter,** and **Plymouth,** ending at **Penzance.** Frequent trains connect London to Bath, Bristol, and Salisbury. Branch lines connect **St. Ives, Newquay, Falmouth,** and **Barnstaple** to the network. As elsewhere, day return fares are often only slightly more than single fares. A variety of rail **Rover passes** can be used in the region: the **Freedom of the Southwest Rover** covers all of Cornwall, Devon, Somerset, and parts of Avon and Dorset (8 days out of 15 £71.50). The **Devon Rail Rover** is bounded by and includes travel on the Taunton-Exmouth line on the east and the Gunnislake-Plymouth line in the west (3 days out of 7 £30, 8 out of 15 £46.50). The **Cornish Rail Rover** is bounded by the Gunnislake-Plymouth line (£25.50/£40).

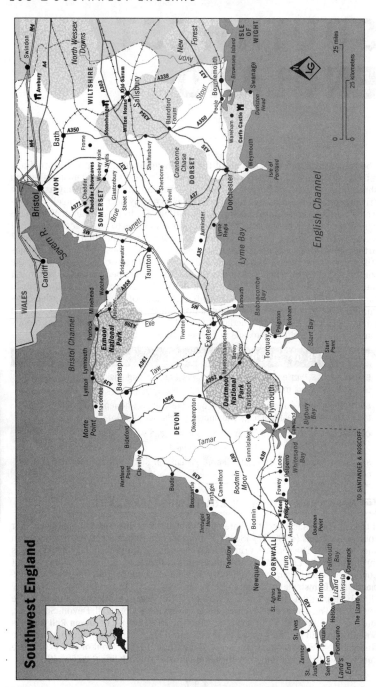

SOUTHWEST ENGLAND

Southwest England

Buses can be few and far between. **National Express** (☎ (08705) 808 080) runs to major points along the north coast via **Bristol** and to points along the south coast (including **Penzance**) via **Exeter** and **Plymouth.** For journeys within the region, local buses routes are usually less expensive and more extensive than trains. **First** is the largest bus company in the area. The comprehensive **Traveline** service (☎ (0870) 608 2608) can help plan travel to any destination; operators are on-call 7am-5pm daily. **Explorer** and **Day Rambler** tickets (£6, concessions £4.25, families £12.50) allow unlimited travel on all buses within one region. The **Corridor Ticket** (£2.50, children £1.50; £1 more before 8:45am) allows unlimited travel between two points on any route. When traveling to multiple destinations on one route, start at one end and ask the driver for a Corridor ticket to the end of the line, and for the day you'll have unlimited access to all the towns in between. Many tourist destinations are served by trains and buses only seasonally. For off-season transport (Oct.-May), phone Traveline to check routes and schedules.

⬚ HIKING AND BIKING IN THE SOUTHWEST

Distances between towns in southwest England are so short that you can travel through the region on your own steam. The narrow roads and hilly landscape can make biking difficult, but hardy cyclists will find the quiet lanes and country paths rewarding terrain. If you're walking or cycling bring along a large-scale **Ordnance Survey** map and a windbreaker to shield you from foul weather. As always, respect the property of local residents when hiking or biking through the countryside.

The 630 mi. **South West Coast Path,** England's longest coastal path, originates in Somerset (at Minehead, in Exmoor National Park) and passes through North Devon, Cornwall, and South Devon, ending in Dorset (Poole). Winding past cliffs, caves, beaches, and resorts, it takes several weeks to walk in its entirety. However, since the path passes through many towns, is easily accessible by bus, and features B&Bs and hostels at manageable intervals, it's perfect for shorter hikes. Many rivers intersect the path; some can be waded across, but others require ferries—check times carefully to avoid being stranded. Some sections of the trail are difficult enough to dissuade all but the most ambitious, so consult tourist officials before you set out to make sure that the area you want to visit is well-marked. Most TICs sell guides and Ordnance Survey maps covering appropriate sections of the path, which is generally smooth enough to cover by **bike;** rental shops can often suggest three- to seven-day cycling routes.

The path is divided into four parts. The **Somerset and North Devon Coastal Path** extends from Minehead through Exmoor National Park to Bude. The least arduous section, it features the highest cliffs in southwest England and passes the 100 ft. dunes of Saunton Sands and the steep cobbled streets of Clovelly on Hartland Point. The **Cornwall Coast Path,** with some of the most rugged stretches, starts in Bude, where magnificent Cornish cliffs harbor a vast range of birds and marine life, rounds the southwest tip of Britain, and continues along the coast to Plymouth. The **South Devon Coast Path** runs from Plymouth to Paignton, tracing spectacular cliffs, wide estuaries, and remote bays set off by lush vegetation and wildflowers. The final section, the **Dorset Coast Path,** picks up in Lyme Regis and runs to Poole Harbor. For more information, contact the **South West Coast Path Association** (☎ (01364) 73859) or any local TIC.

WILTSHIRE

SALISBURY   ☎ 01722

That all roads in Salisbury lead to its cathedral gates is no accident—the city's small grid of streets was carefully charted by Bishop Poore in the early 13th century. The cathedral is the geographic center of town, and the Salisbury Stake the highest spire in England. If one architectural wonder isn't enough, you might try visiting Stonehenge, a nearby and moderately interesting group of rocks.

▐ TRANSPORTATION

Trains: South Western Rd. (☎(02380) 213 600), west of town across the River Avon. Ticket office open M-Sa 5:30am-8pm, Su 7:30am-8:45pm. Trains (☎(08457) 484 950) from most major towns, including: **London Waterloo** (1½hr., every hr., £22-30); **Southampton** (40min., 2 per hr., £8); **Winchester** (1½hr., every hr., £11.50); **Portsmouth and Southsea** (1½hr., every hr., £11-13).

Buses: 8 Endless St. (☎336 855). Open M-F 8:15am-5:30pm, Sa 8:15am-5:15pm. **National Express** (☎(08705) 808 080) runs from **London** (2¾hr.; 4 per day; £12.20, return £13.10). Buy tickets at the TIC. **Wilts and Dorset** (☎336 855) from **Bath** (X4, 1 per hr. 7am-6pm, £3.95). An **Explorer** ticket is good for a day's worth of travel on **Wilts and Dorset** buses and some **Hampshire, Provincial,** and **Solent Blue** buses (£5.50, seniors £3.85, children £2.60, families £10.50).

Taxis: Cabs cruise by the train station and New Canal. **A and B Taxis** (☎744 744) provides wheelchair-friendly service. **505050 Value Cars** (☎505 050) runs 24hr.

Bike Rental: Hayball Cycles, 26-30 Winchester St. (☎411 378). £10 per day, £2.50 overnight, £60 per week; deposit £25. Open M-Sa 9am-5:30pm. For routes and services call the **Walking and Cycling Hotline** (☎623 255).

▐ PRACTICAL INFORMATION

Tourist Information Centre: Fish Row (☎334 956; www.visitsalisbury.com), in the Guildhall in Market Sq. National Express ticket service. Books rooms for a 10% deposit. Open June-Sept. M-Tu 9:30am-5pm, W-Sa 9:30am-6pm, Su 10:30am-4:30pm; Oct.-Apr. M-Sa 9:30am-5pm; May M-Sa 9:30am-5pm, Su 10:30am-4:30pm. 1½hr. **city tours** leave Apr.-Oct. 11am and 8pm; £2.50, children £1.

Financial Services: Banks are easily found. **Thomas Cook,** 18-19 Queen St. (☎313 500). Open M-Tu and Th-Sa 9am-5:30pm, W 10am-5:30pm.

Launderette: Washing Well, 28 Chipper Ln. (☎421 874). Open daily 7:30am-8:30pm.

Police: Wilton Rd. (☎411 444).

Internet Access: Starlight Internet Cafe, 1 Endless St. (☎349 359) at Market Sq. £1 per 15min. Open Mar.-Aug. daily 9:30am-10pm; Sept.-Feb. 9:30am-7pm. **ICafe,** 30 Milford St. (☎320 050). Funky music and fishtank. £2 per 30min., £2 minimum; 10% student discount. Open M-Sa 10am-8pm, Su noon-8pm. **YHA Salisbury** (see below).

Post Office: 24 Castle St. (☎(08457) 223 344), at Chipper Ln. **Bureau de change.** Open M-Sa 9am-5:30pm. **Post Code:** SP1 1AB.

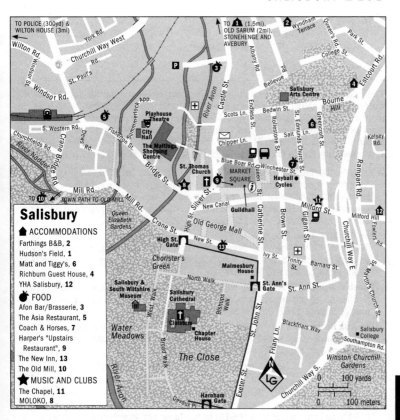

Salisbury

ACCOMMODATIONS
Farthings B&B, **2**
Hudson's Field, **1**
Matt and Tiggy's, **6**
Richburn Guest House, **4**
YHA Salisbury, **12**

FOOD
Afon Bar/Brasserie, **3**
The Asia Restaurant, **5**
Coach & Horses, **7**
Harper's "Upstairs
    Restaurant", **9**
The New Inn, **13**
The Old Mill, **10**

MUSIC AND CLUBS
The Chapel, **11**
MOLOKO, **8**

ACCOMMODATIONS AND CAMPING

Salisbury's proximity to a certain circle o' stones breeds B&Bs, most of them comfortable and reasonably priced, though they fill quickly in summer.

YHA Salisbury, Milford Hill House, Milford Hill (☎327 572; fax 330 446). Tucked into a cedar grove with 74 beds, 4 kitchenettes, TV lounge, Internet access (£2.50 per 30min.), and cafeteria (breakfast £3.40, dinner under £4). Lockout 10am-1pm. The first place to fill in summer; make a reservation. Dorms £11.25, under 18 £8. ❷

Matt and Tiggy's, 51 Salt Ln. (☎327 443), just up from the bus station. A welcoming 450-year-old home with warped floors and ceiling beams and an overflow house nearby; both are remarkably convenient. Mellow, hostel-style, 2-, 3-, and 4-person rooms; no bunk beds. Breakfast £2.50. Sheets £1. Dorms £11-12. ❷

Farthings B&B, 9 Swaynes Close (☎330 749). A peaceful haven with a gorgeous garden, just a 10min. walk from the city center. Singles £23-27; doubles £46-55. ❸

Richburn Guest House, 25 Estcourt Rd. (☎325 189). Ensuite bathrooms and ample space are complimented by warm and efficient service at this upscale-ish B&B. Singles £30; doubles £40-52; family rooms £50-90. ❸

Camping: Hudson's Field, Castle Rd. (☎320 713). Between Salisbury and Stonehenge, 20min. from the city center. Modern, clean, and well located. Vehicle curfew 11pm. £3.50-5 per person. Pitches £5 per night. ❶

📷📺 FOOD AND PUBS

The most jaded pub dweller can find a pleasing venue among Salisbury's 60-odd watering holes. Most serve cheap food ($4-6) and live music (free). **Market Sq.** in the town center fills on Tuesdays and Saturdays, with vendors hawking everything from peaches to posters. (Open 7am-4pm.) A **Sainsbury's** supermarket is at The Maltings. (☎332 282. Open M-Th 8am-8pm, F 8am-9pm, Sa 7:30am-7pm, Su 10am-4pm.) **Salisbury Health Foods,** Queen St., is near the TIC. (Open M-Sa 9am-5:30pm.)

🔲 **Harper's "Upstairs Restaurant,"** 6-7 Ox Rd., Market Sq. (☎333 118). Their slogan is "real food is our speciality," but their true speciality is really *good* food. Inventive English and international dishes (£6-10) make a hearty meal, as does the "8B48" (2 generous courses £8 before 8pm, seniors £6.50). Open M-F noon-2pm and 6-9:30pm, Sa noon-2pm and 6-10pm, Su 6-9pm. AmEx/MC/V. ❷

The Old Mill, Town Path (☎327 517), atop the River Nadder at the end of a scenic 10min. stroll along Town Path through the Harnem Water Meadows. The ideal setting for an outdoor drink, with real ales from Salisbury's Hopback Brewery on tap. Open M-Sa 11am-11pm, Su noon-10:30pm. ❷

Coach & Horses, Winchester St. (☎336 254). Meals and drinks flow nonstop, drawing families during the day and a louder crowd at night to what may be Salisbury's oldest pub, open since 1382. Open M-Sa 11am-11pm. ❶

The Asia Restaurant, 90 Fisherton St. (☎327 628). Indian food so generously spiced it can be smelled from across the street. Appetizers run £2-4, main courses £4-11. Open daily noon-3pm and 5:30pm-midnight. ❷

The New Inn, 41-47 New St. (☎327 679). A trailblazer for nonsmoking pubs in Britain. Enjoy your brew or vegetarian meal (£5.50-7.25) with a cathedral view. Open M-Sa 11am-3pm and 6-11pm, Su noon-3pm and 7-11pm; no food 2-3pm or 10-11pm. ❷

Afon Bar/Brasserie, Mill Stream Approach (☎552 366), off Castle St. Light lunches (£5-11) and romantic dinners (£5-18) for the young and smartly-dressed at this mellow spot overlooking the River Avon. Show your theater tickets for a free bottle of house wine with dinner (M-Th 6:30-7:30pm). Open M-Sa 11am-11pm, Su noon-3pm. ❸

🧭 SIGHTS

🔲 SALISBURY CATHEDRAL

☎555 120. *Open June-Aug. M-Sa 7:15am-8:15pm, Su 7:15am-6:15pm; Sept.-May daily 7:15am-6:15pm. Suggested donation £3.50, concessions £2.50, children £2, families £8. Evensong M-Sa 5:30pm, Su 3pm. Free tours May-Oct. M-Sa 9:30am-4:45pm, Su 4-6:15pm; Nov.-Feb. M-Sa 10am-4pm. 1½hr. roof and tower tours May-Sept. M-Sa 11am, 2, 3pm, Su 4:30pm; June-Aug. M-Sa also 6:30pm; winter hours vary, so call ahead. £3, concessions £2.*

Salisbury Cathedral rises from its grassy close to a neck-breaking height of 404 ft. Built in just 38 years, rather than the usual centuries, the cathedral has a singular and weighty design. The bases of the marble pillars bend inward under the strain of 6400 tons of limestone—if a pillar rings when you knock on it, you should probably move away. Nearly 700 years have left the building in need of repair, and scaffolding shrouds parts of the outer walls where the stone is disintegrating (note the avalanche warning signs). Once inside, head to the wooden tomb of William Longespee, Earl of Salisbury (d. 1226), rare in a universe of stone sarcophagi. The chapel houses the oldest functioning mechanical clock, a strange collection of wheels and ropes that has ticked 500 million times over the last 600 years. A tiny stone figure rests in the nave—legend has it either that a boy bishop is entombed on the spot or that it covers the heart of Richard Poore, founder of the cathedral. The incongruously abstract window at the eastern end, gleaming in rich jewel-like tones, is dedicated to prisoners of conscience, for whom a prayer is said each day.

Much to King John's chagrin, the best-preserved of the four surviving copies of the *Magna Carta* rests in the **Chapter House** and is still legible (to those of you who can read medieval Latin). Ask a guide for a complete list of the relief figures in the stunningly detailed friezes. *(Open June-Aug. M-Sa 9:30am-5:30pm, Su noon-5:30pm; Sept.-May daily 9:30am-5:30pm. Free.)*

SALISBURY AND SOUTH WILTSHIRE MUSEUM. The museum houses a mixture of artwork, including Turner's watercolors of the cathedral, and random oddities like period fashion and doll houses. The worthwhile Stonehenge exhibit shares an extensive amount of history—not bad, seeing as the structure's still utterly baffling. *(65 The Close, along the West Walk. ☎332 151. Open July-Aug. M-Sa 10am-5pm, Su 2-5pm; Sept.-June M-Sa 10am-5pm. £3.50, concessions £2.30, under 16 £1, families £7.90.)*

🎭 🎵 NIGHTLIFE, ENTERTAINMENT, AND FESTIVALS

For a little nightlife, head to **The Chapel,** 30 Milford St., whose sign requests that "no unattractive people" be admitted. Not to worry—don't wear jeans or trainers, and you'll be cute enough for the three huge dance floors. *(☎504 255. W £2; Th £4, ladies free; F-Sa £10. Open W 10:30pm-2am, Th 8pm-2:30am, F-Sa 8pm-3am.)* **MOLOKO,** 5 Bridge St., is a self-styled Russian vodka bar, with red walls and a big red star outside. Choose from an endless list of vodkas, but try not to spill—up to 200 people pack the tiny space on weekends. *(☎507 050. Open Tu-Sa noon-1am.)*

Salisbury's repertory theater company puts on shows at the **Playhouse,** Malthouse Ln., over the bridge off Fisherton St. *(☎320 333. Box office open daily 10am-7pm. £9-14, concessions £2 less. Half-price tickets available same day.)* The **Salisbury Arts Centre,** Bedwin St., offers music, theater, and exhibitions throughout the year. *(☎321 744. Box office open Tu-Sa 10am-4pm. From £5.)* Summertime features free Sunday **concerts** in various parks; call the TIC for info. The **Salisbury Festival** features dance exhibitions, music, and wine-tasting for two weeks in late May and early June. Contact the Festival Box Office at the Playhouse. *(☎320 333; www.salisburyfestival.co.uk. Tickets from £2.50.)*

🔲 DAYTRIPS FROM SALISBURY

OLD SARUM. At Old Sarum, the prehistoric precursor to Salisbury, an Iron Age fort evolved into a Saxon town, then a Norman fortress. In the 13th century, church officials moved the settlement into the neighboring valley, where they built Salisbury Cathedral. Old Sarum was the most notorious of the "rotten boroughs"—districts notorious for the buying and selling of Parliamentary seats—eliminated by the Reform Act of 1832. Now a windswept mound strewn with stone ruins, it is still an atmospheric spot with perfect country views. Look for the annual celestial visitation, heralded by a detailed crop circle imprinted in the wheatfields. *(Off the A345, 2 mi. north of town. Buses #3 and 6-9 run every 15min. from Salisbury. ☎335 398. Open July-Aug. M-Sa 10am-5pm, Su 2-5pm; Apr.-June and Sept.-Oct. M-Sa 10am-5pm; Nov.-Mar. M-Sa 10am-4pm. £2, concessions £1.50, children £1.)*

WILTON HOUSE. Declared by James I to be "the finest house in the land," the home of the Earl of Pembroke showcases paintings—including Rembrandt's portrait of his mother, returned to the Great Ante Room after she was stolen and MIA for eight years, then discovered in the trunk of a London car. The house's impressive—nay, outrageous—interior was designed in part by Inigo Jones. The Tudor kitchen and Victorian laundry shed new light on the domestic arts (complete with automated rat). Before touring the house, watch the award-winning introductory film, narrated by the ghost of a plague-stricken 14th-century nun. *(3 mi. west of Salisbury on the A30; take bus #60 or 61 (M-Sa every 10min., Su 1 per hr.) ☎ 746 720. Open Easter-Oct. daily 10:30am-5:30pm; last admission 4:30pm. House and grounds £7.25, concessions £6.25, children £4.50, families £20. Grounds only £3.75, children £2.75.)*

NEAR SALISBURY

STONEHENGE

> You may put a hundred questions to these rough-hewn giants as they bend in grim contemplation of their fellow companions; but your curiosity falls dead in the vast sunny stillness that shrouds them and the strange monument, with all its unspoken memories, becomes simply a heart-stirring picture in a land of pictures.
> —Henry James

Surely these gentle giants will fascinate us for millennia to come. A ring of colossi amid swaying grass and indifferent sheep, Stonehenge stands unperturbed by the winds whipping across the flat Salisbury plain. The present 22 ft. stones comprise the fifth temple constructed on the site—Stonehenge, it seems, was already ancient in ancient times. The first arrangement probably consisted of an arch and circular earthwork furrowed in 3050 BC, and was in use for about 500 years. Its relics are the **Aubrey Holes** (white patches in the earth) and the **Heel Stone** (the rough block standing outside the circle). The next monument used about 60 stones imported from Wales around 2100 BC and marked astronomical directions. The present shape, once a complete circle, dates from about 1500 BC.

Though fantastical attributions of Stonehenge to sources ranging from Merlin the Magician to little green men have helped build an attractive mythology, the more plausible source—Neolithic builders—is perhaps the most astonishing of all. The incredible motivational drive and era-defying technology required to erect these 45-ton stones (many of which came from hundreds of miles away) make Stonehenge an incomparable monument to human achievement.

Many peoples have worshipped at the Stonehenge site, from late Neolithic and early Bronze Age chieftains to contemporary mystics. In 300 BC, Druids arrived from the Continent and claimed Stonehenge as their shrine. Today, Druids are permitted to enter Stonehenge on the summer Solstice to perform their ceremonial exercises. In the last few years, however, new-age mystics have beaten them to the spot; in 1999 this led to conflicts with the police and eventual arrests, but the past three celebrations have proved considerably more peaceful.

◪ **TRANSPORTATION.** Getting to Stonehenge, 8 mi. northwest of Salisbury, doesn't require much effort—as long as you don't have a 45-ton rock in tow. **Wilts and Dorset** (☎ 336 855) runs several **buses,** including daily service from the Salisbury train station (#3, 40min., return £5.25). The first bus leaves Salisbury at 8:45am (Su 10:35am), and the last leaves Stonehenge at 6:30pm (Su 5:45pm). An **Explorer** ticket (£5) is cheaper than a Salisbury-Stonehenge return; it allows you to travel all day on any bus, including those stopping by **Avebury,** Stonehenge's less-crowded cousin (see below), and Old Sarum (see p. 203). **Guide Friday,** with Wilts and Dorset, runs a **tour bus** from Salisbury (3 per day, £6-12.50).

The most scenic walking or cycling route from Salisbury is the **Woodford Valley Route** through Woodford and Wilsford. Go north on Castle Rd., bear left just before Victoria Park onto Stratford Rd., and follow the road over the bridge through Lower, Middle, and Upper Woodford. After about 9 mi., turn left onto the A303 for the last mile. If Stonehenge isn't enough rock for you, keep your eyes peeled to your right in Wilsford for the Jacobean mansion that belongs to singer Sting.

◙ **ON THE ROCKS?** Admission to Stonehenge includes a 40min. audio tour that uses handsets resembling cell phones. The effect may be more haunting than the rocks themselves—a bizarre march of tourists who seem engaged in business calls. Nonetheless, the tour is helpful, and includes arguments between a shepherd and his mother about the stones' origins. English Heritage also offers free guided tours (30min.). From the roadside or from Amesbury Hill, 1½ mi. up the A303, you can get a free view of the coterie of giants looming in the distance. (☎(01980) 624 715. Open June-Aug. daily 9am-7pm; mid-Mar. to May and Sept. to mid-Oct. 9:30am-6pm; mid-Oct. to mid-Mar. 9:30am-4pm. £4.40, concessions £3.30, children £2.20, families £11.)

AVEBURY

The small village that has sprouted within the **stone circle** at Avebury lends an intimate feel to this sight, a far cry from the sightseeing mobs storming Stonehenge, 18 mi. to the south. Visitors can amble among the megaliths and the sheep, and even picnic in their midst. With stones that date from 2500 BC, Avebury's sprawling titans are older than their favored (and smaller) cousins at Stonehenge. Built over the course of centuries, the circle has remained true to its original form and a mystery to the archaeologists, mathematicians, and astronomers who have studied it so stubbornly. Just outside the ring, curious **Silbury Hill** rises from the ground. Europe's largest manmade mound has stumped researchers, and its date, 2660 BC, was only determined by the serendipitous excavation of a flying ant. The **Alexander Keillor Museum** details the history of the stone circle and its environs. (Buses #5 and 6 run from Salisbury, 6 per day, £3.90. ☎(01672) 539 250. Open Apr.-Oct. daily 10am-6pm; Nov.-Mar. 10am-4pm. £2.50.) **The Circle Restaurant**, just beside the museum, serves sandwiches, soups, and desserts for £3-6. Locate the Avebury **tourist information centre** by following the signs from the bus stop through the carpark. (☎(01672) 539 425. Open W-Sa 10am-5pm, Su 10am-4pm.)

SOMERSET AND AVON

BATH   ☎01225

On a perfect day, Bath is one of the most beautiful spots in England—a trip to this sophisticated spa town is a must for visitors longing for Italian vistas. Early in their occupation of Britain, the Romans built an elaborate complex of baths to house the curative waters at the town they called Aquae Sulis. In 1701, Queen Anne's trip to the hot springs reestablished the city as a prominent meeting place for artists, politicians, and intellectuals. Bath quickly became a social capital second only to London, its scandalous scene immortalized by authors as diverse as Fielding, Austen, and Dickens. The city's Georgian architecture, heavily bombed in WWII, has been painstakingly restored so that today's thoroughfares remain utterly elegant, even if graced by more hair salons than literary salons.

SOUTHWEST ENGLAND

TRANSPORTATION

Trains: Bath Spa Station, Railway Pl., at the south end of Manvers St. Ticket office open M-F 5:30am-8:30pm, Sa 6:30am-8:30pm, Su 7:20am-8:30pm. Travel center open M-F 8am-7pm, Sa 9am-6pm, Su 9:30am-6pm. **Trains** (☎ (08457) 484 950) from: **Birmingham** (2½hr., every hr., £23); **Bristol** (15min., 4 per hr., £4.60); **Exeter** (1¼hr., every hr., £22); **London Paddington** (1½hr., 2 per hr., £32); **London Waterloo** (2¼-3hr., 3 per day, £21); **Salisbury** (1hr., every hr., £10); **Plymouth** (2-3hr., every hr., £32).

Buses: Station at Manvers St. (☎464 446). Ticket office open M-Sa 8am-5:30pm. **National Express** (☎(08705) 808 080) from **London** (3hr., every hr., £13) and **Oxford** (2hr., 1 per day, £10.25). **Badgerline** buses (☎464 464) sell a **Day Rambler** ticket for unlimited bus travel in the region (£6, concessions £4.25).

Taxis: Abbey Radio (☎444 444) or **Bath Taxis** (☎484 488).

Bike Rental: Avon Valley Bike Hire (☎442 442), behind the train station. £9 per half-day, £14 per day. Credit card deposit. Open M-W and F-Sa 9am-5:30pm, Th 9am-8pm.

Boat Rental: Bath Boating Station (☎466 407), at the end of Forester Rd., about ½ mi. north of town. Punts and canoes £5 per person first hr., £1.50 each additional hr. Open May-Sept. daily 10am-6pm, Apr. and Oct. 11am-6pm, Nov.-Mar. 2-6pm.

ORIENTATION AND PRACTICAL INFORMATION

The **Roman Baths,** the **Pump Room,** and **Bath Abbey** cluster in the city center. The River Avon flows just east of them, and wraps around the south part of town near the **train** and **bus stations.** Uphill to the northwest, historical buildings lie on **Royal Crescent** and **The Circus.**

Tourist Information Centre: Abbey Chambers (☎477 221; www.visitbath.co.uk). Town map and mini-guide 50p. Pick up *This Month in Bath* (free) for event listings. Books accommodations for £5 plus 10% deposit. Open May-Sept. M-Sa 9:30am-6pm, Su 10am-4pm; Oct.-Apr. M-Sa 9:30am-5pm, Su 10am-4pm.

Tours: The Mayor's Honorary Guides lead free **walking tours** from the entrance to the baths daily at 10:30am and 2pm. The 90min. **Bizarre Bath Walking Tour** (☎335 124) begins at the Huntsman Inn at North Parade Passage. Apr.-Sept. nightly at 8pm. Hysterical guides impart absolutely no historical facts. £5, students £4.50. The 2hr. **Ghost Walk** (☎463 618) begins at 8pm at Nash Bar of Garrick's Head, near Theatre Royal. Apr.-Oct. M-Sa, Nov.-Mar. F. £5, students and children £4. **Bath's Classic** (☎(07721) 559 686) runs hop-on/hop-off bus tours. Every 15min. 9am-4:30pm; £6.50. **Mad Max Tours** (☎325 900) organizes daytrips to Wiltshire, including Stonehenge and the Cotswolds. Departs 8:45am from the end of Cheap St.; £17.50. **CitySafari** (☎(07977) 929 486) does the same but leaves at 10am from the Abbey Hotel; £17.50.

Financial Services: Banks are ubiquitous; most are open M-F 9:30am-5pm, Sa 9:30am-12:30pm. **Thomas Cook,** 20 New Bond St. (☎492 000). Open M-Tu and Th-Sa 9am-5:30pm, W 10am-5:30pm. **American Express,** 5 Bridge St. (☎444 757), just before Pulteney Bridge. Open M-Sa 9am-5:30pm. **Branch** (☎424 416) in the TIC.

Luggage Storage: International Backpackers Hostel (☎446 787) will store for non-guests. £2 per bag. Open daily 8am-midnight.

Launderette: Spruce Goose, Margaret's Buildings, off Brock St. Wash £2-3, dry £2, soap 60p. Open M-F and Su 8am-9pm, Sa 8am-8pm, last wash 1 hr. before closing.

Police: Manvers St. (☎444 343), near the train and bus stations.

Pharmacy: Boots, 1 Marchants Passage, Southgate. Open M-W 9am-5:30pm, Th 9am-6:30pm, F-Sa 8:45am-6pm, Su 11am-5pm.

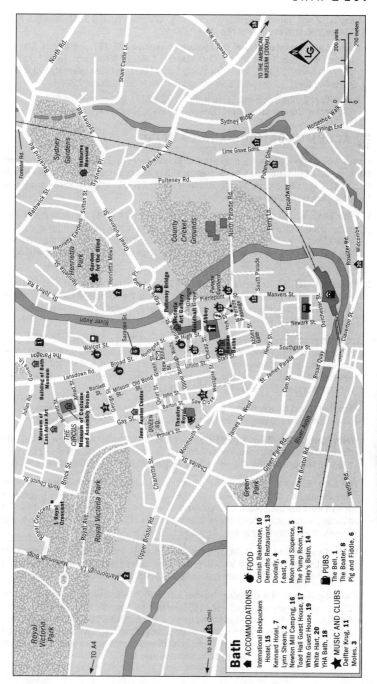

SOUTHWEST
ENGLAND

Bath

▲ ACCOMMODATIONS
International Backpackers
Hostel, **15**
Kennard Hotel, **7**
Lynn Sheam, **2**
Newton Mill Camping, **16**
Toad Hall Guest House, **17**
White Guest House, **19**
White Hart, **20**
YHA Bath, **18**

★ MUSIC AND CLUBS
Delfter Krug, **11**
Moles, **3**

♦ FOOD
Cornish Bakehouse, **10**
Demuths Restaurant, **13**
Doolally, **4**
f.east, **9**
Moon and Sixpence, **5**
The Pump Room, **12**
Tilley's Bistro, **14**

▮ PUBS
The Bell, **1**
The Boater, **8**
Pig and Fiddle, **6**

Hospital: Royal United Hospital, Coombe Park, in Weston (☎428 331). Take bus #14, 20A, or 20C from the train or bus station.

Internet Access: International Backpackers Hostel (☎446 787; see below). 50p per 15min. Open daily 8am-midnight. **Click Internet Cafe,** 13 Manvers St. (☎481 008), is faster but pricier. £1 per 20min. Open daily 10am-10pm. **Ret@iler Internet,** 129 Walcot St. (☎445 999). £3 per hr., £1.50 minimum. Open M-Sa 10:30am-7:30pm.

Post Office: 21-25 New Bond St. (☎(08457) 223 344), across from the Podium Shopping Centre. **Bureau de change.** Open M-Sa 9am-5:30pm. **Post Code:** BA1 1AJ.

ACCOMMODATIONS AND CAMPING

Bath's well-to-do visitors drive up prices. B&Bs cluster on **Pulteney Rd.** and **Pulteney Gdns.** South of the train station, **Widcombe Hill** offers options, as does **Upper Bristol Rd.,** west of the city center. For yet another front of B&Bs, walk west toward Royal Victoria Park onto **Crescent Gdns.**

▨ **Lynn Shearn,** Prior House, 3 Marlborough Ln. (☎313 587; priorhouse@greatplaces.co.uk). Take bus #14 from the train station to Hinton Garage (6 per hr., £1) or walk 15min. Friendly proprietors and inviting rooms, complete with board games and hair dryers. Familial breakfast ensues around a large dining table. Doubles and twins from £45, with bath £50. ❹

▨ **Kennard Hotel,** 11 Henrietta St. (☎310 472; reception@kennard.co.uk), off Great Pulteney St. This 18th-century Georgian townhouse is the epitome of luxury, with gilded mirrors and chandeliers. Rooms with phone and modem connection. Breakfast included. Singles £48-54; doubles £88-110. ❹

International Backpackers Hostel, 13 Pierrepont St. (☎446 787; fax 446 305; info@backpackers-uk.demon.co.uk). Extremely convenient location, up the street from the stations and 3 blocks from the baths. Each room and bed is identified by a music genre and artist. ("I'm sleeping in Classical on Gershwin.") Internet access (see above). Luggage storage £1. Laundry £2.50. Dorms £12. ❷

Toad Hall Guest House, 6 Lime Grove (☎423 254). Friendly B&B with 3 spacious doubles (1 can be let as single) and hearty breakfasts. Single £22-25; doubles £42-45. ❸

White Hart, Widcombe Hill (☎313 985), 5min. from train station. New hostel with friendly staff, satisfying accommodations, and kitchen. Dorm beds, 1 single, 2 doubles, 1 family. Midnight curfew. Dorms £12.50; single £20; doubles £40; families £50. ❷

YHA Bath, Bathwick Hill (☎465 674; bath@yha.org.uk). From North Parade Rd., turn left on Pulteney Rd., right on Bathwick Hill, then climb the endless hill (40min.). Bus #18 or 418 from the bus station goes up every 10min. (return £1.20). Secluded Italianate mansion is distant but comfortable. Internet access (£2.50 per 30min.), lockers, and laundry. Book ahead in summer. Dorms £11.25, under 18 £8. ❷

White Guest House, 23 Pulteney Gdns. (☎426 075). Homey B&B with flower-filled patio. All rooms have TV and bath. Singles £28; doubles £50. Prices lower Nov.-Apr. £2 off if you tell them *Let's Go* sent you; 10% off if you stay 3 or more nights. ❸

Camping: Newton Mill Camping, Newton Rd. (☎333 909; newtonmill@hotmail.com), 2½ mi. west of city center off the A36. Take bus #5 from the bus station (5 per hr., return £1.60) to Twerton and ask to be let off at the campsite. 90 car and caravan sites and 105 tent plots in an idyllic stream-side setting. Shop, laundry, and restaurant. No reservation necessary for individual campers; drivers should book a week ahead. Tents £4.25-12, caravans and cars £11-15. Showers free. ❶

⌐ FOOD

Although most restaurants in Bath are expensive and elegant, reasonably priced cafes and restaurants dot the city. For fruits and vegetables, visit the **Guildhall Market,** between High St. and Grand Parade. (460 808. Open daily 9am-5:30pm.) Find picnic fare at **Waitrose** market's excellent salad bar in the Podium on High St., across from the post office. (☎442 550. Open M-F 8:30am-8pm, Sa 8:30am-7pm, Su 11am-5pm.) Southwest of town is an enormous **Sainsbury's,** at Green Park Station. (☎444 737. Open M-F 9am-midnight, Sa 7:30am-10pm, Su 10am-4pm.)

The Moon and Sixpence, 6a Broad St. (☎460 962), draws a yuppie crowd with simple decor. Locals tout the mouthwatering "modern international cuisine." Lunch £7, dinner £10-15. Open M-Sa 11am-noon and 5:30-11pm, Su 11am-3pm and 6:30-11pm. ❸

Demuths Restaurant, 2 North Parade Passage (☎446 059), off Abbey Green. Creative vegetarian and vegan dishes even a devoted carnivore would enjoy. Chocolate fudge cake (£4.25) is superb. Lunch £5.50-6.50, dinner £11. Open daily 10am-10pm. ❷

Tilley's Bistro, 3 North Parade Passage (☎484 200). Savor Tilley's French creations and English and vegetarian fare (£5-9). Open M-Sa noon-2:30pm and 6:30-11pm. ❷

f.east, 27 High St. (☎331 330), serves fantastic Pan-Asian cuisine from Japanese udon to pad thai to Korean kimchi. Sophisticated decor and bench seating create a relaxed, friendly atmosphere. Noodles £5-8. Open M-Sa noon-11pm, Su noon-5pm. ❷

Cornish Bakehouse, 11a The Corridor (☎426 635), across from Guildhall. Award-winning Cornish pastries £1.40-1.80. Open M-Sa 9am-5:30pm, Su 10am-5:30pm. ❶

Doolally, 51 Walcot St. (☎444 122). A fun, playful atmosphere and small, tasty treats. Desserts 60p-£1.20, sandwiches and salads £2-3. Open M-Tu 8:30am-5:30pm, W-Sa 8:30am-10:30pm, Su 11am-4:30pm. ❶

The Pump Room, Abbey Churchyard (☎444 477). Exercises its monopoly over Bath Spa drinking water (50p per glass) in a palatial Victorian ballroom. Cream tea (£7.50) served after 2:30pm. Lunch £4-15; pricey dinners served July-Aug. (£22-25 for 2-3 courses). Open Apr.-Sept. daily 9:30am-6pm; Oct.-Mar. 9:30am-5pm; last admission 30min. before closing. ❹

THE BIG SPLURGE

BATH CALORIE CRAWL

This sumptuous calorie crawl is a worthy splurge for any traveler who's trekked through Bath—those who've climbed Bathwick Hill deserve a double go.

Fudge connoisseurs should start at **Jim Garrahy's Fudge Kitchen,** 10 Abbey Churchyard. Handmade fudges melt in your mouth and come in over a dozen flavors, including Coffee Walnut, Whiskey Cream, After Dinner Mint, and the sigh-inducing Belgian Chocolate Swirl. At £3 per slice and £11 per box, it may damage your waist more than your wallet. *(☎462 277. Open daily 10am-5:30pm.)*

Take a lengthy stroll to **The Fine Cheese Co.,** 29/31 Walcot St., specializing in decadent English and European cheeses. Prices range from Muenster at £10 per kg. to Roquefort at £27. The *Bath Box* gift set (£23.50) includes crackers, chutney, and local cheeses. *(☎483 407. Open M-F 9:30am-5:30pm, Sa 9am-5:30pm.)*

Hobble back to the city center for dessert. **Whittard,** 10 Stall St., features Lindor chocolates in white, dark, and hazelnut. Buy a whole box (£4) or bite-sized pieces (£1.80 per 100g). *(☎428 684. Open M-Sa 9am-5:30pm, Su noon-5pm.)* With full-sized chocolate soccer and rugby balls (both £13), **Café Cadbury,** 23 Union St., caters to the sporty. *(☎444 030. Open M-Sa 9am-7pm, Su 11am-4pm.)*

SIGHTS

THE ROMAN BATHS. In 1880, sewer diggers inadvertently uncovered the first glimpse of what excavation has shown to be a splendid model of advanced Roman engineering. Bath flourished as a Roman city for 400 years, its hot bubbling springs making the city a pilgrimage site. Most of the outside bath complex, however, is not Roman, but a Georgian dream of what Romans might have built.

The **museum** merits the entrance price with its displays on Roman building design (including central heating and internal plumbing) and excavation finds. Walkways wind through the partially excavated remains of the complex, past bubbling springs that invisibly gurgle up 250,000 gallons a day at 115°F. Read the various recovered curses that Romans cast into the spring; some are deliciously meanspirited. Tradition promised that if a curse floated on the water, it would be visited back upon the curser. The Romans neatly avoided this by writing their ill wishes on lead. *(Stall St. ☎ 477 759. Open July-Aug. daily 9am-10pm; Oct.-Mar. 9:30am-5:30pm; Apr.-June and Sept. 9am-6pm. Last admission 1hr. before close. Hourly guided and audio tours included. £8, concessions £7, children £4.60, families £20.50. Joint ticket to the Baths and the Museum of Costume £10/£9/£5.50/£27.)*

MUSEUM OF COSTUME AND ASSEMBLY ROOMS. This museum hosts a dazzling, albeit motionless, parade of 400 years of catwalk fashions, from 17th-century silver tissue garments to the revealing Versace dresses worn by J.Lo and Geri Haliwell. The collection is so vast that only a fraction of it is displayed. Free audio tours dispel the myth of the 18-inch waist of the late 1800s—it was much closer to a heifer-like 21. *(Bennett St. ☎ 477 789. Open daily 10am-5pm. £5, seniors £4, children £3.50. See above for joint ticket with the Roman Baths.)* The museum is in the basement of the **Assembly Rooms,** which staged fashionable 18th-century events. Although WWII ravaged the rooms, renovations duplicate the originals in fine detail. *(☎ 477 789. Open daily 10am-5pm. Free.)*

BATH ABBEY. On a site that once contained a Saxon cathedral three times as large, the 15th-century abbey still towers over its neighbors at 78 feet. In AD 973, the abbey saw the crowning of King Edgar, "first king of all England." The whimsical west facade sports angels climbing ladders up to heaven...and two climbing down. At the east end, the **Trinity Frontal's** 56 stained-glass windows depict scenes of Jesus's life and flood the abbey with light. Read about the eerie ways various Brits and Yanks met their ends on the memorial plaques covering every possible surface. *(Next to the Baths. ☎ 422 462. Open Apr.-Oct. M-Sa 10am-6pm, Su 8am-8pm; Nov.-Mar. 10am-4pm, Su 8am-8pm. Requested donation £2.)* Below the abbey, the **Heritage Vaults** detail the abbey's history and importance. *(Open M-Sa 10am-4pm, last admission 3:30pm. £2.50, concessions £1.50, under 16 free.)*

JANE AUSTEN CENTRE. Austen lived in Bath (at 13 Queen Sq.) from 1801 to 1806 and thought it a "dismal sight," although she still managed to write *Northanger Abbey* and *Persuasion* here. The center holds nothing that personally belonged to her, but explains Austen's references to Bath and describes the city as it was when she lived here, complete with period furnishings and rare books. *(40 Gay St. ☎ 443 000. Open Apr.-Sept. M-Sa 10am-5:30pm, Su 10:30am-5:30pm; Oct.-Mar. M-Sa 10am-5pm, Su 10:30am-5pm. £4, concessions £3.45, children £2.45, families £11.45.)* Tours of the sights in her novels run daily 1:30pm from Abbey Churchyard. *(£3.50/£2.50/£2/£8.)*

OTHER MUSEUMS AND GALLERIES. The **Victoria Art Gallery** holds a diverse collection of works by Old Masters and British artists, including Thomas Barker's "The Bride of Death"—Victorian melodrama at its sappiest. *(Bridge St., next to the Pulteney Bridge.* ☎ *477 233. Open Tu-F 10am-5:30pm, Sa 10am-5pm, Su 2-5pm. Free.)* The **Museum of East Asian Art** displays objects from 5000 BC onward and has an amazing collection of jade and ceramics. *(12 Bennett St.* ☎ *464 640. Open Tu-Sa 10am-5pm, Su noon-5pm; last admission 4:30pm. £3.50, concessions £1-3, under 6 free, families £8.)* Homesick Yankees will appreciate **The American Museum,** featuring furnished rooms transplanted from historically significant homes, including a cozy Revolutionary War-era kitchen with a working beehive oven. *(Claverton Manor. Climb 2 mi. up Bathwick Hill, or take bus #18 or 418 (£1.20).* ☎ *460 503. Open late Mar. to Oct. Tu-Su 2-5pm. Gardens open Tu-F 1-6pm, Sa-Su noon-6pm; also M in Aug. Museum, grounds, and galleries £6, concessions £5.50, children £3.50.)*

HISTORIC BUILDINGS. Those interested in Bath's architectural history should visit the **Building of Bath Museum,** on the Paragon, which boasts a scale-model of the city and displays on how it was designed. *(☎ 333 895. Open mid-Feb. to Nov. Tu-Su 10:30am-5pm. £4, concessions £3, children £1.50, families £10.)* In the city's residential northwest corner, Beau Nash's contemporaries John Wood, father and son, made the **Georgian rowhouse** a design to reckon with. Walk up Gay St. to **The Circus,** which has attracted illustrious inhabitants for two centuries; greenish-gray plaques proclaim former residents, including Thomas Gainsborough. Proceed from there up Brock St. to the **Royal Crescent,** a half-moon of townhouses. The interior of **1 Royal Crescent** has been painstakingly restored to a near-perfect replica of a 1770 townhouse, authentic down to the last teacup and butter knife. *(☎ 428 126. Open mid-Feb. to Oct. Tu-Su 10:30am-5pm; Nov. Tu-Su 10:30am-4pm. £4, concessions £3.50, families £10.)* For stupendous views, climb the 156 steps of **Beckford's Tower,** 2 mi. north of town. *(Lansdowne Rd.* ☎ *338 727. Take bus #2 or 702 to Ensleigh; otherwise, a 45min. walk. Open Easter-Oct. Sa-Su 10:30am-5pm. £2.50, concessions £2, families £6.)*

GARDENS AND PARKS. Consult a map or the TIC's *Borders, Beds, and Shrubberies* brochure to locate the city's many stretches of cultivated green. Next to the Royal Crescent, **Royal Victoria Park** contains one of the finest collections of trees in the country. Its botanical gardens nurture 5000 species of plants from all over the globe. For bird aficionados, there's also an aviary. *(Open M-Sa 9am-dusk, Su 10am-dusk. Free.)* **Henrietta Park,** laid in 1897 to celebrate Queen Victoria's Diamond Jubilee, was later redesigned as a garden for the blind—only the most fragrant flowers and shrubs were chosen for its tranquil grounds. The **Parade Gardens,** at the base of North Parade Bridge, have lawn chairs and a pleasant green, perfect for relaxing or reading. *(☎ 477 744. Open Apr.-Sept. daily 10am-8pm, Nov.-Mar. 10am-6pm. Apr.-Sept. £1.20, children and seniors 60p; Nov.-Mar. free.)*

🖼🎧 PUBS AND CLUBS

Luring the backpacker contingent, the **Pig and Fiddle,** 2 Saracen St. (☎ 460 868), off Broad St., is the first stop for many pub crawlers, and gathers a young crowd on its generous patio. Friendly and vibrant, **The Bell,** 103 Walcot St. (☎ 460 426), challenges its clientele to talk over the live folk, jazz, blues, funk, salsa, and reggae. **The Boater,** 9 Argyle St. (☎ 464 211), isn't the prettiest pub—galley theme accomplished with tacky high-gloss paint—but overlooks the river with a view of the lit Pulteney Bridge. (All pubs open M-Sa 11am-11pm, Su noon-10:30pm.) At 14 George St., underground **Moles** pounds out a mix of soul, funk, and house. Live bands and cheesy pop nights are popular as well. (☎ 404 445. Cover £5. Open M-Th 9pm-2am, F-Sa 9pm-4am.) **Delfter Krug,** on Saw Close, draws a large weekend crowd to its lively upstairs club, which plays everything from hip hop and R&B to commercial pop and house. (☎ 443 352. Cover £3-5. Open M-Sa noon-2am, Su noon-10:30pm.)

SOUTHWEST ENGLAND

🎵 🌸 ENTERTAINMENT AND FESTIVALS

In summer, buskers (street musicians) fill the streets with music, and a brass band often graces the Parade Gardens. The magnificent **Theatre Royal,** Sawclose, at the south end of Barton St. (Beau Nash's old home), showcases opera and theater. (☎448 844. Box office open M-Sa 10am-8pm, Su noon-8pm. Tickets £8-26, standby £5, £1 less for seniors and students M-Th.)

The renowned **Bath International Music Festival** takes place in late May and early June (May 16 to June 1 in 2003) and features world-class symphony orchestras, choruses, and jazz bands. The **Contemporary Art Fair** opens the festival by bringing together the work of over 700 British artists. For a brochure or reservations, write or call the **Bath Festivals Office.** (2 Church St., Abbey Green, Bath BA1 1NL. ☎463 362. Open M-Sa 9:30am-5:30pm.) The concurrent **Fringe Festival** (☎480 097) celebrates music, dance, and liberal politics with 150 live performances. During the last week of September, the **Bath Jane Austen Festival** features Jane-themed walks, restaurant meals, and movies. (Contact Festival Box Office. Tickets £2.50-8.) The **Literature Festival** in March, the **Balloon Fiesta** in mid-May, and the **Film Festival** in late October are other popular events. Stay abreast of current entertainment news by picking up the weekly *Venue* (£1.90), available at the TIC and around town.

BRISTOL
☎ 0117

A city of pigeon droppings, cigarette butts, and unattractively modern buildings, Bristol seems at first an ugly image of progress gone wrong. Beneath the grimy surface, however, this transportation shrine reveals the history of a city of wealth and advancement, once second only to London. Though the lucrative sugarcane and slave trades are gone and WWII bombs demolished much of the city's architectural might, the city remains the southwest's largest (pop. 401,000). A business center by day, the city springs to life at night, its people-packed streets illuminated by countless late-night eateries, pubs, and clubs. Despite a rebuilt city center and lavish quay front, Bristol remains largely undiscovered by tourists, making its lack of pretension and hopping nightlife one of Britain's best-kept secrets.

⌐ TRANSPORTATION

Trains: Bristol Temple Meads Station. Ticket office open M-Sa 5:30am-9:30pm, Su 6:45am-9:30pm. Trains (☎(08457) 484 950) from: **Bath** (15min., 4 per hr., £4.80); **Cardiff** (50min., 2 per hr., £7.20); **London Paddington** (1¾hr., 2 per hr., £41); **Manchester** (3½hr., every hr., £50). Another station, **Bristol Parkway,** is far, far away—make sure to get off at Temple Meads.

Buses: Marlborough St. Bus Station. Information shop open M-F 7:30am-6pm and Sa 10am-5:30pm. **National Express** (☎(08705) 808 080) from **London** (2½hr., every hr., £13) and **Manchester** (5¾hr., 6-8 per day, £19) via **Birmingham** (2½hr., £14.50). Office open M-Sa 7:20am-6pm, Su 9am-6pm.

Public Transportation: Badgerline (☎955 3231) buses run in the city. An **Explorer** ticket buys unlimited travel for a day (£6, concessions £4.25, families £12.50).

Taxis: Bristol Hackney Cabs (☎953 8638). **Streamline** (☎926 4001).

ORIENTATION AND PRACTICAL INFORMATION

Bristol is a sprawling mass of neighborhoods. The shopping and commerce center is in the **Broadmead** district, while restaurants and clubs fill the heart of the city along **Park St.** and **Park Row** in the **West End**. The student population to the northeast makes **Whiteladies Rd.** (follow Queen's Rd. north) yet another option for restaurants and bars. In the west, the **Suspension Bridge** sits at the edge of the quaint, upscale neighborhood of **Clifton Village**.

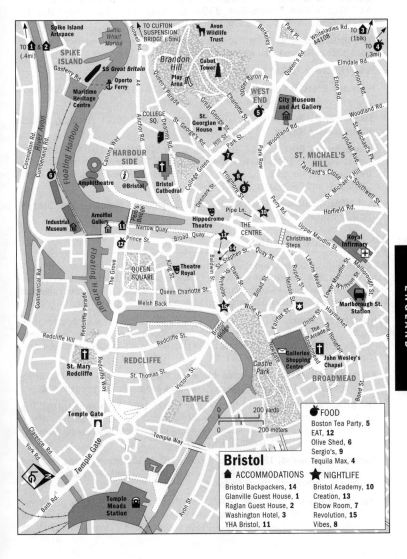

Bristol

SOUTHWEST ENGLAND

♠ ACCOMMODATIONS
Bristol Backpackers, **14**
Glanville Guest House, **1**
Raglan Guest House, **2**
Washington Hotel, **3**
YHA Bristol, **11**

🍎 FOOD
Boston Tea Party, **5**
EAT, **12**
Olive Shed, **6**
Sergio's, **9**
Tequila Max, **4**

★ NIGHTLIFE
Bristol Academy, **10**
Creation, **13**
Elbow Room, **7**
Revolution, **15**
Vibes, **8**

Tourist Information Centre: Harbourside (☎926 0767; www.visitbristol.co.uk). Books accommodations for £3 and a 10% deposit. Sells tickets for local attractions (booking hotline ☎946 2222). **Guided walking tours** (1hr.) Apr.-Oct. £3, children £2. Open Apr.-Oct. daily 10am-6pm; Nov.-Mar. M-Sa 10am-5pm, Su 11am-4pm.

Tours: CitySightseeing (☎(01934) 830 050) runs bus tours from 10am to 4:30pm. £7, students and children £5. **The Bristol Packet** (☎926 8157) runs various boat tours, including daytrips to the Avon Gorge or Bath and tours of the harbor. Runs Apr.-Sept. Sa-Su; call for winter times. £4-15, seniors £3-13, children £2.50-11.

Financial Services: HSBC, 11 Broadmead, is open M-W and F 9am-5pm, Th 9am-7pm, Sa 9:30am-3:30pm. **Thomas Cook,** 93-95 Broadmead (☎948 7900). Open M-W and F-Sa 9am-5:30pm, Th 10am-5:30pm, Su 11am-4pm.

Work Opportunities: When the student population decreases in the summer, bars are a good place to find work. The Wednesday *Evening Post* lists jobs.

Police: Nelson St. (☎927 7777).

Pharmacy: Boots, The Galleries, 59 Broadmead (☎929 3631). Open M-W and F 9am-5:30pm; Th 9am-7pm; Sa 9am-6pm; Su 11am-5pm.

Hospital: Bristol Royal Infirmary, Upper Maudlin St. (☎923 0000). **Frenchay,** in North Bristol near the M32 (☎970 1212).

Internet Access: BristolLife, 27/29 Baldwin St., (☎945 9926). £4 per hr., off-peak £2 per hr. Open M-Th 10am-10pm, F 10am-9pm, Sa-Su 10:30am-9pm. Access is free at the **library,** St. George's Rd., next to Bristol Cathedral. Open M-Tu and Th 9:30am-7:30pm, W and F-Sa 9:30am-5pm, Su 1-4pm.

Post Office: The Galleries, Union St. (☎925 2322), inside the shopping center. Open M-Sa 9am-5:30pm. **Post Code:** BS1 3XX.

▚ ACCOMMODATIONS

B&Bs are difficult to find, and those that exist are far from the city center. A handful of comfortable, cheap, and convenient ones lie south of the Harbour on **Coronation Rd.** Walk west along Cumberland Rd. for 15min., cross the red footbridge and turn right onto Coronation Rd., and then walk a few blocks past Deans Ln.

▨ **Bristol Backpackers,** 17 St. Stephen's St. (☎925 7900; www.bristolbackpackers.co.uk). Hot off the presses, this former newspaper building is now a backpacker's dream, in the heart of nightlife action. Power showers and sturdy bunks. Internet access 3p per min. ID required. Dorms £13. ❷

Raglan Guest House, 132 Coronation Rd. (☎966 2129). Kind proprietress offers comfy beds and family atmosphere. Singles £22; doubles and triples £15 per person. ❸

YHA Bristol, Hayman House, 14 Narrow Quay (☎922 1659; bristol@yha.org.uk). This 88-bed hostel boasts an excellent city-center location, free luggage storage (bring a padlock), and laundry facilities. Arrange for post-midnight entry. Book ahead, especially July-Sept. Dorms £12.75, under 18 £8.75. ❷

Glanville Guest House, 122 Coronation Rd. (☎963 1634), advertises "hot and cold water," but offers simple but cozy lodgings as well. Book 1-3 weeks ahead. Singles £16; doubles and triples £13.50 per person. ❷

Washington Hotel, St. Paul's Rd., (☎973 3980). Walk west on Queen's Rd. past Whiteladies Rd., turn right at Victoria Rooms, and right again at St. Paul's Rd. 10min. from the City Museum and Park St. Singles £40-53; doubles £52-67. Lower on weekends. ❹

FOOD

Posh restaurants line **Park St.** and **Whiteladies Rd.** Try **Tesco Metro,** conveniently located on Broadmead, for groceries. (☎948 7400. Open continuously M 7am to Sa 10pm, also Su 11am-5pm.)

▨ **Boston Tea Party,** 75 Park St. (☎929 8601). Lunch options include a bevy of fresh homemade soups, quiches, and sandwiches (try the chilli hummus sandwich for £1.75). Entrees £4-7. Open M 7am-6pm, Tu-Sa 7am-10pm, Su 9am-7pm. ❶

Olive Shed, Princes Wharf (☎929 1960), next to the Industrial Museum. Reminiscent of a seaside resort with outdoor waterfront seating and bright decor. Great veggie fare and gourmet seafood. Tapas, salads, and soups run £3-5; dinner entrees £8.50-14. Open Tu-Sa 10am-late, Su 10am-6pm. ❸

EAT, Prince St. (☎908 4166), behind the YHA and across the street. Tasty tapas and sandwiches (£1.80-3.30). English breakfast £1.95. Open M-Sa 9:30am-2pm. ❶

Sergio's, 1-3 Frogmore St. (☎929 1413). Hunger-inducing smells pour into the street from this tiny but rowdy Italian eatery. Entrees average £7. Open M-Sa from 5:45pm. ❷

Tequila Max, 109 Whiteladies Rd. (☎466 144). Mexican food at its searing best, with great enchiladas (£10). The upstairs bar has a salsa DJ. Open for lunch M-Sa noon-2:30pm; dinner M-Th 5-11pm, F-Sa 5pm-midnight. ❸

◉ SIGHTS

▨ **@BRISTOL.** The two buildings that make up Bristol's newest attraction have been widening visitors' eyes since July of 2000. **Explore** features interactive exhibits, from a planetarium to the virtual journey of an egg-bound sperm. **Wildscreen** holds two main attractions: the four-storey **IMAX theater** and the biology museum **Wildwalk,** with a biodome housing a living rainforest and displays on everything from fungus to pollution. (Anchor Rd., Harbourside. ☎915 5000. Explore and Wildwalk open daily 10am-6pm; IMAX M-W 10am-4:45pm, Th-F 10am-8:30pm, Sa-Su 12:30-8:30pm. Single sight £6.50-7.50, children £4.50-5; 2 sights £11-12/8-9; all 3 £16.50/11.45.)

BRANDON HILL. Just west of Park St. lies one of the most peaceful and secluded sights in Bristol. Pathways snake through flower beds up to Cabot Tower, a monument commemorating the 400th anniversary of explorer John Cabot's arrival in North America. Ascend the 108 steep steps for a stunning view. (☎922 3719. Open daily until dusk. Free.)

CLIFTON SUSPENSION BRIDGE. Isambard Kingdom Brunel, famed engineer of London's Paddington Station, also created the architectural masterpiece that spans the Avon Gorge. The Visitor's Centre, nearby on Sion Pl., explains the finer points of Brunel's genius, which revolutionized Victorian technology. (☎974 4664. Take bus #8 or 9. Open Apr.-Oct. daily 10am-5pm; Nov.-Mar. M-F 11am-4pm, Sa-Su 11am-5pm. £1.90, seniors £1.70, under 16 £1.30, families £5.)

S.S. GREAT BRITAIN. Also a Brunel production, this ship was the largest in the world when it was built (in the 1840s) and also the first to be made of metal. The luxury liner, although not exactly on the scale of the *Titanic*, was notably more successful at crossing the Atlantic. (☎929 1843. Open Apr.-Oct. daily 10am-5:30pm; Nov.-Mar. 10am-4:30pm. £6.25, seniors £5.25, children £3.75, families £16.50.)

OTHER MUSEUMS. The **City Museum and Art Gallery** covers all the bases from minerals to mummies. (Queens Rd. ☎922 3571. Open daily 10am-5pm. Free.) From April to October, the museum opens various **Victorian sights** throughout the city, including the Georgian House and Industrial Museum. (Contact City Museum for info. All free.) The new **Arnolfini Gallery** by the Harbour has an impressive collection of contemporary art. (16 Narrow Quay. ☎929 9191. Open daily 10am-5pm. Free.)

SOUTHWEST ENGLAND

CHURCHES. Visitors can tell by the smell that **John Wesley's Chapel,** which now sits incongruously in the midst of Bristol's shopping district, is the world's first and oldest Methodist building. Note the chair fashioned from an inverted elm trunk. (☎ 926 4740. Open M-Sa 10am-4pm. Free.) Built in 1140, the **Bristol Cathedral** features a beautiful Norman Chapter House with a quilt-like roof. The surrounding College Green receives swarms of students, skateboarders, and suntanners. (☎ 926 4879. Open daily 8am-6pm. Evensong 5:15pm. Suggested donation £2.)

🎵 🌾 ENTERTAINMENT AND FESTIVALS

Britain's oldest theater, the **Theatre Royal** was rebuked for debauchery until King George III finally approved the actors' antics. (King St. ☎ 987 7877. Tickets £7-20, students £2 discount. Open M-Sa 10am-8pm.) The **Hippodrome,** St. Augustine's Parade, presents the latest touring productions and musicals. (Box office open M-Sa 10am-8pm, 10am-6pm when no show. Call Ticketmaster ☎ (0870) 607 7500 or go to the box office.) In late July, the popular **Bristol Harbour Festival** (☎ 922 3719) explodes with fireworks, raft races, street performances, live music, hundreds of boats, and a French market. The **Bristol International Balloon Fiesta,** the first or second weekend in August, welcomes half a million visitors. Hot-air balloons fill the sky while acrobatics and motorcycle teams perform at ground level. (☎ 953 5884.)

🎆 NIGHTLIFE

On weekend nights, virtually the entire city turns out in clubwear. Bristol's fluorescent venues pump the finest techno through the city's heart, and thousands of university students sustain the energetic vibe.

Bristol Academy, Frogmore St. (☎ 927 9227). This seductive, factory-style space holds 1700 partiers, lures big-name DJs, and hosts bands like Counting Crows and Stereophonics. Live bands M-W. Cover £10-20 M-W, £3-4 Th, £5-10 F-Sa. Open M-W 7-11pm, Th 10pm-3am, F-Sa 10pm-4am.

Creation, 13-21 Baldwin St. (☎ 922 7177). The silver-tube metallic entrance draws trendy club-goers, college students, and sometimes Fatboy Slim. Weekend queues are long, so arrive early. Cover £5-15. Open Th 10pm-2:30am, F-Sa 10pm-4am.

Revolution, St. Nicholas St. (☎ 930 4335). Any dissent in this completely packed, Red-tinted bar drowns in the liquid goodness of exotic vodkas. Live DJs nightly. No cover. Open M-Sa noon-2am, Su noon-12:30am.

Elbow Room, 64 Park St. (☎ 930 0242). Slightly removed from the chaotic party center, this relaxed bar features pool tables, moody purple and blue lighting, and window seating looking out onto the street. Open M-Sa noon-2am, Su noon-12:30am.

Vibes, 3 Frogmore St. (☎ 934 9076). A new gay-friendly venue with neon lights and modern décor. Different rooms play different music, from cheesy pop to hard house. Cover £1-4. Open M-Th 9pm-2am, F-Sa 9pm-3am.

WELLS ☎ 01749

Named for the natural springs at its center, Wells (pop. 10,000) is humbled by its magnificent cathedral. Charming, if self-consciously classy, England's smallest city is lined with petite Tudor buildings and golden sandstone shops.

TRANSPORTATION

Trains leave Wells enough alone, but **buses** stop at the **Princes Rd. Depot.** (☎673 084. Office open M-Tu and Th-F 9am-5pm, W 9am-noon and 1-5pm, Sa 9am-1pm.) **Bakers Dolphin** (☎679 000) runs fast buses from **London** (2hr., 1 per day, £17). **First** runs from **Bath** (☎(01225) 464 446; #173; 1¼hr.; M-Sa every hr., Su 3 per day; £3.60) and **Bristol** (☎(01934) 429 336, #376, 1hr., every hr., £3.60). If you'll be skipping around in the area, buy a **Day Rambler** (£6, concessions £4.25). **Wookey Taxis** (☎678 039) and **A Taxis** (☎672 200) scurry through the cramped streets. Rent bicycles at **Bike City**, 31 Broad St. (☎671 711. £7 per half-day, £9 per day, £40 per week. Deposit £50. Open M-Sa 9am-5:30pm.)

PRACTICAL INFORMATION

The **tourist information centre**, on Market Pl., at the end of High St., books rooms for a 10% deposit and has bus timetables. Exit left from the bus station, then turn left onto Priory Rd., which becomes Broad St. and eventually merges with High St. (☎672 552; fax 670 869. Open Apr.-Oct. daily 9:30am-5:30pm; Nov.-Mar. 10am-4pm.) Other services include: **banks** on High St.; **Thomas Cook**, 8 High St. (☎313 000; open M-Sa 9am-5:30pm); **Wells Launderette**, 39 St. Cuthbert St. (☎(01458) 830 409; wash £3, dry 50p per 10min.; open daily 7am-8pm, last wash 7pm); **work opportunities** at JobCentre, 46 Chamberlain St. (☎313 200; open M-W and F 9am-4:30pm, Th 10am-4:30pm); the **police**, Glastonbury Rd. (☎(01275) 818 181); **Wells and District Cottage Hospital**, St. Thomas St. (☎673 154); and the **post office**, Market Pl. (☎(08457) 223 344; open M-F 9am-5:30pm, Sa 9am-12:30pm). **Post Code:** BA5 2RA.

ACCOMMODATIONS

Most B&Bs offer only doubles and run £22-30, so making Wells a daytrip from Bristol or Bath may be a better option. The closest YHA hostel and campgrounds are 10 mi. away, near Wookey Hole and Cheddar (see **Near Wells**, p. 218).

Richmond House, 2 Chamberlain St. (☎676 438). From the bus station, exit right on Princes Rd.; turn right on Chamberlain St. Brass mirrors and an antique fireplace—and that's just the bathroom. English breakfast with French croissants and fresh fruit. Singles £25; doubles £46. ❸

Canon Grange, Cathedral Green (☎671 800). Follow directions to TIC, but from High St., turn left on Sadler. Superb accommodations in an amazing location. More frills than similarly priced options. Singles £25-35; doubles £48. ❸

Number Nine, 9 Chamberlain St. (☎672 270). Same directions as Richmond House. Rose-ringed Georgian house has enormous rooms. Singles £21-25; doubles £40. ❸

The Old Poor House, 7a St. Andrew St. (☎675 052, mobile (07831) 811 070). Tidy rooms just up the street from the cathedral. £22 per person, with bath £25. ❸

FOOD

Assemble a picnic at the **market** behind the bus stops (open W and Sa 8:30am-4pm), or purchase groceries at **Tesco**, across from the bus station. (☎(01749) 313 400. Open continuously M 8am to Sa 10pm, also Su 10am-4pm.) Find great home-cooked pizzas (£1.85 per slice), quiches (£1.70), and vegetarian options at **The Good Earth ❶**, 4 Priory Rd. Delicious soups (£1.65-2.20) and salads (£2.50-3.40) are available at the adjoining takeaway. (☎678 600. Open M-Sa 9am-5pm.) A city jail in the 16th century, the **City Arms ❸**, 69 High St., now serves delicious meals (entrees £5-14) like halibut steak and veggie burgers in a flower-filled outdoor veranda. (☎673 916. Open M-F 7:30am-10pm, Sa 8am-10pm, Su 9am-9pm.)

SIGHTS

WELLS AND MENDIP MUSEUM. The museum contains archaeological finds of the Mendip area and remnants of the cathedral's decor. The statues look ill-proportioned but are designed to appear normal when viewed from below. Also on display are the milking pot, goats (what's left of them), and bones of an elderly woman believed to be the legendary "Witch of Wookey Hole." Her "crystal ball" looks like your average rock but is made from alabaster, which isn't native to the area. *(8 Cathedral Green. ☎ 673 477. Open Easter-Oct. daily 10am-5:30pm, mid-July to mid-Sept. until 8pm; Nov.-Easter W-M 11am-4pm. £2.50, concessions £2, children £1, families £6.)*

CATHEDRAL CHURCH OF ST. ANDREW. The 13th-century church at the center of town anchors a fantastically preserved cathedral complex, with a bishop's palace, vicar's close, and chapter house. The facade of the cathedral comprises one of England's greatest collections of **medieval statues,** featuring a resurrection theme with Jesus at the top, the apostles in the middle, and the saints below. Atop the 14th-century **astronomical clock** in the north transept, a pair of jousting mechanical knights duke it out every 15min. The **Wells Cathedral School Choir**—one of the best in the country—sings services from September to April; visiting choirs assume the honor through summer break. Pick up the leaflet *Music in Wells Cathedral* at the cathedral or TIC. *(☎ 674 483. Open Mar.-Sept. daily 7:15am-8:30pm if there's no concert; Oct.-Feb. until 6pm. Free tours 10:15, 11:15am, 12:15, 2:15, 3:15pm. Evensong M-Sa 5:15pm, Su 3pm. Suggested donation £4.50, concessions £3, children £1.50.)*

BISHOP'S PALACE. A humble parish priest's abode, the palace was built in the 13th century. The swans in the moat pull a bell-rope when they want to be fed—the first swan to learn (now stuffed... in a different sense) was consistent to the hour, but the new swans aren't as punctual. Visitors are encouraged to feed them brown and wholemeal bread (but not white—they get sick). The palace **gardens** surround the springs that give the city its name and make an ideal setting for a picnic. *(Near the cathedral. ☎ 678 691. Open Aug. daily 10:30am-5pm; Apr.-July and Sept.-Oct. Tu-F 10am-5pm, Su 1-6pm. Palace and gardens £3.50, students £1.50, seniors £2.50, children £1.)* **Vicar's Close,** behind the cathedral, is reputedly Europe's oldest street of houses, some dating back to 1363. **St. Andrew's Well** produces 40 gallons of spring water per second. Bishop Beckynton harnessed the flow in the 15th century, and the water still runs through the city streets today.

NEAR WELLS: WOOKEY HOLE AND CHEDDAR

A short journey from Wells brings you to a vale of cheese, in every sense of the word. Two miles northwest, a 20min. tour takes visitors through the **Wookey Hole Caves,** a miracle-of-nature-turned-kitschy-tourist-attraction, with colored lights and contrived commentary. Appropriately enough, the caves have been co-opted as a filming location for a few movies, including *Harry Potter.* Admission includes a visit to the **Papermill,** where visitors can witness the miracle of papermaking, and a room of **gaudy carnival attractions,** with wooden horses and funhouse mirrors. *(☎ 672 243. Open Apr.-Oct. daily 10am-5pm; Nov.-Mar. 10:30am-4:30pm. £8, children £5.)* **Camp** beside a brook at nearby **Homestead Park ❶.** *(☎ (01749) 673 022. £3-4 tent or caravan, £2.50-3.50 per additional person. Electricity £2.)*

Seven miles northwest of Wells, the town of **Cheddar** lies near a large hill leading to the **Cheddar Gorge,** a stunning sight carved by the River Yeo (YO). Starting at the base of the hill, an open-top **bus** travels to and around the gorge. Along the hill huddle the **Cheddar Showcaves,** England's finest; travel as far as a quarter mile into the Earth to see stalactites, stalagmites, and Cheddar Man, a 9000-year-old skeleton typical of the Stone Agers who settled in the Gorge. Also along the hill, **Jacob's Ladder,** a 274-step lookout over the hills and plains, is the start of a 3 mi. **clifftop gorge walk.** (☎ (01934) 742 343. Open May to mid-Sept. daily 10am-5pm; mid-Sept. to Apr. 10:30am-4:30pm. Caves, Jacob's Ladder, and bus ride £9, children £6, families £24; Ladder only £2.80, children £2.30; discount tickets available from Wells TIC.) **The Cheddar Gorge Cheese Co.,** at the hill's base, features cheese-making, cider-tasting, and fudge-eating. (☎ (01934) 742 810. Open Apr.-Oct. 10am-5pm. £1.50, seniors £1.25, children £1, families £4.50. Shop open all year Sa-Su 10am-5pm.)

From Wells, **buses** travel to **Wookey Hole** (#172 or 670, 10-15min., M-Sa 8 per day, return £1.95) and **Cheddar** (#126 or 826; 25min.; M-Sa every hr., Su 7 per day; return £3.90), but no bus service connects the two towns. If you plan to see both, you'll have to travel to and from Wells; a **Day Rambler** is useful (see p. 216). Cheddar's **tourist information centre** is at the base of the hill. (☎ (01934) 744 071. Open Easter-Nov. daily 10am-5pm; Dec.-Easter Su 11am-4pm.) The **YHA Cheddar ❷** is ½ mi. from Cheddar Gorge. From the bus stop, walk up Tweentown Rd. away from the gorge, turn left on The Hayes, and right at Hillfield. (☎ (01934) 742 494. Curfew 11pm. Open July-Aug. daily; May-June and Sept.-Oct. M-Sa; Mar.-Apr. Tu-Sa; Feb. and Nov.-Dec. F-Sa. Dorms £11.25, under 18 £8.) For caravaning and camping, try **Broadway House ❶,** 2 mi. west of the caves. (☎ (01934) 742 610. £7-15 for 2 people.)

GLASTONBURY   ☎ 01458

The reputed birthplace of Christianity in England and a seat of Arthurian myth, Glastonbury (pop. 6900) is an idiosyncratic intersection of mysticism and religion. According to legend, King Arthur, Jesus, Joseph of Arimathea, and Saints Augustine and Patrick all came here (not together, sadly). While one myth claims the stark Glastonbury Tor is the resting place of the Holy Grail and the spot where the Messiah will return, another holds that it's the Isle of Avalon, where King Arthur sleeps; yet another claims it's a passage to the underworld. Glastonbury's shops partake in all these myths, selling everything from crosses to crystals to curative herbs. Grow your hair, suspend your disbelief, and join hands with Glastonbury's subculture of hippies and spiritualists.

⬛ TRANSPORTATION. Glastonbury has no train station; **buses** stop at the town hall in the town center. **First** buses run to **Bristol** (1hr.; #376, M-Sa every 40min., change at Wells for Su service) and **Wells** (15min.; M-Sa

LOVE, BEAUTY, AND AVALON

In 2002, Let's Go interviewed a 25-year resident of Glastonbury, who owns a bookstore and runs "mystical tours."

Q: What exactly is your favorite part of Glastonbury?

A: Well, I love every part of it. Glastonbury is so beautiful. Its mystically sculptured landscape invites and invokes so much wonderful, romantic, historical feeling.

Q: I've noticed that everyone is really friendly. What is it about the city that makes that happen?

A: I think it's in the land. The land is very powerful. And it's very beautiful countryside. And that lifts the spirits of the people. Gives them contentment. Inspires them. Makes them friendly. And, also, many people have shared interests here in the alternative lifestyle.

Q: I've heard a lot about how Glastonbury is where Avalon used to be, and that's a legend, right?

A: Glastonbury *is* the Isle of Avalon. It still is the Isle of Avalon. Avalon is a place of the other world and the veil is very thin between this world and the next in Glastonbury. And so Avalon is the place of the fountain of youth, the elixir of life, and where the Holy Grail is to be found. Figuratively speaking, it means it's the search for enlightenment. It is a place in your heart and your mind you feel most inspired. And the other world—the Isle of Avalon is where you can find that.

#29, 163, 377, every 15min.; Su #929 and 977, every hr.; £2.70). Direct service to **Bath** only operates on Sundays (1¼hr.; #173 and 969; 8 per Su; change at Wells for M-Sa service). Travel to **Yeovil** (1hr.; M-Sa #377, every hr.; Su #977, 7 per day; £3.30) to connect to destinations in the south, including **Lyme Regis** and **Dorcester** (£2.60). **Explorer Passes** let you travel a full day on all buses (£6, concessions £4.25).

█ ▪ ▐ ORIENTATION AND PRACTICAL INFORMATION. Glastonbury is 6 mi. southwest of Wells on the A39 and 22 mi. northeast of Taunton on the A361. The town is bounded by **High St.** in the north, **Bere Ln.** in the south, **Magdalene St.** in the west, and **Wells Rd.** in the east. The **tourist information centre,** The Tribunal, 9 High St., books rooms for £3 and a 10% deposit; after hours find the B&B list behind the building in St. John's carpark. (☎832 954. Open Apr.-Sept. Su-Th 10am-5pm, F-Sa 10am-5:30pm; Oct.-Mar. Su-Th 10am-4pm, F-Sa 10am-4:30pm.) Other services include: **banks** on High St., including **Barclays,** 21-23 High St. (☎582 203; open M-Tu and Th-F 9:30am-4:30pm, W 10am-4:30pm); the **police,** in nearby Street, at 1 West End (☎(01275) 818 181); **Internet access** at **Visionscape,** 1 Northload St. (☎835 373; 50p per 15min; open M-F 9:30am-1pm, 2-5pm; Sa 11am-3pm); and the **post office,** 35 High St. (☎831 536; open M-F 9:30am-5:30pm, Sa 9am-1pm). **Post Code:** BA6 9HG.

▐ ACCOMMODATIONS. Single rooms are rare in Glastonbury. The nearest YHA hostel is the **YHA Street ❶,** The Chalet, Ivythorn Hill St., off the B3151 in Street. Take Badgerline bus #376 to Marshalls Elm, and walk 1 mi. (☎442 961. Lockout 10am-5pm. Curfew 11pm. Open July-Aug. daily; Apr.-June and Sept. W-Su. Dorms £9.50, under 18 £6.75.) Buses stop nearly in front of the ▨**Glastonbury Backpackers ❷,** at the corner of Magdalene St. and High St.; the attached sandwich shop and friendly staff complement a great location. Lucky "Bridal Suite" guests get jungle-print sheets and ceiling mirror. (☎833 353. Dorms £10; doubles £26-30.) **Hawthorns Hotel ❸,** 8 Northload St., offers upscale lodgings in the heart of town. (☎831 255. Singles £25-30; doubles £50-70.) Walk uphill to the end of High St. and turn right onto Lambrook, which becomes Chilkwell St.; a few blocks bring you to **The Bolt Hole ❷,** 32 Chilkwell St., opposite the Chalice Well. (☎832 800. £19-22 per person.)

▐ FOOD. Find tasty baguettes (£1.65) and other picnic foods at the **Truckle of Cheese** deli, 33 High St. (☎832 116; open M-Sa 9am-5:30pm), or buy groceries at **Heritage Fine Foods,** 34 High St. (open M-W 7am-10pm, Th-Sa 7am-9pm, Su 8am-9pm). ▨**Spiral Cafe ❶,** 24 High St., makes tasty soups, salads, quiches, and veggie burgers (£3-5) with organic ingredients. (☎(01458) 834 633. Open Tu-Th and Su noon-5pm, F-Sa noon-8pm.) The vegetarian and wholefood menu at **Rainbow's End ❶,** 17a High St., changes with the chef's creative whims; if available, try the roasted red pepper and sweet potato flan. Soups, salads, and quiches are £1.50-6. (☎833 896. Open daily 9am-4pm.) **Elaichi Tandoori ❷,** 62 High St., serves delectable Indian cuisine; entrees run £4.50-12. (☎833 966. Open daily noon-3pm, 5:30-11:30pm.) **Burns the Bread ❶,** 14 High St., doesn't, baking cheap chocolate muffins (65p) and pasties (85p) instead. (☎831 532. Open M-Sa 7am-5pm, Su 11am-5pm.)

◉ ▨ SIGHTS AND THE FESTIVAL. A 15min. hike from the base of the 521 ft. **Glastonbury Tor** brings visitors to the huge mound's windy top, a pilgrimage site since the 6th century. To reach the Tor, turn right at the top of High St. on Lambrook, which becomes Chilkwell St.; turn left at Wellhouse Ln., and follow the path uphill. Once an island, the Tor is reputedly the site of the Isle of Avalon, where King Arthur lies snoozin', ready to awaken when his country needs him. The hill now features a simple tower, built in 1360. In summer, the **Glastonbury Tor Bus** takes weary pilgrims from the city center (St. Dunstan's carpark, on Magdalene St.) to a shorter climb on the other side of the Tor (£1, children 50p).

On the way to the Tor, a tiered garden of flowers and climbing vines on Chilkwell St. houses **Chalice Well,** the purported resting place of the Holy Grail. Legend once held that the well ran with Christ's blood; in these post-Nietzsche days, it's admitted that the red tint comes from rust deposits at the bottom of the stream. Ancient mystics interpreted the iron-red water's mingling with clear water from nearby **White Well** (which now runs through a cafe across the street) as a symbol of balance between the divine feminine and divine masculine. (Open Apr.-Oct. daily 10am-6pm; Feb.-Mar. and Nov. 11am-5pm; Dec.-Jan. 11am-4pm. £2.30, seniors £1.60, children £1.20.) The crumbling ruins of **Glastonbury Abbey** mark England's oldest Christian foundation, and once its most important abbey, dedicated to Mary and visited by Jesus himself. The abbey has also claimed two national patron saints as its own, **St. Patrick** of Ireland and **St. George** of England—Patrick is said to be buried here and George to have slain his dragon just around the corner. New-age religion finds an outlet in the open-air masses periodically held among the ruins. (☎ 832 267. Open June-Aug. daily 9am-6pm; Sept.-May 9:30am-4:30pm. £3.50, concessions £3, children £1.50, families £8.) Southwest of the town center rests **Wearyall Hill,** where legend has it that the staff of St. Joseph of Arimathea bloomed and became the **Glastonbury Thorn,** which dates back to Saxon times. The tree still blooms each year at Christmas and Easter.

Modern day rockers make the pilgrimage to Pilton, 5 mi. east, the site of the annual **Glastonbury Festival** (☎ (0115) 912 9129; www.glastonburyfestivals.co.uk), Britain's largest summer music festival. The week-long event takes place at the end of June and has featured some of the world's biggest bands.

THE DORSET COAST

BOURNEMOUTH ☎ 01202

Only 190 years old, Bournemouth (pop. 150,000) is an infant among English cities. In summer months, the seaside resort, made popular by its healing pine scents and curative sea-baths, is invaded by daytrippers and active retirees for its expansive beach and coastal ravines. Come nightfall, clubs and boardwalk entertainment attract families and students.

▐▀ **TRANSPORTATION.** The **train station** lies on Holdenhurst Rd. (Travel center open M-F 8am-7pm, Sa 9am-6pm, Su 9am-5:30pm; ticket office open M-Sa 5:40am-9pm, Su 6:40am-9pm.) **Trains** (☎ (08457) 484 950) serve: **Birmingham** (3½hr., 8 per day); **Dorchester** (40min., every hr., £7.40); **London Waterloo** (1¾hr., 2 per hr., £30.40). **National Express buses** (☎ (08705) 808 080) pull up at The Square and serve: **Birmingham** (5hr., 3 per day, £31); **Bristol** (3½hr., 1 per day, £12.50); **London** (3hr., every hr., £11). Get tickets at the TIC. **Wilts and Dorset** (☎ 273 555) runs local buses, including #150 to Swanage via Studland, #151 to Poole via Compton Arms, and #142 from Swanage to Poole via Corfe Castle. Purchase an **Explorer** ticket (£5.50, children £2.75, families £11) for unlimited travel. **United Taxi** (☎ 556 677) runs 24hr.

▐ **PRACTICAL INFORMATION.** The **tourist information centre,** Westover Rd., has free bus schedules, books rooms for a 10% deposit, and leads free 1½hr. **guided walks.** (☎ (0906) 802 0234; walks June-Sept. M-F 10:30am, Su 2:30pm. Open July-Aug. M-Sa 9:30am-7pm, Su 10:30am-4pm; Sept.-June M-Sa 9:30am-5:30pm.) John Walker runs themed tours like the **Murder Walks** (☎ 265 436). Other services include: **banks** in The Square; **Thomas Cook,** on Richmond Hill (open M-Sa 9am-5:30pm); **American Express,** in the Christchurch Rd. pedestrian area (open M-F

9:30am-5:30pm, Sa 9am-5pm); **launderette,** 172 Commercial Rd. (wash £2.40, dry £1.50; open daily 8am-10pm, last wash 9pm); **work opportunities,** especially seasonal work, at **JobCentre,** 181-187 Christchurch Rd. (☎(0845) 601 2001; open M-Th 9am-4:30pm, F 9:30am-4:30pm); the **police,** Madeira Rd. (☎552 099); **Bournemouth Hospital,** Castle Land East, Littledown (☎303 626); **Internet access** at **Click 'n' Link,** 248 Old Christchurch Rd. (☎780 999; £2 per hr., students £1 per hr.; open M-Sa 10am-midnight, Su 11am-midnight); and the **post office,** Post Office Rd., off Richmond Hill (open M-Sa 9am-5:30pm). **Post Code:** BH1 2BU.

⌐⌐ ACCOMMODATIONS AND FOOD. B&Bs are rare in Bournemouth, which is full of hotels catering to businessmen and convention-goers. In the **Boscombe** neighborhood, a string of family villas have been converted into affordable B&Bs; follow signs from the train station (20min.). **⬛Bournemouth Backpackers ❶,** 3 Frances Rd., a friendly independent hostel, has the most reasonable rates. The proprietor is an area expert. (☎299 491. Kitchen. Reception June-Aug.; call beforehand other months. Dorms £9-16; doubles £42; less for longer stays.) **Sweet Briar ❸,** 12 Derby Rd., offers affordable rooms near the station. Exit left from the station, cross Holdenhurst Rd. to St. Swithuns, and turn left on Frances Rd. (☎553 028. Singles £20; doubles £40-44.) **Campers** enjoy **Merley Court Park ❶,** Merley, Wimborne, 8 mi. north on the A341. (☎881 488. Open Mar.-Dec. Caravans and tents £8-14.)

Christchurch Rd. boasts diverse food offerings, and international students living north of Bournemouth make **Charminster Rd.** a center of great ethnic cuisine and cheap Internet cafes. At **CH₂ ❷,** 37 Exeter Rd., modern decor, inexpensive lunch specials (£5.50), and Mediterranean cuisine make a reactive combination. (Open Tu-Sa noon-2:30pm and 6-10:30pm.) **Eye of the Tiger ❸,** 207 Old Christchurch Rd., serves delicious Indian entrees for £6-11. (☎780 900. Open daily noon-2pm and 5pm-midnight.) The best in creamy goodness, **Shake Away ❶,** 7 Post Office Rd., serves tasty takeaway and over 120 flavors of milkshake (£1.69-2.29), from marshmallow to rhubarb. (☎310 105. Open M-Sa 9am-5:30pm, Su 10:30am-5:40pm.)

◙◪ SIGHTS AND BEACHES. The city center holds few interesting attractions. The **Russell-Cotes Art Gallery and Museum,** East Cliff, houses a remarkable private collection of Victorian art, sculptures, and artifacts from all over the world. (☎451 820. Open Tu-Su 10am-5pm. Free.) On the corner of Hilton Rd. and St. Peter's Rd., **St. Peter's** parish church holds the remains of Mary Shelley, author of *Frankenstein*. Most visitors, however, come for **Bournemouth Beach** (☎451 781), a 7 mi. sliver of shoreline barely wide enough to hold the inflatable slides. Cheap amusements have spoiled the area surrounding **Bournemouth Pier,** but a short walk takes sunbathers to quieter spots, where they can rent bungalows and deck chairs.

Instead of staying in Bournemouth, travel the shore for more stunning sights. A 95 mi. stretch of the Dorset and East Devon coast, dubbed the **Jurassic Coast,** was recently named a World Heritage Site for its famous fossils and unique geology (www.jurassiccoast.com). Beautiful **Studland Beach** sits across the harbor, reachable by bus #150 (50min., every hr.). A **nude beach** awaits just down the shore. Take bus #150 or 151 (25min., 2 per hr.) to reach the themed landscapes of **Compton Acres,** featuring a stunning Italian garden with Roman statues and a sensory garden designed for the blind. (☎700 110. Open Mar.-Oct. daily 10am-7:30pm; Nov.-Feb. 9am-5:30pm. £6, seniors £5.45, children £3.25.) Thousand-year-old **Corfe Castle** is no gently weathered pile of ruins: Parliamentarian engineers were ordered to destroy the castle during the English Civil War. What remains is a testament to its incredible strength. (☎418 294. Open Apr.-Oct. daily 10am-6pm, Mar. 10am-5pm, Nov.-Feb. 10am-4pm. £4.30, children £2.15, families £10.80.) To get to the castle, travel to Poole (bus #151) or Swanage (#150) to catch bus #142 (every hr.).

⚡🎭 ENTERTAINMENT AND FESTIVALS. Swarms of foreign-language students and young vacationers have revitalized Bournemouth's nightlife. Most start their nights at the roundabout up the hill from **Firvale Rd.**, working their way downhill through the numerous bars on **Christchurch Rd.** The bar **Circo** and downstairs club **Elements**, on Firvale Rd., attract large crowds. (☎311 178. Circo open M and W-Sa 7-11pm, Su 7pm-12:30am; Elements cover £3-7, open M and W-Sa 9:30pm-2am.) Far, far away, **The Opera House**, 570 Christchurch Rd., a former theater, has become the best (and priciest) club in town. (☎399 922. Drinks £4. Cover £5-12. Open Th-Su 9pm-3am.) In a tradition dating back to 1896, 15,000 candles light up the Lower Gardens every summer Wednesday during the **Flowers by Candlelight Festival.** Bournemouth's **music festival** (☎451 702) is in late June.

DORCHESTER ☎01305

Every city has its favorite children, but in Dorchester, Thomas Hardy is an only son, and the locals indulge his spirit to the point of spoiling it. Pub regulars will share time-worn stories about the author whose sober statue overlooks the town's main street, and most businesses, from inns to shoe stores, manage to incorporate "Hardy" into their names. Those travelers not Hardy-hooked will hardly be hooked by Dorchester. The sleepy city that inspired the fictional "Casterbridge" has seen more prosperous times, though Dorchester *is* far from the madding crowd.

🚆 TRANSPORTATION

Most **trains** (☎(08457) 484 950) come to **Dorchester South,** off Weymouth Ave. (Ticket office open M-F 6:05am-8pm, Sa 6:40am-8pm, Su 8:40am-7pm.) Trains run from **Bournemouth** (40min., every hr., £7.40) and **London Waterloo** (2½hr., every hr., £33.40). Some trains arrive at the unstaffed **Dorchester West,** also off Weymouth Ave., including those from **Weymouth** (15min., 20 per day, £2.70). Dorchester lacks a bus station, but **buses** stop frequently at Dorchester South train station. **National Express** (☎(08705) 808 080) serves **Exeter** (2hr., 1 per day, £8.75) and **London** (3½hr., 1-3 per day, £16); tickets are sold at the TIC. **Wilts & Dorset** (☎673 555) bus #184 goes to **Salisbury** via **Blandford** (2hr., 6 per day, £4.50). **First** bus #212 serves **Yeovil** (1½hr., every hr., £3.30), which connects to destinations farther south. **Coach House Travel** (☎267 644) provides local service. **Rent bikes** at **Dorchester Cycles,** 31a Great Western Rd. (☎268 787. £5 per half-day, £10 per day, £50 per week. £100 credit card deposit or passport. Open M-Sa 9am-5:30pm.)

🏙🚩 ORIENTATION AND PRACTICAL INFORMATION

The intersection of **High West** with **South St.** (which eventually becomes **Cornhill St.**) serves as the unofficial center of town. The main **shopping district** extends southward along South St. The **tourist information centre,** 11 Antelope Walk, on Trinity St., stocks walking maps (including the free Hardy Trail pamphlet), books accommodations for a 10% deposit, and sells bus tickets. (☎267 992. Open Apr.-Oct. M-Sa 9am-5pm, Su 10am-3pm; Nov.-Mar. M-Sa 9am-4pm.) General **walking tours** leave at erratic times from the TIC (July to mid-Sept. £3-5), while the **Thomas Hardy Experience,** also booked through the TIC, guides visitors over every inch of town remotely connected to the author (Aug.-Sept. £7-10). Other services include: **Barclays,** 10 South St. (☎326 700; open M-Tu and Th-F 9am-5pm, W 10am-5pm); **Lara's Launderette,** 16c High East St. (wash £2.60-3, dry 20p per 10min.; open daily 8am-7pm); the **police,** Weymouth Ave. (☎251 212); **West Dorset Hospital,** Williams Ave. (☎251 150); free **Internet access** at the **library,** Colliton Park, off The Grove (☎224 448; open M 10am-7pm, Tu-W and F 9:30am-7pm, Th 9:30am-5pm, Sa 9am-4pm); and the **post office,** 43 South St., including a **bureau de change** (☎(08457) 223 344; open M-Sa 9am-5:30pm). **Post Code:** DT1 1DH.

▐ ACCOMMODATIONS AND CAMPING

The White House, 9 Queens Ave. (☎266 714), off Maumbury Rd. In Dorchester's posh area. Quite possibly the largest guest rooms in southern England. £20. ❸

Junction Hotel, 42 Great Western Rd. (☎268 826), offers spacious ensuite rooms and a cottage atmosphere, adjacent to The Junction pub. Singles and doubles £45. ❹

Maumbury Cottage, 9 Maumbury Rd. (☎266 726). Close to both train stations. Kind Mrs. Wade lets 1 single, 1 double, and 1 twin. Lucky guests get homebaked bread with breakfast. £19 per person. ❷

YHA Litton Cheney (☎(01308) 482 340), 10 mi. west. Take bus #31 to Whiteway; follow the signs 1½ mi. Open Jan.-Sept. Tu-Su. Dorms £10.25, under 18 £7. ❷

Camping: Giant's Head Caravan and Camping Park, Old Sherborne Rd. (☎(01300) 341242), Cerne Abbas, 8 mi. north of Dorchester. Head out of town on The Grove and bear right onto Old Sherborne Rd. Showers, laundry, and electricity. Open Apr.-Sept. ❶

▐ ▌ FOOD AND PUBS

The eateries along **High West St.** and **High East St.** provide a range of options. Find groceries at the **market,** in the carpark near South Station (☎(01202) 841 212; open W 8am-3pm, Su 8am-1pm), or at **Waitrose,** in the Tudor Arcade, off South St. (☎268 428. Open M-W and Sa 8:30am-7pm, Th-F 8:30am-8pm; in summer also Su 10am-4pm). **The Potter Inn ❶,** 19 Durngate St., puts orchards into their apple cake (£1.20) and serves towering sandwiches and small meals (£2.25-4.25) on a sunny, secluded patio. (☎260 312. Open M-Sa 10am-4:30pm.) **The Celtic Kitchen ❶,** 17 Antelope Walk (☎269 377), near the TIC, serves delicious homemade cornish pasties (£1.50-2.10), from veggie to chicken and tarragon. For a nice sit-down meal, try **The Mock Turtle ❸,** 34 High West St., where veggie risotto (£8.75) and seafood dishes (£8-12) star. (☎264 011. Open Tu-F noon-2:30pm, M-Sa 6:30-9:30pm.)

Dorchester barely dabbles in nightlife, but find a good pint among the friendly alternative crowd at **The Old George,** at the bottom of Trinity St. (☎263 534. Open M-Th 11am-11pm, F-Sa 11am-midnight, Su noon-10:30pm.) Heed the warning to "duck or grouse" when entering the **King's Arms,** 30 High East St., and then drink and be merry at the historic inn, featured in Hardy's *Mayor of Casterbridge.* (☎265 353. Open M-Sa 11am-11pm, Su noon-10:30pm.)

◉ SIGHTS

Dorchester's half-dozen Hardy attractions can't quite compete with the compelling sights in the hills just outside of town. East of town, Hardy-related sites hint at the poet-novelist's inspiration for Wessex, a fictional region that roughly corresponds with the Dorchester area; west of town, remnants of Roman Britain are partially buried, but still visible. Negotiate both areas in a day with a bike or a bus schedule.

Hardy designed the home **Max Gate,** 1 mi. southwest of town off Arlington Rd., and lived there from 1885 to his death in 1928, penning *Tess of the D'Urbervilles* and *Jude the Obscure* in the interim. (☎262 538. Drawing room and garden open Apr.-Sept. M, W, and Su 2-5pm. £2.30, children £1.20.) Hardy adventurers will also appreciate the tiny **Stinsford Church,** 2 mi. northeast of town in Stinsford Village. Hardy was christened in the church, and the yard holds his family plot, where both his first and second wives are buried. Only Hardy's heart is buried here—his ashes lie in Westminster Abbey (see p. 111). Nearby rests classicist Cecil Day-Lewis (Daniel's dad), who asked to be buried near the author. Take bus #184 (every 2hr., 80p) from Trinity St. toward Puddletown; ask to be dropped off near the church. Or walk 40min. east on London Rd. (which becomes Stinsford Hill) to Church Ln. Turn right; the churchyard is just over the hill.

On the other side of town, scattered ruins (all free and always open) recall Dorchester's status as a former Roman stronghold. The most significant of these is **Maiden Castle**, a fortification dating to 3000 BC and seized by the Romans in AD 44. The "castle" was actually a fortified hilltop, today patrolled by sheep. Take local shuttle #2 (M-Sa 5 per day, 80p) to Maiden Castle Rd., ¾ mi. from the hill. Alternatively, hike a scenic 2 mi. from the town center down Maiden Castle Rd. Roman sights within Dorchester are not as spectacular, but still merit a visit. Archaeologists have unearthed the complete foundation and mosaic floor of a first-century **Roman Town House,** at the back of the County Hall complex. (Walk north on The Grove until it intersects with Northernway, where steep stairs lead to the entrance.) The only remaining fragment of the **Roman Wall** hides just 5min. south, on Albert Rd. Just past the South Station entrance sprawl the **Maumbury Rings,** a Bronze Age monument with a grassy, gaping maw used as a Roman amphitheater.

In town, the **Dorset County Museum,** 66 High West St., explores Roman and Hardy history and then some, with a replica of Hardy's study and relics of the city's other keepers—Druids, Romans, and Saxons. (☎262 735. Open M-Sa 10am-5pm; May-Oct. also Su 10am-5pm. £3.75, concessions £2.45, children £1.75, families £9.) One of the few non-Roman, non-Hardy sights in town, the **Keep Military Museum of Devon and Dorset,** Bridport Rd., collects uniforms and memorabilia from the Devon and Dorset regiments. See what might be Hitler's desk, swiped by British soldiers from his chancellery in 1945. (☎264 066. Open Apr.-Sept. M-Sa 9:30am-5pm, Oct.-Mar. Tu-Sa 9:30am-5pm.; July-Aug. also Su 10am-4pm. £3, concessions £2, families £9.)

LYME REGIS   ☎01297

Known as the "Pearl of Dorset," Lyme Regis (pop. 3500) huddles at the bottom of a coastal hillside. Steep climbs, startling views, and rocky shores entice travelers to this quiet hamlet, where seagull calls and the sigh of waves mingle with the bustle of the main road. The stark coast and curving Cobb have inspired many: Jane Austen worked and vacationed here, Whistler painted, and Meryl Streep filmed *The French Lieutenant's Woman*, written by native John Fowles.

🖅🚆 TRANSPORTATION AND PRACTICAL INFORMATION. Lyme Regis is a fine daytrip from Exeter. Take the **train** (☎(08457) 484 950) to **Axminster** (40min., 9 per day), 5 mi. north of Lyme, and transfer to **First** (☎(01305) 783 645) bus #31 or X31 (25min.; every hr.; £1.90, return £2.15). **Southern National** bus X53 goes directly to Lyme from **Exeter** (1½hr., 5 per day, £5.40). The **tourist information centre,** Church St., downhill from the bus stop, locates lodgings and stocks walking guides. (☎442 138. Open M-Sa 10am-5pm.) Historian Richard J. Fox conducts 1½hr. **history tours** and **ghost tours.** (☎443 568. History tours Tu and Th 2:30pm, from Guildhall; ghost tours Tu and Th 7pm, from the top of Broad St. £3, children £2.) Paleontologist Steve Davies leads a 2hr. **hunting walk,** which roams the shores in search of fossils. (Contact the Dinosaur Museum for times. £4.50, seniors £4.20, children £2.50, families £13.) Numerous companies on the Cobb run **boat tours** (£7, children £5). Other services include: **banks** on Broad St., including **Lloyds TSB,** 54 Broad St. (open M-Tu and Th-F 9am-4:30pm, W 9:30am-4:30pm); **Internet access** at **LymeNet,** Church St., through a small archway opposite the Parish Church (☎444 570; £1 per 30min.; open M-Tu 9am-8pm, W-F 9am-5pm, Sa 10am-1pm); a **launderette,** Lyme Close (☎443 461; wash £2, dry 50p per 10min.; open M-Tu and Th-F 2-9pm, W and Sa-Su 8am-10pm); the **police,** Hill Rd. (☎442 603); **Axminster Hospital,** Chard Rd. (☎32071), Axminster; and the **post office,** 37 Broad St. (☎442 836; open M-F 8:30am-5:30pm, Sa 8:30am-6pm). **Post Code:** DT7 3QF.

SOUTHWEST ENGLAND

⬛⬜ ACCOMMODATIONS AND FOOD. Lyme is full of **B&Bs**, all pricey and busy during the summer. A 10min. hike up Broad St. (veer right onto Silver St.) brings travelers to **Woodmead Rd.**, which intersects **View Rd.**; both streets offer cheaper options. **Westwood Guest House ❸**, 1 Woodmead Rd., has comfortable lodgings and low prices. (☎442 376. £20 per person.) **Camp** at **Hook Farm ❶**, Gore Ln., in the town of Uplyme. (☎442 801. Open Mar.-Nov. £2 per person, £5.90-11.50 per pitch, £1 per tent or car.) Coffee shops and costermongers line **Broad St.**, the town's main strip, and **Coombe St.** has a handful of quieter cafes and sit-down restaurants. Fish and chips sizzle on **Marine Parade** near the Cobb; the seafood (£5) is excellent at the **Cobb Arms ❷** pub. (☎443 242. Open daily 11am-11pm; food served until 9pm.) For delicious pizzas (£4.50-9) and pastas (£4.95-5.50), visit **The Italian Place ❷**, Drake's Way, in a quaint alley off Broad St. (☎444 788. Open Apr.-Oct. Tu-Sa 6-9:30pm; Nov.-Mar. Th-Sa.) **Café Sol ❶**, 1a Coombe St., fixes tasty baguettes, sandwiches (£2.80-3.50), and organic drinks (£1.40-1.85), featuring local produce. (☎442 404. Open Apr.-Oct. daily 10am-5pm.)

⬛⬜ SIGHTS AND ENTERTAINMENT. The Cobb, a 10 to 20 ft. high rock seawall, curves out from the land to cradle the small harbor. In Jane Austen's *Persuasion*, Louisa Musgrove suffered an unfortunate (or fortunate, if you're rooting for the good guys) fall here. The **Marine Aquarium** on the Cobb exhibits a limited collection of sea critters. (☎333 106. Open May-Oct. daily 10am-5pm; later in July-Aug. £2, concessions £1.50.) The **Lyme Regis Philpot Museum,** Bridge St., two doors down from the TIC, chronicles Lyme's geological and cultural histories and houses local fossils, including a 200-million-year-old ichthyosaurus. (☎443 370. Open Easter-Oct. M-Sa 10am-5pm, Su 11am-4pm; Nov.-Easter Sa-Su only. £1.60, concessions £1.30, families £3.80.) For more fossil facts, see paleontologist Steve Davies at the **Dinosaur Museum,** Coombe St., which features his private fossil collection. (☎443 541. Open daily 10am-5pm. £3.50, seniors £3.20, children £2.50, families £11.)

Langmoor Gardens, accessible from Pound St. and Marine Parade, sits on a hill above Marine Parade, overlooking the ocean. Another peaceful retreat is garden- lined **Riverside Walk,** a short path flanked on both sides by the River Lym and accessible from Coombe St., off Bridge St. A stone archway housing a well marks where the Lepers' Hospital once stood. The TIC stocks information on longer hikes, including **footpaths** that wind along the coast toward Seaton and over clifftops to Charmouth. In summer, **festivals** visit Lyme Regis—particularly popular are the **Jazz Festival** (early July), **Lifeboat Week** (late July), and **Regatta Carnival** (early Aug.).

DEVON

EXETER ☎01392

In 1068, the inhabitants of Exeter earned the respect of William the Conqueror, holding their own against his forces for 18 days. When the wells within the city ran dry, the Exonians used wine for cooking, bathing, and (of course) drinking, which might explain why the city finally fell. As years went by, Exeter's cathedral made it the religious center of the southwest and eventually the county seat of Devon, only to be flattened by three days of Nazi bombing in 1942. Frantic rebuilding has made Exeter (pop. 110,000) an odd mixture of the venerable and the banal.

▐ TRANSPORTATION

Exeter is a convenient gateway to the rest of Devon and Cornwall.

Trains: St. David's Station, St. David's Hill. 20min. from town. Ticket office open M-F 5:45am-8:40pm, Sa 6:15am-8pm, Su 8am-8:40pm. Trains (☎(08457) 484 950) to: **Bristol** (1hr., every hr., £15); **London Paddington** (2½hr., every hr., £41); **Salisbury** (2hr., every 1-2hr.). **Central Station,** Queen St. Ticket office open M-F 7:50am-6:15pm, Sa 8:50am-6pm, Su 9:15am-4:25pm. To **London Waterloo** (3hr., 6 per day, £40.10).

Buses: Bus station, Paris St. (☎427 711). Ticket office open M-Sa 8:30am-6pm. **Lockers** (24hr., £1-2). **National Express** (☎(08705) 808 080) to **Bristol** (2hr.; 4-6 per day; £10.25, return £15.50) and **London** (4-5hr.; 9 per day; £14.50, return £26).

Public Transportation: An **Exeter Freedom Ticket** (£3 per day, £10 per week) allows unlimited travel on city **minibuses.** Daytrippers may want an **Explorer Ticket,** allowing unlimited travel on **Stagecoach** buses (☎427 711; £6 per day, £20.65 per week).

Taxis: Capital (☎433 433) and **City Central** (☎434 343).

Bikes and Canoes: Available at the Exeter Quayside next to the footbridge.

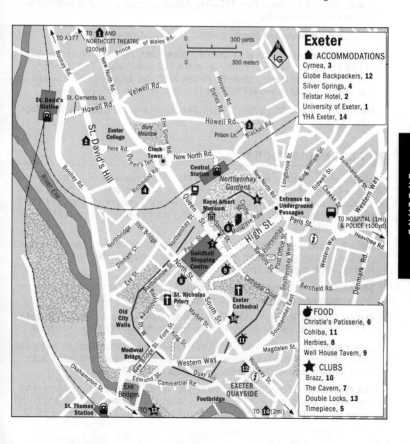

Exeter

🏠 **ACCOMMODATIONS**
Cyrnea, **3**
Globe Backpackers, **12**
Silver Springs, **4**
Telstar Hotel, **2**
University of Exeter, **1**
YHA Exeter, **14**

🍴 **FOOD**
Christie's Patisserie, **6**
Cohiba, **11**
Herbies, **8**
Well House Tavern, **9**

⭐ **CLUBS**
Brazz, **10**
The Cavern, **7**
Double Locks, **13**
Timepiece, **5**

SOUTHWEST ENGLAND

▓ PRACTICAL INFORMATION

Tourist Information Centre: At the Civic Centre, Paris St. (☎ 265 700). Books accommodations for a 10% deposit. Open M-Sa 9am-5pm; July-Aug. also Su 10am-4pm.

Tours: The best way to explore this idiosyncratic city is by taking one of Exeter City Council's (☎ 265 203) free 1½hr. **themed walking tours,** including Murder and Mayhem, Ghosts and Legends, and Medieval Exeter. Most walks leave from the front of the Royal Clarence Hotel off High St.; some depart from the Quay House Visitor Centre on the Quay. (Apr.-Oct. 4-5 per day, Nov.-Mar. 11am and 2pm.)

Financial Services: Banks are easy to find. **Thomas Cook,** 9 Princesshay (☎ 601 300). Open M-W and F-Sa 9am-5:30pm, Th 10am-5:30pm.

Work Opportunities: JobCentre, Queen St. (☎ 606 000). Open M-Tu and Th 9am-4:30pm, W 9:45am-4:30pm, F 9am-4pm.

Launderette: St. David's Launderette, 24 St. David's Hill (☎ 274 459), at the corner of Richmond Rd. Wash £2, dry 20p per 4min, soap 30p. Open daily 8am-9pm.

Police: Heavitree Rd. (☎ (08705) 777 444), 3 blocks past the junction of Heavitree Rd., Western Way, and Paris St.

Hospital: Royal Devon and Exeter (Wonford), Barrack Rd. (☎ 411 611).

Internet Access: Hyperactive, 1a Central Station Buildings, Queen St. (☎ 201 544). £2.50 per 30min., students £2.25. Open M-F 10:30am-7:30pm, Sa 10am-6pm, Su noon-6pm. **Central Library,** Castle St. (☎ 384 206). Free for the first 20min., then £1 per 20min. Open M-Tu and Th-F 9:30am-7pm, W 10am-5pm, Sa 9:30am-4pm.

Post Office: Bedford St. (☎ (08457) 223 344). Open M-Sa 9am-5:30pm. **Post Code:** EX1 1AA.

▗ ACCOMMODATIONS

A handful of inexpensive **B&Bs** lie near the **Clock Tower** roundabout north of Queen St., especially on **St. David's Hill** between St. David's Station and the center of town. From Easter to October, the **University of Exeter** (☎ 211 500) offers limited accommodations, including B&B at **The Old Library ❷,** Prince of Wales Rd. (☎ 215 566. Reservations required. £12.50 per person.)

▨ **Globe Backpackers,** 71 Holloway St. (☎ 215 521). Friendly surroundings and fantastic showers. Guests get their own front door key. Free luggage storage. Dorms £11 first night, £10 per night thereafter. ❷

Silver Springs, 12 Richmond Rd. (☎ 494 040). Cozy and luxurious Georgian townhouse conveniently near both train stations. Singles £25-32; doubles £50-65. ❸

Cyrnea, 73 Howell Rd. (☎/fax 438 386). Open atmosphere; ensuite rooms. If Mr. Budge is home when you call, he may pick you up from the station. £17-19 per person. ❷

Telstar Hotel, 77 St. David's Hill (☎ 272 466; reception@telstar-hotel.co.uk). Family-run B&B with large, comfortable rooms. Full breakfast includes fresh fruit salad. Book 1 week ahead in summer. Singles £22-30; doubles £40-60. ❸

YHA Exeter, 47 Countess Wear Rd. (☎ 873 329; fax 876 939), 2 mi. southeast of the city center. Take minibus K or T from High St. to the Countess Wear post office (£1.10); follow signs to the spacious, cheery hostel (10min.). Dorms £11.25, under 18 £8. ❷

FOOD

Get groceries at **Sainsbury's,** in the Guildhall Shopping Centre. (☎ 217 129. Open M-W and F 8am-6:30pm, Th 8am-7pm, Sa 7:30am-6pm, Su 10:30am-4:30pm.) **Herbies ❷,** 15 North St., has a wide variety of veggie delights, with light dishes ringing up at £3-4, dinner entrees £6-7. (☎ 258 473. Open M-Sa 11am-2:30pm, Tu-Sa also 6-9:30pm.) **Cohiba ❸,** South St., serves delicious tapas (£4) and Mediterranean main dishes (£8-13) with a mellow mix of jazzy Latin tunes. (☎ 678 445. Open daily noon-late.) Find hefty, made-to-order sandwiches (£1.20-2) and savories (most under £1) with a vegetarian spin at **Christie's Patisserie ❶,** 29 Gandy St. (☎ 423 003. Open M-F 8am-5pm, Sa 8am-5:30pm.) For pub grub, try **Well House Tavern ❷,** on Cathedral Close, an annex of the ancient and blue-blood-haunted Royal Clarence Hotel. (☎ 223 011. Open M-Sa 11am-11pm, Su noon-10:30pm; food served noon-2:30pm.)

⊙ SIGHTS

EXETER CATHEDRAL. The west front features five rows of weather-beaten statues, starting at the bottom with angels, then warriors, kings, apostles, and St. Peter at the top as a virile, naked fisherman. The cathedral is home to the 60 ft. **Bishop's Throne** (made without nails), which was disassembled and taken to the countryside in 1640 and again during WWII to save it from destruction. Less fortunate was the chapel, hit by a German bomb in 1942. The cathedral also contains an intricate 15th-century clock; when it strikes one, look for the tiny hole where the bishop's cat once ran in after mice (hence "Hickory Dickory Dock"). The Bishop's Palace refectory holds a collection of manuscripts known as the **Exeter Book**—the world's richest treasury of early Anglo-Saxon poetry. (☎ 255 573. Cathedral open daily 7am-6:30pm. Library open M-F 2-5pm. Evensong M-F 5:30pm, Sa-Su 3pm. Free guided tours Apr.-Oct. M-F 11:30am and 2:30pm, Sa 11am. Requested donation £3, seniors £2, families £5.)

THE UNDERGROUND PASSAGES. Six hundred years ago, the clergy built underground passages to deliver clean water to the church community. Not to be outdone, wealthy merchants built their own subterranean piping network. Although the pipes are long since pilfered, visitors can now take a 30min. tour of the incredibly narrow passages (2 ft. by 6 ft., and decidedly not for the claustrophobic), which contain doors built by Cavaliers during the Civil War to keep out besieging Roundheads. (Romangate Passage, off High St. ☎ 265 887. Open July-Sept. M-Sa 10am-5:30pm; Oct.-June Tu-F 2-5pm, Sa 10am-5pm. Tours start every 30min., last tour 4:30pm. £3.75, concessions £2.75, families £11.)

THE ROYAL ALBERT MEMORIAL MUSEUM. This museum's thorough exploration of local history, from Roman occupation to WWII attacks, is part of a diverse collection. World culture galleries feature everything from totem poles and Egyptian tombs to exotic butterflies and a stuffed Kenyan elephant. (Queen St. ☎ 665 858. Open M-Sa 10am-5pm. Free.)

GARDENS. Upon penetrating the city, William the Conqueror built Rougemont Castle to keep the locals in check. Today, only the castle walls remain, and, due to security at the adjacent court building, tourists can only view the ruins from a non-photogenic angle in the surrounding **Rougemont Gardens.** Follow the path along the castle walls through immaculate flowerbeds to reach the expansive 17th-century **Northernhay Gardens** next door. (Accessible from Castle St. Open daily dawn-dusk. Free.)

SOUTHWEST ENGLAND

🔊 🎵 NIGHTLIFE AND ENTERTAINMENT

Exeter boasts a growing nightlife scene, with bars and clubs in the small alleys off High St. and near Exeter Cathedral. **Gandy St.** has a number of decent bars. Street signs make for funky decor at **Timepiece,** Little Castle St., which draws a rowdy crowd to its upstairs club. (☎493 096. Cover £2-5. Open M-W 7pm-1am, Th-Sa 7pm-1:30am, Su 7pm-12:30am.) Hardcore clubbers go to **The Cavern,** 83-84 Queen St., in a brick cellar, which hosts up-and-coming bands nightly; check the kiosks plastered in fluorescent paper on High St. for details. (☎495 309. Cover free-£8. Open Su-Th 8:30pm-1am, F-Sa 8:30pm-2am.) Along the river, 1½ mi. south of the city center, is ever-popular **Double Locks,** on Canal Banks. (☎256 947. Open M-Sa 11am-11pm, Su noon-10:30pm.) Those too lazy or incapacitated to walk can take the **White Heather boat,** which runs between Canal Banks and Exeter Quay (3 per day; £2.50, return £4.50). **Brazz,** 10-12 Palace Gate, is closer but more chichi. (☎925 2000. Open M noon-11pm, Tu-F 11am-11pm, Sa 10am-11pm, Su noon-10:30pm.)

The professional **Northcott Theatre** company performs throughout the year. (Stoker Rd. ☎493 493. Box office open M-Sa 10am-6pm, until 8pm on show nights. Tickets £10-15; students £2 discount M-Th, standbys £6.) Tickets can also be booked at the **Arts Booking and Information Centre** (☎211 080), just off High St., which supplies monthly listings of cultural events in the city. The **Exeter Festival** (July 4-20 in 2003) features concerts, opera, dance lessons, standup comedy, and an explosion of theater. For details and tickets (£5-15), contact the **Festival Box Office,** Civic Centre, Paris St. (☎213 161. Open M-F 9:30am-6pm, Sa 10am-2pm.)

EXMOOR NATIONAL PARK

Once a royal hunting preserve, Exmoor is among the smallest of Britain's national parks, covering 265 sq. mi. on the north coast of the island's southwestern peninsula. Dramatic sea-swept cliffs fringe moors cloaked in purple heather where sheep and cattle graze. Wild ponies still roam, and England's last herds of red deer graze in woodlands between the river valleys. Although over 80% of Exmoor is privately owned, the territory is accommodating to respectful hikers and bikers.

🏃 GETTING THERE

As always, **Traveline** (☎(0870) 608 2608) is the most helpful resource for planning public transport. For specific questions about **Somerset buses,** call ☎(01823) 251 151. Exmoor's western gateway is **Barnstaple.** The **train station** serves **Exeter St. David's** (1¼hr.; M-Sa 9-11 per day, Su 5 per day; £10.40). **National Express buses** (☎(08705) 808 080) connect Barnstaple to **Bristol** (3hr., 3 per day, £15.50) and **London** (5½hr., 3-4 per day, £23.50). To reach **Exeter,** take **First DevonBus** (☎(01271) 345 444) #315 (2¼hr.; M-Sa 4-5 per day, Su 2 per day; £3.70, return £5). To reach **Plymouth,** take #86 (3¼hr.; M-Sa 7 per day, Su 2 per day; £4.50) or the more direct DevonBus X85 Saturday service (2¾hr., 1 per Sa, £4.50).

Exmoor's eastern gateway is **Minehead,** accessible via **Taunton,** whose train station connects to bigger cities like **Exeter** (25min., every hr., £7). To reach Minehead from Taunton, take bus #28, 298, or 300 direct (1¼hr.; M-Sa every hr., Su 9 per day; £3.75) or get off at **Bishops Lydeard** (20min.), then take a **West Somerset Railway** (☎(01643) 704 996) train to Minehead (1¼hr., Apr.-Oct. 4-8 per day). Drivers sell combined bus and train tickets (£11.55, seniors £9.65, children £5.75).

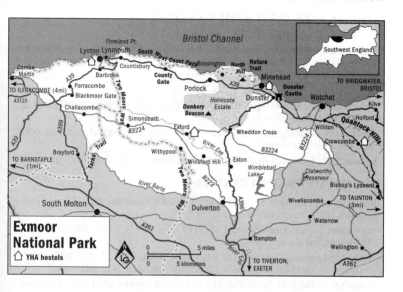

Exmoor National Park
⌂ YHA hostels

LOCAL TRANSPORTATION

Although getting to the outskirts of Exmoor by public transportation is relatively easy, bus service within the park is erratic. You'll get around Exmoor with fewer gray hairs if you grab a copy of the *Exmoor and West Somerset Public Transportation Timetable*, free at TICs, which provides bus schedules as well as vague but well-meaning walking maps. *Accessible Exmoor*, free from National Park Information Centres (NPICs), provides a thorough guide for disabled visitors.

Nearly all **buses** in the area are run by **First**. Since single fares are about £2, it's wise to purchase **First Day Plus** (£5, children £3.50) or **First Week Plus** (£20/£10) tickets, which allow unlimited travel on all area First buses. The more limited **First Day** (£2.50/£1.50) and **First Week** (£11/£7) **Corridor** tickets allow unlimited travel on a particular route and are cheaper than many return tickets.

Bus #300 runs east to west along the coast, from Taunton to Barnstaple via Dunster, Minehead, Porlock, Lynton, and Ilfracombe. Listed prices are for off-peak hours (purchased after 8:45am). Buses from **Barnstaple** run to: **Ilfracombe** (#3, 30; 40min.; M-Sa 4 per hr., Su 1-2 per hr.; £1.90); **Lynmouth** (#309-310, 1¼hr., M-Sa 3 per day, £1.95); **Lynton** (#309-310, 1hr., M-Sa every hr., £1.95); and **Minehead** (#300; 2¾hr.; 1 per day; £2.90, return £4.20). Buses from **Minehead** run to: **Dunster** (#15, 28, 39, 300, 398, 927-928; 10min.; M-Sa 2 per hr., Su 1-2 per hr.; £1.50); **Ilfracombe** (#300, 2hr., M-F 3 per day, £4.70); **Lynton** (#300, 1hr., 3 per day, £1.95); and **Porlock** (#38, 300; 15min.; M-Sa 3 per day, Su 10 per day; £2.10).

PRACTICAL INFORMATION

NPICs are experts on the park while TICs are geared toward villages and can book beds. Both stock Ordnance Survey maps (£6), the *Public Transport Timetable*, and the invaluable *Exmoor Visitor* newspaper, which lists events, accommodations, and free guided walks, and has a useful map and articles on the area's geography. This information can also be found at www.exmoor-nationalpark.gov.uk.

NATIONAL PARK INFORMATION CENTRES
From November to March, all NPICs are open weekends only.

Combe Martin: Seacot, Cross St. (☎/fax (01271) 883 319), 3 mi. east of Ilfracombe. Open July-Aug. daily 10am-7pm; Apr.-June and Sept. 10am-5pm; Oct. 10am-noon.

County Gate: on the A39, Countisbury (☎(01598) 741 321), 7 mi. east of Lynton. Open Apr.-Sept. daily 10am-5pm; Oct. 10am-4pm.

Dulverton: Dulverton Heritage Centre, The Guildhall, Fore St. (☎(01398) 323 841). Open Apr.-Oct. daily 10am-5pm.

Dunster: Dunster Steep Car Park (☎(01643) 821 835), 2 mi. east of Minehead. Open Apr.-Oct. daily 10am-5pm.

Lynmouth: The Esplanade (☎(01598) 752 509). Open Apr.-Oct. daily 10am-5pm.

TOURIST INFORMATION CENTRES

Barnstaple: 36 Boutport St. (☎(01271) 375 000). Open Apr.-Oct. M-Sa 9:30am-5:30pm; Nov.-Mar. M-Sa 9:30am-5pm.

Ilfracombe: The Landmark Seafront (☎(01271) 863 001). Open Easter-Sept. daily 10am-8pm; Nov.-Easter 10am-5pm.

Lynton and Lynmouth: Town Hall, Lee Rd., Lynton (☎(01598) 752 225). Also has info on Lynmouth. Open Easter-Oct. daily 9:30am-6pm; Nov.-Mar. M-Sa 10am-4pm.

Minehead: 17 Friday St. (☎(01643) 702 624). Open July-Aug. M-Sa 9:30am-5:30pm; Sept.-Oct. and Apr.-June 9:30am-5pm; Nov.-Mar. 10am-4pm.

Porlock: West End. High St. (☎(01643) 863 150). Open Easter-Oct. M-Sa 10am-5pm, Su 10am-1pm; Nov.-Easter Tu-F 10:15am-1pm, Sa 10am-2pm.

⛰ ACCOMMODATIONS

Rain or shine, **hostels** and **B&Bs** (£18-20) fill up quickly; check listings and the *Exmoor Visitor* at the TIC. At busy times, **camping** may be the easiest way to see the park. The *Exmoor Visitor* lists several caravan parks and camping barns that accept tents, but campsites that don't advertise are easy to find, especially near coastal towns. Most land is private; before pitching a tent, ask the owner's permission. The **YHA hostels** below all have daytime lockouts (usually 10am-4pm).

Crowcombe (☎(01984) 667 249). A large house in the woods on the Taunton-Minehead Rd., 1½ mi. from Crowcombe Heathfield below Quantock Hills. Take bus #28 or 928 from Taunton toward Minehead, get off at Red Post. Turn onto the road marked "Crowcombe Station & Lydeard St. Lawrence"; the hostel is ¾ mi. down, on the right. Open Apr.-June M-Sa; July-Sept. daily. Dorms £9.50, under 18 £6.75. ❶

Elmscott (☎(01237) 441 367). Bus #119 from Barnstaple goes to Hartland; from the west end of Fore St. a footpath leads 3½ mi. through The Vale to the hostel. Difficult to find—a map is a must. Dorms £10.25, under 18 £7. ❷

Exford Withypoole Rd. (☎(01643) 831 288), Exe Mead, Exford. Take bus #178 (F) or 285 (Su) from Minehead. The hostel is next to the River Exe bridge, the first road on the left, in the center of the moorland. Laundry facilities. Open July-Aug. daily; mid-Feb. to June and Sept.-Oct. M-Sa. Dorms £11.25, under 18 £8. ❷

Ilfracombe 1 Hillsborough Terr. (☎(01271) 865 337), Ilfracombe. Take bus #1, 2, or 30 from Barnstaple to Ilfracombe bus station, ½ mi. from the hostel. Georgian house with a view of Wales. Family rooms available. Open late Feb., Apr.-Sept., and late Oct. daily. Dorms £10.25, under 18 £7. ❷

Lynton (☎ (01598) 753 237), Lynbridge, Lynton. Take bus #309 or 310 from Barnstaple to Castle Hill Car Park, or #300 from Minehead. A former Lyn West valley hotel. Open July-Aug. daily; Apr.-June M-Sa; Sept.-Oct. Tu-Sa. Dorms £10.25, under 18 £7. ❷

Minehead (☎ (01643) 702 595), Alcombe Combe, Minehead. Halfway between the town center and Dunster (2 mi. from either), 3hr. walk to Dunkery Beacon. From Minehead, follow Friday St. as it becomes Alcombe Rd., turn right on Brook St. and follow to Manor Rd. (30min.). From Taunton, take bus #28 to Minehead or 928 to Alcombe; the bus stops 1 mi. from the hostel. Laundry facilities. Open July-Aug. daily; mid-Apr. to June M-Sa. Dorms £10.25, under 18 £7. ❷

Quantock Hills (☎ (01278) 741 224), Sevenacres, Holford, Bridgwater. Buses #15, 915, and 927 from Bridgwater to Minehead stop at Kilve. Take Pardlestone Ln. opposite the post office (1 mi.). Country house overlooking Bridgwater Bay. Open late July to Aug. daily. Dorms £9.50, under 18 £6.75. ❶

🄢 🄜 HIKING AND OTHER ACTIVITIES

With wide-open moorland in the west and wooded valleys in the east, Exmoor has a varied landscape best toured on **foot** or **bike.** Local residents run numerous free walks, but the **Exmoor National Park Rangers** (☎ (01398) 323 665) also lead free nature and moorland walks, as well as horseback riding trips. **NPICs** offer 1½-10 mi. themed walks (see p. 232). **National Trust** (☎ (01643) 862 452) leads walks with various focuses, including summer birds, butterflies, and archaeology (£2.50, children £1). More themed walks (£3-5) are listed in the *Guided Walks and Events* pamphlet (free at NPICs and TICs). **Heritage Coach Tours** (☎ (01643) 704 204) operates day, half-day, and evening bus tours.

Although Barnstaple, just outside the park, isn't the only suitable hiking base, it is the largest town in the region, a transport center, and the best place to get gear. Two good points to start woodland traipsings are **Blackmoor Gate,** 11 mi. northwest of Barnstaple, or **Parracombe,** 2 mi. farther northwest. Both are on Barnstaple-Lynton bus #309 route. The **Tarka Trail** starts in Barnstaple and traces a 180 mi. figure-eight, 31 mi. of which are bicycle-friendly. **Biketrail Cycle Hire** (☎ (01598) 763 263) will deliver wheels to you, while **Tarka Trail Cycle Hire,** at the Barnstaple train station, is conveniently located at the trailhead (☎ (01271) 324 202; £9 per day, children £6, families £17; open daily 9:30am-5pm).

Only 1 mi. from the park's eastern boundary, **Minehead** is also a good place to start hiking. The commercialized little town boasts an informative **nature trail** with labeled vegetation as well as other well-marked paths that weave through **North Hill.** The 630 mi. **South West Coast Path** (see p. 199) starts in Minehead and ends in Poole; the 70 mi. portion running through Exmoor passes through Porlock, Lynmouth, Lynton, Ilfracombe, and Barnstaple. Once used by coast guards to monitor smuggling activity, the well-worn path covers every cove and inlet on England's gorgeous southwest shores. For more information, contact the South West Coast Path Association (☎ (01364) 73859). The trailhead is on Quay St.—follow the signs for "Somerset and North Devon Coastal Path."

Porlock, 9 mi. along the South West Coast Path from Minehead, nestled in wooded valleys, offers good hiking and horseback riding. The TIC sells *13 Walks from Porlock* (£1.50), which includes a scenic route to Lynton and Lynmouth (14 mi.), a 2 mi. hike to **Weir–Culborne Church,** England's smallest parish church, and an 8 mi. trek to Exmoor's highest point, **Dunkery Beacon.** The TIC also has a list of local stables, including **Burrowhays Farm Riding Stables,** 1 mi. east of Porlock off the A39. (☎ (01643) 862 463. Open Easter-Oct. M-F and Su. 30min. pony rides £5, 1-2hr. trips £10 per hr., half-day trips for experienced riders £34.50.)

Dubbed England's Little Switzerland, the twin villages of **Lynton** and **Lynmouth** sit atop the coast and promise good sailing and boat trips. Call the Lynmouth Quay (☎ (01598) 753 207) for weather conditions. The **Cliff Railway** (☎ (01598) 753 366), a Victorian-era water-powered lift, shuttles visitors between the two villages. Just upstream from the Harbour, **Glen Lyn Gorge,** at the Lynmouth Crossroads, affords beautiful views of the tumbling water. (Open Easter-Oct. ₤3, concessions ₤1.50)

Dunster, a tiny village of cobblestone sidewalks, 2½ mi. east of Minehead, is worth a visit for its only sight, **Dunster Castle.** Home to the Luttrell family for six centuries, the enormous residence towers over the village. Its elaborate interior includes a 16th-century portrait of a half-naked Sir John Luttrell—as well as what's reputed to be the oldest bathroom in England, made in 1868. One gallery features floor-to-ceiling paintings on leather that tell the story of Antony and Cleopatra. (☎ (01643) 821 314. Open Apr.-Sept. Sa-W 11am-5pm; Oct. 11am-4pm. Gardens open Mar.-Sept. daily 10am-5pm; Oct.-Feb. 11am-4pm. ₤6.20, children ₤3.10, families ₤15.50. Gardens only ₤3/₤1.50/₤7.50.)

DARTMOOR NATIONAL PARK

Dartmoor National Park, south of Exmoor and 10 mi. west of Exeter, is strewn with remnants of the past, from oddly balanced granite tors to Neolithic rock formations. Ramblers through the 367 sq. mi. of green hills and gray skies may also find the skeleton of a once-flourishing tin-mining industry and the heavily guarded Princetown prison. Dartmoor's rough terrain and harsh climate have allowed the park to remain largely untouched for centuries, save by sheep and wild ponies.

▌ TRANSPORTATION

Buses are infrequent: plan ahead, and pick up the invaluable *Discovery Guide to Dartmoor* (free at TICs), which has comprehensive bus and train schedules as well as a useful map and hiking suggestions. **Explorer** tickets allow unlimited travel on one company's buses (**Stagecoach** ₤6, concessions ₤5.15, families ₤12.45; **First** ₤6/₤4.50/₤13), while a **Sunday Rover** allows unlimited travel on all buses (₤6/₤4.50/₤12). A few routes run one or two more trips on Sundays. The **First Day Plus** ticket, which is cheaper than some return fares, allows unlimited travel between two points on First buses regardless of route number (₤2.50, children ₤1.50).

To reach the middle and northeast part of the park, **First** DevonBus #82, a.k.a. the **Transmoor Link** (late May to Sept. M-Sa 3 per day; Su 5 per day; ₤5) connects **Plymouth** in the southwest to **Exeter** in the northeast, passing straight through the park and hitting **Yelverton, Princetown, Postbridge, Moretonhampstead,** and **Steps Bridge.** Bus #359 also connects **Exeter** to **Moretonhampstead** (40min., M-Sa every 2hr., First Day Plus ticket ₤2.50). In the middle of the park, bus #98 shuttles between **Princetown** and **Postbridge** (15min., 3 per day, ₤1.40).

To access the western and northern part of the park, take a bus from **Plymouth** to **Tavistock** and **Yelverton** in the west (#83-84, 86; 1hr.; 4 per hr.) or **Okehampton** in the north (#86, 118; 1½-2hr.; M-Sa every hr., Su 5 per day). Reach Okehampton more quickly from **Exeter** (X9-10; 1hr.; M-Sa every hr., Su 4 per day). Within the park, a bus connects **Okehampton** and **Moretonhampstead** (1hr., 1 per day, ₤2.45).

To reach the park's southern towns, try **Stagecoach Devon** (☎ (01392) 427 711) bus #39 and X39 (M-Sa 8 per day, Su 6 per day; ₤4.85), which also link **Plymouth** and **Exeter,** but pass through the park's southern towns, including **Ivybridge, Buck-**

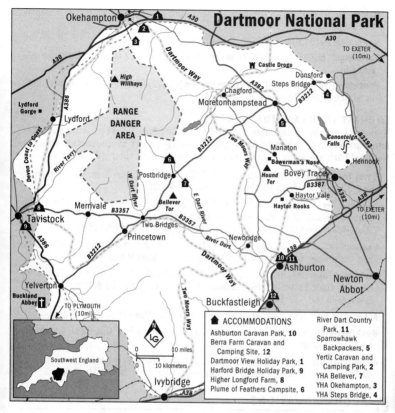

Dartmoor National Park

ACCOMMODATIONS
Ashburton Caravan Park, **10**
Berra Farm Caravan and
  Camping Site, **12**
Dartmoor View Holiday Park, **1**
Harford Bridge Holiday Park, **9**
Higher Longford Farm, **8**
Plume of Feathers Campsite, **6**

River Dart Country
  Park, **11**
Sparrowhawk
  Backpackers, **5**
Yertiz Caravan and
  Camping Park, **2**
YHA Bellever, **7**
YHA Okehampton, **3**
YHA Steps Bridge, **4**

fastleigh, Ashburton, and **Bovey Tracey. First** buses X80 and 88 also run to **Ivybridge** (1-2 per hr.) from **Plymouth** (30min., £2.70) and **Torquay** (1¼hr., £3.40).

For more information on transportation, call **Traveline** (☎ (0870) 608 2608), which operates daily from 7am to 5pm, or any NPIC (see below). Once you've reached the park's perimeter, explore by foot or bike, since most sights are not accessible by main roads; buses serve larger villages, but these are of little interest beyond being good hiking bases. In winter, snow often renders the park and its tortuous roads impassable. **Hitchhikers** report that rides are easy to get, but *Let's Go* does not recommend hitchhiking as a safe mode of transport.

PRACTICAL INFORMATION

All NPICs and TICs stock the indispensable *Dartmoor Visitor* newspaper, which has a detailed map and listings on events, activities, accommodations, and guided walks (see hiking information below).

NATIONAL PARK INFORMATION CENTRES

All NPICs listed below have the same hours (Easter-Oct. daily 10am-5pm; Nov.-Easter Sa-Su 10am-4pm). The Princetown NPIC serves as the main visitors center for the entire park, and has free exhibitions about the area.

Haytor: (☎(01364) 661 520), near Leonard's Bridge. In the bottom end of a carpark just off the B3387.

Newbridge: (☎(01364) 631 303), in the Riverside carpark.

Postbridge: (☎(01822) 880 272), in a carpark off the B3212 Moretonhampstead-Yelverton Rd.

Princetown (High Moorland Visitor Centre): (☎(01822) 890 414), in the former Duchy Hotel, The Square, Tavistock Rd.

TOURIST INFORMATION CENTRES

Numerous villages in Dartmoor have TICs. The first four listed below are gateways into Dartmoor; the last three are towns whose TICs work in conjunction with the National Park Authority and are staffed by volunteers familiar with the area.

Bovey Tracey: Lower Car Park (☎(01626) 832 047). Open Easter-Sept. M-F 10am-4pm, Sa 9:30am-3:30pm, Su 10:15am-12:45pm and 2-4:30pm.

Ivybridge: (☎(01752) 897 035). Books accommodations within 10 mi. for a 10% deposit, beyond 10 mi. for an additional £3 fee. Open Easter-Oct. M-F 9am-5pm, Sa 10am-4pm, July-Aug. also Su 9am-2pm; Nov.-Easter M-Tu and F-Sa 10am-4pm.

Okehampton: 3 West St. (☎(01837) 53020), in the courtyard adjacent to the White Hart Hotel. Open Easter-Oct. M-Sa 10am-5pm; Nov.-Easter M and F-Sa 10am-4:30pm.

Tavistock: Town Hall, Bedford Sq. (☎(01822) 612 938). Books accommodations for £3-3.50. Open Easter-Oct. M-Sa 9:30am-5pm, July-Aug. also Su 9:30am-5pm; Nov.-Easter M-Tu and F-Sa 10am-4pm.

Ashburton: Town Hall, North St. (☎(01364) 653 426). Open M-Sa 9am-4:30pm.

Buckfastleigh: The Valiant Soldier (☎(01364) 644 522). Open Apr.-Oct. M-Sa 10:30am-4:30pm.

Moretonhampstead: 11 The Square (☎(01647) 440 043). Books accommodations for £2.50 and 10% deposit. Open Easter-Oct. daily 10am-5pm; Nov.-Easter F-Su.

▐ ACCOMMODATIONS

B&B signs often appear on pubs and farmhouses along the roads. All NPICs provide accommodations lists, and all TICs book rooms. The hostels in the park are:

YHA Bellever (☎(01822) 880 227), 1 mi. southeast of Postbridge village. Bus #98 from Tavistock stops in front. #82 from Exeter or Plymouth stops in Postbridge; from there, walk west on the B3212 and turn left on Bellever (20-25min.). In the heart of the park—very popular. Friendly staff has reams of local knowledge. Open July-Aug. daily; Mar.-June and Sept.-Oct. M-Sa. Dorms £10.25, under 18 £7; private rooms £40. ❷

YHA Okehampton, Klondyke Rd. (☎(01837) 53916; okehampton@yha.org.uk). 15min. walk from the town center. From the TIC, turn right on George St., veer right onto Station Rd. just before Simmons Park, and continue uphill and under the bridge. Open Feb.-Nov. Dorms £11.25, under 18 £8; doubles £40. **Camping** available all year £5.70. ❷

YHA Steps Bridge (☎(01647) 252 435; fax 252 948), 1 mi. southwest of Dunsford on the B3212, near the eastern edge of the park. Take bus #359 from Exeter (£2.35), get off at Steps Bridge, and hike up the steep drive. Open July-Aug. daily; Apr.-June M-W and F-Su. Dorms £8.75, under 18 £6. ❶

Sparrowhawk Backpackers, 45 Ford St., Moretonhampstead (☎(01647) 440 318). 5min. from the village center. From the bus carpark, walk toward the church, veer left at the fork; turn left at Fore St. Tasty vegetarian breakfasts available. £10 per person. ❷

CAMPING

Although official **campsites** and **camping barns** exist, many travelers camp on the open moor. All of Dartmoor is privately owned, so ask permission before camping. Backpack camping is permitted on non-enclosed moor land more than ¾ mi. from the road or out of sight of inhabited areas and farmhouses. Pitching is prohibited in common areas used for recreation. Campers may only stay for one night in a single spot. Don't build fires in the moors or climb fences or walls unless posted signs say you may do so. Many areas are restricted for camping; it's best to check www.dartmoor-npa.gov.uk or www.discoverdartmoor.com before heading for the moor. When using official campsites, call ahead for reservations, especially in summer. For general information on camping, see p. 47.

Ashburton: River Dart Country Park ❶, Holne Park (☎ (01364) 652 511), ½ mi. off the A38. Follow signs. Lush surroundings and a boating lake. Open Easter-Sept. Tent or caravan £9.50-14. **Ashburton Caravan Park ❶,** Waterleat (☎ (01364) 652 552), 1½ mi. from town; head north on North St. and follow signs; bear right at the bridge. July-Aug. 1 person and tent £6, 2 people £10, £2.25 each additional; Easter-June and Sept.-Oct. £4/£8/£1.50. Caravans £300 per week.

Buckfastleigh: Berra Farm Caravan and Camping Site ❶, Colston Rd., (☎ (01364) 642 234), 2 mi. from town center. Follow the signs for the Otter Park, continue 200 yd. past the entrance, and walk 1½ mi. down Old Totnes Rd. Tents £3.25.

Okehampton: Dartmoor View Holiday Park ❶, Whiddon Down (☎ (01647) 231 545), 5 mi. from town. Head east toward Exeter; stay on the smaller road. Open Mar.-Oct. 2-person tent £9.75; caravans £275-325 per week. **Yertiz Caravan and Camping Park ❶,** Exeter Rd. (☎ (01837) 52281). 1 mi. east of Okehampton, off the A30. Take the B3260 toward Okehampton; 50 yd. past Moorcroft Inn. Tents £6-7; caravans £8-9.

Princetown: Plume of Feathers Campsite ❶ (☎ (01822) 890 240), behind the Plume of Feathers Inn, opposite the NPIC. £3 per person.

Tavistock: Harford Bridge Holiday Park ❷ (☎ (01822) 810 349), on the River Tavy. Follow signs from town. Open Mar.-Nov. 2-person tents and caravans £10.50. Electricity £2. **Higher Longford Farm ❶,** Moorshop (☎ (01822) 613 360). 2½ mi. from Tavistock toward Princetown on B3357. Office open daily 10am-5pm. Tents and caravans £8-12.

HIKING AND OTHER ACTIVITIES

Visitors should not underestimate Dartmoor's moody **weather** and treacherous terrain. Ordnance Survey Outdoor Leisure Map #28 (1:25,000; £7), a compass, and waterproof garb are essential. Stick to marked paths, and call ☎ (0891) 500 404 to check the weather before heading for the moor; mists may descend without warning, especially in non-summer months, and there is no shelter away from the roads. The **Dartmoor Rescue Group** is on call at ☎ 999. (See **Wilderness Safety,** p. 49.)

The rugged terrain of Dartmoor, with remnants of the Bronze Age dotting its sweeping moorland, offers unparalleled **hiking.** The National Park Authority conducts guided walks (1-6hr.; £3-5, free if arriving at starting point by public transport), which are listed in the *Dartmoor Visitor.* Those who'd rather trek on their own will find a wealth of information and advice as well as various guidebooks (free-£10) at NPICs and TICs. A good option for short hikes is the *Transmoor Link Self Guided Bus Walks* (free), which details four hikes along the #82 Transmoor Link bus route (see p. 234). Long-distance trails are numerous. **Dartmoor Way** is a 90 mi. circular route that hits the park's main towns, running through river valleys and rural lakes. The 180 mi. **Tarka Trail** runs from Okehampton to Exmoor National Park in the north (see p. 233). The 100 mi. **Two Moors Way** also connects the two parks, running through Lynmouth and Ivybridge.

The park's highest land is near Okehampton. The area is crowned by several peaks, the highest of which is **High Willhays** (2038 ft.). The peak is accessible only by foot; a 4 mi. hike from Okehampton traverses hilly country and ventures into Dartmoor's danger area. Tiny **Lydford Church** sits atop an extinct volcano near Lydford, accessible only by foot. A mile from the town rests the 1½ mi. ravine **Lydford Gorge**. Walk along the top of the gorge to reach the fantastic 90 ft. **White Lady Waterfall**. (☎ (01822) 820 320. Open Apr.-Sept. 10am-5:30pm; Oct. 10am-4pm; Nov.-Mar. 10:30am-3pm. £3.70, children £1.85.) A wealth of **Bronze Age structures,** the remains of Neolithic civilization, cluster near Merrivale. The knee-high stone circles, hut circles, burial chambers, and long stone rows date back 3500 years. Merrivale is on the #98 and #172 (summer only) bus routes. Haytor Vale, near Bovey Tracey, boasts numerous tors, including the massive **Haytor Rocks** and the celebrated medieval ruins at **Hound Tor,** where excavations unearthed the remains of 13th-century huts and longhouses. Venture several miles north (1 mi. from Manaton) to discover the 40 ft. **Bowerman's Nose** tor, named after the man who first recognized the tor's resemblance to the human proboscis. Also near Bovey Tracey is the 220 ft. **Canonteign Falls,** England's highest waterfall. (☎ (01647) 252 434. Open Mar.-Oct. daily 10am-5:30pm; Nov.-Feb. Sa-Su 10:30am-dusk. £4.)

Dartmoor's roads are hilly but good for **cycling.** Passing through Okehampton and Ilfracombe, the 102 mi. **Devon Coast to Coast** runs along rivers and through rural countryside. **Dartmoor Way** is also suitable for bikes, though the cycling route is slightly different from the hiking route. **Okehampton Cycle Hire,** Garden Centre, rents bikes. From Fore St., go uphill on North St., which becomes North Rd., then bear left off the main road, continuing downhill to the T junction; follow signs for the garden center. (☎ (01837) 53248. Open daily 9am-5pm. £9-16.50, children £6.)

Dartmoor also boasts breathtaking sites for canoeing, horseback riding, rock climbing, hang gliding, fishing, and golf. **Canoeing** season on the River Dart is from October to February; contact Mr. Chamberlain, **Mountain Stream Activities,** Hexworthy (☎ (01364) 646 000). For **horseback riding,** the best bridleways are in the middle of the moor, although the outskirts are worthwhile as well; NPICs can refer you to stables. Those looking to get themselves aloft should contact the **South Devon Hang Gliding and Paragliding Club** (☎ (01364) 73255). More information on outdoor activities is best obtained from NPICs.

 WARNING. The Ministry of Defense uses much of the northern moor for **target practice;** consult the *Dartmoor Visitor* or an Ordnance Survey map for the boundaries of the danger area. Call the Dartmoor Rangers (☎ (800) 458 4868) for weekly firing schedules, which are also posted in NPICs; post offices; police stations; and some hostels, campsites, and pubs; and published in Friday's *Western Morning News.* Danger areas, marked by red-and-white posts, change yearly, so be sure your information is up-to-date.

⊙ SIGHTS

The harsh Dartmoor landscape stretches across roughly 400 sq. mi. of wide open moorland. Scattered through the area are Bronze Age burial mounds, knee-high stone rows, and stone circles. Also prevalent are **tors,** which may look manmade, but are actually the result of thousands of years of geological activity. Granite pushed to the surface develops cracks over time from the wind; hence the stack-like effect. (Although the Glastonbury tor is a large mound of earth, in Dartmoor, "tor" refers to rock structures, originating from the Celtic "tawr" or "tower.")

CASTLE DROGO. England's last castle was built between 1910 and 1930 atop a gorge by tea baron Julius Drewe. Convinced that he was a direct descendant of a Norman who had arrived with William the Conqueror, Drewe constructed this granite fortress in the style of his supposed ancestor. From the castle, easy 3-4 mi. hikes can be made to the **River Tein** and its well-known **Fingle Bridge,** as well as to the picturesque town of **Drewsteignton.** *(☎(01647) 433 306. Take bus #173 from Moretonhampstead. Open Apr.-Oct. Sa-Th 11am-5:30pm. Grounds open daily 10:30am-dusk. £5.70, children £2.85, families £14.20. Grounds only £2.90.)*

BUCKLAND ABBEY. A few miles south of Yelverton, this abbey was built by Cistercian monks in 1273 and later bought by Sir Francis Drake, who was born here. While the interior is rather lusterless, the exterior and grounds make for an interesting wander. The huge Tithe Barn houses Drake's drum. It is said that if ever the drum is lost, England will go to ruins. *(Milton Combe Rd. ☎(01822) 853 607. Take Citybus #55 from Yelverton. Open Apr.-Oct. M-W and F-Su 10:30am-5:30pm; Nov.-Mar. Sa-Su 2-5pm; last admission 45min. before close. £4.70, children £2.85, families £11.70. Grounds only £2.50, concessions £1.10.)*

PRINCETOWN PRISON. Dartmoor's forbidding maximum-security prison, still in use today, is not a tourist attraction but does have an interesting history. Frenchmen from the Napoleonic Wars and Americans who fought to annex Canada in 1812 once languished within its walls. The bleak moorland surrounding the prison is the setting for Sherlock Holmes's famed escapade, *The Hound of the Baskervilles,* which emerged from an ancient Dartmoor legend of a gigantic, glowing pooch. The tiny **Prison Museum** nearby features a gallery of weapons and objects made by creative inmates, including pipes, a knife made of matchsticks, and brass knuckles. *(Tavistock Rd. ☎(01822) 890 305. Open Easter-Oct. daily 9:30am-4:30pm.; Nov.-Easter Tu-Sa 9:30am-4:30pm. £2, concessions £1.)*

TORQUAY ☎01803

The largest city in the Torbay resort region—the self-proclaimed "English Riviera"—Torquay isn't quite as glamorous as the French original, but does have friendly beaches, abundant palm trees, and stimulating nightlife. Agatha Christie schemed up her supersleuths here, and it was in Torquay that the fictional Basil Fawlty ran his madcap hotel. Semi-tropical when it doesn't rain, Torquay serves as a base for exploring the sunnier parts of the southwestern English coast.

SOUTHWEST ENGLAND

▐▌ TRANSPORTATION AND PRACTICAL INFORMATION. Torquay's **train station** is off Rathmore Rd., near the Torre Abbey gardens. (Ticket office open M-Sa 7:10am-5pm, Su 10am-5pm.) Trains (☎(08457) 484 950) arrive from: **Bristol** (2hr., 4 per day, £21); **Exeter** (45min.; 1 per hr.; £6.60, return £7.30); **London Paddington** (3½hr., 2-3 per day, £52.50); **London Waterloo** (4hr., 2-5 per day, £52.50); **Plymouth** (1hr.; 2 per day; £7.30, return £7.70). **Buses** depart from **The Pavilion,** the roundabout where Torbay Rd. meets The Strand. The **Stagecoach** office, next to the TIC, provides info on its buses, which predominate in Torquay. (☎664 500. Open M-F 9am-5pm, Sa 9am-1pm.) Bus #85 runs to **Exeter** (1½hr.; M-Sa every 15min., Su 3 per hr.; £3.70, return £5.50), as does the more direct X46 (1hr.; M-Sa every hr., Su 7 per day; £4.55, return £5.80). **First** X80 runs to **Plymouth** (1¾hr.; every hr.; £3.50, return £5.80). **Taxis** (☎211 611) are available 24hr.

The **tourist information centre,** Vaughan Parade, arranges theater bookings, discounted tickets for nearby attractions, and accommodations for a 10% deposit. (☎(0906) 680 1268; fax 214 885. Open Easter-Oct. M-Sa 9:30am-6pm, Su 10am-6pm; Nov.-Easter M-Sa 9:30am-5pm.) **Cruise Tours** (1hr.; £4, children £2) leave Princess Pier for **Brixham** (Western Lady Ferry Service ☎297 292) and **Paignton** (Mariner ☎528 555). Other services include: **banks** on Fleet St.; **Thomas Cook,** 54 Union St.

(☎352 100; open M and W-Sa 9am-5:30pm, Tu 10am-5:30pm); a **launderette,** 63 Princes Rd., off Market St. (☎293 217; wash £2.40; open M-F 9am-7pm, Sa 9am-6pm, Su 9am-3pm); the **police,** South St. (☎(08705) 777 444); **Torbay Hospital,** Newton Rd. (☎614 567); **Internet access** at the **library,** Lymington Rd. (open M, W, F 9:30am-7pm; Tu 9:30am-5pm; Th 9:30am-1pm; Sa 9:30am-4pm); and the **post office,** 25 Fleet St. (open M-Sa 9am-5:30pm). **Post Code:** TQ1 1AD.

🛏📖 ACCOMMODATIONS AND FOOD. Unlike the hotel in *Fawlty Towers,* most accommodations in Torquay promise budget-busting prices rather than side-splitting humor. As this is a resort town, book well in advance for July and August. Find less expensive **beach hotels** on **Babbacombe Rd.,** including **Torwood Gardens Hotel ❸,** 531 Babbacombe Rd., with spacious rooms 5min. from the surf. (☎298 408. Apr.-Oct. £25 per person; Nov.-Mar. £15 per person.) Cheaper **B&Bs** line **Abbey Rd.** and **Morgan Ave.** Ever-accommodating Jane fosters a friendly atmosphere at **Torquay Backpackers ❷,** 119 Abbey Rd. From the train station, turn left and walk down Torbay Rd., continuing straight uphill on Shedden Hill Rd., then turn left on Abbey Rd. (☎299 924. Dorms £12 first night, £10 thereafter; doubles £20-24.) Continue down Abbey Rd. and turn right at the first street to find amiable **Rosemont Guest House ❷,** 5 Morgan Ave. (☎295 475; £15-16 per person) or cozy **Aries House ❷,** 1 Morgan Ave. (☎404 926; singles £16-18; doubles £32).

Buy groceries at **Somerfield,** Union Square. (Open M-Sa 8:30am-8pm, Su 10am-4pm.) **Number Seven Fish Bistro ❸,** Beacon Terr., at the top of Beacon Hill, is the place to splurge for dinner. This ichthyo-obsessed bistro serves superb seafood (£10-15) in a simple setting. (☎295 055. Open W-Sa 12:45-1:45pm and 6-9:45pm; Su-Tu 7-9:45pm.) For cheaper comestibles (fish and chips £2.40-3.30), try nearby **Chandlers Chippy ❶,** 31 Victoria Parade, Torquay Harbourside, a local favorite. (☎215 213. Open daily 9am-10pm.) **Jingles ❷,** 34 Torwood St., serves delicious cajun grill, chimichangas, and enchiladas (£7-13), and is a fantastic non-fish choice. (☎293 340. Open M-Sa from 6pm, Su 7pm.) Stock up on sandwiches and baguettes (£1.35-2.50) at **Picknics ❶,** 2 Fleet St. (☎200 444. Open daily 10am-3pm.)

🏖📷 SIGHTS AND BEACHES. To get out of the sun (or rain), head for **Torre Abbey,** Kings Dr. Founded as a monastery in 1196, the abbey was converted into a private mansion in the 16th century. It now features a collection of 18th-century watercolors, a scroll on local history from 1830 to 1991, and a re-creation of Agatha Christie's study. The **Spanish Barn** is reputed to be haunted by the Spaniards kept there as captives hundreds of years ago. (☎293 593. Open Easter-Oct. daily 9:30am-6pm, last admission 5pm. No stilettos. £3, concessions £2.50, children £1.50, families £7.25.) For more on Agatha and Torquay's history, visit the **Torquay Museum,** 529 Babbacombe Rd. (☎293 975. Open M-Sa 10am-5pm, Easter-Oct. also Su 1:30-5pm. £3, seniors £2, children and students £1.50.)

There are clear distinctions between the English Riviera and its more established French cousin—the weather, for one. Yet spotty skies lend Torquay beaches a beauty of their own, and the slightest hint of sun thrills waiting crowds. **Torre Abbey Sands** draws the hordes, but visitors can reach better beaches by bus (5-20min., every 30min.). Just southeast of Torquay, **Meadfoot** boasts beach huts, deck chairs, and sandy, pebbly shores (bus #155-156, 70p). Take bus #85 north to slightly rockier **Oddicombe,** hidden under a cove (95p, return £1.45), or much farther north to peaceful and near-deserted **Maidencombe** (£1.50, return £2.35) and **Watcombe** (£1.30, return £2.05).

🎭🎪 NIGHTLIFE AND FESTIVALS. When the sun dips and beaches empty, nightlife options wake. The best place to get a drink is **Mojo,** Palm Court Hotel, Torbay Rd., a friendly seaside hangout with Torquay's latest bar hours. (☎294 882. Open M-Sa 11am-1am, Su 11am-12:30am.) **The Piazza,** Braddons Hill, off Fleet St., has a lively atmosphere and livelier bands that keep locals loyal. (☎295 212. Open M-Sa 11am-11pm, Su 11am-10:30pm.) Nightclub **Claires,** Torwood St., stands out with popular house music. (☎292 079. Cover £3-5. Open Th-Sa 9pm-2am.)

Summer brings two big festivals. The last week of August features the **Torquay Regatta** (☎316 618), while early July tries to **Kick Up the Arts** (contact the TIC).

PLYMOUTH ☎01752

Immortalized by those hasty to leave it behind—the English fleet that defeated the Spanish Armada in 1588, explorers Sir Francis Drake and Captain Cook, the Pilgrims, and millions of emigrants to the United States and New Zealand—Plymouth (pop. 250,000) is no longer a point of immediate departure. Massive air raids during WWII left the city only the cracked shell of a naval capital, but among its rectilinear rows of buildings and awkward modern thoroughfares, patches of Plymouth's rich history still merit a day's exploration.

🇫🇮 GETTING THERE AND SAILING AWAY

Plymouth lies on the southern coast between Dartmoor National Park and the Cornwall peninsula, on the London-Penzance train line.

Trains: Plymouth Station, North Rd. Ticket office open M-F 5:30am-8pm, Sa 5:30am-7pm, Su 9:30am-8pm. Buses #5 and 6 run to the city center. (It's a long walk—take a bus.) Trains (☎(08457) 484 950) arrive from: **Bristol** (3hr., 2 per hr., £32); **London Paddington** (4hr., 2 per hr., £57.50); **Penzance** (2hr., 2 per hr., £13.80).

Buses: Bretonside Station, First National Office (☎(01752) 254 542). Office open M-Sa 8:30am-6pm, Su 9am-5pm. **Lockers** £1-3. **National Express** (☎(08705) 808 080) from **Bristol** (2½hr., £21.50) and **London** (5hr., 7-8 per day, £23.50). **Stagecoach** buses X38, 39, and X39 run to **Exeter** (1¼-1¾hr., 12-13 per day, £5) as does **First** #82 via Dartmoor (late May to Sept.; M-Sa 3 per day, Su 5 per day; £5).

Ferries: Brittany Ferries, at Millbay Docks (☎(08750) 360 360). Follow signs to "Continental Ferries," 15min. from the town center. Taxi to the terminal (£4). Buy tickets 24hr. ahead, though foot passengers may need to arrive only 2hr. early. Check in 45min. before departure, disabled travelers 1-1½hr. To **Roscoff, France** (6hr., 12 per week, £25-50) and **Santander, Spain** (24hr., 1 per week, return £60-150).

Public Transportation: Citybus (☎222 221) buses from Royal Parade (40p-£1.80).

Taxis: Plymouth Taxis (☎606 060).

Bike Rental: Plymouth Cycle Hire, Tamar Bldg., Queen Anne's Battery Marina (☎258 944), 250 yd. east of the Aquarium. Credit card or ID deposit. £12.50 per day, £7.50 per half-day. Open daily 9am-5pm.

🔣 ORIENTATION AND PRACTICAL INFORMATION

The commercial district formed by **Royal Parade, Armada Way,** and **New George St.** is Plymouth's city center. South of here is the **Hoe** (or "High Place"), which boasts little more than simple greenery and a quiet Promenade. The **Royal Citadel,** home to many a man in uniform, is flanked by the Hoe to its west and, to its east, **The Barbican,** where cobbled streets quake with tourists, shoppers, and diners.

Tourist Information Centre: Island House, 9 The Barbican (☎304 849; fax 257 955). In a building said to have housed the Pilgrims just before their departure on the *Mayflower* (look for a list of those on the boat). Books accommodations for 10% deposit. Free map. Open Easter-Oct. M-Sa 9am-5pm, Su 10am-4pm; Nov.-Easter M-F 9am-5pm, Sa 10am-4pm. Another **branch** on Crabtree at the Plymouth Discovery Centre is open July-Sept. and has the same hours.

THE HIDDEN DEAL

THE CONTINENT FOR CHEAP

If you're tired of sandy beaches, nauseated by fish and chips, and just generally sick of this island, it may be time for a jaunt across the Channel. Plymouth is the ferry gateway to France and Spain, but last-minute tickets can cost a pretty penny. Those who are flexible with their schedules, however, and not too anxious to hop that ship may end up saving a good pocketful of pounds.

If you're planning ahead, the best time to book a ticket from Brittany Ferries is in mid-November, when prices are first published. Call then to reserve as much as a year before you actually take the trip. And if you're not in a hurry, opt instead to cross the Channel at Dover. The ferry from there travels to Calais, France, just a stone's throw from Paris. The Dover-Calais crossing is the shortest between England and France, so the fare may be as little as a quarter of the Plymouth-Roscoff fare. Dover is a 6hr. bus trip from Plymouth, but the slow chug along the southern coast may turn out to be a great sightseeing adventure that tops off your stay in England.

Of course, it's always wise to research before deciding on a trip. Contact a few ferry companies to compare prices: **P&O Ferries** (☎(0870) 600 0600) and **Hoverspeed** (☎(0870) 524 0241) are two that run trips across the ocean. (See **By Ferry,** p. 28.)

Tours: The Plymouth Mayflower (see p. 244) runs **Discovery Trails** around the Barbican and harbor (1hr.; 2 per day; £1.50, children 50p). **Guide Friday** bus tours leave every 30min. from stations near the Barbican and the Hoe. (Apr.-Sept. daily, except mid-Apr. to mid-May Sa-Su only; £6, concessions £5, children £2, families £12.) **Plymouth Boat Cruises** (☎822 797) depart sporadically from Phoenix Wharf. (1-2hr.; £6-7.50, children £3-4, families £14-18.)

Financial Services: Banks are plentiful along Old Town St., Royal Parade, and Armada Way. **Thomas Cook,** 9 Old Town St. (☎612 600). Open M-Sa 9am-5:30pm. **American Express,** 139 Armada Way (☎502 706). Open M and W-Sa 9am-5pm, Tu 9:30am-5pm.

Work Opportunities: JobCentre, Buckwell St. (☎616 021) or Hoegate St. (☎616 163). Open M-Th 9am-4:30pm, F 9am-4pm.

Launderette: Hoegate Laundromat, 55 Notte St. (☎223 031). Wash £2.30, soap 70p. Open daily 8am-8pm, last wash 1hr. before close.

Police: Charles Cross (☎(08750) 777 444), near the bus station.

Hospital: Derriford Hospital (☎777 111). In Derriford, about 5 mi. north of the city center. Take bus #42 or 50 from Royal Parade.

Internet Access: Web-U-Like, Pannier Market, New George St. (☎269 710). £1 per 30min. Open M-Tu and Th-Sa 8:30am-5:30pm, W 8:30am-4:30pm. The **library,** Northhill (☎305 907), has free access. Open M-F 9:30am-5:30pm, Sa 9am-4pm.

Post Office: 5 St. Andrew's Cross (☎(08457) 740 740). Open M-Sa 9am-5:30pm. **Post Code:** PL1 1AB.

ACCOMMODATIONS AND CAMPING

Inexpensive B&Bs grace **Citadel Rd.** and its side streets. Rooms tend to be small but cheap (£15-20 per person).

Riviera Hotel, 8 Elliot St. (☎/fax 667 379), a family-run hotel with numerous amenities: all rooms have baths, phones, and hairdryers. Singles £25-35; doubles £50. ❸

Seymour Guest House, 211 Citadel Rd. E. (☎667 002), where Hoegate St. meets Lambhay Hill. Comfy lodgings practically on The Barbican. Singles £16; doubles £30. ❷

Westwinds Hotel, 99 Citadel Rd. (☎601 777; fax 662 158). Veggie breakfasts and professional service. Singles £15-18, with bath £22-30; doubles £32-38/£40-44. ❷

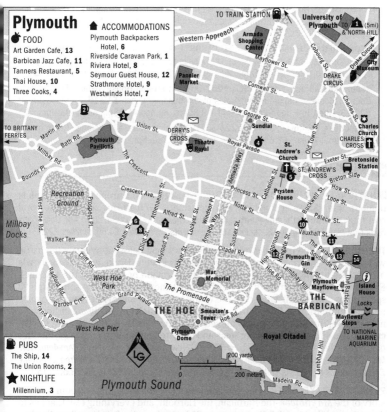

Plymouth

● FOOD

Art Garden Cafe, **13**
Barbican Jazz Cafe, **11**
Tanners Restaurant, **5**
Thai House, **10**
Three Cooks, **4**

▲ ACCOMMODATIONS

Plymouth Backpackers
Hotel, **6**
Riverside Caravan Park, **1**
Riviera Hotel, **8**
Seymour Guest House, **12**
Strathmore Hotel, **9**
Westwinds Hotel, **7**

● PUBS

The Ship, **14**
The Union Rooms, **2**

★ NIGHTLIFE

Millennium, **3**

SOUTHWEST ENGLAND

Strathmore Hotel, Elliot St. (☎662 101; fax 223 690), a brightly lit hotel with spacious rooms, some with large bay windows. Singles £45; doubles £55; family rooms £65. **❹**

Plymouth Backpackers Hotel, 172 Citadel Rd. (☎225 158). Friendly albeit slightly unkempt lodgings. Free showers; baths £1.50. Laundry service. Smoking allowed downstairs. Dorms £10, 3 days £25, weekly £55; singles £15; family rooms £45. **❷**

Camping: Riverside Caravan Park, Longbridge Rd., Marsh Mills (☎344 122). 5 mi. northeast of the city center. Take any bus to Exeter, or head toward Exeter on the A38. £3.75 per adult, £1.50 per child. **❶**

◐ ◪ FOOD AND PUBS

The largest supermarket in town is **Sainsbury's,** in the Armada Shopping Centre. (☎674 767. Open M-Sa 8am-8pm, Su 11am-4pm.) Pick up picnic fixings at **Pannier Market,** an indoor bazaar at the west end of New George St. (☎264 904. Open M-Tu and Th-Sa 8am-5:30pm, W 8am-4:30pm.)

Barbican Jazz Cafe, 11 The Parade (☎672 127). This local favorite serves up live music and Continental flavor in a fantastic, relaxed atmosphere. Open daily 7pm-2am. **❷**

Thai House, 63 Notte St. (☎661 600). Named "the best Thai restaurant in Devon," Thai House compensates for Plymouth's dearth of fine dining options. Main courses £6-14. Open Tu-Su from 6pm. ❷

Art Garden Cafe, Parade Quay Rd. (☎224 987). Standing out among the seaside cafes, this colorful restaurant offers filling sandwiches (£1.95-2.50). Take a seat on the patio or enjoy the artwork inside. Open M-F 9am-5pm, Sa 9am-6pm, Su 9:30am-6pm. ❶

Tanners Restaurant, Finewell St. (☎252 001), in Prysten House, behind St. Andrew's Church. Medieval dining in Plymouth's oldest building. Lunch £12-15, 3-course dinner £20-23. Open Tu-F noon-2:15pm and 7-9:30pm, Sa noon-1:30pm and 7-9:30pm. ❹

Three Cooks, 38 Royal Parade (☎224 352). Cheap breakfast all day long. 7-item breakfast £2 until 11am, £1.65 after 2pm. Open M-Sa 7am-5pm. ❶

🜨 SIGHTS

🜨NATIONAL MARINE AQUARIUM. Britain's largest and Europe's deepest tank is home to four sharks at this high-tech aquarium, also featuring an immense coral reef tank and **Britain's only giant squid.** *(The Barbican. ☎220 084. Open Apr.-Oct. 10am-6pm; Nov.-Mar. 10am-4pm. £8, seniors £6.50, students £6, children £4.50, families £22.)*

THE HOE. The Hoe provided tremendous views long before it oversaw the battle with the Spanish Armada. Legend has it that Sir Francis Drake was playing bowls on the Hoe in 1588 when he heard that the Armada had entered the Channel. English through and through, he finished his game before hoisting sail. Climb 93 spiral steps and leaning ladders to the windy balcony of **Smeaton's Tower** for a magnificent impression of Plymouth and the Royal Citadel. Originally a lighthouse 14 mi. offshore, the 72 ft. tower was moved to its present site in 1882. Nearby, the **Plymouth Dome** employs plastic dioramas and story-telling actors to relate Plymouth's past, from the Armada to WWII. *(☎603 300. Tower open Apr.-Oct. daily 10am-4pm; Nov.-Mar. Tu-Sa 10am-4pm. Dome open Apr.-Oct. daily 10am-5pm. Tower £2, children £1. Dome £4.50, concessions £3.50, children £3, families £12. Tower and Dome £6/£5/£3.50/£15.)*

PLYMOUTH MAYFLOWER. One of Plymouth's newer sights, this museum tells the story of the *Mayflower,* the Barbican, the Harbour, and everything else that has to do with the Pilgrims. *(3-5 The Barbican. ☎306 330. Open Apr.-Oct. 10am-6pm; Nov.-Mar. 10am-5pm; last admission 30min. before close. £4, concessions £3, children £2, families £10. Joint ticket with Discovery Trail tour £5/£4/£2.25/£13.)*

ST. ANDREW'S CHURCH. Built in 1087, St. Andrew's has been a Christian meeting site for nearly 1200 years. When three days of bombing in 1941 left it roofless, the church was rebuilt according to plans that are now on display in the **Prysten House,** Plymouth's oldest complete building. Ask to be let in to this 15th-century structure, the lower level of which is now a restaurant. *(Royal Parade. ☎661 414. Open M-F 9am-4pm, Sa 9am-noon, Su 9am-5pm.)*

OTHER SIGHTS. The still-in-use **Royal Citadel** gives a tour of its battlements and garrison walls, historic guns, and church, all built 300 years ago by Charles II. *(Easter-Oct. Tu 2:30pm. £3.)* At the **Mayflower Steps,** on The Barbican, a plaque and American flag mark the spot from which the Pilgrims set off in 1620 for their historic voyage; subsequent departures have been marked as well, including Sir Humphrey Gilbert's journey to Newfoundland, Sir Walter Raleigh's attempt to colonize North Carolina, and Captain Cook's expedition to Australia and New Zealand. The blackened shell of **Charles Church,** destroyed by a bomb in 1941, now stands in the middle of the Charles Cross traffic circle as a memorial for victims of the Blitz. The **Plymouth Gin,** 60 Southside St., is England's oldest active gin distillery, at it since 1793. Tours (45-50min.) scour the distillery and dispense historical tidbits. (☎ 665 292. Open Easter-Dec. M-Sa 10:30am-4pm. Shop open M-Sa 10:30am-3:30pm. Tours Mar.-Dec. £2.75, seniors £2.25, families £7, free with aquarium ticket; £1 discount on gin with ticket.)

🔊 📭 BEACHES AND ENTERTAINMENT

To enjoy the sun, ferry to the other side of the harbor to **Kingsand** and **Cawsand,** twin villages with small but pretty slips of sand. (Cawsand Ferry ☎ (07833) 936 863; 1hr.; 4 per day; £2.50, children £1.)

The biggest **club** in town is **Millennium,** 34-36 Union St., with three rooms of music and crowds of revelers. (☎ 266 188. Open Th-Sa 10pm-3am.) **The Union Rooms,** 19 Union St., is a popular bar; selected pints are £1.09 on Monday nights. (☎ 288 321. Open M-Sa 11am-11pm, Su noon-10:30pm.) The student crowd heads to North Hill for late-night reveling at **Cuba** and **Ride.** Closer by, **The Ship,** almost at the end of Quay St. in The Barbican, serves seaside spirits with some fishing nets hanging about. (☎ 667 604. Open M-Sa 11am-11pm, Su 11am-10:30pm.)

The **Theatre Royal,** on Royal Parade, has one of the West Country's best stages, featuring ballet, opera, and West End touring companies, including the Royal National Theatre. (☎ 267 222. Box office open M-Sa 10am-8pm, 6pm if no show. Musicals and ballets £27.50-30, opera £41, plays £16; student £3-5 discount M-Th evenings, standbys on limited shows 30min. before curtain.)

Plymouth's festivals revolve around its harbor. In late August of every other year (2004, 2006, etc.), the **Plymouth Navy Days** celebrates Plymouth's great ships. (☎ 266 031. Tickets go on sale in June. £9.50, £12.50 at the door; concessions £5/6.50; families £19/25.) The **Armed Forces Show** (☎ 501 750), in the second weekend of July, features exhibitions by the Royal Navy, Army, and Air Force. The **British National Fireworks Championship** explodes in mid-August, while **Powerboat Championships** take place in late July. Call the TIC for more information.

📭 DAYTRIP FROM PLYMOUTH

LOOE AND POLPERRO

Looe is about 1½hr. from Plymouth by bus, and Polperro is another 20min. from there. Take First bus #81A (2 per day, £2.70) or City Bus X77 or A77 (Su 3 per day; £3.50, return £4.50). Seeing both towns in one day is the best bargain—the villages are on the same bus route and First Corridor (£2.50, children £1.50) and City Bus Country (£4.50) tickets allow unlimited travel between them.

The small coastal villages of Looe and Polperro, though heavily touristed, make an enjoyable daytrip. Both towns boast redundant shops of Cornish ice cream, fish and chips, and cheap souvenirs. There are no incredible sights to see, but quaint bustle and small-town hubbub make them worth a short visit.

The larger of the two, **Looe** is split in half by a wide estuary. Far from the sandy shores and into the sea lies mile-wide **Looe Island,** the only privately owned island in the UK. Visitors can take a boat to the island and have a look around (£6.50); many believe that Jesus and Joseph of Arimathea landed here too. **Speedboat** operates tours around the coast and bay (£4, children £2-3). Those who'd rather stay on land should visit the **Discovery Centre,** on Looe's west side, which stocks the free *Looe Valley Line Trails from the Track,* a packet of ten hiking trails. (☎ (01503) 263 266. Open Easter-Sept. M-F and Su 10am-6pm, Sa 11am-3pm; Oct.-Dec. and Mar.-Easter daily 10am-4pm.) The **tourist information centre,** Fore St., East Looe, books rooms for £1 and a 10% deposit. (☎ (01503) 262 072. Open May-Sept. daily 10am-5pm; Oct.-Apr. 10am-5pm. Unmanned except M-F 10am-noon.)

SOUTHWEST ENGLAND

Farther east is tiny **Polperro**, once England's most notorious smuggling bay—the village's proximity to the Channel Islands made it a perfect port for illegal alcohol and tobacco transport. Before a new road (named, uh, "New Rd.") was built in 1840, the village was incredibly remote and nearly impossible to enter undetected, but even when The Law arrived, villagers supported their smugglers. Visit the **Polperro Heritage Museum of Smuggling and Fishing,** which displays photos of smugglers, a sword of a smuggler, stories about smugglers, and also some pictures of a flood. (☎ (01503) 272 423. Open Easter-Oct. 11am-5pm. £1.50, children £1, families £4.) Get off land and you may see dolphins while taking a **boat trip** around the harbor (☎ (01503) 272 476. £3, children £2). The **tourist information centre,** Talland St., is at end of New St. (☎ (01503) 272 320. Open Easter-Oct. M-Sa 9:30am-4:30pm.)

CLOVELLY   ☎ 01237

Once a tiny fishing village, Clovelly (pop. 155) is now one of England's most distinctive tourist towns. Its torturously steep main street—170 treacherous cobbled steps poking from the ground—has long been a site of tourist pilgrimages. To visit Clovelly, privately owned by the Rous family for 700 years, visitors pay a fee that goes toward keeping the village in its time-capsule-like state. Indeed, little has changed in the past 50 years. Land rovers have replaced the donkeys that once carried visitors up the leg-cramp-inducing hill, and a visitors center was built in 1987 to replace the admission-collecting huts of days gone by; but beyond that, the quaint charm remains, making Clovelly a fascinating destination of living history.

After paying the town admission fee, all sights are free. In the village center, the **Fisherman's Cottage** is a restored 1930s cottage. Next door, the **Kingsley Museum and Shop** celebrates Charles Kingsley, Christian Socialist, author of *Westward Ho!,* and (briefly) resident of Clovelly. (Both open 9am-4:45pm.) Near the carpark, visitors can make their own pottery (£1.50) at **Clovelly Pottery,** which also displays the work of local artists. (☎ 431 042. Open M-Sa 10am-6pm, Su noon-5:30pm.) **Clovelly Silk,** Lower Yard, features designer hand-painted, hand-rolled silk scarves (£14.75). Make your own print for £30. (☎ 431 033. Open 10:30am-5:30pm.) During the colder months, a short walk east along the shore brings trekkers to a surging **waterfall,** which slows to a stream in warmer months. **Boat trips** from the harbor run to **Lundy Island** (☎ 431 042. 1hr. sailing and 6hr. onshore; £22.50, children £20; £3.50 admission to the island.) 20min. **moorboat trips** around the coast cost £3 per person.

Getting to Clovelly by public transport can be trying. **First bus** #319 connects Clovelly to **Bideford** (40min.; M-Sa 5 per day, Su 2 per day; £1.60, return £2.30) and continues to **Barnstaple** (1hr., £1.80). Buses #119 and 128 run from **Bude** (45min.; Tu and F 4 per day; £1.40, return £2.10). The **land rovers** that shuttle visitors between the bottom of Clovelly and the carpark run every 10min. (£1.60, return £2.50). Children can ride one of the **donkeys** stabled beside the carpark (£1.50). The **Clovelly Visitor Centre,** at the carpark, is where visitors pay admission to the village. (☎ 431 781. Open daily Easter-Oct. 9am-6:30pm; Nov.-Easter 10am-4pm. £3.50, children £2.50.)

The village only has two hotels and five B&Bs, but Higher Clovelly, 1 mi. uphill, has many more B&Bs. For heart-warming hospitality and excellent showers, head for ▧**Pillowery Park ❸,** on Burscott St., in Higher Clovelly. (☎ 431 065. Singles £23; doubles £36.) Closer and on the main road is friendly **Boathouse ❷,** Sierra Hill, Higher Clovelly. (☎ 431 398. Singles £16; doubles £30.) In Clovelly, **New House ❹,** High St., offers only comfortable doubles. (☎ 431 303. £38-45.)

CORNWALL

Cornwall's ethereal landscape doesn't quite feel like England. With its turquoise seas and golden beaches, cultivated fields of lush minty green, rough and rugged moorland, and England's best sun, it's no wonder the Celts chose to flee here in the face of Saxon conquest. Today, the westward movement continues in the form of surfers and sun worshipers, hikers and family vacationers. Penzance, St. Ives, and Newquay boast some of northern Europe's sandiest and surfiest beaches, with a friendly atmosphere to boot. Cornwall may have England's most precarious economy, but it's hard to tell in a region so rich in history and good humor—not to mention in shops serving up a good pasty, the region's ubiquitous stuffed turnover (see **The Pasty's Past,** below). History, beauty, and temptation all turn up in Cornwall, and no trip to England is complete without a stopover here.

TRANSPORTATION

Penzance is the southwestern terminus of Britain's **trains** (☎ (08457) 484 950) and the best base from which to explore the region. The main rail line from **Plymouth** to **Penzance** bypasses coastal towns, but connecting rail service reaches **Newquay, Falmouth,** and **St. Ives.** A **Rail Rover** ticket may come in handy for those touring the area (3 days in 7 £25.50, 8 in 15 £40).

The **First bus** network is thorough, although the interior is not served as well as the coast. Buses run from **Penzance** to **Land's End** and **St. Ives** and from **St. Ives** to **Newquay,** stopping in the smaller towns along these routes. Pick up timetables at any Cornwall bus station. Many buses don't run on Sundays, and often operate only May-September. **Traveline** (☎ (0870) 608 2608; daily 7am-5pm) can help you get anywhere you want to go. **Explorer tickets** allow unlimited travel on all buses and are of excellent value to those making long-distance trips or hopping from town to town (£6, seniors £4.50, children £4, families £13). A **First Day Plus** (£5, children £3.50) or **Week Plus** (£20, £10) offers unlimited travel on First buses, the predominant carrier in this area. Whenever a fare exceeds £2.50, purchase the **Corridor Ticket** (£2.50, children 1.50), which allows unlimited travel on one bus route.

Cyclists may not relish the narrow roads, but the cliff paths, with their evenly spaced hostels, make for easy **hiking.** Serious trekkers can try the famous **Land's End-John O'Groats** route, running from Britain's tip to top.

THE PASTY'S PAST First-time visitors to Cornwall may be daunted by the mysterious pasty (PASS-tee), its flaky shell hiding a variety of savory or sweet ingredients. Even the devil, according to legend, had concerns about the piping hot pastry pockets—he dared not venture into Cornwall for fear of being diced and baked into them by local housewives. An important part of Cornish history, pasties were once a source of crucial sustenance in mining towns. Originally baked rock-hard so they wouldn't break if dropped down a mine shaft, pasties provided miners a balanced meal. Their ridged crusts made a perfect grip for dirty fingers, allowing workers to eat the soot-free filling and toss the crust later.

FROM THE ROAD

EXTREME ENGLAND

Avid adventurers may bypass England to trek the Amazon jungles, crocodile-wrestle in Bangkok, or navigate the New Jersey Turnpike. Prim and proper can't be adventurous, they say. But which of these wide-eyed wanderers can claim to have gone to the beach, legs pasty and unshaven after four months of wearing jeans in the British rain? Now that, I assure you, is sheer social convention-breaking, taboo-committing bravery. That particular incident may not impress, but I do believe England has offered me enough adventure for one summer, if not half a lifetime.

Any visitor to Newquay should try to surf, if not for the perfectly foamy waves, then at least to brag about it. So here I will commence bragging: I met those treacherous turquoise blue waters head-on, paddled ceaselessly to put myself in the face of a massive wave, struggled onto my board, and, mere seconds later, gently coasted right back to shore. Surfing is very difficult. In an hour of paddling and wading, I only actually stood on my board three or four times—and only once for more than the count of two. But in those two seconds, I felt like I had achieved the miraculous, something on par with surviving natural childbirth and climbing Everest all at once. I left thinking I wouldn't accomplish anything more satisfying in my trip. But sometimes adventure just falls into your lap.

On the bus to Camelford, I meet a friendly local who turns out to be a flight instructor. After a brief chat, he offers me a flight around the area. I sit

BODMIN MOOR

Bodmin Moor is high country, containing Cornwall's loftiest points—Rough Tor (1311 ft.) and Brown Willy (1377 ft.). The region is rich with ancient remains, such as the stone hut circles that litter the base of Rough Tor. Some maintain that Camelford, at the moor's northern edge, is the site of King Arthur's Camelot, and that Arthur and his illegitimate son Mordred fought each other at Slaughter Bridge, a mile north of town. A mere glimpse of this seemingly untouched terrain explains how it can inspire such romantic stories.

▐ TRANSPORTATION

Bodmin town sits at the southern edge of Bodmin Moor, which spreads all the way north to coastal (but non-beach) **Tintagel** and **Camelford. Trains** (☎ (08457) 484 950) stop at **Bodmin Parkway** from: **London Paddington** (4hr., 9 per day, £60.80); **Penzance** (1½hr., 1-2 per hr., £9.10); **Plymouth** (40min., 1-2 per hr., £6.80). The station is open M-Sa 6am-7pm, Su 10am-7:30pm. **National Express buses** (☎ (08705) 808 080) arrive from **Plymouth** (1½hr., 2 per day, £4). Book tickets at **Let's Go Travel,** 4 Market House Arcade. (☎ (01208) 75206. Open M-Sa 10am-5pm.)

Bodmin town is served directly by buses from **Padstow** (#55, M-Sa 10 per day, £3.50) on the north coast and **St. Austell** (#29, M-Sa 12 per day, £2.50) to the south. **First** X4 service arrives at the TSB bus stop, in the center of town, from **Tintagel** via **Camelford** (1-2hr., every hr., £3.50). From Bodmin, a bus tour runs into the center of the moor twice a week (Tu and Th 1 per day, return £3.50).

Since Bodmin is not a national park, it lacks National Park Information Centres dedicated to the area; visit local TICs instead. **Hiking** is convenient from Camelford, and is the only way to reach the tors, which give grand views of the boulder-strewn expanse. Bodmin town, however, is not a good place to start hiking. **Bikes** can be hired in surrounding towns. **Hitchhiking** is dangerous, especially on the narrow A roads, which leave drivers with only six inches of road shoulder space. *Let's Go* never recommends hitchhiking.

▐ ACCOMMODATIONS

B&Bs can be booked through the Bodmin TIC (☎ (01208) 76616). **Jamaica Inn ❸,** Bolventor, Launceston, smack in the middle of the moor, has only double rooms. Buses from Bodmin stop right in front. (☎ (01566) 86250. £25-38 per person.) Just 3 mi. from there, **Barn End ❸,** Ninestones Farm, Common Moor, Liskeard, also offers doubles. (☎ (01579) 321 628. Open Mar.-Dec. £22 per person.) The nearest **YHA hostels** are on the beautiful northern coast of Cornwall, a few miles northwest of the moor; both have a 10am-5pm lockout and 11pm curfew. **YHA Boscastle Harbour ❷,** Palace Stables, Boscastle Harbour, is set among steep green hills and flowery riverbanks. Take bus X10 from Exeter, or #55, 122, or 125 from Bodmin or Wadebridge. From the bridge on B3263, walk toward the harbor along the river. (☎ (01840) 250 287; fax 250 615. Self-catering. Open Apr.-Sept. daily. Dorms £10.25, under 18 £7.) For directions to **YHA Tintagel,** see p. 250.

BODMIN   ☎ 01208

The town of Bodmin (pop. 14,500), ancient capital of Cornwall, is the last supply stop before venturing out to Arthurian stomping grounds. For hiking or cycling, the 17 mi. **Camel Trail** starts in Padstow and passes through Bodmin on the way to Poley's Bridge, with views of the River Camel, quarries, and tea shops. A former railway track, the trail is mostly smooth and level (no humps).

In town, a few sights are of interest. The **Military Museum** displays George Washington's Bible and account book (which reveals a missing $3000), pilfered by the Duke of Cornwall's infantry during the Revolutionary War. (St. Nicholas St. ☎ 72810. Open M-F 10:30am-5pm, July-Aug. also Su. £2, children 50p.) Built in 1776, the **Bodmin Jail,** with its 3 ft. thick granite walls, was the safekeep for the crown jewels and Domesday book during WWII. (Berrycombe Rd. ☎ 76292. £3.90, concessions £3.30, children £2.) In the 1800s, after a harsh winter, men would sell their wives at the **Old Cattle Market,** now the Market House Arcade.

Hidden in Bodmin's surrounding forests, the stately mansion **Lanhydrock,** built in the 1650s and gutted by fire in 1881, is surrounded by elaborate formal gardens. Inside, magnificent plasterwork ceilings portraying scenes from the Old Testament overhang plush Victorian furnishings. From Bodmin, take **First** bus #55 (£2.50) or **DAC Coaches** #269 (£2.90), or walk 2½ mi. southeast of Bodmin on the A38. (☎ 73320. House open Apr.-Oct. Tu-Su 11am-5:30pm. Gardens open daily Dec.-Sept. 10am-6pm; Oct.-Nov. 10am-5pm. £7, children £3.50, families £17.50. Grounds only £3.80, children £1.90, Nov.-Jan. free.)

Elmsleigh ❷, 52 St. Nicholas St., is a cozy B&B with spacious rooms, just uphill from the TIC. (☎ 75976. £16 per person.) A mile north of town, camp at the

unbelieving for a millisecond before taking him up on his offer. In less than an hour, I am wearing a flight suit, geared up with a helmet and headset, and making myself comfortable in an aircraft that appears to consist of two chairs and a pair of wings. Off we go, hunkering past clusters of wandering sheep, slowly building up speed on a WWII air strip before zooming up, up, and away.

From the air, the biggest mining quarry in the world looks like a single-serving pudding cup, the sheep seem like tiny confectionery sprinkles, and 1311 ft. Rough Tor reminds me of a pancake dusted with chocolate shavings. Of course, there's more to flying than everything looking edible. We cruise over a misty cloud we've just flown straight through, and I see a magnificent circular rainbow inside the puffy whiteness.

After 40min. of sky wandering, we return to the ground, back to the meandering sheep, and I feel ready to climb a mountain... which I do later that day. Well, it's more like a tiny cliff, but that's my kind of adventure. And England, despite its staid reputation, modern conveniences, and luxurious bubble baths to return to at the end of your exploring, is full of opportunities for these personal wanderings.

— Angie Sun

Camping and Caravanning Club ❶, Old Callywith Rd., with laundry, showers, and a shop. Head north of town on Castle St., which becomes Old Callywith Rd. (☎73834. Open Mar.-Oct. £2.85-4.20 per person. £4.50 per pitch. Electricity £1.75.)

The **tourist information centre**, Shire Hall, Mount Folly, sells Ordnance Survey maps for £6. (☎76616. Open M-Sa 10am-5pm.) To rent a car, contact **Bluebird Car Hire** (☎77790), a.k.a. Rent-a-Wreck. Other services include: **banks** on Fore St.; the **police** (☎(08705) 777 444), up Priory Rd.; and the **post office**, St. Nicholas St., uphill from the TIC (☎(08457) 223 344; open M-F 9am-5:30pm, Sa 9am-12:30pm). **Post Code:** PL3 1AA. To reach town from the **Bodmin Parkway Station,** 3 mi. away on the A38, take Western National **bus** #55 (every hr., £1.70) or call **ABTaxis** (☎75000; £4.50 between station and town). The **Bodmin General Station**, St. Nicholas St. (☎73666), serves **Bodmin & Wenford Railway's** private trains, which run to Bodmin Parkway and Boscarne Junction, near Wadebridge. (Apr.-Sept. 4-7 per day; entire route £8, children £4.50, families £23; Bodmin General to Boscarne Junction £5/£3/£14.50; Bodmin General to Bodmin Parkway £6/£3.50/£16.50).

CAMELFORD ☎01840

Warning: those who imagined Camelot as a pinnacled and pennanted citadel will be disappointed by miniscule Camelford, 13 mi. north of Bodmin. Those who came looking for challenging treks into rugged Bodmin Moor, however, will be duly satisfied. The **tourist information centre,** in the North Cornwall Museum, gives good hiking advice. (☎212 954. Open Apr.-Sept. M-Sa 10am-5pm.)

From the center of town, **Rough Tor** (RAO-tor) is a 1¼hr. walk amid mist and skittish sheep; take Rough Tor Rd. to the end. The climb is not arduous until the 300 ft. ascent at the top, where stacked granite boulders form steps and passageways, offering a wind-ravaged lookout over the moor. Keep going past the tor, and find your way around an electric fence to climb **Brown Willy,** another 1hr. hike. Much closer to town (1½ mi. north), tiny **Slaughter Bridge** is inlaid with hunks of petrified wood and marks the site where Arthur supposedly fell. The nearby **Arthurian Centre** is a tourist trap with a play area, shops, and Arthur's Stone—a big rock with inscriptions on it. (☎212 450. Open Easter-Oct. daily 10am-5pm. £2.50, children £1.50.) To view it all without moving a muscle, head for ▓**Moorland Flying Club,** at Davidstow Airfields, 3 mi. from Camelford (£5 by taxi); a surreal 20min. flight in a two-seat glider through clouds and over harbors will do the job. (☎261 517. Lessons or flights £5 plus £1 per min.)

It's relatively easy to reach Camelford by **bus. First** #56 runs to **Bodmin** (1hr., M-Sa 5-7 per day, £2.80); #122 and 125 to **Wadebridge** (30min., M-Sa 7 per day, £2.10); and X10 to **Exeter** (2¼hr., M-Sa 4 per day).

TINTAGEL ☎01840

More enjoyable than Camelford, Tintagel, 6 mi. northwest, is a dusty little village just 1 mi. from the magnificent ruins of ▓**Tintagel Castle** of Arthurian legend. Roman and medieval rubble piles atop a headland besieged by the Atlantic, with some chunks having already disappeared into the sea. Below, **Merlin's cave** is worth the climb, but check for low-tide times and be careful on the steep cliffs. Even if you don't buy into the legends, the views are haunting. (☎770 328. Open July-Aug. daily 10am-7pm; Apr.-June and Sept. 10am-6pm; Oct. 10am-5pm; Nov.-Mar. 10am-4pm. £3, concessions £2.30, children £1.50.)

Inland, **King Arthur's Great Hall of Chivalry,** Fore St., was once headquarters of the Round Table of King Arthur, founded in 1927 by millionaire Frederick Thomas Glasscock to spread the Arthurian order of chivalry in response to WWI. Once boasting 17,000 supporters, membership has dwindled to 250. The Great Hall has two rooms: an antechamber with a 10min. light show telling Arthur's story, and the great hall which houses not one, not two, but *three* Round Tables. (☎ 770 526. Open summer daily 10am-5pm; winter 10am-dusk. £2.75, children £2.)

Escape gaudy homages to Arthur on a 1½ mi. walk through ◙St. Nectan's Glen to its cascading 60 ft. waterfall, a spiritual healing center in times past. From the Visitor Centre, head toward Bossiney for about 1 mi., then follow signs along the footpath to your right; numerous paths lead to the glen. (☎ 770 760. Open Easter-Oct. daily 10:30am-6:30pm; Nov.-Easter only F-M and W. £2, children 75p.) The **Tintagel Visitor Centre**, Bossiney Rd., offers hiking and coastal walk suggestions. (☎ 779 084. Open daily Mar.-Oct. 9am-5pm; Nov.-Feb. 10:30am-4pm.)

Buses X10, 122, and 125 come from **Camelford** (15min., M-Sa 4-8 per day, £1.60). Overnight visitors can find lodgings at **Castle Villa ❸**, Molesworth St., opposite the bus stop, with cozy rooms and a bright garden. (☎ 770 373. Doubles £30.) The **YHA Tintagel ❷**, at Dunderhole Point, is ¾ mi. from Tintagel. Head east out of town ¼ mi. past St. Materiana's Church, then bear left through the cemetery and keep close to the shore. After 250 yd., look for the chimney, in a hollow by the sea. You'll find a kitchen, spectacular sea views, and one happy owner. (☎ 770 334. Lockout 10am-5pm. Open mid-Mar. to Oct. daily. Dorms £10.25, under 18 £7.)

BOSCASTLE ☎ 01840

Flanked by two grassy hills, tiny Boscastle is the prettiest town in the Bodmin Moor area. A sparkling river flows to the harbor and winds into the ocean. High cliffs guard the harbor, and climbing the eastern cliff affords expansive sea views. The **National Trust Information Center**, The Old Forge, Boscastle Harbour, offers good hiking suggestions. (☎ 250 353. Open Apr.-Oct. 10:30am-5:30pm.) The **Valency Valley** above the village invites exploration, with scenic River Valency coursing through wooded vales. From there, a 2½ mi. hike leads to **St. Juliot's Church,** where Thomas Hardy met his second wife. Hikes along the headland cliffs provide spectacular views. In town, the **Museum of Witchcraft** displays an extensive collection of artifacts and stories, from definitions of various spirits, fairies, and shape-shifting boogies to biographies of living witches. (☎ 250 111. Open Easter-Halloween M-Sa 10:30am-5:30pm, Su noon-5:30pm. £2, concessions £1, naughty children and little monsters £10.) **Buses** X10, 122, and 125 come to Boscastle from **Tintagel** (10min.; M-F every hr., Sa 5 per day; 70p) and continue to **Bude** (30min.; M-F every hr., Sa 3 per day; £2.50). Bus #124 heads to **Newquay** (3hr., 1 per day). The **YHA Boscastle Harbour ❷** has an incredible location in the town center, alongside the river. (☎ (0870) 241 2314. Lockout 10am-5pm. Open Apr.-Sept. £10.25, under 18 £7.) For B&B, try the **Riverside Hotel ❸**, The Bridge. (☎ 250 216. £20-23.50 per person.)

PADSTOW ☎ 01841

A tiny seaside resort town nestled beside a picturesque harbor, Padstow is a popular destination among sailboated yuppie families and sun-seeking retirees. The town isn't visited for any particular sight, but Padstow itself offers a quaintness rarely matched. **Clifftop walks** along the estuary are pleasant and not too difficult. Cyclists converge in Padstow for the start of the **Camel Trail** (see p. 249) and the **Saints' Way**, which follows the route of the Celtic saints who landed here from Ireland and Wales. **Rent bikes** at **Padstow Cycle Hire,** South Quay, in the carpark. (☎ 533 533. Open daily 9am-5pm. £5-10 per half-day, £8-12 per day; children £3-5/£5-7.)

Numerous nearby beaches are perfect for exploring, surfing, and sunbathing. Take bus #555 or 556 (5min.; M-Sa 7 per day, Su 4 per day) to cave-pocked **Trevone Beach.** Bus #556 continues to remote **Constantine Bay** (15min., M-Sa 5 per day), with great surfing, and **Porthcothan Beach** (30min., 4-6 per day), a relaxing spot for tanning. Take lessons at **Harlyn Surf School,** 16 Boyd Ave. (☎ 533 076. £25 per half-day, £35 per day.) Fishing and boating trips depart from the Harbour. **Cornish Bird** (☎532 053) takes passengers to shipwrecks around the bay (£3) and operates mackerel and reef fishing trips (2-8hr., £8-24). Book at the Harbour or at **Sport&Leisure,** North Quay (☎532 639). **Ferries** chug across the bay to nearby **Rock,** where visitors will find sailing, waterskiing, windsurfing, and golfing (10-15min.; Easter-Oct. daily, Nov.-Easter M-Sa; £1 each way). The **National Lobster Hatchery,** South Quay, was built to aid the ailing fishing industry. Expectant lobster moms are brought here to lay their eggs, and visitors can see the insectlike babies in various stages of development. (☎533 877. Open May to mid-Sept. daily 10am-6pm; mid-Sept. to Apr. M-Sa 10am-4pm. £2.50, concessions £1.50, families £6.)

The **tourist information centre,** Red Brick Bldg., North Quay, books accommodations for £3 and a 10% deposit. (☎533 449. Open Easter-Oct. daily 9am-5pm; Nov.-Easter M-F 10am-4pm.) **First bus** #55 (every hr.) comes to Padstow from **Bodmin** (45min., return £3.15) and **Wadebridge** (20min., return £2.40); **Western Greyhound** (☎(01736) 871 871) bus #556 arrives from **Newquay** (1½hr., 4-5 per day, return £4).

Lodgings in Padstow are pleasant but sparse and pricey (£25-30). Find inviting rooms and a wealth of knowledge at the home of **Peter and Jane Cullinan ❹,** 4 Riverside, along the harbor as you walk into town. (☎532 383. Doubles £45-56; triples £51-57.) **North Point ❸,** Hill St., a short uphill walk from the harbor, affords spectacular views. (☎532 355. £25 per person.) Farther uphill, **Ms. Anne Humphrey ❸,** 1 Caswarth Terr., offers cozy rooms. (☎532 025. Singles £25; doubles £38.) The nearest hostel, the **YHA Treyarnon Bay ❷,** is 4½ mi. from Padstow, on Tregonnan in the small town of Treyarnon. It's off the B3276; take bus #56. (☎(0870) 770 6076. Open July-Aug. daily; Apr.-June and Sept.-Oct. M-Sa. £10.25, under 18 £7.) **Trevean Farm Caravan and Camping Park ❶,** St. Merryn, is just outside town. (☎/fax 520 772. Tents and caravans £7-8.) Splurge at **St. Petrocks Bistro ❹,** New St., for mouthwatering seafood at £14-20 per dish. (☎532 700. Open daily noon-2pm and 7-9:30pm.) Get cheap pasties and budget eats at **Victorian Tea Room ❶,** 22 Duke St. (☎533 161. Open Easter-Oct. daily 9:30am-6pm.) Lanadwell St. is home to the classic pubs **Golden Lion** and **London Inn.** (Both open M-Sa 11am-11pm, Su noon-10:30pm.)

NEWQUAY   ☎01637

At Newquay (NEW-key) station, a range of hairstyles disembark: bald, bleach blonde, blue. Sheathed boards strapped to their backs, serious surfers head straight for the beach. Others, imposter kahunas in Airwalks, race to the pubs. Partiers here, families there, tackiness everywhere, Newquay (pop. 30,000) swells to 100,000 in summer with holiday-makers. Europe's best surf and parties throbbing late into the night make this a favorite spot for England's youth.

▉ TRANSPORTATION

The unmanned train station is on Cliff Rd.; buy tickets at the **Western National** office. (Open M-F 9am-4pm, Sa 9am-3:45pm.) All **trains** (☎(08457) 484 950) come from **Par** (50min.; M-Sa 4-5 per day, July-Aug. also Su 4 per day; £4.30), where they connect to **Penzance** (1¾hr., every hr., £10.30) and **Plymouth** (1hr., 15 per day, £8.10). **National Express buses** (☎(08705) 808 080) arrive from London (6hr., 1-3 per day, £30.50). The First bus office, 1 East St. (open June-Sept. M-F 9am-7pm, Sa 8:30am-5:30pm, Su 9am-1pm and 2-7pm; Oct.-May M-F 9am-4pm, Sa-Su 9am-1pm) receives #21 and 21B from **St. Austell** (1hr.; M-F every hr., Sa every 2hr.; return £3.50), some continuing to **Bodmin** (2hr., 3 per day, £5) and **St. Ives** (2hr., June-Sept. 1 per day, £5). X89 and X90 go to **Falmouth** (£3.30).

🔃 PRACTICAL INFORMATION

The **tourist information centre,** Marcus Hill, a block from the bus station, sells street maps for 50p and *What's On in Newquay* for £1. (☎ 854 020; fax 854 030; info@newquay.co.uk. Open Easter-Oct. M-Sa 9:30am-5:30pm, Su 9:30am-4:30pm; Nov.-Easter M-F 9:30am-4:30pm, Sa 9:30am-12:30pm.) **Western Greyhound,** 15 East St., runs **bus tours** to the Eden Project (see p. 257) and popular nearby coastal towns. (☎ 871 871. 5½-7½hr.; 1-4 tours per day; £5-13, concessions £5-11.50.) **First** operates similar tours (☎ 722 625; 5-7hr.; 1-3 per day; £5-13, children £3.40-10); both can be booked at the TIC. Other services include: **banks** on (appropriately) Bank St. (most open M-Tu and Th-F 9am-4:30pm, W 10am-4:30pm); **work opportunities** at a very busy **JobCentre,** 32 East St. (☎ 894 900; open M-Th 9am-4:30pm, F 9:30am-4:30pm); **luggage storage** at **Station Cafe** (£1 per item; no overnight storage; open May-Sept. 7am-5pm; Oct.-Apr. 8am-2pm); a **launderette,** 1 Beach Parade, off Beach Rd. (☎ 875 901; wash £2.30-3, dry 20p per 4min., soap 45p; open M-F 9:30am-5pm, Sa 10am-3pm; last wash 1hr. before closing); **Newquay Hospital,** St. Thomas Rd. (☎ 893 600); **Internet access** at **@CTS,** Seymour Ave., opposite the TIC (☎ 875 114; open M-F 1-4pm; £1.50 per hr.); and the **post office,** 31-33 East St. (☎ (08457) 223 344; open M-F 9am-5:30pm, Sa 9am-12:30pm). **Post Code:** TR7 1BU.

🔃 ACCOMMODATIONS AND CAMPING

Hordes of **B&Bs** are near the TIC (£18-20), while numerous **backpacker hostels** (£12-16) gather on **Headland Rd.** and **Tower Rd.** at the top of Fore St. near Fistral Beach. When surfing competitions come to town, accommodations swell with visitors, who often book weeks in advance; so call first, especially in summer.

The Danes, 4 Dane Rd. (☎ 878 130), at the very top of Fore St., offers beautiful seaside views and immaculate rooms. Borrow a parking pass. Singles £25; doubles £36. ❸

Original Backpackers, 16 Beachfield Ave. (☎ 874 668), fantastically located off Bank St. near Central Sq., facing the beach. £12 per person; £50 per week. ❷

Seagull Cottage, 98 Fore St. (☎ 875 648). Friendly proprietress pampers guests with hospitality and comfy beds a scone's throw from town. Singles £18; doubles £30. ❷

Newquay International Backpackers, 69-73 Tower Rd. (☎ 879 366; backpacker@dial.pipex.com). International crowd parties late into the night. Guests get clean dorms; pub, club, and restaurant discounts; and free shuttle service to the sister hostel in St. Ives. Internet access £1 per 15min. Dorms £12-14. ❷

Together Guest House, 33 Trebarwith Cres. (☎ 871 996), on the street just behind the bus station, has bright rooms. £20 per person. ❸

Camping: Trenance Chalet and Caravan Park, Edgcumbe Ave. (☎ 873 449). A campsite miraculously located in town. From the train station, turn right on Cliff Rd., then right on Edgcumbe, a 5min. walk total. ❶ **Trencreek Farm Holiday Park** (☎ 874 210), 1½ mi. southeast of the city center off the A392, has numerous facilities, even a swimming pool. Take bus #21 toward St. Austell; watch for the sign. ❶

🔃 FOOD AND PUBS

Restaurants in Newquay tend to be quick, bland, and costly. For a cheap alternative, head for pubs with dinner specials between 5-7pm or craft a meal at **Somerfield** supermarket, at the end of Fore St. (☎ 876 006. Open M-Sa 8am-8pm, Su 10:30am-4:30pm; July-Aug. closes 1hr. later.)

SOUTHWEST ENGLAND

Ye Olde Dolphin, 39-47 Fore St. (☎874 262). Newquay's abysmal restaurants count at least one jewel. Meals can be a bit dear, but take advantage of the 6-8pm specials, including a 3-course meal for £10. Open daily 6-11pm. ❸

Prego Prego, 4 East St. (☎852 626). A gem of a cheapie, serving a variety of fresh panini (£3) and baguettes (£1.75-2.65), from sun-dried tomato and mozzarella to chicken pesto and peppers. Specialty coffees £1-1.65. Open daily 7:30am-6pm. ❶

The Shack, 52 Bank St. (☎875 675). Friendly, family-oriented sit-down with a beach theme and tasty dishes (£3-8), from vegetarian and Caribbean plates to the popular Shack Wraps (£4.25). Open daily Mar.-Sept. 9am-11:30pm; Oct.-Feb. 9am-3pm. ❷

🅑 BEACHES

After their 3000 mi. trip across the Atlantic, winds descend on **Fistral Beach** with a vengeance, creating what most consider the best surfing conditions in Europe. The shores are less cluttered than the sea, where throngs of wetsuited surfers pile in between the troughs and crests. Ominous skies often forecast the liveliest surf, which can tumble from heights of 12 ft. Just in case the waters get too fierce, lifeguards roam the white sands May through September 10am-6pm. On the bay side, the sands are divided into four beaches: **Towan Beach** and **Great Western Beach** are thronged with families lured by tamer waters, while enticing **Tolcarne Beach** and **Lusty Glaze Beach** attract beach-goers of all ages.

Sunset Surf Shop, 106 Fore St., rents all the surf paraphernalia you needs to bust the rippingest British tubes, mate. (☎877 624. Boards £5-10 per day, £12-25 per 3 days, £25-40 per week; wetsuits or bodyboards £4-5/£10-12/£20. Open Apr.-Oct. daily 9am-6pm.) Larger **Fistral Surf,** with three branches in Newquay (main one at 19 Cliff Rd.) also rents equipment; call them for surf condition updates. (☎850 808. Board £5 per day, £25 per week; wetsuit £5/£20. Open daily 9am-6pm; June-Sept. until 10pm.) Learn the ropes from **West Coast Surfari,** the oldest school in town. Meet at Watergate Beach, or get free transportation from 27 Trebarwith Cres., behind the bus station. Hardcore surfers can join surf tour packages (1-4 weeks; £325-600) to France, Morocco, and South Africa. (☎876 083 or book through surf shops in town. Lessons £20 per half-day, £30 per day, £55-75 per weekend, £110 per week.)

🅒 NIGHTLIFE

The party beast stirs at 9pm and roars uncontested through the wee hours of the morning. The trail of surfer bars begins on North Quay Hill at the corner of Tower Rd. and Fore St. All spots listed below exceed critical density in late July and early August.

Tall Trees, Tolcarne Rd. Park (☎850 313). From the train station, walk away from the town center, turn right at Tolcarne Rd., and veer right at the seeming end. 2 floors and big crowds make the 15min. walk worth it. Cover £2-6, £1 less before midnight. Open mid-Mar. to mid-Sept. M-Sa 9pm-2am; mid-Sept. to mid-Mar. W-F and Sa only.

Central Inn, 11 Central Sq. (☎873 810), in the town center. Outdoor seating facing the busy bustle, crowded all day long. Open M-Sa 11am-11pm, Su noon-10:30pm.

Bertie's, East St. (☎870 370). Newquay's biggest club packs in surfers and booty shakers. Bar open 11am-11pm, Su 11am-10:30pm. Club cover £5-7, open daily 9:30pm-2am.

Sailors, 115 Fore St. (☎872 838). 2 levels, 4 bars, and no dearth of tanned flesh. Dress is smart, but still casual. Cover £3-6 before 11pm, up to £10 on busy nights. Open June-Sept. M-Sa 9:30pm-2am, Su 9:30pm-12:30am; Oct.-May Th-Sa 9:30pm-2am.

The Red Lion, North Quay Hill (☎872 195), at Tower Rd. and Fore St. Surfers and a young international crowd jam at this traditional first stop on the clubbing tour. Open M-Sa 11am-11pm, Su 11am-10:30pm.

FALMOUTH ☎01326

The bustling port town of Falmouth (pop. 18,300) is guarded against sea invaders by two circular battlements. With seven rivers flowing into its harbor, Falmouth was the perfect entry point into Cornwall for Spanish and French invaders of centuries past; although today's invasions (of the tourist variety) are staged from the landside, the 450-year-old fortresses of Pendennis and St. Mawes still eye each other across the narrow harbor. Though its busy main street of shops and restaurants is crowded with traffic and pedestrians, Falmouth still maintains a quaint and friendly atmosphere.

▮ TRANSPORTATION

Trains: Falmouth has 3 unmanned **train stations. Penmere Halt** is near cheap B&Bs, **Dell-Falmouth Town** is uphill from the busy town center, and **Falmouth Docks** is nearest to Pendennis Castle. Purchase tickets at **Newell's Travel Agency,** 26 Killigrew St., next to the TIC. (☎312 620. Open M-F 9am-5:30pm, Sa 9am-4pm.) Trains (☎(08457) 484 950) from: **Exeter** (3-3½hr., 6-10 per day, return £19.20); **London Paddington** (5½hr., 12 per day, £68); **Plymouth** (2hr.; M-Sa 17 per day, Su 9 per day; £9.70, return £10.50); **Truro** (22min.; every 1-2hr.; £2.60, return £2.80).

Buses: All buses stop near the TIC. **National Express** (☎(08705) 808 080) from: **London** (8hr., 2 per day, £34.50) and **Plymouth** (2½hr., 2 per day, £5.25); schedules and tickets at Newell's Travel Agency (see above). **First** buses #2 and 2A run to **Penzance** (2hr., 5-6 per day, £2.90) via **Helston** (50min.; M-Sa 7 per day, Su 5 per day; return £3.20), while #88A, 89, X89, and X90 go to **Newquay** (1¼hr., M-Sa every hr.) via **Truro** (45min.; M-Sa every 20min., Su every hr.; £2.70, return £3.30). **Truronian** (☎(01872) 273 453) sends buses to the **Lizard Peninsula** (see p. 258).

Ferries: All ferries leave from both Prince of Wales Pier and Custom House Quay. **St. Mawes Ferry Co.** (☎313 201) runs to **St. Mawes** between 9:30am and 5:30pm

Falmouth

⬧ ACCOMMODATIONS
Boscovean, **9**
Castleton Guest House, **2**
Dolvean Hotel, **11**
Lyonesse Guesthouse, **8**

🍴 FOOD
Harbour Lights, **7**
Pipeline, **5**
Sea Farers, **6**

🍺 PUBS
The Cork and Bottle, **3**
The Grapes Inn, **4**
Pirate Inn, **10**

★ MUSIC AND CLUBS
Remedies, **1**

SOUTHWEST ENGLAND

(20min., 2 per hr., return £4.60). Boats also run to **Smugglers Cottage** and **Truro** (45min.-1hr., 7 per day, £3).

Taxis: Falmouth & Penryn Radio Taxi (☎315 194).

Bikes: Cycle Hire, 18-19 High St. (☎317 679). £5 per half-day, £7-8 per day, £30-40 per week. Open July-Sept. daily 9:30am-6pm.

Scuba Diving: Cornish Diving, Bar Rd., (☎313 178), near Falmouth Docks. Lessons £49 per day, children £30. Open M-Sa 9am-5:30pm, Su 9:30am-4:30pm.

Sailing: Britons Slip Sailing School, 40 High St. (☎211 100).

ORIENTATION AND PRACTICAL INFORMATION

The rail line runs along the highest parts of Falmouth, and streets from there to the sea are steep. **The Moor** is Falmouth's main square. The main street extends from there, changing names five times, and covers the entire commercial area. The **tourist information centre,** 28 Killigrew St., The Moor, books beds for a 10% deposit and has information on the Lizard Peninsula. (☎312 300; fax 313 457. Open Apr.-Sept. M-Sa 9:30am-5:30pm, July-Aug. also Su 10am-2pm; Oct.-Mar. M-F 9:30am-5:30pm.) From the Prince of Wales Pier, numerous companies run **cruises** on River Fal to the north and Helford River to the southwest (1-2hr.; £5-7). **K&S Cruises** (☎211 056) offers fishing trips (2½-4hr., 3 per day, £8-16). Other services include: **banks** on Market St.; **Bubbles Laundry,** 99 Killigrew St. (☎311 291; wash £1.80-3.50, dry 20p per 4min., soap 50p; open M-F 8am-7pm, Sa 9am-7pm, Su 10am-3pm); the nearest **police station** (☎213 432), in Penryn; **Falmouth Hospital,** Trescobeas Rd. (☎434 700); **internet access** at the library, the Moor (☎314 901; 75p per 15min., £2 per hr.; open M-Tu and Th-F 9:30am-6pm, Sa 9:30am-4pm); and the **post office,** on The Moor (☎(0845) 601 1022; open M-F 9am-5:30pm, Sa 9am-12:30pm). **Post Code:** TR11 3RB.

ACCOMMODATIONS

Western Terr. has a wealth of B&Bs at a wide range of prices (£15-45 per person), while lodgings on **Cliff Rd.** and **Castle Dr.** promise great views for a pretty penny. The plushest (and priciest) B&B in town, **Dolvean Hotel ❹,** 50 Melvill Rd., boasts superior service and luxurious beach vistas. (☎313 658; fax 313 995. Singles £40-45; doubles £80-90. AmEx/MC/V.) Guest requests, from veggie breakfasts to a spare umbrella, are always met at **Castleton Guest House ❸,** 68 Killigrew St. (☎311 072. Singles £22; doubles £36-46.) **Lyonesse Guesthouse ❷,** 17 Western Terr., celebrates the color pink in its cozy rooms. (☎313 017. Singles £19, with bath £25; doubles £38/£44.) **Boscovean ❷,** 3 Western Terr., offers simple, comfortable lodgings for the best price in town. (☎/fax 212 539. Open Easter-Oct. £15 per person.) If you're **camping,** you'll find the nearest site at **Penance Mill** (☎(01326) 312 616).

FOOD

To create your own meals, pick up groceries at **Tesco,** The Moor. (☎437 400. Open M-Sa 7am-8pm, Su 10am-4pm.) Otherwise, Falmouth has lots of options for quality eats, from cheap pasties to outrageously priced lobsters. **Harbour Lights ❶,** Arwenack St., is arguably Cornwall's best chippy. Fish and chips start at £3.40; the Moby Dick Giant Cod is worth the £4.70. (☎316 934. Open daily 9am-10pm, takeaway until 2am.) **Pipeline ❸,** 21 Church St., serves Mediterranean and Cajun fusion fare (£8-13) and has playful seaside decor. (☎312 774. Open Tu 6-9:45pm, W-Sa noon-2:15pm and 6-9:45pm, Su 10am-3pm and 7-9:15pm.) Beach-themed **Sea Farers ❸,** 33 Arwenack St., is the perfect setting for mouthwatering seafood. Light dishes are £4.25-6, main courses £11-20. (☎319 851. Open Su-Th 6-10pm, F-Sa 6-10:30pm.)

📷 🎧 SIGHTS AND BEACHES

Pendennis Castle, built by Henry VIII to keep French frigates out of Falmouth, now features a walk-through diorama that assaults the senses with waxen gunners bellowing incoherently through artificial fog. Find better views and ventilation on the battlements. (☎316 594. Open July-Aug. daily 9am-6pm; Apr.-June and Sept. 10am-6pm; Oct. 10am-5pm; Nov.-Mar. 10am-4pm. £4, concessions £3, children £2.) A 25min. ferry across the channel (see p. 255) ends among thatched roofs and aspiring tropical gardens in **St. Mawes** village. A 10min. uphill walk from the ferry drop-off point leads to the village's only attraction, **St. Mawes Castle,** actually a circular battlement. Built by Henry to blow holes through any Frenchman spared by Pendennis's gunners, the six-storey structure of numerous stairs and narrow passages is the perfect playground for the castle's schoolchild visitors. Though the tower is worth climbing, Pendennis wins the battle for superior views. (☎270 526. Open Apr.-Sept. daily 10am-6pm; Oct. 10am-5pm; Nov.-Mar. W-Su 10am-1pm and 2-4pm. 1hr. audio tour included. £2.90, concessions £2.20, children £1.50.)

To taste the surf, head to one of Falmouth's three beaches; if morning skies are gray, wait until noon, when the Cornish weather might surprise you. **Castle Beach,** on Pendennis Head, is too pebbly for swimming or sunbathing, but low tide reveals a labyrinth of seaweed and tidepools. **Gyllyngvase Beach** and **Swanpool Beach** are both sandy, and have areas suitable for windsurfing and jet skiing.

📺 🎵 NIGHTLIFE AND ENTERTAINMENT

For a smallish town, Falmouth has a surprisingly vibrant social scene. Swill some rum at the **Pirate Inn,** Grove Pl., where local bands perform live every night. (Open M-Th 9pm-midnight, F-Sa 9pm-2am.) The town's hottest club, **Remedies,** The Moor, is best on weekends when crowds groove to rock and chart. (☎314 454. Pints £2.10-2.30. Cover Tu-F £2, Sa £3, Tu-Th before 10:30pm £1. Open daily 6pm-2am.) Friday and Saturday nights, the bacchanalian crowd at **The Cork and Bottle,** 6-7 Church St. (☎316 909) vies to match that of **The Grapes Inn** (☎314 704), across the road at 64 Church St. (Both open M-Sa 11am-11pm, Su noon-10:30pm.) The **Falmouth Arts Centre,** Church St., hosts exhibitions, concerts, theater, and films. (☎212 300. Box office open M-Sa 10am-2pm. Exhibitions free, theater and concert tickets £5-10.) **Regatta Week,** in mid-August, is Falmouth's main sailing event, with boat shows and music performances. The **Oyster Festival,** during the first weekend of October, features oyster tasting, cooking demonstrations, and craft fairs.

▶ DAYTRIP FROM FALMOUTH

▨ THE EDEN PROJECT

Bodelva, St. Austell. Reach Eden Project from St. Austell, which connects to Truro and Falmouth via Truronian bus T9 or First bus #21A. From St. Austell, take DAC Coaches (☎(01822) 834 571) #269 (20min.; M-Sa 5 per day, Su 2 per day) or Truronian (☎(01872) 273 453) T9 (20min., every hr.). From the north, take First bus #55 from Padstow (1¼hr., 7-9 per day), which passes through Wadebridge (1hr.) and Bodmin (40min.). Signposted from the A390, A30, and A391. ☎(01726) 811 911; www.eden-project.com. Open Apr.-Oct. 10am-6pm, last admission 5pm; Nov.-Mar. 10am-4:30pm, last admission 3pm. Buy advance tickets at any TIC to avoid long lines. £9.80, seniors £7.50, students £5, children £4, families £23; cyclists get a £3 discount, child cyclists free.

"A global garden for the 21st century," the Eden Project is one of England's most unique and fascinating sights. Popular, too—the brand-new project welcomed nearly two million visitors in its first year. Once a clay mining quarry, the area is now home to three massive biodomes: one open and two covered. (The special foil that covers the domes lets in UV rays, making sunburns possible—come prepared.) The **Warm Temperate Biome** mimics the weather of South Africa and California, with olive groves and citrus trees. The **Humid Tropics Biome** is the world's largest greenhouse, and houses a living rainforest. The 30-acre **Roofless Biodome** features hemp, sunflowers, tea, and other plants that thrive in a European climate. A fourth biome, the Desert Environ, is currently in the works. Those who want to see the natural wonders of the world can do it efficiently here; it takes roughly 4hr. to walk through all three domes.

THE LIZARD PENINSULA

The Lizard Peninsula offers peaceful hiking trails despite the growing numbers of tourists. Jutting into the ocean just southwest of Falmouth, the peninsula has a breathtaking coast of rocky cliffs and sandy coves; hikes along the **South West Coastal Path** (see p. 199) afford fantastic sea views. Although the name may daunt the herpetophobic, visitors need not worry about encountering reptilia—"Lizard" is a corruption of Old Cornish "Lys ardh," meaning "the high place." Coincidentally enough, however, the **serpentine rocks** found (and sold) in this area look remarkably like reptile skin, crafted into shiny chess pieces and jewelry cases.

The tiny village of **The Lizard** has been particularly keen on this roaring (or at least hissing) trade. Visitors pass a quiet street full of souvenir shops before reaching the tip of the peninsula, **⬛Lizard Point.** Pink flowers climb the rocky cliff of England's southernmost point, which hangs perilously above the brilliant blue sea. The **National Trust Information Centre** here stocks books and maps and offers hiking suggestions. (Open Easter-Oct. 10am-4pm.) **⬛Kynance Cove,** 1 mi. west of Lizard Point along the coast, is one of those gorgeous hiking destinations, with golden sands, shallow shores, and turquoise waters. Farther north is rocky **Mullion Cove,** where steep but climbable cliffs await. **Mullion Island,** 250 yd. off the cove, is home to hundreds of seabirds. The cove is a 3-4hr. hike from Lizard Point but a more comfortable 1½ mi. from Mullion village.

In the middle of the peninsula, 7 mi. from Helston, is **Earth Station Goonhilly,** the world's largest satellite station. Over 60 satellites grace the premises, where a visitors center features exhibits, films, live web cams, and a shuttle tour through the satellites' perimeters. (☎(0800) 679 593. Open July-Sept. Su-Th 10am-6pm; Apr.-June and Oct. 10am-5pm. £5, concessions £4, children £3.50.) The **National Seal Sanctuary,** Europe's leading marine sanctuary and home to sea lions, otters, and seal pups, is 5 mi. farther north, in the town of Gweek. (☎(01326) 221 874. Open daily 9am-4pm.) Truronian **buses** run from Helston to both Goonhilly (T2, 20min., 4-6 per day, return £2.40) and Gweek (T2, T4; 20-30min.; 5 per day; return £2.20).

To reach Lizard Point, bus riders must first get to **Helston,** 11 mi. north of the point. **First** buses #2 and 2A makes the trip to Helston from **Falmouth** (50min., 5-6 per day) or **Penzance** (1hr.; M-Sa 2 per hr., June-Sept. also Su every hr.; £3), but does not serve Lizard Point. **Truronian** (☎(01872) 273 453) buses do both, running from Falmouth to Helston (T4, 1¼hr., 4 per day) and from there to **Lizard** (T1; 40min.; £1.90, return £3) or **Mullion** (T1; 30min.; every hr.; £1.35, return £2.30). To make multiple stops in a day, buy a **Day Rover** (£5.50, seniors £4.50, children £3.50, families £12.50). **Driving** access is via the A3083 from the A394.

The **tourist information centre,** in front of the Trengrouse bus stop in Helston, books accommodations for a 10% deposit. (☎565 431. Open M-F 10am-1pm and 2-

4:30pm, Sa 10am-1pm, July-Aug. also Sa 2-4pm.) Stock up on cash in Helston—elsewhere, **banks** and **ATMs** are rare. **YHA Coverack ❷,** 12 mi. northeast of Lizard Point, is the peninsula's only hostel; take Truronian bus T3 (1hr., 3 per day) from Helston or T34 from the Redruth train station to Coverack village. (☎(01326) 280 687; fax 280 119. Open Apr.-Oct. daily. £10.25, under 18 £7.) For **campsites,** consult the numerous listings in the free *Map and Guide to the Lizard Peninsula,* available at TICs in nearby towns. **Sea Acres ❶,** Kennack Sands, Ruan Minor, in Helston, overlooks a sandy beach. (☎(0845) 458 0064. Caravans and tents £10.)

PENZANCE ☎ 01736

Penzance is the very model of an ancient English pirate town: water-logged and unabashed. The city's armada of souvenir shops wages countless raids on tourist doubloons and sometimes makes Penzance feel as authentic as the wooden pirates on a Disney ride. But with glorious sunsets and mildly bawdy pubs, it's difficult not to enjoy such an irreverent, swashbuckling town.

⬛ TRANSPORTATION

Trains: Wharf Rd., at the head of Albert Pier. Ticket office open M-Sa 6:15am-6pm, Su 8:15am-5:30pm. Trains (☎(08457) 484 950) from: Exeter (3hr., every hr., £19.10); London (5½hr., every hr., £56); Newquay via Par (2hr., 6 per day, £10.30); Plymouth (2hr., every hr., £10.30); and St. Ives (direct: 25min., 4-5 per day, £2.80; via St. Erth: 40min.-1hr., every hr., £2.80).

Buses: Wharf Rd. (☎(01209) 722 625), at the head of Albert Pier. Ticket office open M-F 8:30am-4:45pm, Sa 8:30am-1:30pm, Easter-Oct. also Su 9:30am-12:30pm; Nov.-Easter 8:30am-noon, 1-4:45pm. **National Express** (☎(08705) 808 080) from: **London** via **Heathrow** (8hr., 8 per day, £28.50) and **Plymouth** via **Truro** (3hr., 2 per hr., £6).

Taxis: Nippy Cabs (☎366 666).

⬛ ⬛ ORIENTATION AND PRACTICAL INFORMATION

Some refer to Penzance as the "nine mile town"—it's 9 mi. from the Lizard Peninsula, 9 mi. from Land's End, and 9 mi. from St. Ives. The train station, bus station, and TIC cluster conveniently on **Wharf Rd.,** adjacent to the harbor and town. **Market Jew St.** (a corruption of the Cornish "Marghas Yow," meaning "Market Thursday") is laden with well-stocked bakeries and ill-stacked bookstores. It mutates into **Alverton St.,** then **Alverton Rd.,** then becomes the A30, the road to Land's End. **Chapel St.,** a cobblestone row of historic buildings turned touristy shops, descends from the town center into a welter of alleys near the docks.

Tourist Information Centre: Station Rd. (☎362 207), between the train and bus stations. Books beds for a 10% deposit. Free Penzance map. Open May-Sept. M-Sa 9am-6pm, Su 10am-1pm; Oct.-Apr. M-F 9am-5pm, Sa 10am-1pm.

Tours: Anyone interested in Cornish history, touring with a folk band, or riotous jokes about Neolithic man should try ▧ **Harry Safari,** a corny trip through the Cornish wilds. (☎711 427 or book at TIC; www.harrysafari.co.uk. 4hr., Su-F 1 per day, £15.) **National Express, Western National,** and **Cornwall** buses also offer guided tours of Cornwall. **First** (☎(01209) 719 988) tours include weekly trips to King Arthur sights near Bodmin Moor (F 9:30am; £8, children £6), fishing villages Looe and Polperro (W 9:30am, £8/£6), and the Lizard Peninsula (M 11am, £6.50/£4.50). From the TIC, **Ghost Walks** has a pair of 1hr. tours of town, the Hair Raiser and Spine Chiller. (☎331 206. July-Aug. Th and Su 8:30pm and 10:15pm; Apr.-June and Sept. 8:30pm. £3, children £2.)

SOUTHWEST ENGLAND

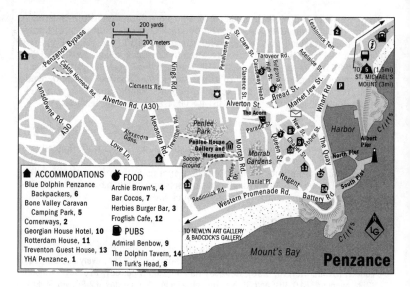

ACCOMMODATIONS
Blue Dolphin Penzance
  Backpackers, **6**
Bone Valley Caravan
  Camping Park, **5**
Cornerways, **2**
Georgian House Hotel, **10**
Rotterdam House, **11**
Treventon Guest House, **13**
YHA Penzance, **1**

FOOD
Archie Brown's, **4**
Bar Cocos, **7**
Herbies Burger Bar, **3**
Frogfish Cafe, **12**

PUBS
Admiral Benbow, **9**
The Dolphin Tavern, **14**
The Turk's Head, **8**

Penzance

Financial Services: Barclays, 8-9 Market Jew St. (☎362 271). Open M-Tu and Th-F 9am-5pm, W 10am-5pm, Sa 9:30am-noon.

Launderette: Polyclean, 4 East Terr. (☎364 815), opposite the train station. Wash £2.20-3, dry 20p per 3min, soap 20p. Open daily 7:30am-8:30pm, last wash 7:30pm.

Police: Penalverne Dr. (☎(0870) 577 744), off Alverton St.

Hospital: West Cornwall Hospital, St. Clare St. (☎874 000). Take bus #10, 10A, 11, 11A, or 11D.

Internet Access: Polyclean (see above) has access for 5p per min., available 9am-8:30pm, while **Penzance Public Library,** Morrab Rd. (☎363 954) charges an equivalent 75p per 15min. (Open M-F 9:30am-6pm, Sa 9:30am-4pm.)

Post Office: 113 Market Jew St. Open M-F 9am-5:30pm, Sa 9am-12:30pm. **Post Code:** TR18 2LB.

🔨 ACCOMMODATIONS AND CAMPING

Penzance's fleet of **B&Bs** (£16-23) are most concentrated on **Alexandra Rd.,** a 10min. walk from the town center. Many buses run from the station to Alexandra Rd. (50p). **Morrab Rd.,** between Alverton St. and Western Promenade Rd., also has a handful. **Camping** areas blanket the west Cornwall peninsula.

▨ **Blue Dolphin Penzance Backpackers,** Alexandra Rd. (☎363 836; fax 363 844; pzback-pack@ndirect.co.uk). Relaxed and well-kept, with an ample lounge. Internet access (8p per min.) and laundry (£3 per load). Dorms £10; doubles £24. ❷

YHA Penzance, Castle Horneck (☎362 666; penzance@yha.org.uk). Walk 20min. or take a taxi from the train or bus stations (£2.50-3.50). Restored 18th-century mansion with classy lounge, kitchen, and laundry. Reception 3-11pm. Lockout 10am-1pm. Dorms £11.25, under 18 £8; doubles £29. **Camp** for £5 and use hostel facilities. ❷

Cornerways, 5 Leskinnick St. (☎364 645), behind the train station. Friendly and cozy; all rooms are ensuite. Veggie breakfast available. Book weeks ahead. Singles £23; twins £40; triples £54. Mention *Let's Go* for a 10% discount. ❸

Rotterdam House, 27 Chapel St. (☎/fax 332 362). Offers smoked haddock for breakfast. Book well ahead, especially in summer. £17 per person. ❷

Georgian House Hotel, 20 Chapel St. (☎365 664). A beautiful family-run option in the heart of town. Singles £28; doubles £46. ❸

Treventon Guest House, (☎363 521), at the bottom of Alexandra Rd. Simple but pleasant rooms at bargain prices. Singles £16; doubles £36-40. ❷

Camping: Bone Valley Caravan Camping Park, Heamoor, Penzance (☎360 313). Family-run site 1½ mi. from the city center. July-Aug. £3 per person; Sept.-June £2.50 per person. £3.50 per pitch. ❶

FOOD

Expect to pay around £10-15 to dine at one of Penzance's excellent seafood spots along **The Quay.** The best buys are in coffee shops and local eateries on smaller streets and alleys near **Market Jew St.** A **farmers market** (☎365 336) convenes every Saturday at the Wharfside Shopping Centre.

▨ **Herbies Burger Bar,** 56 Causeway Head (☎362 850). Fish made to order and fried to perfection. Cod and chips £2.95. Open M-Sa 11:30am-7pm. ❶

Archie Brown's, Bread St. (☎362 828), above Richard's Health Food Store. Heralded by a colorful banner, this bustling vegetarian cafe makes creative meals, including falafel wrap with salad (£4.50), the daily vegan soup (£3), and homity pie (£5). Open M-Sa 9:30am-5pm, also F for pricier dinners (£15). ❶

Frogfish Cafe, Chapel St. (☎332 555), under the Penzance Art Club. Serves über-fresh seafood (caught daily by the chef), including seared yellowfish tuna, scallops with lemon and coriander, and monkfish in pesto dressing. Starters £5-7, entrees £9-17. Open on the chef's whims for dinner only. ❸

Bar Cocos, 12-13 Chapel St. (☎350 222). Busy, colorful tapas bar. Tapas £4-4.50, Mediterranean entrees £8-12. Open M-Sa 10am-10pm, Su 6-10pm. ❷

SIGHTS

Penzance has no large museums but does boast an impressive number of **art galleries,** which pop up on every other block. The *Cornwall Gallery Guide* booklet (£1) is a comprehensive listing of the best galleries in Penzance and nearby cities.

ST. MICHAEL'S MOUNT. Archangel St. Michael is said to have appeared to some fishermen on Marazion, just offshore from Penzance, in AD 495—reason enough to build a Benedictine monastery on the spot. Today, St. Michael's Mount has a church and castle at its peak and a village at its base; at low tide, visitors can stroll there via a lumpy, seaweed-strewn causeway. The castle's interior is unspectacular (try to spot Ollie Cromwell's bib); but the grounds are lovely, and the 30-storey views captivating. Joachim von Ribbentrop, Hitler's foreign minister, had it picked out as his personal residence after the conquest of England. *(Walk 3 mi. from the TIC to Marazion Sq. or take bus #2, 2A, 17A, or 32 (return £1.10). The Mount is accessible by ferry (£1, children 50p) and sometimes by foot (5-10min.); for ferry and tide info, call ☎710 526. Cas-*

SOUTHWEST ENGLAND

THE HIDDEN DEAL

BARGAIN BOOTY

Smell your way to hidden deals at Penzance's **Antiques Arcade,** 61-62 Chapel St., where the musky scent of age promises that you're going to buy something really cheap. With two levels of nameless shops selling antique bric-a-brac, this quiet antique mall has huge potential as a bargain bonanza.

Straining eyes will discover all sorts of fancy items of eclectic interest. Whether it's clocks or perfume bottles or a porcelain merry-go-round horse, visitors are bound to find something worthy of purchase—even if it means offending the sensible taste of others. *(☎ 338 121. Open M-Sa 9:30am-5pm.)*

Venture downstairs for an even bigger smorgasbord of odds and ends at the **Flea Market,** where artwork (£5), porcelain plates (20p-£7), jewelry (£2), and small furnishings cover the floors and walls. *(Open Th-Sa 9am-4:30pm.)* After you've hoarded various cheapie souvenirs for yourself, don't forget to pick up the guides to other antique markets.

tle ☎ 710 507. Open Apr.-Oct. M-F 10:30am-5:30pm, also July-Aug. most Sa-Su. Last admission 4:45pm. Nov.-Mar. M, W, F by tour only. £4.60, children £2.30, families £13.)

NEWLYN ART GALLERY. Penzance is famed for the Newlyn school of art, which began here in the late 19th century. Exhibits, which rotate monthly, feature local as well as British and international works, including pen sketches, modern sculpture, and abstract paintings. *(New Rd. Walk west on Western Promenade Rd., which becomes New Rd. ☎ 363 715. Open M-Sa 10am-5pm. Free.)*

PENLEE HOUSE GALLERY AND MUSEUM. The gallery is internationally known for its impressive collection of Newlyn school art, while the museum upstairs has an eclectic collection of historical artifacts, including the 18th-century Scold's Bridle, a menacing discouragement of loose lips. *(Morrab Rd. ☎ 363 625. Open May-Sept. M-Sa 10am-5pm; Oct.-Apr. 10:30am-4:30pm. £2, concessions £1, children free; free to all Sa.)*

OTHER ART GALLERIES. The following galleries are among the larger and more interesting in Penzance. The curator of the **Rainy Day Gallery,** 116 Market Jew St., compiles the *Cornwall Gallery Guide.* *(☎ 366 077. Open M-Sa 10am-5pm.)* Other galleries worth a visit include **Badcock's Gallery,** The Strand, Newlyn *(☎ 366 159; open M-F 10:30am-6pm, Sa 11am-6pm)*; the three-floor **Tony Saunders Gallery and Antiques,** 14 Chapel St. *(☎ 366 620; open M-Sa 9am-5:30pm)*; and **Shears Gallery,** 58 Chapel St. *(☎ 350 501; open M-Sa 10am-5pm).*

🎭🎵 NIGHTLIFE AND ENTERTAINMENT

Good pubs are in abundance in Penzance. All have the same hours (M-Sa 11am-11pm, Su 11am-10:30pm). **The Turk's Head,** 49 Chapel St. *(☎ 363 093)*, dating from the 13th century, is Penzance's oldest pub and was sacked by Spanish pirates in 1595. Nearby **Admiral Benbow,** 46 Chapel St. *(☎ 363 448)*, is a pleasant local haunt, while a sea captain's ghost is said to haunt **The Dolphin Tavern,** The Quay *(☎ 364 106)*. The Dolphin also has the dubious distinction of being the first place tobacco was smoked in Britain.

A highly-touted theater and music venue, **The Acorn,** Parade St., features everything from tribute bands to jazz bands and from comedy clubs to the rather dark productions of **Kneehigh Theatre,** Cornwall's best-known theater company. *(☎ 365 520. Box* office open Tu-F 11am-5pm, Sa 10am-3pm. Tickets £3-15.) Bacchus visits the city in June during the pagan **Golowan Festival,** featuring bonfires, fireworks, and the election of the mock Mayor of the Quay.

DAYTRIP FROM PENZANCE

▨ MINACK THEATRE

9 mi. southwest of Penzance, in the town of Porthcurno. Take First bus #1A or 1C from the bus station (30min.; M-Sa 8 per day, Su 4 per day; return £2.50), or Sunset Coaches #345 from YHA Penzance or the TIC (40min., M-F 1 per day). Car access is via the B3283. Visitors center ☎ 381 081; www.minack.com. Open Apr.-Sept. 9:30am-5:30pm; Oct.-Mar. 10am-4pm. £2.50, seniors £1.80, children £1. Ticket office ☎ 810 181. Open mid-May to Sept. M-F 9:30am-8pm, Sa-Su 9:30am-5:30pm; closed noon-4:30pm during matinees. Performances M-F 8pm, also W and F 2pm. £5.50-7, children £2.75-3.50. £1-2 charge for phone booking. Arrive 1¼hr. before curtain.

For seventeen weeks during the summer, natives and tourists flock to the stunning open-air ▨**Minack Theatre,** which puts on various performances, from *Richard III* to *Pride and Prejudice* to the inevitable *Pirates of Penzance*. Hacked into a cliffside at Porthcurno, Minack reportedly appeared in a dream to Rowena Cade, who constructed the surreal amphitheater "with her own hands," literally. The 750 stone seats rise high up on a hill facing a curved stage and the open sea. Perched on a cliff, the theater affords spectacular views of the surrounding waters and cliffs; on a clear day, visitors can see the Lizard Peninsula to the southeast, nearly 20 mi. across the bay.

ST. IVES ☎ 01736

As I was going to St. Ives, I met a man with seven wives.
Each wife had seven sacks, each sack had seven cats,
Each cat had seven kits. Kittens, cats, sacks, and wives,
How many were going to St. Ives?

Only one, of course. But medieval St. Ives (pop. 11,100), perched 10 mi. north of Penzance on a spit of land edged by pastel beaches and azure waters, has attracted visitors for centuries. The cobbled alleyways, colored by overflowing flowerpots, drew a colony of painters and sculptors in the 1920s; today, their legacy fills the windows of countless local art galleries, including a branch of the Tate. Virginia Woolf, too, was bewitched by the energy of the Atlantic at St. Ives: her masterpiece *To the Lighthouse* is thought to refer to the Godrevy Lighthouse in the distance, disappearing and reappearing in the morning fog.

▣▨ TRANSPORTATION AND PRACTICAL INFORMATION. Trains (☎ (08457) 484 950) to St. Ives pass through or change at **St. Erth** (15min., 2 per hr., £3), though you can go direct from St. Ives to **Penzance** (25min.; M-F 7 per day, mid-May to Sept. also Sa-Su 3 per day). **National Express buses** (☎ (08705) 808 080) stop in St. Ives (4 per day) between **Plymouth** (3hr.) and **Penzance** (20min.). For Penzance, it's cheaper to take much more frequent **First** bus #16, 16B, or 17 (30-40min., 2 per hr., £2.50). Buses #57 and 57D run to **Newquay** (2¼hr., 3 per day, £2.50).

St. Ives is a jumble of alleys and tiny streets—you'll want to pick up a map. The TIC gives out free xerox copies that include a street index and are much more detailed than the 20p brochure. As a general rule, always walk downhill to reach the sea and town center. The **tourist information centre** is in the Guildhall. From the bus or train station, walk to the foot of Tregenna Hill and turn right on Street-an-

Pol. (☎ 796 297. Open Easter-Sept. M-Sa 9:30am-6pm, Su 10am-1pm; Oct.-Easter M-F 9am-5pm.) A **guided walk** weaves through alleys and explores the town's history. (☎810 287. 1½hr. June-Aug. Tu and Th 8pm. £3, concessions £2.) **Columbus Walks** run longer 4-8 mi. hikes through the area (☎(07980) 149 243; M-Th £3-8, plucky children free). **Ghost Walks** leave from the TIC. (☎331 206. 1hr. July-Aug. M-W 8:30 and 10:15pm; June and Sept. M-Tu 8:30pm; Mar.-May and Oct. Tu 8:30pm. £3; children £2.) Other services include: **banks** along High St., including **Barclays** (☎362 261; open M-Tu and Th-F 9:30am-4:30pm, W 10am-4:30pm); free **luggage storage** at the **St. Ives International Backpackers** (see below); **Internet access** at **C+ Computers,** Chapel St., behind the post office (☎798 166; 50p per 15min.; open M-F 9am-5pm, Sa 9am-3pm); and the **post office,** Tregenna Pl. (☎795 004; open M-F 9am-5:30pm, Sa 9am-12:30pm). **Post Code:** TR26 1AA.

⌂ ACCOMMODATIONS. B&Bs (£20-30) are dotted throughout St. Ives. Pricier ones are near the town center on **Parc Ave.** and **Tregenna Terr.** Walk uphill on West Pl., which becomes **Clodgy View** and **Belmont Terr.,** where B&Bs offer fine sea views and will take a few pounds off (10min.). The fantastically located **Hobblers House ❸,** on the corner of The Wharf and Court Cocking, offers spacious rooms practically right on the beach. (☎796 439; fax 798 178. Single £30; doubles £45.) **Garlands Guest House ❷,** 1 Belmont Terr., may be a tedious hike from the town center, but offers veggie breakfasts, delightful decor, and a "real 'chilled out' experience." (☎798 999. £18-22 per person.) The sparkling new **Nancherrow Cottage ❺,** 7 Fish St., off The Wharf, is right in the heart of town. (☎798 496. Doubles £65.) **St. Ives International Backpackers ❷,** The Stenmack, three blocks inland from the TIC, funkifies a 19th-century Methodist church. There's a free shuttle service for those staying at its sister hostel in Newquay. (☎/fax 799 444. Linens £1.50. Laundry £2.50. Dorms £12, off-season £8; weekly £39-49.) For camping or caravaning, **Ayr Holiday Park ❶** is the closest site. Walk to the end of Bullans Ln. (off The Stennack), turn left at Alexandra Rd., continue past the carpark, and veer right when the road splits. (☎795 855. £4.50-7.) Alternatively, take B3306 toward Zennor to reach **Hellesveor Farm Caravan and Camping ❶** (☎ 795 738), only 1 mi. out of town.

🍴🍺 FOOD AND PUBS. Get groceries at **Co-op,** Royal Sq., two blocks uphill from the TIC. (☎796 494. Open 8am-11pm.) A **farmers market** (☎365 336) takes place every Friday at the Parish Rooms. Miniscule **Ferrell & Son Bakery ❶,** 64 Fore St., does all its making and baking on-site; its pasties (£1-2) and saffron buns (40p) are touted by many as Cornwall's best. (☎797 703. Open M-Sa 11am-5:30pm.) A newly opened restaurant of growing popularity, **Tides Café ❸,** 6 The Digey, serves creative fusion dishes guaranteed to satisfy taste buds. (☎799 600. Lunch £7, dinner £12. Open Easter-Sept. Tu-Su 11am-4pm and 7pm-late; Oct.-Easter only W-Sa.) Try a tasty falafel (£3-5) at the bright and inviting **Beach Hut ❶,** 7 Tregenna Hill, the epitome of a beach cafe, right down to the sandy floors. (☎799 977. Open daily 8:30am-9:30pm.) **The Cafe ❷,** Island Sq., is a good option for vegetarian meals, around £9-10. (☎793 621. Open daily 11am-3pm and 6:30-10pm.)

🏛 GALLERIES. Famed as an **art colony** by the sea and renowned for its superb lighting, St. Ives was once an artists' pilgrimage site. The town's art community is still strong. Pick up a copy of the *Cornwall Galleries Guide* (£1) to navigate your way to the dozens of art galleries littered throughout St. Ives' maze-like alleys.

Like its sister, the Tate Modern in London (see p. 134), the **Tate Gallery** on Porthmeor Beach focuses on abstract art. Exhibits rotate every three months and feature local and international artists. (☎796 226. Open Tu-Su 10am-5:30pm; July-Aug. also M. Free 1hr. tours M-F 2:30pm; shorter tours 11am. £4.25, students £2.50, concessions free.) Under the protective wing of the Tate, the **Barbara Hepworth Museum and Sculpture Garden** allows visitors to view the famed 20th-century sculptor's former home, studio, and garden of artfully placed abstractions. (Same hours as Tate. £4, students £2.25, children and seniors free. Same-day admission to both museums £7/£4/free.) To view works in the St. Ives school style, try **Belgrave Gallery**, 22 Fore St., associated with the Belgrave Gallery London (☎794 888; open M-Sa 10am-1pm and 2-6pm), or **Wills Lane Gallery,** Wills Ln. (☎795 723; open M-Sa 10:30am-5pm). Also of interest are **St. Ives Ceramics,** Fish St. (☎794 930; open daily 10am-5pm) and **Printmakers Gallery,** 8 Tregenna Hill (☎796 654; open daily 10am-5pm), which feature beautiful ceramic and silk art, respectively.

◪ **BEACHES AND WATER SPORTS.** St. Ives's ◪**beaches** are arguably England's finest. Expansive stretches of sand slowly descend into the sea, making for shallow shores perfect for romantic strolls. Follow the hill down from the train station to **Porthminster Beach,** a magnificent stretch of golden sand and tame waves. To escape the crowds of toasting flesh, head for quieter **Porthgwidden Beach,** hugged by the jutting arms of the island. **Porthmeor Beach,** below the Tate, attracts surfers but has less appealing sands. Farther east, **Carbis Bay,** 1¼ mi. from very similar Porthminster, is less crowded and easily accessible by train or bus.

Beach activities at St. Ives are numerous. **Wind An Sea Surf Shop,** 25 Fore St., rents surfboards and wetsuits. (☎794 830. £5 per day, £25 per week; £5 deposit. Open Easter-Oct. daily 9:30am-10:30pm; Nov.-Easter until 9:30pm.) Beginners can start with a lesson at **Surf School.** (☎755 556. £20 per half-day, £30 per day.) **Dive St. Ives,** 25 The Wharf, offers diving lessons among shipwrecks, reefs, sea anemones, and sometimes even dolphins and sharks. (☎799 229. 3-day course July-Aug. £250, Sept. and June £200; 4-5 day course £350/£300.) The less athletically inclined may prefer **boat trips,** which leave from the harbor. **Pleasure Boat Trips** heads to Seal Island and around the bay. (☎797 328. 1½-4hr. £5-7, children free-£5.) Numerous boat companies head to bewitching **Godrevy Lighthouse** (£7, children £4.50). Rent a speedboat at **Mercury Boats.** (☎620 045. £7 per 15min., £10 per 30min., £15 per hr.)

🌙 **NIGHTLIFE** Beer has flowed at **The Sloop,** on the corner of Fish St. and The Wharf, since 1312. (☎796 584. Open daily 9am-11pm, Su 9am-10:30pm.) Nearby, **Lifeboat Inn,** Wharf Rd., has outdoor seating and a friendly atmosphere. (☎794 123. Open M-Sa 10:30am-11pm, Su 10:30am-10:30pm.) **The Sheaf of Wheat,** Chapel St., uphill from the cinema, is the locals' favorite pub. (☎797 130. Open M-Sa 11am-11pm, Su noon-10:30pm.) **Isobar,** at the corner of Street-an-Pol and High St., is St. Ives's busiest club. On Wednesdays, first drinks are free, and subsequent imbibing only costs £1 per round. (☎798 042. Bar open daily 6pm-2am, upstairs club W-Sa 10pm-2am. Cover free-£7.)

PENWITH PENINSULA

ZENNOR. Legend holds that a mermaid drawn by the singing of a young man in this tiny village returned to the sea with him in tow. On misty evenings, locals claim to see and hear the happy pair; a mermaid is carved on one of the benches of the local church. The immaculate **Old Chapel Backpackers Hostel ❷** is close to hiking and 4 mi. from the beaches at St. Ives. (☎(01736) 798 307. Dorms £12.) Zennor is accessible by bus #15 from St. Ives en route to St. Just and Land's End.

ST. JUST. On Cape Cornwall, 4 mi. north of Land's End, the craggy coast of St. Just (pop. 2000) remains fairly untouched by tourism. Derelict copper and tin mines define this former mining center, while the ever-present Neolithic stone circles poke unobtrusively out of the landscape. The dramatic **cliff path,** part of the South West Coast Path (see p. 199), unveils the best of Cornwall.

Just about every route to Land's End passes through St. Just. **Buses** #10, 10A, 10B, 11, and 11A run from **Penzance** (35min., every hr., £2.50); some continue to **St. Ives.** The one-woman **tourist information centre,** at the library opposite the bus park, carries *Ancient Sites in West Penwith* (£4), which outlines good walks from St. Just. (☎ (01736) 788 669. Open June-Aug. Su-W and F 10am-5pm, Sa 10am-1pm.) The **YHA Land's End ❷,** at Letcha Vean, occupies three pristine acres. From the bus station's rear exit, turn left and follow the lane to its end, a 15min. walk. (☎ (01736) 788 437; fax 787 337. Lockout 10am-5pm. Open July-Aug. daily; Sept.-Oct. Tu-Sa; Apr.-June M-Sa. Dorms £10.25, under 18 £7.) Much closer and just opposite the town's school, tiny four-bed **St. Just Backpackers ❷,** Queen St., off Cornwall Rd., includes breakfast. (☎ (01736) 788 088. £13.50 per person.)

SENNEN COVE. Just 2 mi. from Land's End along the coast, or 9 mi. from Penzance on the A30, ◪**Sennen Cove** is a gorgeous mile-long coastline where the land seems to melt into the gleaming sea. **First buses** stop at both the cove and the town; #15 from **St. Just** (35min.; M-Sa 4 per day, Su 6 per day; £2.10) continues toward **Land's End** (10min., £1.60); #1 and 1A come from **Penzance** (45min., every 1-2hr., £2.50). For lodgings, walk ¾ mi. uphill and turn left at the main road to reach tiny Sennen, where ◪**Land's End Backpackers and Guest House ❷,** White Sands Lodge, dazzles with colorful wall art and communal spirit. Give 'em a ring and they may pick you up from the Penzance bus or train station. (☎/fax (01736) 871 776. Dorms £11; singles £18; doubles £36, with bath £42. **Camping** £6.50.) Their adjoining **restaurant ❶** whips up an array of meals in a cozy, well-decorated setting. (Open 8am-10pm. English or vegetarian breakfast £4.50.)

LAND'S END. The Penwith Peninsula meets the Celtic Sea at **Land's End,** England's westernmost point. Visitors may be disturbed by the area's kitschy tourist attractions and stale museums encasing cheesy plastic dioramas, but the money these attractions generate funds the pleasant greenery and well-maintained roads that bring them here. Travelers need not contribute any quid, however, to stand atop the point and look out on dramatic granite cliffs and sea. First buses #1 and 1A run to Land's End from Penzance (40min., every 1-2hr., return £2.50) and St. Ives (35min., 3 per day, £2). For those unafraid of hills and hell-bent drivers, biking affords glimpses of sparkling coastlines. The **Visitors Centre** sells tickets for local attractions (£2.50-4.50, children £1.50-2.50) and offers hiking suggestions. (☎ (0870) 458 0044. Open daily July-Aug. 10am-6pm, Sept.-June 10am-5pm.)

ANCIENT MONUMENTS. Inland on the Penwith Peninsula, some of the least-tarnished Stone and Iron Age monuments in England lie along the Land's End-St. Ives bus route. Once covered by mounds of earth, the quoits (also called cromlechs or dolmens) are thought to be burial chambers from 2500 BC. The **Zennor Quoit** is named for the village. The **Lanyon Quoit,** off the Morvah-Penzance road about 3 mi. from each town, is one of the area's most impressive megaliths.

The famous stone near Morvah (on the Land's End-St. Ives bus route) has the Cornish name **Mên-an-Tol,** or "stone with a hole through the middle." The donut is allegedly endowed with curative powers: climbing through the aperture supposedly remedies backaches, assures easy childbirth, or induces any alteration in physiology your heart desires. The best-preserved Iron Age village in Britain is at **Chysauster,** about 4 mi. from both Penzance and Zennor. Take First bus #16 or 16B from Penzance or St. Ives. (20min. in either direction, M-Sa every hr., £1.80) or the 2½ mi. footpath off the B3311 near Gulval.

THE HEART OF ENGLAND

The patchwork pastures and half-timbered houses that characterize the countryside west of London are the stuff stereotypes are made of. Many of England's heaviest hitters are here: medieval Oxford, Britain's oldest university town; charming Stratford-upon-Avon, Shakespeare's home; and the impossibly picturesque villages of the Cotswolds, scattered among river-riven hills. It takes a wily traveler to avoid the touring hordes in this too-perfect landscape, but whether you're pestered by schoolchildren in a cottage garden or find yourself amidst a chorus of oohs and aahs in front of a Tudor facade, you'll always know just where you are. England. At the heart of it.

HIGHLIGHTS OF THE HEART OF ENGLAND

OXFORD Chat with the gargoyles in a university town rich in architectural flights-of-fancy and bizarre traditions (p. 272).

WINDSOR Feel your jaw drop while exploring one of the world's most divine royal residences (p. 270).

STRATFORD-UPON-AVON The playwright's the thing in Shakespeare's hometown, where tourist trails honor the Bard's footsteps and the Royal Shakespeare Company venerates his every syllable (p. 284).

ST. ALBANS
☎ 01727

From the Catuvellauni tribe to Julius Caesar, William the Conqueror to the royal houses of York and Lancaster, everyone who was anyone has wanted to set St. Albans on fire or make it their magnificent capital—usually a little of both. The first English Christian martyr, the Roman soldier Alban, was beheaded here for sheltering a priest; his consolation prize was eternal salvation and, better still, having Britain's second most significant Roman town named for him.

⌨ TRANSPORTATION. St. Albans has two **train stations;** City Station, the main one, is not to be confused with Abbey Station, which runs a single-schedule local service. **Trains** (☎ (08457) 484 950) enter City Station from **London King's Cross** (20min., 4 per hr., £7). To get from City Station to the town center, turn right out of the station and then right onto Victoria Rd., or avoid the long uphill hike by hopping any "Into Town" bus (60p). **National Express** (☎ (08705) 808 080), which arrives from **London** several times per hr. (30-45min., £5.40) and local **Sovereign** (☎ 854 732) **buses** usually stop at both City Station and along St. Peter's St.

⬛🔼 ORIENTATION AND PRACTICAL INFORMATION. Leaving City Station, **Hatfield Rd.** to the left and **Victoria St.** to the right both head uphill to the town center; the two streets are intersected perpendicularly by the main drag, which morphs from **St. Peter's St.** to **Checquer St.** to **Holywell Hill** to **St. Stephen's Hill** as it descends the slope. The columned **tourist information centre (TIC),** Market Place, St. Peter's St., has a free map and a sights-filled miniguide (25p); book

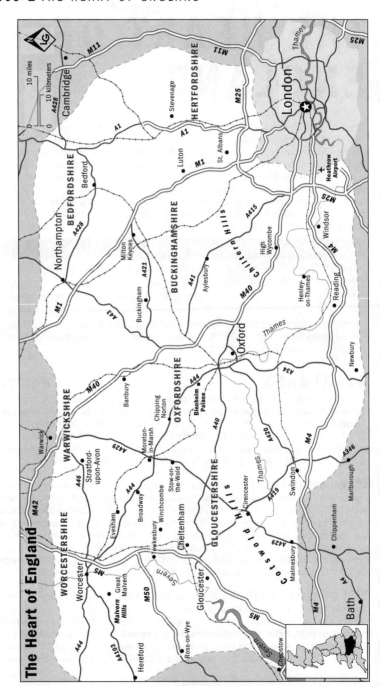

The Heart of England

your accommodations for £2.60. (☎ 864 511; fax 863 533; www.stalbans.gov.uk. Open Apr.-Oct. M-Sa 9:30am-5:30pm; July-Sept. also Su 10:30am-4pm; Nov.-Mar. M-Sa 10am-4pm.) Other services include: major **banks** along St. Peter's St.; the **police,** on Victoria St. (☎ 796 000); **Internet access** (£5 per hr.) at the **library,** The Maltings, near the TIC (☎ 860 000; call ahead to reserve a slot; open M, W 9:30am-7:30pm, Tu 9:30am-5:30pm, Th 9:30am-1pm, F 10:30am-7:30pm, Sa 9am-4pm); and the **post office,** 2 Beaconsfield Rd. (☎ 860 110). **Post Code:** AL1 3RA.

⛺▤ ACCOMMODATIONS AND FOOD. Reasonable lodgings, mainly **B&Bs** (around £25), are scattered and often unmarked. The saints at the TIC offer a free accommodations guide. By City Station, **Mrs. Murphy ❸,** 478 Hatfield Rd., keeps rooms graced by small touches of luxury. (☎ 842 216. Singles £25; doubles and twins £40-50; family rooms £40-60.) **Mrs. Nicol ❸,** 178 London Rd., the next road over from Victoria St., opens her beautiful old home to guests, with cable TV to boot. (☎ 846 726. Singles £30; doubles and twins £45.)

Pick your fruit and veggies at the famous **market** (W and Sa by the TIC); otherwise head to **Iceland,** 144 Victoria St., for daily staples. (Open M-W 9am-7pm, Th-F 9am-8pm, Sa 8:30am-6pm, Su 10am-4pm.) For lunch, a pint, or pure curiosity's sake, visit **Ye Olde Fighting Cocks ❶,** a stroll down Abbey Mill Ln. under the arch by the cathedral. This bizarre octagonal building, with 7th-century foundations, is the oldest pub in England, and among the liveliest. Underground tunnels, used by monks to flee Henry VIII's thugs, run from cathedral to pub. (☎ 865 830. Open M-Sa noon-11pm, Su noon-10:30pm.) Flowers tumble into the lazy River Ver and assertive ducks waddle at the **Waffle House ❶,** St. Michael's St., toward the Roman quarter. Choose from a host of creative meat-lover, veg-head, or sweet-tooth toppings for £3.50-5.50. (☎ 853 502. Open Apr.-Oct. M-Sa 10am-6pm, Su 11am-6pm; Nov.-Mar. M-Sa 10am-5pm, Su 11am-5pm.) St. Albans is home to the **Campaign for Real Ale** (to pay homage, go to 230 Hatfield Rd. or www.camra.org.uk), meaning pubs are plentiful and good ale even more so.

◘ SIGHTS. The Saxon-Norman-Gothic-Victorian ▧**Cathedral of St. Alban** is one-of-a-kind. Built on the foundations of a Saxon parish, the 1077 Norman design still dominates. At 300 ft., the medieval nave is the longest in Britain, and the splendid wooden roof one of the largest. The tower ceiling features the white and red roses of the houses of York and Lancaster, allegedly the first time both were depicted together: it was painted while the outcome of the battle between the two was uncertain and the abbot in charge wasn't a betting man. In defiance of Henry VIII and Cromwell stands the shrine of St. Alban, its fragments at long last reassembled. (☎ 860 780. Open M-Sa 10:30am-5pm, Su 1-5pm. Suggested donation £2.50.)

From the cathedral, take a 10-15min. walk down Fishpool St., over the river and uphill as it becomes St. Michael's St. to visit the ▧**Verulamium Museum.** Homes of the rich and poor of Roman Britain have been painstakingly recreated around mosaics and painted wall plasters discovered in the area. (☎ 751 810. Open M-Sa 10am-5:30pm, Su 2-5:30pm; last admission 5pm. £3.30, concessions £2, families £8.) Barely a block away huddle the remains of one of five **Roman theaters** built in England. The lucky will catch archaeologists working on further excavations. (☎ 835 035. Open daily 10am-5pm. £1.50, concessions £1, children 50p.)

The **Gardens of the Rose** in Chiswell Green is the "flagship garden" of the Royal National Rose Society. Over 30,000 roses conquer sweeps of field and scale tall buildings in a single bound. (2 mi. south of St. Albans. ☎ 850 461. Open June-Sept. M-Sa 9am-5pm, Su 10am-6pm. £4, seniors £3.50, children £1.50, families £10.)

HEART OF ENGLAND

⚡ DAYTRIP FROM ST. ALBANS

HATFIELD HOUSE

Bus S06 links St. Albans and Hatfield House (20min., 1-3 per hr., return £1.90). Hatfield train station, across from the main gate, makes the house easily accessible from destinations other than St. Albans itself. ☎(01707) 262 823. House open late Mar. to late Sept. daily noon-4pm. Grounds open late Mar. to late Sept. daily 11am-5:30pm. Excellent free tours Tu-F. £6.60, children £3.30. Grounds only £4/£3. Prices rise for "Connoisseurs Friday," when tours are longer and more gardens are open: £10, grounds only £6.

The Bishop of Ely and Henry VIII, among others, were early inhabitants of Hatfield House, but it is Queen Elizabeth I with whom its history is most associated. It was here that she spent her turbulent childhood; here she was placed under house arrest for suspected treason by her sister, Queen Mary; and finally, here she ascended to the throne and held her first Council of State. Hatfield boasts two famous portraits of Elizabeth I, and, though the silk stockings attributed to her are fakes, the gloves are real. Keep an eye out for the queen's 22 ft. long family tree, tracing her lineage to Adam and Eve via Noah, Julius Caesar, King Arthur, and King Lear. All that remains of Elizabeth's palace is the Great Hall; the rest was razed to make way for the magnificent mansion that dominates the estate today, which, in a final homage to Liz, was designed in the shape of an 'E.'

WINDSOR   ☎01753

The town of Windsor and the attached village of Eton are entirely overshadowed by their two bastions of the British class system, Windsor Castle and Eton College. Residential Windsor spread out from the castle in the Middle Ages and is now thick with specialty shops, tea houses, and pubs, all of which wear a certain charm. Time is far better spent, however, at the stupendous sights nearby.

▐ TRANSPORTATION

Two train stations lie near Windsor Castle, and signs point the way into town. **Trains** (☎(08457) 484 950) pull into **Windsor and Eton Central** from **London Victoria** and **Paddington** via **Slough** (50min., 2 per hr., day return £6.90). Trains arrive at **Windsor and Eton Riverside** from **London Waterloo** (50min., 2 per hr., day return £6.90). **Green Line** (☎8668 7261) **buses** #700 and 702 arrive at **Central** from London's Eccleston Bridge (1-1½hr., day return £5.50-6.70).

✳ ⚡ ORIENTATION AND PRACTICAL INFORMATION

Windsor village slopes in a crescent from the foot of its castle. **High St.** spans the hilltop, then becomes **Thames St.** at the statue of Queen Victoria and moves downhill to the river; the main shopping area, **Peascod St.,** meets High St. at the statue. The **tourist information centre,** at 24 High St. near Queen Victoria, sells maps and guides (50p-£1.50) and has free brochures. (☎743 900; www.windsor.gov.uk. Open May-June daily 10am-5pm; July-Aug. M-F 9:30am-6pm, Sa 10am-5:30pm, Su 10am-5pm; Sept. M-Sa 10am-5pm, Su 10am-4pm; Oct.-Apr. Su-F 10am-4pm, Sa 10am-5pm.) The **police** are on Alma Rd. (☎50600; head down Peascod St., turn right on St. Marks Rd.) Access the **Internet** at **Central Station** (open M-Sa 9:30am-5:30pm), **Tower Records,** Peascod St. (open M-Sa 9am-6pm, Su 10am-5:30pm), or **YHA Windsor;** all have slot-machine Internet access stations (£2.50 per 30min., minimum 50p).

ACCOMMODATIONS AND FOOD

Windsor is best seen as a daytrip from London, but if you decide to stay, the TIC will locate **B&Bs** for a £5 fee (☎743 907; windsor.accommodation@rbwm.gov.uk). Just across the street from the police station, at 56 Alma Rd., **Alma House ❹** offers you breakfast in a light-filled, white-tableclothed dining room. (☎862 983. Singles £45; doubles £60; family rooms £75.) The newly refurbished **Clarence Hotel ❹**, at 9 Clarence Rd., includes a lounge/bar area, steam sauna, and spacious rooms. (☎864 436; fax 857 060. Singles £45-£65; doubles/twins £50-£67; family rooms £60-£89.) Unfortunately, nothing in Windsor comes much cheaper.

Fast-food joints dominate the downhill end of High St. **The Waterman's Arms ❶**, Brocas St., is just over the bridge to Eton, next to the boat house. Founded in 1542, it's still a local favorite. Cod and chips are £4.50; sandwiches run £2-3. (☎861 001. Open M-Sa noon-2:30pm and 6-11pm, Su noon-3pm and 7-10pm.) Tiny **Crooked Tearoom ❷** lists decidedly to its right at 52 High St. Splurge on high tea (£7), sample a tea fruit infusion (£1.70), snack on cakes and sandwiches (under £5), or make a meal (£5-7) of pasta or potatoes. (☎857 534. Open M-Sa 10am-5:30pm. MC/V.)

◉ SIGHTS

WINDSOR CASTLE

24hr. info ☎831 118. Audio tours (£3.50) and multilingual guidebooks (£4.50) available. Open Apr.-Oct. daily 10am-5:30pm, last entry 4pm; Nov.-Mar. 10am-4pm, last entry 3pm. Allow roughly 2hr. £11.50, seniors £9.50, children £6, families £29.

The largest and oldest continuously inhabited castle in the world, Windsor features some of the most sumptuous rooms in Europe and some of the rarest artwork in the Western tradition. Windsor was built high above the Thames by William the Conqueror as a fortress rather than as a residence, and 40 reigning monarchs have since left their mark. As this is a working castle, members of the royal family often stay here for weekends and special ceremonies. The Queen is officially in residence for the month of April and a week in June; when she visits, the Royal Standard flies over the tower instead of the Union Jack. As a practical consequence of the Royals' residence, large areas of the castle will be unavailable to visitors, usually without warning. The steep admission prices are lowered on these occasions, but it is wise to call before visiting. Visitors can watch the **Changing of the Guard** in front of the Guard Room at 11am (summer M-Sa; winter alternate days M-Sa). The Guards can also be seen at 10:50am and 11:30am as they march to and from the ceremony through the streets of Windsor.

UPPER WARD. Reach the upper ward through the Norman tower and gate. Stand in the left line to enter the ward (it's worth the wait) to detour past **Queen Mary's Doll House**, a replica of a grand home on a 1:12 scale, with tiny classics in its library handwritten by their original authors, as well as functional plumbing and electrical systems. Continue to the opulent **state apartments**, used for ceremonial events and official entertainment. The rooms are decorated with art from the prodigious Royal Collection, including works by Holbein, Rubens, Rembrandt, van Dyck, and Queen Victoria herself. The **Queen's Drawing Room** features portraits of Henry VIII, Elizabeth I, and Bloody Mary, but don't miss smaller details like the silver dragon doorknobs. A fire on the Queen's anniversary in 1992 destroyed the **Lantern Room,** the **Grand Reception Room,** and the stunning **St. George's Hall,** now fully restored.

MIDDLE AND LOWER WARD. The middle ward is dominated by the **Round Tower** and its moat-cum-rose-garden. A stroll to the lower ward brings you to **St. George's Chapel,** a 15th-century structure with delicate vaulting and an exquisite wall of stained glass dedicated to the Order of the Garter. Used for the marriage of Sophie and Prince Edward, the chapel is the repository of the bones of Edward's ancestors. Ten sovereigns lie here, including Charles I. Henry VIII rests beneath a remarkably humble stone.

OTHER SIGHTS

ETON COLLEGE. Eton College, founded by Henry VI in 1440 as a college for (get this) paupers, is England's preeminent public—which is to say, private—school. The Queen is the sole (honorary) female Old Etonian. The boys still wear tailcoats to class and solemnly raise one finger in greeting to any teacher they pass. Despite its position at the apex of the British class system, Eton has shaped some notable dissidents and revolutionaries, including Aldous Huxley, George Orwell, and former Liberal Party leader Jeremy Thorpe. Wander the schoolyard, a central quad where Etonians have gamboled for centuries under the gaze of a statuesque Henry VI. The quad is circled by 25 houses for approximately 1250 students. King's Scholars, selected for full scholarship based on exam scores, live in the house known as "College," in the courtyard of College Chapel. *(10-15min. walk down Thames St., across Windsor Bridge, and along Eton High St. ☎671 177. Tours daily 2:15 and 3:15pm; £4, under 16 £3.10. Open late Mar. to mid-Apr. and July-Aug. daily 10:30am-4:30pm; other months 2-4:30pm; schedule depends on academic calendar. £3, under 16 £2.25.)*

LEGOLAND WINDSOR. A whimsical and expensive addition to the town, this imaginatively landscaped amusement park will wow the 11-and-under set with its rides, playgrounds, and circuses. Adults are wowed in turn by Miniland, which took 100 workers three years and 25 million blocks to craft. The replica of the City of London includes a 6 ft. St. Paul's, as well as every other major city landmark. The Lego buses that motor along the reduced streets are a marvel. *(☎(08705) 040 404. Open mid-July to Aug. 10am-7pm; Mar. to mid-July and Sept. to early Nov. daily 10am-5pm or 6pm; consult schedule. Tickets available at the Windsor TIC. £23, off season £19; children £20/£16; seniors £17/£13. Shuttle from the castle £2.50, children £1.30, under 5 free.)*

OXFORD ☎01865

Oxford has been home to a near-millennium of scholarship—25 British prime ministers and numerous other world leaders have been educated here. A scholarly community formed in the 11th century, but the actual university, Britain's first, was founded by Henry II in 1167. After a tiff with Thomas à Becket, Henry ordered the return of English students from Paris so that "there may never be wanting a succession of persons duly qualified for the service of God in church and state." Today trucks barrel, buses screech, and bicycles scrape past the pedestrians stuffing the streets. Despite the touring crowds, Oxford has an irrepressible grandeur and pockets of sweet quiet that lift the spirits: the basement room of Blackwell's Bookshop, the impeccable galleries of the Ashmolean, the serene lily ponds of the Botanic Garden, and the perfectly maintained quadrangles of Oxford's 39 colleges.

⌐ TRANSPORTATION

Trains: Botley Rd. (☎794 422), down Park End. Ticket office open M-F 6am-8pm, Sa 6:45am-8pm, Su 7:45am-8pm. Trains (☎(08457) 484 950) from **Birmingham** (1½hr., every hr., £22-29); **Glasgow** (6hr., 8 per day, £86); **London Paddington** (1hr., 2-4 per hr., day return £14.80); **Manchester** (3hr., 8 per day, £49).

Buses: Bus Station, Gloucester Green. **Stagecoach** (☎(01604) 620 077) runs from **Cambridge** (3hr.; every hr.; day return £8.75, concessions £6.50) and operates the **Oxford Tube** (☎772 250) to **London** (2hr., every 12min., next-day return £8.50). The **Oxford Bus Company** runs **CityLink** (☎785 400) from: **London** (1¾hr., 3 per hr., next-day return £9); **Gatwick** (2hr.; every hr. daytime, every 2hr. at night; £22); **Heathrow** (1½hr, 2 per hr., day return £12). **National Express** (☎(08705) 808 080) travels from **Cambridge** (4hr., every 2 hr., £16) and **London** (1¾hr., 3 per hr., £8).

Public Transportation: Most local services board around Carfax. The **Oxford Bus Company Cityline** (☎785 410) and **Stagecoach Oxford** (☎772 250) offer swift and frequent service to Iffly Rd. (#4, 4A, 4B, 4C), Banbury Rd. (2A, 2B, 2C, 2D), Abingdon Rd. (16, 35, 35a), Cowley Rd. (5, 5A, 52), and elsewhere. Fares are low (most 80p).

Taxis: Radio Taxi (☎242 424). **ABC** (☎770 681).

▓ ⑦ ORIENTATION AND PRACTICAL INFORMATION

Queen St. becomes **High St.**, and **Cornmarket St.** becomes **St. Aldates** at **Carfax Tower**, the center of the original city. Oxford extends some 3 mi. around the colossal tower, but the colleges are all within a mile of each other, mainly east of Carfax along High St. and Broad St. The pamphlet *Cycle into Oxford*, free at the TIC, is an excellent guide for both cyclists and pedestrians who wish to explore the city.

Tourist Information Centre: 15-16 Broad St. (☎726 871; fax 240 261; www.visitoxford.org). A pamphleteer's paradise. The busy staff books rooms for £3 and a refundable 10% deposit. Visitors' guide £1, monthly *In Oxford* guide free, accommodation list £1.10, restaurant guide 50p. Open M-Sa 9:30am-5pm, Su 10am-3:30pm.

Tours: The 2hr. official Oxford University **walking tour** (☎726 871) leaves from the TIC, and provides access to some colleges otherwise closed to visitors. Daily 11am and 2pm; in summer also 10:30am and 1pm. £6-7, children £3. **Blackwell's** (☎333 3606) offers literary walking tours. £6, concessions £5. **Bus tour** companies allow hop-on/hop-off access all day. **Guide Friday** (☎790 522) departs from the train station every 15min. from 9:30am-5:30pm for a 1hr. tour. £9, concessions £7.50, children £2.50. The **Oxford Classic Tour** (☎(01235) 819 393) provides multilingual earphones and runs every 20min. from 10:10am-5:50pm. £8, concessions £6, children £3.

Budget Travel: STA Travel, 36 George St. (☎792 800). Open M-W and F 9am-5:30pm, Th 10am-5:30pm, Sa 11am-5pm.

Financial Services: Banks line Cornmarket St. **Marks and Spencer,** 13-18 Queen St. (☎248 075), has a **bureau de change** upstairs in the back, no commission. Open M-W and F 8am-7pm, Th 8am-8pm, Sa 7:30am-7pm, and Su 11am-5pm. **American Express,** 4 Queen St. (☎207 101), open M-F 9am-5:30pm, Sa 9am-5pm. **Thomas Cook,** 5 Queen St. (☎447 000), open M-Sa 9am-5:30pm, Su 10:30am-4:30pm.

Launderette: 66 St. Aldates. Open daily 7am-10pm, last wash 9pm. Wash £2-3, dry £1.

Police: St. Aldates and Speedwell St. (☎266 000).

Hospital: John Radcliffe Hospital, Headley Way (☎741 166). Bus #13B or 14A.

Internet Access: Pickwick Papers, 90 Gloucester Green (☎722 849). Adjacent to the bus station. £1 per 30min. Open M-Sa 5am-9pm, Su 8am-8pm.

Post Office: 102-104 St. Aldates (☎(08457) 223 344). Open M-Sa 9-5:30pm. **Bureau de change. Post Code:** OX1.

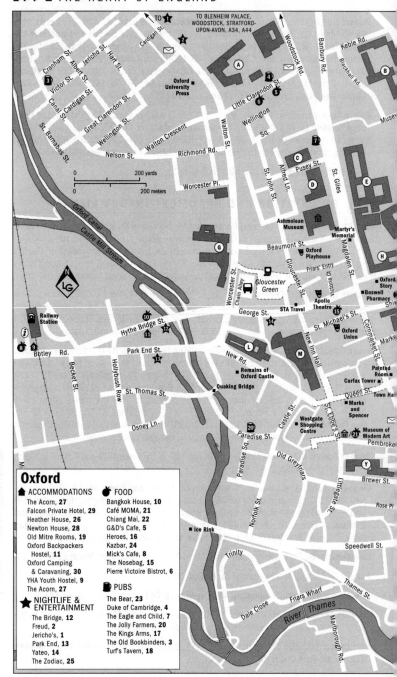

TO BLENHEIM PALACE, WOODSTOCK, STRATFORD-UPON-AVON, A34, A44

Oxford University Press

Oxford Canal

Castle Mill Stream

Railway Station

Ashmolean Museum

Martyr's Memorial

Oxford Playhouse

Friars' Entry

Gloucester Green

STA Travel

Apollo Theatre

Oxford Story

Boswell Pharmacy

Oxford Union

Remains of Oxford Castle

Quaking Bridge

Painted Room

Carfax Tower

Town Hall

Marks and Spencer

Westgate Shopping Centre

Museum of Modern Art

Pembroke

Ice Rink

River Thames

Oxford

▲ ACCOMMODATIONS
The Acorn, **27**
Falcon Private Hotel, **29**
Heather House, **26**
Newton House, **28**
Old Mitre Rooms, **19**
Oxford Backpackers
 Hostel, **11**
Oxford Camping
 & Caravaning, **30**
YHA Youth Hostel, **9**
The Acorn, **27**

★ NIGHTLIFE & ENTERTAINMENT
The Bridge, **12**
Freud, **2**
Jericho's, **1**
Park End, **13**
Yateo, **14**
The Zodiac, **25**

● FOOD
Bangkok House, **10**
Café MOMA, **21**
Chiang Mai, **22**
G&D's Cafe, **5**
Heroes, **16**
Kazbar, **24**
Mick's Cafe, **8**
The Nosebag, **15**
Pierre Victoire Bistrot, **6**

● PUBS
The Bear, **23**
Duke of Cambridge, **4**
The Eagle and Child, **7**
The Jolly Farmers, **20**
The Kings Arms, **17**
The Old Bookbinders, **3**
Turf's Tavern, **18**

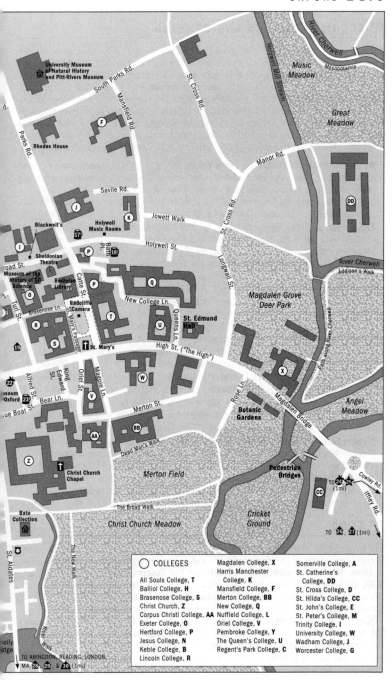

University Museum of Natural History and Pitt-Rivers Museum

South Parks Rd.

St. Cross Rd.

Music Meadow

Mesopotamia

Great Meadow

Parks Rd.

Rhodes House

Mansfield Rd.

Manor Rd.

Savile Rd.

F

J

K

Jowett Walk

St. Cross Rd.

DD

Blackwell's

Holywell Music Rooms

17

Holywell St.

River Cherwell
Addison's Walk

I

Sheldonian Theatre

P

18

Bath Pl.

road St.

Museum of the History of Science

O

Bodleian Library

Catte St.

P

Q

New College Ln.

Magdalen Grove Deer Park

Turf St.

Radcliffe Camera

Mary's Passage

T

U

Queens Ln.

St. Edmund Hall

Longwall St.

Brasenose Ln.

R

S

St. Mary's

High St. ("The High")

Path along River Cherwell

19

Alfred St.

22

useum Oxford

23

King Edward St.

W

V

Magpie Ln.

X

Angel Meadow

Bear Ln.

ue Boar St.

Oriel St.

Merton St.

Rose Ln.

Magdalen Bridge

Z

AA

BB

Dead Man's Walk

Botanic Gardens

Christ Church Chapel

Merton Field

Pedestrian Bridges

TO 24 25 (1mi)

Cowley Rd.

Iffley Rd.

CC

Bate Collection

The Broad Walk

Christ Church Meadow

Cricket Ground

TO 26 27 (1mi)

St. Aldates

The New Walk

River Walk

olly dge

TO ABINGDON, READING, LONDON, M4, 28 29 & 30 (1mi)

○ **COLLEGES**

All Souls College, **T**
Balliol College, **H**
Brasenose College, **S**
Christ Church, **Z**
Corpus Christi College, **AA**
Exeter College, **O**
Hertford College, **P**
Jesus College, **N**
Keble College, **B**
Lincoln College, **R**

Magdalen College, **X**
Harris Manchester College, **K**
Mansfield College, **F**
Merton College, **BB**
New College, **Q**
Nuffield College, **L**
Oriel College, **V**
Pembroke College, **Y**
The Queen's College, **U**
Regent's Park College, **C**

Somerville College, **A**
St. Catherine's College, **DD**
St. Cross College, **D**
St. Hilda's College, **CC**
St. John's College, **E**
St. Peter's College, **M**
Trinity College, **I**
University College, **W**
Wadham College, **J**
Worcester College, **G**

⌐ ACCOMMODATIONS AND CAMPING

Book at least a week ahead from June to September, especially for singles, and be prepared to mail in a deposit or give a credit card number. B&Bs line the main roads out of town and are reachable by bus (or a 15-45min. walk for the energetic). The 300s on Banbury Rd. north of town are reachable by buses #2A, 2C, and 2D. Cheaper B&Bs lie in the 200s and 300s on Iffley Rd. (buses #3 or 4 to "Rose Hill"), and on Abingdon Rd. in South Oxford (bus #16). Wherever you go, expect to pay at least £25 per person. If it's late and you're homeless, call the **Oxford Association of Hotels and Guest Houses** at one of the following numbers: ☎721 561 (East Oxford), ☎862 280 (West Oxford), ☎554 374 (North Oxford), or ☎244 268 (South Oxford).

Oxford Backpackers Hostel, 9a Hythe Bridge St. (☎721 761). Between the bus and train stations, this lively independent hostel nurtures the best of backpacker social life with an inexpensive bar, pool table, constant music, and colorful murals. Linens provided, but no towels. Laundry facilities (£2) and Internet access (£1 per 15min.). Guests must show passport. Dorms £12. ❷

YHA Oxford, 2a Botley Rd. (☎727 275; fax 769 402). An immediate right from the train station onto Botley Rd. Superb location and bright surroundings. Generous rooms and facilities include kitchen, breakfast, lockers (£1) and lockable wardrobes in every room, towels (£1), laundry (£3), Internet (50p per 10min.), and 24hr. security. 4- and 6-bed dorms £18.50, under 18 £13.50; twins £41; families £51-92. Students £1 off. ❷

Heather House, 192 Iffley Rd. (☎/fax 249 757). A 20min. walk from Magdalen Bridge, or take the bus marked "Rose Hill" from the bus or train stations or Carfax Tower. Proprietress Vivian offers sparkling, modern rooms and valuable advice. TV, phone, coffee, and tea in every room. Singles and doubles £33 per person. Lower for longer stays. ❹

Falcon Private Hotel, 88/90 Abingdon Rd (☎511 122). A great place to nest while exploring Oxford. Recently refurbished with an impressive slew of conveniences: TV, phone, alarm clock, shower, tea/coffee. Singles £36; twins £56; doubles £58-68. ❹

The Acorn, 260 Iffley Rd. (☎247 998). ¼ mi. east of Heather House. Limited amenities explain lovely price. Singles £29; doubles and twins £52, with bath £58; triples £72. ❸

Old Mitre Rooms, 4b Turl St. (☎279 800; fax 279 963), between Mahogany hair salon and Past Times Stationery. Lincoln College dorms. Open July to Sept. Especially packed during weekends, so book ahead. Singles £27; doubles and triples also available. ❸

Newton House, 82-84 Abingdon Rd. (☎240 561), ½ mi. from town. Take any Abingdon bus across Folly Bridge. Affable proprietress and dark wardrobes await Narnia fans. Recently renovated; all rooms have TV and phone. Doubles £58-64; twins £66. ❹

Camping: Oxford Camping and Caravaning, 426 Abingdon Rd. (☎244 088, 8:30am-8pm), behind the Touchwoods camping store. Toilet and laundry facilities. £3.80-5 per person; nonmember charge £4.50. 3-night max. stay for backpackers. ❶

◖ FOOD

The proprietors of Oxford's swank, bulging eateries know they have a captive market: students fed up with fetid college food are easily seduced by a bevy of budget options. If you're cooking for yourself, try the **Covered Market** (open M-Sa 8am-5:30pm) between Market St. and Carfax, which has fresh produce, deli goods, breads, and even shoe leather. **⊠Gloucester Green Market** (open W 6am-3:30pm) abounds with tasty treats, well-priced wares, and fabulous trinkets.

Across Magdalen Bridge, cheap restaurants along the first four blocks of Cowley Rd. serve Chinese, Lebanese, and Polish food, as well as good ol' fish 'n' chips. Try the funky **Hi-Lo Jamaican Eating House,** 70 Cowley Rd. (☎725 984) or the Bangladeshi cuisine of **Dhaka,** 186 Cowley Rd. (☎202 011). Near Somerville College, seek out **Jamal's Tandoori Restaurant,** 108 Walton St. (☎310 102). Keep an eye out for after-hours **kebab vans,** usually at Broad St., High St., Queen St., and St. Aldates.

Kazbar, 25-27 Cowley Rd. (☎202 920). This newly opened tapas bar is a local favorite. Spanish-style decor and mood lighting create a posh atmosphere, and cozy bench seating lines large windows. Tasty tapas (£2-4.50); try the Patatas con Chorizo. £5 lunch deal includes 2 tapas and drink (M-F noon-4pm). ❶

The Nosebag, 6-8 St. Michael's St. (☎721 033). Cafeteria-style service in a 15th-century stone building, with great vegan and vegetarian options and tasty homemade soups. Lunch under £6.50, dinner under £8. Open M-Th 9:30am-10pm, F-Sa 9:30am-10:30pm, Su 9:30am-9pm. **The Saddlebag Cafe** on the ground floor sells sandwiches and salads (£3-5.25). Open M-Su 9:30am-5:30pm, sandwiches served until 5pm. ❷

Chiang Mai, 130a High St. (☎202 233), tucked in an alley; look for the small blue sign. Broad Thai menu in half-timbered surroundings. Adventurous? Try the jungle curry with wild rabbit (£7). Appetizers £5-7, entrees £7-10. Open M-Sa noon-2pm and 6-11pm, Su noon-1pm and 6-10pm. F-Sa seatings at 6 and 9pm; reservations recommended. ❷

Bangkok House, 42a Hythe Bridge St. (☎200 705), has an outdoor feel with carved roof eaves, candles, fresh flowers, and a noisy crowd. Entrees £5.50-9. Beware: prawn crackers on your table are not complimentary. Open M-Sa noon-3pm and 5:30-11pm. ❷

G&D's Cafe, 55 Little Clarendon St. (☎516 652). Superb ice cream and sorbet (£1.65-3.45), tasty pizza bagels (£2.40-4), and their incongruous intersection— ice cream bagels. All served in a boisterous atmosphere. Open daily 8am-midnight. ❶

Mick's Cafe, Cripley Rd. (☎728 693), off Botley Rd. next to the train station. A little diner with big breakfasts of bigger value. Combination platters (choice of eggs, sausage, bacon, beans, toast, and more for £1.20-5) and a distinct ambience (murals of the staff) make Mick's popular with locals and students. Open M-F 6am-2pm, Sa 7am-1pm, Su 8am-1pm. ❶

Heroes Sandwich Bar, 8 Ship St. (☎723 459). Where students dine on sandwiches, freshly baked breads, and a plethora of fillings (£1.90-3.65). Best for takeaway, but there's a small eat-in area. Open M-F 8am-9pm, Sa 8:30am-6pm, Su 10am-5pm. ❶

Café MOMA, 30 Pembroke St. (☎813 814), under the Museum of Modern Art. What regulars call the "taste of Oxford." Features an almost entirely vegetarian menu, with delicious salads, quiches, and soups in an informal, family-friendly setting. Desserts £1.10-2.50. Open Tu-Sa 11am-6pm, Su noon-5:30pm. ❷

THE BIG SPLURGE

PIERRE VICTOIRE BISTROT

With its quaint brick walls, French countryside furniture, and warm candle lighting, the cozy **Pierre Victoire Bistrot,** 9 Little Clarendon St., offers the perfect ambience for a relaxed night of fine French dining. The people are friendly, the service is superb, and the delicious food is the epitome of gourmet.

Specials change daily, but the chef's whims are certain to satisfy the most discriminating of tastebuds. The lunch menu features 1 course for £5.90, 2 for £6.90, and 3 for £7.90. At dinner, appetizers run £2-5 and entrees are £7-17. A special pre-theater dinner is available Su-Th for a reasonable £7.90. But it's the desserts that will have you drooling even after your meal, with sorbets and cakes topping the menu. Try the vanilla crème brûlée (£3.50). Champagne, at £16.50 per bottle, is the appropriate accompaniment to a luxurious evening.

The restaurant is bustling even on weekdays, so it may be a good idea to make reservations. (☎316 616. Open M-Sa noon-2:30pm and 6-11pm, Su noon-3:30pm and 6-10pm.)

PUBS

Pubs far outnumber colleges in Oxford—some even consider them the city's prime attraction. Most open by noon, begin to fill around 5pm, and close at 11pm (10:30pm on Sundays). Food is sometimes served only during lunch and dinner hours (roughly noon-2pm and 6-8pm). Be ready to pub crawl—many pubs are so small that a single band of merry students will squeeze out other patrons, while just around the corner, others have several spacious rooms.

Turf's Tavern, 4 Bath Pl. (☎243 235), off Holywell St. Arguably the most popular student bar in Oxford (they call it "the Turf"), this 13th-century pub is tucked in the alley of an alley, against ruins of the city wall. Choose from 11 ales. Open M-Sa 11am-11pm, Su noon-10:30pm; hot food served in back room noon-7:30pm.

The Old Bookbinders, 17/18 Victor St. (☎553 549), walk up Walton St., left on Jericho St. until Victor St. This crowded little pub features low ceilings, a young crowd, and lots of noise. Occasional beer fests feature over 25 ales. Open M-Sa until 11pm.

Duke of Cambridge, 5-6 Little Clarendon St. (☎558 173). Oxford's choice cocktail lounge, where sophisticated decor gets lost in the buzz of happy hour bliss. Cocktails (£3.25-5) half-off during happy hour (daily 5-8:30pm), after which the bar empties out. Open M-F noon-11pm, Sa 10am-11pm, Su 10am-10:30pm.

The Bear, 6 Alfred St. (☎728 164). Over 5000 neckties from famous patrons and Oxford students cover nearly every flat surface of this tiny pub, established in 1242. During the day, the clients are older than the neckwear, and the young sit out back. Open M-Sa noon-11pm, Su noon-10:30pm.

The Kings Arms, 40 Holywell St. (☎242 369). Oxford's unofficial student union. The coffee room at the front lets quieter folk avoid the merry masses at the back. Open M-Sa 10:30am-11pm, Su 10:30am-10:30pm; coffee bar closes 5:30pm.

The Eagle and Child, 49 St. Giles (☎302 925). One of Oxford's most historic pubs, this archipelago of paneled alcoves welcomed C.S. Lewis and J.R.R. Tolkien. *The Chronicles of Narnia* and *The Hobbit* were first read aloud here. Beer £2.50. Open M-Sa 11am-11pm, Su 11am-10:30pm; food served noon-2:30pm and 5-7:30pm.

The Jolly Farmers, 20 Paradise St. (☎793 759). One of Oxfordshire's first gay and lesbian pubs. Crowded with students and twentysomethings, especially on weekends; significantly more sedate in the student-free summer. Steamy pictures of chiseled men grace the walls. Open M-Sa noon-11pm, Su noon-10:30pm.

◉ SIGHTS

Oxford first earned its name as a place where oxen could ford the Thames, and two of **Oxford University's** famous sons, Lewis Carroll and C.S. Lewis, later sat near the stone-bridged waters of the Isis (as the Thames is known here) dreaming of crossings through mirrors and wardrobes. The university has also been a breeding ground for England's leaders. Christ Church College alone has produced 13 prime ministers, while St. John's College was home to collegiate rocker Tony Blair.

The TIC sells a map (£1) and the *Welcome to Oxford* guide (£1) listing the colleges' visiting hours, but these can be rescinded without explanation or notice. Some colleges charge admission. Don't bother trying to sneak into Christ Church outside opening hours, even after hiding your backpack and copy of *Let's Go:* bouncers sporting bowler hats (affectionately known as "bulldogs") and stationed 50 ft. apart will squint their eyes and kick you out. Other colleges have been found less vigilant near the back gates. Coddle the porters or you will get nowhere.

OXFORD MADE EASY Oxford undergraduates study for three years, each year consisting of three eight-week terms; more time is spent on holiday than at school. The university itself has no official, central campus. Though central facilities—libraries, laboratories, and faculties—are maintained by the university, Oxford's independent colleges, where students live and learn simultaneously (at least in theory), are scattered throughout the city. Students dress in formal wear called **sub fusc** for all official university events, including exams; carnations are obligatory. At the end of their last academic year, students from all the colleges assemble for degree examinations, a grueling three-week ordeal in the Examination Schools on High St. in late June and early July. Each year university authorities do their best to quell the vigorous post-examination celebrations. Each year they fail. The authorities, that is.

CHRIST CHURCH COLLEGE

Just down St. Aldates St. from Carfax. ☎ *286 573. Open M-Sa 9:30am-5:30pm, Su noon-5:30pm; in winter closes at 4:30pm. Chapel services are Su 8, 10, 11:15am, and 6pm; weekdays 7:15, 7:35am, 1, and 6pm. £4, concessions £3.*

An intimidating pile of stone, "The House" has Oxford's grandest quad and its most socially distinguished students. Charles I made Christ Church his capital for three and a half years during the Civil Wars, escaping dressed as a servant when the city was besieged. Charles Dodgson first met Alice, the dean's daughter, here; today, the dining hall and Tom Quad serve as shooting locations for the Harry Potter films. In June, hush while navigating the narrow strip open to tourists, lest you be rebuked by irritable undergrads prepping for exams.

CHRIST CHURCH CHAPEL. In AD 730, Oxford's patron saint, St. Frideswide, built a nunnery here in honor of two miracles: the blinding of a troublesome suitor and his subsequent recovery. A stained-glass window (c. 1320) depicts Thomas à Becket kneeling moments before being gorily dispatched in Canterbury Cathedral. A rather incongruous toilet floats in the background of a window showing St. Frideswide's death; the White Rabbit frets in the stained glass of the hall.

TOM QUAD. The site of undergraduate lily-pond dunking, Tom Quad adjoins the chapel grounds. The quad takes its name from Great Tom, the seven-ton bell in Tom Tower, which has faithfully rung 101 strokes (the original number of students) at 9:05pm (the original undergraduate curfew) every evening since 1682. Nearby, the fan-vaulted college hall displays portraits of some of Christ Church's most famous alums—Sir Philip Sidney, William Penn, John Ruskin, John Locke, and a bored-looking W.H. Auden in a corner by the kitchen.

OTHER SIGHTS. Through an archway (to your left as you face the cathedral) lie **Peckwater Quad** and the most elegant Palladian building in Oxford. Look here for faded rowing standings chalked on the walls and for Christ Church's library, closed to visitors. Spreading east and south from the main entrance, **Christ Church Meadow** compensates for Oxford's lack of "backs" (the riverside gardens in Cambridge). Housed in the Canterbury Quad, the **Christ Church Picture Gallery** is a swell collection of Italian, Dutch, and Flemish paintings, starring Tintoretto and Vermeer. *(Enter on Oriel Sq. and at Canterbury Gate; visitors to the gallery only should enter through Canterbury Gate off Oriel St.* ☎ *276 172. Open Apr.-Sept. M-Sa 10:30am-1pm and 2-5:30pm, Su 2-5:30pm; Oct.-Mar. closes at 4:30pm. £2, concessions £1.)*

HEART OF ENGLAND

OTHER COLLEGES

MERTON COLLEGE. Merton has a fine garden and a library housing the first printed Welsh Bible. Tolkien lectured here, inventing the language of Elvish in his spare time. The college's **Mob Quad** is Oxford's oldest and least impressive, dating from the 14th century, but nearby **St. Alban's Quad** has some of the university's best gargoyles. Residents of Crown Prince Narahito's native Japan visit daily to identify the rooms he inhabited in his Merton days. *(Merton St. ☎ 276 310. Open to tours only, M-F 2-4pm, Sa-Su 10am-4pm. Free.)*

UNIVERSITY COLLEGE. This 1249 soot-blackened college vies with Merton for the title of oldest, claiming Alfred the Great as its founder. Percy Bysshe Shelley was expelled for writing the pamphlet *The Necessity of Atheism* but has since been immortalized in a prominent monument, to the right as you enter. Bill Clinton spent his Rhodes days here; his rooms at 46 Leckford Rd. are a tour guide's endless source of smoked-but-didn't-inhale jokes. *(High St. ☎ 276 676. Open to tours only.)*

ORIEL AND CORPUS CHRISTI COLLEGES. Oriel College (a.k.a. "The House of the Blessed Mary the Virgin in Oxford") is wedged between High St. and Merton St. and was once the turf of Sir Walter Raleigh. *(☎ 276 555. Open to tours only, daily 2-5pm. Free.)* South of Oriel, **Corpus Christi College,** the smallest of Oxford's colleges, surrounds a sundialed quad. The garden wall reveals a gate built for visits between Charles I and his queen, residents at adjacent Christ Church and Merton during the Civil Wars. *(☎ 276 693. Open to tours only, daily 1:30-4:30pm. Free.)*

ALL SOULS COLLEGE. Only Oxford's best are admitted to this prestigious graduate college. Candidates who survive the admission exams are invited to dinner, where it is ensured that they are "well-born, well-bred, and only moderately learned." All Souls is also reported to have the most heavenly wine cellar in the city. **The Great Quad,** with its fastidious lawn and two spare spires, may be Oxford's most serene. *(Corner of High St. and Catte St. ☎ 279 379. Open M-F 2-4pm; closed Aug. Free.)*

QUEEN'S COLLEGE. Around since 1341, Queen's was rebuilt by Wren and Hawksmoor in the 17th and 18th centuries in the distinctive Queen Anne style. A trumpet call summons students to dinner, where a boar's head graces the table at Christmas. The latter tradition supposedly commemorates an early student who, attacked by a boar on the outskirts of Oxford, choked his assailant to death with a volume of Aristotle. Alumni include starry-eyed Edmund Halley, the more earthly Jeremy Bentham, and the celebrated Mr. Bean. *(High St. ☎ 279 121. Open only to tours.)*

MAGDALEN COLLEGE. With extensive grounds and flower-laced quads, Magdalen (MAUD-lin) is considered Oxford's handsomest college. The college boasts a deer park flanked by the Cherwell and Addison's Walk, a circular path that touches the river's opposite bank. The college's decadent spiritual patron is alumnus Oscar Wilde. *(On High St. near the Cherwell. ☎ 276 000. Open daily noon-6pm. £3, concessions £2.)*

TRINITY COLLEGE. Founded in 1555, Trinity has a splendid Baroque chapel with a limewood altarpiece, cedar lattices, and cherubim-spotted pediments. The college's series of eccentric presidents includes Ralph Kettell, who would come to dinner with a pair of scissors and chop anyone's hair that he deemed too long. *(Broad St. ☎ 279 900. Open daily 10am-noon and 2-4pm. £1.50.)*

BALLIOL COLLEGE. Students at Balliol preserve the semblance of tradition by hurling abuse over the wall at their conservative Trinity College rivals. Matthew Arnold, Gerard Manley Hopkins, Aldous Huxley, and Adam Smith were all sons of Balliol's mismatched spires. The interior gates of the college bear scorch marks from the immolations of 16th-century Protestant martyrs and a mulberry tree planted by Elizabeth I still shades slumbering students. *(Broad St. ☎ 277 777. Open daily 2-5pm during term, Su only in summer. £1, students and children free.)*

NEW COLLEGE. This is the self-proclaimed first *real* college of Oxford; it is here William of Wykeham in 1379 dreamed up a college that would offer a comprehensive undergraduate education under one roof. The bell tower has gargoyles of the Seven Deadly Sins on one side, the Seven Virtues on the other, all equally grotesque. Former warden Rev. William Spooner is remembered as the inventor of "spoonerisms"; he rebuked a student who had "hissed all the mystery lectures" and "tasted the whole worm." *(New College Ln. ☎ 279 555. Open daily Easter to mid-Oct. 11am-5pm; Nov.-Easter 2-4pm, use the Holywell St. Gate. £1.50 in the summer, free otherwise.)*

SOMERVILLE COLLEGE. Somerville is Oxford's most famous once-women's college, with alumnae including Indira Gandhi and Margaret Thatcher, though women were not granted degrees at all until 1920—Cambridge held out until 1948. Today, all of Oxford's colleges are coed except St. Hilda's, which remains women-only. *(Woodstock Rd. From Carfax, head down Cornmarket St. which becomes Magdalen St., St. Giles, and finally Woodstock Rd. ☎ 270 600. Open daily 2-5:30pm. Free.)*

OTHER SIGHTS

▓ASHMOLEAN MUSEUM. The grand Ashmolean, the finest collection of arts and antiquities outside London, was Britain's first public museum when it opened in 1683. It houses sketches by Michelangelo and Raphael, the gold coin of Constantine, and the Alfred Jewel, as well as works by favorites da Vinci, Monet, Manet, van Gogh, Rodin, and Matisse. Greek pottery, Roman jewelry, and Egyptian artifacts are stunning. *(Beaumont St. ☎ 278 000. Themed tours £1.50. Open Tu-Sa 10am-5pm, Su 2-5pm. Th open until 7:30pm in summer. Free.)*

BODLEIAN LIBRARY. Oxford's principal reading and research library has over five million books and 50,000 manuscripts, and receives a copy of every book printed in Great Britain. Sir Thomas Bodley endowed the library's first wing in 1602—the institution has since grown to fill the immense **Old Library** complex, the **Radcliffe Camera** next door, and two newer buildings on Broad St. Admission to the reading rooms is by ticket only. If you can prove you're a scholar (a student ID may be sufficient, but a letter of introduction from your college is encouraged), present two passport photos, and promise not to light any fires, the Admissions Office will issue a two-day pass (£3). No one has ever been permitted to take out a book, not even Cromwell. Well, especially not Cromwell. *(Catte St. ☎ 277 224. Library open M-F 9am-6pm, Sa 9am-1pm. Tours leave from the Divinity School, across the street; in summer M-F 4 per day, Sa 2 per day; in winter 2 per day. Tours £3.50.)*

SHELDONIAN THEATRE. This Roman-style auditorium was designed by a teen-aged Christopher Wren. Graduation ceremonies, conducted in Latin, take place in the Sheldonian, as do everything from student recitals to world-class opera performances. *The Red Violin* and *Quills*, as well as numerous other movies, were filmed here. Climb up to the cupola for an inspiring view of Oxford's scattered quads. The ivy-crowned stone heads on the fence behind the Sheldonian do not represent emperors: they are a 20th-century study of beards. *(Broad St. ☎ 277 299. Open roughly M-Sa 10am-12:30pm and 2-4:30pm; in winter, until 3:30pm. £1.50, under 15 £1. Purchase tickets for shows (£15) from Oxford Playhouse.)*

BLACKWELL'S BOOKSTORE. Guinness lists it as the largest four-walled space devoted to bookselling anywhere in the world; the staff boasts of six miles of bookshelves. The basement room swallows the building and underpins the foundations of Trinity College next door. *(53 Broad St. ☎ 333 606. Open M and W-Sa 9am-6pm, Tu 9:30am-6pm, Su 11am-5pm.)*

CARFAX TOWER. The tower marks the center or the original city. A hike up its 99 (very) narrow spiral stairs affords a fantastic city vista from the only present-day remnant of medieval St. Martin's Church. *(Corner of Queen St. and Cornmarket St. ☎ 792 653. Open Apr.-Oct. M-Sa 10am-5pm, Su 11am-5pm, weather permitting. £1.20, under 16 60p.)*

THE BOTANIC GARDEN. Green and growing things have flourished for three centuries here in the oldest botanic garden in the British Isles. The path connecting the garden to Christ Church Meadow provides a view of the Thames and cricket grounds on the opposite bank. *(From Carfax, head down High St.; the Garden is on the right. ☎ 286 690. Open Apr.-Sept. daily 9am-5pm; Oct.-Mar. 9am-4:30pm. Glasshouses open daily 10am-4pm. Last admission 4:15pm. Apr.-Aug. £2, children free; free the rest of the year.)*

THE MUSEUM OF OXFORD. From hands-on exhibits to a murderer's skeleton, the museum provides an in-depth, if self-congratulatory, look at Oxford's birth and growth. *(St. Aldates. Enter at corner of St. Aldates and Blue Boar. ☎ 252 761. Open Tu-F 10am-4:30pm, Sa 10am-5pm, Su noon-4pm. £2, concessions £1.50, children 50p.)*

THE OXFORD STORY. This painfully slow-moving ride hauls visitors in medievalized seats through dioramas that recreate Oxford's 800-year past. Share the pleasures of a 13th-century student making merry with a wench. *(6 Broad St. ☎ 728 822. 45min. ride. Open July-Aug. daily 9:30am-5pm; Sept.-June M-Sa 10am-4:30pm, Su 11am-4:30pm. £6.50, concessions £5.50.)*

BEST OF THE REST. Behind the **University Museum of Natural History** *(Parks Rd.; ☎ 272 950; open daily noon-5pm; free)*, the **Pitt-Rivers Museum** has an eclectic archaeology and anthropology collection, including shrunken heads, rare butterflies, and bong-like artifacts. *(☎ 270 927. Open M-Sa noon-4:30pm, Su 2-4:30pm. Free.)* The **Museum of the History of Science** recently reopened after a three-year refurbishing, and boasts countless clocks and astrolabes, as well as Einstein's blackboard. *(Broad St. ☎ 277 280. Call for hours and tours, £1.50. Admission free.)* The **Museum of Modern Art** hosts solid international shows. *(30 Pembroke St. ☎ 722 733. Open Tu-W and F-Sa 11am-5:30-pm, Th 11am-8pm, Su noon-5:30pm. £2.50, concessions £1.50, under 16 free. Free to all Th.)* The **Bate Collection of Historical Instruments** rests in the Faculty of Music. *(St. Aldates St., before Folly Bridge. ☎ 276 139. Open M-F 2-5pm. Free.)*

▨ CLUBS

Like pubs, public transit in Oxford shuts down sometime after 11pm, but nightlife can last until 3am. After happy hour at the pubs, head up **Walton St.** or down **Cowley Rd.** for late-night clubs and a jumble of ethnic restaurants and exotic shops.

Freud, 119 Walton St. (☎ 311 171). In former St. Paul's Church. Cafe by day, collegiate cocktail bar by night. Open M-Tu until midnight, W-Th 1am, F-Sa 2am, Su 10:30pm.

The Zodiac, 190 Cowley Rd. (☎ 420 042). Big dance floor, with crazy themes nightly and the city's best live gigs. Headliners have included Rage Against the Machine and Dido. Cover £4-10. Closes at 2am.

Jericho's (☎ 311 775), on Walton St., north of Freud. Casual and cozy, with 2 pool tables and cheery lighting. Open M-Sa until 11pm, Su 10:30pm.

Park End, on Park End St., is a flashy student and local favorite, cranking out commercial techno and house on 3 floors. Smart clubwear, please. Cover £2-8.

Yates, 41-43 George St. (☎ 723 790), features a chic crowd that mingles by the bar. Tu karaoke 8:30-11pm. Licensed to serve alcohol past 11pm; open M-W until 11pm, Th 1am, F-Sa 2am, Su midnight.

The Bridge (☎ 242 526), on Hythe Bridge St. Erratically frequented by big student crowds. Cover £5-7.

🎭 ENTERTAINMENT

Check *This Month in Oxford* (free at the TIC) for upcoming events. *Daily Information*, posted in the TIC, most colleges, some hostels, and online (www.dailyinfo.co.uk) provides pointers.

Music: Centuries of tradition give Oxford a quality music scene. Attend a concert or an Evensong service at a college—**New College Choir** is one of the best boy choirs around. Performances at the **Holywell Music Rooms** (on Holywell St.) are worth checking out; **Oxford Coffee Concerts** feature renowned musicians and ensembles every Su. Call Oxford Playhouse (below) for tickets (£6-7). The **City of Oxford Orchestra**, the professional symphony orchestra, plays a subscription series at the Sheldonian and in college chapels during summer. (☎744 457. Tickets £12-18.) The **Apollo Theatre**, George St. (☎(0870) 606 3500), features a wide range of performances, from lounge-lizard jazz to musicals to the Welsh National Opera. Tickets from £10; student and senior discounts.

Theaters: The **Oxford Playhouse**, 11-12 Beaumont St. (☎798 600) hosts amateur and professional plays as well as music and dance performances. Box office opens M-Tu and Th-F at 9:30am, W at 10am, and closes after curtain. The playhouse also sells tickets at an 85% discount for venues all over city (☎305 305; www.ticketsoxford.com). The **Oxford Union**, St. Michael's St. (☎778 119), puts up substantial theater productions. Tickets £8, concessions £5. The university itself offers marvelous entertainment; college theater groups often stage productions in gardens or cloisters.

Punting: A traditional pastime in Oxford is **punting** on the Isis or the Cherwell (CHARwul). Before venturing out, punters receive a tall pole, a small oar, and an advisory against falling into the river. Our own advisories: avoid creating an obstacle course for irate rowers and don't be surprised if you come upon **Parson's Pleasure**, a riverside area where men sometimes sunbathe nude. **Magdalen Bridge Boat Co.**, Magdalen Bridge (☎202 643), is just under the bridge (follow the ice cream sign) and rents M-F £9 per hr., Sa-Su £10 per hr. Deposit £20 plus ID. Open Mar.-Nov. daily 10am-9pm.

Festivals: The university celebrates **Eights Week** at the end of May, when the colleges enter crews in bumping races and beautiful people sip pim (a liqueur mixed with lemonade) on the banks. In early September, **St. Giles Fair** invades one of Oxford's main streets with an old-fashioned carnival. Daybreak on **May Day** (May 1) cues one of Oxford's sweetest moments: the Magdalen College Choir sings madrigals from the top of the tower, and the town indulges in morris dancing, beating the bounds, and other age-old rituals of merry men—pubs open at 7am.

🏰 DAYTRIP FROM OXFORD: BLENHEIM PALACE

In the town of Woodstock, 8 mi. north of Oxford. Stagecoach (☎772 250) bus #20 runs to Blenheim Palace from Gloucester Green bus station (30-40min., every 30min. 8:15am-5pm, return £3.60). ☎(01993) 811 091. House open mid-Mar. to Oct. daily 10:30am-5:30pm. Last admission 4:45pm. Grounds open year-round 9am-9pm. £10, concessions £7.50, children £5, families £26. Free tours every 5-10min.

The largest private home in England (and one of the loveliest), Blenheim Palace (BLEN-em) was built in honor of the Duke of Marlborough's victory over Louis XIV at the 1704 Battle of Blenheim. The 11th Duke of Marlborough now calls the palace home. His rent is a single French franc, payable each year to the Crown—not a bad deal for 187 furnished rooms. High archways and marble floors accentuate the artwork inside, including wall-size tapestries of 17th- and 18th-century battle scenes. Winston Churchill, a member of the Marlborough family, spent his early years here before being packed off to boarding school; he returned to propose to his wife, and now rests in the nearby village churchyard of **Bladon**. The grounds consist of 2100 glorious acres, circumscribing fantastic gardens, roaming sheep, and a lake, all designed by landscaper **"Capability" Brown** (well, except the sheep—he wasn't *that* capable). Blenheim is on display in Kenneth Branagh's 4hr. film of *Hamlet* (1996); less recently, Geoffrey Chaucer lived in neighboring Woodstock.

STRATFORD-UPON-AVON ☎ 01789

The remarkable thing about Shakespeare is that he is really very good—in spite of all the people who say he is very good.
— Robert Graves, British poet and novelist

Shakespeare lived here. This fluke of fate has made Stratford-upon-Avon a major stop on the tourist superhighway. Knickknack huts hawk "Will Power" T-shirts, and proprietors tout the dozen-odd properties linked, however tenuously, to the Bard and his extended family. Though all the perfumes of Arabia may not sweeten the exhaust from tour buses, behind their sound and fury there still survives a town worthwhile in its own right for the grace of the weeping Avon and for the pin-drop of silence before a soliloquy in the Royal Shakespeare Theatre.

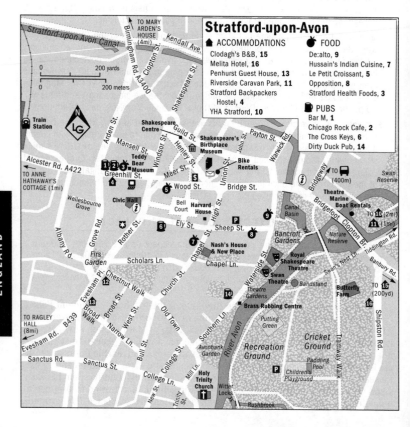

Stratford-upon-Avon

♦ ACCOMMODATIONS
Clodagh's B&B, **15**
Melita Hotel, **16**
Penhurst Guest House, **13**
Riverside Caravan Park, **11**
Stratford Backpackers
  Hostel, **4**
YHA Stratford, **10**

♦ FOOD
De:alto, **9**
Hussain's Indian Cuisine, **7**
Le Petit Croissant, **5**
Opposition, **8**
Stratford Health Foods, **3**

♦ PUBS
Bar M, **1**
Chicago Rock Cafe, **2**
The Cross Keys, **6**
Dirty Duck Pub, **14**

▆ HENCE, AWAY!

Trains: Station Rd., off Alcester Rd. Office open M-Sa 6:20am-8pm, Su 9:45am-6:30pm. **Thames Trains** (☎(08457) 484 950) from: **Birmingham** (1hr., every hr., £3.80); **London Paddington** (2¼hr., 7 per day, £22.50); **Warwick** (25min., 7 per day, £2.80).

Buses: Riverside Coach Park, off Bridgeway Rd. near the Leisure Centre. **National Express** (☎(08705) 808 080) from **London** (3hr., 3 per day, £12). Tickets at the TIC.

Public Transportation: Local **Stagecoach** bus services stop on Wood St. and Bridge St. from **Birmingham** (1hr.; M-Sa 9 per day, Su 6 per day; £5.50); **Coventry** (2hr., 3-4 per hr., £3-4); **Warwick** (20-40min., every hr., £2.55).

Taxis: 007 Taxis (☎414 007) or **Main Taxis** (☎415 514).

Bike Rental: Pashley's Store, Guild St. (☎205 057). Moulton bikes £10 per day, £5 per half-day. Open Tu-Sa 9am-5pm.

Boat Rental: Theatre Marine, Clopton Bridge (☎(07970) 289 114), rents rowboats (£7 per hr.) and motorboats (£12 per hr.). Open Apr.-Sept. daily 10am-7pm.

▋ WHO IS'T THAT CAN INFORM ME?

Tourist Information Centre: Bridgefoot (☎293 127). Maps, guidebooks, tickets, and accommodations list. Books rooms for £3 and 10% deposit. Open Apr.-Oct. M-Sa 9am-6pm, Su 10:30am-4:30pm; Nov.-Mar. M-Sa 9am-5pm. Another **branch** in the Civic Hall, 14 Rother St. (☎299 866).

Tours: 2hr. **walking tours** given by Shakespearean actors start at the Royal Shakespeare Centre (☎403 405). £6, concessions £5, children free. **Guide Friday,** Civic Hall, 14 Rother St. (☎294 466). Transport to Bard-related houses. 4-5 tours per hr. £8.50, concessions £7, children £3.50. Also to the **Cotswolds** (£17.50/£15/£8) and **Warwick Castle** (£17.50/£15/£8; castle admission included). Office open daily 9am-5:30pm.

Financial Services: Barclays, Market Cross (☎(08457) 555 555); open M-Tu and Th-F 9:30am-4:30pm, W 10am-4:30pm, Sa 9:30am-noon. **Thomas Cook,** 37 Wood St. (☎293 582); open M and W-Sa 9am-5:30pm, Tu 10am-5:30pm. **American Express** in the TIC (☎415 856; fax 262 411); same hours as TIC.

Launderette: Sparklean (☎269 075), corner of Bull St. and College Ln. Bring change. Wash £2.70-3.20, dry 20p per 4min or £1 per hr. Open daily 8am-9pm, last wash 8pm.

Police: Rother St. (☎414 111).

Hospital: Stratford-upon-Avon Hospital, Arden St. (☎205 831), off Alcester Rd.

Internet Access: Book days in advance for 30min. and 1hr. slots on 1 computer at the **Central Library,** 12 Henley St. (☎292 209). Open M and F 9:30am-7pm, Tu-W 9:30am-5:30pm, Th 9:30am-5pm, Sa 9:30am-4pm. **Cyber Junction,** 28 Greenhill St. (☎263 400). £3 per 30min., £5 per hr.; concessions £2.50/£4. Open M-Th and Sa 10am-5:30pm, F and Su 10am-5pm.

Post Office: 2-3 Henley St. (☎(08457) 223 344). **Bureau de change.** Open M-Tu 8:45am-6pm, W-Sa 9am-6pm. **Post Code:** CV37 6PU.

▐ TO SLEEP, PERCHANCE TO DREAM

To B&B or not to B&B? This hamlet has tons of them, but singles are hard to find. B&Bs in the £18-26 range line **Evesham Pl., Evesham Rd.,** and **Grove Rd.** Or try **Shipston Rd.** across the river, a 15-20min. walk from the station.

Stratford Backpackers Hostel, 33 Greenhill St. (☎/fax 263 838). 3-storey hostel for sociable pilgrims, near restaurants, pubs, and the Bard's birthplace. Lounge, pool table, TV room, kitchen, and storage. Photo ID required. Dorms £12. ❷

YHA Stratford, Wellesbourne Rd., Alveston (☎297 093; stratford@yha.org.uk), 2 mi. from Clopton Bridge. Follow the B4086 35min. from the town center, or take bus X18 from Bridge St. (10min., every hr., day return £2.30). Large, attractive grounds and a 200-year-old building with RSC photos. Includes B&B amenities like breakfast, and with bus fare costs nearly as much. Kitchen and Internet access (£2.50 per 30min.). Security on-duty after midnight lockout. Dorms £16, under 18 £11.75; dinner £5 extra. ❷

Clodagh's B&B, 34 Banbury Rd. (☎269 714; clodagh@lycosmail.com). Amazing value. Once Clodagh takes you in, you'll be tempted to stay longer than planned. Superb showers and free Internet. Only 2 rooms, so book early. Single £17; double £34. ❷

Melita Hotel, 37 Shipston Rd. (☎292 432). Upscale B&B with gorgeous garden and retreat-like atmosphere. Guests relax on the sunny patio. Singles £39; doubles £69. ❹

Penhurst Guest House, 34 Evesham Pl. (☎205 259), a 10min. walk down Evesham. The hallways may not be impressive, but the clean and smoke-free rooms are bright and spacious with comfortable beds. Singles £18-24; doubles £30-46. ❸

The Hollies, 16 Evesham Pl. (☎266 857). From mint walls to creeping ivy, green prevails. Hosted by a warm and attentive proprietor. Doubles £35, with bath £45. ❸

Camping: Riverside Caravan Park, Tiddington Rd. (☎292 312), 30min. east of town on the B4086. Sunset views on the Avon, but often crowded. Village pub is a 3-4min. walk. Showers. Open Easter-Oct. Tent and 2 people £8, each additional person £1. ❶

CRAZY AS A DANE

1999 marked the passing of David Sutch, founder of the **Official Monster Raving Loony Party (OMRLP).** Screaming Lord Sutch founded the OMRLP in 1980—a party initially dismissed as a "Shakespearean antic for the TV age," but one which enjoyed surprising success in the 1990 by-election, beating the Social Democrats in one whole constituency. Alan "Howling Lord" Hope fought for a parliament seat in 1999, while Baron von Thunderclap (previously the spokesman for transport, saving the dodo, and decimal time) has assumed temporary leadership. Oliver Hewitt—who at age 13 chained himself to the railings of Downing St., protesting the forcing of algebra on children—is being groomed to take over. Despite past hoopla, however, the only news today about the OMRLP is that it still exists.

🍴 FOOD OF LOVE

Baguette stores and bakeries are scattered like itinerant minstrels, while a **Safeway** supermarket beckons from Alcester Rd., past the train station and just across the bridge. (Open M-W and Sa 8am-9pm, Th-F 8am-10pm, Su 10am-4pm.)

Opposition, 13 Sheep St. (☎269 980), receives rave reviews from locals. Low 1500s-style ceilings and candles make for a classy-yet-cozy ambience. Try some lasagne (£8.50), lamb steak (£11.50), or grilled goat cheese and tomato salad (£8.65). Open M-Sa noon-2pm and 5-10pm, Su noon-2pm and 6-9pm. ❸

De:alto, 13 Waterside (☎298 326). A trendy anachronism in this historical town, De:alto's decor will make the New Yorker in you feel at home. Pizzas £5-7, salads and pastas £6-8. Open M-Th noon-10pm, F-Sa noon-11pm, Su 2-9:30pm. ❷

Hussain's Indian Cuisine, 6a Chapel St. (☎267 506). Stratford's best Indian menu, and a favorite of Ben Kingsley. A slew of tandoori prepared as you like it; the chicken tikka masala is fabulous. 3-course lunch £6. Main courses £6.50 and up. 15% discount for takeaway. Open M-W 5pm-midnight, Th-Su 12:30-2:30pm and 5pm-midnight. ❷

Le Petit Croissant, 17 Wood St. (☎ 292 333). A great place for breakfast or lunch, with delicious baked treats such as tarts, baguettes, croissants, and quiches (from 52p). Sandwiches are sold in back (£1.80-2.50). Open M-Sa 8am-6pm. ❶

Stratford Health Foods, 10 Greenhill St. (☎ 292 353). The "Whole Food Takeaway" includes vegan sausage rolls (49p), veggie samosas (57p), and "healthy" desserts like freshly baked brownies (65p). Open M-Sa 9am-5:30pm. ❶

DRINK DEEP ERE YOU DEPART

Bar M, 1 Arden St. (☎ 297 641). A pub by day; the silvered staircase leads to a clubby dance area at night. Various promotions, such as £1 drinks with £5 cover M and Th. Open M and Th noon-1am, Tu-W noon-midnight, F-Sa noon-2am.

Dirty Duck Pub, Waterside (☎ 297 312). Originally called "The Black Swan," but rechristened by alliterative Americans during WWII. River view outside, huge bust of Shakespeare within. Theater crowds abound, and the actors themselves make frequent entrances. Pub lunch £5; entrees £7-15. Open M-Sa 11am-11pm, Su noon-10pm.

The Cross Keys, Ely St. (☎ 293 909). Low-key locale for a quiet drink with friends. Open M-Sa 11am-11pm, Su 11am-10:30pm; food served noon-3pm.

Chicago Rock Cafe, 8 Greenhill St. (☎ 293 344). Modern and popular with locals; hosts tribute bands like Rolling Clones and Z U2. Specials most nights, like Tu "Sin Night" and Th half-price cocktails. Open Tu-Th 6pm-11:30pm, F-Sa 6pm-1am, Su 7pm-12:30am.

THE GILDED MONUMENTS

TO BARD...

Stratford's Will-centered sights are best seen before 11am, when the daytrippers arrive, or after 4pm, when the hurly-burly's done. Bardolatry peaks at 2pm. The five official **Shakespeare properties** are Shakespeare's Birthplace, Mary Arden's House, Nash's House & New Place, Hall's Croft, and Anne Hathaway's Cottage. Opening hours are listed by season: winter (Nov.-Mar.); midseason (Apr.-May and Sept.-Oct.); summer (June-Aug.). Diehards should get the **All Five Houses** ticket (☎ 204 016; £12, concessions £11, children £6, families £29). Those who don't want to visit every shrine can get a **Three In-Town Houses** pass, covering the Birthplace, Hall's Croft, and Nash's House & New Place (£8.50/£7.50/£4.20/£20).

SHAKESPEARE'S BIRTHPLACE. The only in-town sight directly associated with Him includes an exhibit on His father's glove-making, aside from the requisite life-and-works celebration. Join such distinguished pilgrims as Charles Dickens by signing the guestbook. *(Henley St. ☎ 204 016. Open winter M-Sa 10am-4pm and Su 10:30am-4pm; mid-season M-Sa 10am-5pm and Su 10:30am-5pm; summer M-Sa 9am-5pm and Su 9:30am-5pm. £6.50, concessions £5.50, children £2.50, families £15.)*

SHAKESPEARE'S GRAVE. The least crowded way to pay homage to the institution Himself is to visit His little, little grave inside the quiet, riverside **Holy Trinity Church**—though groups still pack the arched door at peak hours. Rumor has it that Shakespeare was buried 17 ft. underground by request, so that He would sleep undisturbed; a curse on the epitaph (said to be written by the man Himself) ensures skeletal safety. The church also harbors the graves of wife Anne and daughter Susanna. *(Trinity St. £1, students and children 50p.)*

HEART OF ENGLAND

MARY ARDEN'S HOUSE. This farmhouse in Wilmcote, 4 mi. from Stratford, was only recently determined to be Mary Arden's—originally, historians thought the more stately building next door was Shakespeare's rich mum's childhood home. A brief history recounts how Mary fell in love with Shakespeare, Sr. The house hosts two big events: **The Big Sheep Show** (second Su of June) features sheepdogs and sheep and **Apple Day** (first Su of Oct.) celebrates cider-making. *(Connected by footpath to Anne Hathaway's Cottage. ☎ 293 455. Open winter M-Sa 10am-4pm and Su 10:30am-4pm, mid-season M-Sa 10am-5pm and Su 10:30am-5pm; summer M-Sa 9:30am-5pm and Su 10am-5pm. £5.50, concessions £5, children £2.50, families £13.50.)*

NASH'S HOUSE AND NEW PLACE. Crazed tourists flock to the home of the first husband of Shakespeare's granddaughter Elizabeth, last of His descendants. Perhaps they're drawn to the fascinating local history collection of Nash's House. More likely, they want to see the adjacent **New Place,** Shakespeare's retirement home, and at the time Stratford's finest house. Today only the foundations remain—a disgruntled 19th-century owner named Gastrell razed the building to protest taxes. He was run out of town, and, to this day, Gastrells are not allowed in Stratford. *(Chapel St. Open winter M-Sa 11am-4pm and Su noon-4pm; mid-season daily 11am-5pm; summer M-Sa 9:30am-5pm and Su 10am-5pm. £3.50, concessions £3, children £1.70, families £8.50.)* Down Chapel St. from Nash's House, the sculpted hedges, manicured lawn, and abundant flowers of the **Great Garden of New Place** offer a peaceful respite from the mobbed streets. *(Open M-Sa 9am-dusk, Su 10am-dusk. Free.)*

AY, THERE'S THE RUB. Watching the serene rowers on the River Avon, you'd never guess that about six million buses rumble down the road behind you. In the free **Royal Shakespeare Theatre Gardens,** south of the theater, the RST Summer House runs a **brass-rubbing studio.** *(☎ 297 671. Open Apr.-Sept. daily 10am-6pm; Oct.-Mar. 11am-4pm. Rubbing plates 95p-£4 and higher; materials included.)*

HALL'S CROFT. Dr. John Hall married Shakespeare's oldest daughter Susanna. He also garnered fame in his own right as one of the first doctors to keep detailed records of his patients. The Croft features an exhibit on Hall and medicine in Shakespeare's time—frogs were a frequent prescription. *(☎ 292 107. Open winter M-Sa 11am-4pm and Su noon-4pm; mid-season daily 11am-5pm; summer M-Sa 9:30am-5pm and Su 10am-5pm. £3.50, concessions £3, children £1.70, families £8.50.)*

ANNE HATHAWAY'S COTTAGE. The birthplace of Shakespeare's wife, about a mile from Stratford in **Shottery,** is probably the fairy-tale, thatched-roof cottage you saw on the travel agent's poster. It boasts very old original Hathaway furniture and a very new hedge maze (the "maze" part will be more effective once the hedge breaks 3 ft.). Entrance entitles you to sit on a bench He may or may not have also sat on. *(Take the ill-marked footpaths north. ☎ 292 100. Open winter M-Sa 10am-4pm and Su 10:30am-4pm; mid-season M-Sa 10am-5pm and Su 10:30am-5pm; summer M-Sa 9am-5pm and Su 9:30am-5pm. £5, concessions £4, children £2, families £11.)*

...OR NOT TO BARD

Non-Shakespearean sights *are* available (if not particularly exciting) in Stratford.

TEDDY BEAR MUSEUM. The museum boasts thousands of stuffed, ceramic, and painted bears. Though most went to children in Yugoslavia, 12 of the "Diana bears" (left in front of Kensington Palace) rest near the original Fozzie, a gift from Jim Henson. *(Exit, pursued by a bear. 19 Greenhill St. ☎ 293 160. Open daily 9:30am-5pm. £2.50, concessions £1.95, children £1.50, families £7.50.)*

STRATFORD-UPON-AVON ■ 289

STRATFORD BUTTERFLY FARM. A weyr of butterflies flutters through tropical-ized surroundings (and past one singularly unbutterfly-like iguana-at-large); less appealing creepy-crawlies—like the Goliath Bird-Eating Spider—hang out in glass boxes in the neighboring room. *(Off Swan's Nest Ln. at Tramway Walk, across the river from the TIC. ☎ 299 288. Open in summer daily 10am-6pm; winter 10am-dusk. Last admission 30min. before closing. £4.25, concessions £3.75, children £3.25.)*

HARVARD HOUSE. Period pieces and pewter punctuate this authentic Tudor building, vaguely connected with the man who lends his name to the American college that owns it—his mother lived here. *(High St.; look for the stars-and-stripes flying outside. ☎ 204 507. Open July-Sept. M, Th, F-Su 11:30am-4:30pm; May-June and Oct. F-Su only. £1.50, children 50p, free for holders of multiple-site tickets.)*

RAGLEY HALL. Eight miles from Stratford on Evesham Rd. (A435), Ragley Hall houses the Earl and Countess of Yarmouth. Set in a stunning 400-acre park, the estate has an art collection and a captivating maze. *(Take bus #25 or 26 (M-Sa 5 per day) to Alcester Police Station, walk 1 mi. to the gates, then ½ mi. up the drive. ☎ 762 090. House open Apr.-Sept. Th-Su noon-5pm, park until 6pm. £6, concessions £5, children £4.)*

🎭 THE PLAY'S THE THING

THE ROYAL SHAKESPEARE COMPANY

The box office in the foyer of the Royal Shakespeare Theatre handles the ticketing for both theaters. ☎ 403 403, 24hr. ticket hotline ☎ (0870) 609 1110; www.rsc.org.uk. Open M-Sa 9:30am-8pm. Tickets for £5-40. Both theaters have £5 standing room tickets; under 25 get half-price same-day tickets; and £8-12 student and senior same-day standbys exist in principle—queue 1-2hr. before curtain and be ready to pounce. Matinee tickets are easier to get. **Disabled travelers** *should call in advance to advise the box office of their needs; some performances feature sign language interpretation or audio description.*

One of the world's most acclaimed repertories, the **Royal Shakespeare Company** sells well over one million tickets each year, and claims Kenneth Branagh and Ralph Fiennes as recent sons. In Stratford, the RSC performs in two connected theaters. The bard was born on Henley St., died at New Place, sleeps in Holy Trinity, and lives on at the **Royal Shakespeare Theatre**, across from Chapel Ln. on the Waterside. Designs are currently in the works for a major re-vamping of the flagship stage (likely to be finished round about 2008). The RSC took the shell of burnt-out Memorial Theatre and renovated it as **The Swan Theatre.** A smaller and more intimate space than the attached RST, it resembles Shakespeare's Globe and stages plays by lesser wordsmiths. The RSC conducts **backstage tours** that cram groups into the wooden "O"s of the theaters. *(☎ 403 405. Tours daily 5:30pm, 11am on matinee days, and also M-Sa 1:30pm and Su noon, 1, 2, 3pm. £4, concessions £3.)*

🎪 OUR RUSTIC REVELRY

Every Friday and every other Saturday, a **traditional town market** is held on Rother St. in Market Place. On Sundays from June through August, a **craft market** takes place along the river. (Both markets 9am-5pm; ☎ 267 000.) Stratford's biggest festival begins on the weekend nearest April 23, **Shakespeare's birthday.** The modern, well-respected **Shakespeare Centre**, Henley St., hosts a **Poetry Festival** every Sunday evening in July and August; cameos include Seamus Heaney, Ted Hughes, and Derek Walcott. (☎ 204 016. Open M-F 9am-5pm. Tickets £7.)

WORCESTER

☎ 01905

Worcester (WUH-ster) sits over the Severn between Cheltenham and Birmingham, but lacks the former's gentility and the latter's pace. The city's name has been made famous by Worcestershire sauce and Worcester porcelain, and the city itself was the site of the Civil Wars' final battle and birthplace of the composer Elgar. Beyond the beautiful cathedral, however, Worcester's sights are lackluster.

□ TRANSPORTATION. Foregate St. Station, at the edge of the town center on Foregate St., is the city's main train station. (Ticket window open M-Sa 6am-9pm, Su 9am-5pm. Travel center open M-Sa 9am-4pm.) **Shrub Hill Station,** just outside of town, serves Cheltenham but has less frequent service to London and Birmingham. (Ticket window open M-Sa 5:30am-9pm, Su 7am-7pm.) **Trains** (☎ (08457) 484 950) travel to Worcester from: **Birmingham** (1hr., 2 per hr., £5.70); **Cheltenham** (30min., every 2hr., £5); **London Paddington** (2½hr., every 1½hr., £23.80). The **bus station** is at Angel Pl. near the Crowngate Shopping Centre. **National Express** (☎ (08705) 808 080) runs from: **Birmingham** (1½hr., every 30min., £3.95); **Bristol** (2hr., 4 per day, £10.75); **London** (4hr., 2 per day, £16.50). **Midland Red West** (☎ 763 888) is the regional bus company; their **Day Rover** allows unlimited one-day travel within Worcestershire (£4.60, seniors £3.60, children £3.10, families £9.20). **Associated Radio Taxis** is at ☎ 763 939. **Peddlers,** 46-48 Barbourne Rd., rents **bikes.** (☎ 24238. £8 per day, £30 per week. Deposit £50. Open M-Sa 9:30am-5:45pm.)

◼️🛈 ORIENTATION AND PRACTICAL INFORMATION. The city center is bounded by the train station to the north and the cathedral to the south. A fickle main street runs between the two, switching names from **Barbourne Rd.** to **The Tything** to **Foregate St.** to **The Foregate** to **The Cross** to **High St.** To reach the TIC from Foregate St. station, turn left onto Foregate St. It's a 15min. walk from Shrub Hill: turn right onto Shrub Hill Rd., then left onto Tolladine Rd. (which becomes Lowesmoor); continue to St. Nicholas St., which intersects The Foregate. From the bus station, turn left onto **Broad St.** and right onto **The Cross.**

The **tourist information centre,** The Guildhall, High St., sells the *Worcester Visitor* guide (75p) and books beds for a 10% deposit. (☎ 726 311. Open M-Sa 9:30am-5pm.) 1½hr. **tours** leave from the TIC. (May-Sept. W 11am and 2:30pm. Oct.-Apr. ghost walks F-Sa 8pm. £3, children free.) Other services include: **Barclays,** 54 High St. (☎ 684 828; open M-Tu and Th-F 9am-5pm, W 10am-5pm, Sa 9:30am-1pm); **Severn Laun-Dri,** 22 Barbourne Rd. (wash £2-3, dry £1; open daily 9am-8pm, last wash 7pm); the **police,** Castle St. (☎ (08457) 444 888), off Foregate; **Worcestershire Royal Hospital,** Newtown Rd. (☎ 763 333; bus #29D or #31A); free Internet access at the **library,** in the City Museum (☎ 765 312; open M and F 9:30am-7pm, Tu-Th 9:30am-5:30pm, Sa 9:30am-4pm); the **post office,** 8-10 Foregate St., next to the train station, with **bureau de change** (☎ (08457) 223 344; open M-Sa 9am-5:30pm). **Post Code:** WR1.

🏠 ACCOMMODATIONS AND CAMPING. B&B prices in Worcester are high, as proprietors cater to businessmen or to Londoners weekending in the country. Try your luck on **Barbourne Rd.,** the fifth manifestation of High St., a 15-20min. walk north from the city center. The nearest **YHA hostel** is 7 mi. away in the town of Malvern, 12min. by train (see p. 292). Visitors will sleep like logs at **Osbourne House ❸,** 17 Chestnut Walk, with TVs and electronic, touch-operated showers in every bedroom, three types of cookies on the nightstand, and brilliant marmalade. (☎/fax 22296. Doubles £40, with bath £45; available as singles for £24-40.) Monty Python fans will appreciate the name of the **Shrubbery Guest House ❸,** 38 Barbourne Rd. Everyone else will appreciate the expert way Mrs. Law makes guests feel at home. (☎ 24871; fax 23620. TVs. Singles £23; doubles £44, with bath £48.) The newly refurbished **City Guest House ❸** is at 36 Barbourne Rd. (☎24695. Singles £20-25; doubles £40-50.) Riverside **Ketch Caravan Park ❶**, Bath Rd., has toilets and showers. Take the A38 2 mi. south of Worcester or local bus #32, every 10min. (☎820 430. Open Easter-Oct. £6-8 per tent, £8 per caravan. Electricity £1.75.)

🏠🍴 FOOD AND PUBS. A **Sainsbury's** is tucked into the Lynchgate Shopping Centre off High St. (☎21731. Open M-Sa 8am-6pm.) Cheap sandwich shops and good Indian restaurants fill **The Tything,** at the north end of the city center—the best is **Monsoon ❷**, with entrees around £6 and excellent service. (☎726 333. Open Su-Th 6pm-midnight, F-Sa 6pm-1am.) **The Lemon Tree ❸**, 12 Friar St., has a pricey but fantastic Mediterranean menu with chargrilled marinated lamb and fishcakes. The average lunch costs £10 and dinner entrees run £8-15. (☎27770. Open Tu-F noon-2:30pm, Th-F also 6:30-10pm, Sa 11:30am-3pm and 6:30-10pm.) **Natural Break ❶**, in The Hopmarket, near the corner of Foregate St. and Sansome, provides coffee and scones (£1.60) and organic sandwiches and quiches from £2.75. (☎26654. Open M-Sa 9am-5pm.) At **Clockwatchers ❶**, 20 Mealcheapen St., farm-fresh sandwiches start at £1.25 for takeaway (sit-down £3-4), and bagels are only 75p. (☎611 662. Open M-Sa 8:30am-5pm.) For pint-sized entertainment, the pub scene on **Friar St.** is popular. **The Conservatory,** 34 Friar St., has modern decor, a lively crowd, and most importantly, ales at £1.40-2.25. (☎26929. Open M-Sa 11am-11pm.)

📷 SIGHTS. Worcester Cathedral, founded in AD 680, towers majestically by the River Severn at the southern end of High St. Over the years, the buttresses supporting the central nave have deteriorated, and the central tower is in danger of collapsing. Renovation attempts are perpetually underway, but even steel rods set in the tower's base don't detract from the building's awe-inspiring Norman detail. To the delight of schoolchildren and *Let's Go* researchers, Bishop Freake has his tomb in the south wall. The **quire** contains intricate 14th-century misericords and King John's tomb; copies of the *Magna Carta* are displayed outside. **Wulston's Crypt** is an entire underground level, with the narrow exit its creepiest attraction. (☎28854. Open daily 7:30am-6:30pm; Evensong M-F 5:30pm, Su 4pm. Free tours May-Sept.; £2 tower tours Sa, late July also M-Th. Suggested donation £2.50.)

Relive the 1651 Battle of Worcester at the **Commandery,** Sidbury Rd. Sit in on the trial of Charles I and choose whether to sign the death warrant—your vote counts. (☎36182. Open M-Sa 10am-5pm, Su 1:30-5pm. £4, concessions £2.85, families £10.) The **Royal**

THE HIDDEN DEAL

THE MUSEUM OF PORCELAIN'S CLEARANCE SHOP

Looking for a souvenir for Mum but would rather spend your quid on yourself? Wondering if you could possibly find something more "English" than a Prince Albert postcard? Look no further than veritable bargain bonanza **The Clearance Shop,** next door to Worcester's **Museum of Porcelain,** where you can nab discontinued porcelain items at an average of 62% off.

Whether it's a gorgeous teapot (originally £80, marked down, way down, to £20), simple cream jug, or that elusive "odd lid" you know has been causing your mother to ransack the cupboards every week, this shop has a wide variety of brilliantly priced wares. You can find beautiful plates going for as little as £1 apiece, while teacups sell for an average of £2-10.

It's well worth the space it'll take in your pack and the resulting pain in your back. Much prettier than Albert and far cheaper than the "real" thing—Mum won't know the difference. *(☎746 000. Open M and W-Sa 9am-5:30pm, Tu 9:30am-5:30pm, Su 11am-5pm.)*

Worcester Porcelain Company, southeast of the cathedral on Severn St., manufactures the famous blue-red-and-gold-patterned bone china on which the royal family has been served since George III. Crockery junkies can visit the adjacent **Worcester Museum of Porcelain,** which holds England's largest collection. (☎23221. Open M-Sa 9am-5:30pm. Tours M-F 4 times per day; £5, no children under 11. Museum £3, concessions £2.25, under 5 free. Museum and tour £8/£6.75.) The highlight of the **Worcester City Museum and Art Gallery,** Foregate St., near the post office, is Hitler's clock, found in his office when it was captured by the Worcester Regiment in 1945. (☎25371. Open M-F 9:30am-5:30pm, Sa 9:30am-5pm. Free.)

Three miles south of the train station, **Elgar's Birthplace Museum** is filled with manuscripts and memorabilia. Midland Red West bus #419/420 stops 1 mi. away at Crown East Church (10min., 2 per day, return £2.20). From the bus stop walk 15min. to the museum. Otherwise, cycle 6 mi. along the Elgar trail. (☎333 224. Open daily 11am-5pm, closed Dec. 23-Jan. 31. £3.50, concessions £3, children £1.75, families £8.75.)

NEAR WORCESTER: MALVERN ☎01684

The name Malvern refers collectively to the contiguous towns of Great Malvern, West Malvern, Malvern Link, Malvern Wells, and Little Malvern, all of which hug the base and the eastern side of the Malvern Hills. The tops of the Malvern Hills peek over the A4108 southwest of Worcester and offer 8 mi. of trails and quasi-divine visions of greenery. **Great Malvern,** a Victorian spa town, was built around the 11th-century **Malvern Priory** on Abbey Rd. Benedictine monks rebuilt the structure in the 15th century, sprucing it up with stained-glass windows. (Suggested donation £1.) On the steep hillside a 20min. hike above town, **St. Ann's Well** supplies the restorative "Malvern waters" that fueled Great Malvern's halcyon days. The beautifully redone **Malvern Theatres** on Grange Rd., 10min. from the train station, host plays. (☎892 277. Box office open M-Sa 9:30am-8pm. Tickets £10-20, student discounts £1-9 less.)

The **Worcestershire Way** slips through the Malverns for 45 mi. to Kingsford County Park in the north. **Trains** (15min.; every 30min.; £2.70, day return £3.50) and **Midland Red West** buses (40min., 1-2 per hr., £2.60) come from **Worcester.** The **tourist information centre,** 21 Church St., by the post office, assists with advice and pamphlets. (☎892 289; fax 892 872. Open daily 10am-5pm.) The **YHA Hatherly ❷,** 18 Peachfield Rd., in Malvern Wells, holds 59 beds and a TV lounge. Take Citibus #42 from Great Malvern or walk 20min. from the train station. (☎569 131. Breakfast £3.40. Lockout 10am-5pm. Curfew 11pm. Open mid-Feb. to Oct. daily; Nov.-Dec. F-Sa. £10.25, under 18 £7.)

CHELTENHAM ☎01242

Cheltenham (pop. 107,000) wears a carefree sophistication; its visitors wear patternless skirts and pressed khakis. A yuppie spa town of manicured gardens and stylish shops, Cheltenham is a peaceful stop for weary sojourners—its quiet refinement is a break from touristy Bath and Stratford and the industrial megaliths of the Midlands—as well as a useful launching pad for the Cotswolds. The student population brings pubs and clubs to semi-life at night.

▐▀ TRANSPORTATION

Cheltenham lies 43 mi. south of Birmingham, on the northeastern outskirts of the Cotswolds. The free *Getting There* pamphlet from the TIC details bus services.

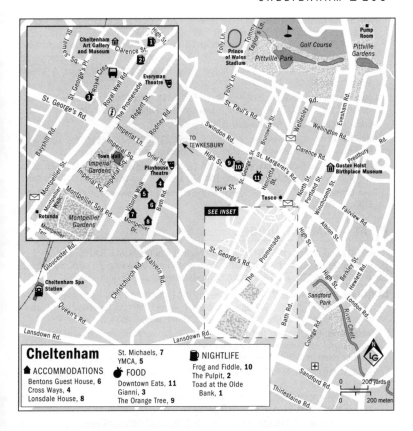

Cheltenham

♠ ACCOMMODATIONS
Bentons Guest House, **6**
Cross Ways, **4**
Lonsdale House, **8**

St. Michaels, **7**
YMCA, **5**
🍴 FOOD
Downtown Eats, **11**
Gianni, **3**
The Orange Tree, **9**

🍷 NIGHTLIFE
Frog and Fiddle, **10**
The Pulpit, **2**
Toad at the Olde
    Bank, **1**

0   200 yards
0   200 meters

Trains: Cheltenham Spa Station, on Queen's Rd. at Gloucester Rd. Ticket office open M-F 5:45am-8:15pm, Sa 5:45am-7:15pm, Su 8:15am-8:15pm. Trains (☎(08457) 484 950) from: **Bath** (1½hr., every hr., £11); **Birmingham** (45min., 2 per hr., £12.50); **London** (2hr., every hr., £36.30); **Worcester** (25min., every 2hr., £5).

Buses: Royal Well Roundabout. Office open M-F 9am-4:30pm, Sa 8:30am-4pm. Lockers £1-2. **National Express** (☎(08705) 808 080) to: **Bristol** (1¼hr., 3 per day, £5.50); **Exeter** (4hr., 3 per day, £17.50); **London** (3hr., every hr., £13). **Swanbrook Coaches** (☎(01452) 712 386) to **Gloucester** (25min., 4-5 per day, £1.70) and **Oxford** (2hr., 4-5 per day, £5.50). Buses to **Tewkesbury** leave from Clarence St.

Taxis: A to B Taxis (☎580 580). **Starline Taxi** (☎250 250). Free phone in train station.

🏳🛈 ORIENTATION AND PRACTICAL INFORMATION

What little goes on in Cheltenham happens on or near **High St.** and **The Promenade,** intersecting pedestrian-only walkways. The train station is at the western edge of town—walk 20min. or catch bus F or G (5min., every 10min., 90p).

Tourist Information Centre: Municipal Offices, 77 The Promenade (☎522 878; accommodations booking 517 110; fax 255 848; www.visitcheltenham.gov.uk). Well-organized staff sells National Express tickets and posts B&B vacancies outside after hours. Open M-Tu and Th-Sa 9:30am-5:15pm, W 10am-5:15pm.

Financial Services: Banks are easy to find. Most are open M-F 9am-4:30pm, W 10am-4:30pm, and Sa 9am-12:30pm.

Launderette: Soap-n-Suds, 312 High St. (☎512 107), across from the Orange Tree Restaurant. Wash £1.60-2.40, dry £1-2. Open daily 8am-8pm, last wash 7pm.

Police: Holland House, 840 Lansdown Rd. (☎521 321).

Hospital: Cheltenham General, Sandford Rd. (☎222 222). Follow Bath Rd. southwest from town and turn left onto Sandford Rd. Emergency entrance on College Rd.

Internet Access: Central Library, Clarence St. (☎532 688), next to City Museum. Sign up for 2hr. Free. Open M, W, F 10am-7pm; Tu and Th 10am-5:30pm; Sa 9:30am-4pm.

Post Office: 225-227 High St. (☎526 056). **Bureau de change.** Open M-Sa 9am-5:30pm. **Post Code:** GL50 1AA.

ACCOMMODATIONS

Standards and prices (£25-40) tend to be high at Cheltenham's B&Bs. A handful of B&Bs can be found in the **Montpellier** area and along **Bath Rd.,** a 5 min. walk from the town center. The TIC books accommodations for a 10% deposit.

Bentons Guest House, 71 Bath Rd. (☎517 417; fax 577 772). English countryside decor and every imaginable creature comfort, from hair dryers to towel warmers. Platter-sized plates can barely hold the breakfast. £25 per person. ❸

Cross Ways, 57 Bath Rd. (☎527 683; fax 577 226; crossways@btinternet.com). The proprietor's experience as an interior designer is apparent in this Regency home's sophisticated furnishings. Rooms as comfy as they are lavish. £26-30 per person. ❸

YMCA, Vittoria Walk (☎524 024; fax 232 365). A backpacker's paradise: some singles even have a full kitchen. Men and women accepted. Breakfast included. Internet 50p per hr. Office open 24hr., but arrive before 9:30pm if you want breakfast. Porter admits guests after 11pm. Book ahead. £16 per person. ❷

Lonsdale House, 16 Montpellier Dr. (☎232 379; lonsdalehouse@hotmail.com). Large home with a bounty of singles. Comfortable, spacious rooms stocked with TVs and English literary classics. Singles £23; doubles with bath £52. ❸

St. Michaels, 4 Montpellier Dr. (☎513 587). Luxurious B&B with great service and spacious ensuite rooms. Singles £42.50; doubles £55; triples £72. ❹

FOOD

A handful of fruit stands, butchers, and bakeries dot **High St.,** while down the road, **Tesco,** 233 High St., has it all under one roof. (☎847 400. Open continuously M 8am to Sa 10pm, also Su 11am-5pm.) A Thursday morning **market** on Henrietta St. sells cheap fruits, meats, and other wares.

Gianni, 1 Royal Well Pl. (☎221 101), just south of the bus stops on Royal Well. Huge portions of Italian food in a fun, lively atmosphere. Appetizers £1.50-7, entrees £6-14. Open daily noon-2pm and from 6:30pm; last order M-F at 10:30pm, Sa-Su at 11pm. ❸

The Orange Tree, 317 High St. (☎234 232). Proudly health-conscious and potentially romantic. The chef recommends wild organic mushroom stroganoff or cashew nut and sesame seed patties with tikka masala sauce (both £8.50); complement either with organic beer. Weekend reservations recommended. Open M 9:30am-4pm, Tu-Th 9:30am-9pm, F-Sa 9:30am-10pm, Su 11am-3pm. ❷

Downtown Eats, 291 High St. (☎516 388). Simple takeaway sandwiches (80p-£2) perfect for picnicking. Open M-F 8am-3:30pm, Sa 9am-3:30pm. ❶

NIGHTLIFE

Frog and Fiddle, 315 High St. (☎701 156). Chill on the big blue couches or play pool and arcade games upstairs. Students fill the pub's cavernous back rooms. M and W drink special: pints £1.50. Open M-Sa 11am-11pm, Su noon-10:30pm.

Toad at the Olde Bank, 15-21 Clarence St. (☎230 099). A mixed crowd frequents this relaxed bar. 2 for 1 drinks M-Tu and Su all day, W-F 8-9pm. Live DJ Tu-Sa. Cover £1-4. Open M-Sa 11am-11pm, Su noon-10:30pm.

The Pulpit, Clarence Parade (☎269 057). Look for yellow signs proclaiming "Scream." This huge space fills with a younger crowd on weekends. Open daily noon-11pm.

SIGHTS AND FESTIVALS

Cheltenham possesses the only naturally **alkaline water** in Britain—George III and the Duke of Wellington both took the waters here. You, too, can enjoy its diuretic and laxative effects—if "enjoy" is the right word—at the **town hall.** (Open M-F 9:30am-5:30pm. Water tasting free.) The less-than-fascinating **Cheltenham Art Gallery and Museum,** on Clarence St., specializes in the Arts and Crafts movement (see p. 80) and has an extensive pottery collection and an exhibit on England's urban prosperity. (☎237 431. Open M-Sa 10am-5:20pm, Su 2-4:20pm. Free.) The **Gustav Holst Birthplace Museum,** 4 Clarence Rd., opposite Pittville Park, portrays the composer's early life in his Regency home. (☎524 846. Open Tu-Sa 10am-4pm. £2.50, concessions £2.) Downtowners and dogs sunbathe among exquisite blooms at the **Imperial Gardens,** north of the town center on The Promenade.

The indispensable *What's On* poster, displayed on kiosks and at the TIC, lists concerts, plays, tours, sporting events, and hotspots. The **Cheltenham International Festival of Music** (three weeks in July) celebrates modern classical works. The concurrent **Fringe Festival** organizes jazz, big band, and rock performances. The **International Jazz Festival** takes place in the beginning of May, while October heralds the fortnight-long **Cheltenham Festival of Literature.** Full details on these festivals are available from the box office, Town Hall, Imperial Sq. (☎227 979), or online, at www.cheltenhamfestivals.co.uk. The **National Hunt,** a horseracing event, starts in the winter and culminates in March, causing the population of Cheltenham nearly to double at its peak. (☎513 014, bookings 226 226 or www.cheltenham.co.uk. Tickets sold Sept.-Feb., usually sold-out by Feb. Tickets £12-60.) The **Cheltenham Cricket Festival,** the oldest in the country, commences in mid-July. Inquire about match times at the TIC, or call (☎(0117) 910 8000); purchase tickets at the gate.

⚡ DAYTRIP FROM CHELTENHAM: TEWKESBURY

Ten miles northwest of Cheltenham, at the confluence of the Rivers Avon and Severn, Tewkesbury has cultivated suburban quaintness, making it an optimal senior citizen hangout. The town merits an excursion for its stately **abbey,** with resplendent high ceilings and fat, round Norman ("English Romanesque") pillars. The abbey is fantastically bright, illuminated by 14th-century stained glass. First consecrated in 1121, it was reconsecrated after the Battle of Tewkesbury, when Yorks killed the abbey's monks for attempting to protect refuge-seeking Lancastrians. (☎(01684) 850 959. Open Apr.-Oct. M-Sa 7:30am-6pm, Su 7:30am-7pm; Nov.-Mar. daily 7:30am-5:30pm. Services Su at 8, 9:15, 11am, and 6pm. Requested donation £2.) The **Little Museum,** 45 Church St., is a merchant's cottage built in 1450 and

FROM THE ROAD

ROADS LESS TRAVELED

The Cotswolds are an inspiring destination. Even the bus ride into this region of rolling hills and inert sheep arouses a sense of dreamy stupor. As my bus rumbled past pastures colored a hundred shades of green, for a moment, if just a fleeting moment, I didn't feel like smacking the kid in the back of the bus who'd been crying and screaming the whole way. The Cotswolds are indeed full of miracles.

This vision of beauty encourages more adventurous attitudes toward traveling. When attempting to visit the small village of Chedworth and its romantic-sounding Roman villa, a mile from the main highway, hikers have two options: taking that well-worn, asphalt-paved road, or finding a shortcut through the fields. In theory, Robert Frost's choice seems a sound option, but practically speaking, he forgot the important details, including hiking boots and insect repellent.

After wandering through rolling fields for nearly an hour, my adventurous spirit has been broken. My jeans are rolled up to my knees, my shoes are caked in red field mud, and my clothes smell oddly of fish. Insects bite my ankles, which are already sore from tripping in a hole. I wonder if I should give up and head home.

The journey continues through rocks and stones, high grass, and endless fields until I finally see a house and a live human being. "How do I get to Chedworth?!" I yell. "You're in it!" she laughs. I nearly wet myself. And that's why one must always, always opt for the road less traveled.

— Angie Sun

restored in the 1960s, when developers added modern conveniences to the whole row of 15th-century buildings, the longest in the UK. (☎(01684) 297 174. Open Apr.-Oct. Tu-Sa 10am-5pm. Free.) The charmingly petite **Tewkesbury Town Museum,** 64 Barton St., has an exhibit on the 1471 Battle of Tewkesbury. (☎(01684) 292 901. Open daily 10am-4pm. £1, concessions 75p, children 50p.)

Tewkesbury makes a leisurely daytrip from Cheltenham and can be adequately visited in a few hours. **Stagecoach** (☎(01242) 522 021) bus #41 departs from Cheltenham (25min.; M-Sa every 30min., Su every 2hr.; return £2.70). The **tourist information centre,** in the Town Museum, sells a 10p map and 20p pamphlet outlining walks through Tewkesbury's alley-like streets. (☎(01684) 295 027. Open M-Sa 9am-5pm, Su 10am-4pm.) **Lloyds TSB,** 19 High St. (☎(01684) 850 995), is open M-Tu and Th-F 9am-5pm, W 9:30am-4pm. The **post office** is at 99-100 High St. (☎(01684) 293 232. Open M-F 9am-5:30pm, Sa 9am-4pm.) **Post Code:** GL20 5JZ. **Crescent Guest House ❹,** 30 Church St., is next to the bus stop. (☎293 395. £40 per spartan room.)

THE COTSWOLDS

The Cotswolds have deviated little from their etymological roots—"Cotswolds" means "sheep enclosure in rolling hillsides." Grazing sheep and cattle roam 800 square miles of vivid, verdant hills, which enfold tiny towns with names longer than their main streets. Saxon villages and Roman settlements, hewn straight from the famed Cotswold stone, link a series of trails accessible to walkers and cyclists. The Cotswolds are not just for outdoors enthusiasts, however; anyone with an interest in rural England will find something here.

⌐ TRANSPORTATION

Public transport to and within the Cotswolds is notoriously infrequent, so planning ahead is a must. The whimsically-named villages of the picturesque "Northern" Cotswolds (Stow-on-the-Wold, Bourton-on-the-Water, Moreton-in-Marsh) are more easily reached via Cheltenham, while the more remote and less touristed "Southern" Cotswolds (Slimbridge and Painswick) are served more frequently from Gloucester. TICs in these starting-point cities stock helpful pamphlets, including the free *Explore the Cotswolds by Public Transport.*

Train stations in the Cotswolds are few and far between, and service is infrequent. **Moreton-in-Marsh**

(open M-F 6am-7:45pm, Sa 6:15am-1pm, Su 9:15am-4pm) runs trains to London (1½hr., every hr., £24) and Oxford (30min., every hr., £7.80). The same train passes through tiny **Charlbury,** between Moreton-in-Marsh and Oxford. In the Southern Cotswolds, **Cam and Dursley** (3 mi. from Slimbridge) runs to Gloucester (15min., 9 per day) and London (2½hr., 7 per day).

It's far easier to reach the Cotswolds by **bus.** The Cheltenham TIC's free *Getting There* pamphlet is fantastically comprehensive, while the *Pulham's Bus Services* booklet (50p) details that company's routes. **Pulham's Coaches** (☎ (01451) 820 369) run from Cheltenham to Moreton-in-Marsh (1hr.; M-Sa 7 per day, Su daily; £2) via Bourton-on-the-Water (35min., £1.50) and Stow-on-the-Wold (50min., £1.55). **Castleway's Coaches** (☎ (01242) 602 949) go from Cheltenham to Broadway (50min., M-Sa 4 per day, £1.80) via Winchcombe (20min., £1.60); **Stagecoach** #165 also runs this route (Th and Sa-Su 4 per day). In the Southern Cotswolds, **Beaumont Travel** (☎ (01452) 309 770) B7 runs from Gloucester to Slimbridge (30min.; 5 per day; single £2, return £3). **Coach tours** cover the Cotswolds from Cheltenham, Gloucester, Oxford, Stratford-upon-Avon, Tewkesbury, and other neighboring cities.

The easiest way to explore is by car, but the best way to experience the Cotswolds is on **foot** or **bike. The Toy Shop,** on High St. in Moreton-in-Marsh, rents bikes with lock, map, and route suggestions. (☎ (01608) 650 756. £10 per half-day, £12 per day. Credit card deposit. Open M and W-Sa 9am-1pm and 2-5pm.) Hoof it

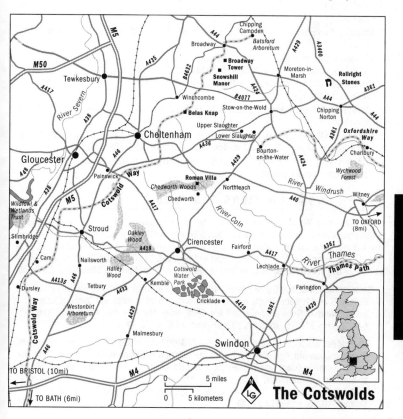

The Cotswolds

with the help of **local buses.** (☎ (01452) 425 543. Day rover £3, concessions £1.50.) #55 runs from Cirencester to Moreton-in-Marsh via Northleach, Bourton-on-the-Water, and Stow-on-the-Wold (M-Sa 6 per day, Su 2 per day); M21 and M22 from Moreton run to Stratford via Broadway and Chipping Campden (3 per day).

✈ 🛈 ORIENTATION AND PRACTICAL INFORMATION

The Cotswolds lie mostly in Gloucestershire, bounded by **Cheltenham** in the north, **Banbury** in the northeast, **Malmesbury** in the south, and **Bradford-on-Avon** in the southwest. The range hardly towers—the average Cotswold hill reaches only 600 ft.—but the rolling hills can make hiking and biking strenuous. The best bases from which to explore are **Cheltenham, Cirencester,** and **Moreton-in-Marsh.**

TOURIST INFORMATION CENTRES
All provide maps and pamphlets and book beds, usually for £1-3 and a 10% deposit.

Bath: See p. 206.

Bourton-on-the-Water: Victoria St. (☎ (01451) 820 211). Open Apr.-Oct. M-Sa 9:30am-5pm, Su 10am-4pm; Nov.-Mar. M-Sa 9:30am-4:30pm, Su 10am-1pm.

Broadway: 1 Cotswold Court (☎ (01386) 852 937). Open Mar.-Oct. M-Sa 10am-1pm and 2-5pm.

Cheltenham: See p. 293.

Chipping Campden: Old Police Station, High St. (☎ (01386) 841 206). Open Apr.-Oct. daily 10am-5:30pm; Nov.-Mar. 10am-5pm.

Cirencester: Corn Hall, Market Pl. (☎ (01285) 654 180; fax 641 182). Open Apr.-Dec. M 9:45am-5:30pm, Tu-Sa 9:30am-5:30pm; Jan.-Mar. daily 9:30am-5pm.

Gloucester: 28 Southgate St. (☎ (01452) 396 572). Open M-Sa 10am-5pm; July-Aug. also Su 11-3pm.

Moreton-in-Marsh: District Council Bldg. (☎ (01208) 650 881). Open Easter-Oct. M-F 9am-5pm.

Stow-on-the-Wold: Hollis House, The Square (☎ (01451) 831 082). Open Easter-Oct. M-Sa 9:30am-5:30pm, Su 10:30am-4pm; Nov.-Easter M-Sa 9:30am-4:30pm.

Winchcombe: Town Hall (☎ (01242) 602 925). Open Apr.-Oct. M-Sa 10am-5pm, Su 10am-4pm; closed 1-2pm.

🏠 🍴 ACCOMMODATIONS AND FOOD

The *Cotswold Way Handbook and Accommodation List* (£2) details **B&Bs,** which usually lie on convenient roads a 5-10min. walk from small villages. If you're not hiking, pick up the cheaper *Cotswolds Accommodation Guide* (50p), which lists B&Bs in or near larger towns. Expect to pay £20-30 per night, unless you stay at one of the **YHA hostels,** both of which serve meals and have a 10am-5pm lockout:

Stow-on-the-Wold: The Square (☎ (01451) 830 497), near Stow TIC; Pulham's bus will drop you at the door. Bright rooms with wooden bunks, most with bath. Kitchen and helpful warden. Book ahead. Open Apr.-Sept. daily; Mar. and Oct. M-Sa; Nov. and Feb. F-Sa. Dorms £12.75, students £11.75, under 18 £8.75. ❷

Slimbridge: Shepherd's Patch (☎ (0870) 770 6036). Off the A38 and the M5, 4 mi. from the Cotswold Way and ½ mi. from the Wildfowl & Wetlands Trust Centre. The nearest train station (Cam and Dursley) is 3 mi.; it's easier to take bus B7 from Gloucester to Slimbridge Crossroads, 2 mi. from the YHA. 56 beds, small store, ponds, and lots of birds. Open Aug. daily; Sept.-July daily for groups, F-Sa only for individual travelers. Dorms £10.25, under 18 £7. ❷

Campsites cluster close to Cheltenham, but there are also convenient places to rough it within the Cotswolds. **Moreton-in-Marsh** is one of these; try **Fosseway Farm B&B** (see p. 300) or the **Caravan Club Site ❷**, on Bourton Rd. (☎(01608) 650 519. £5 nonmember fee. £3.50-4.50 per adult and £1.20 per child, £6-8 per tent. Electricity £1.50-2.25.) The *Gloucestershire Caravan and Camping Guide* (free at local TICs) lists numerous options. Larger towns like Cirencester and Stow-on-the-Wold are home to supermarkets, takeaways, and full-fledged restaurants, while smaller towns have butchers, bakers, and tiny convenience stores. Country pubs crop up along the way.

🖉 HIKING THROUGH COTSWOLD VILLAGES

Experience the Cotswolds as the English have for centuries—by treading well-worn footpaths from village to village. Speed-walkers may be able to cruise through numerous towns in a day, but average folk can adequately explore only three or four. To see more than just rolling hills, thatched roofs, and sheep, pick up a free *Cotswold Events* booklet at a TIC. It lists music festivals and antique markets, as well as woolsack races and cheese-rolling opportunities.

TIC shelves strain under the weight of various **walking** and **cycling guides.** The *Cotswold Map and Guidebook in One* (£5) is detailed enough to plan bike routes and short hikes. For more intense hiking or biking, the *Ordnance Survey Outdoor Leisure Map* #45 shows altitude and the most obscure of trails (1:25,000; £7). The directionally challenged can opt for a **guided walk.** The **Cotswolds Voluntary Warden Service** (☎(01452) 425 674) conducts free walks, some with themes (1½-7½hr.). All walks are listed in the Programme Guide section of the bi-annual *Cotswold LION* newspaper (free at the TIC); show up at the designated Ordnance Survey point. To see the Cotswolds without exerting any energy, try the **Cotswold Experience,** a full-day bus tour that starts in Bath and visits five of the most scenic and touristed villages. Earth-friendly buses use bio-diesel fuel. (☎(01225) 325 900. T, Th, Sa-Su 10am-6pm. £23.50, students £19.50.)

Long-distance hikers can choose from a handful of carefully marked trails. B&Bs and pubs lie conveniently within reach of the Cotswold Way and the Oxfordshire Way. The more extensive **Cotswold Way** spans just over 100 mi. from Bath to Chipping Campden, has few steep climbs, and can be done in a week. The trail passes through pasture lands and the remains of ancient settlements. Note that pockmarks and gravel make certain sections unsuitable for biking or horseback riding. Consult the **Cotswold Way National Trail Office** (☎(01452) 425 637) for details. The **Oxfordshire Way** (65 mi.) runs between the popular hyphen-havens Bourton-on-the-Water and Henley-on-Thames, site of the famed annual regatta (see p. 89). A comprehensive *Walker's Guide* can be found in TICs. Mince over cowpats while wending from Bourton-on-the-Water to Lower and Upper Slaughter along the **Warden's Way,** a half-day hike. Adventurous souls can continue on to Winchcombe for a total of about 14 mi. The **Thames Path Walk** starts on the western edge of the Cotswolds in Lechlade and follows the Thames 184 mi. to Kingston, near London. The section from the Cotswolds to Oxford is low-impact and particularly peaceful. Contact the **National Trails Office** (☎(01865) 810 224) for details. Local roads are perfect for **biking;** rolling hills welcome both casual and hardy cyclers. Tiny villages boast little more than pretty houses, so hit a few larger watering holes as well. Parts of the Oxfordshire Way are hospitable to cyclists, if slightly rut-ridden.

WINCHCOMBE. A convenient daytrip before heading into the Cotswolds, Winchcombe sits 6 mi. north of Cheltenham on the A46 and features the impressive **Sudeley Castle,** a 10min. walk from the town center. Once the manor estate of King

Ethelred the Unready, the castle was a prized possession in the Middle Ages, with lush woodland and a royal deer park. Today, the estate is home to Lord and Lady Ashcombe, who welcome you and your admission fee to their home and 14 acres of gardens. Sudeley also holds seasonal events, including jousting tournaments and chocolate Easter egg hunts. **St. Mary's Chapel** contains the tomb of Henry VIII's Queen #6, Katherine Parr. (☎(01242) 602 308. Open Mar.-Oct. daily, castle 11am-5pm, last admission 4:30pm, gardens 10:30am-5:30pm. Castle and gardens £6.50, seniors £5.50, children £3.50. Gardens only £5/£4/£2.75.)

MORETON-IN-MARSH. With train station, frequent bus service, and bike shop, Moreton is a convenient base from which to explore the northern Cotswolds. Little else in the town is of great interest. A 10min. walk northeast, however, leads to **Batsford Arboretum,** 55 enchanting acres of anti-Cotswold, including a waterfall, a Japanese rest house, a lake, trees, and more trees. (☎(01386) 701 441. Open Feb. to mid-Nov. daily 10am-5pm, mid-Nov. to Jan. Sa-Su 10am-4pm. £4, concessions £3, children £1.) Three miles east of Moreton on the A24, visitors to the **Longborough Farm Shop** can pick their own fruit, or buy it pre-picked. (☎(01451) 830 413. Open M-Sa 9am-6pm, Su 10am-6pm. Self-picking June-Sept., pre-picked Apr.-Dec.) **Warwick House B&B ❸,** London Rd., offers numerous creature comforts, including access to a nearby leisure center. (☎(01608) 650 773; www.snoozeandsizzle.com. Book ahead. £25 per person, £20 for more than 2 nights.) **Fosseway Farm B&B ❸,** Stow Rd., 5min. east of town, has gorgeous views of rolling fields. (☎(01608) 650 503. Caravaning available. Singles £25-30; doubles £38-45.)

BROADWAY. Only 4 mi. southwest of Chipping Campden, restored Tudor, Jacobean, and Georgian buildings with traditional tile roofs rise high on each side of Broadway's main street, giving the town a stately, museum-like air. **Broadway Tower,** a 20-40min. uphill hike, enchanted the likes of decorator-designer-poet William Morris and his pre-Raphaelite comrade Dante Gabriel Rossetti. Built in the late 1700s in a superfluous attempt to intensify the beauty of the landscape, the tower affords a view of 12 counties. (☎(01386) 852 390. Open daily Apr.-Oct. 10:30am-6pm, Nov.-Mar. 10:30am-5pm. £3, concessions £2.50, children £1.50.) **Snowshill Manor,** 2½ mi. southwest of Broadway, was once home to a collector of everything and anything; it now features about 20,000 random odds and ends. (☎(01386) 852 410. Open Apr.-Oct. W-Su noon-5pm. £5, families £15.)

CHIPPING CAMPDEN. Years ago, quiet Chipping Campden was the capital of the Cotswold wool trade: the village became a one-time market center ("chipping" means "market"). **Market Hall,** in the middle of the main street, attests to a 400-year history of commerce. The Gothic **Church of St. James,** a signposted stroll from High St. (5min.), provides some architectural diversity. Currently, the town is famous for its **Cotswold Olympic Games** in the first week of June, featuring wheelbarrow racing and Wellington-throwing contests. The games take place on **Dovers Hill,** a short uphill climb from the town center, which offers arguably the most breathtaking view in the Cotswolds, with unpenned sheep to boot.

STOW-ON-THE-WOLD. The self-proclaimed "Heart of the Cotswolds" hides languidly in the hills. Despite the 24hr. **Tesco** supermarket (open continuously M 8am to Sa 10pm, also Su 10am-4pm), it still exudes Cotswold quaintness. Three miles downhill, on the B4077, **Donnington Trout Farm** lets visitors do more than just fish for trout—feed them (20p), eat them (£1.50-2), or just gaze soulfully at them (free tour if staff is not too busy). Staff can smoke (in the culinary sense) just about anything, even pigeons. (☎(01451) 830 873. Open Apr.-Oct. daily 10am-5:30pm, Nov.-Mar. Tu-Su 10am-5pm.) The **YHA hostel** (see p. 298) stands near the stocks. For more comfortable lodgings and a mouthwatering breakfast, stay with the Cotswolds' most endearing couple at ▓**Beeches ❷,** Fosse Ln., on the street just past Tesco. (☎(01451) 870 836. £18 per person.) Rugged simplicity defines **Pear Tree Cottage ❹**, on High St., in an old stone house with comfortable rooms. (☎ (01451) 831 210. Singles £35-40; doubles £40-45.)

THE SLAUGHTERS. Like the proverbial lamb, you can travel to the Slaughters (Upper and Lower), a few miles southwest of Stow. A tiny version of Bourton-on-the-Water, complete with bubbling stream and centuries-old footbridges, the less touristed and infinitely more charming Slaughters are connected by quaint footpaths. The **Old Mill**, on Mill Ln. at Lower Slaughter, scoops water from the river that flows placidly past. The antique and souvenir shop is worth a look. (☎ (01451) 820 052. Open summer daily 10am-6pm, phone for winter hours. £1.25, children 50p.)

BOURTON-ON-THE-WATER. Inexplicably touted as the "Venice of the Cotswolds" (no gondolas, just the picturesque River Windrush and a series of footbridges), Bourton is also a stop for hikers. The Oxford Way trailhead is here, as is the convergence of other trails, including Wardens Way, Heart of England Way, Windrush Way, and Gloucestershire Way. Follow signs to the **scale model of Bourton,** a miniature labor of patience. Between the olfactory heaven and hell of rose-laden gates and dung-strewn fields, **The Cotswold Perfumery,** on Victoria St., features fragrant flowers and a theater equipped with "Smelly Vision," which releases actual scents as they're mentioned on screen. (☎ (01451) 820 698. Open M-Sa 9:30am-5pm, Su 10:30am-5pm; closes around 6pm in summer. £2, concessions £1.75.)

CIRENCESTER. One of the larger towns, and sometimes regarded as the capital of the region, Cirencester (SI-ruhn-ses-ter) is the site of Corinium, a once-important Roman town founded in AD 49. Although only scraps of the amphitheater remain, the **Corinium Museum,** on Park St., has a formidable collection of Roman paraphernalia. (☎ (01285) 655 611. Closed for renovations until Oct. 2003. £2.50, concessions £1-2.) The **world's highest yew hedge** bounds Lord Bathurst's mansion in the town center; the garden is scattered with Roman ruins. **Cirencester Parish Church** (Gloucestershire's largest) is a "wool church," meaning it was built on the wealth of the wool trade. (☎ (01285) 653 142. Open daily 10am-5pm. Services M-Sa 3 per day; Su 8, 10, 11:30am, 12:15, 6pm. Donation requested.) A short bus ride from Cirencester, and 3½ mi. south of Tetbury, **Westonbirt Arboretum,** the National Arboretum, features 17 mi. of gorgeous tree-lined paths. (☎ (01666) 880 220. Open daily 10am-8pm or until dusk. £4.50, seniors £4, children £1.) An **antique market** arrives on Fridays (☎ (0171) 263 6010; 9am-3pm in Corn Hall near the TIC); smaller **crafts fairs** appear Saturdays, from 10am-4:30pm.

CHEDWORTH. Tucked in the hills southwest of Cheltenham, Chedworth contains a well-preserved **Roman Villa,** equidistant from Cirencester and Northleach off the A429. The villa's famed mosaics came to light in 1864 when a gamekeeper noticed tile fragments revealed by clever rabbits. The site displays a water shrine and two bathhouses just above the River Coln. (☎ (01242) 890 256. Open Apr.-Oct. Tu-Su 10am-5pm; Mar. and Nov. Tu-Su 11am-4pm. £3.80, children £1.90, families £9.50.)

SLIMBRIDGE. Slimbridge, 12½ mi. southwest of Gloucester off the A38, is the site of the largest of seven **Wildfowl & Wetlands Trust** centers in Britain. Sir Peter Scott has developed the world's biggest collection of wildfowl, with over 180 different species. All six varieties of flamingos nest here, and white-fronted geese visit from Siberia. In the tropical house, hummingbirds skim through jungle foliage. The visitor center has exhibits and food. (☎ (01453) 891 900. Open Apr.-Oct. daily 9:30am-5:30pm; Nov.-Mar. 9:30am-5pm; last admission 30min. before close. £6.30, seniors £5.50, children £3.80, families £16.40.) **YHA Slimbridge** (p. 298) benefits from Sir Peter's ornithological efforts, hosting flocks of its own.

Six miles southwest of Slimbridge, off the A38 between Bristol and Gloucester, rises massive **Berkeley Castle** (BARK-lay), 850-year-old ancestral home of the founders of the California university. The stone fortress boasts impressive towers, a dungeon, the cell where King Edward II was murdered, Queen Elizabeth I's bowling green, and a timber-vaulted Great Hall, where barons of the West Country met before forcing King John to sign the *Magna Carta*. (☎(01453) 810 332. Open July-Aug. M-Sa 11am-5pm, Su 1-5pm; June and Sept. Tu-Sa 11am-5pm, Su 2-5pm; Oct. Su 2-4:30pm; Apr.-May Tu-Su 2-5pm; Easter weekend 2-5pm. £5.70, seniors £4.70, children £3.10, families £15.50. Tours free and frequent.)

PREHISTORIC REMAINS. Archaeologists have unearthed some 70 ancient habitation sites in the Cotswolds. **Belas Knap,** a 4000-year-old burial mound, stands 1½ mi. southwest of Sudeley Castle, accessible from the Cotswold Way. The **Rollright Stones,** off the A34 between Chipping Norton and Long Compton (a 4½ mi. walk from Chipping Norton), are a 100 ft. wide ring of 11 stones. Consult Ordnance Survey maps (£4-7) or ask at TICs for other sites.

HEREFORD ☎01432

A square of activity in the bucolic patchwork of the Wye River region, Hereford (HAIR-eh-fuhd; pop. 60,000) was for centuries an important market town. Rural wares are still sold in its busy center, from cider pressed in its orchards to white-faced Hereford cattle and sheep in the livestock market on Wednesdays. Wide, pedestrian streets and narrow (though car-accessible) ways make Hereford a town best seen on foot, while excellent bus and rail connections make it a springboard westward into the Wye Valley on the Welsh-English border (see p. 472).

⎚ TRANSPORTATION. The **train** and **bus stations** are on Commercial Rd. Trains (☎(08457) 484 950) arrive from: **Abergavenny** (25min., 2 per hr., £5.60); **Cardiff** (1hr., every hr., £11.70); **Chepstow** via **Newport** (1½hr., every 2hr., £13.20); **London Paddington** (2¾hr., every hr., £33); **Shrewsbury** (1hr., every hr., £11.20). **National Express** (☎(08705) 808 080) runs buses from **Birmingham** (2hr., 1 per day, £8.25) and **London** (4hr., 3 per day, £16.50). The **bus stop** for local services is a few steps along Broad St. past the TIC. **Kelly's Coaches** (☎271 789) bus #20 connects Hereford with **Abergavenny** (30min., M-F 1 per day). Bus #39 comes from **Brecon** via **Hay-on-Wye** (1¾hr., M-Sa 6 per day, £5). On Sundays, **Yeoman's** bus #40 takes over (4 per day). For bus info, pick up the *Herefordshire Public Transport Map and Guide* or the *Monmouthshire County Council Local Transport Guide* at the TIC. **Rent bikes** from **Phill Prothero Cycles,** near Union St. (☎359 478. Open M-Sa 8:30am-5:30pm, closed Th 8:30am-noon. £10, includes lock, helmet, and repair kit.)

🛂 PRACTICAL INFORMATION. The **tourist information centre,** 1 King St., in front of the cathedral, books beds for £1.50 and a 10% deposit. (☎268 430. Open M-Sa 9am-5pm; June-Oct. also Su 10am-4pm.) **Walking tours** leave from the TIC. (90min. Mid-May to mid-Sept. M-Sa 11am, Su 2:30pm. £2.) **Cathedral Cruises** runs 40min. **river tours.** (☎358 957. Mar.-Oct., subject to weather.) Other services include: **Barclays,** Broad St. (open M-W and F 9am-5pm, Th 10am-5pm, Sa 9:30am-noon); **Thomas Cook,** St. Peter's St., near the Old House (☎422 500; open M-Tu and Th-Sa 9am-5:30pm, W 10am-5:30pm); the **Coin-op Launder Centre,** 136 Eign St. (☎269 610; open M-Sa 7:30am-6:15pm, Su 8:30am-6:15pm, last wash 1hr. before closing); and the **post office,** 13-15 St. Peter's St., by the bus stop (☎275 221; open M-F 9am-5:30pm, Sa 9am-4pm). **Post Code:** HR1 2LE.

🏠 ACCOMMODATIONS AND FOOD. Cheap lodgings in Hereford are scarce; your best bet is to walk to the **B&Bs** at the T-junction at the end of **Bodenham Rd** (from £20). **◼Rita Ford's Bed and Breakfast ❷,** 63 Edgar St., offers bright, airy rooms and, during summer months, an intimate flower garden with patio chairs. (☎270 227. £18 per person.) **Bourvrie House ❸,** 26 Victoria St., offers an array of room options and is a short walk from downtown. (☎266 265. Singles £21; doubles £19.50 per person; family room £55.) Farther from the town center, the **Holly Tree ❸,** 19-21 Barton Rd., has reasonable prices. (☎357 265. No smoking. Singles £22; doubles £24.) **Tesco,** Newmarket St., has all your picnic needs covered. (Open continuously M 8am to Sa 10pm.) Birds of pray will appreciate divine muffins (85p), scones (85p), and salads (£5.65) at the **Cafe@All Saints ❶**, in All Saints' Church on High St. (☎370 415. Open M-Sa 8:30am-5:30pm.) Scrumptious pastries come courtesy of the **Antique Teashop ❶**, 5a St. Peter's St., which also serves top-of-the-line tea. (☎342 172. Open M-Sa 9:45am-5pm, Su 10:15am-5pm.) Locals gather at the **Black Lion Inn ❶**, 31 Bridge St., for friendly conversation, lunch, and a beer… sometimes just the beer. (☎354 016. Open M-Sa noon-11pm, Su noon-10:30pm. Food served Tu-Sa noon-8pm, Su noon-3pm.)

◎ ▢ SIGHTS AND SHOPS. Majestic and imposing, **Hereford Cathedral** will make believers and non-believers alike regret lying about their ages, stepping on ants, and hiding from small children selling candy bars. Assuage your guilty self in the cathedral gift shop. The fascinating **Mappa Mundi** dates from back when the world was flat and missing half its continents (the 13th century). In the **Chained Library,** 1400 rare books are linked to the shelf by slender chains, incarcerated for your viewing pleasure. (☎374 209. Cathedral open daily until Evensong. Mappa Mundi and Library open May-Sept. M-Sa 10am-4:15pm, Su 11am-3:15pm; Oct.-Apr. M-Sa 11am-4pm. Cathedral admission free; Mappa Mundi and Library £4, concessions £3.50, families £10.) Fully intact, the 17th-century **Old House,** High Town, offers a glimpse of lifestyles past. (☎260 694. Open Apr.-Sept. Tu-Sa 10am-5pm, Su 10am-4pm; Oct.-Mar. Tu-Sa 10am-4pm. Free.) The educational-sounding **Cider Museum,** Pomona Pl., provides an excuse to sample the wares. (☎354 207. Open Apr.-Oct. M-Sa 10am-5:30pm; Nov.-Dec. M-Sa 11am-3pm. £2.60, students £2.10.) Ritzy shops in the **High Town** shopping area will help you unload some £20 notes. Those in reduced circumstances may prefer **Chapters,** 17 Union St., where used books go for mere pence. (☎352 149. Open M-Sa 9:30am-4:30pm.) **⧉Dinosaur Market,** off Union St., promises "Wild Clothes, Odd Things," and delivers eclecticness extending from robots to severed hands. (☎353 655. Open M-Sa 10am-5:30pm.)

⚑ NIGHTLIFE. Hereford offers decent if unspectacular options. **Play,** 51-55 Blueschool St., with a young crowd and eclectic mix, is the place to be on weekend nights. (18+ Th and Sa-M, 20+ and smart dress F. £10 cover, open bar. Open Th 9:30pm-1am, F-Sa 9pm-1:30am, Su 9pm-12:30am, M 9pm-1am.) **Booth Hall** on East St., where St. Peter's St. meets High Town, is a pub that cranks up the music in the evenings and brings in a DJ on Sunday nights. Other days, sip drinks in the courtyard. (☎344 487. Open M-Sa 11am-11:30pm, Su 7-10:30pm.)

THE BIG SPLURGE

FLOODGATES RESTAURANT DESIRE, DINNER, AND DESOLATION

The classy restaurant Floodgates may be the ideal place to bring a date, unless the incredible food succeeds in seducing your partner away. It would not be surprising to see the following scene take place: Suavely rakishly, he seated her at the romantically lit table. Sleek and colorful Floodgates was the perfect place to make the final move. His shy Swansea girl gazed coyly at him over the plate of grapes and cheese (£5.45) as he casually mentioned the Tuscan villa his future at the firm, his knowledge of conversational French, and meeting his parents...

Ever so slowly (and he thought sexily), he poured more wine (£20) as his object of desire savored the glazed duck (£12.95). Feeling triumphant, he polished off his smoked sirloin (£13.25), flashing her the smouldering matinee idol smile he'd practiced all morning. Now came the serious ammunition: his love of cats, appreciation of her mother, and tolerance of small, screaming children.

As she bit into her dessert, however, his siren was no longer receptive to wanton gazes. Her eyes had found new love: the beautifully orchestrated white chocolate cake (£4.95). As she seductively licked the ice cream from her spoon, cold chills ran along her spine. Entreaties were useless; she could no longer hear him. Muttering curses, he went and joined all the other forlorn men huddled around the bar.... *(Bridge St. ☎349 009. Open M-Sa 10am-10pm, Su 10am-9pm.)*

THE
MIDLANDS

Mention "the Midlands," and you'll invariably evoke images grim, urban, and decidedly sunless. But *go* to the Midlands and you may be surprised by the unique heritage and quiet grandeur of this smokestacked pocket. Warwick's storybook castle and Lincoln's breathtaking cathedral are two of Britain's standout attractions, while the entire towns of Shrewsbury and Stamford are considered architectural wonders. Even Birmingham, the region's much-maligned center, has its saving graces, among them lively nightlife and the Cadbury chocolate empire. But perhaps Ironbridge and its museums best personify the Midlands: deep in the Severn Valley, this World Heritage Site commemorates the region's innovative role in 18th-century iron production, a history rich with soot and fascinatingly gray.

HIGHLIGHTS OF THE MIDLANDS

IRONBRIDGE Admire the world's first cast-iron bridge and explore living museums at this monument to Britain's Industrial Revolution (p. 310).

LINCOLN Climb your way to Lincoln's cathedral, once Europe's tallest building and now the stunning centerpiece of this city-on-a-hill (p. 321).

STAMFORD Stroll through the streets of this impeccable stone town on your way to Burghley House, one of Britain's most lavish stately homes (p. 315).

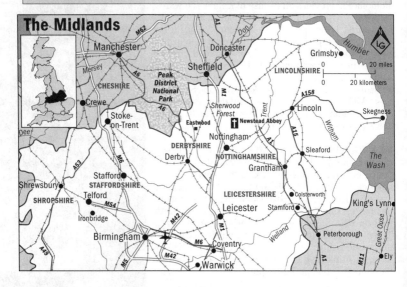

The Midlands

WARWICK ☎ 01926

Small and rather uninspiring on its own, Warwick (WAR-ick) exists as a tourist draw only for the sake of its famous castle, which can make the city a rewarding daytrip from Birmingham or Stratford. Those with an odd fascination for the Great Fire of 1694 may be inclined to stay the night for the town's unique architectural heritage, with buildings that pre- and post-date the fire.

TRANSPORTATION AND PRACTICAL INFORMATION. The Warwick **train station** sits on Coventry Rd. (Ticket office open M-Sa 6am-7:30pm, Su 10am-5pm.) Trains (☎ (08457) 484 950) run daily from: **Birmingham** (40min., 2 per hr., £3.70); **London Marylebone** (2hr., 2 per hr., £20.50); **Stratford** (20-40min., every 2 hr., £2.70). **National Express buses** (☎ (08705) 808 080) stop in Old Square from **London** (3hr., 3 per day, £11); **Flightlink** buses (☎ (08705) 757 747) go to Warwick rail station from **Birmingham** (1hr., 2 per day, £6) and **Heathrow** (1½hr., every 3hr., £20) airports; buy tickets at **Co-op Travel**, 15 Market St. (☎ 410 709), behind the Warwickshire Museum. **Local buses** X16 and X18 (3-4 per hr., £2.55-2.85) both stop at Market Place from **Coventry** (55min.) and **Stratford** (20min.). **Warwickshire Traveline** (☎ 412 987) has local bus info. For cabs, try **B&R Taxi** (☎ 495 000).

The **tourist information centre,** Court House, Jury St., books rooms for £2.50 plus a 10% deposit, and stocks a 30p guided map and a free town map. (☎ 492 212; www.warwick-uk.co.uk. Open daily 9:30am-4:30pm.) **Tours** leave from the TIC (£3; Su 10:45am, some Sa 2:30pm). Other services include: **Barclays,** 5 High St. (☎ 303 000; open M-Tu and Th-F 9:30am-4:30pm, W 10am-4:30pm); **Warwick Hospital,** Lakin Rd. (☎ 495 321); the **police,** Priory Rd. (☎ 410 111); and the **post office,** Westgate House, 45 Brook St. (☎ 491 061). **Post Code:** CV34 4BL.

ACCOMMODATIONS AND FOOD. A stay near the castle can be pricey, but Emscote Rd. has cheaper options. From the train station, turn right on Coventry Rd. and left at the Crown & Castle Inn on Coten End, which becomes Emscote Rd. The humorous young proprietor maintains a laid-back atmosphere at **Westham Guest House ❸,** 76 Emscote Rd., 10min. from the Crown & Castle. (☎ 491 756; westhamhouse@aol.com. Singles £20; doubles £34, with bath £38-42.) All rooms are ensuite at the newly renovated and fabulously decorated **Avon Guest House ❸,** 7 Emscote Rd. (☎ 491 367. Singles £23; doubles £46.) The friendly folks at **Chesterfields ❷,** 84 Emscote Rd., offer cozy lodgings. (☎ 774 864. Singles £20; doubles £35-40.) **Agincourt Lodge Hotel ❹,** 36 Coten End, features fantastically huge rooms, some with four-poster beds. (☎/fax 499 399. Singles £40-50; doubles £52-70.)

Fanshawe's ❷, 22 Market Pl., serves mouthwatering meals, from roasted lamb (£10) to spinach and ricotta cheese Wellington (£6). Top it off with gourmet desserts (£2-4) like crème brûlée or walnut cake. (☎ 410 590. Open M-Sa 6pm-10pm.) The **Crown & Castle Inn ❶,** 4-6 Coventry Rd., has sandwich-and-chips lunch specials (from £2) and dinners (burgers £4.50) in a traditional pub. (☎ 492 087. Open M-Sa 11am-11pm, Su noon-10:30pm.) For quick, tasty, and cheap eats, try **The Coffee Shop ❶,** 11 Old Market Sq., near St. Mary's Church. (☎ (07968) 114 915. Sandwiches £1-2.) At the other end of the dining spectrum, Warwick Castle hosts a five-course **medieval banquet ❺** with unlimited wine and ongoing entertainment, every night from 8-11pm. (☎ 406 602. Call for reservations. Jan.-Oct. £39.50; Nov.-Dec. £46.)

SIGHTS. Many medievalists, architects, and fire-breathing dragons regard **Warwick Castle** as England's finest. Climb 530 steps to the top of its towers and see the countryside unfold like a fairytale kingdom. The dungeons are manned by life-size wax soldiers preparing for battle, while "knights" and "craftsmen" discuss their trades in the festival village. You'll also find medieval games, storytelling by the Red Knight, and seasonal events like summer jousting tournaments and winter Christmas festivals. (☎495 421, 24hr. recording 406 600. Open Apr.-Sept. daily 10am-6pm; Oct.-Mar. 10am-5pm. May to mid-Sept. £12.50, seniors £9, students £9.40, children £7.40, families £33; mid-Sept. to April £1-2 less.)

Warwick also features cheaper, less impressive sites, like **St. Mary's Church,** on Church St., which keeps the grave of Sir Fulke Greville, who's said to haunt the castle's Watergate Tower. (☎403 940. Open daily 10am-6pm. Services Su 8, 10:30am, 6:30pm.) In 1571, Elizabeth I gave Lord Leycester the buildings of the **Lord Leycester Hospital,** 60 High St., to house 12 old soldiers who had fought with him in the Netherlands; today, seven retired veterans still live inside. More interesting to see may (or may not) be the building's Regimental Museum and Brethren's Kitchen. (☎491 422. Open Tu-Su Easter-Oct. 10am-5pm; Nov.-Easter 10am-4pm. £3.25, concessions £2.70, children £2.20.) The **Warwickshire Museum,** in the Market Hall, has displays on archaeology and natural history. (☎412 501. Open Tu-Su 10am-5pm, except Oct.-Mar. Su 11:30am-5pm. Free.)

NEAR WARWICK: COVENTRY   ☎024

Twelve miles northeast of Warwick swells Coventry, bombed during WWII and quickly rebuilt into the dull splotch of modernity that it is today. The city is united around its two stately **cathedrals**—the destroyed and the resurrected, both beautifully decorated with high stained glass windows. Shards of the old cathedral are visible through the glass "west wall" (actually the south) of the new. (☎7622 7597. Open Easter-Oct. daily 9:30am-6pm; Nov.-Easter until 5:30pm. Requested donation £3.) The tourist season commences around the first and second weekends of June during the **Lady Godiva Festival,** which honors Countess Godgifu (who would buy chocolates with a name like that?) of Coventry. See the newest incarnation of Lady Godiva at the annual parade, a celebration of nekkidness that in previous years has featured the stuntriders of *Braveheart.* For less scandalous ways of getting from place to place, try the **Museum of British Road Transport,** Hales St. The museum displays the largest collection of British cars (400) in the world. (☎7683 2425. Open daily 10am-5pm. Last admission at 4:30pm. Free.) If all that movement makes you want to settle down for the night, visit the **Coventry Tourism Centre,** Bayley Ln., which books accommodations for an 8% deposit. (☎7622 7264; fax 7622 7255. Open year-round Sa-Su 10am-4:30pm; Easter-Oct. M-F 9:30am-5pm and Nov.-Easter until 4:30pm.)

BIRMINGHAM   ☎0121

Castle-scouring, monument-seeking history buffs, move on—no great battles were fought in Birmingham, and no medieval landmarks are situated here. In fact, many outside busy "Brum" may grimace at the mention of the industrial heart of the Midlands, a transport hub girdled in ring roads and a mecca for convention-seeking three-piece suits. But a walk through Britain's second most populous city (pop. 1,000,000 and climbing) will reveal some efforts at overcoming its reputation for unfriendly ugliness—witness the elegant fountain of Victoria Sq. or the chichi cafes along redeveloped canal banks. Cadbury World offers some sweet daytime diversion, but it isn't until night that the city, fueled by world-class entertainers and a young university crowd, truly comes alive.

▉ TRANSPORTATION

Birmingham snares a clutch of train and bus lines between London, central Wales, southwest England, and points north.

Flights: Birmingham International Airport (☎ 767 5511). Free transfer to the nearby Birmingham International train station for connections to New St. Station and London.

Trains: New St. Station serves trains (☎ (08457) 484 950) from: **Liverpool Lime St.** (1½hr., 1-2 per hr., £18.50); **London Euston** (2hr., 2 per hr., £29.60); **Manchester Piccadilly** (2½hr., every hr., £16.50); **Nottingham** (1¼hr., 2-4 per hr., £9.20); **Oxford** (1¼hr., 1-2 per hr., £16.50). Others pull into **Moor St.** and **Snow Hill** stations. Follow signs to get from New St. to Moor St. Station (10min. walk).

Buses: Digbeth Station, Digbeth. Open 24hr. Luggage storage £1-3. **National Express** (☎ (08705) 808 080; office open M-Sa 7:15am-6pm, Su 8:15am-6pm) from: **Cardiff** (3hr., 3 per day, £17.80); **Liverpool** (2½hr., every hr., return £11.75); **London** (3hr., every hr., £11.50); **Manchester** (2½hr., every 2hr., return £13). Buses also stop at Colmore Row and Bull Ring.

Birmingham

▲ **ACCOMMODATIONS**
Cook House, **9**
Grasmere Guest House, **10**
Ibis, **13**
Wentworth Hotel, **11**
Woodville House, **8**
🍴 **FOOD**
Lasan, **1**

Style Cafe, **12**
Thai Edge, **6**
Warehouse Cafe, **3**
Wine Republic, **2**
★ **NIGHTLIFE**
Bar2Sixty, **7**
Nightingale, **14**
Rat and Parrot, **4**
Stoodibakers, **5**

Public Transportation: Information at **Centro** (☎200 2700), in New St. Station. Stocks local transit map and bus schedules. Bus and train day pass £5; bus only £2.50, children £1.70. Open M-Tu and F 8:30am-5:30pm, W-Th and Sa 9am-5pm.

◪ PRACTICAL INFORMATION

Tourist Information Centre: 2 City Arcade (☎643 2514; fax 616 1038). Books rooms (10% deposit); sells theater and National Express tickets. Open M-Sa 9:30am-5:30pm. **Branches:** at 130 Colmore Row, Victoria Sq. (☎693 6300), open M-Sa 9:30am-6pm, Su 10am-4pm; and in the International Convention Centre (☎665 6116), open M-Th 9:45am-6pm, F 9:45am-4:45pm.

Tours: City Sightseeing (☎(01789) 299 123) runs 2hr. hop-on/hop-off bus tours, departing from the TIC on Corporation St. daily every hr. 11am-5pm.

Financial Services: Banks in the city center. **American Express,** Bank House, 8 Cherry St. (☎644 5533). Open M-F 8:30am-5:30pm, Sa 9am-5pm. **Thomas Cook,** 99 New St. (☎252 2600). Open M-W and F-Sa 9am-5:30pm, Th 10am-5:30pm, Su 11am-5pm.

Police: Lloyd House, Colmore Circus, Queensway (☎626 5000).

Internet Access: Central Library, Chamberlain Sq., has free web access on the 2nd floor but there's usually a wait. Open M-F 9am-8pm, Sa 9am-5pm. **Internet Exchange** (☎233 2230), also on the 2nd floor of the library, charges £1 per 30min., £1 per hr. with £2 membership. Open M-F 9am-8pm, Sa 10am-5pm.

Post Office: 1 Pinfold St., Victoria Sq. (☎643 5561). **Bureau de change.** Open M-F 8:30am-5:30pm, Sa 9am-5pm. **Post Code:** B2 4AA.

◪ ACCOMMODATIONS

Despite its size, Birmingham has no hostels; the TIC does, however, have good B&B listings. For a bevy of beds, catch bus #9, 109, or 139 to **Hagley Rd.,** where you can drift off to the music of passing traffic.

Grasmere Guest House, 37 Serpentine Rd., Harborne (☎/fax 427 4546). Take bus #22, 23, or 103 from Colmore Row to the Harborne swimming bath (20min.). Turn right off Harborne Rd. onto Serpentine Rd.; it's on the left at the end of the street. Lovely and smoke-free, with board games in lounge and tea and biscuits every night at 9:30pm. Singles £15, with bath £25; doubles £30. ❷

Wentworth Hotel, Wentworth Rd. (☎427 2839). From Harborne swimming bath, turn right on Lonsdale Rd.; Wentworth Rd. is at the end on the left. Luxurious bath in every room. Kind proprietors offer B&B-style hospitality. Singles £32; doubles £54. ❹

Ibis, Arcadian Centre, Ladywell Walk (☎622 6010; fax 622 6020), just east of the Hippodrome Theatre, offers the professional service of a bigger hotel for a smaller price. All-you-can-eat breakfast 6-10am. M-Th £47 per room, F-Su £37. ❹

Cook House, 425 Hagley Rd. (☎429 1916). Take bus #9 or 139 from Colmore Row and ask the driver to stop before the Quantum Pub (20min.), then walk back a few minutes. Informative owner welcomes travelers into his large Victorian home. Bright rooms contrast with dark halls. £21 per person; doubles £36. ❸

Woodville House, 39 Portland Rd., Edgbaston (☎ 454 0274), 1 mi. from the city center. Take bus #128 or 129 from Colmore Row (15min.). Comfortable and well located. Ring bell for late-night entry. All rooms with TV. Singles £18; doubles £30, with bath £35. ❷

FOOD

Birmingham is most proud of **balti,** a Kashmiri-Pakistani cuisine invented here by immigrants from the subcontinent and cooked in a special pan. Brochures at the TIC map out the city's numerous balti restaurants. Most of the best are southeast of the city center in the "Balti Triangle."

Thai Edge, 7 Oozells Sq. (☎ 643 3993), off Broad St. Bamboo poles and minimalist furniture give this reputed Thai restaurant a chic look. Entrees £6-15. ❸

Warehouse Cafe, 54 Allison St. (☎ 633 0261), off Digbeth, above the Friends of the Earth office. A mostly vegan, organic menu. Chill atmosphere and lunchtime veggie burgers (£2) keep locals loyal. Also hosts pricier dinners on special nights; call for more info. Open M-F noon-2:30pm, Sa noon-3pm. ❶

Style Cafe (☎ 643 4780), a tiny shop near Holloway Circus. Pedestrians can smell the delicious sandwiches (£1.60-2.80) from a block away. ❶

Lasan (☎ 212 3664), on the corner of Brook St. and James St. A posh, cozy restaurant serving modern fusion cuisine with Indian flavor. Full entrees £8, small dishes £2-3. Open M-F noon-3pm and 6pm-midnight. ❷

Wine Republic, Centenary Sq. (☎ 644 6464), next to Symphony Hall. Free tapas in outdoor dining area 5:30-9:30pm. Sandwiches, salads, and pastas £4-7, entrees £7-13, over 40 wines. Open M-Sa 11am-11pm, also Su when there's a show. ❷

SIGHTS

The **Birmingham Museum and Art Gallery,** Chamberlain Sq. off Colmore Row, supports **Big Brum,** northern cousin to London's Big Ben, and houses costumes, pre-Raphaelite paintings, and William Blake's illustrations of Dante's *Inferno.* (☎ 303 2834. Open M-Th and Sa 10am-5pm, F 10:30am-5pm, Su 12:30-5pm. Free.) The **Barber Institute of Fine Arts,** in the University of Birmingham on Edgbaston Park Rd., displays works by heavyweights like Rubens, Renoir, Matisse, Gauguin, and Degas. (Bus #61, 62, or 63 from the city center. ☎ 414 7333. Open M-Sa 10am-5pm, Su noon-5pm. Free.) Signs point northwest to the more than 100 shops lining the **Jewellery Quarter,** which hammers out almost all the jewelry in Britain. The **Museum of the Jewellery Quarter,** 75-79 Vyse St., Hockley, lets visitors tour an old factory and watch skilled gemsmiths. (5min. from the Jewellery Quarter train station. ☎ 554 3598. Open M-F 10am-4pm, Sa 11am-5pm. £2.50, concessions £2, families £6.50.)

The **National Sea Life Centre,** The Waters Edge, Brindleyplace, is home to over 3000 creatures and has the world's first fully transparent 360° underwater tunnel. (☎ 643 6777. Open daily 10am-5pm. £8, students £6, concessions £5.50.)

■ **CADBURY WORLD.** Twelve minutes south of town by rail or bus lies Cadbury World, a cavity-prompting celebration of the chocolate firm. Sniff your way through the story of chocolate's birth in the Mayan rainforests, but be prepared to fend off swarms of schoolchildren. Afterwards, fork over £2.35 and indulge in a 400g (big!) chocolate bar. *(By train from New St. to Bournville, or bus #83, 84, or 85 from the city center. Bus tours also make 30min. stops here every hour. ☎ 451 4159. Open daily 10am-3pm; closed certain days Nov.-Feb. £8.25, concessions £6.75, children £6.25, families £24.25, oompa-loompas free.)*

🔊 🎵 NIGHTLIFE AND ENTERTAINMENT

Streets beyond the central district can be dangerous. As always, take care at night.

BARS AND CLUBS

Broad St. is lined with trendy cafe-bars and clubs. A thriving gay-friendly scene has arisen in the area around **Essex St.** Pick up the bimonthly *What's On* to discover the latest hotspots. Clubbers on a budget should grab a guide to public transport's Night Network from the Centro office in New St. Station—**night buses** generally run hourly until 3:30am on Friday and Saturday nights.

Bar2Sixty, 160 Broad St. (☎633 4260). Funky lighting complements big, snazzy furniture. Selected drinks £1.50. M (Disco Inferno) and Su (Soul Jam). Cover £5, free before 9pm. Open M and Th-Sa until 2am, Tu-W until 1am, Su until 12:30am.

Stoodibakers, 192 Broad St. (☎643 5100). The alluringly dark decor of this futuristic warehouse prompts much drinking and posturing, as well as occasional dancing. Dress trendy. Cover £4 F-Sa after 9:30pm.

Rat and Parrot, 200 Broad St. (☎643 7130). The fashionable sip, step, and survey. No trainers, jeans, or sportswear in this bar. Turns clubby Th-Sa 9pm-1am. No cover.

Nightingale, Essex House, Kent St. (☎622 1718). 2 frenzied dance-floors, jazz lounge, and billiard room attract a predominantly gay crowd from all over the UK. Cover £5 weekends, free on weekdays. Open Tu-W 10pm-2am, F-Sa 9pm-4am, Su 9pm-1am.

MUSIC AND THEATER

City of Birmingham Symphony Orchestra (☎780 3333) plays in superb Symphony Hall, at the ICC on Broad St. Box office open M-Sa 10am-8pm; closes 5pm Sa if no performance; Su hours depend on concert times. Tickets £5-33; concessions and group discounts; student standbys after 1pm on concert days £3-5.

Hippodrome Theatre, Hurst St. (☎(0870) 730 1234). Originally a music hall featuring big-name vaudeville artists, the theater now stages West End musicals and quality ballet. Open M-Sa 10am-9pm. Tickets £4-44, £10 last-minute student tickets.

Birmingham Repertory Theatre, Centenary Sq. (☎236 4455), on Broad St. A less grandiose, but still celebrated, theater. Open M-Sa 10am-8pm. Tickets £5-17; discount standby tickets for students, seniors, and jobseekers (with UB40 cards).

The Birmingham Jazz Festival (☎454 7020) brings over 200 jazz bands, singers, and instrumentalists to town during the first 2 weeks of July; book through the TIC.

IRONBRIDGE   ☎01952

Pretty towns shouldn't have such deceptively ugly names. It's hard to believe that this small tree- and river-lined settlement was the birthplace of the Industrial Revolution—'twas a local chap who discovered a method of smelting iron ore with coal residue instead of charcoal. Aside from historic exhibits, nary a trace of the smoke-belching inferno remains today. Instead, cheery boutiques look out on tourist-busy streets, museums wait on every corner, and scenic hikes abound.

🚆 **TRANSPORTATION.** The nearest **train** station is at **Telford,** 20min. from Shrewsbury on the Birmingham-Shrewsbury-Chester line (M-Sa 1-4 per hr., Su every hr.). The best (well, only) way to reach Ironbridge directly is by **bus.** Timetables are notoriously temperamental; even the *Rural Bus Network*, a free booklet available at TICs, is not always up-to-date. For bus information, call the TIC or the **Telford Travelink** (☎200 005). **Midlands North** (☎(08457) 056 005) #96 stops at Ironbridge from **Telford** (15min., M-Sa 6 per day) and **Shrewsbury** (40min.; M-Sa 6 per day, Su 5 per day). Most buses to Ironbridge do not run beyond 5 or 6pm. The Sunday bus from Shrewsbury also stops at **Coalbrookdale, Blists Hill,** and **Coalport. Arriva** (☎(08456) 015 395) bus #99 runs on the Wellington-Bridgnorth route, stopping at **Ironbridge** and **Coalbrookdale** from **Telford** (25min., M-Sa 16 per day). Arriva #76 (20min., M-Sa 5 per day) and #77 (20min., M-Sa 4 per day) provide crucial, albeit spotty, service between **Coalbrookdale** and **Coalport** (both home to YHA hostels), stopping at the Ironbridge Museum of the Gorge en route. Not all buses begin or terminate in Coalport; get a timetable (and a sympathetic ear) at the TIC.

■ ⁊ **ORIENTATION AND PRACTICAL INFORMATION.** Ironbridge is the name of both the river gorge around which several villages cluster and the village at the center. The nine **Ironbridge Gorge Museums** huddle on the banks of the Severn valley in an area covering 6 sq. mi. Some are difficult to reach without a car—buses stop only at selected points and bike rental shops are conspicuously absent. There are three main groupings of museums. Central **Ironbridge** is home to the TIC and the Iron Bridge and Tollhouse; the Museum of the Gorge is ½ mi. to the west. Some 2 mi. northwest of the bridge is **Coalbrookdale,** where you'll find the Coalbrookdale Museum of Iron and the Darby Houses. Two miles east of the bridge, past the Jackfield Tile Museum, the village of **Coalport** is home to the Coalport China Museum and the Tar Tunnel. A mile north of Coalport is Blists Hill Victorian Town.

The friendly staff at the **tourist information centre,** the Wharfage, in Ironbridge, provides the free 66-page tome that is the *Ironbridge Gorge Visitor Guide*, books accommodations for a 10% deposit, and commiserates over bus schedules. (☎432 166, toll-free (0800) 590 258; fax 432 204; www.ironbridge.org.uk. Open M-F 9am-5pm, Sa-Su 10am-5pm.) Ironbridge has **no banks** or **ATMs.** The **post office** is on The Square in Ironbridge. (Open M-Tu and Th-F 9am-1pm and 2-5:30pm, W 9am-1pm, Sa 9am-12:30pm.) **Post Code:** TF8 7AQ.

⋔ ⊓ **ACCOMMODATIONS AND FOOD.** The two buildings of the **YHA Ironbridge Gorge** ❷ grace the valley's opposite ends, 3 mi. apart. The one in **Coalbrookdale** inhabits a remodeled schoolhouse and is near the Ironbridge TIC. Walk past the Museum of the Gorge and turn right toward Coalbrookdale; it's on your right. The other, in **Coalport,** next to the Coalport China Museum, is a renovated china factory equipped with laundry facilities, Internet access, and a restaurant. Both buildings are reached by Arriva bus #76; Coalbrookdale is also a stop on #77. (☎588 755 for both; ironbridge@yha.org.uk. Dorms £11.50, children £8.25.)

Otherwise, budget accommodations are few. Area **B&Bs** charge upwards of £22 per person, and solo travelers can expect to pay at least £30 for a single room. With a prime location in Ironbridge village, **Eley's of Ironbridge** ❹, 13 Tontine Hill, has rooms with baths, color TVs, and great views of the bridge. (☎432 541. Singles £36-42; doubles £49-57.) **The Library House** ❹, Severn Bank, greets guests with wine. The ensuite rooms have video players that will keep you up half the night and enormous breakfasts that will make you happy to wake up. (☎432 299. Singles £45-55; doubles £55-60; family rooms £75-85.) **Coalbrookdale Villa** ❹, Paradise St., is a stunning Gothic house 10min. from Ironbridge. The kind proprietress strives to supply every cereal you could desire. (☎/fax 433 450. Singles £46; doubles £54-58.) The nearest campsite is the **Severn Gorge Caravan Park** ❶, 3 mi. from Ironbridge and 1 mi. north of the Blists Hill Victorian Town, on Bridgnorth Rd. in Tweedale. (☎684 789. 1-person tent £7.65, 2-person tent £10.90. Electricity £2.45-2.75. Showers free.)

Find lunch and light snacks at the parasol-bedecked **Victorian Tea Room** ❷, 6 Tontine Hill. A home-baked snack will set you back £1-3, while meals are £6-8. (☎432 690. Open May-Sept. daily 10am-6pm; Oct.-Apr. M-F 10am-5pm.) **Oliver's Vegetarian Bistro** ❷, 33 High St., offers a varied menu (entrees £4-7) in a cozy setting. (☎ 433 086. Open Tu-F 7-11pm, Sa 11am-3pm and 7-11pm, Su 11am-5pm. Last orders 9:30pm.) Walk 5min. from Ironbridge toward Madeley for the steak-and-kidney pie (£5.25) at the **Horse and Jockey ❶** pub, 15 Jockey Bank, said to be Britain's best. (☎ 433 798. Open daily noon-2:30pm and 7-11pm; food served until 9:30pm.)

🏛 **MUSEUMS.** There's not much more to Ironbridge than the **Ironbridge Gorge Museums,** but you'd be hard-pressed to find a better portrayal of Britain's unique industrial heritage. Count on spending at least two days to cover the lot. If visiting all nine, buy an **Ironbridge Passport** from any of them, which admits you once to each of the museums on any dates you choose (£10.50, seniors £9.50, students and children £6.50, families £32.50). The major museums are open year-round daily 10am-5pm, while smaller collections such as the Darby Houses, the Iron Bridge Tollhouse, and the Broseley Pipeworks are open only limited hours from November through March; call the TIC for more information.

The **Iron Bridge,** built in 1779 by Abraham Darby III to world-wide attention, crosses a deep gorge of the River Severn. At its southern end, a small exhibit in the **Tollhouse** describes the bridge's history and how even royals had to (and still have to) pay the toll. (☎ 884 391. Open Easter-Oct., hours vary. Free.) A 10min. walk from Ironbridge village, the **Museum of the Gorge** provides a brief introduction to the area's history and is a good place to begin the day's exploring. (☎ 432 405. £2, seniors £1.50, students and children £1.) In Coalbrookdale to the northwest, the **Coalbrookdale Museum of Iron,** once a great warehouse, recreates the furnace of Abraham Darby I (where the whole brouhaha began), traces the history of iron use through millennia, and exhibits iron products beyond your wildest imagination. (☎ 433 418. £5/£4.20/£2.90.) Nearby, the **Darby Houses** model the pleasant quarters of a 19th-century ironmaster. (☎ 432 551. £3.15/£2.90/£1.60.) In Coalport to the west, the **Coalport China Museum** and **Jackfield Tile Museum** show the products of the industries that moved in when iron production tailed off; both offer demonstrations and workshops. (China ☎ 580 650; Tile 882 030. Both £4.20/£3.90/£2.40.) Don a hard-hat at the eerie **Tar Tunnel,** constructed to connect the Blists Hill mines to the Severn, where surprised workers discovered smudgy natural bitumen dripping from the walls. (☎ 580 827. £1.10/90p/55p.) After communing with a lot of iron, which, quite frankly, tends not to hold up its end of the conversation, make haste to the open-air **Blists Hill Victorian Town,** where you can chat with real actors going about their make-believe business, and exchange your silly 21st-century money for serious Victorian shillings and brass farthings to buy ale. (☎ 582 050. £8/£7.50/£5.)

SHREWSBURY
☎ 01743

Brightly arrayed hatter's windows, cushy boutiques, and crooked ancient roads make Shrewsbury (SHROWS-bree; pop. 60,000) a popular destination for shoppers and those with a weakness for stereotypically English streetscapes. True history buffs will want to take a roll in the historic Shrewsbury dirt—the semi-circular patch of land was first settled by pugnacious Saxons, who decided to call it Scrobbesbyrig, and then by Roger de Montgomery, second-in-command to William the Conqueror, who sashayed up from Hastings in the 11th century.

▐ TRANSPORTATION

The **train station,** a splendid neo-Gothic building, is at the end of Castle St. (Ticket office open M-Sa 5:30am-10pm, Su 7:30am-8:30pm.) **Trains** (☎ (08457) 484 950) run from: **Aberystwyth** (2hr.; M-Sa 8 per day, Su 5 per day; £11.50); **London** (3hr., 1-2 per hr., £33.50); **Swansea** (3½hr.; M-Sa 4 per day, Su 1 per day; £15.80); **Wolverhampton**

(40min., 2 per hr., £5.90); and most of North Wales via **Wrexham General** and **Chester** (1hr.; M-Sa 14 per day, Su 6 per day; £6.30). The **bus station** is on Raven Meadows, which runs parallel to Pride Hill. (☎244 496. Office open M-F 8:30am-5:30pm, Sa 8:30am-4pm.) **National Express buses** (☎(08705) 808 080) arrive from: **Birmingham** (1½hr., 2 per day, £4.25); **Llangollen** (1hr., 1 per day, £3.25); **London** (4½hr., 2 per day, £14). The *Shrewsbury Public Transport Guide* is free at the bus station and TIC. **Taxis** queue in front of the train station, otherwise call **Access Taxis** (☎344 444).

🔆 🄷 ORIENTATION AND PRACTICAL INFORMATION

The **River Severn** circles Shrewsbury's town center in a horseshoe shape, with the curve pointing south. The town's central axis runs from the train station in the northeast to Quarry Park in the southwest: first **Castle Gates,** the road becomes **Castle St.,** then pedestrian-only **Pride Hill,** then **Shoplatch,** and finally **St. John's Hill.**

Tourist Information Centre: Music Hall, The Square (☎281 200; fax 281 213; www.shrewsburytourism.co.uk), across from the Market Bldg. Get free town maps, buy National Express tickets, and book accommodations for £1.50 and a 10% deposit. Oversized town trail leaflets (95p), the new *Shrewsbury Guide* (£2.50), and piles of brochures. Open May-Sept. M-Sa 10am-6pm, Su 10am-4pm; Oct.-Apr. M-Sa 10am-5pm.

Tours: Historic 30min. **walking tours** from the TIC pass through Shrewsbury's "shuts" (closeable lanes) and reveal the etymology of Grope Lane. May-Sept. daily 2:30pm; Oct. M-Sa; Nov.-Apr. Sa only. £2.50, children £1.

Financial Services: Barclays, corner of Castle St. and St. Mary's St. Open M-Tu and Th-F 9am-5pm, W 10am-5pm, Sa 9:30am-1pm. **Thomas Cook** (☎842 000), corner of Pride Hill and Butcher Row. Open M-Tu and Th-Sa 9am-5:30pm, W 10am-5:30pm.

Launderette: Stidgers Wishy Washy, Monkmoor Rd. (☎355 151), off Abbey Foregate. Self-service Sa-Su only. Wash £3, dry 20p per 3min.; service £7.50 per load. Open M-F 7:30am-5pm, Sa 10am-4pm, Su 10am-2pm; last wishy washy 1hr. before close.

Police: Raven Meadows (☎232 888). Open M-Sa 9am-5pm. Also Clive Rd., Monkmoor.

Hospital: Shrewsbury Hospital, Mytton Oak Rd. (☎261 138).

THE HIDDEN DEAL

ST. MARY'S CHURCH CAFE

According to Shrewsbury law, sheep can graze anywhere—a number infiltrate the churchyard at **St. Mary's Church.** Wander with the woollies to find the peaceful pews of St. Mary's, a 12th-century respite from the city's bustling streets.

Saxon architecture meets beautiful German stained glass and colorful Victorian tiles at this historic church on St. Mary's St. in the heart of town. The small **cafe,** a hidden oasis of much-needed calm and caffeine, refreshes tired shoppers and way-worn tourists. If only a few coins rattle in your threadbare pockets, settle in to sip coffee (50p) or tea (45p) and to soak up some medieval ambience and ecclesiastical tranquility.

Should a few moments' rest inspire recklessness, take a moment to read the sobering tale of a parish rope-walker in the literature displayed. The unfortunate daredevil used to entertain the parish by attaching a length of rope to the steeple (one of England's highest) and skipping along it; sadly, his knot-tying ability wasn't as well developed as his balancing talent. (☎357 006. *Church free. Open M-F 10am-5pm, Sa 10am-4pm.*)

Internet Access: PC+, 11 Abbey Foregate (☎ 242 135), over the English Bridge. £2 per 30min. Open M-Sa 9am-5pm, sometimes later. **Shrewsbury Library,** Castle Gates (☎ 255 300). £1 per 15min. ID required. Open M, W, F 9:30am-5pm, Tu and Th 9:30am-7:30pm, Sa 9:30am-4pm.

Post Office: St. Mary's St. (☎ (08457) 740 740), just off Pride Hill. **Bureau de change.** Open M-Sa 9am-5:30pm. **Post Code:** SY1 1DE.

ACCOMMODATIONS AND FOOD

Shrewsbury accommodations are truly crunched, and singles are hard to find—reserve several weeks ahead during summer. Shrewsbury's YHA hostel closed in December 2002; the reopening at a new downtown site won't happen for a couple of years. Several **B&Bs** (£18-28) lie between **Abbey Foregate** and **Monkmoor Rd.** A taxi (£3) lets you skip the considerable hike from the bus and train stations. Bask in the kindness of strangers at the beautifully decorated **Trevellion House ❸,** 1 Bradford St., off Monkmoor Rd. (☎ 249 582. £22-27 per person.) Comely **Glyndene ❸,** Park Terr., has an elaborate bell-pull and tasteful rooms with TVs. From the bridge, follow the road left of the abbey. (☎ 352 488; www.glyndene.co.uk. £20-22 per person.) Two doors down, **Allandale ❸** hangs its walls with prints of wide-eyed babies and cityscapes. (☎ 240 173. £20 per person.) **Abbey Lodge ❷,** 68 Abbey Foregate, has standard rooms with TVs. (☎/fax 235 832. Singles £18; doubles with bath £42.50.)

Tucked in St. Alkmund's Sq., by Butcher Row, ▨**The Bear Steps Coffee House ❶** offers a unique, relaxing atmosphere, complete with piano and harp music tinkling in the background. Gnaw quiche with bread and butter (£5) or treacle tart and cream (£2.25) under the low beams of this 600-year-old house. (☎ 244 355. Open M-Sa 10am-4pm.) **The Good Life Wholefood Restaurant ❶,** Barracks Passage, off Wyle Cop, serves vegetarian vittles in a 14th-century building near the Lion Hotel. (☎ 350 455. Open M-Sa 9:30am-4:30pm.) At the **King's Head ❶** pub, Mardol St., try the roast dinner (£3.45) and admire a medieval painting of the Last Supper. (☎ 362 843. Open M-Sa 10:30am-11pm, Su noon-11pm; food served M-Sa 11am-7pm, Su noon-7pm.)

SIGHTS

Shrewsbury's biggest attraction is undoubtedly its architecture. Tudoresque houses dot the central shopping district and rally in full force at the **Bear Steps,** which start in the alley on High St. across from the Square. At the end of Castle St., the riverside acres of **Quarry Park** explode with bright flowers. Shrewsbury also makes a point of honoring its native sons, and memorials pepper the city. Check out **Darwin's statue** opposite the castle, the colossal **Lord Hill Column** at the end of Abbey Foregate, and the **Clive of India** outside Market Sq.

The original earth-and-timber version of **Shrewsbury Castle,** near the train station, was constructed in 1083 by Conquerin' Will's buddy Roger de Montgomery, who demolished 50 Saxon houses to make way for it. It's since been replaced by the Great Hall, a more durable stone building, now home to the **Shropshire Regimental Museum.** Climb **Laura's Tower** for a grand view of town. (☎ 358 516. Museum and tower open Easter-Sept. Su-M 10am-4pm, Tu-Sa 10am-5pm; Oct.-Easter W-Sa only. Grounds open Easter-Sept. daily 9am-5pm; Oct.-Easter M-Sa only. £2, seniors £1, students and children free. Grounds free.) The **Shrewsbury Museum and Art Gallery,** Barker St., off Shoplatch, displays Iron Age log boats and a silver mirror from AD 130. An interesting prehistory exhibit details the age when hippos roamed the shire. (☎ 361 196. Open Easter-Sept. Tu-Sa 10am-5pm, Su-M 10am-4pm; Oct.-Easter Tu-Sa 10am-4pm. Free.) Beyond the English Bridge, the 919-year-old **Shrewsbury Abbey** holds the remains of a shrine to St. Winefride, a 7th-century princess who was beheaded, then miraculously re-capitated to become an abbess and patroness of North Wales and Shrewsbury. Peculiar displays include a shrine to vanity and a sculpture of Jesus on the cross with his flesh rotting; a memorial to local WWI poet Wilfred Owen lies in the garden. (☎232 723. Open Easter-Oct. daily 9:30am-5:30pm; Nov.-Easter 10:30am-3pm.)

STAMFORD ☎01780

The finest scene between London and Edinburgh.
　　—Sir Walter Scott

The Conqueror built a castle at Stamford—destroyed in a string of nasty sieges and now the site of a bus station. Renegade scholars abandoned Oxford in 1333 and came here to found a new school—it floundered, and two years later the rebels sulked home. Despite such pitfalls, this sweetly tiny city lures travelers with its architecture. Norman arches frame crooked alleys between Georgian facades, earning Stamford its reputation as the most splendid stone town in England.

🖅🔁 TRANSPORTATION AND PRACTICAL INFORMATION. Stamford teeters on the edge of Lincolnshire, with Cambridgeshire ready to break its fall. **Trains** (☎(08457) 484 950) stop at **Stamford Station,** at the southern end of town, calling from: **Cambridge** (1hr., 1-2 per hr., £12.40); **Lincoln** (1½hr., every hr., £16.70); **London King's Cross** (2hr., 1-2 per hr., £36.50). **Buses** gather at Sheepmarket, off All Saints' St. (☎554 571. Office open M-Sa 9am-5:30pm.) **National Express** (☎(08705) 808 080) makes the trip from **London** (2½hr., 1 per day, £13.50).

To reach the **tourist information centre,** in the Stamford Arts Centre on St. Mary's St., follow Garrett Rd. from the train station over the River Welland and continue uphill to a right at Castle St., which becomes St. Mary's St. The TIC has a town map (£2) and *Town Trail* guide (75p), and books beds for free. (☎755 611. Open M-Sa 9:30am-5pm; Apr.-Oct. also Su 11am-4pm.) Other services include: **banks** along High St.; the **police,** North St. (☎752 222); **Internet access** at **Rush** (see below); and the **post office,** 9 All Saints' Pl. (☎763 294). **Post Code:** PE9 2EY.

🔂🔃 ACCOMMODATIONS AND FOOD. Beauty is priceless, at least in Stamford; consider daytripping from Cambridge or Lincoln to avoid high prices. Budget **B&Bs** stay on the outskirts; call ahead, and you may get a lift. Try **Birch House ❸,** 4 Lonsdale Rd., 20min. from the train station, where each room is decorated with artful zest. (☎754 876. £20 per person.) **The Candlesticks Hotel ❹,** 1 Church Ln., convenient to the city center and to Burghley House, surrounds its gourmet restaurant with elegant, ensuite rooms. (☎764 033. Singles £35-40; doubles £55-60.)

For groceries hit **Tesco,** 46-51 High St. (☎683 000. Open M-W and Sa 7:30am-5:30pm, Th-F 7:30am-6:30pm, Su 10am-4pm.) Gobble creative sandwiches (under £3) and check e-mail (£3 per hr.) between rounds of giant outdoor chess at **Rush ❶,** St. Mary's St. (☎767 874. Open M-Th 9am-6pm, F-Sa 9am-8pm, Su 10am-6pm.) Savor a pot of tea (95p) or an afternoon special (£3-5.25) with your favorite bear at **Paddington's ❶,** Ironmonger St. (☎751 110. Open M-Sa 9am-5:30pm.) Once the Midlands's most famous coaching inn, **The George ❷** commands High St. St. Martin's. (☎750 700. Food served noon-2:30pm.)

🎦🔳 SIGHTS AND ENTERTAINMENT. Stamford's main point of interest is 🔲**Burghley House,** England's largest Elizabethan mansion. It's a 1 mi. walk from Stamford along Burghley Park; signposted from High St. St. Martin's. Thickly wooded forests, home to a herd of fallow deer, give way to the white palace, poised on rolling lawns and ringed with gardens (of Capability Brown's design). The house was the prized creation of William Cecil, Lord High Treasurer of England and advisor to Queen Elizabeth I. The famous **Heaven Room** and infamous **Hell Staircase** are masterworks of Antonio Verrio: giant murals of spectacular ancient gods ascend the walls of the former, while sinners of every shape and hue descend the latter. Don't miss Burghley's newest addition, a 12-acre **Sculpture Garden** showcasing rare flowers and contemporary sculpture. (☎752 451. House open Apr.-Oct. daily 11am-4:30pm; by tour only M-F. Sculpture Garden open daily 11am-4pm. Park open daily dawn-dusk. £7.10, seniors £6.50, children free.)

The quirky **Stamford Museum,** Broad St., charts the town's history from Saxon days through the Georgian high period. One exhibit (of dubious taste and complete with wax figures) concerns Daniel Lambert, England's fattest man, who died in Stamford. Vaudeville novelty Tom Thumb came to Stamford to perform while standing in the armhole of Lambert's waistcoat. (☎766 317. Open M-Sa 10am-5pm; Apr.-Sept. also Su 2-5pm. Free.) On the way to Burghley House, pay a visit to Lambert and the Cecil family, who slumber in their Romanesque tombs beneath **St. Martin's Church,** High St. St. Martin's. (☎751 233. Open daily 9am-4pm. Free.)

The **Stamford Arts Centre,** St. Mary's St., hosts local productions and national touring companies. (☎763 203. Box office open M-Sa 10am-5pm.) The famous **Stamford Shakespeare Festival** is based at Elizabethan **Tolethorpe Hall** from June to August. (☎756 133. Box office open M-Sa 9:30am-8pm; tickets also available from the Stamford Arts Centre. M-Th £10, concessions £9; F-Sa £13, no concessions.)

NOTTINGHAM ☎0115

Nottingham (pop. 262,000) maintains its age-old tradition, created by the mythical Robin Hood, of taking from the rich. The modern city uses its favorite rogue as an economic tool, luring tourists with little substance but plenty of thrill. Don't be fooled: Nottinghamshire has produced more famed residents than its socially conscious outlaws, including Lord Byron, D.H. Lawrence, and Jesse Boot, whose name appears on pharmacies nationwide. Navigating Nottingham today, you'll more likely see savvy urban youths (some of the city's 20,000 university students) than either merry men or club-footed poets.

▐ TRANSPORTATION

Trains: Nottingham Station, Carrington St., south of the city, across the canal. Trains (☎(08457) 484 950) from: **Lincoln** (1hr.; M-Sa 32 per day, Su 7 per day; £5.90); **London St. Pancras** (2hr., every hr., £42.50); **Sheffield** (50min., every hr., £7.30).

Buses: Broad Marsh Bus Station (☎950 3665), between Collin St. and Canal St. Ticket and info booth open M-F 9am-5:30pm. **National Express** (☎(08705) 808 080) from **London** (3hr., 7 per day, £15) and **Sheffield** (1¼hr., every hr., £5.25). **Victoria Bus Station** is at the corner of York St. and Cairn St. **Nottinghamshire County Council Buses** link points throughout the county.

Public Transportation: For short urban journeys, hop on a **Nottingham City Transport** bus (40-90p). All-day local bus passes £2.50. For public transit info call **Nottinghamshire Buses Hotline** (☎924 0000). Open daily 7am-8pm.

⚡ ⁊ ORIENTATION AND PRACTICAL INFORMATION

Nottingham is a busy city and its streets are confusing. Its hub is **Old Market Sq.,** a plaza near the Council House (beware the pigeons).

Tourist Information Centre: 1-4 Smithy Row (☎ 915 5330), off Old Market Sq. Many reference guides, tour and **job listings,** a free city map, and the free *What's On* entertainment guide. Books rooms (before 4:30pm) for £3 and a 10% deposit. Open M-F 9am-5:30pm, Sa 9am-5pm, Aug.-Sept. also Su 10am-3pm.

Tours: Nottingham Experience (☎ (0410) 293 348) leads 30min. tours, leaving from the castle gatehouse. Easter-Oct. daily 10am-4pm; £3, concessions £2.50.

Financial Services: Trip over a **bank** every 5 feet. **Thomas Cook,** 4 Long Row (☎ 909 3000). Offers budget travel services. Open M-Tu and Th-Sa 9am-5pm, W 9:30am-5:30pm. **American Express,** 2 Victoria St. (☎ (08706) 001 060). Open M-Tu and Th-F 9am-5:30pm, W 9:30am-5:30pm, Sa 9am-5pm.

Launderette: Brights, 150 Mansfield Rd. (☎ 948 3670), near the Igloo hostel. Open M-F 8:30am-7pm, Sa 8:30am-6pm, Su 9:30am-5pm. Last wash 1hr. before close.

Police: North Church St. (☎ 967 0999).

Nottingham

🏠 **ACCOMMODATIONS**
Bentinck Hotel, **11**
Igloo, **1**
The Lace Market Hotel, **9**
YMCA, **2**

🍴 **FOOD**
Balti House, **6**
Casa, **8**
Hart's, **4**

🍺 **PUBS**
Ye Olde Trip to
Jerusalem, **10**

⭐ **MUSIC AND CLUBS**
Market Bar, **7**
Rock City, **3**
The Social, **5**

Hospital: **Queen's Medical Center,** Derby Rd. (☎924 9924).

Internet Access: Alphacafe, 4 Queen St. (☎956 6988). 16+ terminals, stylish setting. £2 per hr. before noon, £4 per hr. after. Open M-F 9:30am-8:30pm, Sa 10am-7pm.

Post Office: Queen St. (☎947 4311). Open M-Sa 9am-5:30pm. **Post Code:** NG1 2BN.

ACCOMMODATIONS

Guest houses (£18-22) cluster on **Goldsmith St.** (near Nottingham Trent University).

Igloo, 110 Mansfield Rd. (☎947 5250; reception@igloohostel.co.uk), on the north side of town (High St. becomes Mansfield Rd. after 2 blocks); from the train station, take bus #90. Homey hostel operated by an experienced backpacker. Lively orange and green walls. TV lounge, kitchen, and 2 black cats. Curfew 3am. £12 per person. ❷

Bentinck Hotel, Station St. (☎958 0285), directly across from the train station. Great location more than makes up for worn carpets. Clean rooms with TVs, and a late bar downstairs. £19.50 per person, with bath £23.50. ❷

The Lace Market Hotel, 19-31 High Pavement (☎852 3232). A worthy target for Robin Hood. Chic, upscale rooms with all the requisite luxuries for a weekend (or weekday) splurge. Massive beds, satellite TV, CD players, and well-stocked minibars. The bathrooms are wonders unto themselves. Singles £89; doubles £99-120. MC. ❺

YMCA, 4 Shakespeare St. (☎956 7600). Large building with bland decor on a busy street. Breakfast included. Key deposit £5. Dorms £11; singles £18. ❷

FOOD

Quick, inexpensive bites are easily found on **Milton St.** and **Mansfield Rd.** Gaggles of sandwich shops, trendy cafes, and ethnic eateries line **Goosegate.** Find a **Tesco** supermarket in the Victoria Shopping Centre. (☎980 7500. Open M-Tu and Th-Sa 8am-7pm, W 8am-8pm, Su 11am-5pm.)

Casa, 12-18 Friar Ln. Fine service in expansive surroundings. Size up stylish patrons and passersby as you munch fresh sandwiches (£4-6) and creatively topped pastas (£6-8). Open daily noon-10:30pm. ❷

Ye Olde Trip to Jerusalem, 1 Brewhouse Yard (☎947 3171). Yet another claimant to the title "Oldest Inn in England," this one pulled its first drink in 1189 and served soldiers en route to the Crusades. Locally known as "The Trip," the pub is carved into Nottingham Castle's sandstone base. 6 ft. ceilings—mind your head. Open M-Sa 11am-11pm, Su noon-10:30pm; food served M-F 9am-5pm, Sa-Su noon-6pm. ❶

Hart's, Standard Court, Park Row (☎911 0666). Perfect for those who prefer their dishes braised and glazed, offering complicated variations on traditional English cuisine. Sleek but not snooty surroundings. Entrees £10-14; pre-theater set dinner £17.50. Open M-Su noon-2pm and 7pm-11pm. ❹

Balti House, 35 Heathcote St. (☎947 2871). This tandoori treasure trove sizzles above and beyond the throngs of Indian dives around town. Open daily 6-10pm. ❶

SIGHTS

GALLERIES OF JUSTICE. This is an innovative museum experience at its interactive best. Visitors can explore special exhibitions, like displays of original evidence from the 1963 **Great Train Robbery,** at their leisure before being submitted to the worst of historical English "justice" in the **Crime and Punishment Galleries.** You'll be convicted of one trumped-up charge or another before a merciless judge, then assigned a convict number and shoved into the dungeons by whip-wielding guards—don't be surprised if you end up in Australia. Return to the side of the righteous in the **Police Galleries**, where a series of exhibits explore the historical and modern societal role of British "coppers." *(High Pavement. ☎ 952 0558; www.galleriesofjustice.org.uk. Open Tu-Su 10am-5pm. Allow 2hr. Last admission to Crime and Punishment 3pm, Police Galleries 4pm. £7, concessions £6, children £5.25, families £20.)*

NOTTINGHAM CASTLE. Constructed in 1068 by William the Conqueror, Nottingham's castle (well, its ruins, anyway) top a sandstone rise south of the city center. In 1642, Charles I raised his standard against Parliament here, kicking off the Civil Wars. For his troubles, the king was beheaded and the castle destroyed. What's left now houses the ◪**Castle Museum and Art Gallery,** a refreshing collection of historical exhibits, Victorian art, silver, and the regimental memorabilia of the Sherwood Foresters. *(☎ 915 3700. Open Mar.-Oct. daily 10am-5pm; Nov.-Feb. Sa-Th 10am-5pm. Admission M-Th free; Sa-Su £2, concessions £1, families £5, free for disabled visitors.)* While you're there, check out **Mortimer's Hole,** the underground passageway that leads from the base of the cliff to the castle. *(☎ 915 3700. 50min. tours daily at 2 and 3pm from the Castle Museum entrance. £2, concessions £1.)*

THE UNDERGROUND SCENE. You'd never know it, but Nottingham is riddled with hundreds of caves. As early as the 10th century, dwellers dug homes out of the soft and porous "Sherwood sandstones" on which the city rests. Even in medieval times, the caves were often preferred to more conventional housing—they required no building materials and incurred lower taxes. While subterranean residency dwindled during the Industrial Revolution, Nottingham citizens (and pub owners) continued to use some for storage, and during WWII many were converted to air-raid shelters. Visitors can tour one cave complex, surreally situated beneath the Broad Marsh Shopping Centre. *(☎ 924 1424. Open M-Sa 10am-5pm, Su 11am-5pm. 40min. audio tour. £3.75, concessions £2.75, families £11.50.)*

TALES OF ROBIN HOOD. Cable cars will carry you and your five-year-old through Robin's amusement-park version of Sherwood Forest. Exorcise your inner outlaw at a **medieval banquet**—where you'll pay £35 per person for costume, four courses, and lots of beer—or, yes, that's right, a **medieval murder mystery**—£23.50 per person for three courses and a chance to figure out who killed the Sheriff's bride-to-be. *(30-38 Maid Marian Way. ☎ 948 3284. Open daily 10am-6pm, last admission 4:30pm. £6.50, concessions £5.25, children £4.50, families £20.)*

THE LACE INDUSTRY. Local myth holds that there are five women for every Nottingham man, an unlikely ratio springing from the lace industry that employed thousands of young women in the mid-19th century. The **Museum of Nottingham Lace**, 3-5 High Pavement, demonstrates a working 1850s spinning machine to show how the material was woven into the social fabric of the city. (☎989 7365. Open Apr.-Oct. Tu-Su 10am-5pm; Nov.-Mar. 10am-4pm. 50min. audio tour with £2 deposit. Demonstrations 11am-1pm and 1:30-3:30pm. £3, concessions £2.50, children £2.)

🎭 🎵 NIGHTLIFE AND ENTERTAINMENT

Thirty-plus clubs, and even more pubs, blanket the city. Covers and crowds vary, but students can be found everywhere. Live bands, primarily of the punk and indie variety, play to a casual student crowd on one of the two floors at **The Social**, 23 Pellham St., where theme nights abound. (☎950 5078. Open M-Tu 5pm-11pm, W-F 5pm-2am, Sa 11am-2am.) **Rock City,** 8 Talbot St., hosts local bands and mainstream rock. "Damaging" Thursday nights offer metal appreciation, and Saturdays are alternative. (☎950 0102. Cover £3-4. Open M-Sa 8:30pm-2am.) The stylish set salsas on Sundays at the **Market Bar,** 16-22 Goosegate, Hockley (☎924 1780), when most other clubs are closed. Stage fare can be found at the **Theatre Royal,** Theatre Sq. (☎989 5555), and **Nottingham Playhouse,** Wellington Circus (☎941 9419).

🏛 DAYTRIPS FROM NOTTINGHAM

🏚 **NEWSTEAD ABBEY.** The ancestral estate of Lord Byron stands north of Nottingham in the village of **Linby.** Byron took up residence as a 10-year-old and remained here until forced to sell. Many of his personal effects stayed behind, including a replica of "Byron's skull cup"—an ancient human cranium unearthed at Newstead in 1806, which the poet coated in silver, inscribed with verse, and filled with wine. The original was reinterred in 1863. Lively peacocks hold court in the gracious gardens, and the staff stands ready to enlighten those who step indoors. (Bus #757 travels from Nottingham Victoria Station to the abbey gates (35min., 2 per hr., return £3.25), 1 mi. from the house and grounds. ☎(01623) 793 557. House open Apr.-Sept. daily noon-5pm. Grounds open year-round 9am-dusk. House and grounds £4, concessions £2, under 16 £1.50. Grounds only £2, concessions £1.)

SHERWOOD FOREST. To the north spreads famed Sherwood Forest, considerably thinned since the 13th century. The **Sherwood Forest Visitor Centre** has a small museum, but beware the legions of children armed with mini-archery sets. To escape the crowds, take the signposted 3½ mi. walk, making sure to stop at the "Major Oak," which, at 33 ft. in girth, reputably served as Robin's hideout. In August, the medieval **Robin Hood Festival** stages a jousting tournament. (Buses #33 and 36 leave Nottingham Victoria Station (1hr., every 2hr., £4.50). ☎(01623) 823 202. Centre open Apr.-Oct. daily 10:30am-5pm; Nov.-Mar. 10:30am-4:30pm. Forest open dawn-dusk. Free.)

EASTWOOD. D.H. Lawrence was an Eastwood native and schoolteacher who went on to write controversial poetry and prose. Once he was banned from the bookshelves, now he's buried in Westminster Abbey. The **D.H. Lawrence Birthplace Museum** fills his childhood home. (8A Victoria St., near Mansfield Rd. ☎(01773) 717 353. Open Apr.-Oct. daily 10am-5pm; Nov.-Mar. 10am-4pm. £2, concessions £1.20.) The **Sons and Lovers Cottage,** where young D.H. lived from 1887 to 1891, is free and open by appointment. (28 Garden Rd. ☎(0151) 653 8710. Eastwood is 6 mi. west of Nottingham. Rainbow bus #1 (40min., £3.50) leaves frequently from Nottingham Victoria Station.)

LINCOLN   ☎ 01522

Medieval streets climb their cobbled way past half-timbered homes to Lincoln's dominating 12th-century cathedral, itself a relative newcomer in a town built for retired Roman legionnaires. Lincoln, often thought of as a cold industrial town, does not draw tourists, but those who do make the trip will delight in the bustling marketplace and (after a steep uphill climb to the city's peak) sweeping views.

🚃 TRANSPORTATION

Lincoln's **Central Station** is on St. Mary's St. (Office open M-Sa 5:45am-7:30pm, Su 10:30am-9:20pm; travel center open M-Sa 9am-5pm.) **Trains** arrive from: **Leeds** (2hr., every 2½hr., return £17.70); **London King's Cross** (2½hr., every 1-2hr., return £40.50); **Nottingham** (1hr.; M-Sa 2 per hr., Su 7 per day; return £5.85). Opposite is **City Bus Station**, Melville St. (Open M-F 8:30am-5pm, Sa 9am-1:45pm.) **National Express** comes from: **London** (5hr., 2 per day, £18) and **Nottingham** (1¼hr., 1-2 per hr., £13). For information on Lincolnshire bus services, contact the **Lincolnshire Roadcar** station on St. Mark St. (☎ 522 255. Open M-F 8:30am-5pm, Sa 8:30am-4:30pm.) For other inquiries, try the **Travel Hotline** (☎ 553 135; M-Th 8am-5:15pm, F 8am-4:45pm.)

✳ ❓ ORIENTATION AND PRACTICAL INFORMATION

Roman and Norman military engineers were attracted to the summit of **Castle Hill**; later railway engineers preferred its base. Thus, Lincoln has an affluent acropolis to the north and a cottage-filled lower town near the tracks. The TIC and major sights lie at the junction of **Steep Hill** and Castle Hill.

Tourist Information Centre: 9 Castle Hill (☎ 529 828; www.lincoln-info.org.uk). Books rooms for 10% deposit. Pick up a map (free) and miniguide (25p). Open M-Th 9:30am-5:30pm, F 9:30am-5pm, Sa-Su 10am-5pm. **Branch** (☎ 579 056), on the corner of Cornhill and High St. Same hours M-Sa, closed Su.

Tours: 1hr. tours depart from the TIC July-Aug. daily 11am and 1:30pm; Sept.-Oct. and Apr.-June only Sa-Su. £1.50. **Guide Friday** (☎ 522 255) runs hop-on/hop-off bus tours every 30min. 10am-4pm in summer. £6, concessions £4.50, children £2.50.

Financial Services: Major **banks** line High St. **Thomas Cook,** 4 Cornhill Pavement (☎ 346 400). Open M-Tu and Th-Sa 9am-5:30pm, W 10am-5:30pm.

Police: West Parade (☎ 882 222), near the town hall.

Hospital: Lincoln County Hospital, Greenwell Rd. (☎ 512 512).

Internet Access: Central Library, Free School Ln. (☎ 510 800), between Saltergate and Silver St. 1 terminal must be reserved ahead (£3 per hr.); 2 are for drop-in use (£1 per 15min.). Open M-F 9:30am-7pm, Sa 9:30am-4pm. **Sun Cafe,** 7a St. Mary (☎ 579 067). £4 per hr. Open M-Sa 9am-6pm, Su noon-5pm.

Post Office: Cornhill (☎ 532 288), just off High St. **Bureau de change.** Open M-F 9am-5:30pm, Sa 9am-5pm. **Post Code:** LN5 7XX.

🏠 ACCOMMODATIONS

B&Bs sprinkle **Carline** and **Yarborough Rd.,** west of the castle, most for £17-20 per person. Consult the accommodations list in the window of the branch TIC.

Mayfield Guest House, 213 Yarborough Rd. (☎/fax 533 732). Entrance behind house on Mill Rd., a 20min. walk from the station (or spare yourself and take bus #7 or 8). Near a working windmill. Bright Victorian mansion with large rooms and fluffy quilts. Panoramic breakfast-room view. No smoking. £22 per person. ❸

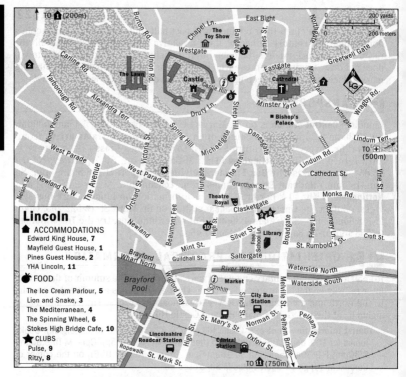

Lincoln

♠ ACCOMMODATIONS

Edward King House, **7**
Mayfield Guest House, **1**
Pines Guest House, **2**
YHA Lincoln, **11**

🍴 FOOD

The Ice Cream Parlour, **5**
Lion and Snake, **3**
The Mediterranean, **4**
The Spinning Wheel, **6**
Stokes High Bridge Cafe, **10**

★ CLUBS

Pulse, **9**
Ritzy, **8**

Pines Guest House, 104 Yarborough Rd. (☎/fax 532 985). 15min. northwest of the train station; walk or take bus #7 or 8 to Yarborough Rd. Large, thickly carpeted B&B. All rooms have TV, but you'll probably spend your time hanging out in the game room at the pool table and bar. Singles from £16; twins and doubles £32, with bath £36. ❷

Edward King House, Minster Yard (☎528 778; enjoy@ekhs.org.uk), near the Bishop's Palace. Run by the diocese; bibles in every room. Views are divine, breakfast room and building immaculate (and smoke-free), and city center location miraculous. Continental breakfast included, English breakfast £3. Singles £20; twins £37. ❸

YHA Lincoln, 77 South Park Ave. (☎522 076). From the station, turn right on Pelham Bridge (becomes Canwick Rd.), and again on South Park Ave. 46-bed Victorian villa. Lockout 10am-5pm. Curfew 11pm. Open Feb.-Oct. Dorms £10.25, under 18 £7. ❷

🗋 FOOD

The **market,** at Sincil St. near the TIC branch, sells local fruits, veggies, and oddities. (Open M-F 9am-4pm, Sa 9am-4:30pm.) A variety of restaurants, tearooms, and takeaways grace **High St.,** while pubs line **Bailgate St.,** on the other side of the hill.

⊠ **The Ice Cream Parlour,** at the base of Bailgate. This tiny, traditional shop scoops out first-rate homemade ice cream and sorbet. A cone of ginger chocolate chip is £1.20. Open M-Th 10:30am-6pm, F-Su 9:30am-sunset.

The Mediterranean, 14 Bailgate St. (☎546 464). Snappy decor, candy-colored wrought-iron tables, and fresh flowers accompany inventive dishes from around the world. Starters and lunches £6-8, dinner entrees £9-15. Open M-F noon-2:30pm and 6-10:30pm, Sa noon-3pm and 6-10:30pm, Su noon-4pm and 6-10:30pm. ❸

Stokes High Bridge Cafe, 207 High St. (☎513 825). Busy tearoom in a Tudor-style house-cum-bridge, displayed on many a postcard. Watch swans float by on the green canal and nibble steak pie (£4.50). 2-course lunch (£5.40) served 11:30am-2pm; tea served 9:30am-5pm. Coffee shop downstairs, open daily 9am-5pm. ❶

Lion and Snake, 79 Bailgate St. (☎523 770), by the cathedral. Pub with picnic tables for a restorative pint and 2-course meal (£4). Famed daily roast £4.25. Open M-Sa 11am-11pm, Su noon-10:30pm; food served M-F noon-6pm, Sa-Su noon-3pm. ❶

The Spinning Wheel, 39 Steep Hill (☎522 463), a block south of the TIC in a leaning, half-timbered building. Tea (80-90p) and vegetarian dishes (£4-5) are nicely priced; others are a bit steeper, but filling (from £6). Open daily 11:30am-10pm. ❷

🔆 SIGHTS

🔳 **LINCOLN CATHEDRAL.** While the rest of Lincoln endured a millennium of rumblings and crumblings in which Roman barricades, bishops' palaces, and conquerors' castles were erected and destroyed, the magnificent cathedral remained king of the hill. Begun in 1072 but not completed until three centuries later, it once towered over Europe as the continent's tallest building. Its many enduring and endearing features include the imp in the Angel Choir, who turned to stone while attempting to chat with seraphim. A treasury room displays sacred silver and a shrine to child martyr Sir Hugh. Rotating exhibits reside in a **library** designed by Christopher Wren. (☎544 544. Open June-Aug. M-Sa 7:15am-8pm, Su 7:15am-6pm; Sept.-May M-Sa 7:15am-6pm, Su 7:15am-5pm. Tours May-Aug. daily 11am, 1, 3pm; Sept.-Apr. Sa only. Cathedral £3.50, concessions £3. Library M-F free; Sa-Su £1, children free.)

LINCOLN CASTLE. Home to one of four surviving copies of the *Magna Carta*, this 1068 castle was also the house of pain for inmates of Victorian Castle Prison. A cheerful guide leads the "Prison Experience," among other tours. (☎511 068. Open Apr.-Oct. M-Sa 9:30am-5:30pm, Su 11am-5:30pm; Nov.-Mar. M-Sa 9:30am-4pm, Su 11am-4pm. Tours Apr.-Oct. 11am-2pm. £2.50, concessions £1.50, children £1, families £6.50.)

BISHOP'S PALACE. The medieval Bishop's Palace was originally wedged between the walls of the upper and lower Roman cities. Thanks to 12th-century cleric Bishop Chesney, a passageway through the upper city wall links the palatial remains to the cathedral. The palace itself—in Chesney's time the seat of England's largest diocese—is now an English Heritage sight with peaceful ruins, vineyards, and long views. (☎527 468. Open Apr.-Oct. daily 10am-6pm; Nov.-Mar. Sa-Su 10am-4pm. £2.50, concessions £1.90, children £1.30.)

THE INCREDIBLY FANTASTIC OLD TOY SHOW. This humble museum is the perfect setting for a child's fantasy or a horror movie, with a collection of antique toys and modern market marvels. (26 Westgate. ☎520 534. Open Apr.-Sept. Tu-Sa 11am-5pm; Oct.-Dec. Sa 11am-5pm, Su noon-4pm. £2.20, concessions £1.80, children £1.20.)

🎸 🎵 NIGHTLIFE AND ENTERTAINMENT

Clubs are usually open from 9pm to 2am and charge a £1-3 cover. On the corner of Silver St. and Flaxengate, **Pulse** (☎522 315) has a range of theme nights. Next door, **Ritzy** (☎522 314) is popular, meaning more techno and dance and longer lines. For less strenuous entertainment, pick up the monthly *What's On* at the TIC, or ask at the cathedral about choral and organ performances. The **Theatre Royal,** Clasketgate at the corner of High St., stages drama and musicals. (☎525 555. Box office open M-Sa 10am-6pm. Tickets £7-16.50.) **The Lawn,** on Union Rd. by the castle, hosts regular outdoor music and dancing. (☎560 306. Open Apr.-Sept. M-F 9am-5pm, Sa-Su 10am-5pm; Oct.-Mar. M-F 9am-4:30pm, Sa-Su 10am-4pm. Free.) Late July brings **Medieval Weekend** and August sports the relatively new **Lincoln Early Music Festival.**

▶ DAYTRIPS FROM LINCOLN

GRANTHAM. Young Sir Isaac Newton attended the **King's School** in Grantham and left a carving of his schoolboy signature in a windowsill. *(Brook St. ☎(01476) 563 180. By appointment only. Free, donations accepted.)* The **Grantham Museum** has exhibits on Newton's life and work and a video exhibit on another of Grantham's illustrious progeny, Margaret Thatcher. *(Museum on St. Peter's Hill, by the TIC. ☎(01476) 568 783. Open M-Sa 10am-5pm. Free. Grantham is 25 mi. south of Lincoln; 45min. by train (every hr., day return £2.50). Lincolnshire Roadcar (☎522 255; 1¼hr.; M-Sa every hr., Su less frequent; day return £4) bus #601 runs from St. Mark St. station.)*

COLSTERWORTH. At Colsterworth stands **Woolsthorpe Manor,** Newton's birthplace. Young Isaac scribbled his early intellectual musings on the wall, a habit Mama Newton must have found adorable, since visitors can still peep at genius-graffiti. Whether he was actually bonked by one of the apple tree's inspirational fruits is debatable, but this is the site of his "what goes up, must come down" deliberations. The barn holds the new **Sir Isaac Newton Science Discovery Centre,** a fantastic hands-on exhibit that clarifies Newtonian ideas for the non-mathematically-inclined. *(7 mi. south of Grantham; 15min. by train (every hr., return £3.20). Lincolnshire Roadcar runs from Grantham (20min., every 2-3hr., return £2.50). ☎(01476) 860 338. Open Apr.-Oct. W-Su 1-5pm. Manor £3.30, children £1.60, families £8.20. Discovery Centre £2/£1/£5.)*

EAST ANGLIA

The rich farmland and watery flats of East Anglia stretch northeast from London, cloaking the counties of Cambridgeshire, Norfolk, and Suffolk, as well as parts of Essex. Literally England's newest landscape, the vast plains of the fens were drained as late as the 1820s. From Norwich east to the English Channel, the water that once drenched enormous medieval peat bogs was channeled into the maze of waterways known as the Norfolk Broads, now a national park. Continental-style windmills helped maintain the drained fens, and some survivors still mark the marshes. Farther inland and 800 years earlier, Norman invaders made their way to the elevated mound at Ely, building a stunning cathedral from stone transported by boat across then-flooded fenland. In the 15th century, in a village to the south, renegade scholars from Oxford set up shop along the River Cam. Eventually granted a royal imprimatur, they built a university. Farther northeast, the imposing houses and magnificent "wool churches" of small towns in Norfolk and Suffolk stand as testament to their past as thriving wool centers. But despite the obvious impact humans have made on this region, much of the rustic beauty that inspired the landscape paintings of natives Constable and Gainsborough remains.

HIGHLIGHTS OF EAST ANGLIA

CAMBRIDGE Stroll among the colleges (but keep off the grass!) in this picturesque university town, one of the world's best-known reserves of scholarship (p. 326).

ELY CATHEDRAL Gaze skyward at a medieval masterwork, still breathtaking as it towers over former fenland (p. 337).

NORWICH Mind your map in this twisting, wool-trading town, once the largest in Anglo-Saxon England, where markets and festivals have endured for centuries (p. 348).

TRANSPORTATION IN EAST ANGLIA

The major rail operator is **Anglia Railways** (☎ (01603) 724 880). A **combined** Anglia Plus Pass (about £60), available only at stations within East Anglia, entitles you to a week's unlimited travel on all **train** routes in the region. A **regular** Anglia Plus Pass allows a week of unlimited travel within either Norfolk or Suffolk (£29). Both zones are covered by their own one- and three-day passes (£9 and £20). All Anglia Plus passes also grant free travel on various lines of the Norwich, Ipswich, and Great Yarmouth local **bus** services. The **Out 'n' About** ticket allows unlimited day travel on Stagecoach Cambuses (£6, students £4.60, children £4). You may end up paying with your time, however; buses run infrequently.

East Anglia's flat terrain and relatively little rainfall please **cyclists** and **hikers**, though rental bikes can be difficult to procure outside of Cambridge and Norwich. The area's two longest and most popular walking trails, together covering 200 mi., are the **Peddar's Way,** which runs from Knettishall Heath to Holme and includes the **Norfolk Coast Path,** and the **Weaver's Way,** an extended trail that traverses the north coast from Cromer to Great Yarmouth. Both cross a town with a train or bus station about every 10 mi. For the Peddar's Way, pick up *Peddar's Way and Norfolk Coast Path.* TICs in Norwich, Bury St. Edmunds, and several Suffolk villages issue guides for the Weaver's Way.

East Anglia

○ SIGHTS

Anglesey Abbey, **7**
Audley End, **12**
Blakney Point
  Seal Colony, **3**
Castle Rising, **4**
Holkham Hall, **2**
Holme Bird Observatory, **1**
Houghton Hall, **6**
Ickworth House, **9**
Kentwell Hall, **10**
Melford Hall, **11**
Sandringham, **5**
Wimpole Hall, **8**

CAMBRIDGESHIRE

CAMBRIDGE   ☎ 01223

It is the quintessence of England: gray, white and silvery stone, rose-red and rust-colored brick, embowered in greenery, ancient lawns running down to the water, and in spring starred with a million daffodils.
—A.L. Rowse, "Cambridge through Oxford Eyes"

In contrast to museum-oriented, metropolitan Oxford, Cambridge is determined to retain its pastoral academic robes—the city manages, rather than encourages, visitors. No longer the exclusive preserve of upper-class sons, the university has at long last opened its doors to women and state school pupils. Some old upper-crust traditions are slipping, too: now students only bedeck themselves in gown and cravat once a week. At exams' end, Cambridge explodes with Pimms-soaked glee, and May Week (in mid-June, naturally) launches a swirl of cocktail parties and balls in celebration of pending graduation ceremonies.

TRANSPORTATION

Bicycles are the primary mode of transportation in Cambridge, a city which claims more bikes per person than any other place in Britain. A series of one-way streets and an armada of foreign teenagers used to riding on the wrong side of the road complicate summer transport. If riding, use hand signals and heed road signs; if walking, look both ways—and behind, above, and under—twice before crossing.

Trains: Station Rd. Ticket office open daily 5am-11pm. **Trains** (☎ (08457) 484 950) run from **London King's Cross** (45min., 2 per hr., £15.10) and **London Liverpool St.** (1¼hr., 2 per hr., £15.10).

Buses: Drummer St. Station—more street than station. Ticket booth open daily 8:45am-5:30pm; tickets also often available on board. **National Express** (☎ (08705) 808 080) from **London** (2hr., 17 per day, from £8). **Jetlink** coach service runs hourly shuttles from: **Gatwick** (3hr., £20); **Heathrow** (2hr., £21); **Stansted** (45min., £9). **Stagecoach Express** (☎ (01604) 676 060) runs from **Oxford** (2¾hr., 10-12 per day, from £6).

Public Transportation: Cambus (☎ 423 554) zooms from the train station to the city center (£1) and around town (£1-2). **Whippet Coaches** (☎ (01480) 463 792) runs day-trips. **Cabco** (☎ 312 444) and **Camtax** (☎ 313 131) taxis are both 24hr.

Bike Rental: Mike's Bikes, 28 Mill Rd. (☎ 312 591). £8 per day, £10 per week; reduced prices for extended rentals. £50 deposit. Lock, light, and basket included. Open M-Sa 9am-6pm, Su 10am-4pm. The TIC lists other bike shops.

ORIENTATION AND PRACTICAL INFORMATION

Cambridge has two main avenues, both suffering from multiple personality disorder. The main shopping street starts at **Magdalene Bridge** and becomes **Bridge St., Sidney St., St. Andrew's St., Regent St.,** and **Hills Rd.** The other—alternately **St. John's St., Trinity St., King's Parade,** and **Trumpington St.**—is the academic thoroughfare. The two cross at St. John's College. From the **Drummer St.** bus station, a stroll down **Emmanuel St.** will land you in the shopping district near the TIC. To get to the heart of things from the **train station,** turn right onto Hills Rd.

Tourist Information Centre: Wheeler St. (☎ 322 640; www.tourismcambridge.com), 1 block south of Market Sq. Mini-guide 40p, maps 20p, *Cambridge: The Official Guide* £3.95. Cycling maps £4. Books rooms for £3 and 10% deposit. Advance booking hotline (at least 5 days; ☎ 457 581; M-F 9:30am-4pm). Open Apr.-Oct. M-F 10am-5:30pm, Sa 10am-5pm, Su 11am-4pm; Nov.-Mar. M-F 10am-5:30pm, Sa 10am-5pm.

Tours: Informative 2hr. **walking tours** of the city and a college or two (usually King's) leave from the TIC (call for times). £7.25, children £4.25. Special **Drama Tour** in July and Aug. led by guides in period dress (Tu 6:30pm; £4.50). **Guide Friday** (☎ 362 444) runs 1hr. hop-on/hop-off **bus tours** every 15-30min. Apr.-Oct. £8.50, concessions £7, children £2.50, families £19.50.

Budget Travel: STA Travel, 38 Sidney St. (☎ 366 966). Open M-W and F 9am-5:30pm, Th 10am-5:30pm, Sa 11am-5pm.

Financial Services: Banks line Market Sq. and St. Andrew's St. **Thomas Cook,** 8 St. Andrew's St. (☎ 366 141). Open M-Tu and Th-Sa 9am-5:30pm, W 10am-5:30pm. **American Express,** 25 Sidney St. (☎ (08706) 001 060). Open M-Tu and Th-F 9am-5:30pm, W 9:30am-5:30pm, Sa 9am-5pm.

Work Opportunities: Blue Arrow, 40 St. Andrews St. (☎ 323 272). Year-round temp work in domestic and food service. Arrange early for summer jobs—demand is high.

EAST ANGLIA

OODLES OF NOODLES: DOJO'S NOODLE BAR

Dojo's is the salvation of Cambridge's starving student population, whipping out almost comically enormous plates of noodles—some of which are vegetarian, none of which is fried—at warp speed. The selection of more than 30 different concoctions is a pantheon of noodle possibilities drawing on Japanese, Chinese, Thai, Vietnamese, Korean, and Malaysian influences. And, more importantly, not a single heap of noodles, no matter how you stack it and spice it, will ever exceed £6.

Pull up a bench and have a seat at the table/counter contraptions against the wall. In the lengthy wait between ordering and receiving your food (somewhere in the neighborhood of about five minutes), you can watch the birth of your meal in the open kitchen.

Words of wisdom from the fictional "Noodfucius" headline every page of the menu: "To be fulfilled, man must satisfy the hunger within." Even the deepest cravings will be satisfied for at least a day (or two, or three) after polishing off one of these plates. *(1-2 Mill Ln. ☎363 471. Open M-Th noon-2:30pm and 5:30-11pm, F-Su noon-4pm and 5:30-11pm.)*

Launderette: Clean Machine, 22 Burleigh St. (☎578 009). Open daily 8am-8pm.

Police: Parkside (☎358 966).

Hospital: Addenbrookes, Hills Rd. (☎245 151). Catch Cambus #4, 5, or 5a from Emmanuel St. (£1) and get off where Hills Rd. intersects Long Rd.

Internet Access: International Telecom Centre, 2 Wheeler St. (☎357 358). £1 for first 33min., then 3-4p per min.; £1 minimum. As low as 50p per hr. with student ID. Open daily 9am-10pm. **CB1,** 32 Mill Rd. (☎576 306). Sip cappuccinos and browse the used book selection between e-mail sessions. 5p per min. Open daily 10am-8pm.

Post Office: 9-11 St. Andrew's St. (☎323 325). Open M-Sa 9am-5:30pm. **Post Code:** CB2 3AA.

◤ ACCOMMODATIONS AND CAMPING

Rooms are scarce, which makes prices high and quality low. Most B&Bs aren't in the town center; many around **Portugal St.** and **Tenison Rd.** house students during the academic year and are open to visitors in July and August. If one is full, ask about others nearby, as they're often unmarked. Pick up a guide from the TIC (50p) or check the list in the window after hours. Cheaper accommodations can be found in nearby **Ely** (see p. 337).

🏠 **Tenison Towers Guest House,** 148 Tenison Rd. (☎566 511). Blue is the word at Tenison Towers, where fresh flowers grace airy rooms 2 blocks from the train station. Mrs. Chance keeps an impeccable house, and breakfast includes her homemade bread and marmalade. Singles and doubles £20-25 per person. ❸

Home from Home B&B, 78 Milton Rd. (☎323 555). A 20min. walk from the city center. Rooms are sweetly scented and well-stocked with biscuits, cocoa, and hotel-style mini-toiletries. B&B £25-30 per person; apartments with decked-out kitchens and enormous lounges £350 per week. ❸

YHA Cambridge, 97 Tenison Rd. (☎354 601; cambridge@yha.org.uk). A relaxed, welcoming atmosphere, though more showers wouldn't hurt. 100 beds, mostly 3-4 per room; a few doubles. Rock music pervades the well-equipped kitchen. Laundry, Internet (£5 per hr.), luggage storage, and TV lounge. **Bureau de change.** Breakfast £3.50, packed lunch £2.80-3.65. Call well ahead. Dorms £15.10, under 18 £11.40. ❷

Netley Lodge, 112 Chesterton Rd. (☎363 845). Plush red carpets and a conservatory lush with greenery welcome you. Roses inside and out of large and tastefully decorated rooms. Singles £28; doubles £45-55. ❸

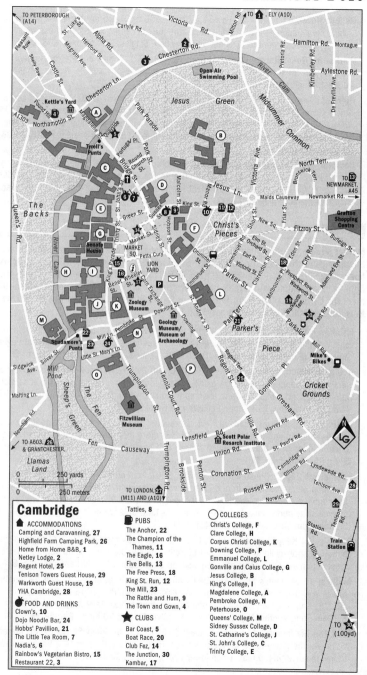

TO PETERBOROUGH (A14)
TO ELY (A10)

Victoria Rd.
Carlyle Rd.
Alpha Rd.
Hamilton Rd.
Montague
Hertford St.
Chesterton Rd.
Pretoria Rd.
Kimberley Rd.
Aylestone Rd.
De Freville Ave.
Magrath Ave.
Pleasant Row
Shelly Row
Castle St.
Pound Hill
Kettle's Yard
A1303
Northampton St.
Chesterton Ln.
Open Air Swimming Pool
Jesus Green
River Cam
Midsummer Common
Park Parade
Magdalene St.
Quayside
North Terr.
Brunswick Terr.
TO NEWMARKET, A45
Tyrell's Punts
Portugal Pl.
Round Church St.
Park St.
Jesus Ln.
Victoria Ave.
Maids Causeway
Newmarket Rd.
Fitzroy St.
Grafton Shopping Centre
Burleigh St.
The Backs
Bridge St.
St. John's St.
Malcolm St.
King St.
Short St. New Sq.
Friar St.
Eden St.
Adam and Eve St.
Queen's Rd.
Green St.
Sussex St.
Hobson St.
Christ's Pieces
Elm St.
Orchard St.
City Rd.
Trinity St.
Market St.
Sidney St.
Drummer St.
Emmanuel Rd.
Earl St.
Clarendon St.
Prospect Row
Warkworth St.
Senate House
King's Parade
MARKET SQ.
Petty Cury
LION YARD
Emmanuel St.
Parker St.
East Rd.
Walkworth Terr.
East St.
Benet St.
Wheeler St.
Corn Exchange
Emmanuel St.
St. Andrew's St.
Zoology Museum
Downing St.
Geology Museum / Museum of Archaeology
Pembroke St.
Mill Ln.
Downing Pl.
Park Terr.
Parker's Piece
Parkside
Mill Rd.
Mike's Bikes
Scudamore's Punts
Silver St.
Little St. Mary's Ln.
Trumpington St.
Regent Terr.
Gonville Pl.
Cricket Grounds
Sidgwick Ave.
Mill Pond
Sheep's Green
The Fen
Tennis Court Rd.
Regent St.
Gresham Rd.
Malting Ln.
Newnham Rd.
Fen Causeway
Fitzwilliam Museum
Lensfield Rd.
Scott Polar Research Institute
Harvey Rd.
St. Paul's Rd.
TO A603 & GRANTCHESTER,
Llamas Land
Brookside
Union Rd.
Coronation St.
Cambridge Pl.
Glisson Rd.
Lyndewode Rd.
Tenison Ave.
Station Rd.
Hills Rd.
Train Station
TO LONDON, (M11) AND (A10)
Penton St.
Russell St.
Norwich St.
Tenison Rd.
TO (100yd)

0   250 yards
0   250 meters

Cambridge

ACCOMMODATIONS
Camping and Caravanning, **27**
Highfield Farm Camping Park, **26**
Home from Home B&B, **1**
Netley Lodge, **2**
Regent Hotel, **25**
Tenison Towers Guest House, **29**
Warkworth Guest House, **19**
YHA Cambridge, **28**

FOOD AND DRINKS
Clown's, **10**
Dojo Noodle Bar, **24**
Hobbs' Pavillion, **21**
The Little Tea Room, **7**
Nadia's, **6**
Rainbow's Vegetarian Bistro, **15**
Restaurant 22, **3**

Tatties, **8**

PUBS
The Anchor, **22**
The Champion of the Thames, **11**
The Eagle, **16**
Five Bells, **13**
The Free Press, **18**
King St. Run, **12**
The Mill, **23**
The Rattle and Hum, **9**
The Town and Gown, **4**

CLUBS
Bar Coast, **5**
Boat Race, **20**
Club Fez, **14**
The Junction, **30**
Kambar, **17**

COLLEGES
Christ's College, **F**
Clare College, **H**
Corpus Christi College, **K**
Downing College, **P**
Emmanuel College, **L**
Gonville and Caius College, **G**
Jesus College, **B**
King's College, **I**
Magdalene College, **A**
Pembroke College, **N**
Peterhouse, **O**
Queens' College, **M**
Sidney Sussex College, **D**
St. Catharine's College, **J**
St. John's College, **C**
Trinity College, **E**

Regent Hotel, 41 Regent St. (☎351 470; fax 566 562). 25 luxurious, ensuite rooms overlooking Parker's Piece, a 5min. walk from the city center. Perfect for those who want privacy, but don't want to miss out on the action. Singles £77; doubles £96. ❺

Warkworth Guest House, Warkworth Terr. (☎363 682). Sunny, ensuite rooms near the bus station for those wishing to skip the walk to the city center. Packed lunch on request. Singles £35; twins £55-60. ❹

Highfield Farm Camping Park, Long Rd., Comberton (☎262 308). Head west on the A603 (3 mi.), then right on the B1046 to Comberton (1 mi.), or take Cambus #118 (every 45min.) from Drummer St. Spacious, tree-lined field with flush toilets and laundry. Open Apr.-Oct.; call ahead. £7 per tent, with car £8.75; off-season £6.25/£7.25. Showers included. ❶

Camping and Caravanning Club Site, 19 Cabbage Moor, Great Shelford (☎841 185). Head 3 mi. south on the M11, then left onto the A1301 for ¾ mi., or take Cambus #102 or 103 to Westfield Rd. Excellent site with facilities for the disabled. Open Mar.-Oct. Call ahead. Pitches £4-5. ❶

🔲 FOOD

Market Square (M-Sa 9:30am-4:30pm) has bright pyramids of fruit and vegetables, cheaper than those in supermarkets. Students get beer and cornflakes at **Sainsbury's,** 44 Sidney St. (☎366 891. Open M-F 8am-9pm, Sa 7:30am-9pm, Su 11am-5pm.) Cheap Indian and Greek fare sates hearty appetites (make sure you don't meet the Christ's College football club out for its ritual curry night). South of town, **Hills Rd.** and **Mill Rd.** brim with good, budget restaurants.

Rainbow's Vegetarian Bistro, 9a King's Parade (☎321 551). Duck under the rainbow sign on King's Parade. A tiny, creative burrow featuring delicious international vegan and vegetarian fare, all for £6.95. Open M-Sa 11am-11pm, last order 10:30pm. ❷

Hobbs' Pavillion, Parker's Piece (☎367 480), off Park Terr. Renowned for imaginative, rectangular pancakes. Feels like a stylish living room, with a view across Parker's Piece, jaunty jazz, and a Mars Bar and ice cream pancake (£4). Dinners are standard English fare (£9-14). Open Tu-Sa noon-2:15pm and 6-9:45pm. ❸

Tatties, 11 Sussex St. (☎323 399). Dedicated to one of England's most popular dishes—the terrific jacket potatoes (£2-5.75) more than make up for fast-food ambience. Fillings from butter to Philly cheese and smoked salmon. Open M-Sa 8:30am-7pm, Su 10am-5pm. ❶

Restaurant 22, 22 Chesterton Rd. (☎351 880). Pretend to be celebrating something (perhaps, say, graduation from a local university) to justify shelling out for 3 courses of the continually rotating, carefully thought-out menu (£24.95). Only 8 tables lend an air of exclusivity and necessitate reservations. As hard to leave as it is to get in. Open Tu-Sa from 7pm, food served until 9:45pm. ❺

Clown's, 54 King St. (☎355 711). Cheerful staff adds the final dash of color to this humming spot—children's renderings of clowns plaster the walls, as do adoring odes by local regulars. Cakes, toasties, even lasagna £1-6. Open daily 7:30am-midnight. ❶

Nadia's, 11 St. John's St. (☎460 961). An uncommonly good bakery with reasonable prices and divine smells. Wonderful flapjacks and quiches (80p-£1.25). Sandwiches (£1.75) and muffins (75p) are a brunch unto themselves. Takeaway only. Open daily 8:30am-5pm. Another Nadia resides at 16 Silver St. and 20 King's Parade. ❶

The Little Tea Room, 1 All Saints' Passage (☎366 033), off Trinity St. Hopelessly pretentious, yet *the* place to be for afternoon tea. Heroic waitstaff navigate 2 tightly packed rooms to serve tip-top teas. Open M-Sa 10am-5:30pm, Su 1-5:30pm. ❶

PUBS

King St. has a diverse collection of pubs and used to host the King St. Run, in which contestants ran the length of the street stopping at each of the 13 pubs to down a pint (the winner was the first to cross the finish line on his own two feet). Most pubs are open 11am-11pm (Su noon-10:30pm). The local brewery, Greene King, supplies many of them with the popular bitters IPA and Abbott.

The Mill, 14 Mill Ln. (☎357 026), off Silver St. Bridge. Patrons infiltrate the riverside park on spring nights for punt- and people-watching. In summer, clientele include the odd remaining student and hordes of international youth.

The Eagle, 8 Benet St. (☎505 020). Cambridge's oldest pub. Watson and Crick rushed in breathless to announce their discovery of DNA–the barmaid insisted they settle their 4-shilling tab before she'd serve them a toast. British and American WWII pilots stood on each other's shoulders to burn their initials into the ceiling of the RAF room.

The Town and Gown, Poundhill (☎353 791), just off Northampton St. Gay men gather in this classically English pub. Strong community feel and a warm welcome. Open M 6:30-11pm, Tu-Sa 11:30am-2:30pm and 6:30-11pm, Su noon-5pm.

The Anchor, Silver St. (☎353 554). Another undergrad watering hole crowded day and night. Savor a pint while watching amateur punters collide under Silver St. Bridge. Open M-Sa 11am-11pm, Su 1-10:30pm.

King St. Run, King St. (☎328 900). The quintessential college pub, but with club hours; packs in the student crowd amid university kitsch. Open M-Sa 11am-1am, Su noon-10:30pm.

The Rattle and Hum, 4 King St. (☎505 015). A prerequisite for Clubbing 101, with a DJ spinning dance tunes from 9pm, 7 nights a week. Th karaoke night.

Five Bells, 126-128 Newmarket Rd. (☎314 019). A primarily gay and lesbian clientele fills the beer garden for buzzing afternoons and lively nights. Open M-F 11am-3pm and 7-11pm, Sa 11am-11pm, Su noon-10:30pm.

The Champion of the Thames, 68 King St. (☎352 043). The size of a broom closet and filled with regulars. Making new friends is pretty much unavoidable in a space like this.

The Free Press, Prospect Row (☎368 337), behind the police station. Named after an abolitionist newspaper, now mostly a local haunt. No smoking, and, even more revolutionary... leave your mobile phone at the door!

⬡ COLLEGES AND OTHER SIGHTS

Cambridge is an architect's fantasia, packing some of England's most breathtaking monuments into less than a single square mile. The soaring **King's College Chapel** and St. John's postcard-familiar **Bridge of Sighs** are sightseeing staples, while more obscure college courts veil undiscovered treats. Most historic buildings are on the **east bank** of the Cam between Magdalene Bridge and Silver St. The gardens, meadows, and cows of the **Backs** lend a pastoral air to the **west bank.**

The **University of Cambridge** has three eight-week terms: Michaelmas (Oct.-Dec.), Lent (Jan.-Mar.), and Easter (Apr.-June). Visitors can gain access to most colleges daily from 9am to 5:30pm, though many close to sightseers during Easter term, and virtually all are closed during exams (mid-May to mid-June); your best bet is to call ahead (☎331 100) for hours. If you have time for only a few colleges, **King's, Trinity, Queens', Christ's, St. John's,** and **Jesus** should top your list. Porters (plump bowler-bedecked ex-servicemen) maintain security. Those who look like undergrads (no traveler's backpack, no camera, and definitely no Cambridge sweatshirt) can often wander freely through the grounds after hours. The fastest way to mark yourself as a target for the porters is to trample the sacred **grass** of the court-yards, a privilege granted only to senior members. In summer, most undergrads skip town, leaving it to PhD students and mobs of foreign teenagers.

KING'S COLLEGE

King's Parade. ☎331 100. Chapel and grounds open M-Sa 9:30am-4:30pm, Su 9:30am-2:30pm. Listing of services and musical events (£1) available at porter's lodge. Evensong 5:30pm most nights. Contact TIC for tours. £3.50, concessions £2.50, under 12 free.

King's College was founded by Henry VI in 1441 as partner to a school he had established near Windsor, and it wasn't until 1861 that students from schools other than Eton were allowed to compete for scholarships. But King's is now the most socially liberal of the Cambridge colleges, drawing more of its students from state schools than any other; the college was also the site of the student riots of 1968. As a result, Cambridge's best-known college is its least traditional—there are no formal dinners or white-tie balls, and interior corridors are coated with lurid graffiti.

Little of this is noticeable to visitors, who descend in droves on the Gothic spectacle that is **King's College Chapel.** If you stand at the southwest corner of the court-yard, you can see where Henry's master mason left off and work under the Tudors began—the earlier stone is off-white. The elaborate wall that separates the college grounds from King's Parade was a 19th-century addition; originally the chapel and grounds were hidden behind a row of shops and houses. The chapel's interior is a single chamber cleft by a carved choir screen whose design was destroyed by its Italian creators, fearful of replication. Heralding angels hover against the world's largest fan-vaulted ceiling, described by Wordsworth as a "branching roof self-poised, and scooped into ten thousand cells where light and shade repose." The chapel also houses a few works of sacrilege—look for the 15th-century graffiti on the wall to the right of the altar and the devilish portrait of a craftsman's estranged wife on the choir screen.

Behind the altar hangs Rubens's *Adoration of the Magi* (1639). The canvas has been protected by an electronic alarm since an attack by a crazed chisel-wielder several years ago. Free musical recitals often play at the chapel; schedules are kept at the entrance. As you picnic by the riverbank, think of those who have gone before you: John Maynard Keynes, E.M. Forster, and Salman Rushdie all felt the college's grounds beneath their feet. In mid-June, university degree ceremonies are held in the Georgian **Senate House** opposite the King's College chapel.

TRINITY COLLEGE

Trinity St. ☎338 400. Chapel and courtyard open daily 10am-5pm. Wren Library open M-F noon-2pm, Sa 10:30am-12:30pm. Easter-Oct. £1.75, Nov.-Easter free.

Henry VIII, not to be outdone by the earlier Henry, intended the College of the Holy and Undivided Trinity (founded 1546) to be the largest and richest in Cambridge. The college has amply fulfilled his wish, being today Britain's third largest landowner (after the Queen and the Church of England); legend holds that it is possible to walk from Cambridge to Oxford without stepping off Trinity land. The alma mater of Sir Isaac Newton, who lived in E staircase for 30 years, the college's illustrious alumni include: literati Dryden, Byron, Tennyson, A.E. Housman, and Nabokov; atom-splitter Ernest Rutherford; philosopher Ludwig Wittgenstein; and Indian statesman Jawaharlal Nehru.

The heart of the college is the aptly named **Great Court,** the world's largest enclosed courtyard, reached from Trinity St. through **Great Gate.** The castle-like gateway is fronted by a statue of Henry VIII grasping a wooden chair leg—a student prankster stole the original scepter years ago. On the west side of the court stand the dour **chapel** and the **King's Gate tower.** The **fountain** in the center of the court is the only one in Cambridge; Lord Byron used to bathe nude in it. The eccentric poet also kept a bear as a pet (college rules only forbade cats and dogs) and claimed it would take his fellowship exams for him. The south side of the court is home to the palatial **Master's Lodge** and the cathedral-like **Great Hall,** where students and dons dine under the hundreds of grotesque carved faces.

On the other side of the Hall is the exquisite Renaissance facade of **Nevile's Court.** Newton measured the speed of sound by timing the echo in the cloisters that lead to Sir Christopher's **Wren Library.** While the college's collection has long outgrown the building, it still houses old books and precious manuscripts; those on view include alumnus **A. A. Milne's** original handwritten copies of *Winnie the Pooh* and Newton's own copy of his *Principia.* Pass through the drab, neo-Gothic **New Court** (Prince Charles's former residence), adjacent to Nevile's Court, to get to the Backs, where you can rent **punts** or simply enjoy the view from **Trinity Bridge.**

E A S T   A N G L I A

DUCKING AND DINING While you're wondering at the height of the ceiling in Trinity's Great Hall, take time to search for a fake duck hanging from the rafters. While no one is sure how the tradition started, it has become a challenge for undergraduates to try to scale the ceiling and move the duck around. Success is rewarded with membership in the ultra-secretive Mallard Society; failure (if you're discovered mid-mallard moving), with immediate expulsion from the college. While the College disapproves of this risky pastime, student lore claims that the president of the society is none other than the Dean—the very man who expels those caught in the act.

OTHER COLLEGES

ST. JOHN'S COLLEGE. Established in 1511 by Lady Margaret Beaufort, mother of Henry VIII, St. John's centers around a paved plaza rather than a grassy courtyard. The **Bridge of Sighs** connects the older part of the college to the towering neo-Gothic extravagance of **New Court,** whose silhouette has been likened to a wedding cake. The **School of Pythagoras,** a 12th-century pile of wood and stone thought to be the oldest complete building in Cambridge, hides in St. John's Gardens. The college also boasts the longest room in the city—the Fellows' Room in Second Court spans 93 ft. and was the site of some D-Day planning. *(St. John's St. ☎ 338 600. Open daily 10am-4:45pm. Evensong 6:30pm most nights. £2, concessions £1.20, families £4.)*

QUEENS' COLLEGE. Founded not once, but twice—by Queen Margaret of Anjou in 1448 and Elizabeth Woodville in 1465—Queens' College has the only unaltered Tudor courtyard in Cambridge. The **Mathematical Bridge,** despite rumors to the contrary, always included screws and bolts: even Cambridge students didn't have the skills to build it relying purely on mathematical principles. *(Silver St. ☎ 335 511. Open Mar.-Oct. daily 10am-4:30pm. £1.)*

CLARE COLLEGE. Clare's coat-of-arms—golden teardrops ringing a black border—recalls the college's founding in 1326 by thrice-widowed, 29-year-old Lady Elizabeth de Clare. Misery has not shrouded the college indefinitely, however, for Clare has some of the most cheerful **gardens** in Cambridge; they lie across elegant Clare Bridge. Walk through Wren's **Old Court** for a view of the University Library, where 82 mi. of shelves hold books arranged according to size rather than subject. *(Trinity Ln. ☎ 333 200. College open daily 10am-5pm. Old Court also open during exams after 4:45pm to groups of 3 or fewer. £2, under 10 free.)*

CHRIST'S COLLEGE. Founded as "God's-house" in 1448 and renamed in 1505, Christ's has since won fame for its gardens and its association with John Milton. Charles Darwin studied at Christ's before dealing a blow to its religious origins—his rooms (unmarked and closed to visitors) were on G staircase in First Court.

New Court, on King St., is one of Cambridge's most modern structures; its symmetrical concrete walls and dark windows make it look like the amalgam of a pyramid, Polaroid camera, and typewriter. Bowing to pressure from aesthetically offended Cantabrigians, a wall was built to block the view of the building from all sides except the inner courtyard. *(St. Andrews St. ☎ 334 900. Gardens open summer M-F 9:30am-noon; term-time M-F 9am-4:30pm. Free.)*

JESUS COLLEGE. Jesus has preserved an enormous amount of medieval work on its spacious grounds. Beyond the high-walled walk called the "Chimny" lies a three-sided court fringed with colorful flowerbeds. Through the arch on the right sit the remains of a gloomy medieval nunnery. *(Jesus Ln. ☎ 339 339. Courtyard open daily 9am-6pm; open during exams to groups of 3 or fewer.)*

MAGDALENE COLLEGE. Inhabiting a 15th-century Benedictine hostel, Magdalene (MAUD-lin), sometime home of Christian allegorist and Oxford man C.S. Lewis, has retained its religious emphasis. (It also retained its men-only status until 1988.) Take a peek at **Pepys Library,** in the second court; the library displays the noted statesman and prolific diarist's collections. *(Magdalene St. ☎ 332 100. Library open Easter-Aug. 11:30am-12:30pm and 2:30-3:30pm; Sept.-Easter M-Sa 11:30am-12:30pm. Free.)*

SMALLER COLLEGES. Thomas Gray wrote his *Elegy in a Country Churchyard* while staying in **Peterhouse College,** Trumpington St., the oldest and smallest college, founded in 1294. *(☎ 338 200.)* In contrast, the Modern Medieval brick pastiche of **Robinson College,** across the river on Grange Rd., is the newest. In 1977, local self-made man David Robinson founded it for the bargain price of £17 million, the largest single gift ever received by the university. *(☎ 339 100.)* **Corpus Christi College,** Trumpington St., founded in 1352 by the common people, contains the dreariest and oldest courtyard in Cambridge, aptly named Old Court and unaltered since its enclosure. The library, however, maintains the snazziest collection of Anglo-Saxon manuscripts in England. Alums include Sir Francis Drake and Christopher Marlowe. *(☎ 338 000.)* The 1347 **Pembroke College,** next to Corpus Christi, harbors the earliest architectural efforts of Sir Christopher Wren and counts Edmund Spenser, Ted Hughes, and Eric Idle among its grads. *(☎ 338 100.)* A chapel designed by Wren dominates the front court of **Emmanuel College,** St. Andrews St., known as "Emma." John Harvard, benefactor of his own university, studied here, but an alum with more tangible accomplishments is John Cleese. *(☎ 334 200.)*

MUSEUMS AND CHURCHES

■ **FITZWILLIAM MUSEUM.** A welcome break from the academia of the colleges, the museum fills an immense Neoclassical building, built in 1875 to house Viscount Fitzwilliam's collection. The mosaic floors could be a display of their own. A goulash of Egyptian, Chinese, Japanese, and Greek antiquities bides its time downstairs, joined by a muster of 16th-century German armor. Upstairs, five galleries feature works by Italian, French, British, and Dutch artists, including Rubens, Monet, and Brueghel. The **Founder's Library** is a must-see, housing an intimate collection of French Impressionists. The drawing room shows William Blake's books and woodcuts. *(Trumpington St. ☎ 332 900. Open Tu-Sa 10am-5pm, Su 2:15-5pm. Guided tours Sa 2:30pm. Call about lunchtime and evening concerts. Suggested donation £3. Tours £3.)*

OTHER MUSEUMS. ■ **Kettle's Yard,** at the corner of Castle St. and Northampton St., keeps early 20th-century art. The gallery exhibits rotate, but the house, created in 1956 by Tate curator Jim Ede as "a refuge of peace and order," is a quiet constant. Visitors can wander the house and admire the eclectic collection as though it were their own. *(☎ 352 124. House open Apr.-Sept. Tu-Sa 1:30-4:30pm, Su 2-4:30pm; Oct.-Mar. Tu-Su 2-4pm. Gallery open year-round Tu-Su 11:30am-5pm. Free.)* The **Scott Polar**

Research Institute, Lensfield Rd., commemorates icy expeditions with photographic and artistic memorabilia. (☎336 540. *Open M-Sa 2:30-4pm. Free.*)

CHURCHES. The **Round Church (Holy Sepulchre),** where Bridge St. meets St. John's St., is one of five surviving circular churches in England, built in 1130 (and later rebuilt) on the pattern of the Holy Sepulchre in Jerusalem. (☎311 602. *Free.*) It merits comparison with **St. Benet's,** a rough Saxon church on Benet St., built in 1050 and the oldest structure in Cambridge. It once had a spire, but spire-building was a technology the Normans lacked, so they spitefully knocked it down. (☎353 903. *Free.*) The tower of **Great St. Mary's Church,** off King's Parade, allows the best view of the broad greens and the colleges. Pray that the 12 bells don't ring while you're ascending the 123 tightly packed spiral steps. (*Tower open M-Sa 9:30am-5pm, Su 12:30-5pm. £1.85, children 60p, families £4.20.*)

🎵 🌿 ENTERTAINMENT AND FESTIVALS

PUNTING. Punting on the Cam is a favored form of hands-on entertainment in Cambridge. Punters take two routes—one from Magdalene Bridge to Silver St., the other from Silver St. to Grantchester. On the first route (the shorter, busier, and more interesting of the two), you'll pass the colleges and the Backs. Beware that punt-bombing—jumping from bridges into the river alongside a punt, thereby tipping its occupants—is an art form. You can rent at **Tyrell's,** Magdalene Bridge (☎(01480) 413 517; £10 per hr. plus a £40 deposit), or **Scudamore's,** Silver St. Bridge (☎359 750; £12 per hr. plus a £60 deposit). Student-punted **tours** (about £20) are another option. Inquire at the TIC for a complete list of companies.

THEATER. The Arts Box Office (☎503 333) handles ticket sales for the **Arts Theatre,** staging traveling productions around the corner from the TIC on Pea's Hill, and the **ADC Theatre** (Amateur Dramatic Club; ☎359 547), Park St., which offers student-produced plays as well as term-time movies and the Folk Festival. You can get an earful at the **Corn Exchange,** at the corner of Wheeler St. and Corn Exchange St. across from the TIC, a venue for band, jazz, and classical concerts. The box office also has info about other local events. (☎357 851. Open M-Sa 10am-6pm, until 9pm on performance evenings; Su 6-9pm performance days only. £7.50-24, student standbys 50% off day of show.) The **Cambridge Shakespeare Festival,** in association with the festival at that other university, features plays in open-air repertory through July and August. Tickets are available from the Arts Box Office or at the Corn Exchange (£10, concessions £7).

NIGHTLIFE. At dusk, **Evensong** begins at King's College Chapel, a breathtaking treat for day-worn spirits—not to mention a good way to sneak into the college grounds free of charge. (M-Sa 5:30pm, Su 3:30pm. Don't forget Evensong at other colleges, notably St. John's, Caius, and Clare.) **Pubs** constitute the core of Cambridge nightlife (see p. 331), but clubs and bars are also on the curriculum. Students, bartenders, TIC brochures, and the latest issue of the term-time *Varsity* (20p) are always good sources of information. Small, dim **Kambar,** 1 Wheeler St., attracts crowds with the only regular indie night in town (Sa) as well as garage, goth, electronica, and drum'n'bass during the week. (☎357 503. Open M-Sa 10pm-2:30am.) **Club Fez,** 15 Market Passage, offers music ranging from Latin to trance to dance in Moroccan-themed surroundings, complete with comfy floor cushions. (☎519 224. Show up early to avoid £2-8 cover. Open M-Tu 9pm-2:30am, W-Sa 9pm-2am, Su 8pm-midnight.) **The Junction,** Clifton Rd., is a music/theater/dance venue that turns into a club on weekends. A rotating schedule includes 7-11pm "teen nights" as well as a monthly gay/lesbian night. (☎357 503; www.junction.co.uk.) The **Boat Race,** 170 East Rd., a packed and popular joint near the police station, features live music every evening. (☎508 533. Usually free. Open from 8pm.) **Bar Coast,** Quayside, offers free, frequent dance nights, from disco to "uplifting house and garage." (☎556 961. Opens 8-9pm.)

MAY WEEK. During the first two weeks of June, students celebrate the end of the term with May Week, crammed full of concerts, plays, and elaborate balls followed by recuperative riverside breakfasts. The college boat clubs compete in an eyebrow-raising series of races known as the **bumps.** Crews line up along the river (rather than across it) and attempt to ram the boat in front before being bumped from behind. May Week's artistic height is the famous **Footlights Revue,** a collection of comedy skits; performers have included then-undergrads, future Monty Python members John Cleese, Eric Idle, and Graham Chapman.

FESTIVALS. Midsummer Fair, dating from the 16th century, appropriates the Midsummer Common for five days in the third week of June. The free **Strawberry Fair** (☎560 160), on the first Saturday in June, attracts a crowd with food, music, and body piercing. Address inquiries to the TIC. **Summer in the City** and **Camfest** brighten the last two weeks of July with a series of concerts and special exhibits culminating in a huge weekend celebration, the **Cambridge Folk Festival** (☎357 851). Book tickets well in advance (about £38); camping on the grounds is £5-18 extra.

▓ DAYTRIPS FROM CAMBRIDGE

GRANTCHESTER

To reach Grantchester Meadows from Cambridge, take the path following the river. Grantchester village lies 1 mi. from the meadows; ask the way at a shop or follow the blue bike-path signs (45min. by foot). If you have the energy to pole or paddle your way, rent a punt or canoe. Or hop on Stagecoach Cambus #118 (9-11 per day, return £1.50).

In 1912, Rupert Brooke wrote "Grantchester! Ah Grantchester! There's peace and holy quiet there." His words hold true today, as Grantchester is a mecca for Cambridge literary types. The gentle Cam and swaying seas of grass rejuvenate after the university's bustle. Brooke's home at the **Old Vicarage** is now owned by novelist and erstwhile London-mayor-wannabe Jeffrey Archer and closed to the public. The weathered 14th-century **Parish Church of St. Andrew and St. Mary,** on Millway, is beautifully intimate and not to be missed. The main village pub, the **Rupert Brooke,** 2 Broadway, will reward the famished for their efforts. (☎840 295. Open M-F 11am-3pm, Sa 11am-11pm, Su noon-10:30pm.) Or wend your way to the idyllic **Orchard Tea Gardens ❶** on Mill Way, once the leisurely Sunday haunt of the "neo-Pagans," a Grantchester offshoot of the famous Bloomsbury Group. Outdoor plays are occasionally performed on summer evenings; ask at the Cambridge TIC. (☎845 788. Light lunches £3-6. Open daily 10am-7pm; indoor and outdoor seating.)

ANGLESEY ABBEY

6 mi. from Cambridge on the B1102 (signposted from the A14). Buses #111 and 122 run from Drummer St. (25min., every hr.); ask to be let off at Lode Crossroads. ☎/fax 811 200. House open Easter to mid-Oct. W-Su and bank holidays 1-5pm; gardens open 10:30am-5:30pm. Last admission 4:30pm. £6.25, children £3.10.

Northeast of Cambridge, 12th-century Anglesey Abbey has been remodeled to house the priceless exotica of the first Lord Fairhaven. One of the niftiest **clocks** in the universe sits inconspicuously on the bookcase beyond the library's fireplace, but don't worry if you miss it—there are 55 other timepieces to enjoy along with a multitude of bizarre tokens and trifles. In the 100-acre gardens, trees punctuate lines of clipped hedges and manicured lawns.

OTHER DAYTRIPS

WIMPOLE HALL. Cambridgeshire's most elegant mansion lies 10 mi. southwest of Cambridge. The hall holds works by Gibbs, Flitcroft, and Joane; outside, an intricate Chinese bridge crosses a lake set in 60 acres of **gardens** designed by Capability Brown. *(Bus #175 from Drummer St. (35min., £2).* ☎*207 257. Open Apr.-Nov. Tu-Th and Sa-Su 1-5pm. £6.20, children £2.80.)* **Wimpole's Home Farm** brims with Longhorn and Gloucester cattle, Soay sheep, and Tamworth pigs. *(*☎*208 987. Open Apr.-Nov. Tu-Th and Sa-Su 10:30am-5pm. Farm £4.90, children £2.80. Hall and farm £9/£4.50.)*

AUDLEY END AND SAFFRON WALDEN. The house "too big for a king" proves that even the monarchy has its limits. The magnificent Jacobean hall is but a quarter of Audley End's former size—it once extended down to the river, where part of the Cam was rerouted by the capable Capability Brown. The grand halls display case after case of stuffed critters, including some extinct species. *(Trains leave Cambridge every hr. for Audley End.* ☎*(01799) 522 842. House open Apr.-Sept. W-Su and bank holidays noon-5pm; Oct. W-Su 11am-4pm. Grounds open Apr.-Sept. 11am-6pm; Oct. 11am-4pm. Last admission 1hr. before close. £7, concessions £5.20, children £3.50, families £17.40. Grounds only £4/£3/£2/£10. Free 15min. talk in the Great Hall.)* One signposted mile east of Audley End is ancient market town **Saffron Walden**, best known for the "pargetting" (plaster molding) of its Tudor buildings and its two mazes, a Victorian hedge maze and an ancient earthen maze. Ask your questions at the **tourist information centre**, Market Sq. (☎(01799) 510 444; open Apr.-Oct. M-Sa 9:30am-5:30pm; Nov.-Mar. M-Sa 10am-5pm), and rest your head at the **YHA hostel ❷**, 1 Myddylton Pl. (☎(01799) 523 117. Lockout 10am-5pm. Curfew 11pm. Open July-Aug. daily; Apr.-June and mid-Sept. to Oct. Tu-Sa; Mar. F-Sa. £10, under 18 £7.50.)

ELY
☎**01353**

The prosperous town of Ely (EEL-ee) was an island until its fens, now rich flatlands, were drained in the 17th century. Legend has it that the city got its name when St. Dunstan transformed local monks into eels for their lack of piety. The more likely story claims that "Elig" (Eel Island) was named for the slitherers that once infested the surrounding waters. Though some might view this quiet town as merely a base for seeing surrounding Cambridgeshire, Ely's spectacular cathedral is a destination in its own right.

TRANSPORTATION AND PRACTICAL INFORMATION. Ely is the junction for **trains** (☎(08457) 484 950) between **London** and various points in East Anglia, including **Cambridge** (20min., every hr., day return £3.40) and **Norwich** (1½hr., every hr., £10.80). **Cambus** (☎(01223) 423 554) X9 arrives at Market St. from **Cambridge** (30min., every hr., £3.40).

Ely's two major streets—**High St.** and **Market St.**—run parallel to the cathedral; the Cromwell House and some shops trail behind on **St. Mary's St.** To reach the cathedral and **tourist information centre** from the train station, walk up Station Rd. and continue up Back Hill. The TIC shares and operates the Cromwell House, 29 St. Mary's St. Staffers book rooms for £1 and a 10% deposit; call at least two days ahead. (☎662 062. Open Apr.-Sept. daily 10am-5:30pm; Oct.-Mar. M-Sa 10am-5pm.) They also sell a combination admission ticket, the **Passport to Ely**, that lets you into Ely Cathedral, Cromwell House, Ely Museum, and the Stained Glass Museum (£9, concessions £7, children free). Other services include: the **police**, Nutholt Ln. (☎(01223) 358 966); **Internet access** at **Ely Computer Supplies**, 17 Broad St. (☎668 863; £2.50 per 30min.), and the **library**, 6 The Cloisters, just off Market Pl. (☎662 350; free, but often a long wait); and the **post office**, in Lloyd's Chemist on 19 High St. (☎669 946). **Post Code:** CB7 4LQ.

☎ ☐ ACCOMMODATIONS AND FOOD. B&B options include **The Post House ❸**, 12a Egremont St., which has elegant rooms and a sinfully strong shower. (**☎** 667 184. From £20 per person.) Close to the train station and river, **Mr. and Mrs. Friend-Smith's ❸**, 31 Egremont St., lets double and twin rooms with garden views. (**☎** 663 118. From £25 per person.) At **Jane's B&B ❸**, 82 Broad St. (**☎** 667 609), stay in a homey flat complete with kitchen for only £20 per person. Camp among spuds and sugar beets with a cathedral view at **Braham Farm ❶**, Cambridge Rd., off the A10, 1 mi. from the city center. (**☎** 662 386. £3 per tent. Electricity £1.50.)

Most shops close on Tuesday afternoons in winter. Stock up on provisions at the **market** in Market Pl. (Th and Sa 8am-4pm). **Waitrose Supermarket,** Brays Ln., hides behind a Georgian facade. (**☎** 668 800. Open M-Tu and Sa 8:30am-6pm, W-Th 8:30am-8pm, F 8:30am-9pm, Su 10am-4pm.) **The Almonry ❷**, just off the corner of High St. and Brays Ln., serves well-heeled basics for £6-7; eat outside for a stunning garden and cathedral vista. (**☎** 666 360. Open M-Sa 10am-5pm, Su 11am-5pm.) Firehoses and rubber boots have been replaced with art exhibits at **The Old Fire Engine House ❸**, 25 St. Mary's St., which prepares local produce in creative ways. Appropriately enough, smoking is not allowed. (**☎** 662 582. Entrees £12-14. Open M-Sa 10:30am-9pm, Su 10:30am-5:30pm.) **The Steeplegate ❶**, 16-18 High St., serves tea and snacks (£3-7) in two rooms built over a medieval undercroft. (**☎** 664 731. Open June-Oct. daily 10am-5pm, Nov.-May M-F 10am-4:30pm and Sa 10am-5pm.) The **Minster Tavern ❶**, Minster Pl., opposite the cathedral, is popular for lunches. (**☎** 652 901. Meals £3-7. Open M-Sa 11am-11pm, noon-10:30pm.)

◘ SIGHTS. The towers of massive **▨Ely Cathedral** are impossible to miss. The cathedral was founded in 1081, on the spot where St. Ethelreda had formed a religious community four centuries before, and was redecorated in the 19th century, when the elaborate ceiling above the nave and many of the stained-glass windows were completed. In 1322, the original Norman tower collapsed, later replaced by the present **Octagon Altar,** topped by the lantern tower. The eight-sided cupola appears to burst into mid-air but is in fact held up by eight stone pillars. In the south transept lies the tomb of Dean of Ely, Humphrey Tyndall, an eternal PR boost for the monarchy: heir to the throne of Bohemia, Humphrey refused the kingship, saying he'd "rather be Queen Elizabeth's subject than a foreign prince." Riiight. Don't overlook the tiled **floor maze,** at your feet as you enter. Keep an eye out, too, for the tomb of one of Ely's former bishops, who strikes a pose more becoming of a Playgirl model than a servant of God. (**☎** 667 735. Open Easter-Sept. daily 7am-7pm; Oct.-Easter M-F 7:30am-6:30pm, Su 7:30am-5pm. Evensong M-Sa 5:30pm, Su 3:45pm. Octagon tours May-Sept. 3 per day, £2.50. Free West Tower tours July-Aug. 4 per day. Free grounds tours 4 per day. £4, concessions £3.50.)

The brilliant **Stained Glass Museum** overlooks the cathedral's nave and details the history of the art form while displaying over a hundred of its finest examples. (**☎** 660 347. Open Easter-Oct. M-F 10:30am-5pm, Sa 10:30am-5:30pm, Su noon-6pm; Nov.-Easter M-F 10:30am-4:30pm, Sa 10:30am-5pm, Su noon-4:30pm. £3.50, concessions £2.50, families £7.) The **brass rubbing center** is free, but materials cost £1.70-8.70. (Open July-Aug. daily 10:30am-4pm, Su noon-3pm.) Monastic buildings around the cathedral are still in use: the **infirmary** houses one of the resident canons, and the **bishop's palace** is a home for disabled children. The other buildings are used by the **King's School,** one of England's older public (read: private) schools.

For an architectural tour of Ely, follow the path outlined in the TIC's free *Town Trail* pamphlet. **Ely Museum,** at the Old Gaol on the corner of Market St. and Lynn Rd., tells the story of the fenland city, highlighting the saga of the swamp-draining project that created the present landscape. (**☎** 666 655. Open summer 10:30am-5:30pm; winter 10:30am-4:30pm. £2, concessions £1.25.) **Oliver Cromwell's House,** 29

St. Mary's St., has been immortalized with wax figures, 17th-century decor, and a "haunted" bedroom. Fish and chips will look positively gourmet after perusal of Lady Cromwell's recipes. (☎ 662 062. Open Apr.-Sept. daily 10am-5:30pm; Oct.-Mar. M-Sa 10am-5pm, Su 11am-3pm. £3.50, concessions £3, families £8.50.)

NORFOLK

KING'S LYNN   ☎ 01553

King's Lynn was one of England's foremost 16th-century ports. Four hundred years later, the once mighty current of the Great Ouse (OOZE, as in slime) river has slowed to a leisurely flow, and the town has slowed its pace to match. This dockside city borrows its Germanic look from trading partners such as Hamburg and Bremen; the earth tones of the flat East Anglian countryside meet with somber red-brick facades. The town slumbers early and heavily, and the sights can be dry, but King's Lynn makes a perfect stopover for hikers exploring the region and anyone in search of rest and relaxation.

▐▓ TRANSPORTATION AND PRACTICAL INFORMATION. Trains (☎ (08457) 484 950) steam into the **station** on Blackfriars Rd. from: **Cambridge** (1hr., 23 per day, return £8.30); **London King's Cross** (1½hr., 24 per day, day return £25.20); **Peterborough** (1hr., 6 per day, return £9). **Buses** arrive at the **Vancouver Centre** (☎ 772 343; office open M-F 8:30am-5pm, Sa 8:30am-noon and 1-5pm). **First Eastern Counties** (☎ (01603) 660 553) buses travel from **Norwich** (1½hr., 16 per day, £3.70) and **Peterborough** (1¼hr., 13 per day, £3.70). **National Express** (☎ (08705) 808 080) runs twice daily from **London** (4-5hr., £11).

The **tourist information centre,** in the Custom House, on the corner of King St. and Purfleet, books rooms for a 10% deposit and provides bus and train info. The TIC is 10min. from the train station: walk down Waterloo St. until the bus station, then veer left onto New Conduit St., which turns into Purfleet. (☎ 763 044. Open M-Sa 9:15am-5pm, Su 10:15am-5pm.) Buy National Express tickets from **West Norfolk Travel,** 2 King St. (☎ 772 910. Open M-Sa 9am-5pm.) Other services include: the **police** (☎ 691 211), at the corner of St. James and London Rd.; the **hospital** (☎ 613 613), on Gayton Rd.; and the **post office** (☎ (08457) 223 344), at Baxter's Plain on the corner of Broad St. and New Conduit St. **Post Code:** PE30 1YB.

▐ ACCOMMODATIONS. The quayside ▓YHA King's Lynn ❶, a short walk from the train and bus stations (keep your eyes peeled—it's easy to miss), occupies part of 16th-century Thoresby College, on College Ln., opposite the Old Gaol House. The location, river view, and friendly staff make this your best bet. It often fills, so call ahead. (☎ 772 461; fax 764 312. No smoking. Lockout 10am-5pm. Curfew 11pm. Open May-Aug. daily; Apr. and Sept.-Oct. W-Su. £9.25, under 18 £6.40.) **B&Bs** are a hike from the city center; the less expensive ones span **Gaywood Rd.** and **Tennyson Ave.** Eight gracious rooms comprise Victorian **Fairlight Lodge ❷,** 79 Goodwins Rd. (☎ 762 234. £18-25 per person.) Super-soft beds dominate the (nearly all ensuite) rooms at **Maranatha Guest House ❷,** 115-117 Gaywood Rd., and a pool table livens up the lounge. (☎ 774 596. £18 per person.)

▐ FOOD. King's Lynn restaurants operate on their own sweet time, and many close on Sunday. Several mega-supermarkets congregate in the area around the Vancouver Centre. For fresh fruit, visit the markets held at larger **Tuesday Market Pl.,** on the north end of High St., or at **Saturday Market Pl.** Traditionally costumed servers present aromatic Thai dishes (£10-15) at **The Thai Orchid ❸**, 33-39 St. James St. (☎767 013. Open M-Sa noon-2pm and 6-11:30pm, Su noon-2pm and 6-10:30pm.) Inexpensive Italian meals (£4-7) await at **Antonio's ❷**, on Baxter's Plain, off Tower St. (Open Tu-Sa noon-3pm and 6:30-11pm.) Quiet **Archers ❶**, a few steps up Purfleet from the TIC, serves tasty lunches (£3-6) and teas. (☎764 411. Open M-Sa 9am-5pm.) The **Seven Sisters ❶** pub presides at the top of Extons Rd., nicely out of the way. (Open M-Sa 11am-11pm, Su noon-10:30pm.)

☉ ᠍᠍ SIGHTS AND ENTERTAINMENT. The sights of King's Lynn pale in comparison to those of neighboring Norwich, but a **walking tour** (30p, from the TIC) is rewarding on a fine day. At the **Tales of the Old Gaol House,** Saturday Market Pl., an audioguide tells of Lynn's murderers, robbers, and witches; try out the stocks or climb up to the stake for a taste of 17th-century justice. The Regalia Room displays the 14th-century "King John Cup" and other treasures. (☎774 297. Open Apr.-Oct. daily 10am-5pm; Nov.-Mar. F-Tu only. £2.40, concessions £1.70.) **St. Margaret's Church,** also on Saturday Market Pl., was built in 1101. Peaceful **Tower Gardens** ensconce Greyfriars Tower on one side of St. James' St., while **The Walks,** on the other side, stretch away from the town center. **The Town House Museum of Lynn Life,** 46 Queen St., leads you through medieval, Tudor, Victorian, and 1950s reconstructions of life in King's Lynn. (☎773 450. Open May-Sept. M-Sa 10am-5pm, Su 2pm-5pm; Oct.-Apr. M-Sa 10am-4pm. £2.40, concessions £1.75.)

The **Corn Exchange** at Tuesday Market Pl. sells tickets for music, dance, and theater events. (☎764 864. Open M-Sa 10am-6pm and at evening showtimes, Su 1hr. prior to show. Shows usually 8pm.) The 15th-century **Guildhall of St. George,** 27-29 King St., near Tuesday Market Pl., is said to be the last surviving building where Shakespeare appeared in one of his own plays; it now hosts the **King's Lynn Arts Centre.** There are no tours or plaques or any such nonsense; just wander around. (☎774 725 or 764 864. Open M-F 10am-2pm. Free.) The Guildhall also brings the **King's Lynn Festival** to town (July 24-Aug. 2 in 2003), an orgy of classical and jazz music, along with ballet, puppet shows, and films. Get schedules at the Festival Office, 5 Thoresby College, Queen St. (Info ☎767 557, tickets 764 864. Box office open M-F 10am-5pm, Sa 10am-1pm and 2-4pm. Tickets £3-10.)

᠍᠍ DAYTRIPS FROM KING'S LYNN

SANDRINGHAM. Sandringham has been a royal home since 1862. The Edwardian interior includes halls lined with weaponry, ornate ceilings, and detailed Spanish tapestries, while the grounds boast flowing lawns, neat gardens, and a lovely lake. The museum touts the big-game trophies of George V and royal cars owned by Edward VII in 1900, Prince Charles in 1990, and Princes William and Harry today. George once described the site as "dear old Sandringham, the place I love better than anywhere else in the world." Its 600 acres are open to the public when not in use by the royals. It's usually closed in June; ask at the King's Lynn TIC. The best time to visit, though, is during the **flower show** in the last week of July. *(10 mi. north of King's Lynn. First Eastern Counties bus #411 arrives from King's Lynn (25 min.; M-Sa 9 per day, Su 5 per day; return £3.35). ☎(01553) 772 675. Open Apr.-Sept. 11am-4:45pm. £6, concessions £4.50, children £3.50, families £15.50. Museum and grounds only £5/£4/£3/£13.)*

CASTLE RISING. Closer to King's Lynn, this solid keep set atop massive earthworks sheltered Queen Isabella, "She-Wolf of France," after she plotted the murder of her husband, Edward II. The beautiful view, navigable ruins, and informative tour make the easy trip worthwhile. *(First Eastern Counties buses run from King's Lynn (#410 and 411, 15min., M-Sa 22 per day; #415, 15min., Su 11 per day; return £2). ☎(01553) 631 330. Open Apr.-Oct. daily 10am-6pm; Nov.-Mar. W-Su 10am-4pm. Admission and audio tour £3.25, concessions £2.50, children £1.60, families £9.)*

HOUGHTON HALL. Built in the mid-18th century for Robert Walpole, England's first prime minister, Houghton Hall is a magnificent example of Palladian architecture. Its rooms, designed and decorated by James Gibbs and William Kent, were intended to reflect the grandeur of Walpole's office, and still include original tapestries, paintings, a famous model soldier collection, and "the most sublime bed ever designed." *(14 mi. northeast of King's Lynn. Take First Eastern Counties bus #411 (45min., M-Sa 2 per day, return £3.75). ☎(01485) 528 569. Open Easter to late Sept. Th, Su, and bank holidays 2-5:30pm; gate closes 5pm. £6, children £2.)*

THE NORTHERN NORFOLK COAST

The northern Norfolk Coast is a blissfully tranquil expanse of British seashore. The occasional windmill or mansion punctuates untamed beaches, sand dunes, and salt marshes, while sailboats slumber and wading birds balance in boggy harbors. Those with eight to twelve days can traverse the linked 93 mi. of the **Norfolk Coast Path** and **Peddar's Way** (see p. 325). The **National Trail** begins 16 mi. north of King's Lynn at **Hunstanton,** stretches east to **Wells-next-the-Sea** and then **Sheringham** and the **Norfolk Broads** (see p. 347), finishing near **Cromer.** The trail and its villages are also fine daytrips. The **Norfolk Coast Hopper,** Norfolk Green Coach #36, makes daily stops between Hunstanton and Sheringham. (☎(0845) 300 6116. 1½hr.; every hr. in summer, fewer in winter; all-day ticket £4.) Non-hikers can see the coast via alternative modes of transportation: **Coastal Voyager** runs seatrips from Southwold (☎(07887) 525 082; £6-25, children half-price) and **Skyride Balloons** (☎(07000) 110 210) offers the best seaviews of all.

The highlight of the coast is the boisterous ■**Blakeney Point Seal Colony.** Though accessible by a 4 mi. footpath from Cley-next-the-Sea, the seals would much rather their admirers visit by boat; **Temple's Ferry Service** runs trips from Morston Harbour. (☎(01263) 740 791. 1-1½hr. £5, children £3.50.) In Hunstanton, on the Southern Promenade, the **Hunstanton Sea Life Sanctuary** rehabilitates injured grown-up seals and (cute, sleepy) abandoned baby seals in its **Seal Hospital.** (☎(01485) 533 576. Open summer daily 10am-5pm; call for winter hours. £5.50, children £3.75.) The **Norfolk Coast Hopper** runs from Hunstanton to **Holme's Crossing** (12min.)— close by are the superb **Scolt Head Island Reserve** and **Holme Bird Observatory.** To visit Scolt Head Island, go via Brancaster Staithe, 10 mi. east along the A149.

For a taste of luxury, visit **Holkham Hall,** 2 mi. west of Wells-next-the-Sea, the Palladian home of the Earl of Leicester. Marvel at the massive marble hall before getting lost in the amusing **Bygones Museum,** which assembles over 4000 knick-knacks from the family's past. The labyrinthine grounds attract all sorts of wildlife, from heron to deer to Manhattanite tourists. (☎(01328) 710 227. Open Apr.-Sept. Su-Th 1-5pm. Hall and museum £8, children £4. Hall or museum each £5/£2.50.)

The Norfolk Coast makes an easy daytrip from **King's Lynn,** though **Hunstanton,** at the western edge, is a more intimate touring base. Buses #410 and 411 run from Vancouver Centre in King's Lynn to Hunstanton (45min.; M-Sa 2 per hr., Su every 2hr.; £2.80, return £3.70). For details on the Northern Norfolk Coast, maps, and bus schedules, consult the Hunstanton **tourist information centre,** Town Hall, The Green. (24hr. ☎(01485) 532 610. Open Apr.-Sept. daily 9:30am-5pm; Oct.-Mar. 10:30am-4pm.) *Walking the Peddars Way and Norfolk Coast Path with Weavers Way* is a decent guide and accommodations list (£2.70); more extensive (and expensive) details of the trail can be attained from the *National Trail Guides Book* (£12.70). The **National Trail Office,** 6 Station Road, Wells-next-the-Sea, has expert advice on hiking the Norfolk Coast Path. (☎(01328) 711 533. Open daily 9am-5pm.) Budget accommodations along the coast are rather scarce, but the kind folks at the King's Lynn or Hunstanton TICs can help you find something suitable for a 10% deposit. On the coast, your best bet is Hunstanton's **YHA hostel ❷,** 15 Avenue Rd., a well-signposted, 5min. walk from the bus station—take Sandringham Rd. south, then turn right on Avenue Rd. A comfortable TV lounge, laundry facilities, and a well-kept patio await. (☎(01485) 532 061. Open July-Aug. daily; Easter-June M-Sa; Sept.-Oct. Tu-Sa. Dorms £10.25, under 18 £7.25.)

NORWICH   ☎01603

In the mood to lose your way? Try navigating the dizzying medieval streets of Norwich (NOR-idge) as they wind willy-nilly outwards from the Norman castle, past the cathedral, and to the scattered fragments of the 14th-century city wall. But though Norwich retains the hallmarks of an ancient city, a university and active art community ensure that it is also thoroughly modern. One sign of the times: Norwich once had a church for every Sunday and a pub for every day of the year, but now only 36 churches coexist with 380 pubs. Clearly, the hum of "England's city in the country" has not yet abated, with a daily market almost a millennium old still thriving alongside busy art galleries and nightlife.

▐ TRANSPORTATION

Easily accessible by bus, coach, or train, Norwich makes a decent base for touring both urban and rural East Anglia, particularly the Norfolk Broads.

Trains: Station at the corner of Riverside and Thorpe Rd., 15min. from the city center (bus 40p). Ticket window open M-Sa 4:45am-8:45pm, Su 6:45am-8:45pm. Information open M-Sa 9am-7pm, Su 10:15am-5:30pm. **Anglia Railways** (☎(08457) 484 950) from: **Great Yarmouth** (30min.; M-Sa 1 per hr., Su 14 per day; return £4-5.30); **London Liverpool St.** (2hr., M-Sa 30 per day, £34.50); **Peterborough** (1½hr.; M-Sa 15 per day, Su 12 per day; return £11.60-15.10).

Buses: Station (☎660 553) on Surrey St., off St. Stephen St., southwest of the castle. Information center and ticket desk open M-F 8am-5:30pm, Sa 9am-5:15pm. **National Express** (☎(08705) 808 080) from **London** (3hr., 6 per day, £13.25). **Cambridge Coach Services** (☎(01223) 423 900) from **Cambridge** (#74; 2hr.; 4 per day; £9.10, concessions £7, children £4.65). **First Eastern Counties** (☎(08456) 020 121) travels to **King's Lynn, Peterborough,** and other Norfolk towns; **Ranger tickets** give 1 day of unlimited travel (£6, seniors £4.70, children £4, families £11.50).

Taxis: Express Taxis (☎767 626). 24hr. Call ☎300 300 for wheelchair taxi (limited availability). **Canary Taxis** (☎414 243) has a 24hr. wheelchair taxi.

▐▐ ORIENTATION AND PRACTICAL INFORMATION

The best way to find your way around Norwich is to get a map and pray. The city planner must have had a wobbly hand, for although sights are fairly close together and walking is an efficient way to get around, the twisty streets are guaranteed to confuse. Take care in the center of town after dark, when getting lost is most probable and few pedestrians (aside from other poor lost souls) are around to assist.

Tourist Information Centre: The Forum, Millennium Plain, Bethel St. (☎666 071; www.norwich.gov.uk). Books rooms for £3 and a 10% deposit. Open June-Sept. M-Sa 9:30am-5pm; Oct.-May M-F 9:30am-4:30pm, Sa 9:30am-1pm and 1:30-4:30pm. **Walking tours** (1½hr.) Apr.-Oct.; £2.50, children £1.

Financial Services: Banks on London St. and Bank Plain. **Thomas Cook,** St. Stephen's St. (☎241 200). Open M-Tu and Th-F 9am-5:30pm, W 10am-5:30pm, Sa 10am-4pm.

Launderette: Laundromat, 179a Dereham Rd. (☎626 685). Change and soap (20p) available. Open M-Sa 8am-8pm, Su 10am-7pm; last wash 1½hr. before closing.

Police: Bethel St. (☎768 769).

Hospital: Norfolk and Norwich Hospital (☎286 286), at the corner of Brunswick Rd. and St. Stephen's Rd.

Internet Access: Norwich's cyber cafes are quick to kick the cyberbucket; get an up-to-date list at the TIC. **Cybercand,** 14 Bank St. (☎619 091). Open M-F 9am-7pm, Sa 1-6pm. £4 per hr., £2 per hr. with £5 membership. **Library,** next to the TIC (☎774 774). Free access upstairs, at regular terminals, and downstairs at 6 "Express Terminals." Library open M and W-F 9am-8pm, Tu 10am-8pm, Sa 9am-5pm. Express open M and W-F 9am-10:30pm, Tu 10am-10:30pm, Sa 9am-8:30pm, and Su 10:30am-4:30pm.

Post Office: 84-85 Castle Meadow Walk (☎761 635). **Bureau de change.** Open M-F 9am-5:30pm, Sa 9am-6pm. **Branches** at Queen St. (☎220 278) and 13-17 Bank Plain (☎220 228). **Post Code:** NR1 3DD.

⬛ ACCOMMODATIONS AND CAMPING

Cheap (£17-20) and convenient lodgings are located on **Stracey Rd.,** a 5min. walk from the train station. Turn left onto Thorpe Rd., walk two blocks away from the bridge, and go right onto Stracey Rd. Many pleasant B&Bs in the £18-24 range line **Earlham Rd.** and **Unthank Rd.,** but they're at least 20min. west of downtown and even farther from the train station. B&Bs can also be found along **Dereham Rd.:** follow St. Benedict's St., which eventually becomes Dereham Rd.

The Abbey Hotel, 16 Stracey Rd. (☎/fax 612 915), 5min. from the train station up Thorpe Rd. A TV and wash basin await in every quiet room of this clean, yellow building—as do cocoa and biscuits. Singles £20-29; doubles £40-54. ❸

Earlham Guest House, 147 Earlham Rd. (☎459 469). Take bus #26 or 27 from the city center and ask to get off at The Mitre pub. Friendly hosts Mr. and Mrs. Wright's guest house stands out for its cozy lounge and refreshing garden. The tasteful, color-coordinated rooms are kept to an unearthly standard of cleanliness. No smoking. Singles £25-28; doubles and twins £23-26 per person. ❸

Beaufort Lodge, 62 Earlham Rd. (☎/fax 627 928). This new B&B promises plushly-carpeted, wide-windowed rooms with comfortable furnishings, TV, and plenty of space. The lovely hosts feed you tea, coffee, and cookies after fetching you from the station. No smoking. Singles £40-45; doubles from £50. ❹

Camping: Lakenham campsite, Martineau Ln. (☎620 060; before 8pm), 1 mi. south of the city center; buses #9, 29, and 32 stop nearby. No cars after 11pm. Toilets and showers; handicapped facilities. July-Aug. £4, children £2; Easter-June £3.80/£1.80; Sept.-Easter £3/free. Pitch fee £3.50. Family deals available.

THE HIDDEN DEAL

THE WAFFLE HOUSE

waffle [intrans. v.]. To equivocate. To vacillate. To hesitate. Synonyms: yo-yo; flip-flop.

Do none of the above when faced with the opportunity to nab a cheap lunch at Norwich's Waffle House. Just a few blocks from the market, at 39 St. Giles Street, the smell of freshly baked waffles hangs in the air. Behind the nondescript storefront and nondescript sign, friendly Waffle House staff smother crisp, buttery Belgian waffles (both wholemeal and white) with everything from ham and cheese to tuna and bean sprouts to ice cream with chocolate fudge.

Diners may be permitted a slight tizzy of equivocation when faced with the smorgasbord of waffle possibilities, but they can wash down any lingering uncertainty with a tall glass of homestyle lemonade or a variety of super-thick milkshakes—a decidedly perfect accompaniment.

As if all this wasn't reason enough for you to make up your mind, a 20% student discount and weekday lunch deal mean you can walk out with a two-course meal in your stomach for just £5.50. Indecision ends here. (☎612 790. Open M-Th 10am-10pm, F-Sa 10am-11pm, Su 11am-9pm.)

🍴🍺 FOOD AND PUBS

In the heart of the city and just a stone's throw from the castle spreads one of England's largest and oldest **open-air markets.** (Open M-Sa roughly 8:30am-4:30pm.) Feast on everything from fresh fruits and cheeses to ice cream (jewelry, gewgaws, and gimcracks are harder to digest). **Tesco Metro** is alongside the market square on St. Giles St. (Open M-Sa 7:30am-8pm, Su 11am-5pm.)

🌿 **The Treehouse,** 14 Dove St. (☎ 763 258). Eat fresh vegetarian cuisine on earthenware plates while stuffed parrots eye you hungrily from their perches. Daily menu with creative meals of the main (£6.40) and snack (£4.90) variety... though the gargantuan "snack meals" are deceptively named. The store downstairs sells healthy victuals. Open M-W 11:30am-5pm, Th-Su 11:30am-9pm. ❷

The Orgasmic Cafe, Queen St. (☎ 760 650). Stuffs freshly baked bread from its open kitchen with moan-worthy fillings like salmon with creme fraiche and rogan josh curry (£4.50-5.50). Pizzas (£4.50-8) have similarly creative toppings. The stylish bar and clientele, coupled with a looong wine list, might induce you to make a new friend. Open M-Sa 10:30am-11pm, Su 11am-10:30pm. ❷

Adlard's, 79 Upper Giles St. (☎ 633 522). Norwich's #1 place for fine food. Set dinner of superbly prepared French-English fusion cuisine is well worth £25. Decor evokes a comfortable living room, with friendly waitstaff adding to the homey feeling. Zillions of wines, decadent desserts. Reserve ahead. Open M 7:30-10:30pm, Tu-Sa 12:30-1:45pm and 7:30-10:30pm. ❺

Take 5, St. Andrews Hill (☎ 763 099), off St. Andrews St. One of the best spots for an evening drink in town isn't even a pub—it's a cafe, restaurant, and exhibition center in a fantastic 14th-century building with a cobblestone courtyard. Organic and veggie dishes appeal to the health-conscious (£5.20-6.80). Open M-Sa 11am-11pm. ❷

Bar Tapas, 16-20 Exchange St. (☎ 764 077). Experience the rhythm of South America and the spirit of Spain. Try the authentic *Tortilla Española to Brochetta da Gambas* (£3-5). Entrees £8.25-12. Open M-W 10:30am-6pm, Th-Sa 10:30am-11pm. ❷

The Adam and Eve, Bishopgate (☎ 667 423), behind the cathedral at the Palace St. end of Riverside Walk. Norwich's first pub (est. 1249) is older than sin and still one of its most pleasing watering holes. Open M-Sa 11am-11pm, Su noon-10:30pm; cheese-drenched potatoes and other treats served noon-7pm. ❶

👁 SIGHTS

🏛 **ORIGINS.** This brand-new, ultra-interactive history complex has three floors of exhibits offering an extensive—and fascinating—history of Norfolk. Settlers as diverse as Vikings and WWII American soldiers are treated with equal measures of humor and hard fact, and a 20min. panoramic film shows all the parts of Norfolk you might never get to see for yourself. *(In the Forum, next to the TIC. ☎ 727 920. Open M-Sa 10am-6pm and Su 10:30am-4:30pm. £5, concessions £4, children £3.50, families £13.50.)*

NORWICH CASTLE MUSEUM AND ART GALLERY. The original Norwich Castle was built in 1089 by a Norman monarchy intent on subduing the Saxon city. Its current exterior dates from an 1830s restoration, though last year's £12 million refurbishment was the largest in the castle's history. The Castle Museum in the keep has a hands-on exhibit that brings new life to Norman rule, while the archaeology gallery displays relics of 🏛**Queen Boudicca,** a first-century feminist who rebelled against Roman rule. The art gallery contains a collection of oil paintings and watercolors. *(☎ 493 636. Open July-Aug. M-Sa 10am-7pm, Su noon-5pm; Sept.-June M-Sa 10am-5pm, Su 2-5pm. £4.70, concessions £4.10, children £3.50, families £13.90.)*

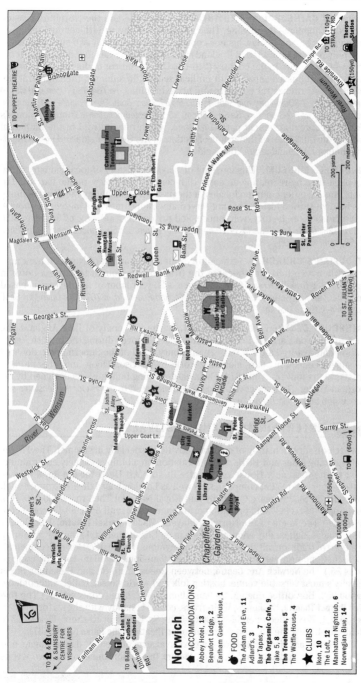

TO PUPPET THEATRE

TO **1** & **2** (.6mi)
& SAINSBURY
CENTRE FOR
VISUAL ARTS

TO **16** (110yd)
STRACEY RD.

Thorpe
Station

Thorpe Rd.

Riverside Rd.

TO **15** (150yd)

River Wensum

Bishop's
House

St. Martin at Palace Plain

Bishopgate

Bishopgate

Hook's Walk

Lower Close

Lower Close

Recorder Rd.

Whitefriars

Cathedral and Tombland

St. Faith's Ln.

Cathedral St.

Palace St.

Pigg St.

Upper Close

Erpingham Gate

St. Ethelbert's Gate

Prince of Wales Rd.

Mountergate

Quay Side

Wensum St.

Tombland

Upper King St.

Rose St.

Rose Ln.

King St.

Fishergate

Magdalen St.

St. Peter Hungate Museum

Princes St.

Queen St.

Bank St.

Rose Ave.

Cattle Market St.

St. Peter Parmentergate

Elm Hill

Redwell St.

Bank Plain

Rouen Rd.

Riverside Walk

Friar's

St. George's St.

St. Andrew's Hill

London St.

Castle Meadow

Castle Museum and Art Gallery

Farmers Ave.

Bell Ave.

Market Ave.

TO ST. JULIAN'S CHURCH (160yd)

Golden Ball St.

Ber St.

Colgate

Bridewell Museum

Bedford St.

NORBIC

Castle St.

Davey Pl.

Timber Hill

Westlegate

Oak St.

Duke St.

St. John's Alley

Exchange St.

Dove St.

Royal Arcade

White Lion St.

Red Lion St.

Surrey St.

River Wensum

Charing Cross

Maddermarket Theatre

Gentleman's Walk

Guildhall

Market

St. Peter's St.

Haymarket

St. Peter Mancroft

Briggs St.

Rampant Horse St.

Matthouse Rd.

TO **17** (60yd)

Westwick St.

St. John's

Upper Goat Ln.

City Hall

The Forum

i

Origins

Brigg St.

St. Benedict's St.

St. Giles St.

Theatre St.

Chantry Rd.

TO (550yd)

St. Stephen's St.

TO EATON RD. (900yd)

St. Margaret's St.

Pottergate

Willow Ln.

Upper St. Giles St.

Bethel St.

Chapel Field N.

Chapel Field Gardens

Chapel Field E.

Ten Bell Ln.

Norwich Arts Centre

Cow Hill

St. Giles Church

Millennium Library

Theatre Royal

Grapes Hill

Cleveland Rd.

St. John the Baptist Catholic Cathedral

Earlham Rd.

Unthank Rd.

TO B&Bs

N

LG

Norwich

♦ ACCOMMODATIONS
Abbey Hotel, **13**
Beaufort Lodge, **2**
Earlham Guest House, **1**

● FOOD
The Adam and Eve, **11**
Adlard's, **3**
Bar Tapas, **7**
The Orgasmic Cafe, **9**
Take 5, **8**
The Treehouse, **5**
The Waffle House, **4**

★ CLUBS
Ikon, **10**
The Loft, **12**
Manhattan Nightclub, **6**
Norwegian Blue, **14**

200 yards
200 meters
0
0

NORWICH CATHEDRAL AND TOMBLAND. The castle and the Norman Norwich Cathedral dominate the skyline. The cathedral, built by an 11th-century bishop as penance for having bought his episcopacy, features unusual two-storey cloisters (the only ones of their kind in England) and flying buttresses that help support the second-tallest spire in the country (315 ft.). Use the mirror in the nave to examine the overhead bosses carved with biblical scenes. In summer, the cathedral frequently hosts orchestral concerts and art exhibitions. (☎ 764 385. Open mid-May to mid-Sept. daily 7:30am-7pm; mid-Sept. to mid-May 7:30am-6pm. Evensong M-F 5:15pm. Free tours May-Oct. M-F 2-3 per day, Sa-Su 3:30pm. £3 suggested donation.) Though it sounds like a macabre amusement park, **Tombland,** which runs in front of the Cathedral Park, is the burial site of thousands of victims of the Great Plague and now a nightclub hotspot. Coincidence? You decide.

BRIDEWELL MUSEUM. This museum displays the history of local industry, turning back time by recreating an early 19th-century pharmacy, public bar, and tap room, among other common locales of the past. The enchanting medieval building has its own storied history, having served at various times as a merchant's house, mayor's mansion, factory, warehouse, and prison. (Bridewell Alley, off St. Andrew's St. ☎ 667 228. Open Apr.-Sept. M-Sa 10am-5pm, Su 2-5pm. £2.50, concessions £2, children £1.50, families £6.50.)

ST. JULIAN'S CHURCH. A 14th-century nun named Julian of Norwich took up a cell of her own here and became the first known woman to write a book in English. Her *Revelations of Divine Love*, a 20-year labor of divine love, is based on her mystic experiences. (Between King St. and Rouen Rd. ☎ 767 380. Open May-Sept. daily 8am-5:30pm; Oct.-Apr. 8am-4pm. Free.)

SAINSBURY CENTRE FOR VISUAL ARTS. At the University of East Anglia, 3 mi. west of town on Earlham Rd., this center was destroyed during the English Reformation and restored after WWII. Sir Sainsbury, Lord of the Supermarket, donated his superb collection of art, including works by Picasso, Bacon, and other modern artists, to the university in 1973. The award-winning building was designed by Sir Norman Foster. (Take any university-bound bus, such as #26, and ask for the Constable Terr. stop. ☎ 456 060. Open Tu-Su 11am-5pm. £2, concessions £1.)

🎵 🎐 ENTERTAINMENT AND FESTIVALS

Norwich offers a rich array of cultural activities, especially in summer. The TIC, as well as many cafes and B&Bs, has information on all things vaguely entertaining. Next to the Assembly House on Theatre St., the Art Deco **Theatre Royal** houses touring opera and ballet companies, as well as London-based theater troupes such as the Royal Shakespeare Company and Royal National Theatre. (☎ 630 000. Box office open M-Sa 9:30am-8pm, non-performance days until 6pm. £3-17, some concessions.) The home of the Norwich Players, **Maddermarket Theatre,** 1 St. John's Alley, stages high-quality amateur drama in an Elizabethan-style theater. Adhering to a bizarre tradition, all actors remain anonymous. (☎ 620 917. Box office open M-Sa 10am-9pm; non-performance days M-F 10am-5pm, Sa 10am-1pm. £7, concessions £5.) The **Norwich Arts Centre,** between Reeves Yard St. and Benedicts St., is the city's most versatile venue, hosting folk and world music, ballet, and comedy. (☎ 660 352. Box office open M-Sa 9am-10pm. £4-12, some concessions.) The **Norwich Puppet Theatre,** St. James, Whitefriars, comes in handy with shows for all ages. (☎ 629 921. Box office open M-F 9:30am-5pm, Sa 1hr. prior to show. Tickets £5-6, children £4.) Ask the TIC about free summer **Theatre in the Parks** (☎ 212 137).

The **Norfolk and Norwich Festival**—an extravaganza of theater, dance, music, and visual arts—explodes in mid-October. **Picture This,** in mid-June, offers two weeks of open artists' studios around the county. (Ask at the TIC or call ☎ 764 764 for info and tickets.) July welcomes the (mostly contemporary) **LEAP Dance Festival.** Norwich's outdoor parks also host a stream of other **festivals** and **folk fairs** in summer.

⚑ NIGHTLIFE

Many Norwichian pubs and clubs offer live music. On **Prince of Wales Rd.**, near the city center, five clubs within two blocks jockey for social position. **The Loft,** on Rose St., is a relaxed, gay-friendly club with live music downstairs and soul and funk wafting from the loft. (☎ 623 559. 18+, occasional 16+ nights. Open Th-F 10:30pm-2am, Sa 10pm-3am, Su 8:30pm-midnight.) **Manhattan Nightclub,** on Dove St., with its Sunday night "Exclusive Chilled-out Zone," is another hotspot. (☎ 629 060. 18+. Open F-Sa 9pm-4am, Su 9pm-2am.) The Riverside has several clubs and bars to choose from, notably, **Norwegian Blue,** with decor inspired by Norway's fjords and IKEA's minimalist style. A 30 ft. waterfall behind the bar splashes over troughs of their 27 different vodkas. (☎ 618 082. Open M-Sa noon-11pm, Su noon-10:30pm.) **Ikon,** on Tombland across from the Maid's Head Hotel, goes retro on Wednesday, party on Friday, and no-nonsense dance on Saturday. (☎ 621 541. 18+. Cover £1-4. Open W 10pm-2am, F-Sa 9:30pm-2am.) The **City Rail Link,** a service of First Eastern Counties (☎ (08456) 020 121), whisks tired partiers between the university and the train station, stopping close to most of the above venues (1-2 per hr.; all night Tu-Sa, last bus Su-M 2:30am; 80p-£1.50).

⚐ DAYTRIP FROM NORWICH

NORFOLK BROADS NATIONAL PARK

To reach the Broads, take a train from Norwich, Lowestoft, or Great Yarmouth to the smaller towns of Beccles, Cantley, Lingwood, Oulton Broad, Salhouse, or Wroxham. From Norwich, First Eastern Counties buses go to: Horning (#723 or 726, 45min., 4 per day, £3.20); Potter Heigham (#723-726, 1hr., 4 per day, return £3.30); Strumpshaw (#30-33, 30min., M-Sa 8 per day, return £2.20); Wroxham (#54, 40min., every 1-2hr., return £2.70); other Broads towns (#705, M-F 1 per day).

Though London and other southern towns have pirated away much of northern East Anglia's marine commerce, folk around here still seek out seafaring adventures. Birds and beasts flock to the **Norfolk Broads,** a soggy maze of navigable marshlands, where traffic in narrow waterways hidden by hedgerows conjures the surreal image of sailboats floating through fields. The landscape didn't occur naturally, but was formed in medieval times when peat was dug out to use for fuel. Over the centuries, water levels rose and the shallow lakes or "broads" were born. Exercise care when mucking about the Broads, designated an environmentally sensitive area and subject to continual abuse by humans.

Among the many **nature trails** that pass through the Broads, **Cockshoot Broad** lets you birdwatch, a circular walk around **Ranworth** points out the various flora, and **Upton Fen** is popular for its bugs. Hikers can challenge themselves with the 56 mi. long **Weaver's Way** between Cromer and Great Yarmouth. By collecting stamps along the trek, the hardy receive an exclusive woven patch upon completion. (Girl Scouts, eat your heart out.) The small village of **Strumpshaw** has a bird reserve popular among birdwatchers. (☎ (01603) 715 191. Open daily 9am-9pm or dusk. £3.25.)

Numerous companies offer **cruises** around the Broads. **Broads Tours** of Wroxham, on the right before the town bridge, runs river trips and rents dayboats. (☎ (01603) 782 207. Office open daily 9am-5:30pm. Tours July-Aug. 7 per day, Sept.-June 11:30am and 2pm; £5-6.80, children £3.70-5.40. Dayboat rentals £10-12 per hr.) **Southern River Steamers,** 65 Trafford Rd., cruises from Norwich to Surlingham

Broad, leaving from quays near the cathedral and train station. (☎(01603) 624 051. 30min.-3¼hr. excursions leave periodically May-Sept. 11am-5:30pm. £1.60-6.70, children 80p-£4.30.) Certain areas of the Broads are accessible only by car or bike; the pamphlet *Broads Bike Hire*, available at the Wroxham TIC, lists rental shops. The most convenient place to rent a cycle is **Camelot Craft** in Wroxham, though it's best to call ahead; follow Station Rd. to the river and take a left onto The Rhond. (☎(01603) 783 096. £5 per half-day, £8 per day. Open daily 9am-5pm.)

Wroxham, 10min. from Norwich by train, is the best base for information-gathering and preliminary exploration of some of the area's most pristine wetlands. To reach the **Wroxham and Hoveton Broads Information Centre** from the train station and bus stop, turn right on Station Rd. and walk about 90 yd. Knowledgeable Broads rangers answer questions and supply maps, guides, and contact information. Pick up free copies of *The Broadcaster*, which outlines local happenings; *The Broad Sheet*, for more recent Broads news; and *The Broad Miniguide*, which recommends sights and includes a map. The office also lists boat rental establishments and campsites throughout the area, and books guest houses and hotels around the park. (☎/fax (01603) 782 281. Open Easter-Oct. M-Sa 9am-1pm and 2-5pm.)

SUFFOLK AND ESSEX

BURY ST. EDMUNDS ☎01284

In AD 869, Viking invaders tied the Saxon monarch King Edmund to a tree, used him for target practice, and then beheaded him. Approximately 350 years later, 25 barons met in the Abbey of St. Edmund to sow the seeds of democracy, swearing to force King John to sign the *Magna Carta*. From these two defining moments in English history, Bury came to be known as "shrine of a king, cradle of the law," and is now a charmingly intimate town.

⬛ TRANSPORTATION. Bury makes a good daytrip from either Norwich or Cambridge, especially if you include a jaunt to Lavenham, Sudbury, Long Melford, or any of the other historic villages in Western Suffolk. **Trains** (☎(08457) 484 950) arrive from: **Cambridge** (45min., every 1-2hr., return £6.50); **Colchester** (1hr., every 1½hr., return £12.75); **Felixstowe** (1¼hr., 2 per hr., return £12); **London Liverpool St.** (2hr., every 1-2 hr., return £32.30). A **National Express bus** (☎(08705) 808 080) comes from **London** (2hr., 2 per day, £11). **R.W. Chenery** (☎(01379) 741 221) sends an express bus from **London Victoria** (1 per day, £14). **Cambus** (☎(01223) 423 554) X11 runs from Drummer St. in **Cambridge** (55min.; M-Sa every 1-2hr., Su every 4hr.; return £4.50). The area around Bury is explorable by **bike,** but rentals are difficult to come by. Try **Barton's Bicycles,** 5 Marrio's Walk, Stowmarket; call a few days in advance. (☎(01449) 677 195. £8 per day, £35 per week. Open M-Sa 9am-5:30pm.)

⬛⬛ ORIENTATION AND PRACTICAL INFORMATION. Laid out according to the original 12th-century plan, Bury's streets are easier to untangle than those of neighboring towns. The folks at the **tourist information centre,** 6 Angel Hill, will happily supply you with maps, accommodations lists, and copies of *What's On.* (☎764 667; fax 757 084. Open Easter-Oct. M-Sa 9:30am-5:30pm, Su 10am-3pm; Nov.-Easter M-F 10am-4pm, Sa 10am-1pm.) To reach the TIC from the train station, follow Northgate St. through the roundabout; turn right onto Mustow St. and walk up to Angel Hill. From the bus station, follow St. Andrew's St. to Brentgovel St., turn right at Lower Baxtel St. and then left onto Abbeygate St. The TIC runs 1½hr. **walking tours** of the city (June-Sept. Su-F 2:30pm; £2.50). Other services include: **banks,** such as **Lloyds,** 9 Buttermarket St. (☎ (0845) 072 333; open M-Tu and Th-F 9am-5pm, W 9:30am-5pm, Sa 9:30am-12:30pm); **Thomas Cook,** 43b Cornhill St. (☎ 351 000; open M-Th and Sa 9am-5:30pm, F 10am-5:30pm); and the **post office,** 17-18 Cornhill St. (☎ (08457) 223 344; open M-F 9am-5:30pm, Sa 9am-12:30pm). **Post Code:** IP33 1AA.

▐▞ ▐▌ ACCOMMODATIONS AND FOOD. The TIC books B&Bs in town or on nearby farms (£18-25). Sling that heavy pack over your shoulder with a smile: the charming home of **Mrs. Montanari ❸,** 6 Orchard St., is a mere 2min. from the bus station. Turn right out of the station, left past the library, and then left again onto St. John's St.; Orchard St. is the first right. (☎ 750 191. Singles £20; doubles £36.) **Mrs. Norton ❷,** 16 Cannon St., provides a warm welcome on a quiet, centrally located street. (☎ 761 776. Singles £18; twins £32.) For groceries, head down Cornhill St. from the post office to the **Iceland** supermarket. (☎ 750 570. Open M-W and Sa 8:30am-6pm, Th-F 8:30am-7pm.) Quiet Bury bustles on **market** days (W and Sa 9am-4pm). A crowd of locals leads the budget eater into **The Baker's Oven ❶,** 11 Abbeygate St., where you can munch on scrumptious toasties filled with tomatoes, ham, and eggs, and a side salad for under £3. (☎ 754 001. Open M-Sa 10:30am-5pm.) Pints go for £1.80 at the pint-sized **Nutshell ❶,** Abbeygate at the Traverse (☎ 764 867), Britain's smallest pub. The hostess speaks with reverence about her entry in the pages of the *Guinness Book of World Records,* earned when the 15-by-17 ft. pub speezed 102 people and one dog between its tiny walls.

◙ SIGHTS. A few hours of whimsical wandering reveal Bury's prized charms. Along Crown St., across from the TIC on the soggy banks of the River Lark, lie the beautiful and extensive ruins of the 11th-century **▨Abbey of St. Edmund,** where the 25 *Magna Carta* barons met in 1214 to discuss their letter to the king, and now home to cadres of foraging ducks. The weathered, massive pillars look like stone refugees from Easter Island; the formal gardens next to the remains are at their fragrant best in late June. Be sure to see the aviary and the Olde English Rose Garden of Frances Hodgson Burnett's dreams. (Ruins and garden open until sunset. Free.) At the TIC, pick up an audio tour of the ruins to hear a 12th-century monk named Jocelin tell executioners' stories with slightly too much glee. (45min. tour £1.50, concessions £1.)

Next door, the interior of the delightful 16th-century **St. Edmundsbury Cathedral** is bathed in magnificent color; look heavenward and admire the wooden ceiling designed in East Anglian style, as well as the shields of the *Magna Carta* barons, which hang above the High Altar. The cherub overhanging the entrance, allegedly pilfered years before, was "rediscovered" by a Bury businessman in a Belgian antique shop. (☎ 754 933. Open June-Aug. daily 8:30am-8pm; Sept.-May 8:30am-6pm. Evensong W-Sa 5:30pm, Su 3:30pm. Suggested donation £2.)

The **Manor House Museum** borders the abbey gardens to the south. This elegant Georgian house, a must-see if you're cuckoo for clocks, contains dozens of synchronized timepieces. Clotheshorses will enjoy the impressive costume collection. (☎ 757 076. Open W-Su 11am-4pm. £2.50, concessions £1.50.) The **Moyses' Hall Museum,** Corn Hill in the marketplace, is hopelessly devoted to its collection of macabre flotsam, including a mummified cat and a violin made of a horse's skull. Superstitious highlights include artifacts from the 1828 murder of local Maria Marten, including a book covered with the murderer's skin. (☎ 757 488. Open M-F 10:30am-4:30pm, Sa-Su 11am-4pm. £2, concessions £1.50, families £6, free after 4pm.) Bury is eminently visitable in mid-May, when the annual three-week **festival** brings music, street entertainment, and fireworks.

▓ DAYTRIPS FROM BURY ST. EDMUNDS

ICKWORTH HOUSE. Three miles southwest of Bury in the village of Horringer, the capacious home of the Marquis of Bristol is a Neoclassical oddity. Dominated by a 106 ft. rotunda, the opulent state rooms are filled with 18th-century French furniture and more portraits than you could possibly absorb, including some by Titian, Velasquez, and Gainsborough. The classical Italian garden is splendid, and the manor's sheep quite cordial. (*First Eastern Counties buses (#141-144, M-Sa 9 per day, return £3.10) leave Bury's St. Andrew's Station. ☎(01284) 735 270. House open late Mar. to Oct. Tu-W, F-Su, and bank holidays 1-5pm. Gardens open daily 10am-5pm. Park open daily 7am-7pm. £5.70, children £2.50. Gardens and park only £2.50/80p.*)

MELFORD. Turrets and moats await those who visit **Long Melford,** a mile-long Suffolk village graced by two Tudor mansions. **Melford Hall,** the more impressive of the two, has retained much of its original Elizabethan exterior and panelled banquet hall. Peek at the Victorian bedrooms before exploring the well-manicured lawns and colorful gardens. (*☎(01787) 880 286. Open May-Sept. W-Th and Sa-Su 2-5:30pm; Apr. and Oct. Sa-Su 2-5:30pm. £4.40.*) More amusing than stately, **Kentwell Hall** is filled with authentically costumed guides; visitors too are sometimes asked to come in Tudor costume. (*☎(01787) 310 207. Open July-Aug. daily noon-5pm; Mar.-May and Sept.-Oct. Su noon-5pm. £5.50, seniors £4.70, students £3.40.*) While in the area, stop by the **Long Melford Church,** between the two mansions, erected in 1484 with funding from affluent wool merchants. (*Long Melford is accessible from Bury by H.C. Chambers bus #753; catch it near the train station.*)

HARWICH AND FELIXSTOWE

Continent-bound travelers head south to **Harwich** (HAR-idge), a ferry depot for trips to Holland, Germany, and Scandinavia, and to **Felixstowe,** where boats sail to Belgium (see **By Ferry,** p. 28). Both are easily accessible by train and bus. Call the Harwich **tourist information centre,** Iconfield Park, Parkeston, for details about ferries. (*☎(01255) 506 139. Open Apr.-Sept. daily 9am-7pm; Oct.-Mar. M-Sa 9am-4pm.*) The Felixstowe **TIC** is on the seafront. (*☎(01394) 276 770. Open M-F 9am-5:30pm, Sa-Su 9:30am-5:30pm.*)

COLCHESTER ☎01206

England's oldest recorded town, Colchester (pop. 89,000) has been so thoroughly beaten on so many occasions it's a wonder everyone hasn't packed up and left. The people of the Trinovantes tribe, the town's first inhabitants, were conquered by the Romans, who were slaughtered by the Iceni (led by ▓**Queen Boudicca**), who were pillaged by the Saxons, who were finally flogged by the Normans. Now dominated by a pedestrian-only shopping center, Colchester's historical sites pale somewhat in comparison to those of other towns. Nonetheless, this oldest of settlements entices with England's largest castle keep and musketball-ridden pubs.

▓▓ TRANSPORTATION AND PRACTICAL INFORMATION. Colchester is best visited as a daytrip from London or nearby East Anglian towns. **Trains** (☎(08457) 484 950) pull into **North Station** from **Cambridge** (2hr., 2 per hr., £29) and **London Liverpool St.** (45min., every 30min., £25). North Station lies a good 2 mi. from town (as opposed to Town Station, which nabs local trains); buses frequently make the uphill trip (#1 is a good choice, 80p). **Buses** from **Cambridge** (2hr., 1 per day, £8) and **London** (2¼hr., 3 per day, £8.25) trundle into the **Bus Authority,** Queen St. (☎282 645), around the corner from the TIC. Said **tourist information centre,** 1 Queen St.,

across from the castle, books rooms two days in advance for a 10% deposit and leads 2hr. city **tours**. (June-Sept. 11am. $2.50, concessions $2, children $1.25.) Pick up a free map and copies of local magazines *The Sticks* and *The Grapevine*, which list music in pubs. (☎282 920. Open Easter-Nov. M-Tu and Th-Sa 9:30am-6pm, W 10am-6pm, Su 10am-5pm; Dec.-Easter M-Sa 10am-5pm.) Other services include: **banks** on High St.; the **police,** 10 Southway (☎762 212); **Internet access** at **Compuccino,** 17 Priory Walk, three blocks south of the TIC (☎519 090; $2 per hr.); and the **post office,** 68-70 North Hill (☎(08457) 223 344). **Post Code:** CO1 1AA.

ⓇⒸ ACCOMMODATIONS AND FOOD. Since the YHA hostel packed up and left town many moons ago, Colchester has had no substitute for the penny-pinching traveler. The cheapest place to stay is in one of the large and spotless rooms at the **Scheregate Hotel ❸**, 36 Osborne St. (☎573 034. Breakfast included. Singles $20-35; twins and doubles $35-45.) The **Sainsbury's** is on Priory Walk, off Queen St. (Open M-Sa 8am-6:30pm.) Surprisingly elegant, **The Thai Dragon ❷**, 35 East Hill, has a full lunch for only $5.50. Dinner is pricier ($4-8), but the traditional dishes are quite tasty. (☎863 414. Open M-Sa noon-2:30pm and 6-11pm, Su noon-2:30pm and 6-10:30pm.) **Jackpots ❶**, along Red Lion Walk off High St., satisfies with jacket potatoes ($3-5.50) and a $4 "classic dish" of lasagna, vegetarian chilli, or "macaroni cheese" with a side potato. (☎549 990. Open M-Sa 8am-5pm.)

◗ SIGHTS. A Norman fortress built by William the Conqueror upon the ruins of a Roman temple, **Colchester Castle** now houses the dynamic (and morbid) **▨Castle Museum,** where interactive displays help you see, touch, and hear history. Act out a short scene behind Roman theater masks, try on battle gear, and experience a chilling witch confession in the dungeon. A tour takes you to the depths of the Roman foundations and the heights of the Norman towers. (☎282 939. Castle open M-Sa 10am-5pm; Mar.-Nov. also Su 11am-5pm. Last admission 4:30pm. 5 tours per day $1.20, children 60p. Castle $3.90, concessions $2.60, families $10.50.)

The castle is flanked by two lesser museums. In a 1718 Georgian townhouse, the freshly renovated **Hollytrees Museum** displays a cache of 18th-century knick-knacks from toys and games to musical instruments and scientific equipment, as well as (somewhat) more modern amusements in the nostalgic "1950s living room." (☎282 939. Open M-Sa 10am-5pm, Su 11am-5pm. Free.) Marveling at the fine collection of 18th-century grandfather clocks in **Tymperleys Clock Museum,** off Trinity St., is a decent way to pass the time. Tick. That is, unless constant ticking drives you mad. Tock. (Open M-Sa 10am-5pm, Su 11am-5pm. Free. Tick.)

EAST ANGLIA

NORTHWEST ENGLAND

The decline of heavy industry affected Northwest England as it did the rest of urban Britain, but this region has embraced post-industrial hipness with a fresh, funky youth culture. Our story begins in the 19th century, when coal clouds and satanic mills revolutionized quiet village life; prosperity followed where smokestacks led, making the cities of the northwest the world's wool and linen workshops. The last few decades have been difficult, but the cities have met challenges with gritty determination and reenergizing spunk. Today their innovative music and arts scene are world famous: Liverpool and Manchester alone produced four of *Q* magazine's ten biggest rock stars of the century. Add a large student population and through-the-roof nightlife, and you'll begin to understand the reinvigorated northwest. If you need a break from the frenetic urbanity, find respite in the Peak District to the east and Cumbria to the north, where the Lake District promises the stunning crags and waters that send poets into pensive meditation.

HIGHLIGHTS OF NORTHWEST ENGLAND

LIVERPOOL Don't miss Liverpool, Beatles fans: virtually every pub, restaurant, and corner claims some connection to the Fab Four (p. 357).

MANCHESTER Revel in the wealth of Manchester nightlife, where trendy cafe-bars morph into late-night venues for dancing and drinking (p. 370).

PEAK DISTRICT AND LAKE DISTRICT Roam the hills, groughs, and moors of urban England's backyard (p. 374), then explore the dramatic mountains and sparkling lakes that inspired Wordsworth, Coleridge, and Romantics everywhere (p. 382).

NORTHWEST CITIES

CHESTER ☎01244

With fashionable chain stores behind mock-medieval facades, tour guides in Roman armor, a town crier in full uniform, and a Barclays bank in a wing of the cathedral, Chester resembles an American theme-park pastiche of Ye Olde English Towne. Built by Romans, the city was later a base for Plantagenet campaigns against the Welsh—old town law states that Welshmen wandering the streets after 9pm can be beheaded—and developed trading connections throughout continental Europe. Silt blocked the River Dee in the 17th century, and Chester, crowded but lovely, commercial but lively, was left to turn its archaism into a selling point.

▐ TRANSPORTATION

Chester serves as a rail gateway to Wales via the North Wales line. The train and bus stations both lie 15min. to the north, outside the city walls.

Trains: City Rd. Office open M-Sa 5:30am-12:30am, Su 8am-midnight. Trains (☎(08457) 484 950) from: **Birmingham** (1¾hr., 1-2 per hr., £10.90); **Holyhead**

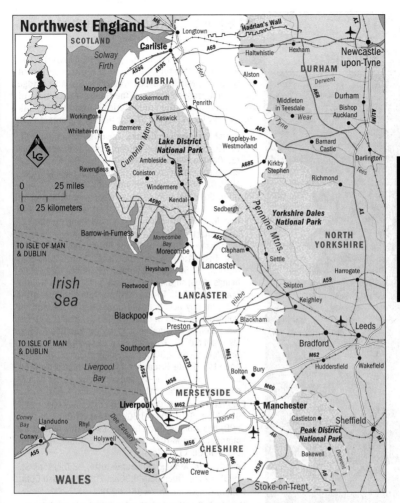

Northwest England

SCOTLAND

NORTHWEST ENGLAND

(1½hr.; M-F every hr., Sa-Su 9 per day; £17); **London Euston** (2½hr., 1-2 per hr., £50); **Manchester Piccadilly** (1hr., 1-2 per hr., £8.90). Frequent **Merseyrail** service makes Chester an easy daytrip from **Liverpool** (1½hr., 1-2 per hr., £3.60).

Buses: Delamere St. (☎381 515), north of the city wall off Northgate St. Office open M-Sa 8:30am-5pm. **National Express** (☎(08705) 808 080) from: **Birmingham** (2hr., 5 per day); **Blackpool** (3½hr., 3-4 per day); **London** (5½hr., 5-6 per day, £16.50); **Manchester** (1¼hr., 3 per day). **Huxley Coaches** (☎(01948) 770 661) bus C56 to Foregate St. from **Wrexham** (M-Sa).

Public Transportation: Call ☎602 666 for local bus info (daily 8am-8pm). Routes are detailed in 12 *Bus Times* booklets, available free at the TIC. The **Chester women's safe transport service** (☎310 585) operates a women-only bus M-Sa 6:30pm-midnight.

Taxis: Radio Taxis (☎372 372).

THE BIG SPLURGE

THE CHESTER GROSVENOR

The biggest splurge of them all, the Chester Grosvenor is the stuff weary wayfarers' dreams are made of. Dapper doormen, a cozy drawing room, a sumptuous mahogany library (complete with grand piano and snack and drink service), and suites named after their royal occupants create an inimitable old-school English ambience.

Gourmets and gourmands alike can sip sherry to the sounds of weekend live music at **La Brasserie** cafe. Established residents, as well as nonguests looking for a smaller splurge, can dress for dinner at **The Arkle** restaurant, named for a famous racehorse. The over-the-top menu caters to those Francophiles who know what "vichyssoise" and "mousseline" are, though diners of all vintages will appreciate the distinctly rich atmosphere. (£32-75 per person, depending on your culinary fetish.)

The charms of this centrally-located Victorian hotel don't end there. Eighty-five individually decorated rooms ooze amenities—refrigerators, trouser presses, and fine toiletries among them—and suites boast their own private menus. Work it off at the on-site sauna and gym, or take advantage of complimentary membership at (and taxi service to) a nearby country club.

If you have to ask, you can't afford it. But luxury lovers with deep pockets and heiresses accustomed to royal treatment will be duly dazzled by the five-star splendor. (Eastgate St. ☎ 324 024; fax 313 246; www.chestergrosvenor.co.uk. From £400 per night.)

ORIENTATION & PRACTICAL INFORMATION

Chester's center is bounded by a **city wall** breached by seven gates. **Chester Cross** is at the intersection of **Eastgate St., Northgate St., Watergate St.,** and **Bridge St.,** which crosses the Dee. **The Groves** hugs a mile of riverbank. From the train station, take the Citylink bus (every 6min., free with rail ticket) to **Foregate St.**

Tourist Information Centre: Town Hall, Northgate St. (☎402 111; www.chestertourism.com). **Chester Visitor Centre,** Vicar's Ln. (☎402 111; fax 403 188), opposite the Roman amphitheater. Both open May-Oct. M-Sa 9am-5pm, Su 10am-4pm; Nov.-Apr. M-Sa 10am-5pm, Su 10am-4pm. Both book accommodations for £3 and sell city maps for £1. Pick up What's On in Chester (free) for information on upcoming events.

Tours: Chester has more tours than Roman columns. A legionnaire in full armor leads the **Roman Tour** (June-Aug. Th-Sa 1:45pm from the Visitor Centre, 2pm from the TIC; £2.50, concessions £2, families £7), while beings ghoulish and ghastly lurk on the **Ghost Hunter Trail** (June-Oct. Th-Sa 7:30pm from the TIC; after 5:30pm, buy tickets at the Coach and Horse pub on Northgate St.; £3.50, concessions £3, families £9). For a run-down of Chester's history, try the **Pastfinder Tour,** also from the TIC. (May-Oct. daily 10:45am and 2:30pm; Nov.-Apr. Sa-Su 2:30pm. £3, concessions £2.50.) The open-top **Guide Friday** (☎347 457) buses do their usual schtick with hop-on/hop-off service. (4 per hr. £7, concessions £5.50, children £2.50, families £16.50.)

Financial Services: Barclays, 35 Eastgate St. Open M-F 9am-5pm, Sa 9:30am-3:30pm. **Thomas Cook** (☎593 500) has 2 branches on Bridge St., 1 with a **bureau de change.** Open M-Tu and Th-Sa 9am-5:30pm, W 10am-5:30pm, Su 11am-4pm.

Launderette: Monogram Launderette, 93 Dicksons St. (☎380 216). Open daily 8:30am-7pm, last wash 6pm.

Police: Grosvenor Rd. (☎350 222).

Hospital: Countess of Chester (West Chester) Hospital, Liverpool Rd. (☎365 000). Take bus #40A from the station or #3 from the Bus Exchange.

Internet Access: Library, Northgate St., beside the Town Hall (☎312 935). First hr. free, £1 per hr. after. Open M and Th 9:30am-7pm, Tu-W and F 9:30am-5pm, Sa 9:30am-1pm. **i-station,** Rufus Ct. (☎401 680). £2 per 30min., rates vary. Open 8am-10pm.

Post Office: 2 St. John St. (☎348 315), off Foregate St. **Bureau de change** and photo booth. Open M-Sa 9am-5:30pm. **Branch,** 122 Northgate St. (☎326 754). Open M-F 9am-5:30pm, Sa 9am-12:30pm. **Post Code:** CH1 1AA.

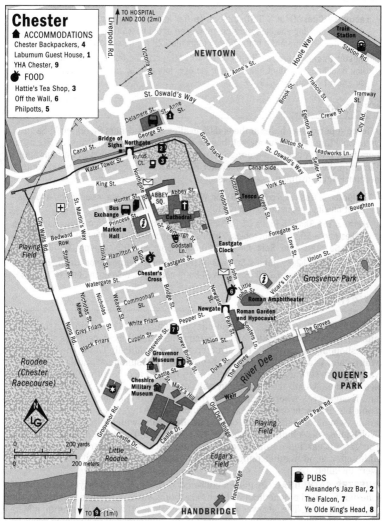

Chester

🏠 ACCOMMODATIONS
Chester Backpackers, 4
Laburnum Guest House, 1
YHA Chester, 9

🍴 FOOD
Hattie's Tea Shop, 3
Off the Wall, 6
Philpotts, 5

TO HOSPITAL AND ZOO (2mi)

NEWTOWN

Train Station

St. Anne's St.

St. Oswald's Way

Liverpool Rd.

Victoria Rd.

Delamere St.

St. Anne St.

George St.

Canal St.

Bridge of Sighs

Northgate

Rufus Ct.

Water Tower St.

King St.

Hunter St.

Bus Exchange

Princess St.

Market Hall

Bedward Row

St. Martin's Way

Stanley St.

Nicholas St. Mews

Nicholas St.

Grey Friars

Black Friars

Nuns Rd.

City Walls Rd.

Playing Field

Roodee (Chester Racecourse)

Little Roodee

Castle Dr.

Grosvenor Rd.

Castle Dr.

Bridge St.

Trinity St.

Hamilton Pl.

Weaver St.

White Friars

Cuppin St.

Grosvenor St.

Lower Bridge St.

Grosvenor Museum

Cheshire Military Museum

St. Mary's Hill

Watergate St.

Commonhall St.

Chester's Cross

Godstall Ln.

Eastgate St.

ABBEY SQ.

Abbey St.

Cathedral

St. Werburgh St.

Gorse Stacks

Milton St.

St. Oswald's Way

Canal Side

York St.

Victoria Pl.

Frodsham St.

Queen St.

Tesco

Eastgate Clock

Foregate St.

St. John

Newgate St.

Little St. John St.

Vicar's Ln.

Grosvenor Park

Roman Amphitheater

Newgate

Roman Garden and Hypocaust

Pepper St.

Park St.

Albion St.

Souter's Ln.

Duke St.

The Groves

The Groves

River Dee

QUEEN'S PARK

Queen's Park Rd.

Weir

Playing Field

Old Dee Bridge

Edgar's Field

Handbridge

HANDBRIDGE

TO 9 (1mi)

Hoole Way

Station Rd.

Brook St.

Francis St.

Egerton St.

Crewe St.

Tramway St.

City Rd.

Leadworks Ln.

Seller St.

Boughton

Union St.

Love St.

N

PUBS
Alexander's Jazz Bar, 2
The Falcon, 7
Ye Olde King's Head, 8

🏠 ACCOMMODATIONS

B&Bs (from £20) are concentrated on **Hoole Rd.**, a 5min. walk from the train station (turn right from the exit, climb the steps to Hoole Rd., and turn right over the train tracks), and **Brook St.** (right from the train station exit, then the first left). Bus #53 (6 per hr.) runs to the area from the city center.

YHA Chester, 40 Hough Green (☎ 680 056), 1½ mi. from the city center. Cross the river on Grosvenor Rd. and turn right at the roundabout (40min.); buses #7 and 16 come from the Bus Exchange, #4 from the train station. Renovated Victorian with laundry and Internet access. Breakfast included. Reception 7am-10:30pm. Open mid-Jan. to mid-Dec. Dorms £15, under 18 £12. Twins and family rooms available. ❷

Laburnum Guest House, 2 St. Anne St. (☎/fax 380 313), across from the bus station. 4 large, sparkling ensuite rooms comprise one of the best values in the kingdom. Only a minute's walk from the north gate. A fantastic £22 per person. ❸

Chester Backpackers, 67 Boughton (☎400 185). 10min. from the train station. Feels like a laid-back student flat. Luggage storage, lounge, and no curfew. Dorms £12.50; singles £17; doubles £29. ❷

◢ FOOD

A **Tesco** supermarket hides at the end of an alley off Frodsham St. (Open M-Sa 7am-9pm, Su 11am-5pm.) The **market,** beside the Bus Exchange on Princess St., numbers fruit and vegetables among its bargains. (☎402 340. Open M-Sa 8am-5pm.) Picnic in the shade of lovely **Grosvenor Park**—its sloping, flowered acres contain neither Roman artifacts nor tourists.

Philpotts, 2 Goss St. (☎345 123), off Watergate St. Stuffs tuna, sweet corn, and Somerset brie into baguettes (£1.60-2.30). Open M-Sa 8am-2:30pm. ❶

Hattie's Tea Shop, 5 Rufus Ct. (☎345 173), off Northgate St. Scrumptious homemade cakes and a £5.25 "giant topless" ham salad sandwich. Open July-Aug. M-Sa 9:30am-5pm, Su 11am-4pm; Sept.-June M-Sa 9:30am-5pm, Su 10:30am-4pm. ❷

Off the Wall, 12 St. John's St. (☎348 964). Typical pub exterior. Crispy barbecue chicken with cheese £3.75. Food served Su-Th noon-4pm, F-Sa noon-5pm. ❶

◉ SIGHTS

ARCHITECTURE. Chester's faux-medieval architecture is its main attraction, although the wannabe Tudor buildings fail to hide that the city center is a vast outdoor shopping mall. While a few structures are authentically Tudor, the black-and-white paint is a strictly Victorian phenomenon. On summer Saturdays a bizarre variety of street musicians, from cowpoke trios to accordion-wielding matrons, sets up shop. Climb the famous **city walls** or the **rows** of Bridge St., Watergate St., and Eastgate St., where walkways provide access to another tier of storefronts. Some historians theorize that Edward I imported the tiered design from Constantinople, which he visited while crusading. **Northgate,** which offers a fine view of Welsh hills, was rebuilt in 1808 to house the city's jail. The **Bridge of Sighs** is outside the gate; it carried doomed convicts from jail to chapel for their last mass, although a good number jumped into the canal and swam for it before railings were installed.

CHESTER CATHEDRAL. In 1092, a guilt-ridden Hugh Lupus, newly named Earl of Chester, founded a Benedictine abbey here, hoping that the monks would pray for his naughty soul. The site was that of a church dedicated to St. Werburgh, a Mercian princess who passed up royal comfort for a nunnery and resurrected geese as a hobby. Intersecting stone arches—"The Crown of Stone"—support the tower, and stained-glass windows blaze throughout. The quire showcases 14th-century woodwork and an enormous pipe organ. Find peace in the cloister, a monastic courtyard with a lovely fountain. *(Off Northgate St. ☎324 756. Free guided tours May-Oct. daily. Open 8am-6pm. Suggested donation £3.)*

ROMAN SIGHTS. The Romans had conquered most of Britannia by AD 43, and Deva (modern-day Chester) was a strategic outpost of considerable importance; at the **Grosvenor Museum,** watch the animated video to see how the Romans lived. *(27 Grosvenor St. ☎402 008. Open M-Sa 10:30am-5pm, Su 2-5pm. Free.)* At the edge of Grosvenor Park, just outside the city wall, lie the scant remains of the largest **Roman amphitheater** in Britain. Lions were specially shipped up for the bloody gladiatorial bouts. *(Always open. Free.)* Next door, the **Roman Garden and Hypocaust** offers a great picnic space on shaded grass lined with stunted Roman columns.

OTHER SIGHTS. Chester Zoo, one of Europe's largest, features frolicking baby elephants, saucy-faced camels, and human-sized prairie dog tunnels. Avoid the weekend crowd or you'll spend the whole day pram-dodging. *(Take Crosville bus #8 or 8X from the Bus Exchange (return £2). ☎ 380 280. Open high season 10am-7pm, last entry 5pm; off season until 5:30pm, last entry 3:30pm. £10.50, concessions £8.50, families £36.50.)*

🎵 🎶 NIGHTLIFE AND ENTERTAINMENT

Chester's nightlife is all **pubs,** all the time—just ask the desperate teenagers roaming the streets in search of clubbing spots. Many of the city's 30-odd pubs parrot Olde English decor, and almost all are open Monday through Saturday from noon to 11pm and Sunday from noon to 10:30pm. Watering holes group on **Lower Bridge St.** and **Watergate St.** Jazz and blues waft into the night on cool breezes from **Alexander's Jazz Bar,** Rufus Court, off Northgate St., on summer Thursdays and some other evenings. Chortles and guffaws follow on Saturday, comedy night. (☎ 340 005. Cover £5-6. Open M-Th 11am-midnight, F-Sa 11am-12:30am, Su 11am-10:30pm.) Traditionalists head to **Ye Olde King's Head,** 48-50 Lower Bridge St. (☎ 324 855), where an assortment of steins hangs from the beams of a restored 17th-century house. For a cheap pint, try upstairs at **The Falcon,** 6 Lower Bridge St., where the black-and-white timbers tilt a little too precariously. (☎ 342 060. Meals £4-5.)

On sporadic spring and summer weekends, England's oldest **horse races** are held on the **Roodee,** former site of medieval "football." Team sizes were unlimited and players brought props (swords and maces) to enhance their athletic prowess. When such fun was banned, men began trying to push each other off galloping racehorses. But we digress. Lodgings fill quickly on race weekends; contact the TIC for schedules and booking. (☎ 304 600. Entrance from £4.) At the end of June and beginning of July, a river carnival and raft race herald the **Sports Festival** (☎ 348 365). The **Chester Summer Music Festival** draws classical musicians to the cathedral in late July. (Box office ☎ 320 700. Ticket prices vary.) Check the TIC's free monthly *What's On in Chester* for other events.

LIVERPOOL ☎ 0151

Mad, mad, mighty Liverpool. Behind its beat loom memories of dark trades, big bombs, and hard knocks, but a brazen and brilliant feeling courses through its clubs and cathedrals, wrecks, ruins, and redevelopment. Free museums, a raucous nightlife, and restaurants on every block make Liverpool a great destination. Scousers—as Liverpudlians are colloquially known—are usually happy to introduce you to their dialect and humor, and to discuss the relative merits of Liverpool's two football teams. Oh, yeah—and some fuss is made over the Beatles.

🎫 TICKET TO RIDE

Trains: Lime St. Station. Ticket office open M-Sa 5:15am-12:30am, Su 7:15am-12:30pm. Trains (☎ (08457) 484 950) from: **Birmingham** (1¾hr.; M-F 5 per day, Sa 2 per day, Su 3 per day; £18.50); **Chester** (45min., 2 per hr., £3.20); **London Euston** (3hr.; M-Sa every hr., Su 10 per day; £48.40); **Manchester Piccadilly** (1hr., 2-3 per hr., £7.40). The smaller **Moorfields, James St.,** and **Central** stations serve mainly as transfer points to local **Merseyrail** trains (including service to Chester).

Buses: Norton St. Station receives **National Express** (☎ (08705) 808 080) from: **Birmingham** (2½hr., 5 per day); **London** (4½hr., 5 per day, £16.50); **Manchester** (1hr., 1-2 per hr.). Other buses stop at **Queen Sq.** and **Paradise St.** stations. If you don't

THE HIDDEN DEAL

PENNY (PINCHING) LANE: COUNTRY KITCHEN

As budget globetrotters know, certain things in life are of great and enduring beauty. Things like transcendental artwork and perfect celestial spheres. Things like dirt cheap food after a long day of hefting your backpack through a budget-busting town.

Country Kitchen, Drury Ln., may be the answer to said globetrotter's prayers. Wedged in on a bitsy little side street, it's hidden from the tourist trails. But locals know where to find the restaurant that puts Picassos and planets to shame, dishing out cheap eats like nobody's business. In this clean little shop, toasties, salads, and pasta cost a mere £1. Even gentler on the wallet: soup is just 75p, tea cakes are only 40p, and coleslaw will only leave you 20p lighter.

Service is speedy and efficient—it'd have to be to handle the crowds of hungry Liverpudlians that throng this tiny shop for their daily fix of inexpensive edibles. (☎236 0509. Open daily 7:30am-3:30pm.)

mind traveling at off-peak hours, the 1-day **Mersey Saveaway** can you save a chunk of change (£1.80, children £1.20).

Ferries: Liverpool Sea Terminal, Pier Head, north of Albert Dock. Open daily 9am-5pm. The **Isle of Man Steam Packet Company** (☎(08705) 523 523) runs ferries from Princess Dock to the **Isle of Man** and **Dublin** (see p. 396).

Local Transportation: Private buses blanket the city and the Merseyside area. Consult the transport mavens at **Mersey Travel** (☎236 7676) in the TIC. Open M and W-Sa 9am-5:30pm, Tu 10am-5:30pm, Su 10:30am-4:30pm.

Taxis: Scouser taxis are cheap, efficient, and amiable. Try **Mersey Cabs** (☎207 2222).

✈ ▮ HELP!

Liverpool's central district is surprisingly pedestrian-friendly. There are two clusters of museums: on **William Brown St.,** near Lime St. Station, and at **Albert Dock,** on the river. These flank the central shopping district, whose central axis comprises **Bold St., Church St.,** and **Lord St.**

Tourist Information Centre: Queen Square Centre (☎(0906) 680 6886; fax 707 0986; www.visitliverpool.com), in Queen Sq. Sells the handy *Visitor Guide to Liverpool and Merseyside* (£1). Books beds for a 10% deposit. Open M and W-Sa 9am-5:30pm, Tu 10am-5:30pm, Su 10:30am-4:30pm. **Branch: Atlantic Dock Centre,** Atlantic Pavilion, Albert Dock (☎(0906) 680 6886). Open daily 10am-5:30pm.

Tours: Expert guide **Phil Hughes** (☎228 4565, mobile (07961) 511 223) runs personalized Beatles tours for the lucky 8 who fit in his van. The same lucky 8 get half-price Beatles Story tickets. (3-4hr.; 1-2 per day; £11, private tours £65.) The yellow-and-blue **Magical Mystery Tour** (☎709 3285) bus takes 40 fans to Fab Four sights, leaving the Queens Sq. TIC and picking up outside Beatles Story 15min. later. (2hr.; mid-July to Aug. 2 per day, Sept. to mid-July 1 per day; £11.) For those interested in non-Beatles sights (if such people exist), **Liverpool Duck Tours** (☎708 7799) waddles 'round the city center in amphibious WWI-era vehicles. (Mid-Feb. to Oct. 8 per day, Nov.-Dec. call for details; £10, concessions £8, children £7, families £27.) Numerous other **bus tours** (from £5) and **walking tours** (£4, concessions £3) run in summer; ask the TIC.

Financial Services: American Express, 54 Lord St. (☎702 4505), has a **bureau de change.** Open M and W-F 9am-5:30pm, Tu 9:30am-5:30pm, Sa 9:30am-5pm.

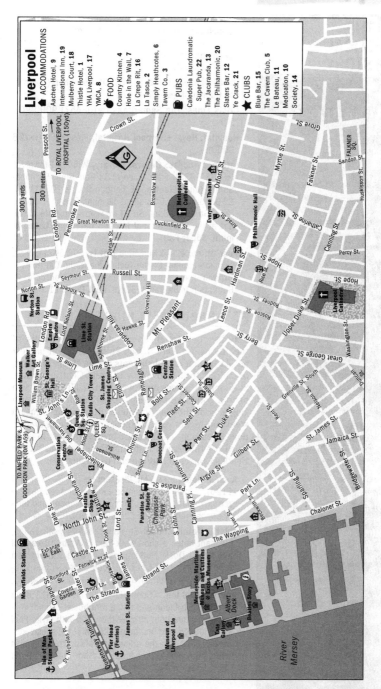

Liverpool

ACCOMMODATIONS
Aachen Hotel, 9
International Inn, 19
Mulberry Court, 18
Thistle Hotel, 1
YHA Liverpool, 17
YMCA, 8

FOOD
Country Kitchen, 4
Hole in the Wall, 7
La Crepe Rit, 16
La Tasca, 2
Simply Heathcotes, 6
Tavern Co., 3

PUBS
Caledonia Laundromatic
Super Pub, 22
The Jacaranda, 13
The Philharmonic, 20
Slaters Bar, 12
Ye Crack, 21

CLUBS
Blue Bar, 15
The Cavern Club, 5
Le Bateau, 11
Medication, 10
Society, 14

THE LOCAL STORY

MEET THE BEATLES

In the summer of 2002, Let's Go interviewed Allan Williams, owner of The Jacaranda Coffee Bar in Liverpool and first manager of the world's favorite mopheads. Williams regaled us with tales of a simpler time... When the Beatles were coffee shop bums, skipping lectures to hang out at The Jac, eating their beloved "bacon-butty" sandwiches and listening to the music they would come to dominate... When Pete Best kept the beat (not that Ringo interloper) and the group had to be smuggled into Hamburg as "students" (and then deported when a 17-year-old George Harrison was busted for hanging out at 18+ clubs). Here are just a few of his memories.

LG: So tell me how you first met the Beatles.

AW: My wife and I had a coffee bar club... and because I was a rock 'n' roll promoter, all the groups used to come to my place, mainly because I let them rehearse for free in the basement... I only knew [the Beatles] as coffee bar layabouts—they were always bumming free coffee off of *anybody*... I had complaints about the obscene graffiti that the girls were writing about the groups, and here these lads were from the art school and they could paint. I said, "Will you decorate the ladies' toilets for me?" And the way they decorated them, I'd have preferred the graffiti, to be honest with you. They were just *throwing* paint on them as if they were Picassos.

Launderette: There are no launderettes downtown, though the **YHA**, next to Albert Dock, often allows non-residents to use its facilities. Alternatively, head to the **Caledonia Laundromatic Super Pub** and do your wash in style (see **Come Together,** below).

Police: Canning Pl. (☎709 6010). **Cop Shop** (outpost) on Church St. (☎777 4147).

Crisis Lines: The Samaritans (☎(08457) 909 090). 24hr.

Hospital: Royal Liverpool Hospital, Prescot St. (☎706 2000).

Internet Access: Central Library, William Brown St. (☎233 5835). Free. Open M-Sa 9am-5pm, Su noon-5pm. **Planet Electra,** 36 London Rd. (☎708 0303). £2 per 30min.; 50p student discount. Open M-F 10am-8pm, Sa 10am-6pm, Su 11am-6pm. Also **Café Latténet** at the **International Inn** and **Caledonia Laundromatic Super Pub.**

Post Office: 42-44 Houghton Way (☎709 6971), in St. John's Shopping Centre (below the Radio City Tower). **Branch** in the splendid Lyceum building on Bold St. Both open M-Sa 9am-5:30pm. **Post Code:** L1 1AA.

A HARD DAY'S NIGHT

Your best bets for cheap accommodations lie east of the city center. **Lord Nelson St.** is lined with modest hotels; similar establishments are on **Mount Pleasant,** one block from Brownlow Hill and Central Station. Stay only at places approved by the TIC, and if you need a good night's sleep, consider springing for a single. Some hostels host herds of clubbing teens on weekend nights—shrill Agents of Slink and men in dogged pursuit. Demand for beds is highest in early April for the Grand National Race and during the Beatles Convention at the end of August.

Aachen Hotel, 89-91 Mt. Pleasant (☎709 3477 or 709 1126). Winner of numerous awards, and it's easy to see why. Clean rooms, chatty bar, pool room, and family atmosphere. Singles £28-38; twins £46-54. ❸

Thistle Hotel, Chapel St. (☎227 4444). Mid-range, pleasant hotel, a short walk from downtown Liverpool and Albert Dock. Nothing crazy or different, but in a town like this, that can be a good thing. Singles £50-100. Call ahead to ask about special rates. ❹

International Inn, 4 South Hunter St. (☎709 8135), off Hardman St. Clean *and* fun, a rare hostel combo. Welcomes visitors from all over the world with style. Pool table, lounge, and enormous kitchen at the guests' disposal, as well as the adjoining **Café Latténet,** which offers "hot coffee, hot food, and hot mail." (£1 per

30min. Cafe open M-F 8am-6pm, Sa 8am-2pm, Su 9am-noon.) Dorms £15; twins £36. ❷

YHA Liverpool, 25 Tabley St. (☎709 8888; liverpool@yha.org.uk). Upscale digs on 3 Beatles-themed floors, next to Albert Dock. Rooms with double beds suitable for families. Laundry, kitchen, Internet access, currency exchange, and restaurant. Breakfast included. Dorms £19, under 18 £14.50. ❷

YMCA, Mt. Pleasant (709 9516). Clean, spartan, and near-unbeatable prices. Laundry. £2 key deposit. Singles £16; twins £20; triples £42. ❷

University of Liverpool: Mulberry Court, Oxford St. (☎794 3298). Self-catering rooms with bath. The university conference office (☎794 6440) has information on other halls open to travelers. Available July-Aug. £15-16 per person. ❷

SAVOY TRUFFLE

Trendy cafes and well-priced Indian restaurants line **Bold St.** and **Hardman St.,** while takeaways crowd **Hardnon St.** and **Berry St.** Many are open until 3am.

Simply Heathcotes, 25 The Strand, Beetham Plaza (☎236 3536). Simply elegant. Sweeping walls of glass and flickering candles complement beautiful dishes. Breaded veal escallop or seared fillet of salmon about £15. Open M-Sa noon-2:30pm and 6pm-10pm. ❹

Tavern Co., Queen Sq. (☎709 1070), near the TIC. Hearty burritos and creative taco salads (£5-7) in a popular wine-bar atmosphere. Open M-Sa noon-11pm, Su 10:30am-10:30pm; food served until 10pm. ❷

La Tasca, Queen Sq. (☎709 7999). With candles, throw pillows, and Spanish music, the most vibrant tapas bar in town. *Queso Manchego* (£3.45) or *Pollo al Ajillo* (£3.25) are agreeable starters. Lively crowds arrive in late evening. Open daily noon-11pm. ❷

La Crepe Rit, 20-21 The Colonnades (☎709 9444), Albert Dock. Slave to your own desire, seek immediate gratification here. Crepes of all varieties run £3.25-5, with lots of creamy fillings. ❶

Hole in the Wall, School Ln. (☎709 7733). This self-described "coffee lounge" serves sandwiches and sweets (£3-4.50). Open M-Sa noon-5pm. ❶

▼ COME TOGETHER

Two of the Liverpool's most notable products—football fans and rock musicians—were born of pub culture, and the city has continued to incorporate these traditions in its pub renaissance. **Slater St.** in particular brims with £1 pints.

LG: Sort of Pollock-style...

AW: Heh. Yeah...

LG: And how did you become their manager?

AW: I put this big rock 'n' roll show on. They came and saw me the next day and said, "Hey Al? When are you going to do something for us like?" And I said to them, "Look, there's no more painting to be done." And they said, "No, we've got a *group.*" I said, "I didn't know that." And they said, "Well, will you manage us?" By then I had got to know them, and they were quite nice personalities—very witty. And I go, "Oh yeah, this could be fun." And then I managed them.

Williams told us how it was their stint in Hamburg, and not Liverpool, that made the Beatles. He then described his falling out with the group, over (what else?) contract disputes and general rock star ingratitude.

AW: I wrote them a letter saying that they appeared to be getting more than a little swell-headed, and, remember, "I managed you when nobody else wanted to know you. But I'll fix it now so that you'll never ever work again."

LG: Uh-oh.

AW: Heh-heh. So that's my big mistake, yeah. Heh. And on that note, we'll finish.

▨ **The Philharmonic,** 36 Hope St. (☎ 707 2837). John Lennon once said the worst thing about being famous was "not being able to get a quiet pint at the Phil." Non-celebrities among us can still get that silent beer. Open M-Sa noon-11pm, Su noon-10:30pm.

The Jacaranda, 21-23 Slater St. (☎ 708 9424). The site of the first paid Beatles gig, the Jac's basement was painted by John and original Beatle Stu Sutcliffe. Live bands play, and a small dance floor lets you kick loose. Open M-Sa noon-2am, Su noon-10:30pm.

Caledonia Laundromatic Super Pub (☎ 709 9567), corner of Catharine St. and Caledonia St. Half-launderette, half-pub, this funky multi-tasker *wasn't* visited by the Beatles—boy did they miss out. 2 computers with free Internet squat atop clothes driers-turned-fishbowls. £3 buys wash, dry, and coffee. Cheap food and pints. DJs nightly. Open noon-11pm; food served noon-8pm. Closes when business is slow.

Slaters Bar, 26 Slater St. (☎ 708 6990). Cheap drinks (pints start at £1.10) and a young crowd by the jukebox. Open M-Sa 11am-2am, Su noon-10:30pm.

Ye Crack, 13 Rice St. (☎ 709 4171). Where Lennon used to finish off lathery pints; ask about how he later got banned. A grizzled, older crowd. Ethnic food theme nights M-Th and fabulous beer garden out back. Open M-Sa 11:30am-11pm, Su noon-10:30pm.

◎ MAGICAL MYSTERY TOUR

With first-rate museums, unusual churches, and the twin religions of football and the Beatles, tourists find Liverpool in their ears and in their eyes. **Hope St.,** southeast of the city center, connects Liverpool's two 20th-century cathedrals. Most other sights are located on **Albert Dock,** an open rectangle of Victorian warehouses now stocked with offices, restaurants, and museums.

THE BEATLES STORY. Walk-through recreations of Hamburg, the Cavern Club (complete with "basement smells"), and a shiny Yellow Submarine trace the rise and—sigh—fall of the band. Audiovisuals will leave you nostalgic and primed for the gift shop. *(Albert Dock. ☎ 709 1963. Open Apr.-Oct. daily 10am-6pm; Nov.-Mar. 10am-5pm; last admission 1hr. before close. £8, concessions £5.45, children £4.95, families £19.)*

MORE BEATLES. For other Beatles-themed locales, get the **Beatles Map** (£2.50) at the TIC. To reach **Penny Lane,** take bus #86A, 33, or 35 from Queen's Sq.; for **Strawberry Fields,** take #176 from Paradise St. Souvenir hunters can raid the **Beatles Shop,** stuffed with memorabilia on Beatles-packed Mathew St., below a small shrine to the boys. *(31 Mathew St. ☎ 236 8066. Open M-Sa 9:30am-5:30pm, Su 11am-4pm.)*

MERSEYSIDE MARITIME MUSEUM. Liverpool's heyday as a major port has passed, but the six impressive floors of this museum allow you to explore the cramped hull of a slave trader's ship or a dimly lit dockside street. Fans of a certain movie starring Leonardo DiCaprio can see items recovered from the "unsinkable" ship. Attached to the Maritime Museum is the **H.M. Customs and Excise Museum,** with an intriguing array of confiscated goods from would-be smugglers, including a fountain pen that shoots chilli powder and a teddy bear full of cocaine. *(Albert Dock. ☎ 478 4499. Open daily 10am-5pm. Free.)*

TATE GALLERY. The intimate Liverpool branch of the now-national institution contains a select range of 20th-century artwork. Works by international artists dominate the ground floor, while the next level shows a rotating collection from the gallery's archives. A special exhibit in summer 2003 will feature the work of Paul Nash. By prior arrangement, the staff will fit the visually impaired with special gloves and allow them to touch some of the art. *(Albert Dock. ☎ 702 7400. Open Tu-Su 10am-6pm. Free; some special exhibits £4, concessions £3.)*

LIVERPOOL CATHEDRAL. Begun in 1904, completed in 1978, this vast Anglican cathedral echoes with superlatives, featuring the highest Gothic arches ever built

(107 ft.), the largest vault and organ (9765 pipes), and the world's highest and heaviest bells. Take two lifts and climb 108 stairs for a view stretching to Wales. *(Upper Duke St. ☎709 6271. Cathedral open daily 8am-6pm; tower open M-Sa 11am-4pm, weather permitting. Suggested cathedral donation £2.50. Tower admission £2, children £1.)*

METROPOLITAN CATHEDRAL OF CHRIST THE KING. Dubbed "Paddy's Wigwam" by locals, the city's Roman Catholic church looks more like an upside-down funnel than a house of worship. A step inside proves you can't judge a cathedral by its resemblance to a kitchen utensil. Neon-blue stained glass casts a glow over the circular interior, and modern sculptures fill niches and chapels. But the cathedral sticks to most traditions—the organists weren't allowed to play popular music until the 1981 memorial service for John Lennon. *(Mt. Pleasant. ☎709 9222. Open summer M-F 8am-6pm, Sa-Su 8:30am-6pm; winter M-F 8am-6pm, Sa 8:30am-6pm, Su 8:30am-5pm. Free.)*

THE MUSEUM OF LIVERPOOL LIFE. This museum tells Liverpool's history of stormy labor struggles and race relations, as well as its sports and soap-operas. Footage from legendary football matches between Liverpool and Everton runs, while a plaque commemorates Grand National-winning horses. *(Albert Dock. ☎478 4080. Open daily 10am-5pm. Free.)*

WALKER ART GALLERY. This stately gallery reopened in February 2002, after more than a year's renovation. The huge collection includes medieval works and a variety of impressive post-Impressionist and pre-Raphaelite paintings. *(William Brown St. ☎478 4199. Open M-Sa 10am-5pm, Su noon-5pm. Free.)*

CONSERVATION CENTRE. A small interactive museum below the conservation studios and labs for the National Museum and Galleries of Merseyside, the Centre provides insight into the processes of art restoration and preservation. Hands-on exhibits are particularly engaging for children. *(Whitechapel. ☎478 4999. Tours W and Sa 2 and 3pm (W £2, Sa £1). Open M-Sa 10am-5pm, Su 11am-5pm. Free.)*

LIVERPOOL AND EVERTON FOOTBALL CLUBS. If you're not here for the Beatles, you're probably here for the football. The rivalry between the city's two main teams is deep and passionate. **Liverpool** and **Everton** offer tours of their grounds (Anfield and Goodison Park, respectively) and match tickets when available. Book both in advance. *(Both can be reached by bus #26 from the city center. Liverpool ☎260 6677. Everton ☎330 2277. Liverpool tour, including entrance to their museum, £8.50, concessions £5.50, families £23. Everton tour £5.50, concessions £3.50. Match tickets from £14.)*

🎵 HIPPY HIPPY SHAKE

Consult the *Liverpool Echo*, sold by street vendors, for up-to-date information, especially the *What's On* section of Friday editions (32p). **Quiggins,** 12-16 School Ln. (☎709 2462), and the **Palace,** 6-10 Slater St., sell crazy hipster paraphernalia and have tons of flyers detailing the club scene. For alternative events, check the bulletin board in **Everyman Bistro,** 9-11 Hope St., where bohemian happenings often occur in the attached **Third Room.** (☎708 9545. Open M-Th noon-midnight, F-Sa noon-2am.) Inquire about gay and lesbian events at **News From Nowhere,** 96 Bold St., a feminist bookshop run by a women's cooperative. (☎708 7270. Open M-Sa 10am-5:45pm.)

On weekend nights, the downtown area, especially **Mathew St., Church St.,** and **Bold St.,** overflows with young pubbers and clubbers. Window-shop venues to find what you like, and dress smartly to avoid provoking the army of bouncers. Also try to avoid wandering into dark alleys, as high concentrations of drunken revelers make prime targets for street theft. Bars and clubs clustered around **Albert Dock** tend to appeal to the older, well-groomed set—sophisticated dress and quite a bit of cash required.

CLUBS AND BARS

Medication, Wolstonholme Sq. (☎709 1161), off Parr St. Baby, *behave.* It's the biggest, wildest student night in town, as desperate university blokes dance crazy, talk crazy, and get crazy, while the girls ignore them. House, pop, and indie rooms. Students only; bring ID. Cover £5. Open W 10am-2am.

The Cavern Club, 10 Mathew St. (☎236 9091). Still coasting on their Fab Four fame, these narrow, brick-lined premises draw locals for live bands (Th-F 8pm-2am, Sa 2-11pm). No cover until 10pm, £2 10-11pm, £4 11pm-2am. Club open Th-F 6pm-2am, Sa 6pm-3am; pub open M-Sa from noon, Su noon-11:30pm.

Le Bateau, 62 Duke St. (☎709 6508). **Uptight,** on the top level, swings with 60s music; a mellow club downstairs relaxes things. Cover £5. Open roughly F-Sa 10pm-3am.

Society, 47 Fleet St. (☎258 1230). Faithfuls call it "sexy, yet laid back." Dance music fills the early hours. Catch one of the legendary theme nights, when there's no such thing as going overboard. Cover £5. Dress chic. Open F 10:30pm-3am.

Blue Bar, Albert Dock (☎702 5835). Where tanned Brit-flick stars discuss the latest deal while their girlfriends pout. Or vice-versa. Sleek, sparkly, and chill; people-watching doesn't get any better. Find (or fake) your inner chic and head on over. Open M-Th 11am-1am, F-Sa 11am-2am, Su noon-1am. Beneath, the **Rawhide Comedy Club** (box office ☎726 077) offers stand-up comedy Th-Su nights.

MUSIC, THEATER, AND FESTIVALS

■ **Bluecoat Centre** (info line ☎709 5297, box office 707 9393), off School Ln. Begun in 1717 as a charity school and now Liverpool's performing arts center. An art-school atmosphere permeates the exhibition spaces. Workshops in music, dance, and art. Linger in the cafe and used bookstore. Open M-Sa 9am-5:30pm; box office open M-F 11am-5pm; gallery open Tu-Sa 10:30am-5pm.

Philharmonic Hall, Hope St. (☎709 3789). The **Royal Liverpool Philharmonic,** one of England's better orchestras, performs here along with an array of others, including jazz and funk bands. Box office open M-Sa 10am-5:30pm, Su noon-5pm. Tickets from £15; student prices as low as £10; concessions half-price day of show.

Liverpool Empire Theatre, Lime St. (☎(0870) 606 3536). Hosts a variety of dramatic performances, welcoming such famed troupes as the Royal Shakespeare Company. Box office open M-Sa 10am-8pm on performance days, otherwise M 10am-6pm, Tu-Sa 10am-8pm, Su 1hr. before show. Tickets normally £10-45, concessions available.

Everyman Theatre (☎709 4776), at Hope St. and Oxford St. Adventurous contemporary productions. Box office open M-F 10am-6pm, Sa noon-6pm. Tickets from £10.

Festivals: Liverpool hosts numerous conventions and festivals, ranging from the **Mersey River Festival** (mid-June) to the **International Street Theatre Festival** (early Aug.). At the end of August, a week-long **Beatles Convention** draws Fab Four devotees and bewildered entomologists from all over.

MANCHESTER   ☎0161

The Industrial Revolution transformed the unremarkable village of Manchester into a northern hub, now Britain's second-largest urban area. A center of manufacturing in the 19th century, the city became a hotbed of liberal politics, its deplorable working-class conditions arousing the indignation of everyone from Frederic Engels (who called it "Hell on Earth") to John Ruskin (who called it a "devil's darkness"). Now a hotbed of electronic beats and post-industrial glitz, Manchester has risen, phoenix-like, from factory soot to savor its reputation as one of the hippest spots in England. Though dodgy in parts, the city is undergoing a gradual gentrification and is accessible to the street smart. Thousands are drawn to its vibrant arts and nightlife scenes, proving that it's not just the pretty who are popular.

▐ TRANSPORTATION

Flights: Manchester International Airport (☎ 489 3000; international arrivals (0839) 888 747, domestic arrivals (0839) 888 757, both 50p per min.). Trains (15-20min., 6-7 per hr., £2.35) and buses #44 and 105 run to Piccadilly Station.

Trains: Manchester Piccadilly, London Rd., serves mostly trains from the south, east, and Scotland. Travel center open M-Sa 8am-8:30pm, Su 11am-7pm. Trains (☎ (08457) 484 950) from: **Birmingham** (1¾hr., 2 per hr., £16.50); **Chester** (1hr., every hr., £9); **Edinburgh** (4hr.; every hr.; £46 via Carlisle, £51.50 via York); **London Euston** (2½-3hr., every hr., £49); **York** (40min., 2 per hr., £18). **Manchester Victoria,** Victoria St., serves mostly trains from the west and north. Ticket office open daily 6:30am-10pm. From **Liverpool** (50min., 2 per hr., £7.40). The stations are connected by Metrolink.

Buses: Chorlton St. Coach Station, Chorlton St. Office open M-F 7:15am-7pm, Sa-Su 7:15am-6:15pm. Lockers £1-3. **National Express** (☎ (08705) 808 080) from: **Leeds** (1hr., every hr., £5.75); **Liverpool** (50min., every hr., £4.75); **London** (4-5hr., 7 per day, £17); **Sheffield** (1½hr., 6 per day, £5.75).

Public Transportation: Piccadilly Gardens is home to about 50 bus stops. Pick up a free route map from the TIC. **Buses** generally run until 11:30pm, some lines until 2:30am on weekends. Office open M-Sa 7am-6pm, Su 10am-6pm. All-day ticket £3.30. **Metrolink** trams (☎ 205 2000) link 8 stops in the city center with **Altrincham** in the southwest, **Bury** in the northeast, and **Eccles** in the west (every 6-15min., 50p-£4.60). Combined bus and tram ticket £4.50. For more information, call ☎ 228 7811 (8am-8pm) or visit www.gmpte.gov.uk.

Taxis: Mantax (☎ 236 5133) or **Radio Cars** (☎ 236 8033).

▐▐ ORIENTATION AND PRACTICAL INFORMATION

The city center is an odd polygon formed by **Victoria Station** to the north, **Piccadilly Station** to the east, the canals to the south, and the **River Irwell** to the west. The area is fairly compact, but the many byways can be tricky to navigate. Most central streets bear illuminated, poster-sized maps, and Mancunians are generally helpful.

Tourist Information Centre: Manchester Visitor Centre, Town Hall Extension, Lloyd St. (☎ 234 3157, 24hr. info (0891) 715 533). Staff books accommodations (£2.50 plus 10% deposit) and can sometimes get better rates or special prices. Free literature includes the *Manchester Pocket Guide*, the *Greater Manchester Network Map*, and *What's On*, which lists local events. Open M-Sa 10am-5pm, Su 10:30am-4:30pm.

Financial Services: Thomas Cook, 23 Market St. (☎ 910 8787). Open M-W and F-Sa 10am-6pm, Sa 9am-5:30pm, Su 11am-5pm. **American Express,** 10-12 St. Mary's Gate (☎ 833 0121). Open M-F 9am-5:30pm, Sa 9am-5pm.

Work Opportunities: Visa holders can contact **Manpower,** 87-89 Mosley St. (☎ 236 8891) for placement in office work.

Police: Chester House, Bootle St. (☎ 872 5050).

Crisis Lines: Samaritans, 72-74 Oxford St. (☎ 236 8000 or 24hr. (08457) 909 090).

Pharmacy: Boots, 32 Market St. (☎ 832 6533). Open M-F 9am-6pm, Sa 9:30am-6pm, Su 10am-4pm.

Hospital: Manchester Royal Infirmary, Oxford Rd. (☎ 276 1234).

Internet Access: Central Library, (☎ 234 1966), free for first hr. **easyEverything,** 8-10 Exchange St., (☎ 832 9200), in St. Ann's Sq. £1 per 40min., £3 for 24hr., £5 for 7 days, £12 for 20 days. Open daily 7am-11pm. **Internet Exchange,** 1-3 Piccadilly Sq. (☎ 833 8111), on the 2nd floor of Coffee Republic. £1 per 15min., £1 per hr. with £2 membership. Open M-F 7:30am-6:30pm, Sa 8am-6:30pm, Su 9:30am-5:30pm.

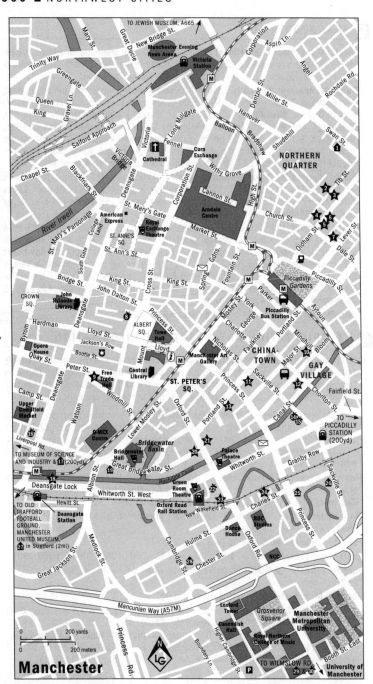

TO JEWISH MUSEUM, A665

New Bridge St.

Great Ducie

Manchester Evening News Arena

Victoria Station

Corporation

Aspin Ln.

Ardel

Rochdale Rd.

Mary St.

Trinity Way

Greengate

Queen

King

Gravel Ln.

Salford Approach

Victoria

Long Millgate

Fennel

Balloon

Hanover

Bradshaw

Dantzic St.

Miller St.

Shudehill

Swan St.

NORTHERN QUARTER

Tib St.

Lever St.

Chapel St.

Victoria Bridge

Cathedral

Corn Exchange

Withy Grove

Cannon St.

High St.

Church St.

Oldham

Dale St.

River Irwell

St. Mary's Parsonage

Blackfriars St.

Deansgate

St. Mary's Gate

American Express

Royal Exchange Theatre

ST. ANNE'S SQ.

St. Ann's St.

Arndale Centre

Market St.

Spring Gdns.

Fountain St.

Piccadilly St.

Piccadilly Gardens

CROWN SQ.

John Rylands Library

Bridge St.

King St.

Cross St.

King St.

Deansgate

John Dalton St.

Princess St.

Mosley St.

York

George

Charlotte

Parker

Piccadilly Bus Station

Piccadilly Station

Portland St.

Minshull

Bloom

Aytoun

Hardman

Byrom

Opera House

Quay St.

Lloyd St.

Jackson's Row

Bootle St.

ALBERT SQ.

Town Hall

Lloyd

Mount

Nicholas St.

Manchester Art Gallery

CHINA-TOWN

Major St.

GAY VILLAGE

Camp St.

Peter St.

Free Trade Hall

Central Library

ST. PETER'S SQ.

Princess St.

Sackville St.

Fairfield St.

Upper Campfield Market

Windmill St.

Oxford St.

Portland St.

Chorlton St.

Canal St.

TO PICCADILLY STATION (200yd)

Liverpool Rd.

TO MUSEUM OF SCIENCE AND INDUSTRY (200yd)

G-MEX Centre

Watson

Lower Mosley St.

Bridgewater Basin

Bridgewater Hall

Great Bridgewater St.

Granby Row

Sackville St.

Deansgate Lock

Albion St.

Whitworth St. West

Green Room Theatre

Palace Theatre

Whitworth St.

Hewitt St.

Oxford Road Rail Station

New Wakefield St.

Charles St.

BBC Studios

Oxford Rd.

TO OLD TRAFFORD FOOTBALL GROUND, MANCHESTER UNITED MUSEUM, in Stretford (2ml)

Deansgate Station

Medlock St.

Hulme St.

Dance House

Great Jackson St.

Cambridge St.

Chester St.

NCC

Mancunian Way (A57M)

Loxford Towers

Cavendish Hall

Grosvenor Square

Royal Northern College of Music

Manchester Metropolitan University

Boundary Ln.

Higher Cambridge St.

TO WILMSLOW RD.

University of Manchester

29 & 30

0   200 yards
0   200 meters

N

LG

Manchester

Manchester

🏠 ACCOMMODATIONS

Burton Arms, **1**
Ibis, **25**
Jurys Inn Manchester, **19**
Manchester Conference
    Centre and Hotel, **26**
Manchester Backpackers
    Hostel and Guest House, **27**
Student Village, **28**
University of Manchester
    Lodgings, **29**
YHA Manchester, **17**

🍎 FOOD

Camel One, **30**
Cornerhouse Cafe, **22**
Dimitri's, **16**
Gaia, **14**
Tampopo Noodle House, **8**
Tribeca, **15**

⭐ NIGHTLIFE

The Attic, **23**
Churchills, **12**
Copacabana, **7**
Cord, **2**
Cruz 101, **11**
Dry Bar, **6**
Essential, **10**
Fab Cafe, **13**
Infinity, **9**
The Lass O'Gowrie, **24**
Matt and Phred's, **3**
Music Box, **21**
Night and Day Cafe, **5**
Revolution, **18**
Simple Bar & Restaurant, **4**
Temple of Convenience, **20**

Post Office: 26 Spring Gdns. (☎839 0687). Open M-Tu and Th-F 8:30am-6pm, W 9am-6pm, Sa 8:30am-7pm. Poste Restante (☎834 8605) has a separate entrance. Open M-F 6am-5:30pm, Sa 6am-12:30pm. **Post Code:** M2 1BB.

🏠 ACCOMMODATIONS

Cheap stays in the city center are hard to find, though summer offers the possibility of decently priced **student housing.** The highest concentration of budget lodgings is 2-3 mi. south in the suburbs of **Fallowfield, Withington,** and **Didsbury;** take bus #40, 42, or 157. Browse the free booklet *Where to Stay* (at the TIC) for listings.

🏨 **Jurys Inn Manchester,** 56 Great Bridgewater St. (☎953 8888), voted Hotel of the Year by *Manchester Life.* Enormous rooms, luxurious baths, and professional service. A double and single bed in every room. Hardly a deal for solo travelers, but a bargain for those with companions. £65 per room. £45 weekend special, subject to availability. ❺

YHA Manchester, Potato Wharf, Castlefield (☎839 9960; fax 835 2054). Take the metro to G-Mex Station or bus #33 from Piccadilly Gardens toward Wigan to Deansgate. Raising hosteling to swanky heights. Friendly staff and good security. Lockers £1-2. Laundry £1.50. Internet access 50p per 6min. Reception open 7am-11pm. Dorms £18.50, under 18 £13.50; £1 student discount. ❷

THE HIDDEN DEAL

LOWRY DESIGNER OUTLET

Instead of spending your pounds on King St., home to DKNY, Versace, D&G, Diesel, and Tommy Hilfiger, opt for the **Lowry Designer Outlet** (☎848 1848) in Salford Quays. Finding a good deal in Manchester may take some effort, but it's far more likely here than anywhere else. Boyfriends with bags and husbands with prams linger outside the outlet's 84 shops, which peddle high-end designer merchandise at 20-70% off.

Proibito (☎877 4287) stocks DKNY ladies' jeans (£19), Valentino blouses (£30), and men's Hugo Boss t-shirts (£17.50), as well as pricier Versace and D&G items. The **Reiss** outlet (☎877 5051) slashes 30-50% off original prices, charging an average of £30-40 for trendy slacks and shirts. Perusing the **Karen Millen** store (☎877 8801) may reveal £110 trousers marked down to £10. *(Take the Metrolink to Harbour City Station, cross the monstrous pink bridge, and follow the signs to the colossal outlet mall; no more than a 10min. walk. Open M-F 10am-8pm, Sa 9am-7pm, Su 11am-5pm.)*

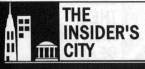

THE INSIDER'S CITY

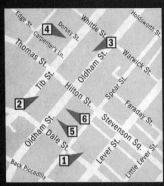

OLDHAM ST. STUMBLE

By day, the Northern Quarter is home to alternative record shops and funky clothes. By night, the Oldham St. area buzzes with nightlife. Evenings churn out many a disoriented reveler, but luckily, Piccadilly Station is only 5min. south (approx. 15min. staggering).

1 Shimmy at **Copacabana**, Dale St. (☎237 3441), host to rumba and salsa dancing and a lively bar.

2 Get happy at **Simple Bar & Restaurant**, 44 Tib St. (☎835 2526). Open daily 11am-11pm.

3 Relax at **Matt and Phred's**, 85 Oldham St. (☎661 7494), an all-jazz venue. Open M-Sa 8pm-2am.

4 See corduroy meet chic at **Cord**, 8 Dorsey St. (☎832 9494). Open M-Sa noon-11pm, Su 3-10:30pm.

5 Dance to retro and hip-hop at **Night and Day Cafe**, 26 Oldham St. (☎236 4597). Cover £3. Open M-Sa 11am-2am.

6 Cavort at the sultry **Dry Bar**, 28-30 Oldham St. (☎236 9840). Too cool for a sign; look for big wooden doors. Open M-Sa noon-2am, Su noon-10:30pm.

Student Village, Lower Chatham St. (☎236 1776). Nothing outstanding about these 1039 rooms but the price. Singles £17, students £15. ❷

Ibis, Charles St., (☎272 5000; fax 272 5051). Simple hotel with sparkling bathrooms. Large rooms resemble cruiseship lodgings. Doubles M-Th £45, F-Su £40. ❹

Manchester Conference Centre and Hotel, Sackville St. (☎955 8000; fax 955 8050), is connected to university rooms. Open mid-June to Sept. Singles £65; doubles £75; less on weekends. ❺

University of Manchester: Call the **University Accommodation Office** (☎275 2888, open M-F 9am-5pm) to find out which dorms are available for lodging during summer vacation (mid-June to mid-Sept). 1 week minimum stay. Reserve a week or more in advance with deposit. £50 per week. Dorms offering lodgings include **Langdale Hall** (☎224 1385), **Hardy Farm** (☎861 9913), and **St. Gabriel's Hall**, 1-3 Oxford Pl., Victoria Park (☎224 7061). ❶

Burton Arms, 31 Swan St. (☎/fax 834 3455). Basic rooms above a pub on a busy street. A 15min. walk from both train stations and St. Peter's Sq. Full English breakfast £3. £19.50 per person, with bath £30. ❸

Manchester Backpackers Hostel and Guest House, 64 Cromwell Rd. (☎865 9296), a 20min. walk from the Metro's Stretford station. Take a left out of the station and walk 5 blocks past the traffic lights. Basic accommodations at a budget price. Dorms £11; twins and doubles £16; triples £14; quads £13. ❷

▣ FOOD

Outwit the pricey Chinatown restaurants by eating the multi-course "Businessman's Lunch" offered by most (M-F noon-2pm, £4-8, with or without briefcase and masculine gender). Better yet, visit **Curry Mile,** a stretch of Asian restaurants on Wilmslow Rd., for quality eats. Come evening, hip youths and yuppies wine and dine in the cafe-bars (see p. 370). A **Tesco** supermarket is at 55-66 Market St. (☎941 9400. Open continuously M 7am to Sa 10pm, also Su 11am-5pm.)

▨ **Tampopo Noodle House,** 16 Albert Sq. (☎819 1966). This spartan noodle house is one of Manchester's favorites. Noodles from Thailand, Malaysia, Indonesia, and Japan are well-priced (£3-8), quick, and delicious. Open M-Sa noon-11pm, Su noon-10pm. ❷

Gaia, 46 Sackville St. (☎228 1002). Skilled chefs prepare brilliant British fusion cuisine with Mediterranean flavor. Renaissance decor features velvet curtains and candlelight. Appetizers £3-5, entrees £8-13. Open M-Th and Su noon-midnight, F-Sa noon-2am. ❸

Camel One, 107 Wilmslow Rd. (☎257 2282). A simple eatery with an extensive Indian menu. Banner claims "Voted #1 in England." Kebab sandwiches made to order. Dishes £2-5.50. Open daily 10am-7am. ❶

Tribeca, 50 Sackville St. (☎236 8300), serves a wide variety of cuisines, from BBQ ribs to bangers and mash. Take your meal on one of the seductively decorated beds downstairs. Appetizers £4-7, entrees £7-11. Open M-Tu noon-midnight, W-Th noon-1am, F-Sa noon-2am, Su noon-12:30am. ❸

Cornerhouse Cafe, 70 Oxford St. (☎200 1508). Part of the Cornerhouse Arts Centre; features 1 bar, 3 galleries, 3 arthouse cinemas, and trendy crowds. Flavors from gourmet pizza to cajun chicken. Entrees £4-6, desserts around £1.50. Open daily 11am-11pm; hot meals served until 10pm; bar open M-Sa noon-11pm, Su noon-10:30pm. ❷

Dimitri's, Campfield Arcade, Tonman St. (☎839 3319), in an alley off Bridgegate St. Greek delicacies for plebeians and soap-opera divas alike (there's a TV studio next door). 2 appetizers make a meal (£3.65-5.45). 20% off drinks during happy hour (5-7pm). Open daily 11am-midnight. ❸

SIGHTS

Few of Manchester's buildings are notable—postcards mostly portray the fronts of trams—but an exception is the neo-Gothic **Manchester Town Hall,** at St. Peter's Sq. Behind the Town Hall Extension, the **Central Library** is the city's jewel. One of the largest municipal libraries in Europe, the domed building has a music and theater library, a language and literature library, and the UK's second-largest Judaica collection. The **Library Theatre Company** puts on small productions and plays. (Library ☎234 1966; theater 236 1913. Open M-Th 10am-8pm, F-Sa 10am-5pm.) The **John Rylands Library,** 150 Deansgate, keeps rare books; its most famous holding is the St. John Fragment, a piece of New Testament writing from the 2nd century. (☎834 5343. Open M-F 10am-5:30pm, Sa 10am-1pm. Free. Tours W at noon £1.)

Reopened in June 2002 after a three-year, £35 million renovation, the **Manchester Art Gallery** holds Rossetti's stunning *Astarte Syriaca* among its gigantic art collection. (☎235 8888. Open Tu-Su and bank holidays 10am-5pm. Admission free. Free audio tours.) In the **Museum of Science and Industry,** Liverpool Rd. in Castlefield, working steam engines and looms provide a dramatic vision of the power, danger, and noise of Britain's industrialization. (☎832 1830. Open daily 10am-5pm. Museum free, special exhibitions £3-5.) The Spanish and Portuguese synagogue-turned-

IN RECENT NEWS

RE-CLASSIFIED INFORMATION

On July 10, 2002, British Home Secretary David Blunkett announced Britain's decision to reclassify marijuana as a Class C drug, downgrading it from more serious Class B. When the change is made (it's expected to take effect in July 2003), carrying a small amount of dope (i.e., not a truckload) will no longer be an arrestable offense, and will earn offenders little more than a slap on the wrist. While Blunkett stressed that the change, which is intended to free the police to focus on more serious crimes, does not amount to a decriminalization of pot (dealing will still incur harsh penalties), opponents and supporters alike interpreted it as a step in that direction.

In Manchester, evocative smells signify that you've arrived in a fast-paced metropolis—hot dogs steam at portable stands, aromatic black coffee sharpens the morning, perfumed air wafts from beauty shops, and tell-tale whiffs of marijuana aren't uncommon. To assist visitors in experiencing the joy of city smells more fully, **Dr. Hermans** offers professional, friendly service, personal attention, and lots of bongs. At this fully stocked store, you could, hypothetically, purchase all the paraphernalia you would need to get on your way to committing a misdemeanor. *(57 Church St., between Tib St. and Oldham St. ☎834 1130. Open daily 10am-5:30pm.)*

Jewish Museum, 190 Cheetham Hill Rd., traces the history of the city's sizeable Jewish community and offers city tours. (☎834 9879. Open M-Th 10:30am-4pm, Su 10:30am-5pm. £3.65, concessions £2.75, families £8.95.) Loved and reviled, Manchester United is England's reigning football team. The **Manchester United Museum and Tour Centre,** Sir Matt Busby Way, at the Old Trafford football stadium (follow signs up Warwick Rd. from the Old Trafford Metrolink stop), displays memorabilia from the club's inception in 1878 to its recent trophy-hogging success. The museum's religious fervor may just convert you. (☎868 8631. Open daily 9:30am-5pm. Tours every 10min., 9:40am-4:30pm. Museum £5.50, concessions £3.75; with tour £8.50/£5.75.)

♫ MUSIC, THEATER, AND FESTIVALS

Besides those listed below, the **Manchester Evening News (MEN) Arena** (box office ☎930 8000; www.men-arena.com), behind Victoria Station, hosts concerts and sporting events.

Royal Exchange Theatre (☎833 9333) has returned to St. Ann's Sq., a few years after an IRA bomb destroyed the original building. The theater stages Shakespeare and premieres of original works. Box office open M-Sa 9:30am-7:30pm. Tickets £7-25, concessions £6.50 when booked 3 days in advance.

Bridgewater Hall, Lower Mosley St. (☎907 9000). Manchester's premier venue for orchestral concerts and glass-and-metal home of the Hallé Orchestra. Open M-Sa 10am-8pm, Sa noon-8pm. Tickets £7-30.

Palace Theatre, Oxford St. (☎228 6255). Caters to classical tastes in theater, opera, and ballet. Box office open M-Sa 10am-6pm, until 8pm performance days.

The Manchester Festival (www.the-manchester-festival.org.uk) runs all summer long, with dramatic, musical, and multimedia events. Call the Central Library (☎234 1944) for information. The Gay Village hosts a number of festivals, most notably late August's **Mardi Gras** (☎237 3237), which raises money for AIDS relief.

◧ NIGHTLIFE

CAFE-BARS

Many of Manchester's excellent lunchtime spots morph into pre-club drinking venues, or even become clubs themselves.

The Lass O'Gowrie, 36 Charles St. (☎273 6932). Traditional pubs aren't at all passé when the evening crowd is this lively. BBC personalities trickle in from the neighboring studio. Good food at amazing prices (£2-5). Open M-Sa 11am-11pm, Su noon-10:30pm; food served 11am-7pm.

Fab Cafe, 111 Portland St. A "TV Movie Theme Bar" with an upbeat atmosphere. Open M and W-Th 5pm-2am, Tu 5pm-11pm, F-Sa noon-2am, Su 5pm-10:30pm.

Temple of Convenience, on Bridgewater St., literally. An entrance in the middle of the street leads downstairs to a small, smoky bar, once home to a toilet. Locals squeeze in for drinks before heading out clubbing.

CLUBS

Manchester's clubbing and live music scene remains a national trendsetter. Centered around **Oldham St.,** the **Northern Quarter** is the city's youthful outlet for live music, its alternative vibe and underground clothing and record shops drawing a hip crowd. On **Oxford St.,** a bigger party crowd comes for clubbing and reveling.

Don't forget to collect flyers—they'll often score you a discount. **Affleck's Palace,** 52 Church St., supplies paraphernalia from punk to funk; the walls of the stairway are postered with event notices. (☎ 839 6392. Open M-F 10am-5:30pm, Sa 10am-6pm.) Just up Oldham St., **Fat City** sells drum'n'bass, hip-hop, reggae, funk, and jazz records and various tickets and passes to clubbing events. (☎ 237 1181. Open M-Sa 10am-6pm, Su noon-4:30pm.)

At night, streets in the Northern Quarter are dimly lit. If you're crossing from Piccadilly to Swan St. or Great Ancoats St., use Oldham St., where the bright late-night clubs (and their bouncers) provide reassurance. There's no shame in short taxi trips at night in this town.

🖾 **Music Box,** on Oxford Rd. (☎ 273 3435), an underground warehouse club that hosts enormously popular parties. Check posters outside for details; monthly Electric Chair and events by Mr. Scruff receive rave reviews from local partiers. Cover £5-8. Open Th-Sa 10pm, closes between 3am and 6am, depending on the event.

Infinity, Peter St. (☎ 839 1112). Circular lights form an electric halo over a decadent dance-floor. Garage, house, and trance complete the £3 million refurbishment. Dress supersmart. Open M-W 9am-2am (cover £2-4), Th-Sa 9pm-3am (Th £4, F-Sa £6-8).

Revolution, Deansgate Locks (☎ 839 7569), on Whitworth St. West. Revolution leads an army of upstart bars and clubs on Deansgate. Red decor (look for the bust of Lenin) is a tasteful backdrop to funk, house, old school, and R&B tunes. 150 vodkas. No cover unless special promotion. Open daily 11am-2am.

The Attic, 50 N. Wakefield (☎ 236 6071), under the bridge on Oxford Rd. Revelers from the connected Thirsty Scholar bar (happy hour 4-7pm) are herded upstairs to this sparsely decorated dance club at 10:30pm. Open Th-Su until 2 or 3am.

THE GAY VILLAGE

Gay and lesbian clubbers will want to check out the Gay Village, northeast of Princess St. Evening crowds fill the bars lining **Canal St.,** in the heart of the area, which is also lively and lovely during the day. When weather cooperates, the bars are busy but empty, with patrons flooding the sidewalk tables.

Essential, 8 Minshull St. (☎ 237 5445), at Minshull and Bloom St., off Portland St. Arguably the most popular and highly frequented club in the Gay Village.

Cruz 101, 101 Princess St. (☎ 237 1554). Fun and sexy cruisers teach a lesson in attitude. Commercial dance gets bodies moving. Dress smart casual. Cover M £2, Tu-Th free, F £3, Sa £5. Open M-Sa 10:30pm-2:30am.

Churchills, 37 Chorlton St. (☎ 236 5529), a brand new club with lot of promise. Upbeat music and bright lighting make for a fun night out. A portrait of Churchill grimaces in the corner. Open M-Sa noon-2am, Su noon-12:30am.

BLACKPOOL ☎ 01253

Once a resort for the well-to-do, Blackpool has embraced its modern fame as King of Tack. The present gaudy era began with the railways built in the mid-1800s, along with the introduction of open-air dancing and electric street lighting. By the end of the 19th century, droves of working-class Brits were arriving for raucous holidays. Today, the town's amusements are numbingly numerous—seven miles of hyperactive promenade with roller coasters, palm-readers, arcades, cheap souvenir shops, donkey rides, fun palaces, and the occasional beach. With its unabashed tackiness (or, more likely, because of it), this boardwalk city stands unrivaled worldwide as a tasteless dispenser of uninhibited fun.

⌐ TRANSPORTATION

Trains: Blackpool North Station (☎620 385), 4 blocks down Talbot Rd. from North Pier. Travel center open daily 8am-6:30pm. Trains (☎(08457) 484 950) arrive from: **Birmingham** (3hr., 5 per day, £15); **Leeds** via **Bradford** (3½hr., 2 per day, £7.75); **Liverpool** (1½hr., every 2 hr., £11.30); **London Euston** via **Preston** (4hr., every hr., £55); **Manchester** (1¼hr., 2 per hr., £10).

Buses: Talbot Rd. Travel center open M-Sa 9am-5pm (closed 1:15-2pm). **National Express** (☎(08705) 808 080) from **Birmingham** (4hr., every 2hr., £10.75) and **London** (6½hr., 6 per day, £21). **Stagecoach** from **Manchester** (2hr., every hr., £6).

Public Transportation: Local trains use Blackpool South and Pleasure Beach stations. **Local bus** info is available at Talbot Rd. station. Bus #1 covers the Promenade every 10min.; **vintage trams** run this route more frequently. A 1-day **Travelcard** (£4.75) buys unlimited travel on trams and local buses; otherwise a ride costs £1.

⑦ PRACTICAL INFORMATION

Tourist Information Centre: 1 Clifton St. (☎478 222; fax 478 210). Books beds for £3 plus 10% deposit, books local shows for £1.50, and sells street maps for £1. (But find the same map in their free accommodations listings.) Open May-Oct. M-Sa 9am-5pm, Su 10am-4pm; Nov.-Apr. M-Sa 8:45am-4:45pm. **Branch** (☎478 222) on the Promenade near the Tower, open M-Sa 9am-5pm and Su 10am-3:30pm.

Financial Services: Banks are easy to find, especially along **Corporation St.** Most are open M-F, roughly 9am-4:30pm.

Launderette: Corner of Albert Rd. and Regent Rd. Open M-F 9am-7pm, Sa 10am-4pm, Su 10am-3pm. Last wash 1hr. before closing.

Internet Access: Blackpool Public Library (☎478 111), on the corner of Queen St. and Abingdon St. Free with ID and small deposit, 1hr. limit. Open M and F 9am-5pm, Tu and Th 9am-7pm, W and Sa 10am-5pm.

Post Office: 26-30 Abingdon St. (☎622 888). Open M-F 9am-5:30pm. **Post Code:** FY1 1AA.

⌐ ACCOMMODATIONS

With over 3500 guest houses and 120,000 beds, you won't have trouble finding a room, except on weekends during the Illuminations (see below). Budget-friendly B&Bs dominate the blocks behind the Promenade between the North and Central Piers (£10-20, less for longer stays). Pick up the free Bible-sized *Blackpool Have the Time of Your Life* at the TIC for an impressive list.

■ **Raffles Hotel,** 73/75 Hornby Rd. (☎294 713), is a 20min. walk from the bus and train stations, 5min. from the Promenade and Tower. From either station, head ocean-ward on Talbot Rd., turn left on Topping St., left on Church St., right on Regent Rd., and right onto Hornby Rd. Luxuriously decorated rooms and expert service. Breakfast included. Only twins, doubles, and family rooms. £21-24 per person, Illuminations £28. ❸

Manor Grove Hotel, 24 Leopold Grove (☎625 577). Follow the Raffles directions, but turn right at Church St., left onto Leopold Grove, and walk 1 block. Familial atmosphere, professional service. Spacious rooms are modem accessible, with TV, phone, and bath. Hearty English breakfast. £19-20 per person; £6 more for singles. AmEx/MC/V. ❷

York House, 30 South King St. (☎ 624 200). Follow the Raffles directions, but turn right onto South King St. after the left on Church St. Bay windows, high ceilings, and aristocratic red decor. Breakfast included. Rooms with TV and bath, £17 per person. ❷

Silver Birch Hotel, 39 Hull Rd. (☎ 622 125). From the bus or train station, head down Talbot Rd. to the ocean, take a left on Market St., pass the Tower, and turn left onto Hull Rd. Maternal proprietress Susan has spoiled guests with warm Irish hospitality for 25 years. Breakfast £3. £12 per person, with bath £15. ❷

FOOD

You know you're in Blackpool when McDonald's starts looking like class. The **Iceland** supermarket, 8-10 Topping St., is on the same block as the bus station. (☎ 751 575. Open M-W 8:30am-6pm, Th-F 8:30am-7pm, Sa 8am-5:30pm, Su 10:30am-4:30pm.) The quaint and cozy **Coffee Pot ❶,** 12 Birley St., serves big portions; try the roast beef dinner ($4.95), which comes with Yorkshire pudding, boiled potatoes, and two vegetables. (☎ 751 610. Open June-Nov. daily 8am-6pm, Dec.-May 8am-4:30pm.) Blackpool's branch of **Harry Ramsden's ❶,** on the corner of the Promenade and Church St., is a step up from most fast food fare. Boxes of scrumptious fish and chips ($2-4.30) make for fast outdoor takeaway. (☎ 294 386. Open Apr.-Nov. M-Th and Su 11:30am-9pm, F-Sa 11:30am-10pm; Dec.-Mar. M-Th and Su 11:30am-7:30pm, F-Sa 11:30am-9pm.)

👁 📷 SIGHTS AND ENTERTAINMENT

No fewer than 36 nightclubs, 38,000 theater seats, several circuses, and a rumbling of roller coasters squat along the **Promenade,** traversed by Britain's first electric tram line. Even the three 19th-century piers are stacked with ferris wheels and chip shops. The only thing the hedonistic hordes don't come for is the ocean.

PLEASURE BEACH. Around 7.1 million people visit this sprawling 40-acre amusement park annually, second in Europe only to EuroDisney. Pleasure Beach is known for its historic wooden roller coasters—the twin-track **Grand National** (c. 1935) is something of a mecca for coaster enthusiasts and the **Big Dipper** was invented here. Thousands of thrill-seekers line up for the aptly named **Big One,** and aren't disappointed as the 235 ft. steel behemoth, tall enough to merit aircraft warning lights, sends them down a heartstopping 65° slope at 87 mph. Although admission to the themeless park is free, the rides themselves aren't—the pay-as-you-ride system does mean queues are shorter than at other amusement parks. Daypasses are available. By night, Pleasure Beach features illusion shows and Las Vegas style theater and dance performances. *(Across from South Pier. ☎ (0870) 444 5566. Opens daily at 10 or 11am; closing time varies. £2-5 per ride. Daypass £25, 2-day £40, senior daypass £18, family daypass £70-100.)*

BLACKPOOL TOWER. When a London businessman visited the 1890 Paris World Exposition, he returned determined to erect Eiffel Tower imitations throughout Britain. Only Blackpool embraced his enthusiasm, and in 1894 the 560 ft. Tower graced the city's skyline. Unfortunately, it looks more like a rusty junkheap find than France's sleek symbol of modernism. The five-storey **Towerworld** in its base is a bizarre microcosm of Blackpool's eclectic kitsch, with a motley crew of attractions: a neon-blue aquarium, a motorized dinosaur ride, an insanely large jungle gym, arcade games, and a casino. An overly ornate Victorian ballroom hosts sedately dancing senior citizens during the day and live swing band performances at night (8pm). Towerworld's circus, named the UK's best, runs up to four shows per day and features mesmerizing tightrope walking, dance, and stunt acts in a rather gaudy and amateur performance arena. Mooky the Clown was also voted Britain's best. *(☎ 622 242. Open May-Oct. daily 10am-11pm; Nov.-Apr. 10am-6pm. Easter-Oct. £11, concessions £7; Nov.-Easter £6, children £4. Tickets allow admission all day.)*

THE ILLUMINATIONS. Blackpool, the first electric town in Britain, consummates its love affair with bright lights in the orgiastic Illuminations. The annual display takes place over 5 mi. of the Promenade from September to early November. In a colossal waste of electricity, 72 mi. of cables light up the tower, the promenade, star-encased faces of Hollywood actors, corporate emblems, and garish placards.

NIGHTLIFE. Between North and Central Piers, Blackpool's famous **Golden Mile** shines with more neon than gold, hosting scores of sultry theaters, cabaret bars, and bingo halls. Blackpool's two most frequented clubs are on the Promenade. **Heaven & Hell** (☎ 625 118), on Bank Hey St., is one block south of the Tower, and **Waterfront & Time,** 168-170 Promenade (☎ 292 900), is much farther north at the corner of the Promenade and Springfield Rd. Cover charges rarely exceed £4.

PEAK DISTRICT NATIONAL PARK

Named Britain's first national park in 1951, the Peak District boasts 555 sq. mi. of ambitious slopes. Devoid of mountains, the area derives its name from the Old English *peac*, meaning "hill." In the **Dark Peak** area to the north, deep groughs (gullies) gouge the hard peat moorland below gloomy cliffs, while friendlier footpaths wicker the rocky hillsides and village clusters of the **Northern Peak** area. The rolls of the southern **White Peak** cradle abandoned millstones and stately country homes. A green cushion between the hard industrial giants of Manchester, Sheffield, and Nottingham, the park serves as playground for its urban neighbors. Trampled trails attest to the Peaks' popularity—20 million visitors stop by each year. The southern regions accommodate hikers with gentler terrain and better transport links, but solitude-seekers should point their compasses toward the bleaker northern moors, beyond the reaches of commuter railways.

▐ TRANSPORTATION

Trains (☎ (08457) 484 950) seem intimidated by the park's rustic splendor: only three lines enter its boundaries, and only one dares to cross. One train travels from **Derby** to **Matlock,** on the park's southeastern edge (M-Sa 13-14 per day, Su 6 per day). Another runs from **Manchester** to **Buxton** (1hr., every hr., £5.70). The **Hope Valley line** (1½hr.; M-Sa 15-17 per day, Su 9 per day) goes from Manchester across the park via **Edale** (£6.70), **Hope** (near Castleton), and **Hathersage,** terminating in **Sheffield** (£11). Both lines from Manchester enter the park at **New Mills**—the Buxton line at Newtown Station and the Hope Valley line at Central Station. A 20min. signposted walk separates the stations.

A sturdy pair of legs is more than sufficient for inter-village journeys, but if you must depend upon the rare train or the infrequent bus, Derbyshire County Council's *Peak District Timetable* (60p) is invaluable. The timetable includes all bus and train routes as well as a large map and information on various day-long bus tickets, cycle hire, hostels, TICs, and hospitals.

Buses make a noble effort to connect the scattered towns of the Peak District, and **Traveline** (☎ (0870) 608 2608) offers solutions and sympathy. Coverage of many routes actually improves on Sundays, especially in summer. **Trent** (☎ (01773) 712 2765) bus TP, the "Transpeak," winds for 3hr. between **Manchester** and **Nottingham,** stopping at Buxton, Bakewell, Matlock, Derby, and other towns in between. **First PMT** (☎ (01782) 207 999) X18 runs from **Sheffield** to **Bakewell** (45min., M-Sa 5 per day) and **Buxton** (1¼hr., M-Sa 5 per day) en route to **Keele** (3¼hr.; M-Sa 5 per day, Su 4 per day). **First Mainline** (☎ (01709) 515 151) #272 and **Stagecoach East Midland** (☎ (01246) 211 007) #273 and 274 both reach **Castleton** from **Sheffield** (40-55min.; 15 per day, Su 12 per day). Stagecoach also runs between **Sheffield** and **Buxton** via **Eyam** (#65-66; 1¼hr.; M-Sa 5 per day, Su 3 per day) and from **Bakewell** to **Castleton** (#173; 45min.; M-Sa 4 per day, Su 3 per day).

Peak District National Park

⌂ **YHA Hostels**

If you're going to use public transport, pick one of the half-dozen bargain day tickets available; they're clearly explained in the *Timetables* booklet, and several have their own brochures at the TIC. The best deal is the **Derbyshire Wayfarer** (£7.25, concessions £3.65, families £12), which allows one day of train and bus travel through the Peak District north to Sheffield and south to Derby. The plain **Wayfarer** (£7.50/£3.75/£12), covers one day's unlimited travel within Greater Manchester and the Peak District as far east as Matlock (including Buxton, Bakewell, Castleton, Edale, and Eyam). Both passes are sold at the Manchester train stations and at National Park Information Centres (NPICs).

◪ PRACTICAL INFORMATION

Daytime facilities in the Peak District generally stay open through the winter due to the proximity of large cities. Some B&Bs and youth hostels welcome travelers until December. Most TICs book accommodations for a 10% deposit.

NATIONAL PARK INFORMATION CENTRES
The **Peak District National Park Office,** Aldern House, Barlow Rd., Bakewell, Derbyshire (☎(01629) 816 200; www.peakdistrict-npa.gov.uk) is a useful contact. All NPICs carry detailed walking guides and provide fun facts on the park.

Bakewell: Old Market Hall (☎(01629) 813 227; fax 814 782), at Bridge St. From the bus stop, walk a block down Bridge St. with the Rutland Arms hotel behind you and Bath Gardens on your left. Doubles as the TIC. Good selection of maps and books accommodations. Open Mar.-Oct. daily 9:30am-5:30pm; Nov.-Feb. 10am-5pm.

Castleton: Buxton Rd. (☎/fax (01433) 620 679). From the bus stop, follow the road past the post office into town and look right. Open Apr.-Oct. daily 10am-1pm and 2-5:30pm; Nov.-Mar. Sa-Su 10am-5pm.

Edale: (☎(01433) 670 207; fax 670 216), Fieldhead, between the rail station and village. Open Apr.-Oct. daily 9am-1pm and 2-5:30pm; Nov.-Mar. closes at 5pm.

Fairholmes: (☎(01433) 650 953), Upper Derwent Valley, near Derwent Dam. Open Apr.-Oct. daily 9:30am-5pm; Nov.-Mar. Sa-Su 9:30am-4:30pm.

TOURIST INFORMATION CENTRES
Ashbourne: 13 The Market Pl. (☎(01335) 343 666; fax 300 638). Open Mar.-Oct. daily 9:30am-5:30pm; Nov.-Feb. M-Sa 10am-4pm.

Buxton: The Crescent (☎(01298) 25106). Open Mar.-Aug. daily 9:30am-5:30pm; Sept. 9:30am-5pm; Oct.-Feb. noon-4pm.

Matlock: Crown Square (☎(01629) 583 388). Open Mar.-Oct. daily 9:30am-5pm; Nov.-Feb. 10am-4pm.

Matlock Bath: The Pavilion (☎(01629) 55082), along the main road. Open Mar.-Oct. daily 9:30am-5pm; Nov.-Feb. Sa-Su 10am-4pm, though hours vary.

◪ ACCOMMODATIONS

NPICs and TICs distribute free park-wide and regional accommodations guides; a camping guide costs 30p. **B&Bs** are plentiful and cheap (from £15 in the countryside, from £20 in towns), as are **hostels** (around £8). **Bakewell** and **Matlock Bath** are particularly well stocked with B&Bs. Most hostels are not open every day of the week. Many farmers allow **camping** on their land, sometimes for a small fee; remember to ask first and leave the site as you found it.

YHA HOSTELS

The Peak District has almost 20 hostels, many of which are listed below, but don't let numbers fool you—most fill quickly with enthusiastic school groups, so call ahead to reserve a space. Hostels lie within a day's hike of one another and sell maps detailing routes to neighboring hostels. Alternatively, the *Peak District Timetables* (60p at TICs) lists both YHAs and the bus services to them. Unless noted, the hostels serve meals and have a 10am-5pm lockout and 11pm curfew. Most offer a £1 **student discount.** Three of the smaller ones (Bretton, Langsett, and Shining Cliff) book through the central **YHA Diary** office (☎(01629) 592 707); only call the hostels directly for general information or for lodging within the following week.

Bakewell: Fly Hill (☎/fax (01629) 812 313). A 5min. walk from the town center. A homely hostel with 28 beds, kind staff, board games, and huge meals. Open Mar.-Oct. M-Sa; Nov.-Feb. daily. Dorms £10.25, under 18 £7. ❷

Bretton: (☎(01433) 631 856). Self-catering hostel 2 mi. from Eyam atop Eyam Edge (1250 ft.). Take bus #65-66 to Foolow. Face the pub and follow the sign to Bretton up the hill on the left. A heck of a view. Open mid-July to Aug. daily; Sept.-Oct. and Easter to mid-July F-Sa. Dorms £8.75, under 18 £6. ❶

Buxton: Sherbrook Lodge, Harpur Hill Rd. (☎/fax (01298) 22287). From the train station, follow Terrace Rd. as it becomes London Rd.; turn right at the sign (25min.). If your pack's too heavy, take bus #185 or 186 toward Harpur Hill (5min., 2 per hr.). Open Apr.-Oct. M-Sa; Nov.-Dec. M and Th-Su; Feb.-Mar. F-Sa. Dorms £8.75, under 18 £6. ❶

Castleton: Castleton Hall (☎(01433) 620 235). Pretty country house and attached vicarage in the heart of town. The vicarage has nicer rooms with baths and no curfew. Internet access. Very popular—book 2-3 weeks ahead. Open Feb. to late Dec. daily. Dorms £11.50, under 18 £8.25; vicarage dorms £14, under 18 £10. ❷

Crowden-in-Longdendale: (☎/fax (01457) 852 135), Crowden, Hadfield, Hyde. Take bus #350 to Crowden (3 per day); the hostel is 200 yd. away. Open Apr.-Aug. Th-Tu; Sept.-Oct. F-Tu; early and mid-Nov. F-Sa. Dorms £9.50, under 18 £6.75. ❶

Edale: (☎(01433) 670 302; fax 670 243), Rowland Cote, Nether Booth, Edale, 1 mi. east of Edale village. From the train station, turn right and then left onto the main road; follow to Nether Booth, where a sign points the way. Includes a climbing tower. No lockout. Open year-round. Dorms £11.25, under 18 £8. ❶

Elton: Elton Old Hall, Main St. (☎/fax (01629) 650 394). Take bus #172, which runs from Matlock to Bakewell, to the Elton stop (M-Sa 7-9 per day). Self-catering. Open Easter-Oct. Tu-Sa. Dorms £8.75, under 18 £6. ❶

Eyam: (☎(01433) 630 335; fax 639 202), Hawkhill Rd. Walk down the main road from the square, pass the church, and look right for the sign. With turret and oaken door, it's more castle than hostel. Internet access. Open Aug. daily; Sept.-Oct. and mid-Feb. to July M-Sa; Nov. F-Sa. Dorms £11.25, under 18 £8. ❷

Hartington Hall: Hall Bank (☎(01298) 84223), Hartington. From the A515, turn at Ashbowl and follow signs; no bus service. 122 beds in a 17th-century manor house. Bonnie Prince Charlie once slept here, *sans* YHA membership. Internet, laundry, restaurant, TV lounge, and playground. Open year-round. Dorms £14, under 18 £9.50. ❷

Hathersage: Castleton Rd. (☎(01433) 650 493). Stone building with white-framed windows and creeping ivy. Open Apr.-Oct. M-Sa. Dorms £10.25, under 18 £7. ❷

Langsett: (☎(01226) 761 548). 5 mi. from Penistone. Be grateful for Yorkshire Traction buses #23, 23a, 24, and 24a, which stop outside the hostel on their circular routes to and from Barnsley (M-Sa every hr., Su 15 per day). Self-catering. Open mid-July to Aug. daily; Sept. to mid-July F-Sa. Dorms £8.75, under 18 £6. ❶

Matlock: 40 Bank Rd. (☎(01629) 582 983). Conveniently located in a regional train and bus hub. Rooms named after popular Peak sights. Internet and laundry facilities. No lockout. Open Feb.-Oct. daily; Nov.-Jan. Tu-Sa. Dorms £11.25, under 18 £8. ❷

Ravenstor: (☎(01298) 871 826), ½ mi. from Millers Dale. Bus #65 (Buxton-Sheffield) and #66 (Buxton-Chesterfield) will stop here (both M-Sa 10 per day, Su 7 per day). Includes Internet access, bar, TV, and games room. Open mid-July to Aug. daily; Feb. to mid-July and Sept.-Nov. F-Sa and school holidays. Dorms £11.25, under 18 £8. ❷

Shining Cliff: (☎/fax (01629) 760 827), Shining Cliff Woods, 2 mi. from Ambergate. 1 mi. from the road in a pristine forest; call for directions. Trains and buses reach Ambergate. A poor local woman raised her family in a tree near the hostel, reportedly giving rise to "rock-a-bye, baby, in the treetop." Self-catering. Bring a flashlight. Open mid-July to Aug., Easter holiday, and bank holidays only. Dorms £8.75, under 18 £6.10. ❶

Youlgreave: Fountain Sq. (☎/fax (01629) 636 518). Bus #170 from Bakewell stops nearby. Open Apr.-Oct. M-Sa; Nov. to mid-Dec. and Feb.-Mar. F-Sa. Dorms £11.50, under 18 £8.25. ❷

CAMPING BARNS

The 13 YHA-operated **camping barns** ❶ are simple shelters, providing sleeping platform, water tap, and toilet (£3.60 per person); bring a sleeping bag and camping equipment. You must book and pay ahead through the **Camping Barns Reservation Office,** 6 King St., Clitheroe, Lancashire BB7 2EP (☎(01200) 420 102; fax 420 103; campbarnsyha@enterprise.net). You can pay over the phone with a credit card, or they'll hold your reservation for five days while you mail a booking form; forms are available in camping barn booklets, distributed free at NPICs and available on the YHA website (www.yha.org.uk). Barns can be found in: **Abney,** between Eyam and Castleton; **Alstonefield,** between Dovedale and Manifold Valley; **Birchover,** near Matlock off the B5056; **Butterton** (two barns), near the southern end of the park, along the Manifold track; **Edale** village; **Gee** (formerly Upper Booth), near Edale; **Losehill,** near Castleton; **Middleton-by-Youlgreave; Nab End,** in Hollinsclough; **One Ash Grange,** in Monyash; **Taddington,** on Main Rd.; and **Underbank,** in Wildboarclough.

🔏 HIKING AND BIKING

The central park is marvelous territory for rambling. Settlement is sparser and buses fewer north of Edale in the land of the Kinder Scout plateau, the great Derwent reservoirs, and the gritty cliffs and peat moorlands. From Edale, the **Pennine Way** (see p. 407) runs north to Kirk Yetholm, across the Scottish border. Be advised that warm clothing and the customary supplies and precautions should be taken (see **Wilderness Safety,** p. 49). The land is privately owned, so be respectful and stay on designated paths. Ramblers' guidebooks and the park's invaluable free newspaper, the *Peakland Post*, are available at NPICs (see p. 376).

The park authority operates six **Cycle Hire Centres.** They can be found in **Ashbourne** (☎(01335) 343 156), on Mapleton Ln.; **Derwent** (☎(01433) 651 261), near the Fairholmes NPIC; **Hayfield** (☎(01663) 746 222), on Station Rd. in the Sett Valley; **Middleton Top** (☎(01629) 823 204), at the visitor center; **Parsley Hay** (☎(01298) 84493), in Buxton; and **Waterhouses** (☎(01538) 308 609), in the Old Station Car Park between Ashbourne and Leek on the A523. (£8 per 3hr., £12 per day. £20 deposit. Tandem bike £22 per 3hr., £100 deposit. Helmet included. 10% discount for YHA members, seniors, and Wayfarer ticket holders. Most open Apr.-Sept. daily 10am-6pm; Oct.-Mar. call for hours.) *Peak Cycle Hire*, available at NPICs, includes opening hours and locations.

CASTLETON ☎ 01433

For such a small town, Castleton (pop. 705) lays claim to an unnatural amount of natural beauty—drawing an equally unnatural number of tourists. The town's main attraction is the **caverns** carved by Ice Age rivers, once mined for lead and later for Blue John, a semi-precious mineral found only in these hills. Buses don't serve the caves on weekdays, but on weekends #260 makes a loop between Edale and Castleton, stopping at Blue John, Speedwell, and Treak Cliff Caverns (Sa-Su 8-9 per day). The entrances are all within walking distance of one another. As you leave town on Cross St. (which becomes Buxton Rd.), formerly the A625, you'll pass a large sign for Peak Cavern. Road signs for the others appear within 10min.

Although it's not the first on the road out of Castleton, **⬛Treak Cliff Cavern** is the one most worth visiting, with Blue John seams coursing through its ceilings and fantastical chambers of stalagmites and stalagtites. The tour is excellent. (☎ 620 571. Admission by 40min. tour only, every 15-30min. Open Easter-Oct. daily 10am-4:45pm; Nov.-Feb. 10am-3:20pm; Mar.-Easter 10am-4:20pm. £5.50, seniors £5, students and YHA members £4.50, children £3.) Just outside Castleton, in the gorge beneath the castle ruins, **Peak Cavern** features the largest aperture in Britain. Decorously known in the 18th century as the "Devil's Arse," the cavern now features tours by guides pale and wry-humored from long days in Old Harry's Sphincter. (☎ 620 285. Open Easter-Oct. daily 10am-5pm; Nov.-Easter Sa-Su 10am-5pm; last tour 4pm. 1hr. tours £5.50, concessions £4.50, children £3.50, families £16.) **Speedwell** and **Blue John** involve very steep stair-climbs, and some consider the tours inferior. Be advised that all caverns are the temperature of your average refrigerator.

William Peveril, son of William the Conqueror, chose a visually arresting and defensively ideal setting in which to build **Peveril Castle**. Not much of the 11th- and 12th-century edifice remains, but the ruins, including a hollowed keep, crown a dramatic peak overlooking the town. (☎ 620 613. Open Apr.-Oct. daily 10am-6pm; Nov.-Mar. W-Su 10am-4pm. £2.50, concessions £1.90, children £1.30.)

Castleton lies 2 mi. west of the **Hope** train station (don't ask for Castleton Station, or you'll end up in a suburb of Manchester), and **buses** arrive from Sheffield, Buxton, and Bakewell (see p. 374). Hikers looking for a challenge can set off southward from town on the 26 mi. **Limestone Way Trail** to Matlock. Castleton's **NPIC** (see p. 376) stocks maps and brochures on local walks (most under £1). The nearest **bank** lies 6 mi. east in **Hathersage;** the Cheshire Cheese Hotel, How Ln., has an **ATM**. Ramblers preparing to assault the moorlands should visit the **Peveril Outdoor Shop,** off the marketplace by the hostel. (☎ 620 320. Open M-F 9:30am-5pm, Sa-Su 9:30am-6pm.) The **post office**, How Ln., near the bus stop, is in a convenience store. (☎ 620 241. Open M-Tu and Th-F 9am-1pm and 2-5:30pm, W 9am-12:30pm, Sa 9am-12:30pm.) **Post Code:** S33 8WJ.

The super **YHA Castleton** and its torrential showers wait by the castle entrance (see p. 377). Those seeking B&B privacy can try ivy-walled **Cryer House ❸**, Castle St., where Mr. and Mrs. Skelton keep two lovely rooms and a tea shop. (☎/fax 620 244; FleeSkel@aol.com. £24.50 per person.)

EDALE AND THE NORTHERN DARK PEAK AREA ☎ 01433

The deep dale of the River Noe cradles a collection of hamlets known as **Edale.** The area offers little in the way of civilization besides a church, rail stop, cafe, pub, school, and hostel. Its environs, however, are among the most spectacular in northern England. The northern **Dark Peak** area is wild hill country, with vast moors like **Kinder Scout** and **Bleaklow** left undisturbed by motor traffic. In these mazes of black peat hags and groughs, paths are scarce and weather-worn. The rare town huddles in the crook of a valley, with provisions and shelter for weary walkers. Less experienced hikers should stick to Edale and southern paths.

On summer weekends Edale brims with hikers and campers preparing to tackle the **Pennine Way** (which begins with a 3- to 4-day stretch through the Peaks; see p. 407), or to trek one of the shorter (1½-8½ mi.) trails detailed in the National Park Authority's *8 Walks Around Edale* (£1.20). The relatively undemanding 3½ mi. path to **Castleton** begins 70 yd. from the TIC down the road toward the town and affords a breathtaking view of the Edale Valley (Dark Peak) and the Hope Valley (White Peak). A flagstone detour with still more spectacular views runs along the ridge between these valleys to **Mam Tor**, a well-touristed decaying Iron Age fort. The hill is known locally as the "shivering mountain" for its shale sides; one such shudder left the road below permanently blocked. Cliffs on three sides beckon fearless hang-gliders from near and far.

Edale lies on the **Hope Valley rail line** and is served by trains every 1-2hr. (from **Manchester** 45min.; **Sheffield** 35min.). Stop at the huge **NPIC** (see p. 376), near the train station, for weather forecasts and training with a map and compass. Unless you reserve ahead, your tent could be your best friend in this town; the popular **YHA Edale** (p. 377) is the only place to stay. Campers can try **Fieldhead ❶**, behind the TIC. (☎670 386. £3.50 per person, children £2.75, cars £1.50. Showers 50p.)

BAKEWELL ☎01629

Fifteen miles southwest of Sheffield and 30 mi. southeast of Manchester, Bakewell makes the best spot from which to explore the region and to transfer to connecting bus routes. Located near several scenic walks through the **White Peaks**, the town is best known as the birthplace of **Bakewell pudding,** created in the 1860s when a flustered cook at the Rutland Arms Hotel tried to make a tart by pouring an egg mixture over strawberry jam instead of mixing it into the dough. Bakewell's stone buildings are huddled around a handful of narrow streets and a central square bursting with flowers, wrapped by a lazy bend in the River Wye. Ducks scuttle beneath the five graceful arches of the **medieval bridge** (c. 1300). On the hill above town, **All Saints Church** lies in a crowded park of gravestones and carven cross fragments. In the south transept, three very curious human gargoyles guard the remains of Anglo-Saxon and Norman headstones. Nearby, a 16th-century timber-frame house encased in stone shelters the **Old House Museum,** which displays a modest collection of 19th-century toys, blacksmith equipment, and early 20th-century cameras. (☎813 165. Open July-Aug. daily 11am-4pm; Apr.-June and Sept.-Oct. 1:30-4pm. £2.50, children £1, under 5 free.)

Buses arrive in Rutland Sq. from: **Manchester** via **Buxton** (TP, 1½hr., 6 per day); **Matlock**, site of the nearest train station (#172, R61, TP; 40-50min.; 1-3 per hr.); **Sheffield** (X18 and 240; 1hr.; M-Sa 13-14 per day, Su 10-12 per day). Bakewell's **NPIC**, at the intersection of Bridge St. and Market St., doubles as a **tourist information centre** (see p. 376). Other services include: **HSBC bank,** Rutland Sq. (open M-F 9:30am-5pm); **camping supplies** at Yeoman's, 1 Royal Oak Pl., off Matlock St. (☎815 371; open M-Sa 9am-5:30pm, Su 10am-5pm); **Bakewell Launderama,** Water St., off Rutland Sq. (open daily 7:30am-7pm, last wash 6pm); the **police,** Granby Rd. (☎812 504); free **Internet access** at **Bakewell Public Library,** Orme Court, above the swimming pool (☎812 267; open M-Tu and Th 9:30am-5pm, W and F 9:30am-7pm, Sa 9:30am-4pm); and the **post office,** in the Spar on Granby Rd. (☎815 112; open M-F 8:30am-6pm, Sa 8:30am-3pm). **Post Code:** DE45 1ES.

The comfy **YHA Bakewell,** on Fly Hill, is a short walk from the TIC (see p. 377). **B&Bs** are plentiful considering the village's size, but expect to pay about £20 per person; *The Derbyshire Dales Accommodation Guide,* free at the TIC, lists B&Bs in the area. Truly elegant stays await at the **Rutland Arms Hotel ❹**, The Square, where Austen, Byron, and Wordsworth all rested their pens. Beds have no right to be so soft, and the breakfasts are amazing. (☎812 812. Singles £47-54;

doubles £79-89. Special rates sometimes available.) Entire villages pour into Bakewell's **market,** held since 1330, off Bridge St. (Open M 9am-4pm; follow the doomed mooing of 3000 cows.) The **Extra Foodstore** peddles groceries at the corner of Granby Rd. and Market St. (Open M-Sa 8am-10pm, Su 10am-4pm.) Cafes aim to cash in on the town's confectionery reputation. **The Old Original Bakewell Pudding Shop ❶,** Rutland Sq., sells sinful desserts under a vaulted ceiling. Skip lunch and order the full afternoon tea (£5), which includes sandwiches, two fruit scones with jam and cream, and a Bakewell pudding. (☎812 193. Open July-Aug. daily 8:30am-9pm; Sept.-June M-Th 9am-6pm, F-Sa 8:30am-9pm.) Enjoy mouthwatering panini (£4.50) or sandwiches (£3.50) under swooping, leafy grapevines at the **Treeline Cafe ❶,** Diamond Court, Water St. (☎813 749. Open Easter-Oct. daily 10am-5:30pm; Nov.-Easter F-W 10am-5:30pm.)

NOT FROM NOTTINGHAM Robin Hood fans may have thought that Kevin Costner's portrayal of the Prince of Thieves as some sort of American prospector was a unique travesty, but Kev isn't the only one confused about the origin of Robin and his merry men. The band of crusading ruffians didn't come from Nottingham, as often supposed, but from the Peak District, a more plebeian base for sporadic and fruitful strikes on nearby Nottingham. "Little John" (the study of his remains has proved him a physical giant) is buried in Hathersage, where a corner pub is now emblazoned with his name.

🗺 DAYTRIPS FROM BAKEWELL

🏰 CHATSWORTH HOUSE

Take bus #179 directly to the house (2 per day) or ask the TIC about other buses that stop close by. ☎(01246) 565 300. 1½hr. audio tour £3. Open Apr.-Dec. daily 11am-5:30pm, last admission 4:30pm. £7, concessions £5.50, children £3, families £17.25. Gardens only £4.50/£3.50/£2/£11.

Near Bakewell unfold the 100 breathtaking acres of Chatsworth House, home of the Duke and Duchess of Devonshire. The rolling grounds beg for a walk, with their cascade fountain—each step designed to make a different sound—hedge maze, and lagoon. The house's 26 ornate rooms are decorated with works of art, including late 17th-century paintings by Laguerre detailing the life of Julius Caesar. Between 1570 and 1581, Mary stayed in the **Queen of Scots Rooms** while under the custody of the 6th Earl of Shrewsbury; admission is an extra £1.

HADDON HALL

From Bakewell, walk down Matlock St. as it becomes Haddon Rd. and then the A6, or take one of the buses that stops outside the gate (#171, 172, 179, TP, and others; ask the TIC for details). ☎812 855. Open Apr.-Sept. daily 10:30am-5pm; Oct. M-Th 10:30am-5pm. £6.75, seniors £5.75, children £3.50, families £18.

Visitors may recognize the Duke of Rutland's Haddon Hall, 2 mi. southwest of Bakewell, as the setting of several movies, including *The Princess Bride,* Franco Zefferelli's 1996 *Jane Eyre,* and *Elizabeth.* The house lends itself to cinematic romance because it has been little altered since the reign of Henry VIII, preserving the wood-lined Long Gallery and frescoed chapel. Think about springing £2.50 for a guidebook, as the infrequent wall text tends to be unsatisfying.

EYAM

Take bus #175 from Bakewell, stand D (20min., 3-4 per day) or #65/66 from Buxton (40min., M-Sa 11 per day).

Just 5 mi. north of Bakewell, the hamlet of Eyam (EE-yum) underwent a self-imposed quarantine when the plague spread here from London in 1665, during which a supposed 259 of its 350 residents died a bubonic death. Plaques on old houses tally the number that succumbed in each, and makeshift graves lie in strangely vibrant gardens (victims were buried quickly to prevent the disease's spread). The first three victims perished in the flower-ringed **Plague Cottages,** Edgeview Rd. The tiny **Eyam Museum,** on Hawkhill Rd., commemorates all the grisly details, including touching final letters and heroic stories. (☎(01433) 631 371. Open Apr.-Oct. Tu-Su 10am-4:30pm. ₤1.50, concessions ₤1, families ₤4.25.) **Eyam Hall,** on Edgeview Rd., 100 yd. west of the church, traces the owner's family history in a 17th-century manor house. The hall boasts a wall-to-wall tapestry room, an eight-line love stanza carved into the library window, and a 1675 pop-up human anatomy textbook. (☎(01433) 631 976. Open June-Aug. W-Th and Su 11am-4pm. ₤4.50, concessions ₤4, children ₤3.25, families ₤14.50.) Eyam's **YHA hostel** plants its flag 800m above the town on Hawkhill Rd. (see p. 377).

CUMBRIA

LAKE DISTRICT NATIONAL PARK

There are temples of Nature, temples built by the Almighty, which have still higher claim to be left unviolated.
—Wordsworth, on the preservation of the Lakes

Quite possibly the most lovely place in England, the Lake District owes its beauty to a thorough glacier-gouging during the last ice age. Jagged peaks and windswept fells stand in desolate splendor. Water trickles through them as hillside torrents and gurgling peat-filled rivers, pooling into serene mountain lakes. The shores are busy, but less packed than one would expect for a region where tourism employs 85% of the local population—and has since the Lake District became England's largest national park in 1951. Little development blights the landscape: on only one lake, Windermere, can visitors zoom around in noisy motorboats. Though summertime hikers, bikers, and boaters almost equal sheep in number (and with four million sheep, that's quite a feat), there is always some lonely upland fell or quiet cove where your footprints will seem the first for generations.

✈ INTERCITY TRANSPORTATION

Trains: By train, **Oxenholme,** on the West Coast Mainline, is the primary gateway to the lakes. Trains (☎(08457) 484 950) to Oxenholme from: **Birmingham** (2½hr., 1-2 per hr., £41.50); **Edinburgh** (2½hr., 6 per day, £41.50); **London Euston** (4-5hr.; M-Sa 16 per day, Su 11 per day; £101); **Manchester Piccadilly** (1½hr.; M-F 6 per day, Sa 5 per day, Su 7 per day; £17). A branch line covers the 10 mi. to **Windermere** from Oxenholme (20min., every hr., £3.10). Direct service runs to Windermere from **Manchester Piccadilly** (2hr., 3-4 per day, £19.80).

Buses: National Express (☎(08705) 808 080) arrives in **Windermere** from **Birmingham** (4½hr., 1 per day, £24.50) and **London** (7½hr., 1 per day, £26), continuing north through **Ambleside** and **Grasmere** to **Keswick. Stagecoach** has 2-3 buses a day connecting **Keswick** with **Carlisle** (1¼hr.).

⌷ LOCAL TRANSPORTATION

Public Buses: Stagecoach in Cumbria is the primary operator of bus services in the region. A complete timetable (*The Lakeland Explorer*) is available free from TICs. Major routes include: **"Lakeslink"** bus #555 from **Kendal** to **Keswick**, stopping at **Windermere, Ambleside,** and **Grasmere** (M-Sa 11 per day; Su 5 per day; £4), and the open-top **"Lakeland Experience"** bus #599 between **Bowness** and **Grasmere** (30min.; Apr.-Oct.; M-Sa 11 per day, Su 5 per day). An **Explorer** ticket offers unlimited travel on all area Stagecoach buses. The 4-day pass usually saves money even for 2- or 3-day stays. 1-day £7, children £5; 4-day £16/£12. Explorer tickets may be purchased on board buses; 4-day also at TICs. Also consult *Getting Around Cumbria and the Lake District* (free from TICs) or **Traveline** ☎ (0870) 608 2608.

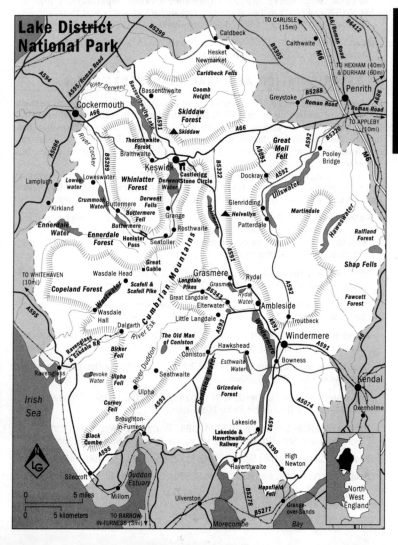

National Trust Shuttles: On summer Su, the National Trust operates buses to popular sights not ordinarily accessible by public transport. ☎(017687) 73780 for more info.

YHA Shuttle: The **YHA Ambleside** provides a minibus service (☎(015394) 32304) for hikers (or just their packs) between hostels in **Coniston Holly How, Elterwater, Grasmere, Hawkshead, Langdale,** and **Windermere** (2 per day, £2.50; schedules available at hostels), plus a daily service to **Patterdale.** Trips from Windermere train station to Windermere and Ambleside hostels are free.

Tours: For those who wish to explore with minimal effort, **Mountain Goat** (☎(015394) 45161), downhill from the TIC in Windermere, does the climbing for you in off-the-beaten-track, half- and full-day themed bus tours (£22-26). They also have an office in Keswick (☎(017687) 73962). Windermere's **Lakes Supertours,** 1 High St. (☎(015394) 42751), in the Lakes Hotel, runs similar half- and full-day tours, with witty local drivers (£17-27.50). Free pickup in the Bowness-Ambleside area.

Boats: Boat transport is available on **Windermere** (p. 387), **Coniston Water** (p. 390), **Derwentwater** (p. 392), and **Ullswater** (p. 394).

■ ⚡ ❷ ORIENTATION AND PRACTICAL INFORMATION

The major lakes diverge like spokes of a wheel from **Grasmere,** south of **Keswick** and north of **Ambleside** on the A591. **Derwentwater** is one of the most beautiful lakes, **Windermere** the largest (and most developed), and western lakes like **Buttermere** and **Crummock Water** the most bewitchingly wild. The towns of Windermere/Bowness, Ambleside, Grasmere, and Keswick make good touring bases, but stay elsewhere and you'll have more elbow room.

The following **National Park Information Centres (NPICs)** dispense information and maps, secure fishing licenses, book accommodations (10% deposit for local; non-local an additional £3), offer guided walks, and often exchange currency.

National Park Visitor Centre: (☎(015394) 46601). In Brockhole, halfway between Windermere and Ambleside. Most buses stop here. An introduction to the Lake District with exhibits, talks, films, and special events in this recently renovated house. Open Easter-Oct. daily 10am-5pm, plus most weekends in winter.

Ambleside Waterhead: On the pier (☎(015394) 32729; fax 31728). From town, walk south on Lake Rd. or Borrans Rd. Open Easter-Oct. daily 9:30am-5:30pm.

Bowness Bay: Glebe Rd. (☎(015394) 42895). Open July-Aug. daily 9am-6pm; Apr.-June and Sept.-Oct. 9am-5:30pm; Nov.-Mar. F-Su 10am-4pm.

Coniston: Ruskin Ave. (☎(015394) 41533; fax 41802), behind the Tilberthwaite Ave. bus stop. Open Easter-Oct. daily 9:30am-5:30pm; Nov.-Easter Sa-Su 10am-3:30pm.

Glenridding: Main Carpark (☎(017684) 82414). Open Easter-Oct. daily 9am-6pm; Nov.-Easter F-Su 9:30am-3:30pm.

Grasmere: Redbank Rd. (☎(015394) 35245; fax 35057). Open Easter-Oct. daily 9:30am-5:30pm; Nov.-Easter Sa-Su 10am-4pm.

Hawkshead: Main Carpark (☎(015394) 36525). Open July-Aug. daily 9:30am-6pm; Easter-June and Sept.-Oct. 9:30am-5:30pm; Nov.-Easter Sa-Su 10am-3:30pm.

Keswick: Moot Hall, Market Sq. (☎(017687) 72645). Open Sept.-July 9:30am-5:30pm.

Pooley Bridge: The Square (☎(017684) 86530). Open Easter-Oct. daily 10am-5pm.

Seatoller Barn: Borrowdale (☎(017687) 77294), at the foot of Honister Pass. Open Easter-Oct. daily 10am-5pm.

ACCOMMODATIONS

Though B&Bs line the streets, and there's a hostel around every bend, lodgings in the Lake District fill in July and August; reserve well in advance for weekend stays. Hostels, in particular, can be full all summer long; call ahead. TICs and NPICs book rooms. Twenty-six **YHA hostels** provide accommodations in the park, but can differ radically in facilities and style. Reception is usually closed 10am-5pm, though public areas and restrooms are accessible throughout the day. The **YHA shuttle** travels between the bigger hostels (see p. 383). YHA also operates 12 wilderness **camping barns** in the Lakes; to reserve call ☎017687 72645 or e-mail KeswickTIC@lake-district.gov.uk. **Campgrounds** are scattered throughout the park. The following is a selection of park hostels; see the YHA handbook or their website (www.yha.org.uk) for others.

■ **Ambleside:** Waterhead, Ambleside (☎(015394) 32304), 1 mi. south of Ambleside on the Windermere Rd. (A591), 3 mi. north of Windermere on the lake's northern shore. Bus #555 stops in front of this mother of all hostels. 245 beds in a superbly refurbished hotel. Distinctive country-club feel—you can even swim off the pier. Books tours, rents mountain bikes, and exchanges currency. Internet £2.50 per 30min. Mar.-Oct. no curfew; Nov.-Feb. midnight. Dorms £13.50, under 18 £9.50. ❷

Black Sail: Black Sail Hut, Ennerdale, Cleator (☎(0411) 108 450). Splendidly set in the hills, 3½ mi. from Seatoller. 18 beds. Outdoor showers; no heat or electricity in dorms. Open July-Aug. daily; Apr.-June and Sept.-Oct. Tu-Sa. Dorms £9.25, under 18 £6.50. ❶

Borrowdale: Longthwaite, Borrowdale (☎(0870) 770 5706). Take bus #79 from Keswick. Comfortable riverside hostel. Open mid-Feb. to Oct. daily; Nov. to mid-Feb. F-Sa. Dorms £11.25, under 18 £8. ❷

Buttermere: King George VI Memorial Hostel, Buttermere (☎(017687) 70245; fax 70231), ¼ mi. south of the village on the B5289. Tranquil setting with lounges, dining room, and kitchen. 70 beds. Lockout 10am-1pm. Open Apr.-Aug. daily; Sept.-Dec. and Feb.-Mar. Tu-Sa; Jan. F-Sa. Dorms £11.25, under 18 £8. ❷

Cockermouth: Double Mills, Cockermouth (☎/fax (01900) 822 561), in the town center, off Fern Bank at Parkside Ave. Converted 17th-century water mill. 28 beds. Open Apr.-Oct. daily. Dorms £8.75, under 18 £6. ❶

Coniston Coppermines: Coppermines House (☎/fax (015394) 41261), 1¼ mi. northwest of Coniston along the Churchbeck River. No need to venture into the hills; the rugged journey to the hostel is itself a scenic challenge. 28 basic beds in the mine manager's house, overlooking the water. Open June-Aug. daily; Apr.-May and Sept.-Oct. Tu-Sa. Dorms £9.50, under 18 £6.75. ❶

Coniston Holly How: Far End, Coniston (☎(015394) 41323), just north of the village at the junction of Hawkshead Rd. and Ambleside Rd. Modernized country house is a good base for walking and watersports. 60 beds. Curfew 11pm. Open Apr. and July-Sept. daily; May-June, Oct.-Nov., and mid-Jan. to Mar. F-Su. Dorms £10.25, under 18 £7. ❷

■ **Derwentwater:** Barrow House, Borrowdale (☎(017687) 77246; fax 77396), 2 mi. south of Keswick on the B5289; take bus #79. Worth the inconvenience to stay in this 90-bed, 200-year-old house with its own waterfall. Open Feb. to early Oct. daily; Jan.-Dec. F-Sa. Dorms £11.25, under 18 £8. ❷

Elterwater: (☎(0870) 770 5716). Farmhouse popular with walkers. Open Apr.-Sept. daily; Feb.-Mar. and Oct.-Dec. Tu-Sa; Jan. F-Sa. £10.25, under 18 £7. ❷

Eskdale: (☎(019467) 23219). In a quiet valley 1½ mi. east of Boot on the Ravenglass-Eskdale railway, adjacent to Hardknot Pass. 50 beds. Open July-Aug. daily; Apr.-June M-Sa; Mar. and Sept.-Oct. Tu-Sa. Dorms £10.25, under 18 £7. ❷

Grasmere: (☎(015394) 35316). 2 buildings. **Butterlip How,** 150 yd. down Easedale Rd. 80-bed Victorian house. Open Mar.-Oct. daily; Nov.-Feb. F-Sa. £12.75, under 18 £8.75. **Thorney How.** Follow Easedale Rd. ½ mi. and turn right at the fork; hostel is ¼ mi. down on the left. 48-bed farmhouse with a kindly staff. Open Apr.-Oct. daily; £10.25, under 18 £7. ❷

Hawkshead: Esthwaite Lodge (☎(015394) 36293), 1 mi. south of Hawkshead. Bus #505 from Ambleside stops at the village center. Follow Newby Bridge Rd. to this Regency mansion overlooking Esthwaite Water. Caters to families. 115 beds. Open Feb.-Oct. daily; Nov.-Dec. F-Sa. Dorms £11.25, under 18 £8. ❷

Helvellyn: Greenside, Glenridding. (☎(0870) 770 5862) 1½ mi. from Glenridding on a route toward Helvellyn. Open July-Aug. daily; mid-Feb. to Mar. and Sept.-Oct. Tu-Sa; Nov. and Jan. to mid-Feb. F-Sa; Apr.-June M-Sa. £10.25, under 18 £7. ❷

Honister Hause: (☎/fax (017687) 77267), near Seatoller. Gray building at the summit of imposing Honister Pass, 9 mi. south of Keswick. Bus #77 from Keswick (May-Oct.); #79 stops within 1½ mi. Continue along Honister Pass and follow the signs. 26 beds. Open June-Aug. daily; Apr.-May and Sept.-Oct. F-Tu. Dorms £9.50, under 18 £6.75. ❶

Keswick: Station Rd. (☎(017687) 72484). From the TIC, bear left down Station Rd.; YHA sign on the left. 91 beds in a former hotel with balconies over a river, clean rooms, and a decent kitchen. 6 showers, laundry facilities, TV, and game room. Curfew 11pm. Open year-round daily. Dorms £11.25, under 18 £8. ❷

Landgdale: High Close. Bookings through Ambleside YHA (see above). 1 mi. from Elterwater village. Victorian mansion in a beautiful setting. Open Mar.-Oct. F-Sa, daily in Aug. and select other times. £10.25, under 18 £7. ❷

Patterdale: (☎(017684) 82394). ¼ mi. south of Patterdale village, on the A592 to Kirkstone Pass. Open Apr.-Aug. daily; Sept.-Oct. and mid-Feb. to Mar. Th-M; Nov. to mid-Feb. F-Sa. £11.25, under 18 £8. ❷

Wastwater: Wasdale Hall, Wasdale (☎(019467) 26222; fax 26056), ½ mi. east of Nether Wasdale. A climber's paradise; 50 beds in a half-timbered house on the water. Open Apr.-Oct. daily; Nov.-Dec. F-Sa; Jan.-Mar. Th-M. Dorms £10.25, under 18 £7. ❷

Windermere: High Cross, Bridge Ln. (☎(015394) 43543), 1 mi. north of Windermere off the A591. Catch the YHA shuttle from the train station. Spacious, 73-bed house with panoramic views. Mountain bikes for rent. Internet £6 per hr. Open mid-Feb. to Oct. daily; Nov. to mid-Feb. F-Sa. Dorms £11.25, under 18 £8. ❷

⚠ HIKING, BIKING, AND CLIMBING

Outdoor enthusiasts run (and walk and climb) rampant in the Lakes. NPICs have guidebooks for all occasions—mountain-bike trails, pleasant family walks, tough climbs, and hikes ending at pubs. Most also offer guided walks throughout the summer. Hostels are also an excellent source of information, with large maps and posters on the walls and free advice from experienced staff.

The Lake District offers some of the best **hiking** in Britain. While there are many trails, be aware that they can be hard to follow—even on popular routes. If you plan to go on a long or difficult outing, check first with the Park Service, call **weather information** (24hr. ☎(017687) 75757; YHAs also post daily forecasts), and leave a route plan with your B&B proprietor or hostel warden before setting out. Steep slopes and reliably unreliable weather can quickly reduce visibility to 5 ft. A good map and compass (and the ability to use them) are necessities. Ordnance Survey Outdoor Leisure Maps #4-7 detail the four quadrants of the Lake District

(1:25,000; £6.50), while Landranger Maps #89-91 and 96-98 chart every hillock and bend in the road (1:50,000; £5.25).

The Lakes are also fine **cycling** country. Several long-distance routes (part of the National Cycling Network; ☎ (0117) 929 0888) traverse the park. There are excellent short routes, too; *Ordnance Survey One Day Cycle Rides in Cumbria* (£10) is a helpful guide. Bike rental is available in many towns, and staffers can often suggest routes. Any cyclist planning an extensive stay should consider investing in the *Ordnance Survey Cycle Tours* (£10), which provides detailed maps of on- and off-trail routes. The circular **Cumbria Cycle Way** tours some of Cumbria's less-traveled areas via a 259 mi. route from Carlisle in the north and around the park's outskirts. Pick up *The Cumbria Cycle Way* (£6) from a TIC for details.

The Lake District is popular for **rock climbing.** A good source for climbing info is **Rock & Run,** Fishereck Mill, Old Lake Road, Ambleside (☎ (15394) 32855).

WINDERMERE AND BOWNESS   ☎ 015394

The largest tourist center in the Lake District, Windermere and its sidekick, Bowness-on-Windermere (combined pop. 10,000), fill to the gills with vacationers in July and August when sailboats and water-skiers swarm the lake. Both towns are popular with families, as much for their year-round celebration of Peter Rabbit as for their gangs of belligerent swans.

NORTHWEST ENGLAND

█▐ TRANSPORTATION AND PRACTICAL INFORMATION. The **train station** and **bus depot** are in Windermere; Bowness, flanking the lake, is an easy 1½ mi. walk south. From the station, turn left onto High St., then right on Main St.; walk through town to New Rd., which becomes Lake Rd., leading pierward. **Bus #599** runs from the station to Bowness pier (3 per hr., £1). For information on getting to Windermere, see p. 382. Try **Windermere Taxis** (☎ 42355) for a cab, or rent bikes from **Country Lanes Cycle Hire,** at the station. (☎ (015394) 44544. £9 per half-day, £14 per day; £2 discount with train ticket. Open Easter-Oct. daily 9am-5:30pm.)

The Windermere **tourist information centre,** next to the train station, stocks guides to lake walks (30p), books National Express tickets, sells Stagecoach four-day tickets, books accommodations, and exchanges currency. (☎ 46499. Open July-Aug. daily 9am-7:30pm; Easter-June and Sept.-Oct. 9am-6pm; Nov.-Easter 9am-5pm.) The **Bowness Bay NPIC** provides similar services and has a display on the Lake District's topology (see p. 384). **Banks** are in both towns; Windermere services include: **luggage storage** at **Darryl's Cafe,** 14 Church St. (☎ 42894; £1 per bag; open W-M 8am-7pm); **launderette** on Main Rd. (wash £2, dry 20p per 4min.; open M-F 9am-6pm, Sa 9am-5pm); the **police,** Lake Rd. (☎ (01539) 722 611); **Internet access** at **Triarom,** Birch St. (☎ 44639; £1 per 10min., £5 per hr.; open M-Sa 9:30am-5:30pm); and the **post office,** 21 Crescent Rd. (☎ 43245; open M-F 9am-5:30pm, Sa 9am-12:30pm). **Post Code:** LA23 1AA.

▐▐ ACCOMMODATIONS AND FOOD. Windermere and Bowness have flocks of **B&Bs,** but booking ahead is still advisable during peak periods. Windermere's **YHA hostel** is 1 mi. north of town (see p. 386). To reach the **Lake District Backpackers Hostel ❷,** exit the train station and turn left on High St.; look for the sign on the right as you descend the hill. The friendly hostel has a great common room and lively atmosphere. (☎ 46374. Reception 9am-1pm and 5-9pm. Dorms £12-14.) The best choices among Windermere's B&Bs include: **Brendan Chase ❷,** 1-3 College Rd., with attractive rooms in two Edwardian townhouses (☎ 45638; £12.50-25 per person); the warm **Ashleigh Guest House ❸,** 11 College Rd. (☎ 42292; no smoking; £20-25 per person); and homey **Greenriggs ❷,** 8 Upper Oak St. (☎ 42265; £16-27 per person). A step up is spacious and well-furnished **Newstead** ❸, New Rd. (☎44485. No smoking. £25-32.50; May-Sept. £5 extra for singles.) In Bowness, **Laurel Cottage** ❸, St. Martins Sq., is a 400-year-old building with a great location, just steps from the pier. (☎45594. No smoking. £23-36 per person.) The closest camping is at lovely **Park Cliffe** ❷, Birks Rd., 3 mi. south of Bowness. Take bus #618 from Windermere station (☎015395) 31344. £10-12.80 per tent.)

In Windermere, **Booths Supermarket** is in the Old Station at the end of Cross St. (☎46114. Open M-F 8:30am-8pm, Sa 8:30am-7pm, Su 10am-4pm.) Get fresh fruit (and liquor) at **Booker's,** on Lake Rd. in Bowness. (☎88798. Open daily 8am-10pm.) **Gibby's** ❷, 43 Crescent Rd., Windermere, is a pleasant small restaurant with decently priced meals. (☎43267. Open daily noon-9:30pm.) At **Wild Oats** ❶, Main Rd., sandwiches with salad are £2 and breakfast is served all day. (☎43583. Open daily 10am-9pm.) Bowness has more options for evening dining. **Jackson's** ❸, St. Martins Sq., serves well-prepared modern British cuisine; a three-course meal costs £13. (☎46264. Open from 6pm.)

🅖 🅝 **SIGHTS AND HIKING.** A **lake cruise** is a good way to appreciate Windermere's surroundings, and a number of sightseeing boats depart from Bowness pier. **Windermere Lake Cruises** (☎43360) is the main operator, with trips north to Waterhead Pier in Ambleside (30min.; return £6.20, children £3.20) and south to Lakeside (40min., £6.40/£3.30). Nonstop sightseeing cruises are also available (45min., £4.80/£2.40). On all routes, departures are frequent between April and October, reduced the rest of the year. The Freedom of the Lake pass allows unlimited one-day travel (£11, children £5.50). A cruise to **Lakeside,** at Windermere's southern tip, lets you visit fish-under-glass at the **Aquarium of the Lakes** (☎(015395) 30153; open Apr.-Sept. daily 9am-6pm, Oct.-Mar. 9am-5pm; £5.50, children £4.20) or take a ride on the 4 mi. steam-powered **Lakeside and Haverthwaite Railway** (☎(015395) 31594; Easter-Oct.; £3.90). At the Bowness and Ambleside piers you can buy tickets that combine the lake cruise with one or both of these attractions.

In-town sights are less remarkable than the lake's offerings, but children (or big-time Jemima Puddleduck fans) will enjoy **The World of Beatrix Potter,** an outdoor recreation of scenes from the author's stories in the Bowness Old Laundry Theatre complex. (☎88444. Open Easter-Sept. daily 10am-5:30pm; Oct.-Easter 10am-4:30pm. £3.75, children £2.25.) At the **Windermere Steamboat Museum,** 1 mi. north of Bowness on Rayrigg Rd., the prize possession is the world's oldest mechanically powered boat. (☎45565. Open Apr.-Oct. 10am-5pm. £3.40, children £2.15.)

PROTO-POWERBARS About the only thing more common in Lakeland than lakes is the hiking essential known as **mint cake.** The marbled white snack assumes myriad forms, but the original recipe dates back to 1913, when a certain James Wilson of Kendal (an inventive but undoubtedly cavity-ridden chap) boiled sugar, peppermint oil, and a touch of salt to create the most saccharine of power foods. Since then, Kendal Mint Cakes have accompanied English expeditioners to the top of Everest and deep into the Sahara—and at 95 grams of sugar per serving, they'll have you bounding through the Lakes like a mountain goat who forgot his Ritalin.

The short but steep climb to **Orrest Head** (1½ mi. round-trip) is moderately difficult, but affords one of the best views in the Lake District; it begins opposite the the TIC on the other side of A591 (signposted). Guides to this and many other area hikes are available at TICs and NPICs.

AMBLESIDE
☎ 015394

Set in a valley a mile north of Windermere's waters, Ambleside is an attractive village with convenient access to the southern lakes. It's popular with hikers, who are drawn by its location—or perhaps by its absurd number of outdoors shops.

⌂⚥ TRANSPORTATION AND PRACTICAL INFORMATION. Buses (☎ 32231) stop on Kelsick Rd. Bus #555 runs from **Grasmere, Windermere,** and **Keswick** (every hr., £2-6.50). Buses #505 and 506 join the town to **Hawkshead** and **Coniston** (M-Sa 1 per hr., Su 3 per day; £2.55). **Rent bikes** from **Ghyllside Cycles,** The Slack. (☎ (015394) 33592. From £14 per day. Open daily 9am-5:30pm; Nov.-Apr. closed Tu.) The **tourist information centre** is in the Central Building on Market Cross. It offers identical services to the TIC in Windermere (see p. 387). Book accommodations online at www.amblesideonline.co.uk. (☎ 31576. Open daily 9am-5:30pm.) There's also a **NPIC** at Waterhead (see p. 384) Other services include: **banks** on Market Pl.; **launderette,** across from the bus station on Kelsick Rd. (open M-F 10am-7pm, Sa 10am-6pm); and the **post office,** Market Pl. (☎ 32267; open M-F 9am-5:30pm, Sa 9am-12:30pm). **Post Code:** LA22 9BU.

⌂⚥ ACCOMMODATIONS AND FOOD. Ambleside's ⬛**YHA hostel** resides near the steamer pier at Waterhead, a pleasant 1 mi. walk from the town center (see p. 385). The brand-spankin' new **Ambleside Backpackers ❷,** Old Lake Rd., offers 82 bunks in a comfortable, airy house. (☎ 32340. Apr.-Sept. £13.50; Oct.-Mar. £11.) **B&Bs** cluster on Church St. and Compston Rd., while others line the busier Lake Rd. leading in from Windermere. **Shirland, Linda's B&B ❷,** on Compston Rd., has four rooms with TV, cramped attic space for three, and a private, hostel-style bunkhouse. (☎ 32999. No singles. £14-15 per person, without breakfast £10.) Hospitable Mr. and Mrs. Richardson run **3 Cambridge Villas ❷,** on Church St. next to the TIC. (☎ 32307. £16 per person, with bath £20.) Across the street, the Irelands have hotel-style lodgings at **Melrose Hotel ❷,** Church St. (☎ 32500. £15-27 per person.)

Forage for your trail snacks at the Wednesday **market** on King St. or at the **Co-op Village Store,** Compston Rd. (☎ 33124. Open M-Sa 8:30am-6pm, Su 10am-4pm.) **Pippin's ❶,** 10 Lake Rd., serves great sandwiches (BLT £3.95), all-day breakfasts, and pizza—plus it's open late. (☎ 31338. Open Su-Th 8:30am-10pm; F-Sa 8:30am-11pm.) A more upscale choice is the **Glass House ❸,** Ryndal Rd., serving Mediterranean and modern British cuisine. (☎ 32137. Open for lunch and dinner, closed M in winter.) One good turn deserves a stop at the **Golden Rule ❶,** on Smith Brow (☎ 32257), which taps good local beer; try the Consiton Brew (£2).

◨⚥ SIGHTS AND HIKING. Lake cruises depart from the **Waterhead Pier** (see p. 388), where you can also rent boats. As in Windermere, the non-lake sights lack luster. At tiny **Bridge House,** off Rydal Rd., bridge and house are one and the same. It shelters a (cramped) National Trust Information Centre. (☎ 32617. Open Apr.-Oct. daily 10am-5pm. Free.) The **Ambleside Museum,** Rydal Rd., pays homage to lakeland literary figures. (☎ 31212. Open daily 10am-5pm. £2.50, children £1.80.) If you're feeling homesick for the city, head for the **Homes of Football Photographic Gallery,** 100 Lake Rd., where panoramic photos of urban soccer shrines grace the walls. (☎ 34440. Open daily 10am-6pm. Free.) Great **hikes** extend in all directions from Ambleside. Splendid views of higher fells can be had from the top of **Loughrigg** (a moderately difficult 7 mi. round-trip). An easy mile from town is the fascinatingly named **Stockghyll Force** waterfall. Area TICs have guides to these and other walks; as always, make sure you have appropriate supplies and clothing, and enough food to keep you on your feet.

GREAT LANGDALE VALLEY ☎ 015394

The spectacular **Great Langdale** valley, a horseshoe-shaped glacial scar dominated by the towering Langdale Pikes, begins 3 mi. west of Ambleside. In a
grove of trees at the center of the valley, the tiny town of **Elterwater** is happily
overwhelmed by its surroundings. The village stands ½ mi. from its namesake
water. This is great **hiking** country—one possibility is the terrific and only moderately difficult walk connecting Elterwater with Grasmere (4 mi.). Another
delightful option is a circuit of the valley beginning from Elterwater village (6
mi.). Hard-core trekkers won't be able to resist the siren song of the **Pikes.** Several popular ascents begin from the Old Dungeon Ghyll Hotel (see below), at
road's end 6 mi. from Ambleside. The path up to the summit of the **Pike of
Blisco** is only 2½ mi. (and 2000 ft. up, but hey, who's counting?). Seasonal **bus**
#516 travels from Ambleside to the Old Dungeon Ghyll Hotel via Elterwater
(Apr.-Oct.; M-Sa 6 per day, Su 5 per day). There are two **YHA hostels** in the area:
Elterwater (see p. 385), in town, and **Langdale** (p. 386), beautifully set 1 mi.
away. The **Britannia Inn ❹,** in Elterwater village, has traditional, comfortable
accommodations. (☎37210. Open Apr.-Dec. ₤36-42 per person.) The wonderfully atmospheric **Old Dungeon Ghyll Hotel ❹,** where the road from Ambleside
ends, keeps well-heeled hoofers holed up in cozy rooms and welcomes weary
walkers to its Hikers' Bar. (☎37272. ₤44.50-47.75 per person; B&B ₤54-57.)

CONISTON ☎ 015394

Less touristed than its nearby counterparts, Coniston retains the rustic feel of the
region's past; fells to the north and **Coniston Water** to the south make it popular
with hikers and cyclists. The town is also known for the former residency of
writer-artist-philosopher-critic-social-reformer John Ruskin—the **John Ruskin
Museum,** on Yewdale Rd., displays the sketches, photographs, and geological hammers of said writer-etc.-etc., as well as general exhibits on the history and geology
of Coniston. (☎41164. Open Easter to mid-Nov. daily 10am-5:30pm; mid-Nov. to
Easter W-Su 10am-3:30pm. ₤3, children ₤1.75, families ₤8.50.) Ruskin's **gravestone**
is in St. Andrew's Churchyard. Pretty **Brantwood,** Ruskin's manor from 1872, looks
across the lake at Coniston and the Old Man (see below); it holds his art and prose
collections. (☎41396. Open mid-Mar. to mid-Nov. daily 11am-5:30pm; mid-Nov. to
mid-Mar. W-Su 11am-4:30pm. ₤4.50, students ₤3, children ₤1. Gardens only ₤2.)

The easiest way to reach Brantwood is by water: the National Trust offers trips
on the elegant and very cool **Victorian steam yacht** *Gondola* (☎63850. Apr.-Oct. 5
per day. Return ₤4.80, children ₤2.80.) The *Coniston Launch* also cruises to
Brantwood, and offers other lake excursions. (☎36216. 8-11 per day. Brantwood
return ₤3.80, children ₤1.90.) Hikers can explore the abandoned **Coppermines** area
in search of the "American's stope"—an old copper mine shaft named in honor of
a Yankee who leapt over it twice successfully and survived a 160 ft. fall the third
time. (*Let's Go* does not, needless to say, recommend 160 ft. falls, but does
approve the moderately difficult 4½ mi. hike.) Another popular walk is to **Tarn
Hows** (see below; from Coniston 5 mi. round-trip). The more ambitious can take on
the surprisingly feisty 2628 ft. **Old Man** (5 mi. round-trip). The TIC, as any good TIC
would, has more information on these walks.

Bus #505 travels between Ambleside and Coniston, with some trips originating
in Windermere (45min.; M-Sa 13 per day, Su 3 per day). Buses stop at the corner of
Tilberthwaite and Ruskin Ave. Coniston's **tourist information centre**-cum-**NPIC** is on
Ruskin Ave. (see p. 384). The town has **no ATM,** but does offer bike rental at **Summi-
treks,** 14 Yewdale Rd. (☎41212; ₤5 per hr.) and mail facilities at the **post office,** Yewdale Rd. (☎41259; open M-F 9am-12:30pm and 1:30-5:30pm, W closes at 5pm, Sa
9am-noon). **Post Code:** LA21 8DU.

A LITTLE LAKE DISTRICT... If you stick around for a few days, you're bound to hear this trivia question from locals: How many lakes are there in the Lake District? (Hint: The map's at the beginning of the Cumbria section.)

Accommodations are available at Coniston's two **YHA hostels—Holly How** (see p. 385) or the rugged **Coppermines** (see p. 385). The **Beech Tree Guest House ❸**, Yewdale Rd., is a comfortable B&B, and the best in its price range. (☎41717. £19-25 per person.) Outdoorsfolk will find their ideal hosts in the ice-, rock-, and mineshaft-climbing proprietors of **Holmthwaite ❷**, on Tilberthwaite Ave. Large rooms and lots of advice make for excellent resting and hiking. (☎41231. £18.50-20 per person.) The fine **Coniston Lodge Hotel ❹**, Station Rd., has lovely rooms and top-notch dinners. (☎41201. £32.50-47 per person, meals extra.)

NEAR CONISTON
☎015394

In the hamlet of **Hawkshead,** 4 mi. east of Coniston, you can imagine yourself pulling Wordsworth's hair and passing him notes at the **Hawkshead Grammar School,** Main St., where the poet studied from 1779 to 1787. (Open Easter-Oct. M-Sa 10am-12:30pm and 1:30-5pm, Su 1-5pm. £1, children free.) Also on Hawkshead's main street is the **Beatrix Potter Gallery.** Housed in offices once used by her husband, the gallery displays sketches and watercolors from her beloved children's stories. (☎36355. Open Apr.-Oct. Su-Th 10:30am-4:30pm. £3, children £1.50, families £16.) Potter lived 2 mi. from Hawkshead, on her farm at **Hill Top.** The house, which was featured in many of the author's stories, remains exactly as she left it. Here you can make like Peter Rabbit and cavort in Mr. McGregor's garden—but be prepared to wait for the privilege, as lines can be long. Clever bunnies book ahead. (☎36269. Open June-Aug. Sa-W 10:30am-5pm; Mar.-May and Sept.-Oct. Sa-W 11am-4:30pm.) **Tarn Hows,** a pond surrounded by a grove of pine trees, is a peaceful (though popular) picnic spot. This charming scene, 2½ mi. from both Hawkshead and Coniston, is almost entirely manmade—the trees were planted, the tarn enlarged.

Bus #505 stops in Hawkshead on its way between Ambleside and Coniston (M-Sa 13 per day; Su 3 per day). From April to September, **Mountain Goat** offers a combined boat and bus shuttle to Hill Top from Bowness, as well as a bus service from Hawkshead. (☎45164. 8 per day; return from Bowness £5.80, children £3.60.) On summer Sundays, the National Trust (☎ (017687) 73780) offers a **shuttle** to Tarn Hows from Coniston and Hawkshead. You can get trail advice and other fun stuff at the Hawkshead **NPIC** (see p. 384).

GRASMERE
☎015394

With a lake and a canonized poet all to itself, the attractive village of Grasmere has its share of camera-clicking tourists. The sightseers crowd in at midday to visit sights pertaining to William Wordsworth's life, death, and afterlife, but in the quiet mornings and evenings the peace that the poet so enjoyed graciously returns. Guides provide 30min. tours of the early 17th-century ▧**Dove Cottage,** where Wordsworth lived with his wife Mary and his sister Dorothy from 1799 to 1808, and which is almost exactly as he left it. Next door, the outstanding **Wordsworth Museum** includes pages of his handwritten poetry and all the dirt on his Romantic contemporaries. The cottage is 10min. from the center of Grasmere. (☎35544. Open mid-Feb. to mid-Jan. daily 9:30am-5pm. Cottage and museum £5.50, students and YHA members £4.70, seniors £4.90, children £2.50. Museum only £2.75, children £1.25.) **Wordsworth's grave** is in town at St. Oswald's churchyard.

Another 1½ mi. southeast of Grasmere is ▧**Rydal Mount,** the penwright's home from 1813 until his death in 1850. The small hut in which he frequently composed

...HUMOR Answer: Only one, Bassenthwaite Lake. The rest are known only by name, or are followed by "Water," or "mere," which means the same thing. No one ever said the locals were funny.

verses lies across the garden terrace, designed by the man himself. (☎ 33002. Open Mar.-Oct. daily 9:30am-5pm; Nov.-Feb. W-M 10am-4pm. £3.75, concessions £3.25, children £1.75.) Down Grasmere's Redbank Rd., hydrophiles can get a pot of tea and gaze (Romantically, of course) across the water at the fells, or hire **rowboats** and strike out onto the deep green lake. (Open summer daily 10am-5pm. £2-4 per person depending on size of group; £10 deposit.)

Grasmere is a good place for daffodil-seeking Wordsworthians to begin their rambles. A steep, strenuous scramble (4 mi. round-trip) leads to the top of **Helm Cragg,** dubbed "the lion and the lamb." The 6 mi. **Wordsworth Walk** circumnavigates the two lakes of the Rothay River, passing the poet's grave, Dove Cottage, and Rydal Mount. The combined **TIC** and **NPIC** is in town on Redbank Rd. (see p. 384).

There are two **Grasmere YHA hostel** buildings within an 8min. walk: **Butterlip How** and **Thorney How** (see p. 386). Or perhaps the **Glenthorne Quaker Guest House ❸,** ¼ mi. up Easedale Rd. and past the Butterlip How hostel, has a place for thee. Most rooms are clean, spacious singles. (☎ 35389. B&B £21, full board £39.50.) **The Harwood ❸,** Red Lion Sq., has eight comfortable rooms right in the center of town. (☎ 35248. 2-night minimum stay on weekends. £24.50-32.50 per person.) **Newby's Deli ❶,** Red Lion Sq., packs superb sandwiches from £1.25. (☎ 35248. Open M-Sa 9am-5:30pm.) **Sara's ❷,** Broadgate, serves teas and sandwiches during the day and then magically transforms into a bistro in the evening. (☎ 35266. Open daily 10am-4pm and 6-9pm.) Sarah Nelson's famous Grasmere Gingerbread, a staple since 1854, is a bargain at 22p in **Church Cottage,** outside St. Oswald's Church. (☎ 35428. Open Easter-Nov. M-Sa 9:15am-5:30pm, Su 12:30-5:30pm; closes earlier in winter.)

KESWICK ☎ 017687

Sandwiched between towering Skiddaw peak and the northern edge of Derwentwater, Keswick (KEZ-ick) rivals Windermere as the Lake District's tourist capital. However, with an appealing town center and a beautiful lake just a stroll away, Keswick surpasses its competitor in tranquil charm.

🛈 PRACTICAL INFORMATION. For information on how to get to Keswick, see p. 383. The **NPIC** is in Moot Hall, behind the clock tower in Market Sq. (see p. 384). **Keswick Mountain Bikes,** just out of town in Southey Hill Industrial Estate, rents cycles. (☎ (017687) 75202. £10 per half-day, £13 per day. Open daily 9am-5:30pm.) Other services include: **banks** here and there; **launderette,** Main St., west of the mini-roundabout (open daily 7:30am-7pm); the **police** (☎ (01900) 602 422), Bank St.; **Internet access** at **U-Compute,** 48 Main St., above the post office (☎ 75127; £2.75 per hr.; open M-Sa 9:30am-6pm, Su 9:30am-4:30pm); and the **post office** itself (☎ 72296; open M-F 9am-5:30pm, Sa 9am-1pm, Su 11am-4:30pm). **Post Code:** CA12 5JJ.

🛏️ ACCOMMODATIONS, FOOD, AND PUBS. The **Keswick** and **Derwentwater YHA hostels** grace the town (see p. 385). The area between Station St., John St. (the Ambleside road), and Penrith Rd. has more **B&Bs** than anyone could want—walk by in the morning and smell the breakfasts wafting out of many a window. Good bets include **Bluestones ❷,** 7 Southey St. (☎ 74237; £15-19 per person) and **Dorchester House ❷** (☎ 73256; £18-22 per person). **Badgers Wood ❷,** 30 Stanger St., is friendly, comfortable, and has rooms named after trees. (☎ 72621. £18-23 per person.) Set apart from the fray, between town and lake, **Howe Keld ❸,** 5-7 The Heads, is noted for its superb breakfasts. (☎ 72417. £25-30 per person.)

Sundance Wholefoods, 33 Main St., sells nature-friendly groceries. (☎74712. Open summer daily 9am-6pm; winter roughly 9am-5pm.) For meatless treats, grab sandwiches (£3) at **Lakeland Pedlar ❶,** in an alley off Main St. (☎74492. Open July-Sept. daily 9am-8pm; Oct.-Apr. 10am-4pm; May-June M-F 10am-4am, Sa-Su 9am-4:30pm.) **Brysons ❶,** 42 Main St., is an excellent bakery with an upstairs tea room. (Open M-Sa 9am-5:30pm, Su 9am-4:30pm.) Those in the know frequent the lively **Dog & Gun ❶,** past Moot Hall on Market Pl., for above-average pub grub. (☎73463. Open M-Sa 11am-11pm, Su noon-10:30pm; food served noon-9pm.) **Ye Olde Queen's Head,** behind the Queen's Hotel on Main St., is perfect for unwinding over a pint. (☎73333. Open M-Sa 11am-11pm, Su 11am-10:30pm; happy hour 6-7pm.)

◙ ♫ SIGHTS AND ENTERTAINMENT. The best sight in Keswick is **Derwentwater,** undoubtedly one of the prettiest in a land o' lakes. The lapping waves are only a 5min. walk south of the town center along Lake Rd. The **Keswick Launch** sends cruises to other points on the lake, has boats for hire at the marina, and starts off a handful of trails around the shore. (☎72263. Mid-Mar. to Nov. 6-11 cruises per day, Dec. to mid-Mar. 3 per day; return £6.) Always wanted to know more about pencils? No? Well… go to the **Cumberland Pencil Museum** anyway. The No. 2 *was* invented here, after all, and displays include the world's largest specimen. The museum is west of the town center on Main St. (☎73626. Open daily 9:30am-4pm. Free.) The **Keswick Museum and Art Gallery,** in Fitz Park on Station Rd., has an interesting grab-bag of Victorian artifacts. (☎73263. Open Apr.-Oct. 10am-4pm. £1, concessions 50p.) For rainy day mopers, the culture-starved, and everyone else, **Theatre by the Lake** (by the, uh, lake) features a year-round program of repertory theater, music, and dance. (☎74411. Discount tickets available.)

◪ HIKES. A standout 4 mi. amble from Keswick crosses slopeside pastures and visits the **Castlerigg Stone Circle,** a neolithic henge dating back nearly 5000 years. Archaeologists believe this stunted Stonehenge may have been used as a place of worship, astronomical observatory, or trading center. The resident sheep think it's just swell. Another short walk hits the beautiful **Friar's Crag,** on the shore of Derwentwater, and **Castlehead,** a viewpoint encompassing town, lakes, and peaks beyond. Both these walks are by-and-large easy on the legs, with only a few moderately tough moments. Maps and information on these and a wide selection of other walks are available at the TIC.

BORROWDALE ☎017687

One of Lakeland's most beautiful spots (yes, that's saying a lot), the valley of Borrowdale gracefully winds its way south from the tip of Derwentwater. There are relatively few settlements in this serpentine, tree-filled valley—that, naturally, is no small part of its appeal. Postcard-ready **Ashness Bridge,** in the north, is worth a look, but lies some distance from the main road (and thus from public transportation, though small van tours do tend to stop there). The hamlet of **Rosthwaite** has several hotels and B&Bs. Towering above all is **Scafell Pike,** the highest mountain in England (3,205 ft.). Second bananas are the almost-as-lofty **Scafell** and **Great Gable.** Treks up these begin from **Seatoller,** at the head of the valley, which is home to a **NPIC** (see p. 384). Walks to the summits are popular, but very strenuous and not to be taken lightly—Scafell Pike is 4 mi. to the top and a 3100 ft. climb; Great Gable is also 4 mi., though not so steep.

Bus #79 runs from Keswick to Seatoller via Rosthwaite (55min., 8-20 per day). Accommodations are scattered throughout the valley. **YHA Burrowdale** is in the valley itself, while **Derwentwater** and **Honister Hause** are nearby (see p. 385). In Rosthwaite, **The How ❷** has simple rooms from £19 to £20.50. (☎77692.

Open Mar.-Nov.) Wanderers with heavier purses might try the elegant-yet-laid-back **Scafell Hotel ❹**, which also has a pub with perfectly passable grub. (☎77208. £41.50-59 per person.)

LIAR, LIAR, PINT'S ON FIRE Every third Thursday in November at Santon Bridge, near Eskdale in the Western Lake District, noses grow a little when the local pub hosts the "Biggest Liar in the World" competition. The contest was started in the 1920s by one William Rishden, proprietor of the Wasdale Head Inn and the self-styled Greatest Liar in the World. (Many a weary traveler would come to the Inn, spend a comfortable night, and then get hopelessly lost the next day due to Rishden's entirely fictional directions and hiking suggestions.) One year, after taking part in the contest for over a decade, Rishden refused to enter. Curious, his competitors asked him why. "I cannot tell a lie," he answered. He was promptly awarded first prize.

BUTTERMERE AND CRUMMOCK WATER ☎017687

The dramatic Buttermere Valley encompasses two lakes: Buttermere and Crummock Water. There's a genuine sense of isolation here—the road through the valley is one lane at times—and a harsher, bleaker beauty than that found at the more visited lakes. The stark mountains (bare rather than the more typical soft green) seem to plummet right into the lakes. Miniscule **Buttermere** village lies between the two waters; the shore of each is a few minutes' walk from town. Good **hikes** range from a stroll around Buttermere (4½ mi.) and a visit to a waterfall on Crummock Water (4 mi.), to a no-joke climb over the **Buttermere Fells** (10 mi.). The drive in and out of Buttermere Valley is beautiful on its own; southbound it passes the striking **Honister Pass,** a big, green half-pipe filled with scattered rocks.

Seasonal **bus** #77/77A serves Buttermere from Keswick (55min., Apr.-Oct. 8 per day). **YHA Buttermere** is a mere quarter-mile south of the village (see p. 385), while the uniquely situated **Honister Hause** sits atop Honister Pass (p. 386). In the village itself, **Trevene ❸** is the lone **B&B** (☎70210; £20 per person); the well-appointed **Bridge Hotel ❹** is another option (☎70252; £38-50 per person). **Skye Farm ❶** has basic camping. (☎70222. £5 per person.)

ULLSWATER ☎017684

Ullswater, in the northeast of lakeland, has great beauty, and one of its delights is that it doesn't reveal itself all at once. Around each rocky outcrop or grassy bank, a new corner of the lake is visible. The main settlements, **Glenridding** and **Patterdale,** are on the southern tip of the water, and either can be a departure point for the popular climb up 3114 ft. **Helvellyn.** For those planning the ascent, one possible route begins in Glenridding and takes about six strenuous hours to complete (9¼ mi.). Departing from Glenridding, the **Ullswater Steamers** cut across the lake with stops at Howtown and Pooley Bridge. (☎82229. 7-9 per day, fewer in winter. From £5 return.) For an outstanding lakeshore walk, take a steamer to Howtown and then walk 6½ mi. back to Glenridding. Another Ullswater attraction is **Aira Force**—the most accessible waterfall in the Lakes—just off the A5091 toward Keswick.

Public transport to Ullswater is limited. The only year-round **bus** service is #108 from **Penrith** (on the West Coast main rail line and connected by bus to Keswick). Two additional services operate seasonal schedules: #517 from **Bowness/Windermere** to **Glenridding** (55min.; Apr.-July Sa-Su and bank holidays 3 per day; Aug. daily) and #208 from **Keswick** to **Patterdale** via Aira Force and Glenridding (45min.; Aug. daily, June-July Sa-Su and bank holidays 5 per day). The **YHA shuttle** (see p. 384) makes a daily trip from the southern lakes to Patterdale. A **NPIC** camps out in the main carpark in Glenridding (see p. 384), and you'll find a number of options for resting your head in town: B&Bs include comfortable **Moss Crag ❸** (☎82500; from £20.50) and **Beech House ❷** (☎82037; from £18). **YHA Helvellyn** is 1½ mi. from Glenridding on the way up the peak (see p. 386). **YHA Patterdale** is a basic hostel outpost (p. 386), and Patterdale village has several guest houses, including **Ullswater View ❸** (☎82175; from £20). Those interested in dropping some serious pounds (you'd be at least £130 lighter) can try the extremely upscale hotels on the lake itself.

CARLISLE   ☎01228

Cumbria's principal (that is, only) city, Carlisle was once nicknamed "The Key of England" for its strategic position in the Borderlands between England and Scotland. The likes of Emperor Hadrian, Mary, Queen of Scots, Robert the Bruce, and Bonnie Prince Charlie have all played lord of the land from here. Today, Carlisle remains an ideal stopover for more peaceful border crossings, as well as a good base for examining **Hadrian's Wall** (see p. 447).

⌸ TRANSPORTATION. Carlisle's **train station** lies on Botchergate, diagonally across from the castle. (Ticket office open M-Sa 5am-11:30pm, Su 9:30am-11:30pm.) **Trains** arrive from: **Edinburgh** (2hr., every hr., £26.50); **Glasgow** (2½hr., every hr., £26.50); **London Euston** (4hr., every hr., £101); **Newcastle** (1½hr.; M-Sa every hr., Su 9 per day; £9.30). Get tickets at the **bus station,** on the corner of Lowther St. and Lonsdale St. (Open M-Sa 8:30am-6:30pm, Su 9:45am-5:30pm.) **National Express** (☎(08705) 808 080) arrives from **London** (9½hr., 1 per day, £26). **Stagecoach in Cumbria** bus #555 drives in from **Keswick** in the Lake District (1¼hr.; M-F 2 per day, Sa-Su 3 per day; £4.85). **Bike rental** is available at **Scotby Cycles,** 30 Bridge St. (☎(0800) 783 2312. £12 per day. £20 deposit. Open M-Sa 9am-5:30pm.)

⌸ ⌷ ORIENTATION AND PRACTICAL INFORMATION. Carlisle's city center is a pedestrian zone formed by **English St., Scotch St.,** and **Bank St.** The **tourist information centre** lies in the middle of this triangle at the Old Town Hall. To get there from the train station, turn left and walk about three blocks (Botchergate becomes English St.), then cross the Old Town Square. To get to the TIC from the bus station, cross Lowther St., walk through the shopping center, and go right. The TIC **exchanges currency,** has day-long **luggage storage** (75p), and books rooms. (☎625 600; fax 625 604. Open July-Aug. M-Sa 9:30am-6pm, Su 10:30am-4pm; May-June and Sept. M-Sa 9:30am-5pm, Su 10:30am-4pm; Mar.-Apr. and Oct. M-Sa 9:30am-5pm; Nov.-Feb. M-Sa 10am-4pm.) Other services include: many **banks; Internet access** at **Laserquest,** Victoria Viaduct (☎511 155; £2 per hr.; open M and F-Sa 11am-9pm, Tu-Th 11am-10pm, Su 10am-7pm); and the **post office,** 20-34 Warwick Rd., which also has a **bureau de change** (☎512 410; open M-Sa 9am-5:30pm). **Post Code:** CA1 1AB.

⌸⌷ ACCOMMODATIONS AND FOOD. The **Old Brewery Residences ❷,** Bridge Ln., offers inexpensive dormitory accommodations in July and August. (☎597 352. £13.50, under 18 £9.) Warwick Rd., running east out of the city, is cluttered with **B&Bs.** Top picks include: the relatively large **Cornerways Guest House ❷,** 107 Warwick Rd. (☎521 733; £15-16 per person, with bath £18); Victorian **Howard House ❷,** 27 Howard Pl. (☎529 159; £18-25 per person); and the nicely furnished **Langleigh House ❸,** 6 Howard Pl. (☎530 440; £20-30 per person).

The fairground interior of the **Market Hall,** off Scotch St., holds fresh fruit, veggies, and baked goods. (Open M-Sa 8am-5pm.) Carlisle's best eating is on Warwick Rd. **Casa Romana ❷,** 44 Warwick Rd. (☎591 969), is esteemed among the many Italian restaurants; dishes start at £3.20 for lunch and before 7pm. **David's ❹,** 62 Warwick Rd., has a well-regarded menu. (☎523 578. Entrees around £15. Open daily noon-1:30pm and 6:30-9pm.) In the evening, students, regulars, and tourists mix in the plush, blue-and-maroon interior of **The Board-room,** Paternoster Row, by the cathedral. Jukebox tunes and occasional live music lend an upbeat atmosphere. (☎ 527 695. Open M-Sa 11am-11pm, Su noon-10:30pm; food served 11am-8pm.)

◑ **SIGHTS.** The **Tullie House** museum and art gallery on Castle St. houses exhibits on Hadrian's Wall and other areas of local history, plus a collection of old shoes large enough to make Imelda Marcos jealous. (☎ 534 781. Open Apr.-Oct. M-Sa 10am-5pm, Su noon-5pm; Nov.-Mar. closes 4pm. £3.75, concessions £2.75, students £2.25.) Built by William II with stones from Hadrian's Wall, **Car-lisle Castle** looms in the northwest corner of the city. Mary, Queen of Scots, was imprisoned here until Elizabeth I decided she wanted her a wee bit farther from the border. Hundreds incarcerated in the dungeons of the castle after the 1745 Jacobite rebellion stayed alive by slurping water that collected in the trenches of the dark stone walls. Observe these "licking stones" as you learn about forms of torture employed against the Scots. (☎ 591 922. Open Apr.-Sept. daily 9:30am-6pm; Oct. 10am-6pm; Nov.-Mar. 10am-4pm. Guided tours June and Sept. Su 12:30 and 2pm, July also Su 11am; £1.40, children 70p. Admission £3.10, concessions £2.30, children £1.60.)

Carlisle's **cathedral,** founded in 1122, contains some fine 14th-century stained glass and the Brougham Triptych, a beautifully carved Flemish altar-piece. Sir Walter Scott married his French sweetheart on Christmas Eve, 1797, in what is now called the **Border Regiment Chapel.** (☎ 548 151. Open M-Sa 7:30am-6:15pm, Su 7:30am-5pm. Evensong during school year M-F 5:30pm. Suggested donation £2.)

ISLE OF MAN   ☎ 01624

No man is an island, but the Isle of Man is a speck of earth (33 mi. by 13 mi.) in the middle of the Irish Sea. While the 75,000 Manx swear allegiance to Queen Elizabeth, they are not a part of the UK and have their own government, flag, currency, and language. Vikings landed on Man in the 9th century and established the Isle's parliament, Tynwald Court. After the last Viking king died in 1266, Scottish and English lords struggled for power; in 1405 the English "Lords of Man" took control and ended home rule. Smugglers contributed to an economic boom until England's Isle of Man Purchase Act (1765) sent the island spinning into poverty. Rejuvenation began in 1828, when self-government was restored, and today Man controls its own internal affairs while remaining a crown possession.

Ringed by cliffs and sliced by valleys, Man can be explored in a few days. The island caters more to families than backpackers, but draws all types when motor-cyclists descend for the famous **T.T. races.** Much of the fauna is unique, including multi-horned **Manx Loghtan sheep** and tail-less **Manx cats.** Man's most famous (and odorous) delicacy is the **kipper,** herring smoked over oak chips. The **Manx lan-guage,** a cousin of Irish and Scots Gaelic, is heard when Manx laws are proclaimed each year on July 5, and the **three-legs-of-Man** emblem appears on every available surface, asserting the proud and singular identity of this tiny island nation.

◖ **GETTING THERE**

Flights: Ronaldsway Airport (☎ 821 600), 10 mi. southwest of Douglas on the coast road. Buses #1, 1C, and 2 connect to Douglas (25min., 1-3 per hr.), while others stop at points around the island. **Manx Airlines** has been purchased by **British Airways**

(☎(0845) 773 3377; www.britishairways.com), and began operating as part of BA on September 1, 2002. Flights come from Birmingham, Dublin, Glasgow, London Gatwick, Manchester, and other airports in Britain and Ireland. **British European** (UK ☎(08705) 676 676, Ireland (1890) 925 532; www.british-european.com) also serves the Isle.

Ferries: Douglas Sea Terminal. Travel Shop open M-Sa 9am-5pm, and at sailings. The **Isle of Man Steam Packet Company** (☎646 645 or (08705) 523 523; www.steam-packet.com) runs the only ferries to the isle, from: **Belfast** (2¾hr.; Apr.-Oct. 2 per week usually M and F, July-Aug. also W); **Dublin** (2¾hr.; Apr.-Oct. 2-3 per week); **Heysham,** Lancashire (2½-3½hr., 2-3 per day); **Liverpool** (2½hr.; Apr.-Oct. 1-3 per day, Nov.-Mar. 3 per week). Fares are highest in summer and on weekends (£26-30, return £47-54).

⊏ LOCAL TRANSPORTATION

The Isle of Man may have more cars per person than anywhere else in the world except Los Angeles, but it also has an extensive system of public transportation, run by **Isle of Man Transport** (☎663 366) in Douglas. Their **Travel Shop,** on Lord St. next to the bus station, has details on all government-run transportation, including free maps and schedules and discount tickets. (☎662 525. Open M 10am-12:30pm and 1:30-5:45pm, Tu-F 8am-5:45pm, Sa 8am-3:30pm.) The Travel Shop and the Douglas TIC sell **Island Explorer tickets,** which provide unlimited travel on most Isle of Man Transport bus and train services, as well as on horse trams (1-day £8, 3-day £18, 5-day £26, 7-day £32; children half-price). Pick up a free copy of the *Isle of Man Transport Timetables* at the TIC for all bus and train info.

Trains: Isle of Man Railways (☎663 366) runs along the east coast from Port Erin to Ramsey (Easter-Oct., limited service in winter). The 1874 **Steam Railway** runs from Douglas to Port Erin via Castletown. The 1899 **Electric Railway** runs from Douglas to Ramsey. The **Mountain Railway** runs to **Snaefell,** the island's highest peak (2036 ft.); trains #1 and 2 are the oldest in the world.

Buses: Frequent buses connect every hamlet. **Douglas** is the center of the bus empire.

Tours: Isle of Man Bus Tour Company, Central Promenade (☎674 301), in Douglas, provides several tours, including the popular "Round the Island" departing from Douglas W and Su at 10:15am and returning at 5pm (£15, children £7.50). Office open 45min. before tour departures.

Bicycling: The island's size makes it easy to get around by bike. The southern three-quarters of the Isle are covered in challenging hills—manageable, but worthy of Man's status as professional terrain. TICs provide a map of 6 1-day cycle trails.

⊓ PRACTICAL INFO

Manx **currency** is equivalent in value to British currency but not accepted outside the Isle; notes and coins from England, Scotland, and Northern Ireland can be used in Man. Manx coins are reissued each year with different and often bizarre designs—we're talking dirtbikes and cell phones, here. When preparing to leave the island, you can ask for your change in UK tender and usually get it. **Manx stamps** are also unusual (the eagle-eyed will notice that the Queen's head bears no crown). BT phonecards don't work on Man; post offices and newsagents sell Manx Telecom **phonecards** instead. The Isle shares Britain's **international dialing code,** 44. In an **emergency,** dial ☎999 or 112.

Isle of Man

HIKING AND WALKING

The government maintains three long-distance trails. **Raad ny Foillan** ("Road of the Gull") is a 90 mi. path around the island marked with seagull signs. The **Port Erin to Castletown route** is a spectacular hike (12 mi.) offering the best of the island's south: sandy beaches, cliffs, and splashing surf. **Bayr ny Skeddan** ("The Herring Road"), once used by Manx fishermen, covers the less spectacular 14 mi. between Peel in the west and Castletown in the east. It overlaps the **Millennium Way,** which goes from Castletown to Ramsey along the 14th-century Royal Highway for 28 mi., ending 1 mi. from Ramsey's Parliament Sq. For a shorter walk, follow signs in **Port Erin** to the nature trail, which leads to a coastal peak; this easy climb offers a terrific view of the island and of the **Calf of Man,** the small bird sanctuary off the isle's southern tip. The Douglas TIC has maps and free leaflets detailing island walks.

EVENTS

The island's economy relies heavily on tourism, so frequent festivals celebrate everything from jazz to angling. The TIC stocks a calendar of events; ask for *What's On the Isle of Man* or surf over to www.isleofman.com. The first two weeks of June turn Man into a merry motorcycling beast for the **T.T. (Tourist Trophy) Races.** The population doubles, the Steam Packet Co. schedules extra ferries, and Manx Radio is replaced by its evil twin, "Radio T.T." The races originated in 1904 when the tourist-hungry government passed the **Road Closure Act,** allowing roads to be closed and speed-limits lifted for a motor race. The circuit consists of 38 mi. of hairpin turns and mountain climbs, and the winner's name and make of motorcycle are engraved on the same silver "tourist trophy" that has been used since 1907. Today, 600 racers and 40,000 fans gather for a fortnight of nonstop partying.

The **Isle of Man International Cycling Week** usually occurs around the T.T. Race weeks and uses the same tracks. Established in 1936, it's now the most respected bicycle race in the British Isles. **Southern "100" Motorcycle Races** (☎ 822 546) take place over three days in mid-July: more bikers, more fun, and based in Castletown, the self-proclaimed "Road Racing Capital of the World." The Isle also celebrates during **Tynwald Fair,** which sees the pronouncement of new legislation on July 5, **Manx National Day.** Representatives don British wigs and robes to read the laws, but they do so in the Manx tongue upon a remote hill of ancient significance. The holiday takes place as part of the week-long **Manx Heritage Festival.**

DOUGLAS ☎ 01624

Recent capital of an ageless island, Douglas (pop. 22,000) has leveled the natural landscape under a square mile of concrete promenades and narrow Victorian townhouses. In the last century, Douglas bloomed as a seaside resort, but today it profits from the savvy businessmen who hurry down The Promenade from nine to five. It remains a solid spot from which to explore the island's more scenic parts.

🖪 TRANSPORTATION. Ferries arrive at the **Sea Terminal,** at the southern end of town, near the bus station. **Isle of Man Transport,** Banks Circus (☎ 663 366), runs local trains and buses (see **Local Transportation,** p. 397). Slow but inexpensive horse-drawn **trams** clip-clop down The Promenade between the bus and Electric Railway stations in summer. Stops are posted every 200 yd. or so. (☎ 663 366. Runs June-Aug. daily 9:10am-8:50pm; Sept.-May 9:10am-6:30pm.) Motorized **buses** also run along The Promenade, connecting the bus and Steam Railway stations with the Electric Railway (65p). For taxis, call **A-1 Taxis** (☎ 663 344) or **Telecabs** (☎ 621 111), both open 24hr. Several car rental companies are based in Douglas; the TIC has fliers. **Eurocycles,** 8a Victoria Rd., off Broadway, rents **bikes.** (☎ 624 909. Call ahead in summer. £10 per day. ID deposit. Open M-Sa 9am-6pm.)

🖪🖪 ORIENTATION AND PRACTICAL INFORMATION. Douglas stretches for 2 mi. along the seafront, from **Douglas Head** to the **Electric Railway** terminal. Douglas Head is separated from town by the **River Douglas,** which flows into the harbor. The ferry and bus terminals lie just north of the river. **The Promenade** bends from ferry terminal to the Electric Railway terminal along the beach. **Nobles Park** boasts recreation facilities and the start of the T.T. course. The shopping district spreads around pedestrianized **Strand St.** The **tourist information centre,** Sea Terminal Bldg., books beds. (☎ 686 766; www.visitisleofman.com. Open Easter-Sept. daily 9:15am-7pm; Oct.-Easter M-Th 9am-5:30pm, F 9am-5pm.) Other services include: **Lloyds TSB,** 78 Strand St. (open M-F 9:30am-4:30pm, Sa 9:30am-12:30pm); **Thomas Cook,** 7/8A Strand St. (☎ 626 288; open M-W and F-Sa 9am-5:30pm, Th 10am-5:30pm); a **launderette,** 24 Broadway (☎ 621 511; open Easter-Aug. daily 8:30am-4pm, Sept.-Easter closed Th); the **police,** Glencrutchery Rd. (☎ 631 212); **Nobles Isle of Man Hospital,** Westmoreland Rd. (☎ 642 642); **Internet access** at **Feegan's Lounge,** 22 Duke St. (☎ 679 280; £1 per 15min.; open M-F 9am-7pm, Sa 9am-5pm); and the **post office,** Regent St. (☎ 686 141; open M and W-F 9am-5:30pm, Tu 9:30am-5:30pm, Sa 9am-12:30pm). **Post Code:** IM1 2EA.

THE HIDDEN DEAL

O'NEILL'S SANDWICH BAR

He'll only eat his cheese sandwich with onions—no tomato, no pickle, and definitely no coleslaw. She guards her pence like a jealous dragon hoarding treasure. Fortunately, both the finicky and the frugal can be satisfied at **O'Neill's Sandwich Bar,** where there are more menu items than square feet of floor space and baps and baguettes come at bargain prices.

The sandwiches (£1.10-1.95) are simple, but come in a cornucopia of mouthwatering combinations, including cheese and coleslaw, ham and tomato, corn beef salad, and egg mayo and sausage. Jacket potatoes are available with every imaginable topping—basic butter is £1.25, while tuna mayonnaise and sweetcorn runs £2.25, and chicken tikka costs £2.55. Hot toasties (from £1.40) and Cornish pasties (85p) round out the menu, while various soups and sweets are always available.

A simple sum for the numerically-inclined: 83 menu choices, 68 of which cost less than £2. Factor in the delicious, fresh ingredients, and add it all up to find it equals an excellent deal for the thrifty traveler. *(1 Howard St. ☎ 663 381. Open M-Sa 8am-3pm.)*

ACCOMMODATIONS AND FOOD. Douglas is overrun with B&Bs and hotels. During T.T. race weeks, they raise their rates and fill a year in advance. The **Welbeck Hotel ❹**, Mona Dr., offers above-average rooms—all ensuite and some with stately views. (☎675 663. From £40-60 per person.) The **Glen Mona ❸**, 6 Mona Dr., is a family-run hotel up The Promenade with 17 pleasant rooms. (☎676 755. Singles £22; other rooms £20 per person.) Top-of-the-line treatment awaits at the **Sefton Hotel ❺**, Harris Promenade, where ritzy rooms, excellent service, and a swimming pool cushion the blow to your wallet. (☎645 500. Singles from £68; doubles and twins from £79.) **Grandstand Campsite ❶** is behind the T.T. races' start and finish line. (☎621 132. Office open M-F 9am-5pm. Open

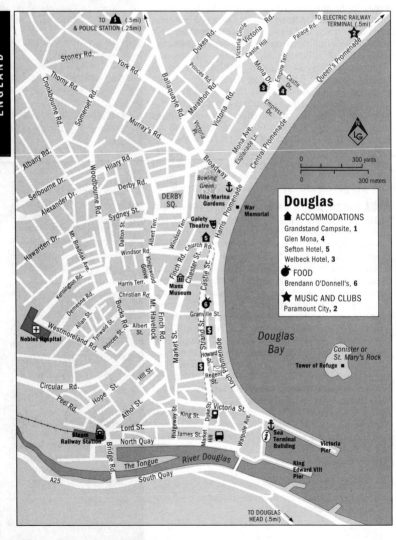

Douglas

🛖 ACCOMMODATIONS
Grandstand Campsite, 1
Glen Mona, 4
Sefton Hotel, 5
Welbeck Hotel, 3

🍎 FOOD
Brendann O'Donnell's, 6

★ MUSIC AND CLUBS
Paramount City, 2

mid-June to mid-Aug. and Sept. £6 per pitch. Laundry £2. Showers £1.) It's closed during the T.T. races and Grand Prix week, but other campsites open then—ask the TIC for a list.

Grill and chip shops proliferate along **The Promenade, Duke St., Strand St.,** and **Castle St.** The **Safeway** is on Chester St. (Open M-W 8:30am-8pm, Th-F 8:30am-9pm, Sa 8am-8pm, Su 9am-6pm.) At **Brendann O'Donnell's,** 16-18 Strand St., Guinness posters and traditional music remind you of the owner's loyalty and the Isle's proximity to Ireland. The place is as Irish as all get out—but none of the patrons are. (☎621 566. Open Su-Th noon-11pm, F-Sa noon-midnight.)

◨ ▣ SIGHTS AND ENTERTAINMENT. From the shopping district, signs point to the Chester St. parking garage, where an elevator ride to the roof leads you across a footbridge to the entrance of the **Manx Museum.** This eclectic gallery chronicles the history of the island since the Ice Age, with geological and taxidermical displays, folk crafts, and a pair of arguing rocks. (☎648 000. Open M-Sa 10am-5pm. Free.) Past the Villa Marina Gardens on Harris Promenade sits the **Gaiety Theatre.** Designed in 1900 and recently restored, the theater shone during Douglas's seaside resort days. Take a tour to see the nifty antique machinery. (☎625 001. 1½hr. tours Sa 10:15am, July-Aug. also Tu and Th 1:45pm. £4, children £2; advance booking recommended. Performances Mar.-Dec. Box office open M-Sa 10am-4:30pm and 1hr. before curtain. Tickets £13-15; discounts for seniors and children.) The distant sandcastle-like structure in Douglas Bay is the **Tower of Refuge,** built as an offshore hope for shipwreck survivors, but closed to the non-shipwrecked public.

Most of the **clubs** in Douglas are 21+ and some are free until 10 or 11pm, with a £2-5 cover thereafter. **Paramount City,** Queen's Promenade (☎622 447), houses two nightclubs: the upstairs **Director's Bar** plays faves from the 50s to the 90s, while the downstairs **Dark Room** pumps chart and dance. (No t-shirts or sportswear. Cover £3-4. Open F-Sa 10pm-3:15am.)

PEEL ☎01624

The "cradle of Manx heritage" and headquarters of the kipper industry, Peel is a beautiful fishing town on the west coast of Man. Twisting streets and salt-soaked stone buildings remain practically unchanged since the days when fishermen sailed from here to the Hebrides. Romantic **▨Peel Castle,** situated atop the height of **St. Patrick's Isle,** is easily reached from the mainland by a pedestrian causeway. Although not as grand as its British counterparts, the castle has served the Lords of Man quite nicely for centuries. Sinners were punished in the eerie **Bishop's Dungeon.** Footpaths ring the ruins before dipping to a stretch of beach and skimming the rocks of **Peel Hill.** (Open Easter-Oct. daily 10am-5pm; winter hours vary. £3, children £1.50, families £7.50; includes audio tour.) Across the narrow harbor is the impressive **House of Manannan,** a link in the island-wide Story of Man museum series, emphasizing the role of the sea in Manx history with engaging reconstructions and informative videos. (☎648 000. Open daily 10am-5pm, last admission 3pm. £5, children £2.50, families £12.50.) Catch a whiff of **Moore's Traditional Curers,** on Mill Rd. off East Quay, one of Peel's two **kipper factories.** The largest of its kind in Europe, this 1880 structure once produced 250,000 of the smoked fishies a day. Alas, the kipper industry isn't what it used to be. (☎843 622. Tours run Apr.-Oct. daily 2 and 3:30pm. £2, children £1.)

Buses (☎662 525) come to the station on Atholl St. from **Douglas** (#4, 5A, 6, 6A, 7; 35min.; M-Sa 1-2 per hr., Su 11 per day; return £3) and **Port Erin** (#8; 55min.; M-Sa 3 per day, Su 2 per day; return £3.10). Some buses leave from around the corner outside the town hall on Derby Rd., and all buses do so on Sundays and after 6pm on weekdays. The **tourist information centre** is a window in the Town Hall, Derby Rd. (☎842 341. Open M-Th 8:45am-5pm, F 8:45am-4:30pm.)

Large ensuite rooms await at **Kimberley House ❸**, 8 Marine Parade. (☎844 763. From ₤23 per person.) **Peel Camping Park ❶**, Derby Rd., has laundry facilities and showers. (☎842 341. Open May to mid-Sept. ₤3.75 per person.) The two **Shoprite** grocery stores are on Derby Rd. (open M-F 8:30am-8pm, Sa 8am-6pm) and in the center of town on Michael St. (open M-Th 8:30am-6:30pm, F 8:30am-8pm, Sa 8am-6:30pm, Su 10am-5pm). The **Harbour Lights Cafe and Tearoom ❷**, Shore Rd., provides the chance to try a Peel kipper. (☎897 216. Main courses ₤6-8. Kipper ₤5.50. Open Tu-Su 10am-5pm.) At **Davidson's Ice Cream Parlour ❶**, Shore Rd., two enormous scoops of ice cream cost an unheard-of ₤1.20. *Let's Go* sampled six flavors in a scientific tastefest and heartily recommends Raspberry Ripple. (☎844 761. Open Apr.-Sept. daily 10am-9pm; Oct.-Mar. 10am-7:30pm.)

CREGNEASH   ☎01624

The oldest village on the island, home to an open-air museum, makes a great daytrip from either Douglas or Peel. The **Cregneash Village Folk Museum** is a living, working illustration of a 19th-century Manx crofting town, complete with thatching, wool-dying, and blacksmithing demonstrations. (☎648 000. Open Apr.-Oct. daily 10am-5pm. ₤4.25, children ₤2.25, families ₤10.75.) Man's most beautiful **walks** also begin in this corner of the island. **Bus** #1 runs to Cregneash from **Douglas** (1¼hr., M-Sa 2 per day) and, more frequently, from **Port Erin** (20min., M-Sa 5-6 per day). Those wishing to stay in the area can try **Anchorage Guest House ❸**, Athol Park, in Port Erin, where the super-friendly owner bends over backwards to accommodate. (☎832 355. From ₤20 per person.)

NORTHEAST ENGLAND

With Scotland to the north and the North Sea to the east, this corner of England has always been border country. Hadrian's Wall sketches a history of skirmishes with fierce northern neighbors, and the area's three national parks, some of the most removed countryside in England, retain their frontier ruggedness. No trail tests hikers like the Pennine Way, Britain's first and longest official long-distance path. An extensive network of shorter trails accommodates ramblers of all levels, crisscrossing the heather-flecked moors of a Brontëan imagination and the rolling dales beloved by James Herriot. The isolation of the northeast testifies to its agricultural bent; even the main industry (textile manufacturing) sprang from the pervasive presence of sheep. But while the principal urban areas of Yorkshire and Tyne and Wear (including Leeds, York, and Newcastle) may have grown out of the wool and coal industries, bearing 19th-century scars to prove it, today their refurbished city centers have turned their energies to accommodating visitors.

HIGHLIGHTS OF NORTHEAST ENGLAND

YORK MINSTER Don't miss Britain's largest Gothic cathedral, which contains the largest medieval glass window in the world (p. 420).

NATIONAL PARKS Wander the emerald valleys and stone walls of the **Yorkshire Dales** (p. 414), brave the winds and haunting sweeps of the **North York Moors** (p. 426), or seek solitude in rough-hewn **Northumberland** (p. 449).

NEWCASTLE BY NIGHT Sample the famed brown ale of this gritty city, home to crowded dance floors, lively locals, and legendary nightlife (p. 441).

HADRIAN'S WALL Admire the remains of Hadrian's massive construction, which once delineated the northernmost border of the Roman Empire (p. 447).

YORKSHIRE

SHEFFIELD ☎ 0114

Sheffield (pop. 530,000) rose to fame in a flurry of chopping, scooping, carving, and spreading. While Manchester was clothing the world, Sheffield was setting its table, first with hand-crafted flatware, then mass-produced cutlery, and eventually stainless steel (invented here). As 20th-century industry moved elsewhere, economic depression, made familiar by *The Full Monty*, set in. Though a dearth of city-center accommodations foils any budget traveler's overnight aspirations, Sheffield, with its three new town squares and numerous art galleries, represents the last bastion of urbanity and nightlife before the Peak District.

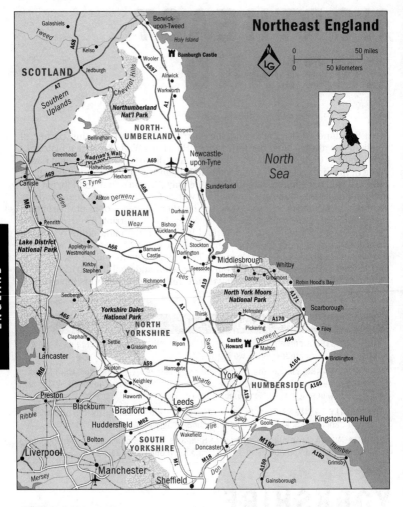

Northeast England

SCOTLAND

Galashiels
Tweed
Kelso
Jedburgh
Southern Uplands
Berwick-upon-Tweed
Holy Island
Bamburgh Castle
Wooler
Chevriot Hills
Alnwick
Warkworth
Northumberland Nat'l Park
NORTH-UMBERLAND
Bellingham
Morpeth
Greenhead
Hadrian's Wall
Haltwhistle
Hexham
Newcastle-upon-Tyne
Carlisle
S Tyne
Sunderland
Alston
Derwent
DURHAM
Wear
Durham
Bishop Auckland
Penrith
Lake District National Park
Appleby-in-Westmorland
Barnard Castle
Stockton
Darlington
Kirkby Stephen
Richmond
Tees
Teesside
Battersby
Middlesbrough
Danby
Grosmont
Whitby
Robin Hood's Bay
Sedbergh
North York Moors National Park
Yorkshire Dales National Park
Thirsk
Helmsley
Scarborough
NORTH YORKSHIRE
Pickering
A170
Filey
Clapham
Settle
Grassington
Ripon
Castle Howard
Derwent
Malton
Lancaster
Skipton
Harrogate
Bridlington
Preston
Keighley
Wharfe
York
HUMBERSIDE
Haworth
Blackburn
Bradford
Leeds
Ribble
Huddersfield
Selby
Goole
Kingston-upon-Hull
Bolton
Wakefield
SOUTH YORKSHIRE
Doncaster
Grimsby
Liverpool
Mersey
Manchester
Sheffield
Don
Gainsborough
Humber

North Sea

0   50 miles
0   50 kilometers

TRANSPORTATION AND PRACTICAL INFORMATION

Sheffield lies on the M1 motorway, about 30 mi. east of Manchester and 25 mi. south of Leeds. **Midland Station** (☎(08457) 221 125) is on Sheaf St., near Sheaf Sq. **Trains** (☎(08457) 484 950) arrive from: **Birmingham** (1½hr., 1-2 per hr., £18.50); **Liverpool** via Stockpool (1¾hr., every hr., £13.90); **London St. Pancras** (2-3hr., 1-2 per hr., £46); **Manchester** (1hr., every hr., £10.75); **York** (1¼hr., every hr., £12.80). The major **bus station** in town is the **Interchange,** between Pond St. and Sheaf St. (☎275 4905. Open M-F 8am-5:30pm. Lockers £1-2.) **National Express** (☎(08705) 808 080) travels from: **Birmingham** (2½hr., 6 per day, £13.25); **London** (3½hr., 8 per day, £12.75); **Nottingham** (1¼hr., every hr., £5.25). The **Supertram,** Sheffield's modern transport system, covers the city. (☎272 8282. Daily pass £1.90, weekly £6.30.)

Sheffield's **tourist information centre,** 1 Tudor Sq., off Surrey St., books rooms for a 10% deposit. Ask for a free copy of *It's Happening In Sheffield.* (☎221 1900, bookings 201 1011; www.sheffieldcity.co.uk. Open M-Th 9:30am-5:15pm, F 10:30am-5:15pm, Sa 9:30am-4:15pm.) Other services include: **banks** on Pinstone St. and Church St.; **police,** West Bar (☎220 2020); **Northern General Hospital,** Herries Rd. (☎243 4343); **Internet access** at **Havana Bistro** (see below); and the **post office,** Fitzalan Sq. (☎733 525; open M 9am-5:30pm, Tu-Sa 8:30am-5:30pm). **Post Code:** S1 1AB.

ACCOMMODATIONS AND FOOD

Sheffield doesn't exactly roll out the red carpet, nor even a worn welcome mat, for the budget traveler. If you don't mind the 30min. commute by train, try the **YHA hostel** in **Hathersage** (see p. 377). Unless you opt to nest above a pub, expect a hilly westward hike from the city, where **B&Bs** cost at least £18.

Rutland Arms ❸, 86 Brown St., near the train and bus stations, offers clean rooms above a friendly pub, all with bath. (☎272 9003; fax 273 1425. Breakfast included. Singles £23.50; doubles £37; family room £47.) **The Bristol Hotel ❺,** Blonk St., embraces post-industrialism with sand-blasted windows, sparely decorated rooms, talking elevators, and silver shower curtains. (☎220 4000. M-Th £69.50 per room, F-Su £52.50.) On the other hand, the **House of Elliott ❸,** 465 Manchester Rd.,

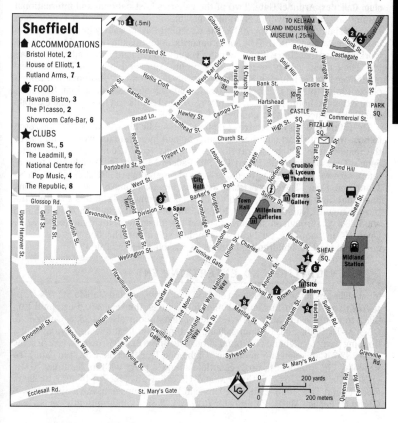

NORTHEAST ENGLAND

will make you forget you're in Industria with its thick carpets and free rides on the rocking horse. Take bus #51 from the City Hall or Leopold St. to Crosspool. (☎268 1677. Continental breakfast. £20 per person, £18 additional nights.)

Cheap nourishment in the city center is hard to come by; head for the student haunts on **Ecclesall Rd.** or the ubiquitous cafe-bars on **Division St.** and **Devonshire St.**, where clubbers prepare for the evening. The **Spar** supermarket, at the intersection of Holly St. and Division St., is open 24hr. The minimalist **Showroom Cafe-Bar ❷**, 7 Paternoster Row, draws the wear-black, drink-wine crowd. Lounge on the couch over large and tasty chicken dishes, burgers, and stir-fry (£7-10) before watching one of the arthouse flicks next door. (☎275 3588. Open M-Sa 11am-11pm, Su noon-10:30pm.) **Havana Bistro ❶**, 32-34 Division St., concocts out-of-the-ordinary cyber fare, such as chicken goujons and melted brie for £3.50. (☎249 5452. Internet access £1 per 15min. Open M-Th 10am-10pm, F-Sa 10am-7pm, Su 11am-6pm.) **The P!casso Restaurant and Bar ❹**, on the second floor of the Bristol Hotel (see above), pays homage to the Master of Modernity with nouvelle cuisine (£10-15) and colorful furnishings. (☎220 4000. Open M-Sa 9am-11pm, Su 9am-9pm.)

◎ SIGHTS

Sheffield's cultural reputation has been energized by the opening of the ◪**Millennium Galleries,** Arundel Gate. Two of the galleries host national and international exhibitions, with the works of John Constable, followed by "Flower Power" and "Pleasureland," lined up for 2003. The excellent **Ruskin Gallery** has its roots in a museum established in 1875 by Victorian critic John Ruskin, intended to show the working class that "life without industry is guilt, and industry without art is brutality." The current gallery merges nature, architecture, and industry. The final permanent gallery celebrates **Metalwork.** Stifle that groan of boredom and take a closer look—this isn't shop class. (☎278 2600. Open M-Sa 10am-5pm, Su 11am-5pm; extended hours for special exhibits. General admission free. Special exhibits usually £4, concessions £3, children £2, families £9.)

The ◪**Graves Gallery,** on Surrey St. above the public library, dedicates one room to post-war British art, another to Romantic and Impressionist works, and leaves the remaining six open for traveling exhibitions. (☎278 2600. Open M-Sa 10am-5pm; off season closed M. Free.) The **Site Gallery,** 1 Brown St., is dedicated to contemporary works including media art and photography. (☎281 2077. Open Tu-Su 11am-5pm. Free.) The **Kelham Island Industrial Museum,** Alma St., studies the strong hand and dirty glove of Sheffield's industrial movement. Take bus #53 from the Interchange to Nursery St.; turn left on Corporation St., right on Alma St., and wind 200 yd. through an industrial park to the museum on the right. (☎272 2106. Open M-Th 10am-4pm, Su 11am-4:45pm; last admission 1hr. before close. £3.50, concessions £2.50, children £2, families £8, disabled visitors free.)

▣ ♫ NIGHTLIFE AND ENTERTAINMENT

Most **clubs** are in the southeastern section of the city, around **Matilda St.;** *It's Happening in Sheffield* has current nightlife listings. **The Leadmill,** 6 Leadmill Rd., plays to almost every taste in two student-packed rooms. (☎221 2828. Cover £2-5. Open M-Th 10pm-2am, F 10pm-2:30am, Sa 10pm-3am.) Sandwiches by day and a hopping party by night can be found at buzzing **Brown St.,** 60 Brown St. (☎279 6959. Cover £2-7. Cafe open M-F noon-4pm. Club open Th-F 9pm-3am, Sa 9pm-4am.) **The Republic,** 112 Arundel St., hosts Sheffield's largest party with its Saturday "Gatecrasher" bash. (☎276 6777. Cover M and Th £2-3, F £3-5, Sa £10-15 after 10:30pm. Open M and Th-F 10pm-2am, Sa 10pm-6am.) Once a museum, the garish **National Centre for Popular Music,** Paternoster Row (☎249 8885), intermittently serves as a nightclub. For nightlife without a backbeat, visit the **Crucible** and **Lyceum Theatres,** both in Tudor Sq. and sharing a box office on Norfolk St., which stage musicals, plays, and dance shows, many of them West End transfers. (☎ 249 6000. 20% concessions discount; same-day tickets £5.)

PENNINE WAY

The Pennine Peaks arch up the center of Britain like a spine, from the Peak District National Park to the Scottish border. Britain's first long-distance trail, the 268 mi. Pennine Way begins at Edale, traverses the boggy plateau of **Kinder Scout,** then passes into the **Yorkshire Dales** at Malham to reemerge at the 2273 ft. peak of Pen-y-ghent. The northern section crosses the **High Pennines,** a 20 mi. stretch from below Barnard Castle to Hadrian's Wall, terminating at Kirk Yetholm in Scotland. The moorland of this often desolate landscape has fostered a rebellious population. They erected chapels in defiance of Canterbury, embraced socialism in the face of textile barons, and broke the will of private-property absolutists by winning public right-of-way access for these very trails.

◪ HIKING THE PENNINE WAY

Hikers have completed the Way in as few as ten days, but most spend three weeks on the trail. The less ambitious can make brief but rewarding forays on well-traveled walkways from major towns. The unusual limestone formations in the Yorkshire Dales and the lonely moor of Kinder Scout are Way highlights. The Pennines do not, however, coddle hikers. Sudden storms can reduce visibility to under 20 ft., leave low-level paths swampy, and sink you knee-deep in peat. Those in the know recommend that all save the most hardcore types stay away from the Pennines in the winter. Bring a map and compass and know how to use them. Rain gear, warm clothing, and extra food are also essential. (Consult **Wilderness Safety,** p. 49.) Wainwright's *Pennine Way Companion* (£10), a pocket-sized volume available from bookstores, is a worthwhile supplement to Ordnance Survey maps (£6-8), all available at National Park Information Centres (NPICs) and TICs. Comprehensive coverage of the route comes in the form of two National Trail Guides, *Pennine Way North* and *Pennine Way South,* each £12. Those wishing to see some of the Way without hoofing the whole thing should get hold of the *Pennine Way Public Transport Guide,* free at NPICs.

◪ ACCOMMODATIONS AND CAMPING

YHA hostels are spaced within a day's hike (7-29 mi.) of each other. The handy YHA **Pennine Way Package** allows you to book a route along the Way (50p per hostel) and provides useful advice on paths and equipment. Send a self-addressed envelope to YHA Northern Region, P.O. Box 11, Matlock, Derbyshire DE4 2XA (☎ (01629) 825 850). Any NPIC or TIC can supply details on trails and alternate accommodations. The *Pennine Way Accommodations Guide* (90p) is invaluable, as is the YHA website (www.yha.org.uk).

YHA HOSTELS

The following hostels are arranged from south to north, with the distance from the nearest southerly hostel listed. Unless otherwise noted, reception is open from 5pm, and breakfast and evening meals are served.

Edale: in the Peak District. See p. 377.

Crowden-in-Longdendale: 15 mi. from Edale in the Peak District. See p. 377.

Mankinholes: Todmorden (☎/fax (01706) 812 340), 24 mi. from Crowden. Shop in hostel. Open Apr.-Oct. M-Sa. Dorms £10.25, under 18 £7. ❷

Haworth: Just outside the town. 18 mi. from Mankinholes. See p. 410.

Earby: 9-13 Birch Hall Ln., Earby (☎/fax (01282) 842 349), 15 mi. from Haworth. Open Apr.-Oct. Dorms £9.50, under 18 £6.75. ❶

Malham: 15 mi. from Earby in the Yorkshire Dales. See p. 416.

Stainforth: 8 mi. from Malham in the Yorkshire Dales. See p. 416.

Hawes: 19 mi. from Stainforth in the Yorkshire Dales. See p. 416.

Keld: 9 mi. from Hawes in the Yorkshire Dales. See p. 416.

Baldersdale: Blackton, Baldersdale (☎/fax (01833) 650 629), 15 mi. from Keld in a converted stone farmhouse overlooking Blackton Reservoir. Open July-Aug. daily; Apr.-June and Sept.-Oct. Tu-Sa. Dorms £9.50, under 18 £6.75. ❶

Langdon Beck: Forest-in-Teesdale (☎(01833) 622 228; fax 622 372), 15 mi. from Baldersdale. Has a small shop. Open Apr.-Aug. M-Sa; Feb.-Mar. and Sept.-Oct. Tu-Sa; Nov. F-Sa. Dorms £10.25, under 18 £7. ❷

Dufton: Redstones, Dufton, Appleby (☎(017683) 51236; fax 53798), 12 mi. from Langdon Beck. Has a small shop. Open July-Aug. Th-Tu; Apr.-June and Sept.-Oct. Th-M. Dorms £9.50, under 18 £6.75. ❶

Alston: The Firs, Alston (☎/fax (01434) 381 509), 22 mi. from Dufton. Open Apr.-Aug. daily; Sept.-Oct. F-Tu. Dorms £9.25, under 18 £6.75. ❶

Greenhead: 17 mi. from Alston. See p. 447.

Once Brewed: 7 mi. east of Greenhead. See p. 447.

Bellingham: 14 mi. from Once Brewed in Northumberland. See p. 450.

Byrness: 15 mi. from Bellingham in Northumberland. See p. 450.

Kirk Yetholm (SYHA): 27 mi. from Byrness. See p. 568.

CAMPING BARNS

In the High Pennines, the YHA operates three **camping barns,** hollow stone buildings on private farms with wooden sleeping platforms, (very) cold water, and a toilet. The telephone numbers below are for confirming arrival times *only;* to book, call ☎(01200) 420 102 or e-mail campbarnsyha@enterprise.net. You can also get information on the YHA website (www.yha.org.uk) and in the free *Camping Barns in England,* available at TICs.

Holwick Barn: Mr. and Mrs. Scott, Low Way Farm, Holwick (☎(01833) 640 506), 3 mi. north of Middleton-in-Teesdale. Sleeps 20. £5 per person. ❶

Wearhead Barn: Mr. Walton, Blackcleugh Farm, Wearhead (☎(01388) 537 395), 1 mi. from Cowshill. No electric lights. Sleeps 12. £4 per person. ❶

Witton Barn: Witton Estate, Witton-le-Wear (☎(01388) 488 322), just off the Weardale Way. Sleeps 15. £4 per person. ❶

SOUTH PENNINES

Prepared by their dog-eared copies of *Wuthering Heights* for bleak and isolated vistas, visitors to the South Pennines may be surprised by the domesticated feel of this landscape. The quaint villages of Hebden Bridge and Haworth nestle in the gorse-strewn moorlands. Between them, heathery slopes of greenery unfold quietly, patterned into well-cultivated fields and grazed upon by impassive sheep.

⌨ TRANSPORTATION

The proximity of the South Pennines to Leeds and Bradford makes **train** transport (☎ (08457) 484 950) fairly easy. **Arriva's** Transpennine Express reaches Hebden Bridge directly from Blackpool and Leeds (M-Sa every hr. 7am-9pm, every 2 hr. on Su). **Metro's** Airedale Line, from Leeds, stops at **Keighley** (KEETH-lee), 5 mi. north of Haworth. From there, reach Haworth by the **Keighley and Worth Valley Railway's** private steam trains (☎ (01535) 645 214). **Bus** travel will take you through smaller cities. Travel to **Halifax** to get to Hebden Bridge, and Keighley to get to Haworth; both cities are convenient destinations from **Leeds**. Local buses make the half-hour journey from these cities to Hebden Bridge and Haworth; for more information, see below or contact **Metroline**. (☎ (0113) 245 7676. Open daily 9am-8pm.)

TICs have a wide selection of trail guides. The **Worth Way** traces a 5½ mi. route from Keighley to Oxenhope; ride the steam train back to your starting point. From Haworth to Hebden Bridge, choose a trail from the TIC's *Two Walks Linking Haworth and Hebden Bridge* (30p), which guides visitors on the dark and verdant paths that inspired the Brontë sisters.

HEBDEN BRIDGE   ☎ 01422

An historic gritstone village on a hillside, Hebden Bridge lies close to the Pennine Way and the circular 50 mi. **Calderdale Way**. Originally a three-farm cluster, the medieval hamlet stitched its way to modest expansion in the booming textile years of the 18th and 19th centuries, and many of the trademark "double-decker" houses of this period are still standing. Today, Hebden Bridge has few sights; most visitors use it as a starting point for day (or longer) hikes.

One of the most popular hiking destinations is the National Trust's **Harcastle Crags** (☎ 844 518), a ravine-crossed wooded valley of picture-book greenery known locally as Little Switzerland, 1½ mi. northwest along the A6033; pick up a free guide from the TIC. You can also take day hikes to the villages of **Blackshaw Head, Cragg Vale**, or **Hepstonstall**. Hepstonstall holds the remains of Sylvia Plath and the ruins of the oldest Methodist house of worship in the world. **Calder Valley Cruising** gives horse-drawn boat trips along the Rochdale Canal. (☎ 845 557. Office open M-F 10am-noon; Easter-Oct. also Sa-Su 11am-5pm. 2-3 trips per day in summer. £6, concessions £5, children £3, families £14.)

Hebden Bridge lies about halfway along the Manchester-Leeds rail line. **Trains** pass through at least hourly, and sometimes as frequently as every 10min. (☎ 845 476. Manchester £6.30, Leeds £3.) **Buses** stop at the train station and on New Rd. The **tourist information centre**, 1 Bridge Gate, offers the popular *Walks Around Hebden Bridge* (40p) and a mass of other walking guides. (☎ 843 831. Open mid-Mar. to mid-Oct. M-F 9:30am-5:30pm, Sa-Su 10:30am-5pm; mid-Oct. to mid-Mar. M-F 10am-5pm, Sa-Su 10:30am-4:15pm.) **Internet access** is free for the first hour at the **library,** on the corner of Cheetham and Hope St. (☎ 842 151. Open M and W 9:30am-7:30pm, Tu 9:30am-1pm, Th-F 9:30am-5pm, Sa 9:30am-4pm.) Alternatively, try the **Java Lounge**, 23 Market St. (☎ 845 740. £1 for 30min. Open M-W 11am-7pm, Th 11am-8pm, F-Su 11am-5pm.) The **post office** is on Holme St. (☎ 842 366. Open M-Sa 6am-noon.) **Post Code:** HX7 8AA.

At the **B&B** of photographer **Claire McNamee ❷**, 1 Primrose Terr., and her painter husband, simply furnished rooms are hung with original works of art. (☎ 844 747. £16 per person.) **Angeldale Guest House ❹**, a large Victorian at the north end of Hangingroyd Ln., has lovely, spacious rooms. (☎ 847 321. Singles £35; doubles £44-52.) Purchase groceries at the **Coop**, 41 Market St. (☎ 842 452. Open M-Sa 8am-9pm, Su 10am-4pm.) For award-winning scones (£1.35), visit the **Watergate Tea Room ❶**, 9 Bridge Gate. (☎ 842 978. Open Su-F 10:30am-5pm,

Sa 7am-9:30pm.) Satisfying pizzas and pastas (£5-8) are served up at local favorite **Hebdens ❷,** on Hangingroyd Ln., just across the bridge from St. George Sq. (☎843 745. Open W-Th 4:30-10pm, F-Sa 4:30-10:30pm, Su 4:30-9:30pm.)

HAWORTH   ☎01535

I can hardly tell you how the time gets on at Haworth. There is no event whatever to mark its progress. One day resembles another...
   —Charlotte Brontë

Haworth's (HAH-wuth) *raison d'être* stands at the top of its hill—the parsonage that overlooks Brontëland. A cobbled main street milks all association with the ill-fated literary siblings, with numerous tearooms and souvenir shops lining the uphill climb to the Brontë home. The village today wants for wandering heroines, but a moving echo of the windswept moors remains.

▐▀ ▐▟ TRANSPORTATION AND PRACTICAL INFORMATION. The **train station** (☎645 214) only serves the **Keighley and Worth Valley Railway's** private steam trains, which run to and from **Keighley** (25min.; 4-10 per day, no weekday service Sept. to mid-June; return £9, children £4.50). **Metroline buses** (☎603 284) #663-665 and 720 also reach Haworth from **Keighley** (15min., every 15-30min., £1-3). Bus #500 will take you to and from **Hebden Bridge** (30min., 4-5 per day, £1), or you can pick up a guide from the TIC (30p) and hike there (6-8 mi. trails).

The **tourist information centre,** 2-4 West Ln., at Main St.'s breathless summit, provides the useful *Three Walks from the Centre of Haworth* (30p) and the town's mini-guide (35p), and books beds for a 10% deposit. (☎642 329; fax 647 721. Open Easter-Oct. daily 9:30am-5:30pm; Nov.-Easter 9:30am-5pm.) The **post office,** 98 Main St., is the only place to **exchange currency.** (☎644 589. Open M and W-F 9am-1pm and 2-5:30pm, Tu 9am-1pm, Sa 9am-12:30pm.) **Post Code:** BD22 8DP.

▐▛ ▐▙ ACCOMMODATIONS AND FOOD. The elegant **YHA Haworth ❷** is in a Victorian mansion, a 15min. hike from the train station up Lees Ln.; turn left on Longlands Dr. (☎642 234; fax 643 023. Meals £3-5.25. Open mid-Feb. to Oct. daily; Nov. to mid-Dec. F-Sa. Dorms £10.25, under 18 £7.) Built by the doctor who attended Charlotte Brontë's death, **▨Ashmount ❸,** 5min. from the TIC on Mytholmes Ln., has sweeping views and an enchanting family atmosphere. (☎645 726. Singles £29; doubles £42; triples £55.) More **B&Bs** (£15-30) await on West Ln. and Main St.; the cheaper, quainter ones are downhill. **▨The Old Registry ❸,** 2-4 Main St., has gorgeous, spacious rooms, each with a theme. (☎646 503. Singles £30; doubles and twins £50; triples £70.) For groceries, try **Spar Shop** on Station Rd. (☎647 662; open daily 7am-10:30pm). **The Fleece Inn ❶,** 67 Main St. (☎642 172), Haworth's most popular pub, has a friendly atmosphere that draws crowds of locals. **The Black Bull ❶,** once frequented by the errant Branwell Brontë, is a stone's throw from the TIC. (Open M-Sa noon-11pm, Su noon-10:30pm.) Diverse restaurants line **Mill Hey,** just east of the train station. Most only open for dinner (5:30-11pm). **Haworth Tandoori ❷,** 41 Mill Hey (☎644 726) is a local favorite.

◪ SIGHTS. Down a tiny lane behind the village church, the site where Charlotte got married and under which all but Anne are buried, the tasteful **Brontë Parsonage** details the lives of Charlotte, Emily, Anne, Branwell, and their infamously irascible father. Quiet rooms, including the dining room where the sisters penned *Wuthering Heights, Jane Eyre,* and *The Tenant of Wildfell Hall,* contain original furnishings and mementos like Char's minuscule boots and mittens. An exhibition traces the Brontës' humble origins in Ireland. (☎642 323. Open Apr.-Sept. daily

10am-5pm; Oct.-Mar. 11am-4:30pm; closed in Jan. £4.80, concessions £3.50, children £1.50, families £10.50.) A footpath behind the church leads uphill toward the pleasant (if untempestuous) **Brontë Falls**, a 2 mi. hike.

LEEDS ☎ 0113

Leeds (pop. 700,000) blossomed with textile-based prosperity in the ornate Victorian period, and today its building facades feature a curious cast of stone lions, griffins, and cherubs. Although most textile jobs have moved overseas, Britain's fourth-largest city has experienced a glamorous economic revival. The birthplace of Marks & Spencer now sports blocks of swanky shops, a dynamic arts scene, extravagant restaurants, and numerous nightlife venues, making this young professionals' hub worth a few days' exploration.

TRANSPORTATION AND PRACTICAL INFORMATION

Trains: City Station, City Sq. Ticket office open M-Sa 8am-8pm, Su 9am-6pm. Luggage storage £3.50-5. Trains (☎ (08457) 484 950) from: **London King's Cross** (2½hr., every hr., £56); **Manchester** (1½hr., 3 per hr., £10); **York** (30min.-1hr., 5 per hr., £6.50).

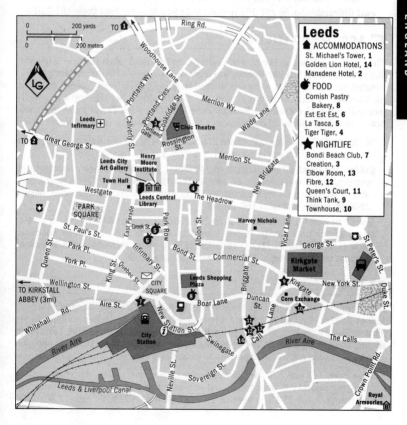

Leeds

▲ ACCOMMODATIONS
St. Michael's Tower, 1
Golden Lion Hotel, 14
Manxdene Hotel, 2

🍴 FOOD
Cornish Pastry Bakery, 8
Est Est Est, 6
La Tasca, 5
Tiger Tiger, 4

★ NIGHTLIFE
Bondi Beach Club, 7
Creation, 3
Elbow Room, 13
Fibre, 12
Queen's Court, 11
Think Tank, 9
Townhouse, 10

NORTHEAST ENGLAND

Buses: York St., next to Kirkgate Market. Office open M-F 8:30am-5:30pm, Sa 8:30am-4:30pm. Luggage storage £2. **National Express** (☎(08705) 808 080) serves Leeds from most major cities, including **Birmingham** (3-4hr., 4-6 per day, £18.50); **Edinburgh** (7hr., 2 per day, £31.50); **Glasgow** (7hr., 1 per day, £31.50); **Liverpool** (2hr., every hr., £8.25); **London** (5-6hr., 9 per day, £17.50); **Manchester** (1hr., every hr., £5.75); and **York** (45min., 3 per day, £3.75). **Metroline** (☎245 7676) runs local buses to **Bradford** (1hr., every 30min., £1) and **Hull** (1¾hr., 7 per day, £3.50).

Tourist Information Centre: Gateway Yorkshire, in the train station (☎242 5242; fax 246 8246) books rooms for £2; call ☎0800 808 050. Open M-Sa 9am-5:30pm, Su 10am-4pm. **Branch** in the bus station. Open M-F 9am-5:30pm, Sa 9am-4:30pm.

Financial Services: Every conceivable **bank** lies on Park Row. Most close at 5:30pm weekdays and 1:30pm Sa.

Police: Millgarth (☎(0845) 606 0606), north of the bus station.

Pharmacy: Boots, on Bond St. (☎243 3551), in the Leeds Shopping Plaza. Open M-F 8am-6pm, Sa 8:30am-6pm, Su 11am-5pm.

Internet Access: Leeds Central Library, the Headrow (☎247 8911), across the street from Town Hall. Free. Open M and W 9am-8pm, Tu and F 9am-5:30pm, Th 9:30am-5:30pm, Sa 10am-5pm. **Internet Exchange,** 29 Boar Ln. (☎242 1093). Fast connections at £1 per 30min. Open M-F 9:30am-7pm, Sa 10:30am-7pm, Su 11:30am-6pm.

Post Office: City Sq. (☎237 2858). Open M-Sa 9am-5:30pm. **Post Code:** LS1 2UH.

ACCOMMODATIONS

There are no hostels in Leeds, and finding a budget B&B often requires a lengthy bus ride into a suburb like **Headingly.** To get to Headingly's B&B-rich **Cardigan Rd.,** (singles average £30), take any bus toward Headingly from Infirmary St., get off at St. Michael's Church (20min.), then walk 5min. down St. Michael's Ln. Well-located hotels offer weekend discounts; the TIC's free *Visit Leeds* guide lists such hotels and their specials. Lower prices also abound during school holidays.

St. Michael's Tower, Cardigan Rd. (☎275 5557). One of the less extravagant Cardigan Rd. options, with a bright lounge and TVs. Singles £25-33; doubles £38-43. ❸

Golden Lion Hotel, 2 Lower Briggate (☎243 6454). This attractive, newly restored hotel pampers guests with room service, satellite TV, and a convenient location. Book rooms at www.laterooms.com for a discount (£49 per room) on weekends. Otherwise, singles £50-99; doubles and twins £60-110. ❹

Manxdene Hotel, 154 Woodsley Rd. (☎243 2586), a 20min. walk from the city center. Head east on Great George St., which becomes Clarendon Rd.; turn left on Woodsley. More easily accessible by bus (#56) or cab (£5). All rooms are standard with washbins. Includes breakfast. Singles £27; twins and doubles £40. ❸

FOOD

Butchers and bakers proffer their wares at **Kirkgate Market,** Europe's largest indoor market. (At Call Ln., where it becomes New York St. Indoor stalls open M-Tu and Th-Sa 9am-5pm, W 9am-1pm; outdoor stalls close 30min. earlier.) For posh dining, walk along **Greek St.** between East Parade and Park Row. **Vicar Ln.,** north of Headrow, boasts a few less expensive restaurants.

Tiger Tiger, 117 Albion St. (☎236 6999). If there were such a thing as gourmet British food, this would be it. Open terrace and alcoves of comfy snugs make for a chic dining experience. Lunch £5-10, entrees £8-15. Open M-Sa noon-2am, Su noon-12:30am. ❸

La Tasca, 4 Russell St. (☎244 2205). Warm and inviting, with a tasteful Spanish theme. Serves tasty tapas (£2-4) and paellas (£9) beneath romantic candlelit chandeliers. ❷

Est Est Est, 31-33 East Parade (☎246 0669). Features pasta and pizzas (£6-8) in an open and casual setting. ❷

The Cornish Pastry Bakery, 54 Boar Ln. (☎242 0121). Caters to students and business types. Hot pastry pockets with assorted fillings (70p-£2). Open daily 8am-8pm. ❶

◉ ⌂ SIGHTS AND SHOPPING

The much-touristed ◪**Royal Armouries** has one of the world's best collections of arms and armor. A warmonger's Graceland, the museum features war, tournament, shooting, and self-defense galleries, with interactive battle simulations, recreations of battle scenes, and demonstrations by staff in period dress. Bring the kids. (From the bus station, walk south under the overpass, veer left at the traffic circle, and turn right at Crow Bridge. Take a left at Armouries Way, just over the bridge. ☎220 1999. Open daily 10am-5pm. Free.)

Leeds's massive **library** and two art museums, clustered adjacent to the Victorian **Town Hall,** form the city's artistic center. The **Leeds City Art Gallery,** on The Headrow, features one the best collections of 20th-century British art outside London, from Victorian paintings to contemporary water colors. (☎247 8248. Open M-Tu and Th-Sa 10am-5pm, W 10am-8pm, Su 1-5pm. Free.) The adjacent **Henry Moore Institute** holds excellent traveling sculpture exhibitions. (☎234 3158. Open M-Tu and Th-Su 10am-5:30pm, W 10am-9pm. Free.) The well-maintained ruins of 12th-century **Kirkstall Abbey,** 3 mi. west of the city center on Kirkstall Rd., inspired artist J.M.W. Turner. (Take buses #732-736; disembark when you see the abbey on your left. ☎230 5492. Open daily 9am-dusk. Free.)

Leeds is widely known for its shopping, and some of the malls and stores are sights in their own right. **Cornmarket Exchange,** at the corner of Duncan St. and Call Ln., houses three balconied floors of shops with the latest in hipster-, alterna-, and clubwear. (Open M-F 9am-5:30pm, Sa 9am-6pm, and Su 10:30am-5pm.) The only British branch of **Harvey Nichols** (Hahvey Nicks, dahling!) outside of London awaits in the posh Arcade Shopping Centre on Briggate, the trendiest street in town.

◪ NIGHTLIFE

Trendy clubgoers flock to Leeds to partake in neon nights of commercial dance, house, indie-rock, and hip-hop music. Find up-to-date club listings in the monthly *Absolute Leeds,* available at the TIC.

Creation, 55 Cookridge St. (☎242 7272). Spins house, retro, and mainstream dance music on its 3 floors and outdoor balcony. Smart casual dress. Cover £4-8, free before 10pm. Open M-Th until 2am, F-Sa 3am, and Su 1:30am.

Elbow Room, 64 Call Lane, 3rd/4th fl. (☎245 7011). Stylish pool hall and bar, with funk music and a big crowd. Half-off cocktails Th-F. Pool £5-8 per hr. Cover (£3-5, free before 10pm) on Sa only. Open M-Sa noon-2am and Su noon-12:30am.

Townhouse, Assembly St. (☎2194 0040). Lines start to form around 10pm at this well-known 3-floor club. Cocktail bar on the 2nd floor and DJ every night on the 3rd floor. No cover. Open M-Sa 11:30-2am.

Think Tank, 2 Call Ln. (☎234 0980). Punk and indie rock in a dark, cozy basement. Casual dress. Cover £3-6. Open W-Sa 10pm-2am.

Queen's Court, 167 Lower Briggate (☎245 9449), under the overpass on Briggate. Leeds's premier gay club and occasional host to drag queen competitions. Cover £3. Open M and F-Sa until 2am. Next door, gay-friendly bar **Fibre** (☎234 1304) draws a young, trendy crowd. Open M-W until midnight, Th 1am, F-Sa 2am, and Su midnight.

Bondi Beach Club, Queens Bldg. at City Sq. (☎243 4733). Surfboards, bikini-clad girls, and a revolving dance floor simulate beach culture in what doorman Pat calls a "cheesy theme bar." Cover £2-5. Open M-Sa until 2:30am.

YORKSHIRE DALES

A swath of verdant hills and valleys, the Yorkshire Dales are liberally laced with sparkling rivers, subterranean caverns, and stone walls. The beauty of the dales (valleys formed by swift rivers and lazy glacial flows) is enhanced by traces of earlier residents: abandoned castles and stone farmhouses are scattered among tiny villages. Bronze and Iron Age tribes blazed winding "green lanes," footpaths that remain up on the high moorland; Romans built straight roads and stout forts; and 18th-century workers pieced together the countless stone walls. As with most British national parks, the land is not purely recreational—99% is privately owned and used for farming or other purposes. Most property owners, however, are perfectly willing to share the wealth of such marvelous countryside.

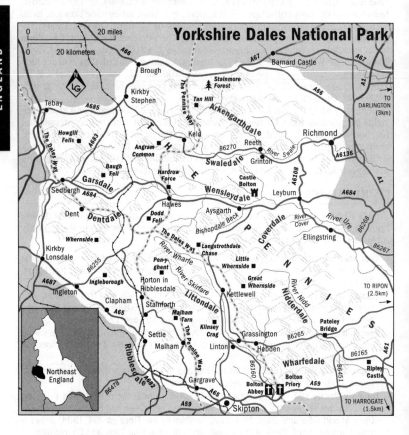

Yorkshire Dales National Park

TRANSPORTATION

Skipton is the most convenient place to enter the park. **Trains** (☎ (08457) 484 950) run there from: **Bradford** (40min., 2 per hr., £3.70); **Carlisle** (2hr., every 2hr., £13.50); **Leeds** (40min., 2 per hr., £4.80). The **Settle-Carlisle Railway** (☎ (01729) 822 007), one of England's most scenic routes, slices through **Skipton, Garsdale,** and **Kirkby Stephen** (Settle to Carlisle 1¾hr., £13.40). **National Express buses** (☎ (08705) 808 080) run to **Skipton** from **London** (1 per day, £12.40). **First Leeds** (☎ (0113) 242 0922) travels from **Leeds** (#84, 1¼hr., every hr., £2).

For those without a car and not keen on hiking long distances, good luck. The *Dales Connection* timetable (free at TICs and NPICs) helps demystify public transport. **Traveline** (☎ (0870) 608 2608) also answers transportation questions. Plan your journey in advance, as many inter-village **buses** run only a few times per week and tend to hibernate in winter. **Pride of the Dales** (☎ (01756) 753 123) connects **Skipton** to **Grassington,** sometimes continuing to **Kettlewell** (#72; M-Sa every hr., Su 3 per day; return £4.50). **Pennine Bus** (☎ (01756) 749 215) connects **Skipton** to **Settle** (#580, M-Sa every 1-2hr., return £6.90) and **Malham** (#210; M-Sa 4 per day, in summer also Su; return £6). Other villages are served less regularly, but **postbuses** run once per day to scheduled towns. **Hitchhikers** complain that pickups are infrequent; *Let's Go* does not recommend hitching.

ORIENTATION AND PRACTICAL INFORMATION

Sampling the Dales requires several days, a pair of sturdy feet, and careful planning. In the south of the park, **Skipton** serves as a transport hub and provides goods and services not available in the smaller villages. **Grassington** and **Linton,** just north, are scenic bases for exploring southern Wharfedale. **Malham** is a sensible starting point for forays into western Wharfedale and Eastern Ribblesdale. To explore Wensleydale and Swaledale in the north, move out from **Hawes** or **Leyburn.**

The following **National Park Information Centres (NPICs)** are staffed by Dales devotees. Pick up the invaluable annual park guide, *The Visitor*, and *The Yorkshire Dales Official Guide* (both free), along with numerous maps and walking guides. In addition, most towns have TICs.

Aysgarth Falls: (☎ (01969) 663 424), in Wensleydale, 1 mi. east of the village. Open Apr.-Oct. daily 9:30am-5:15pm; Nov.-Mar. Sa-Su 10am-5pm.

Clapham: (☎ (015242) 51419), in the village center. Open Apr.-Oct. daily 10am-5pm.

Grassington: Hebden Rd., Wharfedale (☎ (01756) 752 774). 24hr. info terminal. Open Apr.-Oct. daily 9:30am-5:15pm; off-season hours vary.

Hawes: Station Yard, Wensleydale (☎ (01969) 667 450). 24hr. info terminal. Open Apr.-Oct. daily 10am-5pm; some off-season weekends.

Malham: Malhamdale (☎ (01729) 830 363), at the southern end of the village. Open Apr.-Oct. daily 9:30am-5:15pm; Nov.-Mar. Sa-Su 10am-4pm.

Reeth: (☎ (01748) 850 252), in the Green. Open Apr.-Oct. daily 10am-5pm; off-season weekends with reduced hours.

Sedbergh: 72 Main St. (☎ (01539) 620 125). Open Apr.-Oct. daily 9:30am-5:15pm; Nov.-Mar. F-Sa 10am-4pm.

ACCOMMODATIONS AND CAMPING

Hostels, converted barns, tents, and B&Bs are all good options in the Dales. The free *Yorkshire Dales Accommodation Guide* is available at NPICs and TICs.

The Yorkshire Dales area hosts 12 **YHA hostels.** Hawes, Keld, and Malham lie on the Pennine Way (see p. 407), while Linton, Stainforth, Kettlewell, Dentdale, Aysgarth Falls, and Grinton Lodge sit a few miles off the Way. Ingleton, on the western edge of the park, is a good jumping-off point for the Lake District. Ellingstring, near Ripon, and Kirkby Stephen, north of Hawes, are both served by rail, but are set a little farther from the hiking trail. Hostel employees will often call other YHA hostels to help you find a bed for the next night.

Aysgarth Falls: (☎(01969) 663 260), ½ mi. east of Aysgarth on the A684 to Leyburn. Reception from 5pm. Lockout 10am-1pm. Open Apr.-Oct. daily; Nov.-Mar. Sa-Su. Dorms £10.25, under 18 £7.50. ❷

Dentdale: (☎(015396) 25251), Cowgill, on Dentdale Rd. 6 mi. east of Dent, 2 mi. from the Hawes-Ingleton road. A former shooting lodge on the River Dee. Lockout 10am-5pm. Open July-Aug. daily; Sept.-Oct. and Mar. F-Tu; Nov.-Feb. Sa-Su; Apr.-June F-W. Dorms £11.25, under 18 £8. ❷

Ellingstring: Lilac Cottage (☎(01677) 460 216), in the village. 18 beds. No smoking. Self-catering. Lockout 10am-5pm. Curfew 11pm. Open July-Aug. daily; Apr.-June and Sept.-Oct. M-Th, groups only F-Su. Dorms £7, under 18 £5. ❶

Grinton: Grinton Lodge (☎(01748) 884 206), on the "Herriot Way," ¾ mi. south of town on the Reeth-Leyburn road. Reception from 5pm. Lockout 10am-5pm. Curfew 11pm. Open Apr.-Sept. daily; Oct. M-Sa; Nov.-Mar. F-Sa. Dorms £11.25, under 18 £8. ❷

Hawes: Lancaster Terr. (☎(01969) 667 368), west of Hawes on Ingleton Rd., uphill from town. 54 beds. Enthusiastic staff. Meals £3-4. Curfew 11pm. Open July-Aug. daily; Apr.-June and Sept.-Oct. Tu-Sa; Mar. and Nov.-Dec. F-Sa. Dorms £10.25, under 18 £7. ❷

Ingleton: Greta Tower (☎(015242) 41444), downhill from Market Sq. 58 beds. Reception closed noon-5pm. Open Apr.-Aug. daily; Sept.-Oct. M-Sa; Nov.-Mar. F-Su. Dorms £11, under 18 £7.90. ❷

Keld: Keld Lodge (☎(01748) 886 259), Upper Swaledale, west of Keld village. 38 beds. No smoking. Lockout 10am-5pm. Curfew 11pm. Open Apr.-Aug. daily; Sept.-Oct. W-Su; Jan.-Mar. and Nov. F-M. Dorms £9.50, under 18 £6.75. ❶

Kettlewell: Whernside House (☎(01756) 760 232), in the village center. 43 beds. No smoking. Lockout 10am-5pm. Curfew 11pm. Open Apr.-Sept. daily; Oct.-Mar. F-Su. Dorms £10.25, under 18 £7. ❷

Kirkby Stephen: Market St. (☎(017683) 71793). In a former chapel, complete with pews and stained glass. 44 beds. Kitchen (meals available). Laundry facilities. Lockout 10am-5pm. Curfew 11pm. Open July-Aug. daily; Apr.-June and Sept.-Oct. Th-M. Dorms £9.25, under 18 £6.40. ❶

Linton: The Old Rectory (☎/fax (01756) 752 400), Linton-in-Craven, next to the village green, in a 17th-century stone rectory. Take Skipton-Grassington bus #71 or 72. Friendly staff. Lockout 10am-5pm. Open June-Aug. daily; Apr.-May and Sept.-Oct. M-Sa; Jan.-Feb. and Nov. to mid-Dec. M-Th. Dorms £10.25, under 18 £7. ❷

Malham: John Dower Memorial Hostel (☎(01729) 830 321), at Malham Tarn. Well-equipped, hiker-friendly. 82 beds. Dorms £11.25, under 18 £8. ❷

Stainforth: Taitlands (☎(01729) 823 577), 2 mi. north of Settle, ¼ mi. south of Stainforth. Georgian house, walled garden. Lockout 10am-5pm. Curfew 11pm. Open Apr.-Oct. daily; Feb.-Mar. and Nov. F-Sa. Dorms £11.25, under 18 £8. ❷

Numerous **Dales Barns ❶,** converted barns split up into hostel-style bunk rooms, cost £5-7 per night. Most have showers, kitchens, and drying rooms. Book weeks ahead and get specific directions and locations along the trails. **Airton Quaker Hostel** (☎ (01729) 830 263; £6, under 16 £3.50); **Barden Bunk Barn** (☎ (01756) 720 330; £6); and **Grange Farm Barn** (☎ (01756) 760 259; £8, under 18 £6) are all a few miles from Skipton. **Hill Top Farm** (☎ (01729) 830 320; £7.50) is in Malham. **Craken House Farm** (☎ (01969) 622 204; barn £5; B&B £25; camping £3.50) stands ½ mi. south of Leyburn. Complete lists of Dales Barns are available at TICs.

Campgrounds are difficult to reach on foot, but farmers may let you use their stretches of dale. In Skipton, try **Howarth Farm Camping and Caravan Site ❶.** (☎ (01756) 720 226. £6 per 2-person tent.) In Grassington, try **Wood Nook ❶.** (☎ (01756) 752 412. £9.60 per 2-person tent.) Near Hawes, **Bainbridge Ings ❶** is ½ mi. out of town on the Old Gale back road. (☎ (01969) 667 354. Open Apr.-Oct. £7.50 per 2-person tent and car, £1 per additional person. Showers 50p.) **Brompton-on-Swale Caravan Park ❶** is in Richmond. (☎ (01748) 824 629. Open Apr.-Oct. £9 per 2-person tent.) In Aysgarth, try **Street Head Caravan Park ❶.** (☎ (01969) 663 472. £8 per 2-person tent and car.) Ask area TICs about other caravan and camping sites.

HIKING IN THE DALES

> **ALL SHOOK UP.** Be aware that the Dales are filled with **shake holes:** small, often unmarked depressions, similar to grassy potholes, that indicate underground caverns. They can give way, and the fall could be deadly. Ordnance Survey maps and a compass are essential, especially on smaller, unmarked trails. See **Wilderness Safety,** p. 49, for other important tips.

Since buses are infrequent and the scenery breathtaking, hiking remains the best way to see the Dales. The park's seven NPICs can help you prepare for a trek along one of three long-distance footpaths. The challenging 268 mi. **Pennine Way** (see p. 407) curls from Gargrave in the south to Tan Hill in the north, passing Malham, Pen-y-ghent, Hawes, Keld, and most of the major attractions of the Dales. The more manageable 84 mi. **Dales Way** runs from Bradford and Leeds past Ilkley, through Wharfedale via Grassington and Whernside, and by Sedbergh on its way to the Lake District; it crosses the Pennine Way near Dodd Fell. The 190 mi. **Coast-to-Coast Walk** stretches from Richmond to Kirkby Stephen.

The park authority encourages visitors to keep to designated walks and to avoid falling into hidden mineshafts. Definitely take a **map** and **trail guide;** stone walls and hills all look similar after a while. Don't forget to leave gates as you find them, lest you unleash throngs of hungry, dimwitted livestock. **Ordnance Survey** maps are available for most smaller paths and can be purchased at any NPIC or outdoors supply store (£4.50-8). Good ones for specific regions include *Outdoor Leisure* #2, 21, 30, and 34, and *Landranger* #91 and 98; *Touring Map and Guide* #6 covers the Dales in general. NPICs sell leaflets (£1) covering over 30 short routes. YHA produces its own series of leaflets (30p) on dayhikes between hostels, and many hostel employees are avid walkers, so ask for suggestions. **Cyclists** can ask at NPICs for a list of rental stores and buy route cards plotting the **Yorkshire Dales Cycleway,** a series of six 20 mi. routes connecting the dales (£2.50). Bicycles are forbidden on public footpaths. If you're worried your pack may hold you back, the **Pennine Way/Dales Way Baggage Courier** will lighten your load. (☎ (01729) 830 463, mobile (0411) 835 322. £5-10 per bag.) If you'd rather not walk at all, **▧Cumbria Classic Coaches** runs various trips around the Dales in vintage coaches. (☎ (01539) 623 254; www.cumbriaclassiccoaches.co.uk. Regular trips £8 per person; special trips with accommodations around £90.)

SKIPTON
☎ 01756

Skipton is a transfer or sleeping point; once you've gathered your gear, skip town and strike for the Dales. Empty **Skipton Castle** is the main sight, and one of the most complete medieval castles in England, much to the chagrin of the Parliamentarians, whose three-year civil-war siege—the longest in British history—came to nought. (☎792 442. Open Mar.-Sept. M-Sa 10am-6pm, Su noon-6pm; Oct.-Feb. closes 4pm. £4.60, concessions £4, children £2.30.)

Skipton's **train station** is ¼ mi. west of the city center on Broughton Rd. **Buses** stop on Keighley St. between Hirds Yard and Waller Hill, behind Sunwin House. Rent and repair bikes at **Dave Ferguson Cycles,** 1 Brook St., off Gargrave Rd. (☎795 367. £8 per half-day, £14 per day. £40 deposit. Open daily 9am-5:30pm.) Car rental is available from **Skipton Self Drive,** Otley Rd. Garage. (☎792 911. From £28 per day, less for longer rentals.) Sample the Dales from the water with **Pennine Cruisers of Skipton,** The Boat Shop, 19 Coach St. (☎795 478), which rents dayboats on the Leeds and Liverpool Canal for £60-185. **Airborne Adventures Ltd.** (☎730 166) sends balloons aloft over the Dales from both Skipton and Settle. The **tourist information centre,** 35 Coach St., books accommodations for a 10% deposit. (☎792 809. Open M-F 10am-5pm, Sa 9am-5pm, Su 11am-3:30pm.) Get **camping supplies** at **George Fisher's,** by the TIC on Coach St. (☎794 305. Open M and W-Sa 9am-5:30pm, Tu 10am-5:30pm, Su 10am-4pm.) Other services include: **HSBC bank,** 61 High St. (open M-F 9:30am-4:30pm); **Internet access** at **Profile Computers,** 16 Swadford St. (☎796 622; £2 per hr.); and the **post office** in a supermarket at Sunwin House, 8 Swadford St. (☎792 724; open M-F 9am-5:30pm, Sa 9am-4pm). **Post Code:** B23 1JH.

B&Bs are moderately priced and easy to find—just look along Keighley Rd. The affable Hardings let rooms at **Carlton House ❸,** 46 Keighley Rd., where blue vases and canopy beds reign supreme. (☎700 921. Singles £25; doubles £40; off season £18 per person.) Nearly next door, **Westfield Guest House ❷,** 50 Keighley Rd., offers huge breakfasts and huge beds for small prices. (☎790 849. £18-20 per person.) Load up on fresh gooseberries and cheese at the **market,** which floods High St. (Open M, W, and F-Sa.) **Healthy Life,** 10 High St., near the church, peddles revitalizing snacks, including veggie haggis; the cafe upstairs, **Herbs ❶,** serves sandwiches for £2. (☎790 619. Store open M and W-Sa 8:30am-5:30pm, Tu 10am-5pm; cafe open M and W-Sa 9:30am-4:45pm.) The renowned **Bizzie Lizzies ❷,** 36 Swadford St., serves exceptional fish and chips for £5-7. (☎793 189. Open summer M-F 11:30am-10pm, Su noon-10pm; winter M-F 11:30am-8pm, Su noon-8pm.) Scrumptious French dinners are available at **La Cascade ❹,** 21 Keighley Rd.; make sure to hit the apple tart à la mode for dessert. (☎794 803. Open M-Sa 6pm-11pm.)

WHARFEDALE AND GRASSINGTON
☎ 01756

The valley of Wharfedale, created by the River Wharfe, is best explored using lovely **Grassington** as a base. Spectacular **Kilnsey Crag** lies 3½ mi. from Grassington toward Kettlewell, through a deep gorge and Bronze Age burial mounds; let *Wharfedale Walk #8* (available at the NPIC) be your guide. The **Stump Cross Caverns,** adorned with stalagmites and glistening rock curtains, are 5 mi. east of Grassington. Dress warmly—it gets chilly down under. (☎752 780. Open Mar.-Oct. daily 10am-4pm; Nov.-Feb. Sa-Su 10am-4pm. £4.60, children £2.40.)

Pride of the Dales **bus** #72 arrives from **Skipton** (M-Sa every hr., Su 4 per day; day return £4.50). The **NPIC,** Hebden Rd. (see p. 415), stocks the useful *Grassington Footpath Map* (£1.30), standard park trail guides (£1), and gives occasional **guided walks** (Mar.-Oct. £2-3, children £1-1.50). **The Mountaineer,** Pletts Barn Centre, at the top of Main St., sells outdoor gear. (☎752 266. Open daily 10am-5pm.) Find **Barclays** at the corner of Main St. and Hebden Rd. (open M-Tu and Th-F 9:30am-3:30pm, W 10am-3:30pm), and the **post office** at 15 Main St. (☎752 226; open M-F 9am-5:30pm, Sa 9am-12:30pm). **Post Code:** BD23 5AD.

Raines Close ❸, 13 Station Rd., lets comfortable ensuite rooms close to the center of Grassington. (☎752 678. £25-28 per person, reduced rates for longer stays.) **Burtree ❷,** a few steps from the NPIC, on the corner of Hebden Rd. and Sedber Ln., is a cottage with a glorious garden. (☎752 442. £18 per person.) Pubs and tea shops pack Main St., including **Picnic's Cafe ❶,** 10 Main St., which serves traditional hot meals for £2-6. (☎753 342. Takeaway available. Open daily 10am-5:30pm; off season closes at 3:30pm.)

MALHAMDALE AND INGLETON

Limestone cliffs and gorges slice the pastoral valley of Malhamdale, creating spectacular natural sights within easy walking distance of one another. A 4hr. hike from the NPIC will take you past the stunning, stony swath of **Malham Cove,** a massive limestone cliff, to **Malham Tarn,** Yorkshire's second-largest natural lake. Two miles from Malham village is the equally impressive **Gordale Scar,** cut in the last Ice Age by a rampaging glacier. Catch all of these beauties in *A Walk in Malhamdale* (#1), available from Malham's **NPIC** (see p. 415), while staying at the superior-grade **YHA hostel** (see p. 408), populated by Pennine Way followers. **Townhead Farm ❶,** Cove Rd., the last farm before Malham Cove, provides tent sites with showers (50p) and toilets. (☎(01729) 830 287. £3 per person; £1 per tent; £1.50 per car.)

North of Malham, the high peaks and cliffs of Ingleborough, Pen-y-ghent, and Whernside form the **Alpes Penninae.** The 24 mi. **Three Peaks Walk** connecting the Alpes begins and ends in **Horton in Ribblesdale** at the clock of the **Pen-y-ghent Cafe,** a hiker's haunt that serves as the local TIC. (☎(01729) 860 333. Open Apr.-Oct. daily 9am-5:30pm; Nov.-Mar. W-Su 9am-5pm.) The best place to break your journey is **Ingleton,** near the middle of the trek. The village's **tourist information centre,** in the community center carpark, books rooms. (☎(015242) 41049. Open Apr.-Oct. daily 10am-4:30pm.) The 4½ mi. walk through the **Ingleton Waterfalls** is one of the park's most popular routes. Pick up the walk leaflet from the TIC or check out the Ingleton town trail sign in the village center. Ingleton has a **YHA hostel** (see p. 416). Several small **B&Bs** on Main St. charge around £15; a 1 mi. walk brings you to **Stacksteads Farm ❶,** Butterthorne Rd., which offers B&B and a bunk barn with 22 beds. (☎(015242) 41386. Self-catering. B&B £20; barn £9.)

WENSLEYDALE AND HAWES ☎01969

The northerly Wensleydale landscape (a mouthful of potholes, caves, clints, and grikes) melts into a broad sash of fertile dairyland. Base your ventures in **Hawes,** which has an NPIC (see p. 415). Fork over 40p at the Green Dragon Pub to access the trail to the **Hardrow Force** waterfall (1 mi. north on the Pennine Way). If you tire of natural landscapes, visit the **Dales Countryside Museum,** in the same building as the NPIC, which chronicles the history of "real Dalespeople." (☎667 450. Open Apr.-Oct. daily 10am-5pm; winter 10am-4pm. £2, concessions £1, children free.) The solid form of **Castle Bolton** graces Wensleydale—explore it from dungeon to battlements. (☎623 981. Open Mar.-Nov. daily 10am-5pm. £4, concessions £3.) The castle is a nice day's walk from **YHA Aysgarth Falls,** while the **YHA Hawes** (see p. 416) is in town, and **B&Bs** (£17-21) line Main St.; check the list outside town hall each afternoon. Pubs, takeaways, and a **Barclays** (open M, W, F 9:30am-3:30pm; Tu 9:30am-4:30pm; Th 10am-4:30pm) are also along Main St.

Farther north, **Swaledale** is known for picture-perfect barns and meadows. Also worthwhile are **Aysgarth Falls** to the east—rolling in tiers down the Yoredale Rocks—and the natural terrace of the **Shawl of Leyburn.** Both Aysgarth and Leyburn are served by United **buses** #156-157 from Hawes to Northallerton (30-40min., every hr., return £3.90). Aysgarth's **NPIC** idles in the carpark above the falls (see p. 415), and **Leyburn** has a **tourist information centre.** (☎623 069. Open Easter-Sept. daily 9:30am-5:30pm; Oct.-Easter M-Sa 9:30am-noon and 1-4pm.)

NORTHEAST ENGLAND

YORK

☎ 01904

The history of York is the history of England.
—King George VI, then Duke of York

With a pace suitable for ambling and its tallest building a cathedral, York is as different from nearby Leeds as it is from its new American namesake. Although the well-preserved city walls have foiled many, they fail to impede present-day tourist hordes. In AD 71, the Romans founded Eboracum as a military and administrative base for Northern England; the town remained important as Anglo-Saxon "Eoforwic" and Viking "Jorvik." William I permitted York's Archbishop to officiate at his consecration, and York thanked him by joining with the Danes in 1069 to massacre 3000 men in the Conqueror's garrison, producing just some of the ghosts in the self-proclaimed "most haunted city in the world." Current marauders, brandishing zoom lenses, come seeking York's compact collection of rich historical sights—including one monster of a cathedral—and the city manages to put itself on display without sacrificing the authenticity of its heritage.

▐ TRANSPORTATION

Trains: York Station, Station Rd. Travel center open M-Sa 8am-7:45pm, Su 9am-7:45pm. Ticket office open M-Sa 5:45am-10:15pm, Su 7:30am-10:10pm. **Luggage storage** £2-4; open M-Sa 8:30am-8:30pm, Su 9:10am-8:30pm. Trains (☎(08457) 484 950) from: **Edinburgh** (2-3hr., 2 per hr., £52.50); **London King's Cross** (2hr., 2 per hr., £65); **Manchester Piccadilly** (1½hr., 2 per hr., £16.10); **Newcastle** (1hr., 2 per hr., £15.50); **Scarborough** (50min., 2 per hr., £10.60).

Buses: (☎551 400). Stations at Rougier St., Exhibition Sq., the train station, and on Piccadilly. **National Express** (☎(08705) 808 080) from: **Edinburgh** (5hr., 2 per day, £26.50); **London** (4½hr., 6 per day, £19.50); **Manchester** (3hr., 6 per day, £7.25).

Local Transportation: First York (☎622 992, timetables 551 400). Ticket office open M-Sa 8:30am-4:30pm. **Yorkshire Coastliner** (☎(0113) 244 8976 or (01653) 692 556) runs buses from the train station to **Castle Howard** (see p. 426).

Taxis: Station Taxis (☎623 332 or 628 197). 24hr.

Bike Rental: Bob Trotter, 13 Lord Mayor's Walk (☎622 868). From £8 per day; £50 deposit. Open M-Sa 9am-5:30pm, Su 10am-4pm.

▐▐ ORIENTATION AND PRACTICAL INFORMATION

Today, York's streets present a greater obstacle than the ancient walls ever did. They're winding, short, rarely labeled, and prone to name-changes. Fortunately, most attractions lie within the **city walls,** so you can't get too lost, and the towers of the **Minster,** visible from nearly everywhere, provide easy orientation. The **River Ouse** (rhymes with "muse") cuts through the city, curving west to south. The city center lies between the Ouse and the Minster; **Coney St., Parliament St.,** and **Stonegate** are the main thoroughfares. The **Shambles,** York's quasi-medieval shopping district, lies between Parliament St. and Colliergate.

Tourist Information Centres: Exhibition Sq. (☎621 756; www.york-tourism.co.uk). Books rooms for £3 plus a 10% deposit. The *York Visitor Guide* (50p) has a detailed map. *Snickelways of York* (£5) is an offbeat self-tour. Open June-Oct. daily 9am-6pm; Nov.-May 9am-5pm. **Branch** in the train station. **Bureau de change.** Open June-Oct. M-

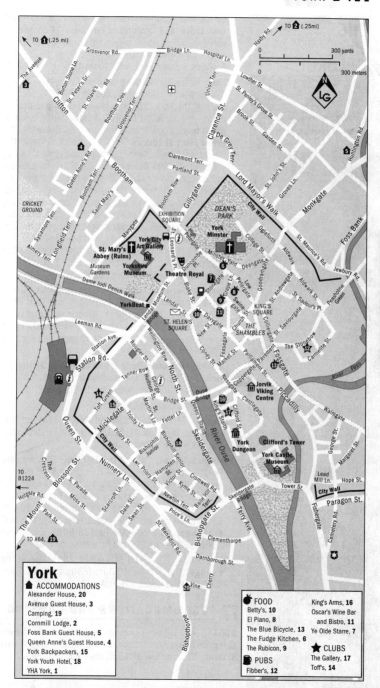

TO 1 (.25 mi)

TO 2 (.25mi)

Grosvenor Rd.
Bridge Ln.
Hospital Ln.
Haxby Rd.

0   300 yards
0   300 meters

The Avenue
3
Clifton
Burton Stone Ln.
St. Peter's Gr.
St. Olave's Rd.
Grosvenor Terr.
Bootham Cres.
Union Terr.
Lowther St.
Clarence St.
De Grey Terr.
St. Penley's Grove St.
Brook St.
Garden St.
Monkgate
5
Huntington Rd.

Queen Anne's Rd.
4
Bootham Terr.
Bootham
Saint Mary's
Claremont Terr.
Portland St.
Bootham Row
Gillygate
Lord Mayor's Walk
DEAN'S PARK
City Wall
St. John's St.
Groves Ln.
St. Maurice's Rd.
Aldwark
Foss Bank

CRICKET GROUND
Sycamore Terr.
Almery Terr.
Longfield Terr.
Marygate
St. Leonard's Pl.
EXHIBITION SQUARE
High Petergate
Duncombe Pl.
York Minster
College St.
Minster Yard
6
Deangate
Ogleforth
St. Andrewgate
St. Saviour's Pl.
Jewbury Rd.
Peasholme Green

St. Mary's Abbey (Ruins)
York City Art Gallery
Museum Gardens
Yorkshire Museum
Dame Judi Dench Walk
Theatre Royal
Low Petergate
Stonegate
7
8
Grape Ln.
Swine-gate
KING'S SQUARE
Colliergate
Collier St.
Goodramgate

YorkBoat
Lendal Museum St.
Lendal Bridge
ST. HELEN'S SQUARE
New St.
Davygate
9
10
11
THE SHAMBLES
Church St.
Saviourgate
The Stonebow
Carmelite St.
12

Leeman Rd.
Wellington Row
Coney St.
Market St.
Parliament St.
Pavement
Fossgate
13
River Foss

Station Ave.
Station Rd.
Rougier St.
Tanner Row
George Hudson St.
North St.
Bridge St.
Ouse Bridge
King's Staith
Coppergate
Castlegate
Jorvik Viking Centre
Piccadilly
Walmgate

Queen St.
Micklegate
15
City Wall
Tanner Row
Martin's Ln.
Trinity Ln.
Fetter Ln.
Queen's Staith
River Ouse
16
Clifford St.
York Dungeon
Clifford's Tower
York Castle Museum
George St.
Margaret St.

TO B1224
Blossom St.
S. Parade
Moss St.
Priory St.
Bishophill Junior
Bishophill Senior
Cromwell Rd.
18
Skeldergate
Lead Mill Ln.
Hope St.

The Crescent
The Mount
Park St.
Holgate Rd.
Nunnery Ln.
Scarcroft Ln.
Dale St.
Swan St.
Hampden St.
Victor St.
Kyme St.
Newton Terr.
Balie Hill Terr.
Price's Ln.
Skeldergate Bridge
Terry Ave.
Tower St.
City Wall
Paragon St.
Fishergate

TO A64
19
St. Benedict Rd.
Clementhorpe
Darnborough St.
Bishopthorpe
Cemetery Rd.

Vine
Cherry
20

York

▲ ACCOMMODATIONS
Alexander House, **20**
Avenue Guest House, **3**
Camping, **19**
Cornmill Lodge, **2**
Foss Bank Guest House, **5**
Queen Anne's Guest House, **4**
York Backpackers, **15**
York Youth Hotel, **18**
YHA York, **1**

☕ FOOD
Betty's, **10**
El Piano, **8**
The Blue Bicycle, **13**
The Fudge Kitchen, **6**
The Rubicon, **9**

King's Arms, **16**
Oscar's Wine Bar and Bistro, **11**
Ye Olde Starre, **7**

🍺 PUBS
Fibber's, **12**

★ CLUBS
The Gallery, **17**
Toff's, **14**

THE BIG SPLURGE

VIVE LA FRANCE: CONTINENTAL DINING AT THE BLUE BICYCLE

The Blue Bicycle wants you to forget about England for awhile. And no matter what degree of anglophilism followed you in, by the time you're finished with dinner, you might be planning your next holiday... on the other side of the Channel.

Smooth-talking French waiters rush flowerpots (yes, flowerpots) of freshly baked bread to each table, then delight oenophiles by pouring oversize glasses from an absurdly long wine list. Flickering candlelight glancing across wooden tables makes for an atmosphere straight out of "A Year in Provence," or the Loire Valley, or whichever portion of the French countryside you prefer. The food, centered around fresh produce and careful preparation (rather than the more typical creams and sauces), is at once simple and filling (entrees £11-18).

The downstairs area is a bit more risqué than its rustic upstairs: intended to recall Fossgate's former glory days as York's red light district, the decor includes overstuffed pillows and oversize mirrors. *(34 Fossgate. ☎ 673 990. Open M-Su noon-2:30pm and 6pm-10pm.)*

Sa 9am-8pm, Su 9am-5pm; Nov.-May daily 9am-5pm. **York Visitor and Conference Bureau,** 20 George Hudson St. (☎ 554 455), offers similar services. Books rooms for £4 plus a 10% deposit. Open M-Sa 9am-5:30pm; in summer also Su 10am-4pm.

Tours: A free 2hr. **walking tour** is offered daily by the Association of Voluntary Guides (☎ 630 284). Meet in front of the York City Art Gallery; tour times posted across the street at the TIC. A bewildering array of **ghost tours** all offer similar experiences. Brave the 1hr. **Ghost Hunt of York** (☎ 608 700), which meets at the Shambles daily 7:30pm. £3, "boils and ghouls" (a.k.a. children) £2. **York Pullman** (☎ 622 992) runs a variety of half- and full-day tours of the Yorkshire Dales and Moors (£7-20). **Guide Friday** (☎ 640 896) leads its familiar hop-on/hop-off bus tours. £6, concessions £4, families £12. Several companies along the **River Ouse** near Lendal, Ouse, and Skeldergate Bridges offer 1hr. **boat cruises,** including **YorkBoat,** Lendal Bridge (☎ 628 324). Office open from 10:30am. Easter-Oct. 2 trips per hr.; Feb.-Mar. and Nov. at least 2 per day, call ahead. £6, seniors £5.50, children £3.

Financial Services: Banks fill Coney St. **Thomas Cook,** 4 Nessgate (☎ 881 400). Open M-W and F-Sa 9am-5:30pm, Th 10am-5:30pm. **American Express,** 6 Stonegate (☎ 676 501). Open M-F 9am-5:30pm, Sa 9am-5pm; in summer **bureau de change** also open Su 10:30am-4:30pm.

Launderette: Haxby Road Washeteria, 124 Haxby Rd. (☎ 623 379). Open M-F 8am-6pm, Sa 8am-5:30pm, Su 8am-4:30pm. Last wash 2hr. before close.

Police: Fulford Rd. (☎ 631 321).

Hospital: York District Hospital (☎ 631 313), off Wigginton Rd. Take bus #1, 2, 3, or 18 from Exhibition Sq. and ask for the hospital stop.

Internet Access: Cafe of the Evil Eye, 42 Stonegate (☎ 640 002). Vends cocktails, coffees, and Internet access (£2 per hr.). After 6pm, 1 free hr. of webtime for every drink you buy. **Gateway Internet Cafe,** 26 Swinegate (☎ 646 446). 50p quick check, £1.50 per 15min., £4 per hr; 20% student discount. **Internet Exchange,** 13 Stonegate (☎ 638 808). £1.50 per 15min., £5 per hr; 99p per hr. with student ID.

Post Office: 22 Lendal St. (☎ 617 285). **Bureau de change.** Open M-Tu 8:30am-5:30pm, W-Sa 9am-5:30pm. **Post Code:** YO1 8DA.

▐ ACCOMMODATIONS AND CAMPING

B&Bs (from £18) are concentrated on the side streets along **Bootham** and **Clifton,** in the Mount area down **Blossom St.,** and on **Bishopthorpe Rd.,** due south of town. Book weeks ahead in summer, when competition for inexpensive beds is fierce; the TICs and the Visitor and Conference Bureau may help.

▨ **York Backpackers,** 88-90 Micklegate (☎/fax 627 720; yorkbackpackers@cwcom.net). Fun atmosphere in a stately 18th-century mansion. Kitchen and laundry facilities. TV lounge. Internet access £2.50 per 30min. "Dungeon Bar" open 3 nights per week, long after the pubs close. Dorms £9-14; doubles £30. ❶

▨ **Avenue Guest House,** 6 The Avenue (☎620 575; www.avenuegh.fsnet.co.uk), off Clifton on a quiet, residential side street. Enthusiastic hosts provide immaculate rooms surrounding an impressive spiral staircase. Soft beds and plush towels make it a step up without being pricey. All rooms with TV. Some ensuite family rooms. Singles £18-20; doubles £34-38, with bath £38-44. ❷

Alexander House, 94 Bishopthorpe Rd. (☎625 016). Just outside the city walls and barely 5min. from the train station. King-sized beds in 4 luxurious ensuite doubles adorned with paintings and fresh flowers. Sparkling bathrooms have toiletries and fluffy towels. Doubles £32.50-34.50 per person; as single £55-59. ❹

Cornmill Lodge, 120 Haxby Rd. (☎620 566; cornmill_lodge@hotmail.com). From Exhibition Sq. go up Gillygate to Clarence St. and then Haxby Rd., or take bus A1 from the station. Purify body and soul in this quiet, vegetarian B&B. Clean, convivial rooms with TV. Singles £20-30; doubles £40-60. ❸

Queen Anne's Guest House, 24 Queen Anne's Rd. (☎629 389), a short walk out Bootham from Exhibition Sq. Spotless singles and doubles with TVs; some doubles with bath. Friendly proprietors serve regal breakfasts. Singles from £18-20; doubles £32-40; discount for *Let's Go* users. ❷

YHA York, Water End (☎653 147), Clifton, 1 mi. from town. From Exhibition Sq., walk ¾ mi. on Bootham and turn left at Water End; from the train station follow the river path "Dame Judi Dench" (connects to Water End); or take a bus to Clifton Green and walk ¼ mi. Bedroom lockout 10am-1pm. Open mid-Jan. to mid-Dec. Dorms £16, under 18 £12; singles £18.50; twins £37; family rooms £52-78. ❷

Foss Bank Guest House, 16 Huntington Rd. (☎635 548). Walk or take bus #13 from the train station. Comfortable beds and wooden desks in clean rooms by the River Foss. Doubles are particularly luxurious. All rooms with shower and sink, some with bathtub and TV. No smoking. Singles £25; doubles £46-52; discount for *Let's Go* users. ❸

York Youth Hotel, 11-15 Bishophill Senior (☎625 904; info@yorkyouthhotel.com). Well-located hostel catering primarily to groups. Bar open 9pm-1am. Laundry facilities. Key deposit £3. Reception 24hr. Dorms £10-13; singles £20-25; twins £15-17. ❷

Camping: Riverside Caravan and Camping Park (☎705 812), Ferry Ln., Bishopthorpe, 2 mi. south of York off the A64. Take bus #23 and ask the driver to let you off at the campsite (2 per hr., return £1.30). July-Aug. £8 per 2-person tent; Sept.-June £7. ❶

FOOD AND PUBS

Greengrocers peddle at **Newgate Market** between Parliament St. and Shambles. (Open M-Sa 9am-5pm; Apr.-Dec. also Su 9am-4:30pm.) There are more **pubs** in the center of York than gargoyles on the Minster's east wall. Most are packed on weekend nights, and all serve bar meals during the day.

Oscar's Wine Bar and Bistro, 8 Little Stonegate (☎652 002), off Stonegate. This popular pub has a swank courtyard, varied menu, and lively mood. Live jazz and blues M nights. Hearty grub in massive portions (£6-8) will keep you going for a week. Happy hour Su-M 4pm-close, Tu-F 5-7pm. Open daily 11am-11pm. ❷

The Fudge Kitchen, 58 Low Petergate (☎645 596). Over 20 scrumptious flavors of gooey fudge, from Vintage Vanilla to Banoffee (slices £2.50-3). Nibble a free sample while the sweet goodness is made before your very eyes. Open M-Sa 10am-5:30pm. ❶

El Piano, 15 Grape Ln. (☎ 610 676). Laid-back atmosphere and low lighting make this ideal for an hour or so of relaxation. Latin flavors infuse fresh veggie dishes (tapas £3, entrees around £8). Open M-Sa 10am-midnight. ❷

The Rubicon, 5 Little Stonegate (☎ 676 076), off Stonegate. Vegetarian restaurant has creative options (£3.50-6.50), such as butterbean and hazelnut pâté, and sandwiches (£4.50) for upscale, ladies-who-lunch clientele. Generously portioned dinners £7-9. Vegan and gluten-free options. Open daily 11:30am-10pm. ❷

Ye Olde Starre, 40 Stonegate (☎ 623 063). The city's oldest pub, with a license that dates back to 1644. Pub meals (£4-7), with sumptuous *chili con carne*, bursting Guinness pie, and giant Yorkshire puddings, plus a pleasant inner courtyard. Open M-Sa 11am-11pm, Su noon-3pm and 7-10:30pm. ❶

Betty's, 6-8 St. Helens Sq. Traditional cream teas (£5-9 for scones, finger-sandwiches, clotted cream, etc...) are served in a terrifically refined atmosphere. Also serves lunch and dinner (£3-12). Live piano music daily 6-9pm. Open daily 9am-9pm. ❷

⬛ SIGHTS

The best introduction to York is a walk along its **medieval walls** (2½ mi.), especially the northeast section. Beware the tourist stampede, which weakens only in early morning and just before the walls close at dusk.

▨ YORK MINSTER

You can't miss it. ☎ 639 347. *Open summer daily 7am-8:30pm; winter 7am-6pm. Evensong M-F 5pm, Sa-Su 4pm. Tours 9:30am-3:30pm. Requested donation £3.*

Everything (and everyone) in York converges at its Minster, and justifiably so: the largest Gothic cathedral in Britain is sure to awe even the most jaded of cathedral hounds. Within this building, Miles Coverdale translated the first complete printed English Bible in 1535. If the interior seems to glitter, it's because an estimated half of all the medieval stained glass in England holds the walls together. The **Great East Window,** constructed from 1405 to 1408 and depicting both the beginning and the end of the world in over a hundred small scenes, is the largest single medieval glass window in the world—it's as big as a tennis court. Also world-famous, although nobody seems to know why, is the **Monkey's Funeral,** the fifth pane to the left upon entering the cathedral (look in the bottom right corner).

CENTRAL TOWER. It's a mere 275 steps up to the top of the tower, but ascents are only allowed during a 5min. period every 30min., as the staircase won't allow passing traffic. *(Open June-Sept. daily 9:30am-6:30pm; May 10am-6pm; Apr. and Oct. 10am-5:30pm; Mar. and Nov. 10am-4:30pm. £3, children £1.)*

FOUNDATIONS, CRYPT, AND TREASURY. Displays narrate how the Minster's central tower began to crack in 1967. You can tour the huge concrete and steel foundations inserted by engineers, remnants of the previously unearthed buildings, and treasured items of the cathedral. Plunge to the **Roman level** to explore the remains of the Roman headquarters and town, including the spot where Constantine the Great was proclaimed emperor. Along the way, duck into the **crypt,** which isn't a crypt at all but rather the altar of the Saxon-Norman church, with the shrine of **St. William** and the 12th-century **Doomstone** upon which the cathedral was built. *(Open June-Sept. daily 9:30am-6:30pm; May 10am-6pm; Apr. and Oct. 10am-5:30pm; Mar. and Nov. 10am-4:30pm. £3, concessions £2.60, children £1, families £6.50.)*

CHAPTER HOUSE AND LIBRARY. If you fancy grotesque medieval carvings, the **Chapter House** is the place to be. Every minute figure is unique, from mischievous demons to a three-faced woman; keep an eye out for the tiny Virgin Mary, so small she went unnoticed by Cromwell's idol-smashing thugs. Pick up the safari guide (20p) on your way in to help your hunt. **Minster Library,** designed by Christopher Wren, guards manuscripts at the far corner of the grounds. *(Chapter House open June-Sept. daily 9:30am-6:30pm; May 10am-6pm; Apr. and Oct. 10am-5:30pm; Mar. and Nov. 10am-4:30pm. £1, concessions 80p. Library open M-Th 10am-4pm, F 10am-noon. Free.)*

OTHER SIGHTS

◪**YORK CASTLE MUSEUM.** Housed in a former debtor's prison, the huge York Castle Museum lives up to its billing as Britain's premier museum dedicated to everyday life. Fascinating and extensive, the exhibits were the brainchild of the eccentric Dr. John Kirk, who began collecting items during his housecalls from the 1890s to the 1920s. The many era-themed rooms include **Kirkgate,** an intricately reconstructed Victorian shopping street complete with carriage, and **Half Moon Court,** its Edwardian counterpart. *(Between Tower St. and Piccadilly St. ☎653 611. Open Apr.-Oct. daily 9:30am-5pm; Nov.-Mar. 9:30am-4:30pm. £6.75, concessions £4, families £18.)*

◪**JORVIK VIKING CENTRE.** This is one of the busiest places in the city; arrive early or late to avoid lines, or book at least a day ahead. Visitors ride through the York of AD 948 in floating "time cars," past artifacts, painfully accurate smells, and eerily life-like, mobile mannequins. Watch out for the evidence that Vikings, too, had bodily functions. *(Coppergate. ☎643 211; advance bookings 543 403. Open Apr.-Oct. daily 9am-5:30pm; Nov.-Dec. 10am-4:30pm; Jan.-Mar. Su-F 9am-3:30pm, Sa 9am-4:30pm. Last admission 1hr. before close. £9, concessions £7.50, children £6, families £23.)*

CLIFFORD'S TOWER. This tower is one of the last remaining pieces of York Castle, and a chilling reminder of the worst outbreak of anti-Semitic violence in English history. In 1190, Christian merchants tried to erase their debts to Jewish bankers by destroying York's Jewish community. On the last Sabbath before Passover, 150 Jews took refuge in a tower that previously stood on this site and, faced with the prospect of starvation or butchery, committed suicide. Visitors can read informative storyboards along a wall walk with panoramic views. *(Tower St. ☎601 901. Open July-Aug. daily 9:30am-7pm; Apr.-June and Sept. 10am-6pm; Oct. 10am-5pm; Nov.-Mar. 10am-4pm. £2.10, concessions £1.60, children £1.10, families £5.30.)*

YORKSHIRE MUSEUM AND GARDENS. Hidden in ten gorgeous acres of gardens, the Yorkshire Museum presents Roman, Anglo-Saxon, and Viking artifacts, as well as the £2.5 million **Middleham Jewel** (c. 1450), an enormous sapphire set in a gold amulet engraved with the Trinity and the Nativity. In the gardens, children chase pigeons into lovers reclining among the haunting ruins of **St. Mary's Abbey,** once the most influential Benedictine monastery in northern England. *(Enter from Museum St. or Marygate. ☎551 800. Open daily 10am-5pm. £4, concessions £3, families £11.50. Gardens, pigeons, and ruins free.)*

BEST OF THE REST. The **York City Art Gallery,** on Exhibition Sq. across from the TIC, has an uneven collection of Continental work, a better selection of English painters (including William Etty, York native and pioneer of the English painted nude), and a spattering of pottery. *(☎551 861. Open daily 10am-5pm, last admission 4:30pm. £2, concessions £1.50.)* The morbidly inclined should try **York Dungeon,** 12 Clifford St. Learn the story of Guy Fawkes and Dick Turpin, stare at sore-ridden bodies in the Plague exhibit and mangled wax figures in the Torture exhibit. *(☎632 599. Open Apr.-Sept. daily 10am-5:30pm; Oct.-Mar. 10am-4:30pm. £7, concessions £5, children £4.50.)*

◧ ▒ NIGHTLIFE AND FESTIVALS

For help planning your attack of after-hours York, consult the monthly *What's On* and *Artscene* guides (available at the TIC), which have listings of live music, theater, cinema, and exhibitions. A **ghost tour** makes a lively start to the evening (see p. 422), while calmer twilight activities take place in **King's Square** and on **Stonegate,** where barbershop quartets share the pavement with jugglers, magicians, and soapboxers. The 250-year-old **Theatre Royal,** next to the TIC on St. Leonards Pl., offers stage fare. (☎ 623 568; 24hr. info 610 041. Box office open M-Sa 10am-8pm. £6-30, student standbys £4.) Have a pint at the **King's Arms,** King's Staith (☎ 659 435), a constantly packed pub with outdoor seating along the Ouse—except during floods. Highwater markers inside the pub glorify the forces of nature. York's dressy new club, **The Gallery,** 12 Clifford St., has two dance floors and six bars. (☎ 647 947. No trainers. Cover £1.50-4. Open F-W 9:30pm-2am, Th 10pm-2am.) The excellent **Toff's,** 3-5 Toft Green, plays mainly dance and house. (☎ 620 203. No trainers. Cover £3.50, F free before 10:30pm. Open M-Sa 9pm-2am.) **Fibber's,** Stonebow House, the Stonebow, doesn't lie about the quality of live music playing nightly at 8pm. (☎ 466 148. Check *What's On* for events.)

The Minster and local churches host a series of **summer concerts.** July's **York Early Music Festival** celebrates Purcell and friends. (☎ 658 338 for more information.) The city recently revived a tradition of many centuries past, performing the medieval **York Mystery Plays** in the nave of the Minster during June and July every few years— the next performances will be in 2004. (☎ 635 444 for more information.)

▶ DAYTRIP FROM YORK

▒ CASTLE HOWARD

15 mi. northeast of York. Yorkshire Coastliner bus #842 runs half-day excursions (5 per day, return £4.50); reduced admission with bus ticket. ☎ (01653) 648 333. Open mid-Mar. to Nov. daily 11am-4:30pm; gardens 10am-6:30pm. 10min. chapel services Sa-Su 5:15pm. £7.50, concessions £6.75, children £4.50. Gardens only £4.50, children £2.50.

Castle Howard, still inhabited by the Howard family, made its TV debut in the BBC adaptation of Evelyn Waugh's *Brideshead Revisited.* Grand halls (including a spectacular entrance with marble floors) and stairways are cluttered with Roman busts and festooned with portraits of Howard ancestors in full regalia. The **long gallery** is a dwarfing promenade between enormous windows and shelves stuffed with books. Head to the **chapel** for the kaleidoscopic stained glass. More stunning than the castle itself are its 999 acres of glorious **grounds,** including luxurious rose gardens, fountains, and lakes, all roamed by raucous peacocks. Be sure to see the domed **Temple of the Four Winds,** whose hilltop perch offers views of rolling hills, still waters, and lazy cows. Kids can entertain themselves at the **Lakeside Adventure Playground,** should architecture and landscaping fail to hold their attention.

NORTH YORK MOORS

Imagining Heathcliff and Dracula upon Yorkshire's windy moors requires no suspension of disbelief: these heathered expanses and cliff-lined coasts have changed little since inspiring Emily Brontë and Bram Stoker. The North York Moors easily ranks as one of the country's most splendid national parks. Among its attractions: lonely hills cheered by the largest swath of heather in England (flowering from July to early September), deep-sided valleys, two superb scenic railways, an impossibly dramatic coastline, and endearing towns.

North York Moors National Park

National Park Information Centre
(i) Tourist Information Centre
The Cleveland Way

North Sea

Northeast England

FROM THE ROAD

SHOWER POWER

Most travel guides spend pages telling you how to purchase traveler's checks and keep clear of European stinging nettles, when, really, how to avoid exhibitionary nakedness and evade plumbing disasters are much more pertinent (and interesting) topics. In Britain, the bathing establishment has an unsettling habit of building showers in front of large windows. It also has a habit of "accidentally" forgetting to put curtains on those windows. Then there's the building code, which apparently says it's okay to build houses so close that you can inspect your neighbor's dental work without leaving home.

A B&B I stayed at recently (quite a nice one, mind you: big fluffy beds, an affectionate Burmese cat happily drooling on my hand, and a kindly owner plying me with tea and cakes) had one of these shameless showers. It was late evening and completely dark outside when I walked into the shower-room like the heroine of a decadently twisted film noir (okay, a lame, boring film noir). The shower was, as expected, in front of the window, and as usual, the window was curtainless.

Feeling Terribly Clever, I turned the light off and set about figuring out the shower. It consisted of two pull strings, two twisting knobs, one button, and one switch, as well as a soap dispenser I decided not to mess with. I turned the most likely looking knob and was pelted with icy cold water. Twisting the knob all the way to the right didn't change the temperature. I yanked one of the pull cords.

▆ TRANSPORTATION

The primary gateways to the North York Moors are **York** to the south and **Middlesbrough** to the north. Middlesbrough is a short train ride from **Darlington** (every hr., £3.10), which is on the main London-Edinburgh rail line. The *Moors Connections* pamphlet, free at TICs and National Park Information Centres (NPICs), covers bus and rail service in glorious detail—service varies by season and is significantly reduced in winter. **Traveline** also provides timetables (☎ (0870) 608 2608).

Three **train** lines serve the park. There's frequent service between **York** and **Scarborough** (45min., 2 per hr., £9.30). The scenic **Esk Valley Line** runs from **Middlesbrough** to **Whitby** via **Danby** and **Grosmont** (1½hr., 4-7 per day, £7.30). The tourist-oriented **North Yorkshire Moors Railway** (reservations ☎ (01751) 472 508; timetables (01751) 473 535) links the north and south, chugging from **Pickering** to **Grosmont** (1hr., 3-7 per day, no service during some off-season times; see p. 433).

Buses cover more turf and run more frequently than trains. Many of the operators mentioned here offer daily or weekly passes; it's worth inquiring, as these can save money. Yorkshire Coastliner (☎ (0113) 244 8976) #840 travels between **Leeds, York, Pickering,** and **Whitby** (3hr., 5 per day) while #843 runs between **Leeds, York,** and **Scarborough** (3hr., every hr.). Arriva bus #93/93A journeys between **Middlesbrough, Whitby, Robin Hood's Bay** (93A only), and **Scarborough** (2hr., 2 per hr.). Scarborough and District (☎ (01723) 503 020) bus #128 covers **Scarborough, Pickering,** and **Helmsley** (1½hr., every hr.). The national park operates the **Moorsbus**, with routes throughout the park; schedules are available at all TICs (☎ (01845) 597 426; www.moorsbus.net; Apr.-Oct. Su and bank holidays; all-day pass £2.50).

✳ ORIENTATION

North York Moors National Park is 30 mi. north of York. Toward the park's southwest corner, quiet, appealing **Helmsley** has several worthwhile sights and good access to hiking, particularly when the park's Moorsbus shuttle is operating (see above). To the east, centrally-located **Pickering** is the starting point for the scenic **North Yorkshire Moors Railway,** a sweat-free way to see the park. The **Esk Valley,** cutting across the north of the park and served by another beautiful railway, the Esk Valley Line, is good terrain for hikers. The seaside resort towns **Whitby** and **Scarborough** are often flooded with summer vacationers and feel removed from the park proper. **Robin Hood's Bay,** just south of Whitby, is a picturesque coastal village.

🛈 PRACTICAL INFORMATION

The *Moors & Coast* visitor guide (50p), available at any TIC or NPIC, is particularly useful.

NATIONAL PARK INFORMATION CENTRES

Danby: The Moors Centre (☎(01287) 660 654). From the Danby train station, turn left after you pass the gate, and right at the crossroads before the Duke of Wellington Pub; the Centre is ½ mi. ahead on the right (20min.). The Moors' largest NPIC. Open Apr.-Oct. daily 10am-5pm; Nov.-Dec. and Mar. 11am-4pm; Jan.-Feb. Sa-Su 11am-4pm.

Sutton Bank: (☎(01845) 597 426), 6 mi. east of Thirsk on the A170. Open Apr.-Oct. daily 10am-5pm; Mar. and Nov.-Dec. 11am-4pm; Jan.-Feb. Sa-Su 11am-4pm.

TOURIST INFORMATION CENTRES

Goathland: The Village Store and Outdoor Centre (☎(01947) 896 207). Open Easter-Oct. daily 10am-5pm; Nov.-Easter M-W and F-Su 10am-4pm.

Great Ayton: High Green Car Park (☎(01642) 722 835). Open Apr.-Oct. M-Sa 10am-4pm, Su 1-4pm.

Guisborough: Priory Grounds, Church St. (☎(01287) 633 801). Open Apr.-Sept. Tu-Su 9am-5pm; Oct.-Mar. W-Su 9am-5pm. Closed daily noon-12:30pm (F noon-1pm).

Helmsley: Town Hall, Market Pl. (☎(01439) 770 173), in the town center. Open Mar.-Sept. daily 9:30am-6pm; Oct. 9:30am-5:30pm; Nov.-Feb. F-Su 10am-4pm.

Pickering: The Ropery (☎(01751) 473 791), beside the library. Open Mar.-Oct. M-Sa 9:30am-6pm, Su 9:30am-5:30pm; Nov.-Feb. M-Sa 10am-4:30pm.

Scarborough: see p. 432.

Whitby: see p. 434.

🛏 ACCOMMODATIONS AND CAMPING

Local TICs book beds for a small fee and 10% deposit. **B&Bs, hotels,** and **caravan parks** in or near the national park are listed under the appropriate towns. The following **YHA hostels** provide lodging in the Moors. As always, reservations are not a bad idea. Clearly named bus stops are rare; tell drivers where you're headed.

The entire tub began shaking violently and water spurted two feet up the sides. I yanked desperately at the other cord. The light burst on, the neighbor looked up, and I stopped, dropped, and rolled into a towel. Something under the tub made a high pitched, warning-like whistle. Envisioning my editors gaping at a bill for one new tub, one new shower head, one re-tiled wall, and one new ceiling, I jumped up and managed to turn the whole dang thing off. The next half hour was spent drying the soaking wet opposite wall. Travel writing is every bit as glamorous as they say.

How to avoid this sort of situation: In general, the pull cord farthest from the shower operates the fan and/or lightswitch. Closer pull cords often turn the hot water on. Turning the swivel-knob won't do a bit of good until the heat's on. Be sure NOT to turn it all the way over before turning on the hot water—third-degree burns aren't as cool as they sound. Some showers have only one pull cord, which might serve either function.

Other showers have a cord that turns on the tub jets, while a wall switch turns the light on. Still others possess small white boxes with a button that turns the shower on and off and two knobs, marked "temperature" and "pressure," but which may control the opposite features. Be wary of soap vs. shampoo dispensers—I have twice Dove-soaped my hair.

Also, many apparently curtainless windows have small grooves along the top, concealing the Wily Shade.

— Jenny Pegg

Boggle Hole: (☎(01947) 880 352; fax 880 987), Mill Beck, Fylingthorpe. Easy access to the Cleveland Way and Coast-to-Coast trails. Seaside 19th-century mill, 1 mi. south of Robin Hood's Bay along the beach or (during high tides) cliffs. Reception opens 1pm. Curfew 11pm. Open Feb.-Oct. daily; Nov. F-Sa. Dorms £10.25, under 18 £7. ❷

Helmsley: (☎/fax (01439) 770 433). From Market Pl. take Bondgate Rd., turn left onto Carlton Rd., and left again at Carlton Ln.; hostel is on the left. Lockout 10am-5pm. Curfew 11pm. Open Apr.-Aug. daily; Sept.-Oct. Tu-Sa. Dorms £9.50, under 18 £6.75. ❶

Lockton: The Old School (☎(01751) 460 376), off the Pickering-Whitby Rd. 2 mi. from the North Yorkshire Moors Railway station at Levisham. 4 mi. north of Pickering; take Coastliner bus #840 toward Whitby. Self-catering. Reception opens 5pm. Open July-Aug. daily; June and Sept. M-Sa. Dorms £7.75, under 18 £5.50. ❶

Osmotherley: (☎(01609) 883 575; fax 883 715), Cote Ghyll, Northallerton. Between Stockton and Thirsk, just northeast of Osmotherley. Reception opens 1pm. Open Mar.-Oct. daily; Feb. F-Sa. Dorms £10.25, under 18 £7. ❷

Scarborough: The White House, Burniston Rd. (☎(01723) 361 176; fax 500 054), 2 mi. from Scarborough. Bus #3 from the train station, or follow the signs on Royal Albert Dr. ½ mi. past the Promenade. In a former mill on a river, 10min. from the sea. Lockout 10am-5pm. Open Mar.-Aug. daily; Sept.-Oct. M-Sa. Dorms £10.25, under 18 £7. ❷

Whitby: (☎(01947) 602 878). 12th-century stone building next to the abbey, atop 199 mossy steps. Moors-bound school groups often fill the place until mid-July; call ahead. Family rooms available. Lockout 10am-5pm. Curfew 11pm. Open Apr.-Aug. daily; Sept.-Oct. M-Sa; Jan.-Mar. and Nov. F-Sa. Dorms £10.25, under 18 £7. ❷

The YHA operates four **camping barns** (see p. 408) in the Moors: in **Farndale**, Oakhouse farmyard (☎(01751) 433 053); **Kildale**, on the Cleveland Way (☎(016427) 221 35); **Sinnington**, on the edge of the park between Pickering and Helmsley (☎(01751) 473 792); and **Westerdale**, in Broadgate Farm (☎(01287) 660 259). Reservations must be made in advance; call ☎(01200) 420 102 or e-mail campbarnsyha@enterprise.net. The barns all cost £5 per person or less.

🏔 HIKING AND BIKING

Hiking is the best way to travel these vast tracts of moor. Wrapping fully around the national park, the 93 mi. **Cleveland Way** is the yellow brick road of the North York Moors. A particularly well-marked and breathtaking portion of the Way is the 20 mi. trail between Whitby and Scarborough (the less eager might only go as far as Robin Hood's Bay, 5½ mi. from Whitby)—wavering hills on one side, tranquil sea on the other, and miles of shoreline cliffs stretching ahead and falling behind. Ambitious hikers might consider tackling the 79 mi. **Wolds Way,** a stunning coastal hike that extends from Scarborough southward to the sandstone cliffs of Filey, or the shorter and unofficial **White Rose** (37 mi.). There are excellent day hikes from stations on the park's two scenic **railways,** the Esk Valley Line (see p. 428) and the North Yorkshire Moors Railway (see p. 433). Good short walks also surround the towns of **Helmsley** and **Danby.** Since trails are not always marked or even visible, all hikers should carry a detailed map and compass (see **Wilderness Safety,** p. 49).

The amount of **tourist literature** on the moors is astounding. The National Park Authority's *Waymark* guides (30-40p) detail short (up to half-day) walks starting from villages or points of interest. Before hitting the trails, consult more expensive books (£3-6) and get good advice (£0) from tourist officials. The Ordnance Survey Tourist Map #2 (£4.25) covers the whole park, but may be too general for hikers; Outdoor Leisure #26-27 (1:25,000; £6) are more precise. **Disabled travelers** should call the Disablement Action Group (☎(01947) 821 001) for guidance.

The Moors are steep, and **cycling** around them a challenge, but the paths on the plateaus are pleasant. The **Whitby to Scarborough Coastal Railtrail** (guidebook 30p), with sea views, refreshment stops, and sections for all skill levels, is especially popular. You can rent bikes at **Trailways** (☎(01947) 820 207), in Hawsker, 2 mi. south of Whitby on the A171. TICs and NPICs offer lists of other cycle hire stores, as well as several guides to cycling in the Moors (£1.80-7).

The Moors can be horribly hot or bitterly cold in the summer. Call the Danby NPIC (☎(02187) 660 654; see p. 429) for the **weather forecast** before setting out, but be aware that it reports on all of the northeast. Conditions can vary dramatically even within the park, and it *is* England—bring raingear.

HELMSLEY ☎01439

Its tourist-oriented shops notwithstanding, picturesque Helmsley feels happily stuck in the past. The town centers around the cobbled Market Place, site of a Friday market. **Helmsley Castle** was built around 1120 in case the Scots ever got restless. They did, but the castle didn't see military action until the Civil War, when Ollie Cromwell blew the place in half—explaining its present-day shattered profile. (☎770 442. Open Apr.-Sept. daily 10am-6pm, Oct. 10am-5pm, Nov.-Mar. 10am-1pm and 2-4pm. £2.50, concessions £1.90, children £1.30.) The **Walled Garden** behind the castle contains over a hundred varieties of clematis, which, statistically speaking, is England's favorite flower. (☎771 427. Open Apr.-Oct. daily 10:30am-5pm; Nov.-Mar. F-Su noon-4pm. £2, concessions £1, children free.) **Duncombe Park**, ¾ mi. south of Market Pl. on Buckingham Sq., is a large landscaped park and nature reserve home to the lavish 18th-century villa of Lord and Lady Feversham. Informative guides point out family portraits, but you may spot the noble twosome themselves. (☎770 213. By hourly tour only. Gardens open May-Oct. Su-Th 11am-5:30pm; house noon-5pm. £6, concessions £5, children £3. Gardens only £3.60.)

An enjoyable 3½ mi. walk out of town along the beginning of the Cleveland Way (or, when the Moorsbus is running, a quick ride to the Cleveland Way stop) leads to the stunning 12th-century ◪**Rievaulx Abbey** (REE-vo). Established by monks from Burgundy, the abbey was an aesthetic masterpiece until Thomas Mannus, first Earl of Rutland, initiated a swift decay, stripping it of valuables (including the roof). It is now one of the most spectacular ruins in the country. (☎798 228. Open Apr.-Sept. daily 10am-6pm, Oct. 10am-5pm, Nov.-Mar. 10am-1pm and 2-4pm. £3.60, concessions £2.70, children £1.80.) Just uphill, the **Rievaulx Terrace & Temples** features two 18th-century temples and a huge lawn with superb views of the abbey. (☎748 283. Open Apr.-Sept. daily 10:30am-6pm, Oct.-Nov. 10:30am-5pm. One temple closed 1-2pm. £3.30, children £1.50.)

Buses (including the seasonal **Moorsbus**) stop on Market Pl., where you'll find Helmsley's **tourist information centre** (see p. 429). Auto-less, footsore travelers might choose to catch a **taxi** to the nearby sights (☎770 817; about £4 to Rievaulx). Other services include: **banks**, on Market Pl., and the **post office**, Bridge St., just off Market Pl. (open M-Tu and Th-F 9am-12:30pm and 1:30-5:30pm, W and Sa 9am-12:30pm). **Post Code:** YO6 5BG.

Helmsley has a comfortable **YHA hostel** (see p. 430) and B&Bs. **Stillworth House ❸**, 1 Church St., lets attractive, large rooms in a Georgian townhouse near the main square. (☎(01439) 771 072. £22.50-30 per person.) There are **pubs** on Market Pl., and **Nice Things ❶**, 10 Market Pl., does its name justice with a homemade quiche, jacket potato, and side salad for the kind price of £4. (☎771 997. Open M-F 9:15am-5:30pm, Sa-Su 9:15am-6:30pm.)

PICKERING
☎ 01751

The attractive market town of Pickering is best known as the starting point for the popular **North Yorkshire Moors Railway,** though it could also serve as a convenient base for exploring the national park. Originally built in fear of Northern invasions, **Pickering Castle** soon became a favorite royal hunting spot. Remnants of the Norman castle still command an inspiring view. (☎ 474 989. Open Apr.-Sept. daily 10am-6pm; Oct. 10am-5pm; Nov.-Mar. W-Su 10am-1pm and 2-4pm. £2.50, concessions £1.90, children £1.30.) The **Parish Church of St. Peter and St. Paul** is a squat Norman building with a 15th-century gothic spire. Its medieval frescoes are in surprisingly good condition. (Open dawn-dusk. Suggested donation £1.)

Pickering's **tourist information centre** is at The Ropery (see p. 429). Other services include: **banks,** on Market Pl.; **Internet access** at the **library,** next to the TIC (open M-T and Th 9:30am-5pm, F 9:30am-7:30pm, Sa 9:30am-12:30pm); and the **post office,** 7 Market Pl., inside Morland's Newsagents, with a **bureau de change** (☎ (0845) 223 344; open M-F 9am-5:30pm, Sa 9am-12:30pm). **Post Code:** YO18 7AA.

The nearest hostel to Pickering is the **YHA Old School** in Lockton (see p. 430). Among a number of B&Bs, **Clent House ❸** is a restored 18th-century guest house on a picturesque street near the castle. (☎ 477 928. Singles £20; doubles £32.) An excellent small hotel in the town center, **The White Swan ❹,** Market Place (☎ 472 288), has well-appointed rooms (from £35) and fine food (entrees around £10). **Wayside Caravan Park ❶,** Wrelton, 2½ mi. down the Pickering-Helmsley road, is a well-maintained site with beautiful park views. (☎ 472 608. £7.50-9 per night.)

SCARBOROUGH
☎ 01723

It all started in 1626 when Mrs. Tanyzin Farrer stumbled upon natural springs under a cliff near town. They tasted bitter but seemed to cure minor ailments, and soon "taking the water" became a medically accepted prescription—and popular pastime. English families and retirees still flock to Scarborough, one of the country's first seaside resorts. During the summer months, when it feels as if all of England has fled to the coast, lively pubs entertain hikers after a day in the moors and the colorful boardwalk offers plenty of amusement. The town is large and often tacky, but it is graced with a beautiful setting—a castle-topped rocky headland separating two grand stretches of beach.

⌗ ⏚ ORIENTATION AND PRACTICAL INFORMATION. A cliff crowned by Scarborough Castle divides **North Bay** and **South Bay,** each of which is fronted by a long stretch of beach. The **train station** is on **Westborough,** the main shopping street. Regional **buses** arrive and depart from several locations on Westborough; National Express services stop behind the train station. The **tourist information centre** is on the corner of Westborough and Valley Bridge Rd., across from the train station. (☎ 373 333. Open May-Sept. daily 9:30am-6pm; Oct.-Apr. 10am-4:30pm.) Other services include: **banks,** along Westborough; the **police** (☎ 500 300); **Internet access** at **Complete Computing,** 14 Northway (☎ 500 501; £1 per 15min.; open M-Sa 9am-5pm); and the **post office,** 11-15 Aberdeen Walk (☎ 381 311; open M-F 9am-5:30pm, Sa 9am-12:30pm). **Post Code:** YO11 1AB.

⌗ ⏚ ACCOMMODATIONS AND FOOD. YHA Scarborough is 2 mi. from town (see p. 430). Reasonable **B&Bs** (£17-20) can be found along Blenheim Terr., Rutland Terr., and Trafalgar Sq. **Kerry Lee Hotel ❷,** 60 Trafalgar Sq., is welcoming, spotless, and well-priced. (☎ 363 845. No smoking. From £13 per person, with bath £15.) Nearby, but overlooking the sea, **Whiteley Hotel ❸,** 99 Queen's Parade, is a fine choice for its well-kept ensuite rooms and tasty breakfasts. (☎ 373 514. June-Sept.

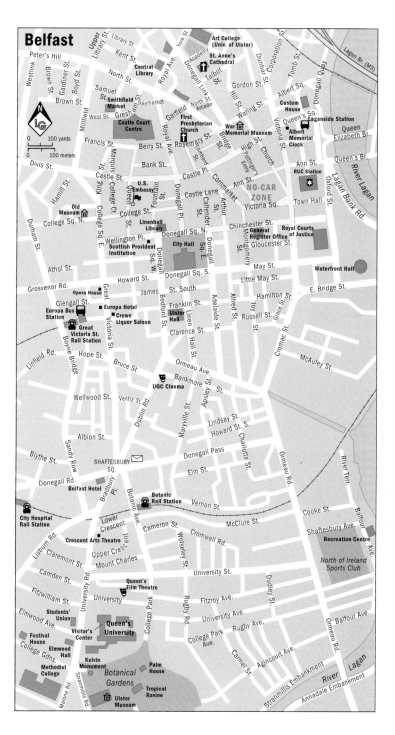

Dublin

0 200 yards
0 200 meters

North Circular Rd.
Drumalee Rd.
Prussia St.
Grangegorman Upper
Royal Canal Bank
Phibsborough Rd.
Auburn St.
We
For
Western
Dominic

Aughrim St.
Ross St.
Oxmantown Rd.
Ben Edar Rd.
Hallidy Rd.
Harold Rd.
Manor St.
Grangegorman Lower
Constitution Hill
Prebend St.
King's Inns

O'Devaney Gdns.
Ivar St.
Manor Pl.
Mt. Temple Rd.
Sitric Rd.
Stoney Batter
Kirwan St.
Linenhall Ter.
Lisburn St.

Brunswick St. N
North King St.
North King
Anne St. N
Halston St.
Cuckoo Ln.

Arbour Hill
Decorative Arts Museum
Blackhall Pl.
Queen St.
Smithfield St.
Church St. Upper
Beresford St.
Mary's Ln.

Montpelier Hill
TO PHOENIX PARK
Benburb St.
Bow St.
Ceol
Old Jameson Distillery
St. Michan's
Greek St.
Markets

Wolfe Tone Quay
Ellis Quay
Chancery St.
Heuston Station
Victoria Quay
Arran Quay
Church
Inns Quay
The Four Courts

St. James Gate Brewery
Island St.
Bridgefoot St.
Usher's Quay
St. Augustine St.
Bridge St.
Merchants Quay
O'Donov. Rossa Br
Wood

Steevens La.
Watling St.
Bonham St.
Oliver Bond St.
Winetavern St.
Ci Office

St. James's St.
Thomas St.
Cook St.
St. Audoens
High St.
Christ Chu Cathedra

TO KILMAINAM GAOL,
ROYAL HOSPITAL
Guiness Storehouse
Cornmarket
Back Ln.
John Dillon St.
Nicholas St.
Ross F
Bridge

Basin St. Lwr.
Portland St. W
Rainsford St.
Bellevue St.
Hanbury Ln.
Earl St.
Thomas Ct.
Meath St.
Swift's Alley
Francis St.
Bull A

Bond St.
Newport St.
Pim St.
Marrowbone Ln.
Summer St.
Pimlico
Meath Pl.
Carman's Hall
Patrick St.
St. Pat Cathe

Grand Canal Bank
Lourdes Rd.
Rosary Rd.
Cork St.
Cameron St.
Ardee St.
The Coombe
Dean St.
Kevin Se

Reuben Ave.
Reuben St.
St. Theresa Gdns.
Donore Ave.
Brickfield Ln.
Brown St. S
St. Thomas Rd.
Chamber St.
Ward's Hill
Newmarket St.
New Rd.
New St. S
Fumbally Ln.

Donore Rd.
Susan Terr.
O'Curry Rd.
St. Thomas Rd.
Clarence Mangan Rd.
O'Donovan Rd.
Mill St.
Blackpits
Clanbrassil St. Lwr.
Malpas St.
Lor

Marty Pl.
Vern

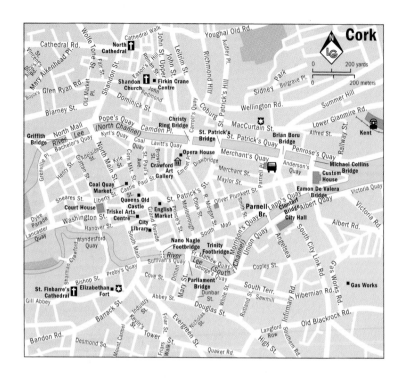

Cork

N LG

0 ___ 200 yards
0 ___ 200 meters

Cathedral Rd.
Cathedral Walk
St. Vincent's Viad.
Mary Aikenhead Pl.
Boyce's
Wolfe Tone St.
Fair St.
North John St.
John St. Upper
Leitrim St.
Youghal Old Rd.
Richmond Hill
Audley Pl.
Sidney Park
Belgrave Pl.
North Cathedral
Glen Ryan Rd.
Blarney St.
Old Market Pl.
Shandon St.
Shandon Church
Firkin Crane Centre
John Redmond
Dominick St.
Coburg St.
Carroll's Quay
St. Patrick's Hill
Wellington Rd.
MacCurtain St.
Summer Hill
Lower Glanmire Rd.
Alfred St.
Railway St.
Kent
Pope's Quay (North Channel)
Camden Pl.
Christy Ring Bridge
St. Patrick's Bridge
St. Patrick's Quay
Brian Boru Bridge
Penrose's Quay
Griffith Bridge
North Mall
River Lee
Bachelor's Quay
Kyrl's Quay
Lavitt's Quay
Coal Quay
Merchant's Quay
Anderson's Quay
Michael Collins Bridge
Custom House
Grenville Pl.
Henry St.
Gratton St.
North Main St.
Corn Mkt. St.
St. Paul's Ave.
Emmet Pl.
Opera House
Crawford Art Gallery
Merchant St.
Maylor St.
Oliver Plunkett St.
Parnell St.
Eamon De Valera Bridge
Victoria Quay
Coal Quay Market
Castle St.
Browne St.
Drawbridge
Parnell Br.
Victoria Rd.
Adelaide St.
Liberty St.
Queens Old Castle
St. Patrick's St.
Cook St.
R. Morgan St.
Caroline St.
Marlborough St.
Lapp's Quay
Clontarf Bridge
Albert Quay
Albert Rd.
Sheares St.
Court House
Triskel Arts Centre
English Market
City Library
Prince's St.
South Mall
Morrison's Quay
Union Quay
City Hall
Angelsea
South City Link Rd.
Dyke Parade
Lancaster Quay
Washington St.
Hanover St.
Grand Parade
Nano Nagle Footbridge
Trinity Footbridge
Fr. Mathew Quay
George's Quay
Copley St.
Wandesford Quay
Sharman Crawford
Bishop St.
Proby's Quay
Cove St.
Mary St.
Drinan St.
River Lee (South Channel)
Sullivan's Quay
South Terr.
Gas Works Rd.
Hibernian Rd.
Gas Works
St. Finbarre's Cathedral
Gill Abbey
Elizabethan Fort
Abbey St.
Parliament Bridge
Dunbar St.
White St.
Rutland St.
Sawmill
Old Blackrock Rd.
Barrack St.
Industry St.
Kevin's St.
Friar St.
Nicholas St.
Evergreen St.
Douglas St.
Langford Row
Southern Rd.
High St.
Bandon Rd.
Desmond Sq.
Mount Carmel
Kevin's Tower
Friar's Walk
Quaker Rd.

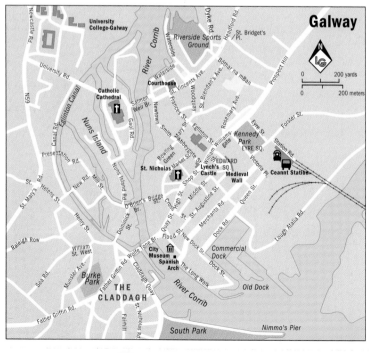

Galway

N LG

0 ___ 200 yards
0 ___ 200 meters

Newcastle Rd.
University College-Galway
River Corrib
Dyke Rd.
Headford Rd.
St. Bridget's Pl.
University Rd.
Waterside
Riverside Sports Ground
Bóthar na mBan
Prospect Hill
N59
Eglinton Canal
Canal Rd.
Catholic Cathedral
Salmon Weir Br.
Courthouse
St. Vincents Ave.
Woodquay
St. Brendan's Ave.
Rosemary Ave.
Eyre St.
Forster St.
Station Rd.
Nuns Island
Presentation Rd.
Gaol Rd.
Newtown Smith
Frances St.
Mary St.
Eglinton St.
St. Williams Gate
Williams Pl.
Kennedy Park
EYRE SQ.
Ceannt Station
St. Mary's Rd.
St. Helens St.
New Rd.
Mill St.
Nuns Island St.
Bowling Green
Abbeygate St.
Market St.
Shop St.
EDWARD SQ.
Lynch's Castle
Medieval Wall
Victoria Pl.
St. Nicholas
Middle St.
St. Augustine St.
Queen St.
Lough Atalia Rd.
Raleigh Row
O'Brien's Br.
Dominick St.
Bridge St.
Cross St.
Quay St.
Merchants Rd.
Dock Rd.
Helens St. West
Henry St.
Wolfe Tone Br.
Flood St.
New Dock St.
Commercial Dock
Sea Rd.
William St. West
Munster Ave.
Father Griffin Rd.
Claddagh Quay
City Museum
Spanish Arch
The Long Walk
Dock St.
Old Dock
Burke Park
THE CLADDAGH
River Corrib
Fairhill
St. Nicholas Rd.
South Park
Nimmo's Pier

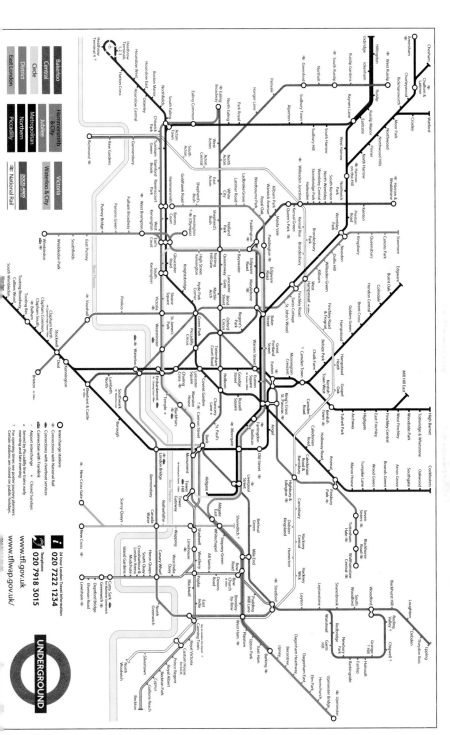

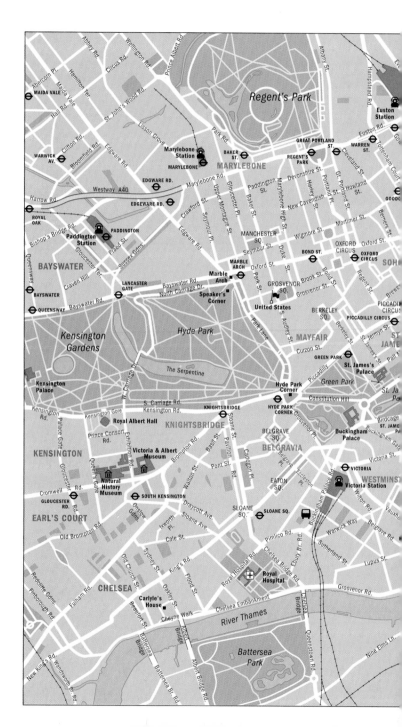

London Overview

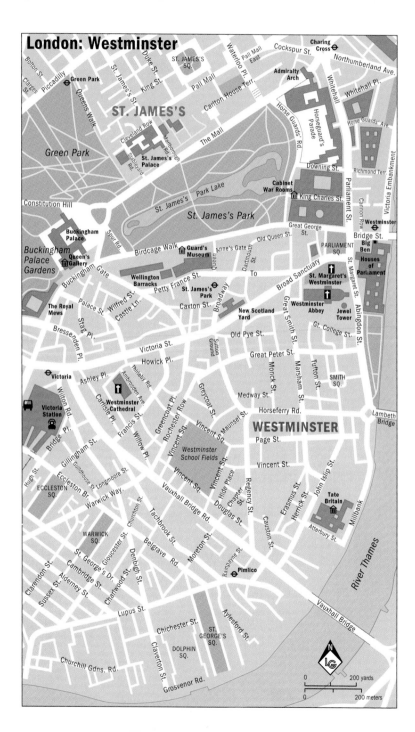

London: Westminster

Bolton St.
Piccadilly
Berkeley Sq.
Green Park
Queens Walk
Green Park

Duke St.
King St.
St. James's St.
ST. JAMES'S SQ.
Pall Mall East
Cockspur St.
Charing Cross
Northumberland Ave.

Pall Mall
Carlton House Terr.
Admiralty Arch
Whitehall
Whitehall Pl.
Horse Guards' Ave.

ST. JAMES'S
Cleveland Row
Marlborough Rd.
Stafford Rd.
St. James's Palace

The Mall
Horse Guards' Rd.
Horseguard's Parade
Downing St.
Richmond Terr.
Victoria Embankment

Constitution Hill
Spur Rd.
St. James's Park Lake
Cabinet War Rooms
King Charles St.
Parliament St.
Cannon Row
Westminster

Buckingham Palace
Queen's Gallery
Buckingham Palace Gardens

St. James's Park
Great George St.
Bridge St.
PARLIAMENT SQ.
Big Ben
Houses of Parliament

Birdcage Walk
Guard's Museum
Anne's Gate
Old Queen St.
St. Margaret's Westminster
St. Margaret St.

Buckingham Gate
Wellington Barracks
Petty France St.
Queen Anne's Gate
Dartmouth St.
To
Broad Sanctuary
Westminster Abbey
Jewel Tower
Abingdon St.

The Royal Mews
Palace St.
Wilfred St.
Castle Ln.
St. James's Park
Caxton St.
New Scotland Yard
Great Smith St.
Gt. College St.

Bressenden Pl.
Stag Pl.
Broadway
Old Pye St.
Great Peter St.
Tufton St.
SMITH SQ.

Victoria St.
Howick Pl.
Sutton Ground
Monck St.
Marsham St.

Victoria
Ashley Pl.
Thirleby Rd.
Medway St.
Horseferry Rd.
Lambeth Bridge

Wilton Rd.
Ambrosden Ave.
Westminster Cathedral
Carlisle Pl.
Greycoat Pl.
Rochester Row
Vincent Sq.
Maunsel St.
WESTMINSTER
Page St.

Victoria Station
Bridge Pl.
Francis St.
Willow Pl.
Greencoat Pl.
Westminster School Fields
Vincent Sq.
Hide Place
Vincent St.

Gillingham St.
Guildhouse St.
Longmoore St.
Churchton St.
Vauxhall Bridge Rd.
Chapter St.
Regency St.
Erasmus St.
Herrick St.
John Islip St.
Tate Britain

ECCLESTON SQ.
Eccleston Br.
Warwick Way
Tachbrook St.
Douglas St.
Causton St.
Atterbury St.
Millbank

Hugh St.
WARWICK SQ.
Gloucester St.
Denbigh St.
Belgrave Rd.
Moreton St.
Rampayne St.
Pimlico

Clarendon St.
St. George's Dr.
Cambridge St.
Charlwood St.
Sussex St.
Alderney St.
Lupus St.

Chichester St.
ST. GEORGE'S SQ.
Aylesford St.
River Thames

Churchill Gdns. Rd.
DOLPHIN SQ.
Claverton St.
Grosvenor Rd.
Vauxhall Bridge

N
LG
0   200 yards
0   200 meters

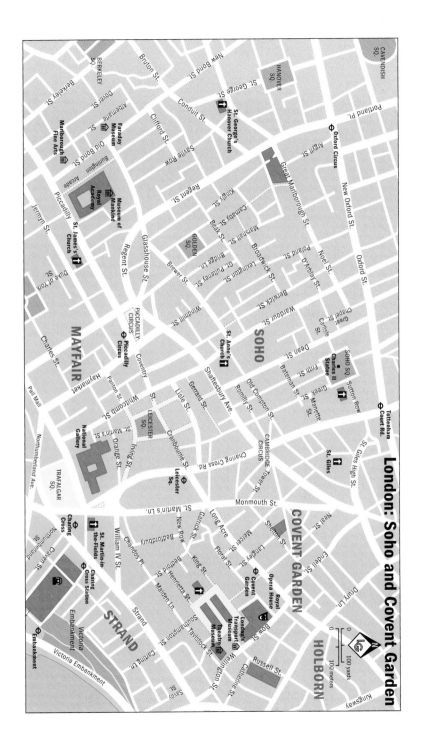

London: Soho and Covent Garden

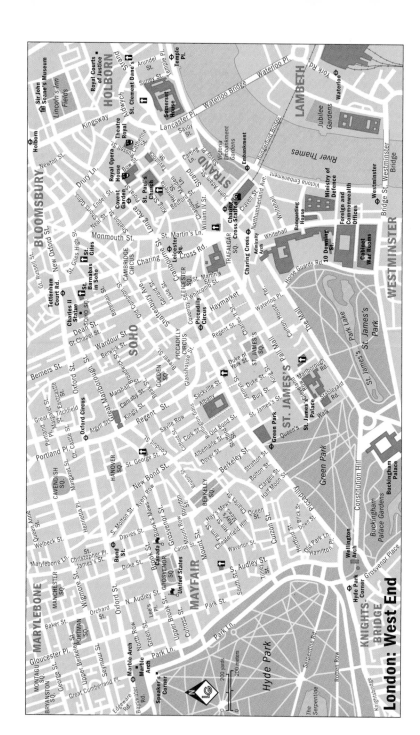

London: West End

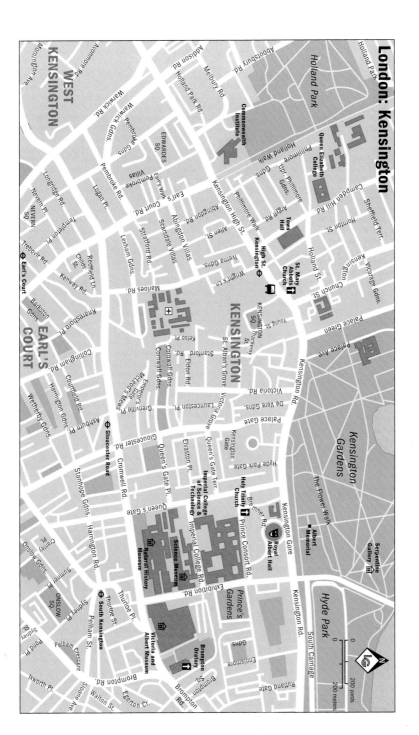

London: Kensington

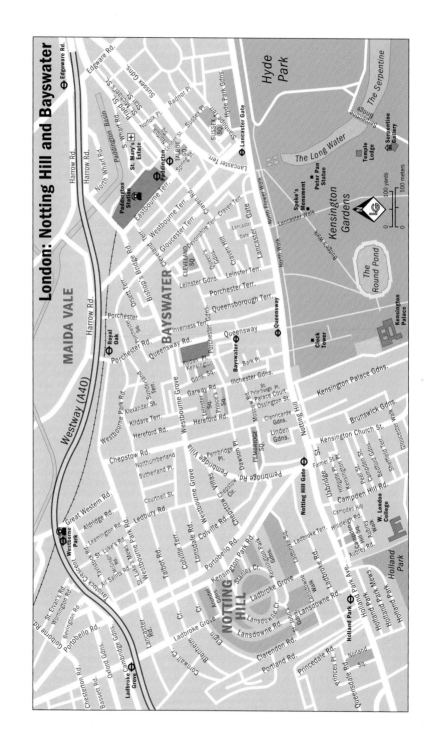

London: Notting Hill and Bayswater

£23 per person; Oct.-May £21.50; sea view £2 extra.) An old-fashioned but pleasant place, **Parmelia Hotel ❸**, 17 West St., is in an enjoyable neighborhood near the beach, just south of town center. (☎361 914. £19.50 per person, with bath £21.50.) The clean, friendly **Terrace Hotel ❷**, 69 Westborough, awaits the lazy just two blocks from the train station. (☎374 937. £18 per person.)

You haven't truly been to Scarborough until you've had its fish and chips. The best in town? Many locals swear by **Mother Hubbards ❶**, 43 Westborough. (☎376 109. Haddock with bread and butter and tea or coffee £4.95. Open M-Sa 11:30am-6:45pm.) The **Golden Grid ❶**, 4 Sandside, in an airy dining room along the boardwalk, is another serious contender. (☎360 922. Cod and chips £4.95. Open daily 11am-9pm.) Probably Scarborough's best restaurant, **Laterna ❹**, 33 Queen St., serves outstanding Italian cuisine with an emphasis on local seafood. (☎363 616. Dover sole £16.50, starters £6. Open M-Sa evenings.) If an inexpensive indoor market is more to your wallet's liking, head to the **Public Market Hall,** just off Westborough between Friargate and Cross St. (Open roughly 9am-5pm.)

🔲 🔲 **SIGHTS AND ENTERTAINMENT.** Scarborough's beach and boardwalk amusements occupy many a visitor's time. Beyond the sand, a glimpse at the cliffs separating North and South Bay makes clear why the city was long a strategic stronghold. ▨**Scarborough Castle** was built by Henry II around 1160 on a site once home to a Roman signal station and Viking fort. The fascinating history of stubborn sieges and defiant defenses is more than matched by tremendous views over town and sea. (☎372 451. Open Apr.-Sept. daily 10am-6pm; Oct. 10am-5pm; Nov.-Mar. W-Su 10am-4pm. £2.30, concessions £1.70, children £1.20; includes 40min. audio tour.) Just down the hill, the cemetery of 12th-century **St. Mary's Parish Church**, across Church Ln., holds the grave of Anne Brontë. (☎500 541. Open May-Sept. M-F 10am-4pm, Su 1-4pm.) The **Stephen Joseph Theatre** (☎370 541), on the corner of Westborough and Northway, premiered much of Alan Ayckbourn's work, including *How the Other Half Loves*. As an actor in the theater, Ayckbourn often complained about his parts. And when the director told him to write a better play, he usually did. A wide range of productions are staged here.

NORTH YORKSHIRE MOORS RAILWAY

One of the region's most popular tourist attractions, the steam-pulled North Yorkshire Moors Railway (NYMR) chugs its way across 18 scenic miles of the national park. The railway was completed in 1835 and its carriages pulled by horses until 1847, when the first steam engine arrived. Today the NYMR operates as a heritage railway, with brilliantly restored steam engines and carriages. The train passes superb scenery on its route between **Pickering** and **Grosmont.** Most visitors make a round-trip of it and just enjoy the views, but stations along the way open up some good **hiking;** pick up *Walks from the Train* (80p) at a TIC.

Traveling north from Pickering, the railway soon reaches **Levisham;** the pretty village is 1½ mi. east of the station. Nearby **Lockton** has a self-catering **YHA hostel** (see p. 430). The second stop (by request only), **Newton Dale,** is near many backcountry walks. The most popular stop is **Goathland,** largely because the postcard-perfect village featured in the British TV series *Heartbeat.* (The train also appeared as the "Hogwarts Express" in the first *Harry Potter* film, so be prepared for wannabe wizards in search of Platform 9¾.) The NYMR terminates at **Grosmont,** also a stop on the Whitby-Middlesbrough Esk Valley Line. (NYMR information: ☎(01751) 472 508; talking timetable 473 535. 3-7 return trips late Mar. to Oct. daily; Nov.-Dec. most weekends; Jan.-Feb. select holidays. All-day rover tickets £10, children £5, seniors £8.50, families from £23. Single tickets also available.)

WHITBY ☎01947

Straddling a harbor between two desolate headlands, the beautiful seaside resort town of Whitby has been the muse for more than its share of history-makers and literary greats. Here Caedmon sang the first English hymns, Bram Stoker conjured evil, and Lewis Carroll wrote *The Walrus and the Carpenter* while eating oysters. And this former whaling outpost (one of two English ports where the midsummer sun can be seen both rising and setting over the sea) inspired Captain James Cook to set sail for Australia in the 18th century. True, Whitby has all the diversions required of any self-respecting English beach town—slot-machines, fish-and-chip huts, and the like—but it seems somehow more timeless than all that. Perhaps it's the narrow cobblestone streets, or the gentle clanging of the working harbor, or the famed ruins of Whitby Abbey, looming above.

■■ ORIENTATION AND PRACTICAL INFORMATION. Whitby populates the west and east banks of the River Esk; the North Sea lies, quite conveniently, to the north. The carcass of Whitby Abbey stands atop 199 steps on the east bank of the river. **Trains** and most **buses** stop at **Station Sq.** on Endeavour Wharf, on the west side of the river; you can also flag Scarborough-bound buses along **Langborne Rd.** (Station Sq. office ☎602 146. Luggage storage £1. Open daily 9am-5pm.) Whitby's **tourist information centre** is at Station Sq. across Longhorne Rd. (☎ (01947) 602 674. Open May-Sept. daily 9:30am-6pm; Oct.-Apr. 10am-12:30pm and 1-4:30pm.) Other services include: **banks**, on Baxtergate near the bridge; **Internet access** at **Digi Internet Lounge,** 41 Baxtergate (☎603 017; £3 per hr.; open daily 9am-10pm); and the **post office** inside the North Eastern Co-Op next to the train station. (Post office ☎602 327; open M-W and Sa 8:30am-5:30pm, Th-F 8:30am-7pm. Store ☎600 710; open M-Sa 8am-8pm, Su 10am-4pm). **Post Code:** YO21 1DN.

■■ ACCOMMODATIONS AND FOOD. The **YHA Whitby,** located hilltop right next to Whitby Abbey, has incredible views (see p. 430). Another hostel, **Harbour Grange ❶,** has a dockside patio, kitchen, and homey decor for a great price. It's 10min. from the TIC—cross the bridge to the east side of the river, walk south on Church St. and look right just after Green Ln. (☎600 817. No smoking. Sheets £1. Curfew 11:30pm. Dorms £8.) **B&Bs** mass on the **western cliff,** along Royal Crescent, Crescent Ave., Abbey Terr., and nearby streets. The **Ashford Guest House ❸,** 8 Royal Crescent, is a meticulous, well-furnished place with fine sea views. (☎602 138. No smoking. Aug.-Sept. £24 per person; Oct.-July from £22; discounts for longer stays.) Camp at the **Northcliffe Caravan Park ❶,** 3 mi. south of town in High Hawkser. Take bus #93A from the bus station (£1), or head south on the A171 and turn onto the B1447. (☎880 477. Laundry facilities. July-Aug. £10.50 for tent and car; Apr.-June and Sept. £7; Oct.-Mar. £6. Showers free. Electricity £2.)

The town has a twice-weekly **market** (Tu and Sa 9am-4pm). Pubs and snack shacks abound. Rumor has it that the **Magpie Cafe ❷,** 14 Pier Rd., serves the best fish and chips in all Britain, if not the world. (☎602 058. Open daily 11:30am-9pm.) For superb food in a relaxed atmosphere, **The Vintner ❸** vints at 42a Flowergate. Specials run £8-9; try the leek and roquefort canneloni. (☎601 166. Open M-Tu 5:30-9:30pm, W-Sa noon-2:30pm and 5:30-9:30pm, Su noon-8:30pm. Reduced hours Nov.-Mar.) On the east side of the river, **Sanders Yard Restaurant ❶,** 95 Church St., in the back of the Shepherd's Purse market, serves tasty vegetarian morsels (sandwiches £3.50) in a funky cafe and tea garden. (☎820 228. Open daily 10am-5pm.)

■■ SIGHTS AND ENTERTAINMENT. Enjoying marvelous views of the bay below, the ruins of ■**Whitby Abbey** sit atop a hill buffeted by shrieking winds. Bram Stoker was a frequent visitor to Whitby, and the abbey and graveyard are believed to have inspired *Dracula*. The abbey's nonfictional history begins in AD 675 when

St. Hilda founded a monastery here. It was burned by Vikings in 867; the present structure dates to 1078. (☎603 568. Open Apr.-Sept. daily 10am-6pm; Oct.-Mar. 10am-4pm. £3.60, concessions £2.70, children £1.80.) Next to the abbey, the medieval **St. Mary's Church** has an impressive interior noted for its box pews. (☎603 421. Open July-Aug. daily 10am-5pm; closes 2pm in winter. Suggested donation £1.)

Westward from Station Sq. on Bagdale, **Pannett Art Gallery and Whitby Museum,** in Pannett Park, has model ships, domestic bygones, and a good fossil collection. (Open May-Sept. M-Sa 9:30am-5:30pm, Su 2-5pm; Oct.-Apr. Tu 10am-1pm, W-Sa 10am-4pm, Su 2-4pm. Museum £2.50, children £1, families £5. Gallery free.) At East Terr., above the pier, a bronze **statue of Captain Cook** overlooks the harbor. Maps in his left hand, sextant in his right, he squints toward Australia, the continent he charted. Nearby, the self-explanatory **Whalebone Arch** pays tribute to the 17th-century cetacean-killing industry. The **Captain Cook Memorial Museum** is at Grape Ln. on the east side of the river. In a historic home where the Cap'n once stayed, the museum contains original letters, drawings, and navigational instruments. (☎601 900. Open Apr.-Oct. daily 9:45am-5pm. £2.80, children £2, seniors £1.80.)

Whitby has a thriving **live music** scene; pubs like the popular **Tab & Spile,** New Quay Rd. (☎603 937), across from the train station, have performances most nights. The town takes particular pride in the August **Folk Festival** (☎708 424) and its 200 hours of dance, concerts, and workshops. The *What's On* brochure at the TIC and the *Whitby Gazette* (published Tu and F) list events around town.

ROBIN HOOD'S BAY ☎01947

No Sherwood Forest, but rather a stunning coastal village where red-roofed buildings and steep, stepped streets seem to spill gently into the sea. There's little to do in Robin Hood's Bay (which locals often call Baytown) beyond soak in the surroundings, but for many visitors, that's attraction enough. The winding cobbled lanes, their edges softened by encroaching gardens, are pedestrian-only—automobiles are restricted to a carpark just north of the village. The bay itself is a cliff-ringed arc, sheltered and quiet enough to be a perfect smugglers' haunt (which, mind you, it most certainly was). You can ramble along the beach or scramble up for views inland across the moors. Robin Hood's Bay is 6 mi. south of Whitby; **Arriva** bus #93A stops here en route from Scarborough to Whitby. The popular **YHA Boggle Hole** is 1 mi. from town (see p. 430). Hotels and B&Bs are also available, but it's essential to book ahead in summer. One possibility is **Ravenswood ❸,** with sea views from its perch in the village and four-course breakfasts in the morning. (☎880 690. Singles £25; doubles £20 per person, with bath £22.50.)

DANBY AND THE ESK VALLEY

The gorgeous Esk Valley cuts across the northern reaches of North York Moors National Park. Outstanding views can be had without ever leaving the railcars of the **Esk Valley Line** (see p. 428) as they travel the Valley between Whitby and Middlesbrough. It's well worth stopping off, however—this is a splendid place for **hiking,** and there are marked trails leaving from almost every station along the rail route. TICs and NPICs can provide further details and literature; *Walks in the Esk Valley* (£1.90), for example, outlines five 3-9 mi. trails. At the small town of **Grosmont,** the Esk Valley Line connects with another scenic train journey, the **North Yorkshire Moors Railway** (see p. 433). Farther west in the Valley, rolling hills give way to some of the national park's finest moorland. **Danby** is blessed with a particularly spectacular setting. The Moors Centre, the mother of all NPICs (see p. 429), is the perfect place to research excellent nearby walks. Among them: an ascent of the 981 ft. **Danby Beacon,** which affords outstanding views in clear weather, and an easy hour-long jaunt to **Danby Castle,** a roofless jumble of 14th-century stones attached to a working farm. **Fox & Hounds ❸,** near the Danby train station, has comfortable rooms. (☎(01287) 660 218. From £27 per person.)

COUNTY DURHAM

DURHAM
☎ **0191**

The commanding presence of England's greatest Norman cathedral lends grandeur to the small city of Durham (pop. 90,000). For 800 years, the Bishops of Durham ruled the county, with their own currency, army, and courts. In the 1830s, new rulers, otherwise known as Durham University undergrads, took over the hilltop city. Though the stream of students dries during during the summer, a transfusion of tourists and festival-goers flows steadily through the narrow streets.

▐ TRANSPORTATION

Durham lies 20 mi. south of Newcastle on the A167 and an equal distance north of Darlington. The **train station** is on a steep hill west of town. (☎ 232 6262. Ticket office open M-F 6am-9pm, Sa 6am-8pm, Su 7:30am-9pm. Advance ticket sales M-Sa 8:30am-5:45pm, Su 10am-5:45pm.) **Trains** (☎ (08457) 484 950) arrive from: **Edinburgh** (2hr., frequent, £35.50); **London King's Cross** (3hr., every hr., £83); **Newcastle** (20min., 2 per hr., £3.40); **York** (1hr., 2 per hr., £15.50). The **bus station** is on North Rd., across Framwellgate Bridge from the city center. (☎ 384 3323. Office open M-F 9am-5pm, Sa 9am-4pm.) **National Express** (☎ (08705) 808 080) runs from: **Edinburgh** (4½hr., 1 per day, £18.50); **Leeds** (2½hr., 3 per day, £11.75); **London** (5½hr., 5-6 per day, £26.50). **Go Northern** and **Arriva** run a joint service from the Eldon Sq. station in **Newcastle** (#723, 1hr., frequent, £3.50). **Arriva** buses serve most local routes. **Rent bikes** at the bright yellow **Cycle Force**, 29 Claypath. (☎ 384 0319. £12 per day. £35 deposit. Open M-W and F 9am-5:30pm, Th 9am-7pm, Sa 9am-5pm.)

▐ ▼ ❷ ORIENTATION AND PRACTICAL INFORMATION

The **River Wear** coils around Durham, creating a partial moat crossed by a handful of footbridges. With its cobbled medieval streets, Durham is pedestrian-friendly, though hills are not heavy-pack-friendly. The **tourist information centre** is in Millennium Place, just north of the Millburngate Bridge. (☎ 384 3720; fax 386 3015. Open July-Aug. M-Sa 10am-5:30pm, Su 11am-4pm; June and Sept. M-Sa 10am-5:30pm; Oct.-May M-Sa 10am-5pm.) Other services include: **banks** in Market Pl.; the **police**, New Elvet (☎ 386 4222); **Internet access** at **Reality-X Durham**, 1 Framwellgate Bridge (☎ 384 5700; £3 per 30min.; open daily 10am-8pm) or at **Saints**, Back Silver St. (☎ 386 7700; £2.50 for 30min.; open daily 10am-6pm); and the **post office**, 33 Silver St. (open M-Sa 9am-5:30pm). **Post Code:** DH1 3RE.

▐ ❖ ACCOMMODATIONS AND FOOD

Durham's accommodations can fill quickly; reserve ahead during busy times (especially during university graduation in late June) or take advantage of the TIC's free booking service. Durham is without hostels, but the large supply of inexpensive and often beautiful **dormitory rooms** is a boon for summer travelers. Others merely tour it, but you can pretend to be lord or lady of Durham Castle in the ▨**University College** ❸ dorms. (☎ 374 3863; fax 374 7470. Breakfast included. From £20.50 per person.) On a cobbled street behind Durham Cathedral, **St. John's College** ❸, 3 South Bailey, also offers accommodations. (☎ 374 3598; fax 374 3573. From £20 per person.) The dorms are available July-Sept. and around Easter and Christmas; contact the **Durham University Conference and Tourism Office** (☎ 374 7360).

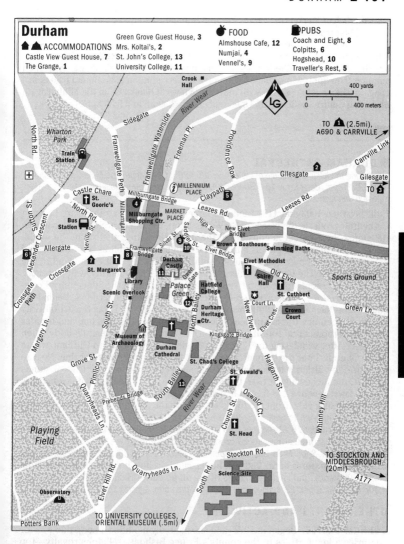

Durham

▲▲ ACCOMMODATIONS
Castle View Guest House, 7
The Grange, 1

Green Grove Guest House, 3
Mrs. Koltai's, 2
St. John's College, 13
University College, 11

🍎 FOOD
Almshouse Cafe, 12
Numjai, 4
Vennel's, 9

🍺 PUBS
Coach and Eight, 8
Colpitts, 6
Hogshead, 10
Traveller's Rest, 5

NORTHEAST
ENGLAND

There are inexpensive **B&Bs** along Gilesgate; among the most appealing are **Green Grove Guest House ❷,** 99 Gilesgate (☎ 384 4361; from £18.50 per person) and **Mrs. Koltai's ❷,** 10 Gilesgate, where you can have your breakfast options explained in English and Spanish (☎ 386 2026; £16 per person). **Castle View Guest House ❹,** 4 Crossgate, lives up to its name and has comfortable rooms and a well-tended garden. (☎ 386 8852. Singles £45; doubles £58.) **Camp** at the **Grange ❶,** Meadow Ln., 2½ mi. away in Carrville, on the A690 off the A1. Take bus #220 to Rumpsite Hotel; follow the signs to the campground. (☎ 384 4778; fax 383 9161. Office open 8:30am-8pm. £4.20 per person, £9.60 per car. Laundry facilities. Showers free.)

At the **Indoor Market** off Market Pl., find butcher, baker, and candlestick maker. (Open M-Sa 9am-5pm.) Students congregate over sandwiches or pastas (£2.50-4) in the 16th-century courtyard of **Vennel's ❶**, next to Waterstone's in Saddler's Yd. (Open daily 9:30am-5pm.) The crowded **Almshouse Cafe and Restaurant ❷**, 10 Palace Green, near the cathedral, serves delicious specials for £4-6. (☎ 361 1054. Open summer 9am-8pm; winter 9am-5:30pm; meals served noon-2:30pm and 5:30-8pm.) Dine on Thai cuisine (£7-10) with unrivaled views at **Numjai ❸**, in the Millburngate Shopping Centre. (☎ 386 2020. Open daily noon-2:30pm and 5:30-8pm.)

◉ SIGHTS

▨ DURHAM CATHEDRAL

Crowning the hill in the middle of the city. ☎ 386 4266. Open June-Sept. M-Sa 9:30am-8pm, Su 12:30-8pm; Oct.-May M-Sa 9:30am-6pm, Su 12:30-5pm. Tours available June-Sept. Suggested donation £3.

Built between 1093 and 1133 (and still largely intact), the extraordinary Durham Cathedral stands, in the words of Sir Walter Scott, as "half church of God, half castle 'gainst the Scot." It is considered the finest Norman cathedral in the world. There are explanatory panels sprinkled throughout, as well as a more detailed pamphlet for purchase (60p). The stunning **nave** was the first in England to use pointed arches. The beautiful **Galilee Chapel** features 12th-century wall paintings. Nearby is the simple tomb of the Venerable Bede, author of the 8th-century *Ecclesiastical History of the English People*, the first history of England. Behind the quire is the **tomb of Saint Cuthbert,** who died in AD 687 and was buried on Holy Island; 9th-century Danish raiders sent the island's monks packing, and besides their prayerbooks and toothbrushes, they brought along the saint's body when they fled. After wandering for 120 years, a vision led the monks to Durham, where White Church (later the cathedral) was built to shelter the saint's shrine. Next to the quire, the **Bishop's throne** has been the subject of intense criticism—it stands nearly three inches higher than the Pope's throne at the Vatican. The cathedral's central **tower** reaches 218 ft. and is supported by intricately carved stone pillars. The spectacular view from the top is well worth the 325-step climb it takes to get there. *(Open mid-Apr. to Sept. daily 9:30am-4pm; Oct. to mid-Apr. M-Sa 10am-3pm, weather permitting. £2, under 16 £1, families £5.)* The **Monks' Dormitory** off the cloister houses pre-Conquest stones and casts of crosses under an enormous 600-year-old timber roof. *(Open Apr.-Sept. M-Sa 10am-3:30pm, Su 12:30-3:15pm. 80p, children 20p, families £1.50.)* The **Treasures of St. Cuthbert** holds saintly relics, holy manuscripts dating back 1300 years, and rings and seals of the all-powerful Bishops. *(Open M-Sa 10am-4:30pm, Su 2-4:30pm. £2, concessions £1.50, children 50p, families £5.)*

OTHER SIGHTS AND ACTIVITIES

DURHAM CASTLE. Begun in 1072 (and substantially modified since), this was for centuries a key fortress of the county's Prince Bishops (religious royalty—top brass among bishops and with oodles of power). Today it's a splendid residence for university students or summer sojourners. *(Next to the cathedral. ☎ 374 3800. Call for tour times, or visit the info booth at the gates. Admission by guided tour only. Mar.-Sept. daily 10am-12:30pm and 2-4pm; Oct.-Feb. M, W and Sa-Su 2-4pm. £3, children £2, families £6.50.)*

BEST OF THE REST. On the river bank between Framwellgate Bridge and Prebends Bridge, the **Museum of Archaeology** showcases an impressive collection of Roman stone altars alongside finds from the prehistoric period to the present. *(☎ 374 3623. Open Apr.-Oct. daily 11am-4pm; Nov.-Mar. M and Th-F 12:30-3pm, Sa-Su 11:30am-3:30pm. £1, concessions 50p, families £2.50.)* Across the river and off South

Rd. on Elvet Hill lies the interesting **Oriental Museum.** (*374 7911. Open M-F 10am-5pm, Sa-Su noon-5pm. £1.50, concessions 75p, students free.)* A stroll along Framwellgate Waterside reaches **Crook Hall,** Frankland Ln. Built in the 13th century, this humble medieval manor occupies an enchanting position on the banks of the Wear. (*384 8023. Open May-Sept. Su 1-5pm; late July to early Sept. also M-F 1-5pm. £3.75, concessions £2.75, families £9.75.)* **Brown's Boathouse Centres,** Elvet Bridge, rents rowboats in which you can trace the river's horseshoe curve. (*386 3779 or 386 9525. £2.50 per hr., children £1.25. Deposit £5.)* For a less arduous journey, the center runs a 1hr. cruise on the **Prince Bishop River Cruiser.** (*Easter-Sept. daily; times depend on weather and university boating events. £3.50, children £1.50.)*

⚑ ❀ NIGHTLIFE AND FESTIVALS

After-hours entertainment in Durham is closely tied to university life; when students depart for the holidays, most nightlife follows suit. The intersection of **Crossgate** and **North Rd.,** across Framwellgate Bridge, is a good place to be at 10pm. A young crowd fills the popular **Hogshead** pub, 58 Saddler St., which has a fine selection of wines and a wall filled with the theatrical history of Durham. (*386 9550. Open M-Sa 11am-11pm, Su noon-10:30pm.)* The sporty riverside **Coach and Eight,** Bridge House, Framwellgate Bridge, is enormous and has a giant-screen TV to match. (*386 3284. Disco W and F-Su. Open M-Sa noon-11pm, Su noon-10:30pm.)* **Traveller's Rest,** 72 Claypath, offers a quiet sanctuary with an alluring selection of ales. (*386 5370. Open daily noon-3pm and 6-11pm.)* **Colpitts,** Colpitts Terr., is perfectly suited to live music. Mondays are Irish, Thursdays folk, and local acts and an open mic fill the weekends. (*386 991. Open M-Sa noon-11pm, Su noon-10:30pm.)*

The TIC stocks the free pamphlet *What's On,* a great source of information on festivals and local events. Durham holds a **folk festival** in August with singing and clog dancing. Many events are free; others cost £2-7. **Camping** is free along the river during festival weekends (F-Su). Other major events include the **Durham Regatta** in the middle of June, held since 1834, and a sodden **beer festival** (the second largest in the country) in early September.

⚐ DAYTRIP FROM DURHAM

BEAMISH OPEN AIR MUSEUM. One of the region's most popular attractions, Beamish is a re-creation of 18th- and early 19th-century life in North England. It features period villages with costumed actors, a farmhouse, a manor house, and an 1825 replica railway. The highlight is the tour into the depths of a former **drift mine.** There's quite a lot to see; plan on spending about four hours in the summer and two in the winter—some attractions only operate in high season. (*Beamish, on the A693, is 8 mi. northwest of Durham. Go-Northern bus #720 travels from Durham to the museum gates (30min., every hr.); #709 offers service from Newcastle (50min., every hr.).* ☎*(0191) 370 4000. Apr.-Oct. daily 10am-5pm; Nov.-Mar. Tu-Th and Sa-Su 10am-4pm, last admission 3pm. Closed late Dec. £12, children £6, seniors £9; all visitors £4 in winter.)*

BARNARD CASTLE   ☎ 01833

Twenty miles southwest of Durham along the River Tees, Barnard Castle, the name of both a peaceful market town and its Norman ruins, is the best base for exploring the castles of Teesdale and the peaks of the North Pennine Hills.

⬛ 🔊 TRANSPORTATION AND PRACTICAL INFORMATION. To reach Barnard Castle from Durham, take **Arriva** bus #5 from Durham to **Bishop Auckland** (40min., every hr., £2.50), and then change to **Go-Northern** bus #8 to Barnard Castle (50min.,

IN RECENT NEWS

THE NEW NEWCASTLE

In the 19th century Newcastle was a thriving center of coal export and shipbuilding. But as the 20th century dawned, those industries went into rapid decline—and so, too, did Newcastle. Such tales are familiar across the UK, but the decline was particularly harsh here: the northeast remains England's most impoverished region. Little wonder, then, that local leaders are trying hard to reinvent and reinvigorate this gritty city on the Tyne. A tidy sum has been poured into Newcastle (and neighboring Gateshead), resulting in flashy new construction like the International Centre for Life, the Gateshead Millennium Bridge, the BALTIC Centre for Contemporary Art, and the Music Centre Gateshead.

Britain's turn to name one of its cities the European Capital of Culture comes in 2008, and the winner gets more than bragging rights—promoters of Newcastle's bid have claimed that winning the title could generate £700 million extra in tourism and create up to 17,000 jobs. Newcastle's competitors—Belfast, Birmingham, Bradford, Brighton, Bristol, Canterbury, Cardiff, Inverness, Liverpool, Norwich, and Oxford—range from other recovering industrial centers to old standbys to relative unknowns. Finalists were chosen from that list in September 2002; the winner will be declared in March 2003. Whatever the outcome of the contest, however, it remains to be seen whether Newcastle's changing cityscape will be enough to change the grim realities facing many of its citizens.

10 per day, £2.55). Five gracious and witty women manage the well-stocked **tourist information centre,** Woodleigh, Flatts Rd. (☎630 262; fax 690 909. Open Apr.-Oct. daily 10am-6pm; Nov.-Mar. 11am-4pm.) **Guided walks** of town leave from here. (1½hr.; late July to early Sept. Th 2:30pm. £1.50, concessions 75p.) **Banks** line Market Pl. The **post office,** 2 Galgate, has a **bureau de change.** (☎638 247. Open M-F 9am-5:30pm, Sa 9am-12:30pm.) **Post Code:** DL12 8BE.

ACCOMMODATIONS AND FOOD. Barnard Castle has no hostel, but is blessed with superb **B&Bs,** many of which line Galgate. **Mrs. Kilgarrif ❸,** 98 Galgate, offers satellite TV, an exercise room and sauna, and an impressive knick-knack collection. (☎637 493. £21 per person, with bath £25.) The **Homelands ❸,** 85 Galgate, is another excellent choice. (☎638 757. Singles £25, with bath £32; doubles with bath £49.) The **Hayloft,** 27 Horsemarket, is an eclectic indoor market, with fruit and vegetables and a couple of cafes. **Stables Restaurant ❶,** in the Hayloft, satisfies with sandwiches and salads (£3), along with other meals for under £4. (☎690 670. Open daily 8:30am-5:30pm.)

SIGHTS. Along the river, the remains of a Norman **castle** sprawl across six acres. (☎638 212. Open Apr.-Sept. daily 10am-1pm and 2-6pm; Oct. 10am-1pm and 2-5pm; Nov.-Mar. M-Sa 10am-1pm and 2-4pm. £2.50, concessions £1.90, children £1.30; includes audio tour.) Past Newgate, the remarkable **Bowes Museum** was built in the 19th century by John and Josephine Bowes to bring continental culture to England. The gallery now houses the couple's extensive and often curious private collection, including the largest gathering of Spanish paintings in Britain—El Greco's magnificent *Tears of St. Peter* among them—and a life-size mechanized silver swan (activated every day at 2 and 4pm) fancied by Mark Twain. (☎690 606. Open daily 11am-5pm. Tours May-Aug. Tu-Sa 2 per day, Sept.-Oct. Sa-Su 1 per day. £4, concessions £3, families £12.) Dickens fans can follow the **Dickens Drive,** a 25 mi. route that traces the path Chaz took in 1838 while researching *Nicholas Nickleby.* Pick up the free *In the Footsteps of Charles Dickens* from the TIC. The ruins of 12th-century **Egglestone Abbey,** in a lovely spot overlooking the River Tees, are a pleasant 1½ mi. walk southeast of town. Arriva bus #79 from Barnard Castle will also drop you there. (Open daylight hours. Free.)

Northeast of Barnard Castle on the A688, **Raby Castle** (RAY-bee) is an imposing 14th-century fortress with a deer park. Take bus #75-76 (20min., 2 per hr., £1.50) toward Darlington. (☎660 202. Open July-Sept.

M-F and Su 1-5pm; May-June W and Su 1-5pm; park and gardens open same days 11am-5:30pm. £5, concessions £4, children £2, families £12. Park and gardens only £3, concessions £2.)

TYNE AND WEAR

NEWCASTLE-UPON-TYNE ☎ 0191

The largest city in the northeast, Newcastle (pop. 278,000) is trying hard to shed its image as a faded capital of faded industry. This city of firsts contributed the world's first steam locomotive, hydraulic crane, beauty contest, and dog show, not to mention Sting (the first person to invoke Nabokov in a pop song), but has rarely been first on tourist itineraries. Yet it's increasingly worth a look: ambitious building efforts—from a restoration of the central historical district to a new world-class music hall—have lent the city genuine energy and even occasional beauty. Things really heat up at night, when locals, students, and tourists throng to Newcastle's (in)famous pubs and clubs. Best of all, perhaps, are the people: Newcastle Geordies are proud of their accent, very proud of their football club, very, very proud of their brown ale, and usually happy to show you around.

> **THE GEORDIES** What exactly is a Geordie (JOR-die)? Anyone born in Northumberland, Durham, or Tyne and Wear can claim Geordie status. But possessive as these sturdy Northerners are of their nickname, its origins are debatable; try any of the following explanations. During the Jacobite Rebellion of 1745, Newcastle's denizens supported George I, the reigning king, and were deemed "for George" by the Jacobites. In 1815, George Stephenson invented the miner's lamp, which quickly gained favor among Northumberland miners. The lamps, and eventually the miners, became known as Geordies. In 1826, Stephenson spoke before the Parliamentary Commission of Railways, and his dialect amused the snooty southerners, who began to call all keelmen carrying coal to the Thames "Geordies."

NORTHEAST ENGLAND

▐▀ TRANSPORTATION

Newcastle is the last English stronghold before the Scottish border. The city lies 1½hr. north of York on the A19 and 1½hr. east of Carlisle on the A69. Edinburgh is straight up the coast along the A1, or through pastures and mountains via the A68.

Trains: Central Station, Neville St. Travel center sells same-day tickets daily 5:40am-9:15pm and advance tickets M-F 7am-7:50pm, Sa 7am-6:50pm, Su 8:40am-7:50pm. Trains (☎(08457) 484 950) from: **Carlisle** (1½hr.; M-Sa 15 per day, Su 9 per day; £9.30); **Durham** (20min., 3 per hr., £3.40); **Edinburgh** (1½hr.; M-Sa 23 per day, Su 16 per day; £33.50); **London King's Cross** (3hr., every hr., £83).

Buses: Gallowgate Coach Station (☎232 7021), off Percy St. Ticket office open M-Sa 8am-6pm. **National Express** (☎(08705) 808 080) from **Edinburgh** (3hr., 3 per day, £13) and **London** (6hr., 6 per day, £23). **Haymarket,** by the Metro stop, is the gateway for local and regional service. Ticket office open M-F 8:30am-5:30pm, Sa 9am-4pm.

Ferries: International Ferry Terminal, Royal Quays. 7 mi. east of Newcastle. **Fjord Line** (☎296 1313) and **DFDS Seaways** (☎(0900) 333 000) offer ferry service to **Norway, Sweden,** and the **Netherlands** (see p. 28). Bus #327 serves all departures, leaving Central Station 2½hr. and 1¼hr. before each sailing. Take the Metro to Percy Main (£1.30) and walk 20min. to the quay, or catch a cab (£12).

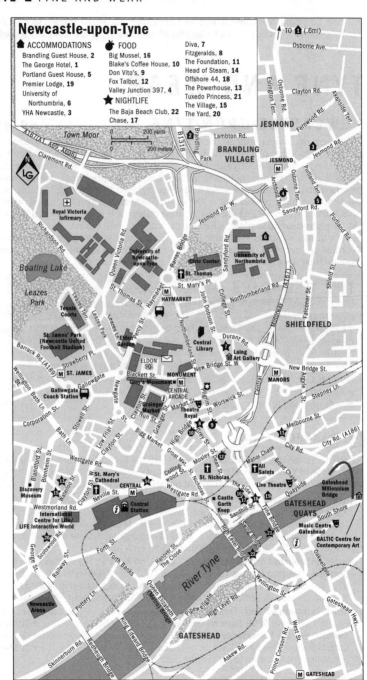

Newcastle-upon-Tyne

🏠 ACCOMMODATIONS
Brandling Guest House, **2**
The George Hotel, **1**
Portland Guest House, **5**
Premier Lodge, **19**
University of
Northumbria, **6**
YHA Newcastle, **3**

🍎 FOOD
Big Mussel, **16**
Blake's Coffee House, **10**
Don Vito's, **9**
Fox Talbot, **12**
Valley Junction 397, **4**

⭐ NIGHTLIFE
The Baja Beach Club, **22**
Chase, **17**

Diva, **7**
Fitzgeralds, **8**
The Foundation, **11**
Head of Steam, **14**
Offshore 44, **18**
The Powerhouse, **13**
Tuxedo Princess, **21**
The Village, **15**
The Yard, **20**

Public Transportation: Call **Traveline** (☎(0870) 608 2608) for complete details. The **Metro** subway system runs from the city center to the coast and the airport, with only a few stops in the city center. Tickets are purchased beforehand and checked on board. Single journeys from 50p. The **DaySaver** allows 1 day of unlimited travel (£3). First train around 6am; last around 11:30pm. Local **buses** stop throughout the city, but main terminals are near Haymarket Metro and the Eldon Square Shopping Centre. A **Day Rover,** available at TICs and Metro and bus offices, offers unlimited travel on all Tyne & Wear public transport (£3.70).

Bike Rental: Newcastle Cycle Centre, 11 Westmorland Rd. (☎230 3022). £10 per day, £35 per week. £50 deposit. Open M-Sa 9am-5:30pm.

ORIENTATION AND PRACTICAL INFORMATION

The free, full-color map of Newcastle available at the TIC is essential—streets shift direction and name without batting an eye. When in doubt, remember that the waterfront is at the bottom of every hill. The center of town is **Grey's Monument** (dedicated to Charles, Earl of Grey, responsible for the 1832 Reform Bill and for mixing bergamot into Britain's tea), an 80 ft. stone pillar in **Monument Mall,** directly opposite **Eldon Sq. Gateshead** is the city across the Tyne (rhymes with "mine") from Newcastle, home to some of the area's attractions, restaurants, and clubs.

Tourist Information Centre: Newcastle Information Centre, Central Exchange Bldgs., 132 Grainger St. (☎277 8000), facing Grey's Monument. Books rooms for 10% deposit. Open M-W and F-Sa 9:30am-5:30pm, Th 9:30am-7:30pm; June-Sept. also Su 10am-4pm. **Branch** at Central Station. Open June-Sept. M-F 10am-8pm, Sa 9am-5pm; Oct.-May M-F 10am-5pm, Sa 9am-5pm.

Tours: The TIC offers various walking and coach tours. £2-6.50. **Citysightseeing Newcastle** (☎(01708) 866 000) operates a hop-on/hop-off tour. Departures every 30-60min., originating at Central Station.

Financial Services: Thomas Cook, 6 Northumberland St. (☎219 8000). Open M-Tu and F-Sa 9am-5:30pm, W 10am-5:30pm, Th 9am-8pm.

Launderette: Clayton Rd. Launderette, 4 Clayton Rd., Jesmond (☎281 5055), near the YHA hostel. Open M-Sa 8am-6pm, Su 8am-1pm.

Police: (☎214 6555), on the corner of Market St. and Pilgrim St.

Hospital: Royal Victoria Infirmary, Queen Victoria Rd. (☎232 5131).

Internet Access: Internet Exchange, 26 Market Pl. (☎230 1280). £1 per 15min. Open M-F 9:30am-8pm, Sa 10am-8pm, Su 11am-6pm.

Post Office: 24-26 Sidgate (☎(0345) 223 344), in the Eldon Sq. Shopping Centre. **Bureau de change.** Open M-Sa 9am-5:30pm. **Post Code:** NE1 7AB.

ACCOMMODATIONS

Inexpensive lodgings can be in short supply in Newcastle; it's advisable to call ahead. Pickings are slim in the city center, but the YHA hostel and several guest houses are within reasonable walking distance (or a short Metro ride). The biggest cluster of guest houses and small hotels is in residential **Jesmond,** on or near **Osborne Rd.,** 1 mi. from the city center; take the Metro to West Jesmond.

YHA Newcastle, 107 Jesmond Rd. (☎281 2570; fax 281 8779). Metro: Jesmond. 15min. walk from city center. 58 beds in a comfortable townhouse. Friendly staff. Often full; call several days in advance. Internet access. Lockout 10am-5pm. Open Feb.-Dec. daily; Jan. F-Su. Dorms £11.25, under 18 £8. ❷

University of Northumbria, Coach Ln. (☎227 4024). Accommodations office in Student Services in the library, St. Mary's Pl. Standard dorm bed-basin-desk combos, but proximity to the city center a definite plus. Shared bathrooms. Breakfast included. Open late Mar. to mid-Apr. and June to mid-Sept. Singles £18.75; doubles £35. ❷

Portland Guest House, 134 Sandyford Rd. (☎232 7868). Metro: Jesmond. 10min. walk from city center. Cheapest, most convenient guest house in town, offering a range of clean rooms. Continental breakfast included. Singles £18-30; doubles £36-40. ❷

Brandling Guest House, 4 Brandling Park (☎281 3175). 9 spacious rooms on a quiet block of Jesmond. Singles and doubles £21-45. ❸

The George Hotel, 88 Osborne Rd., Jesmond (☎281 4442). Metro: West Jesmond. One of the best-priced choices along lively Osborne Rd. Friendly, with ensuite rooms and breakfast included. Singles from £35; doubles £46-50. ❸

Premier Lodge, Quayside (☎(0870) 700 1504). A fairly standard incarnation of this value hotel chain (hence comfortable, nondescript rooms), with a great city-center location near all the Quayside action. All rooms £50. ❹

 FOOD

Every other restaurant in Newcastle has inexpensive pizza and pasta, and those in between serve everything from tandoori chicken to veggie burgers. Chinese eateries form a small Chinatown along **Stowell St.** near Gallowgate; all-you-can-eat specials for £4-6 are common. Many of the restaurants lining **Dean St.** serve cheap lunch specials. The **Grainger Indoor Market** is between Grainger St. and Grey St. near the monument. (Open M and W 7am-5pm, Tu and Th-Su 7am-5:30pm.)

Don Vito's, 82 Pilgrim St. (☎232 8923). Stands out among Italian eateries with generous pizzas and pastas for £4.75, replete with great toppings and inventive sauces. Try the *gnocchi.* Open M-F 11:45am-2pm and 5-10pm, Sa 11:45am-10:30pm. ❶

Blake's Coffee House, 53 Grey St. (☎261 5463). Popular daytime hangout, with a range of good coffees and teas plus lunches (meals £4-5). Open until 5:30pm. ❶

Valley Junction 397, Archbold Terr. (☎281 6397), in the old station near the Jesmond Metro terminal. Sample Bengali-influenced cuisine while dining in an antique railway car. The Indian lager Kingfisher (£3.25) blends well with spinach-based paneers (£6-7). Vegan fare available. Open Tu-Sa noon-2pm and 6-11:30pm, Su 6-11:30pm. ❷

Big Mussel, 15 The Side, Quayside (☎232 1057). Shows off its mussels (and other seafood) in a busy, 2-level dining room. Dinner around £10, with £5 lunch specials and early-bird deals. Open M-Sa noon-2pm and 5:30-10pm, Su 5:30-10pm. ❸

Fox Talbot, 46 Dean St. (☎230 2229). The earth tones and sheet-metal art may look too chichi for your budget, but this upscale eatery has terrific lunch deals: 2 courses and a glass of wine under £5. Roast kangaroo, sweet potato chips, and red onion marmalade await the adventurous (£12). Open M-Sa 11am-11pm. ❸

◎ SIGHTS

A combination of hoary old and resilient new, Newcastle's monuments blend with the city. Between Central Station and architectural masterpiece **Tyne Bridge** lingers **Castle Garth Keep.** The keep, at the foot of Dean St., is all that remains of the 12th-century New Castle. It was constructed on the site of an earlier castle, built in 1080 by Robert Curthose, bastard son of William the Conqueror. Oddly enough, the "New Castle" from which the city derives its name is the older Curthose structure. (☎232 7938. Open Apr.-Sept. daily 9:30am-5:30pm; Oct.-Mar. 9:30am-4:30pm. £1.50, concessions 50p.) Uphill on Mosley St., the **Cathedral Church of St. Nicholas** is topped with an elegant set of small towers around a double arch, meant to resemble Jesus's crown of thorns. (Open M-F 7am-6pm, Sa 8am-4pm, Su 7am-noon and 4-7pm. Free.) The ▣**Laing Art Gallery,** on New Bridge St., showcases an excellent collection of local art and a selection of fresh temporary exhibitions in a cutting-edge setting. (☎232 7734. Open M-Sa 10am-5pm, Su 2-5pm. Free.)

Newcastle has spearheaded its recent urban renewal with major projects showcasing science, technology, and the arts. New in 2000, **LIFE Interactive World,** Times Sq., on Scotswood Rd. by the train station, is an enjoyable hands-on science museum. Covering topics from the origin of life to baboon lovemaking, it's just like biology class—well, biology class with a motion simulator and 3-D movies. It's part of the ambitiously-named **International Centre for Life.** (☎243 8223, booking hotline 243 8201. Open daily 10am-6pm. £7, concessions £5.50, children £4.50, families £20.) The **Gateshead Millennium Bridge** is the only rotating bridge in the world, opening like a giant eyelid to allow ships to pass and giving pedestrians access to the **Gateshead Quays,** site of major new development. Here, the brand-new **BALTIC Centre for Contemporary Art** (☎478 1810), housed in a mid-century grain warehouse, is the largest center for contemporary visual art outside London, with 3 sq. km. of exhibition space. Nearby, the unmissably metallic **Music Centre Gateshead,** set to open in 2003, will contain two concert halls and be a permanent home for Northern Sinfonia, the Northumberland regional orchestra, and Folkworks, an agency dedicated to promoting traditional music. Heading south from Newcastle by rail or road, you can't miss the massive **Angel of the North,** 5 mi. from the city off the A1. Quite the conversation piece, the 200-ton steel sculpture is 20m tall and wider than a jumbo jet.

◪ ♫ NIGHTLIFE AND ENTERTAINMENT

Home of the nectar known as brown ale, Newcastle's pub and club scene is legendary throughout Britain. Nightlife is divided into distinct areas. **Bigg Market** is a rowdy Geordie haven with England's highest concentration of bars. Be cautious in this area—here stocky footballer Paul "Gazza" Gascoigne was beaten up *twice* for deserting Newcastle, and underdressed student-types are frowned upon. **Quayside** (KEY-side), which is slightly more relaxed, attracts the younger local crowd. (Note that some Quayside establishments are across the river, in neighboring Gateshead.) **Osborne Rd.,** in Jesmond, a mile north of the city center, is also popular for bar-hopping. The gay and lesbian scene centers around the corner of **Waterloo St.** and **Sunderland St.** in the city's southwest. *The Crack* (published monthly; free) is the best source for music and club listings. No matter what your plans, finish the night Newcastle-style with a kebab and extra chilli sauce.

PUBS

Pubs are generally open Monday to Saturday 11am-11pm and Sunday noon-6pm. Most offer happy hours Monday to Saturday 4-8pm and Sunday 7-8pm.

Chase, 10-15 Sandhill (☎245 0055), Quayside. Neon lights and a fluorescent bar give this hopping pub a trendy rep. Designer drinks in a designer location under Tyne Bridge.

Offshore 44, 40 Sandhill (☎261 0921), Quayside. Bearing an uncanny resemblance to a pirate's lair, this riverside pub blasts rock classics amid treasure chests, candles, and palm trees. Popular with the student crowd, *yar.*

Head of Steam, 2 Neville St. (☎232 4379). This split-level venue features the best in live soul, funk, and jazz reggae, as well as local DJs. Look for special mixing contests.

Fitzgeralds, 58-60 Grey Street (☎230 1350). An old-fashioned pub with a wood interior near the entertainment district, perfect for an afternoon cocktail or pre-theater tipple.

CLUBS

Opening hours and special events vary with season. Clubs are 18+ unless noted.

Tuxedo Princess, Hillgate Quay (☎477 8899), Gateshead. The city's hottest dance club is located on a decommissioned cruise ship under Tyne Bridge. The gentle river won't make you seasick, but the rotating dance floor might. Open M and W-Sa 7:30pm-2am.

The Foundation, 57 Melbourne St. (☎261 8985). A flashy crowd fills this gutted factory warehouse with posh neon lighting and suspended balcony. Open M-Sa 7:30pm-2am.

The Baja Beach Club, Pipewellgate (☎477 6205), Gateshead. Nothing says Northeast England like sand and scantily-clad beach babes, right? Apparently, the folks behind this hugely-popular club know something you don't. Open M-Sa 8pm-2am.

Diva, New Bridge St. (☎261 2526), attached to the club Ikon. Home to the local punk scene, this small, rambunctious club spins James, the Charlatans, and the Roses. Very loud. 21+ on Sa. Open M-Sa 7:30pm-2am.

GAY AND LESBIAN

The Powerhouse, Waterloo St. (☎272 3621). The only exclusively gay club in all of Northeast England. Theme nights range from "Cheap Booze" to "Classic Rock." Open M and Th 10pm-2am, Tu-W 11pm-1am, F-Sa 10am-3am.

The Village, Sunderland St. (☎261 8874), next to The Powerhouse. Described by locals as the "Champion Gay Bar," this pre-Powerhouse hangout has a 7hr. "happy hour" starting at noon. Open M-Sa noon-11pm and Su noon-6pm.

The Yard, 2 Scotswood Rd. (☎232 2037). An attractive 2-level bar, with a trendier feel upstairs. Open Su-Th 1-11pm, F-Sa noon-midnight.

THEATER

For seated entertainment, treat yourself to an evening at the lush gilt-and-velvet **Theatre Royal,** 100 Grey St. (☎232 2061). **The Royal Shakespeare Company** makes a month-long stop here, beginning the last week in September. **Live Theatre,** 27 Broad Chare (☎261 2694), Quayside, emphasizes local writers and new talent.

SPORTING EVENTS

St. James' Park, home of the **Newcastle United Football Club,** is a prominent feature of the city skyline (and testament to how seriously the Geordies take their football). Tickets (☎201 8400) can be hard to come by, but it's worth a shot.

HADRIAN'S WALL

When Emperor Hadrian ordered that a wall be built in AD 122, the official word went out that he wanted to define his boundaries. But everyone knew he was just scared of the folks to the north. Hadrian's unease created a permanent monument on the Roman frontier—first a V-shaped ditch 27 ft. wide, then a stone barrier 15 ft. high and 8-9 ft. across. Eight years, 17 milecastles (forts), 5500 cavalrymen, and 13,000 infantrymen later, Hadrian's Wall stretched unbroken for 73 mi. from modern-day Carlisle to Newcastle. The years have not been kind to the emperor's pet project. Most of the stones have been carted off and recycled into surrounding structures, and the portions of wall that remain stand at only half their original height. The highest concentration of ruins is along the western part of the wall, at the southern edge of Northumberland National Park (see p. 449).

▐ TRANSPORTATION. The wall is best accessed by car; failing that, **buses** are available. **Stagecoach in Cumbria** sends the **Hadrian's Wall Bus,** a.k.a. **#AD122** (who knew public transport had a sense of humor?) from **Carlisle** to **Hexham,** stopping at the wall's major sights (2¼hr., 6 per day June-Aug., 70p-£4.30; 1 daily bus extends to **Newcastle**). Bus #185 offers year-round service between **Carlisle** and **Housesteads,** stopping at the **Roman Army Museum, Haltwhistle,** and the **Once Brewed Visitor Centre** (1¼hr., M-Sa 3 per day). Bus #685 runs year-round between **Newcastle** and **Carlisle** via **Hexham, Haltwhistle, Greenhead,** and other wall towns (2hr.; M-Sa 11 per day, Su 4 per day). A **Hadrian's Wall Bus Whole Day Rover ticket,** available from TICs or bus drivers, is a good idea for those planning to make several stops in one day (£5.50, children £3, families £11). Another option is the **Hadrian's Wall Rover,** a 2-out-of-3-day ticket valid between Sunderland and Carlisle on the Tyne Valley train line, the Hadrian's Wall Bus, and the Tyne & Wear Metro (£12.50, children £6.25).

Trains (☎ (08457) 484 950) run frequently between **Carlisle** and **Newcastle,** but stations all lie 1½-4 mi. from the wall; be prepared to hike to the nearest stones. Trains depart about every hour and stop at: **Brampton,** 2 mi. from Lanercost and 5 mi. from Birdoswald; **Haltwhistle,** 2 mi. from Cawfields; **Bardon Mill,** 2 mi. from Vindolanda and 4½ mi. from Housesteads; and **Hexham.**

▐▐ ORIENTATION AND PRACTICAL INFORMATION. Hadrian's Wall stands between Carlisle to the west and Newcastle to the east, spanning Cumbria, Northumberland, and Tyne and Wear. The towns of **Greenhead, Haltwhistle, Once Brewed, Bardon Mill, Haydon Bridge, Hexham** (the hub of Wall transportation), and **Corbridge** lie somewhat parallel to the wall from west to east. For general information, phone the **Hadrian's Wall Information Line** (☎ (01434) 322 002). Useful publications and accommodation bookings are available at the Hexham **tourist information centre,** at the bottom of the hill across from the abbey on Hallgate Rd. (see p. 448), and the **National Park Information Centre** in Once Brewed, on Military Rd. (☎ (01434) 344 396 or 344 777. Open June-Aug. daily 9:30am-6pm; Apr.-May and Sept.-Oct. 9:30am-5pm; Nov.-Mar Sa-Su 10am-3pm.)

▐ ACCOMMODATIONS. Both **Carlisle** and **Hexham** have abundant **B&Bs** and make good bases for daytrips to the wall. Other towns near the wall, such as **Corbridge** and **Haltwhistle,** also have accommodations. Two hostels lie along the Hadrian's Wall Bus route. **YHA Greenhead ❶,** 16 mi. east of Carlisle, is a converted chapel with modern facilities, just steps from the wall. (☎/fax (016977) 47401. Lockout 10am-5pm. Open July-Aug. daily; Apr.-June M-Sa; Sept.-Oct. F-Tu. Dorms £9.50, under 18 £6.75.) **YHA Once Brewed ❷,** Military Rd., Bardon

Mill, has a central location—2½ mi. northwest of the Bardon Mill train station, 3 mi. from Housesteads Fort, 1 mi. from Vindolanda, and ½ mi. from the wall itself. (☎(01434) 344 360. Laundry and Internet. Lockout 10am-1pm. Open Apr.-Aug. daily; Sept.-Oct. M-Sa; Mar. F-Sa. Dorms £11.25, under 18 £8.) An independent hostel, the isolated **Hadrian Lodge ❷** makes a good base for serious walkers; take a train to Haydon Bridge, then follow the main road uphill for 2½ mi. (☎(01434) 688 688. Breakfast £1.50-3.50. Kitchen and laundry. Dorms £10; singles £23-28; doubles £42-45.)

◙ **SIGHTS.** All sights listed below are accessible by the Hadrian's Wall Bus. If you have limited money or time, be sure to visit ◙**Housesteads,** the most complete Roman fort in Britain, 5 mi. northeast of Bardon Mill on the B6318. The well-preserved ruins are set high on a ridge and adjoin one of the best sections of the wall. (☎(01434) 344 363. Open Apr.-Sept. daily 10am-6pm; Oct. 10am-5pm; Nov.-Mar. 10am-4pm. £3, concessions £2.30, children £1.50.) Constructed of stones "borrowed" from the wall, the **Roman Army Museum** at Carvoran, ¾ mi. northeast of Greenhead, presents impressive stockpiles of artifacts, interactive stations, and a faux Roman Army recruiting video. (☎(016977) 47485. Open Apr.-Sept. daily 10am-6pm; Mar. and Oct. 10am-5pm; Nov.-Feb. 10am-4pm. £3.10, concessions £2.70, children £2.10; discount with Vindolanda.) Well-preserved milecastles and bridges dot the area between Greenhead and **Birdoswald Roman Fort.** The fort itself, 15 mi. east of Carlisle, is the site of recent excavations, and offers views of wall, turret, and milecastle. An interactive visitor center introduces the Wall and traces Birdoswald's 2000-year history. (☎(016977) 47602. Open Mar.-Nov. daily 10am-5:30pm; reduced hours in Nov. Museum and wall £2.50, concessions £2, children £1.50, families £6.50. Wall only £1, children 50p.) **Vindolanda,** 1½ mi. north of Bardon Mill and 1 mi. southeast of Once Brewed, is a fort and civilian settlement predating the wall. Excavations have revealed hundreds of inscribed wooden tablets that illuminate details of Roman life. (☎(01434) 344 277. Same hours as the Army Museum. £3.90, concessions £3.30, children £2.80.) Dramatically situated on the cliffs of Maryport next to the fort, the **Senhouse** museum houses Britain's oldest antiquarian collection, with exhibits on Roman religion and warfare. (☎(01900) 816 168. Open July-Oct. daily 10am-5pm; Nov.-Mar. F-Su 10:30am-4pm; Apr.-June Tu and Th-Su 10am-5pm. £2, children 75p.) From Chollerford, 3 mi. north of Hexham, Britain's best-preserved cavalry fort, **Chesters,** can be reached by a footpath leading ¼ mi. west. The extensive remains of a bath house spot the fort's riverside setting; a museum houses altars and sculptures from the wall. (☎(01434) 681 379. Open Apr.-Sept. daily 9:30am-4pm; Oct. 10am-5pm; Nov.-Mar. 10am-4pm. £2.90, concessions £2.20, children £1.50.)

HEXHAM ☎01434

West of Newcastle on the A69, well-heeled Hexham makes a fine base for exploring Hadrian's Wall, but also charms with its own sights. The cobbled town center coils around the impressively kept **Hexham Abbey.** Built by Augustinian canons, it houses the 7th-century bishop's throne of St. Wilfrid. (☎602 031. Open May-Sept. daily 9am-7pm; Oct.-Apr. 9am-5pm. Suggested donation £2.) Facing the abbey, the substantial 14th-century **Gatehouse Tower** recalls Hexham's turbulent past. For more corporeal evidence, sample the punishments of the **Border History Museum,** behind Market Pl. in the Old Gaol House. Built in 1332, this early prison includes a dungeon and interactive stocks and pillory. (☎652 349. Open Apr.-Oct. daily 10am-4:30pm; Feb.-Mar. and Nov. M-Tu and Sa 10am-4:30pm. Free.)

Hexham's **train station** is a 10 min. walk from the Abbey and the center of town (see **Transportation,** p. 447). The **tourist information centre** stands between the train station and town center, in the carpark behind Safeway. (☎652 220. Open mid-May to Sept. M-Sa 9am-6pm, Su 10am-5pm; Apr. to mid-May and Oct. M-Sa 9am-5pm, Su 10am-5pm; Nov.-Mar. M-Sa 9am-5pm.) Other services include: the **police,** Shaftoe Leages (☎604 111); the **General Hospital,** Corbridge Rd. (☎655 655); **Internet access** at **NBS The Computer Shop,** 10b Hencotes (☎600 022; £1 per 10min.; open M-F 9:30am-5:30pm, Sa 9:30am-4:30pm); and the **post office,** Priestpopple Rd., hidden within Robbs of Hexham department store (☎602 001; open M-Tu, Th, and Sa 8:30am-5:30pm, W 9am-5:30pm, F 8:30am-6pm). **Post Code:** NE46 1NA.

    West Close House ❸, Hextol Terr., off Allendale Rd., is a comfortable and quiet B&B. (☎603 307. £21-26 per person.) The **YHA Acomb ❶,** 2 mi. from Hexham, tucks backpackers into a converted stable. Take bus #880, 881, or 882 from the Hexham railway station. (☎602 864. Open July-Aug. daily; June Tu-Sa; Apr.-May and Sept.-Oct. W-Su; Nov.-Mar F-Sa. Dorms £7, under 18 £5.) **Bunters Cafe/Athena's ❷,** 10 Hallgate, serves a well-priced mix of English standards and Greek specialties. (Open Tu-Sa 10am-4:30pm and 6:30-9:30pm, Su 10:45am-4:30pm, M 10am-4:30pm.)

NORTHUMBERLAND

NORTHUMBERLAND NATIONAL PARK

Perched at the edge of the Scottish frontier, these desolate hills were once the site of skirmishes involving first territorial Romans, then Anglo-Saxons. Today, Northumberland National Park's 400 sq. mi. stretch south from the grassy Cheviot Hills near the border to the dolomitic crags of Whin Sill, including part of Hadrian's Wall. Visitors are guaranteed a struggle with its poor public transport network, but this least-populated and roughest-edged of England's national parks is blissfully free from tourist legions.

TRANSPORTATION

Public transportation is limited. **Bus #880** runs from **Hexham** to **Bellingham** (45min.; M-Sa 11 per day, Su 3 per day). One daily bus runs between **Newcastle** and **Rothbury,** with additional service summer weekends. Otherwise, take a bus from Newcastle to **Morpeth,** then take #516/416 on to **Rothbury** (30min.; M-Sa 11 per day, Su 3 per day). Also change at Morpeth if traveling to Rothbury from **Alnwick.** From **Wooler,** bus #470 heads to **Alnwick** (1½hr., M-Sa 8 per day) and #267 to **Berwick** (1hr.; M-Sa 7 per day, Su 2 per day). Twice-weekly bus #710 connects **Wooler** with **Newcastle** and the **Scottish Borders** (W and Sa 1 per day). **National Express's** once-daily Newcastle-Jedburgh-Edinburgh bus #383 cuts through the park and stops at **Byrness.** Bus #714 travels from **Gateshead** (across the river from Newcastle) via **Bellingham** to **Kielder/Kielder Water** (2hr.; June-Oct. Su 1 per day, Aug. also W 1 per day). Year-round, **Postbus #815** journeys from **Hexham** to **Kielder** via **Bellingham** (2½hr., M-Sa 1 per day) while regular bus #814 travels from **Bellingham** to **Kielder** (during school terms M-F 5 per day;

school holidays Tu and F 3 per day). For current schedules, call **Traveline** (☎ (0870) 608 2608) or obtain the 256-page *Northumberland Public Transport Guide* (£1), available at TICs and bus stations.

ⓘ ORIENTATION AND PRACTICAL INFORMATION

There are few roads or settlements in the park, which begins at **Hadrian's Wall** (see p. 447) and stretches north to the Scottish border. **Bellingham, Rothbury,** and **Wooler** are small towns near the park's eastern edge which offer accommodations and good access to walking routes. In the southwest is the large reservoir of **Kielder Water,** surrounded by planted pines (the **Kielder Forest**) and popular for water sports. The military operates a Live Firing Range in the middle of the park; needless to say, walkers should heed the warning signs.

Northumberland National Park operates three **National Park Information Centres (NPICs)** which can advise on hikes and activities and make accommodation bookings. Throughout the warmer months, they offer ranger-led talks and walks. There are also several **tourist information centres** in the area.

NATIONAL PARK INFORMATION CENTRES

Ingram: (☎(01669) 578 248). Open June-Aug. daily 10am-6pm; Apr.-May and Sept. 10am-5pm; Oct. Sa-Su 10am-3pm.

Once Brewed: for Hadrian's Wall; see p. 447.

Rothbury: Church St. (☎(01669) 620 887). Open June-Aug. daily 10am-6pm; Apr.-May and Sept.-Oct. 10am-5pm; Jan.-Mar. Sa-Su 10am-3pm.

TOURIST INFORMATION CENTRES

Bellingham: Main St. (☎(01434) 220 616). Open Easter-Oct. M-Sa 10am-1pm and 2pm-5pm, until 6pm mid-May to Sept.; also Easter-Sept. Su 1pm-5pm.

Kielder Forest: In Kielder Castle (☎(01434) 250 209). Open Apr.-Oct. daily 10am-5pm, Aug. until 6pm.

Tower Knowe (Kielder): Visitor Centre, Falstone (☎(01434) 240 398). Open Apr.-Oct. daily 10am-5pm; Nov.-Mar 10am-4pm.

Wooler: Cheviot Centre (☎(01668) 282 123). Open July-Aug. M-Sa 10am-6pm; Apr.-June and Sept. M-Sa 10am-5pm; Oct. M-Sa 10am-4pm; Su 10am-2pm; closed 1-2pm. Call for limited winter hours.

⌂ ACCOMMODATIONS

Bellingham, Rothbury, and **Wooler** have B&Bs and hotels. The following **YHA hostels** offer accommodations in or near the park:

Bellingham: Woodburn Rd. (☎(01434) 220 313). Self-catering cedarwood cabin. Reception from 5pm. Open July-Aug. daily; Apr.-June and Sept.-Oct. Tu-Sa. Dorms £8.75, under 18 £6. ●

Byrness: 7 Otterburn Green (☎(01830) 520 425). National Express bus #383 Newcastle-Edinburgh via Jedburgh will stop here. Basic, self-catering hostel. Reception from 5pm. Open Apr.-Sept. daily. Dorms £7, under 18 £5. ●

Kielder: Butteryhaugh, Kielder Village (☎(01434) 250 195). Spacious new facility. Open July-Aug. daily; Apr.-June M-Sa; Sept.-Nov. Th-M. Dorms £10.25, under 18 £7. ❷

Wooler: 30 Cheviot St. (☎(01668) 281 365). 5min. walk up Cheviot St. from the bus station. Comfortable hostel. Reception from 5pm. Open July-Aug. daily; Apr.-June M-Sa; Sept.-Oct. Tu-Sa; Mar. F-Sa. Dorms £9.50, under 18 £6.75. ❶

🥾 HIKING

The **Pennine Way** (see p. 407) traverses the park, entering along Hadrian's Wall, passing through Bellingham and near The Cheviot peak, and leaving near Kirk Yetholm, Scotland. Another long-distance route crossing the park is **St. Cuthbert's**

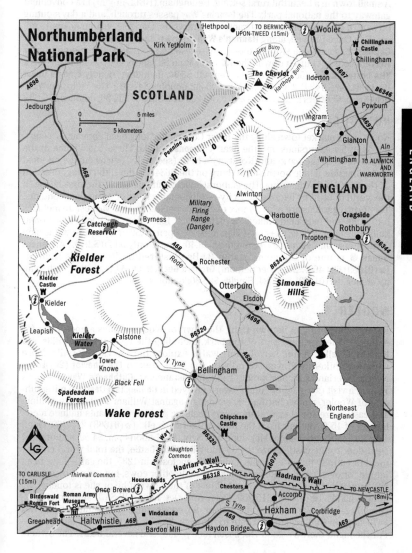

(see p. 407)

Way, which passes through the Cheviot Hills and Wooler on its way between Melrose, Scotland and Holy Island. There are shorter trails, too, though they can be difficult to reach without private transport. Good possibilities include the **Simonside Hills,** near Rothbury, and the **Cheviot foothills** near Wooler. The area's isolation is a good reason to walk here, but it's also a good reason to be prepared—maps and proper equipment are essential (see **Wilderness Safety,** p. 49). NPICs and TICs can provide hiking suggestions.

BELLINGHAM.

A small town in a beautiful rural setting, Bellingham (BELL-in-jum) is a convenient gateway to the national park. The **Pennine Way** passes through, and a day's outing on part of that trail promises attractive countryside. One fine section heads 18 mi. south to Once Brewed, along **Hadrian's Wall.** In town, the 12th-century **Church of St. Cuthbert** has a unique stone-vaulted roof—designed so that pesky raiding Border Reivers couldn't burn it down. The **TIC** is on Main St. (see p. 450). Bellingham has a **YHA hostel** (see p. 450) and several pleasant **B&Bs,** including friendly **Lyndale Guest House ❸.** (☎ (01434) 220 361. Singles £25-30; doubles £47-50.) The Victorian **Westfield House ❸** offers nice views. (☎ (01434) 220 340. Singles £28-30; doubles £56-60.)

ROTHBURY

Rothbury, a market town along the River Coquet, has long been popular as a starting point for excursions into the nearby **Simonside Hills.** These boast some of the finest views in the park, and Rothbury's **NPIC** (see p. 450) gives advice on local trails. **Cragside,** a mile north of Rothbury on the B6341, is the 19th-century creation of the first Lord Armstrong. His elaborate Victorian mansion—the first house in the world to be lit by hydro-electricity—still contains most of its original contents. The formal gardens are a lovely mix of exotic species, and the vast estate includes footpaths and man-made lakes. (☎ (01669) 620 150. Open Apr.-Oct. House open daily 1-5:30pm, last admission 4:30pm; estate open 10:30am-7pm, last admission 5pm. House and estate £6.70, children £3.40; estate only £4.20/£2.10.) **Alexandra House ❸** is one of the comfortable B&Bs clustered on Rothbury's High St. (☎ (01669) 621 463. £20-22 per person.) **Orchard Guest House ❸** is another high-quality choice. (☎ (01669) 620 684. Singles £25-30; doubles £46-50.)

WOOLER

Rather uninspiring in its own right, the town of Wooler makes a good base for exploring the northern part of the park, including the nearby **Cheviot Hills** and **Harthorpe Valley.** A number of short walks explore the Cheviot foothills. More ambitious hikers will want to take on the 7 mi. trek to **The Cheviot** (2674 ft.), Northumberland's highest point. The long-distance **St. Cuthbert's Way** also pays Wooler a visit (see p. 451). King Edward I stayed in **Chillingham Castle,** 6 mi. southeast of Wooler, while charting his campaign against William Wallace's rebellion. The castle is restored in a rather quirky fashion; present occupants include a collection of 15 ft. antlers from the now-extinct Irish elk. (☎ (01668) 215 359. Open July-Aug. daily noon-5pm; May-June and Sept. W-M noon-5pm. £4.50, seniors £4.) Next door to the castle graze the 60-odd **Wild White Cattle,** the total world endowment of entirely purebred cattle. Originally enclosed in 1235, the cattle have been inbred for over seven centuries. They resemble other cows, but cannot be herded, will attack humans, and may even kill one of their own if he or she is touched by human hands. (☎ (01668) 215 250. Open Apr.-Oct. M and W-Sa 10am-noon and 2-5pm, Su 2-5pm. Warden-led tours 1-1½hr. £3, concessions £2.50, children £1.) **Bus** #470 stops in Chillingham en route to Alnwick. Wooler also has a **TIC** (see p. 450). For the night, there's a good **YHA hostel** (see p. 450) and several **B&Bs.** The owners of **Loreto Guest House ❷**, 1 Ryecroft Way, are hiking mavens. (☎(01668) 281 350. £18-21 per person.) You might also try **Winton House ❸**, 39 Glendale Rd. (☎(01668) 281 362. Singles £25-28; doubles £38-44.)

ALNWICK AND WARKWORTH ☎01665

About 31 mi. north of Newcastle off the A1, the tiny town of **Alnwick** (AHN-ick) settles quietly beside the magnificently preserved ◪**Alnwick Castle,** a former Percy family stronghold and now home to the Duke and Duchess of Northumberland. This rugged Norman-fortification-turned-stately-home, featured in the films *Elizabeth* and *Harry Potter*, gives way to an ornate Italian Renaissance interior, circled by three small museums. (☎510 777. Open Easter-Oct. daily 11am-5pm, last admission 4:15pm. £6.75, concessions £5.75, children £4.)

The **bus station** is at 10 Clayport St. Buses #505/515/525 connect Alnwick with **Berwick** (1hr.; M-Sa 9 per day, Su 5 per day) and **Newcastle** (1¼hr.; M-Sa every hr., Su 8 per day). The **tourist information centre** is at 2 The Shambles, Market Pl. (☎510 665; fax 510 477. Open July-Aug. M-Sa 9am-6:30pm, Su 9am-5pm; reduced hours during off season.) **Barter Books,** a huge secondhand bookshop, also provides **Internet access** under the circling tracks of a model train. (☎604 888. £1.50 per 15min. Open July-Aug. daily 9am-7pm; Sept.-June M-W and F-Su 9am-5pm, Th 9am-7pm.) The **post office** is at 19 Market St. **Post Code:** NE66 155.

Stay with Mrs. Givens and her affectionate mutt at **The Tea Pot ❷**, 8 Bondgate Without. Yes, that's a street name. (☎604 473. £17-18 per person; £1 off if you mention *Let's Go*.) Nearby, **Bondgate House Hotel ❸**, 20 Bondgate Without, is a slightly cushier option. (☎602 025. £24-25 per person.) Get groceries at **Safeway,** beside the bus station. (☎510 126. Open M-Th 8:30am-10pm, F 8am-10pm, Sa 8am-9pm, Su 9am-5pm.) **The Town House ❷** vegetarian restaurant, 15 Narrowgate, serves baguettes (£2.15) and other creative meals (£5-8) in a warm atmosphere. (☎606 336. Open M-F 10:30am-3pm, Sa 10am-4pm, Su from noon; F-Sa also from 6:30pm.)

Seven miles southeast of Alnwick, the evocative ruins of 12th-century **Warkworth Castle** guard the mouth of the River Coquet. The extraordinary keep, foundation rubble, and largely intact curtain wall come to life in an excellent audio tour. (☎711 423. Open Apr.-Sept. daily 10am-6pm; Oct. 10am-5pm; Nov.-Mar. 10am-1pm and 2-4pm. Adults £2.60, concessions £2, children £1.30.) Shakespeare set much of *Henry IV* in Warkworth; the 14th-century **hermitage** carved from the Coquet cliffs is the reputed site of Hotspur's baptism. The castle staff will row you there. (Open Apr.-Sept. W and Su 11am-5pm. £1.70/£1.30/90p.) **Buses** #420/422/518 make frequent trips between Alnwick and Warkworth (25min.).

BERWICK-UPON-TWEED ☎01289

Just south of the Scottish border, Berwick-upon-Tweed (BARE-ick) has changed hands more often than any town in Britain—14 times between 1100 and 1500 alone. The town's taste for strife has helped propagate the local legend that Berwick was at war with Russia for over 50 years—supposedly Queen Victoria used her full title in the 1854 declaration of war, "Queen of Great Britain, Ireland, Berwick-upon-Tweed, and the British dominions beyond the sea," but neglected to include Berwick in the peace treaty. Most of the **castle** is buried beneath the train station, although the 13th-century **Breakneck Stairs,** opposite the terminal, can still be ascended for ocean views. (Open M-Sa 6:30am-7:50pm, Su 10:15am-7:30pm. Free.) For a sense of Berwick's turbulent history, traverse the 16th-century **Elizabethan Walls,** built to encircle the Old Town. The town's most substantial sight is the tongue-twisting **Berwick Barracks,** on the corner of Parade and Ravensdowne. The early 18th-century structures now contain a museum on military life, a crowded exhibit on Berwick's history, and a terrific contemporary art gallery. (☎304 493. Open daily 11am-5pm. ₤2.70, concessions ₤2, children ₤1.40.)

Berwick has good transport connections. It's on the East Coast Main Line and has frequent **rail** service to **Edinburgh** (50min.), **London King's Cross** (3¾hr.), and **Newcastle** (50min.). From the train station, it's a 10min. walk down Castlegate to the town center. Most **buses** stop on the corner of Castlegate and Marygate, at **Golden Sq.** Bus #505/525 makes frequent trips to **Newcastle** (2¼hr.) via **Alnwick** (1hr.). For the Scottish Borders, take #23 to **Kelso** (55min.; M-F 11 per day, Sa 7 per day, Su 3 per day) or #60 (M-F 7 per day, Sa-Su 5 per day) to **Galashiels** (1¾hr.) via **Melrose** (1½hr.). The **tourist information centre,** 106 Marygate, books rooms for a 10% deposit. (☎330 733; fax 330 448. Open M-Sa 10am-6pm, Su 11am-4pm.) The **post office** (☎307 596) is down the street. **Post Code:** TD15 1BH.

Berwick Backpackers ❶, 56-58 Bridge St., is a small, comfortable hostel in the middle of town. (☎331 481. Dorms from ₤9.) For B&B, try the well-tended **Clovelly House** ❷, 58 West St. (☎302 337; ₤19-25 per person), or **Deravig Guest House** ❸, 1 North Rd., just north of the train station (☎332 321; from ₤20). Stock up on foodstuffs at the **North Eastern Co-op,** 15 Marygate. (☎302 596. Open M-Sa 9am-5:30pm.)

HOLY ISLAND AND BAMBURGH CASTLE

Ten miles from Berwick-upon-Tweed, wind-swept ▦**Holy Island,** at low tide connected to the mainland by a causeway, rises just off the coast, an ideal day-trip for the romantically inclined. Seven years after Northumberland's King Edwin converted to Christianity in AD 627, the missionary Aidan arrived from the Scottish island of Iona to found England's first monastery, **Lindisfarne Priory,** the ruins of which still stand. (☎(01289) 389 200. Open Apr.-Oct. daily 10am-6pm; Nov.-Mar. 10am-4pm. ₤2.90, concessions ₤2.20, children ₤1.50.) The hill beyond the priory provides a good view of the remains and will save you some shillings. Also on the island, **Lindisfarne Castle** is a 16th-century fort later converted into a private residence. The castle's hilltop perch is spectacular from the outside, though its interior contains only a standard display of 19th-century furnishings. (☎(01289) 389 244. Open Apr.-Oct. M-Th and Sa-Su noon-3pm, possibly 1½hr. earlier or later depending on tides. ₤4.20, families ₤10.50.) Tiny **Saint Cuthbert's Island,** marked by a wooden cross 220 yd. off the coast of the priory, is where the famed hermit-saint took refuge when even the monastery proved too distracting. The blend of fermented honey and white wine known as **Lindisfarne Mead,** a local concoction dating back to the Middle Ages, is still made by the island's monks.

You can cross the 4 mi. causeway only at low tide; check the tide tables at a TIC before you go. **Bus** #477 runs from Berwick to Holy Island (Aug. daily; Sept.-July W and Sa only; schedules vary). Jim of **Jim's Taxis** (☎(01289) 302 814, mobile (0977) 143 530) can drive you over the causeway before the tide sweeps in. If the waves trap you, the island does have a few accommodations, but call ahead as they often fill up. The welcoming **Britannia House** ❸ has the best prices (☎(01289) 389 218; open Mar.-Nov.; ₤20-22 per person), while **The Bungalow** ❸ offers slightly more in the way of comfort (☎(01289) 389 308; ₤25-27.50 per person).

▧**Bamburgh Castle,** a stunning Northumbrian landmark, straddles a rocky outcropping 25 mi. from Berwick. The castle's renovation began in the 1890s when it was acquired by the first Baron Armstrong. Today, the sumptuous interior contains one of the largest armories outside London. The public tour includes a glimpse of the ornate, vaulted ceilings of **King's Hall** and the eerie **catacombs** and **dungeon.** (☎ (01668) 214 515. Open Apr.-Oct. daily 11am-5pm. £4.50, seniors £3.50, children £1.50.) Reach the castle and surrounding village by **bus** #411 or 501 from Berwick (40min.; M-Sa 8 per day, Su 4 per day). Holy Island and Bamburgh Castle can be seen in a single day, though the tides make scheduling tight.

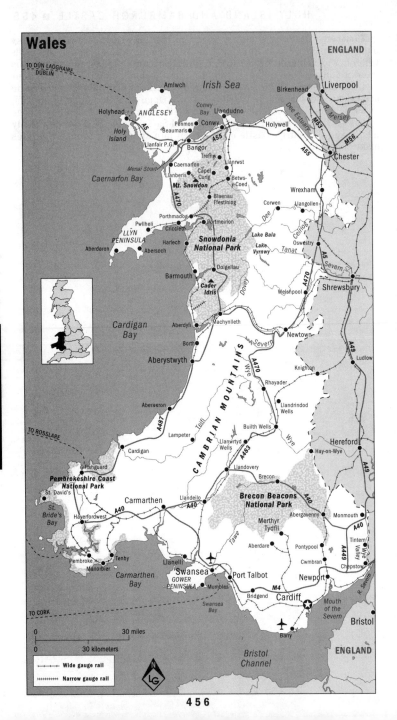

Wales

WALES (CYMRU)

Brooded over by mist more often than swirled about by cloud, drizzled rather than storm-swept, on the western perimeter of Europe lies the damp, demanding and obsessively interesting country called by its own people Cymru... and known to the rest of the world, if it is known at all, as Wales...

—Jan Morris, *The Matter of Wales*

Wales borders England, but if many of the nearly 3 million Welsh people had their druthers, they would be floating miles away. Since England solidified its control over the country in 1282 with the murder of Prince Llywelyn ap Gruffydd, relations between the two have been marked by a powerful unease. Wales clings steadfastly to its Celtic heritage, continuing a centuries-old struggle for independence, and the mellifluous Welsh language endures in conversation, commerce, and literature. As churning coal, steel, and slate mines fell victim to Britain's faltering economy, Wales turned its economic eye from heavy industry to tourism. Travelers today are lured by miles of sandy beaches, grassy cliffs, dramatic mountains, and numerous brooding castles, remnants of long battle with England. Against this striking backdrop, the Welsh express their nationalism peacefully in the voting booths and in celebrations of their distinctive culture and language.

TRANSPORTATION

GETTING THERE

Most travelers reach Wales through London. **Flights** to Cardiff International Airport originate within the UK and from a few European destinations, though direct flights from London to Cardiff are nonexistent. **British Airways** (☎ 0845 773 3377) flies to Cardiff from Aberdeen and Dublin; the new airline **Air Wales** (☎ 01792 200 250) connects Cardiff to Cork and Dublin. **Ferries** criss-cross the Irish Sea, shuttling travelers between Ireland and the docks of Holyhead, Pembroke, Fishguard, and Swansea (see p. 40). Frequent **trains** (as often as half-hourly) leave London for the 2hr. trip to Cardiff; call **National Rail** (☎ 08457 484 950) for schedules and prices. **National Express buses** (☎ 08705 808 080) are the slightly slower, cheaper way to get to Wales: a trip from London to Cardiff takes just over 3hr. and costs £15-20.

GETTING AROUND

BY TRAIN

BritRail passes are accepted on all trains, except narrow-gauge railways, throughout Wales. The **Freedom of Wales Flexipass,** which allows a certain amount of rail travel as well as daily bus travel for the duration of the pass (4 days in 8 of rail £45-55, 8 days in 15 of rail £75-92), is valid on the entire rail network and for most major buses. Pass holders also receive discounts on some narrow-gauge trains, bus tours, and tourist attractions. The **Freedom of Wales Rover** allows train travel in Wales and along the Abergavenny-Chester line (4 consecutive days £39-49, 8 days in 15 £75-92). The **North and Mid Wales 3-in-7-Day Flexi Rover** (£29) and **7-Day Rover** (£43) cover rail travel (and some buses) north of Aberystwyth, while the **South Wales Flexi Rover 3-in-7** (£27-32) covers three days of rail travel in the south. Day-trippers may find that various **Day Ranger** passes make their rail travel less costly. Call **National Rail** (☎ 08457 484 950) for information. **Narrow-gauge railways** tend to be tourist attractions rather than actual means of transport, but trainspotters can purchase a **Great Little Trains of Wales Wanderer** ticket, which allows unlimited travel on eight narrow-gauge lines (4 days in 8 £36, 8 days in 15 £46).

BY BUS

Navigating the overlapping routes of Wales's numerous bus operators makes pronouncing your destination properly look easy. Most of these are local services—almost every region is dominated by one or two companies. **Cardiff Bus** (timetables ☎08706 082 608, other inquiries 029 2066 6444) blankets the area around the capital. **TrawsCambria** #701, the main north-south bus route, runs from Cardiff and Swansea north to Machynlleth, Bangor, and Llandudno. **Stagecoach** (☎01452 527 516) buses serve routes from Gloucester and Hereford in England west through the Wye Valley, past Abergavenny and Brecon, while **First Cymru** covers the Gower peninsula and the rest of southwest Wales, including Pembrokeshire Coast National Park. **Arriva Cymru** (☎01492 592 111) provides service throughout most of North Wales. Life-saving regional public transport guides, available free at TICs, exist for many areas, but for some you'll have to consult an array of small brochures. The very useful *Wales Bus, Rail, and Tourist Map and Guide* provides information on routes, but not timetables. Local buses often **don't run on Sunday;** some special tourist buses, however, run *only* on summer Sundays. Bus schedules and prices commonly change twice a year, and four changes in a year aren't unusual—confirm in advance to avoid unpleasant surprises. The **National Enquiry Line** (☎0891 910 910) is open daily from 6am to 9pm; **Traveline** (☎08706 082 608; www.traveline.org.uk) can also help plan public transportation journeys. Above all, however, be flexible in your travel schedule—missed buses are perfect opportunities to discover new people, places, and pubs.

BY FOOT, BICYCLE, AND THUMB

Wales has numerous beautiful and well-marked footpaths and cycling trails; the **Offa's Dyke Path** (see p. 473) and the **Pembrokeshire Coast Path** (see p. 493) are particularly popular. The Wales Tourist Board maintains the websites **Walking Wales** (www.walking.visitwales.com) and **Cycling Wales** (www.cycling.visitwales.com), which provide links to tour operators and other useful sites, and publishes print guides of the same names. The **Countryside Council for Wales** (☎01248 385 500; www.ccw.gov.uk) may also be helpful. *Let's Go* does not recommend **hitchhiking,** but many people choose this form of transport, especially in the summer and in cases of bungled bus schedules. Cars stop most readily for hitchers who stand in lay-by (pull-off) areas along narrow roads.

LIFE AND TIMES

HISTORY

CELTS, ROMANS, AND NORMANS. As the western terminus of many waves of emigration, Wales has been influenced by a wide array of peoples since prehistoric times. Stone, Bronze, and Iron Age inhabitants left their mark on the Welsh landscape in the form of stone villages, earth-covered forts, *cromlechs* (standing stones also known as menhirs and dolmens), and partially subterranean burial chambers. It is the early **Celts,** however, who make Wales most distinct from her neighbors today. The 4th and 3rd centuries BC witnessed two waves of Celtic immigration, the first from northern Europe and the second from the Iberian peninsula. By the time the **Romans** arrived in AD 50, the Celts had consolidated into four main tribes, with links to each other and to Celts in Ireland and Brittany. By AD 59, the Romans had invaded and established a fortress at Segontium (present-day **Caernarfon**, p. 513), across the Menai Straits from **Ynys Môn (Isle of Anglesey,** p. 522), the center of druidic, bardic, and warrior life in northern Wales. Although the Romans achieved a symbolic conquest, wily Celtic resistance compelled them to station two of their four legions in Britain along the modern-day Welsh border.

When the Romans departed Britannia in the early 5th century AD, they left not only towns, amphitheaters, roads, and mines, but also the Latin language and the seeds of Christianity, both of which heavily influenced further development of Welsh scholarship and society. For the next 700 years, the Celts ruled themselves, doing their best to hold invading Saxons, Irish, and Vikings at bay, their efforts perhaps spearheaded by the legendary **King Arthur.** Yet they were not, in the end, successful: in the 8th century, Anglo-Saxon **King Offa** and his troops pushed what Celts remained in England into Wales and other corners of the island (including Cornwall and Scotland). To make sure they stayed put, Offa built **Offa's Dyke,** a 150 mi. earthwork that still roughly marks the border between England and Wales (see p. 473). However, seeing as the Dyke kept the English out as well as the Welsh in, *Let's Go* imagines there were no few Welshmen helping in construction. At this point, Wales consisted of Celtic kingdoms united by language, customary law, a kinship-based social system, and an aristocracy, but the kingdoms did not achieve political unity until the time of **Llywelyn ap Gruffydd** in the 11th century.

THE ENGLISH CONQUEST. Within 50 years of William the Conqueror's invasion of England, one-quarter of Wales had been subjugated by the **Normans.** The newcomers built a series of castles and market towns, introduced the feudal system (gee, thanks), and brought with them a variety of Continental monastic orders. The English **Plantagenet Kings** invaded Wales throughout the 12th century, and in 1282 a soldier of **Edward I** killed Prince Llywelyn ap Gruffydd, ending what was left of Welsh independence. Edward, through sheer trickery, had his son appointed "Prince of Wales," and in 1284 dubbed the Welsh **English subjects** (boo, hiss). To keep these perennially unruly "subjects" in check, Edward constructed a series of massive castles at strategic spots throughout Wales. He may have been a steel-fisted tyrant, but boy, could he build a castle—the magnificent surviving fortresses at **Conwy** (p. 527), **Caernarfon** (p. 520), **Harlech** (p. 507), and **Beaumaris** (p. 523) stand testament to his efforts.

In the early 15th century, the bold insurgent warfare of **Owain Glyndŵr** (Owen Glendower) temporarily freed Wales from English rule. Reigniting Welsh nationalism and rousing his compatriots to arms, Glyndŵr and his followers captured the castles at Conwy and Harlech, threatened the stronghold of Caernarfon, and convened a national parliament at Machynlleth. Glyndŵr created the ideal of a **unified Wales** that has captured the country's collective imagination ever since. Unfortunately, poverty, war, and the plague were ravaging his country, and, despite support from Ireland, Scotland, and France, the rebellion was soon reduced to a series of guerrilla raids. By 1417 Glyndŵr had disappeared into the mountains, leaving only legend to guide his people. Though Wales placed her hope in Welsh-born **Henry VII,** who emerged victorious from the Wars of the Roses and ascended the throne in 1485 (see p. 71), the Tudors kept none of their campaign promises.

The 1536 **Act of Union** granted the Welsh the same rights as English citizens and returned the administration of Wales to the local gentry, symbolizing full integration with England. However, the price of power was assimilation. The act banished the distinctive Welsh legal and administrative system, officially "united and annexed" the country, and sought to "extirpate all and singular the sinister usages and customs differing." Thus began the rise of English in Wales, which quickly became the language of the courts, government, and gentry.

WALES

METHODISM AND THE INDUSTRIAL REVOLUTION. Religious shifts changed Welsh society in the 18th and 19th centuries. As the church became more anglicized and tithes grew more burdensome, the Welsh were ripe for the appeal of new Protestant sects. Nonconformists, Baptists, and Quakers all gained a foothold as early as the 17th century, but it was the 18th-century **Methodist revolution,** with its fiery preachers and austere lifestyle, that was most influential (by 1851, 80% of the people were Methodist). Life centered on the chapel, where people created tight local communities through shared religion, heritage, and language. Chapel life remains one of the most distinctive features of Welsh society; the Sabbath closure of stores in parts of Wales (particularly in the north) is but one lasting effect.

The 19th century brought the **Industrial Revolution** to Wales, as industrialists from within and without sought to exploit coal veins in the south and iron and slate deposits in the north. New roads, canals, and—most importantly—**steam railways** were built to transport these raw materials, and the Welsh population grew from 450,000 to 1.2 million between 1750 and 1851. Especially in the south, pastoral landscapes were transformed into grim mining wastelands, and the workers who braved these dangerous workplaces faced lives of taxing work, poverty, and despair. Early attempts at unionism failed, and workers turned to violence to improve conditions. The discontent was channeled into the **Chartist Movement,** which asked for political representation for all male members of society; its highest point was an uprising in Newport in 1839. Welsh society became characterized by two forces: a strongly **leftist political consciousness**—aided by the rise of organized labor—and large-scale **emigration.** Welsh miners and religious outgroups replanted themselves in America (founding particularly vibrant settlements in Pennsylvania), and in 1865 a group founded **Y Wladfa** (The Colony) in the Patagonia region of Argentina. Rural society was hardly more idyllic, and tenant farmers led the **Rebecca Riots** between 1839 and 1843.

The strength of the Liberal Party in Wales bolstered the career of **David Lloyd George,** who rose from being a homegrown rabble-rouser to Britain's Prime Minister (1916-22). Numerous Welshmen went to fight **World War I;** over 35,000 never returned. This loss of a generation, combined with Winston Churchill's violent quelling of a Welsh **coal-miners' strike** and the **economic depression** of the 1930s (which spurred further emigration), led to growing dissatisfaction.

TODAY

Long home to a distinct culture and a distinct people, Wales now faces the challenges and opportunities of a distinct political entity. Just as **devolution** begins to give the Welsh a taste of their long-sought self-determination, greater independence from Westminster is impeded by the intimate bonds between the two countries—unlike Scotland, Wales shares its educational and legal systems with England. The wobbly Welsh **economy** resists any sort of quick fix—the coal and steel industries, which built up the country during the Industrial Revolution, have sharply declined in the last few decades, causing poverty and unemployment more severe than that endured by the rest of Britain. **Economic rebuilding** is particularly difficult for a nation that has never had diversified industries, especially as it seeks to avoid basing its new economy on low-quality, low-paying jobs. A recent upsurge in **tourism** is promising, however, and visitors are discovering a Wales that outshines its grimy, industrial past. **Cardiff** (p. 465), which was named the Welsh capital in 1955, has dubbed itself "Europe's Youngest Capital" and is trying particularly hard to reinvent itself as a cultural center.

MODERN POLITICS. Welsh politics in the late 20th century has been characterized by nationalism and a vigorous campaign to retain one of Europe's oldest living languages. The establishment of Welsh language classes, publications, radio stations, and even a Welsh television channel (known as Sianel Pedwar Cymru, "Channel 4 Wales," or S4C for short), indicates the energy invested in Welsh. In 1967, the **Welsh Language Act** established the right to use Welsh in the courts, while the **1988 Education Reform Act** ensured that all children would be introduced to the language of their forebears. The **1993 Welsh Language Act** went even farther, stipulating that Welsh and English should be regarded as equal in the conduct of public business—allowing the people to use their preferred tongue in the public realm.

Besides the fight to preserve the Welsh language, politics sees other nationalist movements: **Plaid Cymru**, the Welsh Nationalist Party, was founded in 1925 and consistently garners seats in Parliament. In the 1950s, a **Minister for Welsh Affairs** was made part of the national Cabinet, but Tory rule in the 1980s brought the legitimacy of governing from London into question, despite the fact that most of the Welsh seats were held by Labour and Plaid Cymru. On September 18, 1997, the Welsh voted in favor of **devolution,** but unlike their Scottish counterparts support for the idea was tepid, with only 50.3% voting "yes" despite major governmental backing. Still, this was enough to lead to elections for the 60-seat **Welsh Assembly** (held in May 1999), a parliamentary body that now controls Wales's budget (see p. 470). A meager 46% voter turnout saw Labour take home a 28-seat plurality, and Plaid Cymru doing unexpectedly well with 17 seats.

CULTURE AND CUSTOMS

Though modernity may be the future of Wales, and Cardiff's cosmopolitan bustle rivals that of other major international cities, the real Wales comes through in its rural towns and villages, where pleasantries are exchanged across garden hedges, locals swap gossip over post office counters, and a visitor can expect to remain anonymous for all of, oh, three minutes. Welsh **friendliness** and **hospitality** seem to bubble up from a never-ending spring—long conversations and cheerful attention tend to be the rule more than the exception.

The **Welsh language** (see p. 462) is an increasingly important part of everyday life, and visitors can expect to find road signs, pamphlets, and timetables written both in English and in Welsh. Nearly all Welsh speakers are fluent in English, and while a well-timed burst of Welsh may earn a smile, the monolingual should not expect to encounter discrimination or discomfort. **Nationalism** runs deep in Wales and may surface at unexpected moments—above all, avoid the supreme faux pas of calling a Welshman "English" or his country "England."

> ## GAG ME WITH A SPOON
> Some suitors bring flowers, others serenade with a guitar and ballad, but in Wales, olde-tyme wooing often involved a large wooden spoon. Making a **lovespoon** for one's sweetheart is a centuries-old Welsh custom. The romantic utensils, popular during the 18th and 19th centuries, were carved to pass the time on long winter evenings. Gentlemen translated their affections into fancy designs, making for some ridiculously elaborate ladles. Acceptance of the spoon meant courting could begin in earnest. Although the custom has languished, lovespoons can still be found in homes and tourist traps across Wales.

Wales has long been a country defined by its customs, and **folk culture** has always been at its heart. Chances to partake in the distinctly and uniquely Welsh—witnessing an **eisteddfod** (see p. 464), listening to a traditional male choir, or tast-

WALES

ing homemade baked goods—should not be passed up. Welsh national symbols are the **red dragon,** the **leek,** and the **daffodil. St. David's Day,** the observance of Wales's patron saint, is celebrated March 1, and is one opportunity to see the Welsh **national costume**—a long red cloak and tall black hat.

LANGUAGE

Let me not understand you, then; speak it in Welsh.
—William Shakespeare, *Henry IV, Part 1*

The word "Welsh" comes from the Old English *wealh,* or "foreigner," and the language does seem alien to most English speakers. Though modern Welsh borrows from English for vocabulary, as a member of the **Celtic family** of languages, *Cymraeg* is based on a grammatical system more closely related to **Cornish** and **Breton.** After a sharp decline since 1900 (when about 50% of the population spoke Welsh), the language is undergoing a powerful resurgence. Today, more than 500,000 people speak the country's mother tongue; just over half of those are native speakers. Welsh-speaking communities are especially strong in the north and west.

Though English suffices nearly everywhere in Wales, it's a good idea to familiarize yourself with the language and avoid the laughter of bus drivers when you try to approximate the name of your destination. Welsh shares with German the deep, guttural **ch** heard in "Bach" or "loch." **Ll**—the oddest Welsh consonant—is produced by placing your tongue against the top of your mouth, as if you were going to say "l" and blowing. If this technique proves baffling, try saying "hl" (hlan-GO-hlen for "Llangollen"). **Dd** is said either like the "th" in "there" or the "th" in "think" (hence the county of Gwynedd is pronounced the same way as Gwyneth Paltrow's first name). **C** and **g** are always hard, as in "cat" and "golly." **W** is generally used as a vowel and sounds either like the "oo" in "drool" or "good." **U** is pronounced like the "e" in "he." Tricky **Y** changes its sound with its placement in the word, sounding either like the "u" in "ugly" or the "i" in "ignoramus." **F** is spoken as a "v," as in "vertigo," and **ff** sounds exactly like the English "f." Emphasis nearly always falls on the penultimate syllable, and there are (happily) no silent letters.

Most Welsh place names are derived from prominent features of the landscape. *Afon* means river, *betws* or *llan* church or enclosure, *caer* fort, *llyn* lake, *mynydd* mountain, and *ynys* island. The Welsh call their land *Cymru* (KUM-ree) and themselves *Cymry* ("compatriots"). Because of the Welsh system of letter mutation, many of these words will appear in usage with different initial consonants. *Let's Go* provides a delicious mouthful of **Welsh Words and Phrases** on p. 813.

THE ARTS

LITERATURE

The Welsh prefer philosophy to philology; music and poetry to both.
—T. Charles Williams

In Wales, as in other Celtic countries, much of the national literature stems from a vibrant **bardic tradition.** The earliest extant poetry in Welsh comes from 6th-century northern England, where the **cynfeirdd** (early poets), including the influential poet **Taliesin,** composed praiseful oral verse for their patron lords. The *Gododdin,* a series of lays attributed to the poet **Aneirin,** is a celebration of valor and heroism from this period. The 9th through 11th centuries brought emotional poetic sagas focusing on pseudo-historical figures, including poet **Llywarch Hen, King Arthur,** and **Myrddin** (Merlin). Ushering in the most prolific period in Welsh literature, 12th-century monastic scribes compiled Middle Welsh manuscripts. Most notable is the

Mabinogion, a collection of eleven prose tales drawing on mythology and heroic legend. In the 14th century, **Dafydd ap Gwilym** developed the flexible poetic form *cywydd*. Often called the greatest Welsh poet, he turned to love and nature as subjects, and influenced the work of later poets such as **Dafydd Nanmor** and **Iolo Goch** well through the 17th century. A growing anglicization of the Welsh gentry in the 18th century led to a decline in the tradition of courtly bards. Poets found their venues mainly at *eisteddfodau* (see p. 464) and local poetry competitions.

Modern Welsh literature has been influenced by Bishop William Morgan's 1588 **Welsh translation of the Bible**, which helped standardize Welsh and provided the foundation for literacy throughout Wales. A circle of Welsh romantic poets, **Y Beridd Newydd** (the New Poets), including T. Gwynn Jones and W.J. Gruffydd, developed in the 19th century, while the horrors of WWI produced an anti-romantic poetic voice typified in the work of **Hedd Wyn**. The work of 20th-century Welsh writers (in both Welsh and English) features a compelling self-consciousness in addressing questions of identity and national ideals. The incisive poetry of **R.S. Thomas** treads a fine line between a fierce defense of his proud heritage and a bitter rant against its claustrophobic provincialism, while **Kate Roberts's** short stories and novels, such as *Feet in Chains*, dramatize fortitude in the face of dire poverty. The best-known Welsh writer is Swansea's **Dylan Thomas**, whose emotionally powerful poetry, as well as popular works like *A Child's Christmas in Wales* and the radio play *Under Milk Wood*, describe his homeland with nostalgia, humor, and a tinge of bitterness. Wales's literary heritage is preserved in the **National Library of Wales** in Aberystwyth (p. 502), which receives (by law) a copy of every Welsh-language book published in the UK.

MUSIC

Music has always occupied an important place in this land of song. The Welsh word **canu** means both "to sing" and "to recite poetry," suggesting an intimate historical connection between the sung and the spoken word. Though little Welsh music from before the 17th century has survived, three traditional medieval instruments are known: the **harp**, the **pipe** (hornpipe or bagpipe), and the **crwth**, a six-stringed bowed instrument. Welsh indigenous musical tradition began to disappear when England's 16th-century Tudor court incorporated Welsh harpists; traditional playing died out by the 17th century. The 18th-century rise of chapels led to an energetic singing culture, as Welsh folk tunes were adapted to sacred songs and hymn-writers such as **Ann Griffiths** made their mark. Their works, sung in unison in the 18th century, became the basis for the harmonic **choral singing** of the 19th and 20th centuries, now Wales's best-known musical tradition. While many associate the all-male choir with Wales, both single-sex and mixed choirs are an integral part of social life, and choral festivals like the **cymanfa ganu** occur throughout Wales.

Today's musical life includes much more than the chorus. Cardiff's **St. David's Hall** (one of the finest venues in Britain) regularly hosts both Welsh and international orchestras, and the **Welsh National Opera**, featuring renowned tenor **Bryn Terfel**, has established a worldwide reputation. Modern Welsh composers, including **Alun Hoddinott** and **William Mathias**, have won respect in the classical genre. Young soprano **Charlotte Church** earned international attention with her 1998 debut, *Voice of an Angel*. **Rock music** (in both English and Welsh) is the voice of youth, although the most famous Welsh pop music exports are the no-longer-youthful **Tom Jones** and **Shirley Bassey**. Current bands combine Britpop sounds with a (sometimes fierce) nationalism, led by the **Manic Street Preachers**. Other bands with their share of hits include **Catatonia, Stereophonics,** and the **Super Furry Animals**.

WALES

FOOD

Traditional Welsh cooking relies heavily on leeks, potatoes, onions, dairy products, lamb (considered the best in the world), pork, fish, and seaweed. Soups and stews are ubiquitous. **Cawl** is a complex broth, generally accompanied by bread; most soups brim with leeks and generous helpings of lamb or beef. **Welsh rarebit** (also called "Welsh rabbit") is buttered toast topped with a thick, cheesy, mustard-beer sauce. But the baked goods tempt most—Wales is famed for unique, tasty **breads. Welsh cakes** are buttery, scone-like treats, studded with currants and golden raisins and traditionally cooked on a bakestone or griddle. The adventurous should sample **laverbread,** a cake-like slab made of seaweed, while the sweet-toothed will love **bara brith,** a fruit and nut bread served with butter, and **teisennau hufen,** fluffy doughnut-like cakes filled with whipped cream. **Cwrw** (beer) is another Welsh staple; **Brains S.A.** is the major brewer.

FESTIVALS

The most significant of Welsh festivals is the **eisteddfod** (ice-TETH-vod), a competition of Welsh literature (chiefly poetry), music, and arts and crafts. Hundreds of local *eisteddfodau* (the plural) are held in Wales each year, generally lasting one to three days. The most important of these is the **National Eisteddfod** (Eisteddfod Genedlaethol Cymru; see below). The **International Musical Eisteddfod,** held in Llangollen (p. 532) in July (July 8-13 in 2003), draws folk dancers, singers, and choirs from around the world for performances and competitions.

> ## THE NATIONAL EISTEDDFOD
> The National Eisteddfod of Wales was established in 1568 by Elizabeth I to address her concern over the "intolerable multitude of vagrant and idle persons calling themselves minstrels, rhymers, and bards." Today's National Eisteddfod is a grand festival held the first week of August, alternating yearly between locations in North and South Wales. Its present incarnation owes much to the fancy of Iolo Morgannwg, poet and writer, who invented a "tradition" reaching back into the Druidic past. He created the *Gorsedd Beirdd*—an honorary group of great poets—who parade in white, green, and blue robes at two ceremonies, officiated by the "Archdruid," at which the winners of the two main poetry prizes are introduced to the crowd amid much pomp. In recent years, Eisteddfod events, which are conducted in Welsh, have made translations available for non-Welsh speakers.
>
> In 2003, the National Eisteddfod will be in Montgomeryshire and The Marches, near the village of Meifod, from August 2 to 9. Your best bets for reaching the bards and bands commemorating this most prominent of celebrations of Welsh culture are the base cities of Welshpool (8 mi. away), on the Aberystwyth-Birmingham rail line, and Llanfair Caereinion (5 mi. away). Arriva Cymru bus #75 stops in Welshpool between Llanidloes and Shrewsbury. For info, contact Eisteddfod Genedlaethol Cymru, 40 Parc Ty Glas, Llanisien, Cardiff CF4 5WU (☎(029) 2076 3777; www.eisteddfod.org.uk).

SOUTH WALES

Marauding peoples have found the south of Wales attractive for millennia. Irresistibly drawn by the lush curves of her landscape and her sweetly rushing streams, they have repeatedly battled to win her hand. The English have held it for centuries now, but many Welsh consider it a forced marriage. Travelers today find themselves falling under her spell—intrigued by the quilted pastures and silhouetted peaks of the ancient landscape, welcomed by the friendly people, and charmed by the odd encounter with a sweet, shaggy pony.

HIGHLIGHTS OF SOUTH WALES

CARDIFF Plunge into the vibrant cultural scene of one of Europe's youngest capitals, then scale majestic castle battlements north of the city (p. 465).

VALES AND HILLS Hike the Wye Valley for a fine view of **Tintern Abbey** (p. 474) and proceed north to the land of wild ponies in **Brecon Beacons National Park** (p. 479).

HAY-ON-WYE Browse the shelves in a literary wonderland that boasts the largest secondhand bookstore in the world (p. 478).

ST. DAVID'S Savor the soft light in Britain's holiest city, at the tip of the cliff-happy **Pembrokeshire Coast National Park** (p. 495).

CARDIFF (CAERDYDD) ☎029

Independent. Aspiring. Vibrant. Words that wouldn't once have described Wales now evoke its rapidly changing capital. Formerly the main port of call for Welsh coal, Cardiff (pop. 325,000) is now the port of arrival for a colorful international mix—you're as likely to hear Urdu as Welsh on a street corner. Theaters and clubs spill out from the city center, where ten paces in any direction will find you tripping over a pint or a plate. Don't let gray, rainy days dampen your view—Cardiff's reinvention is far from complete, but in this self-styled "Youngest Capital" of Europe, a visitor might soon become a believer.

▣ TRANSPORTATION

Trains: Central Station, Central Sq., south of the city center, behind the bus station. Ticket office open M-Sa 5:45am-9:30pm, Su 6:50am-9:30pm. Trains (☎(08457) 484 950) from: **Bath** (1-1½hr., 1-3 per hr., £12.20); **Birmingham** (2¼hr., 1-3 per hr., £21.80); **Bristol** (45min., 3 per hr., £7.20); **Edinburgh** (7hr., 7 per day, £105); **London Paddington** (2hr., every hr., £46.80); **Swansea** (1hr., 1-3 per hr., £8.20).

Buses: Central Station, on Wood St. National Express booking office and travel center. Show up at least 15min. before closing to book a ticket. Open M-Sa 7am-5:45pm, Su 9am-5:45pm. **National Express** (☎(08705) 808 080) from: **Birmingham** (2½hr., 8 per day, £12.50); **London** (3½hr., 6 per day, £12.50); **London Heathrow** (3½hr., 11 per day, £24); **London Gatwick** (4½hr., 11 per day, £26.50); **Manchester** (5½hr., 4 per day, £19.50). Avoid confusion by picking up timetables from the bus station and a *Wales Bus, Rail, and Tourist Map and Guide* at the TIC.

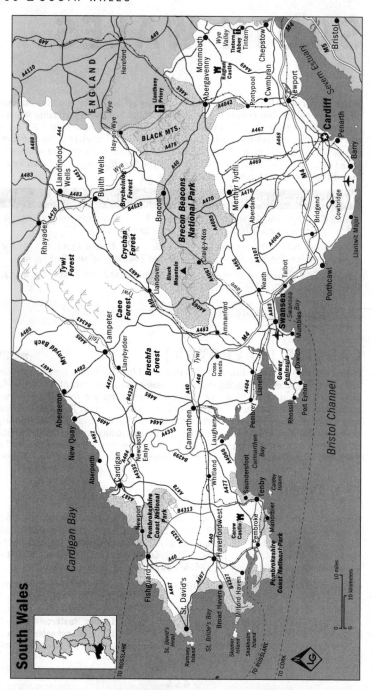

South Wales

Local Transportation: Cardiff Bus (Bws Caerdydd), St. David's House, Wood St. (☎2066 6444; office open M-F 8am-6:30pm, Sa 9am-4:30pm). Runs a 4-zone network of green buses in Cardiff and surrounding areas. Stops are often shared with **Stagecoach** and other carriers. Show up at the stop 5-10min. early; schedules can be unreliable. Service ends M-Sa 11:20pm, Su 11pm. Fares 60p-£1.50; reduced fares for seniors and children. Week-long **Multiride Passes** available (£15.95, children £9.60). **City Rider** tickets allow 1-day unlimited travel in the greater Cardiff area and can be purchased from drivers (£3.20, children £2.20, families £6.50). Pick up *A Guide to Bus Fares in Cardiff* from the bus office or TIC.

Taxis: Premier (☎2077 7777) and **Dragon** (☎2033 3333).

◼◼ ◼ ORIENTATION AND PRACTICAL INFORMATION

Cardiff Castle stands in the city center, with **Bute Park** stretching behind it along the River Taff. Eastward along Park Pl. are the Civic Centre, university buildings, and the National Museum. Shops, pedestrian walks, and arcades cluster between **St. Mary St.** and **Queen St.**, southeast of the castle. The bus and train stations lie south of the center, by the River Taff; developing **Cardiff Bay** is still farther south. Like any city, Cardiff has its sketchy pockets; stay alert and be cautious at night.

Tourist Information Centre: 16 Wood St. (☎2022 7281; www.visitcardiff.info), opposite the bus station. Home to a knowledgeable and friendly staff. Free accommodations list and map. Books rooms for £1 and a 10% deposit. Ask about **walking tours.** Open July-Aug. M-Sa 9am-6pm, Su 10am-4pm; Sept.-June M-Sa 9am-5pm, Su 10am-4pm.

Tours: Leisurelink 1hr. hop-on/hop-off bus tour departs every 20-30min. (10am-4pm, later if enough demand) from the main gate of Cardiff Castle. Purchase tickets from driver. £7, concessions £5, children 15 and under free. **Cardiff Cats** (☎2071 2693) water buses tour Cardiff Bay, the River Taff, and the River Ely year-round, departing from Mermaid Quay on Cardiff Bay. Call for schedules and prices.

Financial Services: Banks line Queen St. and St. Mary St. **Thomas Cook,** 16 Queen St. (☎2042 2500). Open M-Th and Sa 9am-5:30pm, F 10am-5:30pm. **American Express,** 3 Queen St. (☎(0870) 6001 0601). Open M-F 9am-5:30pm, Sa 9am-5pm. No commission currency exchange at **Bakers Dolphin** travel agency, 2-4 Royal Arcade (☎2038 7757). Open M-F 9am-5:30pm.

Work Opportunities: Bars, restaurants, and shops occasionally seek short-term help, especially during big rugby weeks. Employers often post notices on the bulletin board at the Cardiff International Backpacker (see below).

Launderette: Drift In, 104 Salisbury Rd. (☎2023 9257), northeast of Cardiff Castle. Open M-F 9am-9pm, Sa 9am-6pm.

Police: (☎2022 2111) King Edward VIII Ave.

Hospital: University Hospital of Wales, Heath Park, North Cardiff (☎2074 7747).

Internet Access: Internet Exchange, 8 Church St. (☎2023 6048), by St. John's Church. £4 per hr., minimum £1. Open M-Th 9am-9pm, F-Sa 9am-8pm, Su 11am-7pm.

Post Office: 2-4 Hill's St. (☎2022 7305), off The Hayes. Open M-Sa 9am-5:30pm. **Bureau de change.** Money Gram wiring service. **Post Code:** CF10 2ST.

◼ ACCOMMODATIONS AND CAMPING

"Budget accommodation" is a Cardiff city center oxymoron, but the TIC lists reasonable B&Bs (£18-20) on the outskirts. Many of the B&Bs on lovely **Cathedral Rd.,** a short ride on bus #32 or a 15min. walk, are expensive (£25 and up); better bargains await on side streets. Between June and September, **Cardiff University Student Housing** (☎2087 4864) lets out dorm rooms (from £9.40) to students; call ahead.

▨ **Cardiff International Backpacker,** 98 Neville St. (☎2034 5577; fax 2023 0404). Three steps to a young backpacker's heaven: from Central Station, go west on Wood St., turn right onto Fitzhamon Embankment just across the river, then left onto Despenser St; the hostel is the purple building. Inside beckon a kitchen, cable TV, pool table, bar, small store, Internet (£1 per 15 min.), and bike rental (£7.50 per day; £5 deposit for helmet and lock). International students only in summer, assuring a diverse scene. Curfews vary. 4- to 8-bed single-sex dorms £14.50; doubles £35; triples £43. ❷

YHA Cardiff, 2 Wedal Rd., Roath Park (☎2046 2303). Take bus #28 or 29 from Central Station (30 min., 1 per hr., 90p) and ask to be let off at the YHA. Hostel has lounge, kitchen, Internet (£2.50 per 30min.), and breakfast; nearby Roath Park Conservatory

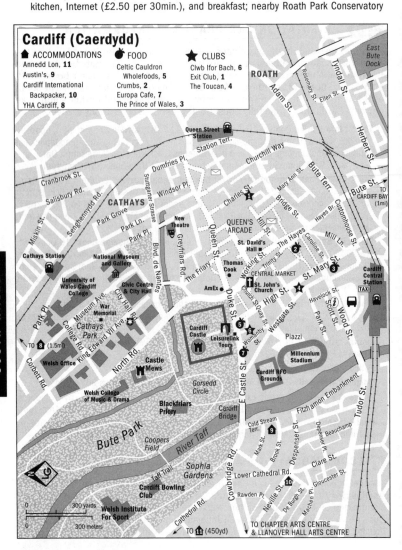

Cardiff (Caerdydd)

🏠 ACCOMMODATIONS
Annedd Lon, **11**
Austin's, **9**
Cardiff International
  Backpacker, **10**
YHA Cardiff, **8**

🍴 FOOD
Celtic Cauldron
  Wholefoods, **5**
Crumbs, **2**
Europa Cafe, **7**
The Prince of Wales, **3**

★ CLUBS
Clwb Ifor Bach, **6**
Exit Club, **1**
The Toucan, **4**

offers a pretty, über-British walk. Reception 7am–11pm. Check-out 10am. £14, under 18 £10.50; international travelers and nonmembers £2 extra, students £1 off. ❷

Annedd Lon, 157-159 Cathedral Rd. (☎2022 3349; fax 2064 0885). Conjoined Victorian houses (built in 1894) provide a peaceful respite from the city. No smoking. Rooms in 159 are big and quiet (singles £20; doubles £40); rooms in 157, the upscale half, include bath and British breakfast (singles £25; doubles £45). ❸

Austin's, 11 Coldstream Terr. (☎2037 7148; austins@hotelcardiff.com). 5min. from the castle and downtown area. Laugh (nicely, of course) at the unfortunates paying £40 more just across the river. Simple singles £20-25; doubles £30-39. ❸

Camping: Acorn Camping and Caravanning, Rosedew Farm, Ham Ln. South, Llantwit Major (☎(01446) 794 024). 1hr. by bus X91 from Central Station, 15min. by foot from the Ham Ln. stop. Mar.-Nov. £7 per night, Dec.-Feb. £6.50. Electricity £2. ❶

🍴🍺 FOOD AND PUBS

Budget travelers scavenge the stalls of Victorian-style **Central Market,** between St. Mary St. and Trinity St., where merchants sell tasty treats of all sorts and everything from wigs to Bibles. (*Let's Go* does not recommend eating wigs or Bibles.) The suave chat it up at the shiny new restaurants on **Mill Ln.** (£10-20), while the steely-stomached satisfy late-night hunger pangs with fish and chips or kebabs at shops on **Caroline St.** (most open M-W until 3am and Th-Sa until 4am).

⬛ Europa Cafe, 25 Castle St. (☎2066 7776), across from the castle, toward the river. Europa offers coffeehouse intellectualism, with writers' group meetings and mellow live music. Curl up on a comfy sofa with a hot chocolate (£1.50) or hang out by the bookshelf and talk Chaucer or Rand. Open W-Sa 11am-11pm; M-Tu and Su 11am-6pm. ❶

⬛ Celtic Cauldron Wholefoods, 47-49 Castle Arcade (☎2038 7185), across from the castle. Don't miss this authentic and untouristy option. Delicious Welsh cakes are 40p; an entire meal runs less than £5. Hours vary. ❶

⬛ The Prince of Wales, (☎2064 4449), at St. Mary St. and Wood St. Big helpings, a big menu, and a big clientele make the Prince fun. Pick a table and order food at the bar. Horrify the vegetarian in your life by ripping into the mixed grill (£6). Desserts start at £2. The boisterous evening scene feeds off the free-flowing beer (£1.09 special M). Open M-Sa 11am-11pm, Su noon-10:30pm; food served until 1hr. before close. ❷

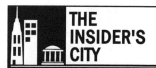

THE INSIDER'S CITY

CARDIFF BAY

Newly developed Cardiff Bay sports new and popular shops, restaurants, and attractions. Take Cardiff bus #7 or 8 to the bay shopping area.

1 Taste Turkish cuisine at waterfront **Bosphorus** (☎2048 7477).

2 For a night of comedy, try the **Glee Club** (☎(0870) 241 5093).

3 Craving raspberry? Mint? Run to **Cadwalader's World Famous Ice Cream** (cones £1, sundaes £3.50).

4 Admire handmade Welsh crafts at **The Makers Guild in Wales,** Craft in the Bay (☎2048 4611).

5 The telescope-shaped **Bay Visitor Centre** provides sight-seeing materials and souvenirs (☎2046 3833).

6 Get artsy at the **Norwegian Church Arts Centre** (☎2045 4899).

7 Let loose at hands-on museum **Techniquest** (☎2047 5475).

8 Browse displays on the Welsh National Assembly at the historic **Pierhead Building** (☎2089 8200).

9 Enjoy murals and a monolithic fountain at the **Oval Basin Plaza.**

Crumbs, 33 David Morgan Arcade (☎ 2039 5007). Tucked between St. Mary St. and The Hayes. Locals gather for friendly conversation at this pleasant veggie hangout. Stun the carnivore in your life by savoring a salad (£2.80-4) or delicious curry and brown rice (£4.25). Open M-F 10am-3pm, Sa 10am-4pm. ❷

◉ SIGHTS

▨ **CARDIFF CASTLE.** The interior of Cardiff Castle is no less flamboyant than the strutting peacocks within its gates. The third Marquess of Bute employed William Burges, the most lavish of Victorian architect-designers, to restore his home in mock-medieval style. Visit the museums of the **Welsh Regiment** and **1st Queen's Dragoon Guards,** enjoy a medieval supper, watch falconry demonstrations featuring owls Billy and Floyd, and climb the remnants of the Norman keep for a sweeping view. *(Castle St. ☎ 2087 8100. Open Mar.-Oct. daily 9:30am-6pm; Nov.-Feb. 9:30am-4:30pm. Last entry 1hr. before closing. Free tours Mar.-Oct. every 20min.; Nov.-Feb. 5 tours daily. Last tour 5pm. £5.50, students £4.20, concessions £3.30, families £15.50.)*

NATIONAL MUSEUM AND GALLERY. A dazzling audiovisual exhibit on the evolution of Wales speeds you through millennia of geological transformation. The fine collection of European art and variety of ancient Welsh artifacts are also worth a look. *(☎ 2039 7951. Open Tu-Su 10am-5pm. Free.)*

CIVIC CENTRE. The stately Cardiff Civic Centre is set against the lawns of **Cathays Park.** Find the Functions Office, upstairs in **City Hall,** to pick up a brochure or inquire about tours. In the Hall of Welsh Heroes, St. David, patron saint of Wales, is flanked by Owain Glyndŵr, the rebel leader who razed Cardiff in 1404. *(North Rd. across from the castle. ☎ 2087 1727. Open M-F 9am-6pm. Free.)*

NATIONAL ASSEMBLY. The temporary location of the **National Assembly of Wales,** next to the construction site for its permanent home, is open for tours. Observe assembly in session on Tuesday and Wednesday. Information and exhibitions are in the nearby Pierhead Building. *(☎ 2089 8688 for tours, 2089 8477 for general information. Book tours in advance. Free.)*

◪ ♫ NIGHTLIFE AND ENTERTAINMENT

CLUBS

Cardiff's nightlife centers around the compact downtown area—there's never much of a walk between clubs. Hotspots shift quickly, so pick up the *Itchy Insider's Guide* at Castle Welsh Crafts, across from the castle, and the *City Nights* guide at Thomson House, near the TIC—or just find **St. Mary St.** and follow the crowd. Clubs start jumping after 11pm. After dark, hail a cab if you're leaving the city center.

The Toucan, 95-97 St. Mary's St. (☎ 2037 2212). This colorful, live music venue is a club for everyone from the timid beginner to the addict looking for a laid-back change of pace. Acoustic, hip-hop, funk, Latin, salsa, and more make this the most varied club in town. Music and dancing on the second floor; awesome food, bar, and comfy seating at the ground level. Open Tu-Su noon-2am; food served noon-11pm, club from 9pm.

Clwb Ifor Bach (a.k.a. the **Welsh Club**), 11 Womanby St. (☎ 2023 2199). This manic 3-tiered club offers everything from Motown tunes to video games. Bands such as Catatonia got their start performing here. Theme nights include Tu "rock inferno," W student night, and F hip-hop. Local lore has it that knowledge of Welsh can help you get in the door—but mind that accent. Cover £2-8. Open M-Th until 2am, F-Sa until 3am.

Exit Club, 48 Charles St. (☎2064 0101). Where Cardiff's gay crowd dances to chart faves. No cover before 9:30pm, £2-3 after. Open M-Sa 6pm-1am, Su 6pm-2am.

ARTS

Bursting onto the international scene, Cardiff is experiencing an arts renaissance, with an influx of new blood and a renewed interest in Welsh vocal, theatrical, and artistic traditions. The TIC offers brochures for local craft shops and art events.

New Theatre, Park Pl. (☎2087 8889), off Queen St. Home to the **Welsh National Opera** and features children's theater, plays, and dance by local and visiting groups. Box office open M-Sa 10am-8pm. Tickets £6-47. Some student standby tickets available.

St. David's Hall, The Hayes (☎2087 8444). One of Britain's top concert venues; hosts the **BBC National Orchestra of Wales,** with several performances each week.

Chapter Arts Centre, Market Rd., Canton (☎2030 4400). An elegant building featuring a mix of film, gallery shows, dance, and drama.

Llanover Hall Arts Centre, Romilly Rd., Canton (☎2063 1144). Offers adult summer school classes (1 day to 1 week) in everything from batik to glass-firing.

Life Bar Cafe, St. Mary's St. (☎2066 7800). Latin dance classes (W 7:30-10pm, £2).

SPORTS

The gew-gaws gracing the **John Bachelor Statue,** at the corner of Hill's St. and The Hayes, are a gauge of Cardiff's festive atmosphere. Scarves, hats, and a clumsily grasped can of Brains S.A. signify sport-induced bacchanalia. **Rugby** matches are played at **Millennium Stadium,** Cardiff Arms Park, a 73,000-seater with retractable roof. If you're lucky enough to catch the city in the fervor of a local match (fall is rugby season), call the Welsh Rugby Union (☎2039 0111) for tickets. The **WHR Shop** (☎2082 2040), on Wood St., by the bus station, peddles rugby paraphernalia.

◪ DAYTRIPS FROM CARDIFF

Cardiff Bus whisks travelers to nearby **Barry Island** to visit the fairgrounds and bask on sandy beaches (bus #353-355, 30min. ferry, 1 per hr.). For those seeking pastoral diversion, the 55 mi. **Taff Trail** winds from Cardiff Bay through the Taff Valley to the heart of Brecon Beacons National Park (see p. 478).

◪ CAERPHILLY CASTLE. Eight miles north of Cardiff, this stunning castle will have romantics and history buffs alike in dreamy trances. Begun in 1268 by Norman warlord Gilbert de Clare, its stone walls, pivoting drawbridges, water defenses, and (re-created) catapults still amaze today. Tempt fate by posing for a picture under the precariously leaning main tower. *(Take the train (30min., M-Sa 2 per hr., £2.60), or hourly bus #24 or 25 from Central Station stand C1, and step off in the shadow of a massive curtain wall across the moat. ☎2088 3143. Open June-Sept. daily 9:30am-6pm; Apr.-May and Oct. 9:30am-5pm; Nov.-Mar. M-Sa 9:30am-4pm, Su 11am-4pm. Last admission 30min. before closing. £2.50, concessions £2, families £7.)*

MUSEUM OF WELSH LIFE. Four miles west of Cardiff in **St. Fagan's Park,** the open-air museum (Amgueddfa Werin Cymru in Welsh) is home to more than 40 authentic buildings from all corners of Wales, some nearly 500 years old. Reassembled throughout the 100 acres of park and staffed by traditionally garbed craftspeople, they act as an interactive history lesson. A guidebook ($1.95) is useful for those intent on seeing everything; others can simply take a day to wander the grounds. Stop by **St. Fagan's Castle,** and listen for Sarah, the Welsh-singing ghost said to wander the place. *(Bus #320 runs to the museum from Central Station (20min., 1 per hr., £1.20). ☎2057 3500. Open daily 10am-5pm. Free.)*

LLANDAFF CATHEDRAL. Two miles northwest of the city center, near the River Taff, the cathedral stands unassumingly amid stone paths and wildflowers. Built by Normans, used by Cromwell as an alehouse, and gutted by a German bomb, it is now an architectural mince pie—a stern and solid 12th-century arch behind the altar is overshadowed by an intrusive 1957 concrete arch. Ask gift shop workers for Llandaff stories—some remember the bombing. Nearby lie the ivy-covered ruins of the **Castle of the Bishops of Llandaff.** *(Take bus #60 or 62 from Central Station to the Black Lion Pub (15min.) and walk up High St. Or walk down Cathedral Rd. and through Llandaff Fields, turn left on Western Ave., right on Cardiff Rd., and right on High St. ☎2056 4554 for tours or questions (10am-3pm). Open daily 7:30am-7pm. Evensong daily 6pm. Free.)*

CASTELL COCH. Like its cousin in Cardiff, this 13th-century castle bears the ornate signature of Lord Bute and his renovator Burges, with butterflies on one ceiling, lascivious monkeys another, scenes from *Aesop's Fables* a third. Unlike the other Cardiff fortresses, Castell Coch occupies a secluded forest hillside and offers hikers connections to the Taff Trail. *(Take bus #24 (25min., every hr.) from Central Station to Tongwynlais, get off across from the post office, and walk 15min. up Mill St. ☎2081 0101. Open Mar.-May daily 9am-5pm; June-Sept. 9:30am-6pm; Oct. 9:30am-5pm; Nov.-Mar. M-Sa 9:30am-4pm, Su 11am-4pm. £3, concessions £2.50, families £8.50; audio tour 50p.)*

WYE VALLEY

Crossing and recrossing the oft-troubled Welsh-English border, the Wye River (Afon Gwy) cuts through a tranquil valley, with legend-rich castles, abbeys, and trails on its banks. Its towns and clusters of homes and farms retain a fresh, honest feel—from Tintern Abbey to the George Inn Pub, the past is palpable.

▐▛ TRANSPORTATION

The valley is best entered from the south at Chepstow. **Trains** (☎(08457) 484 950) chug to Chepstow from **Cardiff** and **Newport** (40min., 7-8 per day). **National Express buses** (☎(08705) 808 080) go to Chepstow from: **Cardiff** (50min., 7 per day); **London** (2¼hr., 10 per day); **Newport** (1hr., 10 per day). **Stagecoach Red and White** buses #65 and 69 loop between **Chepstow** and **Monmouth** (8-9 per day); bus #69 stops in Tintern. **Glyn Williams Travel** (☎(01495) 229 237) bus #83 careens from **Monmouth** to **Abergavenny** (1hr., 4 per day). One-day **Network Rider** passes (£4.50, concessions £2.50, families £9; available on Stagecoach buses) might save you money. There is little Sunday bus service in the valley. Consult the indispensable *Wales Bus, Rail and Tourist Map and Guide*, or the even more indispensable *Discover the Wye Valley on Foot and by Bus* (30p), in area TICs, for schedules. **Hitchhikers** try their luck on the A466 in the summer; some stand near the entrance to Tintern Abbey or by the Wye Bridge in Monmouth. *Let's Go* does not recommend hitchhiking.

◤ HIKING

Those who follow the Wye's example and wander the woods are rewarded with stunning vistas of the valley. Two main trails follow the river on either side: the Wye Valley Walk and Offa's Dyke Path. TICs disperse pamphlets and sell Ordnance Survey maps (1:25,000; £7) to long-distance hikers.

Wye Valley Walk (77 mi.). West of the river, this walk treks north from Chepstow via Hay-on-Wye to Prestatyn along wooded cliffs and farmland, eventually ending in Rhayader. From **Eagle's Nest Lookout**, 3 mi. north of Chepstow, 365 steps descend steeply to the riverbank. At **Symond's Yat**, 15½ mi. north of Chepstow, the hills drop away to a panorama of the Wye's horseshoe bends, seven counties, and a cliff where peregrine falcons make their eyrie every spring. *(Bus W73 from Coleford Square DIY Shop, 6 per day.)*

Offa's Dyke Path (177 mi.). East of the river, this beautiful path starts in Sedbury's Cliffs and winds along the Welsh-English border before finishing in Prestatyn; depending on who you ask, it was a trench originally dug to keep the Welsh in or the English out. Consult trail maps (available at TICs) before beginning a walk, as some paths change grade suddenly and without warning. For info, consult the **Offa's Dyke Association,** based halfway up the trail in Knighton (☎(01547) 528 753; www.offasdyke.demon.co.uk).

Royal Forest of Dean. This 20,000-acre forest, once the hunting grounds of Edward the Confessor and Williams I and II, is across the English border and allows pleasant hikes. Contact **Forest Enterprise,** Bank St., in Coleford, England, across the river from Monmouth (☎(01594) 833 057; open M-Th 8:30am-5pm, F 8:30am-4pm) or the **Coleford tourist information centre,** High St. (☎(01594) 812 388; open M-Sa 10am-5pm).

CHEPSTOW (CAS-GWENT)   ☎01291

Chepstow's strategic position at the mouth of the River Wye and the base of the Welsh-English border made it an important fortification in Norman times and a frontier town during the English Civil Wars. While not necessarily a year-round vacation destination, Chepstow does offer a fun downtown shopping area, Britain's oldest stone **castle** (built by Earl William, Norman companion of Conquerin' Will), a Sunday market at the race course, and the famed **Chepstow Festival,** a three-week spectacular featuring a light show, mock armed battles, and musical and theatrical entertainment. The festival takes place every other year (next in July 2004; www.chepstow-festival.co.uk), with smaller exhibitions in the odd years (in Tintern in 2003). Book accommodations far in advance during festive times.

Chepstow's **train station** is on Station Rd., and **buses** stop above the town gate in front of the Somerfield supermarket. Both stations are unstaffed. Train and bus tickets are bought onboard, except those for bus travel to major cities, which must be purchased at **The Travel House,** 9 Moor St. (☎623 031, M-Sa 9am-5:30 pm).

The **tourist information centre** faces the castle from Bridge St. Ask about hikes, book accommodations, or pick up a copy of *What's On Chepstow*. (☎623 772; www.chepstow.co.uk. Open Apr.-Oct. daily 10am-5:30pm; Nov.-Mar. 10am-4:30pm.) Other services include: **Barclays**, Beaufort Sq. (☎(016) 3320 5000; open M-Tu and Th-F 9am-4:30pm, W 10am-4:30pm); **Neptune Laundry Services**, 36 Moor St., near the bus station (☎626 372; wash £2.80, dry 20p, soap £1.10; open M-F 8:30am-7pm, Sa 9:15am-5:30pm, Su 10am-4pm); the **police**, Moor St. (☎623 993), across from the post office; the **Community Hospital** (☎636 637, 24hr.), west of town on Mounton Rd.; **Internet access** at the **Chepstow Library** on Manor Way in the town center (☎635 730; 30min. free; open M and F 9:30am-5:30pm, Tu 10am-5:30pm, W and Sa 9:30am-4pm, Th 9:30am-8pm); and the **post office**, Albion Sq. (☎622 607; open M-F 9am-5:30pm, Sa 9am-12:30pm). **Post Code:** NP16 5DA.

Tesco, Mill Ln., is open 24hr., but closes Su. The nearest **YHA hostel** is at **St. Briavel's Castle**, in England (see **Tintern**, below). In Chepstow, stay at lovely **Langcroft ❸**, 71 Kingsmark Ave., where a simple room, long chats, and personal attention await. (☎/fax 625 569, £20 per person.) Or visit **Mrs. Presley ❸**, 30 Kingsmark Ave., who has beautiful rooms and a conservatory. (☎624 466; £20 per person.)

TINTERN   ☎01291

Five miles north of Chepstow on the A466, the village of Tintern stretches along a half mile of road above the curving Wye. At ◪**Tintern Abbey**, see the cliffs and haunting arches which, as Wordsworth wrote, "connect the landscape with the quiet of the sky." Built by Cistercian monks in the 12th and 13th centuries as a center for religious austerity, the abbey was the richest in Wales until Henry VIII dissolved it and it fell into romantic ruin. The windows now provide an intimate connection to the nearby hills and dense trees. Arrive in the morning to avoid hoards of tourists and Wordsworth devotees. (☎689 251. Open June-Sept. daily 9:30am-6pm; Apr.-May and Oct. 9:30am-5pm; Nov.-Mar. M-Sa 9:30am-4pm, Su 11am-4pm. £2.50, concessions £2, families £7. 45min. audio tours £1 plus £5 deposit.) If crowds overwhelm, get a copy of *Popular Walks Around Tintern* (£3) from the gift shop and head for the hills, or ask the gift shop employees for directions to the **Monk's Path** (2¼hr.) that winds around Tintern and the surrounding area. A 1½hr. hike will get you to **Devil's Pulpit**, a huge stone from which Satan is said to have tempted the monks as they worked in the fields.

A mile north of the abbey, on the A466, lies Tintern's **Old Station**. Once a stop on the Wye Valley Line, the out-of-service train station now holds a series of railway carriages, one of which houses the **tourist information centre**. Book accommodations for a £1 fee. (☎/fax 689 566. Open Apr.-Oct. daily 10:30am-5:30pm.) The nearest **YHA hostel** is **St. Briavel's Castle ❷**, 4 mi. northeast of Tintern across the English border. Once King John's hunting lodge, later a fortress against the marauding Welsh, the 12th-century castle maintains its medieval character. 15th-century graffiti marks one dorm wall. From the A466 (bus #69 from Chepstow) or Offa's Dyke, follow signs for 2 mi. from Bigsweir Bridge. (But be forewarned—that's a boot camp-worthy 2 mi. uphill hike.) Bus L12 runs from Monmouth to St. Briavel's on Wednesday only. (☎(01594) 530 272; fax 530 849. Meals £3-5. Lockout 10am-5pm. Curfew 11:15pm. Dorms £11.25, under 18 £8.) B&Bs are strung along the A466 throughout the village, many with river views. Try the cozy **Holmleigh House ❷** near the Sixpence and Moon pub on the A466 (☎689 521; £16.50 per person.) **Campers** can use the **field ❶** next to the old train station. (£1.50 per person. Parking 50p per 3hr. No showers.) Near St. Briavel's Castle hostel lies the ◪**George Inn Pub ❶**, a 16th-century local favorite, with original timber, low ceilings, and dim lighting straight out of a medieval story. *Let's Go* recommends the death by chocolate cake with vanilla ice cream. (Open M-Sa 11am-2:30pm and 6:30pm-11pm.)

LET THEM EAT CHEESE Don't be alarmed if you wake from an afternoon nap at St. Briavel's youth hostel to a rhythmic chant. The villagers gathered across the street leaping at flying chunks of cheese aren't preparing to storm the castle, but rather engaging in a mysterious ceremony unique to this tiny village.

In the 17th century, the English Earl of Hereford withdrew the local villagers' right to gather wood, but when his compassionate wife protested, the Earl backed down. As a gesture of thanks, his wife suggested that each villager contribute a penny to feed the poor. The ritual has since evolved from its charitable roots, and now residents from all social strata feast on hurled cheese. (There are some things not even *Let's Go* can explain.) Every Whitsunday (the seventh Sunday after Easter), bread and cheese are distributed outside the Roman church to this chant: "St. Briavel's water and Whyrl's wheat are the best bread and water King John ever eat."

HAY-ON-WYE (Y GELLI) ☎ 01497

More than 40 bookshops, dozens of antique dealers, and numerous cafes spill from alleyways onto the bustling narrow lanes of Hay. The 1961 appearance of Booth's Books (now the world's biggest secondhand bookstore, with 400,000 titles) sparked the development of this bibliophile's nirvana. This smallest of towns contains the largest of literary festivals in June, when book fever threatens to ignite the surrounding grassy farmlands.

☎🔁 TRANSPORTATION AND PRACTICAL INFORMATION. The closest **train station** is in Hereford, England (see p. 302). **Stagecoach Red and White bus** (☎(01633) 838 856) #39 stops at Hay between **Hereford** and **Brecon** (1hr. from Hereford, 40min. from Brecon; M-Sa 5 per day; £3.10-4.45). On Sundays, **Yeoman's** (☎(01432) 356 202) bus #40 runs the same route twice (£4-5). The **tourist information centre,** Oxford Rd., by the bus stop, books beds for £2. To find your dream book, pick up the *Hay Bookworm* (£2) or the *Secondhand & Antiquarian Booksellers & Printsellers* map and brochure (free), or search over a million titles at www.haybooks.com. (☎820 144; www.hay-on-wye.co.uk. Open Apr.-Oct. daily 10am-1pm and 2-5pm; Nov.-Mar. 11am-1pm and 2-4pm.) Other services include: **Barclays,** Broad St. (open M-F 10am-4pm); a **launderette,** near the bus stop on Bell Bank (☎820 360; open M-Sa 8am-9pm; £4 per load, soap 20p); **Internet access** at **Hay Design & Print,** 4 High Town (☎821 058; £3 per hr.; open M and W-F 10am-5pm); and the **post office,** 3 High Town (open M, W, F 9am-1pm and 2-5:30pm, Tu 9am-1pm, Th 9am-5:30pm, Sa 9am-12:30pm). **Post Code:** HR3 5AE.

☎🔁 ACCOMMODATIONS AND FOOD. The **YHA hostel** nearest to Hay-on-Wye is 8 mi. from town at Capel-y-Ffin (see p. 482). Delightful stays await at ◪**The Bear ❸,** Bear St., a 16th-century coaching inn that couples inglenook fireplaces with bright rooms. Gracious hosts Sue and Jon serve breakfast; order *crempog las* (vegetarian Welsh pancakes) the night before. (☎821 302; www.thebear-hay-on-wye.co.uk. Rooms from £24.) **Camp** along the **Wye Valley Walk** or **Offa's Dyke** (see p. 472). **Radnor's End Campsite ❶,** on a tiny valley plateau, is closest to town; cross Bridge St. and go 500 yd. to the right toward Clyro. (☎820 780. £3 per person.)

At **The Granary ❷,** Broad St., enjoy generous portions and a fine vegetarian selection. (☎820 790. Entrees from £8.25. Open mid-July to Aug. daily 10am-9pm; Sept. to mid-July 9am-5:30pm.) **Oscars ❷,** High Town, offers scones and pastries (£1-1.50) as well as tasty meals. (☎821 193. Open M-Su 10:30am-4:30pm.) A sign calls for "wine, women, mirth and laughter" at the **Wheatsheaf Inn ❶,** Lion St., where the locals hang out. (☎820 186. Happy hour M-F 4-6pm; drinks 30% off. M-Sa 11am-11pm, Su noon-10:30pm; food served daily noon-2:30pm, M-F also 6-8:30pm.) The **Tipple 'n' Tiffin ❶,** The Pavement, caters to couples, with specialized seats and dishes for two. (☎821 932. Open M-F noon-2:30pm and 7-9:30pm.)

HAY'S DAY Hay-on-Wye straddles the England-Wales border. This indeterminate status, and the compelling logic that the independent city-states of ancient Greece and Renaissance Italy were the world's greatest civilizations, led to Richard Booth's grand April Fool's joke: a declaration of Hay's independence on April 1, 1977. Booth, owner of Booth's Books (which acquires more books than all of Wales's universities and public libraries combined), made his proclamation as an attack on bureaucracy and big government. Now he and his wife preside as King and Queen of Hay Castle. Arrive around April 1 to join the Independence Day celebrations.

■ **SIGHTS.** After eight centuries of wars, fires, and neglect, Hay's **Norman castle** has been conquered by countless unruly first editions, courtesy of the castle branch of Richard Booth's bookshop. (Open summer daily 9:30am-6pm; winter 9am-5:30pm.) The town's myriad other shelves are a browser's paradise. Some specialize, like the **Poetry Bookshop,** Brook St. (☎821 812), while others *specialize*, notably B&K Books, dedicated to apiculture. Most vend a hodgepodge of used volumes, selling century-old editions for under £20. The annual 10-day **literary festival** brings the literati to town (recently, Harold Pinter, Toni Morrison, and Paul McCartney) to give readings. (May 23-June 1 in 2003; £1-10.) Book accommodations early. For less cerebral pursuits, **Celtic Canoes,** Newport St., rents canoes and gives lessons. (☎847 422; mobile (07966) 505 286. £16 per half-day, £25 per day.)

ABERGAVENNY (Y FENNI) ☎01873

The market town of Abergavenny (pop. 10,000) styles itself as the traditional gateway to Wales. Savvy visitors take this literally and travel straight through town on their way to the hills—the Black Mountains in the eastern third of Brecon Beacons National Park and the Seven Hills of Abergavenny.

TRANSPORTATION. Trains (☎(08457) 484 950) run from: **Bristol** (1¼hr., every 2hr., £7.60); **Cardiff** (40min., every hr., £7.60); **Chepstow** (1hr., every 2hr., £8.30); **Hereford** (25min., 2 per hr., £5.60); **London** (2½hr., every hr., £33-44); **Newport** (20min., 2 per hr., £4.80). To get to town from the train station, turn right at the end of Station Rd. and walk 15min. along Monmouth Rd. The **bus station** is on Monmouth Rd., by the TIC. **Stagecoach Red and White** (☎(01633) 838 856) buses roll in from: **Brecon** (#21, 1hr., 5 per day, £3.50); **Cardiff** (X30, 1½hr., every hr., £4.50); **Hereford** (#X4, 1hr., every 2hr., £4.50); **Newport** via **Cwmbran** (X23 and X30, 45min., 2 per hr., £4). **Lewis Taxis** (☎854 140) are clean and cheap.

PRACTICAL INFORMATION. The well-stocked **tourist information centre** (☎857 588; www.abergavenny.co.uk; open Apr.-Oct. daily 10am-5:30pm; Nov.-Mar. 10am-4pm) shares space with the **National Park Information Centre** on Lower Cross St. (☎853 254; open Apr.-Oct. daily 9:30am-5:30pm). Purchase camping supplies at **Crickhowell Adventure Gear,** 14 High St. (☎856 581. Open M-Sa 9am-1:30pm and 2:30-5:30pm.) Other services include: **Barclays,** 57 Frogmore St. (open M-Tu and Th-F 9am-4:30pm, W 10am-4:30pm); the **police,** Tudor St. (☎852 273); the **hospital,** Nevill Hall on Brecon Rd. (☎732 732); **Internet access** at the **Public Library,** Library Sq., Baker St. (☎735 980; free; open M-F 9:30am-5:30pm, Sa 9:30am-4pm) and **Celtic Computer Systems,** 39 Cross St. (☎858 111; £5 per hr.; open M-Sa 9:30am-5pm); and the **post office,** St. John's Sq., where Tudor St. abuts Castle St., with a **bureau de change** (☎223 344; open M-F 9am-5:30pm, Sa 9am-12:30pm). **Post Code:** NP7 5EB.

⌐⌐ ACCOMMODATIONS AND FOOD. Mrs. Bradley ❷, 10 Merthyr Rd., where Frogmore St. becomes Brecon Rd., keeps a simple house with friendly cats. (☎ 852 206. £12 per person with continental breakfast, £14 with cooked breakfast.) More **B&Bs** await on **Monmouth Rd.** and **Hereford Rd.,** 15min. from town. The **Black Sheep Backpackers ❷** offers Internet access (£1 per 15min.), a kitchen, and a pool table. (☎ 859 125. Dorms £10; doubles £13 per person.) On Tuesday, Friday, and Saturday mornings, the bustling **market** in Market Hall on Cross St. (☎ 735 811) offers fruit and vegetables, baked goods, and livestock trading; a flea market hops in on Wednesday. For a tasty pastry (£1-2) or a darn good sandwich (£2.40-3), head to the **Mad Hatters Cafe ❶,** 58 Cross St. (☎ 859 839. Open M-F 9:30am-5:30pm.) The friendly **Hen and Chickens ❶** pub, 7 Flannel St., has family seating. (☎ 853 613. Open daily 10am-11pm.) **Harry's Carvery ❶,** St. John's St., loads crusty baguettes with scrumptious fillings for £1.75 and up. (☎ 852 766. Open M-Su 8:30am-4pm.)

◙ ⚲ SIGHTS AND OUTDOORS. Site of many a medieval intrigue, Abergavenny's **castle** is a ruin, with views of the valley and mountains through the gaps in its walls. A 19th-century hunting lodge on the grounds houses the **Abergavenny Museum.** (☎ 854 282. Museum open Mar.-Oct. M-Sa 11am-1pm and 2-5pm, Su 2-5pm; Nov.-Feb. M-Sa 11am-1pm and 2-4pm. £1, concessions 75p, children free. Grounds open daily 8am-dusk. Free.)

Abergavenny's real attractions lie in the hills that ring it; the excellent *Walks from Abergavenny* pamphlet (£2) details mountain climbs. **Blorenge** (1833 ft.) is 2½ mi. southwest of town and the only word that rhymes with orange. A path begins off the B4246, traversing valley woodlands to the upland area; it climbs the remaining 1500 ft. in 4½ mi. The trail to the top of **Sugar Loaf** (1955 ft.), 2½ mi. northwest, starts a mile west of town on the A40. Many report that it's easy to hitch a ride to the carpark and start hikes from there, though *Let's Go* does not recommend hitchhiking. The path to **Skirrid Fawr** (the Holy Mountain; 1595 ft.) lies northeast of town and starts 2 mi. down the B4521. The TIC has details on **pony trekking** in its comprehensive *Activity Wales* guide. Local companies include **Grange Trekking Centre** (☎ 890 215; £16 per half-day, including instruction; £24 per day), **Wern Riding Center** (☎ 810 899; £10 per hr., £17.50 per half-day, £30 per day), and **Llanthony Riding and Trekking** (☎ 890 359; £14 per half-day, £22 per day).

▶ DAYTRIPS FROM ABERGAVENNY

If traveling to the sights near Abergavenny by bus, a **Network Rider Pass** (£4.50 per day for travel on all Stagecoach Red and White, Phil Anslow, and Cardiff buses) is usually cheaper than return tickets.

▧ BIG PIT NATIONAL MINING MUSEUM FOR WALES. The silent hillsides of Blaenavon, 9 mi. southwest of Abergavenny, overlook a green valley scarred by fields of black. Descend a 300 ft. shaft to the subterranean workshops of a 19th-century coal mine, operative until 1980, where ex-miners guide you with stories as grim as the surroundings. Dress warmly and wear sensible shoes. *(Take bus X4 (13 per day) to Bryn Mawr, then #30 (every 2hr.) to Blaenavon. ☎ (01495) 790 311. Open Mar.-Nov. daily 9:30am-5pm. Underground tours 10am-3:30pm. Free. Under 5 not admitted underground.)*

LLANTHONY PRIORY. All the megaliths in the Black Mountains are said to point toward ruined and relatively untouristed 12th-century Llanthony Priory. Founder William de Lacy doffed hunting gear and aristocratic title, choosing a contemplative life amid humbling natural beauty. The **YHA Capel-y-Ffin** (see p. 482) is another 4 mi. out. *(Take Stagecoach Red and White bus X4 (M-Sa 6 per day) or follow the A465 to Llanfihangel Crucorney, where the B4423 begins. Most walk and some hitch the last 6 mi. to the priory, but Let's Go does not recommend hitchhiking. Always open. Free.)*

RAGLAN CASTLE. Between Abergavenny and Monmouth on the A40, Raglan is a mere 565 years old. Planned as a residence rather than a fortress (as the absence of arrow slits suggests), the castle's design will interest castle fanciers. *(Take Stagecoach Red and White #83 from Abergavenny or Monmouth (20min., 4-6 per day), or #60 from Monmouth or Newport (40min. from Newport, 4 per day, £3-4.20).* ☎ *(01291) 690 228. Open June-Sept. daily 9:30am-6pm; Apr.-May and Oct. 9:30am-5pm; Nov.-Mar. M-Sa 9:30am-4pm, Su 11am-4pm; last admission 30min. before close. £2.50, concessions £2.)*

BRECON (ABERHONDDU)   ☎01874

Just north of the mountains, Brecon (pop. 8000) is the best base for hiking the Brecon Beacons. This quiet market town offers pleasant shops, lovely scenery, and evening strolls along the gentle river pathway. August sees the exceptional **Jazz Festival,** when the streets fill with music and tourists bump into such luminaries as Branford Marsalis, Keb' Mo', and Van Morrison.

■ TRANSPORTATION. Brecon has no bus or train station, but **buses** arrive regularly at **The Bulwark** in the central square (near the large statue). Ask for schedules at the TIC. **National Express** (☎(08705) 808 080) bus #509 runs from **London** (5hr., 1 per day, £19) via **Cardiff** (1¼hr., £3). **Stagecoach Red and White** (☎(01633) 838 856) buses arrive from: **Abergavenny** and **Newport** (#21, M-Sa 6 per day, £3-4.50); **Merthyr Tydfil** (#43; 40min.; M-Sa 6 per day, Su 3 per day); **Swansea** (#63, 1½hr., M-Sa 3 per day, £4-5). To reach Brecon from **Cardiff,** take the X4 or X40 to Merthyr Tydfil and transfer to the #43 (2 per hr., £5-7). Bus #39 comes in from **Hereford** via **Hay-on-Wye** (M-Sa 5 per day, £3.10-4.45); on Sundays, **Yeomans** (☎(01432) 356 202) follows the same route (#40, 2 per day, £4-5).

⑦ PRACTICAL INFORMATION. The **tourist information centre** is located in the Cattle Market carpark, across from Safeway; walk through Bethel Sq. off Lion St. (☎622 485. Open daily 9:30am-5pm.) The TIC stocks an abundance of pamphlets, as does the **National Park Information Centre** in the same building. (☎/fax 623 156. Open Apr.-Sept. daily 9:30am-5:30pm.) **Brecon Cycle Centre,** 10 Ship St., rents mountain bikes and gives advice on maintenance and trails. (☎622 651. £15 per day, £25 per weekend.) **Bikes and Hikes** (see below) also rents equipment and organizes climbing, caving, and other gorge-oriented expeditions. (☎610 071. £10 per half-day, £15 per day.) Other services include: **Barclays,** at the corner of St. Mary's St. and High St. (☎(01633) 20500; open M-Tu and Th-F 9am-4:30pm, W 10am-4:30pm); **Beacons Laundry,** St. Mary's St. (☎979 625; open M-Sa 9am-5:30pm); the **police,** Lion St. (☎622 331); free **Internet access** at **Brecon Branch Library,** Ship St. (☎623 346; call ahead to reserve); and the **post office,** in the Cooperative Pioneer, off Lion St. (☎611 113; open M-F 8:30am-5:30pm, Sa 8:30am-4:30pm). **Post Code:** LD3 9HY.

⚑ ACCOMMODATIONS. Mid-August visitors should book far in advance—the Jazz Festival claims every pillow in town. Pamper yourself at the **George Hotel ❹,** George St., in the town center, a 17th-century inn with a Victorian-era restaurant, where food is cooked on an open stone kiln. (☎623 421; fax 611 579. Breakfast included. Singles £45; doubles £65-75; families £70.) Friendly Mrs. Parkin keeps warmly decorated rooms in a former monks' habitation at **Mulberry House ❷,** 3 Priory Hill, across from the cathedral. (☎624 461. £18 per person.) **Mrs. J. Thomas ❷** has traveled to 27 countries, lived in 18, collected exotic memorabilia from each, and now keeps a signless B&B at 13 Alexandra Rd., behind the TIC. (☎624 551. Open Feb.-Nov. From £17 per person.) **Bikes and Hikes ❷,** the Struet, 2min. from the TIC, lives up to its name: the outdoors-enthusiast owners rent equipment and lead trips. (☎610 071. Pool table, lounge, kitchen. £12.50 per person.)

The nearest **YHA hostel** is **Ty'n-y-Caeau** (tin-uh-KAY-uh) ❷, 3 mi. from Brecon. From the town center, walk down The Watton, continuing to the A40-A470 roundabout. Follow the Abergavenny branch of the A40. Just after the roundabout, take the footpath to the left of **Groesffordd** (grohs-FORTH); then turn left on the main road. Continue 10-15min., bearing left at the fork; the hostel is on the right. A bus runs from Brecon to Groesffordd several times daily; alternatively, the Brecon-Abergavenny bus can drop you at the Groesffordd footpath. The Victorian mansion has gardens, a TV room, and Internet access. Lunch and dinner save guests a trip to town. (☎665 270. Open July-Sept. daily; Nov.-Feb. M-Sa. Dorms £10.25, under 18 £7.) **Camp at Brynich Caravan Park** ❶, 1½ mi. east of town on the A40, signposted from the A40-A470 roundabout. (☎623 325. Open Easter-Oct. £4.50 per person, £9.50 with car.) During the Jazz Festival, additional campsites open on farms.

🔲 **FOOD.** Fill your pack at the **Cooperative Pioneer,** off Lion St. (☎625 257. Open M-Sa 8am-9pm, Su 10am-4pm.) For a taste of the real (Welsh) thing, head to the **Cegin Cymru** ❶ (Welsh Food Centre), in the George Inn courtyard. Jams, honeys, sweets… and beer. (☎620 020. Open Easter-Christmas M-Sa 9am-5pm, Su 10am-4pm.) Peaceful and hearty meals await on the sun-dappled grounds of the cathedral at the **Pilgrims Restaurant and Tea** ❶. (☎610 610. Open daily about 10am-late afternoon.) **St. Mary's Bakery** ❶, 4 St. Mary St., sells yummy filled rolls and meat pasties for 75p-£1. (☎624 311. Open M-F 7am-5pm, Sa 7am-2pm.) When the sun sets over the Beacons, try **The Camden Arms** ❷, 21 The Watton, for drinks and grub. Be it a chip butty bap or a 10 oz. rumpsteak (£9.25), the food here deserves a hearty bottoms-up. (☎625 845. Open Th-Sa 6-11pm; food served 6-9pm.)

🔲🔲 **SIGHTS AND FESTIVALS.** Wearing 900 years of architectural fashion gracefully, **Brecon Cathedral** occupies a grove above the River Honddu. A nearby 16th-century tithe barn houses the **Heritage Centre,** which tells the cathedral's history. (Cathedral ☎623 857, Centre 625 222. Cathedral open daily 10am-Evensong, around 5:30pm. Centre open Mar.-Dec. daily 10:30am-4:30pm.) Those enamored of sharp and pointy objects will enjoy **The Royal Regiment of Wales Museum Brecon,** The Barracks, where military paraphernalia commands all available space. (☎613 310. Open Apr.-Sept. daily 9am-5pm; Oct.-Mar. M-F 9am-5pm, last admission 4:15pm. £3, students and children free.) **Brecknock Museum and Art Gallery,** Captain's Walk, in the 1842 Assize Courthouse, has a full-size diorama of the Victorian Assize Court and other exhibits. (☎624 121. Open M-F 10am-5pm, Sa 10am-1pm and 2-5pm; Apr.-Sept. also Su noon-5pm; Nov.-Feb. closes 4pm. £1, concessions 50p.) Set for the second week of August in 2003, the **Brecon Jazz Festival** (☎625 557; www.breconjazz.co.uk) dubs itself "the only festival in Britain bigger than the town itself." Other events include **antique fairs** (last Sa of the month Feb.-Nov.) and **crafts fairs** in Market Hall (third Sa of the month Easter-Nov.).

BRECON BEACONS

Brecon Beacons National Park (Parc Cenedlaethol Bannau Brycheiniog) encompasses 519 sq. mi. of shorn peaks, well-watered forests, and windswept moorlands. The park divides into four regions: barren **Brecon Beacons,** where King Arthur's mountain fortress is thought to have stood; **Fforest Fawr,** with the spectacular waterfalls of Ystradfellte; the **Black Mountains** to the east; and the remote western **Black Mountain** (singular). The market towns on the fringe of the park, particularly Brecon and Abergavenny, make pleasant touring bases, but hostels allow easier access to the park's inner regions.

TRANSPORTATION

Since crowds in the Brecon Beacons are less dense than in other Welsh parks, public transport is all the scarcer. The **train** line (☎ (08457) 484 950) from **London Paddington** to South Wales runs via **Cardiff** to **Abergavenny** at the park's southeastern corner and to **Merthyr Tydfil** on the southern edge. The **Heart of Wales** rail line passes through **Llandeilo** and **Llandovery** in the more isolated Black Mountain region. **National Express** (☎ (08705) 808 080) bus #509 runs once a day to **Brecon**, on the northern side of the park, from London (£18.50) and Cardiff. **Stagecoach Red and White buses** (☎ (01685) 388 216) cross the park en route to Brecon from: **Abergavenny** (#21, 1hr., M-Sa 5 per day, £3-4.10); **Cardiff** via **Merthyr Tydfil** (X4 or X40, changing to #43; 1½hr.; X4 and X40 2 per hr., #43 M-Sa 6 per day; £5-7); **Hay-on-Wye** (#39, 45min., M-Sa 6 per day, £2.80-4.10); **Swansea** (#6, 1½hr., 2-4 per day, £4). **Yeomans** (☎ (01432) 356 202) #40 runs from **Hay-on-Wye** on Sundays (2 per day, £4-5). **Brecon Bus Service** #760 runs twice on summer Sundays. The free *Brecon Beacons: A Visitor's Guide* details bus coverage and describes walks accessible by public transport. **Brecon Cycle Centre** (see p. 478), among others, rents mountain bikes. **Hitchhikers** say the going is tougher on the A470 than on minor roads, where drivers often stop to enjoy the view. *Let's Go* does not recommend hitchhiking.

> **WARNING.** The mountains are unprotected and often difficult to scale. Cloud banks breed storms in minutes. In violent weather, do not shelter in caves or under isolated trees, which tend to draw lightning. A compass is essential: much of the park is trackless, and landmarks get lost in sudden mists. Never hike alone, and consider registering with the police before setting out. See **Wilderness Safety**, p. 49.

⁇ PRACTICAL INFORMATION

Stop at a **National Park Information Centre (NPIC)** before venturing forth. While TICs are helpful in planning a route by car or bus, NPICs provide advice on hiking and biking. Free maps are available, but Ordnance Survey Outdoor Leisure Maps #12 and 13 (1:25,000; £7) are indispensable for serious exploring and for reaching safety in bad weather. The park staff usually conducts guided walks of varying difficulties between April and November. Centers also stock leaflets on everything from lovespoon carving (see p. 461) to sheepdog demonstrations.

NATIONAL PARK INFORMATION CENTRES

Libanus National Mountain Park Visitor Centre (Mountain Centre): Brecon Beacons (☎ (01874) 623 366). Bus #43 to Libanus, 5 mi. southwest of Brecon (8min., M-Sa 6 per day), then walk 1½ mi. uphill; on Su in July-Aug., take a shuttle to the front door (15min., 6 per day) or Beacons Bus Service #7 (15min., 2 per day), both from Brecon. Open July-Aug. daily 9:30am-6pm; Apr.-June and Sept. M-F 9:30am-5pm, Sa-Su 9:30am-5:30pm; Mar. and Oct. 9:30am-5pm; Nov.-Feb. 9:30am-4:30pm.

Abergavenny: see p. 476.

Brecon: see p. 478.

Craig-y-nos: At the Country Park, Pen-y-cae (☎/fax (01639) 730 395). Silverline Bus #63, the Swansea-Brecon route; ask to be dropped at Craig-y-nos (1½hr., M-Sa 3 per day). Open May-Aug. M-Th 10am-6pm, F-Su 10am-7pm; Mar.-Apr. and Sept.-Oct. M-F 10am-5pm, Sa-Su 10am-6pm; Nov.-Feb. M-F 10am-4pm, Sa-Su 10am-4:30pm.

ENGLAND

Hay-on-Wye

B4348

B4350

TO HEREFORD (21mi)

A438

A4018

Wye

BLACK MOUNTAINS

Offa's Dyke Path

B4423

Honddu

Skirrid Fawr

A465

B4233

Abergavenny

A4042

Capel-y-Ffin

Grwyne Fawr

Llanthony

Cwmyoy

Sugar Loaf

Crug Mawr

Crickhowell

Blorenge

B4246

A4043

Abertillery

Waun Fach

Pen y Gadair Fawr

Pen Cerrig Calch

Iron Age cairn

Canal

A4246

A4046

Brynmawr

Blaenavon

A467

A4048

A479

Talgarth

Tretower

Usk

B4558

B4560

Llangynidr

Ebbw Vale

A469

Llan-gors

A40

Tor y Foel

BRECON MOUNTAIN RAILWAY

Merthyr Tydfil

B4520

Roman fort

Brecon

Llandefaelog

Llanfaes

Libanus

Waun Rydd

Pen-y-Fan

Cribyn

Corn Du

Llyn Cwm Llwch

Storey Arms

BRECON BEACONS

Pontsticill

TO CARDIFF (25mi)

A40

A4215

Iron Age fort

A4059

Hepste

Aberdare

Sennybridge

Fan Fawr

Hirwaun

A465

Trecastle

Llywel

Cral

Fan Llia

Fan Nedd

FFOREST FAWR

Porth-yr-Ogof

Sgwd Ffald Waterfall

Sgwdr Eira Waterfall

Bronze Age monument

Fan Gyhirych

Ystradfellte

A4109

Glyn Neath

Llandovery

Myddfai

Fan Brycheiniog

Llanddeusant

BLACK MOUNTAIN

Dan-yr-Ogof Showcaves

Craig-y-nos

Abercrave

Tawe

A4221

A4109

A4069

A4068

Ystradgynlais

TO SWANSEA (10mi)

A40

Llangadog

A4069

Tawe

Amman

Wales

TO CARMARTHEN (15mi)

Llandeilo

Trapp

Carreg Cennen Castle

Llandybie

A483

Ammanford

SOUTH WALES

0 5 miles
0 5 kilometers

Brecon Beacons National Park

▲ ACCOMMODATIONS

YHA Capel-y-Ffin, **5**
YHA Llanddeusant, **1**
YHA Llwyn-y-Celyn, **3**
YHA Ty'n-y-Caeau, **4**
YHA Ystradfellte, **2**

Llandovery: Kings Rd. (☎(01550) 720 693). Near Black Mountain; take Heart of Wales train or bus #280 from Carmarthen. Open Easter-Sept. M-Sa 10am-1pm and 1:45-5:30pm; Oct.-Easter M-Sa 10am-1pm and 1:45-4pm, Su 2-4pm.

ACCOMMODATIONS

B&Bs are rare; the Brecon TIC's free *Where to Stay in Brecknockshire and Brecon Beacons National Park* lists a few. Scattered about the park are five **YHA hostels,** including **Ty'n-y-Caeau,** near Brecon (see p. 478). The other four are:

Capel-y-Ffin (kap-EL-uh-fin; ☎(01873) 890 650), near River Honddu at the eastern edge of the Black Mountains along Offa's Dyke Path, 8 mi. from Hay-on-Wye. Take Stagecoach Red and White #39 or Yeomans #40 from Hereford to Brecon, stop before Hay, and walk uphill; a taxi from Hay (Border Taxis ☎(01497) 821 266) is £12. The road to the hostel climbs up Gospel Pass. Horseback riding trips by Black Mountain Holidays leave from here. (☎(01873) 890 961; ask for Howard.) Lockout 10am-5pm, daytime access to toilets and bad weather shelter. Open July-Sept. daily; Oct.-Dec. and Mar.-June F-Tu. Dorms £8.75, students £7.75, under 18 £6. **Camping** £5 per tent. ❶

Llanddeusant (HLAN-thew-sont; ☎(01550) 740 218). At the foot of Black Mountain near Llangadog village; take the Trecastle-Llangadog road for 9 mi. off the A40. Lockout 10am-5pm. Curfew 10:30pm. Open mid-Apr. to Aug. Dorms £8.75, students £7.75, under 18 £6. ❶

Llwyn-y-Celyn (HLEWN-uh-kel-in; ☎(01874) 624 261; fax 625 916), 7 mi. south of Brecon, 2 mi. south of Libanus, and 2 mi. north from Storey Arms carpark on the A470. Take Stagecoach Red and White #43 from Brecon or Merthyr Tydfil (M-Sa every 2hr., Su 4 per day). Close to Pen-y-Fan and the Beacons range. Farmhouse near a nature trail. Lockout 10am-5pm, access to lounges and toilets. Curfew 11pm. Open Easter-Aug. daily; Nov. and Feb.-Easter F-Su. Dorms £9.50, students £8.50, under 18 £6.75. ❶

Ystradfellte (uh-strahd-FELTH-tuh; ☎(01639) 720 301), south of the woods and waterfall district, 3 mi. from the A4059 on a paved road; 4 mi. from the village of Penderyn; a 5min. walk from the Porth-yr-Ogof cave. Hard to reach by public transport except on Su in summer. Small 17th-century cottages. Kitchen. Open mid-July to Aug. daily; Apr. to mid-July and Sept.-Oct. F-Tu. Dorms £8.50, students £7.50, under 18 £5.75. ❶

Campsites are plentiful, but often difficult to reach without a car. *Where to Stay in Brecknockshire and Brecon Beacons National Park* lists 14 sites. Many offer laundry and grocery facilities, and all have parking and showers (£3-6 per tent). Farmers may let you camp on their land if you ask first and leave the site as you found it; be prepared to make a donation toward feeding the sheep. *Bunkhouse Accommodations In and Around the Brecon Beacons* (free at NPICs) provides info on more than 18 **bunkhouses.**

REGIONS OF THE PARK

THE BRECON BEACONS

At the center of the park, the Brecon Beacons lure hikers to pastoral slopes and stark peaks. A splendid view of the range complements an exhibit on its history at the NPIC outside Libanus (see p. 480). A pamphlet on walks around the center costs 60p; one stroll among daredevil sheep leads to the scant remains of an **Iron Age fort.** The most convenient route to the top of **Pen-y-Fan** (pen-uh-VAN; 2907 ft.), the highest mountain in southern Wales, begins at **Storey Arms,** a carpark and bus stop 5 mi. south of Libanus on the A470. Paths have eroded over time, and scree (loose rocks) shakes underfoot. A more pleasant hike starts in **Llanfaes,** a western suburb of Brecon. Walk the first 3 mi. from Llanfaes down Ffrwdgrech Rd. (take the middle fork after the first bridge). From the Pont-yr-daff carpark a trail to the peak passes **Llyn Cwm Llwch** (HLIN-koom-hlooch), a 2000 ft. glacial pool in the shadow of **Corn Du** (CORN-dee) peak. An arduous ridge path leads from Pen-y-Fan to other peaks in the Beacons.

The touristy **Brecon Mountain Railway,** Pant Station, Merthyr Tydfil, allows a glimpse of the south side of the Beacons as the narrow-gauge train runs north to Pontsticill. (☎ (01685) 722 988. Runs Mar. to mid-Sept. daily 11am-4pm; mid-Sept. to Oct. Tu-Th and Sa-Su. £6.80, seniors £6.20, children £3.40.)

THE WATERFALL DISTRICT (FFOREST FAWR)

Rivers tumble through rapids, gorges, and spectacular falls near **Ystradfellte,** about 7 mi. southwest of the Beacons. At **Porth-yr-Ogof** ("mouth of the cave"), less than 1 mi. from the YHA Ystradfellte, the River Mellte ducks into a cave at the base of the cliff and emerges as an icy pool. Swimming is decidedly *not* recommended: the stones are slippery, the pool deepens alarmingly, and dipping here has proved fatal in the past. Porth-yr-Ogof provides no solitude, and rubbish crowds the banks. Remote but worth the sweat is the **Sgwdyr Eira** waterfall (on the River Hepste ½ mi. from its confluence with the Mellte); you can stand behind thundering water in a cliff-face hollow, remaining dry as a bone. Follow the marked paths to the falls from Gwaun Hepste. Hikers reach the waterfall district from the Beacons by crossing the A470 near the YHA Llwyn-y-Celyn, climbing Craig Cerrig-gleisiad cliff and Fan Frynych peak, and descending along a rocky Roman road. The route crosses a nature reserve and some of the park's trackless heath.

Near **Abercrave,** between Swansea and Brecon off the A4067, the **Dan-yr-Ogof Showcaves** (☎ (01639) 730 284, 24hr. info 730 801) reveal gargantuan stalagmites. From YHA Ystradfellte, 10 mi. of trails pass **Fforest Fawr** (headlands of the waterfall district) on their way to the caves. (Open Apr.-Oct. daily 10:30am-5pm, last admission 3pm. £7.80, children £4.80, under 4 free.) A **campsite ❶** is nearby (camping £4 per night; caravans £10; electricity free). Relax at **Craig-y-nos Country Park,** ½ mi. away. (☎ (01639) 730 395. Open May-Aug. M-F 10am-6pm, Sa-Su 10am-7pm; Mar.-Apr. and Sept.-Oct. M-F 10am-5pm, Sa-Su 10am-6pm; Nov.-Feb. M-F 10am-4pm, Sa-Su 10am-4:30pm. Free. Parking £2.) **Stagecoach Red and White** #63 (1½hr., 2-3 per day) stops at the hostel, caves, and campsite en route from Brecon to Swansea.

THE BLACK MOUNTAINS

Located in the easternmost section of the park, the Black Mountains are a group of long, lofty ridges offering 80 sq. mi. of solitude. Summits like **Waun Fach,** the highest point (2660 ft.), may seem dull and boggy, but the ridge-walks are unsurpassed. The Ordnance Survey Outdoor Leisure Map #13 (1:25,000; £7) is essential.

Crickhowell, on the A40 and Stagecoach Red and White route #21 between Brecon and Abergavenny (M-Sa every 2-3hr.), is the best starting point for forays into the area. You can also explore by bus: Stagecoach Red and White bus #39 linking Brecon and Hay-on-Wye (see p. 478) descends the north side of the Black Mountains. **Gospel Pass,** the park's highest mountain pass, often sees sun above the cloud cover. Nearby, **Offa's Dyke Path** (see p. 472) sprints down the park's eastern boundary. The ridge valleys are dotted with churches, castles, and other ruins. There is almost no public transportation along valley routes.

SOUTH WALES

SWANSEA (ABERTAWE)   ☎ 01792

Like most good paradoxes, native son Dylan Thomas's assessment of Swansea (pop. 230,000) as "this ugly lovely town" is both logically impossible and very true. Endless rows of box houses creep uphill, offering travelers a worn hello; pedestrian-friendly streets and a wide, sandy beach partially redeem poor first impressions. A haven for night-owls, consumers, and Thomas aficionados, Swansea also serves as a transport hub for voyagers to the Gower and Ireland.

TRANSPORTATION. Swansea has direct connections to most major cities in Britain. At the **train station**, 35 High St., trains (☎ (08457) 484 950) arrive from: **Birmingham** (4hr., every hr., £31.40); **Cardiff** (1hr., 1-2 per hr., £7.80); **London** (3hr., 1-2 per hr., £60). The **Quadrant Bus Station** (☎ 475 511) is near the Quadrant Shopping Centre and the TIC. **National Express** (☎ (08705) 808 080) buses from: **Birmingham** (4hr., 4-5 per day, £22); **Cardiff** (1¼hr., 16 per day, £5); **London** (4¼hr., 5 per day, £17). **First Cymru** (☎ (08706) 082 608) buses cover the Gower Peninsula and the rest of southwest Wales; Monday to Friday a shuttle runs to **Cardiff** (1½hr., 4 per hr., return £8.25). A First Cymru **Day Saver** ticket (£4.70, concessions £3.70, families £9.50) allows unlimited travel for a day in the area; the **Swansea Bay Pass,** purchased on the bus, covers a week of travel on the Peninsula (£12, children and seniors £8.40). **Stagecoach Buses** arrive from smaller towns around Wales, including **Brecon** (1½hr., 3 per day, £4.50). **Taxis** zip around town and down the bay to Mumbles courtesy of **Data Cabs** (☎ 474 747) and **Glamtax** (☎ 652 244). **Swansea-Cork ferries** (☎ 456 116; £27 per person) leave for **Cork, Ireland,** from King's Dock (see **By Ferry,** p. 40). **Cruises** (☎ (01412) 432 224) set sail from Swansea to **Ilfracombe** (£18) and other spots on the Bristol Channel from July to September.

PRACTICAL INFORMATION. On the north side of the bus station, the **tourist information centre** books rooms for £1 and a 10% deposit and stocks events calendars and an excellent city map. (☎ 468 321. Open M-Sa 9:30am-5:30pm, some Su in summer.) Other services include: **Barclays**, the Kingsway (☎ (0800) 400 100; open M-Tu and Th-F 9am-5pm, W 10am-5pm, Sa 9:30am-noon); **American Express,** 28 The Kingsway (☎ 455 188; open M-F 9am-5pm, Sa 9am-4pm); the **police** (☎ 456 999), at the bottom of Mt. Pleasant Hill; **Singleton Hospital** (☎ 205 666), on Sketty Park Ln.; **Internet access** at the YMCA's **Cyber-Cafe,** 1 The Kingsway (☎ 652 032; £1.50 per 30min.; open M-F 10:30am-3pm), or free at the **Swansea Public Library,** Alexandra Rd. (☎ 516 753; book ahead; open M-W and F 9am-7pm, Th and Sa 9am-5pm); and the **post office,** 35 The Kingsway (open M-Sa 9am-5:30pm). **Post Code:** SA1 5LF.

ACCOMMODATIONS AND FOOD. The closest hostel is the popular **YHA Port Eynon,** an hour out of town by bus (see p. 486). Inexpensive **B&Bs** and guest houses line **Oystermouth Rd.,** along the bay, but you won't find any pageant winners here. More comely **Ael-y-Bryn House ❷,** 88 Bryn Rd., has bay views and is worth the walk. (☎/fax 466 707. £18 per person.) **Harlton Guest House ❷,** 89 King Edward's Rd., is a mile out of town. Take bus #37 (1 per hr.) from the bus station, or walk 1 mi. from the city center. (☎ 466 938. £12 per person.) In high season, many travelers **camp** at sites along the Gower Peninsula.

Indian and Chinese takeaways line **St. Helen's Rd.,** and cafes dominate the **Oxford St.** pedestrian zone and **Wind St.'s** busy sidewalks. The city convenes to peruse everything from bread to CDs at the massive **Swansea Market,** on the other side of the Quadrant Shopping Centre from the bus station. (Open M-Th 8:30am-5:30pm, F-Sa 8am-5:30pm.) Self-described as "Hotter than a chilli pepper, smoother than a Latin lover," wildly decorated **¡Mambo! ❷,** 46 The Kingsway, serves funky, but tasty, sit-down dinners. (☎ 456 620. Open 10am-11pm.) Those under 18 will find the

SOUTH WALES

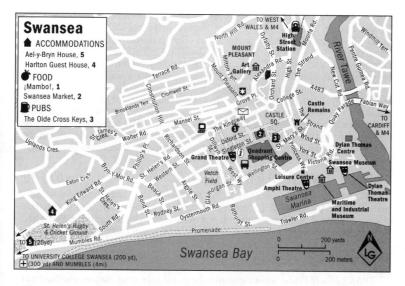

Swansea

ACCOMMODATIONS
Ael-y-Bryn House, 5
Harlton Guest House, 4

FOOD
¡Mambo!, 1
Swansea Market, 2

PUBS
The Olde Cross Keys, 3

doors of many traditional pubs closed, but **The Olde Cross Keys** ❶, 12 St. Mary's St., is a popular place to go with friends. (☎630 921. Open M-Sa 11am-11:30pm, Su noon-11pm; food served M-Th 11am-8pm, F-Sa 8am-5:30pm, Su noon-6pm.)

◙ SIGHTS. The **castle**, reduced to ruins by rebel-hero Owain Glyndŵr, lies between Wind St. and The Strand; it overlooks **Castle Square**, a motley extravaganza of street entertainers and people-watchers. **Swansea Museum**, Victoria Rd., is the oldest in Wales. The collection includes randomness ranging from an Egyptian mummy to a dolphin's skull; the display on area history begins with the days when hippopotami roamed the Gower. (☎653 763. Open Tu-Su 10am-5pm, last admission 4pm. Free.) A pensive and bulbous-nosed **Dylan Thomas** sits at the end of the marina, and a full page of the *Swansea Bay* guide (from the TIC) is devoted to shepherding iambic junkies along the **Dylan Thomas Uplands Trail** and **City Centre Trail**, past the poet's favorite haunts. More detailed guidebooks to the trails (from £1.50) are available at the **Dylan Thomas Centre**, Somerset Pl., which exhibits anything and everything Thomas. In a video, Thomas claims he wasn't the world-class drinker and ladies' man he seemed. The Centre also presents dramatic, cinematic, and literary performances. (☎463 980; box office 463 892. Open Tu-Su 10:30am-4:30pm. Free.) As in Cardiff, recent rebuilding has transformed the **maritime quarter** from decaying dockland to upscale apartment blocks and outdoor cafes. In the **Maritime and Industrial Museum**, vintage cars and tugboat photos share space with an exhibit on the world's first passenger railway, which chugged from Swansea to Oystermouth in 1807. Climb aboard the lightship **Helwick** docked outside and admire the pint-sized bunks. (☎650 351. Museum open Tu-Su 10am-5pm. Boat open June-Aug. Th-Su 10am-4pm. Both free.)

◙◙ NIGHTLIFE AND ENTERTAINMENT. Evenings in Swansea are rowdy affairs, the downtown pedestrian area packed with theater-goers and clubbers. Nightlife centers around The Kingsway, where swarms of students club-hop on weekend nights—just follow their lead. **Time & Envy**, 72 The Kingsway, is one place to start. (☎653 142. Cover £5. Open F-Sa 10pm-2am.) About 5 mi. away, pubs on Gower's Mumbles Rd. are a barfly's magnet (see p. 487).

SOUTH WALES

The bimonthly *What's On*, free at the TIC, lists events around town. The **Dylan Thomas Theatre,** along the marina, stages dramas and musicals. (☎473 238. Tickets £8-38.) The **Grand Theatre,** on Singleton St., puts on operas, ballets, concerts, and comedy. (☎475 715. Box office open 9:30am-8pm. Tickets £8-40, student discounts sometimes available day of show.) The **Taliesin Arts Centre,** University College, hosts films, art shows, and dance. (☎296 883. Box office open M-F 10am-8pm, Sa noon-6pm, performance nights 6-8:15pm.) In mid-August, the village of Pontardawe, 8 mi. north (take bus #120), floods with international folk and rock musicians for the **Pontardawe International Music Festival** (☎830 200). The **Swansea Festival** (☎411 570, bookings 475 715; Oct. 4-18 in 2003) presents a variety of shows, concerts, and family activities. No calendar would be complete without the late October **Dylan Thomas Celebration,** including readings, shows, and lectures.

THE GOWER PENINSULA ☎01792

Surrounded by sparkling waters, the 18 mi. Gower Peninsula is rife with unexpected finds. Ancient burial sites, castles, churches, and other ruins constellate the beautiful land. Expansive white beaches meet crashing water on one side and flower-covered limestone cliffs on the other, while paths above promise breathtaking views. Best of all, the peninsula's proximity to Swansea (5 mi. from Mumbles) means you'll be spared a leg-breaking hike to get there.

▐ TRANSPORTATION. Buses overrun the peninsula from Swansea's **Quadrant Station. First Cymru** (☎(08706) 082 608) buses #2 and 2A leave **Swansea** for Oystermouth Sq. in **Mumbles** (20min., 3 per hr., £1.70) and continue to **Langland Bay** and then **Caswell Bay.** Buses #18 and 18A run to **Oxwich** (40min., every 2hr., return £3), while #18A also lurches through the hills to **Rhossili** via **Port Eynon** (1hr., every 2hr., return £2.90). Bus #14 shuttles to **Pennard** (35min., every hr.). On Sundays, bus travel is difficult: only #18D crosses the peninsula, joined by #48 June through August. The First Cymru **Day Saver** is valid through the Gower and beyond (£4.80, concessions £3.50, families £9), while the **Gower & City Rider** allows a week's unlimited travel around the Peninsula (£12, children £8.20). **A.A. Taxis** (☎360 600) provide on-call transport. **Hitchhiking** is said to be quicker than public transport and allows coastal views. (*Let's Go* does not recommend hitchhiking.) The pleasant **Swansea Bikepath and Promenade** traces the coast from Swansea Bay to Mumbles pier.

▐ PRACTICAL INFORMATION. Most useful services on the Gower can be found in **Mumbles.** The **tourist information centre** stands in a portacabin near the main bus stop on Mumbles Rd. (☎361 302. Open Easter-Oct. M-Sa 9:30am-5:30pm; July-Aug. also some Su.) Other services include: **Barclays,** 16 Newton Rd. (☎492 600; open M-Tu and Th-F 9am-4:30pm, W 10am-4:30pm); **work opportunities,** posted in the window of the meat market at the bottom of Newton Rd.; the **police,** Newton Rd. (☎456 999), near Castle St.; free **Internet access** at **Oystermouth Library,** Dunns Ln., up the street from the TIC (☎368 380; open M-F 9:30am-5:30pm, Sa 9:30am-5pm; closed 1-2pm); and the **post office,** 522 Mumbles Rd. (☎366 821; open M-F 9am-12:30pm and 1:30-5:30pm, Sa 9am-12:30pm). **Post Code:** SA3 4DH.

▐ ACCOMMODATIONS AND FOOD. The farther west you go on the Gower, the more likely you are to find tourist-free accommodations. **B&Bs** in Mumbles charge upwards of £22 and cluster on **Mumbles Rd.** and in the **South End** area (10min. from the TIC); singles are hard to find. **Glenview Guest House ❹,** 140 Langland Rd., a 10min. walk from the TIC, is a Victorian belle with gorgeous ensuite rooms and extra perks, like children's videos in the family room. (☎367 933. Doubles £52; family room £75.) With a prime quayside location, the gabled **Coast House ❸,** 708 Mumbles

Rd., has sunny rooms and sea views. (☎368 702. Most rooms with TV and bath. Single £23; doubles £40-46.) Behind it, comfortable **Rock Villa ➍**, 1 George Bank, claims a prize bay vista. (☎366 794. Doubles £42-44.) Take bus #14 to reach accommodations in nearby **Bishopston.** To camp at **Three Cliffs Bay Caravan Park ➊**, North Hills Farm, Penmaen, take bus #18 from Swansea. (☎371 218. £5 per person; families £11.) Bus #18A runs from Swansea to Port Enyon, west of Mumbles and home to the awesome ⍟**YHA Port Eynon ➊**. This former lifeboat house on the beach offers nice rooms, a clean kitchen, and a cozy common area. Learn to surf or enjoy stunning local cliff hikes. (☎/fax 390 706. Reception 8am-10am and 5pm-10pm. Bedroom lockout 10am-5pm. Security code for entry after 11pm. Open July-Aug. daily; Apr.-June M-Sa; Sept.-Oct. Tu-Sa. £9.50, under 18 £6.75.) Beachside **camping** is also possible in Port Eynon.

In Mumbles, the **Somerfield** supermarket is at 512 Mumbles Rd. (Open daily 8am-10pm.) If a quick and healthy snack is all you need, try **The Choice is Dours** fruit and vegetable shop, Newton Rd., for fresh produce. (Open M-Sa 8:30am-5:30pm.) Head to busy ⍟**Verdi's ➊**, Knab Rock, at the southern end of Mumbles Rd., to savor homemade ice cream (from £1.50) in a people-watching paradise; the pricier restaurant serves pastas from £7. (☎369 135. Open daily 10am-9pm.) Braised duck and king prawns (from £15) await at **Claude's Restaurant ➍**, 93 Newton Rd. (☎366 006. Open Tu-Sa noon-2:30pm and 7pm-9pm, Su noon-3pm.) For a view of the Welsh cliffs, walk 2 mi. along the Bay Footpath to **Rother's Tor Cafe and Restaurant ➊**, where you'll be rewarded with sandwiches (£3) on beachside tables. (Open July-Aug. daily 10am-9pm; Sept.-June 10am-5pm.)

◩◪ SIGHTS AND BEACHES. Perched high above Mumbles, the battlements of 13th-century **Oystermouth Castle**, on Castle Ave. off Newton Rd., are overrun with birds, flowers, and occasional reenactments. (☎368 732. Open Apr. to mid-Sept. daily 11am-5pm. £1, concessions 80p.) Picnickers can attempt the challenging ascent to the 56-acre **Mumbles Hill Nature Reserve,** where scrub, wildflowers, and rock overlook Mumbles and the sea. The endless staircase begins by the George Hotel, 10min. from the Mumbles Rd. bus station. Staff at the **Lovespoon Gallery,** 492 Mumbles Rd., can tell you what to do if a wild-eyed Welshman lurches after you with a wooden spoon—they'll even sell you one of your own for £3-5 (a spoon, that is, not a Welshman; see p. 461). (☎360 132. Open M-Sa 10am-5:30pm.)

On the Gower Peninsula gorgeous **beaches** are a dime a dozen. From Southgate and Pennard, a 30min. walk along the Coast Path brings you to **Three Cliffs,** a secluded, cave-ridden beauty almost completely submerged at high tide. **Langland Bay, Caswell Bay, Oxwich Bay,** and **Port Eynon Bay** are all popular. To reach Langland, walk 45min. along the Bays Footpath that begins around the point of Mumbles Head. Caswell is another 45min., and Oxwich and Port Eynon are several miles beyond; buses #18 and 18A from Swansea sometimes make a stop. On the peninsula's western tip, green cliffs clutch the sexy curve of ⍟**Rhossili Beach,** whose dramatic expanse makes overcrowding unlikely; take bus #18A from Swansea. At low tide, a causeway of tortured rock provides access to **Worm's Head,** a series of crags that looks like Nessie's Welsh cousin lumbering out to sea. **Llangennith Beach,** north of Rhossili, draws surfers from all over Wales.

◩◪ NIGHTLIFE AND FESTIVAL. A fishing-hole by day, **Mumbles** becomes a watering hole at night. The short stretch of **Mumbles Rd.** at Mumbles Head is lined with pubs, some of them Dylan Thomas's former haunts. In University of Swansea parlance, to hang out on Mumbles Rd. is to "go mumbling"; to start at one end and have a pint at each pub is to "do the Mumbles Mile." Flower's, Usher's, Buckley's, and Felin Foel are the local real ales. The **Gower Festival** fills the peninsula's churches with string quartets and Bach chorales during the last two weeks of July. The *What's On* guide, free at the Mumbles TIC, has details.

SOUTH WALES

TENBY (DINBYCH-Y-PYSGOD)   ☎ 01834

"Fair and fashionable" and nicknamed the Welsh Riviera, Tenby lives up to the good and bad implicit in its reputation. Alluring soft-sanded beaches invite you to walk barefoot where shore meets sea. Half of Britain, their children, and their dogs have accepted the invitation already—avoid the crush by visiting in early June or late August. But even during the busiest times, Tenby rewards with history, ghost stories, shady benches, and that perfect patch of sand.

▐ TRANSPORTATION

The five booklets of the *Public Transport Timetables for South Pembrokeshire*, available free at TICs, list buses, trains, and ferries for the area, including Tenby, Pembroke, Saundersfoot, and Manorbier.

Trains: At the bottom of Warren St. Unstaffed. **Tenby Travel** (☎843 214), in the Tenby Indoor Market between High St. and Upper Frog St., books tickets. Open M-Tu and Th-F 9am-5pm, W and Sa 9am-4pm. Trains (☎(08457) 484 950) from: **Cardiff** (2½hr., £13.90); **Carmarthen** (45min., £5.20); **Pembroke** (30min., £3); **Swansea** (1½hr., £8.20). All M-F 8 per day, Sa 10 per day, Su 5 per day.

Buses: Buses leave from the multi-storey carpark on Upper Park Rd., next to Somerfield supermarket. **First Cymru** (☎(01792) 580 580) arrives from **Haverfordwest** via **Pembroke** (#349, every hr. M-Sa until 5:30pm). Or go from **Swansea** to **Carmarthen** (X11 or X30, M-Sa every hr., £3.60) and transfer to **Silcox Coaches** bus #333 (2½hr., M-F 1 per day). A Silcox Coaches office (☎842 189) is in the arcade between South Parade and Upper Frog St., across from the market hall. First Cymru **Day Saver** (£4.80) and **Cleddau Rider** (£11.90) buy unlimited daily or weekly travel west of Carmarthen. **National Express** (☎(08705) 808 080) also runs from **Swansea** (#508).

Taxis: Local Taxis (☎844 603). Taxis also congregate by the bus station, and near pubs on F and Sa nights.

◼⚡ ORIENTATION AND PRACTICAL INFORMATION

The old town is in the shape of a triangle pointing into the bay, with the sides formed by **North Beach** and **Castle Beach,** coming to a point at **Castle Hill,** and the train station along the lower edge. From the station, **Warren St.** approaches town, becoming **White Lion St.** and continuing to North Beach. Off White Lion, **South Parade, Upper Frog St., Crackwell St.,** and **High St.** all lead toward South Beach. **The Croft** runs along North Beach, and the **Old Wall** runs along South Parade.

Tourist Information Centre: The Croft (☎842 404; fax 845 439), overlooking North Beach. Free list of over 30 accommodations. Town maps 15p. Open June to mid-July daily 10am-5:30pm; mid-July to Aug. 10am-9pm; Sept.-May M-Sa 10am-4pm.

Financial Services: Barclays, 18 High St. (☎(01437) 822 400). Open M-W and F 9am-4:30pm, Th 10am-4:30pm. The ATM is hidden on Frog St.

Launderette: Fecci's, Lower Frog St. (☎842 484). Change machine. Wash £1.70-2.60, dry 20p per 5min., soap 20p. Open daily 8:30am-9pm; last wash 8:30pm.

Police: Warren St. (☎842 303), near the church off White Lion St.

Hospital: Tenby Cottage Hospital, Trafalgar Rd. (☎842 040).

Internet Access: Tenby County Library, Greenhill Ave. (☎843 934), is free. Book at least 3 days ahead. Open M and W-F 9:30am-1pm and 2-5pm, Tu 9:30am-1pm and 2-6pm, Sa 9:30am-12:30pm. **Webb-Computers,** 17 Warren St. (☎844 101). £1 per 15min. Open M-Sa 9:30am-5:30pm.

Post Office: Warren St. (☎843 213), at South Parade. Open M-F 8:30am-5:30pm, Sa 8:30am-12:30pm. **Post Code:** SA70 7JR.

ACCOMMODATIONS AND CAMPING

Warren St., outside the town wall near the train station, has loads of B&Bs for £20-26; the side streets of **Greenhill Ave.** and those off the Esplanade and Trafalgar Rd. are almost as well endowed. You can also take a bus to **Saundersfoot** (#352, M-Sa every hr.; #350, Su 4 per day, summer only).

Hazlemere, 13 Warren St. (☎844 691). Comfy house decorated with original artwork by the host. If singing's your thing, ask about the next Tenby Choir concert. June-Aug. £18 per person; Sept.-May £16 per person. £4 extra for singles. ❷

Gwynne House, Bridge St. (☎842 862). Overlooks North Beach, and pampers guests with beautiful ensuite rooms, harbor views, and breakfast. £30 per person. ❸

Lyndale, Warren St. (☎842 836). The comfortable rooms may have you spending more time in bed than on the beach. Summer £25 per person; winter £18-20. ❸

Langdon Guest House, Warren St. (☎843 923). The family energy will recharge your battery. Color TV. £18 per person; Sept.-Easter prices lower. ❷

Camping: Meadow Farm (☎844 829), at the top of The Croft, overlooking the town and North Beach. Open Easter-Sept. £5, children £2.50. Showers free. ❶

FOOD

Tenby has plenty of restaurants, but many are so expensive you'll be tempted to drink the ketchup. Lunch specials can soften the blow, and there's always the fruit-and-candy diet (try **Four Seasons Produce,** Upper Park Rd. and **Tenby Rock and Fudge,** St. George's St., respectively). Buy picnic goods at **Tenby Market Hall** between High St. and Upper Frog St. (open daily 8am-5pm; Oct.-June closed W and Su) or **Somerfield** supermarket, next to the bus station on Upper Park Rd. (☎843 771; open M-Th and Sa 8am-8pm, F 8am-9pm; mid-July to Aug. until 10pm.)

The Plantagenet, Quay Hill (☎842 350). Hidden in an alley connecting Bridge St. and St. Julian's St., though a jungle of flowers betrays it in warmer months. Inside, candles illuminate romantic couples enjoying excellent food (lunch £5-10, dinner from £12). Sit under the 800-year-old, 40 ft. stone chimney, or take friends to the cozy bar downstairs. Open Easter-Sept. daily 9:30am-12:30am; Oct.-Easter F-Su 9:30am-12:30am. ❸

The Country Kitchen, Upper Frog St. (☎843 539). Baguette lovers, fret not—the Kitchen provideth. A wide variety of filled rolls and baguettes (£1.35-2.35) make a perfect beach lunch or snack. Open June-Aug. daily 9:30am-4pm; Sept.-May 9:30am-3pm. ❶

Pam Pam, 2 Tudor Sq. (☎842 946), satiates with their "light meals menu" (£3.55-7) until 5:30pm. Dinner runs £6-16, vegetarian dishes £7-8. Open Easter-Oct. daily 10am-10:30pm; Nov.-Easter 10:30am-9pm. ❷

Shajahan (☎845 045), below the Hilton pub, just beyond the B&Bs on Warren St. Indian food (£4-10) with adventurous menu options. Open Su-Th 5pm-12:30am. ❷

SIGHTS AND BEACHES

The three floors of the **Tudor Merchant's House,** on Quay Hill off Bridge St., detail life in a 16th-century Welsh household. Explore the many uses of a latrine or find out why lefties were forbidden to stir the stew. (☎842 279. Open Apr.-Sept. M-Tu and Th-Sa 10am-5pm, Su 1-5pm; Oct. M-Tu and Th-F 10am-3pm, Su noon-3pm. £2, children £1, families £5.) The ruins of Tenby's **castle** rest at the summit of Castle

Hill, almost fully surrounded by ocean. Views reach across Carmarthen Bay to Worm's Head on the Gower Peninsula, and sometimes all the way to Devon. At night, Tenby's spooks and ghouls share the streets with resort revelers; the 1½hr. **Ghost Walk of Tenby** departs from the Lifeboat Tavern in Tudor Sq. at 8pm. (☎ (07970) 420 734. Mid-June to mid-Sept. daily; mid-Sept. to mid-May advance booking required. £3.50, concessions £3.25, children £2.50, families £11.)

Promenades and clifftop benches afford marvelous views, but most visitors zip straight to the sand. On a sunny day, **North Beach,** by the Croft, and **South Beach,** beyond the Esplanade, swarm with pensioners and naked toddlers. At the eastern tip of Tenby, **Castle Beach** reaches into caves that lure the curious explorer, but only by evading the crowds and heading for rockier, less groomed sand will you find the treasure troves of Tenby seashells. A variety of excursions leave from the harbor; check the kiosks at Castle Beach. **Coastal and Island Cruises** runs boat trips. (☎ 843 545. Open Apr.-Oct. £6, concessions £5, children £3.)

▶ DAYTRIPS FROM TENBY

MANORBIER CASTLE. Get your castle and your beach at the same time! Gerald of Wales wasn't exaggerating (for once) when he called this, his birthplace, "the pleasantest spot in Wales." Between Tenby and Pembroke, superbly preserved Manorbier is home to a family of wax figures who demonstrate 13th-century castle life. *(Trains from Tenby and Pembroke (10 per day). First Cymru bus #349 shuttles between Tenby, Manorbier, Pembroke, and Haverfordwest (M-Sa every hr., summer also Su 6 per day). Castle ☎(01646) 621 500. Open Easter-Sept. daily 10:30am-5:30pm. £2.50, seniors £2, children £1.)* Manorbier has a **YHA hostel** (see p. 492), as well as numerous B&Bs. The national park authorities organize guided walks in the area, outlined in their free seasonal publication *Coast to Coast.*

CAREW CASTLE. Strange, handsome Carew Castle, 5 mi. northwest of Tenby, is an odd mixture of Norman fortress and Elizabethan manor, where mighty stone towers mingle with pretty glass windows. Nearby, one of Britain's three **tidal mills,** dating to 1558, turns by a medieval bridge and an 11th-century cross. Check *Coast to Coast,* free at most TICs, for events at the castle. *(Take Silcox bus #361 from Tenby to the castle (45min., M-Sa 3-4 per day). Castle ☎(01646) 651 782. Open Apr. to early Nov. daily 10am-5pm. Tours usually 11am, noon, 2, 3pm. Castle and mill £2.80, concessions £1.90, families £7.50. Castle or mill only £1.90, concessions £1.50.)*

CALDEY ISLAND. This saffron-sanded island lies 3 mi. south of Tenby. Site of an active monastery founded in the 6th century, the current building is the dogged third coming, as Vikings and Henry VIII sacked the first two. The island hosts a community of seabirds, seals, and 20 enterprising Cistercian monks, who produce perfume and chocolate for the island's several stores. The post office dispenses information and fake souvenir stamps. If the commercialism is too much, take a footpath to the other side of the island. *(Caldey Boats sail from Tenby harbor. ☎842 296. Easter-Oct. M-F 9:45am-5:30pm. Cruises 20min.; 2-4 per hr.; return £7, seniors £6, children £3.)*

DYLAN THOMAS BOAT HOUSE. Dylan Thomas spent his last four years in the boat house in **Laugharne** (LARN) at the mouth of the River Taff, about 15 mi. northeast of Tenby. The boat house, now fairly commercialized, displays Thomas's photographs, art, and books, and the shed where he wrote is just as he left it. *(Take First Cymru bus #351 to Laugharne (45min., every 2hr.). House ☎(01994) 427 420. Open May-Oct. daily 10am-5pm; Nov.-Apr. 10:30am-3:30pm. £3, children £1, seniors £2, under 7 free.)*

PEMBROKESHIRE COAST NATIONAL PARK

The 225 sq. mi. of Pembrokeshire Coast National Park (Parc Cenedlaethol Arfordir Penfro), stretch along the water and are scattered in inland pockets. The park features the wooded Gwaun Valley and prehistoric Celtic remnants deep in the Preseli Hills. But the coast remains the supreme draw: hikers follow 186 mi. of coastal path past secluded inlets, towering rocks, tiny chapels, squat cathedrals, and sheer cliffs that rise from Atlantic surf.

⌐ TRANSPORTATION

The best place to enter the region is **Haverfordwest.** Buses offer more frequent and wider-ranging service than trains. The Dale Peninsula, southwest of Haverfordwest, is not served by public transport at all. While *Let's Go* does not recommend hitchhiking, hitchers rave about the area. Mountain bikes are an excellent means of transport on the one-lane roads. Do not, however, ride on the coastal path itself; it is illegal and extraordinarily dangerous.

Trains: (☎(08457) 484 950). To **Haverfordwest** from **Cardiff** (2½hr., 7 per day) and **London Paddington** (4¾hr.; M-F 7 per day, Sa 5 per day, Su varies). Also to **Fishguard** on the north coast and **Tenby** and **Pembroke Dock,** on the south (change at Whitland).

Buses: Consult the 5 unnamed bus-and-train transport booklets, free at TICs, to sort out the many local providers. **Richards Brothers** (☎(01239) 613 756) runs from **Haverfordwest** to **Fishguard** (1½hr., 5 per day) and **St. David's** (#411, 45min., 13 per day). **First Cymru** (☎(01792) 580 580) runs from **Haverfordwest** to **Milford Haven** (#302; 30min.; M-Sa 1-2 per hr., Su 7 per day) and, with **Silcox Coaches** (☎(01646) 683 143), from **Haverfordwest** to **Broad Haven** (#311, 15min., M-Sa 4-8 per day). A **West Wales Rover Ticket** (£4.80 per day, children £2.60-3.60) gets you virtually unlimited travel in **Pembrokeshire** and neighboring **Carmarthenshire** and **Ceredigion.**

Bike Rental: Voyages of Discovery, Cross Sq. (☎(01437) 721 911), in St. David's, will rent you a bike for a half-day (£8) or a day (£12). Open daily 8:30am-5pm.

Other Rentals: A number of **outdoor activity centers** rent canoes, kayaks, ponies, bikes, and other archaic means of transport (starting at £10 per day); check the *Coast to Coast* newspaper, available at NPICs, for locations. Among the most popular is the excellent **TYF Adventure,** with stores in Tenby and St. David's.

⚡ PRACTICAL INFORMATION

The **National Park Information Centres (NPICs)** listed below sell ten annotated maps covering the coastal path (from 45p each). Park officers will aid your planning for free; ask about the guided walks offered by the park. Write for brochures to National Park Information Services, Pembrokeshire Coast National Park Head Office, Winch Ln., Haverfordwest, Pembrokeshire, SA61 1PY (☎(01437) 764 636; www.pembrokeshirecoast.org). For **weather info,** call any NPIC; in an emergency, contact **rescue rangers** by dialing ☎999 or ☎112.

NATIONAL PARK INFORMATION CENTRES

Haverfordwest: 40 High St. (☎(01437) 760 136). Open Easter-Sept. M 10am-4pm.

Newport, Pembrokeshire: Bank Cottages, Long St. (☎/fax (01239) 820 912). Open Easter-Oct. M-Sa 10am-5:30pm, June-Aug. also Su 9:45am-1:15pm.

St. David's: The Grove (☎ (01437) 720 392). Doubles as the town TIC. Open Easter-Oct. daily 9:30am-5:30pm; Nov.-Easter M-Sa 10am-4pm. Closed 2 weeks in Jan.

TOURIST INFORMATION CENTRES

Fishguard: See p. 496.

Haverfordwest: 19 Old Bridge (☎ (01437) 763 110; fax 767 738). Open Apr.-Aug. M-Sa 10am-5:30pm; Sept. 10am-5pm; Oct.-Mar. 10am-4pm.

Milford Haven: Charles St. (☎ (01646) 690 866). Open Easter-Oct. M-Sa 10am-5pm.

Saundersfoot: The Barbecue, Harbour Car Park (☎ (01834) 813 672; fax 813 673). Open Easter-Oct. daily 10am-5pm.

Tenby: See p. 488.

🏕 ACCOMMODATIONS AND CAMPING

Roads between Tenby, Pembroke, and St. David's teem with **B&Bs** (£15-30), but they are hard to secure in summer. Spaced along the coastal path, the park's **YHA hostels,** listed below, are all within a reasonable day's walk of one another. If you plan well ahead (at least 14 days in advance), you can book all of the hostels by calling ☎ (08702) 412 314. The coast is lined with **campsites,** as many farmers convert fallow fields into summer sites (about £4 per tent); inquire before pitching. The Manorbier and Pwll Deri hostels also allow camping.

Broad Haven: (☎ (01437) 781 688), on St. Bride's Bay off the B4341. Take bus #311 from Haverfordwest to Broad Haven (20min., 4-5 per day) or Puffin bus #400 from St. David's (40min., 2 per day). 75 beds. Washing machine (£1). Lockout 10am-1pm. Curfew 11pm. Open mid-Feb. to Oct. daily. Dorms £11.25, under 18 £8. ❷

Manorbier: Skrinkle Haven (☎ (01834) 871 803; fax 871 101), near Manorbier Castle. From the train station, walk past the A4139 to the castle, make a left onto the B4585, a right up to the army camp (fear not, it's not the hostel), and follow the signs. Vigorous showers and laundry facilities. Lockout 10am-5pm. Curfew 10:30pm. Open Mar.-Oct. daily. Dorms £11.25, under 18 £8. Camping £5.60. ❶

Marloes Sands: (☎ /fax (01646) 636 667), near the Dale Peninsula. Take Puffin bus #400 (1¼hr., 2 per day) from St. David's—ask to be let off at the hostel. A cluster of farm buildings on National Trust Property, with a great board game collection. Lockout 10am-5pm. Curfew 11pm. Open Apr.-Oct. daily. Dorms £7.35, under 18 £5.15. ❶

Pwll Deri: (☎ /fax (0870) 770 6004), on breathtaking cliffs around Strumble Head near Fishguard. Lockout 10am-5pm. Curfew 5pm. Open July-Aug. daily; Sept.-Oct and Apr.-June W-Su. Dorms £8.75, under 18 £6. Camping £4. ❶

St. David's: (☎ (01437) 720 345; fax 721 831), near St. David's Head. Take the 2 mi. path turning right at the Bishop's Palace and look for the red doors. Or, from the A487 (Fishguard Rd.), turn onto the B4583 and follow signs from the golf club. Men stay in the cowshed, women in the stables, with extra rooms in the granary. Lockout 10am-5pm, but daytime access to dining hall. Curfew 11pm. Open mid-July to Aug. daily; Sept.-Oct. and Apr. to mid-July W-Su. Dorms £8.75, under 18 £6. ❶

Trevine: (☎ (01348) 831 414), between St. David's and Fishguard, near pretty walks. Bus #411 stops upon request. Recently renovated. Lockout 10am-5pm. Curfew 11pm. Open July-Aug. daily; Sept.-Oct. and Apr.-June Tu-Sa. Dorms £8.75, under 18 £6. ❶

📝 HIKING

For short hikes, stick to the more accessible **St. David's Peninsula** in the northwest. Otherwise, set out on the 186 mi. **Pembrokeshire Coast Path,** marked with acorn symbols along manageable terrain. It begins in the southeast at Amroth and continues west through Tenby to St. Govan's Head, where worn steps lead to **St. Govan's Chapel** on a patch of cliff over crashing ocean. One myth has it that Arthurian knight Sir Gawain retreated here after the fall of Camelot. The waters of the well are said to heal ills and grant wishes, and no mortal can count the steps.

From here to the impressive **Elegug Stacks,** pinnacles of rock a bit offshore, the path passes natural sea arches, mile-wide lily pools at Bosherston, and limestone stacks. Unfortunately, the stretch from St. Govan's Head to the Stacks (6 mi.) is sometimes used as an artillery range and closed to hikers. Call the **Castemartin Range Office** (☎(01646) 662 367) or the **Pembroke National Visitor Centre** (☎(01646) 622 388) for openings or check at the Tenby TIC. For 10 mi. west of the Stacks the coast is permanently off-limits, and the path veers inland until **Freshwater West.**

From Freshwater West to **Angle Bay,** the coastline walk covers mild and pretty terrain. It breaks slightly at Milford Haven, where it's crossed by a channel running over 25 mi. inland. Geologists call it a "ria," or drowned river valley. From the Dale Peninsula, the path passes by the long, clean beaches of **St. Bride's Bay,** turns up to Newgale, and arrives at ancient **St. David's Head,** the site of pre-Cambrian formations and the oldest named feature on the coast of Wales. The ocean has carved away caves and secluded inlets, and the jagged terrain is awe-inspiring.

🏝 ISLANDS OFF THE PEMBROKESHIRE COAST

GRASSHOLM. On Grassholm, farthest from the shore, 35,000 pairs of gannets raise their young. **Dale Sailing Company** runs guided trips around, but not to, the island from Martin's Haven on the Dale Peninsula, often encountering Manx shearwaters and storm petrels along the way. (☎(01646) 601 636. Times vary; call for information. Reservations required. £20.) The company also sails to the island of **Skomer,** a marine reserve and breeding ground for auks, seals, and puffins. (Apr.-Oct. Tu-Su. £7 boat fee, £6 landing fee; children £5.)

RAMSEY ISLAND. Seals and rare seabirds live on Ramsey Island, off St. David's Peninsula farther up the coast. On the east side of the island lurk the **Bitches,** a chain of rocks that have brought countless sailors to grief. **Thousand Islands Expeditions,** Cross Sq. (☎(01437) 721 686 or (0800) 163 621), in St. David's, sails from Whitesands Bay or St. Justinians around the island. (1½hr.; Easter-Nov. daily, weather permitting; £12, children £6) and offers landing trips from St. Justinians (Easter-Oct. Sa-Th 2 per day; £10/£5). The adventurous can brave the passages between the Bitches on a white-water jetboat trip (1hr.; £25, adults only) or a journey through the island's sea-caves, the longest in Wales (2hr.; £22.50, children £10). **Voyages of Discovery and Ramsey Island Cruises,** Cross Sq., St. David's, also runs tours. (☎(0800) 854 367. Tours £15, concessions £8, under 4 £4.)

PEMBROKE (PENFRO) AND PEMBROKE DOCK ☎01646

Though still bounded by 14th-century walls and a towering Norman castle, Pembroke is not the military stronghold it once was. This former bastion of anti-Cromwell resistance now offers peaceful strolls down medieval streets. Pembroke Dock, about 1½ mi. away, lacks its neighbor's ancestry—the ferry to Rosslare, Ireland, is its greatest attraction. Both towns are stepping stones to the national park, but Pembroke is the more popular place to stay.

E TRANSPORTATION. Pembroke's unstaffed **train station** rests on Lower Lamphey Rd. **Trains** (☎ (08457) 484 950) run to both towns from **Tenby, Swansea,** and points farther east (2hr.; M-F 5 per day, Sa 7 per day, Su varies). In Pembroke, **buses** going east stop outside the Somerfield supermarket; those going north stop at the castle. **National Express** (☎ (08705) 808 080) arrives from **Cardiff** via **Swansea** (3½hr., 2 per day) and **London** (6hr., 2 per day). In Pembroke Dock, buses stop at the **Silcox Garage** (☎683 143; open M-F 8:30am-5:30pm). Be sure to signal your stop to the bus driver. **First Cymru** (☎ (01792) 580 580) stops in Pembroke and Pembroke Dock between **Tenby** and **Haverfordwest** (#349; 35-40 min.; M-Sa 21 per day, Su 2 per day). **Irish Ferries** (☎ (08705) 329 543) and **Stena Sealink** (☎ (08705) 707 070) send ferries from Pembroke Dock to **Rosslare, Ireland** (return £9-22; see **By Ferry,** p. 40).

▣ ⁊ ORIENTATION AND PRACTICAL INFORMATION. Pembroke Castle lies up the hill on the western end of **Main St.;** the street's other end fans into five roads from a roundabout. The **tourist information centre** occupies a former slaughterhouse on Commons Rd. below the town center and has displays on town history. The staff books accommodations for £1 and a 10% deposit and ferries for free, and sells town maps for 10p. (☎622 388. Open Easter-June daily 10am-5pm; July-Sept. 10am-5:30pm.) Other services include: **Barclays,** 35 Main St. in Pembroke (☎ (01437) 822 400; open M and W-F 9am-4:30pm, Tu 10am-4:30pm); the Pembroke Dock **police,** 4 Water St. (☎682 121); the Pembroke Dock **hospital,** Forte Rd. (☎682 114); **Internet access** at the Pembroke Dock **library** (☎686 356; open M and F 10am-7pm, Tu-Th 10am-5pm, Sa 9:30am-12:30pm); and the Pembroke **post office,** 49 Main St. (☎682 737; open M-F 9am-5:30pm, Sa 9am-1pm). **Post Code:** SA71 4JT.

▥ ◨ ACCOMMODATIONS AND FOOD. The nearest **YHA hostel** is in Manorbier on the bus line between Tenby and Pembroke (see p. 492). The few B&Bs in Pembroke are scattered and singles are scarce; try to book ahead. Flower-covered **Beach House ❷,** 78 Main St., has an interior so ornate (complete with full-feathered peacock) and a breakfast so tasty, you'll feel guilty for not paying more. (☎683 740. £15 per person.) Get a bargain at **Somerfield** on Main St. (Open M-Sa 8am-8pm, Su 10am-4pm.) **Haven Coffee Shop ❶,** 1 Westgate Hill, sells cheap sandwiches (£2.85), lunches, and coffees, with garden seating and a play area for tots. (☎685 784. Open M-F 10am-4pm.) Across the Northgate St. bridge and on the right is the **Watermans Arms ❶,** 2 The Green, where you can sit by Mill Pond with a view of swans... not to mention Pembroke Castle. (☎682 718. Open Easter-Oct. daily noon-3pm and 6-11pm; food served noon-1:45pm and 7-9pm. Winter hours vary.)

◙ SIGHTS. ▨**Pembroke Castle,** at the head of Main St., is a mighty fortress, authentically restored and a feast for the imagination. From the hardened history buff to the come-on-a-whim hiker, the castle offers everyone a glimpse of centuries past. Henry VII, founder of the Tudor dynasty, was born in one of these seven massive towers. Scattered displays tell of the castle's history (learn how early land acquisitions were carried out in the dungeon area), while the top of the Norman keep offers a view of the surrounding hills—as well as of the hideous Pembroke Dock smokestacks. Take photos selectively. (☎684 585. Castle open Apr.-Sept. daily 9:30am-6pm; Mar. and Oct. 10am-5pm; Nov.-Feb. 10am-4pm. Gatehouse history exhibit open summer daily 9:30am-5pm; winter 10am-4pm. £3, concessions £2, families £8. Tours May-Aug. 4 per day; 50p, children free.)

ST. DAVID'S (TYDDEWI) ☎01437

An evening walk in St. David's (pop. 1700), once medieval Wales's largest and richest diocese, inevitably leads to the cathedral, where the red-gold glow of sunset creates a moment of magical serenity. In the Middle Ages, it was considered so holy that two pilgrimages here equaled one to Rome, and three equaled one to Jerusalem. Today's pilgrims come for varied reasons: peaceful walks, quiet beaches, outdoor sports, fiery Atlantic sunsets, or to feel something of the divine.

▣⚠ TRANSPORTATION AND PRACTICAL INFORMATION. Pick up *1: Haverfordwest & St. David's Area*, which lists bus services, free at any Pembrokeshire TIC. The **Richards Bros. Haverfordwest-Fishguard bus** (☎(01239) 613 756) hugs the coast, stopping at St. David's from both towns (#411; 50min.; M-Sa 5 per day, Su 2 per day). Other buses terminate at St. David's during the week. A **Day Explorer Pass** may be the cheapest return fare (£3.30, children £2.20). **Tony's Taxis** (☎720 931) come when you call, and **Frank's Cabs** (☎721 731) has minivans. The **National Park Information Centre**, The Grove, doubles as the TIC; the staff stocks maps and books beds for £1 plus a 10% deposit. (☎720 392; www.stdavids.co.uk. Open Easter-Oct. daily 9:30am-5:30pm; Nov.-Easter M-Sa 10am-4pm.) Other services include: **Barclays**, at High St. and New St. (☎822 400; open M-F 10am-4pm); the **police**, High St. (☎720 233); the nearest **hospital** (☎764 545), in Haverfordwest; and the **post office**, 13 New St. (☎720 283; open M-F 9am-5:30pm, Sa 9am-1pm). **Post Code:** SA62 6SW.

⚐▢ ACCOMMODATIONS AND FOOD. The **YHA St. David's** lies 2 mi. northwest of town at the foot of a rocky outcrop near St. David's Head (see p. 492). Beautiful **Alandale ❸**, 43 Nun St., is run by Rob and Gloria Pugh, whose genuine warmth and filling breakfasts will make your stay worthwhile. (☎720 404. £25 per person.) **The Coach House ❷**, 15 High St., at the center of town, has rooms ranging from singles to bunkbeds, all with TVs. An elegant cafe downstairs serves lunch with soft classical background music. (☎720 632. £15-20 per person; July-Aug. £20-25.)

The trendy **Pebbles Yard Gallery & Expresso Bar ❶**, Cross Sq., is popular with the young set. Hearty lunches (sandwiches £3, salads £4.75) are complemented by crazy light fixtures. (☎720 122. Open daily 9:30am-5:30pm.) For excellent Welsh food, head for **Cartref ❷**, also in Cross Sq. Dinner starts at £8, but at lunch a sandwich will only set you back £3.50. Waits can be long. (☎720 422. Open Mar.-May daily 11am-2:30pm and 6:30-8:30pm; June-Aug. 11am-3pm and 6-8:30pm.)

IN RECENT NEWS

THE PIRATE THAT CLAIMED MANHATTAN

New Yorkers, watch out. Descendents of an 18th-century Welsh pirate have laid claim to a sizable chunk of Manhattan—a chunk that includes parts of Wall Street and Broadway and is valued at hundreds of billions of dollars. According to his heirs, pirate Robert Edwards was given a tidy little 77-acre plot on Manhattan island by the British Crown. In 1778 the land was leased for 99 years by associates of Trinity Church... but in the intervening years, Americans grew oddly fond of their little bit of island, and somehow the land never reverted to the pirate's family.

Heirs in the UK have been agitating to reclaim the land for decades, joined by thousands of US members of the Edwards Heirs association. Trinity Church, however, steadfastly denies the pirate's claim, weathering multiple legal challenges, citing a long-passed statute of limitations, and dispatching a form letter to latter-day Edwardses who attempt to inform it of its oversight.

These modern Edwardses are sometimes as interesting as their forebear: in 1999, six former Heirs employees went on trial for stealing over a million dollars from the association for rodeo jackets, Disney World vacations, and other "unidentified" costs. Other opportunists have bilked bunches of credulous Edwardses out of their hard-earned savings, promising them access to their "shares" of the yet-unsubstantiated billions.

■ **SIGHTS.** ■**St. David's Cathedral,** perhaps Wales's finest, stands in a hollow below the village. Remnants of the 6th-century church linger in the 12th-century structure, and tombs of long-dead lords, ladies, and bishops trace the centuries past, as well as your path around the chambers. The reliquary holds the bones of St. David, patron saint of Wales, and his comrade St. Justinian, who was killed on nearby Ramsey Island but, in saintly conscientiousness, carried his own head back to the mainland. In the St. Thomas à Becket chapel, the stained-glass window portrays three surly knights jabbing swords at the martyr. (Open from 6am to around 5:30pm, and for evening services. Suggested donation £2, children £1.) Those with an insatiable love for pealing bells are welcome to sit in on a ringer's practice session in the tower. (W and F 7:45-9pm. Suggested donation £1.)

The **Bishop's Palace,** across a bridged brook, was built in the 14th century by Bishop Henry Gower, back when it was acceptable for a bishop to have the largest palace in Wales. The exhibition details why archaeologists love medieval cesspits. (☎720 517. Open June-Sept. daily 9:30am-6pm; Oct. and Apr.-May 9:30am-5pm; Nov.-Mar. M-Sa 9:30am-4pm, Su noon-2pm. £2.50, concessions £2, families £7.) A half-mile south of town, the walls of **St. Non's Chapel** mark the birthplace of St. David. A precocious child, the saint split a rock poised to fall on his mother at the moment of his birth. Water from the nearby well supposedly cures all ills; take Goat St. downhill and follow the signs to health and happiness. Tours run to **Ramsey Island,** off the coast (see p. 493).

FISHGUARD   ☎01348

Victim of pirate attacks, star of the film *Moby Dick,* and harbor of the late *Lusitania,* modest Fishguard hasn't let its moments of celebrity go to its head. Its roots lie in Lower Town's herring trade, where merchants made the money that moved the town up the cliff to Upper Fishguard. Now a ferry port, rumored passageways from basements to smugglers' caves, cannon balls wedged in walls, and local pride keep Fishguard relatively lively.

■ **TRANSPORTATION.** Trains (☎(08457) 484 950) pull into **Fishguard Harbour,** Goodwick, from **London** via **Bristol, Newport, Cardiff, Swansea,** and **Whitland** (4½hr., 1 per day). **Buses** stop at **Fishguard Sq.,** the town center. Ask at the TIC for *2: Fishguard and Cardigan Area,* a free bus and train timetable. From the north, take **Richards Bros.** (☎(01239) 613 756) buses from **Aberystwyth** to **Cardigan** (#550 or 551, 2hr., M-Sa 10 per day) and then on to **Fishguard** (#412, 45min., M-Sa 13 per day). Take **First Cymru** (☎(01792) 580 580) buses from **Tenby** or **Pembroke** to **Haverfordwest** (#349; 1hr.; M-Sa every hr., Su 2 per day) and from **Haverfordwest** to **Fishguard** (#412, 45min., 1-2 per hr.). Two **ferries** run daily from **Rosslare, Ireland: Stena Sealink** (☎(08705) 707 070; 1¾hr.; 2-4 per day; £13-30, children £12-16) and **Superferry** (☎(08705) 421 107; 2 per day; £10/£6). Call for reservations. (See **By Ferry,** p. 40). **Town bus** #410 shuttles the mile between Fishguard Harbour and Fishguard Sq. (5min., 2 per hr., 45p), and **Merv's Taxis** (☎875 129) are on call 24hr.

■ **PRACTICAL INFORMATION.** The **tourist information centre,** Town Hall, Main St., sells National Express and ferry tickets and books rooms for £1 and a 10% deposit. (☎873 484. Open Easter-Oct. daily 10am-5pm.; Nov.-Easter M-Sa 10am-4pm.) Other services include: **Barclays,** across from the TIC (☎822 400; fax 402 999; open M-Tu and Th-F 9am-4:30pm, W 10am-4:30pm); the **police,** Brodog Terr. (☎872 835); the nearest **hospital** (☎(01437) 764 545), in Haverfordwest; **Dyfed Cleaning,** Brodog Terr. (☎872 140; wash £2.80, dry 85p; open M-Sa 8:30am-5:30pm); **Internet access** at **Cyber Cafe,** The Parrog, in the Ocean Lab building (☎874 737; £2 per 30min.; open 10am-6pm); and the **post office,** 57 West St. (☎873 863; open M-F 9am-5:30pm, Sa 9am-12:30pm). **Post Code:** SA65 9NG.

⌐⌐ ACCOMMODATIONS AND FOOD. Find **B&Bs** (£16-20) on **High St.** and **Vergam Terr.** in Upper Fishguard. Run laps around large rooms at **Avon House ❷**, 76 High St., or chat with the pleasant hostess. (☎874 476. From £17.50 per person.) Near tiny Trefin, **Bryngarw ❸**, Abercastle Rd., 1 mi. off the A487 between St. David's and Fishguard, perches mere feet from a cliff and from country-road rambles. Take bus #412 from Fishguard Sq. (☎831 211. £25-27 per person, singles £5 extra.) **Harlton Guest House and Backpackers Lodge ❷**, 21-23 Hamilton St., is intensely comfortable, with a book-lined TV lounge, toast-and-tea breakfasts, and well-traveled host Steve. (☎874 797; www.fishguard-backpackers.com. Laundry, kitchen, and Internet. Dorms £11; singles and doubles £13 per person.)

Y Pantri ❶, 31 West St., rolls sandwiches, fills baguettes (£1.40), and stuffs corned beef pasties (85p) for uncommonly low prices. Dip into the "free bird bread" bin to gather yourself a devoted flock. (☎872 637. Open M-Sa 9am-5:30pm.) If your dreams are of fish and chips, rest easy: **Bursco's ❶** (☎872 008), Market Sq., fulfills such fantasies for £2-3. **Taj Mahal ❷**, 22 High St., serves a celebrated cardamom-rich curry. Main dishes start at £3.50. (☎874 593. Open M-Su 6-11:30pm, takeaway until midnight.) Not your average pub and converted barn, **The Old Coach House ❷**, High St., has a mammoth menu of British and Italian fare for £3-10. (☎875 429. Open M-Sa 11am-11pm, Su noon-10:30pm; food served noon-2pm and 6-9pm.)

◙ ⌐ SIGHTS AND ENTERTAINMENT. The **Marine Walk**, a paved path undulating along the ocean cliffs, has exquisite overlooks of town and sea, and plaques on the town's rich history. Peer down, as Richard Burton and Gregory Peck did, on Lower Town, where *Under Milk Wood* and *Moby Dick* were filmed. Ramblers can see Goodwick Harbour, where the ill-fated flagship *Lusitania* began its sailings to America, and where the first flight from Britain to Ireland took off.

WEDDING WINE AND WELSH WOMEN The last

invasion of Britain took place in 1797, when two frigates and several smaller boats landed just outside Fishguard. Led by the Irish-American General Tate, this gallant band of 1500 Frenchmen aimed to spread a bit of the revolution that had seized their own country a few years earlier. But when the warriors landed, they set up headquarters in a farmhouse stocked for a wedding; the party favors more than quenched the soldiers' thirst. Tate's force, suddenly a drunken mob, couldn't hold out long enough to recover from the hangover. When the would-be heroes emerged from the farmhouse, they were met by hundreds of red-cloaked women who had assembled to witness the spectacle. Thinking himself vastly outnumbered by British soldiers, Tate surrendered. According to local legend, Jemima Nicholas, a 47-year-old cobbler, captured 12 Frenchmen single-handedly with her pitchfork. *La gloire*, indeed.

In a glassy beachside building, **Ocean Lab**, The Parrog, features a 15min. show by the muppeteers from the Henson Creature Shop. The simulated submarine trip to view prehistoric sea creatures is suitable for most youngsters. Use the cyber cafe while waiting for the show. (☎874 737. Open Easter-Oct. daily 10am-6pm. Call for winter times. Submarine show every 45min.) Next door at **Watersports**, outdoorsy sorts can go windsurfing, canoeing, or sailing. (☎874 803. Weather permitting.) During the day, picnickers and sun gluttons speckle protected **Goodwick Beach.** Inquire at the TIC about day-walks and tours into the **Preseli Hills**, ancient grounds pebbled with stone circles and a mysterious **standing stone.**

If indoor pursuits are more your style, check out the shops near **Upper Fishguard Sq.** Most enigmatic is **Debris**, which offers whale vertebrae, bowls carved from fossil orthoceras pods, and a coffee table and pyramid constructed of the same—all under £1000. (☎874 896. Individual fossils from £3.25. Open M-Sa 9am-4pm.)

Fishguard nightlife is quiet early in the week, but weekends erupt into a pub scene of festival proportions. The **Old Coach House** (above) is the place to be, but all pubs along **High St.** see some action—until 11pm, that is, when the law requires them to close. Some pubs allow patrons to remain past the hour of doom, but shut their doors to potential newcomers. Saturday nights, students stumble onto Brynawelon buses that leave the square at 11pm for the disco at the **Brynawelon Country Hotel,** nearby in Letterston. (☎ 840 307. Cover £3.50. Last hurrah 1am.)

NORTH WALES

Wild and fiercely beautiful, the mountains of the north have long harbored the most fervent Welsh blood. In the 14th century, Welsh rebel leaders plotted campaigns against the English from deep within the jagged peaks of Snowdonia. The English King Edward I designed a ring of spectacular fortresses to keep the rebels in the mountains, but Welsh pride never wavered and remains strong despite (or perhaps due to) centuries of union with England. Tensions continue to run surprisingly high—travelers may still come across signs and graffiti proclaiming "Welcome to Wales: English bastards go home." Yet the north has a kind heart, and villagers are unlikely to let a weary traveler go without food, rest, and a lengthy conversation. To escape the crowds swarming Edward's coastal castles, head to the mountain footpaths, lakes, and hamlets of Snowdonia National Park, which covers the greater part of northwest Wales. To the west, the Llŷn Peninsula beckons with sandy beaches; to the northwest, the Isle of Anglesey is rich in prehistoric remains; and to the east sleep the peaceful villages of the Vale of Conwy.

HIGHLIGHTS OF NORTH WALES

SNOWDONIA Dash (okay, hike) up **Mt. Snowdon,** the most precipitous point south of Scotland and the center of **Snowdonia National Park** (p. 515), land of craggy peaks, high moors, dark pine forests, and deep glacial lakes.

LLYN PENINSULA Go Mediterranean at the Italianate village of **Portmeirion** (p. 509) before heading for the quiet beaches of this unhurried region (p. 509).

CASTLES Survey your holdings from the towers of the majestic fortresses at **Beaumaris** (p. 523), **Caernarfon** (p. 513), **Conwy** (p. 525), and **Harlech** (p. 507).

ABERYSTWYTH ☎ 01970

A strange mix of summer resort destination and college town, Aberystwyth (ahber-RIST-with) is packed with tourists and students. Though salt-stained buildings and a hotel-lined quay draw the camera-toters, it's the would-be scholars who fill seaside flats, raucous pubs, and innumerable veggie cafes. Halfway between St. David's and the Llŷn Peninsula, Aberystwyth is a pleasant stop for travelers heading north toward mountain valleys and craggy peaks.

▣ TRANSPORTATION

A transport hub for all of Wales, Aberystwyth sits at the end of a rail line running from Shrewsbury, England.

Trains: Alexandra Rd. (☎(08457) 484 950). Office open M-F 6:20am-5:25pm, Sa 6:20am-3:20pm, Su varies. Trains from **Machynlleth** (30min.; M-Sa 8 per day, Su 4-5 per day; £4.70) and **Shrewsbury** (2hr.; M-Sa 7 per day, Su 4-5 per day; £11.50-19.80). Machynlleth is the southern terminus of the **Cambrian Coaster** line, which runs to **Pwllheli.** The **Cambrian Coaster Day Ranger** covers travel along the line (£6.80). The **Vale of Rheidol Railway** (☎625 819) runs to mountain sites (see p. 503).

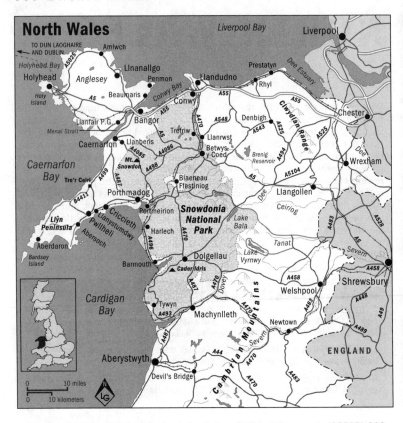

North Wales

TO DUN LAOGHAIRE AND DUBLIN

Liverpool Bay — Liverpool

Holyhead Bay — Amlwch — Llnanallgo

Holyhead — Anglesey — Penmon — Llandudno — Prestatyn — Dee Estuary

Holy Island — Beaumaris — Conwy Bay — Conwy — Rhyl

Llanfair P.G. — Bangor — Denbigh — Chester

Menai Strait — Trefriw — Llanrwst

Caernarfon — Llanberis — Betwys-y-Coed — Brenig Reservoir

Caernarfon Bay — Tre'r Ceiri — Mt. Snowdon — Wrexham

Blaeneau Ffestiniog — Llangollen

Porthmadog — Portmeirion — **Snowdonia National Park** — Lake Bala — Ceiriog

Criccieth — Llanystumdwy — Harlech — Tanat

Llŷn Peninsula — Pwllheli — Abersoch

Aberdaron — Lake Vyrnwy

Bardsey Island — Barmouth — Dolgellau — Cader Idris

Cardigan Bay — Welshpool — Shrewsbury

Tywyn — Machynlleth — Newtown

Aberystwyth — Cambrian Mountains — ENGLAND

Devil's Bridge

0   10 miles
0   10 kilometers

Buses: Alexandra Rd., beside the train station. **National Express** (☎(08705) 808 080) from **London** via **Birmingham** (8hr., 1pm, £22-31). **TrawsCambria** bus #701 from **Cardiff** (4hr., 1-2 per day) and **Holyhead** (4hr., 1 per day). **Arriva Cymru** (☎(08706) 082 608) from **Machynlleth** (#512/514; 50min.; M-Sa 6 per day, Su 2 per day). **Richard Brothers** (☎(01239) 613 756) from **Cardigan** via **Synod Inn** (#550/551, 55min., M-Sa 6 per day); **Arriva Cymru/Summerdale Coaches** (☎(01348) 840 270) runs the same route twice on Su. **Day Rover** tickets (£4.80, children £2.40) are valid on most buses in the Ceredigion, Carmarthenshire, and Pembrokeshire area. The **North and Mid-Wales Rover** (1, 3, or 7 days) is valid on buses and trains north of the imaginary Aberystwyth-Shrewsbury line and on Arriva Cymru buses south of Aberystwyth.

Taxis: Express (☎612 319). 24hr.

◨ PRACTICAL INFORMATION

Tourist Information Centre: Lisburne House, Terrace Rd. (☎/fax 612 125), at the corner of Bath St. Staff doles out B&B photos and rates. Books rooms for £1 plus 10% deposit. Open July-Aug. daily 9am-6pm; Sept.-June M-Sa 10am-5pm.

Financial Services: Most **banks** are along Great Darkgate St. and North Parade.

Launderette: Wash 'n' Spin 'n' Dry, 16 Bridge St. (☎625 406). Wash £2, dry £1, soap 10p. Bring change. Open daily 7am-9pm, last wash 8:30pm.

Police: Blvd. St. Brieuc (☎612 791), at the end of Park Ave.

Hospital: Bronglais General Hospital, Caradog Rd. (☎623 131).

Internet Access: Biognosis, 21 Pier St. (☎636 953). £3.50 per hr., minimum 20min. Open M-Th 10am-7pm, F 10am-5pm, Sa 11am-5pm.

Post Office: 8 Great Darkgate St. (☎632 630). **Bureau de change.** Open M-F 9am-5:30pm, Sa 9am-12:30pm. **Post Code:** SY23 1DE.

ACCOMMODATIONS AND CAMPING

Expensive B&Bs (£16-40) snuggle up with student housing on the waterfront. **Bridge St.** has a small B&B community, and a few cheap establishments are scattered on **South Rd.** and **Rheidol Terr.**

Bodalwyn, Queen's Ave. (☎612 578). Pricey, but darn nice, this guest house is only minutes from the promenade and cliff railway. Singles £30-38; doubles £50-60. ❹

Sunnymead, 34 Bridge St. (☎617 273). Caters to those on a budget. You can't miss the bright yellow facade, and the tidy rooms cheer weary travelers. £17.50 per person. ❷

YHA Borth (☎871 498), 9 mi. north of Aberystwyth. Take the train to Borth or Crosville bus #511 or 512. From the train station, turn right onto the main road and walk 5min. Set near beautiful beaches and often full. Kitchen. Open Apr.-Aug. daily; Sept.-Oct. F-Sa; but some exceptions—call ahead. Dorms £10.25, under 18 £7. ❷

Mrs. Rowley, 28 South Rd. (☎612 115), off Bridge St. Pleasant bedrooms have TVs and washbasins, the bathrooms ring with wind chimes, and the lounge has an assortment of porcine figurines. Ask the proprietress about growing up on a farm. £15 per person. ❷

Camping: Midfield Caravan Park (☎612 542), 1½ mi. from town on the A4120, 200 yd. uphill from the A487 junction. From Alexandra Rd., take any bus to Southgate. Lovely site, with a view of town and hills. £5 per person. Electricity £1.50. Showers free.

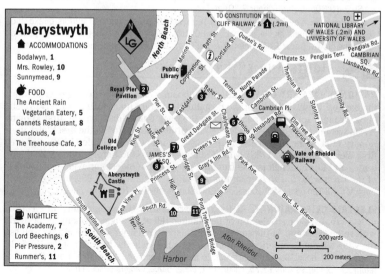

Aberystwyth

🏠 ACCOMMODATIONS
Bodalwyn, **1**
Mrs. Rowley, **10**
Sunnymead, **9**

🍴 FOOD
The Ancient Rain
  Vegetarian Eatery, **5**
Gannets Restaurant, **8**
Sunclouds, **4**
The Treehouse Cafe, **3**

🍷 NIGHTLIFE
The Academy, **7**
Lord Beechings, **6**
Pier Pressure, **2**
Rummer's, **11**

NORTH WALES

◖◗ FOOD

Pier St. takeaways are cheap and open Sunday. The **market** is at Market Hall, St. James Sq. (open M-Sa 8am-5pm), and the 24hr. **Spar**, 32 Terrace Rd., sells sundries.

Sunclouds, 25 North Parade (☎617 750). Yummy 3-cheese pasta (£4.75) and crispy baguettes (£2-2.50) are excellent choices at this comfy cafe with wooden counters and a big picture window. Open M-Sa 10am-4:30pm. ●

The Ancient Rain Vegetarian Eatery, 13 Cambrian Pl. (☎612 363), on the corner of Union St. Serves pancakes (from £2.45) and vegan and vegetarian meals (from £4) in a brightly-decorated seating area. Takeaway available. Open M-Sa 10am-4:30pm. ●

The Treehouse Cafe, 14 Baker St. (☎615 791). Summery tablecloths and wood floors characterize this haven of organic hipness atop the Treehouse Organic Shop. Cool your carnivorous cravings with a beef burger (£4) or terrorize chickpeas the world over by ordering hummus with pita (£1.50). Open M-Sa 9am-5:30pm. ●

Gannets Restaurant, St. James Sq. (☎617 164). Run by a former British Airways catering manager—if only airline food were half so good. Main courses pricey (£6.50-11), but a few starters make a fine meal: try the ravioli au gratin (£1.20) or smoked mackerel (£1.50). Open M and W-Sa noon-2pm and 6-midnight, last orders 9:30pm. ❷

◪◧ PUBS AND CLUBS

Aberystwyth boasts more than 50 pubs; student swarms keep them buzzing.

The Academy, St. James Sq. (☎636 852). In this converted chapel, sports are cast on a 16 ft. screen. Breakfast served all day. Su-Th pints as little as 99p. Open M-F noon-11pm, Sa 11am-11pm, Su noon-10:30pm; food served noon-3pm and 6-8:30pm.

Lord Beechings, Alexandra Rd. (☎625 069). Fit for a king and priced for a poor man; huge meals are £1.50-6. Open M-Sa 11am-11pm, Su 11am-10:30pm; food served M-F 11:45am-2:45pm and 6-8:45pm, Sa-Su all day.

Rummer's, Pont Trefechan Bridge, at the end of Bridge St. A vine-covered beer garden and student revelry make this a choice stop. Open M-Tu 7pm-midnight, W-Sa 7pm-1am, Su 7-10:30pm. Happy hour 9:30pm.

Pier Pressure, The Royal Pier, Marine Terr. (☎136 100). Smashed mirrors quake and smashed clubbers shake. Th rocks to 60s-80s; the weekend "Cheese Factory" pulls a young crowd. Cover £1-5. Open M-W 10:30pm-1am, Th-F 10pm-1am, Sa 9pm-1am.

◉ ♫ SIGHTS AND ENTERTAINMENT

NATIONAL LIBRARY OF WALES. An imposing, classical structure overlooking the bay, off Penglais Rd. past the hospital, the library houses almost every Welsh book or manuscript ever penned. The **Gregynog Gallery** displays the first known Welsh written text (c. 800), the first Welsh printed book (1546), the first Welsh dictionary (1547), the first Welsh map (1573), the first Welsh Bible (1588), and the first Welsh magazine (1735), which managed one issue before folding. Scalded toutes and lusty bachelors rise from the pages of the oldest surviving manuscript of the *Canterbury Tales*, from the early 15th century. (☎632 800; www.llgc.org.uk. Open M-F 9:30am-6pm, Sa 9:30am-5pm. Exhibitions open M-Sa 10am-5pm. Free.)

ELECTRIC CLIFF RAILWAY. At the northern end of the promenade, an electric railcar creaks 430 ft. to the top of **Constitution Hill** at an angle normally associated with roller coasters. At the summit waits a spectacular view of the city as well as the wide lens of a camera obscura. You can also scale the hill by foot. (☎617 642. Open July-Aug. daily 10am-6pm; mid-Mar. to June and Sept.-Oct. 10am-5pm. Trains 6 per hr.; return £2.25, concessions £1.75, children £1, under 5 free. Camera obscura free.)

ABERYSTWYTH CASTLE. South of the Old College on a hilly peninsula, the castle has seen centuries of English oppression and Welsh rebellion. Before Edward I built the present structure in 1277, previous forts had burned down five times, the fifth at the hands of Llywelyn ap Gruffydd. When night falls, the crumbling walls are often silhouetted against fiery sunsets over the Atlantic. *(Always open. Free.)*

PIER. Aberystwyth's fin-de-siecle pier has been battered by the tourist trade. Still, the beachfront and promenade remain much as they were in Victorian times, and pastel townhouses lend the town a tamed, aristocratic air. At the south end of the promenade, the university's **Old College** is a neo-Gothic structure opened in 1877 as a hotel and restored in 1885 as Wales's first university. Prince Charles was drilled in Welsh here before being crowned Prince of Wales in 1969.

OTHER ACTIVITIES. Up Penglais Rd., on the University of Wales campus, the **Aberystwyth Arts Centre** sponsors drama and films in Welsh and English; schedules are available at the TIC. (☎ 623 232. Prices £3.50-20 depending on event. Box office open M-Sa 10am-8pm.) More antsy than artsy? Work off that energy with a ride at nearby **Rheidol Riding Centre.** (☎ 880 863. 4 mi. from Aberystwyth by car.)

⚡ DAYTRIPS FROM ABERYSTWYTH

▨ DEVIL'S BRIDGE
Trains from Aberystwyth run mid-July to Aug. M-Th 4 per day, F-Su 2 per day; Apr. to mid-July and Sept.-Oct. 2 per day. £11, seniors £10.

Originally built to serve the lead mines, the **Vale of Rheidol Railway** (☎ 625 819) chugs and twists its way from Aberystwyth station to the waterfalls and gorges of Devil's Bridge, all on tracks less than 2 ft. apart. The **three bridges** were inexplicably built on top of one another; the lowest bridge, attributed to the Architect of Evil, was probably built by Cistercian monks from the nearby **Strata Florida Abbey** in the 12th century. (☎ (01974) 831 261. Abbey open daily 10am-5pm. Apr.-Sept. £2, concessions £1.50, families £5.50; Oct.-Apr. grounds free, but exhibits closed.) The paths to the bridges are turnstile-operated, so take some change. (☎ 890 233. Trails to bridges £2.50, concessions £2, children £1.25.) The rungs of **Jacob's Ladder** (£1.20) descend into the **Devil's Punchbowl** gorge, cross the torrent on an arched footbridge, and climb back along the waterfall to the road.

MACHYNLLETH ☎ 01654
And so 'twas Machynlleth (mach-HUN-hleth) that briefly—ever so briefly— became the capital of Wales when Owain Glyndŵr, that great 15th-century Welsh rebel, summoned delegates from all over the country to talk revolution. Unfortunately, the rebellion unraveled when the delegates left, and not too much has happened since. Machynlleth remains a pretty little town, however, and is a good starting point for mountain biking or hiking in the nearby hills, or for a taste of traditional Welsh character and ancient Celtic history.

▐ **TRANSPORTATION.** The **train station** (☎ 702 887), Doll St., receives trains (☎ (08457) 484 950) from: **Aberystwyth** (30min., 7-9 per day, £4); **Birmingham** (2¼hr.; M-Sa 8 per day, Su 4 per day; £12.10); **Shrewsbury** (1½hr.; M-Sa 8 per day, Su 5 per day; £10.90). The **Cambrian Coaster Day Ranger** covers routes from **Aberystwyth** (£6.80, £3.80 after 4:30pm). **Buses** stop by the clock tower. **Arriva Cymru** (☎ (08706) 082 608) buses #511, 512, and 514 arrive from **Aberystwyth** (40min.; M-Sa 8 per day, Su 2 per day), and #512 and 514 from **Dolgellau** (30min.; M-Sa 7-8 per day, Su 2 per day). **TrawsCambria** #701 rolls in once per day from

FROM THE ROAD

OF MOUNTAINS AND MADMEN

Legend holds that whoever spends a night atop Cader Idris will come down a poet, a madman, or not at all. I had been joking, somewhat, when I announced to my editors that I wanted to spend a night on the peak. We'd all read *The Dark is Rising* sequence, by Susan Cooper, in which Idris figures prominently. The novelty from our bright, sunny Cambridge office was immense.

But my first night in dark-stoned Dolgellau, the sky swirled with brooding darkness. The malevolent, magical mountain towered above. A man can easily get stuck at the summit in thick mists like that, and bells in surrounding towns toll for the lost. It was assuredly not a sleep-out opportunity. *Too bad, such a pity,* I hummed as I tucked myself into the downy blankets of a valley farmhouse.

Shortly thereafter, however, a series of unfortunate coincidences left me temporarily penniless, and camping began looking like a good option. The day was sunny, the trees green, and even Idris looked welcoming. Legends of men swallowed alive by the bottomless lake below, of the hellhounds racing round the top, of the cairns of long dead kings, and of the malicious Grey King... all those seemed quaint little fairytales.

"Well," I thought, "why *not* Idris? No one will bother me there." When I mentioned my plans to a shopkeeper, however, he furrowed his brow. "Good 'eavens, m'love," interjected his wife, "Idris will'n't be taken lightly. Strange happenings, up on Idris..."

Aberystwyth (35min.) and **Dolgellau** (1hr.); the Dolgellau bus originates in **Holyhead** (3½hr.), while the Aberystwyth bus comes through **Cardiff** (5½hr.). Rent mountain **bikes** at **Greenstiles**, 4 Maengwyn St., across from the clock tower. (☎703 543. £10-12 per half-day, £14-18 per day, £60 per week. 50% discount with Centre for Alternative Technology ticket. Open M-Sa 9:30am-5:30pm; Apr.-Oct. also Su 10am-4pm.)

■ ⓘ **ORIENTATION AND PRACTICAL INFORMATION.** The unmistakable heart of town is the **clock tower,** standing Eiffel-like where **Pentrerhedryn St., Penrallt St.,** and **Maengwyn St.** form a T. From the train station, turn left onto Doll St., veer right at the church onto Penrallt St., and continue until you see the clock tower; Maengwyn St. is on the left. The **tourist information centre,** in the Owain Glyndŵr Centre, Maengwyn St., books rooms for £1 plus a 10% deposit. (☎702 401; fax 703 675. Open M-Sa 9:30am-5:30pm, Su 10am-5pm.) Other services include: **Barclays** under the tall timepiece (open M-W and F 9am-4:30pm, Th 10am-4:30pm); the **police,** Doll St. (☎702 215); **Chest Hospital,** Newton Rd. (☎702 266); **Nigel's Launderette,** New St. (wash £2.50, dry 20p per cycle, no soap or change machine; open M-Sa 8:30am-8pm, Su 9am-7:30pm; last wash 30min. before close); **Internet access** at the **Machynlleth Public Library,** Maengwyn St. (☎702 322; free; open M 5-7pm, Tu-W 10am-1pm and 2-5pm, F 11am-1pm and 2-7pm, Sa 9:30am-1pm), or **Cyberspace,** 6 Penrallt St. (☎703 953; £4 per hr., £1 minimum; open M-Sa 10am-5pm); and the **post office,** 51-53 Maengwyn St., inside the **Spar** grocery (☎702 323; office open M-Th 8:30am-5:30pm, F 9am-5:30pm, Sa 9am-1pm). **Post Code:** SY20 8AE.

🛏️🍴 **ACCOMMODATIONS AND FOOD.** Machynlleth lacks a hostel, but **YHA Corris ❶,** on Corris Rd., is 15min. away by bus #30 or 32. Reminders of nature abound, from the location on the southern side of Cader Idris to the conservation motif. (☎/fax 761 686. Laundry. Lockout 10am-5pm. Open mid-Feb. to Oct. daily; Jan. to mid-Feb. and Nov. F-Sa. Dorms £9.50, under 18 £6.75.) **B&Bs** are few, and fewer are budget-friendly. **Melin-y-Wig ❷,** Aberystwyth Rd., near Celtica, has black-and-white TVs and a voluminous bathtub. (☎703 933. From £17 per person.) **Haulfryn ❷,** next door on Aberystwyth Rd., blooms with large, flowery rooms and a breakfast nook packed with plates from around the world. (☎702 206. £15 per person.) **Campers** can seek out riverside **Llwyngwern Farm ❶,** off the A487 next to the Centre for Alternative Technology. (☎702 492. Open Apr.-Sept. £5 per person, £7.50 per 2 people.)

Craft your own menu at **Spar,** 51-53 Maengwyn St. (open M-Sa 7am-11pm, Su 7am-10:30pm), or at the **market** along Maengwyn St., Pentrerhedryon St., and Penrallt St., dating to 1291—the CDs and alarm clocks are more recent additions (open W 9am-4pm). Super-fresh food makes **Y Bwtri ❶,** Maengwyn St., a local lunchtime favorite. The baked goods are particularly recommended. (☎703 679. Open daily 9am-4pm.) Get cheap sustenance at the **Quarry Shop Cafe and Wholefoods ❶,** 13 Maengwyn St., where the all-vegetarian fare is under £4 and bags of nuts and banana chips are only 70-80p. (☎702 624. Open M-Sa 9am-4:30pm, Th 9am-2pm.) Machynlleth pubs aren't spectacular for affordable gluttony, but tasty dishes are served beside a massive stone hearth at the **Skinners Arms ❶,** 14 Penrallt St., near the clock tower. Main courses in the lounge are £4-8; food at the bar is £1.50-4. Come nightfall, it's the liveliest pub in town. (☎702 354. Open M-Tu noon-11pm, W-Sa 11am-11pm, Su noon-10:30pm; food served M-Sa noon-2pm and 6-8pm.)

◨ **SIGHTS.** From the gargoyled clock tower, a 2min. downhill walk along Aberystwyth Rd. (the A487) brings you to **Celtica,** in Y Plas, the former country home of the Marquess of Londonderry. Now a high-tech multimedia experience tracing the story of the Celtic peoples, the museum features darkened chambers containing an impressive replica village. In a bizarre but entertaining denouement, a druid atop a gnarled tree whisks you on a whirlwind video tour of Celtic history, bringing you back to the present. (☎702 702. Open daily from 10am, last entrance 4:40pm. £5, concessions £4.20, families £15-20. YHA members £3.50 off.)

On a hill 3 mi. north of town along the A487, the **Centre for Alternative Technology** is like a giant summer camp whose counselors never leave. A water-powered funicular railway draws visitors up a 200 ft. cliff into a village of lily ponds, wind turbines, and energy-efficient homes. Learn about those living here communally or climb into the Mole Hole to meet Megan the Mole and walk among giant insect replicas. Take Arriva bus #30 or 34 (5-10min., M-Sa 12 per day) to the entrance, or #32 (5min., M-Sa 7 per day) to Pantperthog and walk 200 yd. north and across a bridge. (☎705 950. Centre open daily 10am-5:30pm. Railway open Easter-Oct. £7, concessions £5, children £3.60, families £20, under 5 free. YHA members, cyclists, pedestrians, and those with proof of train or bus travel get discounts.)

Bringing the present into focus, or sometimes strikingly out of focus, the **Museum of Modern Art, Wales,** in Y Tabernacl on Penrallt St., houses rotating

As I set out through the narrow streets of Dolgellau, my gaze was pulled upward. The stern peak—Pen y Gadair—disappeared into mist known locally as the Brenin Llwyd ("breath of the Grey King"). The sun, however, was still bright, and the fog not heavy.

Cader Idris is steeper than it looks, and the climb was long and lonely. Reddish grass became scree, then rocky outcroppings and stunted grasses. Pockets of mist formed vague shapes, then dissipated.

"P'nawn da, Brenin Llwyd!" I said cheerfully. My voice was muted. I swallowed. It was growing dark, and my small sleeping roll was looking inadequate against the chilling wind. So when I saw the stones rising out of the mists ahead, I smiled triumphantly. Cairns. Perfect, ready-made shelter.

Sleeping in an ancient tomb is not so fun as it sounds. My biscuits fast disappeared. I couldn't sleep. Questions flashed through my head. Why didn't I tell anyone I was coming up here? Are those lichens edible? Where are the public restrooms?

I shivered. Cold rocks bit into my back. Gray mist pressed in, and voices on the wind rose and fell in heinous chorus. "The Brenin Llwyd," Cooper had written in her foreword, "I did not invent." A lone cry came up from below, and I pressed myself against the rocks. Legends can remind you of their factual roots in a most unsettling manner.

More than this I cannot say. Perhaps, if you are brave, or foolhardy...

— *Jenny Pegg*

exhibits. On summer evenings music floats in from the performance hall next door. (☎ 703 355. Open M-Sa 10am-4pm. Free.) The museum and theater are the center of the annual **Machynlleth Festival,** held over a week in August, featuring musical performances and lectures. (Tickets £2-10.) For an informative walk through history, visit the **Owain Glyndŵr Interpretive Centre,** Maengwyn St., which occupies a stone building on the site of Glyndŵr's parliament house. (☎ 702 827. Open Easter-Sept. M-Sa 10am-5pm; Su and winter by appointment. Free.)

DOLGELLAU ☎ 01341

Dark and roughly hewn, the stone buildings of Dolgellau (dol-GECTH-lai) seem appropriate in the imposing presence of Cader Idris and the surrounding wilderness. The town has been populated since Roman times, when three roads met here and legionnaires scoured the hills for gold. In the summer, as the sun peeks through mountain fog and misty legends, Dolgellau becomes a beautiful base from which to hike, ride, and cycle stunning local and mountain paths.

▐█ 🛈 TRANSPORTATION AND PRACTICAL INFORMATION. Buses stop in Eldon Sq. near the TIC. **Arriva** (☎ (08706) 082 608) bus #94 (M-Sa 9 per day, Su 4 per day) arrives from: **Barmouth** (20min.); **Llangollen** (1½hr.); **Wrexham** (2hr.). Arriva bus #2 follows a winding, scenic route through the mountains from **Caernarfon** via **Porthmadog** (1½-2½hr.; M-Sa 6 per day, in summer also Su 4 per day). A lone **Traws-Cambria** bus stops daily from **Cardiff** (Arriva 701; 6hr.).

The **tourist information centre,** Queen's Sq., in Tŷ Meirion by the bus stop, books rooms for £1 plus a 10% deposit and stocks numerous books on Welsh; it doubles as a **Snowdonia National Park Information Centre,** with an exhibit on local mountains and trails. (☎ 422 888. Open Apr.-Sept. 10am-1pm and 2-6pm; Oct.-Mar. Th-M 10am-1pm and 1:30-5pm.) Equip yourself with camping and hiking gear and Ordnance Survey maps (£6-7) from **Cader Idris Outdoor Gear,** at Eldon Sq. (☎ 422 195. Open M-Sa 9am-5:30pm; May-Sept. also Su 10am-4pm.) Other services include: **HSBC bank,** Eldon Sq. (☎ 525 401; open M-F 9am-5pm); **Dolgellau Launderette,** Smithfield St. (wash £2, dry £1, no soap; open W-M 9am-7pm, last wash 6:30pm); **Internet access** at the library, Bala Rd. (☎ 422 771; cross Smithfield St. bridge and turn right, then walk 5min.; open M and F 10am-7pm, Tu and Th 10am-5pm, W 10am-1pm, and Sa 10am-noon); and the **post office,** inside Spar at Plas yn Dre St. (open M-F 9am-5:30pm, Sa 9am-12:30pm). **Post Code:** LL40 1AD.

▐ ▐ ACCOMMODATIONS AND FOOD. The **YHA Kings** is 4 mi. away (☎ 422 392; see p. 517). In Dolgellau, lodging is scarce and expensive, tending to start around £18. Two **B&Bs** with lower rates and spectacular views of the Idris range cling to the hills just north of town. **Arosfyr ❷,** Pen y Cefn, is a working farm with bright, airy rooms and the occasional kitten stalking through the flowers. From the bus stop, with the HSBC on your right, walk down over the bridge, turn left, then right at the school, and follow the steep road until a sign on the right directs you past farm sheds. (☎ 422 355. Singles £17.50; doubles £33.) Comfortable **Dwy Olwyn ❸** keeps horses and serves big breakfasts. Cross the Bont Fawr bridge, turn right, then left onto the unmarked road after the Kwik Save; it's 5min. uphill—follow the signs. (☎ 422 822. Singles £22; doubles £34-38.) **Camping** is available at the hostel and at the deluxe **Tanyfron Caravan and Camping Park ❶,** a 10min. walk south on Arron Rd. onto the A470. (☎/fax 422 638. £6-10. Electricity £2. Showers free.)

Spar is on Plas yn Dre St. (Open daily 8am-10pm.) Knick-knacks, a letter from 10 Downing St., and numerous paintings deck the walls at the **Aber Cottage Tea Room ❷,** Smithfield St., where equally exuberant seating, food, and prices will leave your pocket emptier but your senses *so* much happier. (Lasagne £7.95, scones £1.30. Open daily 10am-5pm.) A heavenly aroma greets those who descend into the

Popty'r Dref ❶ bakery and delicatessen, Smithfield St., just off Eldon Sq., where homemade jams, filled rolls (85p-£2), and spongy pastries (£1-2) crowd the shelves. (☎422 507. Open M-Sa 8am-5pm.) Duck under the low portal at **Y Sospan ❶**, Queen's Sq., behind the TIC, for sandwiches (£2-6) or minty lamb steak (£5.25), but beware—come lunchtime everyone else will have the same idea. (☎423 174. Cafe open daily from 9am; restaurant open F-Sa 7-9pm.)

🔲 **SIGHTS.** The free **Quaker Interpretive Centre**, above the TIC and open the same times, details the history of this hotbed of nonconformity and the circumstances that fueled Quaker emigration to the United States. Once you've completed your history lesson, head for the hills. The famous 3 mi. of **Precipice Walk** reward with views of the Mawddach Estuary and **Cader Idris,** while the 2½ mi. of **Torrent Walk** circle through woodlands and past waterfalls. Pamphlets (40p) are available at the TIC, as is the informative *Local Walks Around Dolgellau* (£4).

CADER IDRIS

The origin of the name Cader Idris ("Chair of Idris") remains a mystery. One story has it that a national hero named Idris was killed in battle by a host of marauding Saxons; another maintains that Idris was a giant who kept house here. This portion of Snowdonia offers scenic walks less crowded than those of Mt. Snowdon to the north, catering to all levels of experience (all cross privately owned farm and grazing land: be courteous and close any gates you open). The 5 mi. pony track from **Llanfihangel y Pennant** is the longest but easiest way to the summit. A rather complicated route, the path climbs steadily after a relatively level first third. The pony track from **Tŷ Nant** begins at Tŷ Nant farm, 3 mi. from Dolgellau. While the trail is eroded in spots, it is not particularly strenuous, and offers the most striking views of the surrounding countryside. The **Minffordd Path** (about 3 mi.) is the shortest but steepest ascent. On its way to the summit, it traverses an 8000-year-old oak wood and rises above the lake of **Llyn Cau.** One story holds that a young man swimming in the lake was ingested by a monster and never seen again; another claims that anyone who sleeps on the mountainside will awaken a poet or a madman. (*Let's Go* does not recommend swimming in monster-infested lakes or sleeping on haunted mountainsides.) Also watch out for the Cwn Annwn (Hounds of the Underworld), said to fly around the range's peaks. Allow 5hr. for any of these walks. Booklets charting each are available at the NPIC in Dolgellau (40p). For longer treks, the Ordnance Survey Outdoor Leisure #23 or Landranger #124 maps (£6-7) are essential. Check with the NPIC for weather forecasts and trail changes.

The 6000-hectare **Coed-Y-Brenin Forest Park** is laced with biking trails along with miles of trails reserved for hikers. Covering the peaks and valleys around the Mawddach and Eden Rivers, the forest is best entered 7 mi. north of Dolgellau off the A470, near the **Coed-Y-Brenin Visitor Centre.** (☎(01341) 440 666. Open Apr.-Oct. daily 10am-5pm; Nov.-Mar. Sa-Su 10am-4pm.) Mountaineers and sporty sorts will find the town of **Dolgellau** (see p. 506) and the **Corris YHA** (see p. 504) convenient spots to rest aching limbs.

HARLECH ☎01766

On the Cambrian coast south of the Llŷn Peninsula and in the foothills of Snowdonia, tiny Harlech clings to a steep hillside, commanding panoramic views of sea, sand, and summits. Harlech's castle, its chief attraction, ranks among the most spectacular in Britain, perched 200 ft. above the sea on an utterly impenetrable promontory. The grassy dunes far below its parapets attract those seeking solitude and sea breezes. While fair weather reveals craggy Snowdonia peaks by day and Llŷn town lights sparkling along the bay by night, frequent mist and rolling dark clouds lend the scene a more haunting texture.

NORTH WALES

TRANSPORTATION. Harlech lies midway on the **Cambrian Coaster** line. The uphill walk to town from the unstaffed **train station** is a calf-burner; follow the signs. **Trains** arrive from **Machynlleth** (1¼-1¾hr.; M-Sa 6 per day, Su 3 per day; £8.20) and connect to **Pwllheli** and other spots on the **Llŷn Peninsula** (M-Sa 6 per day, Su 3 per day). The **Cambrian Coaster Day Ranger** (£6.60, after 4:30pm £3.70) allows unlimited travel on the Coaster line for a day and is cheaper than the single fare from Machynlleth. **Arriva Cymru bus** (☎(08706) 082 608) #38 links Harlech to southern **Barmouth** (M-Sa 7 per day) and northern **Blaenau Ffestiniog** (M-Sa 3-4 per day), stopping at the carpark on Stryd Fawr and the train station.

ORIENTATION AND PRACTICAL INFORMATION. The castle opens out onto **Twtil;** slightly uphill is the town's major street, **Stryd Fawr** (less commonly known as High St.). The **tourist information centre,** 1 Stryd Fawr, near the castle, doubles as a **National Park Information Centre.** The staff stocks Ordnance Survey maps (£6-7) and pamphlets on walks up Snowdon and Cader Idris (40p) and books accommodations for £1 plus a 10% deposit. (☎/fax 780 658. Open July-Aug. daily 10am-6pm; Easter-June and Sept.-Oct. 10am-1pm and 2-6pm.) Other services include **HSBC bank** (open M, W, and F 9:30-11:30am; Tu and Th 12:45-3pm) and the **post office** (☎780 231; open M-Tu and Th-F 9am-12:30pm and 1:30-5:30pm, W and Sa 9am-12:30pm), both on Stryd Fawr. **Post Code:** LL46 2YA.

ACCOMMODATIONS AND FOOD. The closest hostel is **YHA Llanbedr ❶,** 4 mi. south of town; take the train to the Llanbedr stop (10min.) or ride bus #38 and ask to be let off at the hostel. (☎(0870) 770 5926; fax 770 5927. Open Apr.-Oct. Dorms £9.50, under 18 £6.75.) Revel in spacious rooms and Harlech's best views at **Arundel ❷,** Stryd Fawr. Walk past the TIC and take a right before the Yr Ogof Bistro. Energetic Mrs. Stein (pronounced "Steen") will pick you up if the climb from the train station doesn't appeal. (☎780 637. £15 per person.) The **Byrdir Guest House ❷,** a former hotel on Stryd Fawr near the carpark and bus stop, offers comfortable rooms with TVs and washbasins. Slake your horse's thirst at the nearby water trough. (☎/fax 780 316. Singles £17.50-30; doubles £45.) **Camp** at **Min-y-Don Park ❶,** Beach Rd., between the train station and the beach. (☎780 286. Laundry facilities. Open Mar.-Oct. £9 per 2-person tent, £12 for larger tents. Showers 20p.)

Spar, Stryd Fawr, greets travelers next to the Plâs Cafe. (Open daily 8am-8pm; summer until 10pm.) At said **Plâs Cafe ❷,** guests linger over long afternoon teas (with dessert £1-4) and sunset dinners (starting at £7) while enjoying sweeping ocean views from the grassy patio. (☎780 204. Open Mar.-Oct. daily 9:30am-8pm; Nov.-Feb. 9:30am-5:30pm.) **Yr Ogof Bistro ❸,** left from the castle on Stryd Fawr, offers vegetarian dishes for £5-7 and a satisfying three-course Welsh menu for £12. (☎780 888. Open daily 7-9:30pm.) The bar at the **Lion Hotel ❷,** off Stryd Fawr above the castle, is the top place for an evening pint in this virtually publess town. Bar snacks are 70p-£3.50, meals run £5.50-9.50. (☎780 731. Open M-F noon-11pm, Sa 11am-11pm, Su noon-10:30pm; food served until 9pm.)

SIGHTS AND ENTERTAINMENT. **Harlech Castle,** a World Heritage Site and arguably the most spectacularly located of Edward I's many fortresses, retains much of its former glory, with sweeping views of Snowdonia, brown-sugar sand dunes, and the bay. From the outer bailey, 151 absurd steps descend the cliff to the train station, where the sea once lapped at the boat gate. Built in the late 13th century on legendary King Bendigeidfran's favorite resting spot, the castle also served as the insurrection headquarters of Welsh rebel Owain Glyndŵr after he captured the castle from Edward I in 1404. Be careful where you step: many areas lack retaining walls or railings, and the drop is such that one could sing a full rendition of "Men of Harlech" before hitting the ground. (☎780 552. Open June-Sept. M-Sa 9:30am-6pm, Su 9:30am-5pm; May and Oct. daily 9:30am-5pm; Nov.-Mar. M-Sa 9:30am-4pm, Su 11am-4pm. Last admission 30min. before close. £3, concessions £2, families £8.) Public **footpaths** run from Harlech's grassy dunes to the forested hilltops above the town; get recommendations and directions at the TIC. **Theatr Ardudwy,** Coleg Harlech, below the town on the same road as the train station, hosts films, plays, exhibitions, and a big shiny grand piano. It also organizes performances at the castle; pick up a pamphlet at the TIC. (☎780 667. Movies £3.50, concessions £3; other performances from £6, concessions £1-2 less.)

LLŶN PENINSULA (PENRHYN LLŶN)

The Llŷn has been a tourist hotspot since the Middle Ages, when religious pilgrims tramped through on their way to Bardsey Island. Now 25 mi. of sandy beaches along the southern coast draw pilgrims of a different faith: sun worshippers coddled by the uncharacteristically fine weather of the towns between Pwllheli and Abersoch. A hilly region of simple beauty, the Llŷn offers green fields spreading down to the water, bounded by hedges and bright *blodau wylltion* (wildflowers). The farther west you venture, the more unsullied the Llŷn becomes and the scarcer conveniences grow—stock up in Porthmadog, Pwllheli, and Criccieth.

▐▀ TRANSPORTATION

The northern end of the **Cambrian Coaster** (☎(08457) 489 450) train line runs through **Porthmadog** and **Criccieth** to **Pwllheli,** stopping at smaller towns in between. Trains begin at **Aberystwyth** and require a change at **Machynlleth** or **Dyfi Junction** for **Porthmadog** (1½-2hr.; M-Sa 6-7 per day, Su 3 per day) and **Pwllheli** (2-2½hr.). The **Cambrian Coaster Day Ranger** offers unlimited travel along the line (£6.60 per day, after 4:30pm £3.70). The line's western end is at **Blaenau Ffestiniog,** inland east of the peninsula. It continues via **Betws-y-Coed** to **Llandudno,** on the northern coast, and then connects to **Bangor** and **Chester** (M-Sa 6 per day, Su 3 per day).

National Express (☎(08705) 808 080) #545 arrives in **Pwllheli** from **London** via Birmingham, Bangor, Caernarfon, and Porthmadog (10hr., 1 per day). Bus #380 arrives in **Pwllheli** from **Newcastle-upon-Tyne** via Manchester, Liverpool, and Bangor (11hr., 1 per day). **TrawsCambria** bus #701 connects **Porth-**

THE BIG SPLURGE

PORTMEIRION

An eccentric landmark of Italy-fixation the private village of Portmeirion more of a resort compound than traditional village (the adorable bungalows are rental condos), rises from the woods by a quiet estuary 2 mi. east o Porthmadog. Mediterranean court yards, pastel buildings, and the occa sional palm tree provide ar otherworldly contrast to Wale's cas tles and cottages. The mock-village was built between 1925 and 1972 b' Sir Clough Williams-Ellis, who wanted to show "how a naturally beautifu place could be developed withou defiling it." Though the threat of Dis neyfication has been narrowl' averted, it still wouldn't seem out o character if a Munchkin or Oompa Loompa tottered out of a sun-baked building into one of the pooled gar dens. As one of Wales's most popula tourist destinations, the village doe experience Disney-like crowds. To find some semblance of peace, take one of the four color-coded trails tha snakes out from the village.

(The village of Portmeirion is 2 mi. eas of Porthmadog. Bus #98 arrives M-Sa per day—once from Porthmadog er route to Croesor (10min.) and twice back from Croesor (20min.). #98 also stops in Minffordd (6-7 per day), a 30min. walk from Portmeirion and a stop on the Cambrian Coaster train line (M-Sa 6-7 per day). Open daily 9:30am; shops close at 5:30pm. £5.30, concessions £4.20, children £2.60, families £12.60 reduced admission Nov.-Mar.)

madog once a day with **Aberystwyth** (2hr.), **Swansea** (6hr.), and **Cardiff** (7hr.). **Express Motors** (☎(01286) 881 108) bus #1 stops in **Porthmadog** on its winding route between **Blaenau Ffestiniog** (30min.; M-Sa every hr. until 10:15pm, summer also Su 5 per day) and **Caernarfon** (1½hr.). **Berwyn** (☎(01286) 660 315) and **Clynnog & Trefor** (☎(01286) 660 208) run bus #12 between **Pwllheli** and **Caernarfon** (45min.; M-Sa 1 per hr., Su 3-4 per day).

A smattering of bus companies, most prominently **Arriva Cymru** (☎(08706) 082 608), serves most spots on the peninsula with reassuring haste for £1-2. Check bus schedules in *Gwynedd Public Transport Maps and Timetables*, available from TICs. **Arriva** and **Caelloi** (☎(01758) 612 719) share responsibility for bus #3, often open-top in the summer, from **Porthmadog** to **Pwllheli** via Criccieth (30min.; M-Sa 1-2 per hr., Su 6 per day). Arriva buses #17, the circular 17B, and 18 leave Pwllheli to weave around the western tip of the peninsula. A **Gwynedd Red Rover,** bought from the driver, secures a day of travel throughout the peninsula and Gwynedd and Anglesey counties (£4.80, children £2.40).

PORTHMADOG ☎01766

Don't get bogged down by the banal town center of Porthmadog (port-MA-dock); this travel hub, minutes from mountain walks and world-class climbing rocks, is ideally situated for touring the Llŷn Peninsula and hiking into Snowdonia. Its principal attraction is the ■**Ffestiniog Railway,** which departs from Harbour Station on High St. The narrow-gauge railway offers spectacular views as it chugs along the slate-lined hillsides of the Ffestiniog Valley into Snowdonia, terminating in Blaenau Ffestiniog. (☎516 073; www.festrail.co.uk. 1¼hr. June-Aug. 4-10 per day; Apr.-May and Sept.-Oct. 2-4 per day; Nov.-Mar. call for timetables. Day return £14, seniors £11.20, families £28.) At the other end of town, across from the train station, the more modest **Welsh Highland Railway** and Russell, their dogged 1906 locomotive, try to recapture the glory days of rail travel, reconstructing the atmosphere of a 1920s steam line. Once the longest narrow-gauge line in Wales, the track runs ¾ mi. to **Pen-y-mount.** (Info ☎513 402, timetables (08703) 212 402. June-Sept. daily 5 per day; mid-Apr. to May Sa-Su 5 per day; less frequent in Oct. £3, seniors £2.50, children £2, families £7.50.)

From the **train station,** a right turn on High St. leads to town. **Buses** stop on High St., most commonly outside The Australia pub. Holler for **Dukes Taxis** (☎514 799) if you need a lift. **K.K. Cycles,** 141 High St., rents **bikes.** (☎512 310. £2 per hr., £9 per day. Open daily 8:30am-7:30pm.) The **tourist information centre,** High St., by the harbor, books rooms for £1 plus a 10% deposit. (☎512 981. Open Easter-Oct. daily 10am-6pm; Nov.-Easter 10am-5pm.) Other services include: **Barclays,** 79 High St. (open M and W-F 9am-4:30pm, Tu 10am-4:30pm); **Internet access** at the **I.T. Centre,** 156 High St. (☎514 944; £1.50 first 15min., £1 per 15min. thereafter; open M-F 9am-5:30pm; some summer Sa); and the **post office,** High St. and Bank Pl., with a **bureau de change** (☎512 010; open M-F 9am-5:30pm, Sa 9am-12:30pm). **Post Code:** LL49 9AD.

The best place to stay in Porthmadog—well, in the Porthmadog area—is 10min. down Church St. in neighboring **Tremadog.** National Express #545 (to London) and #380 (to Manchester) and local buses stop in Tremadog. The birthplace of Lawrence of Arabia is now the comfortable ■**Snowdon Backpackers Hostel ❷,** complete with TV, fireplace lounge, large dining room, and kitchen. The owners impress with local insight and expert advice on hiking trails. (☎515 354; snowdon@backpackers.fsnet.co.uk. Continental breakfast included. Internet access. Laundry. Apr.-Oct. dorms £12.50; Nov.-Mar. £11.50. Doubles, twins, triples £14.50-16.50 per person.) Signs along **Madoc St.** and **Snowdon St.** in Porthmadog mark **B&Bs.**

Hungry hikers can try the busy **Castle Bakery ❶**, 105 High St., where *bara brith* (a Welsh bread, £1.65), sandwiches (£1.50-2.50), and a variety of salads (90p-£1.50) are freshly made. (☎ 514 982. Open daily 9am-5pm.) Scatter crumbs along the stool-lined counter as you wolf down affordable sandwiches (most £1.35) at **Jessie's ❶**, 75 High St. (☎ 512 814. Open M-Sa 9am-5pm, Easter-Sept. also Su 10am-4pm.) **The Australia ❶**, 31-33 High St., features good grub (£2-6) and a wide-screen TV. (☎ 510 931. Open M-Sa 11am-11pm, Su noon-10:30pm; food served daily noon-2:30pm, M-F also 6-8:30pm; mid-July to Aug. dinner only.)

CRICCIETH   ☎ 01766

Above coastal Criccieth (KRIK-key-ith), 5 mi. west of Porthmadog, the remains of **Criccieth Castle** loom above Tremadog Bay, with views of Snowdonia and Harlech. Built by Llywelyn the Great in 1230, taken by Normans in 1283, destroyed by Owain Glyndŵr in 1404, and now a World Heritage Site, the castle puzzles architectural historians, who debate which walls were English and which walls were Welsh. (☎ 522 227. Open June-Sept. daily 10am-6pm; Apr.-May 10am-5pm. £2.50, concessions £2, families £7. Nov.-Mar. free, unstaffed, and always open; use side gate.)

Cambrian Coaster trains arrive from **Pwllheli** and **Machynlleth** (see p. 509). From the station, turn right on High St. for the town center. **Arriva bus** #3 comes from **Porthmadog** and **Pwllheli** (15-25min.; M-Sa 2 per hr., Su 6 per day). The closest **TIC** is in Porthmadog (see p. 510). To buy your way out of trouble, try **HSBC bank**, 51 High St. (Open M-F 10:30am-1pm.) The **post office** is around the corner from the station. (Open M-Tu and Th-F 9am-5:30pm, W and Sa 9am-12:30pm.) **Post Code:** LL52 OBV.

B&Bs (£15-25) are scattered on **Tan-y-Grisiau Terr.**, across the train tracks from the bus stop, and on **Marine Terr.** and **Marine Cres.**, by the beach near the castle. At **Dan-Y-Castell ❷**, 4 Marine Cres., scaling the edge of the castle hill, the lucky get spacious rooms with sea views, and all marvel at the animal figurines decorating the house. (☎ 522 375. £15 per person.) **Spar**, High St., stocks groceries in a closet-sized space. (Open daily 8:15am-10pm.) Dinner-seekers head to tiny, popular **Poachers Restaurant ❷**, 66 High St., down the road from the bus stop. The three-course meal costs £9; vegetarian options are £7. (☎ 522 512. Open daily 6-9pm; Su reserve ahead.) Branches of **Cadwalader's ❶** ice-cream store dot the Llŷn, but the original lies on Castle St., down the road from the castle's entrance. (Open M-F 10:30am-9pm, Sa-Su 10am-9:30pm.) The beer garden of **Bryn Hir Arms ❶**, High St., is the ideal setting for a quiet pint. (☎ 522 493. Open Easter-Sept. daily noon-11pm; Oct.-Easter M-F 4pm-11pm, Sa-Su noon-11pm. Food served noon-2:30pm and 6pm-9:30pm.)

LLANYSTUMDWY   ☎ 01766

Just 1½ mi. north of Criccieth, tiny Llanystumdwy (HLAN-ih-stim-doo-ee) was the boyhood home of **David Lloyd George**, British Prime Minister from 1916 to 1922—and the town makes sure you know it. The centerpiece **Lloyd George Museum** chronicles the leader's life with relics from his career, among them his working copy of the Treaty of Versailles and the pen he used to sign it. Exit the museum, turn right, and follow the path behind it to **Highgate**, George's boyhood home. The **workshop** features a tape-recorded uncle, who tells long-winded family anecdotes. A trek through the museum carpark and across the street leads to George's striking grave. (☎ 522 071. Open July-Sept. daily 10:30am-5pm; Apr.-June M-F 10:30am-5pm; Oct. M-F 11am-4pm. £3, concessions £2, families £7.) Satisfy your longing for warm fuzzies by petting sheepdog puppies, Shetland ponies, and baby bunnies at **Dwyfor Ranch**, across the bridge from the Lloyd George Museum. (☎ 523 136. Open Easter-Oct. daily 10am-7pm.) Arriva bus #3 stops twice per hour (20min. from Pwllheli, 15min. from Porthmadog, 4min. from Criccieth.)

PWLLHELI   ☎01758

The last stop on the Cambrian Coaster rail line, Pwllheli (poohl-HEL-ly), 8 mi. west of Criccieth, is best known for its bus station, which spews buses to every corner of the peninsula and beyond. Its two **beaches**—sandy Abererch Beach to the east and pebbly South Beach—are hardly spectacular, and both are farther away than the TIC's brochures imply.

The **train station** hugs the corner of Y Maes and Ffordd-y-Cob at Station Sq.; the **bus station** is farther down Ffordd-y-Cob on the right. For **taxis**, call ☎740 999. The **tourist information centre**, Station Sq., books B&Bs for £1 plus a 10% deposit. (☎613 000. Open Apr.-Oct. daily 10am-6pm; Nov.-Mar. M-W and F-Sa 10:30am-4:30pm.) Other services include: **HSBC bank**, at High St. and Penlan St. (☎632 700; open M-F 9am-5pm); **Internet access** in free 30min. shifts at **Pwllheli Library**, in Neuadd Dwyfor (the Town Hall), along Stryd Penlan (☎612 089; open M 2-7pm; Tu, Th, and Sa 10am-1pm; W and F 10am-1pm and 2-7pm); and the **post office**, New St., at the back of a general store (☎612 658; open M-F 9am-5:30pm, Sa 9am-12:30pm).

Bank Place Guest House ❷, 29 High St., safeguards spacious rooms with TVs and huge breakfasts. (☎612 103. £15 per person.) Area **camping** is good; try **Hendre ❶**, 1½ mi. down the road to Nefyn at Efailnewidd. (☎613 416. Laundry. Open Mar.-Oct. £8-12 per tent.) Get Welsh cakes and produce at the open-air **market** in front of the bus station (W 9am-5pm). The **Spar** supermarket is on Y Maes Sq. (☎612 993. Open daily 8am-10pm.) The **Bodawen Cafe ❶**, also on Y Maes, serves tasty sandwiches for £1.75-2.75. (☎612 533. Open M-Su 8:30am-4:30pm, sometimes later.)

ABERDARON AND TRE'R CEIRI   ☎01758

In a sandy cove close to the peninsula's western tip, the peaceful village of **Aberdaron** merges with the mist-blue of sea and sky, where winds brush hillside houses and skittish sheep. By the beach, enter the **Church of Saint Hywyn** through the oldest doorway in northern Wales for ocean views. (Open in summer daily 10am-6pm; winter 10am-4pm.) Water in the **wishing well**, 1½ mi. west of town, stays fresh even when inundated by the tide. Follow road signs from Aberdaron 2 mi. to **Porthor**, where, if conditions are right, the "whistling sands" live up to their nickname. Enjoy an exhilarating horseback ride on the beach with **Parc Dwyros Trekking**. (☎760 580. £14-15 per hr.) The **Bardsey Island Trust Booking Office**, in the center of the village, provides information on boats to **Bardsey Island**. Long a religious site—its first monastery was allegedly built in the 6th century—the "Island of Twenty Thousand Saints" was once so holy that three pilgrimages there equaled one to Rome. Several beautiful walks allow visitors to admire the ruins of the old abbey and hundreds of migratory birds. A **National Trust information point** lodges in a Coast Guard hut overlooking Bardsey at the Uwchmynydd headland, Wales's Land's End. (☎760 667. Trust open Easter-Sept. most weekends. Ferries 15-20min., allowing 4hr. visits; frequency depends on weather and demand. £18.50, children £9.50.)

Bus #17 runs from **Pwllheli** (40min., M-Sa 7 per day); #17B follows a more scenic, coastal route and takes 5min. longer (2 per day). Follow the sign pointing toward Uwchmynydd to the lovely **Bryn Mor ❷**, where elegant rooms have sea views and TVs. (☎760 344. £18 per person.) **Spar** provides groceries. (☎760 234. Open Apr.-Oct. daily 8am-9pm; Nov.-Mar. 8am-5:30pm.) Since 1300, pilgrims to Bardsey have fended off hunger in the small building occupied by the **Y Gegin Fawr ❶** ("The Big Kitchen") cafe. Tear into large salads for £4.20-6 or tasty Welsh rarebit for £3. (☎760 359. Open July-Aug. daily 10am-5pm; Easter-June and Sept.-Oct. 10am-5:30pm.) The **post office** is inside. (Open M-Tu and Th-F 9am-12:30pm and 1:30-5:30pm, W and Sa 9am-noon.) **Post Code:** LL53 8BE.

Tre'r Ceiri (trair-KAY-ree; "town of the giants"), on the peninsula's north shore, is Britain's oldest fortress, dating back some 4000 years. Take the Pwllheli-Caernarfon bus #12 to **Llanaelhaearn,** 7 mi. from Pwllheli (15min.; M-Sa every hr., Su 4 per day), then look for the footpath signposted 1 mi. southwest of town on the B4417 (from the bus stop, go uphill until you hit the B4417, then turn left). At the path's upper reaches, keep to the stony track, which is more or less a direct uphill route (elevation 1600 ft.). The remains of 150 circular stone huts are clustered within a double defensive wall, which, however strong, fails to protect against the windy weather. Wear warm clothes and only attempt the hike in sunny weather.

CAERNARFON ☎01286

Strikingly well-preserved and festively majestic, the walled city of Caernarfon (car-NAR-von) faces the Isle of Anglesey with a world-famous castle at its helm and mountains in its wake. Occupied since pre-Roman times and once the center of English government in northern Wales, Caernarfon has been a hotspot of struggle for regional political control. During a 1294 tax revolt, the Welsh managed to break in, sack the town, and massacre the English settlers. Vestiges of English domination remain (a young Charles, resembling a rabbit caught in headlights, was invested as Prince of Wales at the castle in 1969), but Caernarfon is thoroughly Welsh in character—visitors can hear the town's own dialect used in its flower-bedecked streets and inviting pubs.

▐▄ TRANSPORTATION. The nearest **train station** is in **Bangor** (see p. 520), though Caernarfon is the well-greased pivot for **buses** from mid-Wales swinging north to Bangor and Anglesey, which arrive on Penllyn in the city center. **Arriva Cymru** (☎(08706) 082 608) #5 and 5X come from **Conwy** via Bangor (1¼hr.; M-Sa 2 per hr., Su every hr.), while #5A and 5B come from **Bangor** only (25min.; M-Sa 5-6 per hr., Su every hr.). **Express Motors** (☎881 108) #1 and **Arriva** #2 drift in from **Porthmadog** (45min.-1hr.; M-Sa every hr., Su 5 per day). **Clynnog & Trefor** (☎660 208) and **Berwyn** (☎660 315) run bus #12 from **Pwllheli** (45min.; M-Sa every hr., Su 3 per day). **KMP** (☎870 880) #88 zooms from **Llanberis** (25min.; M-Sa 1-2 per hr., Su every hr. until 10pm), while its **Sherpa** #95 passes **Beddgelert** and several YHA hostels (30min., 5-8 per day). Arriva's **TrawsCambria** bus #701 arrives daily from **Cardiff** (7½hr.) and **Holyhead** (1½hr.). **National Express** (☎(08705) 808 080) #545 arrives daily from **London** via Chester (9hr., 1 per day). A Gwynedd **Red Rover** ticket earns unlimited bus travel in the county (1 day; £4.80, children £2.40); the divine *Gwynedd Public Transport Maps and Timetables* gives info on bus and train routes between major towns. For a **taxi,** try **Vale Cabs,** Palace St. (☎676 161 or 881 345).

▐▄ ORIENTATION AND PRACTICAL INFORMATION. The heart of Caernarfon lies within and just outside the town walls, though the city spreads far beyond. As you face outward from the castle entrance, the TIC is directly across **Castle Ditch Rd. Castle St.** intersects Castle Ditch Rd. perpendicularly at the same point. Reach **High St.** by walking away from the castle on Castle St.

The **tourist information centre** is on Castle St., inside Oriel Pendeitsh. Pick up the illustrated street map in the free *Visitor's Guide to Caernarfon.* (☎672 232. Open Apr.-Oct. daily 10am-6pm; Nov.-Mar. Th-Tu 9:30am-4:30pm.) Get **camping supplies** at **14th Peak,** 9 Palace St. (☎675 124. 10% student discount. Open M-W and F-Sa 9am-5:30pm, Th 9am-5pm, Su 1-4pm.) Other services include: **Barclays,** 5-7 Bangor St. (☎672 900; open M-Tu and Th-F 9am-4:30pm, W 10am-4:30pm); **Pete's Laundrette,** Skinner St., off Bridge St. (☎678 395; open daily 9am-6pm, last wash 5:30pm); the **police,** Maesincla Ln. (☎673 333, ext. 5242); **Internet access** at the **public library,** on the corner of Bangor St. and Lon Pafiliwn (☎671 137; free; 30min. maximum; open M-Tu and Th-F 10am-7pm, W 10am-1pm, Sa 9am-1pm) and at **Dimensiwn 4,** 4 Bangor St. (☎678 777; £1 per 15min.; open M-Tu and Th-Sa 9:30am-6pm, W 9:30am-5pm); and the **post office,** Castle Sq. (☎(08457) 223 344; open M-F 9am-5:30pm, Sa 9am-12:30pm). **Post Code:** LL55 2ND.

NORTH WALES

ACCOMMODATIONS. In a town nearly devoid of affordable rooms, budget travelers can thank their lucky stars for ■**Totter's Hostel ❷**, 2 High St. This Plas-Porth-Yr-Aur ("Grand House of the Golden Gate"), run by friendly Bob and Henryette, has huge rooms with comfortable wooden bunks and a living room equipped with sofas and movies. In the cellar, a medieval stone arch graces a full kitchen and a banquet table perfect for post-pub gatherings. (☎672 963, mobile (07979) 830 470; www.applemaps.co.uk/totters. Free lockers and bikes to borrow. Dorms £12.) **B&Bs,** generally from £20, line **Church St.** inside the old town wall; those on **St. David's Rd.,** a 10min. walk from the castle off the Bangor St. roundabout, are sometimes cheaper. At **Bryn Hyfryd ❸**, St. David's Rd., guests are cared for in style. Rooms have bath and bright flowers, and are *extremely* well lit. (☎673 840. Singles £25; doubles £50. Mid-Sept. to June £20/£40.) **Marianfa ❸**, St. David's Rd., has spacious rooms with stunning views of the Menai. Ask the proprietress about motorbike and sight-seeing packages. (☎674 815; marianfa@aol.com. £18-25 per person.) **Camp** at **Cadnant Valley ❷**, Cwm Cadnant Rd. (☎673 196. From £11.)

⬛🏠 FOOD AND PUBS. Safeway is on the Promenade. (Open M-Th 8:30am-10pm, F 8am-10pm, Sa 8am-8pm, Su 10am-4pm.) On Saturdays and some Mondays, a **market** takes over Castle Sq. (9am-4pm.) Cafes and pubs crowd within the town walls. **Stones Bistro ❸**, 4 Hole-in-the-Wall St., near Eastgate, is famous, candlelit, and crowded. The Welsh lamb (£11) is worth it; vegetarian main courses go for £8.30-10. (☎671 152. Open Tu-Sa 6-11pm.) **Crempogau ❶**, at the corner of Palace St. and High St., cooks savory, lunch-worthy pancakes; try the chicken supreme (£2.20) or nibble the Bavarian apple (£1.70) for dessert. (☎672 552. Open Apr.-Oct. daily 10:30am-4pm.) Climb aboard the **Floating Restaurant ❷**, Slate Quay, where views of strait, castle, and mountains complement seafood steaks (£6-9.45), burgers and salads (£5.10), and a kids' menu from £2. (☎672 896. Open Easter to mid-Sept. 11am-7:30pm.) The stout wooden doors of the **Anglesey Arms ❶** open onto the Promenade just below the castle. Relax outdoors with a pint as the sun dips into the shimmering Menai. (Open M-Sa 11am-11pm, Su noon-10:30pm.)

◩ SIGHTS. In a nod to Caernarfon's Roman past (and, no doubt, to his own ego), Edward I built ■**Caernarfon Castle** in imitation of Byzantine Constantinople, with eagle-crowned turrets and polygonal towers. Starting in 1283, Edward spent a fortune constructing this grandest in his ring of North Welsh fortresses; one resentful Welshman called it "this magnificent badge of our subjection." Despite its swagger, the castle was left unfinished thanks to an empty royal pocket and the distraction of unruly Scots. Summer sees a variety of performances, including scenes from the Welsh epic *The Mabinogi* and reenactments of the American Revolution. Entertaining and cynical tours run hourly for £1.50, and a free 20min. video recounts the castle's history twice hourly. The **regimental museum** of the Royal Welsh Fusiliers, inside the castle, is worth a walk-through. (☎677 617. Open June-Sept. daily 9:30am-6pm; Apr.-May and Oct. 9:30am-5pm; Nov.-Mar. M-Sa 9:30am-4pm, Su 11am-4pm. £4.50, concessions £3.50, families £12.50.)

Most of Caernarfon's 13th-century **town wall** survives, and a short stretch between Church St. and Northgate St. is open for climbing during the same hours as the castle. To see what today's hostels will look like in 2000 years, inspect the ruined barracks at **Segontium Roman Fort.** Plundered to its foundations by zealous builders stealing stones for Caernarfon Castle, the fort impresses with thoughtful displays of archaeological excavations. From Castle Sq., follow signs uphill along Ffordd Cwstenin; the fort is on the left. (☎675 625. Open Apr.-Oct. M-Sa 10am-5pm, Su 2-5pm; Nov.-Mar. M-Sa 10am-4pm, Su 2-4pm. Free.)

SOMEDAY MY PRINCE WILL COME While there is today a Prince of Wales, not since the 1282 slaying of Llywelyn ap Gruffydd has there been a Welsh prince. Fully aware that, no matter how many intimidating castles he constructed along the northern coast, the Welsh would not be settled until they once again had a Welsh prince and English dominion withdrawn, Edward I made them a promise: their very own Prince of Wales, born in Wales, and speaking not a word of English. When his son, later Edward II, was born, Edward I carried the baby to the window of Caernarfon Castle on the Welsh shield, and presented him as the next Prince of Wales: son of an English king, true, but born in Wales, and speaking not a word of English.

The remains of a Celtic settlement scatter atop **Twt Hill,** alongside the Bangor St. roundabout; the jutting peak offers sweeping vistas of town and castle. **Paradox,** a huge nightclub off Castle St. (descend the stairs next to the post office) sponsors 70s nights on the last Thursday of the month and other special events. (☎ 673 100. Smart dress. Cover £2-6. Open 10pm-1:30am.)

SNOWDONIA NATIONAL PARK

What time the splendour of the setting sun
Lay beautiful on Snowdon's sovereign brow,
On Cader Idris, or huge Penmanmaur...
    —William Wordsworth

Rough and handsome, misty purple and mossy green, the highest mountains in Wales dominate horizons across the 840 sq. mi. of Snowdonia National Park (Parc Cenedlaethol Eryri), stretching from forested Machynlleth in the south to sand-strewn Conwy in the north. Known in Welsh as Eryri ("Place of Eagles"), Snowdonia's upper reaches are as powerfully graceful as their name suggests. Where sheep don't blanket the landscape, dark pine forests run into gorges and estuaries flow into sun-pierced coves. Though these lands lie largely in private hands—only 0.3% belongs to the National Park Authority—endless public footpaths easily accommodate its droves of visitors. The second largest of England and Wales's national parks, Snowdonia is also a stronghold of national pride: 65% of its 27,500 inhabitants speak Welsh as their native tongue.

▄ TRANSPORTATION

Trains (☎ (08457) 484 950) stop at larger towns on the park's outskirts, including **Bangor** and **Conwy.** The **Conwy Valley Line** runs through the park from **Llandudno** through **Betws-y-Coed** to **Blaenau Ffestiniog** (1hr. from Llandudno to Blaenau Ffestiniog; M-Sa 7 per day, Su 2-3 per day). **Buses** serve the interior from towns near the edge of the park. The *Gwynedd Public Transport Maps and Timetables* and *Conwy Public Transport Information* booklets, indispensable for travel in the two counties that comprise the park, are both available for free in the region's TICs. **Snowdon Sherpa** buses, usually painted blue, maneuver between the park's towns and trailheads with somewhat irregular service, but will stop at any safe point in the park on request. A Gwynedd **Red Rover ticket** (£4.80, children £2.40) buys unlimited travel for a day on Sherpa buses and all other buses in Gwynedd and Anglesey; a **Snowdon Sherpa Day Ticket** secures a day's worth of rides on Sherpa buses (£2.50, children £1.25). Most routes run every 2hr., and Sunday service is sporadic at best. Ask bus drivers how to make connections.

Narrow-gauge railway lines let you enjoy the countryside in a few select locations without enduring a hike. The **Ffestiniog Railway** (see p. 510) weaves from Porthmadog to Blaenau Ffestiniog, where the mountains of discarded slate rival those of Snowdonia. You can travel part of its route to Minffordd, Penrhyndeudraeth, or Tan-y-bwlch. At Porthmadog, the narrow-gauge rail meets the Cambrian Coaster service from Pwllheli to Aberystwyth; at Blaenau Ffestiniog, it connects with the Conwy Valley Line. The **Snowdon Mountain Railway** and the **Llanberis Lake Railway** both make short trips from Llanberis (see p. 518).

🛈 PRACTICAL INFORMATION

TICs and National Park Information Centres (NPICs) stock leaflets on walks, drives, and accommodations, as well as Ordnance Survey maps. For details, contact the **Snowdonia National Park Information Headquarters,** Penrhyndeudraeth (penrin-DAY-dryth), Gwynedd LL48 6LF (☎(01766) 770 274). The annual *Snowdonia—Mountains and Coast,* free at TICs across North Wales, contains fistfuls of information on the park and accommodations. If you're cyber-savvy, check out www.snpa.co.uk or www.gwynedd.gov.uk. The following are Snowdonia's **NPICs:**

Aberdyfi: Wharf Gdns. (☎/fax (01654) 767 321). Open Easter-Aug. daily 10am-6pm; Sept.-Oct. closed 1-2pm.

Betws-y-Coed: The busiest and best stocked. See p. 530.

Blaenau Ffestiniog: Isallt Church St. (☎(01766) 830 360). In the Ffestiniog Railway's steam clouds. Open Easter-Oct. daily 10am-6pm; Nov.-Easter closed 1-2pm.

Dolgellau: See p. 506.

Harlech: See p. 507.

🏠 ACCOMMODATIONS

This section lists **YHA hostels** in Snowdonia; B&Bs are listed under individual towns. The seven hostels in the mountain area are some of the best in Wales and are marked on the Snowdonia map. All have kitchens, and meals are available except where noted.

Bryn Gwynant: (☎(0870) 770 5732; fax 770 5733), ¾ mi. from the Watkin path, above Llyn Gwynant and along the Penygwryd-Beddgelert road (4 mi. east of Beddgelert). Take Sherpa bus #95 from Caernarfon (40min., M-Sa 5 per day) or Llanberis (20min.; M-Sa 5 per day, Su 3 per day). Sherpa summer express #97A comes from Porthmadog or Betws-y-Coed (30min. each way, June-Sept. 3 per day). Lockout noon-5pm. Curfew 11pm. Open Mar.-Oct. daily. Dorms £10.25, under 18 £7. ❷

Capel Curig: (☎(0870) 770 5746; fax 770 5747), 5 mi. from Betws-y-Coed on the A5. Sherpa buses #19, 96, 96B, and 97A from Betws and Llanberis stop nearby. At the crossroads of many mountain paths; favored by climbers and school kids. Spectacular view of Mt. Snowdon across a lake. Lockout 10am-5pm. Curfew 11:30pm. Open Easter-Sept. daily; Oct.-Dec. Su-Th. Dorms £13.50, under 18 £10.25; doubles £28/£21. ❷

Idwal Cottage: (☎(0870) 770 5874; fax 770 5875), just off the A5 at the foot of Llyn Ogwen in northern Snowdonia, 4 mi. from Bethesda. Within hiking distance of Pen-y-Pass, Llanberis, and Capel Curig. Bus routes here are scarcer—take Sherpa bus #66 from Bangor (20min., every hr.), changing to #96B at Bethesda (10min.; M-Sa 4-5 per day, Su 3 per day), which goes to the hostel. On Su, #7 from Bangor stops at the hostel (30min., 3 per day). Self-catering kitchen. Lockout 10am-5pm. Curfew 11pm. Open mid-Feb. to Aug. daily; Jan. and Sept. to mid-Dec. Su-Th. Dorms £8.75, under 18 £6. ❶

Kings (Dolgellau): (☎(0870) 770 5900; fax 770 5901), Penmaenpool, 4 mi. from Dolgellau. Take Arriva bus #28 from Dolgellau (5min.; M-F 7 per day, Sa 5 per day, Su 3 per day). Endure the uphill walk to this country house in the Vale of Ffestiniog. Open mid-Apr. to Aug. daily. Dorms £9.50, under 18 £6.75. ❶

Llanberis: (☎(0870) 770 5928; fax 770 5929), ½ mi. up Capel Goch Rd., with views of Llyn Peris, Llyn Padarn, and Mt. Snowdon; follow signs from High St. Curfew 11:30pm. Open Apr.-Oct. daily; Nov.-Mar. Su-Th. Dorms £10.25, under 18 £7. ❷

Pen-y-Pass: (☎(0870) 770 5990; fax 770 5991), in Nant Gwynant, 6 mi. from Llanberis and 4 mi. from Nant Peris. Take Sherpa bus #96 from Llanberis or Betws-y-Coed (25min.; late May to Sept. every hr., otherwise M-Sa 6 per day, Su 9 per day) or #19 from Llanberis or Llandudno (May-Sept. 3 per day). 1170 ft. above sea level at the head of the Snowdon Pass. The doors open onto a track to the Snowdon summit. Outdoors shop sells supplies and rents hiking boots, waterproofs, and ice axes. Hostel bar open mid-afternoon to 11pm. Open year-round. Dorms £10.25, under 18 £8. ❷

Snowdon Ranger: Llyn Cwellyn (☎(0870) 770 6038; fax 770 6039).

The base for the Ranger Path, the grandest Snowdon ascent. Take Sherpa bus #95 from Caernarfon (20min.; M-Sa 8 per day, Su 5 per day) directly to the hostel. Lockout 10am-5pm. Curfew 11pm. Open Easter-Aug. daily; Sept.-Oct. W-Su; mid-Feb. to Easter and Nov.-Dec. F-Su. Dorms £10.50, under 18 £7. ❷

In the high mountains, **camping** is permitted as long as you leave no mess, but the Park Service discourages it because of recent and disastrous erosion. In the valleys, the landowner's consent is required to camp. Public campsites dot the roads in peak seasons; check listings below and inquire at NPICs for specific sites.

🏔 OUTDOOR ACTIVITIES

Weather on Snowdonia's exposed mountains shifts quickly, unpredictably, and wrathfully. No matter how beautiful the weather is below, it *will* be cold and wet in the high mountains. Dress as if preparing for a confrontation with the Abominable Snowman: bring a waterproof jacket and pants, gloves, hat, and wool sweater and peel off layers as you descend. The free *Stay Safe in Snowdonia* offers advice and information on hiking and climbing. (See **Wilderness Safety,** p. 49.) Pick up the Ordnance Survey Landranger Map #115 (1:50,000; £6) and Outdoor Leisure Map #17 (1:25,000; £7), as well as individual mountain path guides (40p) at TICs,

NORTH WALES

NPICs, and bookstores. Call **Mountaincall Snowdonia** (☎ (0891) 500 449; 36-48p per min.) for a local three- to five-day forecast and ground conditions. **Weather forecasts** are also tacked outside NPICs. Ask park rangers about guided **day-walks.**

Snowdonia National Park Study Centre, Plas Tan-y-Bwlch, Maentwrog, Blaenau Ffestiniog, conducts three- to seven-day courses on naturalist favorites such as wildlife painting (☎ (01766) 590 324; ₤90-350). **YHA Pen-y-Pass,** Nant Gwynant (see above) puts groups in touch with guides for mountaineering, climbing, and watersports. **Beics Eryri Cycle Tours,** 44 Tyddyn Llwydyn, leads guided trips from Caernarfon for multi-night forays into the park. (☎ (01286) 676 637. From ₤42 per night including bike and accommodations; groups only.) **Snowdonia Riding Stables,** 3 mi. from Caernarfon, off the A4085 near Waunfawr, offers horse treks. Take Sherpa buses #95 or 95A (10min.; M-Sa every hr., Su 7 per day) and ask to be let off at the turn-off road. (☎ (01286) 650 342. ₤13 per hr., ₤28 per half-day, ₤48 per day.) The brave can paraglide off the peaks of Snowdonia with the help of Llanberis-based **Snowdonia Paragliding School.** (☎ (01248) 602 103. 3 flights with instruction ₤75. Weather dependent; call ahead.) Myriad adventures are detailed in the *The Snowdon Peninsula: North Wales Activities* brochure, available in TICs and NPICs.

LLANBERIS   ☎01286

One of the few small villages lively even on Sundays, lovely Llanberis owes its outdoorsy bustle to popular Mt. Snowdon, whose ridges and peaks unfold just south of town, and its idyllic setting upon peaceful Padarn Lake. Hikers can absorb the scenery on a multitude of beautiful trails starting in and around the town.

▐▓ TRANSPORTATION AND PRACTICAL INFORMATION. Situated on the western edge of the park, Llanberis is a short ride from Caernarfon on the A4086. Catch **KMP bus** (☎ 870 880) #88 from **Caernarfon** (25min.; M-Sa 1-2 per hr., Su every hr. until 10pm). **Sherpa** bus #96, operated by Arriva, winds past Pen-y-Pass on its way from **Betws-y-Coed** (late May to Sept. every hr., Oct. to mid-May 6-10 per day). In town, KMP's **Sherpa** #96A does a complete circle around Llanberis, stopping at major sites like the Snowdon Mountain Railway, Parc Padarn, and Electric Mountain (15-30min. round-trip; M-Sa 9 per day, Su 5-8 per day).

The **tourist information centre,** 41b High St., doles out hiking tips and books beds for ₤1 plus a 10% deposit. (☎ 870 765. Open Easter-Oct. daily 10am-6pm; Nov.-Easter W and F-Su 11am-4pm.) Pick up gear, maps, and advice at **Joe Brown's Store,** Menai Hall, High St. (☎ 870 327. Open M-F 9am-1pm and 2-5:30pm, Sa 9am-6pm, Su 9am-5pm.) Other services include: an ATMless **HSBC bank,** 29 High St. (open M-F 10am-2pm); the bankless **Barclays ATM,** at the entrance to Electric Mountain on the A4086; **Internet access** at Pete's Eats (see below); and the **post office,** 36 High St. (open M-Tu and Th-F 9am-5:30pm, W and Sa 9am-7:30pm). **Post Code:** LL55 4EU.

▐▐ ACCOMMODATIONS AND FOOD. Plenty of sheep and cows keep hostelers company at the **YHA Llanberis** (see p. 517), while the **Heights Hotel ❷,** 74 High St., has 24 bunk beds packed into three plain co-ed dorms, as well as more expensive hotel-style rooms with bath. Half the town crowds into the bar on weekends. (☎ 871 179; fax 872 507. June-Aug. dorms ₤12, with breakfast ₤15; Sept.-May ₤10/₤13. Singles ₤30.) **B&Bs** are farther from town and start around ₤15. Those who aren't up to roughing it can enjoy comfortable, mostly ensuite rooms at the grand **Plas Coch Guest House ❸,** High St. (☎ 872 122. From ₤24 per person.) A cozy 19th-century temperance house, **Snowdon Cottage ❷,** Pentre Castell, sits in the shadow of Dolbadarn Castle. Walk 5min. along High St. and its extension, the A4086, toward the park and past the Victoria Hotel. (☎ 872 015. ₤15-20 per person.) **Camping** is 2 mi. north at the **Snowdon View Caravan Park ❶,** which has excellent facilities, including a heated swimming pool. (☎ 870 349. ₤5-10 per tent. Electricity ₤1.50.)

Spar is at the corner of High St. and Capel Goch Rd. (Open M-Sa 7am-1. 7am-10:30pm.) Llanberis's restaurants feed the healthy demands (and app, of hikers. For a relaxed dinner, try **Y Caban ❷,** High St. (☎870 434. Open M-Sa ⌐ 5pm and 6pm-9:30pm, Su 9am-5pm.) Delicious meads, honeys, teas, and ⌐ creams—many locally made—are £1 and up at **Snowdon Honey Farm ❶,** High St. (☎870 218. Open daily 7am-4pm.) At **Pete's Eats ❶,** 40 High St., opposite the TIC, surf the net (£1 per 15min.) while enjoying a vegetarian mixed grill (£5.20), super-hot chilli (£4.85), and tunes from the jukebox. (☎870 358. Open Easter-Oct. M-F 9am-8pm, Sa-Su 8am-8pm; Nov.-Easter M-F 9am-6:30pm, Sa-Su 8am-8pm.)

◙ **SIGHTS.** For a small village, Llanberis brims with attractions; most lie near the fork where the A4086 meets High St. Part self-promotion for Edison Energy, part journey to the center of the earth, **Electric Mountain** takes visitors on a fasci-nating underground tour of the Dinorwig power station. Located deep in the heart of a mountain, the station occupies the largest manmade cavern in Europe (St. Paul's Cathedral would fit comfortably inside), which required the removal of 12 million tons of slate. The riveting bus tour is unfortunately flanked by two promo-tional videos showing how the company's electricity delivers joy to the lives of the elderly and brings multi-racial families together. (☎870 636. Open Easter-Sept. daily 9:30am-5:30pm; Oct.-Dec. 10:30am-4:30pm; Jan.-Easter Th-Su 10:30am-4:30pm. 1hr. tour £5, concessions £3.75, children £2.50, families £12.)

The immensely popular but expensive **Snowdon Mountain Railway** whisks visitors to Snowdon's summit from the terminus on the A4086. The 2½hr. round-trip allows only 30min. at the peak, so snap those panoramic shots quickly. If you miss your return train, you may have to hike to the bottom. Weather and passenger demand dictate the schedule from mid-May to early September; on clear days the first train leaves Llanberis at 9am, with subsequent trains twice per hour until 5pm. (☎870 223. Runs mid-Mar. to Oct., but not always to summit. Return £18, chil-dren £13; single £13/£10. Concessions £3 off each way. Line up early for a ticket.)

Most other attractions lie by the entrance to **Parc Padarn.** The **Llanberis Lake Railway** takes a short, scenic route from Gilfach Ddu station at Llanberis through the woods along the lake. The **Woodland and Wildlife Centre,** at the halfway point, is a nice picnic spot. (Railway ☎870 549. 40min. round-trip. Open M-F, some Sa, most Su 11am-4:30pm; schedule at TIC. £4.50, children £1.60. Centre same hours. Free.) Nearby, the imposing **Welsh Slate Museum** has exhibits on the importance of slate to Welsh history, including a 3-D movie complete with singing rock cutters. The working waterwheel in the Power Hall is a marvel. (☎870 630. Open Easter-Oct. daily 10am-5pm; Nov.-Easter Su-F 10am-4pm. Free.) Follow the road into the park until a footbridge to the right leads to **Dolba-darn Castle,** where Prince Llywelyn of North Wales imprisoned his brother for 23 years. Only a single tower remains, but the grassy hill offers lovely views of the lake and park. (Always open. Free.) For an eye-level view of the waterfall **Ceunant Mawr,** follow the well-marked footpath from Victoria Terr. by the Victoria Hotel (¾ mi.).

MOUNT SNOWDON AND VICINITY

By far the most popular destination in the park, Mt. Snowdon (Yr Wyddfa; "the burial place") is the highest peak in both England and Wales, measuring 3560 ft. Over half a million hikers tread the mountain each year. Future hikes were nearly scuttled in 1998 when a plot of land including Snowdon's summit was put up for sale, but celebrated Welsh actor Sir Anthony Hopkins sprang to the rescue, con-tributing a vast sum to the National Trust to save the pristine peak. Enthusiasts have disrupted Snowdon's ecosystem and eroded some of its face; park officers request that hikers stick to the well-marked trails to avoid further damage. Six principal paths of varying difficulty wend their way up Snowdon; TICs and NPICs stock guides on these ascents.

NORTH WALES

vdon is the main attraction in the northern part of the park,
ers cart pick-axes and ropes to the **Ogwen Valley.** There,
hen (Twll Du), the **Glyders** (Glyder Fawr and Glyder Fach),
'rom **Llyn Ogwen.** Those attempting climbs should pick up
unce Survey maps and get advice on equipment and sup-
folks at **Joe Brown's Store** (see p. 518). Excellent horse-
\d at the **Dolbadarn Trekking Centre,** whose guides can
...es from *Willow* and *Mortal Combat II* were filmed.
... trek £15, 2hr. £25.)

BANGOR ☎ 01248

Crowded into a valley by the Menai Strait, Bangor lures visitors as a transport hub
and as a cheap and convenient base for exploring the Isle of Anglesey. Students
from the University of Wales keep the pubs and clubs raucous until the wee hours.

◼ TRANSPORTATION. Bangor is the transport depot for the Isle of Anglesey
to the west, the Llŷn Peninsula to the southwest, and Snowdonia to the southeast. The **train station** is on Holyhead Rd., up a hill at the end of Deiniol Rd.
(☎ (01492) 585 151. Ticket office open daily 5:30am-6:30pm; off season
11:30am-6:30pm.) **Trains** (☎ (08457) 484 950) arrive from: **Chester** (1hr.; 1-2 per
hr.); **Holyhead** (30min.; M-Sa 1-2 per hr., Su 10 per day); **Llandudno Junction**
(20min.; M-Sa 1-2 per hr., Su 10 per day). The **bus station** is on Garth Rd., downhill from the town clock. **Arriva Cymru** (☎ (08706) 082 608) bus #4 arrives from
Holyhead via **Llangefni** and **Llanfair P.G.** (1¼hr., M-Sa 2 per hr.), while on Sunday
#44 makes the trip; #53, 57, and 58 come from **Beaumaris** (30min.; M-Sa 2-3 per
hr., Su 8 per day). Arriva bus #5 and its cousins 5A, 5B, and 5X journey from
Caernarfon (25min.; M-Sa every 10-20min., Su every hr.); #5 and 5X continue
east to **Conwy** (40min.; M-Sa 2 per hr., Su every hr.). Transfer at **Caernarfon** for
the **Llŷn Peninsula,** including Pwllheli and Porthmadog. **TrawsCambria** bus #701
follows the coast all the way from **Cardiff** (7¾hr., 1 per day) and the other way
to **Holyhead** (1hr., 1 per day). **National Express** (☎ (08705) 808 080) buses come
from **London** (8½hr., 1 per day).

◼ ◼ ORIENTATION AND PRACTICAL INFORMATION. An age-old street plan
and roads that don't advertise their names might leave you scratching your
head. Bangor sprawls over hills, but its two main streets—**Deiniol Rd.** and **High
St.**—run parallel to each other, sandwiching the city. **Garth Rd.** starts from the
town clock on High St. and winds past the bus station, merging with Deiniol
Rd. **Holyhead Rd.** begins its ascent at the train station. The **University of Wales at
Bangor** straddles both sides of **College Rd.,** a right off Holyhead Rd. as it
approaches the summit.

The **tourist information centre,** Town Hall, on Deiniol Rd., near the bus station,
provides a free booklet with an essential town map and books rooms for £1 and
a 10% deposit. (☎ 352 786. Open Easter-Sept. daily 10am-1pm and 2-6pm; Oct.-
Easter F-Sa 10am-1pm and 2-6pm.) Get **camping supplies** at **The Great Arete,** 307
High St. (☎ 352 710. Open M-Sa 9am-5:30pm.) Other services include: **HSBC bank,**
274 High St. (☎ (08457) 404 404; open M-F 9:30am-5pm, Sa 9am-12:30pm); the
police, Garth Rd., across from the bus station (☎ 370 333); the **hospital** (☎ 384
384); **Internet access** at the **YHA hostel** and **Java Cafe** (see below), and at the **library**
across from the TIC (open M and Th-F 10am-7pm, Tu 10am-5pm, W 10am-1pm,
Su 9:30am-1pm); and the **post office,** 60 Deiniol Rd., with a **bureau de change**
(☎ 373 329; open M-F 9am-5:30pm, Sa 9am-12:30pm). **Post Code:** LL57 1AA.

⌐⌐ ACCOMMODATIONS AND FOOD. Finding a room in Bangor during
ation hoopla (the second week of July) is a nightmarish prospect. Book m
ahead. The **YHA Bangor ❷**, Tan-y-Bryn, is ½ mi. from the town center. Follow H
St. to the water and turn right onto the A5122 (Beach Rd.), then right at the sig
Bus #5 (to Llandudno; 2 per hr.) passes the hostel; ask to be dropped off. The rich
wood paneling of the entrance hall and wide-beam ceilings betray its former role
as country estate. Vivien Leigh and Sir Laurence Olivier stayed in what is now
Room 6. (☎353 516. Meals, foosball, and laundry facilities. Internet access £1 per
20min. Open Apr.-Sept. daily; Oct. and Mar. Tu-Sa; Nov. and Jan.-Feb. F-Sa. Dorms
£11.25, under 18 £8.) Quality **B&Bs** are scarce in Bangor; the most agreeable
occupy the Victorian townhouses on **Garth Rd.** and its extensions. **Mrs. S. Roberts
❷**, 32 Glynne Rd., between Garth Rd. and High St., has TVs and 13 choices for
breakfast, including omelettes. (☎352 113. £15 per person.) At **Dilfam ❷**, 10min.
from the TIC down Garth Rd., most rooms are ensuite and all have TVs. (☎353 030.
Singles £18.50; doubles £40.) **Dinas Farm ❶**, on the banks of the River Ogwan,
offers camping. Follow the A5 past Penrhyn Castle and then turn left off the
A5122. (☎364 227. Open Easter-Oct. £3 per person. Electricity £2.)

High St. holds an array of fruit shops and cafes, as well as a **Kwik Save** supermarket toward the water. (Open M-Sa 8am-10pm, Su 10am-4pm.) **Java Cafe ❷**, above a
clothing store of the same name on High St., has plush couches and an international menu. Try a Mexican fajita (£5.75) or delicious pasta (£5) while surfing the
web for £1 per 15min. (☎301 612. Open M-Tu 10am-6pm, W-Sa 10am-10pm.) **Penguin Cafe ❶**, 260 High St., is perfect for munching sandwiches (£2.35-2.95) and people-watching. (☎361 652. Open M-Sa 7am-5:30pm.)

◙ ⫇ SIGHTS AND ENTERTAINMENT. George Hay Dawkins-Pennant's 19th-
century neo-Norman mansion, **Penrhyn Castle**, squats over two acres just outside
Bangor. Walk up High St. toward the bay, then turn right on the A5122 and go
north 1 mi., or catch bus #5 or 5X from town to the grounds entrance (10min.; M-
Sa 2 per hr., Su every hr.); the castle is another mile. Ivy-covered towers guard a
40-acre estate, testament to the staggering wealth of the owners of Gwynedd's
slate quarries. The interior opulence makes Versailles seem understated—the
intricately carved stone staircase took ten years to complete. Ask about Queen
Victoria's eventful stay. (☎353 084 or 363 200. Open July-Aug. W-M grounds 10am-
5:30pm, castle 11am-4:30pm; late Mar. to June and Sept.-Oct. W-M grounds 11am-
5pm, castle noon-4:30pm. Castle and grounds £6, children £3. Grounds only £4/£2.)

Humble and steepleless, **St. Deiniol's Cathedral**, on Gwynedd Rd. off High St., has
been the ecclesiastical center of this corner of Wales for 1400 years; its Bible Garden cultivates plants mentioned in the Good Book. (☎353 983 or 370 693. Open M-
F 8am-6pm, Sa 8am-1pm, Su 7:30am-6pm.) The **Bangor Museum and Art Gallery**, also
on Gwynedd Rd., houses an authentic **man-trap**, used as an anti-poaching device
(but there's no reason it couldn't be more widely applied). (☎353 368. Open Tu-F
12:30-4:30pm, Sa 10:30am-4:30pm. Free.) Watch tides ebb and flow at the long,
onion-domed Victorian **pier** at the end of Garth Rd.; desserts at its tea shop are as
little as 40p. (Tea shop open M-F 8:30am-6pm, Sa-Su 10am-6pm.)

The modern **Theatr Gwynedd**, on Deiniol Rd. at the base of the hill, houses a thriving
troupe that performs in Welsh and English. (☎351 708. Box office open M-F 9:30am-
5pm, Sa 10am-5pm; on performance days M-F 9:30am-8pm, Sa 10am-8pm, Su 6-8pm.
Films £4.30, concessions £3.30, children £2; plays £6-18.) Bangor's students propel
lively clubs, and many pubs along High St. pump up the volume on weekends. Buy
your happiness at **Bliss**, on Dean St. off High St., where Wednesday is student night and
Friday offers cheap drinks. (☎354 977. Smart dress. Cover £3-5. Open W and F-Sa 8pm-
1am.) At **Joop's Night Club**, farther down High St., enjoy a smaller dance-floor and
ample bar without the cover. (☎372 040. Open Th-Sa 8pm-1am, doors close 11pm.)

ANGLESEY (YNYS MÔN)

…nd Wales by the Menai and Britannia Bridges, the flat, green …asts sharply with the tall gray peaks and hills to the south-…ame, Mona mam Cymru (Mona the mother of Wales), hints …eeply in its Celtic past, visible to tourists at ancient rural druidic sites.

⌐PORTATION

Anglesey is difficult to explore properly without a car. The motorless will find, however, that **Bangor**, on the mainland, is the best hub for the island. **Trains** (☎ (08457) 484 950) run on the North Wales line to **Holyhead** from Bangor (45min., 1-2 per hr., from £5); some stop at **Llanfair P.G.** The main **bus** company is **Arriva Cymru** (☎ (08706) 082 608), which spins a web of buses over most of the island; a handful of smaller bus companies fill the gaps. Arriva bus #4 travels north from Bangor to **Holyhead** via **Llanfair P.G.** and **Llangefni** (1¼hr., M-Sa 2 per hr.); on Sundays #44 follows a similar route (1½hr., 6 per day). Buses #53, 57, and 58 hug the southeast coast from Bangor to **Beaumaris** (30min.; M-Sa 2 per hr., Su 8 per day), and some continue to **Penmon** (30-45min.; M-Sa 12 per day, Su 4 per day). Bus #62 journeys to **Amlwch,** on the northern coast, from Bangor (50min.; M-Sa 1-2 per hr., Su 5 per day; £1.75). Bus #42 from Bangor curves along the southwest coast up to **Aberffraw** before continuing north to **Llangefni** (1hr., M-Sa 9 per day); on Sundays, **Aberffraw** is the end of the line (50min., 2 per day). **Lewis y Llan** (☎ (01407) 832 181) bus #61 cruises from **Amlwch** into **Holyhead** (50min.; M-Sa 8 per day, Su 4 per day). **Lewis** #32 shuttles north from **Llangefni** to **Amlwch** (40min.; M-Sa 8 per day, Su 4 per day). The Gwynedd **Red Rover ticket** (£4.80, children £2.40) covers a day's bus travel in Anglesey, as well as Gwynedd, including Bangor. Pick up the map-filled *Isle of Anglesey Public Transport Guide*, free at TICs.

◎ SIGHTS

People have fancied Anglesey since prehistory. Burial chambers, cairns, and other remains are scattered on Holyhead and both the eastern and western coasts. Most ancient monuments sit quietly in farmers' fields, so a map detailing exactly how to reach them is helpful. TICs sell Ordnance Survey Landranger Map #114 (1:50,000; £6) and the more detailed Explorer Maps #262 and 263, each of which cover one half of the island (1:25,000; £7). The eight brochures of the *Circular Walks on the Island of Anglesey* are useful for walkers, while the pamphlet *Rural Cycling on Anglesey* is a must for bikers (both free at TICs).

▨BRYN CELLI DDU. Bryn Celli Ddu (bryn kay-HLEE thee, "The Mound in the Dark Grove") is a burial chamber dating from the late Neolithic period and the most famous of Anglesey's remains. From the outside, this 4000-year-old construction looks like any old mound of earth in the middle of a sheep pasture, but a flashlight (bring your own) helps illuminate the etchings on the walls inside. *(Bangor-Holyhead bus #4 sometimes stops at Llandaniel (M-Sa 9 per day); walk 1 mi. from there. Bus #42 to Plas Newydd also comes within 1 mi. of Bryn. Free.)*

PLAS NEWYDD. The 19th-century country home of the Marquess of Anglesey, 2 mi. south of Llanfair P.G., is now run by the National Trust. The 58 ft. Rex Whistler painting that covers an inside room is impressive, but admission is expensive. *(Take bus #42 from Bangor to the house (15min.; M-Sa 11 per day, Su 2 per day), or catch #4 to Llanfair P.G. (15min., M-Sa 2 per hr.) and walk. ☎ (01248) 714 795. House open Apr.-Oct. Sa-W noon-5pm. Garden open 11am-5:30pm. £4.70, children £2.40. Garden only £2.80/£1.40.)*

NORTH WALES

PENMON PRIORY. The late medieval priory of Penmon is the most readisible of Anglesey's sights. The simple church dates to the 11th century ansesses two elaborately carved cross stands, as well as Europe's largest dove(a set of shoebox-sized nesting holes). From the parking lot, a short train leads6th-century St. Seiriol's Well, reputed to have healing qualities. *(Some buses rudirectly to the Priory; check timetables. Otherwise, take Arriva Cymru bus #57 or 58 from Beau-maris to Penmon (10-20min.; M-Sa 11 per day, Su 4 per day) and follow the sign to Penmon Point; the priory is an additional 25min. walk on the same road.)*

LLANALLGO. Three sets of remains cluster near the town of Llanallgo, but getting to them requires a bit of effort. Follow the minor road (to the left of the Moelfre road) to the ancient **Ligwy Burial Chamber.** Between 15 and 30 people are entombed in this squat enclosure, covered with a 25-ton capstone. Farther on stand the 12th-century chapel **Hen Capel Ligwy** and the remains of the Roman **Din Ligwy Hut Group.** *(Arriva bus #62 hits Llanallgo on its Bangor-Cemaes route (35min.; M-Sa 1-2 per hr., Su 5 per day). Ask the driver to stop at the roundabout heading to Moelfre.)*

LLANFAIRPWLL...

Llanfairpwllgwyngyllgogerychwyrndrobwillllantysiliogogogoch (HLAN-vire-poohl-gwin-gihl—ah, never mind), the longest-named village in the world, is linked to Bangor by the Britannia Bridge. Devised by a 19th-century humorist to attract attention, the name translates roughly as "Saint Mary's Church in the hollow of white hazel near the rapid whirlpool and the Church of Saint Tysillio near the red cave" (or, alternatively, "we-couldn't-find-a-compelling-reason-to-get-you-to-come-here-so-we-just-created-a-ridiculous-name"). Sensibly, the town's war memorial reads **"Llanfair P.G."** so as not to overwhelm the roll call of the dead. The town (pop. 2472) is also known locally as "Llanfairpwll." **James Pringle Woollens Factory,** beside the train station, is mobbed by tourists taking snapshots of the town's emblazoned name. The store houses one of Anglesey's two **tourist information centres.** (☎(01248) 713 177; fax 715 711. Open Apr.-Oct. M-Sa 9:30am-5:30pm, Su 10am-5pm; Nov.-Mar. M-F 9:30am-1pm and 1:30-5pm, Su 10am-5pm.)

BEAUMARIS   ☎01248

Four miles northeast of the Menai Bridge on the A545, the main street of Beaumaris runs quietly along the yacht-dotted harbor. In town, savor the magnificent (albeit unfinished) symmetry of **Beaumaris Castle,** the last of Edward I's Welsh fortresses and now a World Heritage site. Begun in 1295 and built on a marsh, the castle's concentric design renders it virtually impregnable. (☎810 361. Open June-Sept. daily 9:30am-6pm; Apr.-May and Oct. 9:30am-5pm; Nov.-Mar. M-Sa 9:30am-4pm, Su 11am-4pm. £3, concessions £2.50, families £8.50.)

On Bunkers Hill, off Steeple Ln., the cells of **Beaumaris Gaol,** formerly Anglesey's only prison, show what it was like to be incarcerated in Victorian times. Out-of-line inmates faced time on the treadwheel, solitary confinement, or execution at the courtyard gallows. (☎810 921. Open Easter-Sept. daily 10:30am-5pm. Last admission 4:30pm. £2.75, concessions £1.75, families £7.) Leave the kids in lockup and have yourself some fun at the **Museum of Childhood Memories,** 1 Castle St., where legions of tin wind-ups, round-eyed dolls, and pea-shooting piggy banks sing the silly song of nostalgia. Bring 10p coins to try your hand at Depression-era arcade games. (☎712 498. Open Easter-Oct. M-Sa 10:30am-5:30pm, Su noon-5pm; Nov.-Easter Sa-Su 10:30am-5pm. Last admission 45min. before close. £3.25, concessions £2.75, children £2, families £9.50.) *Let's Go,* of course, does not recommend locking children up in old gaols. (They might escape.) Win back their affection with a **catamaran cruise** down the Menai Strait and around **Puffin Island.** Cruises leave from the Starida booth on the pier. (☎810 379; before 10:30am or after 5pm 810 251. Cruises 1¼hr. £4, seniors £3.50, children £3.)

...s careened perilously along the edge of a Welsh cliff. The driver whistled and floored the accelerator, turning onto a twisting one-lane road. I gripped my seat, braced my feet, and looked up. A large brown cow blocked the lane ahead.

It blinked. The bus stopped short.

"Moo," said the cow.

"Ooogh," I said.

"Well, now," said the driver.

Languid brown eyes looked curiously into the bus before the cow went back to munching a bit of clover next to the left front tire. The driver took out a magazine. "Looks like we're a'goin' t' be 'ere for awhile," he said happily, propping his feet up.

We arrived an hour and fifteen minutes late. As Welsh buses go, that's pretty good—sometimes they don't show up at all. I had begun arriving at the stops ten minutes ahead of time, in case my bus was early, or, more often, in the hope that I might catch the previous bus, 50 minutes late. I discovered that a day pass or return ticket is always cheaper than a single, something none of the drivers had told me. I worked a bit harder at faking a Welsh accent. (Disastrous. Don't try it.)

Another ride found me sharing the bus with an entire rugby team, twenty 13-year-olds (there are no separate school buses), two elderly women with five shopping bags apiece, and a very large, very wet sheepdog

Buses stop on Castle St. The **tourist information centre,** Town Hall, on Castle St., provides a free town map and information on accommodations. (☎810 040. Open Easter-Oct. daily 10am-5:30pm.) The **HSBC bank** is also on Castle St. (Open M-F 11am-2pm.) The **post office** is at 10 Church St. (Open M-Tu and Th-F 9am-5:30pm, W and Sa 9am-12:30pm.) **Post Code:** LL58 8AB.

The closest hostel is the **YHA Bangor** (see p. 520). Beaumaris itself appeals little as a place to stay. None of the town's few B&Bs offer singles, and doubles cost around £30; consider sleeping across the strait in Bangor or Caernarfon. Camping is best at **Kingsbridge Caravan Park ❶,** 1½ mi. from town, toward Llangoed. At the end of Beaumaris's main street, follow the coastal road past the castle to the crossroads. Turn left toward Llanfaes; Kingsbridge is 400 yd. on the right. Arriva #57 and 58, running from Bangor through Beaumaris to Glanrafon, stop nearby if you ask. (☎490 636. Open Mar.-Oct. £4 per adult, £2 per child. Electricity £2. Showers free.) Gratify gluttony at **Spar,** 11 Castle St. (Open M-Su 8am-11pm.) Tea shops cluster around the castle; **Sarah's Delicatessen ❶,** 11 Church St., sells delicious gourmet fixings for under £3. (☎811 534. Open M-Tu and Th-Sa 9am-5pm, W 11am-5pm.)

HOLYHEAD (CAERGYBI)   ☎01407

An unattractive town attached to Anglesey by a causeway and a bridge, Holyhead is primarily known as a port for Ireland. **Irish Ferries** and **Stena Sealink** operate ferries and catamarans to **Dublin** and its suburb, **Dún Laoghaire.** Foot passengers check in at the terminal adjoining the train station; cars proceed along the asphalt beside the terminal. Arrive 30min. early and remember your passport. (See **By Ferry,** p. 40.)

In town, the **Maritime Museum,** Beach Rd., occupies the oldest lifeboat house in Wales, and details Holyhead's nautical history. (☎769 745. Open Apr.-Oct. Tu-Su 1-5pm. £2, seniors £1.50, children 50p, families £5.) **St. Gybi's Church,** in the center of town between Stanley St. and Victoria Rd., has lovely stained-glass windows. The **Caer Gybi** that surround the church date to Roman times. (☎763 001. Open May-Sept. daily 11am-3pm; call in winter. Free.) If you have time, explore the many paths of **Holyhead Mountain** near town. Its North and South Stacks are good for bird-watching, and the lighthouse looks longingly to sea. **Caer y Tŵr** and **Holyhead Mountain Hut Group** sit at the mountain's base. The former is an Iron Age hillfort, the latter a settlement inhabited from 500 BC until Roman times.

Reach Holyhead every hour by **train** from: **Bangor** (30min.); **Chester** (1½hr.); **London** (4½-6hr.). **Arriva Cymru bus** (☎(08706) 082 608) #4 comes from **Bangor** via **Llanfair P.G.** and **Llangefni** (1¼hr., M-Sa 2 per hr.); on Sundays #44 journeys from **Bangor,** sometimes stopping in **Ysbyty Gwynedd** (1¼hr., 8 per day). **National Express** (☎(08705) 808 080) hits Holyhead from major cities. **TrawsCambria** #701 arrives from **Cardiff** (9hr., 1 per day). For a **taxi,** call ☎765 000. The **tourist information centre,** in Terminal One of the train and ferry station, books boats and beds for £1 and a 10% deposit. (☎762 622. Open M-Su 8:30am-6pm.) Other services include: **HSBC bank,** on the corner of William St. and Market St. (open M-F 9am-5pm); the **police** (☎762 323); and the **post office,** 13a Stryd Boston, off Market St., with a **bureau de change** (open M-F 9am-5:30pm, Sa 9am-12:30pm). **Post Code:** LL65 1BP.

Holyhead **B&Bs** are accommodating to passengers at the mercy of boat schedules. Owners may arrange to greet you at unusual times if you call ahead, and "B&B" here often becomes B&PL (beds and packed lunches) for ferry riders. To get to **Orotovia ❷,** 66 Walthew Ave., go up Thomas St., which becomes Porth-y-Felin Rd. as it passes the school, and turn right onto Walthew Ave. (not to be confused with Walthew St. or Walthew Ln.); if bogged down with bags, call for a ride from the station. The helpful proprietors enjoy long conversations with guests. (☎760 259. £17.50 per person.) If you fancy something, well, fancier, try beautiful **Hendre ❸,** Porth-y-Felin Rd., where the elegant rooms and warm reception are delightful before or after a long ferry ride. (☎762 929. From £25 per person.) A little way down the road, **Witchingham ❷,** 20 Walthew Ave., features a lovable miniature poodle. Call for a ride from the station at any reasonable hour. (☎762 426. Singles £19; doubles with bath £42.) **Roselea ❷,** 26 Holborn Rd., is the closest B&B to the station and ferries. (☎/fax 764 391. Singles £18; twins £32-34.) Good eats are scarce in Holyhead, but tasty baguettes (£2.05-2.55) and jacket potatoes (£2) await at the **Picnic Hamper ❶,** Market St. (☎762 318. Open M-Sa 8:30am-4:30pm.)

CONWY   ☎01492

With a 13th-century castle towering over narrow lanes and a pleasant quayside, Conwy bears its wearisome role as modern tourist mecca well. Edward I, who seemed never to tire of constructing the damn things, had the town's solemn castle built as another link in his chain of North Wales fortresses. It now stands guard over a fine city wall, elegant houses, and a gaggle of eclectic attractions.

Naturally, the bus was behind schedule. The rugby players huddled around the back seats. One spoke: "...and there were these twins, yeah, *twins,* and they just sidled up to me— I was at the bar, see..." The schoolboys strained to hear the conversation—one nearly fell over his seat.

"SIT DOWN, Owen!" scolded their teacher. A great ruckus erupted among the rugby players. "...didn't know that was possible! Bloody hell! Amazing!" "OWEEEEEEEEN—!" yelped his teacher, dragging him to the front of the bus. The sheepdog yowled.

"Cabbages for brains, they has," whispered one lady. Then, loudly, "I bet none of you are married!" The team muttered; some turned red.

"My dear, are you traveling *alone*?" she asked me. "Mm, yes," I replied. "Hear that, Enid, she's traveling *alone*!" "*Alone,*" her companion nodded vigorously. "You're a brave young lady," she continued, with a dirty look toward the back. "Hope you're not connecting, with the bus late like this, and you all alo—"

"Oh, I'm fine," I said quickly.

The bus stopped, children and rugby players spilling out the door. The elderly women politely (but rather firmly) took my arms. "You *will* join us for tea, won't you, m'love?"

Two hours later, I watched the sun dip behind the hills. *Lousy buses,* I thought, biting into another scone.

— Jenny Pegg

![] TRANSPORTATION

Trains (☎ (08457) 484 950) only stop at **Conwy Station,** off Rosehill St., by request, though it lies on the North Wales line linking Holyhead to Chester. Trains *do* stop at nearby **Llandudno Junction** station, one of the busiest in Wales, which connects to the scenic Conwy Valley line. (Booking office open M-Sa 5:30am-6:30pm, Su 11:30am-6:30pm.) Not to be confused with Llandudno proper (a resort town 1 mi. north; see p. 528), Llandudno Junction is a 20min. walk from Conwy. Turn left on a side road after exiting the station, pass a supermarket on the left, walk under a bridge, and climb the stairs to another bridge leading across the estuary to Conwy castle and town. If you lack the energy, nearly every bus route to Conwy stops at the Junction; the most frequent are #5 and 5X (3min.; M-Sa 2 per hr., Su every hr.).

    Buses are the best way to get directly to Conwy, with the two main stops at Lancaster Sq. and Castle St. before the corner of Rosehill St.; check posted schedules. **National Express** (☎ (08705) 808 080) comes from: **Liverpool** (2¾hr., 1 per day); **Manchester** (4hr., 1 per day); **Newcastle** (10hr., 1 per day). **Arriva Cymru** (☎ (08706) 082 608) #5 and 5X stop in Conwy as they climb the northern coast from **Caernarfon** via **Bangor** toward **Llandudno** (1-1½hr.; M-Sa 2 per hr., Su every hr.). Bus #19 takes in Conwy on its **Llandudno-Llanrwst** journey down the Vale of Conwy (20min.; M-Sa 1-2 per hr., Su 8 per day). The comprehensive *Conwy Public Transport Information* booklet is available free at the TIC.

![] ORIENTATION AND PRACTICAL INFORMATION

The town wall squeezes old Conwy into a roughly triangular shape. The castle lies in one corner; **Castle St.,** which becomes **Berry St.,** runs from the foot of the fortress parallel to the **Quay. High St.** stretches from the Quay's edge to **Lancaster Sq.,** from which **Rosehill St.** circles back to the castle. In the opposite direction, **Bangor Rd.** scrunches northward through a small arch in the wall.

    The **tourist information centre,** Castle Entrance, has street maps and books beds for £1 plus a 10% deposit. (☎592 248. Open Easter-Oct. daily 9:30am-6pm; Nov.-Mar. Th-Sa 10am-4pm.) **Conwy Outdoor Shop,** 9 Castle St., has an extensive, if expensive, selection of gear; with advance notice, they also **rent bikes** for £12.50 per day and tents from £7. (☎593 390. Open daily 9am-6pm.) Other services include: **Barclays,** 23 High St. (☎616 616; open M-F 10am-4pm); the **police,** Lancaster Sq. (☎511 000); **Internet access** at the **library,** Civic Hall, Castle St. (☎596 242; £2.50 per 30min.; open M and Th-F 10am-5:30pm, Tu 10am-7pm, W and Sa 10am-1pm); and the **post office,** Lancaster Sq. at High St., in The Wine Shop (☎573 990; open M-Tu 8:30am-5:30pm, W-F 9am-5:30pm, Sa 9am-1:30pm). **Post Code:** LL32 8DA.

![] ACCOMMODATIONS AND CAMPING

    Bryn Guest House (☎592 449), below the town wall's highest point, amid roses. Big ensuite bedrooms and hearty breakfasts. Singles £23; doubles £40. ❸

    Swan Cottage, 18 Berry St. (☎596 840). One of few B&Bs within the town wall. Cozy rooms with timber ceilings and TVs. Loft room with estuary view. £18 per person. ❷

    YHA Conwy, Larkhill, Sychnant Pass Rd. (☎593 571). From Lancaster Sq., head down Bangor Rd. Turn left on Mt. Pleasant and right at the top of the hill; it's on the left (150 yd.). Self-catering kitchen, laundry, TV room, and lockers (£1). Internet £2.50 per

30min. Bike rental £7.50 per half-day, children £3.75; £12.50/£6.25 per day. Reception 8am-10:30pm. Open mid-Feb. to Dec. Dorms £13, under 18 £9.

Glan Heulog, Llanrwst Rd., Woodlands (☎593 845). Go under the arch near the Visitor Centre on Rosehill St., down the steps, and across the carpark. Turn right and walk 5min. down Llanrwst Rd. Huge house on a hill with TVs, ensuite rooms, and "healthy option" breakfasts. Proprietors allow use of their computer for Internet access, requesting a donation to the charity box. Singles £18-23; doubles and twins £36-44.

Camping: Conwy Touring Park, Llanrwst Rd. (☎592 856). Follow Llanrwst Rd. and posted signs a steep mile out of town. Open Easter-Sept. 2-person tent £4-11. Electricity £1.75-2.80.

🍴 FOOD

Most Conwy restaurants serve ordinary grub, but the name "High St.," along which many are found, might well be a reference to the inflated prices. Fear not, thrifty gourmands, for the ever-reliable **Spar** defends its territory next to Barclays. (Open daily 8am-10pm.) A weekly **market** fills the train station parking lot. (Open summer Tu 8:30am-5pm.) Fine vegetarian and vegan fare (£4-10) awaits at **The Wall Place ❷,** on Chapel St. off Berry St., where traditional Welsh music wafts across the wood floor; on winter afternoons, the cafe hosts creative workshops. (☎596 326. Open Easter to mid-Sept. daily noon-3pm and 6-10pm; mid-Sept. to Easter varies. Music and buffets some Sa.) Put together a top-notch picnic at **Edward's Hot Carvery ❶,** 18 High St., where the variety (from meats to salads to spreads) and quality are superb. (☎592 443. Open M-Sa 7am-5:30pm.) Each evening, the elegant interior of the award-winning **Shakespeare Restaurant ❹,** High St., lights up with romantic tables and laughing dinner parties. (☎582 800. Open daily 7pm-9:30pm.) For light meals (£3.25-5) and sandwiches (from £2), try popular **Pantri Conwy ❶,** Lancaster Sq. (☎592 436. Open Easter-Oct. daily 9am-5pm; Nov.-Easter 9am-4pm.)

👁 SIGHTS

▧ CONWY CASTLE. More compact than Edward I's colossal fortresses at Caernarfon and Beaumaris, Conwy Castle's menacing design was still challenge enough for would-be attackers. The prison tower saw many prominent Normans rot beneath its false bottom, and Richard II was betrayed and deposed in the castle chapel in 1399. Two years later, Welsh rebel Owain Glyndŵr and his band of armed nationalists seized the ramparts. (☎592 358. Open June-Sept. daily 9:30am-6pm; Apr.-May and Oct. 9:30am-5pm; Nov.-Mar. M-Sa 9:30am-4pm, Su 11am-4pm. Last admission 30min. before close. Tours £1. £3.50, concessions £3, families £10.)

PLAS MAWR. Perhaps the best-preserved Elizabethan house in Britain, this 16th-century mansion has been lovingly restored to recall its days as home of merchant Robert Wynn. Climb the watchtower and open one of the small windows for terrific views over the city or stroll the courtyard below. The entrance price includes a free 1hr. audio tour. (☎580 167. Open June-Aug. daily 9:30am-6pm; Apr.-May and Sept. Tu-Su 9:30am-6pm; Oct.Tu-Su 9:30am-4pm. £4.50, concessions £3.50, families £12.50.)

THE SMALLEST HOUSE. Bang your head into what's billed as Britain's smallest house, another of Conwy's oddities. With a frontage of 6 ft., the 380-year-old two-floor edifice housed an elderly couple and then one 6 ft. 3 in. fisherman before it was condemned in 1900. (Head down High St. and onto the Quay. ☎593 484. Open Aug. daily 10am-9pm; Easter-July and Sept.-Oct. 10am-6pm. 50p, concessions 30p.)

TELFORD SUSPENSION BRIDGE. Next to an unsightly rail bridge, Telford's elegant 1826 suspension bridge stretches across the Conwy River from the foot of the castle's grassy east barbican; at the opposite end stands the tollmaster's house, restored as a mini-museum. Both bridge and castle can be seen by boat; vigorous bellowing heralds the departure of the **Queen Victoria** from the quay at the end of High St. *(☎573 282. Bridge and house open July-Aug. daily 10am-5pm; Apr.-June and Sept.-Oct. W-M 10am-5pm. Last admission 4:30pm. £1, children 50p. 30min. cruises £3/£2.)*

TOWN WALL. Almost a mile long, the wall was built at the same time as the castle and shielded burghers with its 22 towers and 480 arrow slits—the 12 latrine chutes may have been useful, too. Climb the Mt. Pleasant side for magnificent views.

TEAPOT MUSEUM. "You'd have to be potty to miss it," proclaims the sign under which two grand British traditions—tea and eccentricity—meet. The one-room museum displays 300 years of teapots—some short, some stout, and some shaped like a craggy Lloyd George, a dour Thatcher, and a roomy Pavarotti. Don't knock over the Humpty Dumpty pot; the nearest savior is the King of Rock 'n' Roll, who warns that only fools rush in this packed little room. Glimpses of *risqué* teapots reward the observant. *(Castle St. ☎593 429. Open Easter-Oct. M-Sa 10am-5:30pm, Su 11am-5:30pm. £1.50, concessions £1, families £3.50. 10% discount for YHA members.)*

OTHER SIGHTS AND ENTERTAINMENT. 14th-century **Aberconwy House,** Conwy's oldest house, served as a sea captain's home and a temperance center, and is now a National Trust sight. *(Castle St. ☎592 246. Open Apr.-Oct. W-M 11am-5pm. £2, children £1, families £5.)* Most of Conwy's tranquility has migrated to **St. Mary's Church,** where the grave that inspired Wordsworth's "We are Seven" lies outside the South Porch. In July, the **North Wales Bluegrass Festival** brings Appalachia to Conwy.

LLANDUDNO ☎01492

Llandudno (hlan-DID-no) consists primarily of two things: touristy stores and Victorian-era guesthouses, in a symbiotic relationship that would make any biologist proud. While dodging postcard racks, cars, and unfriendly dogs can tax the nerves, there are interesting things to see and do, particularly on and about the Great Orme.

⌷ TRANSPORTATION. Llandudno is the northern terminus of several lines of transport. The **train station** is at the end of Augusta Rd. (Ticket office open M-Sa 8:40am-3:30pm, July-Aug. also Su 10:15am-5:45pm.) Trains (☎(08457) 484 950) arrive on the single-track Conwy Valley line from **Blaenau Ffestiniog** via **Betws-y-Coed** (1hr.; M-Sa 5 per day, Su 2 per day). On the North Wales line, trains enter **Llandudno Junction,** 1 mi. south of town, from **Bangor** (20min., 1-3 per hr.); **Chester** (1hr., 1-4 per hr.); **Holyhead** (50min., 18 per day). **National Express buses** (☎(08705) 808 080) hit Mostyn Broadway once per day from: **Chester** (1¾hr.); **London** (8hr.); **Manchester** (4hr.). **Arriva Cymru** (☎(08706) 082 608) #5, 5A, and 5X come from **Bangor** (1hr.); **Caernarfon** (1½hr.); **Conwy** (20min.; M-Sa 2-3 per hr., Su every hr.). Bus #19 arrives from **Llanrwst** in the Vale of Conwy (1hr.; M-Sa 1-2 per hr., Su 7 per day). Bus #96, the Snowdon Sherpa, travels from **Betws-y-Coed** (50min., Sa 2-3 per day); #70 makes the same trip (1½hr., Sa 2 per day). Call **Kings Cabs** (☎878 156) for a **taxi.** Rent **bikes** from **West End Cycles,** 22 Augusta Rd., near the train station. (☎876 891. £10 per day. £25 deposit. Open M-Sa 9am-5:30pm.)

◼⌷ ORIENTATION AND PRACTICAL INFORMATION. Llandudno is flanked by two pleasant **beaches;** the West Shore is less built up than the North, which is decorated with Victorian promenades and tipped by a long pier. A left on Augusta St. as you exit the train station leads to the **tourist information centre,** Chapel St., which houses a library of free pamphlets and books rooms for £1 and a 10% deposit. (☎876 413. Open Easter-Oct. daily 9:30am-5:30pm; Nov.-Easter M-Sa.) Other services include: **Barclays,** on the corner of Mostyn St. and Market St. (open M-Tu and Th-F 9:30am-4:30pm, W 10am-4:30pm, Sa 10am-12:30pm); the **police,** Oxford Rd. (☎517 171); the **General Hospital** (☎860 066), near the Maesdu Golf Course on the West Shore; **Internet access** at the **library,** Mostyn St. (☎574 020; £2 per 30min.; open M-Tu and F 9am-6pm, W 10am-5pm, Th 9am-7pm, Sa 9:30am-1pm); and the **post office,** 14 Vaughn St., with a **bureau de change** (☎(0345) 223 344; open M-F 9am-5:30pm, Sa 9am-12:30pm). **Post Code:** LL30 1AA.

⌨🖰 ACCOMMODATIONS AND FOOD. Designed for visitors, Llandudno overflows with B&Bs, guest houses, and cheap hotels. Budget travelers should seek out B&Bs (£12-15) on **Chapel St., Deganwy Ave.,** and **St. David's Rd.** Conveniently located next to the TIC, **Walsall House ❷,** 4 Chapel St., has rooms with TVs. (☎875 279. £15.50-17 per person, £12.50-14 without breakfast.) The **Empire Hotel ❹,** Church Walks, offers elegance for those looking to do Llandudno in style. (☎860 555; fax 860 791. Singles from £50; doubles from £85.) The popular **YHA Conwy** (see p. 526) is only 20min. away by bus (#5, 5A, and 5X; M-Sa 3 per hr., Su every hr.). Eateries accommodate all appetites. **The Fat Cat Cafe-Bar ❶,** 149 Mostyn St., with a varied menu in a funky academic atmosphere, is one of the most fun eateries in town. Nachos are £3.55, veggie burritos with wild rice £5.85, and steak wraps under £5. (☎871 844. Open M-Sa 10am-11pm, Su 10am-10:30pm. Food served 10am-10pm.) At **The Cambridge ❷,** Mostyn St., look down on the world from your stained-glass lamp-lit table. Most meals cost £5-8.50. (Open M-Sa 10:30am-9pm.) **Habit ❷,** 12 Mostyn St., has an extensive, well-priced menu, with main courses from £4 to £6. (☎875 043. Open daily 9:30am-5:30pm.) **The Cottage Loaf ❶,** down Market St., off Mostyn St. next to Barclays, maintains a village pub atmosphere with a blooming beer garden, and serves up really good grub. (☎870 762. Open M-Sa 11am-11pm, Su noon-10:30pm; food served 11am-8pm.)

◩ SIGHTS. Llandudno's pleasant beaches, the Victorian **North Shore** and the quieter **West Shore,** are both outdone by the looming **Great Orme.** At the 679 ft. summit, wildflowers run amok amid prehistoric remains and a modern visitors center, accessible by foot; the **Great Orme Tramway** departs from Church Walks. (☎876 749. 20min. to summit, around 3 per hr. Runs Apr.-Oct. 10am-6pm. £3, children £2.20; return £4/£2.80.) The two counter-balanced cable cars also stop halfway up at the fantastic **Bronze Age Copper Mines.** Strap on a helmet and bang it against low ceilings as you step through tunnels dug 3500 years ago. The silence of the inner cavern is broken only by dripping water and the occasional hyperactive child. (☎870 447. Open Feb.-Oct. 10am-5pm. £4.50, children £3, families £12.50. Joint tram ticket £7.60/£5.20/£24.) Winter or summer, don't miss the chance to speed down a Welsh mountain in your own luge-like toboggan at **Ski Llandudno.** (☎874 707. Open daily 10am-7:30pm, depending on weather. £3 for 2 runs.) Alice Liddell, muse to Lewis Carroll, spent her childhood summers in Llandudno. Kids might get a kick out of the **Rabbit Hole** at the Alice in Wonderland Centre, 3-4 Trinity Sq., a campy recreation of Wonderland. (☎/fax 860 062. Open M-Sa 10am-5pm, Easter-Oct. also Su 10am-4pm. £2.95, seniors £2.75, children £2.50.)

◪🖰 NIGHTLIFE AND ENTERTAINMENT. Llandudno's two clubs are both a 10min. walk from the town center. **Broadway Boulevard,** Mostyn Broadway, is a versatile venue down Mostyn St. The 70s and 80s groove on Wednesday, Friday is dance, and Saturday a mix. (☎879 614. No trainers. Cover £3-6. W open 9pm-2am, F-Sa 9:30pm-2am. Last admission midnight.) A bit farther down Mostyn Broadway

NORTH WALES

and left on Clarence Rd. is **Washington,** a complex with two venues, **Capital** on the first floor and **Buzz Club** on the second. Capital is lined with portraits of U.S. presidents and caters to an older set; Buzz is a more traditional dance club. (☎877 974. No trainers. Cover £2-3. Capital open W-Sa 7pm-midnight. Buzz open F-Sa 7pm-1am.) **North Wales Theatre,** sandwiched between Mostyn Blvd. and the Promenade, hosts plays and concerts. (☎872 000. Schedules at the TIC. Box office open M-Sa 9:30am-8:30pm, Su 3hr. before performance. Tickets £5-50, concessions available.)

VALE OF CONWY

Watered by river and rain, the lush Vale of Conwy surprises visitors with mossy glens, hidden paths, and chance encounters with wildlife. Hills slope from the foot of Snowdonia's mountains to the tidal Conwy River, and in the thick woods around Betws-y-Coed, tributaries converge to meander north to Llandudno. Cyclists take advantage of the scenic terrain: views are glorious and gear-changes infrequent. Pick up the excellent *Walks from the Conwy Valley Line* at local TICs and train stations for details on the area's splendid hiking opportunities.

▐ TRANSPORTATION

The single-track, 27 mi. **Conwy Valley** line (☎(08457) 484 950) offers unparalleled views. **Trains** hug the river banks between the seaside resort of **Llandudno** and the mountain town of **Blaenau Ffestiniog,** stopping at **Llandudno Junction** and **Betws-y-Coed** (1hr.; M-Sa 6 per day, Su 3 per day). The **North and Mid Wales Rover ticket** is good for nearly unlimited bus and train travel as far south as **Aberystwyth** (1-day £19.50, 3-day £29, 7-day £43). Most **buses** stop at Llanrwst, some also at Betws-y-Coed. The main bus along the Conwy River is **Arriva Cymru** (☎(08706) 082 608) #19, which winds from **Llandudno** and **Conwy** to **Llanrwst** (M-Sa 1-2 per hr., Su 7 per day). From Llanrwst, **Sherpa** #96 continues to **Pen-y-Pas** via Betws-y-Coed (8 per day), while #96A runs from **Betws-y-Coed** to **Llanberis** (50min.; M-Sa 4 per day, Su 7 per day). Bus #97A connects Betws-y-Coed with **Porthmadog** (1hr., 3 per day). Arriva's one-day **Explorer** pass allows unlimited travel on its buses (£5, children £3.50).

BETWS-Y-COED ☎01690

At the southern tip of the Vale of Conwy and the eastern edge of the Snowdonia mountains, the crowded but picturesque village of Betws-y-Coed (BET-oos uh COYD) is one of the few places where small town banter and kindnesses are still exchanged over counters and doorways. At the same time, Betws seethes with adventurism—*everyone* seems to be communing with the great outdoors. Coursing through town, the Conwy and Llugwy rivers crash over rocks and foamy rapids, while brooding pines darken the hills and lend the scene a distinctly Alpine air.

▐ **TRANSPORTATION. Trains** (☎(08457) 484 950) stop in Betws-y-Coed on the Conwy Valley line (see above). **Sherpa** bus #96, operated by Arriva Cymru, connects Betws-y-Coed with **Llanrwst** and **Llandudno,** stopping at most area hostels (M-Sa 4 per day); #96A arrives from **Llanberis** (40min.; direct 4 per day, others require transfer to bus #96 in Snowdon). Arriva bus #70 runs from **Corwen** (2-3 per day, £2.15). Rent **bikes** from the laid-back cyclists at **Beics Betws,** beside the TIC. (☎710 829. £13 per half-day, £17 per day. Open daily 9am-5pm.)

▐▌ **ORIENTATION AND PRACTICAL INFORMATION.** The main (and only real) street is **Holyhead Rd.,** which is also the A5. It runs northwest from the River Conwy, past the park at the town center, and makes a sharp turn to run west out of town toward Swallow Falls. Possibly the busiest **tourist information centre** in North Wales (also a **Snowdonia National Park Information Centre**), the Betws TIC is at the Old Stables, next to a park between the train station and Holyhead Rd. A spirited staff provides timetables and information on sights. (☎ 710 426; www.betws-y-coed.co.uk. Open Easter-Oct. daily 10am-6pm; Nov.-Easter 9:30am-12:30pm and 1:30-4:30pm.) From April to September, **guided walks** around Betws leave from the TIC. (All walks 6-8 mi. and 5-6hr. Th-Su 9:55am. £3.50, children 50p.) A number of outdoor stores line Holyhead Rd. Two **Cotswold** outlets are among them, one next to the Royal Oak Hotel (☎ 710 710), with a wide selection of gear, the other south of town focusing on specific activities such as cycling and climbing. (☎ 710 234. Both open mid-July to Aug. Su-Th 9am-6pm, F-Sa 9am-7pm; Oct.-Apr. Su-Th 9am-5:30pm, F-Sa 9am-6:30pm.) Other services include: **HSBC bank** at the southern edge of Holyhead Rd. (open M 9:15am-2:30pm, Tu-F 9:15am-1pm); the caring officers at the Llanrwst **police** station (☎ (01492) 517 171, ext. 5362); and the **post office,** at the T-junction of Holyhead Rd. and Station Rd., which **exchanges currency** (open M-F 9am-1pm and 2-5:30pm, Sa 9am-7:30pm). **Post Code: LL24 0AA.**

⌐⌐ ACCOMMODATIONS AND FOOD. Two hostels rest conveniently near town: **YHA Lledr Valley** and **YHA Capel Curig** (see p. 516). Most **B&Bs** charge £17.50 or more and cluster along **Holyhead Rd.** For a comfy lounge and fine views of riverside lambs, head for **Glan Llugwy ❷,** on the western edge of town. Make the brief walk along Holyhead Rd. toward Swallow Falls, or call the kind owners for a lift. (☎ 710 592. £18-19.50 per person.) Lovely **Bryn Llewlyn ❸** is a non-smokers' B&B with large, impeccably clean rooms and pleasant hosts. (☎/fax 710 601. Singles £27; doubles £18-25 per person.) Just 2min. past Bryn toward Swallow Falls, take a look at **Pennant Crafts,** where beautiful handmade pottery sells for less than £10. (☎ 710 224. Open Easter-Nov. daily 9am-5:30pm.) **Riverside ❸,** Holyhead Rd., offers comfy beds, TVs, and old-fashioned flavor above a restaurant and gift shop—take a look at the gilt Patagonian jewelry. (☎/fax 710 650; riverside4u@talk21.com. Singles £20; doubles £38, with bath £42.) **Riverside Caravan Park ❶** suns itself by a cemetery behind the train station. (☎ 710 310. Open Mar.-Oct. Tents or caravans £5 per adult, £2.50 per child. Electricity £2.)

For a supermarket experience, head to **Spar** at the northern bend of Holyhead Rd. (☎ 710 324. Open daily 8am-10pm.) Most restaurants in Betws cater to tourists and are priced accordingly. Remarkably good food for remarkably reasonable prices is found at the wild-fruit-and-flower-painted tables of **Caban-y-Pair ❶,** Holyhead Rd. All day breakfast is £3.75; cakes are just £1. (☎ 710 505. Open June-Oct. M-F 9am-6:30pm, Sa-Su 8am-6:30pm; Nov.-May daily 10am-5pm.) A knight guards the door at **Three Gables ❷,** Holyhead Rd., where homemade pizza runs £4.60-6.80, and dinnertime brings plenty o' seafood from £8.75-10.50. (☎ 710 328. Open Easter-Oct. M-Su noon-9:30pm; Nov.-Easter F-Su noon-9:30pm.)

◙ SIGHTS. Betws is known for its eight **bridges,** especially Telford's 1815 cast-iron **Waterloo Bridge** at the village's southern end, built the year the battle ensured Napoleon's political demise. Rather boring from atop, the bridge offers better photo-ops from below. Near St. Michael's Church, the miniature **suspension footbridge,** which sways when trod upon, crosses the Conwy. **Pont-y-Pair Bridge,** "the bridge of the cauldron," crosses the Llugwy to the north. The first bridge was built in 1475; Inigo Jones may have contributed to building the second, which consists of 11 stone arches hopping from rock to rock. Behind the train station, weathered gravestones surround humble 14th-century **St. Michael's Church.**

Two miles west, signposted off the A5, the swift waters of the Llugwy crash over descending rock plateaus at **Swallow Falls.** (Always open. Turnstile-operated. £1.) Sherpa bus #96 between Betws and Snowdon stops at the falls, as do most #96A buses to Llanberis and #97A buses to Porthmadog (4min., 1-3 per hr.). Farther along the A5, "the Ugly House," **Tŷ Hyll,** is named for its unfinished facade. According to local legend, a house constructed in a day and a night (with smoke wafting out the chimney by morning) earned the builder the right to live there. (☎720 287. Open Apr.-Sept. daily 9:30am-5:30pm; winter hours vary. £1, children free.)

VALLEY VILLAGES AND SIGHTS   ☎01492

The Vale of Conwy is still largely untouched by coach-bound tourists, leaving walkers and cyclists free to explore its gorgeous scenery.

TREFRIW. To the south, Trefriw sleeps along the River Crafnant. Lake Crafnant, 3 mi. uphill from town (along the road opposite the Fairy Hotel), is surrounded by some of Snowdonia's highest peaks. North of town, 1½ mi. along the main road, a rust grotto spews the world's only fully licensed medicinal spring water at the **Trefriw Wells Spa.** Originally used to treat rheumatism and skin diseases, today the water eases iron deficiency. A month's supply goes for £6.50. (☎640 057. Open Easter-Oct. daily 9:30am-5:30pm; Nov.-Easter M-Sa 10am-dusk, Su noon-dusk. £3, seniors £2.75, children £2, under 8 free, families £8.50.)

To reach Trefriw, take Arriva **bus** #19 from Conwy, Llandudno, or Llandudno Junction (M-Sa 1-2 per hr., Su 7 per day). **B&Bs** (from £15) line Trefriw's long main street. The rustic **YHA Rowen ❶,** halfway between Trefriw and Conwy, is a superb place to rest your weary bones after the treacherous mile hike uphill from the road; the ascent begins ¼ mi. down from the bus stop, which is served by #70 (M-Sa 3-4 times per day) and sometimes #19. (☎650 089. Lockout 10am-5pm. Open May-Aug. Dorms £8.75, under 18 £6.)

LLANRWST. A useful transit town, Llanrwst has **banks** and a Tuesday **market.** Along the Conwy River, across the 1636 Old Bridge built by Inigo Jones, the 15th-century stone **Tu-Hwnt-i'r-Bont** hides a tearoom; check the timbers for multilingual graffiti. (Open Easter-Oct. Tu-Su 10:30am-5pm.) A 10min. walk past the tea house reaches **Gwydir Castle,** the 16th-century manor of Sir John Wynne. When the home was auctioned in 1921, American newspaper giant William Randolph Hearst acquired Lot 88: the wall panels, doorframe, fireplace, and leather frieze of Gwydir's dining room. In 1994, the castle's new owners traced the room to a storage box in a New York museum, re-purchased it, and unpacked Lot 88 to its former glory. Outside, the grounds shelter peacocks and a selflessly named yew tree. (☎641 687. Open Easter-Oct. daily 10am-4:30pm. £3, children £1.50.)

BODNANT GARDENS. At 80-acre Bodnant Gardens, 8 mi. south of Llandudno, the Chilean Fire Bush flirts shamelessly with eucrypheas and hydrangeas. The gardens host plays and other events on summer evenings. (☎650 460. Open mid-Mar. to Oct. daily 10am-5pm. Last admission 4:30pm. £5.20, children £2.60.) Take Arriva **bus** #25 from Llandudno (40min., M-Sa 10 per day) to the gates or the Conwy Valley train (M-Sa 6 per day, Su 3 per day) to the Tal-y-Cafn stop, 2 mi. away.

LLANGOLLEN   ☎01978

Set in a hollow in the hills near the English border, Llangollen (hlan-GO-hlen) hosts the annual International Musical Eisteddfod, which draws crowds every summer. Apart from this cultural extravaganza, all town attractions are natural. Walkers gently tread the surrounding hills on their way to Horseshoe Pass, and weekends bring whitewater canoeists slashing through neighboring streams and into the River Dee, which tumbles through town under a 14th-century bridge.

⚓⚐ TRANSPORTATION AND PRACTICAL INFORMATION. For a tourist town, Llangollen can be difficult to reach. **Trains** (☎ (08457) 484 950) come to **Wrexham,** 30min. away, from **Chester, Shrewsbury,** and **London.** A closer, though less well served, train station is **Ruabon,** from which B&B owners occasionally fetch weary backpackers. **National Express bus** (☎ (08705) 808 080) #420 comes to Wrexham from **London** (5½hr., 1 per day, £20). To get to Llangollen from Wrexham, take **Bryn Melyn** (☎ 860 701) bus X5 (30min., M-Sa 2 per hr., £2.20). On Sundays, **Arriva Midland** (☎ (01543) 466 124) runs a winding version of bus #5 (40min., 4 per day). Direct service to Llangollen is possible on some buses; **Arriva Cymru** (☎ (08706) 082 608) bus #94 comes from **Barmouth** (2½hr.; M-Sa 7 per day, Su 4 per day; £4.90) and **Dolgellau** (2hr.; M-Sa 8 per day, Su 4 per day; £3.30). Arriva Cymru's bus #70 runs twice a day from **Llanrwst** and **Betws-y-Coed** via **Corwen;** sometimes with a change in Corwen, where buses including the #94 connect to Llangollen (1hr., £2.20).

The **tourist information centre,** Town Hall, Castle St., and the Eisteddfod office (see below) list accommodations; the TIC books rooms for £1 and a 10% deposit. (☎ 860 828; fax 861 563; www.llangollen.org.uk. Open Easter-Oct. daily 10am-6pm; Nov.-Easter 9:30am-5pm.) **Horse-drawn boat trips** depart from Llangollen Wharf. (☎ 860 702. Apr.-Oct. 5-10 per day. £4, children £2.50.) Other services include: **Barclays,** opposite the TIC (open M-Tu and Th-F 10am-4pm, W 10:30am-4pm); **Blue Bay Launderette,** 3 Regent St. (wash £2, dry 20p per 5min.; open 9am-noon and 12:15-7pm, Th closes 6pm); free **Internet access** at the **library,** Parade St. off Castle St. (☎ 860 720; open M 10am-7pm, Tu 10am-5pm, W 10:30am-5pm, F 10:30am-5:30 pm, Sa 9:30am-12:30pm); and the **post office,** 41 Castle St., with a **bureau de change** (open M-F 9am-5:30pm, Sa 9am-12:30pm). **Post Code:** LL20 8RU.

⚐⚑ ACCOMMODATIONS AND FOOD. The **YHA Llangollen ❷,** Tyndwr Hall, Tyndwr Rd., is a Victorian manse 1½ mi. out of town. Follow the A5 toward Shrewsbury, bear right up Birch Hill, and after ½ mi. take a right at the Y-junction. (☎ 860 330. Internet access from £1 per 20min. Open mid-Feb. to Oct. Dorms £10.50, under 18 £7.25.) **B&Bs** (£15-20) are numerous, especially along **Regent St.** Just before Regent St., head up Hill St. to **Danika Guest House ❸** for pleasant rooms with TVs and baths, and a tasty breakfast. (☎ (07931) 855 646. £20 per person.) Near the town center, yet set back from the road, **Oakmere ❹** has clean, expansive rooms promising relaxing evenings. (☎ 861 126. Singles £38-45; doubles £25 per person.) **Campsites** abound; pick up fliers at the TIC, or try **Eirianfa Riverside Holiday Park ❶,** 1 mi. from town. Follow the A5 toward Corwen. (☎ 860 919. 1- or 2-person tent £6, family tent £10. Electricity £2. Laundry and showers.)

Spar, on Castle St., sells fruits, vegetables, and refreshments. (☎ 860 275. Open M-Sa 7am-11pm, Su 8am-10:30pm.) For the most transcendent macaroni and cheese experience of your life, go to the slightly pricey ▧**Corn Mill ❸,** Dee Ln., where the patio hangs low over the river and birds dip and preen on the rocks. If the main courses (£7-12.25) are too hefty, spend a few pounds on a pint and watch the waterwheel spinning frantically outside. (☎ 869 555. Open M-Sa noon-11pm, Su noon-10:30pm; food served noon-9pm.) At **Cafe and Books ❶,** 17 Castle St., thumb hundreds of used volumes upstairs and grab a meal downstairs; the all-day breakfast is £3.85. (☎ 861 963. Open Apr.-Sept. daily 9am-6pm; Oct.-May 9am-5pm.)

◪ SIGHTS. Up Hill St. from the town center, **Plas Newydd** is the former home of two noblewomen who fled Ireland in 1778. Charmed by the area, the "Ladies of Llangollen" settled into village life, dividing their time between self-improvement and the elaborate decoration of the house, evident in the carved-oak walls. As "two of the most celebrated virgins in Europe," their still-undefined relationship appealed to many intellectuals of the time. Wellington and Sir Walter Scott visited, as did Wordsworth, who penned a poem in their honor. (☎861 314. Open Easter-Oct. daily 10am-5pm. Last admission 4:15pm. £2.50, children £1.25, families £6.) Perched on a steep mount high above town are the lyrical ruins of ■**Castell Dinas Brân** (Crow Castle), perfect for picnickers. The panoramic drop-away view spans from the peaks of Snowdonia to the flat English Midlands. Two main paths lead to the castle: a 40min. gravel trail zig-zags directly up the side, while a 1hr. walk runs along a pastoral road and up the grassy hillside. Both are well-marked and steep, scoff at weak shoes, and begin just over the canal bridge, next to Dinbryn Rd. A 30min. amble from Llangollen along Abbey Rd., the ruins of 13th-century **Valle Crucis Abbey** grace a leafy valley. Its empty arches frame trees, sky, and an unfortunate cluster of caravans in the park next door. (☎860 326. Open Apr.-Sept. daily 10am-5pm; Oct.-Mar. 10am-4pm. £2, concessions £1.50, families £5.50; free in winter.)

■ **THE EISTEDDFOD.** Every summer, the town's population of 3,000 swells to 80,000 for the **International Musical Eisteddfod** (ice-TETH-vod), not to be confused with the roaming National Eisteddfod (see **Ffestivals,** p. 464). From July 8-13 in 2003, the hills will be alive with the singing and dancing of competitors from 50 countries—much to the chagrin of groggy livestock. Book tickets and rooms far in advance through the **Eisteddfod Box Office,** Royal International Pavilion, Abbey Rd., or by e-mail at tickets@international-eisteddfod.co.uk. (☎862 000; www.international-eisteddfod.co.uk. Phone bookings M-F 9am-5pm. Box office open from Oct. 2002 M-Th 9am-4pm, F 9am-3pm. Unreserved seat and admission to grounds on day of show £5, seniors £4, children £3, families £12; concert tickets £7-40.)

SCOTLAND

Beautiful, glorious Scotland, has spoilt me for every other country!
—Mary Todd Lincoln

A little over half the size of England but with a tenth the population, Scotland possesses open spaces and wild natural splendor its southern neighbor cannot hope to rival. The craggy, heathered Highlands, the silver beaches of the west coast, and the luminescent mists of the Hebrides elicit any traveler's awe, while farmlands to the south and peaceful fishing villages on the eastern shore harbor a gentler beauty. Scotland at its best is a world apart from the rest of the UK. Its people revel in a culture all their own, from the fevered nightlife of Glasgow to the festival energies of Edinburgh to the isolated communities of the Orkney and Shetland Islands. Before reluctantly joining with England in 1707, the Scots defended their independence, bitterly and heroically, for hundreds of years. Since the union, they have nurtured a separate identity, retaining control of schools, churches, and the judicial system. In 1999, Scots finally regained a separate parliament, which gave them more power over domestic tax laws and strengthened their national identity. While the kilts, bagpipes, and souvenir clan paraphernalia of the larger cities grow tiresome, a visit to the less touristed regions of Scotland will allow you to encounter the inheritors of ancient traditions: a B&B owner speaking Gaelic to her grandchildren, a crofter cutting peat, or a fisherman setting out in his skiff at dawn.

TRANSPORTATION

GETTING THERE

Reaching Scotland from outside Britain is usually easiest and cheapest through London, where the **Scottish Tourist Board,** 19 Cockspur St., SW1 Y5BL (☎020 77930 8661), stocks gads of brochures and books train, bus, and plane tickets.

BY PLANE. Flights are predictably expensive. **British Airways** (☎08457 222 111) sells a limited number of APEX return tickets starting at £70. **British Midland** (☎0870 607 0555) offers Saver fares from London to Glasgow (from £70 return), but you'll need to book as far in advance as you can (2 weeks if possible) for the cheapest fare. Some of the cheapest fares available with the fewest headaches are **easyJet** (☎0870 600 0000; www.easyjet.com) from London Luton or Gatwick (Glasgow or Edinburgh return from £80). Scotland is linked by **ferry** (see p. 40) to Northern Ireland and the Isle of Man.

BY TRAIN AND BUS. From London, **trains** (☎08457 484 950) to **Edinburgh** and **Glasgow** take only 6hr., but fares are steep—around £90 (cheaper APEX tickets require advance booking). On overnight trains you can pay more for sleeper berths. Although the **bus** from London takes more than 7hr., it's significantly cheaper than rail travel. **National Express** (☎08705 808 080) connects England and Scotland via Glasgow and Edinburgh.

Scotland

0 ____ 20 miles
0 ____ 20 kilometers

N

North Atlantic Ocean

TO FAROES, HANSTHOLM, DENMARK

Shetland Islands

Unst
Yell

Mainland

Scalloway
Lerwick

Orkney Islands

Stromness
Kirkwall
Hoy
Burwick

North Sea

Cape Wrath
Durness
Kyle of Tongue
Scrabster
Thurso
John O'Groats
Wick
Helmsdale

Eddrachillis Bay

Stornoway
Lewis
North Minch
Lochinver
Achiltibuie
Ullapool

OUTER HEBRIDES

Tarbert
Harris
Leverburgh
Berneray
North Uist
Lochmaddy
Benbecula
South Uist
Lochboisdale
Barra
Castlebay

Uig
Skye
Gairloch
Ashnasheen
Torridon
Applecross
Broadford
Kyle of Lochalsh
Kyleakin
Armadale

HIGHLANDS

Cannich
Inverness
Drumnadrochit
Loch Ness
Caledonian Canal
Aviemore

Moray Firth
Forres
Elgin
Spey River
Grampian Mts.
Cairngorm Mts.
Tomintoul
Don River
Dee River
Aberdeen
Braemar
Crathie
Stonehaven

Canna
Rum
Eigg
Muck

Mallaig
Fort William
Ben Nevis
Glencoe
Loch Etive
Kilchoan
Tobermory
Mull
Staffa
Treshnish Isles
Iona
Craignure
Oban
Crianlarich
Ben More
Loch Tay
Killin
Aberfeldy
Tay R.
Dunkeld
Birnam
Pitlochry
Montrose
Dundee
Firth of Tay
St. Andrews
Anstruther

INNER HEBRIDES

Coll
Tiree
Colonsay
Port Askaig
Islay
Bowmore
Port Ellen
Jura
Tarbert
Argyll
Inveraray

Trossachs
Loch Lomond
Balloch
Stirling
Perth
FIFE
Kirkcaldy
Firth of Forth

CENTRAL

LOTHIAN
Edinburgh
Berwick-upon-Tweed

Glasgow
Ardrossan
Lochranza
Brodick
Arran
Ayr
AYERSHIRE

Galashiels
Peebles
Selkirk
Melrose
Kelso
Jedburgh
Tweed River
BORDERS
Cheviot Hills

Nith River

DUMFRIES & GALLOWAY
Galloway Forest Park
Dumfries
Castle Douglas
Glencaple
Kirkcudbright
Stranraer
Portpatrick
Luce Bay
Isle of Whithom
Solway Firth

Carlisle
Hexham
Hadrian's Wall
ENGLAND
Penrith
Keswick

NORTHERN IRELAND
Larne
TO BELFAST

SCOTLAND

GETTING AROUND

BY TRAIN AND BUS. In the Lowlands (south of Stirling and north of the Borders), train and bus connections are frequent. In the Highlands, trains snake slowly on a few restricted routes, bypassing the northwest almost entirely, and many stations are unstaffed—buy tickets on board. **Buses** tend to be the best way to travel. They're usually more frequent and far-reaching than trains and always cheaper, though nonsmokers may find them less hospitable than smoke-free railway cars. **Scottish Citylink** (☎ 08705 505 050) runs most intercity routes. Bus service declines in the northwest Highlands and grinds to a halt on Sundays almost everywhere.

A great money-saver is the **Freedom of Scotland Travelpass.** It allows unlimited train travel and transportation on most **Caledonian MacBrayne** ("CalMac") ferries, with discounts on some other ferry lines. Purchase the pass *before* traveling to Britain at any BritRail distributors (see **By Train,** p. 30).

BY BUS TOUR. If you have limited time or if you want to be thrown together with a group of backpackers, a thriving industry of tour companies is eager to whisk you into the Highlands. The two main companies are **MacBackpackers** (☎ 0131 558 9900; www.macbackpackers.com) and **HAGGiS** (☎ 0131 557 9393; www.radical-travel.com). Both cater to the young and adventurous with a number of tours departing from Edinburgh, and both run hop-on/hop-off excursions that let you travel Scotland at your own pace (usually within three months). MacBackpackers, specializing in tours of the hop-on/hop-off variety, guarantees accommodation at any of the associated, super-social **Scotland's Top Hostels** in Edinburgh, Fort William, Skye, Oban, and Inverness. HAGGiS is geared more toward set tours with specific itineraries (some in England and Ireland), slightly more expensive but run by witty and knowledgeable local guides and guaranteeing accommodation at a few favorite stopping points. (See **Bus Tours,** p. 38). **Celtic Connection** (☎ 0131 225 3330; www.thecelticconnection.co.uk) covers Scotland in a variety of three- to seven-day tours, with one-way, return, or hop-on/hop-off options. Other companies, like **Heart of Scotland Tours,** 11 Wellington St. in Edinburgh (☎ 0131 558 3108; www.heartofscotlandtours.co.uk) provide half-, one-, and two-day bus tours.

BY CAR. Though Southern and Central Scotland are well served by public transportation, travel in the Highlands and Islands may be greatly restricted without a car. Driving gives you the freedom to explore Scotland at your own pace and to access some of its most remote quarters without fear of being stranded by complicated bus services. As in the rest of Britain, driving in Scotland is on the left, seatbelts are required at all times, the minimum age to drive with a valid foreign license is 17, and the minimum age to rent is 21, often higher. In rural areas, roads are often **single-track:** both directions of traffic share one lane, and drivers must be prepared to slow to a crawl to negotiate oncoming traffic. Often one car must reverse to a **passing place** (shoulder turn-off) to enable another to pass, as well as to allow same-way traffic to overtake. Many rural roads are also liberally sprinkled with **livestock;** drive slowly and be prepared to wait until the beasties move on.

BY BICYCLE. Scotland's biking terrain is scenic and challenging. You can usually rent bikes even in very small towns and transport them by ferry for little or no charge. Fife and regions south of Edinburgh and Glasgow offer gentle country pedaling, and Orkney, Shetland, and the Western Isles are negotiable by bicycle. In the Highlands, touring is more difficult. Most major roads have only one lane, and locals drive at high speeds—keep your eye out for passing places. Bringing a bike to the Highlands by public transportation can be as difficult as pedaling there, as many trains can carry only four or fewer bikes; reservations are essential. Harry Henniker's *101 Bike Routes in Scotland* (£10) is worth a look before you set out.

BY THUMB. Many hitchhike in Scotland, most often in the Highlands and Islands and less so in the more built-up regions around the larger cities. Hitchers report that drivers tend to be most receptive in the least-traveled areas. Far to the northwest and in the Western Isles, the Sabbath is strictly observed, making it difficult or impossible to get a ride on Sundays. *Let's Go* does not recommend hitchhiking.

BY FOOT. Two long-distance footpaths were planned and marked by the Countryside Commission under the Countryside Act of 1967. The **West Highland Way** begins just north of Glasgow in Milngavie and snakes 95 mi. north along Loch Lomond, through Glen Coe to Fort William and Ben Nevis. The **Southern Upland Way** runs 212 mi. from Portpatrick on the southwest coast to Cockburnspath on the east coast, passing through Galloway Forest Park and the Borders. Most tourist information centres (TICs) distribute simple maps of the Ways as well as a list of accommodations along the routes. For information on these paths, write or call the **Scottish Tourist Board,** 23 Ravelston Terr., Edinburgh EH4 3EU (☎ 0131 332 2433). Detailed guidebooks for both are available at most bookstores.

Mountain ranges like the Cuillins, the Torridons, the Cairngorms, Glen Nevis, and Glen Coe have hostels situated in their midst, providing bases for spectacular hill-walking or biking. You can also walk along mainland Britain's highest **cliffs** at Cape Wrath or ramble across the eerie **moors** of the Outer Hebrides. One of the most attractive aspects of hiking in Scotland is that you can often pick your own route across the heather. However, the wilds do pose certain dangers: stone markers can be unreliable, and expanses of open heather often disorient. Heavy mists are always a possibility, and blizzards may surprise even in July; never go up into the mountains without proper equipment (see **Wilderness Safety,** p. 49). Many trails (even those in national parks) cross privately owned land; be respectful and, when in doubt, ask permission. Leave a copy of your route and timetable at the hostel or nearest rescue station, and if you're out between mid-August and mid-October, be sure to ask about areas in which deer hunters might be at work. For information on walking and mountaineering in Scotland, consult Poucher's *The Scottish Peaks* (£13) or the introductory Tourist Board booklet, *Walk Scotland.*

MUNRO BAGGING Scottish mountaineering is dominated by the frequently obsessive practice of Munro Bagging. Hugh T. Munro compiled the original list of Scottish peaks over 3000 ft. in 1891; today about 280 are recorded. Any addition sends thousands of hikers scrambling up previously unnoticed peaks to maintain their distinction of having "bagged every Munro." Some people accomplish this feat over a lifetime of hiking; others do it in a frenetic six months. Thankfully, only one Munro, the Inaccessible Pinnacle on Skye, requires technical rock-climbing skills. *The Munros* (£18), produced by the Scottish Mountaineering Club, presents a list of the peaks along with climbing information.

LIFE AND TIMES

HISTORY

EARLY TIMES. Little is known of the early inhabitants of Scotland, save that they managed to repel Roman incursions in their land and scared **Emperor Hadrian** so badly that he hid all of Roman England behind a wall (see p. 447). Other invading tribes were more successful, and by AD 600 the Scottish mainland was inhabited by four groups. The **Picts,** originally the most powerful, are also the most mysterious—

only a collection of carved stones and references to them in Latin histories provide information. The Celtic **Scots** arrived from Ireland in the 4th century, bringing the Gaelic language and Christian religion. The Germanic **Angles** invaded Scotland from northern England in the 6th century. In AD 843, the Scots decisively defeated the Picts and formed a joint kingdom. United by the threat of encroaching **Vikings**, various groups were led by the first king of all Scotland, **Duncan** (later killed by a certain Macbeth in 1040). The House of Canmore ("big-headed," after Duncan's son Malcolm, who was cranially well-endowed) reigned over Scotland for 200 years. Allied through marriages with the Norman lords who had come to dominate England, the Scottish monarchs found their independence considerably threatened by the increasingly powerful nation to the south. The 13th century was characterized by an uneasy peace punctuated by periodic skirmishes, while the Scottish kings successfully contained both civil revolts and Scandinavian attacks.

SQUABBLES WITH ENGLAND. King **Alexander III** died in 1286 without an heir, and the ensuing contest over the Scottish crown fueled the territorial ambitions of **Edward I** of England, who promptly seized most of Scotland and kicked off a long history of English oppression—his gentle governing hand earned him the nickname "Hammer of the Scots." The **Wars of Independence** bred heroic figures like William Wallace (yes, the *Braveheart* guy), who bravely, and for a time successfully, led a company of Scots against the English. But it was the patient and cunning **Robert the Bruce** who emerged as Scotland's leader (read: assassinated his way to the throne). Against all odds, Robert led the Scots to victory over Edward II's forces at **Bannockburn** in 1314, winning Scotland her independence. In the next centuries the monarchy set nobles against each other in an attempt to preserve its own waning position, and the Scottish kings frequently capitalized on their **"Auld Alliance"** with France to stave off the English crown.

The reigns of **James IV** (1488-1513) and **James V** (1513-42) witnessed the arrival of both **Renaissance** and **Reformation** (see p. 71). The death of James V left the infant **Mary, Queen of Scots** (1542-67), on the throne. The Queen was promptly sent to France, where she later married the future François II. Lacking a strong ruler during Mary's absence, Scotland was vulnerable to passionate Protestant revolts—nobles and commoners alike were drawn to the appeal of Protestantism, embodied in the form of iconoclastic preacher **John Knox**. In 1560, the monarchy capitulated. The Protestant **Scottish Parliament** denied the Pope's authority in Scotland and established the Presbyterian Church as Scotland's new official church.

In 1561, after the death of her husband, staunchly Catholic Mary returned to Scotland. Never accepted by Scottish nobles or Protestants, Mary's rule fanned the flames of discontent, and civil war resulted in her forced abdication and imprisonment in 1567. She escaped her Scottish captors only to find another set of shackles across the border, where her cousin Elizabeth I ran the show; as the Queen languished in an English prison, her son **James VI** was made King. Nine years later, with Catholic Spain a rising threat, Queen Liz made a tentative alliance with the nominally Protestant James (which didn't stop her executing his mother in 1587).

UNION WITH ENGLAND. Elizabeth's death without an heir in 1603 left James VI to be crowned **James I of England,** uniting both countries under a single monarch. James ruled from London, while his half-hearted attempts to reconcile the Scots to British rule were tartly resisted. Scottish Presbyterians supported Parliamentarian forces against James's successor **Charles I** during the **English Civil Wars** (see p. 72). However, when the Parliamentarians executed Charles, the Scots again switched sides and declared the headless king's son to be King Charles II. **Oliver Cromwell** handily defeated him as well, but in a conciliatory gesture gave Scotland representation in the English Parliament. Though Cromwell (thankfully) went away, the political precedent of Scottish representation in Parliament endured. The Protestant victory of William of Orange over James II in the **Glorious Revolution** (see p. 72) and the **War of the Spanish Succession** (1701-1714) convinced Scotland's Presbyterian leaders that its interests were safer with the Anglicans than with longtime ally Catholic France. (That, and the fact that many Scots were impoverished and famine-stricken after defending their independence for four centuries.) The Scottish Parliament was subsumed by England in the **1707 Act of Union.**

THE JACOBITE REBELLION. Scottish supporters of James II (called **Jacobites**) never accepted the Union, and after a series of unsuccessful uprisings, they launched the **"Forty-Five,"** the uprising of 1745 that has snared the imaginations of Scots and romantics everywhere. James's grandson **Bonnie Prince Charlie** landed in Scotland, where he succeeded in mustering unseasoned troops from various Scottish clans. From **Glenfinnan** (p. 648), B.P. Charlie rallied his troops, marching to Edinburgh, where he kept court and prepared for full rebellion. On the march to London, however, desertions and the uncertainty of help from France prompted a retreat to Scotland. Modest French support did materialize and the Jacobites claimed victories at Stirling and Falkirk in 1746. After that, the rebellion once again collapsed; although Charles eventually escaped back to France, his Highland army fell on the battlefield of **Culloden** (p. 641). The English, not comfortable with the idea of being invaded, enacted a new, harsh round of oppressive measures: the wearing of hereditary **tartans** and the playing of **bagpipes** were forbidden, speaking **Gaelic** was discouraged, and much of traditional Scottish culture was forcibly forgotten. Walter Scott's novel *Waverley*, written sixty years after the Forty-Five, expresses the next generation's nostalgia for the lost way of life.

ENLIGHTENMENT AND THE CLEARANCES. Despite Jacobite agitation and reactionary English counter-measures, the 18th century proved to be one of the most prosperous in Scotland's history. As agriculture, industry, and trading all boomed, a vibrant intellectual environment and close links to Continental **Enlightenment** thought produced such luminaries as **Adam Smith, David Hume,** and **Thomas Carlyle.** In the 19th century, although political reforms did much to improve social conditions, economic problems proved disastrous. The Highlands in particular were affected by a rapidly growing population combined with the lack of available land and food, archaic farming methods, and the demands of rapacious landlords. The subsequent poverty resulted in mass **emigration**—mostly to North America—and the infamous **Clearances.** Between 1811 and 1820, the Sutherland Clearances, undertaken by the Marquis of Stafford, forcibly relocated poor farmers from their lands to the coasts, where farming could be supplemented by fishing, or to smaller landholdings called **crofts.** Resistance to the relocations was met with violence— homes were burned and countless people killed. Other Clearances occurred throughout the Highlands, in many cases evicting entire families from their homes, whereupon they were not just relocated to another area in Scotland, but forcibly packed on boats and shipped overseas. Meanwhile, the **Industrial Revolution** led to urban growth in southern Scotland—Glasgow grew into a gritty manufacturing metropolis—and increasingly poor living conditions for new industrial laborers.

THE 20TH CENTURY. Scotland, like the rest of Britain, lost a generation of young men in the Great War, and suffered the following economic downturn. The **Depression** of the 1930s hit Scotland as hard, if not harder, than the rest of the world. The **Home Rule** (or **Devolution**) movement, begun in 1886 and put on hold during WWI, continued agitation for a separate Parliament in Edinburgh. The **Scottish National Party (SNP)** was founded in 1934 on the strength of Scottish nationalist sentiments. Riding this wave were the four young tartan-blooded agitators who broke into Westminster Abbey on Christmas of 1950 and liberated the **Stone of Scone** (or "Stone of Destiny"), which had been liberated from Scotland previously by Edward "It's All Mine" I (see **Stoned,** p. 112). However successful they were at burglarizing English cathedrals, Home Rulers never managed to score a real victory on the floor of Parliament during the years following WWII. The movement didn't go away; in fact, polls in the 70s indicated as much as three-fourths of Scotland's population favored devolution. The crucial **1979 referendum,** however, failed due to exceptionally low voter turnout. Meanwhile, the **oil industry** had come to eastern Scotland in a big way: North Sea drilling operations gave Aberdeen and Shetland a taste of petroleum-laced prosperity, but provoked new battles over where the black gold was going (overseas, or worse, to England) and who got the revenue.

TODAY

Stands Scotland where it did?
—William Shakespeare, *Macbeth*

CURRENT POLITICS. Today, Scotland has 72 seats in the United Kingdom's House of Commons and is largely integrated into the British economy. The May 1997 elections swept the Scottish Conservatives out of power and accrued support for the SNP, which based its platform on devolution from England. September 1997 brought a victory for the proponents of home rule; Scottish voters supported **devolution** by an overwhelming 3:1 margin, and the first elections for 129 seats in the new **Scottish Parliament** occurred in 1999. Parliament holds court temporarily in a building at the foot of Edinburgh Castle while awaiting its new digs at **Holyrood** (scheduled to be opened in 2003; see p. 557). Though Edinburgh is able to levy taxes and legislate in other areas, Westminster still controls foreign affairs and fiscal policy. Scotland, Wales, and Northern Ireland have all devolved from England by varying degrees, and it's still too soon to say which will succeed and to what extent. On the one hand, even the mention of "Bannockburn" still stirs nationalist feeling among Scots, and the last party supporting union with England has been scourged from the Scottish Parliament. On the other, there are many Scottish politicians more closely tied to London than to their own constituents, and three centuries of economic and social intertwining to combat. Only time will tell whether Scotland is truly on the road to greater independence.

SCOTLAND AT CENTURY'S END. Scotland's **industrial boom** during the World Wars was nurtured during the post-war years by a string of Labour governments, a practice that wedded the Scottish economy to the state, for better or worse. And the rocky times were ahead—**Thatcherism** removed many of the public-funding props sustaining industries in the north of Britain, and Scotland's workforce was reduced by 20% before the 1980s were a year old. The country faced economic downturn and depression similar to, if not more intense than, that of the industrial meccas of Northern England. Nonetheless, by the end of the decade **Glasgow** had reinvented itself and was leading the way out of a sad, sooty past and into a bright new post-industrial morning. Declared **European Capital of Culture** in 1990 and **UK City of Design and Architecture** in 1999, the city on the Clyde continues the fond, fierce rivalry with its sister 45 mi. east. **Edinburgh,** long a cultural magnet, has recently seen its 55-year-old **International Festival** (and attendant events like **The Fringe,** see p. 545) make headlines around the world—today, over 15% of the revelers come from overseas. Edinburgh's festival energies peak during the August madness but fuel the economy all year round, creating hundreds of millions of pounds in revenue and thousands of jobs.

The **cultural tourism** that draws visitors to both cities is a significant part of Scotland's tourist industry—droves of heritage-seekers and Celtic devotees take the country by storm each summer, and many Scottish see attending to them as a replacement for lost manufacturing might. Though the industrial trades still enjoy

Scotland's largest workforce, in holiday spots like the Highlands and Islands, tourism employs more people than any other field. Still others have turned to new technologies as potential economic saviors. On July 5, 1996, **Dolly the sheep** was born in the labs of the Roslin Institute, brought into the world by Dr. Ian Wilmut—the first successful cloning of a mammal is indicative of a booming (30% growth rate) interest in **biotechnology.** Scotland also has a stake in **microtechnologies,** producing nearly half of all the superconductors in the UK. As computers and the Internet filter into the country and trickle down through the social classes, Scotland seems poised to leave its 20th-century woes behind while bringing its older (more profitable) heritage with it into the new millennium.

CULTURE AND CUSTOMS

The cold, drizzly skies of Scotland hang over some of the warmest people on earth. The Scottish reputation for openness and good nature is well-known and well-founded. Reserve and etiquette is somewhat less important here than down in the London megopolis and its over-developed sprawl, but that's no reason to go forgetting your manners. Life is generally slower and less frenetic outside—and even within—the densely populated belt running between Glasgow and Edinburgh. As in the few other unharried corners of the world, **hospitality** and **conversation** are highly valued; most Scots will welcome you with geniality and pride. That is, unless you call them English. In certain areas of the Highlands, **nationalism** runs deep and strong; using the (technically) correct "British" will win you no friends. **Religion** and **football,** and the religion of football, are topics best left untouched if you're not prepared to defend yourself—verbally and otherwise.

A WORD ABOUT KILTS. The kilt is not purely a romanticized, Hollywoodized concept, though it's not likely you'll see all that many during your travels. Originally just Highlands garb, **tartan** plaids denoted the geographic base of the weaver. Proscribed after the Jacobite rebellion, kilts were revived in the mid-19th-century nostalgia for Highland culture. Some Scots do wear kilts in their clan tartans, dressing them up (with tuxedo-ish **Prince Charlie jackets** for formal occasions) or down (with tweed sports coats), but if you see someone in the full Scottish regalia of your mind's eye, it's likely a hired costume.

LANGUAGE

Although the early Picts left no record of their language, settlers in southern Scotland well into the 7th century heard a **Celtic** language related to Welsh. These settlers also brought their native tongues—Gaelic from Ireland, Norse from Scandinavia, and an early form of English (Inglis) brought by the Angles from northern England. By the 11th century, **Scottish Gaelic** (pronounced GAL-ick; Irish Gaelic is GAYL-ick) had subsumed other dialects and become the official language of Scottish law. As the political power of southern Scotland increased, Gaelic speakers migrated to the Highlands and Islands. Inglis, or **Scots,** became the language of the Lowlands and, eventually, of the monarchy. Beginning as a dialectical variation of the English developing in England, Scots (influenced by Flemish, French, and Latin) developed into a distinctive linguistic unit.

While a number of post-1700 Scottish literati, most notably Robert Burns and the contemporary poet Hugh MacDiarmid, have composed in Scots, union with Britain and the political and cultural power of England led to the rise of England's language in Scotland. Today, **standard English** is spoken throughout Scotland, but with a strong Scots influence. In the Highlands, for example, "ch" becomes a soft "h," as in the German "ch" sound. Modern Scottish Gaelic, a linguistic cousin of Modern Irish, is spoken by at least 65,000 people in Scotland today, particularly in the western islands. Recent attempts to revive Gaelic have led to its introduction in the classroom, assuring that some form of the language will continue to exist in Scotland for years to come. (For a **glossary** of Scottish Gaelic and Scots words and phrases, see p. 814; for Gaelic **classes,** see p. 63.)

THE ARTS

LITERATURE. Spanning centuries and including composition in three languages—Gaelic, Scots, and English—Scottish literature embodies a complexity of experience. In a nation where stories and myths have long been recounted by the fireside, **oral literature** is as much a part of literary tradition as novels. Most medieval Scottish manuscripts have unfortunately been lost—not surprising, as raids on monastic centers of learning were fierce and frequent, effectively erasing pre-14th-century records. **John Barbour** is the best-known writer in Early Scots—his *The Bruce* (c. 1375) preceded Chaucer and favorably chronicled the life of Robert I in an attempt to strengthen national unity. **William Dunbar** (1460-1521) composed in Middle Scots and is today considered representative of Scots poetry.

In 1760, **James Macpherson** published the works of **"Ossian,"** supposedly an ancient Scottish bard to rival Homer; Macpherson was widely discredited when he refused to produce the manuscripts that he claimed to be translating. **James Boswell** (1740-95), the biographer of Samuel Johnson (see p. 78), composed Scots verse as well as voluminous journals detailing his travels with the good Doctor. "Scotland's National Bard," **Robert Burns** (1759-96), bucked pressure from the south that urged him to write in English, instead composing in his native Scots. New Year's Eve revelers owe their anthem to him, though most mouth "Auld Lang Syne" without a clue what it means. **Sir Walter Scott** (1771-1832) was among the first Scottish authors to achieve international accolades for his work. The chivalry- and damsel-laden *Ivanhoe* is one of the best-known, if sappiest, novels of all time. Scott was also interested in nostalgia, and his works (including the *Waverley* novels) may have single-handedly sparked the 19th-century revival of Highlands culture. **Robert Louis Stevenson** (1850-94) is most famous for his tales of high adventure, including *Treasure Island* and *Kidnapped*, which still fuel children's imaginations. His *Strange Case of Dr. Jekyll and Mr. Hyde* is nominally set in London, but any Scot would recognize Edinburgh's streets. Another of Edinburgh's authorial sons is **Sir Arthur Conan Doyle** (1859-1930), whose *Sherlock Holmes* series is beloved by mystery fans the world over.

Scotland's literary present is as vibrant as its past. A 20th-century renaissance of Scottish Gaelic, particularly the Lowlands ("Lallands") dialect has had poets—most notably **Hugh MacDiarmid** and **Edwin Morgan**—returning to the language of Burns. James Leslie Mitchell (known as **Lewis Grassic Gibbon;** 1901-1935) had a short but important career—he co-authored *Scottish Scene* with MacDiarmid, a scathing account of what was wrong with their country. **Neil Gunn** (1891-1973) wrote short stories and novels about Highland history and culture. More recent novelists include **Alasdair Gray, Tom Leonard, Janice Galloway,** and **James Kelman,** who won 1995's Booker Prize for his controversial, sharp-edged novel *How Late It Was, How Late.* **Irvine Welsh's** *Trainspotting,* the 1993 novel about Edinburgh heroin addicts and its 1996 film adaptation, have been both condemned as amoral and hailed as chronicles of a new generation.

ART. Scotland has produced fewer visual artists than it has writers and musicians, but a visit to the extraordinary collections of the **galleries** and **museums** of Glasgow and Edinburgh proves that this is a country with a fine aesthetic eye. 18th- and

YOU OUGHTA BE IN PICTURES If Scotland looks familiar, it's probably because you've seen parts of it in a dozen movies. Go figure: grand, sweeping landscapes tend to make nice cinematic backdrops. But the obsessive among us insist on knowing exactly where Mel Gibson, Ewan McGregor, and that dude from Highlander slew Englishmen, shot heroin, and screamed until they were blue in the face. For those who must view life through a movie screen, *Let's Go* provides a handy how-to and where-to on reenacting your favorite celluloid Scotlands:

Highlander: There can be only one castle, and it's **Eilean Donan Castle** (p. 653) at the heads of Lochs Long, Alsh, and Duich, near Kyle of Lochalsh. If you haven't seen the film, you've seen the castle on just about every calendar, postcard, and shortbread tin. Prance around on the photogenic stone bridge and try not to behead any tourists.

Trainspotting: Grab three mates and a bottle of vodka and head out to **Rannoch Moor,** east of Glen Coe (p. 644). Step off the train, walk about 100 ft. toward Buchuaille Etive Mor, and come to the realization that Scotland has been "colonized by wankers." Or run frantically down Princes Street in **Edinburgh** (p. 546) after stealing car radios. (*Let's Go* does not recommend shooting heroin after selling stolen goods. Or before, for that matter.)

Braveheart: Hike out to **Glen Nevis,** east of Fort William (p. 644), and run up to the summit of one of the mountains while a rotating helicopter films a 360° panorama of your striking physique against the horizon. Pretend that the English have killed your father and brother and recently slit your wife's throat, but comfort yourself with the knowledge that you'll get to sleep with a French princess-cum-Bond Girl.

Monty Python and the Holy Grail: Rent a boat and row out to the Castle of the Holy Grail, which is actually **Castle Stalker,** on Loch Linnhe, near Oban (p. 615). You need to ask the family that owns the castle for permission; King Arthur didn't, and he ended up in the back of a paddywagon, didn't he?

Hamlet: To follow in Mel Gibson's footsteps as the famous Dane, climb the dramatic cliffs by **Dunnottar Castle** (p. 630), in Stonehaven south of Aberdeen. Extemporize a soliloquy on suicide and/or revenge, or merely admire the weasly whalish clouds.

19th-century portraitists like **Allan Ramsay** and **Sir Henry Raeburn,** and landscape painter **David Wilkie** are recognized names in the world of art, but the most famous is Glaswegian artist and architect **Charles Rennie Mackintosh** (1868-1928). Mackintosh was part of the Arts and Crafts movement (see p. 80), as well as a leader on the Art Nouveau scene. His elegant designs of Glasgow buildings—like the School of Art and Willow Tea Rooms (see p. 588)—are there for the gawking.

MUSIC. The Gaelic music of western Scotland has its roots in the traditional music of Irish settlers; as in Ireland, **ceilidhs** (KAY-lees), spirited gatherings of music and dance, bring jigs, reels, and Gaelic songs to halls and pubs. Although there are no extant scores of Gaelic music prior to the 17th century, evidence suggests the *clarsach*, a Celtic harp, was the primary medium for musical expression until the 16th century, when the Highlander's **bagpipes** (one of the oldest instruments in the world) and the violin introduced new creative possibilities. Scots musical heritage centers around **ballads**, dramatic narrative songs. The strong folk tradition is evident in the Scottish contribution to popular music: Scotland's sound influenced international rock trends, while the country itself produced **The Proclaimers**, folk-rockers **Belle and Sebastian,** and Britpop entries **Texas** and **Travis.** Glasgow was a thriving exporter of musical talent throughout the 80s, giving us bands like **Simple Minds** and **Tears for Fears.**

FOOD AND DRINK

Another assault by massed calories.
—Israel Shenker, on the food at Culzean castle

The frequenter of B&Bs will encounter a glorious **Scottish breakfast,** including oat cakes, porridge, and marmalade. In general, however, Scottish cuisine greatly resembles English food. Aside from delicious, buttery **shortbread,** visitors are unlikely to take a shine to traditional dishes, the most (in)famous of which is certainly **haggis,** made from a sheep's stomach. The food might be a let-down, but Scotland's **whisky** (spelled without the "e") certainly is not. Scotch whisky is either "single malt" (from a single distillery), or "blended" (a mixture of several different brands). The malts are excellent and distinctive, the blends the same as those available abroad. Raise a glass yourself at the **distilleries** in Pitlochry (p. 605), the Speyside area (p. 636), or on the Isles of Islay and Jura (p. 615). Due to heavy taxes on alcohol sold in Britain, scotch may be cheaper at home or from duty-free stores than it is in Scotland. The Scots do know how to party: they have the highest alcohol consumption rate in Britain, and, no surprise, are more generous in their licensing laws than in England and Wales—drinks are served later and pubs open longer (often until midnight or after).

HAGGIS: WHAT'S IN THERE? Restaurants throughout

Scotland produce steamin' plates o' haggis for eager tourists, but we at *Let's Go* believe all should know what's inside that strange-looking bundle before taking the plunge. An age-old recipe calls for the following ingredients: the large stomach bag of a sheep, the small (knight's hood) bag, the pluck (including lights [lungs], liver, and heart), beef, suet, oatmeal, onions, pepper, and salt. Today's haggis is available conveniently canned and includes lamb, lamb offal, oatmeal, wheat flour (healthy, no?), beef, suet, onions, salt, spices, stock, and liquor (1%). Vegetarian haggis is proof of the Scottish capitulation to certain new-fangled dietary fads.

SPORTING AND MERRYMAKING

The Scottish are as passionate about **football** as their English neighbors, and the intensity of devotion in Glasgow in particular (see **Pitched Battle,** p. 593) rivals any Mancunian fervor. **Rugby** is also popular in its amateur (Union) form (see p. 87). Traditional **Scottish games** originated from competitions under English military oppression, in which participants could use only common objects, such as hammers, rounded stones, and tree trunks. Although **"tossing the caber"** may look easy, it actually does require a good deal of talent and practice to chuck an 18 ft., 180 lb. pine trunk. Weekend clan gatherings, bagpipe competitions, and Highland games occur frequently in Scotland, especially in summer; check for events at TICs and in the local newspapers. In addition, the Scottish Tourist Board publishes the annual *Scotland Events*, which details happenings across Scotland.

Each year a slew of festivals celebrate Scotland's distinctive history and culture. June and July's **Common Ridings** in the Borders (p. 566) and the raucous **Up-Helly-Aa'** in Shetland on the last Tuesday in January (p. 686) are among the best known. Scotland is also famous for its New Year's Eve celebration, known as **Hogmanay.** The party goes on all over the country, taking over the streets in Edinburgh and Glasgow (see www.hogmanay.net for events and locations). Above all events towers the **Edinburgh International Festival** (Aug. 10-30 in 2003; ☎0131 473 2001; www.eif.co.uk), one of the largest in the world. The concentration of musical and theatrical events in the space of three weeks is dizzying; Edinburgh's cafes and shops stay open to all hours and pipers roam the streets. Be sure to catch the **Fringe Festival** (Aug. 3-25 in 2003; ☎0131 226 0026; www.edfringe.com), the much less costly sibling of the International Festival. There are literally hundreds of performances every day, including drama, comedy acts, jazz, and a bit of the bizarre.

SOUTHERN SCOTLAND

Stark contrasts distinguish southern Scotland—from a history of conflict to the changeable landscape. Until the 17th century, southern Scotland was characterized by skirmishes with its southern neighbors, from the Roman-Pict battles to the interminable wars with England. The Borders region to the southeast contains monuments and ruins marking these struggles, and Dumfries and Galloway in the southwest are rich in tales of local-born hero Robert the Bruce, who led Scotland to independence in 1314. Walkers and cyclists enjoy the region's serenity while literary buffs visit sites dedicated to national icon Robert Burns. Isolation and tranquility characterize the lovely Isle of Arran, but just eastward are southern Scotland's true draws: the great cities of Edinburgh and Glasgow. Nearly 80% of all Scots live in the cities' greater metropolitan areas. A fountainhead of the Enlightenment and Scotland's capital, Edinburgh preserves its classical beauty and draws enormous crowds each summer during its festival. Not to be outdone, Glasgow offers formidable art collections, stunning architecture, and kinetic nightlife.

HIGHLIGHTS OF SOUTHERN SCOTLAND

EDINBURGH AND THE FESTIVAL Military fireworks, theater, opera, jazz, and readings by artists the world over enthrall audiences during the city's August Festivities (p. 562).

THE BORDERS Visit Sir Walter Scott's grave at majestic Dryburgh Abbey, one of many haunting ruins peppering the region (p. 566).

GLASGOW Survey magnificent architecture, free museums, hundreds of pubs, and Britain's highest concentration of Indian restaurants (p. 581).

ISLE OF ARRAN Delight in "Scotland in miniature," explore Brodick Castle, or take on the challenge of climbing Goatfell (p. 578).

EDINBURGH ☎ 0131

This profusion of eccentricities, this dream in masonry and living rock is not a drop-scene in a theatre, but a city in the world of reality.
— Robert Louis Stevenson

A city of elegant stone amid rolling hills and ancient volcanoes, Edinburgh (ED-in-bur-ra; pop. 500,000) is the jewel of Scotland. It's impossible to have a poor time here, where friendliness thrives, festivals reign, and rollicking pubs congregate in the regal shadow of the castle. Since David I granted it burgh (town) status in 1130, Edinburgh has been a site of cultural significance. Here was the poetic and musical center of the medieval Stuarts, here the seeds of the Scottish Reformation were sown, here the dim alleys joined Bonnie Prince Charlie's premature victory celebration, and here the brilliant intellectuals of the Scottish Enlightenment fostered a heady, forward-thinking atmosphere. Today's city continues as a cultural

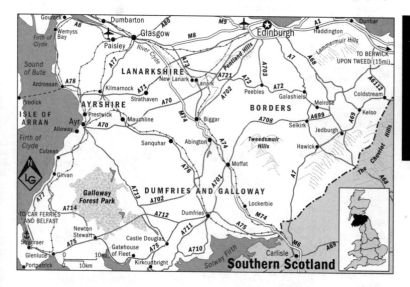

Southern Scotland

beacon, its medieval spires rising above streets infused with cosmopolitan verve. During the August festival-time, the city becomes a theatrical, musical, and literary magnet, drawing international talent and enthusiastic crowds. Motivated largely by tourism, new hostels, museums, and government buildings are springing up city-wide. These are exciting times for Edinburgh, and the fervor is infectious.

✈ INTERCITY TRANSPORTATION

Edinburgh lies 45 mi. east of Glasgow and 405 mi. northwest of London on Scotland's east coast, on the southern bank of the Firth of Forth.

Airport: Edinburgh International Airport (☎333 1000), 7 mi. west of the city. Lothian Buses' **Airlink** (☎555 6363) goes between the airport and Waverley Bridge (25min.; every 10-15min. all day and about every hr. after midnight; £3.30, children £2; return £5). **Airsaver** gives you 1 trip on Airlink plus 1 day unlimited travel on local Lothian Buses (£4.20, children £2.50).

Trains: Waverley Station, in the center of town, straddles Princes St., Market St., and Waverley Bridge. Free **bike storage** at the back of the travel center. Office open M-Sa 8am-8pm, Su 9am-8pm; Su-F until 11pm for same-night travel reservations only. Trains (☎(08457) 484 950) from: **Aberdeen** (2½hr.; M-Sa every hr., Su 8 per day; £31); **Glasgow** (1hr., 2 per hr., £7.40-8.40); **Inverness** (3½hr., every 2hr., £31); **London King's Cross** (4¾hr., 2 per hr., £89.50); **Oban** via Glasgow (4½hr., 3 per day, £25); **Stirling** (50min., 2 per hr., £5.30); **Thurso** (7½hr., M-Sa 1 direct per day, £39.40).

Buses: The new **bus station** is on the eastern side of **St. Andrew's Sq.** Call the local **Traveline** (☎(0800) 232 323) for the latest info. Edinburgh is a major hub of Scotland's bus network. **National Express** (☎(08705) 808 080) from **London** (10hr., 5 per day, £27). **Scottish Citylink** (☎(08705) 505 050) from: **Aberdeen** (4hr., at least every hr., £15); **Glasgow** (1hr.; M-Sa 4 per hr., Su 2 per hr.; £3.80); **Inverness** (4½hr., 8-10 per day, £14.70). A combination bus-ferry route via Stranraer goes to **Belfast** (2 per day, £29-33) and **Dublin** (1 per day, £41).

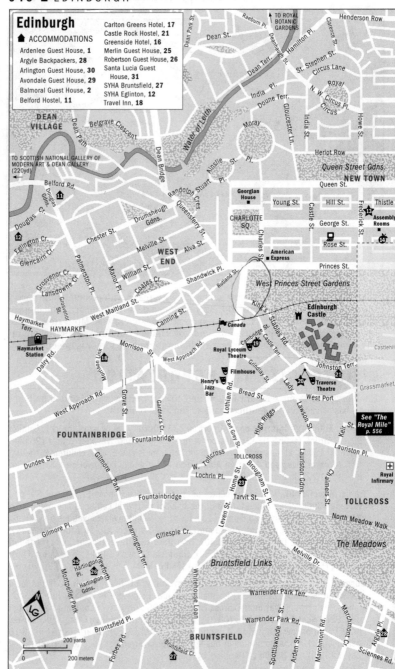

Edinburgh

♦ ACCOMMODATIONS

Ardenlee Guest House, **1**
Argyle Backpackers, **28**
Arlington Guest House, **30**
Avondale Guest House, **29**
Balmoral Guest House, **2**
Belford Hostel, **11**

Carlton Greens Hotel, **17**
Castle Rock Hostel, **21**
Greenside Hotel, **16**
Merlin Guest House, **25**
Robertson Guest House, **26**
Santa Lucia Guest
 House, **31**
SYHA Bruntsfield, **27**
SYHA Eglinton, **12**
Travel Inn, **18**

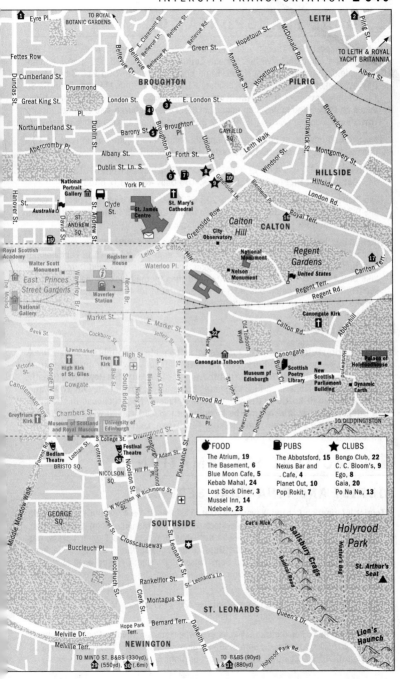

FOOD

The Atrium, 19
The Basement, 6
Blue Moon Cafe, 5
Kebab Mahal, 24
Lost Sock Diner, 3
Mussel Inn, 14
Ndebele, 23

PUBS

The Abbotsford, 15
Nexus Bar and
. Cafe, 4
Planet Out, 10
Pop Rokit, 7

CLUBS

Bongo Club, 22
C. C. Bloom's, 9
Ego, 8
Gaia, 20
Po Na Na, 13

⫶ LOCAL TRANSPORTATION

Public Transportation: Though your feet will usually suffice (and are often faster), Edinburgh has a comprehensive bus system. **Lothian Buses** (☎555 6363; www.lothianbuses.co.uk) provide most services. Exact change required (50p-£1). Buy a 1-day **Daysaver** ticket (all day M-F £2.20, children £1.50; after 9:30am M-F and all day Sa-Su £1.50) from any driver or the **Travelshops** on Hanover St. and Waverley Bridge. **Night buses** cover selected routes after midnight (£2). **First Edinburgh** also operates locally. **Traveline,** 2 Cockburn St. (☎(0800) 232 323), has info on all area public transport.

Taxis: Taxi stands are at both stations and on almost every corner on Princes St. **City Cabs** (☎228 1211). **Central Radio Taxis** (☎229 2468).

Car Rental: The TIC has a list of rental agencies. Generally 21+ or 23+. From £19 per day. **Carnie's Car Hire** (☎346 4155). **Avis,** 100 Dalry Rd. (☎337 6363).

Bike Rental: Biketrax, 11 Lochrin Pl. (☎228 6633). Mountain bikes £15 per day. Open M-F 9:30am-6pm, Sa 9:30am-5pm, Su noon-5pm. **Edinburgh Cycle Hire,** 29 Blackfriars St. (☎556 5560), off High St., organizes cycle tours.

Hitchhiking: Hitchers often take public transit to the city's outskirts. For points south (except Newcastle and northeast England), most grab bus #4 or 15 to Fairmilehead and then thumb a ride on the A702 to Biggar. For Newcastle, York, and Durham, many take bus #15, 26, or 43 to Musselburgh and then try their luck on the A1. Hitchers seeking to go north catch bus #18 or 40 to Barnton for the Forth Rd. Bridge and beyond. *Let's Go* never recommends hitchhiking.

⫶ ORIENTATION

This is a glorious city for walking. **Princes St.** is the main thoroughfare in **New Town,** the northern section of Edinburgh. From there you can view the impressive stone facade of the towering **Old Town,** the southern half of the city. **The Royal Mile** (Castle Hill, Lawnmarket, High St., and Canongate) is the major road in the Old Town and connects **Edinburgh Castle** in the west to the **Palace of Holyroodhouse** in the east. **North Bridge, Waverley Bridge,** and **The Mound** connect Old and New Town. Greater Edinburgh stretches well beyond Old and New Town; **Leith,** 2 mi. northeast, is the city's seaport on the Firth of Forth.

⫶ PRACTICAL INFORMATION

TOURIST AND FINANCIAL SERVICES

Tourist Information Centre: Waverley Market, 3 Princes St. (☎473 3800), on the north side of the Waverley Station complex (look for the blue triangular sign). Slick, helpful, and mobbed. Books rooms (£4); sells bus, museum, tour, and theater tickets; has excellent free maps and pamphlets. **Bureau de change.** Open July-Aug. M-Sa 9am-8pm, Su 10am-8pm; May-June and Sept. closes daily 7pm; Oct.-Apr. open M-W 9am-5pm, Th-Sa 9am-6pm, Su 10am-5pm. In summer, look for yellow-slicker-wearing **City Centre Representatives,** who can answer questions in several languages.

Budget Travel: STA Travel, 27 Forrest Rd. (☎226 7747). Open M-W 9:30am-6pm, Th 9:30am-6pm, F 10am-5:30pm, Sa 11am-5pm.

Financial Services: You'll trip over **banks** everywhere you go. **Thomas Cook,** 52 Hanover St. (☎226 5500). Open M-Sa 9am-5:30pm. **American Express,** 139 Princes St. (☎718 2503 or (08706) 001 600). Open M-F 9am-5:30pm, Sa 9am-4pm.

ACCOMMODATIONS ■ **551**

LOCAL SERVICES

Camping Supplies: Camping and Outdoor Centre, 77 South Bridge (☎225 3339). All the essentials, but no rentals. Open M-Sa 9am-5:30pm.

Bisexual, Gay, and Lesbian Services: Edinburgh has many gay- and lesbian-oriented establishments and events—pick up the *Gay Information* pamphlet at the TIC, or drop by the **Centre for Lesbians, Gays, and Bisexuals,** 58a Broughton St. (☎557 2625). See also **Gay and Lesbian Nightlife,** p. 565.

Disabled Services: TIC has info on access to restaurants and sights, as well as *The Access Guide* and *Transport in Edinburgh.* **Shopmobility** (☎225 9559), The Mound, by the National Gallery, lends free motorized wheelchairs. Open M-Sa from 10am.

Public Showers: In the "Superloo" at the train station. Super clean (for a train station). Shower £2, toilet 20p. Towels for £1 deposit. Open daily 4:15am-1am.

EMERGENCY AND COMMUNICATIONS

Emergency: ☎999 or 112.

Police: 5 Fettes Ave. (☎311 3131).

Hospital: Royal Infirmary of Edinburgh, 1 Lauriston Pl. (emergencies ☎536 4000, otherwise 536 1000).

Internet Access: No place is cheaper than ultra-convenient **easyInternet Cafe,** 58 Rose St. (☎220 3577). £1 per 30min.-3hr., depending on demand. Open M-Sa 7am-11pm, Su 8am-11pm. **e-corner,** Platform 1, Waverley Station. £1 per 20min., £2 per hr. Open M-F 7:30am-9:30pm, Sa-Su 8am-9pm.

Post Office: In the St. James Shopping Centre, New Town (☎556 9546). Open M 9am-5:30pm, Tu-F 8:30am-5:30pm, Sa 8:30am-6pm. **Post Code:** EH1.

⛰ ACCOMMODATIONS

Edinburgh accommodations come in all shapes and sizes, but not all availabilities. **Hostels** and **hotels** are the only city center options; **B&Bs** and **guest houses** begin on the outer edges. It's a good idea to book ahead in summer, and absolutely essential to be well ahead of the game during festival-time (late July to early Sept.) and New Year's. The TIC's booking service can help during busy periods.

HOSTELS AND CAMPING

This backpacker's paradise offers a bevy of cheap and convenient hostels, many of them smack-dab in the middle of town, ranging from the small and cozy to the huge and party-oriented. Expect cliques of long-term residents.

▨ **High St. Hostel,** 8 Blackfriars St. (☎557 3984). Good facilities, party atmosphere, and convenient Royal Mile location—this has long been an Edinburgh favorite. Pool table, movies, continental breakfast (£1.60). With Castle Rock Hostel and Royal Mile Backpackers, part of the **Scotland's Top Hostels** chain (www.scotlands-top-hostels.com). Single-sex dorms £10.50-13. ❷

Castle Rock Hostel, 15 Johnston Terr. (☎225 9666). Just steps from the castle, this large but friendly place has 220 beds in spacious 8- to 12-bed single-sex rooms. Regal views and top-notch common areas. Nightly movies. Internet access (80p per 30min.). Continental breakfast (£1.60). Dorms £10.50-13. ❷

Brodies Backpackers, 12 High St. (☎/fax 556 6770; www.brodieshostels.co.uk). Relaxed, good-times environment at this relatively small Royal Mile hostel. 4 comfy dorms (3 co-ed, 1 all-female); slightly cramped common room. Internet access. Dorms Sept.-July M-Th £10-14, F-Su £12-16; Aug. £17. Weekly £59-89. ❷

Edinburgh Backpackers, 65 Cockburn St. (that's CO-burn; ☎220 1717; www.hoppo.com). Friendly hostel with a great location. 110 beds in co-ed dorms. Common areas are on the small side, but offer pool table, ping pong, and TV. 10% discount at the downstairs cafe. Reception 24hr. Check-out 10am. Dorms £12.50-15. **34a Cockburn St.** has doubles and twins with kitchen access (£42.50-49). ❷

Royal Mile Backpackers, 105 High St. (☎557 6120). Spiffy, communal-feeling 38-bed facility. Guests can use amenities at nearby High St. Hostel. Dorms £10.50-13. ❷

St. Christopher's Inn, 9-13 Market St. (☎226 1446; www.st-christophers.co.uk), across from Waverley Station. Clean and friendly Edinburgh outpost of a chain known for its large London hostels. Dorms £11-17; singles £40; doubles £40-46. ❷

City Centre Tourist Hostel, 5 West Register St. (☎/fax 556 8070; www.edinburghhostels.com). Small, comfortable New Town hostel close to Waverley Station. Super-clean and without an overpowering party atmosphere. Reception 24hr. Dorms £12-20. ❷

Belford Hostel, 6-8 Douglas Gdns. (☎225 6209). Close to Haymarket Station. Self-proclaimed "Scotland's Craziest Church"—Gothic stone ceilings soar over pastel bunk beds. Great bar area and TV room. Dorms £11.50-15; doubles and twins £37.50-45. ❷

Argyle Backpackers, 14 Argyle Pl. (☎667 9991; argyle@sol.co.uk), south of the Meadows and the Royal Mile. Take bus #40 or 41 from The Mound to Melville Dr. 2 renovated townhouses with relaxing patio. An alternative to louder city hostels with B&B-style private rooms, some with TV. Dorms £10-12; doubles and twins £24-40. ❷

SYHA Hostels (www.syha.org.uk). They may not be quite as fun as other hostels, but they're certainly clean.

> **Eglinton,** 18 Eglinton Cres. (☎337 1120). Near Haymarket Station. Attractive though oft-crowded townhouse with 160 beds in 3- to 14-bed dorms. Continental breakfast included, dinner £4.20. Check-out 9:30am. Curfew 2am. Dorms £11.50-15, under 18 £10.25-13.25. ❷

> **Bruntsfield,** 7 Bruntsfield Cres. (☎447 2994). Take bus #11, 16, or 17. Pleasant hostel with tidy dorms. Sony PlayStation access £1. Dorms £11.50-15, under 18 £10.25-13.25. ❷

> **Central,** Robertson's Close, Cowgate (☎556 5566) and **Pleasance,** New Arthur Pl. (☎668 3423). Open July-Aug. only. Singles £16-18.50. ❷

Camping: Edinburgh Caravan Club Site, Marine Dr. (☎312 6874), by the Forth. Take bus #8A from North Bridge. Electricity, showers, hot water, laundry facilities, and shop. £3.75-4.75 per person, £2-3 per pitch. ❶

HOTELS

Most of the city center hotels have stratospheric prices. At the affordable end are budget **chain hotels**—entirely lacking in character, but comfortable and often very well-located. Three sit on prime Old Town real estate: **Premier Lodge** ❹, 94 Grassmarket (☎(0870) 700 1370; www.premierlodge.com; £50 per room); **Hotel Ibis** ❺, 6 Hunter Sq. (☎240 7000); and **Travelodge** ❺, 33 St. Mary's St. (☎(0870) 085 0950; www.travelodge.co.uk; £70). **Travel Inn** ❹, 1 Morrison Link, is near Haymarket Station. (☎0870 238 3319; www.travelinn.co.uk. £55 per room.) It's also worth considering the small hotels near **Calton Hill,** around 10min. from Waverley Station. **Greenside Hotel** ❸, 9 Royal Terr., is a recently refurbished Georgian building with fine views of the Firth from its top floors. (☎557 0022. Singles £25-50; doubles £45-90.) The **Carlton Greens Hotel** ❹, 2 Carlton Terr., is peaceful and pleasant, with views of Arthur's Seat. (☎556 6570. Singles £35-60; doubles £70-90.)

B&BS AND GUEST HOUSES

B&Bs (£20-30) cluster in three well-stocked colonies, all of which are fairly easy to walk to, and served by numerous buses from Princes St. Try Gilmore Pl., Viewforth Terr., or Huntington Gdns. in the **Bruntsfield** district south from the west end of Princes St. (bus #11, 16, or 17 west/southbound); Dalkeith Rd. and Minto St. in **Newington**, south from the east end of Princes St. (bus #37, 7, or 31, among others); or **Pilrig**, northeast from the east end of Princes St. (bus #11 east/northbound).

◪ **Merlin Guest House**, 14 Hartington Pl., Bruntsfield (☎ 229 3864). Just under 1 mi. southwest of the Royal Mile. Comfortable, well-priced rooms in a leafy-green neighborhood. £15-22.50 per person; student discounts in winter. ❷

◪ **Ardenlee Guest House**, 9 Eyre Pl. (☎ 556 2838), at the extreme northern edge of New Town. Walk or take bus #23 or 27 from Hanover St. northbound to the corner of Dundas St. and Eyre Pl. Near the Royal Botanic Garden, this friendly guest house offers large, comfy rooms. No smoking. £26-35 per person. ❸

Robertson Guest House, 5 Hartington Gdns., Bruntsfield (☎ 229 2652). Quiet and welcoming, with top-notch breakfasts. No smoking. Singles £22-50; doubles £44-74. ❸

Balmoral Guest House, 32 Pilrig St., Pilrig (☎ 554 1857; www.balmoralguest-house.co.uk). Wrap yourself in a warm welcome at this comfortable, well-furnished guest house. No smoking. Singles £20-30; doubles £34-60. ❸

Avondale Guest House, 10 South Gray St., Newington (☎ 667 6779). From Waverley Station, turn right on Princes St. and again on North Bridge St., or catch any Newington-bound bus to the corner of Minto St. and West Mayfield. Turn right onto West Mayfield and again onto South Gray St. Friendly proprietors welcome you to their small, smartly decorated house. Free Internet access. Singles £20-30; doubles £36-60. ❸

Arlington Guest House, 23a Minto St., Newington (☎ 667 3967; www.the-arlington.co.uk). Straight down North Bridge a little over 1 mi. south of the city center. Stately but warm house on a major thoroughfare. Singles £18-25; doubles £32-44. ❷

Santa Lucia Guest House, 14 Kilmaurs Terr., Newington (☎ 667 8694). Off Dalkeith Rd.; take bus #14, 21, 33, or 82. Relaxed atmosphere and calm neighborhood, all rooms with TV. £15-25 per person; £2 less without breakfast. ❷

◪ FOOD

Edinburgh boasts an increasingly wide range of cuisines and restaurants. Of course, if it's traditional eats you're after, the capital won't disappoint, with everything from haggis at the neighborhood pub to creative "modern Scottish" preparations at the city's top restaurants. If you're looking for food on the cheap, many **pubs** offer student and hosteler discounts in the early evening, takeaway shops on **South Clerk St., Leith St.,** and **Lothian Rd.** have well-priced Chinese and Indian fare, and there's always **Sainsbury's**, 9-10 St. Andrews Sq. (☎ 225 8400. Open M-Sa 7am-10pm, Su 10am-8pm.)

OLD TOWN

◪ **The City Cafe**, 19 Blair St. (☎ 220 0125). Right off the Royal Mile behind the Tron Kirk, this Edinburgh institution is popular with the young and tightly-clad. Relaxed by day, and a flashy pre-club spot by night. Try the venison burgers (£4-6) or nachos. Incredible shakes, immortalized by *Trainspotting*. Food served M-Th 11am-11pm, F-Su 11am-10pm; drinks until 1am. ❷

Kebab Mahal, 7 Nicolson Sq. (☎ 667 5214). This unglamorous, student-filled hole-in-the-wall will stuff you with authentic Indian food for under £5. Worth the wait. Open Su-Th noon-midnight, F-Sa noon-2am. ❶

THE BIG SPLURGE

EDINBURGH'S TOP TABLES

After extensive, expensive, and delicious research, *Let's Go* has chosen what might just be the two very best restaurants in all the city. Even if our tendency towards superlative is misplaced, this pair won't disappoint.

Restaurant Martin Wishart is the only restaurant in the city to win a Michelin star (that, for the uninitiated, means it's damn good). The eponymous chef has trained with London's top culinary talent, and diners at his minimalist Leith showcase can't stop raving about the exquisite, imaginative modern French cooking. A two-course set lunch is £14.50; two courses from the *a la carte* dinner menu run about £28. *(54 The Shore, Leith.* ☎ *553 3557. Open Tu-F noon-2pm and 7-10pm, Sa 7-10pm.)*

One of Edinburgh's hottest eateries, **The Atrium** dazzles with elegant but creative decor and expert service. The real treat, of course, is the food—modern Scottish cuisine that makes wonderfully inventive use of local ingredients grown, hunted, or yanked from the sea. Two courses at the Atrium cost about £28. Reservations are essential. *(10 Cambridge St.* ☎ *228 8882. Open M-F noon-2pm and 6-10pm, Sa 6-10pm.)*

The Elephant House, 21 George IV Bridge (☎ 220 5355). A perfect place to chill, chat, smoke, or pore over the stack of newspapers, all under the watchful eyes of 600 elephants. Exotic teas and coffees, the best shortbread in the universe, and filling fare for less than £5. Great views of the castle and Old Town from the back room. Happy hour M-Sa 9-10pm. Live music Th 7pm. Open daily 8am-11pm. ❶

The Last Drop, 72-74 Grassmarket (☎ 225 4851). Tourist-friendly pub next to the old gallows (hence the name). "Haggis, tatties, and neeps" in carnivore and herbivore versions. Nearly everything £3 for students and hostelers before 7:30pm. Open 10am-2am. ❶

NEW TOWN

🏠**The Basement,** 10a-12a Broughton St. (☎ 557 0097). The menu of this cheap, high-quality restaurant changes daily, with plenty of vegetarian courses. Well-known for Mexican fare Sa-Su and Thai cuisine on W nights. Draws a lively mix of locals to its candlelit cavern. Make reservations F-Sa. Food served daily noon-10pm; drinks until 1am. ❷

Lost Sock Diner, 11 East London St. (☎ 557 6097). True, launderettes don't usually bring meals to mind. But this 50's-style diner is attached to one—order a delicious dish (£4) while waiting for your clothes dry. Open M 9am-4pm, Tu-F 9am-10pm, Sa 10am-10pm, Su 11am-5pm. ❶

Mussel Inn, 61-65 Rose St. (☎ 225 5979). Locals and tourists alike "muscle" their way "in" (thank you, thank you... we'll be here all night) for fresh, expertly-prepared seafood. Full lunch under £10, dinner under £15. Open M-Sa noon-10pm, Su 1:30-10pm. ❸

Hadrian's Brasserie, 2 North Bridge (☎ 557 5000). Given its suave, inviting decor and location in the swanky Balmoral Hotel, you might expect to pay more for Hadrian's classic British dishes. All-day set menu £10.50, dinner around £14. Open M-Sa 7-10:30am, noon-2:30pm, 6:30-10:30pm; Su 7:30-11am, 12:30-3pm, 6:30-10pm. ❸

ELSEWHERE

🏠**Ndebele,** 57 Home St. (☎ 221 1141), in Tolcross, ½ mi. south from the west end of Princes St. Named for a tribe from Swaziland, this atmospheric restaurant serves generous portions for under £5. Try an avocado, mushroom, and cucumber sandwich (£3), or sample the daily African special. Mind-numbing array of African and South American coffees and fresh juices. Open daily 10am-10pm. ❶

Fishers, 1 The Shore (☎ 554 5666), in Leith, near the water, and long one of the city's most popular restaurants. Outstandingly fresh seafood, with preparations from the exotic to the simple. Service is casual but attentive. Entrees £12-17. Reservations advised. Open M-Sa noon-10:30pm, Su 12:30-10:30pm. ❸

🔍 SIGHTS

TOURS. A boggling array of tour companies tout themselves as "the original" or "the scariest"; the most worthwhile is ◧**McEwan's 80/- Edinburgh Literary Pub Tour** (that's "McEwan's eighty shilling," in case you thought you'd found a glaring typo). Led by professional actors, this 2hr., alcohol-friendly crash course in Scottish literature meets outside the Beehive Inn on Grassmarket. (☎ 226 6665. July-Aug. daily 6 and 7:30pm; June and Sept. daily 7:30pm; Apr.-May and Oct. Th-Su 7:30pm; Nov.-Mar. F 7:30pm. £7, concessions £5.) Or consider a one-on-one encounter with the MacKenzie Poltergeist on the **City of the Dead Tour.** (40 Candlemaker Row. ☎ 225 9044. Daily 8:30 and 10pm. £5, children £4.) The older **Mercat Tours,** leaving from Mercat Cross in front of St. Giles Cathedral, enters Edinburgh's spooky underground vaults. (☎ 557 6464. Groups depart hourly 11am-9pm. £4-6.)

Edinburgh is best explored by foot, but should you get lazy, several separate (but similar) hop-on/hop-off open-top bus tours stop at the major sights beginning at Waverley Bridge. **Lothian Buses'** Edinburgh Tour departs at least every 15min. (☎ 555 6363. £7.50, concessions £6, children £2.50.) Other operators include **Guide Friday** (☎ 556 2244) and **MacTours** (☎ 270 0770).

THE OLD TOWN AND THE ROYAL MILE

Edinburgh's medieval center, the fascinating **Royal Mile** defines **Old Town** and passes many classic houses and attractions. The Old Town once packed thousands of inhabitants into a scant few square miles, with narrow shopfronts and slum buildings towering to a dozen stories.

■**EDINBURGH CASTLE.** Perched atop an extinct volcano and dominating the city center, the castle is a testament to Edinburgh's past strategic importance. Though there were settlements here long before, the oldest surviving building in the complex is tiny 12th-century **St. Margaret's Chapel,** thought to have been built by King David I in memory of his mother. The rest of the castle is the result of centuries of renovation and rebuilding; the most recent additions date to the 1920s. The **Palace,** begun in the 1430s, contains the room where Mary, Queen of Scots, gave birth to King James VI (see **Mary, Mary...** p. 571) as well as the **Scottish Crown Jewels,** older than their counterparts in London. Here, too, is the storied though visually unspectacular Stone of Scone, more commonly known as the **Stone of Destiny** (see **Scone Palace,** p. 602). Other highlights include the 15th-century cannon **Mons Meg,** the **Scottish National War Memorial,** and the magnificent views all the way to Fife, though on the whole the castle is perhaps most impressive from the exterior. The **One O'Clock Gun** fires daily (except Su) at 1pm. Guided tours of the castle are free; a comprehensive audio guide costs £3. (*Looming over the city center.* ☎ 225 9846. *Open Apr.-Sept. daily 9:30am-6pm; Oct.-Mar. 9:30am-5pm. Last admission 45min. before close. £8, seniors £6.50, children £2, under 5 free.*)

THE ROYAL MILE: CASTLE HILL AND LAWNMARKET

CASTLE HILL. The Scotch Whisky Experience at the Scotch Whisky Heritage Centre, 334 Castle Hill, provides a Disney-Worldish tour through the "history and mystery" of Scotland's most famous export. (*Open daily 10am-5pm, extended in summer. £7, concessions £4.75, children £3.40.*) Nearby, the **Outlook Tower** affords incredible city views from a rooftop terrace. Its 150-year-old **camera obscura** captures a moving image of the streets below. (*Open daily 10am-6pm. Tower and camera obscura £4.25.*)

GLADSTONE'S LAND. The oldest surviving house on the Royal Mile (c. 1617) has been carefully preserved, boasts hand-painted ceilings and a fine collection of 17th-century Dutch art, and is staffed with knowledgeable guides. *(477b Lawnmarket. ☎ 226 5856. Open Apr.-Oct. M-Sa 10am-5pm, Su 2-5pm. £5, students £3.75.)*

WRITER'S MUSEUM. This tribute to literary personae, established in Lady Stair's House, contains memorabilia and manuscripts belonging to three of Scotland's greatest wordwrights—Robert Burns, Sir Walter Scott, and Robert Louis Stevenson. *(Through the passage at 477 Lawnmarket. ☎ 529 4901. Open M-Sa 10am-5pm, during Festival also Su 2-5pm. Free.)*

THE ROYAL MILE: HIGH STREET

◪HIGH KIRK OF ST. GILES. The kirk is Scotland's principal church, sometimes known as **St. Giles Cathedral.** From its pulpit, Reformer John Knox delivered the sermons that drove the Catholic Mary, Queen of Scots, into exile. Spectacular stained-glass windows illuminate the structure; its crown spire is one of Edinburgh's hallmarks. Most of the present structure was built in the 15th century, with restorations and additions ongoing since, but parts date as far back as 1126. The impressive 20th-century **Thistle Chapel** honors the Order of the Thistle. St. Giles is flanked on the east by the stone **Mercat Cross,** marking the site of the medieval market (hence, "mercat"), and on the west by the **Heart of Midlothian,** inlaid in the pavement. According to city legend, spitting on the Heart protects you from being hanged in the square. (It can't hurt, right?) The cathedral hosts free organ and choral concerts throughout the year. *(Where Lawnmarket becomes High St. ☎ 225 4363. Open Easter to mid-Sept. M-F 9am-7pm, Sa 9am-5pm, Su 1-5pm; mid-Sept. to Easter M-Sa 9am-5pm, Su 1-5pm. Requested donation in the Thistle Chapel £1.)*

TRON KIRK. A block downhill from St. Giles rises the high-steepled Tron Kirk—built to deal with the overflow of 16th-century religious zealots from St. Giles. Today, it functions as the **Old Town Information Centre,** with local displays and an archaeology exhibit. *(Open July-Aug. daily 10am-7pm; June and Sept.-Oct. 10am-5pm. Free.)*

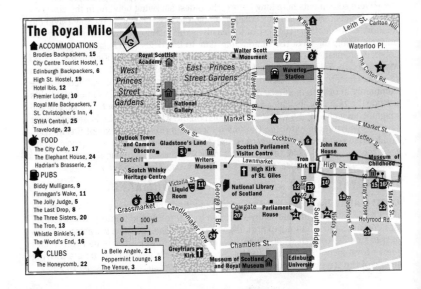

The Royal Mile

🛏 ACCOMMODATIONS
Brodies Backpackers, **15**
City Centre Tourist Hostel, **1**
Edinburgh Backpackers, **6**
High St. Hostel, **19**
Hotel Ibis, **12**
Premier Lodge, **10**
Royal Mile Backpackers, **7**
St. Christopher's Inn, **4**
SYHA Central, **25**
Travelodge, **23**

🍴 FOOD
The City Cafe, **17**
The Elephant House, **24**
Hadrian's Brasserie, **2**

🍺 PUBS
Biddy Mulligans, **9**
Finnegan's Wake, **11**
The Jolly Judge, **5**
The Last Drop, **8**
The Three Sisters, **20**
The Tron, **13**
Whistle Binkie's, **14**
The World's End, **16**

★ CLUBS
The Honeycomb, **22**
La Belle Angele, **21**
Peppermint Lounge, **18**
The Venue, **3**

SCOTTISH PARLIAMENT VISITORS CENTRE. This centre gives background on Scotland's new governing body (instituted 1999). The new Scottish Parliament Building at Holyrood (see below) is scheduled to open in 2003. In the meantime, the parliament debates at the former **Church of Scotland Assembly Hall,** accessible through Mylne's Close, off the Royal Mile and across from Johnston Terr. Visitors can watch from the public gallery; the fiery Thursday afternoon questioning session is especially popular. Tickets can be reserved no more than a week in advance. *(Visitors Centre at the corner of George IV Bridge and Royal Mile. ☎ 348 5000. Open M-F 10-5pm, earlier when Parliament is in session (Sept.-June). Public gallery ☎ 348 5411. Free.)*

THE ROYAL MILE: CANONGATE

Canongate, the steep hill that constitutes the last segment of the Royal Mile, was once a separate burgh and part of an Augustinian abbey. Here, the Royal Mile's furious tourism begins to dwindle.

CANONGATE KIRK. Yet another Royal Mile church, this 17th-century chapel is where royals worship when in residence. Adam Smith, founder of modern economics, lies in its sloping graveyard. Nearby, find the famous joint effort of three literary Roberts: Robert Louis Stevenson commemorated a monument erected by Robert Burns in memory of Robert Fergusson. *(Open Easter to mid-Sept. M-F 9am-7pm, Sa 9am-5pm, Su 1-5pm; mid-Sept. to Easter M-Sa 9am-5pm, Su 1-5pm. Free.)*

SCOTTISH POETRY LIBRARY. A relaxing refuge from the main tourist drag in an award-winning piece of expansive modern architecture, the library treasures a fine collection of Scottish and international poetry. *(5 Crichton's Close. ☎ 557 2876. Open M-F noon-6pm, Sa noon-4pm; longer during Festival. Free.)*

HOLYROOD

PALACE OF HOLYROODHOUSE AND HOLYROOD ABBEY. This Stewart palace abuts Holyrood Park and the peak of Arthur's Seat, and dates from the 16th century. It remains Queen Elizabeth II's official Scottish residence; only parts of the ornate interior are open to the public. It was home to Mary, Queen of Scots, and site of the brutal murder of Mary's secretary, David Rizzio. On the palace grounds lie the 12th-century ruins of **Holyrood Abbey,** ransacked during the Reformation. Only a doorway remains from David I's original construction, begun in 1128; most of the ruins date from the later 12th and 13th centuries. *(At the east end of the Royal Mile. ☎ 556 7371. Open Apr.-Oct. daily 9:30am-6pm; Nov.-Mar. M-Sa 9:30am-4:30pm; last admission 45min. before close. No admission during official residences (often late May and late June to early July). £6.50, seniors £5, children £3.30, families £16.30.)*

NEW SCOTTISH PARLIAMENT BUILDING. The new Scottish Parliament Building, designed by the late Catalan architect Enric Miralles, is scheduled to open in 2003. Until it does, get a preview at the **visitors center** on the construction site. *(Holyrood Rd. Open daily 10am-4pm. Free.)* For more parliamentary doings, visit the official Scottish Parliament Visitors Centre (see above).

ELSEWHERE IN THE OLD TOWN

GREYFRIARS KIRK. Off George IV Bridge, the 17th-century kirk rests in a quiet churchyard that, while lovely, is estimated to contain 250,000 bodies and has long been considered haunted. A few centuries ago, body-snatchers like the infamous Burke and Hare dug up their precious corpses here. The kirkyard's sweeter claim to fame is loyal pooch **Greyfriars Bobby;** the terrier's grave is in front of the kirk, his much-photographed statue at the southwestern corner of George IV Bridge. *(Beyond the gates atop Candlemakers Row. ☎ 225 1900. English services 11am, Gaelic services Su 12:30pm. Open Easter-Oct. M-F 10:30am-4:30pm, Sa until 2:30pm. Free.)*

> **DEAD MAN'S BEST FRIEND** Greyfriars Cemetery's most famous resident may be one John Gray. According to local legend, Gray once lived on the Cowgate with his faithful pooch, Bobby. After Gray's death, Bobby breached the cemetery every night for 14 years to sleep on his master's tombstone. A statue of "Greyfriars Bobby" was erected by the city to commemorate the dog's loyalty. The sweet story has since found its way to books and even a Disney flick, and the statue ranks among Scotland's most photographed monuments. Naysayers claim that the tombstone actually belongs to a *different* John Gray—not Bobby's master—and that the dog's real affection was for a nearby donut shop. Such spoilsports didn't stop Greyfriars Bobby pub from cashing in—one night, pub workers stole out with a screwdriver and reversed the statue's position on its pedestal. Thanks to this maneuver, their pub is now Scotland's most photographed watering hole.

NATIONAL LIBRARY OF SCOTLAND. The library rotates exhibitions from its vast archives, which include a Gutenberg Bible, the last letter of Mary, Queen of Scots, and the only surviving copy of *The Wallace*, a wildly popular epic poem which inspired a certain wildly popular Hollywood movie. (*George IV Bridge.* ☎ *226 4531. Open M-Sa 10am-5pm, Su 2-5pm; during Festival M-F until 8pm. Free.*)

THE NEW TOWN

Edinburgh's New Town is a masterpiece of Georgian design. James Craig, a 23-year-old architect, won the city-planning contest in 1767, and his rectangular grid of three parallel streets (**Queen, George,** and **Princes**) linking two large squares (**Charlotte** and **St. Andrew**) reflects the Scottish Enlightenment's belief in order. Queen St. and Princes St., the outer streets, were built up on only one side to allow views of the Firth of Forth and the Old Town, respectively. Princes St. is also home to the venerable **Jenner's,** the Harrod's of Scotland. On your way in or out, wander through Charlotte Sq., Edinburgh's most elegant 18th-century plaza.

THE WALTER SCOTT MONUMENT. Statues of Sir Walter and his dog preside inside the spire of this Gothic "steeple without a church." Climb 287 winding steps for an eagle's-eye view of the Princes St. Gardens, the castle, and Old Town's Market St. (☎ *529 4068. On Princes St. between The Mound and Waverley Bridge. Open June-Sept. M-Sa 9am-8pm, Su 10am-6pm; Mar.-May and Oct. M-Sa 9am-6pm, Su 10am-6pm; Nov.-Feb. M-Sa 9am-4pm, Su 10am-6pm. £2.50.*)

GEORGIAN HOUSE. Guides staff each room of this elegantly restored home, giving a fair picture of how the well-heeled lived 200 years ago. (*7 Charlotte Sq. From Princes St., turn right on Charlotte St. and then take the second left.* ☎ *226 3318. Open Apr.-Oct. daily 10am-6pm; Nov.-Mar. 11am-4pm. £5, concessions £3.75, children £1.*)

CALTON HILL. This hill at the eastern end of New Town provides as fine a view of the city and the Firth of Forth as Edinburgh Castle (finer, in fact, since you can't see the castle from the castle). Climb 143 steps higher inside the castellated **Nelson Monument,** built in 1807 in memory of the Battle of Trafalgar. (☎ *556 2716. Open Apr.-Sept. M 1-6pm, Tu-Sa 10am-6pm; Oct.-Mar. M-Sa 10am-3pm. £2.*) The hilltop grounds are also home to the **Old Observatory** (1776), the **New Observatory** (1818), **Dugald Stewart's Monument** (1837), and the **National Monument** (1822), affectionately known as "Edinburgh's Disgrace." The structure, an ersatz Parthenon designed by the city to commemorate those killed in the Napoleonic Wars, was scrapped when civic coffers ran dry after a mere 12 columns were erected.

BEYOND THE CITY CENTER

LEITH AND THE BRITANNIA. Edinburgh's port on the Firth of Forth, **Leith** stands 2 mi. northeast of the city center. Incorporated into the capital in 1920, the area went into steep decline following WWII. Since the 1980s, however, Leith has undergone a revival, its ugly council estates and abandoned warehouses replaced (or at least joined) by upmarket flats, restaurants, and bars. It's an interesting neighborhood and a great place to come for a meal, particularly if you're craving seafood. The most ambitious building projects are along the waterfront, a prime example being the new **Ocean Terminal Shopping Centre.** Moored behind the Ocean Terminal is one of Edinburgh's top tourist attractions, the ■ **Royal Yacht Britannia.** Used by the Queen and her family from 1953 to 1997, *Britannia* sailed around the world on state visits and royal holidays before going into permanent retirement here. Visitors can follow a audio tour of the entire ship—all the furnishings have been left as they were when it was last used. The interior is surprisingly subdued, but the tour also reveals the strict etiquette and arduous work required to keep royal standards afloat. *(Entrance inside the Ocean Terminal. ☎ 555 5566. Open Apr.-Sept. 9:30am-4:30pm; Oct.-Mar. 10am-3:30pm. £7.75, seniors £6, children £3.75, families £20.)* Bus #22 from Princes St. and #35 from the Royal Mile travel to Ocean Terminal via Leith town center; #16 also stops in Leith and passes close by the Ocean Terminal. Tour buses to the *Britannia* leave from Waverley Bridge.

DEAN VILLAGE. In a riverside valley west of the city center, Dean Village was once a busy milling community. Many of the mills remain—some now converted into trendy apartments—and the result is one of the city's most picturesque residential areas. The graceful four-arched **Dean Bridge**—a great feat of engineering when it opened in 1832—crosses high above the Water of Leith. A visit to this area might be combined with the **Scottish National Gallery of Modern Art** and **Dean Gallery** (see p. 560), both 10min. west of Dean Village along the scenic Water of Leith walkway. *(To get to Dean Village, walk north on Queensferry St. from the west end of Princes St. Buses #41 and 42 travel up Queensferry St. from The Mound.)*

CRAIGMILLAR CASTLE. This finely-preserved 15th-century castle stands 2½ mi. southeast of central Edinburgh. Mary, Queen of Scots, fled here after the murder of her secretary at Holyroodhouse. While she was here, plans emerged for the murder of her second husband, Lord Darnley. *Let's Go* would not have gone anywhere near Mary, Queen of Scots. *(Take bus #33 from Princes St. to the corner of Old Dalkeith Rd. and Craigmillar Castle Rd., then walk 10min. up the castle road. ☎ 661 4445. Open Apr.-Sept. daily 9:30am-6:30pm; Oct.-Mar. M-W and Sa 9:30am-4:30pm, Th 9:30am-1pm, Su 2pm-4:30pm. £2.20, seniors £1.60, children 75p.)*

EDINBURGH ZOO. At long last, your search for the world's largest penguin pool has come to an end. You'll find it (along with exhibits featuring some 1000 other animals) 2½ mi. west of the city center at the well-regarded Edinburgh Zoo. *(Take buses #12, 26, or 31 westbound from Princes St. ☎ 334 9171. Open Apr.-Sept. daily 9am-6pm; Oct.-Mar. 9am-4:30pm. £7.50, seniors £5, children £4.50.)*

GARDENS AND PARKS

HOLYROOD PARK. Just off the eastern end of the Royal Mile, Holyrood Park is a true city oasis, a natural wilderness replete with hills, moorland, and lochs. At 823 ft., ■ **Arthur's Seat,** the park's highest point, affords stunning views of the city and countryside, extending as far as the Highlands. Considered a holy place by the Picts, Arthur's Seat is probably a debasement of "Ard-na-Saigheid," Gaelic for "the height of the flight of arrows," or possibly of "Archer's Seat." Traces of forts and Bronze Age terraces dot the surrounding hillside. From the Palace of Holyrood, the walk to the summit takes about 45min. **Queen's Drive** circles the park and intersects with Holyrood Rd. by the palace.

PRINCES STREET GARDENS. Located directly in the city center and affording fantastic views of Old Town and the castle, this lush park is on the site of now-drained Nor' Loch, where Edinburghers used to drown their accused witches. The Loch has been replaced with an impeccably manicured lawn, stone fountains, and enough shady trees to provide shelter from the Scottish "sun."

ROYAL BOTANIC GARDENS. Edinburgh's requisite herbaceous oasis has plants from around the world, as well as a shop and cafe. *(Inverleith Row. Take bus #23 or 27 from Hanover St.* ☎ *552 7171. Open Apr.-Aug. daily 9:30am-7pm; Mar. and Sept. 9:30am-6pm; Feb. and Oct. 9:30am-5pm; Nov.-Jan. 9:30am-4pm.)*

🏛 GALLERIES AND MUSEUMS

NATIONAL GALLERIES OF SCOTLAND

☎ *624 6200. All open M-Sa 10am-5pm; Su noon-5pm; longer hours during Festival. All free, except for special exhibits.*

Edinburgh's four galleries form an elite group, all excellent collections housed in stately buildings and connected by a free hourly shuttle.

■ **NATIONAL GALLERY OF SCOTLAND.** Housed in a grand 19th-century building designed by William Playfair, this prize gallery has a superb stash of works by Renaissance, Romantic, and Impressionist masters including Raphael, Titian, Gauguin, Degas, and Monet. The basement houses a fine selection of Scottish art. *(On The Mound between the two halves of the Princes St. Gardens.)*

SCOTTISH NATIONAL PORTRAIT GALLERY. Past the lavishly gilded entrance hall, the gallery features the faces of the famous, including the definitive portraits of wordsmith Robert Burns, renegade Bonnie Prince Charlie, and royal troublemaker Mary, Queen of Scots. *(1 Queen St., north of St. Andrew Sq.)*

SCOTTISH NATIONAL GALLERY OF MODERN ART. In the west end of town, the gallery has an excellent rotating collection that includes works by Braque, Matisse, and Picasso. Take the free shuttle, bus #13 from George St., or walk—several picturesque paths follow the Water of Leith to Belford Rd. *(75 Belford Rd.)*

DEAN GALLERY. The newest addition to the National Galleries and dedicated to Surrealist and Dadaist art, the gallery also has a massive collection of work by landmark sculptor Eduardo Paolozzi, best known for his machine-like human figures. A towering, three-storey Paolozzi statue dominates the museum. *(73 Belford Rd., across from the Gallery of Modern Art.)*

OTHER MUSEUMS AND GALLERIES

MUSEUM OF SCOTLAND AND ROYAL MUSEUM. These two connected museums and their stunning architecture are not to be missed. The superbly designed ■ **Museum of Scotland,** opened in 1998, traces the whole of Scottish history through an impressive collection of treasured objects and decorative art. Highlights include the Monymusk Reliquary, said to have once contained St. Columba's bones and been present at the Battle of Bannockburn, and the Maiden, Edinburgh's pre-French Revolution guillotine, used on High St. around 1565. Gallery tours and audioguides in various languages are free. Less modern and more motley, the **Royal Museum** has exhibits on natural history and international art dating back to the Roman era. The rooftop terrace provides a 360° view of the city. Watch the **Millennium Clock** chime every hour—it's a towering, nightmarish display of mechanized Gothic figures. *(Chambers St. Museum of Scotland* ☎ *247 4422. Royal Museum* ☎ *247 4219. Both open M and W-Sa 10am-5pm, Tu 10am-8pm, Su noon-5pm. Free.)*

OUR DYNAMIC EARTH. Edinburgh is proud of its newest museum, a glitzy, high-tech, high-priced lesson in geology, natural history, and ecology. Part amusement park, part science experiment, it's billed as an "experience." Computerized time machines take you back to various simulated environments, including a prehistoric volcano and an elaborate rainforest. Kids and science buffs should have a blast. Look for the huge white tent-like structure next to the Palace of Holyroodhouse. (Holyrood Rd. ☎ 550 7800. Open Apr.-Oct. daily 10am-6pm; Nov.-Mar. W-Su 10am-5pm. £8, concessions £4.50, families £21-24.)

OTHER MUSEUMS. The Museum of Childhood has an insightful display of old toys, such as the "creeping baby automata." (42 High St. ☎ 529 4142. Open M-Sa 10am-5pm, during Festival also Su 2-5pm. Free.) The picturesque **John Knox House** offers an engaging look at former inhabitants John Knox and James Mossman, and the Protestant-Catholic conflicts that engulfed them. (43 High St. ☎ 556 9579. Open M-Sa 10am-4:30pm; July-Aug. also Su noon-5pm. £2.25, concessions £1.75, children 75p.) **Canongate Tolbooth** (c. 1591), with a beautiful clock face and hangman's hook projecting over the Royal Mile, once served as a prison and gallows for "elite" criminals. Now it houses **The People's Story Museum,** an eye-opening look at "the ordinary people of Edinburgh." (163 Canongate. ☎ 529 4057. Open M-Sa 10am-5pm, during Festival also Su 2-5pm. Free.) Across the street in 16th-century Huntly House, the **Museum of Edinburgh** contains a hodgepodge of artifacts and the original 1638 National Covenant. (142 Canongate. ☎ 529 4143. Open M-Sa 10am-5pm, during Festival also Su 2-5pm. Free.)

SMALLER ART GALLERIES. The City Art Centre houses the city's collection, including modern Scottish work, and hosts international exhibitions. (2 Market St. ☎ 529 3993. Open M-Sa 10am-5pm; during Festival also open Su. Free, except special exhibits.) The **Fruitmarket Gallery** flaunts a variety of Scottish and world art. (Beneath The Mound and down Market St. ☎ 225 2383. Open M-Sa 11am-6pm, Su noon-5pm. Free.)

🎭 ENTERTAINMENT

The summer sees an especially joyful string of events—music in the gardens, plays and films, and ceilidhs—and that's all before the Festival comes to town. In winter, shorter days and the crush of students promote a flourishing nightlife. No one knows it better than The List (£2.20), a comprehensive biweekly guide to events, available from any local newsagent.

THEATER AND FILM

Festival Theatre, 13-29 Nicholson St. (☎ 529 6000). Stages ballet and opera. Box office open M-Sa 10am-6pm and before curtain. Drastically discounted tickets (£5.50) for evening performances sometimes go on sale at 10am. Affiliated **King's Theatre,** 2 Leven St., promotes serious and comedic fare, musicals, opera, and pantomime.

Royal Lyceum Theatre, 30 Grindlay St. (☎ 248 4848). Scottish, English, and international theater. Box office open M-Sa 10am-6pm. Tickets £7-17.50; students half-price.

Traverse Theatre, 10 Cambridge St. (☎ 228 1404). Performs innovative, sometimes controversial drama. Box office open daily 11am-6pm. Tickets £1-2.

Bedlam Theatre, 11b Bristo Pl. (☎ 225 9893). The university theater presents excellent student productions of traditional and experimental drama in a converted church with a bedlam-red door. Box office open M-Sa 10am-6pm. Tickets £4-5.

The Stand Comedy Club, 5 York Pl. (☎ 558 7272). Acts every night, from accomplished headliners and improvisationalists to comedic singers and musical performers. Special 15-shows-per-day program for the Fringe Festival. Tickets £1-7.

The Filmhouse, 88 Lothian Rd. (☎228 2688). European and arthouse films, though quality Hollywood fare appears as well. £3.20-5.20. For mainstream cinema, try **Odeon,** 7 Clerk St. (☎667 0971), or **UGC Fountainpark,** Dundee St., Fountainbridge (☎(0870) 902 0417; bus #1, 28, 34, 35).

LIVE MUSIC

Thanks to an abundance of university students who never let books get in the way of a good night out, Edinburgh's live music scene is alive and well. Excellent impromptu and professional folk sessions take place at pubs (see p. 563), and many of the university houses also sponsor live shows—look for flyers near Bristol Sq. For a run-down of upcoming acts, look to *The List* or *The Gig Guide.* Free live jazz can be found at **Henry's Jazz Bar,** 8 Morrison St. (☎538 7385. Open W-Sa; performances around 8pm, doors open around 6pm.) **The Venue,** 15 Calton Rd. (☎557 3073), and **The Liquid Room,** 9c Victoria St. (☎225 2528; www.liquidroom.com), often host rock and progressive shows. **Ripping Records,** 91 South Bridge (☎226 7010), lists and sells tickets to rock, reggae, and pop performances. **Whistle Binkie's,** 4 Niddry St., off High St., is a subterranean pub with live music most nights. (☎557 5114. Open daily until 3am.)

❄ FESTIVALS

Edinburgh has special events year-round, but the real show is in August, when this city is *the* place to be in Europe. Prices rise, pubs and restaurants stay open later than late, and street performers have the run of the place. What's commonly referred to as "the Festival" actually encompasses a number of independently organized events. **The Edinburgh International Festival** is the original and most highbrow, the **Fringe** the biggest and longest. For more information on all the festivals, check out www.edinburghfestivals.co.uk.

EDINBURGH INTERNATIONAL FESTIVAL

Aug. 10-30 in 2003. Bookings can be made by post, phone, fax, web, or in person at The Hub, Edinburgh's Festival Centre, Castlehill, Edinburgh EH1 2NE. (☎473 2000; fax 473 2003; www.eif.co.uk. Open M-Sa from early Apr.; daily from late July.) Tickets £5-80, 50% off for students and children, 25% off for seniors.

Begun in 1947, the **Edinburgh International Festival** attracts top performers from around the globe, mainly in classical music, ballet, opera, and drama. The most popular single event is the festival's grand finale: a spectacular **Fireworks Concert** with pyrotechnics choreographed to orchestra music. Tickets go on sale in early April, and a full program is published by then. While the biggest events do sell out well in advance, you're not out of luck if you arrive ticketless in August: at least 50 tickets for major events are held back and sold on the day of performance (at The Hub M-Sa 9am, Su 10am; queue early). Throughout the festival, unsold tickets may be purchased at The Hub or at the door an hour prior to showtime. Selected shows are half-price on the day of performance.

▧ FRINGE FESTIVAL

Aug. 3-25 in 2003. Book tickets on the web, by phone, or in person at the Fringe Festival Office, 180 High St., Edinburgh EH1 1QS (☎226 0000; www.edfringe.com. Open mid-July to Aug. daily; mid-June to mid-July M-F limited hours.) Tickets £5-11, some free events.

Around the established festival has grown a less formal **Fringe Festival,** which now includes over 600 amateur and professional companies presenting theater, comedy, children's shows, folk and classical music, poetry, dance, mime, opera, revue, and various exhibitions. Any performer who can afford the registration fee can participate in the Fringe—you may see brilliance, you may see rubbish. Newspapers—led by *The Scotsman*—publish influential reviews, though word-of-mouth can be equally important. The Fringe program is available from mid-June; full listings and review summaries also appear on the Fringe website.

OTHER SUMMER FESTIVALS

May Day sparks the pagan revels of **Beltane,** up on Calton Hill and Arthur's Seat. The following festivities are just a few of the events that take place during the five-week period surrounding the Festival in August.

Military Tattoo: Tattoo Ticket Sale Office, 32 Market St, Edinburgh EH1 1QB (☎225 1188; www.edintattoo.co.uk). A spectacle of military bands, bagpipes, and drums performed in the shadow of the castle. Aug. 1-23 in 2003. Book well in advance by post, phone, fax, or web (from Dec.) or at the office (from Mar.). Tickets £9-27.50.

Edinburgh International Film Festival: Film Festival, The Filmhouse, 88 Lothian Rd., Edinburgh EH3 9BZ (☎229 2550; www.edfilmfest.org.uk). During the 2nd and 3rd weeks of Aug. Box office sells tickets starting at the end of July.

Edinburgh Jazz and Blues Festival: (☎467 5200; www.jazzmusic.co.uk). Runs late July and early Aug. A highlight is the free **Jazz on a Summer's Day** in Ross Theatre. Program available in June; bookings by phone, web, or at The Hub. Tickets £5-27.50.

Edinburgh International Book Festival: Scottish Book Centre, 137 Dundee St. (☎228 5444; www.edbookfest.co.uk). Europe's largest book celebration, early and mid-Aug. in Charlotte Sq. Gardens. Program available mid-June. Tickets £3-9; some free events.

HOGWILD ON HOGMANAY

The party doesn't stop, despite the long, dark winter. The light at the end of the tunnel is the insanity of **Hogmanay,** Edinburgh's traditional New Year's Eve festival, a serious street party with a week of associated events. Hogmanay has deep pagan roots and is observed all over Scotland—it celebrates the turn of the calendar and the return of the sun. (And depends heavily on booze.) For more information, including how to get tickets for the street party, inquire at The Hub or check out www.edinburghshogmanay.org.

ⓜ NIGHTLIFE

PUBS

Edinburgh claims to have the highest density of pubs in Europe, and *Let's Go* doesn't doubt it. (Actually, we started to count, but ended up three sheets to the wind and found ourselves in the wrong bed back at the hostel.) Pubs directly on the **Royal Mile** usually attract an older crowd, while students and backpackers tend to loiter in the **Old Town** just south. Casual pub-goers gallivant to live music on **Grassmarket, Candlemaker Row,** and **Victoria St.** The New Town also has its share of worthy watering-holes, some historical, and most strung along **Rose St.,** parallel to Princes St. Gay-friendly **Broughton St.** is increasingly popular for nightlife, though its pubs are more trendy than traditional. No matter where you are, you'll have to start thinking about finishing your drink somewhere between 11pm and 1am.

▩ **The Tron,** 9 Hunter Sq. (☎226 0931), behind the Tron Kirk. Wildly popular for its incredible deals and location. All pints are always under £2. Students and hostelers get £1 drinks on W nights in term (£1 cover), burgers and a pint for £4 year-round (3-7pm). 3

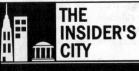

THE INSIDER'S CITY

EDINBURGH UNIVERSITY PUB CRAWL

Students at the prestigious University of Edinburgh enjoy intellectual challenge and scholarly debates. And beer. Lots and lots of beer. Thanks to *Let's Go*'s handy-dandy crash course on some of the students' favorite watering holes, you, too, can get the university experience (minus all those pesky classes and books).

1 Call in at the **Pear Tree House,** and make the most of the elusive Scottish summer in their peaceful beer garden. (38 West Nicholson St. ☎667 7796. Open daily noon-midnight.)

2 At the **Brass Monkey,** kick back in the cinema lounge with *Braveheart* and a pint of McEwan's. Life is good. (14 Drummond St. ☎556 1961. Open daily 10am-1am.)

floors of carousing. Frequent live music. Open daily 11:30am until at least 1am.

The Three Sisters, 139 Cowgate (☎622 6801). Copious space for dancing, drinking, and socializing; attracts a young, boisterous crowd to its 3 themed bars (Irish, Gothic, and Style). Outdoor beer garden. Open daily 9am-1am.

Biddy Mulligans, 96 Grassmarket (☎220 1246). Located in the middle of Grassmarket, an essential stop on any crawl. Kick things off early at this Irish-themed pub, which also serves big breakfasts. Open daily 9am-1am, food until 9pm.

The World's End, 4 High St. (☎556 3628), on the corner of St. Mary's St. Traditional and local-frequented. Open-mic Su (10pm-midnight) with free pints for extroverts willing to take the stage. Great pub food in 3 sizes: wee, not so wee, and friggin' huge. Open M-F 11am-1am, Sa-Su 10am-1am.

The Abbotsford, 3 Rose St. (☎225 5276). Probably the most authentic of the Rose St. pubs. Elegantly built in 1902, it retains the era's ambience. Popular with locals. Open daily 11am-11pm. Above-average pub grub served noon-2:30pm and 5:30-10pm.

Jolly Judge, 7a James Ct. (☎225 2669). Hidden down a close just off the Royal Mile, with a great, cozy atmosphere. Open daily noon-11pm.

Finnegan's Wake, 9b Victoria St. (☎226 3816). Promotes the Irish way with several stouts on tap and live Irish music every weekend. During the summer, broadcasts live Gaelic football and hurling on the big screen. Open daily 1pm-1am.

Pop Rokit (☎556 4272), corner of Broughton St. and Picardy Pl. More London-chic than Edinburgh-cozy, this trendy bar is a favorite pre-club hangout. Black-clad clientele dine on Mediterranean food in a smoked-glass-and-concrete interior. DJs spin house and soft funk Th-Su from 9pm. Open daily 11am-1am. Food served noon-7pm.

CLUBS

Edinburgh may be best known for its pubs, but the club scene is none too shabby. It is, however, in constant flux, with venues continuously closing down and reopening under new management—you're best off consulting *The List*. Clubs tend to cluster around Edinburgh's historically disreputable Cowgate, just downhill from and parallel to the Royal Mile, and most close at 3am.

The Honeycomb, 15-17 Niddry St. (☎530 5540). One of the city's top clubs. Many monthly theme nights and lots of guest DJs, so check what's on. Mostly house music, but also funk, drum 'n' bass, etc. Cover free-£10.

Bongo Club, 14 New St. (☎556 5204), off Canongate. A happily eclectic range of club nights and music; particularly noted for its hip-hop. Cover £4-6.

La Belle Angele, 11 Hasties Close (☎225 7536). Although the exterior is uninspiring, this laid-back venue showcases some of the best hip-hop, trance, and progressive house in the city. One F per month, La Belle hosts the blowout "Manga," known for its penetrating drum 'n' bass vibes. Cover £2-10.

The Venue, 17-23 Calton Rd. (☎557 3073). It's big. 3 dance floors and monthly nights running the whole musical gamut. Also hosts top live gigs; call ahead to get the lineup.

Po Na Na, 26 Frederick St. (☎226 2224). This Moroccan-themed nightclub oozes glam. Parachute ceilings, red velvet couches, and an eclectic blend of disco, funk, and lounge music ensure a lush night. No cover Su-Th, £3 F-Sa.

Peppermint Lounge, Blair St. (☎662 6811), near the Cowgate, around the corner from the Three Sisters. Popular with dedicated partiers not quite ready to go home. Colorful lighting, cozy furnishings, and an impressive selection of cocktails make this a hot stop for students and backpackers. Cover £1, free with student ID.

Gaia, 28 King Stables Rd. (☎229 9438). Worshiped by students for its cheap drink specials. Mostly chart, disco, and house music. Weekly theme nights include "Shagtag" and "Traffic Light" (pick a sticker: red=leave me alone; green=I'll ask your name in the morning). Cover usually under £4.

GAY AND LESBIAN NIGHTLIFE

The Broughton St. area of the New Town (better known as the **Broughton Triangle**) is the center of Edinburgh's gay community. Prepare for a wild night at mello w **Planet Out,** 6 Baxter's Pl. (☎524 0061. Open M-F 4pm-1am, Sa-Su 2pm-1am.) **C.C. Bloom's,** 23-24 Greenside Pl. on Leith St., is a super-friendly, super-fun gay club with no cover. Sunday nights are for karaoke; the rest of the week is for the dance floor. (☎556 9331. Open M-Sa 6pm-3am, Su 8pm-3am.) **Blue Moon Cafe,** on the corner of Broughton St. and Barony St., is a friendly place with great food. (☎557 0911. Open M-F 11am-11:30pm, Sa-Su 9am-12:30am.) The **Nexus Bar and Cafe** is another local favorite, attracting a range of ages. (Open daily 11am-11pm.) The club **Ego,** 14 Picardy Pl. (☎478 7434), hosts several gay nights, including the long-established **Joy** (1 Sa per month; cover £10).

3 **Oxygen Bar** has been around a while, but don't worry, it's still cool. (3-5 Infirmary St. ☎557 9997. Open M-Sa 10am-1am, Su noon-1am.)

4 Bask in reasonable prices, disco beats, good food, and looong hours at **Iguana**. (41 Lothian St. ☎220 4288. Open daily 9am-3am.)

5 A popular, laid-back student hangout, **Negociants** is also a great place to cure those late-night munchies—food is served until 2:15am. (45-47 Lothian St. ☎225 6313. Open M-Sa 9am-3am, Su 10am-3am.)

6 **Greyfriars Bobby.** Yup, it's a tourist trap. But this pup-named pub is also a favorite with students for a pint and a cheap bar meal. (34 Candlemaker Row. ☎225 8328. Open daily 11am-1am.)

7 Sleek, trendy, and creatively decorated, **Beluga Bar** is the "it" spot for the stylish scholar set. (30a Chambers St. ☎624 4545. Open daily 9am-1am.)

🔀 DAYTRIPS FROM EDINBURGH

SOUTH QUEENSFERRY. Eight miles west of central Edinburgh, the town of South Queensferry lies at the narrowest part of the Firth of Forth, where two bridges—the **Forth Road Bridge** and the splendid **Forth Rail Bridge** (or just "Forth Bridge")—cross the waterway. In South Queensferry town center, along High St., the **Queensferry Museum** catalogs the history of the bridges and the community. (☎ 225 3858. Open M and Th-Sa 10am-1pm, Su noon-5pm. Free.) From Hawes Pier, under the Forth Bridge, the **Maid of the Forth** ferries to Inchcolm Island, site of the wonderfully preserved 12th-century **Inchcolm Abbey.** (Ferry ☎ 331 4857. Mid-July to early Sept. sailing daily; Apr.-June and Oct. Sa-Su. Return ticket includes admission to abbey. £10, concessions £8.50, children £4.) To get to South Queensferry from Edinburgh, take First Edinburgh **bus** #88 from the eastern end of Princes St. Alternatively, hop a **train** to nearby Dalmeny.

Two miles farther west of South Queensferry stands one of Scotland's finest stately homes, **Hopetoun House.** The original house was built around 1700 and designed by Sir William Bruce (also responsible for Holyroodhouse). Later in the 18th century, William Adam and his sons Robert and John designed a large and ornate extension. The grounds offer lovely views of the Forth. (☎ 331 2451. Open Apr.-Sept. daily 10am-5:30pm, last entry 4:30pm. £5.30, concessions £4.70, children £2.70.) No public transport runs to Hopetoun; take a **taxi** from South Queensferry.

ROSSLYN CHAPEL. The exotic stone carvings of Rosslyn Chapel, in the village of Roslin, 7 mi. south of Edinburgh's city center, raised eyebrows in late medieval Scotland. Filled with occult symbols, the chapel became important to the Knights Templar, and is one of the dozen-odd British sites claiming to have the Holy Grail squirreled away somewhere. The most famous visible part of the church is the pier known as the **Apprentice Pillar,** supposedly the work of an apprentice later killed by the jealous master mason. Outside the chapel, footpaths lead to the ruined **Roslin Castle** in peaceful Roslin Glen. *(Take Wilson's Bus #315 from Edinburgh's St. Andrews Sq. (M-F every hr., Sa every 2hr., Su 2 per day). ☎ 440 2159. Chapel open M-F 10am-5pm, Su noon-4:45pm. £4, concessions £3.50, children £1.)*

THE BORDERS

From the time Hadrian and his legions were repelled in the second century AD until just 200 years ago, this 1800 sq. mi. region was caught in a tug-of-war between Scotland and England. Relics of past strife remain: fortified houses and castles dot the landscape, and spectacular abbeys at Dryburgh, Jedburgh, Kelso, and Melrose lie in ruins. These grim reminders of war stand in contrast to a countryside where winding roads and fantastic hill paths reward walkers and cyclists, and where gentle rivers inspire the poetic (Sir Walter Scott among them). Still, the tradition of conflict remains strong, if only in the rugby matches for which the Borders are famous, and to which the locals are fanatically devoted.

▐ TRANSPORTATION

There are no **trains** in the Borders, but **buses** are frequent; **First** (☎ (01896) 752 237) is the largest of several operators. Inquire about daily passes, which can be worthwhile. Ask at TICs for the Borders Council's *Travel Guides*, which contain all the bus schedules; the *Central Borders* guide includes most of the relevant routes.

Schedules can also be obtained by calling **Traveline** (☎ (0870) 608 2608). Bus #23 runs from **Berwick** to **Kelso** (55min.; M-F 11 per day, Sa 7 per day, Su 3 per day), while #60 (M-F 7 per day, Sa-Su 5 per day) heads from Berwick to **Galashiels** (1¾hr.) via **Melrose** (1½hr.). The following routes depart **Edinburgh:** #62 (every hr.) to **Peebles** (1hr.) and **Galashiels** (1¾hr.), with #62B continuing to **Melrose** (2¼hr.); #29 to **Jedburgh** (2hr.; M-F 5 per day, Sa-Su 3 per day); #30 to **Kelso** (2hr.; M-Sa 3 per day, Su 1 per day) and **National Express** #383 (1 per day) to **Newcastle** via **Galashiels, Melrose,** and **Jedburgh.** Limited-stop bus #95/X95 (about every hr.) travels from **Galashiels** north to **Edinburgh** (1hr.) and south to **Carlisle** (2hr.). For travel between Borders towns, other useful bus routes include #62/65/66/67 from **Galashiels** to **Kelso** via **Melrose** and #68/71 from **Galashiels** to **Jedburgh** via **Melrose.** Bus #29 connects **Edinburgh** with **Jedburgh** (2hr.).

Hitchhikers report that the lethargy of Border hitching is least painful along the main roads; the A699 runs east-west between Selkirk and Kelso, the A68 connects Edinburgh to Newcastle via Jedburgh, and the A7 runs south through Galashiels and Hawick. The labyrinth of smaller B roads is less traveled. As always, *Let's Go* does not recommend hitchhiking as a safe mode of travel.

⬛ HIKING AND BIKING

The Borders welcome hikers of all levels; take a late afternoon stroll in the hills or wander the wilds for days at a time. Trails weave through the **Tweedsmuirs** (all over 2500 ft.) to the west along the A708 toward Moffat, as well as the **Cheviot Hills** to the southeast. Closer to Edinburgh, the **Moorfoots** and **Lammermuirs** offer gentler day walks. Eighty-two miles of the **Southern Upland Way,** Scotland's longest footpath (212 mi.), wind through the Borders. The Way is clearly marked (with a thistle in a hexagon), and the Countryside Commission for Scotland publishes a free pamphlet with route and accommodations info. **St. Cuthbert's Way** rambles for 62 mi. from Melrose to Lindisfarne on the English coast. Retrace ancient footsteps along **Dere St.** (an old Roman road), **Girthgate** (a pilgrimage from Edinburgh to Melrose Abbey), or **Minchmoor** (a bandit-ridden drove road); for info on the trails, pick up the helpful *Scottish Hill Tracks—Southern Scotland.* Local TICs provide plenty of trail guides, leaflets on walks (45p), and Ordnance Survey maps (1:50,000; £5). The superb *Walking in the Scottish Borders* (free) details many scenic half-day walks. The same series includes booklets on cycling, golf, and fishing.

For on- and off-trail **bikers,** the essential *Cycling in the Scottish Borders,* free from TICs, includes routes, accommodations, cycle shops, and useful contact numbers. The **Tweed Cycleway** is an 89 mi. route that hugs the Tweed River from Biggar to Berwick, while the **Four Abbeys Cycle Route** connects the abbeys at Melrose, Dryburgh, Jedburgh, and Kelso. **Hawick Cycle Centre,** 45 North Bridge St., Hawick, rents bikes (☎ (01450) 373 352; £10 per day, £50 per week, deposit £20 and ID; open M-Sa 9am-5pm), as do shops in **Galashiels** (p. 569) and **Peebles** (p. 569).

⬛ ACCOMMODATIONS

All TICs can help you find a bed, usually for a 10% deposit; make advance bookings at ☎ (0870) 608 0404. The following **SYHA hostels** in the Borders are strategically dispersed—a fourth is in **Melrose** (p. 568).

Broadmeadows (☎/fax (01750) 76262), 5 mi. west of Selkirk off the A708, and 1¼ mi. south of the Southern Upland Way. The first SYHA hostel (opened 1931), close to the

Tweedsmuir Hills. Reception closed 10:30am-5pm. Curfew 10:45pm. Open Apr.-Sept. Dorms £8.75, under 18 £7.50. ❶

Coldingham (☎/fax (01890) 771 298), outside Coldingham at St. Abbs Head, near the ocean. Surveys the eastern Southern Upland Way and coast. Reception closed 10:30am-5pm. Curfew 11:30pm. Open Apr.-Sept. Dorms £9, under 18 £7.75. ❶

Kirk Yetholm (☎(01573) 420 631), at the junction of the B6352 and B6401, near Kelso. Bus #81 runs from Kelso (20 min.; M-F 9 per day, Sa 7 per day, Su 3 per day). Watch hikers collapse at the northern terminus of the Pennine Way. Reception closed 10:30am-5pm. Curfew 11:30pm. Open Apr.-Sept. Dorms £9, under 18 £7.75. ❶

MELROSE   ☎01896

Among the loveliest of the region's towns, Melrose draws many visitors to its abbey and is within convenient reach of Dryburgh Abbey and Abbotsford, Sir Walter Scott's country home. The town's centerpiece, Cistercian ▓**Melrose Abbey** was begun in 1136, destroyed by the English, rebuilt in an ornate Gothic style, then destroyed again by the English in 1549. Some walls remain remarkably intact, while others provide good ventilation. Search the extensive grounds for the tombstone marking Robert the Bruce's embalmed heart. On the lighter side, the monastery's amusing gargoyles include a bagpipe-playing pig and winged cow on the south wall. (☎822 562. Open Apr.-Sept. daily 9:30am-6:30pm; Oct.-Mar. M-Sa 9:30am-4:30pm, Su 2-4:30pm. £3.30, seniors £2.50, children £1.20.) Admission to the abbey includes the **Abbey Museum,** which displays objects unearthed from the abbey and regional Roman forts, and details Sir Walter Scott's life, death, and poetic dishonesty. Come, see, and briskly conquer the one-room **Trimontium Exhibition,** in Market Sq. Straddle the replica Roman saddle—you know you want to. (☎822 651. Open Apr.-Oct. daily 10:30am-4:30pm, Sa-Su closed for lunch. £1.50, concessions £1, families £4.) The Roman fort covered in the museum spanned the three volcanic summits of the **Eildon Hills,** an easy 5 mi. hike from town. Legend has it that King Arthur and his knights lie in an enchanted sleep in a cavern beneath the hills and will wake when the country needs saving. (That is, if they're not in Wales, Glastonbury, or any of the other places making similar claims.) To reach the hills, walk 200 yd. south of Market Sq. on Dingleton Rd.; after passing Newlyn Rd. on the right, look for the footpath on the left.

Buses to Melrose stop at Market Sq. The **tourist information centre** is across from the abbey on Abbey St. (☎822 555. Open July-Aug. M-Sa 9am-6pm, Su 10am-5pm; June and Sept. M-Sa 10am-5:30pm, Su 10am-2pm; Oct. M-Sa 10am-4pm, Su 10am-1pm; Apr.-May M-Sa 10am-5pm, Su 10am-1pm.) A **Bank of Scotland** is at Market Sq. (Open M-Tu and Th-F 9am-12:30pm and 1:30-5pm, W 10:30am-12:30pm and 1:30-5pm.) The **post office** is on Buccleuch St. (☎822 040. Open M-F 9am-1pm and 2-5:30pm, Sa 9am-12:30pm.) **Post Code:** TD6 9LE.

A minute from the town center and the abbey ruins, the **SYHA Melrose** ❶, off High Rd., resembles a stately manor more than a backpackers' abode, with 86 beds, an excellent kitchen, laundry facilities, and a garden. (☎822 521; melrose@syha.org.uk. Continental breakfast included. Reception 7am-11pm. Curfew 11:45pm. Dorms £9.50-11, under 18 £6-9.75.) **Birch House** ❸, High St., has homey, pine-furnished rooms (☎822 391; singles £25; doubles £36-44), while **Dunfermline House** ❸, Buccleuch St., is a comfortable guest house in the former town saddlery (☎822 148; £23-25 per person). **Camp** at the deluxe **Gibson Park Caravan Club Park** ❶, St. Dunstan's Park, off High St., which claims the cleanest campsite bathrooms ever. (☎822 969. £4 per adult, under 17 £1.20; tent and car £3.50.)

NEAR MELROSE

▨ DRYBURGH ABBEY. Those with time and the willingness to walk can reach the real treasure of the area, Dryburgh Abbey, whose serene grounds host extensive ruins and the graves of Sir Walter Scott and WWI commander Earl Haig. The abbey was built in 1150 and inhabited by Praemonstratensian monks for nearly two centuries. When Edward II began removing his English troops from Scotland in 1322, the monks prematurely rang their bells in celebration. Angered, the soldiers retraced their steps and set the abbey afire. If you have wheels, make for **Scott's View,** north of Dryburgh on the B635. Its vistas of the Tweed Valley were much favored by Sir Walter. *(Abbey 5 mi. southeast of Melrose, near St. Boswell's. From Melrose or Galashiels, take bus #67 or 68 (10min., frequent) to St. Boswell's, then walk north 1 mi. along the A68. ☎ (01835) 822 381. Open Apr.-Sept. daily 9:30am-6:30pm; Oct.-Mar. M-Sa 9:30am-4:30pm, Su 2-4:30pm. £2.80, seniors £2, children £1.)*

ABBOTSFORD. Sir Walter Scott wrote most of his Waverly novels in this mock-Gothic estate 3 mi. west of Melrose and died here in 1832. The gaudy house, stuffed with Scott's books, armor, and knickknacks, includes a lock of Bonnie Prince Charlie's hair and a piece of the gown worn by Mary, Queen of Scots, at her execution. *(Frequent buses between Galashiels and Melrose stop nearby. Get off at Tweedbank; the house is a 10min. walk. ☎ (01896) 752 043. Open June-Sept. daily 9:30am-5pm; mid-Mar. to May and Oct. M-Sa 9:30am-5pm, Su 2-5pm. £4, children £2.)*

THIRLESTANE CASTLE. The ancient seat of the Earls and Duke of Lauderdale, Thirlestane Castle stands 10 mi. north of Melrose on the A68, near Lauder. The defensive walls in the Panelled Room and Library are 13 ft. thick, but their beautiful restoration can't hide the castle's bloody history—jealous nobles hanged a host of King James III's low-born supporters here in 1482. *(From Melrose or Galashiels, take bus #61 toward Lauder; ask to be let off at the entrance. ☎ (01578) 722 430. Open Apr.-Oct. M-F and Su 10:30am-5pm, last admission 4:15pm. £5.30, children £3, families £13.)*

GALASHIELS   ☎ 01896

One of the largest towns in the Borders, "Gala" (pop. 16,000), center of the wool-weaving industry since the 13th century, can be thanked for clothing tweedy professors everywhere. Start your visit at **Lochcarron's Scottish Cashmere and Wool Centre,** Huddersfield St., which has a museum and (more interesting) factory tours. (☎ 752 091. Open M-Sa 9am-5pm, June-Sept. also Su noon-5pm. £2.50, children free. Free 40min. tours M-Th every hr. 10:30am-2:30pm, F 10:30 and 11:30am.) Gala's also an important regional transport hub. The **bus station,** across Gala Water, **stores luggage** (50p) during office hours. (☎ 752 237. Open M-F 9am-12:30pm and 1:30-5pm, Sa 9am-noon.) The **tourist information centre** is at 3 St. John's St., off Bank St. (☎ 755 551. Open July-Aug. M-Sa 10am-6pm, Su 11am-1pm; Apr.-June and Sept.-Oct. M-Sa 10am-5pm.) **Gala Cycles,** 38 Island St., **rents bikes.** (☎ 757 587. £5 per half-day, £10 per day. Open M-Tu and Th-F 10am-5pm, W 10am-noon, Sa 10am-5pm.) **Banks** are on Bank St. The **post office** is on Post Office St.... that is, 1 Channel St. (☎ 754 731. Open M-F 9am-5:30pm, Sa 9am-12:30pm.) **Post Code:** TD1 1AA. For a bed, try **Morven Guest House ❸,** 12 Sine Pl. (☎ 756 255. Singles £22; doubles £34-50.)

PEEBLES   ☎ 01721

Eighteen miles west of Galashiels, Peebles overlooks a particularly lovely stretch of the River Tweed. A 20min. sally upstream yields **Neidpath Castle,** a small but sturdy fortress with crumbling rooms, river views (one of the best is from the bathroom), batik art depicting the life of Mary, Queen of Scots, and a tartan display. (☎ 720 333. Open July-Aug. daily 11am-6pm. £3, concessions

£2.50, children £1, families £7.50.) The walk to Neidpath can be combined with a fine jaunt into the nearby hills (5 mi.; brochure available at the TIC). The **Tweeddale Museum and Gallery**, in the Chambers Institute on High St., houses constantly changing exhibitions and copies of Greek friezes. (☎724 820. Open M-F 10am-noon and 2-5pm; Easter-Oct. also Sa 10am-1pm and 2-4pm. Free.)

The **tourist information centre** is at 23 High St. (☎720 138; fax 724 401. Open July-Aug. M-F 9am-8pm, Sa 9am-7pm, Su 10am-6pm; off-season hours vary slightly, but often closed Su.) Other services include: **banks** along High St.; **bike rental** at **Crossburn Caravan Park**, Edinburgh Rd. (☎720 501; open M-Sa 8:30am-6pm; £7 per half-day, £14 per day, £60 deposit); and the **post office**, 14 Eastgate (☎720 119; open M-F 9am-5:30pm, Sa 9am-12:30pm). **Post Code:** EH45 8AA.

Stay with Mrs. Mitchell at **Viewfield ❷**, 1 Rosetta Rd., in a room above her wonderful garden (☎721 232; singles £18.50; doubles £35), or at the tasteful **Rowanbrae ❸**, Northgate (☎721 630; singles £21; doubles from £36). Campers find comfort at the **Rosetta Camping and Caravan Park ❶**, Rosetta Rd., a 10min. walk from town. (☎720 770. Open Apr.-Oct. Tent and car £10.) At **Big Eg's ❶**, 14-16 Northgate, just outside the town center, tasty fish and chips go for £3 takeaway or £4.10 sit-down. The owner's travel advice is free. (☎721 497. Open M-Sa 11:45am-11pm, Su 1-8pm.)

▶ DAYTRIP FROM PEEBLES

TRAQUAIR HOUSE. Twelfth-century ▨ **Traquair House** (TRARK-weer), the oldest inhabited house in Scotland, stands 6 mi. east of Peebles and about 1 mi. south of the A72. Remarkably, many original features remain—the treasures of the Stewarts of Traquair (who have lived here since 1491) are displayed upstairs. Present resident Catherine Stewart makes ale in the 200-year-old brewery and has tastings on summer Fridays—when more visitors than usual find themselves entangled in the hedge-maze on the grounds. *(From Peebles, take bus #62 toward Galashiels and ask to be dropped at the entrance. ☎(01896) 830 323. Open June-Aug. daily 10:30am-5:30pm; mid-Apr. to May and Sept.-Oct. 12:30-5:30pm; £5.30, seniors £5, children £2.80.)*

JEDBURGH   ☎01835

Smack in the heart of Jedburgh (JED-burra; known to locals as "Jethart"), 13 mi. south of Melrose, King David I founded ▨ **Jedburgh Abbey** to show both Englishman and Scot that the monarch was not afraid to place magnificent monuments on the fringes of his realm. The abbey was derisively dismantled in the 1540s by the English Earl of Hertford. The best preserved abbey in the region, its remarkable relics include an intricately decorated ivory comb that lies at the heart of a 12th-century murder mystery. (☎863 925. Open Apr.-Sept. daily 9:30am-6:30pm; Oct.-Mar. M-Sa 9:30am-4:30pm, Su 2-4:30pm. £3.30, seniors £2.50, children £1.20.) For the best free view of the abbey, try Abbey Close St. off Castlegate.

The **Mary Queen of Scots Vistor Centre**, down Smiths Wynd on Queen St., stands in a rare example of a 16th-century fortified house. It provides interesting background on the monarch, who visited Jedburgh in 1566. (☎863 331. Open Mar.-Nov. M-Sa 10am-4:30pm, Su noon-4:30pm. £2.50, concessions £1, children free.) The 19th-century **Jedburgh Castle Jail** looms atop a hill on Castlegate, over the original Jethart Castle, which was destroyed in 1409 to prevent the English from taking it. (☎863 254. Open Apr.-Oct. M-Sa 10am-4:30pm, Su 1-4pm. £1.50, concessions £1.)

Buses stop on Canongate, near the abbey and next to the **tourist information centre**. The TIC books National Express tickets, reserves rooms for a 10% deposit, and **exchanges currency** for free. (☎863 435. Open July-Aug. M-F 9am-8pm, Sa 9am-7pm, Su 10am-7pm; June and Sept. M-Sa 9:30am-6pm, Su 10am-6pm; off-season hours

> **MARY, MARY, QUITE CONTRARY** Mary, Queen of Scots (1542-87), survived a storm of spicy rumors during her lifetime. Her first husband, King François II of France, reportedly was, well, something less than regal in the bedroom. Court wits remarked that if the Queen were to become pregnant, the child could not be his. In any case, Mary experienced a "hysterical" (false) pregnancy during her year as Queen of France before François died. Her later marriage to the wicked Lord Darnley *did* bear fruit. During the agonizing birth, Mary's companion, Lady Reres, moaned and thrashed beside her while a lady-in-waiting supposedly used witchcraft to draw the Queen's pains into her friend. Legend has it that Mary's son was stillborn, and the future King James VI of Scotland (James I of England) was actually another infant smuggled in to replace the dead child—a story made more tantalizing by the discovery (years later) of a tiny wee skeleton hidden in the walls of Mary's apartments.

reduced.) **Banks** are on High St., as is the **post office** (☎ 862 268; open M-F 9am-5:30pm, Sa 9am-12:30pm). **Post Code:** TD8 6DG.

B&Bs pepper the town. At 39 Doune Hill, Mrs. Lowe's **Windyridge ❷** offers panoramic views of castle and abbey (☎ 864 404; singles £18; doubles £38-40), as does **Meadhon House ❸**, 48 Castlegate, with its secluded garden (☎ 862 504; singles £28-30; doubles £40). Stargazers can camp at **Jedwater Caravan Park ❶**, 4 mi. south of the town center off the A68; watch for signs. (☎/fax 840 219. Open Easter-Oct. Tent and 2 people £8, extra adult £1, children 50p.) For groceries, visit the **Co-op Superstore,** on the corner of Jeweller's Wynd and High St. (☎ 862 944. Open M-Sa 8am-8pm, Su 9am-6pm.) At **Simply Scottish ❷**, 6-8 High St., well-prepared specials go for £5-7. (☎ 864 696. Open M-Th 10am-8:30pm, F-Sa 10am-9pm, Su 11am-8:30pm.)

KELSO
☎ 01573

Kelso is an attractive and (relatively) busy market town at the meeting of the Tweed and Teviot rivers. The Duke of Roxburgh resides in the palatial **Floors Castle,** 1 mi. northwest, and Prince Andrew drops by for the annual charity golf tournament. The castle, dating from the 1720s, has scores of turrets, vast grounds, and nearly 400 windows, affording spectacular views of the Tweed. A holly in the gardens marks the site where James II met his noble end—killed while inspecting a cannon. (☎ 223 333. Open Easter-Oct. daily 10am-4:30pm. £5.50, concessions £4.75, children £3.25.) Like Jedburgh's, Kelso's **abbey,** near Market Sq., was King David-raised and Earl of Hertford-razed—but this one didn't hold up as well. (Open Apr.-Sept. M-Sa 9:30am-6pm, Su 2-6pm; Oct.-Mar. M-Sa 9:30am-4pm, Su 2-4pm. Free.) **Mellerstain House,** one of Scotland's finest Georgian homes, is 6 mi. northwest of Kelso on the A6089. Begun in 1725 by William Adam and completed by his son Robert, the house is noted for its exquisite plaster ceilings. Take bus #68 or 89 (10min.; M-F every hr., Su 8 per day; return £1.20) toward Gordon, and ask the driver to drop you near the house. (☎ 410 225. Open Easter-Sept. M-F and Su 12:30-5pm. House and gardens £4.50, concessions £3.50, children £2. Gardens only £2.)

The **bus station** is off Roxburgh St., near Market Sq. (☎ 224 141. **Luggage storage** 50p. Open M-F 8:45am-5pm, Sa 8:45-11am.) Kelso's **tourist information centre,** Market Sq., books rooms for a 10% deposit. (☎ 223 464. Open July-Aug. M-Sa 9am-6pm, Su 10am-5pm; June and Sept. M-Sa 9:30am-5pm, Su 10am-5pm; Oct. M-Sa 10am-4:30pm, Su 10am-1pm; Apr.-May M-Sa 10am-5pm, Su 10am-1pm.) The **post office** is at 13 Woodmarket. (Open M-F 9am-5:30pm, Sa 9am-12:30pm.) **Post Code:** TD5 7AT.

The **SYHA Kirk Yetholm** (see p. 568) is 6 mi. southeast of Kelso. For basic B&B, visit **Mr. Watson ❷**, Clashdale, 26 Inchmead Dr., where you'll be treated like long-lost family. (☎ 223 405. £15 per person.) **Abbey Bank ❹**, The Knowes, is well-furnished and 2min. from town. (☎ 226 550. Singles from £30; doubles from £44.)

Restock at **Safeway,** Roxburgh St. (☎225 641. Open M-W and F 8am-8pm, Th 8am-9pm, Sa 8am-6pm, Su 9am-6pm.) **Home Bakery ❶,** 50 The Square, near Hosemarket, sells pies and sandwiches for around £1.50. (☎226 782. Open daily 7:30am-5pm.)

DUMFRIES AND GALLOWAY

Dumfries and Galloway see relatively little of the tourism enjoyed to the north and south, but offer plenty of sights of their own. This southwest corner of Scotland has castles, abbeys, magnificent gardens, and local heroes like Robert the Bruce and Robert Burns. Here, too, in Scotland's mildest climate, are lush hillsides, lochs, mountains, and 200 mi. of rugged coastline.

GETTING THERE AND STAYING THERE

Trains serve Dumfries and Stranraer. **Buses** reach other towns, although service to isolated areas can be infrequent or nonexistent. Schedule information for the region's several bus operators can be obtained from **Traveline** (☎(0870) 608 2608). A **Day Discoverer Ticket,** available on buses, allows unlimited travel in Dumfries and Galloway, and on Stagecoach buses in Cumbria (£5, children £2). Each town has its own clutch of B&Bs and hotels. The region's thee **SYHA hostels** are probably of most interest to walkers; only one (Minigaff) is reachable by public transport.

Kendoon (☎(01644) 460 680). 20 mi. from Threave Castle. Near Loch Doon, the Corbetts, and the Southern Upland Way. Open Apr.-Sept. £8.75, under 18 £7.50. ❶

Minigaff (☎(01671) 402 211). In the village of Minigaff, across the bridge from Newton Stewart (accessible by bus from Dumfries, Stranraer, and Kirkcudbright). The area is popular with hikers and anglers. Open Apr.-Sept. £9, under 18 £7.75. ❶

Wanlockhead (☎(01659) 74252). In Scotland's highest village, along the Southern Upland Way. Open Apr.-Sept. £9, under 18 £7.75. ❶

HIKING AND BIKING

With a fine coastline and the highest of the **Galloway** and **Moffat** hills, Dumfries and Galloway have much to offer the walker. Many good short trails are detailed in free leaflets at regional TICs. The 30 mi. **Pilgrim's Way** travels the Machars Peninsula from Glenluce Abbey in the north to the Isle of Whithorn, where St. Ninian founded a chapel in the 4th century, at the southern tip. The **Southern Upland Way** (see p. 567) begins at Portpatrick and snakes 212 mi. in a northeasterly direction, passing SYHA hostels in Kendoon, Wanlockhead, Broadmeadows (p. 567), and Melrose (p. 568). The **Galloway Forest Park,** covering 290 sq. mi. of woodland, moorland, and lochs, has excellent walking and camping but is difficult to access using public transport. The park has three visitors centers: **Clatteringshaws** (☎(01644) 420 285), 6 mi. west of New Galloway; **Glen Trool** (☎(01671) 402 420), 12 mi. north of Newton Stewart; and **Kirroughtree** (☎(01671) 402 165), 3 mi. east of Newton Stewart. **Cyclists** will find *Cycling in Dumfries and Galloway* (free at TICs) useful. The Forest Enterprise also puts out leaflets describing on- and off-trail routes in Galloway and other area forests.

DUMFRIES ☎01387

Dumfries (pop. 37,000) hangs its tam on little but the tales of two famous Roberts. In 1306, Robert the Bruce proclaimed himself King of Scotland in Dumfries after stabbing throne-contender Red Comyn at Greyfriars. Beloved Scots-scribbler Robert

Burns made Dumfries his home from 1791 until his death in 1796, and, lest its auld acquaintance be forgot, the town has devoted many (many) a site to him. Along with these historical claims, the central location and transportation connections make this the unofficial (and unexciting) capital of southwest Scotland.

📞 🚆 TRANSPORTATION AND PRACTICAL INFORMATION. Trains (☎ (08457) 484 950) come from: **Carlisle** (35min.; M-Sa every 2hr., Su 4 per day; £6.40); **Glasgow Central** (1¾hr.; M-Sa 8 per day, Su 2 per day; £9.70); **London Euston** (change in Carlisle, 5hr., 9 per day, £101); and **Stranraer** (3hr., 2 per day, £14.90). **Bus** X74 runs from **Glasgow** (2hr.; M-Sa 5 per day, Su 2 per day; £6.40, return £8.70) while #100/X73 travels from **Edinburgh** (2¾hr., same frequency and price).

The Dumfries **tourist information centre**, 64 Whitesands Rd., books accommodations for £1 plus a 10% deposit and sells National Express tickets. (☎ 253 862; fax 245 555. Open June-Sept. M-Sa 10am-5:30pm, Su noon-5pm; Oct.-May M-Sa 10am-5pm, Su 10am-4pm.) Other services include: **banks** along High St.; **Internet access** at **Dumfries IT Centre**, 26-28 Brewery St. (☎ 259 400; £4 per hr.; open M-F 9am-6pm, Sa 10am-5pm); and the **post office**, 7 Great King St. (☎ 256 690; open M-F 9am-5:30pm, Sa 9am-12:30pm). **Post Code:** DG1 1AA.

🛏 🍴 ACCOMMODATIONS AND FOOD. Steps from the railway station, **Torbay Lodge ❸**, 30 Lover's Walk (not as romantic as it sounds), is welcoming and comfortable. (☎ 252 262. Singles £22-30; doubles £40-46.) Nearby is the equally agreeable **Morton Villa ❸**, 28 Lover's Walk. (☎ 255 825. Doubles £40.) Cheaper abodes lie along **Lockerbie Rd.**, north of the city across the tracks. **The Haven ❷**, 1 Kenmore Terr., is a riverfront Victorian home with a do-it-yourself kitchen—though breakfast is still cooked for you. (☎ 251 281. Singles £15; doubles £18-20.) Cafes, bakeries, and fish-and-chip shops line **High St.**, and **Whitesands Rd.** has other cheap dining options. Choices grow scarce after dark; at **The Queensberry Hotel ❶**, 16 English St., listen to the boastings of the local football team as you gulp down a bowl of excellent soup. (☎ 253 526. Open M-Sa 9am-9pm, Su noon-8pm; food served noon-3pm and 5-9pm.) Be like Burns and stop for a pint at **The Globe Inn**, 56 High St., one of the poet's favorite haunts. (☎ 252 335. Open M-Th 10am-11pm, F-Sa 10am-midnight, Su noon-11pm.)

🏛 SIGHTS. It's all Robbie Burns. Pick up a free copy of *Dumfries: A Burns Trail* in the TIC for an easy-to-follow walking tour that covers all the major sights. Across the river, the **Robert Burns Centre**, Mill Rd., contains Burns memorabilia (naturally), including a cast of his skull. A 20min. film runs through a sentimental version of the poet's life; the ten million Burns songs make it worth the small fee. (☎ 264 808. Open Apr.-Sept. M-Sa 10am-8pm, Su 2-5pm; Oct.-Mar. Tu-Sa 10am-1pm and 2-5pm. Centre free. Film £1.50, concessions 75p.) In an ornate mausoleum in **St. Michael's Kirkyard,** St. Michael St., a marble Burns leans on a plow and gazes at the attractive muse hovering overhead. The mausoleum was built in 1815 after admirers decided the poet's former grave was too ordinary. (☎ 255 297. Open M-Sa 9am-8pm, Su noon-6pm. Free.) The Robster died in the wee **Burns House**, Burns St., which now contains many original manuscripts and editions. (☎ 255 297. Open Apr.-Sept. M-Sa 10am-5pm, Su 2-5pm; Oct.-Mar. Tu-Sa 10am-1pm and 2-5pm. Free.)

The top floor of the **Dumfries Museum**, Church St., has panoramic views (weather permitting) from Britain's oldest camera obscura. (☎ 253 374. Open Apr.-Sept. M-Sa 10am-5pm, Su 2-5pm; Oct.-Mar. Tu-Sa 10am-1pm and 2-5pm. Museum free. Camera obscura £1.50, concessions 75p.) The **Old Bridge House Museum**, Mill Rd., packs eclectic paraphernalia into four little rooms. The only thing less appealing than the dentures in the dentistry collection is the nightmarish dental equipment. (☎ 256 904. Open Apr.-Sept. M-Sa 10am-5pm, Su 2-5pm. Free.)

SOUTHERN
SCOTLAND

DAYTRIPS FROM DUMFRIES

CAERLAVEROCK CASTLE. Eight miles southeast of Dumfries, on the B725 just beyond Glencaple, moated, triangular Caerlaverock Castle (car-LAV-rick) is one of Scotland's finest medieval ruins. No one is sure whether this strategic marvel was built for Scottish defense or English offense; it was seized by England's Edward I in 1300 and passed around like a hot kipper thereafter. *(Stagecoach Western Bus #371 runs to the castle from the Loreburn Shopping Centre, off Irish St. in Dumfries (30min.; M-Sa 12 per day, Su 2 per day; £1, return £1.80). ☎(01387) 770 244. Open Apr.-Sept. daily 9:30am-6:30pm; Oct.-Mar. M-Sa 9:30am-4:30pm, Su 2-4:30pm. £2.80, seniors £2, children £1.)*

SWEETHEART ABBEY. This abbey, 8 mi. south of Dumfries along the A710 and now a splendid, well-preserved ruin, was founded in the late 13th century by Lady Devorguilla Balliol in memory of her husband John. She was later buried here with John's embalmed heart clutched to her breast. *(Take MacEwan's bus #372 (45min.; M-Sa 15 per day, Su 5 per day; £1.40, return £2.40) to New Abbey from Dumfries. ☎(0131) 668 8800. Open Apr.-Sept. daily 9:30am-6:30pm; Oct.-Mar. M-W and Sa 9:30am-4:30pm, Th 9:30am-12:30pm, Su 2-4:30pm. £1.80, seniors £1.30, children 75p.)*

RUTHWELL CHURCH. Nine miles southeast of Dumfries, the Ruthwell Church contains the magnificent 7th-century **Ruthwell Cross,** which bears dense carvings of vine scrolls and beasts of Celtic art, plus everyone's favorite Anglo-Saxon poem (and Scotland's oldest surviving fragment of written English), *The Dream of the Rood,* in the margins. Call Mrs. Coulthard (☎(01387) 870 249) to get the key to the church. *(Take a bus to Annan via Clarencefield and get off at Ruthwell (30min.; M-Sa every hr.; Su every 2hr.; £1.40, return £2.55). Free.)*

DRUMLANRIG CASTLE. Eighteen miles north of Dumfries off the A76 is the home of the Duke of Buccleuch. The noted painting collection includes works by Rembrandt and Da Vinci. The good Duke also has formal gardens and a large country park. *(From Dumfries, Stagecoach Western bus #246 (45min.; M-Sa 5 per day, Su 2 per day; £2.45) stops about 1½ mi. away. ☎(01848) 330 248. Castle open by guided tour May-Aug. M-Sa 11am-4pm, Su noon-4pm. Grounds open May.-Sept. £6, concessions £4, children £2, families £14. Grounds only £3, concessions £2.)*

CASTLE DOUGLAS   ☎01556

Halfway between Dumfries and Kirkcudbright, Castle Douglas resembles most every other town in Scotland's southwest. The real reasons to visit are the nearby gardens and castle. One mile west, the 60-acre **Threave Garden** bursts with blooms gingerly pruned by students of the School of Gardening. Buses #500 and 501 between Kirkcudbright and Castle Douglas pass the garden turnoff; ask the driver to stop, then walk 10min. (☎502 575. Garden open daily 9:30am-sunset. Walled garden and greenhouses open daily 9:30am-5pm. £5, concessions £4.) Three miles west of Castle Douglas, the ruins of late-14th century ■**Threave Castle** command an island on the River Dee. Threave (built by the splendidly named Archibald the Grim) was a stronghold of the Earls of Douglas and the last to surrender to James II in 1453. The Kirkcudbright bus can drop you off at the roundabout on the A75; follow signs for Threave Castle on the road that ends at Kelton Mains Farm. Look for the roofless keep: when you ring the ship's bell nearby, a boatman should appear to ferry you across the river. (Open Apr.-Sept. daily 9:30am-6:30pm; last boat 6pm. £2.20, seniors £1.60, children 75p.; ferry included.)

   MacEwan's buses #500 and 501 zip to Castle Douglas from Kirkcudbright (45min., 12 per day, £1.50). For local lodgings, ask the staff at the **tourist information centre,** Market Hill, to help you find a room. (☎502 611. Open June-Aug. M-Sa 10am-5:30pm,

Su 11am-5pm; Apr.-May and Sept.-Oct. M-Sa 10am-5pm.) **Mrs. Laidlaw ❸**, 33 Abercromby Rd., a 5min. walk from town, runs a B&B close to bird-watching, fishing, and walking trails. (☎503 103. Singles £20; doubles £40-45.) Among the several former coaching inns offering accommodation in the town center, **The Crown Hotel ❸**, 25 King St., is the best value. (☎502 031. Singles £24-32; doubles £46-58.)

KIRKCUDBIGHT ☎01557

Attractive and dignified, Kirkcudbright (kir-COO-bree) occupies its coastal spot in the center of Dumfries and Galloway with grace, its old Scottish buildings and Georgian homes lining the angular High St. Such a colorful setting prompted a circle of prominent Scottish artists to take up residence in the 1890s.

📧🚋 TRANSPORTATION AND PRACTICAL INFORMATION. Buses #500, 501, and 505 travel from **Dumfries** (every hr.), and bus #431 comes from **Newton Stewart** (1hr.; M-Sa 7-8 per day, Su 2 per day; £2.85), sometimes beginning in **Stranraer.** The **tourist information centre**, Harbour Sq., books rooms for £1. (☎330 494; fax 332 416. Open mid-June to mid-Sept. daily 9:30am-5:30pm; mid-Sept. to Oct. 10am-4:30pm; Apr. to mid-June 10am-5pm.) Other services include: **Royal Bank of Scotland,** 37 St. Mary St., at the corner of St. Cuthbert St. (☎330 492; open M-Tu and Th-F 9:15am-4:45pm, W 10am-4:45pm); **Shirley's Launderette,** 20 St. Cuthbert St. (☎332 047; wash £2, dry £2); and the **post office,** 5 St. Cuthbert's Pl. (☎330 578; open M-F 9am-12:30pm and 1:30-5:30pm, Sa 9am-12:30pm). **Post Code: DG6 4DH.**

🏠🍴 ACCOMMODATIONS AND FOOD. Parkview ❷, 22 Millburn St., a bright blue house with fountained garden run by fabulous Mrs. McIlwraith, captures the Kirkcudbrian character. (☎330 056. Singles £17; twins £34.) The Georgian townhouse **14 High St. ❸**, right in the town center, is rather more luxurious. (☎330 766. Singles £30; doubles £50.) Get groceries at **Safeway,** 52 St. Cuthbert St., at Millburn St. (☎330 516. Open M-W and Sa 8:30am-6pm, Th-F 8:30am-8pm, Su 10am-4pm.) **The Royal Hotel ❷**, St. Cuthbert St., has an all-you-can-eat lunch buffet (£5), a multicourse seafood dinner (£6.50), and live music on Sunday nights. (Lunch buffet M-Sa noon-2:30pm. Dinner F-Sa 6:30-9pm, Su noon-3pm. Open M-Sa 11am-11pm, Su noon-10:30pm.) Top off your meal with a pint at the **Selkirk Arms ❶**, High St., the inn where Robert Burns wrote the *Selkirk Grace* in 1794. (☎330 402. Open M-Sa 11am-11pm, Su noon-10:30pm; food served M-Sa noon-2:30pm and 6:30-9pm.)

📷 SIGHTS. The **Tollbooth Art Centre,** High St., housed in the oldest surviving tollbooth in Scotland (and one-time prison of navy man John Paul Jones), tells the story of the local artists' colony. In the upper studio, visitors can peek over the shoulders of paint-slingers at work. (☎331 556. Open July-Aug. M-Sa 10am-6pm, Su 2-5pm; May-June M-Sa 11am-5pm; Mar.-Apr. and Sept.-Oct. M-Sa 11am-4pm; Nov.-Feb. Sa 11am-4pm. £1.50, students 75p, children free.) **Broughton House,** 12 High St., displays the artwork (mostly carefree girls cavorting amid wildflowers) of E.A. Hornel, who drew inspiration for his later paintings from the years he spent in Japan. The backyard is everything a garden could hope to be, with emerald lawns, lily ponds, sundials, and greenhouses. (☎330 437. Open July-Aug. daily 11am-5:30pm; Apr.-June and Sept.-Oct. from 1pm. £2.50, concessions £1.70, families £6.70.) **MacLellan's Castle,** a 16th-century tower house, dominates the town from Castle St. Sneak into the "Laird's Lug," a secret chamber behind a fireplace from which the laird could eavesdrop on conversations in the Great Hall. (☎331 856. Open Apr.-Sept. daily 9:30am-12:30pm and 1:30-6:30pm; Oct.-Nov. M-Sa 9:30am-4:30pm, Su 2-4:30pm. £1.80, concessions £1.30.)

STRANRAER   ☎01776

On the westernmost peninsula of Dumfries and Galloway, Stranraer (stran-RAHR) provides ferry access to Northern Ireland—and that's about all. Locals have a unique accent, as most early residents came from Ireland; they are often referred to as the Galloway Irish.

▐▐ 💺 GETTING THERE AND SAILING AWAY. Trains (☎(08457) 484 950) come from **Ayr** (M-Sa 7 per day, Su 2 per day; £10) and **Glasgow** (2½hr.; M-Sa 4-7 per day, Su 2 per day; £15). **Scottish Citylink buses** (☎(08705) 505 050) arrive from: **Ayr** (1½hr., 2 per day, £4.50); **Dumfries** (#500; 3hr.; M-Sa 4-5 per day, Su 3 per day; £4.50); **Glasgow** (#923, 2½hr., 2 per day, £8.50). **National Express** (☎(08705) 808 080) runs from: **Carlisle** (2½hr., £15); **London** (9hr., 2 per day, £33); **Manchester** (5½hr., 1 per day, £27). **Ferries** travel to Northern Ireland across the North Channel. **Stena Line** (☎(08705) 707 070) sails to **Belfast** (1¾hr.-3¼hr.; 9 per day; £14-24, concessions £10-19, children £7-12). Five miles up the coast at **Cairnyan, P&O Ferries** (☎(0870) 242 4777) depart for **Larne** (1-2¼hr., 8 per day, £18-25). Sea passage is sometimes discounted with a rail ticket. (See **By Ferry,** p. 40.)

🛈 PRACTICAL INFORMATION. The **tourist information centre,** Harbour St., books rooms for a 10% deposit. (☎702 595; fax 889 156. Open June-Sept. M-Sa 9:30am-5:30pm, Su 10am-4:30pm; Apr.-May and Oct. M-Sa 10am-5pm; Nov.-Mar. M-Sa 11am-4pm.) **Banks** are everywhere. **Internet access** is available at the **Stranraer Public Library,** North Strand St. (☎707 400. £3 per 25min., £5 per 55min. Open M-W and F 9:30am-7:30pm, Th 9:30am-5pm, Sa 9:30am-1pm and 2-4:30pm.) The **Tesco** on Charlotte St. houses Stranraer's **post office.** (☎702 587. Open M-W 8:30am-6pm, Th-F 8:30am-8pm, Sa 8am-6pm, Su 11am-2pm.) **Post Code:** DG9 74F.

▐▐ ⊟ ACCOMMODATIONS AND FOOD. If you're marooned, check B&Bs on the A75 (London Rd.) toward the castles. The proprietors of the **Jan Da Mar Guest House ❷,** 1 Ivy Pl., on London Rd. between the town center and ferry pier, supply nicely furnished rooms and lively conversation. (☎/fax 706 194. Singles £18-25; doubles £32-40.) The **Harbour Guest House ❸,** Market St., near the west pier, is another good option. (☎704 626. Singles £25-28; doubles £40-50.) The **Tesco** supermarket is on Charlotte St. at Port Rodie near the ferry terminal. (Open M-F 8:30am-8pm, Sa 8am-6pm, Su 10am-5pm.) When the sun starts to fade, head to that creatively named establishment, **The Pub,** 3 Hanover St. (☎705 518. Open M-W 4pm-midnight, Th 4-10pm, F-Sa noon-1am, Su 12:30pm-midnight.)

🖾 SIGHTS. In town, the only sight is the **Castle of St. John,** George St., a 1510 edifice which looks more ill-designed than regal. (☎705 544. Open Apr.-Sept. M-Sa 10am-1pm and 2-5pm. £1.20, children 60p.) Four miles east of Stranraer on the A75, the **Castle Kennedy Gardens** have two castles and lovely landscaping set between a pair of lochs. Frequent buses #430 and 500 from Stranraer pass the castle; it's about a mile off the main road. (☎702 024. Open Apr.-Oct. daily 10am-5pm. £3, concessions £2, children £1.)

WESTERN GALLOWAY

The two peninsulas of Western Galloway are fringed with cliffs, beaches, and great views—those car-less travelers willing to brave the slightly tricky public transport will find worthwhile stopping places, like the **Kirkmadrine Sontes,** gracing a windswept hill at **Sandhead** (south of Stranraer); or the **Galloway Forest Park,** 290 sq. mi. of hikeable peaks, surrounding **Glen Trool** (northeast of Stranraer). Until the mid-19th century, **Portpatrick,** 8 mi. southwest of Stranraer, was the main sailing port for Northern Ireland. Today it's a low-key seaside town, its rocky coastline fronted by comely pastel buildings. The coast-to-coast **Southern Upland Way** (see p. 567) begins here, and there's also a coastal path leading back to Stranraer. The ruins of 16th-century **Dunskey Castle** lie secluded on a spectacular cliff overlooking the ocean, a 20min. walk from Portpatrick harbor. On the left side of the harbor as you face the water, a long flight of steps leads to the castle path. **Bus** #358/367 serves Portpatrick from Stranraer (25min.; M-Sa 16 per day, Su 3 per day). The welcoming **Knowe Guest House ❸**, 1 North Crescent, has comfortable rooms with harbor views. (☎810 441. Singles £20-30; doubles £35-42.)

AYRSHIRE

AYR
☎01292

The spoilsport Scottish weather often dampens the long, sandy beach lining coastal Ayr (as in fresh AIR; pop. 50,000). Most tourists set their sights on Robert Burns's birthplace at Alloway, 3 mi. to the south. Ayr also boasts the top racetrack in Scotland, home to the **Scottish Grand National** in April and the **Ayr Gold Cup** in September. (☎264 179. Tickets £10-25; call for race dates.)

Ayr's **train station** is 10min. southeast of town at the crossroads of Station Rd., Holmston Rd., and Castle Hill Rd. Trains (☎(08457) 484 950) run from **Dumfries** (2 per day, £10.20); **Glasgow** (55min., 2 per hr., £5.30); and **Stranraer** (1½hr.; M-Sa 7 per day, Su 3 per day; £10). The **bus station,** in the town center on Sandgate, receives **Stagecoach** (☎613 500) buses from **Glasgow** (£3.15) and **Stranraer** (£5.70). The nearby **tourist information centre,** 22 Sandgate, **exchanges currency.** (☎288 688. Open July-Aug. M-Sa 9am-6pm, Su 10am-5pm; Sept.-June M-Sa 9am-5pm.) Other services include: **banks** on High St.; **Internet access** at **Carnegie Library,** 12 Main St. (☎618 492; £3 per hr.; open M-Tu and Th-F 10am-7:30pm, W and Sa 10am-5pm); and the **post office,** 65 Sandgate (☎287 264; open M-Sa 9am-5:30pm). **Post Code:** KA7 1AB.

Tramore Guesthouse ❷, 17 Eglinton Terr., has Moroccan decor a pebble's toss from the beach. (☎/fax 266 019. £17 per person.) **Craggallan Guest House ❸**, 8 Queen's Terr., is friendly and comfortable, though it lacks singles. (☎264 998. Doubles £36-44.) The **Safeway** is across from the train station on Castlehill Rd. (☎283 906. Open M-Th 8am-8pm, F 8am-9pm, Sa 8am-6pm, Su 9am-5pm.) Probably the top restaurant in town is **Fouters Bistro ❸**, 2a Academy St., off Sandgate. (☎261 391. Open Tu-Sa for lunch and dinner.) Have a pint at the most popular pub in town, the tartan-filled, proud-to-be-Scottish **◙Chapman Billie's,** on Dallair Rd. at Barnes St. (☎618 161. Open daily 1pm-12:30am.)

▶ DAYTRIPS FROM AYR

ALLOWAY
From Ayr, take bus A1 from Burns Statue Sq. (15min.; M-Sa frequent, Su every hr.) or the hop-on/hop-off Burns Country Open-Top Bus Tour, longer but more scenic.

Two miles south of Ayr, the village of Alloway blazes with Burns sites. Visit the **Burns Cottage and Museum,** built by you-know-who's dad, where guess-who was born. The museum's excellent collection of Burns memorabilia redeems the saccharine tableaux of family life and realistic barnyard smells. (☎(01292) 441 215. Open Apr.-Oct. daily 9am-6pm; Nov.-Mar. M-Sa 10am-5pm, Su noon-4pm. £2.80, concessions £1.40.) The **Tam o' Shanter Experience** presents the life of the poet and a lyrical multimedia reading. (☎ (01292) 443 700. Open Apr.-Oct. daily 9am-6pm; Nov.-Mar. 9am-5pm. £2.80, concessions £1.40. Joint ticket with museum £4.50/ £2.20.) The nearby **Burns Monument and Gardens** are not only free, but divine on a sunny day. A view of the **Brig o' Doon,** a bridge featured in the "Tam o' Shanter" poem, can be had if you climb for it. Stop by ruined **Alloway Kirk,** where, according to Burns, the devil played the bagpipes; for a further taste of historic, haunted Alloway, let **Scruffy Dog Tours** lead you through the Kirk's graveyard with tales of cannibalism and witchcraft. (☎ (0775) 494 1801. Tours M-F 8-10:30pm. £6, children £4.)

■ CULZEAN CASTLE

From Ayr take bus #60 (45min., every 1-2hr.) and tell the driver where you're going. The castle is signposted about 1 mi. from the main road. ☎(01655) 760 274. Castle open Apr.-Oct. daily 10am-5pm. Park open year-round. Free tours July-Aug. daily 11am and 3:30pm. £9, concessions £6.50, families £22. Park only £4.50/£3.50/£12.50.

Twelve miles south of Ayr, Culzean Castle (cul-LANE) perches imposingly on a coastal cliff. According to legend, one of the cliff's caves shelters the Phantom Piper who plays to his lost flock when the moon is full. The castle's famed oval staircase was designed by Robert Adam; although he drafted nearly 40 blueprints for estate homes and constructed over 20 full-scale castles, his efforts at Culzean are considered his finest. The building's top floor was given to Dwight Eisenhower for use during his lifetime—with a presidential budget you can be like Ike and rent his digs for the night (£375; other castle accommodations from £140). Very popular during high season, the castle is surrounded by a 560-acre country park.

ISLE OF ARRAN ☎01770

The glorious Isle of Arran (AH-ren; pop. 4750) justifiably bills itself as "Scotland in Miniature." Gentle lowland hills and majestic Highland peaks coexist on an island less than 20 mi. long. In the north, the crags of Goatfell and the Caisteal range overshadow pine-filled foothills. Near the western coast, prehistoric stone circles rise suddenly out of boggy grass. The eastern coastline winds south from Brodick Castle past Holy Island into meadows and white beaches. On sunny days, the waters turn crystalline, providing an enchanting view of the marine life below.

◀ TRANSPORTATION

To reach Arran, take a **train** (☎ (08457) 484 950) to **Ardrossan** from **Glasgow Central** (45min., 4-5 per day, £4.50), or **bus** #580 from **Ayr** (1hr.; M-Sa 2 per hr., Su 5 per day; £2.75). From Ardrossan, the **CalMac ferry** (☎302 166) makes the crossing to **Brodick** on Arran in sync with the train schedule (1hr.; M-Sa 6 per day, Su 4 per day; £4.55). There's also seasonal ferry service to **Lochranza** on Arran from **Claonaig** on the Kintyre Peninsula (30min.; mid-Apr. to mid-Oct. 9 per day; £4, bikes £1). Pick up a timetable at the Brodick TIC.

The *Area Transport Guide,* distributed free at the TIC and on the ferry, contains all bus and ferry schedules for the island. **Stagecoach Western** (☎302 000; office at Brodick pier) operates a comprehensive **bus** service; a connection to and from every part of the island meets each ferry. A few additional services are run by **Royal Mail** (☎ (01463) 256 200). The **Rural Day Card** grants a full day of bus travel (available on board; £3, children £1.50). During peak season, Stagecoach offers half- and full-day **tours** of the island departing from Brodick pier, though the regular services follow the same routes (full-day £7.50, concessions £5).

✦🔢 ORIENTATION AND PRACTICAL INFORMATION

The A841 runs all the way around the Isle of Arran; the full circuit is 56 mi. Ferries from Ardrossan arrive at **Brodick,** on the western shore; those from Claonaig arrive at **Lochranza,** in the north. In the southwest of the isle are **Lamlash,** the largest settlement, and the pleasant village of **Whiting Bay.** **Blackwaterfoot** is the largest town on the sparsely-populated western shore. Though Brodick has the widest range of tourist services, you'll get a better feel for the island staying elsewhere. Arran's **tourist information centre** is across from the ferry pier in Brodick. It books B&Bs for £1.50 plus a 10% deposit. (☎302 140; fax 302 395. Open June-Sept. M-Sa 9am-7:30pm, Su 10am-5pm; Oct.-May roughly M-F 9am-5pm, Sa 10am-5pm.) A tourist information desk on the Ardrossan-Brodick ferry answers questions from Easter to September. Arran accommodations can fill up quickly; it's best to book ahead.

🔺 HIKING AND BIKING

Despite Arran's proximity and excellent connections to Glasgow, swaths of wilderness in the northwest and southeast remain untouched. The TIC has maps, walking leaflets, and information on high-season guided walks; SYHA wardens can also be invaluable resources. The signposted path up popular ▧**Goatfell,** Arran's highest peak (2866 ft.), begins on the road between the Arran Heritage Museum and Brodick Castle. The 7 mi. round-trip hike averages 4-5hr., but the view from the cold and windy peak is worth it; on a clear day, it stretches from Ireland to the Isle of Mull. An alternative path to the top leaves from the village of **Corrie.** Another fine walk is the 7 mi. **Cock of Arran** route, which departs from Lochranza and circles the northern tip of the island. Well-marked shorter walks depart from, among other places, Whiting Bay and north of Blackwaterfoot (see below).

Biking on the hilly island is a rewarding challenge; pedaling part or all of the 56 mi. ringing the island reveals splendid views, and traffic is light except at the height of tourist season. For **bike rental,** inquire at **Mini-Golf Cycle Hire** in Brodick (☎302 272), 300 yd. from the pier; the **Coffee Pot,** Whiting Bay (☎700 382); the **Lochranza Golf Caravan Camping Site,** Lochranza (☎830 273); or **Blackwaterfoot Garage,** Blackwaterfoot (☎860 277).

BRODICK   ☎01770

Though the town of Brodick lacks any immediate appeal, it's hard to complain about the setting—a peaceful bay set against a backdrop of rugged mountains. Some 2½mi. north of town, ▧**Brodick Castle** surveys the harbor above fantastic wild and walled gardens. Built on the site of an old Viking fort and the ancient seat of the Dukes of Hamilton, the castle contains a fine porcelain collection, paintings, and scores of dead beasties. If you can't manage a visit, look on the back of a Scottish £20 note. (☎302 202. Castle open Apr.-Oct. daily 10am-5pm, Nov.-Dec. Sa-Su 10am-4pm. Castle and gardens £6, concessions £4. Gardens only £2.50/£1.70.) The **Arran Heritage Museum,** 1½ mi. north of Brodick town center, is a small display on the Arran of yesteryear. (☎302 636. Open Apr.-Oct. daily 10:30am-4:30pm. £2.25, seniors £1.50, children £1, families £6.) Any northbound bus from Brodick will pass both the museum and the castle; Stagecoach also operates a vintage coach service (Apr.-Sept. 9 per day; return £2, children £1) direct to the sights.

Brodick's town center is along Shore Rd. just north of the ferry pier; take a right with your back to the water. Services include: **banks** on Shore Rd.; a **launderette** at the northern end of Shore Rd. (☎302 427; open Th-Tu 9am-5pm, W 9am-4pm; last wash 45min. before close); and the **post office,** set back from Shore Rd. on Mayish Rd. (☎302 245; open M-F 9am-5:30pm, Sa 9am-12:45pm; winter closed 12:45-1:45pm). **Post Code: KA27 8AA.**

If you spend the night in Brodick, try the spacious, seafront **Glenfloral Guest House ❷,** Shore Rd. (☎302 707; singles £17; doubles £34-40); sandstone **Carrick Lodge ❸,** left from the ferry pier and a 5min. uphill walk (☎302 550; £21-27 per person); or the well-appointed **Invercloy ❹,** Shore Rd. in town (☎302 225; singles £34-44; doubles £58-88). **Glen Rosa Farm ❶,** 2 mi. north of Brodick, lets campers pitch tents. (☎302 380. Toilets and cold water. £2.50 per person.) The **Co-op** sells groceries across from the ferry terminal. (☎302 515. Open M-Sa 8am-10pm, Su 9am-7pm.) **Stalkers Eating House ❷,** Shore Rd., has decently priced pub grub. (☎302 579. Open Easter-Oct. daily 9am-9pm, Nov.-Easter M-Sa 10:30am-4:30pm.) **Creelers ❸** (☎302 797), a highly regarded, moderately expensive seafood bistro north of town on the way to the castle, opens for lunch and dinner from mid-March to October.

WHITING BAY AND LAMLASH

Southeast Arran is marked by rolling hillsides, swaths of dense forest, and a gentle, beautiful coastline. **Lamlash** is the largest town on the island and, with one of Europe's finest natural harbors, a popular sailing center. Farther south, **Whiting Bay,** a genteel resort town set on a lovely crescent of coast, is an enjoyable place to stay. From a trailhead near the hostel at the southern end of town, two easy, 1hr. walks lead to **Glenashdale Falls** and a viewpoint at **Giant's Graves. Holy Island,** just off the coast of Arran, is visible from both Lamlash and Whiting Bay. The island is presently owned by a group of Tibetan Buddhists—choose your own path to enlightenment, or just follow the trail up to the island's highest point (1030 ft.) A few ferries per day depart for Holy Island from Whiting Bay; a slightly more frequent service departs Lamlash.

SYHA Whiting Bay ❶, at the southern end of town, is a good hostel with lots of lawn. (☎700 339. Open Apr.-Oct. Dorms £9-9.50, under 18 £7.75-8.25.) The **Royal Hotel ❸,** Shore Rd., is welcoming and spacious (☎700 286; £26 per person), while the small, lovely **Swan's Guest House ❸** is uphill on School Rd. (☎700 729; doubles £50-60). Several hotels and pubs serve food; **The Coffee Pot ❶,** toward the southern end of town on the coastal road, makes a good spot for afternoon tea (£1-3) or a bowl of scrumptious homemade soup (£1.50) with a view of Holy Island. (☎700 382. Open daily 10am-5pm; July-Aug. until 6pm.)

LOCHRANZA

Northern Arran is an often spectacular land of bare peaks and rocky coast. Idyllic Lochranza, 14 mi. from Brodick at the island's northern tip, shelters a serene harbor ringed with high hills and guarded by the rubble of a 13th-century **castle.** Pick up the key from the post office and unlock the iron gate to explore the solitary ruins. (Open Apr.-Sept. Free.) The **Isle of Arran Distillery,** at the southern end of town on the road to Brodick, will tour you through its whisky-making wonderland. (☎830 264. Open mid-Mar. to Oct. daily 10am-6pm. Tours every 45min. £3.50, concessions £2.50, under 12 free.) Lochranza is also a popular base for ramblers, many of whom choose to meander 1 mi. down the coast, on the road toward the western isle. There, the fishing village of **Catacol Bay** harbors the **Twelve Apostles,** a dozen connected white houses that differ only in the shapes of their windows.

Lochranza has **no banks or ATMs.** The **post office** is located in Primrose's, the local grocery store, overlooking the erstwhile castle. (☎830 641. Open M-Tu and Th-Sa 8:30am-1:30pm and 2:30-5:30pm, W 8:30am-1:30pm and 5-6pm; supermarket only Su 10am-2pm and 5-6pm.) **Post Code:** KA27 8EU.

Toward the southern end of town on the main road to Brodick, the **SYHA Lochranza ❶** has 68 beds, five showers, two friendly and helpful wardens, and one strict curfew. (☎/fax 830 631. Laundry £2. Kitchen lockout 10:30am-5pm. Curfew 11:30pm. Open Mar.-Oct. Dorms £9.50-10, under 18 £8.25-8.75.) The top-notch, friendly ▧**Apple Lodge** ❹, near the whisky distillery, has Edwardian rooms and fine cooking. (☎830 229. Doubles £62-74.) In the former town church across from the castle, the **Castlekirk B&B** ❸ has high, arched ceilings, a lounge with stained-glass windows, and enchanting quietude. (☎830 202. £20 per person.) Near the Apple Lodge, campers can pitch at the **Lochranza Golf Caravan Camping Site** ❶. (☎830 273. Open Apr.-Oct. £3 per person, £2-4 per tent.) Hungry? The veggie pasta (£5.80) or the lunch baguettes (£3) at waterfront **Lochranza Hotel** ❶ will surely hit the spot. (☎830 223. Open daily 11am-9:45pm.) More upscale is the restaurant at the **Isle of Arran Distillery** ❷. (See above; restaurant open mid-Mar. to Oct. 10am-10pm.)

WESTERN ARRAN

The **Machrie Moor Stone Circle,** a Bronze Age arrangement of upright stones and boulders, is reachable by a farm track 1 mi. south of the village of **Machrie.** Another mile south starts the trailhead to **King's Cave,** where Robert the Bruce allegedly passed time watching the spiders while in hiding. For a good walk you might visit the stones and the cave, and then continue south along the coast to **Blackwaterfoot,** where there are a few places to fill your belly and catch a wink.

GLASGOW ☎0141

Glasgow (pop. 700,000) has been constantly reinventing itself. Like a canvas painted over many times, the city is full of colorful elements, each found in its own unique corner. Scotland's largest urban area rose to prominence during Victoria's reign, exploiting heavy industry to become the world's leading center of shipbuilding and steel production, a sooty past recalled by cranes littering the river Clyde and the blackened stones of Glasgow Cathedral and the Necropolis. Across the river, the daring curves of the new multi-million pound Science Centre shimmer brilliantly. Dozens of free museums, excellent international cuisine, and shopping opportunities second only to London add a splash of cosmopolitan flair. Bustling clubs and pubs, popular with the largest student population in Scotland and football-mad locals, finish off the flavor of this ever-changing modern metropolis.

▐ TRANSPORTATION

Glasgow lies on the Firth of Clyde, 45min. west of Edinburgh. The M8 motorway links the two cities.

INTERCITY TRANSPORTATION

Flights: Glasgow Airport (☎887 1111), 10 mi. west in Abbotsinch. Scotland's major airport, served by **KLM, British Airways,** and others. Scottish Citylink bus 905 runs to the airport from Buchanan Station (25min., every 10min. 6am-midnight, £3.30).

Trains: Bus #88 runs between Glasgow's 2 main stations (4 per hr.; 50p), but it's only a 10min. walk.

   Central Station, Gordon St. U: St. Enoch. Trains from southern Scotland, England, and Wales. Open daily 5:30am-midnight. Travel center open M-F 5:50am-11:50pm, Sa 5:50am-10pm, Su 6:20am-3:20pm. Bathrooms 20p; shower with soap and towel £2; open M-Sa 5am-midnight, Su 6am-midnight. All luggage searched. Trains (☎(08457) 484 950) to: **Ardrossan,** connecting to Arran ferries (1hr., 10-12 per day, £4.40); **Dumfries** (1¾hr.; M-Sa 7 per day, Su 2 per day; £10); **Liverpool** (4hr., every hr., £48.40); **London King's Cross** (5-6hr., every hr., £82); **Manchester** (4hr., every hr., £48.40); **Stranraer** (2½hr.; M-Sa 8 per day, Su 3 per day; £15.50).

Queen St. Station, beside Millennium Hotel, George Sq. U: Buchanan St. Serves trains from the north and east. Open M-Sa 5am-12:30am, Su 7am-12:30am. Travel center open M-Sa 5:15am-10pm, Su 7am-10pm. Bathrooms 20p. All luggage scanned. Trains (☎(08457) 484 950) to: **Aberdeen** (2½hr.; M-Sa every hr., Su 11 per day; £31); **Edinburgh** (50min., 2 per hr., £7.40); **Fort William** (3¾hr., 2-3 per day, £18); **Inverness** (3¼hr., 5 per day, £31).

Buses: Buchanan Station (☎(0870) 608 2608), Hanover St., 2 blocks north of Queen St. Station, stables National Express and Scottish Citylink buses. Ticket office open M-Sa 6:30am-10:30pm, Su 7am-10:30pm.

Byres Rd.

🍴 FOOD
Beanscene, **1**
La Focaccia, **3**
Cul de Sac Restaurant, **2**

Bathrooms 20p. Luggage storage £2-4 per item. Lockers open daily 6:30am-10:30pm. **Scottish Citylink** (☎(08705) 505 050) to: **Aberdeen** (3-4½hr., every hr., £25.50); **Edinburgh** (75min., 2-3 per hr., £5.50); **Perth** (1½hr., every 30min., £10.20); **Inverness** (3½-4½hr., every hr., £25); **Oban** (3hr., 2-3 per day, £10.70). **National Express** (☎(08705) 808 080) arrives daily from **London** (8-10hr.; every hr.; £21.50, return £28).

LOCAL TRANSPORTATION

Travel Center: Strathclyde Transport Authority, St. Enoch's Sq. (☎332 7133), 2 blocks from Central Station. U: St. Enoch. Immensely useful advice, passes, and Underground maps. Open M-Sa 8:30am-5:30pm. **STA Travel,** 184 Byres Rd. (☎338 6000.) Student and budget travel arrangements. Open M-Sa 9am-6pm.

Public Transportation: Glasgow's transportation system includes suburban rail, private local bus services, and the circular **Underground (U)** subway line, a.k.a. the "Clockwork Orange." U trains run M-Sa 6:30am-11pm, Su 11am-5:30pm. 90p, children 50p. **Underground Journey and Season Tickets** are a good deal at £7.50 for 10 trips (children £4), £11.50 for 20 trips (children £6), £8 for 7 days (children £4.50), or £25 for 28 days (children £13); bring a photo and ID to the office at St. Enoch station. The **Discovery Ticket** for 1 day of unlimited travel is valid on the Underground after 9:30am M-F and all day Su (£1.60). For a whirlwind tour, travel fast and far enough to get your money's worth from a **Roundabout Ticket,** which covers 1 day of unlimited Underground and train travel, valid after 9am M-F and all day Sa-Su (£3.50, children £1.75).

Taxis: Wide TOA Taxis (☎429 7070). Handicapped-accessible. **Mick's Taxis** (☎0800 052 9339). Both 24hr.

Bike Rental: Compact and crisscrossed by bike lanes, Glasgow is great for cycling. **West End Cycles,** 16 Chancellor St. (☎357 1344). £15 per day; deposit £50 + credit card.

■ ORIENTATION

George Sq. is the center of town; the stations and TIC are within a few blocks. Sections of **Sauchiehall St.** (SAW-kee-hall), **Argyle St.,** and **Buchanan St.** are pedestrianized, forming busy shopping districts. **Charing Cross,** in the northwest where Bath St. crosses the M8, can be used as a locator. The vibrant **West End** revolves around **Byres Rd.** and **Glasgow University,** a mile northwest of George Sq. The city extends south of the **River Clyde** toward Pollok County and the Science Centre.

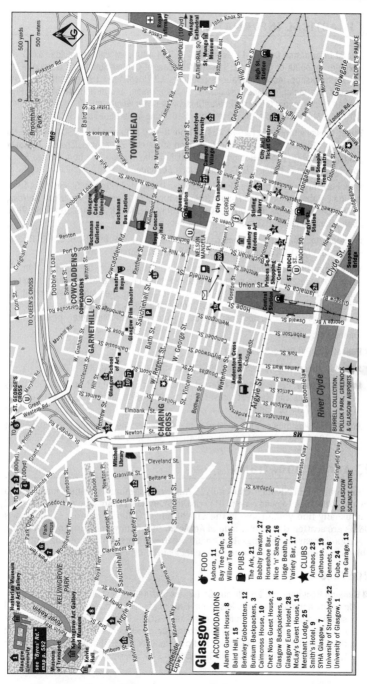

Glasgow

♦ ACCOMMODATIONS
Alamo Guest House, 8
Baird Hall, 15
Berkeley Globetrotters, 12
Bunkum Backpackers, 3
Cairncross House, 10
Chez Nous Guest House, 2
Glasgow Backpackers, 6
Glasgow Euro Hostel, 28
McLay's Guest House, 14
Merchant Lodge, 25
Smith's Hotel, 9
SYHA Glasgow, 7
University of Strathclyde, 22
University of Glasgow, 1

♣ FOOD
Ashora, 11
Bay Tree Cafe, 5
Willow Tea Rooms, 18

📖 PUBS
The Ark, 21
Babbity Bowster, 27
Horseshoe Bar, 20
Nice 'n' Sleazy, 16
Uisge Beatha, 4
Variety Bar, 17

★ CLUBS
Archaos, 23
Cathouse, 19
Bennets, 26
Cube, 24
The Garage, 13

⚑ PRACTICAL INFORMATION

Tourist Information Centre: 11 George Sq. (☎204 4400; www.glasgowguide.co.uk), off George Sq. south of Queen St. Station, northeast of Central Station. U: Buchanan St. Travel bookshop, accommodations bookings £2 (local) or £3 (regional) plus 10% deposit, car rental, CalMac ferry tickets, Western Union, and **bureau de change.** Pick up the free *Essential Guide to Greater Glasgow & Clyde Valley* and *Where to Stay.* Open July-Aug. M-Sa 9am-8pm, Su 10am-6pm; Sept.-June M-Sa 9am-7pm, Su 10am-6pm.

Tours: Glasgow City Walk (☎946 4542). From the TIC M-Tu and Th-F 2:30 and 6pm, Su 10:30am. Historic 1½hr. tours cover the heart of the city. £5, concessions £4. **Discover Glasgow** (☎248 7644). Hop-on/hop-off Guide Friday buses leave from George Sq. 2 per hr. 9:30am-5:30pm. £7.50, concessions £6, under 14 £2.50, families £17.50.

Financial Services: Banks are plentiful. **Thomas Cook,** 15-17 Gordon St. (☎204 4484), inside Central Station. Open M-Sa 8:30am-5:30pm, Su 10am-4pm. **American Express,** 115 Hope St. (☎(08706) 001 060). Open July-Aug. M-F 8:30am-5:30pm, Sa 9am-5pm; Sept.-June M-F 8:30am-5:30pm, Sa 9am-noon.

Launderette: Coin-Op Laundromat, 39-41 Bank St. (☎339 8953). U: Kelvin Bridge. Wash £3, dry £1. Open M-F 9am-7:30pm, Sa-Su 9am-5pm.

Work Opportunities: Glasgow's tourism industry swells during the summer with the arrival of tourist hordes. To meet the needs of these oh-so-active sight-seers, food-eaters, and bed-sleepers, Glasgow's TIC and other popular sites hire seasonal help. In addition, many restaurants, bars, clubs, hotels and B&Bs, especially in the city center, post listings on their windows or place ads in local papers for temporary positions.

Emergency: ☎999.

Police: 173 Pitt St. (☎532 2000).

Hospital: Glasgow Royal Infirmary, 84-106 Castle St. (☎211 4000).

Internet Access: easyEverything Internet Cafe, 57-61 St. Vincent St. (☎222 2365), has 400 computers and the best rates. £1 buys 40min.-3hr., depending on the demand. Open daily 7am-10:45pm.

Post Office: Post offices are sprinkled in the city center; the main one is 47 St. Vincent St. (☎204 3688). Open M-F 8:30am-5:45pm, Sa 9am-5:30pm. **Post Code:** G2 5QX.

⚑ ACCOMMODATIONS

Book your bed in advance, especially in August. Last-minute planners may want to try the **SYHA Loch Lomond** (see p. 611) or the **SYHA New Lanark** (see p. 591). The TIC can usually find you a room in the £16-20 range. Otherwise, most of Glasgow's B&Bs are scattered on either side of **Argyle St.** in the university area or east of the Necropolis near **Westercraigs Rd.** The universities offer summer housing, but available dorms change from year to year; check at the offices listed below.

HOSTELS

▨ **Bunkum Backpackers,** 26 Hillhead St. (☎/fax 581 4481). Just up the hill from Glasgow University and the West End. Reserve ahead—owners Jim and Jean provide advice and a social atmosphere, and it's no wonder their beds fill quickly. Dorm rooms have more space than you can imagine and comfy beds. Common room with TV, large selection of movies, smaller selection of books, and pianola. Lockers (£10 deposit), laundry (wash £1.50, dry 60p for 8min.), and kitchen. Dorms £10; weekly £50. ❷

Berkeley Globetrotters Hostel, 56 Berkeley St. (☎221 7880; fax 204 5470), about 2 blocks west of Charing Cross, just south of Sauchiehall St. Take bus #57 to Berkeley St. Within easy walking distance of the city center and the West End. Rooms are clean and basic. Rock bottom prices and free breakfast make it a good option for the tight budget. Be sure and ask the owner where to go for a good night on the town. Dorms £9.50, £8.50 for longer stays; twins £11. ❶

SYHA Glasgow, 7-8 Park Terr. (☎332 3004; fax 331 5007). U: St. George's Cross. Take bus #44 from Central Station, ask for the first stop on Woodlands Rd. and follow the signs. From Queen St. or Buchanan Station, catch bus #11. Once the residence of an English nobleman and later an upscale hotel frequented by rockstars, this hostel maintains a carefully cultivated air of luxury. Prime location overlooking Kelvingrove Park. All rooms (4-8 beds) with shower. TV and game rooms, bike shed, laundry (£1), Internet access, and kitchen. Dorms £9.50-12. ❶

Glasgow Backpackers Hostel, 17 Park Terr. (☎332 9099; Oct.-June ☎(0131) 220 1869). U: St. George's Cross or Charing Cross. Near the SYHA Glasgow (see directions above). Internet access, self-catering kitchen, and no bunks! Laundry £2.50. Open July-Sept. Dorms £11; twins £25. ❷

Glasgow Euro Hostel (☎222 2828; www.euro-hostels.com), corner of Clyde St. and Jamaica St., opposite Central Station by the river. Convenient location near the city center; if you haven't booked in advance, this is your best chance. Impersonal rooms not the first choice for the social traveler, but facilities are clean and complete. Breakfast included. Internet access, laundry, game room, and kitchen. Dorms £9.75-18.50. ❷

UNIVERSITY DORMS

University of Strathclyde, Office of Sales and Marketing, 50 Richmond St. (☎553 4148). B&B in summer at a number of dorms. **Baird Hall,** 460 Sauchiehall St. (☎332 6415). Furnished rooms in a grand location near the campus village. 1 small kitchen per floor, laundry facilities, and towels. Open mid-June to mid-Sept. Singles £19; twins £33. Also 11 year-round **guest rooms.** Singles £21; twins £35. ❷

University of Glasgow, 3 The Square (☎330 5385; vataion@gla.ac.uk). Enter from University Ave. and turn immediately right into The Square. Summer housing at several dorms. Office open M-F 9am-5pm. **Cairncross House,** 20 Kelvinhuagh Pl. (☎221 9334), offers self-catering housing off Argyle St., near Kelvingrove Park. Tea and coffee, soap, towels, and linen provided. Dorms £14; B&B £17.50. ❷

B&BS

McLay's Guest House, 268 Renfrew St. (☎332 4796; fax 353 0422). Central location near the Glasgow School of Art and Sauchiehall St. With 3 dining rooms and satellite TV and phones in each of the 62 rooms, this posh B&B looks and feels more like a hotel. Singles £24, with bath £26; doubles £40/£48; family room £55/£65. ❸

Merchant Lodge, 52 Virginia St. (☎552 2424; fax 552 4747). Conveniently located in the city center. An upscale B&B, originally a tobacco store and warehouse built in the 1800s by traders from the newly liberated American colonies. Big self-serve breakfast. All rooms with bath. Singles £35; doubles £55; triple £70. ❹

Alamo Guest House, 46 Gray St. (☎339 2395), across from Kelvingrove Park at its southern exit. Beautiful location in the West End; family-run and on a quiet street. Singles £20-22; doubles from £34. ❸

Chez Nous Guest House, 33 Hillhead St. (☎334 2977), just north of Glasgow University. U: Hillhead. Convenient access to West End. Attractive rooms are small but well kept. Free parking. Singles £20-30; doubles £20-25 per person. ❸

Smith's Hotel, 963 Sauchiehall St. (☎339 7674; www.smiths-hotel.com), 1 block east of Kelvingrove Park on Sauchiehall St. in West End. Manager Brian is knowledgeable, gracious, and helpful. Free luggage storage for up to a week. Singles £21-36; doubles £38-52; triples £66; children under 5 free. ❸

❸ FOOD

Glasgow is often called the curry capital of Britain, and for good reason. The area bordered by **Otago St.** in the west, **St. George's Rd.** in the east, and along **Great Western Rd., Woodlands Rd.,** and **Eldon St.** brims with kebab 'n' curry joints. The presence of university students has bred a number of hole-in-the-wall restaurants with excellent food. **Byres Rd.** and **Ashton Ln.,** a tiny hard-to-find cobblestone alley parallel to Byres Rd., thrive with cheap, trendy cafes and bistros. Bakeries along **High St.** below the cathedral serve scones for as little as 20p.

The Willow Tea Rooms, 217 Sauchiehall St. (☎332 0521; www.willowtearooms.co.uk), upstairs from Henderson Jewellers. A Glasgow landmark, restored in 1983 to its original design (by Charles Rennie Mackintosh). Try any of 31 kinds of tea (£1.70 per pot) in the elegantly refined atmosphere, or order a 3-course high tea and sip away the afternoon with sandwich, scone, and cake or pastry for £8.75. Open M-Sa 9am-4:30pm, Su noon-4:15pm. Another Willow Tea Room is at 97 Buchanan St. ❷

Cul-De-Sac Restaurant, 44-46 Ashton Ln. (☎334 4749). Lunch crepes and pastas are good, but try the 3-course dinners (£13-20) of vegetable dishes, meat cassoulets, and haggis. After a filling meal, head upstairs to the **Attic,** a comfortable bar (happy hour 4-8pm) with live local and underground music most days. Lunch M-Sa noon-5pm; brunch Su 12:30-4pm; dinner daily until 10:30pm. ❸

Beanscene, 16 Cresswell Ln. (☎334 6776). 1 block east of Byres Rd. just north of Great George St. A small hole-in-the-wall that serves it all: coffee, juice, bread, cheese, meats, and fruits (£1.40-10). Live music Th 8pm. Open M-Sa 8am-11pm, Su 10am-11pm. ❶

The Bay Tree Cafe, 403 Great Western Rd. (☎334 5898), at Park Rd. This popular, cramped cafe keeps a student crowd fed with a large selection of delicious veggie and meat dishes, complemented by a variety of cakes (75p-£2). Try the Greek hummus with tortilla bread and salad (£5.25). 20% student discount. Open daily 10:30am-10pm. ❶

La Focaccia, 291 Byres Rd. (☎337 1642). Semi-upscale, semi-West End. A small cafe-bistro on busy Byres Rd. People-watch on the sidewalk while sipping coffee and snacking on almond triangle pastries (£1.60). Open M-Sa 7:30am-6pm, Su 9am-6pm. Lunch available for takeaway or sit-in. ❶

❸ SIGHTS

Glasgow is a budget sightseer's paradise, with grand museums, chic galleries, and splendid period architecture. Many of the best sights are part of the **Glasgow Museums** group, whose collections, scattered across the city, are free. *The List,* available from newsagents for £2.20, reviews current exhibitions and lists galleries.

THE CITY CENTER

GEORGE SQUARE. This red-paved, grassy-patched landmark lies in the busiest part of the city. Named for George III, the square's 80 ft. central column was originally designed to support a statue of His Royal Highness; because his royalness tried to quell a rebellion by Glasgow's closest trading partners (an event better known as the American Revolution), Glaswegians replaced the king with a statue of Sir Walter Scott. The author wears his plaid, as always, over the wrong shoulder (the right). The square is populated by statues, one of which sometimes sports an orange traffic cone, courtesy of pranksters from Glasgow's School of Art. The **City Chambers,** on the east side of George Sq., epitomize Victorian confidence: an elaborate Italian Renaissance interior hides behind its dignified stone facade. Pop into the lobby for 30 seconds, or take a free 1hr. tour starting at the main entrance. (☎287 4017. Tours M-F 10:30am and 2:30pm.) The eclectic **Gallery of Modern Art,** south of George Sq. on Queens St., is housed in a beautiful classical building, once the Royal Exchange. (☎229 1996. Open M-Th and Sa 10am-5pm, F and Su 11am-5pm. Free.)

▓ GLASGOW CATHEDRAL AND NECROPOLIS. This dark and imposing Gothic structure was the only large-scale cathedral spared the fury of the 16th-century Scottish Reformation. Its slanted lime-green roof and blackened exterior contrast sharply with the ornate carvings and stonework of the interior. The stained glass is mostly post-war: look for the purple Adam and Eve in the western window, rendered in graphic detail. The Victorians would not have been amused. (Castle St. Walk to the eastern end of Cathedral St., behind Queen St. Station. ☎552 6891. Open Apr.-Sept. M-Sa 9:30am-6pm, Su 2-5pm; Oct.-Mar. M-Sa 9:30am-4pm, Su 2-4pm. Organ recitals held some Tu in July and Aug. at 7:30pm. Free.) The chilling hilltop **necropolis,** where tombstones, statues, and obelisks lie aslant and broken on the ground, is best appreciated on a gloomy, stormy day. A 50 ft. statue of John Knox (leader of the Scottish Reformation) looms atop the hill, taking advantage of amazing views over the city. At night, visit at your own risk and watch out for wandering spirits. (Behind the cathedral over the bridge walkway. Free. And very cool.)

ST. MUNGO MUSEUM OF RELIGIOUS LIFE AND ART. In a striking display of tolerance, the museum surveys every religion you can shake a stick at, from Islam to Yoruba. It features a fascinating exhibit on the intersection of sex, marriage, gender roles, and religion, though its prized possession is Dalí's painting *Christ of St. John's Cross*; both can be pondered in the serene Zen Garden. (2 Castle St. ☎553 2557. Open M-Sa 10am-5pm, Su 11am-5pm. Free.)

SHOPPING. Glasgow, quite simply, is a first-rate place to shop—second only to London in purchasing verve. **Sauchiehall St.** and **Buchanan St.** are both pedestrianized and lined with interesting stores, as well as pubs, cafes, and art galleries; as an old Glasgow saying has it, "if you go up Sauchie and down Bucky, you will have shopped your heart out." **Princes Square** is a high-end shopping mall as classy as Kensington, and the Mackintosh-designed interior

THE HIDDEN DEAL

ASHORA

Haggis. Whisky. Pickled herring. Aloo paratha. Bagara baingan. Tikka masala. What gives? But it's true—this city knows how to do Indian food. Ashora will convince even the staunchest skeptic of Glasgow's fine reputation for cuisine from the Indian subcontinent, and the sub-average prices will woo wallets of any size.

Just west of several hostels on Berkeley St., this family-run establishment claims to be the first Indian restaurant in Britain. While that may be debatable, Ashora's award-winning (back-to-back Best Curry in Britain recipient for 2001 and 2002) food is unassailable.

Fine silverware, bronze napkin rings, a tuxedoed waitstaff, and big band music in the background make the £2.95 all-you-can eat lunch buffet well worth the wee chunk of change you'll fork over. Dinner prices are more expensive but still attractive, with the buffet at £5.95 and sit-down service starting at £6.95. (108 Elderslie St. ☎221 1761. Open 11am-midnight, lunch buffet 11am-2pm.)

makes it well worth the visit, even if you're strapped for cash. *(48 Buchanan St.* ☎ *221 0324.)* A new shopping center, the **Buchanan Galleries,** at the end of Buchanan St., opened to protests in 1999 because of its every-mall appearance, but it remains hugely popular among capitalists and tourists alike (as well as those in need of a public restroom).

OTHER CENTRAL SIGHTS. Built in 1471 (making it the oldest house in Glasgow), **Provand's Lordship** now preserves a collection of antique furniture in its musty rooms. The Renaissance-style garden grows some of Glasgow's finest healing herbs. *(3-7 Castle St., across from the St. Mungo Museum.* ☎ *553 2557. Open M-Th and Sa 10am-5pm, F and Su 11am-5pm. Free.)* In their enthusiasm for the Industrial Revolution, Glaswegians destroyed most of their medieval past, only to recreate it later on the ground floor of the **People's Palace** museum. *(On Glasgow Green by the river.* ☎ *554 0223. Open M-Th and Sa 10am-5pm, F and Su 11am-5pm. Free.)*

THE WEST END

■ **KELVINGROVE PARK, MUSEUM, AND ART GALLERY.** Starting one block west of Park Circus, **Kelvingrove Park** is a genteel, wooded expanse on the banks of the River Kelvin, peppered with statues and fountains. Don't let the daytime calm fool you: be careful at night, as several college students have recently been harassed. Rumored to have been built back to front (the true entrance faces the park, not the street), the spired **Kelvingrove Art Gallery and Museum** occupies the park's southwest corner. The unusual architecture contains an extensive art collection, including works by Rembrandt, Monet, van Gogh, Renoir, and Cezanne. The museum also has a display on arms 'n' armor (from medieval knights to imperial stormtroopers), as well as costume and natural history exhibits. *(On the corner of Argyle St. and Sauchiehall St. U: Kelvin Hall.* ☎ *287 2699. Gallery tours at regular intervals. Open M-Th and Sa 10am-5pm, F and Su 11am-5pm. Free.)*

UNIVERSITY OF GLASGOW. The central spire of the university, a neo-Gothic revival structure, is visible from afar. The main building is on University Ave., which runs into Byres Rd., a busy thoroughfare in the West End. The best overall views of the university buildings are from Sauchiehall St. by Kelvingrove Park, or 226 steps up the spire, but the structures are worth a zoomed-in look as well. Stop by the **Visitor Centre** for a free map and self-guided tour. *(*☎ *330 5511. U: Hillhead. Open M-Sa 10am-4:30pm, Su 2-4:30pm. Free tours M-Sa 2pm. Tower access F 2pm.)* While walking the campus that has churned out 57 Nobel laureates, stop by the **Hunterian Museum.** The oldest museum in Scotland includes a death mask of Bonnie Prince Charlie, the 540-year-old University Mace, and a huge coin collection. *(*☎ *330 4221. Open M-Sa 9:30am-5pm. Free.)* The **Hunterian Art Gallery,** across University St., displays 19th-century Scottish art, the world's second-largest Whistler collection, a variety of Rembrandts, Pissarros, and Rodins, and reconstructed rooms from Mackintosh's house. *(*☎ *330 5431. Open M-Sa 9:30am-5pm, except during exam period. Free.)*

CHARLES RENNIE MACKINTOSH BUILDINGS. Several buildings designed by art nouveau wiz and Scotland's most famous architect are open to the public. Pick up the free *Charles Rennie Mackintosh: Buildings & Tours Guide* at the TIC or any Mackintosh sight and plan your route. The best place to start is the **Glasgow School of Art,** completed in 1898. Here, Mackintosh fused wrought iron, sweeping bay windows, Scottish Baronial styles, and French influences to create a uniquely modern Glaswegian style. *(167 Renfrew St.* ☎ *353 4526. Tours M-F 11am and 2pm, Sa 10:30am; July-Aug. also Sa 11:30am and 1pm, Su 10:30, 11:30am, and 1pm. £5, students £3.)* The Charles Rennie Mackintosh Society is based at the stark **Willow Tea Rooms;** stop by to imbibe both tea and the surroundings (see p. 586).

BOTANIC GARDENS. Colorful gardens with year-round blooms grace the northern end of Byres Rd. and stretch along the River Kelvin. Humid rooms in the **Main Range** hothouse contain a fantastic collection of exotic orchids, ferns, palms, and cacti, while more cool-headed species grow in the native Scottish sections outside. An impressively designed wrought-iron greenhouse, **Kibble Palace** has an elegant fishpond surrounded by neoclassical statues and tropical ferns. *(Great Western Rd. and Byres Rd. ☎337 1642. Tours available if reserved in advance. Gardens open daily 7am-sunset. Kibble Palace and Main Range open Apr. to late Oct. 10am-4:45pm; late Oct. to Mar. 10am-4:15pm; Main Range opens Sa 1pm, Su noon. All free.)*

SOUTH OF THE CLYDE

▓ POLLOK COUNTRY PARK AND BURRELL COLLECTION. The main attraction of Pollok Country Park, a huge wooded area of shady forest paths and colorful flora 3 mi. south of Glasgow, is the famous **Burrell Collection,** which rivals Kelvingrove in variety and quality. The collection was once the private stash of ship magnate William Burrell, reflecting his diverse (but always discriminating) tastes: paintings by Cezanne and Degas, plenty of needlework from European tapestries to Persian textiles, exquisite pieces from Greece and Rome, and fine china from... China. Together, the park and collection are well worth the 15min. bus ride from the city center. *(☎287 2550. Open M-Th and Sa 10am-5pm, F and Su 11am-5pm. Tours 11am, 2pm. Free.)* Also in the park is the less spectacular, more domestic **Pollok House.** See how the other half used to live in a nondescript Victorian mansion with a small collection of Spanish paintings. *(Take bus #45, 56, or 57 (£1.20) from Jamaica St. ☎616 6410. Open Apr.-Oct. daily 10am-5pm; Nov.-Mar. 11am-4pm. Downstairs servants' quarters free. Upstairs £5, students £3.50.)*

GLASGOW SCIENCE CENTRE. Opened in June 2001, the Science Centre is the latest addition to Glasgow's striking architectural tradition, and worthy of the city's high standards. Visible from across the river, the Centre's titanium-clad exterior (the only in the UK) gleams in the sunlight. A full experience of the three different buildings requires three different tickets and three different attitudes. The first houses Scotland's largest screen and only IMAX theater. *(Open Su-Th noon-6pm, F and Sa noon-8pm. £5.50, concessions £4.50.)* The second, shaped like an orange slice turned on its side, contains hundreds of interactive exhibits. *(Open Tu-Su 10am-5pm. £6.50/£4.50.)* Perhaps of greatest interest is the 100m Glasgow Tower, the only building in the world that rotates 360° from the ground up. Scotland's tallest freestanding structure (built as an airfoil to move with the wind), the tower chronicles the city's history and offers breathtaking views 20 mi. in every direction. *(Open Su-Th noon-6pm, F-Sa noon-8pm. £5.50/£4.50.)* The entire complex cost £75 million—one-tenth the cost of London's Millennium Dome but ten times more successful. *(50 Pacific Quay. U: Cessnock, accessible by Bells Bridge. ☎420 5010; www.gsc.org.uk.)*

◪ NIGHTLIFE

Glaswegians have a reputation for partying hard, and visitors seem to be keen on showing them up. Three universities and the highest student-to-resident ratio in Britain guarantee a kinetic after-hours vibe. *The List,* available from newsagents for £2.20, has detailed nightlife and entertainment listings for both Glasgow and Edinburgh while *The Gig* (free at newsstands) highlights the live music scene.

PUBS

You'll never find yourself much more than half a block from a frothy pint in this city. The infamous **Byres Rd.** pub crawl slithers past the Glasgow University area, beginning at Tennant's Bar and proceeding toward the River Clyde. Watch for happy hours, when many pubs significantly reduce prices, but pace yourself for the standard midnight closing time.

■ **Uisge Beatha,** 232 Woodlands Rd. (☎ 564 1596). A Scottish bar with classic wood furnishings and kilt-clad bartenders. "Uisge Beatha" (oos-ga BAY-uh) is Gaelic for "water of life" (read: whisky), and this pub has over 100 malts (£1.60-30). Sip the national drink as you listen to Gaelic tunes (live Tu, W, and Su after 7pm). Open M-Th 11am-11pm, F-Sa 11am-midnight, Su 12:30-11pm. Happy hour daily 4-7pm. Food served M-W noon-5pm, Th-Sa noon-9pm, Su noon-3pm.

■ **Babbity Bowster,** 16-18 Blackfriar St. (☎ 552 5055). The perfect place to come for the Glaswegian experience, pure and simple: fewer kilts and less Gaelic music, but more bonhomie, good drinks, and plenty of football talk. Tasty pub grub offers good value, and the (mercifully) vegetarian haggis isn't half bad (£4.20). Open M-Sa 10am-midnight, Su 11am-midnight.

Nice 'n' Sleazy, 421 Sauchiehall St. (☎ 333 0900). Eclectic live music downstairs M-Sa, £2.50-3. Upstairs, drink at the bar or order some grub. Happy hour Su-Th 5-10pm, F 5-8pm; £6 gets you a 4-pint pitcher. Occasional cover Th-Sa. Open M-Sa 11:30am-midnight, Su 12:30pm-midnight.

Horseshoe Bar, 17-21 Drury St. (☎ 221 3051), in an alley 1 block north of Gordon St., off Reinfield St. This horseshoe-shaped Victorian pub, with etched mirrors and carved wooden walls, boasts the longest continuous bar in the UK. Fortified by happy hour (daily 3-8pm), brave souls sing karaoke M-Sa from 8pm and Su from 5pm. Head upstairs for a hearty 3-course lunch (£2.95; served M-Sa noon-2:30pm) or pantry-style dinner (£2.40; M-Sa 3-7:30pm). Open M-Sa 11am-midnight, Su 12:30pm-midnight.

Variety Bar, 401 Sauchiehall St. (☎ 332 4449). An older man's pub by day, an art student's hangout by night, and always popular for its cheap drinks. No frills, just a solid quality joint where bands occasionally stop by. During happy hour (M-Sa 11am-8pm, Su 12:30-8pm) pints of lager are £1.50; Guinness £1.60; vodka, rum, and whisky dashes £1.25. Open daily 11am-11:45pm.

The Ark, 42-46 North Frederick St. (☎ 559 4331), near George Sq. Come in out of the rain and drink amid the bright colors, funky signs, and human animals (paired off and otherwise). Open daily noon-midnight.

CLUBS

Most clubs are open 11pm-3am, but the bacchanalia reaches its fevered pitch after the pubs close at midnight. Many clubs open nightly, but you can count on a wild, wild party Thursday through Saturday.

Archaos, 25 Queen St. (☎ 204 3189), a next-door stumble from its sister bar, Yang. Has 2 for 1 whiskys and frequent student discounts to pack in the punters. Sa is the busiest student night in Glasgow; wear your best clubbing shoes and your trendiest, tightest duds. Varied music on the domed 3rd floor (Th "old school," F "clubby," Sa dance anthems). Cover £3-7. Open Tu and Th-Su 11pm-3am.

The Cube, 34 Queen St. (☎ 226 8990). Home to some of the longest queues in Glasgow. Arrive early, know someone important, or, better yet, be important yourself. Tu gay night, W R&B. Cover £8, students £6 on Th. Open daily from 10:30 or 11pm.

The Garage, 490 Sauchiehall St. (☎332 1120). Look for the yellow truck hanging over the door, visible from afar. Dance club classics blast downstairs while the **Attic,** upstairs, is indie with the occasional DJ. Cover £2-6; student discounts usually available. Open Sa 10:30pm-3am, Su-F 11pm-3am.

Bennets, 80 Glassford St. (☎552 5761). Come here on "alternative nights" (M-Tu) for £1.50 drinks. The rest of the time (W-Su), this gay club hosts live DJs on both its floors. Cover £3-6, but look for discount flyers nearby. Open daily 11:30pm-3am.

Cathouse, 15 Union St. (☎248 6606). Grunge and indie please mostly younger crowds in this packed popular 3-floor club. The cat roars with disco on F and reels with under-18s Sa. Cover £3-5; students £1-2 less. Open W-Su 11pm-3am.

🎵 🌿 ENTERTAINMENT AND FESTIVALS

The city's dynamic student population ensures constant film, theater, and music events from October to April. The **Ticket Centre,** City Hall, Candleriggs, will tell you what's playing at Glasgow's dozen-odd theaters. The free *City Live* guide has great tips. (☎287 5511. Phones staffed M-Sa 9am-10pm; office open M-Sa 9:30am-9pm.) Theaters include the **Theatre Royal,** Hope St. (☎332 9000) and the **Tron Theatre,** 63 Trongate (☎552 4267). The **Cottier Theatre,** 935 Hyndland St. (☎357 3868) hosts a variety of musical and theatrical events, from avant-garde plays to opera. The **Royal Concert Hall,** Sauchiehall St., is a frequent venue for the Royal Scottish National Orchestra. (☎353 8000. Box office open M-Sa 10am-6pm.) The **Glasgow Film Theatre,** 12 Rose St., screens both mainstream and sleeper hits, while art exhibitions and a bar occupy the main space. (☎332 8128. Box office open M-Sa noon-9pm, Su 30min. before first film. £4.90, concessions £3.50; matinees £3.90/2.50.)

Among Glasgow's constant flow of musical shows, temporary art exhibitions, and festivals is the annual **West End Festival,** in the last half of June, when an already vibrant part of the city comes alive with longer bar hours and guest musicians. **Glasgow International Jazz Festival** (☎552 3552), the first week of July, draws jazz greats from all over the world. During mid-August, over 100 of the top bagpipe bands compete for glory and honor on the Glasgow Green at the **World Pipe Championships** (☎221 5414). Be sure not to miss Glasgow's transformation into the **City of the Rose** during July of 2003.

🔲 DAYTRIP FROM GLASGOW

NEW LANARK

To reach New Lanark, you'll need to go through the town of Lanark. Trains from Glasgow Central (55min., every hr., £4.20) run to Lanark. Stuart's Coaches go to New Lanark from the Lanark TIC (every hr., 55p); otherwise, it's a pleasant 20min. walk. ☎661 345. Open daily 11am-5pm. £4.75, concessions £3.25, families £13-15.

Thirty miles southwest of Glasgow, in the peaceful Clyde valley, the recreated village of **New Lanark**—recently named a World Heritage Site—allows tourists to experience the utopian dreams of the Industrial Revolution. Founded in 1785, New Lanark was the most productive manufacturing site in Scotland for much of the 19th century, partly due to the somewhat socialist tendencies of a cotton-mill owner. Instead of sending 8-year-olds to work 12-hour days, Robert Owen sent them to school. He also paid living wages, founded an Institute for the Formulation of Character, and started the first semi-cooperative village store. Visitors can walk through the restored store, a millworker's house, and Owen's own (surprisingly posh) residence. Admission to New

Lanark includes the **New Millennium Experience,** a ride through scenes in the settlement's colorful history.

The surrounding Clyde valley has lovely hikes—check out displays on the natural wonders at the **Scottish Wildlife Visitor Centre.** (☎ 665 262. Open Apr.-Sept. M-F 11am-5pm, Sa-Su 1-5pm; Feb.-Mar. and Oct.-Dec. Sa-Su 1-5pm. £1, children 50p.) A 1 mi. walk upstream past the hydropower plant leads to the beautiful **Falls of Clyde.**

Although New Lanark is an easy daytrip from Glasgow, a stay at the ▩**SYHA New Lanark ❶,** Wee Row, Rosedale St., is more than worth your while. This restored mill workers' dwelling will treat you right, with river views and modern luxuries only dreamed of by earlier occupants—laundry facilities and attached baths in all rooms. (☎ 666 710. Continental breakfast included. Reception closed 10:30am-5pm. Curfew 11:45pm. Open Mar.-Oct. Dorms £9.75-10.50, under 18 £7.25-8.)

PITCHED BATTLE
Glasgow's "Auld Firm" Football Rivalry

Red Sox versus Yankees, eat your heart out. England versus Argentina? Think again. Rocky Balboa versus Apollo Creed? Get real. When it comes to sporting rivalries, the 111-year-old contest between the Glasgow Rangers and Glasgow Celtic football clubs puts all other contenders to shame, both for the magnificence of its matchups on the pitch, and for the ferocity of the antagonism it engenders.

On the field of play, the "Auld Firm" rivalry (so named because of the aged status of the clubs involved) has been sublime, with homegrown footballing legends like Jim Baxter and Ally McCoist leading Rangers to Scottish soccer's most ever titles, and top-flight internationals like Sweden's Henrik Larsson carrying Celtic to its current championship form. Since 1891 one club or the other has won 86 of 105 possible premier-league titles, their seesawing periods of supremacy infusing nearly every head-to-head match with a sense of urgency rarely witnessed at such a high level of play. 2002 saw the two sides pitted against one another in both of Scotland's Cup competitions, the frenzied excitement of which was surely enough to inspire even the most apathetic of onlookers.

Indeed, off the pitch too, the passion that Auld Firm aficionados expend on the rivalry can scarcely be equaled. A study of any given Rangers-Celtic showdown yields ample proof of their exuberance: the briefest of glances bleacher-wards meets with the spectacle of a stadium bedecked in swaths of Rangers blue and Celtic green, and the stands are rocked by songs and chants which repeatedly reverberate from one supporters' section to the other. Oddities also abound, not the least of which is the bewildering sight—unimaginable elsewhere in this normally nationalistic country, but commonplace on the grounds of Celtic Park and Ibrox—of dyed-in-the-wool Scotsmen waving Irish and even *English* flags, in keeping with club ties to Catholic (Celtic) and Protestant (Rangers) movements at home and in Northern Ireland.

Most of the time the rival revels are meant in a spirit of merriment. At times, however, the good fun can turn bad, even ugly. The dark side of the Auld Firm's association with sectarian strife in Ulster is driven home when, nearly every time the sides do battle on the pitch, Unionist Rangers fans and rival Nationalist Celtic supporters shed each other's blood on the streets of Belfast. A similar style of hooliganism afflicts Scotland itself, where "No Football Colours" signs adorning the doors of Glaswegian pubs don't always succeed in preventing clashes between confrontational fans. And not even an ongoing ban on the sale of alcohol at matches has managed to forestall such appalling exchanges as occurred in March 2002, when Rangers fans directed racist pantomimes at Celtic's French defender Dianbobo Balde, or in September 2001, when a Celtic fan affronted Rangers American midfielder Claudio Reyna by simulating an airplane impacting a building.

Perhaps this Mr. Hyde-like side of an otherwise glorious rivalry has contributed to Scottish football's recent money-motivated threat to oust the Auld Firm from its ranks. But whether Rangers and Celtic will surrender a greater share of their revenue for the right to remain in Scotland, or whether they will choose instead to compete in the more lucrative (and more challenging) English leagues, one thing is certain: wherever the two clubs choose to vest their future interests, their fortunes will be followed by throngs of fans whose devotion ensures that their rivalry will remain a conspicuous aspect of Scottish culture.

Brian Algra, a former researcher for Let's Go: California, *is currently pursuing a doctoral degree in English Literature at the University of Edinburgh.*

CENTRAL SCOTLAND

Less lofty than the Highlands to the north and more subdued than the cities to the south, central Scotland has its draws nonetheless. The eastern shoulder, curving from Fife to the Highland Boundary Fault along the North Sea, is a calm countryside peppered with historical fishing villages and centuries-old communities. To the west, the landscape flattens from snow-covered mountains into the plains of the Central Lowlands, giving the A82 road from Loch Lomond to Glen Coe some of Scotland's best views. Castles of all vintages and sizes—from proud, ancient Stirling to Macbeth's dark, mystical Glamis—testify to the region's strategic importance, while the remote Inner Hebrides, separated by mountains and a strip of sea, are wrapped in their own enchanting beauty.

HIGHLIGHTS OF CENTRAL SCOTLAND

STIRRING STIRLING Admire the 5½ ft. sword of William Wallace and one of Britain's grandest castles in the historic royal seat of Scotland (p. 609).

THE BONNIE, BONNIE BANKS Hike the shores of beautiful **Loch Lomond,** the inspiration for the ballad of same name (p. 611).

ISLE HOPPING Pass through the Isle of Mull's pastel, palm-treed Tobermory (p. 620) on your way to the melodious caves of the stunning Isle of Staffa (p. 622).

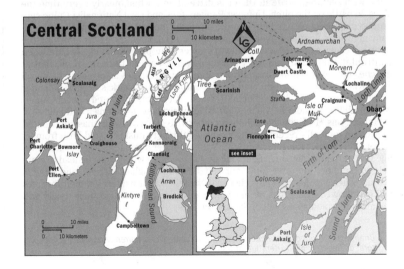

ST. ANDREWS

☎ 01334

Would you like to see a city given over,
Soul and body to a tyrannising game?
If you would, there's little need to be a rover,
For St. Andrews is the abject city's name.
    —Robert F. Murray

The "tyrannising game" of golf overruns the small city of St. Andrews. It was here, at the Royal & Ancient Golf Club, that the rules were formally established, and the club's windows overlook the Old Course, the sport's world headquarters. Shadowed by the game that draws millions of enthusiasts—and the prices they've driven sky-high—are St. Andrews's other glories: the gray stone buildings of Scotland's oldest university, the castle and cathedral ruins attesting to a fascinating religious history, and restored medieval streets leading to the North Sea.

▐ TRANSPORTATION

Trains (☎ (08457) 484 590) from **Edinburgh** stop 5 mi. away in **Leuchars** (LU-cars) on the London-Edinburgh-Aberdeen line (1hr., every hr., £8.10); from Leuchars, buses #94 and 96 run to St. Andrews (6 per hr. 7am-8pm, £1.55). **St. Andrews Bus Station** is on City Rd. (☎ 474 238). **Stagecoach Express Fife Buses** (☎ (01383) 621 249) X59 and X60 come from **Edinburgh** (2hr., M-Sa 2 per hr., £5.70); the X24 leaves **Glasgow** and changes at Glenrothes to X59 before arriving in St. Andrews (2½hr., M-Sa every hr., £5.50). From **Aberdeen, Perth,** and **Inverness,** first take **Scottish Citylink** to **Dundee** (2 per hr.) and then **Stagecoach Fife** #99, 96, or 96A to St. Andrews (1hr., 2 per hr., £2.80, students £1.80). Buses in Fife run reduced service in the evenings and on Sundays, and the schedules are subject to change with little notice—call the **Fife Public Transport Information Line** (☎ (01592) 416 060, M-F 9am-4pm.)

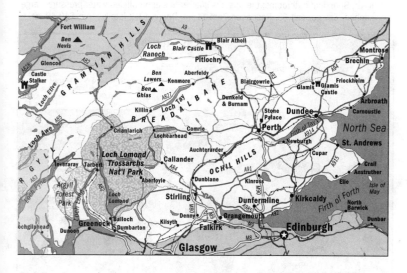

⚡❔ ORIENTATION AND PRACTICAL INFORMATION

The three main streets—**North St., Market St.,** and **South St.**—run nearly parallel to each other and to the sea, terminating near the cathedral at the town's east end.

Tourist Information Centre: 70 Market St. (☎472 021; www.standrews.com). Ask for the *St. Andrews Town Map and Guide.* Books accommodations in Fife for a 10% deposit (£3 more elsewhere). **Bureau de change.** Open July-Aug. M-Sa 9:30am-7pm, Su 10:30am-5pm; Sept. M-Sa 9:30am-6pm, Su 11am-4pm; Oct.-Mar. M-Sa 9:30am-5pm; Apr.-June M-Sa 9:30am-5:30pm, Su 11am-4pm.

Financial Services: Royal Bank of Scotland, 113-115 South St. (☎472 181). **Bureau de change.** Open M-Tu and Th-F 9:15am-4:45pm, W 10am-4:45pm.

Launderette: 14b Woodburn Terr. (☎475 150), outside of town. £5 per load. Open M-Sa 9am-7pm, Su 9am-5pm; last wash 1½hr. before close.

Internet Access: Costa, 83 Market St., across from the TIC. £1 per 20min., £10 per 5hr. Open M-Sa 8am-6pm, Su 10am-5:30pm. **St. Andrews Library,** Church Sq. (☎412 685). Allows disks. £1.75 per 30min. Open Tu-Th 9:30am-7pm, F-M 9:30am-5pm.

Hospital: St. Andrews Memorial, Abbey Walk (☎472 327), southeast of town.

Post Office: 127 South St. (☎(08457) 223 344). **Bureau de change.** Open M-Sa 10am-5:30pm. **Post Code:** KY16 9UL.

📍 ACCOMMODATIONS

The new hostel on **Market St.** is the only reliable budget option. Otherwise, **Murray Park** and **Murray Place,** near the hallowed links, have some expensive B&Bs (£17-24 per person). Summer housing at the university may provide cheap lodging; inquire at the TIC. St. Andrews also makes an easy daytrip from Edinburgh.

St. Andrews Tourist Hostel, St. Mary's Pl. (☎479 911; fax 479 988), above La Posada restaurant; entrance in the alley. From the bus station, turn right on City Rd., then left on St. Mary's Pl. This friendly backpacker haven has good facilities in a great part of town. Sparkling bathrooms; the upstairs shower has unparalleled water pressure. Large kitchen. Key deposit £5. Reception 7am-11pm. Dorms £12; family room £40-48. ❷

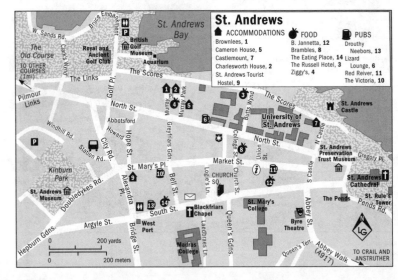

St. Andrews

ACCOMMODATIONS
Brownlees, 1
Cameron House, 5
Castlemount, 7
Charlesworth House, 2
St. Andrews Tourist Hostel, 9

FOOD
B. Jannetta, 12
Brambles, 8
The Eating Place, 14
The Russell Hotel, 3
Ziggy's, 4

PUBS
Drouthy Neebors, 13
Lizard Lounge, 6
Red Reiver, 11
The Victoria, 10

Brownlees, 7 Murray Pl. (☎473 868; www.brownlees.co.uk). Feel like your own clan lord—each room has its own tartan. All with TV. £25-32 per person. ❹

Cameron House, 11 Murray Park (☎472 306). All golf all the time—chat with the owner about it, read about it in the plush living room, dream about it at night. £25-30. ❸

Castlemount, 2 The Scores (☎475 579). Classy and off the B&B block. Castle-view from upstairs dining room and from several of the comfy beds. Open June-Sept. £30. ❸

Charlesworth House, 9 Murray Pl. (☎/fax 476 528; www.charlesworthstandrews.co.uk). Spacious rooms with TV and bath in a professional atmosphere. £23-30. ❸

▣ FOOD

Housing may be pricey, but the university has spawned cheap, greasy takeaways. The **Tesco** supermarket sits at 130 Market St. (☎413 600. Open M-W 8:30am-7:30pm, Th-F 8:30am-8pm, Sa 8am-7pm, Su 10am-6pm.)

Ziggy's, 6 Murray Pl. (☎473 686). Southwestern menu with a sizzling grill; several vegetarian options, including a variety of burritos and fajitas. (And no, you're not misreading—British chilli has 2 L's.) Open M-Sa 10am-9pm, Su noon-9pm. ❷

The Russell Hotel, 26 The Scores (☎473 447). A 2- or 3-course gourmet meal well worth the price (£18.50-22.50). Near the ocean; try reserving the locker room, which pays tribute to every Old Course Open winner. Menu changes bi-weekly for seasonal selections. ❺

Brambles, 5 College St. (☎475 380). Anything but prickly. Vegetarian-friendly menus await in a college-friendly environment. Open M-Sa 9am-10pm, Su 11am-10pm. ❷

The Eating Place, 177-179 South St. (☎475 671). Scottish pancakes—smaller and less sweet than your average flapjack—served all day (under £5) in a friendly diner environment. Open M-Sa 9:30am-5pm, Su 11:30am-5pm. ❶

B. Jannetta, 33 South St. (☎473 285). 52 flavors of award-winning ice cream, including Nutella, prove these "Ice Cream Specialists" mean business. Busy for breakfast and lunch as well. 70p per scoop. Open M-Sa 9am-5pm, Su 10am-5pm. ❶

▣ PUBS

Though the atmosphere ebbs and flows with the stream of college students and tourists, St. Andrews has many decent 19th holes. For a mix of town, gown, and traveler, grab a stool with some **Drouthy Neebors** ("Thirsty Friends," according to Robbie Burns), at 209 South St. (Happy hour Su-Th 8-10pm. Open Sa and M-W 10am-midnight, Th and F 10am-1am, Su 11am-midnight.) **Red Reiver,** 62 Market St., entertains with pool tables in the back, karaoke in the front (F-Su), and happy hour (7:30-9pm) to fill the gaps between. Ask the barman about the pub's name. (☎470 000. Open Su and M-Th 11am-midnight, F-Sa 11am-1am.) In a city without any real clubs, **The Victoria,** 1 St. Mary's Pl., offers the lovelorn a place to ease their lonely hearts, sometimes to the beat of live music. (☎476 964. Happy hour 8-9pm. Open M-W 10am-midnight, Th-Sa 10am-1am, Su noon-midnight.) **The Lizard Lounge,** 127 North St., in the basement of the Inn at North St., offers a more self-consciously stylish atmosphere with frequent live music from the small stage. (☎473 387. Open M-W 11am-midnight, Th-Sa 11am-1am, Su noon-midnight.)

🕐 ⚠ SIGHTS AND ACTIVITIES

GOLF, OF COURSE. If you love golf, play golf, or think that you might ever want to play golf, this is your town. The game was so avidly practiced here that Scotland's rulers outlawed the sport three times, at least once for the sake of national defense ("the men neglected their archery for golf!"). At the northwest edge of town, the **Old Course**, a golf pilgrim's Canterbury, stretches regally along a beach as manicured as the greens. According to the 1568 *Book of Articles*, Mary, Queen of Scots, played here just days after her husband was murdered. Nonmembers must present a handicap certificate or letter of introduction from a golf club. If you weren't old when you made your reservation, you will be when it comes to fruition: book at least a year in advance. You can also enter your name into a near-impossible lottery by 2pm the day before you hope to play, or get in line by the caddie master's hut early (dawn is too late) as a single. *(☎ 466 666; fax 477 036. Apr.-Oct. £90 per round; Nov.-Mar. £56.)* Call the same line to reserve a time at the somewhat less revered (and thus less crowded) **New, Jubilee, Eden,** or **Strathtyrum** courses, or to arrange loaners if you left your clubs at home. *(£20-45 per round. Club rental £20-30 per day.)* The budget option is the nine-hole **Balgove Course** for £7-10. *(Info line ☎ 466 666.)* July 2000 saw the opening of the newest and priciest of the Royal & Ancient courses, the **Kingsbarns Golf Links,** farther east along the coast. *(☎ 880 222; www.kingsbarns.com. £125 per round.)*

BRITISH GOLF MUSEUM. The museum displays everything golf that's imaginable and most of what's not. Their collection includes examples of the earliest spoons (clubs) and feathers (balls). Enthusiasts will find the exhibits fascinating; others, less so. *(Bruce Embankment. ☎ 460 046; fax 460 064. Open Easter-Oct. daily 9:30am-5:30pm; Nov.-Easter Th-M 11am-3pm. £4, concessions £3, children £2.)*

ST. ANDREWS CATHEDRAL. The center of Scottish religion before and during the Middle Ages, this 12th-century church was defaced by iconoclastic Protestants during the Reformation and later pillaged by locals to make their homes. The **St. Andrews Cathedral Museum** houses ancient Pictish carvings and modern tombs. For stunning views, climb the 155 steps of **St. Rule's Tower.** *(☎ 472 563. Open Apr.-Sept. daily 9:30am-5:45pm; Oct.-Mar. 9:30am-3:45pm. Museum and tower £4, seniors £3, children £1.25. Tower only £2.20/£1.60/75p. Cathedral free.)*

ST. ANDREWS CASTLE. Once the local bishop's residence, the castle boasts siege tunnels (not for the claustrophobic), bottle-shaped dungeons (not for anyone), and high stone walls to keep out religious heretics. Overrun in 1546 by Reforming Protestants, it's now stormed daily by tourists and school children. For stellar views, descend the stairs south of the castle fence, where seagulls make their nests in the crags. *(On the water at the end of North Castle St. ☎ 477 196. Free tours daily 11:30am and 3:30pm. Open Apr.-Sept. daily 9:30am-6:30pm; Oct.-Mar. 9:30am-4:30pm. £2.50, seniors £1.90, children £1; joint ticket with cathedral museum £4/£3/£1.25.)*

UNIVERSITY OF ST. ANDREWS. Founded in the 15th century, Scotland's oldest university maintains a well-heeled student body and a strong performing arts program. Following in the footsteps of many Scottish rulers who studied here, Prince William began his undergraduate course in the fall of 2001. While it's possible to meander into placid quads through the parking entrances on North St., only the **official tour** grants access to the building interiors. Buy a ticket from the Admissions Reception, Butts Wynd, beside St. Salvator's Chapel Tower on North St. *(Between North St. and The Scores. ☎ 462 245. 1hr. tours mid-June to Aug. M-F 11am and 2:30pm. £4, concessions £3, under 6 free.)*

OTHER SIGHTS AND ACTIVITIES. The baronial **St. Andrews Museum** codifies the town's theological and political past, testifying that there are religions practiced off the fairways and that golf is but "a small dot" in the town's history. *(Kinburn Park, down Doubledykes Rd. ☎ 412 690 or 412 933. Open Apr.-Sept. daily 10am-5pm; Oct.-Mar. M-F 10:30am-4pm, Sa-Su 12:30-5pm. Free.)* Reproductions of an olde chemist's shoppe and painful-looking dentistry tools are among artifacts of 20th-century everyday life in the tiny **St. Andrews Preservation Trust Museum.** *(North St. ☎ 477 629. Open early June to Sept. daily 2-5pm. Donations welcome.)* The **St. Andrews Aquarium** has oodles of eels, jittery rays, and orphaned seals just a hop, chip, and a jump from the golf museum. *(The Scores. ☎ 474 786. Open daily 10am-6pm. Seal feeding daily 11am and 3pm. £4.50, concessions £3.35-85.)* The **Byre Theatre** recently reopened with shows year-round. *(Abbey St. ☎ 475 000; www.byretheatre.com. Tickets £5-14. Student discounts available.)*

FIFE SEASIDE ☎ 01333

South of St. Andrews, a series of sun-warmed fishing villages cling like barnacles to the coast of Fife, making up The East Neuk ("Neuk" is "Corner" in Scots). With minimal train service and a lack of budget accommodations, Fife's villages may be best seen as daytrips from Edinburgh, Perth, or St. Andrews. The lengthy, scenic **Fife Coastal Walk** strings the villages together, while those with a car can take the A917, which arches from St. Andrews to Elie. Bus service X26 (St. Andrews-Leven) cruises every hour along the A917 with frequent stops, including Crail, Anstruther, Elie, and Pittenween. For the most up-to-date info, call the Fife Public Transport Information Line. *(☎ (01592) 416 060, M-F 9am-4pm.)*

CRAIL. The oldest of Fife's villages, Crail and its harbor offer snap-happy tourists perfect Kodak moments. Lined with white cottages with orange-tile roofs, the town has one of central Scotland's most beautiful stretches of red sand beach—a fitting place to gnaw on freshly caught crab claws. In the last week of July, the **Crail Festival** features concerts, parades, and craft shows from local singers, marchers, and traders. Crail's **tourist information centre,** 62-64 Marketgate, adjoins a small local history museum. *(☎ 450 869. Open June-Sept. M-Sa 10am-1pm and 2-5pm, Su 2-5pm; Apr.-May Sa-Su 2-5pm.)* **Guided walks** of town leave the museum every Sunday at 2:30pm in July and August (1½-2hr., £3).

ANSTRUTHER. The busiest and largest of the seaside towns, Anstruther lies about 5 mi. west of Crail along the A917 (or 9 mi. southeast of St. Andrews along the B9131). Visit the **Scottish Fisheries Museum,** on Shore St., to learn about the occupation that brought Fife to prominence. *(☎ 310 628. Open Apr.-Oct. M-Sa 10am-5:30pm, Su 11am-5pm; Nov.-Mar. M-Sa 10am-4:30pm, Su 2-4:30pm. Last entry 45min. before close. £3.50, concessions £2.50.)* Off the coast, the **Isle of May** nature reserve is home to puffins, gray seals, and Scotland's first lighthouse (built in 1636). From June to August, weather and tide permitting, the *May Princess* sails from Anstruther to the Isle. *(☎ 310 103. 5hr. round-trip. July-Aug. 1 per day, May-June and Sept. W-M 1 per day. £12.50, children £5.50.)* For sailing times, call ahead or check with Anstruther's **tourist information centre,** beside the museum. *(☎ 311 073. Open Apr.-June M-Sa 10am-5pm, Su 11am-4pm; July-Mar. M-Sa 10am-5:30pm, Su 11am-5pm.)* On your way back from the bay and lighthouse, don't stop—no matter how hungry you are—until you reach **Anstruther Fish Bar and Restaurant ❶,** 44-46 Shore St., known for serving Scotland's best fish and chips (Fish & Chip Shop of the Year 2001-02). Only the seals and seagulls have their fish fresher, and they aren't always keen on sharing. *(☎ 310 518. Open daily 11:30am-10pm.)*

(NOT SO) SECRET BUNKER. Halfway between Anstruther and St. Andrews, the **Secret Bunker** burrows beneath a farmhouse and cow pastures. The subterranean shelter, prepared for British leaders in case of nuclear war, contains strategy rooms, an extensive kitchen (for feeding the poor sods who had to work there for four unexciting decades), and two cinemas. Locals claim they knew what it was long before 1993, when the "silence" was broken. Drive past Anstruther or St. Andrews on the A917 and savor the irony of signs pointing to "THE SECRET BUN-KER." Those without a car may be less amused—war buffs only should take bus #61 (Anstruther-St. Andrews), ask to get off at Strathclyde intersection, walk 1 mi. east on B940, then follow a winding single-lane road (½ mi.) to the Bunker. (☎310 301. Open Apr.-Oct. 10am-5pm. ₤7, concessions ₤5.65, children ₤4.)

ELIE. The village of **Elie** (EEL-y), 5 mi. west of Anstruther, has become a posh resort and retirement community, perhaps because of beautiful **Ruby Bay,** named for the garnets occasionally found on its red-tinted sands, or for the crystal waters, perfect for swimming. **Elie Watersports** (☎330 962; www.eliewatersports.com), above the beach and bay, rents windsurfer and sailing dinghies (₤10 per hr.), with lessons for the inexperienced. For a better view of sporting seals and tidal-pool life, walk to the headland by the lighthouse, about 20min. east. Even further east perches **Lady's Tower,** built in the 18th century as a bathing box for Lady Jane Anstruther, who sent a bell-ringing servant through the streets to warn the village of her presence and prevent (promote?) anyone seeing her in her scanties.

FALKLAND. Farther inland in the Kingdom of Fife, **Falkland Palace and Gardens,** once a Stuart hunting lodge (regulars include Mary, Queen of Scots), epitomizes early Renaissance excess in its architecture and furnishings. The royal tennis court, built in 1539, is still in use by the local royal tennis club. (☎(01337) 857 397. Open Mar.-Oct. M-Sa 10am-6pm, Su 1:30-5pm; last entry 1hr. before close. ₤7, concessions ₤5.25, children ₤3.) By car, follow the M90, A92, or A912 from the south or the A91 or A912 from the north and west. Public transportation is trickier: take **Stagecoach Fife Bus** #36 or 66 from **Glenrothes** (40min., 2-4 per day) or #36 from **Perth** (1hr., 2-4 per day). For more information, call **Fife's Council Public Transportation Info Line** (☎(01592) 416 060; M-F 9am-4pm). If stranded, stay in the newly opened **Burgh Lodge ❶**, Back Wynd, tucked behind the Community Hall. (☎(01337) 857 710. Handicapped-accessible. ₤10 per person, ₤9 each additional night.)

PERTH ☎01738

Perth, Scotland's capital until 1452, likes to call itself the "perfect centre" and "the fair city." Beauty is, after all, in the eye of the beholder—though it does successfully blend country with city in its parks and woodlands, Perth is not particularly extraordinary, catering mostly to residents and more sedate types. The beautiful walks in Kinnoull Hill Wood and the historical import of nearby Scone Palace are decent reasons to visit, but travelers short on time should probably move on.

▐ **TRANSPORTATION.** The **train station** is on Leonard St. (Ticket office open M-Sa 6:45am-8:45pm, Su 8:15am-8:25pm.) Trains (☎(08457) 484 950) from: **Aberdeen** (1½hr., 2 per hr., ₤20.70); **Edinburgh** (1½hr., 2 per hr., ₤8.50); **Glasgow** (1hr., every hr., ₤8.50); **Inverness** (2½hr., 8-9 per day, ₤15.80). The **bus station** is a block away on Leonard St. (Ticket office open M-F 7:45am-5pm, Sa 8am-4:30pm.) **Scottish Citylink** (☎(08705) 505 050) buses journey from: **Aberdeen** (2hr., every hr., ₤12.10); **Dundee** (35min., every hr., ₤3.80); **Edinburgh** (1½hr., every hr., ₤5.80); **Glasgow** (1½hr., 2 per hr., ₤6); **Inverness** (2½hr., every hr., ₤10.80); **Pitlochry** (40min., every hr., ₤5.30).

7 PRACTICAL INFORMATION. The **tourist information centre,** Lower City Mills, books local rooms for £1 plus a 10% deposit. It's signposted from the bus station—turn right (north) on Leonard St., jog right then left to South Methven St., and take a left on Old High St. (☎450 600; www.perthshire.co.uk. Open July-Aug. M-Sa 9:30am-6:30pm, Su 11am-5pm; Sept.-Oct. M-Sa 9:30am-5pm, Su 11am-4pm; Nov.-Mar. M-Sa 10am-4pm; Apr.-June M-Sa 9:30am-5:30pm, Su 11am-4pm.) **Guide Friday** runs open-top **bus tours** in summer, making transport to far-off places like Scone Palace and Kinnoull Hill easy. Buy tickets at the TIC or on the bus at the Mill St. stop. (☎(0131) 556 2244. June-Sept. daily every hr. 10am-4pm. £5.50, seniors and students £4, children £2.) Other services include: **banks** by the handful; **Internet access** upstairs at **A.K. Bell Library,** Glasgow Rd. (☎477 949; £2.50 per 30min.; book ahead; open M, W, F 9:30am-5pm; Tu and Th 9:30am-8pm; Sa 9:30am-4pm); and the **post office,** 109 South St. (☎624 413; open M-Sa 9am-5:30pm). **Post Code:** PH2 8AF.

🛏🍴 ACCOMMODATIONS, FOOD, AND PUBS. The last hostel in Perth was scheduled to close in August 2002, but affordable B&Bs line **Glasgow Rd.** Friendly **Mrs. Glennie ❷,** 55 Glasgow Rd., lets comfy rooms. (☎626 723. £16 per person.) For a more upscale experience, **Abercrombie B&B ❸,** 85 Glasgow Rd., is light and airy, with private bathrooms. (☎/fax 444 728. £20-30 per person.) A second cluster of B&Bs is just across the river. Go east across Perth Bridge and immediately turn right, following Main St. north as it turns into Strathmore St. and then Pitcullen Crescent. Start at **Darroch Guest House ❷,** 9 Pitcullen Crescent, where rooms vary from singles to ensuite doubles. (☎/fax 636 893. £16-21.)

An enormous **Safeway** supermarket resides on Caledonian Rd. (☎442 422. Open M-Tu and Sa 8am-8pm, W-Th 8am-9pm, F 8am-10pm, Su 9am-6pm.) Cozy **Brambles Cafe and Restaurant ❶,** 11 Princes St., has a friendly staff serving nicely priced selections, including veggie haggis. (☎639 091. Open M-Sa 10am-4pm, Su noon-2pm.) **Scaramouche ❶,** 103 South St., has a great location and serves cheap, generous portions. (☎637 479. Open M-Th 11am-11pm, F-Sa 11am-11:45pm, Su 12:30-11pm. Food served noon-8pm.) **Mucky Mulligans ❶,** 97 Canal Crescent, hosts live music or DJs on Thursdays and Saturdays. (☎636 705. Occasional cover. Open M-W noon-11:30pm, Th-F noon-1:30am, Sa noon-1am, Su 6-11:30pm.) Visit the **Foundry ❶,** 3 Murray St., for a big bar feel with good bar food and open-air seating in a covered courtyard. (☎836 863. Open M-Th 11am-11pm, F-Sa 11am-midnight, Su 12:30pm-11pm. Food served M-Sa 11am-8pm, Su 12:30-7pm.)

📷🎭 SIGHTS AND ACTIVITIES. In 1559, John Knox delivered an incendiary sermon from the pulpit of **St. John's Kirk,** on St. John's Pl., prompting the destruction of churches and monasteries and sparking the Scottish Reformation. Unfortunately, nothing terribly interesting has happened here since. (☎638 482. Open M-F May-Sept. 10am-4pm.) **The Perth Museum and Art Gallery,** at the intersection of Tay St. and Perth Bridge, provides an idiosyncratic examination of the city. Visitors are invited to sample the medieval toilet seat at the top of the stairs. (Open M-Sa 10am-5pm. Tours M-F in summer by request. Free.) The **Fergusson Gallery,** in the Old Perth Water Works on the corner of Marshall Pl. and Tay St., has excellent works by J.D. Fergusson, a local lad influenced by his companion, dancer Margaret Morris. (☎441 944. Open M-Sa 10am-5pm. Free.) **The Perth Theatre,** 185 High St., hosts shows and concerts year-round. (☎621 031. Box office open M-Sa 10am-7:30pm.) **Balhousie Castle,** off Hay St. north of the city, 16th-century home of the Earls of Kinnoull, now functions as regimental headquarters and houses the **Black Watch Regimental Museum.** It includes weapons, medals, the back-door key to Spandau prison in Berlin, and an occasional real-life member of the Watch. (☎621 281. Open May-Sept. M-Sa 10am-4:30pm; Oct.-Apr. M-Sa 10am-3:30pm. Donation requested.)

THE HIDDEN DEAL

THE WESTER CAPUTH INDEPENDENT HOSTEL

The **Wester Caputh Independent Hostel,** outside of Dunkeld and Birnam, is everything that a hostel could be and everything that a Scottish countryside experience should be. The friendly managers, Iain and Katie (and Katie's mum Mary), make guests feel at home with their cozy fireplace, well-stocked kitchen, old farmhouse decor, and some of Britain's best showers.

Even better than the beds, bathing, and breakfast, however, is the music. Local musicians stop by nightly to play real honest-to-goodness folk tunes on fiddle, guitar, squeezebox, harmonica, and piano. Hostelers are invited, nay, encouraged, to join in the revelry.

Free music and good company make this a required stop for any stay in Perthshire. Be sure to ask the indomitable outdoorsman Iain about nearby hikes and adventure travel.

To reach the hostel, go east out of Dunkeld on the A984 and turn right heading south) after the church in Caputh. Take the next immediate right going west and find the doors of the hostel 150 yards ahead. Call ahead for a pickup from the train or bus station. (☎/fax (01738) 710 617 or 710 449. Breakfast £2.50. Laundry £2-4 per load. Internet access £1 per 15min. Bike rental £6-10. Dorms £8; B&B £10.)

A 20min. walk across the **Perth Bridge** leads to ◪**Kinnoull Hill Woodland Park** and its four signposted nature walks, all of which finish at a magnificent summit with panoramic vistas. Beginners or those with children can try the **Tower Walk,** while hikers in better shape might choose the **Nature Walk,** which winds through the thick of the forest; none of the walks, however, should prove a challenge. Across the **Queen's Bridge,** near the Fergusson Gallery, the mile-long **Perth Sculpture Trail** begins in the Rodney Gardens and surveys 24 pieces of modern art while weaving along the river. The new **Bell's Cherrybank Centre** is famous for its 900-plus types of heather, but also provides a glossy look at Perth and a certain native, Arthur Bell, who took up the whisky business and got a library named after him as a reward. Visitors receive a free dram and free admission to Pitlochry's Blair Athol Distillery (see p. 605). Catch bus #7 from South St. (every 20min.) or walk 20min. uphill along Glasgow Rd. (☎ 627 330. Open Easter-Oct. M-Sa 9am-5pm, Su noon-4pm; Oct.-Easter M-F 10am-4pm. £3, children free.)

◪ DAYTRIPS FROM PERTH

SCONE PALACE. Scone (pronounced SKOON), less than 3 mi. northeast of Perth on the A93, is a regional jewel. Each of Scotland's kings was coronated here at the famous **Stone of Scone** (see **Stoned,** p. 109). The sumptuous grounds are paced by impertinent peacocks while the dazzling interiors are paced by courteous staffers. The palace houses a large collection of ivory statuettes, fine china, and hundred-year-old lace, and is still the home of the Lord and Lady of Mansfield—only a fraction is open for public viewing. Canny travelers may want to picnic in the hidden dells nooked between the trees. Try the **maze,** but beware: maps do exist, but only for those who can find them. (Take bus #3 from South St. (every hr.) and tell the driver where you're going or hop a Guide Friday bus tour. ☎(01738) 552 300; www.scone-palace.co.uk. Open Apr.-Oct. daily 9:30am-4:45pm. £6.20, seniors and students £5.30, under 16 £3.60. Grounds only £3.10/£2.50/£1.70.)

GLAMIS CASTLE. Macbeth's purported home (pronounced GLOMZ), this childhood playground of the Queen Mum noses its dozen handsome turrets into the sky 35 mi. northeast of Perth on the A94. Royal watchers will find a treasure trove of stories and artifacts, and should test drive one of the free tours (every 45min. in summer). The collections of armor, paintings, and furniture inside are significant, but the trek to the castle is inconvenient without a car. (Take Scottish Citylink from Perth to Dundee, then catch Strathtay bus #22 or 22A to Glamis (35min., 5 per day). Call the Perth & Kinross Public Transport Traveline, ☎(0845) 301 1130, for updated info. Castle ☎(01307) 840 393. Open Apr.-Oct. daily 10:30am-5:30pm; Nov.-Mar. call for hours. Last admission 4:45pm. £6.50, concessions £4.80, children £3.20. Grounds only half-price.)

DUNKELD AND BIRNAM   ☎01350

Huddled amid the forested hills of Perthshire on either side of the River Tay, the twin medieval towns of Dunkeld and Birnam (15min. apart by foot) provide easy access to one of Scotland's most isolated regions. The area has long welcomed outdoorsy types for both short day hikes and epic adventures, while artists and musicians energetically contribute to a hidden reserve of Scottish folk culture.

🖪 TRANSPORTATION. The unstaffed **train station** in Birnam is on the Edinburgh-Inverness line. **Trains** run from: **Edinburgh** (2hr., 5 per day, £9.30); **Glasgow** (1½hr., 5 per day, £19.30); **Inverness** (1½hr., 5 per day, £15.40); **Perth** (15min., 5 per day, £4.40). **Scottish Citylink buses** (☎(08705) 505 050) stop by the Birnam train station carpark from: **Edinburgh** (1½hr., 3 per day, £7); **Glasgow** (2hr., 3 per day, £7.50); **Inverness** (2hr., 3 per day, £8.80); **Perth** (22min., 3 per day, £4.10); **Pitlochry** (20min., 5 per day, £5). If you're coming from Perth or Pitlochry, **local buses**, which stop at the Birnam House Hotel, are cheaper and may get you closer to your destination. Grab the essential *Highland Perthshire and Stanley Area Local Public Transportation Guide* (free) from any TIC or call the **Public Transport Traveline** (☎(0845) 301 1130; M-F 8:30am-5pm). **Rent bikes** at **Dunkeld Bike Hire** on Perth Rd. in Birnam. (☎728 744. Bikes £12 per day. £100 deposit. Open daily 9am-5pm.)

🛈 PRACTICAL INFORMATION. Although nearly all public transport arrives in Birnam (a popular Victorian vacation spot), most amenities are in more historic Dunkeld. The Dunkeld **tourist information centre,** by the fountain in the town center, 1 mi. from the train station, books beds for £1 and a 10% deposit. (☎727 688. Open July-Aug. M-Sa 9:30am-6:30pm, Su 11am-5pm; Apr.-June and Sept.-Oct. M-Sa 9:30am-5:30pm, Su 11am-4pm.) Other services include: Dunkeld's **Bank of Scotland,** High St. (☎727 759; open M-Tu and Th-F 9am-12:30pm and 1:30-5pm, W 1:30-5pm); **Internet access** at the Public Bar of the **Royal Dunkeld Hotel,** Atholl St. (£1 per 10min.); and the Dunkeld **post office,** Bridge St. (☎(08457) 223 344; open M-W and F 9am-1pm and 2-5:30pm, Th 9am-1pm, Sa 9am-12:30pm). **Post Code:** PH8 0AH.

🛏🍴 ACCOMMODATIONS AND FOOD. Aside from the nearby and fabulous **🛏Wester Caputh Hostel** (see sidebar), Birnam and Dunkeld have dozens of **B&Bs;** the TIC keeps a complete list with phone numbers outside its door. The happening **Taybank Hotel ❷** (owned by legendary folk musician Dougie Maclean, of "Caledonia" fame) is by the Dunkeld Bridge and offers simple rooms themed around Scottish songsters. (☎727 340; fax 728 606; www.taybank.com. £17.50 per person; singles £5 extra.) **Campers** should head for the **Inver Mill Caravan Park ❶**, on the riverside across from Dunkeld and to the north. (☎727 477. Open Apr.-Oct. £9-11 for 2 people, tent, and car; £1 each additional person. Laundry £4.)

The **Co-op** supermarket, 15 Bridge St., is in Dunkeld. (☎727 321. Open M-Sa 8am-8pm, Su 9am-6pm.) **🎵Maclean's Real Music Bar ❶,** in the Taybank Hotel (see above), serves famous "stovies," baked potatoes packed with meat or veggies (£3.50), and hosts casual gatherings of local and visiting musicians—sometimes even Dougie himself puts in an appearance. Spare instruments hang on the walls—for you to join in the music-making—and there's plenty of space on the outside patio. Thursday and Friday are the best nights for music, with surprise guests and open mic sessions. (☎727 340. Open daily noon-11pm. Cover varies.) For lunch, head to the **Dunkeld Snack Bar ❷**, 5 Atholl St., for fish and chips, pizza, haggis, and other classic choices. (☎727 427. Open M-Sa 11am-6pm, Su noon-6pm.) Take a break for coffee, tea, and mouth-watering homemade shortcake at **Palmerstons ❶**, 10 Atholl St. (☎727 231. Open M-W 11am-6pm, Th-Su 10am-6pm.)

🎥📷 SIGHTS AND ACTIVITIES. Painstakingly restored 18th-century houses line the way to the partially charred **Dunkeld Cathedral,** High St., whose restored quire is now an active parish church. Like other cathedrals, the architecture changed with new additions, making the final product delightfully hodgepodge. (Open Apr.-Sept. M-Sa 9:30am-6:30pm, Su 2-6:30pm; Oct.-Mar. M-Sa 9:30am-4pm, Su 2-4pm. Free.) To the west, over the arched Telford Bridge in Birnam, find a flimsy claim to literary fame: Beatrix Potter spent most of her childhood holidays in the area, drawing on her experiences for *The Tale of Peter Rabbit.* The **Beatrix Potter Garden** and the **Birnam Institute** celebrate her today. (☎ 727 674; www.birnaminstitute.com. Open M-Sa 10am-4pm, Su 2-4pm. Free.) **The Dunkeld and Birnam Festival,** held the last week in June, includes local paintings, plays, and music. (Call ☎ 727 688 for information.)

The TIC's *Dunkeld & Birnam Walks* (50p) provides useful maps of area rambles. Paths lead north from Birnam to the great **Birnam Oak,** remnant of the fabled Birnam Wood that the Ol' Shake wrote about in *Macbeth.* The brisk and savage waterfalls of the **Hermitage** tumble 1½ mi. away, with a well-marked ¾ mi. path passing through all designated photo-ops. The most strenuous hike, the **Birnam Hill Walk,** climbs over 1000 ft. just south of Birnam and rewards with stunning panoramas of the two villages and surrounding countryside. Birdwatchers will enjoy the **Loch of the Lowes,** a wildlife reserve east of Dunkeld and just south of the A923 (20min. on a path from the TIC, detailed in *Dunkeld Walks*). For the past eight years, the Loch has served as a summer retreat for travel-happy ospreys who fly all the way from Gambia. (☎ 727 337. Visitor center open mid-July to mid-Aug. daily 10am-6pm; Apr. to mid-July and mid-Aug. to Sept. 10am-5pm.) Trout season lasts from mid-March to mid-October. Obtain a fishing license (£3-4) for the River Tay from **Kettles,** 15 Atholl St. (☎ 727 556).

NEAR DUNKELD AND BIRNAM: THE CATERAN TRAIL

Highland Perthshire, northeast of Dunkeld and Birnam, is home to the **Cateran Trail,** a terrific 60 mi. hike past the cairns and ruins lining a loop between the Bridge of Cally, Alyth, Blairgowrie, and the Spittal of Glenshee. The well-marked route approximates that of the "Cateran Bands," medieval cattle-rustlers sent to capture and hold herds for ransom on behalf of their clans. ("Blackmail" is originally a Scottish word.) The trail splits into five easy 12 mi. sections, each a day's hike with B&Bs at the finish. Call the **Cateran Trail Company** (☎ (0800) 277 200) to arrange accommodations—for £155, they'll even cart your pack.

LOCH TAY

The most beautiful part of Perthshire is also the most remote. **Aberfeldy,** a low-key base for enjoying the Loch, is accessible by various Perthshire local buses from Pitlochry, Perth, and Dunkeld and Birnam. Schedules vary monthly, but the **Perthshire Public Transport Traveline** (☎ (0845) 301 1130) has the most up-to-date information. Towns around Loch Tay may be reached from Aberfeldy by postbus; however, many only run once per day. The folks at the **Postbus Helpline** (☎ (01246) 546 329) or the Aberfeldy **tourist information centre** can help you sort out the confusion. (☎ (01887) 820 276; fax 829 495. Open July-Aug. M-Sa 9:30am-6:30pm, Su 11am-5pm; Sept.-June M-Sa 9:30am-4:30pm, Su 11am-4pm.)

Just 1 mi. southwest of Pitlochry on the southern shore perches the **Crannog Centre,** a replicated ancient Celtic loch dwelling. Visitors listen to the fascinating history of crannogs in Scotland, walk inside one, and try—usually with modern ineptitude—to use prehistoric tools. (☎ (01887) 830 583. 1hr. tour. Open Mar.-Oct. daily 10am-5:30pm. £4.25, concessions £3.85, children £3.) The tiny village of **Fortingall,** 4 mi. northwest of Kenmore (beyond Aberfeldy on the A827), is notable on two counts: it's home to a 3000-year-old yew tree, the oldest living organism in Europe (and perhaps the world), and is the supposed birthplace of Pontius Pilate, hand-washer extraordinaire, whose father was a Roman soldier stationed here. **Postbuses** arrive from **Aberfeldy** (#211, 55min., M-Sa 9am).

Midway between Kenmore and Killin on the north shore of Loch Tay, the **Ben Lawers Visitor Centre** rests in the shadow of **Ben Ghlas** and **Ben Lawers**, a pair of Munros (see p. 538) and two of Britain's most commanding mountains. (☎(01567) 820 397. Open Easter-Sept. daily 10am-1pm and 2-5pm.) Those with a car enjoy direct access to the Centre, but beware the flocks of sheep who call the mountain home; unlucky pedestrians can brave the 2 mi. hike from the road. A round-trip walk to the top of Ben Ghlas takes about 3hr.; it's 5hr. up and down the farther-off Ben Lawers. Postbus #213 (M-Sa) stops at the bottom of the road that leads to the Visitor Centre on its way from **Aberfeldy** to **Killin**. You might also pack a lunchbox and hop on the school bus that runs to the foot of the hill in the early morning.

At the opposite end of Loch Tay, the village of **Killin** is a good choice for hikers, with reasonably priced B&Bs and a **SHYA hostel ❶**, which, despite spartan amenities, is a well-located base camp for ramblers. (☎(01567) 820 546. Open Mar.-Oct. F-Sa. Dorms £9, under 18 £7.50.) In Killin, the two-room **Breadalbane Folklore Centre** shares a building with the **tourist information centre**, by the Falls of Douchart on Main St. Learn about St. Fillan and the local McGregor clan after gathering information on watersports and countless walks. (☎(01567) 820 254. Open July-Aug. daily 9:30am-6:30pm; June and Sept. 10am-6pm; Oct. and Mar.-May 10am-5pm. Folklore Centre £1.55, concessions £1.05.) A 2hr. hike starts from behind the schoolyard on Main St. and leads to a sheep's-eye view of the loch. On the northern end of Main St., go to the **Killin Library** (☎(01567) 820 571) for free Internet access. **Grant's Laundry** (☎(01567) 820 235) is the only place in town to wash clothes. **Postbuses** (each 1 per day) arrive from: **Aberfeldy** (#213, 3hr.; #839, 1hr.); **Crianlarich** (#025); **Tyndrum** (#025).

PITLOCHRY ☎01796

Emerging from the mists of the Grampian Mountains, Pitlochry is the gateway to the Highlands. Two fine distilleries, famous knitwear, and a web of hill walks introduce travelers to the drinks, clothes, and pastimes of the northern Scottish culture. Surrounded by hills to the north and lowlands to the south, Pitlochry has unique draws: summer theater, a dam and salmon ladder, and friendly locals. The nearby town of **Moulin** takes care of tourist overflow.

▐ TRANSPORTATION. Trains (☎(08457) 484 950) stop near the town center from: **Edinburgh** (2hr., 7 per day, £19.70); **Glasgow** (1¾hr., 7 per day, £19.70); **Inverness** (1¾hr., 9 per day, £13.80); **Perth** (30min., 9 per day, £5). The yellow phone on the platform connects to the office at Inverness Station. **Scottish Citylink buses** (☎(08705) 505 050) stop outside the Fishers Hotel on Atholl Rd. from: **Edinburgh** (2hr., 10 per day, £8); **Glasgow** (2½hr., 8 per day, £8); **Inverness** (2hr., every hr., £8.10); **Perth** (40min., every hr., £5). From Perth, Pitlochry is accessible by various local buses; call the **Public Transportation Traveline** (☎(0845) 301 1130) for up-to-date info. Rent **bikes** at **Escape Route**, 8 West Moulin Rd. (☎ 473 859. Open Su-F 10am-5pm, Sa 9:30am-5pm. £9 per half-day, £15 per day. Book ahead.)

▐ PRACTICAL INFORMATION. Plenty of postcards await at the **tourist information centre**, 22 Atholl Rd., as does the 50p *Pitlochry Walks*. (☎472 215. Open June-Aug. M-Sa 9am-7pm, Su 9am-6pm; Sept.-Nov. and Apr.-May M-Sa 9am-6pm, Su 11am-5pm; Nov.-Mar. M-F 9am-5pm, Sa 10am-2pm.) Other services include: the **Royal Bank of Scotland**, 76 Atholl St. (☎532 200; open M-Tu and Th-F 9am-5pm, W 9:30am-5pm); the **Pitlochry Launderette**, 3 West Moulin Rd. (☎474 044; wash £2.60, dry £1.50; open M-W and F 8:30am-5pm, Th and Sa 9am-5pm); **Internet access** at the **Computer Services Centre**, 67 Atholl Rd. (☎473 711; 8p per min., £4 per hr.; open M-F 9am-5:30pm, Sa 9am-12:30pm) or **MG Technologies Internet Cafe**, 26 Bonnethill Rd. (☎474 141; £1.50 per 15min., £2 per 30min.; open daily 9am-10pm); and the **post office**, 92 Atholl Rd. (open M-F 9am-5:30pm, Sa 1-4pm). **Post Code:** PH16 5AH.

ACCOMMODATIONS AND FOOD. Pitlochry Backpackers ❷, 134 Atholl St., converted from a former hotel, has dorms, twins, and doubles (some ensuite), plus a friendly staff, cheap bike rentals (£5 per half-day), TV, and pool table. (☎470 044. Open Apr.-Oct. £10-12 per person.) Behind the bus station, **Old Bank House Lodge ❷**, 82 Atholl Rd., will give you a clean room and a haircut for a reasonable price. (☎474 022; www.scottishlodge.com. Laundry £1.50. Haircut £9. Dorms £10, with bath £12.) Right across from the TIC, **Atholl Villa ❸**, 29 Atholl Rd., provides comfortable ensuite rooms, a private carpark, award-winning gardens, and spacious family areas. (☎473 820; www.athollvilla.co.uk. £20-28 per person.) The **SYHA Pitlochry ❶**, Knockard Rd. and Well Brae Rd., 15min. from town, is more notable for its magnificent views than its standard dorms and regulations. From the train and bus stations, turn right (east) on Atholl Rd. then go uphill onto Bonnethill Rd., where the hostel is signposted. (☎472 308. Breakfast £2.20. Internet access 50p per 12min. Laundry £2. Reception 7am-11am and 5-11:45pm. Check-out 10:30am. Curfew 11:45pm. Dorms £10, under 18 £8.) Two miles past town on Atholl Rd., camp at picturesque **Faskally Caravan Park ❶**. (☎472 007; www.faskally.co.uk. Open mid-Mar. to Oct. £9.50-11.50 per tent. Extra for electricity, sauna, pool, and jacuzzi.)

On West Moulin Rd., in Pitlochry, the **Pitlochry Co-op** provides groceries. (☎474 088. Open daily 8am-10pm.) The 300-year-old **Moulin Inn ❷**, Moulin Sq., in the wee village of Moulin, brews its own "Braveheart ale" and serves a selection of grub, including various veggie options. (☎472 196. Open Su-Th noon-11pm, F-Sa noon-11:45pm. Food served until 9pm. Brewery tours Th-M noon-3pm.) **Ardchoille Fish & Chip Cafe ❶**, 140 Atholl Rd., serves the cheapest eats in town, and does so with atmosphere. (☎472 170. Open M-Sa 10am-10pm, Su noon-10pm.)

WALKIN' AND DRINKIN'. Hikers should arm themselves with a copy of *Pitlochry Walks*, available at the TIC (50p). For a quick jaunt, take the path over the suspension footbridge in Moulin to the **Pitlochry Dam and salmon ladder.** From the observation chamber, watch as future fillets struggle ceaselessly against the current (Mar.-Oct.). An electronic fish counter keeps tally. (☎473 152. Open Apr.-Oct. daily 10am-5:30pm. Observation chamber and dam free; visitor center £2, students £1.20, children £1.) The opportunistic can get a fishing permit at **Mitchell's of Pitlochry** and head 100 yd. upstream. (☎472 613. £3-5 per day; £6-60 for salmon. Open Jan.-Oct. daily 8:30am-6pm, Nov.-Dec. M-Sa 9:30am-5pm.) Observe other unusual processes at the **HeatherGems Factory and Visitor Centre,** behind the TIC, where craftsmen cut and polish pressurized heather stems into tourist-pleasing jewelry. (☎473 863. Open 9am-5pm.)

Seeing as the word **"whisky"** comes from an old Gaelic term for "water of life" (*uisge beatha*), Pitlochry just might live forever. At the **Blair Athol Distillery,** a ½ mi. from the TIC down the main road, enough alcohol (3,210 liters if *Let's Go's* math is correct) evaporates daily to intoxicate the entire town. Kilted guides take you from flowing water to mashing malt to sampling the wares. (☎472 003. Open Easter-Sept. M-Sa 9:30am-5pm, Su noon-5pm; Oct. M-F 10am-4pm; Nov.-Easter M-F 1-4pm. Last full tour 1hr. before close. £3.) **The Edradour,** Scotland's tiniest (legal) distillery, may only produce 40 bottles a day, but that's enough to feed a happy little fungus that lives off evaporated alcohol. The delightful tour and sample dram are free. The Edradour is a 2½ mi. walk from Pitlochry (past Moulin along the A924); get there before 3pm, when distilling finishes for the day. (☎472 095; www.edradour.co.uk. Open Mar.-Oct. M-Sa 9:30am-5pm, Su noon-5pm.)

ENTERTAINMENT. The glitzy **Pitlochry Festival Theatre,** over the Aldour Bridge, boasts a cinema and international performers. The new season opens May 2003 and continues though October. (☎484 600. Tickets £15-20, students and hostelers half-price.) In the recreation fields southwest of town near Tummel Crescent, **Highland Nights** feature local pipe bands and traditional folk dancing. (May-Sept. M 8pm. Tickets available at the gate; £4, concessions £3, children £1.) Pick up the free *What's On in Perthshire* at the TIC for further entertainment ideas.

◢ DAYTRIPS FROM PITLOCHRY

⬛ BLAIR CASTLE. Seven miles north of Pitlochry on the A9, the white soaring turrets and green tree-lined grounds make Blair Castle seem more like a palace. The interior does not disappoint, with instruments of war arrayed in intricate wall patterns and a well-preserved Victorian bathroom. The castle grounds, frequented by pedestrians and equestrians, are used to train the 10th Duke of Atholl's army, the only private army in Britain. Prepared to fight in both the American Revolution and WWI, the farthest the Atholl troops have ever gone is Ireland. *(Take the train to Blair Athol and walk 10min., or hop on bus #26 or 87 from the West End Car Park. ☎ 481 207; www.blair-castle.co.uk. Open Apr.-Oct. daily 10am-6pm, last admission 5pm. £6.25, seniors and students £5.25, children £4, families £18.)*

HIKING. After legging out a 4hr. hike, visitors can charge up the 2757 ft. **Ben-y-Vrackie,** which gives views of Edinburgh on a clear day. Turn left (north) onto the road directly behind the Moulin Inn in Moulin and follow the curve until you reach a fork (note the standing stones in the field nearby). Take the right-hand road northeast to Ben-y-Vrackie. Continue along the left-hand road (northwest) about 2hr. to explore **Craigower Hill,** which has a view to the west along Loch Tommel and Loch Rannoch to the Glencoe Mountains. A 5 mi. walk from the Pitlochry dam leads to the Pass of Killiecrankie (signposted, and included in *Pitlochry Walks*).

PASS OF KILLIECRANKIE. A few miles north of Pitlochry, the valley of the River Garry narrows into a stunning gorge. In 1689, a Jacobite army slaughtered William III's troops here in an attempt to reinstall James VII of Scotland on the English throne. One stranded soldier by the name of Donald MacBean, preferring to risk the steep fall than surrender (and probably made hardy of heart by *uisge beatha*), vaulted 18 ft. across **Soldier's Leap.** Along with views of the countryside, the area is home to an intriguing array of wildlife and wildflowers, from the buzzard and the Great Tit to the primrose and the Devil's Bit. For information or a guided walk, stop in at the **National Trust Visitors Centre,** down the path from the pass. *(Elizabeth Yule bus #87 runs from the West End Car Park to the pass in summer (4 per day, £1). ☎ 473 233. Centre open Apr.-Oct. daily 10am-5:30pm.)*

STIRLING ☎ 01786

Sitting atop a triangle completed by Glasgow and Edinburgh, Stirling has historically presided over passage through the region—it's been said that he who controlled Stirling controlled Scotland. At the 1297 Battle of Stirling Bridge, William Wallace outwitted and overpowered the English army, enabling Robert the Bruce to lead Scotland to independence 17 years later. Despite recent bustling development, this former capital has not forgotten its heroes. Stirling's moving history and architecture have been rediscovered, and the city now swarms with *Braveheart* fans set on capturing the glorious Scotland of old.

◪ TRANSPORTATION

The **train station** is close to the town center, just off Goosecroft Rd. (Travel center open M-F 6am-9pm, Sa 6am-8pm, Su 8:30am-10pm. Luggage storage £2-4; open M-Sa 10am-6pm.) Trains (☎ (08457) 484 950) arrive from: **Aberdeen** (2hr.; M-Sa every hr., Su 6 per day; £30.90); **Edinburgh** (50min., 2 per hr., £5.30); **Glasgow** (40min.; M-Sa 2-3 per hr., Su every hr.; £5.40); **Inverness** (3hr.; M-Sa 4 per day, Su 3 per day; £30.50); and **London King's Cross** (5½hr., every hr., £44-84). The **bus station** is also on Goosecroft Rd. (☎ 446 474. Ticket office open M-F 8:30am-6pm, Sa 8:30am-5pm. Luggage storage £1; open M-Sa 7am-9pm, Su 12:30-7:30pm.) **Scottish Citylink** (☎ (0870) 505 050) buses run from **Fort William** (2¾hr., 1 per day, £12.90); **Glasgow** (40min., 2-3 per hr., £3.80); and **Inverness** (3¾ hr., every hr., £11.80). **First** (☎ (01324) 613 777) bus M9 runs express to **Edinburgh** (1¼hr., every hr., £4).

ⓘ PRACTICAL INFORMATION

The Stirling **tourist information centre** is at 41 Dumbarton Rd. (☎ 475 019. Open July-Aug. M-Sa 9am-7:30pm, Su 9:30am-6:30pm; June and Sept. M-Sa 9am-6pm, Su 10am-4pm; Oct.-May roughly M-Sa 10am-5pm.) Next to the castle, the **Stirling Visitor Centre** is high-altitude and high-tech with exhibits and a 12min. movie. They'll exchange your currency for a £3 commission and book you a room for a £1 fee. (☎ 462 517. Open July-Aug. daily 9am-6:30pm; Apr.-June and Sept.-Oct. 9:30am-6pm; Nov.-Mar. 9:30am-5pm.) **Guide Friday** operates 70min. hop-on/hop-off bus tours from the castle esplanade throughout town and to the Wallace Monument. (☎ (0131) 556 2244. Daily 10am-5pm. £6.50, concessions £5, children £2, families £15.) Find **Internet access** at the **library**, Corn Exchange (☎ 432 107; £2.50 per 30min., concessions £1.25), and the **post office** at 84-86 Murray Pl. (☎ 465 392; **bureau de change;** open M-F 9am-5:30pm, Sa 9am-12:30pm). **Post Code:** FK8 2BP.

🏠 🍴 ACCOMMODATIONS AND FOOD

At the well-equipped **Willy Wallace Hostel ❷**, 77 Murray Pl., a delightfully witty staff fosters a good-times atmosphere. (☎ 446 773. Dorms £10-14.) The excellent **SYHA Stirling ❷**, on St. John St., halfway up the hill to the castle, occupies the shell of the first Separatist Church in Stirling. Each of the 2- to 5-bed rooms has its own shower and toilet. In July and August, the **Union St. Annex,** known in cooler months as University of Stirling housing, is used for hostel overflow. (☎ 473 442; fax 445 715. Bedroom lockout 10am-2pm. Curfew 2am. Dorms £11-12.50, under 18 £9-11.) **Mrs. Helen Miller's ❷**, 16 Riverside Dr., offers two basic, clean singles—one with a view of the Wallace Monument. (☎ 461 105. £12-14 per person.) Near the train station, **Forth Guest House ❸**, 23 Forth Pl., is a very comfortable Georgian house with ensuite rooms. (☎ 471 020. Singles £20-35; doubles £39-45.)

Tucked down an alley, **The Greengrocer,** 81 Port St., offers some of the freshest fruits and veggies in town. (☎ 479 159. Open M-F 9am-5:30pm, Sa 8:30am-3:30pm.) Fill out your shopping cart at **Iceland,** 5 Pitt Terr. (☎ 464 300. Open M-F 8:30am-

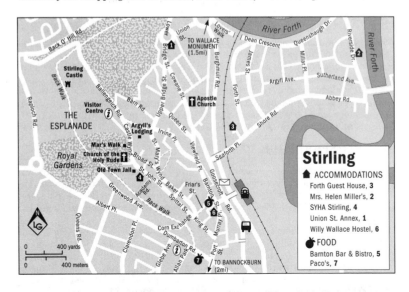

Stirling

⌂ ACCOMMODATIONS
Forth Guest House, **3**
Mrs. Helen Miller's, **2**
SYHA Stirling, **4**
Union St. Annex, **1**
Willy Wallace Hostel, **6**

🍴 FOOD
Barnton Bar & Bistro, **5**
Paco's, **7**

8pm, Sa 8:30am-6pm, Su 10am-5pm.) **Paco's Restaurant ❷**, 21 Dumbarton Rd., has a Tex-Mex dish for every tastebud and a price for every budget, with main courses ranging £4.45-11.45. (☎446 414. Open M-Sa from noon, Su from 5pm.) Popular among pint-swiggers, **Barnton Bar & Bistro ❶**, 3½ Barnton St., serves good, inexpensive light fare. (☎461 698. Open Su-Th 10:30am-midnight, F-Sa 10:30am-1am.)

👁 SIGHTS

▨**STIRLING CASTLE.** Planted on a defunct volcano and embraced on all sides by the scenic Ochil Hills, Stirling's castle has superb views of the Forth Valley and prim gardens that belie its militant history. In an effort to erase the violent memory of English attempts to seize the stronghold, Robert the Bruce ordered the castle's destruction after the Battle of Bannockburn. Nonetheless, it was rebuilt in the 1380s and Robert's statue ironically stands guard in front of the present structure. The castle's hideous gargoyles glowered over the 14th-century Wars of Independence, a 15th-century royal murder, and the 16th-century coronation of the infant Mary, Queen of Scots; its final military engagement came in 1746, when Bonnie Prince Charlie besieged it while retreating from England (and then gave up and kept retreating). Beneath the cannons pointed at Stirling Bridge lie the 16th-century **great kitchens;** visitors can walk among the recreated chaos of cooks, dogs, bakers, and vast slabs of meat. Free 30min. **guided tours,** leaving twice an hour, give background for further exploration. (☎450 000. Open Apr.-Oct. 9:30am-6pm; Nov.-Mar. 9:30am-5pm; last admission 45min. before close. £6.50, seniors £5, children £2.) The castle also contains the **Regimental Museum of the Argyll and Sutherland Highlanders,** a fascinating assemblage of military might. (Open Easter-Sept. M-Sa 10am-5:45pm, Su 11am-4:45pm; Oct.-Easter daily 10am-4:15pm. Free.) **Argyll's Lodging,** a 17th-century mansion on the esplanade, has been impressively restored. (Open Apr.-Sept. 9:30am-6pm; Oct.-Mar. 9:30am-5pm. £3, seniors £2.20, children £1.40; free with castle admission.)

WALLACE MONUMENT. This 19th-century tower offers incredible views to those bravehearted enough to climb its 246-step, wind-whipped spiral staircase. Halfway up, you can catch your breath and admire the 5½ ft. sword William Wallace wielded against King Edward I and contemplate exhibits on Wallace's capture and gruesome execution. (Hillfoots Rd., 1½ mi. from Stirling proper. Guide Friday runs here, as do local buses #62 and 63 from Murray Pl. ☎472 140. Open July-Aug. daily 9:30am-6:30pm; June and Sept. 10am-6pm; Mar.-May and Oct. 10am-5pm; Nov.-Feb. 10:30am-4pm. £4, students £3, seniors and children £2.75, families £10.75.)

SEX, LIES, AND VIDEOTAPE In 1297, a small band of hopelessly outnumbered Scottish clansmen, led by William Wallace, defeated a legion of well-trained English troops at Stirling. We can all thank *Braveheart*'s blue-faced battle scene for bringing the bare bones of this story to the masses. But allow *Let's Go* to give you the meat: although Hollywood depicts the Scots brandishing poles and charging the English heavy cavalry, in reality the clansmen waited quietly for the English to reach Stirling Bridge. Each time the bridge teemed with soldiers—who were forced to break regiment in order to cross it—the Scots attacked and slaughtered the lot, repeating as necessary until the entire army was dead or hostage. While the silver-screen version is known as the Battle of Stirling, the real deal is more appropriately called the Battle of Stirling Bridge. Equally hokum is the steamy Wallace-Princess tryst, considering that Edward II married Isabella of France three years after Wallace was executed. And if you still think Hollywood cannot tell a lie, ask yourself how a 5'9" Aussie could ever wield the Scotsman's 5'6" ft. sword.

THE OLD TOWN. The old center of Stirling, downhill from the castle, contains several worthwhile sights. At **Mar's Walk,** Castle Wynd, an elaborate facade is all that remains of a 16th-century townhouse. Nearby, the high walls and timbered roof of the **Church of the Holy Rude** witnessed the coronation of James VI and shook under the fire and brimstone of John Knox; bullet holes can still be seen in the walls. *(Open May-Sept. daily 10am-5pm; Su service July-Dec. 10am, Jan.-June 11:30am. Frequent organ recitals. Donations requested.)* Next to the church lies 17th-century **Cowane's Hospital,** built as an almshouse for poor members of the merchant guild. *(Open M-Sa 9am-5pm, Su 1-5pm. Free.)* The **Old Town Jail,** St. John St., features excellent reenactments of prison life. Break out onto the roof for its fine views of the Forth Valley. *(☎ 450 050. Open Apr.-Sept. daily 9:30am-6pm; Oct.-Mar. 9:30am-4 or 5pm.)* Stirling's old **town walls** are some of the best-preserved in Scotland; you can follow them along the circular **Back Walk.**

BANNOCKBURN. Two miles south of Stirling at **Bannockburn,** a statue of a battle-ready Robert the Bruce overlooks the field where his men decisively defeated the English in 1314, after which Scotland was independent for 393 years. The **Bannockburn Heritage Centre** screens an audiovisual display on the battle. *(Take bus #51 or 52 from Murray Pl. in Stirling. ☎ 812 664. Centre open Apr.-Oct. daily 10am-5:30pm; Mar. and Nov.-Dec. 10:30am-4:30pm. £2.50, children £1.70. Battlefield open year-round.)*

THE TROSSACHS   ☎ 01877

The gentle mountains and lochs of the Trossachs (from the Gaelic for "bristly country") form the northern boundary of central Scotland. Sir Walter Scott and Queen Victoria praised the region, the only easily accessible Scottish wilderness prior to the 20th century. Just as popular today, the Trossachs are now (with Loch Lomond) Scotland's first national park, and bear the tagline "Rob Roy Country." The A821 winds through the heart of the region between the main towns of **Aberfoyle** and **Callander.** It passes near majestic **Loch Katrine,** the Trossachs' original lure and the setting of Scott's "The Lady of the Lake." A bike- and footpath traces the loch's shoreline, while the popular **Steamship Sir Walter Scott** cruises from the Trossachs Pier. *(☎ 376 316. Mar.-Oct. 11am, 1:45, 3:15pm; W and Sa no 11am sailing; Mar.-Apr. and Oct. no 3:15pm sailing. Return £5.50-6.50, seniors £4, children £3.60.)* Nearby hulks **Ben A'an'** (1207 ft.); the rocky 1hr. hike up begins a mile from the pier, along the A821. In Callander, the **Rob Roy and Trossachs Visitor Centre** is a combined TIC and celebratory exhibit on the 17th-century hero. *(☎ 330 342. Open July-Aug. daily 9:30am-8pm; June 9:30am-6pm; Sept. 10am-6pm; Mar.-May and Oct.-Dec. 10am-5pm; Jan.-Feb. Sa-Su 11am-4:30pm. £3.25, children £2.25.)*

By public transport, access to the Trossachs is easiest from **Stirling. First** (☎ (01324) 613 777) runs up to 11 buses per day from Stirling to **Callander** (45min., £2.90) and up to four per day to **Aberfoyle** (45min., £3.40). From **Glasgow,** reach **Aberfoyle** by changing buses at **Balfron.** During the summer, the useful **Trossachs Trundler** (☎ (01786) 442 707) travels between **Callander, Aberfoyle,** and the Trossachs Pier at **Loch Katrine;** one daily trip begins and ends in **Stirling** (July-Sept. Th-Tu 4 per day; Day Rover £4, concessions £3; including travel from Stirling £8/£5.50). **Postbuses** reach some remoter areas of the region; find timetables at TICs or call the **Stirling Council Public Transport Helpline** (☎ (01786) 442 707). **Katrinewheelz** (☎ 376 248), at Trossachs Pier on Loch Katrine, rents bikes.

Although neither Callander nor Aberfoyle is particularly appealing as a destination in itself, those relying on public transport will likely need to bunk at one or the other. About 1 mi. south of Callander on Invertrossachs Rd., **Trossachs Backpackers ❷** is a comfortable hostel with an attractive setting. (☎/fax 331 200. Dorms £10-15.) In Callander itself, **Abbotsford Lodge ❸,** Stirling Rd., is a private country cottage with a conservatory restaurant. (☎330 066. Singles £19.50-34.75; doubles £39-45.) In Aberfoyle, Ann and John Epps open their secluded home with its stunning views to visitors at **Crannaig House ❸**, Trossachs Rd. (☎382 276. Singles £28-36; doubles £46-55.) Camping is available at the very well-equipped **Trossachs Holiday Park ❶**, just outside Aberfoyle's town center. (☎382 614. Open Mar-Oct. £9.)

LOCH LOMOND AND BALLOCH ☎01389

With Britain's largest lake as its base, the landscape surrounding Loch Lomond is filled with the lush bays, wooded isles, and barren hills immortalized in the famous ballad. Given their proximity to Glasgow, parts of the bonnie banks can get very crowded, but visitors who undertake challenging hikes in such roadless areas as the northeastern edge of the loch are rewarded by stunning views and quiet, untrammeled swaths of space. Hikers adore the **West Highland Way,** which snakes along the entire eastern side of the Loch and stretches 95 mi. from Milngavie north to Fort William. **Balloch,** at the southern tip of Loch Lomond, is the area's largest tourism center, though it's as much suburban town as lakeside resort. Not that it needed more press, but the area has lately seen new tourism developments. More significantly, the loch is now at the heart of Scotland's very first national park, designated **Loch Lomond and The Trossachs.**

▛▊ TRANSPORTATION AND PRACTICAL INFORMATION. The Balloch **train station** is on Balloch Rd., across the street from the TIC. **Trains** (☎(08457) 484 950) arrive from **Glasgow Queen St.** (45min., at least 2 per hr., £3.20). **Scottish Citylink** (☎(08705) 505 050) runs reasonably frequent **buses** from **Glasgow** (40min., £3.60) that drop off about 1 mi. from the town center, at the lay-by north of the Balloch roundabout. These buses then continue along the loch's western shore to **Luss** and **Tarbet. First** (☎(01324) 613 777) sends #204 and 205 to Balloch from Glassford St. in **Glasgow;** First also comes from **Stirling** (1½hr.; M-Sa 3 per day, Su 1 per day; £4.80). To reach the eastern side of the loch, take bus #9 or 309 from Balloch to **Balmaha** (40min., 6 per day, £1.50). Buses #305 and 307 head for **Luss** (15min., 7 per day, £1.90). Balloch's **tourist information centres** are in the Old Station Building (☎753 533; open June-Sept. daily 9:30am-6pm; Apr., May, and Oct. 10am-5pm) and at Loch Lomond Shores (see below).

▛ ACCOMMODATIONS. The ▨SYHA Loch Lomond ❷ is one of Scotland's largest hostels, with 9 entrances, 53 chimneys, and 160 beds in a stunning 19th-century castle-esque structure 2 mi. north of Balloch. From the train station, follow the main road ½ mi. to the roundabout. Turn right, continue 1½ mi., and turn left at the sign for the hostel; it's a short jog up the hill. The high-ceilinged common room is astounding; other amenities include the ghost of Veronica, who, pregnant by a stable boy, leapt from the window of the tower in which her family had locked her. (☎850 226. Book ahead in summer. Dorms £10-12.50, under 18 £8.50-11.) **B&Bs** congregate on Balloch Rd., conveniently close to the TIC. Among these, a good choice is **Norwood Guest House ❸**, overlooking Balloch Castle Country Park. (☎750 309. Singles £20-25; doubles £36-44.)

The **SYHA Rowardennan ❶**, the first hostel along the West Highland Way, has huge windows that put the loch in your lap. (☎(01360) 870 259. Curfew 11:30pm. Open Mar.-Oct. Dorms £9.50-10.50, under 18 £6-8.) To reach the hostel, take the Inverberg **ferry** to Rowardennan. (☎(01301) 702 356. May-Sept. daily; leaves Rowardennan at 10am, 2, 6pm; leaves Inverberg 30min. later. £4, children £1.50.) The **Lomond Woods Holiday Park ❶** is on Old Luss Rd., up Balloch Rd. from the TIC. Soak in a spa or rent mountain bikes at this Club Med of campsites. (☎(01389) 759 475. Reception 8:30am-10pm. Bikes £7.50 per 4hr., £10 per 8hr.; deposit £100. Tent and 2 adults £6.50-9, with car £8.50-12.50; children £1; additional adults £2.)

⬛ SIGHTS. Loch Lomond Shores, Balloch's large new visitor complex, opened in July 2002. Attractions in its centerpiece tower (designed as a "modern-day castle") include a giant-screen film about the loch, a shorter kid-oriented flick taking you on a "journey beneath the loch," and a rooftop outlook from which you can see the loch itself. The complex also contains the ranger-staffed **National Park Gateway Centre:** a NPIC, TIC, and—of course—a shopping mall. Rent bikes or canoes or get a guided hike from **Can You Experience** (☎ 602 576). Loch Lomond Shores is a 10min. walk from the Balloch train station; a shuttle runs every 30min. during the summer. (☎ 721 500. Open Apr.-Sept. 7am-7pm, Oct.-Mar. 10am-5pm. Admission to all 3 attractions £6, concessions £3.75, families £16.50 Individual tickets also available.)

One of the best introductions to the area is **Sweeney's Cruises,** departing from the TIC's side of the River Leven in Balloch. (☎ 752 376. 1hr.; every hr. 10am-4pm; £4.80, children £2.50.) Cruises also sail to **Luss,** with 30min. ashore (2½hr., 2:30pm, £7.50/£3.50), and the evening cruise offers an onboard bar (1½hr., 7:30pm, £6.50/£3). Avert your eyes (or don't) from the nudist colony on one of the islands in the lake's center. **Mullen's Cruises** (☎ 751 481) also offers trips from Balloch. Across the Leven, **Balloch Castle Country Park** provides 200 acres of gorgeous beach lawn, woods, and gardens, as well as a 19th-century castle housing a Visitors Centre and Park Ranger Station. If the weather is good, don't miss the opportunity to look for pixies in **Fairy Glen.** (Park open daily dawn-dusk. Visitors Centre open Easter-Oct. daily 10am-6pm. Free.) The **Glasgow-Loch Lomond Cycleway,** which covers 21 mi. between city and loch, was the first long distance bikepath in Scotland. The route now forms part of the Inverness-Dover "Millennium Route"; get info at any TIC.

INVERARAY   ☎ 01499

The most obvious reason for visiting unpretentious Inveraray is its splendid setting on **Loch Fyne,** though its tourist attractions do make for an entertaining afternoon. Some, certainly, will be fascinated by the **Inveraray Jail,** which welcomes with a "Torture, Death, and Damnation" exhibit. It also houses the Old Prison (1820) and New Prison (1849), stuffed with interactive displays such as the "Crank Machine," which prisoners were required to turn 14,400 times daily as a form of useless labor. Guests are invited to "please try" the Whipping Table. (☎ 302 381. Open Apr.-Oct. daily 9:30am-6pm; Nov.-Mar. 10am-5pm. Last admission 1hr. before close. £4.90, concessions £3.10, children £2.40.) Home to the Duke and Duchess of Argyll, cultivated **Inveraray Castle** contrasts with its rugged mountain backdrop. The present building (built 1745-1785) replaced an earlier fortified keep as a sign of a more peaceful era in British history, but the castle still seems up to its ears in weaponry. (☎ 302 203. Open July-Aug. M-Sa 10am-5:45pm, Su 1-5:45pm; Apr.-June and Sept.-Oct. M-Sa 10am-1pm and 2-5:45pm, Su 1-5:45pm. Last admission 5pm. Castle £5.50, concessions £4.50, children £3.50. Grounds free.) The 126 ft. **Bell Tower** contains some of the world's heaviest bells—climb to the ringers' roost for lochviews. (Open May-Sept. daily 10am-1pm and 2-5pm. £2, concessions 75p.)

Scottish Citylink (☎ (0870) 505 050) connects Inveraray with **Glasgow** (1¾hr., 4-5 per day, £6.90) and **Oban** (1hr., 2-3 per day, £4.90). The small **tourist information centre,** Front St., books accommodations for a £1 fee. (☎ 302 063. Open July to mid-Sept. daily 9am-6pm; Apr. and mid-Sept. to Oct. M-Sa 9am-5pm, Su noon-5pm; Nov.-Mar. M-F 10am-4pm, Sa-Su noon-4pm; May-June M-Sa 9am-5pm, Su 11am-5pm.) A **Bank of Scotland** is at Church Sq. (☎ 302 068. Open M-Tu and Th-F 9:15am-12:30pm and 1:30-4:45pm, W 10:30am-12:30pm and 1:30-4:45pm.) The **post office** is on Black's Land. (☎ 302 062. Open M-Tu and Th-F 9am-1pm and 2-5:30pm, W 9am-1pm, Sa 9am-12:30pm.) **Post Code:** PA32 8UD.

The small **SYHA Inveraray ❶** is just north of town on Dalmally Rd.; take a left through the arch next to the Inveraray Woollen Mill onto Oban Rd. and walk past the gas station. (☎/fax 302 454. Self-catering. 38 beds, 2 showers. Lockout 10:30am-5pm. Curfew 11pm. Open mid-Mar. to Sept. Dorms £9-9.50, under 18 £7.75-8.25.) For B&B, try the **Old Rectory ❷,** Main St. South, which has plush beds and a beautiful glass-ceilinged breakfast room. (☎302 280. £17.50 per person.) Friendly **Newton Hall ❹,** Shore St., is a B&B in a converted church overlooking the loch. (☎302 484. Open Mar.-Dec. Doubles £36-44.)

OBAN ☎ 01631

The busiest ferry port on Scotland's west coast, Oban (OH-ben; pop. 8500) lacks notable attractions of its own, but does have a beautiful harborside setting and good access to nearby islands and the Argyll countryside, and (despite intense summer crowding) has managed to retain a certain small-town charm. As the sun sets over the blue hills of Mull, you can watch the streets of Oban fill with folks strolling along the harbor, chatting with neighbors, or heading to the pub.

◨◪ GETTING THERE AND SAILING AWAY. The **train station** is on Railway Pier. (☎563 083. Ticket office open M-Sa 7am-6:10pm, Su 11am-6:10pm.) **Trains** (☎(08457) 484 950) run from **Glasgow Queen St.** (3hr., 3 per day, £15). Trains also run from **Fort William,** but the bus is much faster. **Scottish Citylink** (☎(08705) 505 050) arrives at the **bus stop,** near the train station, from: **Fort William** (1½hr., M-Sa 4 per day, £7); **Glasgow** (3hr.; M-Sa 3 per day, Su 2 per day; £11.80); and **Inverness** via Fort William (4hr., M-Sa 4 per day).

Caledonian MacBrayne ferries (☎566 688, reservations (08705) 650 000) sail from Railway Pier to the southern Hebrides. Pick up timetables at the ferry station or TIC. Ferries head to: **Craignure,** Mull (45min.; M-Sa 6 per day, Su 5 per day; extra sailings July-Aug.; £3.65); **Lismore** (50min., M-Sa 2-4 per day, £2.55); **Colonsay** (2½hr.; M, W, F 1 per day; £10.10); **Coll** and **Tiree** (2¾hr. to Coll, 3¾hr. to Tiree; 5 per week; £11.70); **Barra** and **South Uist** (5hr. to Barra, 7hr. to South Uist; M and W-Sa 1 per day; £19.20). If you have a car, book ahead and be prepared to pay exorbitant sums. Foot passengers rarely need reservations, but should call to confirm times. Ferry services, like most Highlands transport, are reduced during the winter.

From Oban, several operators offer **day tours** to the isles of **Mull, Iona,** and **Staffa.** Between April and October, **Bowman's & MacDougall's Tours,** 3 Stafford St. (☎563 221) runs daily to Mull and Iona (£23, children £13) and adds Staffa for a bit more (£29-34/£16-18). On Railway Pier, **Gordon Grant Tours** (☎562 842) has similar offerings, while trips with **Turus Mara** (☎(0800) 085 8786) include the **Treshnish Isles.**

◧◪ ORIENTATION AND PRACTICAL INFORMATION. Fronting the harbor, **George St.** is the heart of Oban. **Argyll Sq.,** actually a roundabout, is a block inland, northeast of the pier. **Corran Esplanade** runs along the coast north of town, **Gallanach Rd.** along the coast to the south. A vaulted **tourist information centre** inhabits an old church on Argyle Sq., booking beds for £1 and a 10% deposit. (☎563 122. Open July-Aug. M-Sa 9am-9pm, Su 9am-7pm; Sept. and May-June M-Sa 9am-6:30pm, Su 10am-5pm; Oct. M-Sa 9am-5:30pm, Su 10am-4pm; Nov.-Mar. M-F 9:30am-5pm, Sa-Su noon-4pm; Apr. M-F 9am-5pm, Sa-Su noon-5pm.) **Internet access** is available at the TIC for £1 per 12min. The **post office** is in the **Tesco,** on Lochside St. off Argyll Sq. (☎565 676. Store open M-Th and Sa 8am-8pm, F 8am-9pm, Su 9am-6pm.) **Post Code:** PA34 4AA.

ACCOMMODATIONS. To reach the glorious peach bunks, lively atmosphere, and super-pressure showers of **Oban Backpackers ❷**, 21 Breadalbane St., take George St. from Railway Pier until it forks; the hostel's on the right tine. (☎562 107. Continental breakfast ₤1.60. Internet access ₤5 per hr. Check-out 10:30am. Curfew 2:30am. Dorms ₤10-12.) The mammoth **SYHA Oban ❷**, Rassay Lodge, Corran Esplanade, hugs the waterfront ¾ mi. north of the train station, past St. Columba's Cathedral. Rooms in the **annex** all come with bath but are a bit more expensive. (☎562 025. Lockout 10:30am-1pm. Reception until 11:30pm. Check-out 10:30am. Curfew 2am. Dorms ₤9.50-14, under 18 ₤7-12.50.) The **Oban Waterfront Lodge ❷**, 1 Victoria Cres., near the water and about ½ mi. north of the train station, has comfy beds and amiable staff. (☎566 040. Breakfast ₤1.85. Dorms from ₤10.) A more intimate lodge, the **Jeremy Inglis Hostel ❶**, 21 Airds Cres., has some singles. From the railway station, walk past the TIC and head through Argyll Sq., then take the first right, just before George St. (☎565 065 or 563 064. ₤6.50-12 per person.)

Oban's got B&Bs and guest houses aplenty. Eight rooms, all with bath and TV, welcome you to bright blue **Maridon House ❷**, Dunuaran Rd., where guests have full use of the kitchen. From Argyle Sq., walk to the end of Albany St. and look up. (☎562 670; maridonhse@aol.com. ₤18-22 per person.) Tasteful, comfortable **Glenbervie Guest House ❸**, uphill from town on Dalriach Rd., has fine views of Oban Bay. (☎564 770. ₤22-30 per person.) The tent-and-sleeping-bag set take bus #918 to **Barcaldine**, where the fully-equipped **Camping & Caravanning Club ❶** sits in a walled garden off the A828 coast road. (☎720 348. Open Apr.-Oct. 2-person tent ₤6-8.50.)

FOOD AND PUBS. Harborside **George St.**, beginning near the train station, is Oban's food center and nightlife strip. Seafood shops cluster around the ferry terminal. **Cafe na Lusan ❶**, 9 Craigard Rd., half a block uphill from George St., is a pleasant vegetarian cafe serving light meals and well-priced dinners. (☎567 268. Open Su-Tu 3:30-9:30pm, W-Sa 11:30am-9:30pm.) **McTavish's Kitchens ❶**, 34 George St., has tourist-oriented displays of traditional Scottish song and dance. A downstairs cafeteria serves good, cheap food. (☎563 064. Shows May-Sept. 8:30 and 10:30pm. ₤4, children ₤2. Open summer daily 9am-10pm; winter 9am-6pm.)

O'Donnell's Irish Pub, Breadalbane St., draws the young with live music Thursday through Monday nights. (☎566 159. Open daily noon-1am.) Also competing for local drinkers and cheery hostelers is **Markie Dan's**, next to the Oban Waterfront Lodge on Victoria Cres., just off the Esplanade. Frequent live music, drink specials, plus a friendly bar staff equal a great atmosphere. Step outside for a marvelous view of the water. (Open daily 11am-1am.)

SIGHTS AND ACTIVITIES. The hilltop Colosseum-esque structure dominating the Oban skyline is **McCaig's Tower**. Commissioned in the 19th century by local businessman John Stuart McCaig, it was intended as an art gallery but never completed, and today offers great views over city and harbor. To reach the tower, take the steep Jacob's Ladder stairway at the end of Argyll St., then turn left along Ardconnel Rd. and right up Laurel St. to the grassy entrance. (Always open. Free.) Past the north end of town, the ivy-eaten remains of 7th-century **Dunollie Castle**—Oban's oldest building—loom atop a cliff. Dunollie is the seat of the MacDougall family, who once owned a third of Scotland. From town, walk 20min. north along the water until you've curved around the castle; then take the stinging-nettle-lined path to the right. (Always open. Free.) Just 2½ mi. outside town on Glencruitten Rd., **Achnilarig Farms** offers guided horse treks for all levels of experience. (☎562 745. Open year-round, usually Su-F; hours vary. ₤12 per hr., children ₤10.)

🏃 DAYTRIPS FROM OBAN

KERRERA. Five minutes across the bay from Oban is the beautiful, nearly deserted isle of **Kerrera** (CARE-er-uh). The island has a natural wealth, providing a variety of habitats for seals and puffins, and maintains a no-car policy. A ferry comes to Kerrera from **Ganlochhead,** 2 mi. south of Oban. Turn the board to the black side to signal the ferryman; call for winter sailings. (☎ 563 665. Daily 2 per hr. 10:30am-noon and 2-6pm, also M-Sa 8:45am. Return £3, children £1.50, bikes 50p.) Wander for a day or stay the night at the **Kerrera Bunkhouse** ❶, on the island's south tip, 2 mi. from the pier. (☎ 570 223. Kitchen and bedding available. £8 per person.)

LOCH ETIVE. To the north gapes the mouth of Loch Etive, where the **Falls of Lora** change direction with the shifting of the tides. From **Taynuilt,** off the A85, 7 mi. east of the loch mouth, the family-run **Loch Etive Cruises** sends 1½ and 3hr. tours up the loch into beautiful and otherwise inaccessible countryside. Call the night before you arrive to arrange a free shuttle from your bus to the pier. (☎ (01866) 822 430. May-Sept. M-F 10:30am, noon, and 2pm, Sa-Su 2pm; Apr. and Oct. Su-F 2pm only. £5-8, children £3-5, families £13-23.) **Trains** and Scottish Citylink **buses** traveling between **Oban** and **Glasgow** (or **Edinburgh**) stop here.

Monty Python fans can get a glimpse of Castle Aaaaaaa (actually **Castle Stalker**) on Loch Linnhe; cross Connel Bridge at the mouth of Loch Etive and take the A828 10min. from **Appin** (a bus also goes to Appin from Oban).

ISLE OF ISLAY ☎ 01496

Much like the whisky for which it's famous, the Isle of Islay (EYE-luh) demands subtle and mature appreciation. A barely inhabited outpost and a walker's paradise, Islay's real beauty lies in the nuances of its residents' daily lives. A brief stroll is flavored by the mellow tones of Scottish Gaelic and the heady scent of crofters' new-cut peat, not to mention the intoxicating fumes from some of the world's finest single-malts wafting from the island's numerous distilleries.

🌙 TRANSPORTATION

Ferries leave from **Kennacraig Ferry Terminal,** 7 mi. south of **Tarbert** on the Kintyre Peninsula, running either to Port Askaig or to Port Ellen (M-Tu and Th-Sa 7:15am, 12:50, 6pm; W 8:15am; Su 12:50pm; either route £7.25). To get to Kennacraig, take the **Scottish Citylink** bus that runs between **Glasgow** and **Campbeltown** (M-Sa 3 per day, Su 2 per day). Travelers from **Arran** can catch bus #448 to Kennacraig at the **Claonaig** ferry landing (☎ (01880) 730 253; M-Sa 3 per day, £2.45). Every summer Wednesday, a boat leaves **Oban,** stops on **Colonsay,** and continues to Port Askaig (4hr., £10.35). Ask at TICs for bus and ferry timetables. Most bus schedules follow ferry times quite closely, but call to verify your connection or risk being stranded.

Islay Coaches (☎ 840 273) operates a few daily buses between Islay towns. Bus #451 connects **Port Ellen** and **Port Askaig** via **Bowmore** (M-Sa about 4 per day, Su 1 per day); #450 runs from **Bowmore** to **Port Charlotte** (M-Sa 3 per day). **Postbuses** (☎ (01246) 546 329) also traverse the island a few times a day. Many bus times apply to one day only, so read schedules carefully. Purchase single tickets, as returns aren't cheaper, and tickets on different buses are not interchangeable. For on-call transportation around the island, contact Carol MacDonald at **Minibus & Taxi Service Island Tours** (☎ 302 155, mobile (0777) 578 2155).

THE INSIDER'S CITY

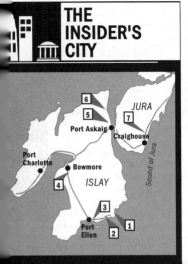

THE WHISKY TRAIL

Islay is renowned for its malt whiskys and boasts seven distilleries (six open to the public); Jura has one more for good measure. The malts are known for their peaty flavor—not surprising, since half of Islay is peat bog. The island's clean, fertile environment and fresh water supply are ideal for a flourishing whisky trail. So what gives each malt its distinctive flavor? A plethora of determinants: water supply, air quality, temperature, type of barley, kind of wood in which the whisky is stored... even the shape of the pot-still (large kettle-like distilling structure) matters. Pick up *The Islay and Jura Whisky Trail*, free at TICs, to aid your quest for the perfect dram. Better yet, use our condensed guide:

1 **Ardberg:** (☎302 244). On the southeast coast, 4 mi. from Port Ellen. The peatiest. Tours 10:30am-3:30pm; call ahead. £2.

2 **Lagavulin:** (☎302 400). 3 mi. from Port Ellen. Islay's classic bestseller. Tours in summer M-F by appointment only. £3.

PORT ELLEN

Port Ellen is useful only as a base for savoring the solitude of the nearby coastline. To the west, the windswept **Mull of Oa** drops dramatically to the sea. For a taste of its beauty, walk along the Mull of Oa road toward the solar-powered **Carraig Fhada lighthouse,** 1½ mi. away. To the east along the A846, a more substantial journey passes the distilleries, standing stones, ruins of the 16th-century **Dunyveg (Dun-Naomhaig) Castle,** and **Loch an t-Sailein** (otherwise known as "Seal Bay" for its breeding colonies). Seven miles east along the A846, **Kildalton Chapel** holds the miraculously well-preserved **Kildalton High Cross,** a piece of carbon blue stone thought to date from the 9th century. Port Ellen's tiny **Kildalton and Oa Information Point,** next to the post office, is not an official TIC, but stocks bus schedules and leaflets on area attractions. (Open Mar.-Dec. M-Sa 9am-noon.)

If you choose to stay in town, Mrs. Hedley's **Trout Fly Guest House ❷,** 8 Charlotte St., has decent rooms. A delicious three-course meal costs £12.50. (☎302 204. Singles £18.50; doubles £41-45.) Three miles away in Kintra, the **Kintra Independent Hostel ❶** stands in solitary coastal splendor on a full-fledged working farm. (☎302 051. Self-catering. Open Apr.-Sept. Dorms £6.50, bedding extra.) Kintra welcomes **camping ❶** as well, at the southern end of Big Strand beach. From Port Ellen, take the Mull of Oa road 1 mi., then follow the right fork, marked "To Kintra." (£2 per person, £2.50 per tent.) In Port Ellen, Frederick Cres. rings the harbor and holds a **Co-op Foodstore.** (☎302 446. Open M-Sa 8am-8pm, Su 12:30-6pm.)

BOWMORE

Bowmore, Islay's largest town, is 10 mi. from both Port Ellen and Port Askaig. Arranged in a grid-like, practical design, Bowmore is not exactly laden with architectural splendors, but it has an undeniable tiny-town charm. The 18th-century **Bowmore Round Church** on Main St. (also called Kilarrow Parish Church) was built perfectly circular to keep Satan from hiding in the corners. (Open daily 10am-5pm. Free.) Behind the town square, **Morrison's Bowmore Distillery,** School St., is the oldest distillery in full operation. The coast between Bowmore and Port Ellen is graced by the **Big Strand,** 7 mi. of white-sand beach.

Islay's only **tourist information centre** calls Bowmore home, and books accommodations for £1. If you plan to explore, pick up *The Isles of Islay, Jura & Colonday Walks* for 50p. (☎810 254. Open July-Aug. M-Sa 9:30am-5:30pm, Su 2-5pm; Apr. and Sept.-Oct. M-Sa 10am-5pm; Nov.-Mar. M-F noon-

4pm; May-June M-Sa 9:30am-5pm, Su 2-5pm.) Other services include: two **banks** with **ATMs;** the only **launderette** on the island, in the **Mactaggart Leisure Centre,** School St., where you can go for a swim (£2.20) while your clothes take a spin (☎810 767; wash £2.80, dry £2.80; open Tu-F 12:30-9pm, Sa 10:30am-4pm, Su 10:30am-5:30pm); and the **post office,** next to the Round Church (☎810 366; open M-W and F 9am-1pm and 2-5:30pm, Th 9am-1pm, Sa 9am-12:30pm). The post office also **rents bicycles** for £10 per day, with discounts for longer rentals. **Post Code:** PA43 7JH.

Among a flock of several similarly priced Bowmore B&Bs, the proprietors of the **Lambeth Guest House ❷,** Jamieson St., offer homey lodgings and good conversation. (☎810 597. £18 per person.) The waterfront **Harbour Inn ❹** is a small, pleasant hotel. (☎810 330. Singles £42-45; doubles £75-85.) **Camp** at **Craigens Farm ❶,** a few miles outside town at Gruinart, by Bridgend. (☎850 256. No facilities. £2 per tent.) A **Co-op Foodstore** is on Main St. (☎810 201. Open M-Sa 8am-8pm, Su 12:30-7pm.) On the expensive side, the **Lochside Hotel ❷,** Shore St., serves large, varied main courses for £6-10, and the bar has a mind-boggling selection of single malt whiskys. (☎810 244. Food served daily noon-2:30pm and 5:30-8:45pm.) Cavort with locals at the only pub in town, the **Bowmore Hotel Pub,** Jamieson St., a.k.a. "Lucci's." Ask for an explanation. (☎810 416. Open daily 11am-1am.)

PORT CHARLOTTE

On the western arm of Islay, across Loch Indaal from Bowmore, Port Charlotte is a lovely village set on a peaceful cove. Probably the most attractive town on Islay, it holds a couple of small museums dedicated to island life. The Islay Natural History Trust's **Wildlife Information Centre** describes the island's famed beasties, including several rare bird species. (☎850 288. Open Apr.-Oct. M-Tu and Th-Sa 10am-3pm, Su 2-5pm. £2, concessions £1.20, children £1.) Across the road, the **Museum of Islay Life** reveals a history of Viking raids, clans, and whisky. (☎850 358. Open Apr.-Oct. M-Sa 10am-5pm, Su 2-5pm. £2, concessions £1.20, children £1, families £5.) The **SYHA Islay ❶,** above the Wildlife Centre, was, appropriately enough, once a distillery. (☎/fax 850 385. Curfew 11:45pm. Open Apr.-Sept. Dorms £9.50, under 18 £8.25.) There are a couple of **B&Bs** near Port Charlotte, but the nicest accommodation by far is the well-furnished, shoreside **Port Charlotte Hotel ❹.** The hotel's **restaurant** is equally good but expensive. (☎850 360. Singles

3 **Laphroaig** (la-FROYG): (☎302 418). Beside Port Ellen. Tours 10:15am and 2:15pm. Free.

4 **Bowmore:** (☎810 441). Right in town. The oldest (est. 1779). Tours year-round M-F 10:30am and 2pm; Apr.-Sept. also M-F 11:30am and 3pm, Sa 10:30am. £2.

5 **Caol Ila** (cool-EE-la): (☎840 207). 1 mi. from Port Askaig. Tours year-round M-Tu and Th-F 10, 11:15am, 1:30, 2:45 pm; W 10 and 11:15am. £3.

6 **Bunnahabhainn** (bunna-HAV-en): (☎840 646). The northernmost. Tours year-round M-Th 10:30am, 1:30, 2:45pm; F 10:30am. Free.

7 **Jura:** (☎820 240). Near Craighouse village. Tours by appointment only.

£55-59; doubles £65-94.) The **Croft Kitchen ❶,** across from the Wildlife Centre, serves tasty seafood. (☎850 230. Open mid-Mar. to mid.-Oct. daily until 8:30pm; no dinner W.)

ISLE OF JURA   ☎01496

Near Islay, the tiny Isle of Jura ("Deer Island"; pop. 50) is isolated and unspoiled, full of rugged hills, wound about by one wee road, and boasts a red deer herd that outnumbers people ten to one. Jura was remote enough to satisfy even conspiracy-theorist-cum-novelist George Orwell, who penned *1984* here in a cottage free from watchful eyes. This is a great place for true wilderness **hiking;** ambitious trekkers tackle the three **Paps of Jura,** a difficult all-day walk that requires advance preparation (try chatting with knowledgeable locals or experienced travelers).

In addition to strong rip currents, the **Corryvreckan Whirlpool,** the third largest in the world and classified as unnavigable by the Royal Navy, churns violently at Jura's northern tip. Its relentless thrashing can be heard over a mile away. Though the distance between Islay and Jura is temptingly short, *Let's Go* definitely does not recommend the breast stroke as a safe mode of transportation. **Jura Ferry** (☎840 681) sends a car ferry across the Sound of Islay from **Port Askaig** to **Feolin** (5min.; summer M-Sa 13-16 per day, Su 6 per day; winter M-Sa 12 per day, Su 2 per day; 90p). During summer and on weekdays during term, a **bus service** (☎820 314 or 820 221) connects **Feolin** with **Craighouse** and other island points (6-8 per day).

CRAIGHOUSE. Jura's only village is a tiny, one-road settlement 10 mi. north of the ferry landing. The 200-year-old **Jura Church** exhibits photographs detailing the history of the island and town. Nearby, the island's only distillery brews **Isle of Jura** whisky (see **Whisky Trail,** p. 616). A short walk from Craighouse leads to the abandoned village of **Keils,** one of the island's oldest settlements. Start from the Craighouse distillery and follow the road along the shore for a mile, then follow the signs for the village left and uphill. From Keils, the path continues past a large barn to a fence gate that leads directly to **Cill Earnadail,** an ancient burial site guarded by a bull. (2 mi. round-trip; roughly 1hr.)

There's one hotel and a handful of B&Bs in Craighouse; **Mrs. Boardman ❷,** 7 Woodside, is a good choice. (☎820 379. £19 per person.) The only restaurant in Craighouse is the **Antlers Tea Room ❶,** where a warm scone and cuppa cost £1. (☎820 366. Open M-F 10:30am-3:30pm, Sa 10:30am-1pm.) A miniscule **post office** resides at the center of the village, sharing its building with a grocery store. (Open M-F 9am-1pm and 2-5:30pm, Sa 9am-12:30pm.) **Post Code:** PA60 7XP.

ISLE OF MULL

Even on the brightest days, mist lingers among Mull's blue hills. Perhaps that's why the island's population clings to the sunnier shoreline. Tiny isles fortify Mull to the west and south, including the captivating Erraid, featured in Robert Louis Stevenson's *Kidnapped.* Wonderfully scenic in its own right—the dramatic mountainscape includes the 3196 ft. Ben More—this most accessible of the Inner Hebrides is also a stepping-stone to the popular isles of Iona and Staffa. Much of Mull's Gaelic heritage has given way to the pressure of English settlers, who now comprise over two-thirds of the population, and to the annual tourist herd (500,000 strong), but local craftsmen and itinerant fishermen keep tradition alive.

TRANSPORTATION

Ferries: CalMac (☎(01631) 566 688) runs a ferry from **Oban** to **Craignure** (45min.; M-Sa 6 per day, Su 5 per day; extra sailings July-Aug.; £3.65). Smaller car and passenger ferries run from **Lochaline** on the Morvern Peninsula, north of Mull, to **Fishnish,** on the east coast 6 mi. northwest of Craignure (15min.; M-Sa 13-14 per day, Su 9 per day; £2.25), and from **Kilchoan** on the Ardnamurchan peninsula to **Tobermory** (35min.; M-Sa 7 per day, June-Aug. also Su 5 per day; £3.50). Winter schedules are reduced. **Day tours** run to Mull from **Oban** (see p. 613).

Buses: Mull's public transport network is fairly limited. **Bowman Coaches** (☎(01680) 812 313) operates the main bus routes. #496 meets the Oban ferry at **Craignure** and goes to **Fionnphort** (1¼hr.; M-F 5 per day, Sa 3 per day, Su 1 per day; return £6.90). #495 runs between **Craignure** and **Tobermory** via **Fishnish** (1hr.; M-F 6 per day, Sa 4 per day, Su 2 per day; return £6.10). **R.N. Carmichael** (☎(01688) 302 220) #494 links **Tobermory** and **Calgary** (45min.; M-F 4 per day, Sa 2 per day; £3.50). You can also jump on friendly **postbuses.** TICs have timetables for most bus companies.

ORIENTATION

Mull's three main hubs, **Tobermory** (northwest tip), **Craignure** (east tip), and **Fionnphort** (FINN-a-furt; southwest tip), form a triangle bounded on two sides by the A849 and the A848. A left turn off the **Craignure Pier** takes you 35 mi. down Mull's main road, along the southern arm of the island, to **Fionnphort.** There, the ferry leaves for **Iona,** a tiny island off the southwest corner. A right turn leads 21 mi. along Mull's northwestern arm to **Tobermory,** Mull's pocket metropolis. Staying in Craignure is convenient for the ferry, but Tobermory is more engaging and offers the island's widest range of accommodations.

CRAIGNURE
☎ 01680

Craignure, Mull's main ferry port, is a wee town with one nameless street. Make like its 10¼ in. gauge miniature **steam train** and toot out of town. (☎812 494. Departs from near the campsite. Apr. to mid-Oct. 5-12 per day 11am-5pm. Return £3.50, children £2.50, families £9.50.) The train rolls one wooded mile south to the inhabited ◾**Torosay Castle,** a Victorian mansion planted amid 12 splendid acres of gardens, filled with Edwardian artifacts, and offering stunning seaviews. It's one of the few castles, furthermore, where commonfolk can actually sit on the furniture. (☎812 421. Open Apr. to mid-Oct. daily 10:30am-5:30pm. Gardens open year-round 9am-dusk. £5, concessions £4, children £1.75, families £12.) Also worthwhile is the spectacular 700-year-old stronghold of Clan MacLean, **Duart Castle,** 3 mi. west of Torosay. Guide yourself through the state bedroom, the dungeon, and the cell where Spanish sailors were held for ransom after the Armada debacle. Take the bus to the end of Duart Rd. and walk the remaining 1½ mi. (☎812 309. Open May to early Oct. daily 10:30am-6pm, Apr. Su-F 11am-4pm. £4, concessions £3.50, children £2, families £9.50.)

To get to **Shielings Holiday Campsite ●** from the ferry terminal, turn left, then left again at the sign opposite the church and pass the dilapidated town hall. It offers tent pitches and hostel-like beds in permanent tents. (☎/fax 812 496. Open Apr.-Oct. 2 people and tent £9.50, with car £11. Bed in permanent tent £9 per person; 2-person private tent £22-33.) For B&B, **Aon a'Dha ❷,** Kirk Terr., near the ferry, will do the trick. (☎812 318. £16 per person.) The **tourist information centre,** also by the ferry, books rooms for £1 and exchanges money for a £3 commission. (☎812 377. Open May-Sept. M-Th and Sa 9am-7pm, F 9am-5pm, Su

10:30am-7pm; Oct.-Apr. M-Sa 9am-5pm, Su 10:30am-5pm.) **Bike** and **car rental** is at **Mull Travel and Crafts,** two doors from the TIC. (☎812 487. Bikes £7 per half-day, £12 per day. Cars 23+; from £27 per day.) The **post office** is in the **Spar.** (☎812 301. Store open M 7:30am-7pm, Tu-F 8:15am-7pm, Sa 8:30am-7pm, Su 10:30-1pm and 2:30-6pm. Post office open M-W and F 9am-1pm and 2-5pm, Th and Sa 9am-1pm.) **Post Code:** PA65 6AY.

TOBERMORY ☎01688

Colorful cafes and pastel houses line an attractive, Mediterranean-style harbor in Tobermory (pop. 1000), Mull's main town. The tiny **Mull Museum** chronicles the island's history with local artifacts and folklore. (Open Easter-Oct. M-F 10:30am-4pm, Sa 10:30am-1:30pm. £1, children 10p.) The **Hebridean Whale and Dolphin Trust,** 28 Main St., has displays on everyone's favorite cetaceans, including kid-friendly interactive exhibits. (☎302 620. Open Apr.-Oct. M-F 10am-5pm, Sa-Su 11am-4pm; Nov.-Mar. M-F 11am-5pm. Free.) Local artists display works at the **An Tobar Arts Centre,** Argyll Terr., which also hosts musical performances. (☎302 211. Open Mar.-Dec. M-Sa 10am-5:30pm; in summer also Su afternoon.) Malts are still made entirely by hand at the **Tobermory Distillery,** on the opposite side of the harbor from the TIC, which conducts 30min. tours and offers generous swigs of the final product. (☎302 645. Tours 2 per hr. Easter-Sept. M-F 10:30am-4pm. Open Easter-Oct. M-F 10am-4pm. £2.50, seniors £1, children free.)

For the freshest in Scottish seafood, rent your own fly rod (£3) from **Tackle and Books,** 10 Main St., a combination angling center and bookstore. They also arrange 3hr. fishing trips in season. (☎302 336. 2-3 trips per week. £15, children £12. Store open July-Aug. M-Sa 9am-5:30pm, Su 11am-4pm; Sept. and June M-Sa 9am-5:30pm.) During the third weekend of April, Tobermory hosts the **Mull Music Festival,** with lively Scottish music, while early July's **Mendelssohn Festival** features oodles of oratorios. The **Mull Highland Games** offer caber-tossing and *ceilidhs* on the third Thursday of July.

The **tourist information centre,** on a pier across the harbor from the bus stop, books rooms for £1 (£3 off-island), and sells boat-tour tickets. (☎302 182. Open July to mid-Sept. M-Sa 9am-6pm, Su 10am-5pm; Apr. and mid-Sept. to Oct. M-Sa 9am-5pm, Su 10am-5pm; May-June daily 9am-5pm.) Other services include: a **CalMac** office next to the TIC (☎302 017; open M-F 9am-6pm; Mar.-Oct. also Sa 9am-4pm); **bike rental** at **Archibald Brown & Son,** 21 Main St. (☎302 020, ask for Bryan; £8 per half-day, £13 per day); **Clydesdale Bank,** Main St., the only bank and **ATM** on the island (bank open M-W and F 9:15am-4pm, Th 9:15am-5:30pm); a full-service **launderette,** by the SYHA hostel (☎302 669; £6; open daily 9am-1pm and 2-5pm, closed some winter Su); **Internet access** at the An Tobar Arts Centre (£1.50 per 15min.; see above); and the **post office,** 36 Main St., on the harbor strip next to the supermarket (open M-Tu and Th-F 9am-5:30pm, W and Sa 9am-1pm). **Post Code:** PA75 6NT.

The small **SYHA Tobermory ❶,** on the far end of Main St. from the bus stop, has a homey kitchen and lounge. (☎/fax 302 481. Lockout 10:30am-5pm. Curfew 11:45pm. Open Mar.-Oct. Dorms £9.50-10.50, under 18 £7.50-8.50.) Beautiful **B&Bs** line the bay. Seafront **Failte Guest House ❸,** Main St., is welcoming and comfortable, and all rooms are ensuite. (☎302 495. Singles £25-35; doubles £40-56.) The **Harbour Guest House ❷,** 59 Main St., conveniently opposite the bus stop, decks its harbor-view rooms in green tartan. (☎302 209. £19.50 per person, with bath £22.) **Ach-na-Craoibh ❸,** on Erray Rd., has a wide range of accommodations. Walk up the footpath by the post office, then follow the road as it curves to the right. (☎302 301. B&B £25 per night. Self-catering rooms from £90 per week.)

The **Co-op** supermarket, Mull's largest, stands by the harbor between hostel and post office. (☎302 004. Open M-W and Sa 8:30am-6pm, Th-F 8:30am-8pm, Su 12:30-6pm.) Many local restaurants cater to wealthy yacht owners; the most established is the **Back Brae Restaurant ❸**, serving local seafood and game. (☎302 422. Most entrees from £10. Open daily from 6pm.) For more affordable cuisine, look to the **Tobermory Fish Company ❶**, Main St., which serves delicious smoked trout sandwiches for £1.45. (☎302 120. Open M-F 9am-5pm, Sa 9am-1pm and 2-5pm.) Fishermen, tourists, and locals crowd the spacious pub at the **Mishnish Hotel ❷**, near the TIC. (☎302 009. Lunch £3-6, dinner £5-12. Live folk music from 9:30pm most summer nights. Open daily 11am-1am. Food served noon-2pm and 6-8:30pm.)

THE TOBERMORY GALLEON
The *San Juan de Sicilia*, a member of the not-so-invincible Spanish Armada, mysteriously sank in Tobermory's harbor in 1588. Soon after the disaster, a explanatory legend emerged: the daughter of King Philip II of Spain came to Tobermory in search of the perfect man. When she found him aboard the *San Juan*, the jealousy-stricken Mrs. Perfect Man blew the ship out of the water. Divers expert and crackpot have long been captivated by the wreck and continually explore it for treasure—perplexing, as there's no reason to expect treasure on a warship. So far they've found a bunch of guns, a cannonball, oak timber, and some coins from the reign of Philip II. The latest search, in 1982, turned up some lead.

IONA, STAFFA, AND TRESHNISH ISLES

The geologic marvels and contemplative isolation offered by these tiny islands off Mull's west coast make them worth the effort to see. **Iona,** a historic cradle of Christianity, is serene and beautiful. **Staffa,** which translates to "Island of Pillars" in Norse, boasts magnificent basalt columns and was immortalized in the music of Mendelssohn. Remote and uninhabited, the **Treshnish Isles** teem with thousands of seabirds and colonies of common and Atlantic gray seals.

CalMac (☎(01631) 566 688) sails to Iona from **Fionnphort** (15min., 2 per hr., £3.50). As there are no other direct ferries between the islands, it's easiest to see them by **tour.** During the summer, **Gordon Grant Tours** (☎(01681) 700 338) and **The Kirkpatricks** (☎(01681) 700 358) offer daily cruises to Staffa from Fionnphort and Iona (2½hr., around £15). Some sailings also include the Treshnish Isles (5½hr., around £25). **Turus Mara** (☎(0800) 858 786) operates similar tours but leaves from the town **Ulva Ferry** on Mull. Day tours also operate from **Oban** (see p. 613).

IONA   ☎01681

The sacred isle of Iona (pop. 150) quivers with purity of color—rocks the hue of Mars and waters in Caribbean tints, all draped with a very Scottish mist. For nearly two centuries after Ireland's St. Columba landed his coracle on the island in AD 563, Iona was one of Europe's most celebrated centers of religious life. Georgian and Victorian Iona-devotees included James Boswell, Samuel Johnson, Sir Walter Scott, John Keats, and Felix Mendelssohn. Every year, more than 140,000 visitors pay homage to this tiny outcropping. The sights can be seen in a few hours, but it's worth staying to savor the serenity once the daytrippers go home.

🗾 **PRACTICAL INFORMATION.** Left of the pier, **Ross Finlay** rents all kinds of **bikes.** (☎700 357. £4.50 per half-day, £8 per day. £10 deposit. Open summer M-Sa 9:15am-6pm, Su 10:15am-6pm; winter daily 11am-1pm and 2-4pm.) The **post**

office, right of the ferry pier, has **Internet access** for £2 per 30min. (☎700 515. Open M-Tu and Th-F 9am-1pm and 2-5pm, W 9am-1pm, Sa 9am-12:30pm.) **Post Code:** PA76 6SJ.

ⓘⒸ ACCOMMODATIONS AND FOOD. The splendidly isolated **Iona Hostel ❷,** on the isle's north end, about 1 mi. from the ferry, has simple, clean dorms. (☎700 781. Dorms £12, children £9.) The island has a sprinkling of **B&Bs,** including some in the small village of **Baile Mor.** The aforementioned **Ross Finlay ❸,** of bike rental fame, lets a reasonable range of rooms. (☎700 357. From £24 per person.) Iona's top lodgings and victuals are at the pleasant **Argyll Hotel ❹,** overlooking the Sound. (☎700 334. £37-48 per person.) At times it's possible to stay with the **Iona Community** (see below) or join a retreat there. (Contact the MacLeod Centre at ☎700 404.) **Spar,** uphill from the ferry, blesses Iona with groceries. (☎700 321. Open Easter-Oct. M-Sa 9am-6pm, Su 10:30am-6pm; Nov.-Easter M-Sa 11am-1pm and 2-4pm.)

Ⓖ SIGHTS. The ecumenical **Iona Community** lies outside the village, where it cleaves to the massive **Benedictine Abbey,** built on the site of St. Columba's original monastery. Walk up through the village and bear right to reach the abbey, the centerpiece of most views from the ferry. Visitors are welcome to attend services. (☎700 512. 10min. services M-Th and Sa 9am and 9pm, F 8:15am and 9pm, Su 10:30am and 9pm; in summer also daily 2pm. Open Apr.-Sept. daily 9:30am-6:30pm; Oct.-Mar. 9:30am-4:30pm. £2.80, concessions £2, children £1.20.) Adjacent to the abbey, gravestones crowd the entrance to a 10th-century chapel. Inside, **St. Columba's Shrine** once contained a relic of Columba and his possessions, making it a popular burial place for local chiefs. Columbites may want to stop at the **Columba Centre,** in Fionnphort, when they cross back to Mull. The sleek exhibition charts the saint's story and the spread of Christianity and monastic life. (☎700 660. Open May-Sept. daily 10am-5:30pm. Free.)

Backtrack from the abbey to find the ruins of a 13th-century **nunnery,** derelict for over 300 years and one of the better-preserved medieval convents in Britain. Signs will get thee from the nunnery to the **Iona Heritage Centre,** located in the "old manse." Here you can learn intriguing snippets about Iona's history, including what happened "the year the potato went away." (☎700 576. Open Easter-Oct. M-Sa 10:30am-4:30pm. £1.50, concessions £1, children free.) To visit the tiny 12th-century **St. Oran's Chapel,** turn right just before the abbey. The surrounding burial ground allegedly contains more than 60 kings of Scotland, Ireland, and Norway, including the pious Macbeth. (Of course, given that the gravestones are over a millennium old, they're a trifle hard to read.) On the far side of the island (a 10min. walk), the **Spouting Cave** blasts salt water when the waves are high enough.

STAFFA

The incredible island of Staffa, composed of hexagonal basalt columns and rimmed with tidal caves, rises 8 mi. north of Iona. The isle owes its wondrous geography to a weak point in the earth's crust, where liquid rock spewed upward and was cooled by ocean water to form columns. Surrounded by treacherous cliffs (particularly slippery in the rain), Staffa is ruled by an imperial council of six sheep and four cows. Puffins nest on the cliff edge and allow the curious to examine their personal space. When the tide is low, you can worship deep inside the natural basalt cathedral known as ▣**Fingal's Cave.** When rough seas roar into the cavern, the sound reverberates around the island; the pounding of wave against rock inspired the surging strings in Mendelssohn's *Hebrides Overture*.

TRESHNISH ISLES

The Treshnish Isles offer sanctuary for large colonies of seals and ferrets, as well as thousands of species of seabirds. Unthreatened by humans, the critters tolerate up-close examination on these most isolated of isles. Wander along the cliffs of **Lunga** as guillemots, razorbills, shags, and other ornithologist favorites land on the only remnant of human inhabitance—a 13th-century chapel. Legend holds that monks from the Iona Abbey buried their library on one of the Treshnish Isles to save it from pillaging during the Reformation. Many have tried digging under the third ferret from the left, as yet without luck.

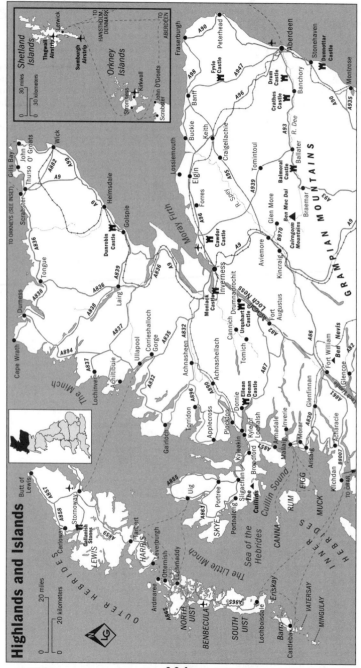

Highlands and Islands

HIGHLANDS AND ISLANDS

Misty and remote, the Scottish Highlands have long been the stuff of fantasy. Yet a trip on the West Highland Railway quickly confirms that these long-romanticized landscapes—often stereotyped as heather-clad outposts doused with the rebellious Scottish spirit—are one of Europe's last stretches of genuine wilderness. Sheep-dotted moors and towering granite mountains are sliced by the narrow lochs of the Great Glen and imposing mountain ranges like the Cairngorms. Off the coast, the pristine Hebrides arch to the west, while the Norse-influenced Orkney and Shetland Islands stretch off Scotland's horn at John O'Groats. The mainland towns of Inverness, Fort William, and Ullapool are access points for further exploration: trains, buses, and ferries stretch outward from bonnie fishing villages and castle-topped cliffsides to rugged islands with seal-strewn shores.

The Highlands haven't always been so unpopulated. Three centuries ago, almost one-third of all Scots lived north of the Great Glen and were members of fierce, clan-based societies. The defeat of the 1745 Jacobite rising (see p. 540), supported by clans opposing the English king, dealt Highland society a heavy blow. Later, profit-seeking landlords turned from tenant farming to sheep farming and evicted entire communities in the infamous 18th- and 19th-century Highland Clearances. Many Scots, forcibly turned out of their homes, emigrated to Canada, Australia, New Zealand, and the United States. The past continues to haunt the nostalgia-steeped Highlands, and the once-universal Gaelic language (see p. 542) is spoken only in the Hebrides. Ironically, driving out the Scots opened the area for tourist exploration in this century, attracting the wayfarers who now provide economic fuel. Highlanders themselves typically make ends meet through self-employment, whether by crofting (independent farming), fishing, or running B&Bs.

HIGHLIGHTS OF THE HIGHLANDS AND ISLANDS

BEN NEVIS Dash up the highest peak in the British Isles, which hides its 4406 ft. head in a layer of clouds. On a clear day, you can see all the way to Ireland (p. 646).

ORKNEY AND SHETLAND ISLANDS Seek the unparalleled wealth of ancient ruins set amid sheep, sky, and ocean (p. 678).

ISLE OF SKYE Explore the mighty Cuillin Mountains and sparkling waters of the most accessible and admired of the Hebrides (p. 652).

NORTHWEST HIGHLANDS Trek far beyond the rail's reaches to find remote sea-lochs slicing deep into rugged mountains (p. 670).

TRANSPORTATION IN THE HIGHLANDS AND ISLANDS

Traveling in the Highlands requires a great deal of planning. Transport services are, as a rule, drastically reduced on Sundays and during the winter, and making more than one or two connections per day on any form of transportation is difficult, even in high season. The *Public Transport Travel Guide* (£1), available from TICs, is absolutely essential for whatever region you plan to travel in. **Trains** (☎ (08457) 484 950), while offering the best views, will only get you so far in the Highlands, and **Scottish Citylink buses** (☎(08705) 505 050) do not travel much beyond the main rail routes. Scottish Citylink's unlimited **Explorer Pass** (from £35 for 3 days) is pricey and not too helpful, though the 50% discount on Caledonian MacBrayne ferry passages may make it worthwhile. Access to more remote and rewarding areas depends on small, local bus companies, listed in the *Public Transport Travel Guide*. Driving in the Highlands is infinitely more convenient but potentially treacherous (see **Driving**, p. 537).

Most **ferries** are operated by **Caledonian MacBrayne**, known as **CalMac** (☎(01475) 650 100; www.calmac.co.uk); their free timetable is widely available. Special 8- to 15-day **Island Rover** tickets provide discounts on ferry trips, but require substantial travel on consecutive days and are not valid on some sailings during peak times. **Island Hopscotch** tickets may provide modest savings for well-planned routes. Bikes can cross without reservations (usually for a £2 fee), but advance booking for cars, which cost significantly more, is highly recommended.

NORTHEASTERN SCOTLAND

ABERDEEN ☎01224

Whoever dubbed Aberdeen (pop. 210,000) "The Granite City" wasn't off the mark: most days, the gray hues of the city's buildings flow seamlessly into the ashy skies. City planners have compromised with the color, surrounding the center with lush parks and building walkways on the sandy beaches. Perpetually haunted by seagulls, this melancholy mecca of the North Sea oil industry nevertheless shelters the din of partying students and an array of pubs, clubs, and museums. Some visitors use Aberdeen solely as a base for exploring the splendid castles nearby, but those who stay longer realize that Scotland's third-largest city—cosmopolitan and melodramatic—should not be ignored.

▐ TRANSPORTATION

Flights: Aberdeen Airport (☎722 331). Stagecoach Bluebird #10 runs to the airport from the bus station (every hr. until 8:40pm, £1.25) and First Aberdeen (☎650 065) #27 runs from Guild St. (every hr. until 5:20pm, £1.45). **British Airways** (☎(08457) 733 377) flies from **London Heathrow** and **Gatwick** (11 per day, £30-£105).

Trains: Guild St. Ticket office open M-F 6:30am-7:30pm, Sa 7am-7pm, Su 8:45am-7:30pm. 24hr. **luggage storage** £2-4. Trains (☎(08457) 484 950) from: **Edinburgh** (2½hr., every hr., £21); **Glasgow** (2½hr., every hr., £28); **Inverness** (2¼hr., every 1½hr., £18.20); **London King's Cross** (7½hr.; 3 per day, 1 overnight sleeper; £27/90).

Buses: Guild St. (☎212 266), next to the train station. Ticket office open M-F 7am-5:45pm, Sa 7am-4:30pm, Su 9:30am-3:30pm. **National Express** (☎(08705) 808 080) from **London** (7 per day, £33). **Scottish Citylink** (☎(08705) 505 050) from **Edinburgh** (4hr., every hr., £15) and **Glasgow** (4hr., every hr., £15). **Stagecoach Bluebird** (☎212 266) #10 from **Inverness** (4hr., every hr., £9).

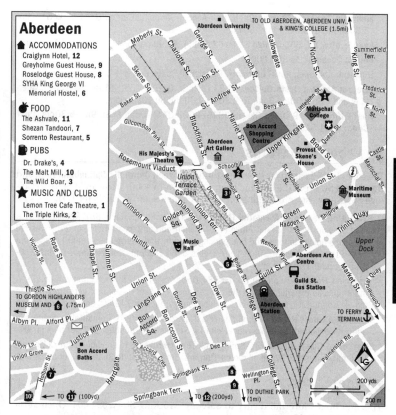

Aberdeen

♠ ACCOMMODATIONS
Craiglynn Hotel, **12**
Greyholme Guest House, **9**
Roselodge Guest House, **8**
SYHA King George VI
   Memorial Hostel, **6**

♦ FOOD
The Ashvale, **11**
Shezan Tandoori, **7**
Sorrento Restaurant, **5**

■ PUBS
Dr. Drake's, **4**
The Malt Mill, **10**
The Wild Boar, **3**

★ MUSIC AND CLUBS
Lemon Tree Cafe Theatre, **1**
The Triple Kirks, **2**

Ferries: Aberdeen Ferry Terminal, Jamieson's Quay (☎572 615). Turn left (south) at the traffic light off Market St., past the P&O Scottish Ferries building. Office open M-F 9am-6pm, Sa 9am-noon. **Northlink Ferries** run to **Kirkwall, Orkney** (5¾hr.; M, W, F 5pm) and **Lerwick, Shetland** (12-14hr.; M, W, F, Su 7pm; Tu, Th, Sa 5pm). Fares aren't cheap (Kirkwall £32-48, Lerwick £43-63).

Car Rental: Major car rental companies have offices at the airport and in town. Arnold Clark Car Hire is one of the cheapest. 23+. (☎249 159. Open M-F 8am-6pm, Sa 8am-5pm, Su 11am-5pm. £22 per day, £110 per week.)

Taxis: Mairs City Taxis (☎724 040). 24hr.

▮ PRACTICAL INFORMATION

Tourist Information Centre: 23 Union St., St. Nicholas House (☎288 828; fax 581 367; www.agtb.org). From the bus station, turn right and head east on Guild St., then left on Market St.; take the second left on Union St. Books rooms for £1.50 and 10% deposit. Open July-Aug. M-Sa 9:30am-7pm, Su 10am-4pm; Sept.-June M-Sa 9:30am-5pm.

Tours: Grampian Coaches (☎650 024) runs various day tours to nearby castles, Royal Deeside, the Whisky Trail, and beyond. July-Sept. £8-12, seniors and children £6-10.

Financial Services: Thomas Cook, Bon Accord Shopping Centre. Open M, W-Sa 9am-5:30pm; Tu 10am-5:30pm; Su noon-5pm.

Launderette: A1, 555 George St. (☎621 211). £3.90 per load. Open daily 10am-6pm.

Police: Queen St. (☎386 000).

Hospital: Aberdeen Royal Infirmary, Foresterhill Rd. (☎681 818).

Internet Access: Costa Coffee, 31-33 Loch St. (☎626 468). £1.80 per 15min. Open M-W and F-Sa 8:30am-6pm, Th 8:30am-7:30pm, Su 10am-5pm.

Post Office: 48-49 Union St. (☎(08457) 223 344). Open M-Sa 9am-5:30pm. **Post Code:** AB11 6AZ.

ACCOMMODATIONS

Reasonable **B&Bs** are near the train station between **Crown St., Springbank Terr.,** and **Bon Accord St.** From the bus and train stations, turn south from Guild St. onto College St., then west onto Wellington Pl. which melds into Springbank Terr.

SYHA King George VI Memorial Hostel, 8 Queen's Rd. (☎646 988). Reachable by a long walk on Union St. and Albyn Pl. or a short ride on bus #14, 15, or 27. Industrial kitchen, smoking lounge, and free parking. Laundry and Internet (£5 per hr.). Reception 7am-11pm. Lockout 9:30am-1pm. Lights out 11:30pm. Curfew 2am. Dorms £10-12.50, under 18 £6-11. ❷

Craiglynn Hotel, 36 Fonthill Rd. (☎584 050; fax 212 225; www.craiglynn.co.uk). A more upscale experience. See the old servants' quarters upstairs or get a room in the old viewing turret facing the sea. Smoking lounge. Singles £42-60; doubles £60-80. ❹

Roselodge Guest House, 3 Springbank Terr. (☎/fax 586 794). Comfortable quarters in a lovely converted home. All rooms with TV. Singles £20; doubles £17 per person. ❸

Greyholme Guest House, 35 Springbank Terr. (☎587 081; greyholme@talk21.com). Tastefully furnished; TVs in all rooms. Carpark. Singles £25; doubles £20 per person. ❸

FOOD

Tins and boxes lure the thrifty to **Safeway,** 215 King St. (☎624 404. Open M-Sa 7:30am-10pm, Su 10am-7pm.)

The Ashvale, 42-48 Great Western Rd. (☎596 981). An Aberdeen institution and 3-time winner of Scotland's "Fish-and-Chip Shop of the Year" award. The fish and chips lunch (£4.45) can't be beat. Takeaway around back. Open daily 11:45am-1am. ❷

Sorrento Restaurant, 20 Bridge St. (☎210 580). Excellent lunch specials (2 courses for £5). Hearty dinners served in Italian-themed ambiance: veal, poultry, and vegetarian dishes for £10-£12. Open M-Sa 11:45am-11pm, Su noon-9:30pm. ❷

Shezan Tandoori, 53 Holburn St. (☎590 810). Friendly staff whip up a mean *korma* and lamb curry specialties. Kebabs starting at £1.70. Open daily 5pm-3am. ❶

SIGHTS

The **Aberdeen Art Gallery,** on Schoolhill, houses changing exhibits of striking 20th-century art alongside older British collections. (☎523 700. Open M-Sa 10am-5pm, Su 2-5pm. Free.) The **Maritime Museum,** on Shiprow, provides a comprehensive history of Aberdeen's long affair with the sea, from fishing to whaling to drilling for oil. (☎337 700; www.aberdeencity.gov.uk. Open M-F 8:15am-5:45pm, Sa 8:15am-4:30pm. Free.) Just up Broad St., **Provost Skene's House** is one of the few 17th-century Aberdonian mansions that has escaped demolition. Its rare and mysterious Painted Gallery boasts grand depictions of the life of Christ. (☎641 086. Open M-Sa

10am-5pm, Su 1-4pm. Free.) Across the street, inside the imposing Gothic hulk of **Marischal College,** the **Marischal Museum** provides a glimpse into Northeast Scotland's prehistoric past and into local lad Robert Wilson's collection of Age of Empire booty. (☎274 301. Open M-F 10am-5pm, Su 2-5pm. Free.)

Aberdeen's must-see architecture is best viewed against a gray sky. For the gloomiest in turrets, visit **Old Aberdeen** and **King's College,** a short bus ride (#1, 2, 5 or 15) from the city center or a long walk along King St. The **King's College Visitor Centre,** off High St., has an exhibit on the history of **Aberdeen University** (which includes both King's and Marischal Colleges) from its 1495 founding. See how the worst can come in small packages in the aptly named "Clatter Vengeance" school bell. (☎273 702. Open M-Sa 10am-5pm, Su noon-5pm. Free.) **King's College Chapel** dates from the 16th century and features intricately carved "misery seats," so called because students were forced to sit in the un-orthopedic chairs for hours. (☎272 137. Open daily 9am-4:30pm. Tours July-Aug. Su 2-5pm. Free.) Twin-spired **St. Machar's Cathedral,** with heraldic ceiling, stained glass, and coffin statues, was built in the 14th century. (☎485 908; www.stmachar.com. Open daily 9am-5pm. Services Su 11am and 6pm.) After visiting, take a walk through grassy **Seaton Park,** where the **Brig O' Balgownie**—a gift from Robert the Bruce—spans the River Don.

Defying the gray conspiracy, Aberdeen is also famous for its greenery, having cinched the Britain in Bloom award ten times since 1963. **Duthie Park** (DA-thee), by the River Dee at Polmuir Rd. and Riverside Dr., accessible by bus #16 and 17, is a grassy escape with an extensive rose garden and the **Winter Gardens Hothouse.** (Hothouse open May-Aug. daily 9:30am-7:30pm; Sept. 9:30am-6:30pm; Apr. and Oct. 9:30am-5:30pm. Free.) The **Gordon Highlanders Museum,** St. Lukes, Viewfield Rd., displays the pomp, circumstance, and bloody heroism of the kilted fighting regiment in a 15min. film and detailed exhibit. (Walk farther down Queens Rd. from the hostel or take bus #14 or 15 from Union St. ☎311 200; www.gordonhighlanders.com. Open Apr.-Oct. Tu-Sa 10:30am-4:30pm, Su 1:30-4:30pm. ₤2.50, concessions ₤1.50, children ₤1.) The aviary, petting zoo, and extensive woodlands of **Hazlehead Park,** off Queen's Rd. 1½ mi. west of the hostel, are worth a quick bus (#14-15) to the city's edge. Aberdeen's sandy **beach** stretches north for about 2 mi. from the old fishing community of **Footdee** (fi-TEE) to the Don estuary. Two **amusement parks** loom over the southern end, while a **golf course** flanks the less disturbed northern sands. Take bus #14 or 15 east to Footdee, for the southern stretch near the amusement parks, or to the Sea Beach stop to be closer to the fairways.

🎭 🎵 NIGHTLIFE AND ENTERTAINMENT

Aberdeen has a pumping nightlife, courtesy of student throngs forced indoors by the cold weather. Pubs frequently host hip bands in an alcohol-friendly atmosphere. **Langstane Pl.,** south of Union St., is the place to prowl for dance clubs. For info on all venues, snag *What's On in Aberdeen* from the TIC or art gallery.

🏛 **Lemon Tree Cafe Theatre,** 5 West North St. (☎642 230), near Queen St. Serves food and drink in front of its mainstage, a sure venue for music most nights and comedy occasional M. Plays and musicals on upstairs stage; tickets £5-9, concessions £2-3.

The Triple Kirks, 12 Schoolhill (☎619 921), just below the Aberdeen Art Gallery. A ruined church that rivals any Glaswegian club. Groove to everything from jazz to disco to techno in its **Exodus Nightclub,** or listen to stand-up at the monthly **Comedy Cafe.** Cover £2-4. Bar open M-Sa 11am-midnight, Su noon-11pm; club Th-Su 10:30pm-2am.

The Wild Boar, 19 Belmont St. (☎625 5357), off Union St. Laid-back bar that pumps jazz tunes by day and turns on the hip-hop and funk at night. Sandwiches and burgers £4-4.75. Homemade desserts; daily specials. Open M-Th 11am-midnight, F and Sa 11am-1am, Su 12:30pm-midnight; food served until 8:45pm, F-Sa until 7:45pm.

Dr. Drake's, 62 Shiprow (☎596 999; www.drdrakesbar.co.uk). A cozy bar with live music every night. Wait for the doctor himself to step up and play. Occasional drink specials. Open Su-Th 5pm-2am, F and Sa 5pm-3am.

The Malt Mill, 82 Holburn St. (☎573 830). Local live music downstairs at least 3 weeknights, bigger names on weekends. Older crowd drinks up top. Student drink specials daily 7-9pm. Open M-Th 11am-midnight, F-Sa 11am-1am, Su 12:30-11pm.

Seagulls aren't the only things to listen to in Aberdeen—five main entertainment venues and other assorted hangouts ensure a steady stream of live music and theater. Obtain tickets and information for all five venues from the friendly folks at the **Aberdeen Box Office,** next to the Music Hall. (☎641 122; fax 627 353. Open M-Sa 9:30am-6pm.) The **Music Hall,** on Union St., features pop bands, musicals, and orchestra recitals. (☎632 080; fax 632 400; www.musichallaberdeen.com.) **His Majesty's Theatre,** Rosemount Viaduct, hosts dance, opera, ballet, and theater. (☎641 122; www.hmtheatre.com.) The **Aberdeen Arts Centre,** 33 King St., stages avant-garde and traditional plays. (Tickets £3-6, concessions £1-2.)

▶ DAYTRIPS FROM ABERDEEN: THE GRAMPIAN COAST

The dramatic Grampian coast is impressive in any weather. With North Sea winds and fury on gray days, waves crash against jutting rocks and roll up sandy shores. In sunlight, the coast sheds its darkness and reveals couples strolling along seaside trails, up and down the rolling green heather.

■ **DUNNOTTAR CASTLE.** Splendidly decrepit Dunnottar Castle stands a romantic 30min. walk from seaside **Stonehaven,** 15 mi. south of Aberdeen. Built in the 14th century by Earl Marischal's family, the castle was the backdrop for the Mel Gibson *Hamlet,* and has witnessed several gruesome historical events (like the burning of an entire English garrison by another Mel incarnation, William Wallace). A photogenic ruin, the castle commands gut-wrenching sea views; if you stoop through the tunnel at the base of the cliff, you'll find a pebbly beach that rattles with the receding waves. *(Trains (20min., 17-25 per day, £2.90) and Bluebird Northern bus #101 (30min., 2 per hr., return £3.65) connect Aberdeen to Stonehaven. ☎(01569) 762 173. Open Easter-Oct. M-Sa 9am-6pm, Su 2-5pm; Nov.-Easter M-F 9am-dusk. £3.50, children £1.)*

■ **FYVIE CASTLE.** Northwest on the inland A947, 25 mi. from Aberdeen, the amazingly intact 13th-century Fyvie Castle endures a brace of curses: in one of the towers, there's a sealed chamber that, when opened, will cause the laird to die and his wife to go blind. For those still in possession of their eyesight, the well-guided interior contains a collection of textiles, furniture, and paintings (including one portrait worth a cool £10 million) while the striking exterior is adorned with five lofty turrets—one added by each family that has owned the castle since the 14th century. *(Stagecoach Bluebird (☎(01224) 212 266) runs from Aberdeen (#305, 1hr., every hr.). ☎(01343) 569 164. Open July-Aug. daily 10am-5:30pm; Apr.-June and Sept.-Oct. Sa-W noon-5pm. Grounds open daily 9:30am-dusk. £7, concessions £5.25, families £19.)*

ROYAL DEESIDE

Between Aberdeen and Braemar, the River Dee meanders through a castle-studded valley. With the Cairngorms to the east and the hills of the Highlands to the north and south, the glen caters to royalty and commoners alike. Queen Victoria made this her Scottish retreat, and tourists have followed suit, tracing the Castle and Victorian Heritage Trails up and down the valley. Although those with title may prefer horseback, cars now hold sway. If you don't have a car, the efficient **Bluebird "Heather-hopper" bus** (☎(01343) 544 222) runs every hour between Aberdeen and Braemar (#201; day rover £7, children £3.50), whisking passengers from

Aberdeenshire, a traditional stronghold of "Lowland" culture, to the edge of the Highlands, where Gaelic no longer thrives, but hill-walking, fishing, and skiing do.

The first stop on the Bluebird route (30min. from Aberdeen), modest **Drum Castle** is pleasantly undertouristed. Drum looks, feels, and *is* ancient; it's been inhabited longer than any other castle (from 1323 to 1975) and may have been built as early as 1286. Hop off the bus at Drumoak and walk a mile to the castle and its **Garden of Historic Roses,** a collection of flowers from the last four centuries. (☎ (01330) 811 204; fax 811 962. Open June-Aug. daily 10am-5:30pm; Apr.-May and Sept. 12:30-5:30pm; Oct. Sa-Su 1:30-5:30pm. Grounds open daily 9:30am-dusk. £5, concessions £3.50, children free. Joint ticket with Crathes Castle available; see below.)

Crathes Castle, a few miles farther down, is considerably more crowded. Grand but not extravagant, the interior contains curiosities like the Horn to Leys, a 1323 gift from Robert the Bruce, and a "trip stair" designed to bungle burglars. A "Green Lady" allegedly haunts the castle, perhaps contributing a thumb to the superlative **gardens,** whose blooms deck ingenious alcoves and hedge-lined passages. (☎ (01330) 844 525; fax 844 797. Castle open Apr.-Sept. daily 10am-5:30pm; Oct. 10am-4:30pm. Last admission 45min. before close. Garden open daily 9:30am-sunset. £8.50, concessions £6.40. Garden or castle only £5/£3.75. Joint ticket with Drum Castle available only at Crathes; £11/£8.)

Another hour along the A93, white **Balmoral Castle and Estate** rests on the southern side of the river, tucked in a valley. The Queen's holiday palace, Balmoral was a gift to Queen Victoria from Prince Albert, who helped design its present form. The traversable landscape is fittingly majestic, but being a royal hideaway, all but the ballroom (containing rotating exhibitions) is closed to the public. (☎ (013397) 42334; www.balmoralcastle.com. Open Apr.-July daily 10am-5pm. £4.50, seniors £3.50, under 16 £1.) **Horseback riding** lends the Estates an antiquated air. (Call ahead for 2hr. pony treks starting at 9:30am and 1:30pm. 12+. £25.)

BRAEMAR ☎ 013397

Situated on the River Dee, Braemar is the southern gateway to the Cairngorms and a hiker's paradise. Brooding 17th-century **Braemar Castle** houses surprises as a 19th-century fire escape (read: rope and pulley) and Great Lakes Native American artifacts. (☎/fax 41219. Open Apr.-Oct. Sa-Th 10am-6pm, also F July-Aug.; last entry 5:30pm. £3.50, concessions £3, children £1.50.) The first Saturday in September, Braemar's population swells from 410 to 20,000 for the one-day **Braemar Gathering,** a Highland Games where the Queen is patron and the Scots are stars. Advance booking is essential for a seat; uncovered stand tickets cost about £12, ringside standing-room £10, climbing a nearby hill and watching through binoculars free. (☎ 55377; www.braemargathering.org) The first full week of July is **Braemar's Gala Week,** featuring such random events as craft fairs, a mountain rescue display, and "Scenic Barbecue and 4x4 Safaris." (Information available at the TIC.)

The only way into (and out of) Braemar by public transportation is the **Bluebird "Heather-hopper" bus** (from Crathie and Balmoral 15min., from Aberdeen 2¼hr.; see p. 630). Rent **bikes** and **nordic skis** from the **Mountain Sports Shop,** at the town's eastern edge, on Invercauld Rd. (☎ 41242. Bikes £15 per day, skis £16. Open M-Th 8:30am-6pm, F-Su 8:30am-7pm.) The **tourist information centre,** Mar Rd., at the Mews, supplies a list of places to sleep and to hike. (☎ 41600. Open July-Aug. daily 9am-7pm; Sept. 10am-6pm; Oct. and Apr. to late May M-Sa 10:30am-1:30pm and 2-5:30pm, Su noon-5pm; Nov.-Mar. M-Sa 10:30am-1:30pm and 2-5pm; late May to June M-Su 10am-7pm.) Stock up on grub at the **Alldays** across the street (☎ 41201; open M-Sa 7:30am-9pm, Su 8:30am-7pm), also home to the **post office** (☎ (08457) 223 344; open M-F 9am-noon and 1-5:30pm, Sa 9am-1pm). **Post Code:** AB35 5YQ.

HIGHLANDS AND ISLANDS

The 64-bed **SYHA Braemar** ❷, 21 Glenshee Rd., occupies a stone house 5min. south of town, surrounded by Scotland's oldest pines. Fear not the 11:30pm curfew and the 11:45pm lockout—most of Braemar is closed by then anyway. (☎41659. Reception 7-10:30am and 5-11pm. Checkout 9:30am. July-Aug. dorms £12, under 18 £8; Sept.-June £9/£6.) The **Rucksacks Bunkhouse** ❶, 15 Mar Rd., behind the TIC, has space for 26, 10 of whom sleep in said bunkhouse and use their own sleeping bags. (☎41517. Laundry £3. Dorms £8.50; bunkhouse £7.) Three doors north of the SYHA, the **Callater Lodge** ❸, 9 Glenshee Rd., has light, airy rooms with a reserved and hospitable Victorian atmosphere. (☎41275; fax 41245. £24-29 per person.) The **Invercauld Caravan Club Site** ❶, 5min. south of the hostel on Glenshee Rd., welcomes tents to its busy premises. (☎41373. Open Dec.-Sept. 9am-6pm. £3.75 per person, £2 per tent. Car £1.50.)

📷 **HIKING NEAR BRAEMAR.** The area around Braemar bristles with signposted hikes for all skill levels, centering around the frothy **Linn of Dee.** Along the river, the leisurely **Derry Lodge Walk** promises red deer, red squirrels, and grouse. The more challenging **Lairig Ghru trail** also starts at the Linn but stretches 20 mi. north to Aviemore. The name means "gloomy pass," which is rather accurate—the path is heartbreakingly desolate as it winds between steep mountainsides and past the often snow-covered **Ben Macdui.** It's also difficult, so don't overestimate your ability or underestimate your need for a map (Ordnance Survey Outdoor Leisure #3). To get to the Linn, drive 20min. east of Braemar on the Linn of Dee Rd., or catch the daily **postbus** from the Braemar post office at 1:30pm (no return). Otherwise, walk or bike the scenic 7 mi. alongside the Linn of Dee road. Hikers should start early to finish the Lairig Ghru in one day; consider spending the previous night at the **SYHA Inverey** ❶, where there are usually more deer than guests. The daily postbus stops at the hostel before swinging by the Linn. (☎ (013397) 41969. No showers. Open mid.-May to Sept. Dorms £8, under 18 £6.75.)

CAIRNGORM MOUNTAINS ☎01479

The towering Cairngorms, 120 mi. north of Edinburgh, are the real deal for Scottish wilderness: misty, mighty, and arctic even in summer. Unfortunately, these mountains have also suffered the deforestation that nearly stripped Scotland of its native pine and birch forests. While the peaks are bare, covered only with heather, reindeer, and, for much of the year, the snow that attracts skiers and dogsledders, the region does contain Britain's largest expanse of nature preserves. With reforestation and wildlife on the rise, the Cairngorms became one of Scotland's first national parks in the summer of 2002.

▶ TRANSPORTATION

The largest town in the Cairngorms, **Aviemore** is conveniently located on the main Inverness-Edinburgh rail and bus lines. The **train station** is on Grampian Rd., just north of the TIC. (☎ (08457) 484 950. Open M-F 7:30am-9:25pm, Sa 7:35am-2:39pm, Su 9:55am-5:35pm.) Trains arrive from **Edinburgh** and **Glasgow** (2¼hr., 7 per day, £32) and **Inverness** (45min., 7-8 per day, £7.20). Southbound **buses** stop at the shopping center north of the train station, northbound buses at the Cairngorm Hotel. **Scottish Citylink** (☎ (08705) 505 050) runs nearly every hour from: **Edinburgh** (3hr., £12.50); **Glasgow** (3½hr., £12.50); **Inverness** (40min., £4.70). **Kincraig**, 6 mi. south of Aviemore on the A9, is accessible by Scottish Citylink #957 from Perth.

The principal path into **Glen More Forest Park**, and the area's prettiest road trip, the **Ski Rd.** begins just south of Aviemore (on the B970) and jogs eastward, merging with the A951. The road passes the sandy beaches of **Loch Morlich** before carrying on to **Glenmore** and ending at the Cairngorm base. From Aviemore's train station, **Highland Country** "Munro Bagger" **buses** #37 and 377 travel the same route, taking in **Kincraig** (10 per day in summer). A similar winter service transports eager skiers.

The **Cairngorm Service Station,** on Aviemore's Main St., rents **cars.** (☎810 596. £34-42 per day, £185-235 per week. Open M-F 8:30am-5pm.) **Bike rental**—including helmet, maps, and breakdown equipment—is available from **Bothy Bikes,** Grampian Rd., north of the train station. (☎810 111. Half-day £10, full day £14. ID required. Open daily 9am-5:30pm.) **Ellis Brigham,** nearby on Grampian Rd., rents skis during the winter and climbing equipment during the summer. (☎810 175. Open M-F 9am-6pm, Sa-Su 8:30am-6pm.) **The Glenmore Shop and Cafe,** just north of the Loch Morlich hostel, rents bikes, skis, and mountain boards downstairs from the cafe area. (☎861 253. Bikes £14 per day, £8 per half-day. Open daily 9am-5pm.)

🔳🇮 ORIENTATION AND PRACTICAL INFORMATION

While the Cairngorms themselves are quiet, their largest town, **Aviemore,** is not. This concrete roadside strip caters to tourists with its clutter of pricey hotels; once you've used its urban amenities, escape to the mountains. **Glenmore** offers the most intimate access, and **Kincraig,** though farther away, sustains visitors with a welcome breath of non-touristed air on the tranquil shores of Loch Insh.

The **Aviemore and Spey Valley Tourist Information Centre,** on Grampian Rd., Aviemore's main artery, books local B&Bs for £3 plus 10% deposit, sells bus tickets, and exchanges currency during peak season. (☎810 363. Open July to mid-Sept. M-Sa 9am-6pm, Su 10am-4pm; mid-Sept. to June M-F 9am-5pm, Sa 10am-4pm.) The **Rothiemurchus Estate Visitors Centre** lies near Inveruie, 1 mi. east on the Ski Rd. from Aviemore. (☎812 345. Open daily 9am-5:30pm.) **Glenmore Forest Park Visitors Centre** offers maps and advice about walks in the valley west of the mountains. (☎861 220; fax 861 711. Open daily 9am-5pm.) **Kincraig Stores** serves as the Kincraig **post office** and unofficial info center. (☎(01540) 651 331. Post office open M-Tu and Th-F 9am-1pm. Store open M-Sa 8am-6pm, Su 8:30am-1pm.) Other services include: **police,** Grampian Rd. (☎810 222); **Bank of Scotland,** Grampian Rd., across from Tesco (☎887 240; open M-Tu and Th-F 9am-5pm, W 9:30am-5pm); **Internet access** for free at **Aviemore Library,** Grampian Rd. behind the Bank of Scotland (☎811 113; open Tu 2-8pm, W 10am-8pm, F 10am-5pm, closed 12:30-2pm and 5-6pm), or £5 per hr. at **SYHA Aviemore** (see below); and the **post office,** Grampian Rd. (☎811 056; open M-F 9am-5:30pm, Sa 9am-noon). **Post Code:** PH22 1RH.

🏠 ACCOMMODATIONS

Check the TIC's *Aviemore & the Cairngorms* publication for a complete list of seasonal hostels and year-round B&Bs (£15-25).

🏚 **Lazy Duck Hostel** (☎821 642; www.lazyduck.co.uk), Badanfhuarain, just east of Nethy Bridge. Catch Highland Country bus #334 from Aviemore (20min., 8 per day). One of Scotland's smallest hostels—bedding 8, tops—is also one of its best. A snug cottage with magical loft and covered garden, congenial ducks and geese, excellent kitchen, and friendly people. Dorms £8.50. ❶

Carrbridge Bunkhouse Hostel (☎(01479) 841 250), Dalrachny House, Carrbridge. A 10min. walk along a marked footpath from Carrbridge train station. Sparely done in outdoorsy fashion, but a perfect haunt for the serious hiker, nature lover, or bargain hunter. Kitchen, hot showers, and sauna, but bring your own sleep sack. Just £7 a night. ❶

SYHA Aviemore (☎810 345), 100 yd. south of the TIC. All the usual SYHA amenities with little to set it apart. 114 beds, 4-8 per room. Breakfast included. Curfew 2am. Dorms £12.25, under 18 £10.75; July-Aug. £1 extra. ❷

Glen Feshie Hostel (☎(01540) 651 323; glenfeshiehostel@totalise.co.uk), 11 mi. south of Aviemore, 5 mi. from Kincraig. Call ahead for a lift from the station; otherwise it's a 9 mi. walk along Loch-an-Eilein. Homey atmosphere and living quarters close to numerous hikes. Linen and porridge breakfast included, meals £5.50-9.50. Dorms £8. ❶

Insh Hall Lodge (☎(01540) 651 272), 1 mi. downhill from Kincraig on Loch Insh; take bus #957 from Kincraig. Basic, sizeable dorms or B&B. Sauna and gym. Stay 2 nights for free use of watersports equipment. From £17.50; full board £35.50. ❷

SYHA Loch Morlich (☎861 238), Glenmore. Take Highland Country Bus from Aviemore station. Lovely lochside setting but impersonal atmosphere and tyrannical 11:45pm lights-out. Curfew 11:30pm. Open Feb.-Sept. Dorms £9.75-10.50, under 18 £8.50. ❶

Camping: Glenmore Forest Camping and Caravan Park ❶ (☎861 271), opposite the SYHA Loch Morlich. Ample space and good facilities, though crowded in summer. Open Dec.-Oct. £4.20-5 per person. **Rothiemurchus Camp and Caravan Park** ❶ (☎812 800), 1½ mi. south of Aviemore on Ski Rd. £4 per person.

FOOD

Several restaurants line Grampian Rd. in Aviemore. For do-it-yourselfers, the local **Tesco** supermarket is north of the train station. (☎887 240. Open M-W 8:30am-8pm, Th-F 8:30am-9pm, Sa 8am-8pm, Su 9am-6pm.) At the Aviemore station, take in high tea (£5.85 for 3 courses) at the modestly titled **Number One Restaurant ❷.** (☎(01479) 811 161. Open M-F 7am-9pm, Sa-Su 7am-10pm.) For a trendier experience, try **Cafe Mambo ❷**, 12-13 Grampian Rd., for their burgers (£5-7) and sinful hot chocolate (£1.50). If you've had one too many "fetish" cocktail pitchers (£11.50), stay to dance it off. (☎811 670. Restaurant and bar open Su-W 11am-11pm, Th-Sa noon-1am; food served until 9pm. Club open F-Sa 10pm-1am.)

HIKING AND SKIING

The Cairngorm region has Scotland's highest concentration of ski resorts. Outdoors enthusiasts, snowbunnies, and tourists converge at **CairnGorm Mountain** (on the mountain Cairn Gorm) for wintertime skiing and summertime hiking, as well as viewing from its newly unveiled **funicular railway.** Sit facing down the mountain for great views on the 5-10min. ride up to **Ptarmigan Centre,** Britain's highest train station (1097m). Those who sit facing uphill can still soak in the scenery (hopefully catching a peak of Ben Nevis to the west) from the observation deck at the top. Due to conservation concerns (which have made the railway a hotly contested topic), railway-goers may not set foot outside the Centre. The only way to wander about on the peak is to do it the old-fashioned way: hiking up from the bottom. (Highland County Bus #37 from Aviemore. ☎861 261; www.cairngormmountain.com. Trains every 15min. Ticket office opens 8:30am, mountain closes between 4:30-5pm. Funicular return £7.50, concessions £6.50, children £5.)

Unfortunately, the funicular railway does not provide access to the popular peak of **Ben MacDui,** Britain's second highest at 4296 ft. To get there, take the **Northern Corries Path** from the carpark to its terminus, and then navigate an unmarked route to Ben MacDui's peak—a 7hr. undertaking suggested only for hikers with some experience, but definitely worth the exertion. Be prepared for all weather, at any time of year, and bring a stock of food. The less ambitious can take the still strenuous but shorter **Windy Ridge Trail** to the top of Cairn Gorm (3-4 hr. round trip). Before setting out, consult the helpful **Cairngorm Rangers** about trail and weather conditions. (Office next to the CairnGorm Mountain carpark. ☎861 703. Open daily 9am-5pm, weather permitting.) Other hikes for all skill levels abound. In the ski area, many signposted trails scour Cairn Gorm—all of which leave from the carpark. The Cairngorm Rangers also host free **guided hikes,** usually on Tuesdays. For forest walks, **Glenmore Visitors Centre** has a few choice trails; the most popular is the easy-going 2½-3hr. **Ryovan Trek** through the woods and along **Green Lochen.** (☎861 220. Open daily 9am-5pm.) Closer to Aviemore, the daunting but renowned **Lairig Ghru** path heads south through 20 mi. of gloomy valleys to Braemar. This one's only for the bravest of souls, so make sure you have your Ordnance Survey Outdoor Leisure map (#3) and a full day's supply of stamina.

> **SAFETY PRECAUTIONS.** Although the Cairngorms rise only 4000 ft., the weather patterns of the **Arctic tundra** characterize the region. Explorers may be at the mercy of bitter winds and unpredictable mists *any day of the year.* Furthermore, many trails are not posted and trekkers must be able to rely on their own proficiency with map and compass. Make sure to use an Ordnance Survey map (Landranger #35 and 36), or preferably, yellow Outdoor Leisure map #3. Both are available at the TIC. Be prepared for **sub-freezing temperatures** no matter what the weather is when you set out. Leave a description of your intended route with the police or at the mountain station, and learn the locations of the shelters (known as bothies) along your trail. See **Wilderness Safety,** p. 49.

For skiers, a day ticket at Cairngorm with rail passes costs £24 (concessions £15-18). Several companies run ski schools and rent equipment; pick up a copy of *Scottish Snow* at the Aviemore TIC for details. Down the hill 3 mi. west of the funicular, the **Cairngorm Reindeer Centre** is home to dozens of velvet-horned sled-pullers. Visitors can pay for a 1½hr. frolic amid the herd. (☎861 228. Open daily 10am-5pm. Visits at 11am; May-Sept. also 2:30pm, call ahead to confirm. £6, seniors and children £3, families £18. Paddock £2/£1/£6.) In summer, the **Highland Country** bus service runs from Aviemore to the funicular and Reindeer Centre. Otherwise, you can do the 10 mi. by hoof or bike. The 269 acres of **Highland Wildlife Park** in Kincraig are dedicated to preserving native beasties. Scottish Citylink #957 stops by from Aviemore en route to Edinburgh, Perth, and Pitlochry. (☎(01540) 651 270; www.kincraig.com/wildlife. Open June-Aug. daily 10am-7pm; Apr.-May and Sept.-Oct. 10am-6pm; Nov.-Mar. 10am-4pm. Last admission 2hr. before close. £7; seniors £6; children, students, and disabled £4.80; families £23.60.)

ELGIN ☎01343

Elgin (whose "g" is pronounced as in Guinness, not gin; pop. 20,000) is a relatively urban town halfway between Aberdeen and Inverness; spectacular **Elgin cathedral** warrants a stopover between the two. Once regarded the most beautiful of Scottish churches, the cathedral was looted and burned by the Wolf of Badenoch in the late 14th century, then further tormented by fire, Edward III, the Reformation, Cromwell's bullets, and townspeople who carted off its deteriorating stones. Half a millennium of neglect has reduced the 200 ft. towers to 90 ft., which still allow a breathtaking view of Elgin and the surrounding country. (☎547 171. Open Apr.-Sept. daily 9:30am-6pm; Oct.-Mar. M-W and Sa 9:30am-4pm, Th 9:30am-noon, Su 2-4pm. £2.50, seniors £1.90, children £1.) Next door, all 104 plants mentioned in the Good Book thrive amidst statues of Jesus and Mary in the **Biblical Garden.** (Open May-Sept. daily 10am-7:30pm. Free.) The **Elgin Museum,** 1 High St., in the city center, traces the history of the Moray area from primordial goo to present times in displays ranging from a 65-million-year-old ammonite to a mummified cat, circa 1471. Me-ouch. (☎/fax 543 675. Open Apr.-Oct. M-F 10am-5pm, Sa 11am-4pm, Su 2-5pm. £2, concessions £1, children 50p, families £4.50.)

The **train station** is 5min. south of the city center at the end of South Guildry St. Ticket office open M-Sa 6:15am-9:30pm, Su 10:30am-5:30pm. Station open M-F

8:30am-5pm, Sa 8:30am-12:30pm and 1-6pm. Trains (☎ (08457) 484 950) hail from **Aberdeen** (1½hr., 10 per day, £11.20) and **Inverness** (45min., 11 per day, £7.40). **Buses** stop behind High St. and the St. Giles Centre. **Stagecoach Bluebird** (☎ (01343) 544 222) #10 arrives at the **bus station,** on Alexandra Rd. across from the Town Hall, from **Aberdeen** (2¼hr., every hr., £7) and **Inverness** (1¼hr., 2 per hr., £7). The **tourist information centre,** 17 High St., books local accommodations for £1.50 and 10% deposit. (☎542 666; fax 552 982. Open July-Sept. M-Sa 9am-6pm, Su 11am-4pm; Mar.-June M-Sa 10am-5pm, Su 11am-3pm; Apr. and Oct. M-Sa 10am-5pm; Nov.-Mar. M-Sa 10am-4pm.) Other services include: free **Internet access** at **Elgin Library** in Cooper Park (☎562 600; open M-F 10am-8pm, Sa 10am-4pm); and the **post office,** with a **bureau de change** (open M-F 8am-8pm, Sa 8am-6pm, Su 10am-5pm) in the **Tesco** supermarket on Batchen Ln. (☎527 400; open M-F 7:30am-8pm, Sa 7:30am-6pm, Su 10am-5pm). **Post Code:** IV30 1LY.

Elgin is full of **B&Bs**, especially on the two blocks just north of the train station between **Moss St., Moray St.,** and **South Guildray St.** Try **Auchmillan Guest House ❸**, 12 Reidhaven St., for its color TVs and hairdryers. (☎(01343) 549 077. Singles £25-30; doubles £36-40.) Grab some grub cheaply and easily at **Romak's Tandoori Take Away ❶**, 47 High St. (☎(01343) 552 266. Open daily 5pm-1am.) Two-course lunches are only £3.25 (noon-2:30pm) at the **Thunderton House ❶** pub, Thunderton Pl. off High St. (☎554 921. Open Su-W until 11pm, Th until 11:45pm, F-Sa until 12:30am.)

NEAR ELGIN

FORRES. Quieter than Elgin and a perennial winner in the cutthroat Britain in Bloom competition, the small town of Forres boasts the magnificent **Sueno's Stone,** a richly carved Pictish cross-slab (Scotland's tallest) viewable day and night in a locked glass house. **Stagecoach Bluebird** #10 makes the 30min. trip to this crossroads, halfway between Elgin and Inverness (2 per hr., £2.40).

LOSSIEMOUTH. Secluded Lossiemouth, 6 mi. north of Elgin on the A941, has two sandy, windswept beaches: **East Beach,** connected to the mainland by a footbridge, and **West Beach,** farther from the town center and sporting a lighthouse. Bus #328 connects "Lossie" to Elgin (20min., 13 per day). Halfway to Lossie, stop off at the derelict **Spynie Palace,** once the digs of the Bishops of Moray, which has the largest surviving tower house in Scotland. (☎(01343) 546 358. Open Apr.-Sept. daily 9:30am-6:30pm; Oct.-Mar. M-Sa 9:30am-4:30pm and Su 2-4:30pm. £2, seniors £1.50, children 75p.) Campers pitch tents under the watchful lighthouse at **Silver Sands Leisure Park ❶**. (☎(01343) 813 262. Open Mar.-Oct. £7.50-12.50 per tent.)

THE MALT WHISKY TRAIL. The world-famous Speyside area has 57 working distilleries, making it prime territory for dram-drinking. The 62 mi. Malt Whisky Trail staggers past seven of them, all of which dispense free booze. **Stagecoach Bluebird** #10 covers Keith, Elgin, and Forres (all key Speyside stop-overs) twice an hour on its way from Aberdeen to Inverness and back. Always tell the driver where you want to go. **Bluebird's Day Rover** ticket earns unlimited one-day travel (☎(01343) 544 222; £11, children £5.50), and the **Off-Peak Day Rover** gets unlimited travel M-F after 9am or all day on weekends (£8/£4).

The self-guided whisky trail starts at **Strathisla Distillery,** the "home and heart" of Chivas Regal, and the Highlands's oldest working distillery (est. 1786). It's a 10min. crawl north along A96 from the Keith bus or train station. (☎(01542) 783 044; fax 783 039; www.chivas.com. Open Apr.-Oct. M-Sa 10am-4pm, Su 12:30-4pm. £4. No charge for under 18.) If you ask the driver, the #336 bus to Glenfiddich will stop at the **Speyside Cooperage,** ¼ mi. south of

Craigellachie on the A941, where visitors can watch casks being handmade—then on to another tasting session. (☎(01340) 871 108; fax 881 437; www.speysidecooperage.co.uk. Open M-F 9:30am-4:30pm. Last admission 4pm. Tours £3, seniors £2.45, children £1.75, families £8.) The best (and only free) tour is at **Glenfiddich Distillery** (glen-FID-ick) in Dufftown, 17 mi. south of Elgin, where bottling is done on the premises. Watch a short video, then walk the rounds with multilingual guides, and end with a generous dram of local origin. Take Bluebird bus #336 from Elgin (40min., 6 per day) to the distillery. (☎(01340) 820 373; www.glenfiddich.com. Open Jan. to mid-Dec. M-F 9:30am-4:30pm; Easter to mid-Oct. also Sa 9:30am-4:30pm and Su noon-4:30pm.)

TOMINTOUL AND THE SPEYSIDE WAY. Rather than nurse a malt, ramblers traipse the **Speyside Way,** an 84 mi. trail along the river from Buckie at Spey Bay to Aviemore in the Cairngorms. For information, call the **Speyside Way Ranger Service** (☎(01340) 881 266) and grab a map (£8-9) and the indispensable *The Speyside Way Long Distance Route* (free) at the Elgin TIC (see p. 635). The trail traverses the Highlands's highest village, **Tomintoul,** which is surrounded by the rolling hills of the **Glenlivet Estate.** Even here you can't escape the water of life—the famous **Glenlivet Distillery,** Ballindalloch, is a 7 mi. hike. (☎(01542) 783 220; www.theglenlivet.com. Open Apr.-Oct. M-Sa 10am-4pm, Su 12:30-4pm. £3, under 18 free.)

If you're not driving, biking, or long-distance hiking, Tomintoul is difficult to reach. **Roberts Buses** (☎(01343) 544 222) runs from Keith and Dufftown (#362, Tu and Sa 1 per day) and Elgin (#363, Th 1 per day, £4). The **tourist information centre,** The Square, dispenses info on various trails and books rooms. (☎(01807) 580 285. Open July-Aug. M-Sa 9:30am-6pm, Su 1-6pm; Apr.-June and Sept.-Oct. 9:30am-1pm and 2-5pm.) Cheap accommodations abound in Tomintoul, including Cathleen Graig's **Alt Na Voir ❷,** Main St., just south of the town center, with friendly service, good breakfast, and cozy beds. (☎(01807) 580 336. £15.)

THE GREAT GLEN

INVERNESS ☎01463

To reach just about anything in the Highlands, you'll have to pass through the transport hub of Inverness, which has shops, pubs, amenities, loads of accommodations, and not much else. Luckily, you don't have to be a Nessie nut to appreciate Britain's largest inland body of water, Loch Ness, only 5 mi. away. And hey, if you don't see the real monster, vendors are all too happy to sell you a stuffed one.

⊫ TRANSPORTATION

Trains: Academy St., in Station Sq. Travel center open M-Sa 6:25am-8:30pm, Su 9:15am-8:30pm. 24hr. **luggage storage** £2-4. Trains (☎(08457) 484 950) from: **Aberdeen** (2¼hr., 7-10 per day, £18.80); **Edinburgh** (3½-4hr., 5-7 per day, £31); **Glasgow** (3½hr., 5-7 per day, £31); **Kyle of Lochalsh** (2½hr., 2-4 per day, £14); **London** (8hr., 3 per day, £84-110); **Thurso** (3½hr., 2-3 per day, £12.50).

Buses: Farraline Park (☎233 371), off Academy St. **Highland Bus and Coach** sells tickets for most companies. Office open M-Sa 8:30am-6:30pm, Su 10am-6:30pm. **National Express** (☎(08705) 808 080) from **London** (13hr., 5 per day, £35). **Scottish**

Citylink (☎(08705) 505 050) from: **Aberdeen** (3½hr., 1 per hr., £9.50); **Edinburgh** (4½hr., 8-10 per day, £14.70); **Glasgow** (4½hr., 10-12 per day, £14.70); **Kyle of Lochalsh** (2½hr., 2 per day, £10.10); **London** (10hr., 1 per day, £34); **Thurso** (3½hr., 4-5 per day, £10.50). Both Citylink and **Rapsons Coaches** (☎(01463) 222 244) from **Ullapool** (1½hr., M-Sa 2-6 per day, £6.50).

Taxis: Inverness Taxis (☎220 222).

Car Rental: Arnold Clark Car Hire, Harbour Rd. (☎713 322). 23+. From £22 per day.

Bike Rental: Barney's convenience store, 35 Castle St. (☎232 249). £8 per half-day, £12 per day. Open M-Sa 7:30am-10:30pm, Su 8am-10:30pm.

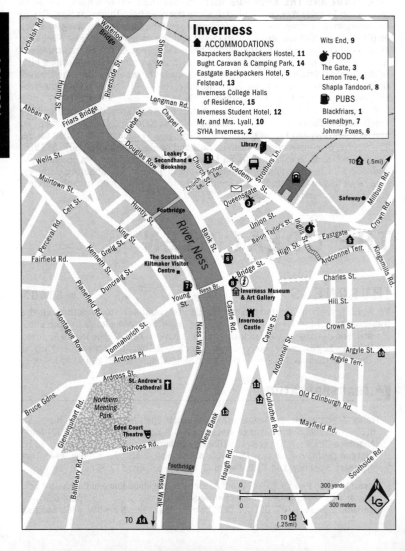

HIGHLANDS AND ISLANDS

Inverness

🏠 **ACCOMMODATIONS**
Bazpackers Backpackers Hostel, **11**
Bught Caravan & Camping Park, **14**
Eastgate Backpackers Hotel, **5**
Felstead, **13**
Inverness College Halls of Residence, **15**
Inverness Student Hotel, **12**
Mr. and Mrs. Lyall, **10**
SYHA Inverness, **2**

Wits End, **9**

🍴 **FOOD**
The Gate, **3**
Lemon Tree, **4**
Shapla Tandoori, **8**

🍺 **PUBS**
Blackfriars, **1**
Glenalbyn, **7**
Johnny Foxes, **6**

🔳 🛈 ORIENTATION AND PRACTICAL INFORMATION

The **River Ness** divides Inverness; most of what you need is on the east bank along **Bridge St.** and the pedestrian area of **High St.** The train and bus stations are to the north on **Academy St.**

Tourist Information Centre: Castle Wynd (☎ 234 353; fax 710 609). Appropriately monstrous, so try not to get lost. The staff helps track Nessie by bus, boat, or brochure, and books non-hostel beds (£3) and CalMac ferries. **Bureau de change** and **Internet access** (£1 per 20min., £2.50 per hr.). Open mid-June to Aug. M-Sa 9am-7pm, Su 9:30am-5pm; Sept. to mid-June M-Sa 9am-5pm, Su 10am-4pm.

Tours: Guide Friday (☎ 224 000). Hop-on/hop-off bus tours leave every 45min. daily May-Sept. from the TIC. Inverness and Culloden tour £7.50, concessions £6, children £2.50. Inverness city tour £5.50/£4/£2.50. **Puffin Express** (☎ 717 181) runs daily summer minibus tours to John O'Groats and the north (£20, children £12) and Cawdor Castle, Clava Cairns, and Culloden (£8). Numerous tours hit **Loch Ness** (see p. 642).

Financial Services: Thomas Cook (☎ 882 200), across from the train station. Open M and W-Sa 9am-5:30pm, Tu 10am-5:30pm.

Work Opportunities: Inverness JobCentre (☎ 888 200 and 888 100), tries to place people where they are needed. Inverness revolves around tourism—in summer, the best bet for jobs is to go knocking on hostel, restaurant, and tourist attraction doors.

Launderette: 17 Young St. (☎ 242 507). Open M-F 8am-8pm, Sa 8am-6pm, Su 10am-4pm; last wash 1hr. before close. Wash £3, dry 20p per 5min.

Police: Old Perth Rd. (☎ 715 555).

Hospital: Raigmore Hospital, Old Perth Rd. (☎ 704 000).

Internet Access: Library, Farraliae Park (☎ 236 463). Just north of the bus station. Provide a passport picture or a British ID for free access. Call ahead to reserve time. Open M and F 9am-7:30pm, Tu and Th 9am-6:30pm, W 10am-5pm, Sa 9am-5pm.

Post Office: 14-16 Queensgate (☎ 243 574). Open M-Sa 9am-5:30pm. Send Post Restante to **Royal Mail Enquiry Office,** Inverness, 7 Strothers Ln. (☎ 256 240). Open M-F 7am-5:30pm, Sa 7am-12:30pm. **Post Code:** IV1 1AA.

🛏 ACCOMMODATIONS

🏅 **Bazpackers Backpackers Hotel,** 4 Culduthel Rd. (☎ 717 663). Down-home atmosphere and great views of the city from the BBQ area. Kitchen, cozy fireplace, co-ed rooms, and clean bathrooms. No smoking, no curfew. Reception 7:30am-midnight. Check-out 10:30am. Mid-June to Sept. dorms £10; doubles £14; Oct. to mid-June £8.50/£12. ❷

Eastgate Backpackers Hostel, 38 Eastgate (☎ 718 756), above a vegetarian restaurant. 38 beds in rooms of 6-8. Relaxed common area with TV and couches. Dorms £8.90; twins £11 per person; less in winter and more in July and Aug. ❶

Felstead, 18 Ness Bank. (☎ 321 634). Location, location, location—along the eastern bank of the Ness River and a 1min. walk south of the city center. Built by a lucky gambler, this B&B antes up spacious rooms, tartan rugs, and comfortable beds. £28-36. ❸

Wits End, 32 Ardconnel St. (☎ 239 909). The owners love backpackers. Soak your cares away in the skylit bathroom, complete with tub. No smoking and no kitchen, but lots of quiet. Dorms £11; twins £24. ❷

Mr. and Mrs. Lyall, 20 Argyle St. (☎ 710 267). Warm welcome and handsome rooms with TV, tea and coffee. Continental breakfast. An eye-popping £12 per person. ❷

SYHA Inverness, Victoria Dr. (☎231 771). From the train station, turn left on Academy St., go up Millburn Rd., and turn right on Victoria Dr. (10-15min.). With card-swipe checkpoints, this state-of-the-art SYHA has an Orwellian feel. 166 beds in rooms of 2-6. Lockers, laundry (£1), kitchen, and TV room. Internet access £5 per hr. Check-out 10:30am. Curfew 2am. Dorms £10.50-12.50, under 18 £9-11. ❷

Inverness Student Hotel, 8 Culduthel Rd. (☎236 556). 6- to 10-bed dorms, free hot chocolate, and great views. Pub crawl with the friendly staff. Breakfast £1.60. Laundry £2.50. Bikes £6.50 per half-day. Internet £5 per hr. Reception 6:30am-2:30am. Check-out 10:30am. July-Sept. £11; Oct.-June £10. ❷

Inverness College Halls of Residence, 23 Culduthel Rd. (☎713 430). Walk 10min. past the castle and Student Hotel or take bus #5 or 7 from the city center. Breakfast £1.50. Open July-Aug. Singles £16; doubles £11 per person. ❷

Camping: Bught Caravan and Camping Park (☎236 920) is closest to town, near the Ness Islands. Open Apr.-Sept. £4.50 per tent, £5.90 per car. ❶

 FOOD AND PUBS

Inverness's restaurants are generally unexceptional. Reach the colossal **Safeway,** Millburn Rd., by going east on Academy St., following it as it veers north. (☎250 260. Open M-W 8am-10pm, Th and F 8am-11pm, Sa 7:30am-9pm, Su 9am-8pm.)

Shapla Tandoori Restaurant, 2 Castle Rd. (☎241 919). Perhaps pricier than usual, but the sizzling curries (£5-9) and river views are worth it. Open daily noon-11:30pm. ❷

Lemon Tree, 18 Inglis St. (☎241 114), north of High St. Folksy, with home-baked goods and fabulous soups (£1.75). Open M-Sa 8:30am-5:45pm. ❶

The Gate, 21 Queensgate (☎711 700). A self-consciously glorified hangout with frothy mochas and Internet. Internet £2.50 per 30min. Food served 11am-6pm. Open M-F 10am-12:45am, Sa 10am-11:45pm, Su noon-11:30pm. ❶

Johnny Foxes, 26 Bank St. (☎236 577). An Irish bar near the main bridge. Live music M-Sa and karaoke Su. Lunch served noon-3pm. Open M-Th 11am-1am, F-Sa 11am-1:30am, Su 12:30pm-midnight. ❶

Blackfriars, 93-95 Academy St. (☎233 881). Purists will appreciate its Scottish spirit: Scottish beer, Scottish whisky, and Scottish folk music (every night but Tu). Food served noon-7pm. Open M-W 11am-midnight, Th-Sa 11am-1am, Su 12:30-11pm. ❶

Glenalbyn, 2 Huntly St. (☎231 637). Soak up more Scottish pride and passion. Occasional live music. Open M-F 11am-1am, Sa 12:30pm-1am, Su 12:30-11pm. ❶

 SIGHTS

With the most popular sights 5 mi. south at the Loch, Inverness has nevertheless tried to snare its share of itinerant Nessie hunters. The interior of **Inverness Castle** is not open to the public, but a 40min. simulation tries to fill the void by recreating life in 1745, complete with a swearing sergeant recruiting volunteers for an army where men are paid 2p a day and women are affectionately called "baggage." (☎243 363; fax 710 755. Simulation Easter-Nov. M-F 10am-1pm and 2-4pm. £3, concessions £2.70, children £2, families £10.) Down the hill, the **Inverness Museum and Art Gallery,** in Castle Wynd, is of interest only for its stylized history of Inverness and its occasional modern art exhibition. A small collection of stuffed birds and animals complements the gallery. West of the TIC, across the river at Bridge St., **The Scottish Kiltmaker Visitor Centre,** 4-9 Huntly St., demonstrates plaid production and answers such burning questions as "how many pleats make it hang properly?" (☎222 781; www.hector-russell.com. Open mid-May to Sept. M-Sa 9am-9pm, Su 10am-5pm; Oct. to mid-May M-Sa 9am-5pm. £2, concessions £1.) **Leakey's Secondhand Bookshop,** at the northern end of Church St. in somber Greyfriar's Hall, claims to be Scotland's largest used bookstore. (☎239 947. Open M-Sa 10am-5:30pm.)

Upstream from the city center, over the Ness Bridge and 10min. along **Ness Walk,** the swift River Ness forks and forks again, forming the **Ness Islands**—narrow islets connected to the banks by small footbridges and blanketed with virgin forest. Picnic here in good weather, and listen to the gurgling river and chirping birds.

🎭 🌸 ENTERTAINMENT AND FESTIVALS

Eden Court Theatre, Bishops Rd., stages sophisticated productions, hosts dance and music shows, and screens films. (☎234 234; www.eden-court.co.uk. Tickets £4-35. Box office open M-Sa 10am-8:30pm.) Dolphins are sometimes spotted on **Moray Firth Cruises,** especially 3hr. before high tide (tidal information available at TIC). Boats leave from the Shore St. quay, downstream from the city center. (☎717 900. 1½hr.; Mar.-Oct. 6 per day; £10, concessions £8, children £7.50, families £36.)

In late July, strongmen hurl cabers during the **Inverness Highland Games** (☎724 264; tickets £3.50, concessions £2), while pipe-and-drum bands dominate the **Inverness Tattoo Festival** (☎235 571; tickets £3-5). In mid-August, the **Marymas Fair** recreates 19th-century street life with craft stalls, concerts, and proletarian strife. (☎715 760.) The **Northern Meeting,** a premier piping competition, comes to Eden Court in early September. (☎234 234; www.edon-court.co.uk. Tickets £16.)

🎒 DAYTRIPS FROM INVERNESS

Those planning to visit numerous spots in a day should invest in either Stagecoach Inverness **Off-Peak Rover** or Highland Country **Tourist Trail Day Rover** tickets. These allow unlimited bus travel to and from Inverness and sights like Culloden Battlefield, Cawdor Castle, Nairn, Fort George, and Castle Stuart. Buses leave from the Inverness bus station or Queensgate. (Both summer only. £6, concessions £4.)

CULLODEN BATTLEFIELD. Though barren, these fields are rich with history. In 1746, Bonnie Prince Charlie, charismatic but no genius in battle, lost 1200 men in a 40min. bloodbath, ending the Jacobite cause. A pretty 1½ mi. south, the stone circles and chambered cairns (mounds of rough stones) of the **Cairns of Clava** recall the Bronze Age. (Highland Country bus #12 (return £2) leaves from the post office at Queensgate. Visitor Centre ☎(01463) 790 607. Open Apr.-Oct. daily 9am-6pm; Nov.-Mar. 10am-4pm. Battlefield free. Centre £3.50, concessions £2.50. Guided tour of the battlefield £5/£3.75.)

CAWDOR CASTLE. The castle has been the residence of the Thane of Cawdor's descendants since the 15th century (long after Macbeth, the best-known Thane) and is still inhabited for much of the year. The late Lord Cawdor IV detailed its priceless items in a series of humorous and witty signs. Don't miss the garden maze, nature walks, and short-hole golf course. (Highland Country bus #12 (return £4.80) leaves from the post office at Queensgate. ☎(01667) 404 615. Open May-Sept. daily 10am-5pm. £6.10, concessions £5.10, children £3.30. Golf £6.)

MONIACK CASTLE. Built in 1580, the home of the hot-blooded Frasers, 7 mi. west of Inverness, still houses the family and their "fruity passions"—wines, liqueurs, and preserves. The castle itself is closed, but guided tours of the winery run every 20min. and culminate in a small tasting. (☎(01463) 831 283; fax 831 419. Open Mar.-Oct. M-Sa 10am-5pm; Nov.-Feb. M-Sa 11am-4pm. £2, children free.)

NEAR INVERNESS: DUNROBIN CASTLE

300 yd. north of Dunrobin station, 1½ mi. north of Golspie. Take a train from Inverness (2hr., 1 per day, £11.40) and request the stop. Stagecoach Inverness sends bus #25X (2hr., 2 per day, £6.50). Castle ☎(01408) 633 177. Open Apr. to mid-Oct. daily 10:30am-5:30pm. Last entry 5pm. £6.25, concessions £5.50, children £4.50, families £17.

The last remnant of aristocracy between Inverness and the northern ferry ports, ▨**Dunrobin Castle,** spectacularly perched above the sea, remains the largest house in the Highlands and offers an extravagant interior, elaborate grounds, and stunning views. Though sections of the mansion date to the 14th century, most of the architecture is ecstatically Victorian, redesigned at the turn of the 20th century in the Scottish Baronial style. Many of the castle's finest rooms are on display, and the ornate grounds, modeled after Versailles, are dramatically situated against the ocean. The castle's curious **museum** assembles a variety of aristocratic collectibles, from animal heads to Pictish stones. Outdoors, the **Falconry Display** allows visitors the opportunity to handle various birds of prey (3 shows per day).

Dunrobin is a bit of a long haul from Inverness, and an all-but-impossible daytrip for those without cars. You can, however, bunk for the night at the simple and relatively nearby **SYHA Helmsdale ❶,** in Helmsdale, 12 mi. from the castle and accessible by train and bus from both Dunrobin and Inverness. (☎(0143) 182 1577. Kitchen. Open Easter-Sept. £8.75, under 18 £7.50.)

LOCH NESS   ☎01456

Unfathomably mysterious, Loch Ness (5 mi. south of Inverness) guards its secrets well. In AD 565, St. Columba repelled a savage sea monster as it attacked a monk; whether a prehistoric leftover, giant seasnake, cosmic wanderer, or product of an overactive saintly imagination, the **Loch Ness monster** has captivated the world ever since. Shaped like a wedge, the loch is 700 ft. deep just 70 ft. from its edge. Its bottom caverns extend down so far that no one has definitively determined how vast it really is, or what life exists at its bottom.

The easiest way to see the loch is with one of the dime-a-dozen tour groups, three of which depart from the Inverness TIC. **Jacobite Cruises,** Tomnahurich Bridge, Glenurquhart Rd., whisks you around any number of ways, to Urquhart Castle or on coach and boat trips. (☎(01463) 233 999. £11-15, students £8.50-11; includes castle admission.) **Kenny's Tours** circles the loch on a minibus. (☎(01463) 252 411. Tours 10:30am-2:20pm and 2:30-5pm. £12.75, concessions £10.) **Guide Friday** runs a 3hr. bus and boat tour. (☎(01463) 224 000; www.guidefriday.com. May-Sept. daily 10:30am and 2:30pm. £14.50, concessions £11.50, children £6.50.) **Scottish Citylink** buses from Inverness to the Isle of Skye (#917, 2hr., 5-6 per day) and Fort William (#919, 2hr., 7-9 per day), which run along the northwest shore of the loch, are another option. A slew of **boat trips** leave from touristy Drumnadrochit, also on the northwest shore; most last 1hr. and cost £8-10.

In **Drumnadrochit,** 13 mi. south of Inverness on the northwest shore of the loch, not one but two visitor centers expound the Nessie legend. The **Original Loch Ness Visitors Centre** (☎450 342; open daily 9am-8pm) falls short, with a monstrous gift shop and a teensy exhibition (£5, concessions £3.50); the **Official Loch Ness Exhibition Centre,** with its 40min. audiovisual display (available in 17 languages) enhanced by smoke and lasers, is the better choice. (☎450 573; fax 450 770; www.loch-ness-scotland.com. Open July-Aug. daily 9am-8pm; June and Sept. 9am-6pm; Oct. 9:30am-5:30pm; Nov.-Easter 10am-5:30pm; Easter-May 9:30am-5pm. £6, concessions £4.50, children £3.50.) Three miles south on the A82, a new exhibition center, with 10min. film, small display, and, naturally, gift shop, completes the impressive, unforgettable ▨**Urquhart Castle** (URK-hart), one of the largest in Scotland before it was blown up in 1692 to prevent Jacobite occupation. Most tours from Inverness stop at the ruins and a number of Nessie photos have been fabricated there. (☎450 551. Open June-Aug. daily 9:30am-6:30pm; Apr.-May and Sept. daily 9:30am-5:45pm; Oct.-Mar. M-Sa 9:30am-3:45pm. £5, seniors £3.75, children £1.20.) The **Great Glen Cycle Route** careens past the loch on its way to Fort William. You can also **bike** along the eastern shore on the narrow B582. Eighteen miles down, the River Foyers empties into the loch in a series of idyllic waterfalls.

Near Drumnadrochit, the hip **Loch Ness Backpackers Lodge ❶,** Coiltie Farm House, East Lewiston, within walking distance of Loch Ness, is served by buses from Inverness (ask for Lewiston) and features cozy cabin-like rooms and a warm fireplace. (☎450 807; hostel@lochness-backpackers.com. Continental breakfast £1.50. Internet access £1 per 20min. 10am checkout. Dorms £9.50; doubles £25.) The more remote **SYHA Loch Ness ❶** stands alone on the loch's western shore, 7½ mi. south of the castle. (☎(01320) 351 274. Laundry £2. Internet £5 per hr. Open mid-Mar. to Oct. Reserve in advance July-Aug. Dorms £9.50-10.50, under 18 £8.25-9.25.) Both hostels lie on the Scottish Citylink bus routes between Inverness and Fort William (#919 and 917, every 2hr., £4.50 from Inverness).

GLEN AFFRIC AND GLEN CANNICH   ☎01456

West of Loch Ness, Glen Affric and Glen Cannich stretch toward the mountains amid one of Scotland's largest indigenous pine forests. Full of hiking opportunities, this remote area has been spared the throngs of tourists attracted by Nessie's tall tales, making it one of the best places to experience Scotland as it used to be.

The main access points for the glens are the villages of **Cannich,** at a turn in the A831, and **Tomich,** farther on. In summer, **Highland Country buses** (☎(01463) 233 371) run from **Inverness** to **Cannich** (1hr.; M-F 3 per day, Sa 1 per day), some extending to **Tomich** (M-F 2 per day). **Ross Minibuses** (☎(01463) 761 250) also run to Cannich from **Beauly** and **Inverness** twice a week and will extend the trip to Tomich upon request. Cannich's two **hostels** stand side by side in nearly identical brown buildings. From the Glen Affric Hotel, head south along the road lined with pine trees, away from the Spar. **Glen Affric Backpackers Hostel ❶** sleeps 70 in mostly double rooms—no bunks. The easygoing wardens are knowledgeable about the area. (☎(01456) 415 263. £7 per person.) With more rules and more expense, the **SYHA Cannich ❶** is a second choice. (☎415 244. Reception 7-10am and 5-11:30pm. Curfew 11:30pm. Open Apr.-Oct. Dorms £8.50, under 18 £7.25. Handicap-accessible.) Next door, the **Cannich Caravan & Camping Park ❶,** rents bikes. (☎415 364. Open Apr.-Oct. Bikes £7.50 per day. Tent pitch £3.50-6.50.) **Slater's Arms ❷,** on the northern end of town, just down the road to Glen Affric, serves standard meals for £4.50-8.25. (☎415 215. Open daily 9am-11pm.) The **Spar** next door is the only shop for miles, and contains the Cannich **post office.** (☎415 201. Open M-Sa 9am-7pm, Su 10am-6pm; post office M-Sa 9-noon.) **Post Code:** IV4 7LN.

Various walks into Glen Cannich depart from behind the Glen Affric Hotel, beside the bus stop. A 4 mi. walk or bike west on the forest road out of Cannich leads to the trailhead for the popular **Dog Falls Forest Walk** on the eastern edge of the **Glen Affric Caledonian Forest Reserve.** Passing by the waterfall, you'll get a good look at the heart of the 400-year-old pine forest, home to red deer, fox, adders, and otters. For more walks in Glen Affric, pick up *A Guide to Forest Walks and Trails: Glen Affric* (50p), or *Fifty Walks Extended to Sixty-Four* (£3), both available at Glen Affric Backpackers or any local hotel.

Tomich offers easier access to the more spectacular Glen Affric, including the breathtaking **Plodda Falls Walk.** Walk or bike 6 mi. east on the forest road out of Tomich to reach the trailhead. Your efforts won't go unrewarded—from a restored bridge spanning the gorge or from a viewing platform above, watch the narrow cascades of Plodda Falls crash 100 ft. down into the gorge below. To ease into the

THE BIG SPLURGE

BATTLE OF THE B&BS: FORT WILLIAM'S BEST AND BRIGHTEST

After a while, most British B&Bs start looking alike. (Particularly when you've seen as many as *Let's Go* has.) But on occasion, one or two really stand out from the crowd. Luxurious furnishings reminiscent of a fine hotel—and yet with a much more personal touch. An owner who seems to anticipate a guest's every need with style and sophistication. Rooms held to an unreal standard of cleanliness. Breakfasts that go well beyond the eggs-and-bacon routine.

Fort William has two such B&B superstars (both recipients of the tourist board's elusive five stars). Their in-own location may be nothing special, but this is bed and breakfast done right—feather-soft beds and fresh flowers in big white-washed Victorian houses, buffered by large swaths of lawn leading up from the street.

The Grange (☎705 516; fax 701 595) and **Crolinnhe** (☎702 709; fax 700 506) are both on Grange Rd. and both open from March through November. At The Grange, which is slightly more formal, you'll breakfast on fine crystal and china. One of its four double rooms runs £86-96 per night. Crolinnhe has a marginally more relaxed feel, only three rooms, and offers single (£76-80) as well as double accommodation (£86-110).

wilderness or back to civilization, stay where sleeping dogs laid—the birthplace of the Golden Retriever at **The Kennels ❸**, 1 mi. west of Tomich on the road to Plodda Falls. Spacious rooms, convenient location, friendly owners, and historic flair mix in a countryside setting. (☎415 400. Singles £25; doubles and twins £20.) The hardy should continue another 3 mi. west to the (extremely) basic **Cougie Lodge ❶**. (☎415 459. Open Apr.-Sept. Dorms £8; camping £5.) Farther in the same direction, the remote but popular **SYHA Glen Affric**, Alltbeithe, is little more than a cabin buried in the mountains, located where trails to Tomich, Ratagan, and Clunie cross. Call the SYHA central reservations line (☎(08701) 553 255) or ask the warden at SYHA Cannich for exact directions. (No phone, showers, laundry, or garbage bin. Open Apr.-Oct. Dorms £9.50, under 18 £8.25.) Bring a sleeping bag when staying at either of these hostels. Ordnance Survey Map Landranger #25 will help you navigate the Glen Affric area successfully.

FORT WILLIAM AND BEN NEVIS   ☎01397

In 1654, General Monck built the town of Fort William among Britain's highest peaks to keep out "savage clans and roving barbarians." Having since let down its guard, today's Fort William is a major center of Highlands tourism. The setting, on the banks of Loch Linnhe, is spectacular, though the town's unappealing layout makes rather poor use of it. No matter—the nearby wilderness easily steals the show. This is the favored base camp for climbs up Ben Nevis, Britain's tallest mountain, and is also convenient to the beautiful Glen Coe valley.

▮ TRANSPORTATION

The **train station** is just beyond the north end of High St. Trains (☎(08457) 484 950) arrive from **Glasgow Queen St.** (3¾hr.; M-Sa 3 per day, Su 2 per day; £18) and **Mallaig** (1½ hr.; M-Sa 4-5 per day, Su 1-3 per day; £7.40) on the magnificent ▧**West Highland Railway.** Built at the turn of the last century, the rail line is a triumph of Victorian engineering, crossing glens, moors, and rivers, and skirting some of Scotland's best scenery. An overnight sleeper train runs to **London Euston** (12hr., 1 per day, £70-96.50). **Buses** arrive next to the Safeway by the train station. **Scottish Citylink** (☎(08705) 505 050) trundles in from: **Edinburgh** (3¾hr., 2 per day, £15.20); **Glasgow** (3hr., 4 per day, £11.90); **Inverness** (2hr., 5-6 per day, £7.20); **Kyle of Lochalsh** (2hr., 3 per day, £10.70); and **Oban** (1½hr., M-Sa 2-4 per day, £6.90). On weekdays, Scottish Citylink/Shiel sends a bus to **Mallaig** (1½hr., M-F 1 per day, £5.70).

Highland Country Buses (☎ 702 373) operates local services. From June to September, #42 departs from the bus station and heads up Glen Nevis to the SYHA hostel and the Ben Nevis trailhead (M-Sa 11 per day, Su 4 per day; £1.10). Bus #45 runs to Corpach from the carpark on Middle St. behind the post office (15min.; M-Sa 3 per hr., Su every hr.; 85p). **Taxis** queue outside the Tesco on High St.; **Alba Taxi** (☎ 701 112) is on-call 24hr. Rent cycles at **Offbeat Bikes,** 117 High St. (☎ 704 008. £10 per half-day, £15 per day. Open M-Sa 9am-5:30pm, Su 10am-5pm.)

🛈 PRACTICAL INFORMATION

From the bus and train stations, an underpass leads to the north end of pedestrianized **High St.,** Fort William's main street. The friendly **tourist information centre,** in Cameron Sq., just off High St., **exchanges currency.** (☎ 703 781. Open mid-July to Aug. M-Sa 9am-8:30pm, Su 9am-6pm; Sept.-Oct. M-Sa 9am-6pm, Su 10am-5:30pm; Nov.-Mar. M-Sa 9am-5pm, Su 10am-4pm; Mar. to mid-June M-Sa 9am-6pm, Su 10am-4pm; mid-June to mid-July M-Sa 9am-7pm, Su 10am-6pm.) **Banks** are on High St. Fort William keeps hikers happy with its outdoors shops; **Nevisport** is at the north end of High St. (☎ 704 921. Hiking and climbing boots £3.50-7.50 per day plus deposit. Open June-Sept. daily 9am-7pm; Oct.-May M-Sa 9am-5:30pm, Su 9:30am-5pm.) Get **Internet access** at the TIC (£2 per 20min., £5 per hr.). The **police** are at the southern end of High St., where you'll find the **mountain rescue post** (☎ 702 361). The **post office** is at 5 High St. (☎ 702 827. Open M-F 9am-5:30pm, Sa 9am-12:30pm.) **Post Code:** PH33 6AR.

🛏 ACCOMMODATIONS

Fort William's accommodations fill up in summer—you'll want to book ahead. Some popular area **hostels** are outside of town. You'll find plenty of **B&Bs** uphill from the train station and the northern end of High St., particularly on **Fassifern Rd.** and **Alma Rd.,** and another cluster just south of town center, near the shore on **Achintore Rd.** and **Grange Rd.**

🏛 **Farr Cottage Lodge and Activity Centre** (☎ 772 315), on the A830 in Corpach. Take Highland Country bus #45 from Fort William. Probably the most atmospheric and comfortable hostel in the area. Comfortable rooms with 4-10 beds and TVs. Congenial staff; activities include history lessons and whisky talks. For a small fee, staff will drive guests to outdoor activities sites. Internet access. Continental breakfast £2. Laundry and kitchen. Dorms £11; cheaper for longer stays. ❷

Fort William Backpackers Guest House, Alma Rd. (☎ 700 711). A 5min. walk from the train station; bear right onto Belford Rd. and head away from the town center. Turn right on Alma Rd. after the hospital and go left at the split; it's uphill on your right. This snug, friendly 38-bed hostel has a convenient location and excellent mountain views. Mac-Backpackers tour buses pull in here. Continental breakfast £1.60. Curfew 2am. Dorms £11; off season £10. ❷

Ben Nevis Bunkhouse, Achintee Farm (☎ 702 240), across the river from the Glen Nevis Visitor Centre, very convenient for climbing Ben Nevis. Take Highland Country bus #42 from Fort William. Sleeps 24 in a 200-year-old barn with full kitchen and bathing facilities. Cafe and Internet access. Lockout 10:30am-4pm. Dorms £9.50-12. ❶

SYHA Glen Nevis (☎ 702 336), 3 mi. east of town on the Glen Nevis road, across from the trail up Ben Nevis; take Highland Country bus #42. Large, straightforward hostel. Continental breakfast included. Reception 24hr. Bedroom lockout 9:30am-12:30pm. Dorms £10-12, under 18 £8.50-10.50. ❷

Bank Street Lodge Bunkhouse, Bank St. (☎ 700 070). Lovely, lazy in-town location; walk 1 block uphill from the post office. No-frills dorm accommodation (singles and doubles available). Small kitchen and TV lounge. Dorms £10-11. ❷

Rhu Mhor Guest House, Alma Rd. (☎ 702 213). A variety of single, double, and triple rooms, on a quiet street with fantastic sunset views over the Nevis Range. Open April-Oct. Book ahead July-Aug. £16-24 per person. ❷

Glen Nevis Caravan & Camping Park (☎ 702 191), on the Glen Nevis road, ½ mi. before the SYHA hostel. Award-winning and highly recommended. Open mid-Mar. to Oct. 2-person tent £7.10, with car £12; less in off season. Showers free. ❶

📷🍴 FOOD AND PUBS

Before striking for the hills, get a packed lunch (£3) at the **Nevis Bakery,** 49 High St. (☎ 704 101), or forage for nuts and berries (and Cadbury Dairy Milk bars) at the **Tesco** supermarket at the north end of High St. (open M-Sa 8am-9pm, Su 9am-6pm). The ground floor of **McTavish's Kitchen ❶,** 100 High St., and the similar **McTavish's Garrison Restaurant ❶,** on the northern end of High St., whip up inexpensive self-service fare, mostly traditional Scottish. (☎ 702 406. Entrees £4-5. Open summer daily 9am-10pm; winter 9am-6pm.) Find Fort William's best dining at the pricey ▧**Crannog Seafood Restaurant ❸,** with a superb location on the town pier and top-notch seafood. (☎ 705 589. Entrees £10-15. Open noon-2:30pm and from 6pm.) Follow the crowd to one of Fort William's few hot nightspots, the justifiably popular **Ben Nevis Bar ❶,** 103-109 High St., which has live music at least once a week. (☎ 702 295. Open M-Sa 11am-12:15am, Su 12:30pm-12:15am; food served noon-10pm.)

🎦🎵 SIGHTS AND ENTERTAINMENT

In Fort William town proper, the only notable sight is the **West Highland Museum,** next to the TIC in Cameron Sq., a rustic treasure with a room full of taxidermy, displays on the mountaineering of yore, and a stirring Bonnie Prince Charlie exhibit. (☎ 702 169. Open M-Sa 10am-5pm; July-Aug. also Su 2-5pm; shorter off-season hours. £2, concessions £1.50, children 50p.) **Seal Island Cruises,** on the town pier, offers 1½hr. boat trips on Loch Linnhe. (☎ 700 714. Apr.-Oct. 4 sailings daily, during peak season also dinner cruise. £6, children £3.) Rock jocks staying in nearby **Corpach** might visit **Treasures of the Earth,** for its fine collection of minerals, gemstones, crystals, and fossils. (☎ 772 283. Open July-Sept. daily 9:30am-7pm; Feb.-June and Oct.-Dec. 10am-5pm. £3, seniors £2.75, children £1.50.)

🧗🏔 HIKING AND OUTDOOR ACTIVITIES

BEN NEVIS. On the 65 days per year that the highest peak in Britain (4406 ft.) deigns to lift its veil of cloud, the unobstructed view spans along Scotland's western coast and all the way to Ireland. The tourist trail up the peak may be well-trodden, but this is not a walk for novices. Essential supplies include an Ordnance Survey **map** (Landranger #41), a compass, sturdy hiking boots (no trainers at Club Nevis), very warm clothing, waterproof gear, food, and water. The hike up takes generally takes around 3-4hr.; the descent 2-3hr. (The round-trip record, set during September's annual **Ben Nevis Race,** is an incredible 82min.) Leave yourself a full 8½hr. of daylight for the 9½ mi. round-trip, check the latest weather before setting out, and be sure to **tell someone your plans.** You can also register with the **mountain rescue post,** at the police station in town (see above). Check with the TIC and local outdoors shops for more info, and see also **Wilderness Safety,** p. 49.

The walk up Ben Nevis starts in **Glen Nevis**—a gorgeous glacial valley about 1½ mi. from Fort William and well worth a look even if you aren't attempting the climb. The **Glen Nevis Visitor Centre** provides info on Ben Nevis and its surroundings. (Open June-Sept. daily 9am-6pm; Apr.-May and Oct. 9am-5pm.) One path to the summit leaves from near Achintee Farm and the Visitor Centre; another from the Glen Nevis SYHA (see above). These two paths join after about a mile. There are several much shorter walks in Glen Nevis; the Visitor Centre or the Fort William TIC can provide leaflets and details. Highland Country **bus** #42 (June-Sept. only) travels to Glen Nevis from town.

NEVIS RANGE SKI AREA. Nevis Range, 7 mi. northeast of Fort William on the slopes of **Aonach Mor** (4006 ft.), is Scotland's highest ski area (if not as large as the one on Cairn Gorm). Throughout the year, Nevis Range's **gondola** propels the lazy man 2150 ft. up to a restaurant, superb views, and hiking trails. (☎705 825. July-Aug. Th-F 9:30am-9pm, Sa-W 9:30am-6pm; Sept. to mid-Nov. and mid-Dec. to June daily 10am-5pm. Return £6.90, children £4.15.) During the summer the lack of snowcover reveals marked **mountain bike trails;** you can rent bikes at the gondola station. During ski season and from July to September, Highland Country **bus** #42A travels to Nevis Range from Fort William (10min.; M-Sa 4 per day, Su 3 per day).

OTHER ACTIVITIES. The **Great Glen Cycle Route** (map available from TICs) runs 80 mostly off-road miles from Fort William to Inverness. Extreme types bored after their conquest of Ben Nevis will find plenty of **adventure sports** offered around Fort William, from canyoning on Inchree Falls to river rafting to hang gliding. Outdoors shops, hostels, and TICs can point adrenaline junkies in the right direction.

GLEN COE ☎01855

Stunning in any weather, Glen Coe is best seen in the rain, when a web of mist laces the valley's innumerable rifts and small silvery waterfalls spill into the River Coe. Only on rare days is the view marred by shining sun—the glen records over 100 inches of rain every year. Glen Coe is infamous as the site of a 1692 massacre, when the Clan MacDonald welcomed a company of Campbell soldiers, henchmen of William III, into their chieftain's home. After enjoying the MacDonalds' hearthside for over a week, the soldiers proceeded to slaughter their hosts, violating the age-old tradition that makes Highland hospitality sacred. Yet neither rain nor bloody history deters hikers and skiers from passing time in this beautiful valley.

◧⊠ TRANSPORTATION AND PRACTICAL INFORMATION. Glencoe village, essentially a single street, rests at the edge of **Loch Leven,** at the mouth of the River Coe and the western end of the Glen Coe valley. The A82 (bound for Glasgow) runs the length of the valley, and **Scottish Citylink buses** (☎(08705) 505 050) between Fort William and Glasgow (4 per day) are a good way to access the valley. A **postbus** (☎(02146) 546 329; M-Sa, call for times) runs from the Fort William post office to some of the more remote parts of Glen Coe. **Highland Country** bus #44 serves Glencoe village from Fort William's Middle St. (30min.; M-Sa 9 per day). For bike rental, try **Mountain Bike Hire,** at the Clachaig Inn, across the river from the Visitor Centre. (☎811 252. £8.50 per half-day, £12 per day.)

The new **Glen Coe Visitor Centre,** off the A82 about 1 mi. south of Glencoe village, has films and extensive displays on the history and natural features of the area. (☎811 307. Open May-Oct. daily 10am-6pm. £3.50, concessions £2.60.) The **Spar** supermarket is the hub of the Glencoe universe, with an **ATM** and **post office.** (☎811 367. Store open M-Sa 8am-9pm, Su 9am-5pm. Post office open M-Tu and Th-F 9am-12:30pm and 1:30-5:30pm, W and Sa 9am-12:30pm.)

ACCOMMODATIONS AND FOOD. The agreeable clapboard **SYHA Glencoe** ❶ rests 1½ mi. southeast of Glencoe village on the minor road into the valley. The 62 beds fill up fast. (☎811 219. Laundry and Internet access. Curfew midnight. Dorms £9-10.50, under 18 £6-9.25.) If you get to the hostel and find it full, backtrack 500 yd. to the white-walled **Leacantium Farm Bunkhouse** ❶. The farm maintains three bunkhouses, from the basic Alpine barn to the super-cozy Ben End suite. (☎811 256. £6.50-7.50 per person, £45 per week.) Follow the painted white rocks to the farm's riverside **Red Squirrel Camp Site** ❶. (£4.50 per person. Showers 50p.) **Clachaig Inn** ❸ is a family-run B&B with views of nearby summits and an attached restaurant. It's in the valley, about 3 mi. southeast of Glencoe; take the minor road from the village or walk across the river from the A82. (☎811 679. £22-36 per person.) The Inn's **public bar** ❷, a lively gathering point and traditional trail's-end pub, also serves the area's best food (£6-10), including some vegetarian dishes. A sign outside bans Campbells on the premises. (☎811 252. Open Su-Th 11am-11pm, F 11am-midnight, Sa 11am-11:30pm; food served noon-9pm.)

HIKING AND ACTIVITIES. Glen Coe provides a range of challenges. Walkers stroll the floor of the magnificent cup-shaped valley, climbers head for the cliffs, and wintertime ice-climbers hack their way up frozen waterfalls. Reaching the trailheads, most several miles beyond Glencoe village in the middle of the valley, requires careful planning or a car. With the right timing, you can use the Scottish Citylink **buses** that travel up the A82. For a small fee, most area hostels will shuttle hikers to the trailheads. Low-impact **camping** is permitted near trails.

The **Coire Nan Lochan** will take you to the summits of the **Three Sisters**, Glen Coe's most distinctive peaks. Well-equipped, sure-footed hikers prepared to use hands, knees, and hindquarters can scramble up the 3766 ft. **Bidean nam Bian** or try the 4 mi. traverse of the **Aonach Eagach** ridge on the north side of the glen. Saner walkers can find the **Lost Valley,** once called the Coire Gubhail ("Corrie of Plunder") because the MacDonalds hid pilfered goods there. The trail follows the stream on the south side of the glen, just west of the Coe Gorge (3hr. round-trip). You can avoid the 1000 ft. climb by taking the **Glen Coe Ski Centre Chairlift,** off the A82 in the middle of Glen Coe. (☎851 226. Open June-Aug. daily 9:30am-4:30pm, weather permitting. £4, seniors £3, children £2.50, families £11. During ski season, daily lift pass £17.50, children £9.50.) When the weather behaves, **Glencoe Cruises & Fishing Trips** (☎811 658) scud across Loch Leven, leaving from the pier in **Ballachulish,** west of Glencoe village, where all buses to Glencoe stop.

ROAD TO THE ISLES

The Road to the Isles (Rathad Iarainn nan Eilean, now the A830), originally traveled by crofters to sell their wares in the larger towns, traverses breathtaking mountains and deep valley lochs on its journey from Fort William to Mallaig. A ride on the **West Highland Railway,** a portion of the ScotRail service running from Glasgow to Mallaig, offers sublime panoramas at a fast clip (3-4 per day, £7.40). In summer, "The Jacobite" steam train chugs from **Fort William** to **Mallaig** (via **Glenfinnan**) in the morning and back in the afternoon; on a rainy day, you won't miss much by taking the cheaper, modern version. (☎(01524) 732 100. Mid-June to Aug. 1 per day. Return £23, children £13. BritRail passes not valid.) **Buses** make the same trip once per day (1½hr.; M-F, July-Sept. also Sa; £5.40).

GLENFINNAN. The road sets off westward from Fort William along Loch Eil, arriving after 12 mi. at spectacular Glenfinnan, on the head of **Loch Shiel**. Trains often stop along the photogenic, trestle-bridged **Glenfinnan Viaduct** to give passengers a sentimental gaze. A **monument** recalls August 19, 1745, the day Bonnie Prince Charlie rowed up Loch Shiel and rallied the clans around the Stewart standard to signal the onset of the "Forty-Five" (see **The Jacobite Rebellion**, p. 540). After you climb the narrow spiral staircase and squeeze through the hatch at the top, a knee-high railing is all that lies between you and the end of your trip—mind the drop. A worthy **Visitor Centre** provides the accompanying history lesson and postcards. (☎ (01397) 722 250. Open mid-May to Aug. daily 9:30am-6pm; Sept.-Oct. and Apr. to mid-May 10am-5pm. £1.50, concessions £1.) Walk up the path just behind the Centre for excellent views of monument, viaduct, and loch. If you're feeling lazy, drift on **Loch Shiel Cruises** as far as **Acharacle**, at the loch's far shore. Trips depart from the Glenfinnan House Hotel, up the road from the Visitor Centre. (☎ (01397) 722 235. 2-2½hr.; departs June-Sept. Tu and Th-F 10:45am, W and Su 2pm; Easter-May and Oct. Th-F 2pm. £10-16, children half-price.)

By **train**, Glenfinnan is 30min. from Fort William (£3.90) and 50min. from Mallaig (£5); by **bus** the trips are roughly the same length (£2.50 and £4). ◼**Glenfinnan Sleeping Car** ❶, a vintage railway-car-turned-hostel at the train station, provides a unique bed. (☎ (01397) 722 295. Bedding £2. Bunk £8.) For a twilight loch view, eat at the **Glenfinnan House Hotel** ❷ pub. (☎ (01397) 722 235. Open M-W 11am-midnight, Th-Sa 11am-1am, Su noon-midnight.)

ARISAIG AND LOCH MORAR. The road finally meets the west coast at the sandy beaches of Arisaig. **Murdo Grant** (☎ (01687) 450 224) operates regular ferries and day cruises from Arisaig to **Rum, Eigg,** and **Muck** and sends charter boats to **Skye, Mull,** and **Canna** (see p. 650). The trips allow for a few hours on the island of your choice. **Dr. Ian Pragnell** rents **bikes** and willingly shares his knowledge of local cycling routes. (☎ (01687) 450 272. £5 per half-day, £10 per day.) For local knowledge and hospitality, stay at **Camus Morar** ❸, a 10min. walk from the A830 in **Morar,** a lochside village halfway between Arisaig and Morar. (☎ (01687) 460 007. Singles £20; doubles and twins £15.) A 3 mi. walk south along the A830 from Arisaig leads to the placid **Camusdarach campsite** ❶, near the beach. (☎ (01687) 450 221. Laundry 50p. £5 per tent; £1 per person. Showers free with £5 key deposit.) Across the road and down a short footpath from the campsite, brilliant white **beaches** afford views of the Inner Hebrides. Rocky outcrops cut across the sand, creating secluded beach coves accessible only by foot. Another fine walk westward follows the banks of **Loch Morar,** Britain's deepest freshwater loch (1017 ft.), complete with a monster named Morag, cousin (by marriage) to a certain Nessie.

MALLAIG   ☎01687

Past Morar sits the relative metropolis of Mallaig (MAL-egg), a fishing village where the railway terminates and where cruises and ferries leave for the Inner Hebrides. **Bruce Watt** (☎ 462 320) runs ferries and day cruises from Mallaig along lovely Loch Nevis to **Tarbet** and **Inverie** (M, W, F; June to mid-Sept. also Tu and Th; £6-13). The only village on mainland Great Britain disconnected from all roads, Inverie sits on the wild **Knoydart Peninsula,** emptied by the Clearances. **CalMac** (☎ 462 403) skips from Mallaig to **Armadale, Skye** (M-Sa 7 per day; June-Aug. also Su 6 per day; £2.90, 5-day return £4.90) and to the **Small Isles.**

If you're land-bound, fill time in town with a visit to **Mallaig Marine World.** You can pet the tops of rays, but avoid their toothy undersides. (☎ 462 292. Open Apr.-Oct. M-Sa 9am-6pm, Su noon-6pm; Nov.-Mar. M-Sa 9am-6pm. £2.75, concessions £2, children £1.50, families £7.50.) The **tourist information centre** is on the waterfront just to the north of the pier. (☎ 462 170. Open July-Aug. M-Sa 9am-8pm, Su 10am-6pm; Apr.-June and Sept.-Oct. daily 10am-6pm; Nov.-Mar. M, W, F 9am-2pm.) Other services include: a **Bank of Scotland,** near the train station (☎ 462 370; open M-Tu and Th-F 9:15am-1pm and 2-4:45pm, W 10am-1pm and 2-4:45pm); **Internet**

access across the street in the **Lochaber College Library** (☎ 460 097; open M 1-5pm, Tu 10am-2pm, W 9:30am-1:30pm, Th 5-8pm, Sa 10am-noon); and the **post office,** in the **Spar,** uphill from Sheena's (☎ 462 419; post office open M-F 9am-5:30pm, Sa 9am-1pm; store open M-Sa 8am-10pm, Su 9:30am-9pm). **Post Code:** PH41 4PU.

Sheena's Backpackers Lodge ❷ fills fast after early train and ferry arrivals in summer, so book ahead. Turn right from the station, and the hostel is past the bank, above the restaurant. (☎ 462 764. Dorms £10.) For more private luxury, continue down the street to the plush **Moorings Guest House ❸,** and ask for a room with a harbor view. (☎ 462 225. £16-20 per person.) The **Fisherman's Mission Cafeteria ❶,** across from the train station, serves cheap, filling grub, including a £4 lasagna with chips and peas. (☎ 462 086. Open M-F 8:30am-10pm, Sa 8:30am-noon; food served M-F 8:30am-1:45pm and 5:30-10pm.) For delicious seafood, head to the **Fishmarket Restaurant ❷,** where they serve up a heaping plate of fish 'n' chips (£6) right in front of the pier. (☎ 462 299. Open daily noon-9:30pm.)

THE INNER HEBRIDES

THE SMALL ISLES   ☎ 01687

Rising from a watery horizon, they form silent gray-green silhouettes—remote, rugged, and seemingly uninhabited. Lacking vehicle-landing facilities and almost untouched by tourism, **Rum, Eigg, Muck,** and **Canna** often require their visitors to jump from their ferry to a small dinghy before setting foot on solid land. Those who make the trip are rewarded with a true taste of island life—jalopies and tractors cruise the roads instead of tourist caravans, electricity is provided by generators, and uninterrupted coastline stretches as far as the eye can see.

CalMac (☎ 462 403) sails from **Mallaig** to Rum, Eigg, Muck, Canna, and back. There are non-landing trips (M-Th 10:30am, F 8:45am and 12:50pm, Sa 6:20am and 1:40pm; £13) and trips that allow time on shore. (**Eigg** M-Tu and Th 10:30am, F 8:45am, Sa 6:20am and 1:40pm; 5-day return £8.55. **Muck** Tu and Th 10:30am, F 8:45am, Sa 6:20am and 1:40pm; 5-day return £13.15. **Rum** and **Canna** M and W 10:30am, F 12:50pm, Sa 6:20am and 1:40pm; 5-day return £12.70-14.15.) For day-trips, look into the more cruise-oriented **Murdo Grant** (☎ 450 224), sailing Easter to September at 11am from **Arisaig** (p. 649) to: **Rum** (Tu and Th, June-Aug. also Sa-Su; return £19, children £9); **Eigg** (daily; return £15/£6); **Muck** (M, W, F; return £15/£6). Murdo Grant also runs summer cruises to **Canna** by request.

RUM. Rum (often spelled Rhum) is the most astounding of the Small Isles, with a mountainous majesty that rivals even neighboring Skye. The largest of the Small Isles, Rum is entirely owned by the National Trust and carefully managed by Scottish Natural Heritage. Deer, highland cattle, golden eagles, and migrating Manx shearwater birds are the main inhabitants; the entire human population emigrated in 1826 during the Clearances. The grand total of full-time residents has today risen to 25. The locals are infectiously friendly, and the island is covered with well-marked hiking trails; the **Loch Scresort Trail** (6hr. round-trip) is most popular. A wealthy Lancashire mill owner built lavish **Kinloch Castle** in 1901 as a private resort. (☎ 462 037. Excellent tours daily in summer, £3.) Because ferry daytrips leave very little time, only an overnight stay can do the island justice—sleep at the back of the castle in **Kinloch Castle Hostel ❷.** (☎ 462 037; advance booking required. £12 per person.) To **camp** on Rum (pitch £1.50), obtain prior permission from the Chief Warden, Scottish Natural Heritage, Isle of Rum PH43 4RR (☎ 462 026).

EIGG. Eigg (pop. 78) shelters the largest human community of the Small Isles amid vertical cliffs, sandy beaches, and green hills. St. Donnan and 52 companions were martyred by the warrior women of the pagan Queen of Moidart at **Kildonnan** in 617; almost a thousand years later, the island's entire population (all 395 Mac-Donalds) were slaughtered by rival MacLeods in **Massacre Cave.** In the summer, ranger John Chester offers weekly **guided walks** from the pier that reveal the island's bloody history. (☎482 477. £3.) A minibus also meets each ferry for a trip across the island to the **Singing Sands,** a perfect beach that sounds out under your footsteps (M-Sa, some Su; return £3). For **bike hire,** look for the shed just north of the grocery store. (☎482 469. £5 per half-day, £10 per day.) If you call ahead, you can stay at the remarkably modern **Glebe Barn ❶.** (☎482 417. Dorms £9.50; twins £22.) For B&B, the best value is **Laig Farm Guest House ❸,** nestled in a private valley with a nearby beach. (☎482 412. £30 per person.) The hostel is 1 mi. from the pier, and the guest house is another 3 mi. beyond. (**Taxis** ☎482 494. £1.50.)

MUCK AND CANNA. Muck, the teensy (1½ mi. by 5 mi.) southernmost isle, is an experiment in communal living. The entire island is a single farm owned by the MacEwens, who handle farming, transport along the Muck 1 road, and shopping on the mainland. Stay at **Port Mor Guest House ❹** (☎462 365; B&B with dinner £35). If you intend to muck about outside, bring food, as supplies are available only sporadically. The miniature isle of **Canna** (Gaelic for "porpoise") offers a few miles of trails for hikers and seabird enthusiasts, but no shops or budget accommodations.

ISLE OF SKYE

Skye is often raining, but also fine: hardly embodied; semi-transparent; like living in a jellyfish lit up with green light. Remote as Samoa; deserted, prehistoric.
—postcard from Virginia Woolf

Often described as the shining jewel in the Hebridean crown, Skye possesses unparalleled natural beauty—from the serrated peaks of the Cuillin Hills to the rugged tip of the Trotternish Peninsula. The island's charms are by no means a secret, as the endless procession of vehicles on the Skye Bridge attests. But most visitors keep to the main roads, and vast swaths of terrain remain unscarred. As elsewhere in the Highlands, the 19th-century Clearances saw entire glens emptied of their ancient settlements, and today, northern migration pushes the English population of Skye toward 40%. Nonetheless, the island resists pandering to tourists. Skye has no fast food chains, only three 24hr. ATMs (in Kyle of Lochalsh, Portree, and Broadford), and a strong Gaelic influence that reveals itself in genealogy centers, bilingual signs, and local music events. Though spotty public transportation may force you to concentrate your travels, Skye's lovely wilds and folk culture ensure that you won't be disappointed.

☾ GETTING THERE

The tradition of ferries carrying passengers "over the sea to Skye" ended with the **Skye Bridge,** which links the island to the mainland's **Kyle of Lochalsh. Trains** (☎(08457) 484 950) arrive at Kyle from **Inverness** (2½hr.; M-Sa 4 per day, Su 2 per day; £15). **Skye-Ways** (☎(01599) 534 328), in conjunction with **Scottish Citylink,** runs **buses** daily from: **Fort William** (2hr., 3 per day, £11); **Glasgow** (5½hr., 3 per day, £19); **Inverness** (2½hr., 2 per day, £10.90). **Pedestrians** can traverse the Skye Bridge's 1½ mi. footpath or take the **shuttle bus** (2 per hr., £1.70). **Cars** no longer wait in ferry lines, but the one-way bridge toll is a weighty £5.70.

From the Outer Hebrides, **Caledonian MacBrayne** ferries sail to **Uig** from **Tarbert** on Harris or **Lochmaddy** on North Uist (1½hr.; M-Sa 1-2 per day; £8.70, 5-day return £14.90; cars £41.50/£71). Ferries also run to **Armadale** in southwestern Skye from **Mallaig** on the mainland (30min.; M-Sa 4 per day, June-Aug. also Su; £2.90, 5-day return £4.90; cars £16/£27.50). For reservations and schedules, call the offices in Tarbert (☎ (01859) 502 444) or Mallaig (☎ (01687) 462 403).

█ LOCAL TRANSPORTATION

Touring Skye without a car takes either effort or cash. To avoid headaches and long unplanned hikes along the highway, pick up the handy *Public Transport Guide to Skye and the Western Isles* (£1) at any TIC.

Buses: Buses on Skye are run by different operators; cherish your transport guide, and be careful not to pay twice when making connections, which are infrequent and some-what pricey (Kyleakin-Uig £8.50; Kyleakin-Armadale £5.50). The only reliable service hugs the coast from Kyleakin to Broadford to Portree on the A87. On **Sundays,** nothing runs except **Skye Ways/Scottish Citylink** and the buses that meet the Armadale ferry.

Biking: Cycling is possible, but be prepared for steep hills, nonexistent shoulders, and rain. Most buses will not carry bikes. To **rent** bikes in Kyleakin, try the **Dun Caan Hostel** (☎ (01599) 534 087; £10 per day); in Broadford, **Fairwinds Cycle Hire** (☎ (01471) 822 270; £7 per day, £5 deposit); in Portree, **Island Cycles** (☎ (01478) 613 121; £10-12 per day); and in Uig, **Uig Cycle Hire** (☎ (01470) 542311; £12 per day).

Car Rental: Sutherland's Garage (☎ (01471) 822 225), Broadford. 21+. Free collection at Kyleakin. From £33 per day; £450 deposit. **MacRaes Car Hire** (☎ (01478) 612 554), Portree. 21+. From £32 per day. £100 deposit or credit card.

Tours: Scottish National Heritage and the Highland Council Ranger Service offer free **walking tours** (☎ (01599) 524 270). For the eager and adventurous, the fantastic ▨**MacBackpackers Skye Trekker Tour,** departing from Kyleakin, offers a 1-day tour emphasizing the mystical-historical side of the island or a 2-day, eco-conscious hike into the Cuillin Hills, with all necessary gear provided plus 1 dinner and £5 for camping grub. (☎ (01599) 534 510, call ahead. Weekly departures Tu 7:30am. 1-day £15, 2-day £45.) For personalized treks, call **A1** in Portree. (☎ (01478) 611 112. £18 per hr.)

Hitchhiking: A very common practice, although one should always consider the risks involved.

♪ ▧ ENTERTAINMENT AND FESTIVALS

Skye's cultural life is vigorous. Snag a copy of the weekly *What, Where, and When* leaflet or *The Visitor* newspaper for a list of special events and check out postings in TICs. Traditional music in both English and Gaelic is abundant, and dances—half folk, half rock—take place frequently in village halls, usually after 11pm. In mid-July, **Feis an Eilein** (☎ (01471) 844 207), on the Sleat Peninsula, is a ten-day celebration of Gaelic culture featuring concerts, *ceilidhs*, workshops, and films. Additional revelry is to be found at the **Highland Games** (☎ (01478) 612 540), a day of bagpipes and boozing in Portree on the first Wednesday of August, and **Highland Ceilidh,** featuring *ceilidhs* in Portree, Broadford, and Dunvegan (☎ (01470) 542 228; June M and W, July-Aug. M-W). Contact a Skye TIC for information.

KYLE OF LOCHALSH AND KYLEAKIN ☎01599

Like a pair of afterthoughts, Kyle of Lochalsh ("Kyle" for short) and Kyleakin (Ky-LAACK-in) bookend the Skye Bridge. The former, on the mainland, has a train station, TIC, and ATM, making it of practical value to travelers. The latter has better capitalized on its fortuitous position—Kyleakin is young and boisterous, a back-packers' hub with three hostels and countless tours.

⊡☎ TRANSPORTATION AND PRACTICAL INFORMATION. The Kyle **train station** is near the pier, and the **bus stop** is just to the west. Highland Country buses meet incoming trains and head for Kyleakin (every 30min., £1.70). The Kyle **tourist information centre**, overlooking the pier from the hill, houses a free phone for accommodations booking. (Open May-Oct. M-Sa 9am-5:30pm.) Other services include: the **last ATM** for miles at Kyle's **Bank of Scotland**, Main St. (☎534 2200; open M-Tu and Th-F 9am-5pm, W 9:30am-5pm); **Internet access** at the chip shop in Kyleakin (open Tu-Sa 5-9:30pm, Su 5-8pm); and the **post office** next door, which sells Citylink bus tickets (☎(08457) 223 344; open M-F 9am-5:30pm, Sa 9am-12:30pm). **Post Code:** IV40 8AA.

☶ ACCOMMODATIONS. In Kyle of Lochalsh, **Cu'chulainn's Backpackers Hostel ❶**, above a popular pub, has the usual amenities and especially cozy beds. (☎534 492. Linens 50p. Laundry £2. £5 key deposit. Dorms £9.) Over the bridge in Kyleakin, a slew of wonderful hostels huddle near the pier. The friendly owners of **▨Dun Caan Hostel ❷** have masterfully renovated a 200-year-old cottage; enjoy a movie in the lounge, relax in your handmade bunk, or concoct a meal spiced with herbs from the garden. (☎534 087; fax 534 795; book ahead. Bike rental £10 per day. No smoking. Dorms £10.) The easygoing warden of the **SYHA Kyleakin ❷**, on the village green, is a top-notch source for outdoors information and a Scrabble whiz to boot. The vibe is young and friendly. (☎534 585. Laundry facilities. Pool table. Internet access £5 per hr. Dorms £10.50-11.50, under 18 £9-10.) At the ultra-social **Skye Backpackers ❷** next door, hit the pubs with the staff or stay in and barbecue out back. (☎534 510. Laundry £2.50. Internet £4 per 30min. Curfew 2am. Dorms £11.) For **B&B**, it's hard to beat **Mrs. Chiffer's ❷** prices. She's on Olaf Rd., three blocks from Skye Backpackers. (☎534 440. £13 per person.) An elegant stay can be had at **Ceol-Na-Mara** (KEY-all na MAH-rah) ❸, on South Obbe St. (☎534 443. Singles £25-32; doubles and twins £20-22 per person.)

⊡▤ FOOD AND PUBS. Grab groceries at the **Co-op**, up the hill to the west of the Kyle bus station. (☎530 196. Open M-Sa 8am-10pm. Su 10am-6pm.) For a taste of local fish, hop off the train at Kyle and into the **Seafood Restaurant ❸**, in the railway building looking into the bay. (☎534 813. Open M-Sa 6-9pm.) Smile back at the staff of the **Pier Coffee Shop ❶** in Kyleakin, who serve toasties for £2, fried haggis for £4, and breakfast (£4.50) all day long. (☎534 641. Open M-F 9am-8pm, Su 10:30am-8pm.) Kyleakin boasts great nightlife, thanks to a steady stream of backpackers and tourists. The **King Haakon Bar ❶**, at the east end of the village green, has a free jukebox and frequent live music on weekend nights. (☎534 164. Open M-Th and Sa 12:30pm-12:30am, F 12:30pm-1am, Su 12:30-11pm. Food served 12:30-8:30pm.) Live music is also common at **Saucy Mary's**, next door to the SHYA hostel. (Open M-Th 5pm-midnight, F 5pm-1am, Sa 5-11:30pm, Su 5-11pm.)

◪ SIGHTS. The **Bright Water Visitor Centre** on the pier offers a kids-oriented look at local history and folklore. (☎570 040. Open Apr.-Oct. M-Sa 9am-6pm. Free.) The center also runs 1½hr. trips to **Eilean Ban**, the island under the Skye Bridge, which sports an old lighthouse and boasts frequent seal and otter sightings. Departure times vary, so call ahead. (M-Sa 3-4 trips per day. £5.50, concessions £4.50, children £3.50.) Quiet **Kyleakin harbor** alights in oranges, pinks, and purples during clear sunsets—for the best views, climb to the memorial on the hill behind the SYHA hostel. A slippery scramble to the west takes you to the small ruins of **Castle Moil**. Cross the little bridge behind the hostel, turn left, follow the road to the pier, and take the gravel path. To stay dry, leave when the tide is lower than the base of the boathouse just east of the pier. According to legend, the original castle on this site was built by "Saucy Mary," who stretched a stout chain across the Kyle Sound and charged ships to come through the narrows. She supposedly flashed those who paid the toll—hence her spicy moniker. (Always open. Free.)

SOUTHERN SKYE   ☎01471

BROADFORD. Situated on a rocky bay 8 mi. west of Kyleakin, Broadford is remarkable only for its 24hr. convenience store and its bus links to the southern half of Skye. The **tourist information centre** sits in a carpark along the bay south of the bus stop. (☎822 361; fax 822 141. Open Apr.-Oct. M-Sa 9:30am-5pm, Su 10am-4pm.) Five minutes north up the road is a blessed **ATM** at the **Bank of Scotland** (☎822 216; open M-Tu and Th-F 9am-5pm, W 9:30am-5pm), while a second post-modern money-tree is by **Skye Surprises,** the 24hr. convenience store/petrol station/car rental/launderette/Internet cafe by the TIC; look for the hairy Highland cow model out front (☎822 225; cars £33 per day, £203 per week; laundry £3.50; Internet £1 per 30min). Broadford also has a **post office.** (☎(08457) 223 344. Open M-Sa 9am-1pm, M-Tu and Th-F also 2-5:30pm.) **Post Code:** IV49 9AB.

The **SYHA Broadford ❶** is the only hostel in the area and has soothing views of the harbor and open sea. Head east on the first road north of the bridge and walk ½ mi. (☎822 442. Laundry £2. Reception 7-10am and 5-11pm. Check-out 9:30am. Curfew midnight. Open Feb.-Oct. Dorms £9.50-10.50, under 18 £8.25-9.) Stock up on munchables at the **Co-op,** next door to Skye Surprises. (☎822 703. Open M-Sa 8am-10pm, Su 10am-6pm.) **The Fig Tree ❷,** near the post office, serves both lunch and dinner, featuring native Scottish salmon for as little as £6.50. (☎822 616. Open M-Sa 10:30am-5:30pm and 6:30-9pm.)

SLEAT PENINSULA AND ARMADALE. Two miles south of Broadford, the single-lane A851 veers southwest through the foliage of the Sleat Peninsula ("slate," like stone), dubbed "The Garden of Skye." Both **Skye-Ways** and **Highland Country** buses run between Armadale and Broadford (4-6 per day, about £3). **Armadale,** 17 hilly miles to the south, sends ferries to Mallaig. In town, the **Armadale Castle Gardens** and **Museum of the Isles** unite a disintegrating MacDonald castle, expansive gardens, and an excellent (if somewhat pro-MacDonald) history of the Isles clans. Its **Study Centre** is one of the best places in Scotland for genealogical research. (☎844 305. Open Apr.-Oct. daily 9:30am-5:30pm. Last admission 5pm. Research from £5 per half-day; first 15min. free. Gardens and museum £4, concessions £3, families £12.) One of today's MacDonalds runs the ◙**Flora MacDonald Hostel ❶,** known for incredible views of the Sound. The extraordinarily friendly Peter will pick you up from the Armadale ferry, perhaps throw back a dram with you, and eagerly tell you about his ancestress, the hostel's namesake. (☎844 272. Kitchen and TV. Dorms £8.) The **SYHA Armadale ❶** has more rules but a more convenient location, overlooking the water across from the pier. (☎844 260. Lockout 10:30am-5pm. Curfew 11:30pm. Lights-out 11:45pm. Open Apr.-Sept. Dorms £8.50, under 18 £7.25.) North of Armadale at **Ostaig,** the famous Gaelic college **Sabhal Mòr Ostaig** teaches the Gaelic language, encourages Gaelic music on Gaelic instruments, throws Gaelic dances, and hosts Gaelic festivals. They also offer summer courses in—you guessed it—all things Gaelic. (☎844 373, answered in Gaelic. Courses £120-200; see p. 63. **B&B ❸** singles £22; twins £18 per person.)

◙ **HIKING IN SOUTHERN SKYE.** Though southern Skye is sometimes abandoned for the more dramatic Cuillins to the north, the graceful landscape here is many an islander's favorite scene. The **Sleat Peninsula** has some of Skye's most verdant landscapes, including the **Kinloch Forest** on the Broadford-Armadale bus route. From the Forestry Commission carpark, a footpath traces a lovely circular route past a deserted settlement called **Letir Fura,** from which **Loch na Dal** is, clouds permitting, visible (2½hr. round-trip). A popular longer hike (3-3½hr. round-trip) reaches Skye's southernmost tip, **The Point of Sleat.** The trailhead begins at the end of the A851, south of **Ardvasar** at the **Aird of Sleat.** After an hour's walk, you'll be rewarded with awesome views of the western island **Rum** from the watery inlet of **Acairseid an Rubha.** Continue another 40min. southwest along the coast to the **Point of Sleat,** with its lighthouse and panorama of the Cuillins to the north. As the path is obscure, the Ordnance Survey Landranger Map #32 is essential, as is a conversation with knowledgeable types like Peter at Flora MacDonald's Hostel (see above).

THE CUILLINS AND CENTRAL SKYE ☎ 01478

Renowned for its hiking and formations of cloud and mist, the Cuillin Hills (COO-leen), the highest peaks in the Hebrides, dominate central Skye from Broadford to Portree. Legend says the warrior Cúchulainn was the lover of the Amazon ruler of Skye, who named the hills for him when the hero returned to Ireland to die. The Kyleakin-Portree road wends its way through the Red Cuillins, which rise at dramatic angles from the road and present a foreboding face to the aspiring hill-walker, meeting the toothed Black Cuillins in Sligachan.

ⓘⓘ ACCOMMODATIONS AND FOOD. Below the mountains at the junction of the A863 to Portree and the A850 to Dunvegan, the village of **Sligachan** (SLIG-a-han) is little more than hotel, pub, and campsite in a jaw-dropping setting. This is a true hiker's hub; the famous trail through Glen Sligachan departs south from here (see below), though there are few budget lodgings in town. Your best bet is the **Sligachan Hotel ❹,** a classic hillwalker's and climber's haunt. (☎ 650 204. Breakfast included. £30-40 per person; singles £10 more.) In society and refreshment, the hotel's **Seumas' Bar ❷** lacks, well, nothing. A broad selection of beers (try their own ale, Slig 80 Shilling, for £2.20), grub (from seafood gratin to lamb casserole, each £5.50) and nearly every malt in existence awaits. (Live music F-Sa. **ATM** available. Open daily 10:30am-11:30pm; food served noon-9pm.) Save your money and become one with the outdoors at the **Sligachan Campsite ❶,** across the road. (☎ (0778) 645 3294. Open May-Sept. £4, children £2.)

The town of **Glenbrittle** can be reached by Highland Country bus #53 from Portree and Sligachan (M-Sa 2 per day, last bus from Portree at noon). Expert mountaineers give tips on exploring the area at the **SYHA Glenbrittle ❶,** near the southwest coast, where a jocular atmosphere compensates for spartan quarters. (☎ 640 278. Open Apr.-Sept. Dorms £8.25, under 18 £7.) Campers should head to **Glenbrittle Campsite ❶,** in a grand setting at the foot of the Black Cuillins. (☎ 640 404. Open Apr.-Sept. Shop open daily 8:30am-8:30pm. £4, children £2.)

ⓘ HIKING AND CLIMBING. The Cuillin Hills are good for both rock climbing and slightly more horizontal trekking. The booklet *Walks from Sligachan and Glen Brittle* (£1 requested donation; available at TICs, campsites, and hostels) suggests routes. Warm, waterproof clothing and Ordnance Survey Outdoor Leisure Map #8 (1:25,000; £7) are essential; see **Wilderness Safety,** p. 49. The treacherously pitted peat is always drenched, so expect sopping wet feet. If you don't want to go it alone, **ⓘMacBackpackers Skye Trekker Tour** (see p. 652) hikes the gorgeous coastal path from Elgol, camping overnight at Camasunary and moving north through Glen Sligachan the next day. A guide, fellow backpackers, and transport to and from trailheads are all part of the deal.

A short but scenic path follows the stream from Sligachan near the campsite to the head of **Loch Sligachan.** After crossing the old bridge, fork right off the main

IKING THE OLD MAN OF STORR: MANO E MANO

Here in the Highlands, deforestation, expanses of placid sheep, a lack of trespassing laws, and field upon open field of heather allow outdoorsy ypes to skip the tourist tracks and amble wherever they like. On the Troternish Peninsula at the northern end of the Isle of Skye, the Old Man of Storr pokes up into the heavens. Being the independent-minded outdoorsman that I am, I decided that I'd avoid the over-peopled trail and find my own way up to the monolith.

Upon reaching the top of the foothill, I stopped to orient myself. I had somehow managed to end up farther west on the bluff than planned, leaving a pleasant-looking field of heather between me and the Old Man. I knew that it would be no trouble to cross the field and—ta da!—there I'd be.

The field turned out to be a moor that's "swamp"), and the heather ended up being tangled camouflage or soggy berns ("streams") and mud-covered rocks ("damn rocks"). By the time I reached the towering basalt column, my feet were soaked, my pants were splattered with gooey mud, and my mood had soured.

On the other hand, I felt the confidence and elation of independence. Standing there, with blue sky over my head, a calm sea in the distance, and the Old Man an arm's length away, I knew that every minute of scrambling had been worth it.

...And then I turned around and followed the tourists back down their straight, smooth, dry trail.

—John Witherspoon

path through the gate and walk upstream along the right-hand bank. The narrow, often boggy path leads past pools and mini-waterfalls, in some places tracing the top of a small cliff (3 mi. round-trip). In 1899, a fit (and barefoot!) Gurkha soldier ascended and descended the 2537 ft. **Glamaig,** an oversized anthill to the south, in just 55min. Set aside your delusions of grandeur, give yourself 3½hr., and even then head up only if you feel at ease on steep slopes with unsure footing. A smaller trail, which branches off the main trail after about 15min., leads up the ridge between the higher peaks, granting views of the ocean and offshore isles.

Experienced climbers might try the ascent to **Sgurr nan Gillean Corrie,** to the southwest of Glamaig, which towers 3167 ft. above a tiny mountain lake. For more level terrain, take the 8 mi. walk down **Glen Sligachan** through the heart of the Cuillins to the beach of **Camasunary,** with views of the isles of Rum and Muck. From Camasunary, you can hike 5 mi. along the coast to **Elgol,** where a less intimate view of the Cuillins unfolds. From there, a sailing trip to **Loch Coriusk** with **Bella Jane Boat Trips** reveals extraordinary panoramas. (☎ (01471) 866 244. Apr.-Oct. M-Sa; call in off season. Reservations recommended. Return £13; maxi return with 4½hr. on shore £19.) From Camasunary beach, you can also hike to the Loch along a coastal trail that traverses steep rocks at the intimidating "Bad Step" (1½hr.). Elgol is 14 mi. southwest of Broadford on the A881—**postbuses** (service 106) rumble in from Broadford (M-F 2 per day, Sa 1 per day).

THE MINGINISH PENINSULA ☎ 01478

Ten miles west of the Cuillins, arresting but less rugged views flank the B8009. This is the Minginish Peninsula, a peaceful realm largely devoid of tourists but packed with flesh-eating midges. **Highland Country Buses** run here from **Portree** and **Sligachan** (M-F 4 per day, Sa 2 per day), stopping at **Carbost,** where some descend to visit the **Talisker Distillery** along serene Loch Harport. The 45min. distillery tour is bland, but the whisky isn't: Skye's only malt packs a fiery finish. (Open Apr.-Oct. M-Sa 9:30am-4:30pm; Nov.-Mar. M-F 2-5pm. £4.) Buses continue to **Portnalong,** where there are two hostels. The **Skyewalker Independent Hostel ❶,** on Fiskavaig Rd., is run in an entrepreneurial spirit that would make George Lucas proud. The manager owns the hostel, a cafe, a post office, several campsites, and offers transportation to and from Sligachan. It's the best licensed cafe on the peninsula; it's also the only one. (☎ 640 250 or (0800) 027 7059. Dorms £7.50. Tent pitch £2.50. **Post office** open M and

W-Th 9-11am. **Post Code:** IV47 8SL.) The **Croft Bunkhouse ❶,** in a converted cow-shed, sleeps 14 in a gigantic two-tiered platform-style bed—bring a sleeping bag—and sports a ping-pong table and dart board. For longer stays, bothies (stone shelters) with more conventional bunks are also available. (☎640 254. Dorms £6.50; bothies £7.) Up the road, the **Taigh Ailean Hotel ❸** offers both bed and breakfast with style and comfort. (☎640 271. From £25 per person.)

PORTREE   ☎01478

Portree lies near the center of Skye geographically, and is central for most other things on the island as well—it's the political capital and major transportation hub, home to the main TIC, a beautiful but bustling harbor, and Skye's largest collection of shops and hotels. Its convenience and importance is overshadowed, however, by its severe bent for tourism—that, and the towering mountains to the north and south, calling out for adventurous souls.

🔢 PRACTICAL INFORMATION. Buses stop at Somerled Sq. from Kyle of Lochalsh (5 per day, £7.80). To reach the **tourist information centre,** Bayfield Rd., from the Square, face the Bank of Scotland, turn left down the narrow lane, and left again onto Bridge Rd. The staff elucidates bus routes and books accommodations for £3 and a 10% deposit. (☎612 137. Open July-Aug. M-Sa 9am-7pm, Su 10am-4pm; Sept.-Oct. and Apr.-June M-F 9am-5pm, Su 10am-4pm; Nov.-Mar. M-Sa 9am-4pm.) Other services include: the **Bank of Scotland,** Somerled Sq. (open M-Tu and Th-F 9am-5pm, W 9:30am-5pm); a **launderette,** in the basement of the Independent Hostel (☎613 737; open M-Sa 9am-9pm); and the **post office,** on Quay Brae by the harbor (☎612 533; open M-Sa 9am-5:30pm). **Post Code:** IV51 9DB.

🔲 ACCOMMODATIONS. The **Portree Independent Hostel ❷,** The Green, has a prime location, a multitude of amenities, a spacious kitchen, enthusiastic staff, and gregarious guests. (☎613 737. Internet £1 per 20 min. Free towels upon request. Dorms £10.50; twins £23.) Comfy beds await at **Portree Backpackers Hostel ❶,** 6 Woodpark, Dunvegan Rd., across from the Co-op. Walk along Bridge Rd. heading west; after the dog-leg south, turn left onto Dunvegan Rd. and continue for 10min. (☎613 641. Laundry facilities. Dorms July-Aug. £9, Sept.-June £8.50; doubles and twins £18.) For true B&B hospitality, stay at the **Harbor Lodge ❸** down by the pier. (☎613 332. £22 per person.)

🔳🔲 FOOD AND PUBS. The **Safeway** on Bank St. feeds budget travelers. (☎612 845. Open M-Sa 8:30am-8pm, Su 10am-5pm.) 🔳**The Bakery ❶,** Somerled Sq., is cheap as dirt but tasty as heaven. These hard-working lasses bake fresh goods daily—try everything from donuts to filled rolls to warm bread. (Open M-F 9am-5pm, Sa 9:45am-4:30pm.) Near the Backpackers Hostel, 15min. from town, the funky cafe at the **An Tuireann Arts Centre ❶** uses local organic produce. (☎613 306. Open M-Sa 10am-5pm. 10% student discount.) Seafood restaurants line the harbor—try the four-star **Bosville Hotel ❷,** Bank St., where you can dine for as little as £6. (☎612 856. Open daily 8am-10pm.) The town's uninspiring nightlife includes the upstairs pub at the **Caledonian Hotel.** (☎612 641. Live music F-Sa. Open M-F 11am-1am, Sa 11am-12:30am, Su 12:30-11:30pm.)

NORTHERN SKYE   ☎01470

Thanks to two scenic roads and miles of pristine shoreline, you can travel northern Skye in blissful ignorance of the thousands of tourists running amok on the island. The northwestern circuit follows the A850 from Portree to Dunvegan Castle, then heads down the A863 along the scenic west coast; the northeastern circuit hugs the A855 and A856 around the Trotternish Peninsula through Uig and Staffin and back to Portree. From Portree, **postbuses** handle the northwest route (M-Sa 9:45am); the northeast is covered by **Highland Country** buses on the Portree-Flodigarry Circular route (M-Sa 4-8 per day, June-Sept. also Su 3 per day; Day Rover £6).

▨ TROTTERNISH PENINSULA. Northeast of Portree, the A855 snakes along the east coast of the Trotternish Peninsula past the **Old Man of Storr,** a finger of black stone, and the **Quirang** rock pinnacles. Geologists may enjoy the backstories to these formations, but the rest can stare slack-jawed at one of Mama Nature's most spectacular canvases. From miles away, the Old Man of Storr seems a towering black monolith, but up close it reveals tiny white crystals—the result of air bubbles trapped in the basalt. The Old Man is accessible by a steep hike (1hr. roundtrip) that begins in the nearby carpark; ask the bus driver to let you off there. The footpath to the Quirang begins in a carpark on the road from Staffin to Uig. It ascends to the **Prison,** loops upward to the **Needle,** and finally arrives at the **Table,** a flat grassy promontory offering some of Skye's best views (3hr. round-trip).

Nearby **Staffin Bay** offers bountiful fossils and remarkable views of Skye and the mainland, while the well-dressed **Kilt Rock** has lava columns that appear pleated above a rocky base crumbling into the sea. Strong, well-shod walkers can try the challenging but magnificent 12 mi. hike along the **Trotternish Ridge,** which runs the length of the peninsula from the Old Man of Storr to Staffin. The less mighty can take the buses from Portree to Staffin.

DUNVEGAN CASTLE. The ancient seat of clan MacLeod and an interesting dose of clan history await here. Highland Country **bus #56** (☎ (01478) 612 622; M-F 3 per day, Sa 1 per day) runs from Portree to Dunvegan Castle. The castle, unusual as one of the few strongholds still owned by a clan chief, contains a smattering of relics, notably the **Fairy Flag,** a 1500-year-old silk, and **Rory Mor's Horn,** capable of holding two liters of claret. Traditionally, the ascending MacLeod chief must drain the horn in one draught "without setting or falling down" to prove his manhood. Present honcho John MacLeod emptied it in just under 2min. (☎ 521 206. Open Apr.-Oct. daily 10am-5:30pm; Nov.-Mar. 11am-4pm. £6, concessions £5.50, children £3.50. Gardens only £4, children £2.50.)

DUNTULM CASTLE. At the tip of the peninsula, Duntulm Castle was the MacDonalds' formidable stronghold until a nurse dropped the chief's baby boy from a window, thereby cursing the house and condemning it to its present state of ruin. (Always open. Free.) Near Duntulm at Kilmuir, the **Skye Museum of Island Life** has preserved an old crofter village of tiny, black, 200-year-old houses. (☎ 552 206. Open Easter-Oct. M-Sa 9:30am-5:30pm. £1.75, students £1.50, seniors £1.25, children 75p.) Along the same turn-off from the highway, **Flora MacDonald's Monument** pays tribute to the Scottish folk hero who sheltered Bonnie Prince Charlie. On a bluff 5 mi. north of **Staffin,** the **Dun Flodigarry Backpackers Hostel ❶** has a small shop, kitchen, and comfortable common area, and is the starting point for many hikes. Take the Staffin bus from Portree and ask to be let off at the hostel. (☎ 552 212. Internet £1 per 15min. Dorms £9.)

UIG ☎ 01470

The town of Uig (OO-ig) flanks a windswept bay on the peninsula's west coast, the terminus for ferries to the Outer Hebrides and the final resting place for most long-distance buses from Glasgow and Inverness. **Highland Country** buses #57A and #57D also run from **Portree** (M-Sa 3-4 per day, £3). While waiting for a ferry, stop by the **Isle of Skye Brewery,** next to the pier. When not busy brewing beer, one of the ten employees will give you a brief tour and tasting. (☎ 542 477. Open M-F 9:30am-

6pm. £2.) The **SYHA Uig ❶** is 30min. from the pier. Facing the sea, turn left on the A586; the large white house will be up the hill on your left. (☎542 211. Reception closed 10am-5pm. Curfew 11pm. Open mid-Mar. to Oct. Dorms £8.25, under 18 £7.25.) More convenient for ferry connections, **Oronsay B&B ❷** is by the pier; all rooms are ensuite and there's **bike rental** 'round back. (☎542 316. Bikes £2 per hr., £12 per day. £16-20 per person.) **The Pub at The Pier ❶** serves standard grub with sides of scenery and an occasional garnish of live music. (☎542 212. Open M-F 11am-midnight, Sa 11am-11:30pm, Su noon-11pm.)

THE OUTER HEBRIDES

The landscape of the Outer Hebrides is extraordinarily beautiful and astoundingly ancient. Much of its exposed rock is more than half as old as the planet itself, and long-gone inhabitants have left behind a rich sediment of tombs, standing stones, and antiquities. The culture and customs of the Hebridean people are rooted in religion and a love of tradition, and scattered family crofts remain the norm on many islands. While television and tourism have diluted old ways of life, you're still more likely to get an earful of Gaelic here than anywhere else in Scotland. On the strongly Calvinist islands of **Lewis, Harris,** and **North Uist,** most establishments close and public transportation ceases on Sundays (though one or two places may assist lost souls with an afternoon pint), while to the south, on **Benbecula, South Uist,** and **Barra,** tight-shuttered Sabbatarianism gives way to Catholic chapels and plates of the Pope on living room walls. While many young Hebrideans seek to escape the isolation of these islands, just as many city-sick "Inlanders" are beginning to migrate westward, seeking seclusion and quiet. Together, the Western Isles remain one of Scotland's most undisturbed and unforgettable realms.

◖ TRANSPORTATION

Three major **Caledonian MacBrayne ferries** (☎(01475) 650 100) serve the Western Isles: from **Ullapool** to Lewis, from **Skye** to Harris and North Uist, and from **Oban** to South Uist and Barra. Once in the archipelago, ferries brave rough sounds and infrequent buses cross causeways to connect the islands. If you know ahead of time which areas you will visit, you'll save money on a month's worth of ferry rides by buying an **Island Hopscotch ticket**—you can even bring your bike along for free. Options are found at the beginning of the invaluable *Discover Scotland's Islands with Caledonian MacBrayne,* free from TICs. You'll also want to pick up the *Lewis and Harris Bus Timetables* (40p) and *Uist and Barra Bus Timetables* (20p). **Cycling** is excellent, provided you like the challenge of windy hills and don't melt in the rain. Though traffic is light, **hitchhikers** report frequent lifts on all the islands. (*Let's Go* does not recommend hitchhiking.) Inexpensive **car rental** (from £20 per day) is possible at several places throughout the isles, but vehicles are usually prohibited from ferries. Except in bilingual Stornoway and Benbecula, road signs are in Gaelic only. TICs often carry translation keys, and *Let's Go* lists Gaelic equivalents after English place names where appropriate.

◤ ACCOMMODATIONS AND CAMPING

Ferries arrive at odd hours; if you plan to stay near a ferry terminal, try to book a bed ahead. Area TICs book **B&Bs** for £1.50. **Camping** is allowed on public land in the Hebrides, but freezing winds and sodden ground often make it a miserable experience. Lewis's remote **SYHA Kershader ❶**, Ravenspoint, Kershader, South

Lochs, is a standard, if small, SYHA, with laundry (£2) and a shop next door at the community center. (☎ (01851) 880 236. Dorms £8.25, under 18 £7.25.) A. Macdonald (☎ (01851) 830 224) runs the W9 **bus** from Stornoway, but you must call ahead.

The Outer Hebrides are home to the unique ◨**Gatliff Hebridean Trust Hostels ❶** (www.gatliff.org.uk), four 19th-century thatched croft houses turned into simple year-round hostels. The atmosphere and authenticity of these hostels make them the ideal way to experience the Western Isles. Enchantingly remote, they accept no advance bookings but very seldom turn travelers away. Aside from basic facilities, all provide cooking equipment, range tops, cutlery, crockery, and hot water. Blankets and pillows are provided, but the hostels have coal fires and are not centrally heated—you'll want a good sleeping bag. All hostels are £7 per person (under 18 £5.25) and offer **camping** with use of hostel facilities for £3.50.

Berneray (Bhearnaraigh), off North Uist. Frequent buses on the W19 and W17 routes shuttle between the hostel, the Otternish pier (where ferries arrive from Harris), the Lochmaddy pier on North Uist, and the Sollas Co-op food store (30min., M-Sa 6-9 per day, £1). A beautifully thatched and white-washed affair near an amazing beach. Watch the sunset while warming yourself at a bonfire on the sands.

Garenin (Na Gearranan), Lewis, 1½ mi. north of Carloway. Buses on the W2 "West Side Circular" route from Stornoway (M-Sa 10-11 per day) go to Carloway, if not Garenin village itself. Free taxi service meets some buses at Carloway. Unsurpassed surroundings: a trail leads along cliff tops to the sandy beaches of Dalmore and Dalberg.

Howmore (Tobha Mòr), South Uist; about 1hr. north of Lochboisdale by foot. W17 buses from Lochboisdale to Lochmaddy will stop at the Howmore Garage (M-Sa 5-8 per day, £1); from there, follow the sign 1 mi. west from the A865. Overlooks a ruined chapel, and near the rubble that was once Ormiclate Castle.

Rhenigidale (Reinigeadal), North Harris. Free minibus from the carpark next to the Tarbert TIC; call ahead. (☎ (01859) 502 221; M-Sa 2 per day; call by 8pm the night before for the morning bus or 3pm for the afternoon.) The bus will take your pack if you want to venture the tough 6 mi. hike along the eastern coast. From Tarbert, take the road toward Kyles Scalpay for 2 mi. and follow the signposted path left to Rhenigidale. The path ascends 850 ft. for stunning views before zig-zagging down steeply (3hr. total). By car, follow the turn-off to Maaruig (Maraig) from the A859 (13 mi. north of Tarbert).

LEWIS (LEODHAS)

Photographs fail time and again to convey Lewis's strange aura. Relentlessly desolate, the landscape is flat, treeless, and speckled with quiet lochs. Drifting mists shroud untouched miles of moorland and half-cut fields of peat, complementing Lewis's many archaeological sites, most notably the Callanish Stones. Somewhat incongruously, the island is also home to "the most consistent surf in Europe" and hosted an international surfing competition in 1999. The passive roads of Lewis are good for biking—Pentland Rd., starting in Stornoway, earns raves. However, check weather forecasts, as a gusty day can bring even strong cyclists to tears. Rent your wheels on a Saturday—otherwise, you'll have nothing to do on Sunday, when virtually everything grinds to a halt.

STORNOWAY (STEORNOBHAIGH) ☎01851

Stornoway, Lewis's main town and the largest in the islands (pop. 8000) is a splash of urban life in the otherwise thoroughly rural Outer Hebrides. Its artificially forested bay, well-kept castle, and industrial and fishing centers contrast vividly with the countryside around it.

⬛�) TRANSPORTATION AND PRACTICAL INFORMATION. CalMac ferries sail from **Ullapool** (M-Sa 2 per day; £13.35, 5-day return £22.85). **Buses** depart from the Beach St. bus station, where the *Lewis and Harris Bus Timetables* are for sale for 40p. (☎704 327. Luggage storage 20p-£1. Open M-Sa 8am-6pm.) Destinations include **Callanish** (Calanais) and **Carloway** (Carlabhaigh; 30min.-1hr. M-F 10-12 per day, Sa 5 per day), **Ness** (Nis; 1hr., M-Sa 8-9 per day), **Tarbert** (An Tairbeart; M-Sa 5 per day, £2.65). Car rental is cheaper than on the mainland: try **Lochs Motors,** across from the bus station. (☎705 857. 21+. From £18 per day. Open M-Sa 9am-6pm.) Rent bikes at **Alex Dan's Cycle Centre,** 67 Kenneth St. (☎704 025. £8.50 per day, £29 per week. Open M-Sa 9am-6pm.)

To get to the Stornoway **tourist information centre,** 26 Cromwell St., turn left (south) from the ferry terminal, then right on Cromwell St. (☎703 088. Open Apr.-Oct. M-Sa 9am-6pm and to meet late ferries; Nov.-Mar. M-F 9am-5pm.) The TIC books **coach tours; Stornoway Trust** organizes free **walks** through town and country, as well as private vehicle tours (☎704 733; Apr.-Oct.). Other services include: **Bank of Scotland,** across from the TIC (☎705 252; open M-Tu and Th-F 9am-5pm, W 10am-5pm); **Thomas Cook,** Cromwell Rd. (☎703 104; open M-W and F-Sa 9am-5:30pm, Th 10am-5:30pm); **Erica's Launderette,** 46 Macaulay Rd., the only one on the island and a bit of a walk (☎704 508; open M-Tu and Th-Sa 9am-3pm); **Internet access** at the **Stornoway Library** (☎708 631; £2 per 30min.; open M-Sa 10am-5pm); and the **post office,** 16 Francis St. (open M-F 9am-5:30pm, Sa 9am-12:30pm). Send **poste restante** to the Royal Mail Delivery Office, Sandwick Rd. **Post Code:** HS1 2AA.

🏠🍴 ACCOMMODATIONS AND FOOD. The best place to lay your head and wax your board is ⬛**Fair Haven Hostel ❷,** a comfortable mecca for wayward kahunas, over the surf shop at the intersection of Francis St. and Keith St. From the pier, turn left (west) onto Shell St., which becomes South Beach, then turn right on Kenneth St. and right again onto Francis St. The fresh cooked meals (freshly caught salmon £8) are better than anything in town. Hostel guests can also get surfing discounts. (☎705 862. Breakfast £2.50. Dorms £10, full board £20.) The **Stornoway Backpackers Hostel ❶,** 47 Keith St., 2min. farther north on Keith St., has free tea and coffee to compensate for somewhat lackluster facilities. (☎703 628. Dorms £9.) Many **B&Bs** oblige early ferries with a crack-of-dawn breakfast. To get to ⬛**Mr. and Mrs. Hill ❷** from the TIC, head north up Church St., turn left on Matheson Rd., and take Robertson Rd., the first street on the right. Enjoy friendly hospitality while wiggling your toes in a sheepskin or snuggling among heaps of pillows and blankets. (☎706 553. £17-19 per person.)

Cheap chow is easy to come by in Stornoway, including groceries at the **Co-op** on Cromwell St. (☎702 703. Open M-Sa 8am-8pm.) For an unexpectedly good taste of Asia, head to ⬛**Thai Cafe ❷,** 27 Church St., where mouth-watering main dishes (£4-6) are served in a lovely, candlelit setting. (☎701 811. Open M-Sa noon-2:30pm and 5-11pm.) The **Bank Street Delicatessen ❶** has everything from curries (£4) to pizza (£3.50); most of the menu is under £2. (☎706 419. Open M-W 11am-11:30pm, Th-F 11am-2am, Sa 11am-11:30pm.) The **An Lanntair Gallery ❶** (see below) also houses the town's best cafe (smoked salmon roll £2.40; closes 30min. before gallery).

◧ SIGHTS. The **An Lanntair Gallery,** in the Town Hall on South Beach St., hosts art exhibits and events including musical and historical evenings. (☎703 307. Open M-Sa 10am-5:30pm. Free.) The **Museum nan Eilean,** Francis St., has fascinating Hebridean exhibitions spanning 9000 years, including an exhibit on the famous Lewis Chessmen. (☎703 773. Open Apr.-Sept. M-Sa 10am-5:30pm; Oct.-Mar. Tu-F 10am-5pm, Sa 10am-1pm. Free.) Meander the grounds of majestic **Lewis Castle,** northwest of town. Built in the 19th century by an opium smuggler, the castle now shelters a college. The entrance is on Cromwell St., but you can admire it from across the water at the end of North Beach St. or from a clearing (turn left after the footbridge from New St.).

NIGHTLIFE AND ENTERTAINMENT. Don't miss out on Stornoway's vibrant nightlife. **Pubs** and **clubs** crowd the area between Point St., Castle St., and the two waterfronts. There's no better place to watch a big-time sporting event than the **Crown Inn** on North Beach St. (☎ 703 181. Open M-W 11am-11pm, Th-F 11am-2am, Sa 11am-11:30pm.) The **Caley Bar,** South Beach St., offers an upbeat local scene (Th and Sa "Karaoke-Disco" nights). **The Heb,** a hip club/bar/cafe, is like nothing you'd ever expect in the Outer Hebrides. (Th-Sa disco from 10pm. 18+. Cover £2. Open M-W 11am-8pm, Th 11am-1am, F 11am-2am, Sa 11am-11:30pm.) The **Hebridean Celtic Festival** in mid-July draws top musical talent from all over Scotland and devotees from all over the world (call ☎ (07001) 878 787 for info).

CHECK, MATE
In 1831, a man was walking along the dunes of West Lewis, bracing himself against a heavy wind. Suddenly a hard gale tripped him up and, as he regained balance, he saw a tribe of small, grim figures rising menacingly from the sand. Dashing off in fright, he returned to tell his family and friends about his perilous encounter in the Kingdom of Fairies. The "tribe" was actually a set of 78 walrus-tooth gamepieces left by Vikings, who apparently were avid chess players when not sacking the country. Today the **Lewis Chessmen** can be seen at the British Museum (see p. 133). A native exhibit on the subject is found in Stornoway's Museum nan Eilean.

LEWIS SIGHTS AND SURF

Most of Lewis's biggest attractions, including the Callanish Stones, Dùn Carloway Broch, and the Arnol Black House, range along the **west coast** and can be reached via the **W2 bus,** which operates on a circuit beginning at the Stornoway bus station (M-Sa 5 per day in either direction). Maclennan Coaches offers a **Day Rover** pass on this route (£5), or a return ticket to see one, two, or three of the sights from May to October (£3.50, £4, and £4.50). Alternatively, travel with a minibus tour company, such as **Out and About Tours** (☎ 612 288; day tours £15) or **Albannach Guided Tours** (☎ 830 433; from £8), both departing from the TIC.

CALLANISH STONES (CALANAIS). The Callanish Stones, 14 mi. west of Stornoway on the A858, are second only to Stonehenge in grandeur and a thousand times less overrun. The speckled, greenish-white stones, hewn from three-billion-year-old Lewisian gneiss, form a small circle with five avenues leading outwards. At least one camp of archaeologists believes that prehistoric peoples used Callanish, coupled with two nearby circles, to track the movements of the heavens, employing complex trigonometry and a level of technical knowledge unavailable to the Greeks 2000 years later. The **Visitor Centre** has a comprehensive exhibit and a short video. (☎ 621 422. Centre open Apr.-Sept. M-Sa 10am-7pm; Oct.-Mar. 10am-4pm. Exhibit and film £1.75, concessions £1.25, children 75p. Stones always open and free.) Local writer Gerald Ponting publishes **guides** to Callanish and neighboring sites with explicit directions (40p-£4; available at the Stornoway TIC).

A mile south of Callanish, postbuses follow the B8011 across the bridge to the island of **Great Bernera** (Bearnaraigh), where the **Bostadh Iron Age House,** one of many, is being excavated from beneath the sands. (Open Tu-Sa noon-4pm. £2, concessions £1, children 50p.) Perhaps more spectacular are the idyllic **white beaches** nearby, but watch out for sheep and signs thereof. Twenty miles farther west stand the surprisingly lush **Glen Valtos** and the expansive beaches at **Timsgarry**, where low tides uncover yards of sand flanked by dozens of deserted islets.

CARLOWAY BROCH (DÙN CHARLABHAIGH). On the A858, 5 mi. north of Callanish, the crofting town of **Carloway** (Carlabhaigh) is dominated by the **Carloway Broch,** an Iron Age tower with a partially intact staircase and breathtaking views of hills and lochs. Once it would have protected farmers and their cattle from Viking raiders; now it shelters tourists from high winds. Still, watch your footing: a sudden gust of wind may give you a closer view of the landscape than you'd like. (Visitor Centre open Apr.-Oct. M-Sa 10am-6pm. Broch always open. Free.) The **Garenin Hebridean Trust Hostel,** 1½ mi. from Carloway (see p. 660), stands within the restored **Gearrannan Blackhouse Village,** a wonderful visit if you haven't seen many traditional croft houses, though there won't be much new here if you have. (☎ 643 416. Open M-Sa 10am-4pm. £2, concessions £1.50, children £1.)

ARNOL BLACK HOUSE. On the A858, beyond **Shawbost,** a small town north of Carloway, stands this restored thatched-roof crofter's cottage. The chimney was intentionally left out, as smoke from the peat fire was supposed to conserve heat and improve the thatch by seeping through the roof—hence the name. Inhale a hearty lungful of peat smoke and get a watery-eyed glimpse of the dim interior. (☎ 710 395. Open Apr.-Sept. M-Sa 9:30am-6:30pm; Oct.-Mar. M-Sa 9:30am-4:30pm. £2.80, seniors £2, children £1.)

SURF'S UP. Beyond scattered villages and grassy moors, the **Butt of Lewis** (Rubha Robhanais) is the island's northernmost point, crowned by a lighthouse on the disintegrating cliffs. At night you can hear the growl of the corncrake, a rare and elusive bird. Just around the corner from the Butt is the **Port of Ness,** home to a popular surf beach. Another occasional option for wave-seekers is **Uig,** the central western area of Lewis. **Kneep Reef** doesn't have much to offer in terms of surf, but the endless deserted beach will cheer those who prefer to work on their tans. Here, or for better results at **Valtos** or **Europie** beaches, search the sands for Neolithic artifacts and the pink shells fabled to be mermaid fingernails. The most frequented surf on the island is at **Dalmor** beach, near the town of **Dalbeg,** site of an international surf competition in 1999 and still a destination for a decent coterie of hang-ten-hopefuls. Head to **Hebridean Surf Holidays** (☎ 705 862), on the corner of Keith St. and Francis St. in Stornoway, and ask for Derek. He offers all-inclusive surfing lessons (from £35 per day), or can rent you equipment and transport you to the beach (from £20). The best swells frequent different beaches depending on wind and tidal cycles, so get your info from boarders in the know.

The handy W2 **bus** route (10-12 per day) runs past Dalbeg and Dalmor beach, while buses operating the W4 route (2-4 per day) from Stornoway and Garynahine pass Kneep Reef and other spectacular surf spots in the Uig district. The Galson Motors bus on the W1 route (M-F 8-9 per day, Sa 6 per day) can whisk you from Stornoway along the northwest coast to the Butt and the Port of Ness.

HARRIS (NA HEARADH)

Harris shares an island with Lewis, but, as the two distinct names suggest, they're entirely different worlds. The deserted flatlands of Lewis, in the north, give way to another kind of desolation, more rugged and spectacular—that of Harris's steely gray peaks. Toward the west coast, the Forest of Harris (ironically, a treeless, heather-splotched mountain range) descends to brilliant crescents of yellow sand bordered by indigo waters and *machair*—sea meadows of soft grass and summertime flowers. In the 19th century, these idyllic shores were cleared for grazing and the islanders moved to the boulder-strewn east coast. Settlers there responded to the complete lack of arable land by developing still-visible "lazybeds," furrowed masses of seaweed and peat compost laid on bare stone. The A859, or "Golden Road" (named for the king's ransom spent in blasting it from the rock), bumps through the mountains from Stornoway to Tarbert, then twists all the way to Harris's southern tip via the desolate east coast, making a harrowing bus trip or grueling bike ride. Small roads branch from Tarbert east to the small fishing community on the island of **Scalpay** (Scalpaigh), connected to Harris by a causeway.

HIKING. Encompassing rocky stretches and heathered slopes, Harris's hiking is near-orgasmic. The largest peaks lie within the **Forest of Harris,** whose main entrances are off the B887 to Huisinish Point, at **Glen Meavaig,** and farther west at **Amhuinnsuidhe Castle** (15 mi. from Tarbert; erected in 1863 and still a private residence). The infrequent summertime W12 bus from Tarbert serves all of these points (Tu and F 3 per day). An excellent 4hr. hike runs down to **Glen Meavaig** from **Ardvourlie** in the north and past **Loch Bhoisimid;** to get to Ardvourlie, take the W10 bus from Tarbert or Stornoway (M-Sa 3-4 per day). If you don't have time for exhaustive exploration, hop any fence near Tarbert and hike up **Gillaval** (1554 ft.; at least 1hr.), which overlooks the town and harbor islands; the trails are unmarked, but the best route to the summit is from the east. A pleasant coastal walk follows the shore from **Taobh Tuath** north to **Horgabost.** Take a bus from Tarbert to Taobh Tuath and pick it up again 2hr. later in Horgabost, after trekking along cliffs and sandy beaches. For the most comprehensive walk, try the **Harris Walkway,** a long but not difficult ramble from **Clisham** in the south to **Scaladal** in the north, via Tarbert. Always carry the proper Ordnance Survey map in these remote parts.

TARBERT (AN TAIRBEART) ☎01859

Tarbert straddles the narrow isthmus that divides Harris into North and South. As the island's center, it has the most amenities, including B&Bs. **Ferries** serve Tarbert from **Uig, Skye** (M-Sa 2 per day; £8.70, 5-day return £14.90). Check with **CalMac** (☎502 444), in Tarbert at the pier, for timetables. **Buses** (☎502 441) run from **Leverburgh** and **Stornoway** (45min., M-Sa 3-5 per day, £2.65) and stop in the carpark behind the TIC. Rent a car from **Gaeltech Car Hire.** (☎520 460. 21+. From £30 per day.) The island's beguiling nothingness is best enjoyed by **bike;** rent from **Paula Williams.** (☎520 319. £10 per day.) When **hiking** in Harris's treeless landscape, there's little risk of getting hopelessly lost. Nevertheless, marked trails are scarce; bring a compass, sturdy boots, and a map.

The **tourist information centre,** Pier Rd. (☎502 011; open Apr. to mid-Oct. M-Sa 9am-5pm and for late ferry arrivals; mid-Oct. to Mar. for ferry arrivals), can give you the hours for **Internet access** at **Sir E. Scott School library,** a cream-colored building 10min. along the A859 to Stornoway (☎502 000; £2 per 30min.). The **Bank of Scotland** is uphill from the pier. (☎502 453. Open M-Tu and Th-F 10am-12:30pm and 1:30-4pm, W 11:15am-12:30pm.) The **post office** is on Main St. (☎502 211. Open M-Tu and Th-F 9am-1pm and 2-5:30pm, W 11:15am-12:30pm.) **Post Code:** HS3 3BL.

The well-located **Rockview Bunkhouse ❶,** Main St., is stuffed with beds less than 5min. west from the pier, on the north side of the street. It's run by two postal clerks, so you can also check in at the post office. (☎502 211. Dorms £9.) Effie MacKinnon keeps a spacious B&B at **Waterstein House ❷,** across from the TIC. (☎502 358. £15 per person.) The **Harris Hotel ❹** has atmosphere and amenities aplenty. (☎502 154. Open Apr.-Oct. £38.50-43.50 per person, with dinner £58-63.) **A.D. Munro,** Main St., serves Tarbert as grocer, butcher, and baker. (☎502 016. Open M-Sa 7:30am-6pm.) The **Firstfruits Tearoom ❶,** next to the TIC, pours hot drinks in a homey setting. (☎502 439. Open Apr.-Sept. 10:30am-4:30pm.) The friendly **Harris Hotel ❷** bar serves food (£5-7) across from the main hotel building.

The menu is standard, but come Sunday, the cheapest meal in town is here: three courses for £21.50. (☎502 154. Bar open M-Tu and Sa 11am-11pm, W-F 11am-midnight. Su dinner 7-8:45pm.) Those interested in local history and culture can check out Bill Lawson's **Evenings of Song, Story, and Slides** at the hotel. (☎502 154. May-Sept. W at 8:30pm. £3.)

RODEL AND LEVERBURGH. After exploring Tarbert and the mountains, head to **Rodel** (Roghadal), at Harris's southern tip, site of **St. Clement's Church.** Peek at three MacLeod tombs; the principal one, built in 1528, portrays the disciples, the Trinity, and MacLeod himself, all hewn from local black gneiss. Up the road is **Leverburgh,** where **CalMac** (☎(01876) 500 337) sails to **Ardmaree, Berneray** (M-Sa 3-4 per day; £4.90, 5-day return £8.30). **Buses** (☎502 441) run from **Tarbert** (45min., M-Sa 7 per day, £3.50). The upscale, funky ▧ **Am Bothan Bunkhouse ❷,** with spacious rooms and a stylish common area, is conveniently located—the bus passes it about ¼ mi. from the pier. (☎(01859) 520 251. Dorms £12.)

THE UISTS (UIBHIST)

Coming from anywhere in the peak-strewn Highlands, the extreme flatness of the Uists (YOO-ists) will be a shock. Save for a thin strip of land along the east coast, these islands are completely level, pocked with so many lochs that it's difficult to distinguish where the land ends and the water begins. A rare shard of sunlight reveals a world of thin-lipped beaches, crumbling black houses, wild jonquils, and quiet streams hiding some of Europe's best salmon-fishing spots.

The population is tiny and decentralized, scattered across small crofts. The main villages of **Lochmaddy** (Loch nam Madadh) on **North Uist** (Uibhist a Tuath) and **Lochboisdale** (Loch Baghasdail) on **South Uist** (Uibhist a Deas) are but glorified ferry hubs. The small island of **Benbecula** (Beinn na Faoghla; bin-BECK-yoo-luh) lies between its two larger neighbors and possesses the Uists' sole airport. If you think this spread-out arrangement will make backpacking difficult, you're absolutely right. There are only five hostels in the Uists, and transportation to them is tricky; prepare to walk. Crossing from North Uist to South Uist, Calvinism gives way to Roman Catholicism. Although Sunday remains a day of church-going, secular public activity is much more acceptable here than in the north.

◖ TRANSPORTATION

CalMac ferries float to **Lochmaddy** from **Uig, Skye** (1¾hr.; 1-2 per day; £8.70, 5-day return £14.90); they also connect with **Tarbert, Harris** (see p. 664). Ferries drift to **Ardmaree, Berneray** from **Leverburgh, Harris** (1¼hr.; M-Sa 3-4 per day; £4.90, 5-day return £8.30) and to **Lochboisdale** from **Oban** (6¾hr.; M and W-Sa 1 per day; £19.20, 5-day return £33). The island council also runs the tiny **Sound of Barra Ferry** from **Eoligarry, Barra** to **Eriskay.** Call ahead to reserve one of the coveted seats. (☎(08151) 701 702. 1hr; M-Sa 4-5 per day, Su 2 per day; £2.50, with car £10.)

All modes of transportation are scarce. **Bus** W17 runs along the main road from Lochmaddy to the airport in **Balivanich** and **Lochboisdale** (M-Sa 5-6 per day, £3.10). W17 and W19 also meet at least one ferry per day in **Ardmaree** for departures to Harris; W17 and W29 go to **Eriskay** in the south for connections to Barra (5-9 per day). If you arrive on a late ferry, there may not be a bus until the next day. Either call ahead to book a B&B that will pick you up or prepare to camp. Get a *Uist and Barra Bus Timetables* (20p) in the Lochmaddy or Lochboisdale TIC. For **car rental,** call **MacLennan's Self Drive Hire,** Balivanich, Benbecula. (☎(01870) 602 191. 21+. From £22 per day. Open M-F 9am-5:30pm, Sa 9am-2pm.) The Uists' few drivers are often friendly to **hitchhikers,**

**IN
RECENT
NEWS**

SUNDAY, BUSTLING SUNDAY

Scratch the surface and there are two different Highlands. There's the awe-inspiring, heather-covered, sheep-grazed mountains and valleys of Protestant Scotland and the awe-inspiring, heather-covered, sheep-grazed mountains and valleys of Catholic Scotland.

This tangle of religion, like everything else in Scotland, has a long and somewhat gory history. The arrival of fiery minister John Knox and the Reformation brought battles, burnings, bloodshed, and other words that start with "B," like bodies, Bibles, and blackened buildings.

The past echoes in the present, stirred up recently by a new ferry service from Oban to the island of North Uist. The traditional Sabbath for many of the staunch Presbyterians who live in the Hebrides, Sunday sees the complete closing of all services in North Uist (and the nearby islands of Harris and Lewis), including public transportation; even driving is frowned upon. Yet CalMac recently began ferrying people and cars on days both sacred and profane. In spite of North Uist's outrage, South Uist—a stronghold of Catholicism, where the Sabbath does not entail so complete a shutdown of public life—welcomes the additional opportunity to travel.

And thus the 16th-century rift remains, perhaps more distinct in such sparsely populated regions. None of this, however, detracts from the reason to visit in the first place: the awe-inspiring, heather-covered, sheep-grazed mountains and valleys.

but it's rude to ask on Sundays. Regardless, one should always consider the risks involved.

⚡ PRACTICAL INFORMATION

Tourist information centres on the piers at **Lochmaddy** (☎ (01876) 500 321; open Apr.-Oct. M-F 9am-5pm, Sa 9:30am-1pm and 2pm-5:30pm) and **Lochboisdale** (☎ (01878) 700 286; open Apr.-Oct. M-Sa 9am-5pm) book accommodations and open late for ferry arrivals. Lochboisdale has a **Royal Bank of Scotland** (☎ (01878) 700 399; open M-Tu and Th-F 9:15am-4:45pm, W 10am-4:45pm), Lochmaddy a **Bank of Scotland** (☎ (01876) 500 323; open M and Th-F 9:30am-4:30pm, W 10:30am-4:30pm), and Benbecula a **Bank of Scotland** (☎ (01870) 602 044; open M-Tu and Th-F 9am-5pm, W 9:30am-5pm); all have **ATMs** and all are closed 12:30-1:30pm. Benbecula also boasts the Uists' sole launderette, **Uist Laundry,** by Balivanich Airport (☎ (01870) 602 876; open M-F 8:30am-4:30pm, Sa 9am-1pm; wash £3, dry £2, kilt £8). **Internet access** is available at **Cafe Taigh Chearsabhagh,** Lochmaddy (50p per 20min.), and at **Past and Present Cafe,** Lochboisdale (£1 per 15min.; see **Food,** below, for both).

🏠 ACCOMMODATIONS

The only **hostel** near Lochmaddy is the **Uist Outdoor Centre ❶,** which also offers courses in rock climbing, canoeing, and water sports for £40 per day. Follow signposts west from the pier for 1 mi. and then turn north. Bring a sleeping bag and book ahead. (☎ (01876) 500 480. Linen £2. Dorms £8.) The other hostels are far from town and reachable only by clever navigation. For the excellent **Taigh Mo Sheanair ❷,** near Clachan, take bus W17 or W18 (20min., 12 per day) from Lochboisdale. The driver can let you off at the Clachan shop on Balishare Rd., from which it's a mile's signposted walk west. (☎ (01876) 580 246. Linen £2. Laundry £3. Dorms £10. Camping £4.) Easier to reach but more primitive is the **Gatliff Hebridean Trust Hostel** on **Berneray** (see p. 660). Another basic Gatliff Trust Hostel is on South Uist at **Howmore** (see p. 660). The bus also passes through **Balivanich,** Benbecula, where the immaculately clean **Taigh-na-Cille Bunkhouse ❷,** 22 Balivanich, just west of the airport, sleeps ten. (☎ (01870) 602 522. Dorms £10-11.)

B&Bs are scarce and difficult to reach. In Lochmaddy, Mrs. Morrison greets guests at the plush and well-located ⬛**Old Bank House ❸,** across the street from the gas station. (☎ (01876) 500 275. £20 per person.) In Lochboisdale, **Mrs. MacLellan's ❷,** Bay View, is above the ferry terminal. (☎ (01878) 700 329. £16-18 per person.) **Mrs. MacDonald's ❷,** Kilchoan Bay, 1 mi.

along the main bus route (W17), is nicer, if you're willing to sacrifice some convenience. (☎(01878) 700 517. £15 per person.) You can camp almost anywhere, but ask the crofters first.

🏠 🍴 FOOD AND PUBS

The cheapest food stores on the islands are the **Co-ops** in **Sollas** (Solas) on North Uist (open M-W and Sa 8:30am-6pm, Th-F 8:30am-7pm) and **Daliburgh** (Dalabrog) on South Uist (☎(01878) 700 326; open M-Sa 8am-8pm), or **MacLennon's Supermarket** in **Balivanich**, Benbecula (open M-W 9am-6pm, Th-F 9am-8pm, Sa 9am-7pm, Su noon-3pm). In Lochboisdale, the ⬛**Past and Present Cafe** ❶ has a varied menu, great cappuccino, and a friendly atmosphere. (☎(01878) 700 820. Open M-W 10:30am-6pm, Th-F 10:30-5pm. Takeaway only Th-Su 5-9pm.) For a sit-down supper in either ferry hub, your only option is pricey but tasty pub grub (£5-10) at the **Lochmaddy Hotel** ❷ (☎(01876) 500 331) or the **Lochboisdale Hotel** ❷. (☎(01878) 700 322. Food served in both noon-2pm and 6-9pm.) Across the street from the Lochmaddy Hotel, the small **Cafe Taigh Chearsabhagh** ❶ sells baked goods and sandwiches for £1-3. (☎(01876) 500 293. Open M-Sa 10am-5pm.) An upscale restaurant for those who take their five-course meals (£20) in all-wood interiors, **Stepping Stone** ❺, awaits in Benbecula. (☎(01870) 603 377. Dinner served M-Sa 6-8:45pm.) If you're going out to Bharpa Langass, follow the signs to **Langass Lodge** (☎(01876) 580 385) for a post-cairn pint. Halfway between Lochmaddy and Clachan, this classy hunting lodge holds some down-and-dirty drinking sessions.

📷 SIGHTS

The vibrant ⬛**Taigh Chearsabhagh Museum and Arts Centre** in Lochmaddy is home to a rotating gallery of contemporary Scottish artists, an extensive photo exhibit on North Uist life, and a gathering room for poetry readings, *ceilidhs*, and small musical performances. The Centre also offers two- to three-day art courses (Sept.-May, from £10 per day) and lets an artist abode (£100 per week) during the summer. (☎(01876) 500 293. Open daily 10am-5pm. Gallery free. Museum £1, concessions 50p, under 12 free.) Elsewhere on North Uist, the A865 runs past wide beaches at **Sollas,** sea-carved arches and a Victorian folly 5 mi. west at **Scolpaig,** and the site of **Sloc a'Choire,** a spouting cave and hollow arch, at **Tigharry.** It's said that a defiant young lass once hid in the arch rather than marry at her parents' demand; listen carefully and you might still hear her echoing cries. Two miles past Locheport Rd. on the A867 is the 3000-year-old chambered cairn **Barpa Langass** and nearby stone circle **Pobull Fhinn.** On North Uist's southern tip at **Carinish** lie the ruins of 13th-century **Trinity Temple,** probably the islands' most noteworthy debris. (Bus W17 from Lochmaddy swings near Langass and Carinish.) Birdwatchers enjoy the **RSPB Balranald Reserve** on western North Uist, north of Bayhead (signposted from the A867). Bus W18 passes by from Lochmaddy (M-Sa 3-4 per day). May and June are the best months for observation, but you'll almost always see lapwings, oystercatchers, and rare red-necked phalaropes. (☎(01870) 620 369. Guided walks May-Aug. Tu 6:30pm and Th 11:30am, £2.50. Visitors Centre always open.)

The A865 (and W17 bus) continues its run southward into Benbecula, where the B892 forks off, passing splendid beaches to the west and arriving at **Nunton,** former spiritual home to nuns massacred during the Reformation. In **Culla Bay,** where the sisters were tied and left to drown, the seaweed clings to the rocks, resisting the pull of the sea.

South Uist has paltry attractions, centered around the birthplace of Highlands heroine **Flora MacDonald** in **Milton,** where her imposing statue perches on a white pedestal up a hill by the A865. The nearby **Kildonan Museum** houses some local artifacts and a showcase for Uist Craft Producers. (☎(01878) 710 343. Open Apr.-Oct. M-Sa 10am-5pm, Su noon-5pm. £1.50, children free.) Access to the **moorland** in the Uists is free, but there are few well-marked footpaths. For vistas of loch and moor, hop over the roadside fence and climb **Blashaval Hill,** a short walk northwest of Lochmaddy on the A865. TICs offer handy *Western Isles Walks* leaflets (50p), as well as a summertime *Out and About* schedule of **guided walks** led by the Southern Isles Amenity Trust. (☎(01870) 602 039. Free-£2.)

NEAR THE UISTS

BERNERAY (BEÀRNARAIGH). The tiny island of Berneray, connected to North Uist's north coast by a causeway, is a rare gem. A favorite retreat of Prince Charles and home to the best-equipped **Gatliff Trust Hostel** (see p. 660), it boasts a gorgeous coast of white sand and *machair* (sea meadow), a thriving seal population, and a friendly human population of 140 that first saw electricity in 1969. You can easily walk the island's 8 mi. circumference, passing a standing stone or two along the way. Berneray is the **ferryport** for Harris arrivals; frequent **buses** W17 and W19 run from Lochmaddy (30min., M-Sa 6-9 per day, £1).

ERISKAY (EIRIOSGAIGH). On February 4, 1941, with strict wartime alcohol rationing in effect, the *S.S. Politician*—carrying 207,000 cases of whisky to America—foundered on a reef off the isle of Eriskay (Eiriosgaigh), between South Uist and Barra. The concerned islanders mounted a prompt salvage operation, and Eriskay hasn't been the same since. The local pub, named after the ship, displays some of the original bottles. The island is perhaps even more notable as the place where Bonnie Prince Charlie first set foot on Scottish soil, at **Prince Charles's Bay.** The unique pink flower that grows on the island is said to have been brought by seedlings stuck to the Prince's shoe. Eriskay is connected to South Uist by a free causeway; **buses** W17 and W29 run from Lochboisdale (45min. 10 per day).

BARRA (BARRAIGH)   ☎01871

Barra, the southern outpost of the Outer Isles, is unspeakably beautiful, a composite of moor, *machair,* and beach. On sunny days, the island's colors are unforgettable: sand dunes crown waters flecked with light-dazzled blue, wreathed below by dimly visible red, brown, and green kelp. Barra is also unspeakably small, and home to a small number of Gaelic-speaking Scots, most of them MacNeils, who preserve the island's unique culture. The best times to visit are May and early June, when the primroses bloom, or in late July during the **Barra Festival,** a celebration of music and craftsmanship. Though beauty and beaches beckon, be forewarned that Barra is not the most easily accessible, or budget-friendly, of the Hebrides.

■ **TRANSPORTATION.** CalMac ferries (☎(01878) 700 288) call at **Castlebay** (Bagh A Chaisteil), Barra's main town, from **Oban** (5hr.; M, W-Th, Sa 1 per day; £19.20) and **Lochboisdale, South Uist** (1¾hr.; Tu, Th-F, Su 1 per day; £5.45). Another ferry runs to **Eoligarry** (Eolaigearraidh) on Barra from **Eriskay.** (☎(08151) 701 702. M-Sa 2 per day; £2.50, cars £10.) Times change daily and the monthly schedule is difficult to read; look to the TIC for help. **Hebridean Coaches** (☎(01870) 620 345) runs buses W17 and W29 to Eriskay from **Benbecula** and **Lochboisdale** (M-Sa 5-9 per day).

You can see almost all of Barra in a day; by far the best way to do so is by **bike.** To rent from **Castlebay Cycle Hire,** drop by the long wooden shed on the main road. (☎810 438. From £8 per day. Open daily 10am-1pm.) You can also take **bus** W32 around the island (☎810 262; 90min. circuit, M-Sa 1-2 per hr.) or rent from **Barra Car Hire** (☎810 243; 25+; from £30 per day). If you tire of dry land, try a guided seakayaking tour with **Chris Denehy,** and take in the surrounding human-deserted islands, populated with seals, otter, eagles, and the occasional basking shark. (☎810 443. £10 per evening, £15 per half-day, £25 per day. Hot drinks and snacks provided; bring a lunch for the full-day trip.)

N PRACTICAL INFORMATION. Castlebay is Barra's primary town, and boasts a helpful **tourist information centre,** around the bend to the east of the pier. They'll find you a B&B (£3), but book ahead—a wedding, festival, or even positive weather forecast can fill every bed on the island. (☎810 336. Open Easter-Oct. M-Sa 9am-5pm, Su 10-11am; also open for late ferries.) Barra has only one **ATM,** at the only **bank,** across from the TIC. (☎810 281. Open M-F 9:15am-12:30pm and 1:30-4:45pm.) **Internet access** is at the **Castlebay School library,** 10min. west of the Castlebay Hotel. (☎810 471. Book ahead. £2 per 30min., £3.50 per hr. Open M and W 9am-4:30pm, Tu and Th 9am-4:30pm and 6-8pm, F 9am-3:30pm, Sa 10am-12:30pm.) The **post office**-cum-shoe store is next door to the bank. (☎810 312. Open M-W and F 9am-1pm and 2-5:30pm, Th 9am-1pm, Sa 9am-12:30pm.) **Post Code:** HS9 5XD.

Ñ Ċ ACCOMMODATIONS AND FOOD. Barra is home to the excellent **⚑Dunard Hostel ❶,** a short walk uphill from the pier and around the bend to the west. Run by one of the few young couples who've remained on the island past childhood, the hostel is a wonderfully social, truly Hebridean experience. (☎810 443. Dorms £10. Camping £7.) Or try **Mrs. Clelland's ❷,** 47 Glen, uphill to the east of the TIC—she runs the cheapest B&B around Castlebay. (☎810 438. £19 per person.) One mile west of Castlebay, the calm of **Nask** (Nasg) hides the airy comfort of **Terra Nova ❸,** a B&B well-managed by Mrs. Galbraith. (☎810 458. Singles £21; doubles and twins £20 per person.) For a drink and a small selection of eats, hit the **Castlebay Bar ❶,** uphill from the harbor. (☎810 223. Live music summer Sa-Su. Open M-Sa 11am-1am, Su noon-midnight.) You can also get **B&B ❹** in one of their large rooms overlooking the castle and bay. (☎810 223. Single £40; twin or double £75.) Just below is the **Co-op** food store. (☎810 308. Open M-W and Sa 8:30am-6pm, Th-F 8:30am-7pm.) If you don't fancy cooking yourself, make someone else do it at the **Castlebay Restaurant ❺,** in the Castlebay Hotel. Savor local salmon (£8.90) or lamb shank (£9.50) while gazing at a confident castle over a calm bay. (Open daily 6-8:45pm.)

◙ SIGHTS. Kisimul Castle, bastion of the old Clan MacNeil, floats in stately solitude in the middle of Castlebay harbor. It lay in ruins for two centuries, and was recently leased to Historic Scotland for 1000 years, for £1 and one bottle of Talisker whisky per year. Take a motorboat from the pier in front of the TIC to the castle gate; inside waits one of the oldest self-flushing toilets in the world. (☎810 313. Open Apr.-Oct. M-Sa 9:30am-6:30pm. £3, concessions £2.30, children £1.) A small sampling of island life and Gaelic culture is found at the rotating exhibits of the **"Dualchas" Barra Heritage and Cultural Centre,** near the school. (☎810 413. Open Apr.-Sept. M-Sa 11am-4pm. £2, concessions £1.50, children £1.) The road west from Castlebay passes the brooding, cloud-topped mass of **Ben Tangasdale** before arching north to an amazing white stretch of beach at **Halaman Bay.** From there the road extends northward past turquoise waters and more white sand. Opposite Allasdale to the north, popular **Seal Bay** makes an excellent picnic spot, so bring some herring and make a flippered friend. A detailed map of Barra can guide you to numerous **standing stones** and **cairns** dotting the hills in the middle of the island.

On the north coast, the expansive beach of **Traigh Mhor** provides a spectacular landing spot for daily Loganair flights; planes land at low tide. Farther north in **Eoligarry** is **Cille Bharra Cemetery.** Still in use, it contains "crusader" headstones thought to have served as ballast in the warship of a clan chief. Inside the neighboring **St. Barr's Church,** step through dusty, candlelit shrines, Celtic crosses, and Norman

FROM THE ROAD

DRIVING ME COURTEOUS

Most people eventually figure out (usually sooner rather than later) how driving in Britain is different than driving in North America, continental Europe, and almost everywhere else: traffic moves on the left side of the road, steering wheels are on the right side of cars, white lines are in the middle of the pavement, and yellow lines are to the outside.

In trying to keep all the changes straight, I've followed some strange advice—I even tried moving my watch to the other wrist, but just ended up losing track of time. The best counsel I've received, however, is about driving etiquette in the Highlands... though I did learn it the hard way.

Up north, single-lane roads lace the countryside. I grew used to keeping one eye watching the pavement ahead of me for oncoming traffic and one eye on the crumbling rock walls and grazing sheep (which were also sometimes ahead of me). Every 200 yards or so, there are small spaces set aside for when oncoming cars meet. One auto pulls into a by-area and the other continues on. In my previous driving life, more aggressive drivers determined the rules of the road and more cautious drivers let them pass.

stones. To see the whole island, follow the single-lane A888, which makes a 14 mi. circle around the rather steep slopes of **Ben Heavel.** An excellent road for **cycling**—if a bit hilly—it follows the coast past more beaches and mountains.

VATERSAY AND MINGULAY. A short causeway connects Barra to **Vatersay** (Bhatarsaigh), the small, southernmost inhabited island in the Outer Hebrides. Lounge on the yellow sand beaches of the southeast coast and visit the nearby monument to the *Annie Jane*, which sank off Vatersay in 1853 while carrying 400 hopeful emigrants to Canada. Buses run to Vatersay from the Castlebay post office, by the pier (M-Sa 3-4 per day). Bird watchers should visit the deserted island of **Mingulay,** still farther south. Call John MacNeil to inquire about boat trips from Castlebay in summer. (☎810 449. 2 per week in good weather, £20.)

THE NORTHWEST HIGHLANDS

If you don't mind comically limited public transportation, the pristine beauty of Scotland's northwest is irresistible. Spectacularly isolated, the region is punctuated by small hamlets, threaded with lochs and waterfalls, dominated by jagged peaks and heather-covered hills, and lapped by ocean waves. Grand expanses of mountain and moor stretch along the coast, from the imposing Torridon Hills to the eerie volcanic formations of Inverpolly near Ullapool and finally to Cape Wrath, where waves crash against the highest cliffs in mainland Britain.

TRANSPORTATION

Without a car, tramping the northwestern coast is tricky in summer and nearly impossible the rest of the year. **Inverness** is the area's main transport hub. **Trains** (☎(08457) 484 950) from Inverness run to **Kyle of Lochalsh** (2½hr., 3 per day, £14) and **Thurso** (3¼hr., 3 per day, £12.50). **Scottish Citylink** (☎(08705) 505 050) and **Rapson Buses** serve the same routes to **Kyle** (2½hr., 2 per day, £10.60) and **Thurso** (3½hr., 2 per day, £10.50), and also go to **Ullapool,** midway up the northwest coast, where ferries leave for the Outer

Hebrides (1½hr., M-Sa 2-4 per day, £6.80). From April to October, the **Northern Explorer Ticket,** available at bus stations, provides decent bus transportation on a route looping from Inverness to Ullapool, Durness, Tongue, and Thurso—if you're lucky, you'll even get a bit of a tour guide for a driver. The ticket covers unlimited travel (3 days out of 6 £35; 5 of 10 £55; 8 of 16 £85), or you can pay somewhat pricey single fares (1 bus per day; Ullapool-Durness £10, Durness-Thurso £7; SYHA and CalMac ferry discounts available). **Postbuses** are another option—as always, consult the public transport guide, or call a local hostel warden for specific routes in outlying regions. Those who **hitchhike** dance with fate. The few locals drive like hell-bats on narrow, winding roads, but pick up any hikers they don't run over. *Let's Go* never recommends hitchhiking.

DORNIE AND NEAR KYLE   ☎01599

Though the tourist mobs rush past to Skye, the region just east of Kyle of Lochalsh is breathtaking in its own right. The made-for-postcard must-see of the area is **Eilean Donan Castle** ("EL-len DOE-nin" or "that KA-sil in HI-lan-der"), the restored 13th-century seat of the MacKenzie family and the most photographed monument in Scotland. For the best snapshots—those that leave out the unattractive motorway and carpark—station yourself on the bridge 200 yd. west on the A87. The views outside are infinitely superior to those inside. (☎555 202. Open Apr.-Oct. daily 10am-5:30pm; Mar. and Nov. 10am-3pm. £4, concessions £3.20, families £10.) The castle stands beside the A87 between Kyle and Inverness; take a Scottish Citylink bus and get off at the sleepy town of **Dornie,** stretched out along Loch Long. If you miss the bus back, stay at the tiny **Silver Fir Dornie Bunkhouse ❷,** which sleeps a cozy four. Walk 10min. heading east along the loch, 200 yd. past the Catholic chapel, and look for a blue fence on your left. (☎555 264. Linen £1. £10 per person.)

Six miles north of the A87 at Camuslunie, Killilan, the ◪**Tigh Iseaball Bunkhouse ❶** is the area's most engaging hostel. With a lovely setting at a mountain's base, the hostel features hiking-knowledgeable wardens, table tennis, billiards, and a basketball hoop. There's no public transportation, but the owner is happy to pick up those who call ahead from Kyle or Dornie. (☎588 205. 2 tasty free-range eggs included. Dorms £7.50.) The trek to the **Falls of Glomach** (the third-largest waterfall in Britain at 370 ft.) is an amazing but tough 1½hr. from Glen Elchig. Farther east, the 3505 ft. **Five Sisters of**

Bearing this in mind, I noticed an old pickup truck rumbling my way. As we closed in on each other, I spotted the nearest side space and tensed to see who would pull into it. The truck flickered its bright headlights at me.

Realizing that he was bigger, stronger, and probably had better insurance, I cowed and pulled aside. But then the truck turned simultaneously into the same small spot, both of us coming to a complete halt. I put my car into reverse, hoping and praying that the large, bearded, and probably kilted driver would not get out. I backed out, re-entered the roadway and sped, carefully, past the truck stopped in the aside.

That night while relating my experience to a wiser and more experienced hand on the road—over a bottle of scotch, naturally—I finally heard the advice that I needed earlier that day. Autos flash their lights to signal that *they* will pull aside, and the *other* car should go ahead.

The larger vehicle had an owner with a larger sense of hospitality, a hospitality that runs, or drives, strong in northern Scotland. Highlanders are rightfully proud of their unique traditions—tartan kilts, wailing bagpipes, warm haggis (okay, *almost* rightfully proud), and family clans—but they take equal pride in their roadside manners.

—John Witherspoon

Kintail tower above the A87, and on the other side of the highway, the spectacular **Mam Ratagan pass** leads to secluded Glenelg.

PLOCKTON   ☎01599

Six miles north of Kyle of Lochalsh, the village of Plockton—blessed with palm trees, a rocky beach, and green mountains bordering a tranquil harbor—deserves the starry-eyed tourists who gasp at its unassuming perfection. The **Leisure Marine Office,** on the waterfront, rents canoes, rowboats, paddleboats, and bikes (£5-12 per hr.). As you relax on the bay's clear waters, keep your eyes peeled for seals, otter, and the occasional porpoise. **Callum's Seal Trips,** at the Main Pier or the Pontoon next to the carpark, are free if no seals show. Signs at both locations indicate the departure point for the next trip. (☎544 306. 1hr. tours Apr.-Oct. daily at 10am, noon, 2, 4pm, and sometimes evenings. £5, children £3.)

Plockton sits on the main Inverness-Kyle of Lochalsh **rail line,** which runs 5-6 trains per day in each direction. It's also served by the Kyle-Plockton-Ardnarff **postbus service** (#119; depart Kyle 9:45am, arrive Plockton 10:35am; depart Plockton 2pm, arrive Kyle 2:55pm). Opposite the train station, the **Station Bunkhouse ❶,** 5min. from the waterfront, has comfortable bedrooms in a renovated two-storey cabin. (☎544 235. Dorms £8.50-10.) The owners run a basic B&B, **Nessun Dorma ❷,** from their house next door. (£15-17 per person; singles £20.)

APPLECROSS   ☎01520

If pleasure is measured in stunning vistas and hair-raising thrills, then the trip to remote Applecross is a white-knuckled joy. The direct route, across the harrowing **Bealach-na-Ba ("Cattle") Pass,** is for the iron-hearted only. At 2054 ft., the steep, single-track Pass is Britain's highest road, punctuated by hairpin turns and livestock with little regard for their own lives and even less for yours. On a clear day, drivers are rewarded with expansive views of Skye and the Small Isles; the rest of the time, vehicles are surrounded by mist and the cliff drop just 5 ft. away is practically invisible. The circuitous **coastal route** is a less-death-defying option, offering its own panoramas from above the rocky seashore.

Applecross itself is a bustling town whose fantastic pub tops off a day of outdoor adventuring. Wander the beach yourself, or check out **Mountain & Sea Guides** for half- and full-day kayaking and trekking trips (£22-35), as well as longer sea kayaking and mountaineering courses. (☎744 393. 3-day to 1-week trips from £145.) From the head of Applecross Bay, a rugged, signposted **hike** rounds the northern peninsula to Kenmore (8 mi.). While still in town, don't miss a meal and a pint at the ◨**Applecross Inn ❷** on the waterfront. The menu rotates but the award-winning food is always delicious, local, and well-priced, especially the Ploughman's Lunch of rich cheeses, pickled toppings, red grapes, and fresh breads (£6.75). Traditional Highland music sessions begin on Friday nights at 9:45pm; join in if you think you've got the stuff. (☎744 262. Open daily 10am-midnight.) The inn also has both **B&B** and **hotel lodgings ❸,** all with free tea and coffee in light, airy rooms (£25-35 a night per person). Pretty **Applecross Campground ❷** is less expensive and uncrowded. (☎744 268. £10 per tent and 2 adults; 1 day free for weekly bookings.) Applecross is served by **postbus** #92 (M-Sa) from **Shieldaig** (11:30am) and **Torridon** (10:30am).

TORRIDON   ☎01445

Just north of the Applecross Peninsula (entire pop. 230), the tiny village of Torridon lies enclosed by Loch Torridon and the Torridon Hills, second in cragginess only to the Cuillins of Skye. This small, beautiful locale draws visitors with its multitude of hikes and climbs. The highest and closest peak is the challenging

Liathach (3456 ft.), considered by some the biggest bully in Britain; this small mountaineering community has grown up in its shadow.

From Inverness, **trains** (☎ (08457) 484 950) run to **Achnasheen** (1¼hr.; M-Sa 4 per day, Su 2 per day); there, **postbus** #91 (12:10pm) connects to Torridon. Buses do not meet every train; call ☎ (01463) 234 111 to confirm times. **Duncan Maclennan** (☎ (01520) 755 239) shuttle buses connect with the Inverness train at **Strathcarron** station (1hr.; June-Sept. M-Sa 12:30pm, Oct.-May M, W, F only; £3). The staff at the **Torridon Countryside Centre,** at the crossroads into Torridon, 100 yd. east of the hostel, possesses an encyclopedic knowledge of the surrounding region and sells guides detailing area walks. (☎ 791 221. Glorified slide show £2, concessions £1, children 50p. Open May-Sept. daily 10am-6pm.)

At the base of the daunting Liathach, the large **SYHA Torridon ❷** offers spartan rooms and a friendly staff, not to mention rowdy hillwalkers trumpeting their latest exploits. (☎ 791 284. Open Mar.-Oct. and Dec.-Jan. Dorms £10.50, under 18 £9.25.) If you're game for some exploring, the remote coastal **SYHA Craig ❶** is 13 mi. west of Torridon along the B8021. It's a 1hr. hike from the western end of the road at **Diabaig,** which **postbus** #91 reaches 8 mi. after Torridon. (Book through SYHA ☎ (0870) 155 3255. No phone or bedding; bring a sleeping bag. Open mid-May to Aug. Dorms £8.50, under 18 £7.) Between the Torridon hostel and the ranger office, the **Torridon Campsite ❶** has an exquisite location at the foot of the hills, although finding an unimpressive one would be difficult in this region. (☎ 791 313. £3 per tent.) The small **general store** 300 yd. west along the road is your lone bet for supplies. (☎ 791 400. Open M-Sa 9:30am-6pm, Su 10am-noon and 4-6pm.)

GAIRLOCH   ☎ 01445

With beautiful coastal scenery and several sandy beaches, the village of **Gairloch** is 20 winding miles north of Torridon. Though somewhat less spectacular than Applecross or Plockton, a trip to Gairloch still rewards with a wide, sandy beach—where an occasional seal surfaces—and the cluttered **Gairloch Heritage Museum,** with such debatable treasures as a carved stone ball ("possibly a symbol of power") and a lighthouse bulb. (☎ 712 287. Open Apr.-Oct. M-Sa 10am-5pm; winter months by arrangement. £2.50, seniors £2, children 50p.) Horseback riders can get their equestrian fix at the **Gairloch Trekking Centre,** across the road just south of the pier. (☎ 712 652. £3.50 per 15min.; lessons available.) Sometimes otters or even minke whales put in an appearance among the usual porpoises and seals on **Sail Gairloch Marine Life Cruises.** (☎ 712 636. Mid-May to Sept. £14, under 16 £12.) Six miles north along the coast road from Gairloch, the **Inverewe Gardens** are a glorious profusion of flowers from all over the world, grown in a tropical microclimate heated by the passing jetstream. Westerbus runs from Gairloch to the gardens at least once per day (M-Sa, £1), but it's best to check the timetable at the TIC (see below) first. (☎ 781 229. Garden open mid-Mar. to Oct. daily 9:30am-9pm; Nov. to mid-Mar. 9:30am-5pm. Visitors center open Apr.-Oct. daily 9:30am-5:30pm. Guided walks mid-Apr. to mid-Sept. M-F 1:30pm. £5, concessions £4.)

Westerbuses runs to Gairloch from **Ullapool** (2¼-2¾hr., M-Sa, £4.40). For £3 and a 10% deposit, the **tourist information centre** books B&Bs in Gairloch and Dundonnell, just east of the Ardessie Gorge. (☎ 712 130. Open June-Aug. M-Sa 9am-5:30pm, Su 10am-4pm; Sept.-Oct. and Easter-June M-Sa 9am-5pm; Nov.-Easter M-Sa 10am-5pm.) Buy grub and other goodies at **Mace supermarket,** on the A832 just south of its intersection with the B8021. (☎ 712 242. Open M-F 7:30am-9pm, Sa 8am-9pm.) Use the only **Internet connection** at the **post office,** 400 yd. west of the A832 on the B8021. (☎ (08457) 223 344. £1 per 15min. Open M-Sa 9am-12:30pm, M-Tu and Th-F also 2-5:30pm.) **Post Code:** IV21 2BZ.

Find a quiet, lochside bed at the **SYHA Carn Dearg ❶**, 2 mi. northwest of town on the B8021. Get off the Gairloch bus at the village of **Strath** and walk toward the sea from there. (☎712 219. Reception 7-10:30am and 5-11:30pm. Curfew 11:30pm. Open mid-May to Sept. Dorms £9.50, under 18 £8.25.) Just ½ mi. west of the hostel, campers can pitch at the beachside **Sands Holiday Centre ❶** (☎712 152; £9-10 per tent) or right in the center of Strath at the **Gairloch Caravan & Camping Holiday Park ❶** (☎712 373; £3.50 per person, £2 per tent).

ULLAPOOL ☎01854

Compared to its neighbors, buzzing Ullapool feels downright cosmopolitan. But while visitors are drawn by amenities, pub life, and transport links to the Outer Hebrides, no amount of tourism-induced ruckus can overpower Ullapool's mountain views and narrow bay. The area is rife with **hikes** long and short, including an excellent ramble through the shaded woodlands of **Ullapool Hill,** where the summit offers impressive views of Glenn Achall. Footpaths are marked with yellow signs and begin through the swinging gates 200 yd. northwest of the school on North Rd. and behind the Royal Hotel on Shore St. (*Ullapool Hill Path* map at the TIC; 2hr. round-trip). The SYHA hostel (see below) provides a free leaflet detailing a longer walk that traverses **Scots Pine** and the **Inverpolly Nature Reserve.** Wardens can also suggest how to **cycle** to nearby hostels in **Carbisdale** and **Achiniver.** For maps and more about area hikes, talk to the helpful folks at the **tourist information centre,** Argyle St. (☎612 135. Open July-Aug. M-Sa 9am-6pm, Su 10am-5pm; Apr.-June and Sept.-Oct. M-Sa 9am-5pm, Su 10am-4pm.) The award-winning **Ullapool Museum,** housed in an old church on West Argyle St., uses audiovisual displays to recount local history; highlighted displays feature local quilts, boat models, and Viking relics. (☎612 987. Open M-Sa 9:30am-5:30pm. £2, concessions £1.50, children free.)

Except for the 1am arrivals, **ferries** from **Stornoway, Lewis** (M-Sa 2-3 per day; £13, 5-day return £22.35) are met by **Scottish Citylink** and **Rapsons Buses** to and from **Inverness** (1½hr., £5.30). **Tim Dearman** also runs buses from Inverness (☎(01349) 883 585; 2hr., 1 per day). **CalMac** (☎612 358) runs a variety of day-long summer **cruise tours** to Lewis (from £18). Smaller boats conduct wildlife tours (£8-15) to the nearby **Summer Isles** (see p. 675); inquire at the booths by the pier. **Scotpackers** (see below) runs half- and full-day minibus tours (£10-15, guests £9-13.50). Access the **Internet** at Scotpackers or at the **library,** in the high school on Mill St. (☎612 543. Free. Open July to mid-Aug. Tu 2-8pm, Th 10am-8pm, F 10am-5pm; closed 1-2pm and 5-6pm.) The **post office** sits at West Argyle St. (☎612 228. Open M-Tu and Th-F 9am-1pm and 2-5:30pm, W and Sa 9am-1pm.) **Post Code:** IV26 2TY.

▨**Scotpackers West House ❶,** West Argyle St., answers all backpacker needs with towering bunks, easy chairs, and a homey lounge. Internet access is free for guests (non-guests £1 per 20min.) and bike rental is £10 per day. (☎/fax 613 126. Dorms £9.25.) The affiliated **Crofton House ❸** has double rooms (£25), but phone the hostel first. The well-situated **SYHA Ullapool ❷,** Shore St., 200 yd. east of the pier, compensates for crowded bunks with outstanding harbor views and amenities. Book ahead. (☎612 254. Laundry £2. Bike rental £6-12 per day. Dorms £10.50, under 18 £8.75.) At the west end of town, pitch your tent for £5 at the **Broomfield Holiday Park ❶** (☎612 026). **Safeway,** west of Quay St. on Latheron Ln., is a true grocery superstore. (☎613 291. Open M-Sa 8am-8pm, Su 9am-6pm.) Steer for ▨**The Seaforth ❷,** by the pier, which has live music on the weekends and a mouth-watering selection of whiskys. After a high-quality meal (£6-10), sample a hard-to-find, startlingly distinctive Laphroaig 15-Year-Old. (☎612 122. Open Su-W 11am-midnight, Th-Sa 11am-1am.) **The Ceilidh Place**

❸, 14 West Argyle St. (☎612 103), is a hotel, cafe, bar, bookstore, and gallery; elegant dinners (£12-18) are served and lively Celtic music is performed several nights a week in summer.

NEAR ULLAPOOL   ☎01854

CORRIESHALLOCH GORGE. Twelve miles south of Ullapool on the A835, the River Broom cascades 150 ft. down the **Falls of Measach** into a menacing gorge. Formed by glacial action, Corrieshalloch slices through the earth like a deep scar. Begin your visit by turning right on the footpath across from the bus stop; about 40 yd. northwest on the path, a short fenced plank thrusts harrowingly over the gorge and serves as a **viewpoint** for the falls upstream to the southeast. Retrace your steps and follow the footpath 100 yd. to the **suspension bridge** (built 1867) that balances over the falls, viewed with a little vertigo directly below. Though it sways unsettlingly with every step, six normal-sized hikers can safely oscillate on the (oft-inspected) relic. The gorge is easily accessible by any Ullapool-Inverness **bus;** double-check that a return trip exists before you set out.

■**ACHILTIBUIE.** Northwest of Ullapool, grander beauty awaits at remote **Achiltibuie,** a small village caught between moody coastal waters and towering rock crags. With a trio of sandy beaches and unique housing, this is the perfect setting for a getaway from beaten tourist paths. Off the coast of Achiltibuie, the lovely **Summer Isles** are so named because local crofters graze their sheep here during high season. The Isles are home to rugged rock formations, radiant beaches, and a seal colony. Tour them from **Ullapool** (see p. 674) or, more thoroughly, on the passenger vessel M.V. *Hectoria* from **Badentarbet Pier** at the western end of Achiltibuie. (☎622 200. Apr.-Oct. 3½hr. tours with 1hr. ashore M-Sa at 10:30am and 2:15pm; £15, children £7.50. 7hr. tour with 4½hr. ashore M-Sa at 10:30am; £20/£15.)

In town, the odd **Hydroponicum** is a self-proclaimed "garden of the future," where produce—including the only native highland banana—is grown without soil. You can also get meals made from the freshest, dirt-free ingredients at the **Lily Pond Cafe ❷.** (☎622 202. Tours depart every hr. Easter-Sept. 10am-5pm. £4.75, concessions £3.50, children £2.75, families £12.50. Cafe open mid-Apr. to Sept. daily 10am-6pm; June-Aug. also Th-Su 7-9pm.) At the **Achiltibuie Smokehouse,** 4 mi. to the northwest in Altandhu, patrons can watch as salmon and other foods are slit, sliced, and smoked. Buy your culinary souvenirs here: 200g of smoked Highland eel is only £18. (☎622 353. Open M-Sa 9:30am-5pm. Free.)

Spa Coaches leave from Ullapool (M-F 2 per day, Sa 1 per day; £2.50). If driving, take the A835 north 10 mi. from Ullapool, then turn west at the well-marked one-lane road and follow it 15 mi. to the coast. The only grocer, **Achiltibuie Store,** is on the main road, right in the middle of town (☎622 496. Open M-Sa 9am-5:30pm.) Another 50 yd. down the road, the **post office** doubles as an information center. (☎622 200. Open M-Sa 9-noon; M-W and F also 1-5:30pm). **Post Code:** IV26 2Y6.

The idyllic **SYHA Achininver ❶,** an old cottage ¼ mi. from a sandy beach and 3 mi. from Achiltibuie, is a short hike from the road. Ask the bus driver to let you off where the hostel is signposted. (☎622 254. Open mid-May to Sept. Dorms £8.75, under 18 £7.50.) Mary King runs the **Vegetarian B&B ❸,** combining two of the finer points in life: vegetables and art. Peek into the gallery of local works when you're not busy eating green. (☎622 426. Singles £20-25; doubles £30-35. Gallery open M-Sa 10am-5pm, by appointment during winter.)

LOCHINVER   ☎01571

Thirty miles up the northwest coast, the unremarkable town of Lochinver is a food-and-petrol outpost for the wild region of **Assynt,** breathtakingly desolate but nearly impossible to penetrate without a car. The **Assynt Visitor Centre** on the waterfront in Lochinver has an informative exhibit on the area, and serves as a TIC. (☎ 844 330. Books rooms for £3. Open Easter-Oct. M-Sa 10am-5pm, Su 10am-4pm.) The **Ranger Service** (☎ 844 654) offers free **guided walks** during summer.

Assynt is known for its treks (8-10hr.) up the imposing mountains of **Suilven** and **Canisp;** though lengthy, these trails are well cleared and accessible to walkers of all levels. Closer to town, you may be able to spot some wildlife. Turn south from the Visitor Centre; the signposted second left turn leads to **Glencanisp Lodge,** where a footpath famed for sightings of deer, otter, and golden eagles skirts the River Inver. At the path's end, retrace your steps to return home (2hr. round-trip). The **Culaig Wood Walk,** starting west of the field near the pier, is shorter (about 1hr. round-trip). From the Achmelvich hostel (see below), a **nature trail** crosses the town of **Alt-na-Bradhan** before reaching the striking rock formation at **Clachtoll** (5hr. round-trip). For longer expeditions, buy a good map—something like Landranger #15, available at the TIC (£6). **Assynt Angling Group** (☎ 844 257) can recommend fishing holes, and the TIC can set you up with a permit (£5 per day, £25 per week).

The only public transport to enter this forbidding country are the **Northern Explorer buses, Rapsons Coaches,** and **Spa Coaches** from Ullapool (1hr., 2-3 per day, £3-4), as well as **postbus** #123 from the Lairg train station (M-Sa 1pm). At the western end of town, just before the pier, the **Royal Bank of Scotland** has an **ATM.** (☎ 844 215. Open M-Tu and Th-F 9:15am-12:30pm and 1:30-4:45pm, W from 10am.) The **Spar** supermarket on the other side of town is managed jointly with the Esso **petrol station.** (☎ 844 207. Open M-Sa 8am-6:30pm, Su 9am-5:30pm.) Just next door is the **post office.** (☎ (08457) 223 344. Open M and W-F 8am-1pm and 2-5pm, Tu 8:30am-1pm.) **Post Code:** IV27 4SY.

The **Ardglas Guest House** ❷, across the stone bridge, is Lochinver's cheapest B&B, with fine views and spacious rooms. (☎ 844 257. Singles and doubles £16 per person.) **Hostels** are far away, but in dramatic locations with great access to hiking and cycling trails. The rugged (read: bare-bones) **SYHA Achmelvich** ❶, Recharn, is 3 mi. west on a stunning footpath, or 20min. by the 11:15am postbus. (☎ 844 480. No showers. Reception 7-10:30am and 5-11pm. Open Apr.-Sept. Dorms £8.75, under 18 £7.50.) Mr. MacLeod runs the nearby **Achmelvich campsite** ❶, beside a beach that can only be described as "Caribbean"—that is, until you sample the icy waters. (☎ 844 393. Tent pitch £7.) Another 13 mi. farther inland, the heart-rending ruins of **Ardvreck Castle** on Loch Assynt sit opposite the social **Inchnadamph Lodge** ❷, Assynt Field Centre, which has endless amenities. Local deer—including three-horned "Freaky"—lurk nearby, waiting for table scraps. (☎ 822 218. Breakfast included. Laundry £1.50. Dorms £10.45; doubles and twins £16.) Ullapool-Lochinver buses, including the Northern Explorer, stop here on request.

DURNESS   ☎01971

A quiet village on Scotland's north coast, Durness combines outstanding natural beauty with plenty of activities, making it a popular stop on a northwest tour. Ten minutes west of town, the yellow sands and pure blue water of secluded **Balnakeil Beach** would seem tropical but for the Atlantic winds and the puffin colony out on **Faraid Head.** A mile up the road from the town center, the ◪**Smoo Caves** take their name from *smuga*, the Viking word for hiding place—legend has it that centuries ago the bastard son of a McKay chieftain hid the bodies of 18 murdered men here. When the eerie caverns aren't flooded after heavy rains, you can float via rubber dinghy past the interior waterfall. (☎ 511 704; ask for Colin. 15min. tours depart from cave entrance Apr.-Sept. daily 10am-5pm. £2.50, children £1.) At the Smoo cave inlet, **Cape Sea Tours** runs 3hr. wildlife boat-watches, taking in Faraid Head and the Cliffs of Moine Schist, with frequent sightings of gray seals, dolphins, minke whales, and the ubiquitous puffins. (☎ 511 284 or 511 259. Easter-Oct. noon and 7pm. ₤7, children ₤3.50.) Britain's highest cliffs soar at **Cape Wrath,** 12 mi. west of Durness. From the Cape Wrath Hotel (1½ mi. west down the road from the town center), a ferry crosses to **Kyle of Durness** (☎ 511 376; 4 per day; return ₤3.80), where it's met by a **minibus** that completes the trip to Cape Wrath (☎ 511 287 or 511 343; return ₤6.50). Together, the ferry and bus operate on demand May through September starting at 9:30am. (Incidentally, the Cape closes every now and then so the Royal Air Force can practice blowing stuff up—call the ferry beforehand.)

To reach Durness, hop **postbus** #104 or 105 from the **Lairg** train station (☎ (01463) 256 228; M-Sa 2 per day). **Highland Country** bus #387 arrives from **Thurso** (2½hr., June to mid-Sept. M-Sa 1 per day, ₤7); **Tim Dearman** coaches pull in from **Inverness** (5hr., 1 per day, ₤14) and **Ullapool** (3hr., 1 per day, ₤8). The **tourist information centre** books B&Bs for ₤3 plus a 10% deposit. (☎ 511 259. Open Apr.-Oct. daily 10am-5pm, Nov.-Mar. 10am-1:30pm.) The **post office** is down the road to the south. (☎ 511 209. Open M-Tu and Th-F 9am-5:30pm, W and Sa 9am-12:30pm.) **Post Code:** IV27 4QF.

The best budget lodgings are provided by the amiable ◪**Lazycrofter Bunkhouse ❶,** whose dull exterior does little justice to its luxurious bunks and nifty showers. (☎ 511 209 or evening 511 366. ₤9 per person.) Simple and well-located, the **SYHA Durness ❶,** 1 mi. north of town along the A838, packs hostelers into bunks. (☎ 511 244. Reception 7-10:30am and 5-11pm. Curfew 11pm. Open Apr.-Sept. Dorms ₤6.75, under 18 ₤6.) Mrs. Conlon provides a less communal respite at her **Smoo Falls B&B ❷,** across the street from the Smoo Caves. (☎ 511 228. Call ahead Dec.-Jan. No smoking. ₤18 per person, with bath ₤20; singles ₤25.) **Sango Sands Camping Site ❶** overlooks the sea next to the visitor center. To the south find a sandy beach; to the north, the campground's own pub. (☎ 551 1726. Reception 9-9:30am and 6-6:30pm. Tent pitch ₤4. Showers 50p.)

THURSO AND SCRABSTER ☎ 01847

A big fish in a very, very small pond, Thurso (bursting its seams with a population of 9000) is considered a veritable Tokyo by the crofters and fishermen of Scotland's desolate north coast. The city has no museums and doesn't seem to care; even the refreshingly frank **tourist information centre,** Riverside Rd., treats the **castle ruins** east of town with casual indifference. (☎ 892 371. TIC open Apr.-Oct. M-Sa 10am-5pm, June-Sept. also Su 10am-4pm.) Thurso's "urban" character is complemented by one of Europe's best **surfing beaches,** near the castle. Rent wetsuits (₤6 per day) and surfboards (₤10) at **Harper's,** 57 High St. (☎ 893 179. Open M-Sa 10am-5pm.) **Scrabster,** 2½ mi. east, is no more than a ferry port for Orkney (see p. 678).

Infectiously friendly, ◪**Sandra's Backpackers Hostel ❶,** 24-26 Princes St., sports TV-blessed dorms, kitchenette, refrigerator, and shower, and the owners provide lifts to Scrabster for noon ferry connections. (☎ 894 575. Continental breakfast included. Internet 75p per 15min. Bike rental ₤8 per day. Dorms ₤8.50; private rooms ₤25.) The **Thurso Youth Club Hostel ❶** is stashed in the echoing halls of a converted mill. From the train station, walk east down Lover's Ln., turn north on Janet St., cross the footbridge over the river, and follow the path to the right. (☎ 892 964. Continental breakfast and linen included. Open July-Aug. Dorms ₤8.)

For good eats, **Sandra's Snack Bar and Takeaway ❶,** beneath the hostel, is a happening backpacker hangout with rock-bottom prices and tasty pizzas, curries, and fish. (☎ 894 575. Open M-F 7:30am-11:30pm, Sa 10am-2am, Su 12:30-10:30pm. 10% discount for hostelers.) A more sophisticated menu waits at **Le Bistro ❷,** 2 Traill St., with window seats for people-watchers. (☎ 893 737. Open M 10am-2:30pm, Tu-F 10am-9pm, Sa 9:30am-4pm and 5:30-9pm.) On Wednesday nights, young and old alike come together to join in singing and performing traditional folk music at **Commercial ("Comm") Bar,** 1 Princes St., Thurso's most popular gathering place. (☎893 366. Open M-Th 11am-midnight, F-Sa 11am-1am, Su noon-11pm.)

JOHN O'GROATS   ☎01955

While you may have heard of the town—it's mainland Britain's northernmost—John O'Groats is hardly memorable, having been robbed of native charm and infiltrated by touristy shops. Fortunately, the surrounding seas have been spared the systematic uglification. **Wildlife Cruises,** run by **John O'Groats Ferries,** leave the docks daily at 2:30pm in July and August to cruise the rugged waters of Pentland Firth, home to razorbills, kittiwakes, great black backs, and other animals you've never heard of. (☎611 353. 1½hr. £12, children £6, families £30, under 5 free.) **Dunnet Head,** halfway from John O'Groats to Thurso, is the true northernmost point on the Isle, but **Duncansby Head,** about 2 mi. east of town, has a better view overlooking the Pentland Firth toward Orkney. The **tourist information centre,** by the pier, helps plan escapes to the more attractive surrounding areas. (☎611 373. Open June-Aug. daily 9am-6pm; Apr.-May and Sept.-Oct. 10am-5pm.) To reach town from the **Wick train station,** take **Highland Country** bus #77 (40min.), which also runs to **Thurso** (1hr., M-Sa 5 per day) and passes the hostel. From May to August, John O'Groats Ferries's **Orkney Bus** rides from **Inverness** (daily 2:20pm, June-Aug. also 7:30am; £12). If stuck on the mainland, stay at the simple but practical **SYHA John O'Groats ❶,** 2½ mi. west in Canisbay. (☎611 424. Reception 7-10am and 5-11:30pm. Curfew 11:30pm. Open Easter-Sept. Dorms £8.25-9.50, under 18 £7.75-8.50.)

ORKNEY ISLANDS

Bjørn was here.
—ancient rune carved into Orcadian standing stone

Orkney Islands

Across the broad and occasionally rough Pentland Firth, the emerald villages, red sandstone cliffs, and iris-studded farmlands of Orkney are remote treasures reserved for the perseverant traveler. Removed from the tourist trail, Orkney's timeless assemblage of paddocks, beaches, and gardens—trod by Orcadians for millennia—are relatively challenging to reach, and even more difficult to travel between once you get there. Still, though public transportation is minimal, and samplings of Orkney's Stone Age sights are visible elsewhere in Scotland, the 70-island archipelago retains some of the best-preserved Pictish and Viking villages, monuments, and burial chambers in Europe. The Pentland Skerries and the islands of Westray, Papa Westray, and ·Copinsay (all pronounced to rhyme with "see") are also sacred to ornithology pilgrims—337 species of birds alight on or inhabit Orkney, and the feathered outnumber the flightless 100 to 1.

Mainland (sometimes called **Pomona**) is Orkney's main island, and holds its two largest towns. The small capital city of **Kirkwall** encases a dramatic 12th-century cathedral, still in use, and a fine medieval and Renaissance palace. Quieter and smaller still, **Stromness** invites visitors to wander down wynds to the waterside, where the cliffs shelter elderducks, fulmar petrels, and the occasional puffin. The southeastern seaside holds more modern secrets as well—at low tide, broken prows and sterns of sunken blockships rear up from the sea foam along the Churchill Barriers, causeways built by POWs during WWII.

◖ GETTING THERE

Ferries connect Orkney to mainland Scotland. **Pentland Ferries** (☎ (01856) 831 226) run the most budget-friendly service, from **Gills Bay,** just west of John O'Groats on the A836, to **St. Margaret's Hope,** on Orkney. From there, a free bus meets the ferry to bring passengers to **Kirkwall.** The bus serving the late ferry operates sporadically during the school year; call ahead to make sure one will be available. (Crossing 1hr.; 9:45am, 1:45, 6:45pm; £10, children £5, under 5 free.) If you're taking a **car** across (£25), be sure to book ahead.

John O'Groats Ferries (☎ (01955) 611 353) travel from **John O'Groats** to **Burwick, Orkney,** where a free bus takes passengers to Kirkwall. (Ferry 45min., bus 35min.; June-Aug. 9, 10:30am, 4, 6pm; May 9am and 6pm; Sept. 9am and 4:30pm; returns to John O'Groats 45min. after arrival; return £28, off-peak £25.) The **Orkney Bus** from **Inverness** (Platform #1) connects with the ferry in John O'Groats. A single ticket purchased in Inverness covers all transportation from Inverness to Kirkwall. (5hr.; Inverness-Kirkwall May 2:20pm, June-Aug. also 7:30am; Kirkwall-Inverness May 9am, June-Aug. also 4:15pm; £28, return £40.) The 7:30am bus must be booked in advance; once in Burwick, travelers have the option of joining a **whirlwind tour** of the archipelago returning in time for the 6pm ferry, ending in Inverness at 9pm. (Reservations ☎ (01955) 611 353. £44, children £22, under 5 free.) **Northlink Ferries** (☎ (01856) 851 144; www.northlinkferries.co.uk) took over the P&O Scottish Ferries routes in the fall of 2002. They run from **Scrabster** (just east of Thurso) to **Stromness** (1½hr.; M-F 3 per day, Sa-Su 2 per day; £27-33). A bus departs from the **Thurso** rail station for Scrabster before each crossing. Northlink also sails from **Aberdeen** to **Kirkwall** (see p. 627).

▣ LOCAL TRANSPORTATION

Orkney Coaches (☎ (01856) 870 555) run between **Kirkwall** bus station and **Stromness Pier Head** (30min., M-Sa 1-2 per hr., £2.20). **Orkney Ferries** (☎ (01856) 872 044) serve the outer islands. Ferries leave from **Kirkwall** to: **Eday** (2hr., 2 per day, £5.40); **North Ronaldsay** (2¾hr., July-Sept. F only, £5.40); **Sanday** (1½hr., 2 per day, £5.40); **Shapinsay** (45min., 5-6 per day, £2.70); **Stronsay** (1½-2hr., 1-2 per day, £5.40); **Westray/Papa Westray** (1½hr., 2-3 per day, £5.40). Ferries leave from **Houton Pier,** accessible from Kirkwall by bus (30min., 5 per day, £1.40), to **Flotta** (M-Sa 3-4 per day, occasional Su service in summer; £2.70) and **Hoy** (20-45min.; M-F 6 per day, Sa-Su 2-5 per day; £2.70). Ferries leave from **Tingwall** (catch a bus from Kirkwall bus station; 35min., 5 per day) to **Rousay/Egilsay/Wyre** (30min., M-Sa 5 per day, £2.70). For exact times, get the *Orkney Public Transportation Guide* (free) from the Stromness or Kirkwall TIC. Winter ferries are far less frequent. It's possible to fly to many of the islands from **Kirkwall Airport;** call **British Airways** (☎ (01856) 872 494).

Car rental, if you can afford it, is by far the most convenient way of getting around Orkney; for rental agencies, try **W.R. Tullock** (☎ 876 262; 21+; from £34 per day) or **Peace's Car Hire** (☎ 872 866; 21+; from £20 per day) in Kirkwall, or **Stromness**

Car Hire (☎850 850; 21+; from £31 per day, £157 per week; open M-F 8am-6pm, Sa 9am-5pm). The less profligate should consider **biking,** though the rain and wind can be problematic. Wheels can be rented in Kirkwall from **Bobby Cycle Centre,** Tankerness Ln., off Broad St. (☎877 777 or (07799) 642 641; £10 per day; open M-F 9am-5pm, Sa 9am-5:30pm) or in Stromness at **Orkney Cycle Hire** (☎850 255; £6 per day, helmet and map included; open daily 8:30am-9pm). Rates are slightly lower in Kirkwall, and the town has better access to the good Mainland sights; consider taking the bus from Stromness.

KIRKWALL   ☎01856

Friendly and self-confident, Kirkwall exists primarily for those who live and work in the islands. Unaccustomed to tourists, the ancient structures of this historic town house the administrative, transportation, and social centers of Orkney, and provide the most convenient base for exploring the islands' mysteries.

🔏 **PRACTICAL INFORMATION.** The Kirkwall **tourist information centre,** 6 Broad St., books B&Bs for £1.50 and distributes invaluable transport info. (☎872 856. Open May-Aug. M-F 8am-5pm, Sa-Su 9am-4pm; Apr. and Sept.-Oct. M-Sa 10am-4pm, Su 10am-3pm; Nov.-Mar. M-Sa 1-3pm; open for late ferry arrivals.) The only **Internet access** in Orkney is at **Support Training Limited,** 2 West Tankerness Ln., one block west of Broad St. (☎873 582. £1 per 10min., £5 per hr. Open M-Tu and Th 9am-5pm, W and F 9am-9:30pm, Sa 10am-5pm.) Other services include: **Bank of Scotland,** 56 Albert St. (☎682 000; open M-Tu and Th-F 9am-5pm, W 9:30am-5pm); **Kelvinator Launderama,** Albert St. (☎872 952; open M-F 8:30am-5:30pm, Sa 9am-5pm); the **police** (☎872 241); and the **post office,** 15 Junction Rd. (☎874 249; open M-Tu and Th-F 9am-5pm, W 9am-4pm, Sa 9:30am-12:30pm). **Post Code:** KW15 1AA.

🔏🎄 **ACCOMMODATIONS AND FOOD.** Kirkwall's **SYHA hostel** ❶ is on Old Skapa Rd. Follow the main pedestrian road south from the TIC for ½ mi. as it evolves from Broad St. into Victoria St. Cross and Union St., heading southwest to Main St., and then High St., where SYHA signs will point you home. Lodgings are unluxurious, but the warm atmosphere more than compensates. (☎872 243. Reception 7:30-10:30am and 5-11:30pm. Lockout 10:30am-5pm. Curfew midnight. Open Apr.-Oct. Dorms £9.50, under 18 £8.25.) If you're catching an early ferry out of Kirkwall and want to be right in the town center, try tiny **Peedie Hostel** ❷, 1 Ayre Rd., across the street from the pier, with tiny bunks, tiny kitchen, and tiny bathroom. (☎875 477. Dorms £10.) At **Mr. and Mrs. Flett's B&B** ❷, Cromwell Rd., climb a ship's staircase to cozy rooms with views of the harbor and sea. (☎873 160. £15-17 per person.) For a more upscale environment, head to the **West End Hotel** ❹, Main St. (☎872 368; fax 876 181. Singles £42; doubles £29 per person.) **Camp** at **Pickaquoy Centre Caravan & Camping Site** ❶, on Pickaquoy Rd. just south of the A965. (☎879 900. £3.60-4.75 per person.) You can also pitch a tent almost anywhere on the islands, as long as you ask the landowner first.

   Safeway dominates the corner of Broad St. and Great Western Rd. (☎228 876. Open M-F 8am-9pm, Sa 8am-8pm, Su 9am-6pm.) **Buster's Diner** ❶, 1 Mounthoolie Ln., is draped in tacky Americana and cooks up pizza and burgers for under £5—all under the front end of a Ford Mustang. (☎876 717. Open M-F noon-2pm and 4:30-10pm, Sa noon-2am, Su 4-10pm.) **Trenabies Cafe** ❶, 16 Albert St., encourages caffeine addictions and tooth decay with cappuccinos and sweet pastries, but can also fill you up with sandwiches and tatties. (☎874 336. Open M-F 8am-6pm, Sa 9:30am-6pm.) Whether you're downing a Dark Island Ale while watching football or sipping a Highland Park whisky and arguing politics with the locals, **The Bothy Bar ❶** is the place to be. (☎876 000. Live folk music Su nights. Open M-W 11am-midnight, Th-Sa 11am-1am, Su noon-midnight; food served until 9:30pm.)

◙ SIGHTS. South of the TIC on Broad St., **St. Magnus Cathedral,** begun in 1137, looms over the town with its blood-red sandstone blocks. Grave markers dating from the 16th and 17th centuries line the aisles. (Open Apr.-Sept. M-Sa 9am-7pm, Su 2-6pm; Oct.-Mar. M-Sa 9am-1pm and 2-5pm. Free.) Across Palace Rd. from the cathedral, the **Bishop's and Earl's Palaces** once housed the Bishop of Orkney (yay!) and his enemy, the wicked Earl Patrick Stewart (boo! hiss!), but became part of the same complex when the earl was executed for treason. (☎871 918. Both buildings open Apr.-Sept. daily 9:30am-6pm; Oct.-Nov. M-Sa 10am-2pm. £2, seniors £1.50, children 75p. Combination ticket allows entry into both palaces plus Skara Brae, Maes Howe, and the Broch of Gurness. £11/£8/£3.50.)

BA'... NOT JUST FOR SHEEP

Amid all the puffin sightings and archaeological digs lurks a more lively Orkney tradition—the Ba'. Best described as a large rugby game with no rules and no limit on time or team size, the Ba' takes place on New Year's Day. Two teams—whose ranks have been known to swell to 400—take to the streets of Kirkwall: the Uppies (from the upper part of town) and the Doonies (you figure it out). The action begins in front of St. Magnus Cathedral, when a specially crafted Ba' ball is thrown to the waiting throngs. The massive scrum can continue for hours, ending at nightfall. There are no time-outs or penalties, although the practice of smuggling the Ba' ball in a car (tried once) is frowned upon. The Uppies quest to chuck the ball into the harbor, while the Doonies labor to hit the side of the town hall: the hardy soul deemed most valuable player gets to keep it.

It's definitely worth your while to visit the **Orkney Museum,** 52 Alfred St., opposite the cathedral, where fun exhibits help contextualize the islands' sights. Ancient artifacts, early photographs, and paintings by native son Stanley Cursiter share space in the house and garden of an Orkney laird, or absentee landowner. (☎873 191. Open Apr.-Sept. M-Sa 10:30am-5pm, Su 2-5pm; Oct.-Mar. M-Sa 10:30am-12:30pm, 1:30-5pm. Free.) The **Highland Park Distillery Visitor Centre** lies 20min. south of town on Holm Rd. Highland Park is the world's northernmost whisky distillery and purveyor of acclaimed single malts. Walk to the southern end of Broad St./Victoria St., turn west on Clay Loan, then south on Bignold Park Rd., and take the right fork onto Holm Rd. (☎874 619; www.highlandpark.co.uk. Open Apr.-Oct. M-F 10am-5pm; May-Sept. also Sa-Su noon-5pm, last tour 4pm; Nov.-Mar. shop open M-F 1-5pm, tours 2pm. £3, concessions £2, children £1.50.)

STROMNESS   ☎01856

Founded in the 16th century as a fishing and whaling port, Stromness is a town of narrow cobblestone streets and beautiful open vistas overlooking a well-mannered bay. The **Pier Arts Centre** heads Victoria St. and merits a walk-through to view the work of contemporary Scottish and international artists. (☎850 209. Open Tu-Sa 10:30am-12:30pm and 1:30-5pm. Free.) The **Stromness Museum,** 52 Alfred St., tackles the history of local boating with artifacts from the whaling and fishing industries. (☎850 025. Open Apr.-Sept. daily 10am-5pm; Oct.-Mar. M-Sa 11am-3:30pm. £2.50, concessions £2, children 50p, families £5.)

The **Northlink Ferry** floats to Stromness from Scrabster (see p. 679); almost everything you'll need is on Victoria St., which parallels the harbor. The **tourist information centre,** in an 18th-century warehouse on the pier, provides free maps. (☎850

THE BIG SPLURGE

BISTRO 76

In a small town, in a small basement, tucked away on a small street, lies the pride of Orkney—The Orca Hotel's Bistro 76. Islanders come from the far reaches of their far-flung archipelago to eat at "the 76," and *Let's Go*, patron of more than a few hidden treasures, can hardly blame them.

In this 300-year-old subterranean escape, candlelit shadows flicker on overhead beams made from the masts of ships. You can feast on native dishes from scallops (£9.80) to Wild Orkney Fillet Breast (£14.75), try a variety of vegetarian options (£7.50-9), or get your spice on with an Orcadian curry (£9).

The menu rotates, and throws a theme night into the mix now and then—a taste of Italy, perhaps, or maybe Austria. There's also an all-you-can-eat buffet on Thursday, Friday, and weekend evenings.

The lengthy wine list (100+) makes for excellent light reading, and the small stage in the dining area often weaves the soothing tunes of live music into the sensuous tapestry of candlelight and delicious smells. The 76 has every right to be proud of its subtly refined atmosphere and warm, friendly service. *(Victoria St. in the middle of Stromness, below Orca's Hotel.* ☎/fax 850 447. Open Tu-Su 5-11pm.)

716. Open May-Sept. daily 8:30am-6pm; Oct.-Apr. M-F 9am-5pm, Sa 10am-12:30pm and 1:30-4pm; open to meet late ferries.) The **library**, 2 Hellihole Rd., is anxiously awaiting free **Internet access**, promised for 2003. (☎850 907. Open M-F 2-5pm and 6-8pm, Sa 10am-1pm and 2-5pm.) The **Bank of Scotland**, on Victoria St., has the only **bureau de change** in town. (☎862 000. Open M-F 9:45am-12:30pm and 1:30-4:45pm, W from 10:45am.) The **post office** is at 37 Victoria St. (☎850 225. Open M-F 9am-1pm and 2-5:15pm, Sa 9am-12:30pm.) **Post Code:** KY16 3BS.

A half-mile from the TIC (turn left onto Victoria St., then right onto Hellihole Rd.), the **SYHA Stromness ❶** is not as infernal as its address suggests. Perched above the pier, it offers comforting sea views, a relaxing dining area, and new beds. (☎850 589. Lockout 10:30am-5pm. Curfew 11:30pm. Open mid-Mar. to Oct. Dorms £8.25, under 18 £7.) **Brown's Hostel ❶**, 45-47 Victoria St., has an easy-going atmosphere and fewer rules, but less space. (☎850 661. £2 key deposit. Dorms £8.) The **Point of Ness Caravan and Camping Site ❶** is a mile from the pierhead. (☎873 535 or 851 235. Laundry and lounge. Open May to mid-Sept. £3.60-5.50 per tent. Electricity £1.85. Showers 20p.) **Orca's Hotel ❸**, 76 Victoria St., offers friendly B&B-style service in the middle of town and keeps a stellar restaurant (see "Bistro 76") hidden down below. (☎/fax 850 447; www.orchotel.com. £21-23 per person.) Across from the pier, **Julia's Coffee Shop ❶**, 20 Ferry Rd., has delicious baked goods and sandwiches for £2-5. Down a creamy hot chocolate, munch a succulent BLT, or tuck into a veggie burger as sunlight pours across the bay waters and into the bay windows. (☎850 904. Open M-Sa 9am-5pm; Easter-Sept. also Su 10am-4pm.)

OTHER MAINLAND SIGHTS ☎01856

Mainland is endowed with an astonishing wealth of Stone Age and Viking remains—not to mention the billowing mist, rocky promontories, and primrose expanses covering the islands. Excellent walks abound, but getting to many sights without a car or superhuman stamina can be tricky, as public transport is either scant or absent. In the summer, **bus** #8A runs twice per day in either direction from Kirkwall to Stromness, hitting the four main archaeological sites: Maes Howe Tomb, the Standing Stones of Stenness, the Ring of Brodgar, and Skara Brae. Despite endless uphills and winds that make even downhills laborious, **cycling** may be the best and cheapest way to do Orkney justice (see p. 679 for rental shops).

If you want guidance, ranger-naturalist Michael Hartley of **Wildabout Tours** squires visitors around

Mainland and Hoy in his minibus on half- and full-day tours. With a vigorous imagination and encyclopedic knowledge of Orkney, Michael helps visitors envision the islands of millennia past. (☎851 011. Tours Mar.-Oct. daily. From £10; student and hosteler discounts.) Orkney native John Grieve leads **Discover Orkney Tours** (☎872 865), which crafts trips to meet your interests (from £10). John will also take you to the other islands—a great way to see them if you lack time or transport (from £29). Both guides leave from the TICs in Kirkwall and Stromness; if you arrange ahead, John Grieve will also pick you up from your ferry, plane, or accommodation.

■**SKARA BRAE.** Dating back 5000 years, Skara Brae was once a bustling Stone Age village. As the ocean crept farther in, waves gradually consumed the village houses; after approximately 500 years of continuous habitation, the villagers abandoned the settlement. Preserved in sand, the village slept quietly until 1850, when a violent storm ripped out the side of the cliff and revealed nine houses, a workshop, and covered town roads, all in perfect condition. While the visitors center is open only during the day, the site remains accessible until nightfall—a trip at dusk avoids tourists and the admission fee. The **Skaill House** is the 17th-century home of the lairds of Breckness, the family who rediscovered the island. *(By the Bay of Skaill.* ☎841 501. *Open Apr.-Sept. daily 9:30am-6:30pm; Oct.-Mar. M-Sa 9am-4:30pm, Su 2-4:30pm. Skara Brae and Skaill House £4.50, seniors £3.30, children £1.30; free tour of Skaill House.)*

RING OF BRODGAR. Six miles east of Skara Brae on the A965, the sedimentary sandstones of the Ring of Brodgar once witnessed gatherings of local chieftains (maybe) or burial ceremonies (perhaps); no two archaeologists agree (though they all discount the *Let's Go* theory of alien hootenannies). The power of the sight's architecture, however, is indisputable. Arranged in a 150 yd. circle, the 36 stones used to number 60 and were surrounded by a deep ditch that would have warded off dogs and wild predators, and which is now filled in for the safety of visitors. The Ring has stayed true to its heritage as a venue for unusual assemblies—drawn by deep amber sunsets that silhouette the stones against a blazing sun, a motley crew congregates annually for the summer solstice.

STANDING STONES OF STENNESS. Less than a mile east of the Ring on the A965, the bern-enclosed Standing Stones of Stenness are somewhat less impressive. A solitary monolith directly between the two monuments causes some to argue that Stenness and Brogdar were once part of the same ceremonial process. By 1760 only four of the original 12 stones remained—no one knows what became of the other eight, but some suggest that they were knocked down by locals angered by the monument's pagan origins.

MAES HOWE TOMB. Halfway between Kirkwall and Stromness on the A965, this tomb may have held the bones of the area's earliest settlers (from approximately 2700 BC). On the 20min. guided tour, watch as a flashlight held up against the wall causes shadows from the carvings to leap off the chamber walls. These later runes, carved by the Vikings, are almost more of an attraction than the tomb itself. This, the largest collection of runic inscriptions in the world, enabled linguists to crack the runic alphabet and translate profound statements such as "This was carved by the greatest rune carver" and "Ingigerth is the most exquisite of women." *(☎761 606; www.maeshowe.co.uk. Open Apr.-Sept. daily 9:30am-6pm; Oct.-Mar. M-Sa 9:30am-4pm, Su 2-4pm. £2.80, seniors £2, children £1.)*

BROUGH OF BIRSAY. An island showing evidence of early Christian and Viking habitation, the Brough is just off the northwest coast of Mainland. Once the administrative and religious center of Orkney, the island's kirkyard holds a Pictish stone engraving of a royal figure with a crown, suggesting that Orcadian kings once ruled from here. The

Brough is accessible by foot only in the hour before and after low tide; tidal charts are available at TICs. Bird-watching is absorbing, but linger too long and the puffins may become your bedfellows. *(Open mid-June to Sept. £1.50, seniors £1.10, children 50p.)*

CHURCHILL BARRIERS AND SCAPA FLOW. In 1939, German U-boats entered the straits leading to the **Scapa Flow** naval anchorage during an exceptionally high tide, sinking a warship, killing 800 seamen, and escaping unscathed. The next year, Prime Minister Churchill erected these massive barriers to seal the seas from attack. The POWs who built the barriers exhausted over a quarter-million tons of rock, and the barrier's **causeways** now provide access from Mainland to the smaller southeast islands of **Lamb Holm, Glimps Holm, Burray,** and **South Ronaldsay.** If you cross the barriers at dusk, look eastwards for one of the sinister oil tankers that patrols the distant North Sea, shrouded in mist.

Scapa Flow witnessed an earlier destructive event: the scuttling of 74 retired German warships in June 1919 by Admiral Ludwig von Reuter, earning him the world record for most ships sunk at one time. To the delight of scuba divers from around the world, seven of the wrecks remain. **Scapa Scuba,** 13 Ness Rd., based in Stromness, offers the non-certified lessons, equipment, and a dive to the wrecks. They also offer more involved tours for experienced divers. *(☎/fax 851 218. Half-day £55.)* If you don't want to get wet, **Roving Eye Enterprises** does the marine work for you via a roaming underwater camera. *(☎811 360. Tours leave Houton Pier daily 1:20pm.)*

SMALLER ISLANDS

BEYOND THE BARRIERS. On **Lamb Holm,** the **Italian Chapel** is all that remains of Camp 60, a prison that held several hundred Italian POWs during WWII. When not at work on the Churchill Barriers, the Italians—using only cement, corrugated iron, and shipwrecked wood—transformed their bare cement hut into a beautiful and brilliant house of worship that is still in use today. (Open Apr.-Sept. daily 9am-10pm; Oct.-Mar. 9am-4:30pm; occasionally closed F afternoon, the traditional time for Orkney weddings. Services first Su of the month. Free.) During the summer, **Causeway Coaches** chug over the Churchill Barriers from Kirkwall to the pier at **St. Margaret's Hope** (☎(01856) 831 444; 3-4 per day). A tiny eight-bed hostel and organic farm, **Wheems ❶,** stands on South Ronaldsay. Call ahead and they might pick you up. (☎(01856) 831 537. Open Apr.-Oct. Dorms £6.50.)

HOY. The landscape of Hoy ("High Island"), the second-largest island in Orkney, is surprisingly rocky and mountainous. All visitors should glimpse its most famous landmark, the **Old Man of Hoy,** a majestic 450 ft. sea stack off the west coast of the island. Hikers can take the steep marked footpath from **Rackwick,** 2 mi. away (3hr. round-trip). The **North Hoy Bird Reserve** offers respite for guillemots and a host of other species. Dedicated puffin-scouts should see several here during breeding season (late June to early July)—the rest of the year, the pudgy little birds rough it on the seas. The **SYHA Hoy ❶** near the pier and the eight beds of **SYHA Rackwick ❶** farther south, 2 mi. from the Old Man of Hoy, offer accommodations and share a telephone number. These hostels do not provide linen, and the island is decidedly sleepingbagless. (☎(01856) 873 535. Hoy open May to mid-Sept.; Rackwick open mid-Mar. to mid-Sept. Dorms £7.50, under 18 £6.50.) Food and supplies are also difficult to procure, especially on Sundays.

SHAPINSAY. A mere 45min. from Kirkwall, with frequent ferry service, Shapinsay is the most accessible of the outer isles. Mostly wide-open space, Shapinsay's relatively flat landscape is defined by **Ward Hill,** the island's highest point at 210 ft. On a clear day you can see almost all the Orkney Islands. An excellent example of the Victorian Baronial style, **Balfour Castle** (built 1848) was formerly home to the influential lairds of Balfour and is now a posh guest house. Romantics can rent the castle and its chapel for weddings. For those without the curiosity or cash to see inside, the castle is perfectly visible from the ferry. (☎(01856) 711 282, tours 872 856. Tours leave Kirkwall pier May-Sept. Su 2:15pm. £15.) **Burroughston Broch,** an Iron Age shelter, lies 5 mi. north of the ferry pier. Archaeology buffs will be thrilled by the crumbling round home, which was excavated in the 1860s. For fans of the feathered, the **Bird Hide,** about a mile north of the pier, looks out over a Royal Society for the Protection of Birds wetland reserve at Mill Dam Pond. For best results, bring binoculars. (Open daily dawn-dusk. Free.) There are no hostels on Shapinsay, but the Kirkwall TIC (see p. 680) can provide information on B&Bs.

PAPA WESTRAY. Now home to a meager 64 Orcadians, the "isle of the priests" once supported an early Christian Pictish settlement. Today's pilgrims content themselves with bird-watching or archaeology. Fly from Kirkwall for £10 (overnight stay required)—if the plane makes a stop at Westray, you can put a certificate for world's shortest commercial flight on your fridge. On the west coast, the **Knap of Howar** is the location of the earliest standing house in northern Europe (c. 3500 BC), built centuries before the pyramids of Egypt. The **Bird Sanctuary** at North Hill sports Europe's largest colony of Arctic terns. Two miles north of the pier, **Beltane House ❶** is open year-round. Hostelers enjoy ensuite dorm rooms while the B&B guests get their own sitting room, but both have access to the only liquor-licensed establishment on the island—a closet full of booze. (☎(01857) 644 267. Dorms £10; B&B £20 per person.) Bring enough food for at least a day, as supplies are difficult to procure on Papa Westray.

WESTRAY. The largest of the outer isles sits just west of Papa Westray, and boasts ruined **Noltland Castle** and the **Knowe O'Burristae Broch,** along with other ancient rubble and magnificent cliffs. Legend holds that the windowless castle is linked underground to the **Gentlemens' Cave,** which hid supporters of Bonnie Prince Charlie. Bird-watchers rejoice on **Noup Head Reserve,** while budget travelers celebrate the two top-notch hostels. **The Barn ❷,** Chalmersquoy, is practically a B&B, minus the second B. (☎(01857) 677 214. £11.75, children £8.80.) **Bis Geos Hostel ❶,** near Pierowall, can arrange a free bus from the ferry pier to the threshold of their heated flagstone floors. (☎(01857) 677 420. Linen £2. Open May-Sept. Dorms £9.)

EDAY. The peat-covered hills of Eday hide Stone Age field walls, chambered tombs like **Vinquoy** and **Huntersquoy Cairns,** the towering **Stone of Setter,** and on the Calf of Eday, the remnants of an Iron Age roundhouse. **SYHA Eday ❶,** London Bay, is on the main north-south road 4 mi. from the pier. (☎(01857) 622 206. Laundry £2. Open Mar.-Oct. Dorms £6.75, under 18 £6. Camping £2.)

ROUSAY. Some will argue that Orkney's finest archaeological sights lie not on Mainland, but here on Rousay. Here the **Midhowe Broch and Cairn** has it all covered, sporting remnants of the Stone, Bronze, and Iron Ages. The **Knowe of Yarso Cairn** stands on a cliff overlooking Eynhallow Sound, and the **Westness Walk** winds past sites from the Neolithic, Pictish, Viking, medieval, and crofting eras. Stay at the **Rousay Hostel ❶** on Trumland Farm near the pier; turn left from the ferry port and walk 5min. down the main road. (☎(01856) 821 252. Bedding £2. Dorms £6.)

NORTH RONALDSAY. The most remote of Orkney's islands is not lacking in archaeological wonders, with the **Broch of Burrian,** the **Brae of Stennabreck,** and an unusual standing stone with a hole through it. Better yet, the island's famous **seaweed-eating sheep** graze on the beaches. Viciously protective nesting birds are all over—take a cue from them and stay at the **North Ronaldsay Bird Observatory Hostel ❶.** (☎(01857) 633 200. Dorms £8; full board £18. Call ahead for a lift from the airport.) Airfares to North Ronaldsay are an unreal £10 if you stay overnight.

SHETLAND ISLANDS ☎01595

Shetland Islands

Shetland and Orkney both became part of Scotland in the 15th century—when King Christian I of Denmark and Norway mortgaged them to pay for his daughter's dowry—but the archipelagoes have little else in common. Shetland, closer to Norway than to Great Britain, seems a country unto itself, looking proudly to a Viking rather than Scottish heritage, an influence lingering in Nordic craftsmanship, Scandinavian architecture, and festivals like the longship-burning Up-Helly-Aa'. Most Shetlanders will look askance if you imply that their homeland is part of the UK—"Scotland," they will tell you, "is down there." Local poet Hugh MacDiarmid aptly described yet another difference between the northern islands: "The Orcadian is a farmer with a boat, the Shetlander is a fisherman with a croft." Indeed, the greatest split may not be genealogical but geological. The true gift of Shetland is the land itself: the rugged hills, peaty fields, jagged cliffs, and windswept valleys found between long fingers of the Atlantic Ocean and North Sea. The hardy people tend hardy crops and hardy animals—peat, ponies, and sheep, sheep, sheep—turning their isolated world into an oasis of relative prosperity.

⚔ ☾ GETTING THERE AND CROSSING THE NORTH SEA

The fastest way to Shetland is by **plane**, assuming the weather cooperates. **Sumburgh Airport** lies on the southern tip of Mainland near the town of Sumburgh. **Leasks** buses run from the airport to **Lerwick** (☎ 693 162. 1hr.; M-F 6 per day, Sa 4 per day, Su 2 per day; £2.10), arriving at the **Viking Bus Station** (☎ 694 100), 5min. from the city center on Commercial Rd. Flights come in from **Orkney,** but prices rise to the hundreds if you don't stay over a Saturday (35min.; M-Sa 1 per day; £88, £74 booked 1 week ahead). **Ridgeway Travel** (☎ (01856) 873 359), by the Kirkwall TIC in Orkney, can get you tickets. **British Airways** (☎ (08457) 773 3377) also flies from **Aberdeen** (£99), **Edinburgh** (£168), and **Glasgow** (£168).

Ferries arrive at **Holmsgarth Terminal,** a 20min. walk northwest of Lerwick's town center, and the smaller **Victoria Pier,** downtown across from the TIC. **Northlink Ferries** (☎ (01856) 851 144) cruise from **Aberdeen** (12-14hr.; M, W, F, Su 7pm; Tu, Th, Sa 5pm; £43-63) and **Kirkwall, Orkney** (7¾hr.; Tu, Th, Sa 11:45pm; £26-39). **P&O Smyril Line** (☎ 690 845) runs mid-May to mid-Sept. from Lerwick to **Bergen, Norway** (13½hr.; M 11:30pm; £68, berth from £77) and to **Iceland** (31hr., W 2am, £150) via the **Faroe Islands** (13hr., £68), with a 10% off-season student discount.

🚃 LOCAL TRANSPORTATION

Infrequent public transport makes getting around Shetland difficult. **Ferries** within the archipelago are heavily subsidized; the longest trips cost about £2. All except those to Fair Isle transport bikes for free. Shetland's main **bus** lines are **John Leask & Son** (☎ 693 162) and **Shetland Coaches** (☎ 880 217). The TIC stocks the vital *Shetland Transport Timetable* (£1) with bus, ferry, and plane schedules. To reach remote areas on Shetland's decent road system, try **Bolts Car Hire,** 26 North Rd. (☎693 636, airport branch (01950) 460 777; 21+; £26 per day) or **Grantfield Garage,** 44 North Rd. (☎692709; 25+; £28 per day). **Eric Brown's Cycle Hire,** on the second floor of Grantfield Garage, rents touring bikes. (☎692 709. £7.50 per day, £45 per week. Helmet £2. Open M-W 8am-9pm, Th-Sa 8am-10pm, Su 11am-9pm.) Remember that strong winds and arduous hills can make biking difficult.

Various **tour** companies offer painfully pricey ways of seeing more of Shetland. The most affordable are the **Leasks Coach Tours,** on the Esplanade in Lerwick. (☎693 162. Mainland tours £9-14, Yell and Unst £25; mid-May to Sept. M-Sa 7:30am-5pm, Su 9:30am-2pm.) More expensive options are the folklore-oriented **Island Trails** (☎(01950) 422 408; May-Sept.), the **Shetland Wildlife Tours** (☎(01950) 422 483), and the artsy **See Shetland** (☎693 434; £25 half-day, £35-45 day).

✳ 🛈 ORIENTATION AND PRACTICAL INFORMATION

Lerwick is on the eastern coast of the main island (called **Mainland**) and is served by the A970, which runs the island's length. The **tourist information centre,** Market Cross, covers all of Shetland and books beds anywhere in the islands for £3 and a 10% deposit. (☎693 434; fax 695 775. Open May-Sept. M-F 8am-6pm, Sa 8am-4pm, Su 10am-1pm; Oct.-Apr. M-F 9am-5pm.) Other services include: **Royal Bank of Scotland,** 81 Commercial St. (☎694 520; open M-Tu and Th-F 9:15am-4:45pm, W 10am-4:45pm); free **Internet access** at the **Shetland Library,** in the church on Lower Hillhead (☎693 868; open M, W-Th 10am-7pm; Tu and F-Sa 10am-5pm); and the **post office,** 46-50 Commercial St. (☎(08457) 223 344; open M-F 9am-5pm, Sa 9am-12:30pm). **Post Code: ZE1 0AA.**

⌂ ACCOMMODATIONS AND CAMPING

The community-run **SYHA hostel ❶,** Islesburgh House, at King Harald St. and Union St., has excellent facilities, elegant curtains, friendly staff, and a cafe, but rules are inflexible. (☎692 114. Reception 9-9:30am, 4-4:30pm, and 9:45-10:15pm; at other times try the neighborly Community Centre. Laundry £1. Curfew 11:45pm. Open Apr.-Sept. Dorms £9.25, under 18 £8.) Lifelong Shetlander **Mrs. Laurenson ❷,** 4 Sands of Sound, runs a quiet B&B overlooking the ocean, a 20min. walk south from Lerwick. (☎696 799. £18-20 per person.) There are three **campgrounds** on Mainland, but you can pitch almost anywhere with the landowner's permission. **Clickimin Caravan and Camp Site ❶** is closest to the Lerwick ferry terminal; turn left (south) on Holmsgarth Rd. (the A970), go through the roundabout, and turn right (west) on North Lochside. (☎741 000. Showers and laundry. Reception 8:30am-10pm. Open May-Sept. Pitches £4.40-8.40.)

Camping **böds ❶** (Old Norse for barns) are a *very* basic accommodations alternative. Mainland's four böds are available from April to September: **Betty Mouat's** near the airport (with hot water and showers), **The Sail Loft** next to the pier in Voe, the **Voe House** in Walls, and **Johnnie Notions** (no electricity) at Hamnavoe, Eshaness, in the far northeast. **Grieve House** is on tiny Whalsay, near Lerwick by bus. The **Windhouse Lodge,** on Yell, is better equipped. All böds cost £5 per night and must be booked in advance through the Lerwick TIC. Bring sleeping bag, camping stove, and 50p coins for electricity (when available); the grass and roof are already there.

🎨 📋 FOOD AND PUBS

Inexpensive eats cluster in the center of **Lerwick.** Head to **D.G. Leslie's** for groceries. (☎ 693 073. Open M-Th 8am-8pm, F-Sa 8am-7pm, Su 10am-7pm.) Jivin' **Osla's Cafe ❶,** on the Esplanade, specializes in pancakes that are worth a stop, no matter what time of day. (☎ 696 005. Open M-W 9:30am-7pm, Th-Sa 9:30am-8:30pm, Su 11am-5pm.) Also on the Esplanade, the **Peerie Shop Cafe ❶** serves sandwiches, baked goods, and organic cider in a bright, lively setting. The Special Hot Chocolate (£1.60) is sinful. (☎ 692 817. Open M-Sa 9am-6pm.) **Raba ❸,** 26 Commercial Rd. (☎ 695 554), offers traditional Indian cuisine in a traditional atmosphere—the all-you-can-eat Sunday buffet is £7.50. Lerwick's most convenient food awaits at the **Islesburgh Community Centre Cafe ❶,** on the first floor of the hostel. (☎ 692 114. Open M-Th 11am-9pm, F-Sa 11am-5pm.) **The Lounge,** 4 Mounthooly St., is the town's busiest pub; a more subdued bar is upstairs. Folks bring their own music-makers to the live sessions on Saturday afternoons and some Wednesday nights. (☎ 692 231. Open M-Sa 11am-1am.) A friendly, eccentric crowd fills **Thule Bar,** near the ferry docks. (☎ 692 508. Open M-Sa 11am-1am, Su 12:30pm-1am.)

🧶 WOOL

Shetland is one of the best places in the world to buy woollens (you may have noticed a few sheep here and there). To avoid paying relatively high prices in tourist shops, get bargains upstairs at the **Shetland Woollen Company,** 68 Commercial St., where you can nab leftover sweaters for as low as £5. (☎ 693 610. Open M-Sa 9am-5pm.) There are also branches in Sandwick, Yell, and Scalloway. Huge piles of cheap sweaters (£11-22) collect at the **Judane Shetland Limited Knitwear Factory,** Blackhill Mills, Gremista Industrial Estate, 1½ mi. north of Lerwick on the A970, opposite the factory stack. Just let yourself in and ask if you can buy anything. (☎ 693 724. Open M-F 8:30am-5pm, Sa 8:30am-3pm.) **The Spider's Web,** 41 Commercial St., showcases its members' high-quality knitwork and will explain their craft upon request. (☎ 693 299. Open M-Sa 9am-5pm, and Su if there is a cruise ship in port.) On northerly **Unst,** you can simultaneously shop for knits and enjoy apple pie at **NorNova Knitwear** in Muness. (☎ (01957) 755 373. Open daily 10am-4pm.)

🔘 MAINLAND SIGHTS

LERWICK. Weather permitting, you can cruise around the bay on the 🌊**Dim Riv,** a full-scale replica of a Viking longship that launches every summer Wednesday at 7pm. Riders may be asked to row. (☎ 693 471. Book ahead at the TIC. Cruises £5, children £2.50.) Not much of a sight in itself, the giant pentagonal **Fort Charlotte,** a Cromwellian-era relic just off Commercial Rd. at the north end of town, offers the best views of Lerwick and its harbor. (Open daily 9am-10pm. Free.) Only a mile west of the city center on Clickimin Rd., the ruins of **Clickimin Broch,** a stronghold from the 4th century BC, loom out of the loch and still look tough enough to repel invaders. (Always open. Free.) Shetland's Norse heritage is on display in longship form at the Up-Helly-Aa' Exhibition in the **Galley Shed,** Saint Sunniva St., Lerwick. (Open mid-May to Sept. Tu 2-4pm and 7-9pm, F 7-9pm, Sa 2-4pm. £2.50, concessions £1.) **The Shetland Museum,** across from the library building on Lower Hillhead, traces local archaeology and marine history on a single, well-designed floor. (☎ 695 057. Open M, W, and F 10am-7pm; Tu, Th, and Sa 10am-5pm. Free.)

SCALLOWAY. There's not much to see in Shetland's ancient capital, 7 mi. west of Lerwick, except 17th-century **Scalloway Castle.** Once home to the villainous Earl

Patrick Stewart, then the sheriff's headquarters, the crumbling edifice can now be yours. Get the key from the Shetland Woolen Company (☎ 880 243; next door) or the Scalloway Hotel. (☎ (01446) 793 191. Castle open M-Sa 9:30am-5pm, Su by appointment only. Free.) **Shetland Coaches** leave from the Viking Bus Station in Lerwick (☎ 880 217; M-Sa 9 per day, return £2.20).

JARLSHOF AND SOUTH MAINLAND. At the southern tip of Mainland, southwest of Sumburgh Airport, **Jarlshof** is one of northern Europe's most remarkable archaeological sites. Layers of human settlement have accumulated here from Neolithic times to the Renaissance, discovered in 1896 when a storm uncovered the tangle of stone walls and artifacts. (☎ 460 112. Open Apr.-Sept. daily 9:30am-6:30pm. £3, seniors £2.20, children £1.50.) A mile up the road, the **Old Scatness Broch** is the fascinating scene of an ongoing excavation. Archaeological remains were discovered in 1975 during airport construction; since then an entire Iron Age village and over 20,000 artifacts have been discovered, all explained in a guided tour, craftsmanship re-enactment, and 5min. video. (☎ 694 688. Open July to mid-Aug. M-Th 10am-5pm, Sa-Su 10:30am-5:30pm. £2, under 16 £1.) On nearby **Sumburgh Head,** thousands of gulls, guillemots, and puffins rear their young on steep cliff walls, cartwheeling into the air at each crashing wave or passing tourist. All South Mainland sights can be reached by the **Leasks bus** that runs to Sumburgh Airport from Lerwick (1hr., 2-4 per day, return £3.80).

NORTH MAINLAND. The northern part of Mainland has the wildest and most deserted coastal scenery, much of which is accessible only by car. At **Mavis Grind,** northwest of Brae, the island is almost bisected; this 100-yard-wide isthmus is flanked by the Atlantic Ocean and the North Sea. Farther northwest stand the imposing volcanic sea-cliffs on ◪**Eshaness.** Try not to get blown away while viewing nesting birds hidden in the crags, ocean-sprayed stacks off in the distance, a deep ravine cutting into the green cliff-side, and the standing arch of **Dore Holm** to the northwest. On Sundays, when buses and ferries are rare, **Leask Coach Tours** runs three different tours of north Mainland. (☎ 693 162. £9.)

▨ SMALLER ISLANDS

BRESSAY AND NOSS. Hourly ferries (5min., £1.50) sail from Lerwick to the west coast of Bressay. Hike to the summit of conical **Ward of Bressay,** referred to by natives as "Da Wart" (742 ft.), for a sweeping view

A CHILDHOOD IN THE ISLANDS

*Facing increasingly older populations, Orcadians and Shetlanders are keen to keep their young people on the islands. How successful have they been? Have opportunities on the islands changed? Let's Go went to the source, learning about daily life from "David" (age 16) and "James" (age 13).**

LG: So what do you think about life on the island?
David: It's boring.
James: It's quite boring.

LG: What did you do last night?
David: We went to the park. There's a wire sheep—you sit on its back and you pull back its head (it's got ears like handles)... You pull its head and it's like you're shaggin' the sheep.
LG: You took pictures of it?!
David: Yeah, we got it on video camera and everything.
LG: What, is this part of a school project or something?
[David and James laugh.]

LG: What do you do during the summer?
[David and James confer.]
James: What do we usually do?
David: Get drunk. Yeah, that'd be it, really.
James: That's boring!
LG: Do you have to work, shearing the sheep or anything?
James: No, we ain't be those kind of people.

Names have been changed.

of the sea to the north, east, and south. From Bressay's east coast, 3 mi. past the Lerwick ferry port (follow the "To Noss" signs), dinghies go to the tiny isle of **Noss;** just stand at the "Wait Here" sign and wave. (National Nature Reserve ☎ 693 345. Mid-May to Aug. Tu-W and F-Su 10am-5pm. Return £3, concessions £1.50.) Great skuas (a.k.a. bonxies), large primeval birds, will tamp up with arctic terns to dive-bomb you at this spectacular **bird sanctuary;** wave a hat, hand, or stick over your head to ward them off. (Noss is open to visitors Tu-W and F-Su 10am-5pm; overnight stays are forbidden.)

MOUSA. The tiny, uninhabited island of Mousa, just off the east coast of Mainland, holds the world's best preserved Iron Age **broch,** a 50 ft. drystone fortress that has endured 1000 years of Arctic storms. Flashlights are provided to help you climb the staircase onto the broch's roof. Catch a Sumburgh-bound Leask bus in Lerwick and ask the driver to let you off at the Setter Junction for Sandsayre (return £2.90); it's a 15min. walk from there to the ferry. (☎ (01950) 431 367. Ferry departs mid-Apr. to mid-Sept. M-Th and Sa noon, F and Su 12:30 and 2pm. £7, children £3.50.) On summer weekdays, **Leask Coach Tours** leads tours of Mousa, leaving from the Lerwick Esplanade. (☎ 693 162. £13, includes 1:30pm ferry.)

ST. NINIAN'S ISLE. Off the southwest coast of Mainland, an unusual **tombolo**—a beach surrounded on both sides by the sea—links St. Ninian's Isle, site of an early monastery, to Mainland, just outside of **Bigton.** Inhabited from the Iron Age to the late 18th century, the isle is now home to a ruined church and plenty of rabbits and sheep. The island is difficult to get to: a **bus** bound for Sumburgh departs Lerwick twice a day (noon and 5:40pm) to meet a shuttle that goes to Bigton; the Lerwick-bound bus returns via Bigton (departs Bigton 8am and 1:50pm). In order to visit St. Ninian's in a day—necessary, since there are no accommodations—the carless have to take the noon bus from Lerwick to Bigton, and the 1:50pm bus from Bigton to Lerwick, which allows about 1¼hr. to explore the beach and island. It's not enough time for a thorough exploration, but worthwhile nonetheless.

YELL. If you tire of bird- and seal-watching on starkly remote Yell, head for the north end of the main road at **Gloup;** a 3 mi. hike from here takes you to the desolate eastern coast. The remains of an **Iron Age fort** on the Burgi Geos promontory have held tenaciously to a perfect defensive position—jagged outcroppings face the sea and a 3 ft. ridge leads between cliffs to the mainland. Killer whales are occasionally spotted in **Bluemull Sound** between Yell and Unst. **Ferries** run from Toft on Mainland to Ulsta on Yell (20min.; 2 per hr.; £1.40, concessions 20p).

UNST. Unst is home to the northernmost everything in Britain. **Muness Castle** was built in the late 16th century; the key-keeper at the white cottage will give you a flashlight to pierce its spooky darkness. At **Haroldswick Beach,** gannets crash into the ocean near crumbling, abandoned air-raid shelters. The celebrated bird reserve at **Hermaness** is graced by a pair of black-browed albatrosses and countless puffins. Ferries from Belmont (Unst) and Gutcher (nothern Yell) divert routinely to Oddsta on the island of **Fetlar,** where birdwatchers view the crimson-tailed finch. To get to Unst, take a **ferry** from **Gutcher** to **Belmont** (10min., 1-2 per hr., £1.25). A daily **Leask** bus leaves Lerwick at 8am and connects with ferries to Haroldswick on Unst (2¼hr). The Baltasound **post office** (open M-Tu and F 9am-1pm and 2-5:30pm, W 9am-1pm and 2-4:30pm, Th and Sa 9am-1pm) lets you experience Britain's northernmost **post code:** ZE2 9DP.

The Leask bus stops along the way at **Gardiesfauld Hostel ❶,** in Uyeasound in the south of Unst, where you'll find a gorgeous coastal view. (☎ (01957) 755 259. No smoking, no pets, no curfew, and no alcohol. Dorms £9.25, under 16 £8.

Tent pitch £6.) Because only one bus runs by the hostel daily, it's easy to get stranded for the day. Those without private means of transport should consider riding the bus to Unst's main town, **Baltasound**, which has a few **B&Bs**.

OTHER ISLANDS. Shetland's outermost islands are the most isolated in Britain. **Planes** depart for the outer islands from **Tingwall** on Mainland, but **ferries,** at an unbelievable £2.15 per single journey (Whalsay is only £1.25), are a cheaper choice. Rooms and transport are hard to come by; booking several weeks ahead is a must. Bring supplies to last at least a week, as ferries often do not operate in inclement weather. Many ferries run from **Walls, Vidlin,** and **Laxo** on Mainland, all of which can be reached by bus from Lerwick (bus generally under 1hr. and £2; consult the *Shetland Transport Timetable*).

Whalsay, a relatively large fishing community (pop. 1000), is accessible by bus and ferry from Lerwick. The **Out Skerries** support 85 hardy fishermen. Planes (5 per week, £20) swoop down from Tingwall, while ferries converge from Lerwick (2½hr., 2 per week) and Vidlin (1½hr., 10 per week). **Papa Stour** (pop. 35) has a frothy coastline with abundant bird life and sea-flooded cliff arches. **Mrs. Holt-Brook's ❸** is the only place to stay. (☎873 238. Breakfast and dinner included, packed lunch £2. £30 per person.) To get to Papa Stour, fly (Tu only, £16) or sail (☎810 460; book ahead; 7 per week, £2.15) from Tingwall.

Far to the west, rugged **Foula** is home to 40 humans, 2000 sheep, and the highest sheer cliff in Britain (1220 ft.). Barely Scottish, the inhabitants of Foula had their own monarch until the late 17th century, spoke the now-extinct Nordic language of Norn until 1926, and still celebrate Christmas and Easter according to the now-defunct Julian calendar. From April to October, **ferries** (☎753 254) drift from Walls (Tu, Sa, and every other Th) and Scalloway (every other Th), while **planes** fly from Tingwall (☎840 246; 15min.; 4-5 per week; £21.30).

Fair Isle, midway between Shetland and Orkney and home of the famous Fair Isle knit patterns, is billed as the most remote island in Britain. In summer, a **ferry** (☎760 222) braves the North Sea's dangerous cliffs every other Thursday from Lerwick and two to three times per week from Sumburgh (Apr.-Sept., £2.15). **Planes** (☎840 246) depart from Tingwall (25min.; Apr. to mid-Oct. M, W and F 2 per day; May to mid-Oct. also Sa 1 per day; £37.20) and Sumburgh (May-Oct. Sa, £37.20). Beds are available at the **Fair Isle Bird Observatory Lodge ❸.** (☎760 258. Open Apr.-Oct. Room and full board £25-40.)

🌺 FESTIVALS

The TIC is an excellent source for info on Shetlandish activities. The **Shetland Folk Festival** (☎741 000; www.sffs.shetland.co.uk), in early May, lures fiddlers from around the world, while the **Shetland Fiddle and Accordion Festival** takes place in Lerwick in mid-October; call the TIC for details. The famous **Up-Helly-Aa' Festival** (www.uphellyaa.com), the last Tuesday in January, begins with the posting of "The Bill" in the Lerwick town square, highlighting the year's gossip, and culminates in a Viking extravaganza with outlandish costumes, a torch-lit procession, and a longship-burning in the town park. Shetlanders plan months in advance for this impressive light-bearing event—after the bonfire dies out, blackness settles in again (with only short reprieves of daylight) until late spring.

NORTHERN
IRELAND

 The phone code for all of Northern Ireland is 028.

Media headlines screaming about riots and bombs have overshadowed the typically calm tenor of life in Northern Ireland. But acts of violence and extremist fringe groups are less visible than is the division in civil society that sends Protestants and Catholics to separate neighborhoods, separate stores, separate pubs, and often separate schools, with separate, though similar, traditional songs and slang. Recent efforts to bring peace culminated in the 1998 Good Friday Agreement, and while both sides have renewed their pledge to make their country safer than before, the change tourists are most likely to see is a greater emphasis on presenting the country's beauty to outsiders. And Northern Ireland *is* beautiful.

Belfast's bursting nightlife gives way to the thatched-cottage fishing villages dotting the strands of the Ards Peninsula, leading to the rounded peaks of the Mournes and the park retreats of Newcastle. The waterfalls and valleys of the glorious Glens of Antrim lie to the north; nearby awaits the eighth wonder of the world, the Giant's Causeway, a volcanic staircase extending out to the Atlantic. The west offers the easily-accessible Sperrin Mountains and the tidy-walled farms of the Fermanagh Lake District. Industrial Enniskillen rests just north, though travelers would do well to continue to Derry, a city rich in both political and historical significance. If this brief taste of the North's charms whets your appetite for more, find expanded coverage in lissome *Let's Go: Ireland 2003*.

HIGHLIGHTS OF NORTHERN IRELAND

BELFAST Discover compelling political murals on a black cab tour (p. 697).

GLENS OF ANTRIM Stroll through tiny villages hiding among the mountains, forests, and lush valleys, then hike along the nearby coast (p. 710).

GIANT'S CAUSEWAY Marvel at 60-million-year-old volcanic rock formations, the stuff of Irish myth and legend (p. 712).

MONEY. The British pound is legal tender in Northern Ireland. Northern Ireland issues its own bank notes, which are equal in value to their British counterparts, but aren't accepted outside Northern Ireland. All British notes, including Scottish bills, are accepted in the North. The Republic of Ireland's euros are generally not accepted in the North, with the exception of some border towns, where shopkeepers will calculate the exchange rate and add a surcharge.

SAFETY AND SECURITY. Northern Ireland has one of the lowest tourist-related crime rates in the world. Although sectarian violence is now dramatically less common than during the Troubles (see p. 694), some neighborhoods and towns still experience turmoil during sensitive political times. It's best to remain alert and cautious during **marching season,** July 4-12 (see **Orange Day,** p. 721). August 12, when the **Apprentice Boys** march in Derry, is also a testy period. In general, be prepared for transport delays and for shops and services to be closed at these times.

Northern Ireland

Vacation areas such as the Glens and the Causeway Coast are less affected. Use common sense, and, as always when dealing with a culture not your own, be respectful of local religious and political perspectives.

Border checkpoints have been removed, and armed soldiers and vehicles are less visible in Belfast and Derry than they once were. **Do not take photographs** of soldiers, military installations, or military vehicles: your film will be confiscated and you may be detained for questioning. Taking pictures of political murals is permissible, though many feel uncomfortable doing so in residential areas. Unattended luggage is always considered suspicious and confiscation-worthy. Hitching is generally unsafe in Northern Ireland. *Let's Go* never recommends hitchhiking.

LIFE AND TIMES

Throughout its turbulent history, Northern Ireland has been steadfast in its resolve to remain divided. The frustrations of recent peace talks only prove how important it is to Northerners to retain their individual cultural identities, even at the cost of lasting stability. The North's 950,000 Protestants are generally **Unionists,** who want the six counties of Northern Ireland to remain part of the UK; the 650,000 Catholics, however, tend to identify with the Republic of Ireland, not Britain, and many are **Nationalists,** who want the North to be part of the Republic. The extremist problem-children on either side are known as **Loyalists** and **Republicans,** respectively, groups who tend to defend their turf with rocks and petrol bombs. This brief history addresses the origins of the modern-day troubles (and Troubles) in the North; for cultural history and historical context, flip over to p. 720.

A DIVIDED ISLAND: IT STARTS. The 17th century's **Ulster Plantation** scattered English and Scottish settlers on what had been Gaelic-Irish land in the island's northeast (see p. 721). French Protestants sought refuge in Ulster, as did merchants and working-class immigrants from nearby Scotland. Institutionalized religious discrimination limited Catholic access to land ownership and other basic rights, but made the North an attractive destination for Scots Protestants, who profited from the cheap land options. Over 300 years, the Ulster Plantation created a working- and middle-class population that identified with the British Empire and didn't support Home Rule. The **Orange Order**—named for William of Orange, who had outwarred arch-nemesis Catholic James II in the 1690s—organized Protestants in local lodges. They ordained July 12th a holiday—**Orange Day**—on which to hold parades celebrating William's victory at the **Battle of the Boyne.** The Order's constituency and radicalism continued to grow despite legislative opprobrium, culminating in explosive opposition to the first Home Rule Bill in 1886 (see p. 721).

Lawyer and politician **Edward Carson,** with trusty sidekick **James Craig,** advocated against Home Rule and sought to make the British elite better understand the arguments against it. In 1914, when Home Rule seemed likely, Carson held a mass meeting, and Unionists signed the **Ulster Covenant of Resistance to Home Rule.** As Home Rule began to appear imminent, the Unionist **Ulster Volunteer Force** (UVF; see p. 721) armed itself. WWI gave Unionists more time to organize and made British leaders realize that the imposition of Home Rule on Ulster would bring havoc: it would cause the UVF to pair off against the **Irish Republican Army** (IRA; see p. 722), who in turn would fight the governing body. The **1920 Government of Ireland Act** created two parliaments for the North and South; it went nowhere in the south and was superseded by the **Anglo-Irish Treaty and Civil War,** but the measure became the basis of the Northern government. The new Parliament met at **Stormont,** near Belfast. Though the Act was intended to be temporary, it underlay the North's government until 1973.

The new statelet encompassed only six of the nine counties of Ulster, excluding Catholic Donegal, Monaghan, and Cavan. This arrangement suited the Protestants in the six counties but threatened the Protestant Unionists living elsewhere on the island and the Catholic Nationalists living within the new Ulster. Orange Lodges and other strongly Protestant groups continued to control politics, and the Catholic minority boycotted elections; anti-Catholic discrimination was widespread. **WWII** gave Unionists a chance to show their loyalty—the Republic stayed neutral while the North welcomed Allied troops and airforce bases. Warship-building invigorated Belfast and allowed Catholics to enter the industrial workforce for the first time. Over the following two decades, a grateful British Parliament poured money into loyal little Ulster. Yet discrimination persisted: the Stormont government neglected to institute social reform, and parliamentary districts were unequally drawn to favor Protestants. As the Republic gained a surer footing, violence (barring the occasional border skirmish) receded on the island (see p. 722).

THE TROUBLES. As time went on, the economy grew, but bigotry and resentment festered. The American civil rights movement inspired the 1967 founding of the **Northern Ireland Civil Rights Association (NICRA),** which worked to end anti-Catholic discrimination in public housing. Protestant extremists arose in response, including the acerbic **Reverend Ian Paisley,** whose **Ulster Protestant Volunteers (UPV)** overlapped in membership with the paramilitary UVF, which had been outlawed. The first NICRA march was raucous but nonviolent. The second, in Derry in 1968, was a bloody mess, disrupted by Unionists and then by the water cannons of the **Royal Ulster Constabulary (RUC)**, the north's Protestant police force.

John Hume and Protestant **Ivan Cooper** formed a new civil rights committee in Derry, but were overshadowed by Bernadette Devlin's radical, student-led **People's Democracy (PD)**. The PD encouraged (and NICRA opposed) a four-day march from Belfast to Derry starting on New Year's Day, 1969. The RUC's physical assault on Derry's Catholic Bogside once the marchers arrived caused the Derry authorities to bar the RUC from the Bogside, making the area **Free Derry**. On August 12, Catholics threw rocks at the annual Apprentice Boys parade along the city walls. The RUC attacked Bogside residents, and a two-day siege ensued. Free Derry remained independent and the violence showed that the RUC alone could not maintain order. The British Army arrived—and hasn't left yet.

Between 1970 and 1972, concessions and crackdowns were alternately instituted, to little effect. The rejuvenated IRA split: while the "Official" faction faded into insignificance, the **Provisional IRA**, or **Provos** (today's IRA), faltered ideologically but gained guns. In 1970, John Hume founded the **Social Democratic and Labour Party (SDLP)**, with the intention of bringing about social change through the support of both Catholics and Protestants; by 1973, it had become the moderate voice of Northern Catholics. But violent strife continued. On January 30, 1972, British troops fired into a crowd of nonviolent protesters in Derry, and 14 Catholics were killed. The British government's reluctance to investigate this **Bloody Sunday** increased Catholic outrage.

Soon after, the British embassy in Dublin was torched, and the IRA bombed a British army barracks. After further bombings in 1973, the Stormont government was replaced by the **Sunningdale Executive**, which split power between Catholics and Protestants. This move was immediately crippled by a massive Unionist work stoppage, and **direct British rule** began. In 1978, 300 Nationalist prisoners began a campaign to have their classification as political prisoners restored. The movement's climax was the ten-man **hunger strike** of 1981. Leader **Bobby Sands** was elected to Parliament from a Catholic district in Fermanagh while he starved. Sands died after 66 days and became a martyr; his face is still seen on murals in the Falls section of Belfast (see p. 703). The remaining prisoners officially ended the strike seven months and two days after it began.

The hunger strikes galvanized Nationalists, and support for **Sinn Féin**, the political arm of the IRA, surged. In 1985, British Prime Minister Margaret

THE LOCAL STORY

IRISH IDENTITY

Let's Go asked Paddy Fitzgerald, of the Omagh Ulster Folk Museum, how he defines his "Irish identity."

PF: Ah, right. It's a very important question. I think it's an issue that everyone in Northern Ireland, and probably in all of Ireland, are obsessed with. I think we spend most of our time belly-button gazing trying to define ourselves. My own identity fluctuates. I used to tell myself that I was "Bri-rish" to negotiate my dual identities. And that's not just a cute way of saying something or nothing at all. The word "Bri-rish" addressed the fact that I was an Ulster Protestant, that I have areas culturally and so on where I feel attached to the British heritage, but that I also have areas where I would see myself relating to an Irish Catholic culture, or an Irish Gaelic culture if you want to use those terms. The word is a way to negotiate the two. I tend to see myself as Irish, even though I am also an Ulster Protestant. Let me give you an example: Gaelic rugby is something I've played since I was a kid. I often find meself screaming in joy at the TV in Belfast when the Irish score a goal against England. So I see meself as Irish, even though I'm also a "Proddie." I mean, there have been people who played on the Irish team and had UVF tattoos. That should give you a good sense of the multi-faceted cultures and identities in the North. I mean, I'm a Northern Irish Protestant named Paddy Fitzgerald. If that doesn't explain the torn identities in Northern Ireland, I don't know what will.

Thatcher and Taoiseach Garret FitzGerald signed the **Anglo-Irish Agreement,** granting the Republic of Ireland (see p. 723) a "consultative role" but no legal authority in the governance of Northern Ireland. Relations between London and Dublin improved, but extremists on both sides were infuriated. In 1992, the **Brooke Initiative** led to the first multi-party talks in the North in over a decade, but the organizers conveniently forgot to invite Sinn Féin. The **Downing Street Declaration,** issued at the end of 1993 by Prime Minister John Major and Taoiseach Albert Reynolds, invited the IRA to participate in talks if they refrained from violence for three months.

THE 1994 CEASE-FIRE. On August 31, 1994, the IRA announced a complete cessation of violence, while Loyalist guerillas cooperated with their own cease-fire. **Gerry Adams,** Sinn Féin's leader, called for talks with the British government. The peace held for over a year. In February 1995, John Major and Irish Prime Minister John Bruton issued the **joint framework** proposal, which suggested a Northern Ireland Assembly that would include the "harmonizing powers" of the Irish and British governments and the right of the people of Northern Ireland to choose their own destiny. Subsequently, the British government began talks with Loyalists and, for the first time, Sinn Féin. Disarmament was the most prominent problem—both sides refused to put down their guns.

The IRA ended their cease-fire on February 9, 1996 with the bombing of a London office building. Despite this, the peace talks went on. Sinn Féin refused to participate because they could not agree to totally disarm. Sinn Féin's popularity had been growing in Northern Ireland, but their credibility was jeopardized on June 15, 1996, when a blast in Manchester injured more than 200 people.

In October 1996, the IRA bombed British army headquarters in Belfast, killing one soldier and injuring 30. In early 1997, the IRA tried to influence upcoming British elections with bomb threats; thoroughly angered, John Major condemned Sinn Féin. The Labour party swept the elections and **Tony Blair** became Prime Minister. Sinn Féin made an impressive showing: Gerry Adams and Martin McGuinness won seats in Parliament but refused to swear allegiance to the Queen and were barred from taking their places. The government ended its ban on talks with the still-uncooperative organization, but hopes for a cease-fire were dashed when a prominent Republican's car was bombed; in retaliation, the IRA shot two members of the RUC.

THE GOOD FRIDAY AGREEMENT. On July 19, the IRA announced an "unequivocal" cease-fire to start the following day, and in September 1997, Sinn Féin joined peace talks. The **Ulster Unionist Party (UUP),** the voice of moderate Protestants, joined shortly thereafter. In January 1998, another dozen lives were lost to extremism. After two Protestants were killed in early February, Unionist leaders charged Sinn Féin with breaking its pledge to support peaceful actions and tried to oust party leaders from the talks. Foreign facilitators continued to push for progress.

The delegates approved a draft of the **1998 Northern Ireland Peace Agreement** (the **Good Friday Agreement**) on April 11. The pact asserted that change in the North could come only with the consent of its citizens and declared that the people must determine individually whether to identify as Irish, British, or both. On May 22, in the first island-wide vote since 1918, the Agreement was made law. A resounding majority (71% of the North and 94% of the Republic) approved the agreement, which divided the governing of Northern Ireland three ways. The main body is a 108-member **Northern Ireland Assembly.** On June 25, the UUP and the SDLP won the most seats, while Sinn Féin garnered more support than ever before. The second strand of the new government, a **North-South Ministerial Council,** serves as the cross-border authority. The final strand, the **British-Irish Council,** approaches similar issues on a broader scale, concerning itself with the entirety of the British Isles.

Then, on August 15, a bombing in religiously mixed **Omagh** killed 29 people and injured 382. A splinter group calling itself the **"Real IRA"** claimed responsibility; their obvious motive was to undermine the Good Friday Agreement. Sinn Féin's Gerry Adams unreservedly condemned the bombing. In October, Catholic John Hume and Protestant David Trimble received the Nobel Peace Prize for their participation in the peace process. The coming year, however, was full of disappointments. The formation of the Northern Ireland Assembly was marred by disagreement over disarmament and the release of political prisoners, and was ultimately assessed as a failure.

CURRENT EVENTS. In December 1999 London returned Home Rule to Northern Ireland after 27 years of British domination. A power-sharing government was formed under the leadership of David Trimble and Seamus Mallon, but the IRA's hidden weapon caches remained a central problem and threatened the collapse of the new assembly, whose four parties included the Democratic Unionist Party, the UUP, the Labour Party, and, to the tune of much controversy, Sinn Féin. In January 2000, Trimble demanded that the IRA put its weapons "beyond use" and predicted a return to British rule if his demands were not met. The IRA's unwillingness to comply hamstrung February peace talks, and the dissident IRA Continuity Group bombed a rural hotel in Irvinestown, an attack condemned by every Irish political group, including Sinn Féin. Though the blast injured no one, it was an unwelcome reminder of the past. Britain suspended the power-sharing experiment just 11 weeks after its implementation and reintroduced direct rule.

On May 29, 2000, Britain restored the power-sharing scheme after the IRA promised to begin disarming. In the Republic, **Bertie Ahern** of the Fianna Fail Party scraped out a "no confidence" victory against the opposition Labour Party. Marching season was a nasty affair, although Blair and Ahern expressed satisfaction over its containment. On July 28, the last political prisoners in **Maze Prison** walked free under the Good Friday provisions, to a mixture of support and outrage.

The story remains the same in the North—political squabbling at the negotiation tables and on the floors of various Parliaments continues, punctuated now and then by bombs or plastic bullets out in the streets. Both sides are making efforts to repair the past—the Bloody Sunday inquiry continues, and the European Court of Human Rights has recently awarded compensation to the families of IRA fighters lost to the British government's "shoot to kill" policy. The slow path to disarmament points to a safer future—in the spring of 2001, the IRA was still dragging its heels but allowed international diplomats a visit to their secret arms dumps. In the June 2001 elections, Loyalist extremists were voted into Parliament in unprecedented numbers, and in July, Catholic schoolchildren in Belfast were targeted by Protestant protesters as they walked to their nearby school. The children suffered mental abuse and physical threats for several months before things calmed down. Then, in 2002, the IRA broke new ground by destroying a small payload of their weapons, a concession that proved conducive to peaceful discussion.

BELFAST (BÉAL FEIRSTE)

Despite the violent associations summoned by the name Belfast, the North's capital feels more neighborly than most visitors expect. The second-largest city on the island, Belfast (pop. 330,000) is Northern Ireland's cultural, commercial, and political center; in stark contrast to the rest of Ireland, the city has been a booming site of mercantile activity for centuries. Today, Belfast's reputation as a thriving artistic center is maintained by renowned writers and an annual arts festival. Such luminaries as Nobel Prize-winner Seamus Heaney and fellow poet Paul Muldoon have given birth to a modern, distinctively Northern Irish literary renaissance that grapples with the area's difficult politics. The Belfast bar scene, a mix of Irish-British pub culture and international trends, entertains locals, foreigners, and a student population as lively as any in the world.

✈ INTERCITY TRANSPORTATION

Flights: Belfast International Airport (☎9448 4848), in Aldergrove, serves **Aer Lingus** (☎(0845) 973 7747), **British Airways** (☎(0845) 722 2111), and **British Midland** (☎9024 1188). **Airbus** (☎9066 6630) runs to Europa and Laganside bus stations in the city center (M-Sa 2 per hr. 5:45am-10:30pm; Su about every hr. 7:10am-8:45pm; £5). **Belfast City Airport** (☎9093 9093), at the harbor, serves **Manx Airlines** (☎(08457) 256 256), though a recent takeover by British Airways may affect service and schedules, and **British European** (☎(1890) 925 532). **Trains** run from City Airport **(Sydenham Halt)** to Central Station (M-Sa 25-33 per day, Su 12 per day; £1).

Trains: Infoline ☎9066 6630. Trains arrive at **Central Station,** East Bridge St. Some also stop at **Botanic Station,** Botanic Ave., in the University area, or **Great Victoria Station,** next to the Europa Hotel. To: **Bangor** (33min.; M-F 39 per day, Sa 25 per day, Su 9 per day; £3); **Derry** (2hr.; M-F 9 per day, Sa 6 per day, Su 3 per day; £6.70); **Dublin** (2hr., 5-8 per day, £20). To get to Donegall Sq., walk down East Bridge St., turn right on Oxford St., and take the first left on May St. A better option for the luggage-encumbered is the **Centrelink** bus service, free with rail tickets (see **Local Transportation,** below).

Buses: Buses traveling to the west, the north coast, and the Republic operate out of **Europa Station,** off Great Victoria St., behind the Europa Hotel (☎9066 6630; inquiries daily 7am-10pm). Buses to **Derry** (1¾hr.; M-Sa 19 per day, Su 6 per day; £7.50) and **Dublin** (3hr., 5-7 per day, £10.31). Buses to Northern Ireland's east coast operate out of **Laganside Station,** off Donegall Quay (☎9066 6630; inquiries daily 7am-10pm).

Ferries: From the ferry terminal, off Donegall Quay, **SeaCat** (☎(08705) 523 523; www.seacat.co.uk) departs for: **Troon,** Scotland (2½hr., 2-3 per day); **Heysham,** England (4hr., Apr.-Nov. 1-2 per day); the **Isle of Man** (2¾hr.; Apr.-Nov. M, W, F 1 per day). Fares £10-30, cheapest if booked 4 weeks in advance. **Norse Merchant Ferries** (☎9077 9090; www.norsemerchant.com) run to **Liverpool,** England. **P&O Ferries** in **Larne** (☎(0870) 242 4777) run to **Cairnryan,** Scotland, and to **Fleetwood,** England. (For more info, see **By Ferry,** p. 40.) Late at night and early in the morning, the docks can be unsafe; take a **taxi** to or from the city center.

▐ LOCAL TRANSPORTATION

Local Transportation: The red **Citybus Network** (☎9024 6485) is supplemented by **Ulsterbus's** suburban "blue buses." Travel within the city center £1.10, concessions 55p. Citybuses going south and west leave from Donegall Sq. East; those going north and east leave from Donegall Sq. West (£1). 4-journey tickets £3.40, concessions £1.70. 7-day **"gold cards"** allow unlimited travel in the city (£12.60), **"silver cards"** permit unlimited travel in either North Belfast, West/South Belfast, or East Belfast (£8.30). The **Centrelink** bus connects Donegall Sq., Castlecourt Shopping Centre, Europa and Laganside Bus Stations, Central Train Station, and Shaftesbury Sq. in the course of its cloverleaf-shaped route. Catch the buses at any of 24 designated stops (every 12min.; M-F 7:25am-9:15pm, Sa 8:30am-9:15pm; 60p, free with bus or rail ticket). **Nightlink** buses shuttle the tipsy from Donegall Sq. West to various small towns outside Belfast F-Sa 1 and 2am; £3, pay on board or at the Donegall Sq. West kiosk.

Taxis: 24hr. metered cabs abound: **Value Cabs** (☎9080 9080); **City Cab** (☎9024 2000; wheelchair-accessible); **Fon a Cab** (☎9023 3333); **Abjet Cabs** (☎9032 0000).

Bike Rental: McConvey Cycles, 183 Ormeau Rd. (☎9033 0322). Open M-Sa 8:30am-6pm. £10 per day, £40 per week. Deposit £50. Panniers £15 per week.

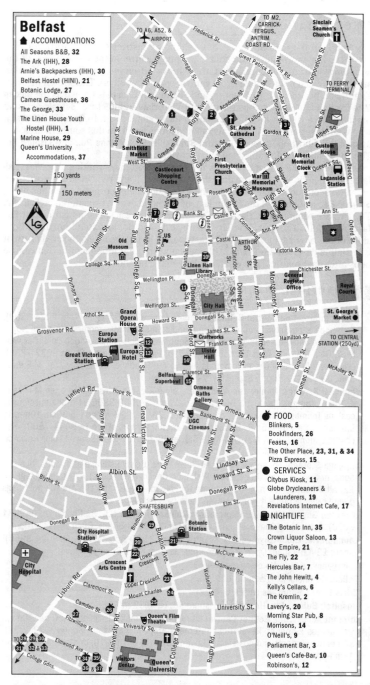

 ORIENTATION

City Hall is in **Donegall Square.** A busy shopping district extends north for four blocks to the enormous Castlecourt Shopping Centre. In the eastern part of the shopping district, the **Cornmarket** area shows off characteristically Belfastian architecture and pubs in its narrow **entries** (small alleyways). The stretch of Great Victoria St. between Europa Station and **Shaftesbury Square** is known as the **Golden Mile** for its highbrow establishments and Victorian architecture. **Botanic Ave.** and **Bradbury Place** (which becomes **University Rd.**) extend south to **Queen's University,** where student pubs and budget accommodations await. In this southern area, the busiest neighborhoods center around **Stranmillis Rd., Malone Rd.,** and **Lisburn Rd.** The city center, Golden Mile, and university are quite safe.

Divided from the rest of Belfast by the **Westlink Motorway,** working class **West Belfast** is more politically volatile than the city center. There remains a sharp division between sectarian neighborhoods: the Protestant neighborhood stretches along **Shankill Rd.,** just north of the Catholic neighborhood, which is centered on **Falls Rd.** The two are separated by the **peace line.** The **River Lagan** splits industrial **East Belfast** from Belfast proper. The city's shipyards and docks extend north on both sides of the river as it grows into **Belfast Lough.** During the week, the area north of City Hall is deserted after 6pm. Although muggings are infrequent in Belfast, use taxis after dark, particularly when pubbing in the northeast.

PRACTICAL INFORMATION

Tourist Information Centre: Belfast Welcome Centre, 47 Donegall Pl. (☎9024 6609). Free booklet on Belfast and info on surrounding areas. Books rooms throughout Northern Ireland and the Republic. Open June-Sept. M-Sa 9am-7pm, Su noon-5pm; Oct.-May M-Sa 9am-5:30pm. **Irish Tourist Board (Bord Fáilte),** 53 Castle St. (☎9032 7888). Provides info and books accommodations in the Republic. Open June-Aug. M-F 9am-5pm, Sa 9am-12:30pm; Sept.-May M-F 9am-5pm.

Financial Services: Banks and **ATMs** are a dime a dozen. Most banks open M-F 9am-4:30pm. **Thomas Cook,** 10 Donegall Sq. West (☎9088 3800). No commission on cashing Thomas Cook traveler's checks, others 2%. Open M-W and F 5:30am-10pm, Th 9am-6pm, Sa 10am-5pm. **Belfast International Airport office** (☎9444 7500) also changes money. Open May-Oct. M-Th 5:30am-8:30pm, F-Sa 5:30am-11pm; Nov.-Apr. daily 6am-8pm.

Luggage Storage: For security reasons, there is no luggage storage at airports, bus stations, or train stations. The **Belfast Welcome Centre** (see above) will store luggage for £2. All 4 **hostels** will hold bags during the day for guests, and **The Ark** will hold bags during extended trips if you've stayed there (see below).

Bisexual, Gay, and Lesbian Information: Rainbow Project N.I., 33 Church Ln. (☎9031 9030). Open M-F 10am-5:30pm. **Lesbian Line** (☎9023 8668). Open Th 7:30-10pm.

Launderette: Globe Drycleaners & Launderers, 37-39 Botanic Ave. (☎9024 3956). About £3-4 per load. Open M-F 8am-9pm, Sa 8am-6pm, Su noon-6pm.

Emergency: ☎999. No coins required.

Police: 65 Knock Rd. (☎9065 0222).

Crisis Line: Samaritans (☎9066 4422).

Hospital: Belfast City Hospital, 9 Lisburn Rd. (☎9032 9241).

Internet Access: The **Belfast Central Library** offers e-mail access at £1.50 per 30min.; web access £2 per hr. **Revelations Internet Cafe,** 27 Shaftesbury Sq. (☎9032 3337). £4 per hr., students and hostelers £3 per hr. Open M-F 10am-10pm, Sa 10am-6pm, Su 11am-7pm.

Post Office: Central Post Office, 25 Castle Pl. (☎9032 3740). Open M-Sa 9am-5:30pm. **Post Code:** BT1 1NB.

ACCOMMODATIONS

Nearly all Belfast's budget accommodations are near Queen's University, south of the city center. Walk 10-20min. from Europa Bus Station or any of the train stations, or catch a **Centrelink** bus to Shaftesbury Sq. or, from Donegall Sq. East, **Citybus** #59, 69-71, or 84-85. Reservations are highly recommended in summer.

HOSTELS AND DORMS

The Ark (IHH), 18 University St. (☎9032 9626). 10min. from Europa Station on Great Victoria St. Great sense of community: strangers gather for meals and Tarantino videos. Internet access. Also **books tours** of Belfast (£8) and Giant's Causeway excursions (£16). Laundry. Curfew 2am. 4- to 6-bed dorms £8.50-9.50; doubles £32. ❶

Arnie's Backpackers (IHH), 63 Fitzwilliam St. (☎9024 2867). A short walk from Europa Station. Impressively clean despite Jack Russell staffers Rosy and Snowy. Closer than the tourist office, the library of travel info here includes bus and train timetables. Key deposit £2 or ID. Luggage storage during the day. 8-bed dorms £7; 4-bed £8.50. ❶

Belfast Hostel (HINI), 22 Donegall Rd. (☎9031 5435; www.hini.org.uk), off Shaftesbury Sq. Foreboding concrete facade belies the inviting interior. Internet access £1 per 20min. Laundry. Reception 24hr. Dorms £8.50-10.50; singles £17; triples £39. ❶

The Linen House Youth Hostel (IHH), 18-20 Kent St. (☎9058 6400), in West Belfast. This converted 19th-century linen factory now houses scores of weary travelers. A new basement common room (open until 1am) with foosball and ping pong almost makes up for the impersonal feel. Laundry. 18-bed dorms £6.50-7; 6- to 10-bed dorms £8.50-9. Singles £15-20; doubles £24-30. ❶

Queen's University Accommodations, 78 Malone Rd. (☎9038 1608). Take bus #71 from Donegall Sq. East; a 25min. walk from Europa Station. University Rd. runs into Malone Rd.; halls are on your left. Typical college dorms available late July to Aug. and Christmas and Easter vacations. Singles for UK students £8.50, with bath £12; for international students £10/£14.50; for non-students £12.40/£17. ❷

B&BS

The B&B universe, just south of Queen's University between Malone Rd. and Lisburn Rd., is one of healthy competition and camaraderie.

Camera Guesthouse, 44 Wellington Park (☎9066 0026). A beautiful, airy, family-run guest house. What differentiates it from others are its breakfasts, which delight with a wide selection of organic options and herbal teas. Also caters to specific dietary concerns. Singles £25, with bath £37; doubles £50/£55. Lower rates in July. ❸

Botanic Lodge, 87 Botanic Ave. (☎9032 7682), on the corner of Mt. Charles Ave. Comfortable and close to the center. Singles £25, with bath £35; doubles £40/£45. ❸

Marine House, 30 Eglantine Ave. (☎9066 2828). A mansion that feels warmer than its size might at first suggest. Singles £35; doubles £48; triples £66. ❹

All Seasons B&B, 365 Lisburn Rd. (☎9068 2814). Farther out, this comfy roost is especially great for those with cars: secure parking is free. Amazingly hospitable family owners and super-strength showers round out the deal. Singles £25; doubles £40; triples £55. ❸

The George, 9 Eglantine Ave. (☎9068 3212). Renowned for its spotlessness. Amenities include fresh fruit at breakfast and saloon-appropriate leather couches in the common room. All rooms with bath. Singles £35; doubles £45. ❹

🔲 FOOD

Dublin Rd., Botanic Rd., and the **Golden Mile** have the most restaurants. Bakeries and cafes dot the shopping areas; nearly all close by 5:30pm, though on Thursdays most of the city center stays open until 8:45pm. **Tesco,** at 2 Royal Ave. (☎9032 3270) and 369 Lisburn Rd. (☎9066 3531), sells slightly cheaper food. (Open M-W and Sa 8am-7pm, Th 8am-9pm, F 8am-8pm, Su 1-5pm.) For fruits and vegetables, plunder the lively **St. George's Market,** East Bridge St., in the big warehouse between May and Oxford St. (Open Th 3-9pm and F 6am-1pm.)

- 🔳 **Bookfinders,** 47 University Rd. (☎9032 8269). Atmospheric bookstore-cafe with mismatched dishes and counterculture paraphernalia. If you push the right door, you may end up in Narnia. Vegetarian options, and even a few for the woebegone vegan. Soup and bread £2.25, sandwiches £2.20-2.50. Open M-Sa 10am-5:30pm. ❶

- 🔳 **Blinkers,** 1-5 Bridge St. (☎9024 3330). An authentic diner—cluttered ashtrays and all—with prices to match. One of the few late-night spots north of City Hall. Quarter-pound burger £2.30. Open M-Th 9am-10pm, F-Sa 9am-10:30pm. ❶

- **The Other Place,** 79 Botanic Ave. (☎9020 7200), 133 Stranmillis Rd. (☎9020 7100), and 537 Lisburn Rd. (☎9029 7300). Reasonably priced all-day breakfast with listed specials. Huge servings and an array of ethnic foods. Open Tu-Su 8am-10pm. ❷

- **Pizza Express,** 25-27 Bedford St. (☎9032 9050). Sounds like your typical franchise, but the spiral staircase and Tuscan decor suggest otherwise. Serves *real* pizza. 1- to 2-person pies £5-7. Open M-Sa noon-11:30pm. ❷

- **Feasts,** 39 Dublin Rd. (☎9033 2787). Pleasant street-side cafe, serving Irish and international farmhouse cheeses in sandwiches (£3.95, take-out £2.95) and other dishes. Makes pasta on the premises (£5-7). Open M-F 9am-6pm, Sa 10am-6pm. ❷

🔲 SIGHTS

If you do one thing in this city, take a 🔳**black cab tour** of the murals and sights of West Belfast, bookable at most hostels. Quality varies; two guaranteed winners are **Original Black Taxi Tours** (passionate; ☎(0800) 032 2003; £7.50) and **Black Taxi Tours** (witty; ☎0800 052 3914; £9). **Citybus** offers several tours of Belfast's sights. (☎9045 8484. Depart from Castle Pl., in front of the post office.)

DONEGALL SQUARE, CORNMARKET, AND EAST BELFAST

BELFAST CITY HALL. The most dramatic and impressive piece of architecture in Belfast is appropriately its administrative and geographic center. Removed from the crowded streets by a grassy square, its green copper dome (173 ft.) is nonetheless visible from nearly any point in the city. Inside, a grand staircase ascends to the second floor, portraits of the city's Lord Mayors somberly line the halls, and glass and marble shimmer in three elaborate reception rooms. In front of the main entrance, an enormous marble **Queen Victoria statue** grimaces formidably. The interior of City Hall is accessible only by tour. (☎9032 0202, ext. 2346. 1hr. tours June-Sept. M-F 10:30, 11:30am, 2:30pm; Sa 2:30pm only; Oct.-May M-Sa 2:30pm. Free.)

LINEN HALL LIBRARY. Originally located across the street in the building that became present-day City Hall, this library moved to its current location in 1894. It contains a famous collection of political documents relating to Northern Ireland. (17 Donegall Sq. North. ☎9032 1707. Open M-F 9:30am-5:30pm, Sa 9:30am-4:30pm.)

CORNMARKET ENTRIES. Though the area is dominated by modern buildings, relics of old Belfast remain in the tiny alleys, or **entries,** that connect some of the major streets. Between Ann St. and High St. runs **Pottinger's Entry.** Off Lombard St. and Bridge St., **Winecellar Entry** hosts Belfast's oldest pub, **White's Tavern.**

ODYSSEY. Belfast's newest mega-attraction is a gigantic center that houses five distinct attractions, including a huge indoor hockey arena, a multiplex cinema and IMAX, and a pavilion of shops, bars, and restaurants—including a Hard Rock Cafe. *(2 Queen's Quay. ☎ 9045 1055.)* Also inside is the new ◪**W5 Discovery Centre,** a science complex that beckons geeks of all ages. *(☎ 9046 7700. Open M-Sa 10am-6pm, Su noon-6pm; last admission 5pm. £5.50, concessions £4, children £3.50, families £15.)*

THE GOLDEN MILE
"The Golden Mile" refers to a strip along Great Victoria St. encrusted with many of Belfast's crown sites. The Golden Mile was once *the* target for IRA bombers.

GRAND OPERA HOUSE. The city's pride and joy was bombed by the IRA, restored to its original splendor, and then bombed again. Come by for a Saturday tour. See p. 705 for information on productions. *(☎ 9024 0411. Tours Sa 11am. £3, concessions £2. Office open M-W 8:30am-8pm, Th 8:30am-9pm, F 8:30am-6:30pm, Sa 8:30am-5:30pm.)*

CROWN LIQUOR SALOON. The National Trust transformed this popular pub into a showcase of the carved (wood), the gilded (ceilings), and the stained (glass). Box-like snugs fit groups of two to ten. (See p. 705.)

QUEEN'S UNIVERSITY AREA
Though the students largely empty out in the summer, their turf, with its city garden oasis, is fun to explore all year round.

BOTANIC GARDENS. Birds do it, bees do it, and on warm days, the majority of the student population does it. You can join them in soaking up in Belfast's occasional sun behind the university. Meticulously groomed, the gardens offer a welcome green respite from the traffic-laden city streets. Inside the gardens lie two 19th-century greenhouses, the **Tropical Ravine House,** and the more temperate **Palm House.** Don't forget to stop and smell the rose gardens. *(☎ 9032 4902. Gardens open daily 8am-dusk. Greenhouses open Apr.-Sept. M-F 10am-noon and 1-5pm, Sa-Su 2-5pm; Oct.-Mar. M-F 10am-noon and 1-4pm, Sa-Su 2-4pm. Free.)*

ULSTER MUSEUM. This first-class museum fills its huge display halls with Irish and modern art, local history, antiquities, and the Mummy of Takabuti. The treasure from a Spanish Armada ship that sank off the Causeway Coast in 1588 is also on display. *(In the Botanic Gardens, off Stranmillis Rd. ☎ 9038 3000 or 9038 1251. Open M-F 10am-5pm, Sa 1-5pm, Su 2-5pm. Free, except for some traveling exhibitions.)*

WEST BELFAST AND THE MURALS
Separated from the rest of the city by the Westlink motorway, the neighborhoods of West Belfast have historically been at the heart of the political tensions in the North. The Catholic area (centered on **Falls Rd.**) and the Protestant neighborhood (centered on **Shankill**) are separated by the **peace line,** a grim, gray, seemingly impenetrable wall. The streets display political murals, which you will encounter as you wander among the houses. It is best to visit the Falls and Shankill during the day, when the murals can be seen. Visit one neighborhood and then return to the city center before heading to the other, as the area around the peace line is desolate and can be unsafe.

THE FALLS. This Catholic neighborhood is much larger than Shankill and houses a younger, growing population. On Divis St., the **Divis Tower,** a high-rise apartment building, was built by optimistic social planners in the 1960s, but soon became an IRA stronghold. The British army still occupies the top three floors, and Shankill residents refer to it as "Little Beirut." Continuing west, Divis St. turns into **Falls Rd.** The **Sinn Féin** office is easily spotted: one side plastered with an enormous portrait of Bobby Sands (see **The Troubles,** p. 694) and an advertisement for the Sinn Féin newspaper, *An Phoblacht.* Continuing down the Falls, several murals feature Celtic art and the Irish language, displaying scenes of traditional music and dance or portraits of Famine victims. Murals in the Falls, unlike those of Shankill, are becoming less militant in nature, though a few remain in the Lower Falls that refer to specific acts of violence.

A PRIMER OF MURAL SYMBOLS

PROTESTANT MURALS

Red, White, and Blue: The colors of the British flag; often painted on curbs and signposts to demarcate Unionist murals and neighborhoods.

The Red Hand: The crest of Ulster Province; used by Unionists to emphasize the separateness of Ulster from the Republic. Symbolizes the hand of the first Norse King, which he supposedly cut off and threw on a Northern beach to establish his primacy.

King Billy/William of Orange: Sometimes depicted on a white horse, crossing the Boyne to defeat the Catholic King James II (see p. 694).

The Apprentice Boys: A group of young men who shut the gates of Derry to keep out the troops of James II, now Protestant folk heroes (see p. 721). The slogan **"No Surrender,"** from the siege, has also been appropriated by radical Unionists.

Lundy: The Derry leader who advocated surrender during the siege; now a term for anyone who wants to give in to Catholic demands.

CATHOLIC MURALS

Orange and Green: The colors of the Irish Republic's flag; often painted on curbs and signposts in Republican neighborhoods.

Saiorsche: "Freedom"; the most common Irish term found on murals.

Éireann go bráth: "Ireland forever"; a popular IRA slogan.

Tiocfaidh ár lá: (CHOCK-ee-ar-LA) "Our day will come."

Slan Abnaile: (slang NA-fail) "Leave our streets"; aimed at the largely Protestant RUC.

Phoenix: Symbolizes united Ireland rising from the ashes of British persecution.

Lug: Celtic god, seen as the protector of the "native Irish" (Catholics).

Green ribbon: IRA symbol for "free POWs."

Bulldog: Symbolizes Britain.

Bowler Hats: Symbolize Orangemen.

SHANKILL. North St., to the left of the TIC, becomes **Shankill Rd.** as it crosses the Westlink and then arrives in Protestant Shankill, once a thriving shopping district. Turning left (from the direction of North St.) on most side roads leads to the peace line. Some murals in Shankill seem to glorify the UVF and UFF more than celebrate aspects of Orange culture. The densely decorated **Orange Hall** sits on the left at Brookmount St. The side streets on the right guide you to the **Shankill Estate** and more murals. Through the estate, Crumlin Rd. leads back to the city center, past an army base, the courthouse, and the jail, which are linked by a tunnel. The oldest Loyalist murals are found here. The Shankill area is shrinking as middle-class Protestants leave, but a growing Protestant population lives on **Sandy Row,** off Donegall Rd. at Shaftesbury Sq. An orange arch topped with King William marks its start.

🎵 ENTERTAINMENT

Belfast's cultural events are covered by the monthly *Arts Council Artslink*, free at the TIC. More listings appear in the daily *Belfast Telegraph* (and its Friday arts supplement) and Thursday's *Irish News*. The **Crescent Arts Centre,** 2 University Rd., supplies general arts info and specific news about its own exhibits and concerts, which take place September through May. The Centre also hosts eight-week courses in yoga, trapeze, writing, trad (traditional music), and drawing. (☎9024 2338. Open M-Sa 10am-10pm. Classes ₤36.) **Fenderesky Gallery,** 2 University Rd., in the Crescent Arts building, hosts contemporary shows year-round. (☎9023 5245. Open Tu-Sa 11:30am-5pm.)

Belfast's theater season runs from September to June. The **Grand Opera House,** 2-4 Great Victoria St. (☎9024 1999), hosts opera, ballet, musicals, and plays. (☎9024 1919, 24hr. info line ☎9024 9129. Tickets from ₤12.50, with occasional student discounts. Open M-W 8:30am-6pm, Th 8:30am-9pm, F-Sa 8:30am-6pm.) **The Lyric Theatre** plays at 55 Ridgeway St. (☎9038 1081. Box office open M-Sa 10am-7pm. Tickets M-Th ₤10, F-Sa ₤12.50.) **The Group Theatre,** Bedford St., brings comedy to Ulster Hall. (☎9032 9685. Box office open M-F noon-3pm. Tickets ₤4-8.)

Music-wise, **Ulster Hall,** Bedford St. (☎9032 3900), brings Belfast everything from classical to pop. Try independent box offices for tickets: **Our Price** (☎9031 3131) or the **Ticket Shop** at Virgin (☎9032 3744). **The Grand Opera House** (see above) resounds with classical vocal music. **Waterfront Hall,** 2 Lanyon Pl., is Belfast's newest concert center, hosting performances throughout the year. (☎9033 4400. Tickets ₤10-35, usually ₤12; student discounts available.)

🍺 PUBS AND CLUBS

Get current nightlife info from *The List*, available at the TIC, hostels, and restaurants. The city center closes early and is deserted late at night; *Let's Go* suggests starting in Cornmarket, visiting old downtown, and finishing near the university.

▧ **Queen's Cafe-Bar,** 4 Queen's Arcade (☎9032 1347), off Fountain St. Friendly, low-pressure atmosphere in a glitzy shopping arcade off Donegall Pl. Mixed, gay-friendly crowd. DJs on Sa nights. Call in advance for private parties.

▧ **Morning Star Pub,** 17-19 Pottinger's Entry (☎9032 3976), between Ann St. and High St. Look for the Victorian wrought-iron bracket hanging above the entry. Award-winning bar food awaits upstairs. Open M-Sa 11:30am-11pm, Su 11:30am-7pm.

▧ **The John Hewitt,** 51 Lower Donegall St. (☎9023 3768). Newish, named after a poet, and suited for business lunches. Run by and for charity. Th trivia, F jazz, much trad.

▧ **O'Neill's,** Joys Entry (☎9032 6711), off High St. Spacious pub by week, crazy club by weekend. 21+. Cover Th ₤5, F-Sa ₤7-8. Open M-Th noon-10pm, F-Sa noon-2am.

White's Tavern, 2-4 Winecellar Entry (☎9024 3080), off Lombard St. and Bridge St.; look for a left turn off High St. Belfast's oldest pub (since 1630). W gay-friendly night. Open M-Tu 11:30am-11pm, W 11:30am-1:30am, Th-Su 11:30am-1am.

Hercules Bar, 61-63 Castle St. (☎9032 4587). Working man's pub with fab local music. Trad F-Sa, blues and jazz other nights. Open M-Th 11:30am-11pm, F-Sa 11:30am-1am.

Morrisons, 21 Bedford St. (☎9024 8458). Painstakingly reconstructed "traditional" atmosphere. Cover ₤3-7. W pub quiz. Gay-friendly one F per month.

Kelly's Cellars, 30 Bank St. (☎9032 4835), off Royal Ave. after the Fountain St. pedestrian area. The oldest (mercifully) unrenovated pub in Belfast. Trad F and Sa afternoons and Sa nights; occasional bands. Open M-W 11:30am-8pm, Th-Sa 11:30am-1am.

Robinson's, 38-40 Great Victoria St. (☎9024 7447). 4 floors of theme bars. Most renowned for **Fibber McGee's** (in the back; incredible trad Tu-Sa twice daily). Non-trad usually F night and Sa afternoons. Decent nightclub upstairs Th-Sa (cover F £5, Sa £8).

Crown Liquor Saloon, 46 Great Victoria St. (☎9024 9476). This National Trust-owned pub had its windows blown in by a bombing, but the inside feels original. Tourist crowd.

Lavery's, 12 Bradbury Pl. (☎9087 1106). 3 unpretentious floors. W live music, DJs weekends, free; disco on 2nd floor £1; 3rd-floor dance club £5. Open until 1am.

The Fly, 5-6 Lower Cres. (☎9050 9750). Belfast's number one club. Very popular; buggy decor. 1st floor for pints, 2nd for mingling, and a lounge on the 3rd. No cover.

The Botanic Inn ("The Bot"), 23 Malone Rd. (☎9066 0460). Huge and popular student bar. Pub grub £4-5. Tu trad, Th-Sa 60s-80s music. 21+. Cover £2. Open until 1am.

The Empire, 42 Botanic Ave. (☎9024 9276). Once a church; now resembles a Victorian music hall. Sept.-June Tu comedy, Th-Su live bands. Cover M-Th and Su £3; F-Sa £4.

GAY AND LESBIAN NIGHTLIFE

On Wednesday nights, Belfast's oldest pub, **White's Tavern,** becomes one of its most progressive. **Queen's Cafe-Bar** always attracts a diverse crowd. (See above.)

The Kremlin, 96 Donegall St. (☎9080 9700). Look for the imposing statue of Stalin. Hot gay nightspot with countless venues and events. Tight security. F theme night. Cover varies, free Su and M. Bar open M-Th 6pm-3am, F-Su 1pm-3:30am. Club open Th-Su.

Parliament Bar, 2-6 Dunbar St. (☎9023 4520), at Talbot St. M pool competition, Tu pub quiz, W *Glitz Blitz*, Th drag disco, Sa *Spank*, Su cabaret. Th-F and Su disco, cover £5-10. Open Th and Su until 1am, F 3am, Sa 4am.

▶ DAYTRIP FROM BELFAST

ULSTER FOLK, TRANSPORT, AND RAILWAY MUSEUMS

Take the Bangor road (A2) 7 mi. east of Belfast to the town of Holywood. Buses and trains stop here on the way to Bangor. ☎9042 8428. Open July-Sept. M-Sa 10am-6pm, Su 11am-6pm; Mar.-June M-F 10am-5pm, Sa 10am-6pm, Su 11am-6pm; Oct.-Feb. M-F 10am-4pm, Sa 10am-5pm, Su 11am-5pm. Folk Museum £4, concessions £2.50. Transport Museum £4/£2.50. Combined admission £5/£3.

The Ulster Folk and Transport Museums stretch over 176 acres in Holywood. Established by an Act of Parliament in the 1950s, the ◪ **Folk Museum** contains over 30 buildings from the past three centuries and all nine Ulster counties. Most of the buildings are transplanted originals, reconstructed stone by stone in the museum's landscape. The Transport Museum and the Railway Museum are across the road. Inside the **Transport Museum,** horse-drawn coaches, cars, bicycles, and trains display the history of moving vehicles. The hangar-shaped **Railway Museum** stuffs in 25 old railway engines.

COUNTIES DOWN AND ARMAGH

NEWCASTLE AND THE MOURNES

On weekends, kids roam the streets in search of fun and entertainment, while the area's beaches draw the rest of the family in July and August. The numerous arcades, joke shops, and waterslide parks of the city's main drag stand in dramatic contrast to the Mourne Mountains which rise just south of town. No road penetrates the center of these majestic mountains, bringing welcome solitude to hikers.

TRANSPORTATION. Newcastle's **bus station** is at 5-7 Railway St. (☎4372 2296), at the end of Main St. away from the mountains. Buses run to: **Belfast** (1¼hr.; M-F 19 per day, Sa 17 per day, Su 10 per day; £5); **Downpatrick** (40min.; M-Sa 10-15 per day, Su 5 per day; £2.30); **Dublin** (3hr.; M-Sa 4 per day, Su 2 per day; £10.31); **Newry** (2hr.; M-F 12 per day, Sa 7per day, Su 2 per day; £5.40). **Rent bikes** at **Wiki Wiki Wheels,** 10b Donard St., beside the Xtra-Vision building left of the bus station. (☎4372 3973. £10 per day, £50 per week; ID deposit. Open M-Th and Sa 9am-6pm, F 9am-8pm, Su 2-6pm.) For a **taxi,** call **Donard Cabs** (☎4372 4100).

ORIENTATION AND PRACTICAL INFORMATION. Newcastle's main road stretches along the waterfront; initially called **Main St.** (where it intersects **Railway St.**), its name subsequently changes to **Central Promenade** and then to **South Promenade.** The **tourist information centre,** 10-14 Central Promenade, is 10min. down the main street from the bus station. Ask for the free map and town guide. (☎4372 2222. Open July-Aug. M-Sa 9:30am-7pm, Su 1-7pm; June and Sept. M-Sa 10am-5pm, Su 2-6pm.) Rent **camping equipment** at **Hill Trekker,** 115 Central Promenade. (☎4372 3842. Open Tu-Su 10am-5:30pm.) Other services include: **First Trust** bank, 28-32 Main St. (☎4372 3476; open M-F 9:30am-4:30pm); **Internet access** at **Anchor Bar**; and the **post office,** 33-35 Central Promenade (☎4372 2418; open M-W and F 9am-5:30pm, Th and Sa 9am-12:30pm). **Post Code:** BT33 0AA.

ACCOMMODATIONS, FOOD, AND PUBS. B&Bs in this summer resort town are plentiful but pricey; fortunately, there's also a hostel. The Mournes are a free and legal camping alternative. Follow Railway St. toward the water and take a right

THE HIDDEN DEAL

THE ANCHOR BAR

Two fierce predators eat away at the wallet of the typical budget traveler in Northern Ireland: the 'net and the pint. Internet access is the cheapest way to keep in touch, but it still commands a premium, while local pub-culture demands that visitors do as the locals do, doling out pounds to the blonde in the black skirt. At the Anchor Bar in Newcastle, however, one payment covers both costs: purchasing a pint (or glass, or even a cup of coffee) earns you *free* time online. How much time? How much do you want?—the friendly staff sets no limit, though courtesy calls for some restraint when others are waiting.

In addition to its fabulous drunk-mailing deals, Anchor has plenty of pints and pastimes to offer the patron less interested in surfing the web. The friendly bartenders and regulars watch football games on the huge flatscreen TV, while others engage in their own matches on the pool table. According to the young manager, a beer garden will soon be appearing out back. For even more of a great deal, stop by for a cheap, filling meal (£2-4), served from noon to 7pm on weekdays, noon to 6pm on Saturday, and 2-7pm on Sundays. *(The Anchor Bar. 9 Bryansford Rd., Newcastle (☎4372 3344). Open M-Sa 11:30am-12:30am, Su 2pm-midnight.)*

at the Newcastle Arms to reach **Newcastle Youth Hostel (HINI) ❷**, 30 Downs Rd. Quarters are tight, but such discomforts are appeased by the prime location and well-lit rooms. (☎4372 2133. Dorms ₤10, under 18 ₤9.) **Drumrawn House ❸**, 139 Central Promenade, a 15min. walk from the bus station, is a Georgian townhouse with marvellous sea views. (☎4372 6847. ₤21.50 per person.) The **camping** is great at **Tollymore Forest Park ❷**, 176 Tullybrannigan Rd., 2 mi. down the A2 or a quick ride on the "Busybus" (10min.; 10am and noon, summer also 4:30pm; 75p) from the Newcastle Ulsterbus station. (☎4372 2428. ₤12 per tent. Electricity ₤1.50.)

The fruitcake-like density of junk food (sweet *and* savory) on the waterfront impresses. ◩**Seasalt ❷**, 51 Central Promenade, is a stylish deli-cafe with a Mediterranean edge. It becomes a delicious, reservations-only, three-course bistro weekend nights. (☎4372 5027. Bistro meal ₤20. Open Su-Tu 9am-6pm, W-Th 9am-10pm, F-Sa 9am-1am.) **Cafe Maud's ❶**, 106 Main St., serves up hipness with a view. (☎4372 6184. Open M-Su 9am-9:30pm.) **The Cookie Jar ❶**, 112 Main St. or in the Newcastle Shopping Centre, serves sandwiches (under ₤2) and pastries. (Open M-Sa 9am-5:30pm.)

◪ **HIKING.** For a taste of the wilderness surrounding Newcastle, stop by the **Tullymore Forest Park**, just 2 mi. west of town at 176 Tullybrannigan Rd. A magical entrance lined with gigantic, gnarled trees leads you toward ancient stone bridges, rushing waters, and well-marked trails. If you're looking for higher peaks and bigger challenges, head to the **Mourne Countryside Centre**, 91 Central Promenade. A friendly and knowledgeable staff leads hikes and offers a broad selection of guides and maps of the Mourne mountains. Those planning short excursions can purchase *Mourne Mountain Walks* (₤6), which describes ten one-day hikes. If you're staying in the Mournes overnight, buy the topographical *Mourne Country Outdoor Pursuits Map* for ₤5. (☎4372 4059. Centre open year-round M-F 9am-5pm.) The **Mourne Heritage Trust,** two doors down, is also worth a stop.

The **Mourne Wall,** built between 1904 and 1923, encircles 12 of the mountains just below their peaks. Walking the 22 mi. wall takes a strenuous 8hr. The Mournes' highest peak, **Slieve Donard** (2788 ft.), towers above Newcastle. The trail up is wide and well maintained (5hr. round-trip). **Donard Park** provides the most direct access to the Mournes from Newcastle; it's convenient to both Slieve Donard and nearby **Slieve Commedagh**. The park lies on the corner of Central Promenade and Bryansford Rd. To hike, follow the dirt path at the back of the carpark as it crosses two bridges and eventually joins the Glen River Path (about 1½ mi.) to reach the Mourne Wall. At the wall, turn left for Slieve Donard or right for Slieve Commedagh. Those seeking a more remote trek might try **Slieve Bernagh** (2423 ft.) or **Slieve Binnian** (2450 ft.), most easily accessed from **Hare's Gap** and **Silent Valley,** respectively. The two craggy peaks, both offering tremendous views, can be combined into a 12 mi. half-day hike.

Wilderness **camping** is popular. Common spots include the **Annalong Valley,** the shores of **Lough Shannagh,** and near the **Trassey River.** While camping around the Mourne Wall is allowed, camping in the forest itself is strictly prohibited due to potential forest fires. Be prepared for weather conditions to change suddenly, and bring warm clothing, as the mountains get cold and windy at night.

ARMAGH (ARD MACHA)

Religious zealotry and violent conflict have long been associated with Armagh. The hilltop fort *Ard Macha* ("Macha's Height") was built in pagan times but converted in the 5th century, supposedly as St. Patrick's base of operations. The city has sought to transcend the sectarian scars of its troubled past by emphasizing its role as the ecclesiastical capital of both the Republic and Northern Ireland.

ⅢⅡ TRANSPORTATION AND PRACTICAL INFORMATION. Buses (☎3752 2266) go to Lonsdale Rd. from **Belfast** (1hr.; M-F 22 per day, Sa 15 per day, Su 7 per day; £5) and **Enniskillen** (2hr., M-Sa 1-2 per day, £5.50). **English St., Thomas St.,** and **Scotch St.** comprise Armagh's city center. To the east lies the **Mall**. West of the city center, two cathedrals sit on neighboring hills. The **tourist information centre** is at 40 English St. (☎3752 1800. Open M-Sa 9am-5pm, Su 1-5pm.) Other services include: **First Trust** bank, English St. (☎3752 2025) and **Ulster Bank,** Market St. (☎3752 2053); **Internet access** at **Armagh Computer World,** 43 Scotch St. (☎3751 0002; £3 per hr.; open M-Sa 9am-6pm); and the **post office,** 31 Upper English St. (☎3751 0313; open M-F 9am-5:30pm, Sa 9am-12:30pm). Poste Restante goes to 46 Upper English St. (☎3752 2856). **Post Code:** BT61 7AA.

Ⅱ ACCOMMODATIONS. Armagh Youth Hostel (YHANI) ❷, behind the Queen's University campus, is huge and squeaky clean. From the TIC, turn left twice, follow Abbey St. for two blocks, and traverse the parking lot; the hostel entrance is in a small abbey. (☎3751 1800. Laundry £3. Reception 8-11am and 5-11pm. Lock-up at 9pm; security code for later access. Dorms £12; private rooms £13.50 per person.) Make a right on Desart Ln., then turn left to reach **Desart Guest House ❸,** 99 Cathedral Rd., a formidable mansion with rooms sunny and plush. (☎3752 2387. Singles £20; doubles £35.) **Maghnavery House ❸,** 89 Gosford Rd., just outside of town, is a converted 19th-century farmhouse perfect for those looking to explore Armagh, Newry, and the Gosford Forest Park. (☎3755 2021. Singles £25-30; doubles £40-50.)

ⅢⅣ FOOD AND PUBS. Finding an eatery in the city center or near the Shambles Market is easy; affording the food is more difficult. Your best bet is to get groceries at **Sainsbury's** in the Mall Shopping Centre, Mall West. (☎3751 1050. Open M-W and Sa 8:30am-8pm, Th-F 8:30am-9pm.) The **Basement Cafe ❶,** under the Armagh Film House on English St., is cheap and chic. (☎3752 4311. Open M-Sa 9am-5:30pm.) **Elichi ❷** promises Italo-Indo-European takeaway, or at least a respectable pizza. (☎3751 8800. Open daily 5pm-midnight.) **Turner's,** on English St. across from the Shambles, is the newest twentysomething hotspot. (☎3752 2028. F live band, Sa DJ.) **The Shambles Lounge,** English St., hosts an older crowd for after-work pints and weekend dinners. (☎3752 4107. Cover £5. Food served 6-9:30pm.)

❺ SIGHTS. Armagh's cathedrals lord it over the city from two opposing hills. To the north, on Cathedral Rd., sits the 1873 Roman Catholic **Cathedral of St. Patrick,** whose imposing exterior contrasts mightily with the ultra-modern sanctuary. (☎3752 4177. Open daily until dusk. Free.) To the south is the **Cathedral of St. Patrick,** or rather, "the Protestant one." Authorities claim that this 13th-century church rests on the site where The Pat founded his main house of worship in AD 445. (☎3752 3142. Open Apr.-Oct. daily 10am-5pm; Nov.-Mar. 10am-4pm. Tours June-Aug. M-Sa 11:30am and 2:30pm. Free.) Up College Hill, north of the Mall, the **Armagh Observatory** (☎3752 2928) was founded in 1790 by Archbishop Robinson. Star-struck tourists can observe a modern weather station and 1885 refractor telescope. More celestial wonders await in the nearby **Planetarium.** (☎3752 3689. 45min. shows July-Aug. daily 3-5 per day; Apr.-June M-F 1 per day. Open M-F 10am-4:45pm, Sa-Su 1:15-4:45pm. Seating limited; book ahead. £3.75, students £2.75.)

Two miles west of Armagh on Killylea Rd. (A28), mysterious **Navan Fort** was the capital of the Kings of Ulster for 800 years. This may look like a grassy mound of dirt, but with imagination, historical knowledge, and a few too many pints, you might see extensive fortifications and elaborate religious paraphernalia strewn across the site. Queen Macha is said to have founded the fort, although it is also associated with St. Patrick, who probably chose Armagh as a Christian center because of its proximity to this pagan stronghold. (Always open. Free.)

NORTHERN IRELAND

COUNTIES ANTRIM AND DERRY

The A2 coastal road skitters along the edge of Antrim and Derry, connecting the scenic attractions of both counties. West of Belfast, stodgy and industrial Larne gives way to lovely seaside villages. The nine Glens of Antrim stimulate scenery fiends. Near the midpoint of the island's northern coast, the Giant's Causeway spills its geologic honeycomb into the ocean. The industrial landscape reappears past the Causeway, with the carnival lights of Portrush and Portstewart. The road terminates at turbulent, fascinating Derry, the North's second-largest city.

LARNE (LATHARNA)

Larne is a working town whose significance to tourists lies in its ferries to and from Scotland. **P&O Ferries** (☎ (087) 0242 4777) operates boats from Larne to **Cairnryan,** Scotland, and **Fleetwood,** England. The **train station** rests adjacent to a roundabout, down the street from the TIC on Narrow Gauge Rd. (☎ 2826 0604. Open daily 7:30am-5:30pm.) The **bus station** is just south of town, on the other side of the A8 overpass. (☎ 2827 2345. Open M-F 9am-5:15pm.)

To reach town from the harbor, take a right outside of the ferry port. It's a good idea to cab it in the evening, as the route passes through a rough neighborhood. The **tourist information centre,** Narrow Gauge Rd., books rooms. (☎ 2826 0088. Open July-Sept. M-F 9am-6pm, Sa 9am-5pm; Oct.-Easter M-F 9am-5pm; Easter-June M-Sa 9am-5pm. 24hr. computerized info kiosk outside.) **Northern Bank** is at 19 Main St. (☎ 2827 6311. Open M 9:30am-5pm, Tu-F 10am-3:30pm, Sa 9:30am-12:30pm.)

Rather than lingering near the ferry port, seek beds down Glenarm Rd., in the more affluent area closer to town. **Inverbann ❷,** 7 Glenarm Rd., has spacious TV- and bath-endowed rooms. (☎ 2827 2524. £15 per person.) The **Co-op Superstore** is on Station Rd., by the bus station. (☎ 2826 0737. Open M-W 9am-9pm, Th-F 9am-10pm, Sa 9am-8pm, Su 1-6pm.) Sandwich shops litter the main street.

GLENS OF ANTRIM

During the last Ice Age, glaciers ripped through the coastline northeast of Antrim, leaving in their wake nine deep scars. Over the years, water collected in these "valleys," spurring the growth of trees, ferns, and other lush flora not usually found in Ireland. The A2 coastal road connects the mouths of these glens and provides entry to roads leading inland, allowing weekenders easy access to the area.

▐ TRANSPORTATION

Two **Ulsterbus** (Belfast ☎ 9032 0011, Larne 2827 2345) routes serve the glens year-round. Bus #156 from **Belfast** stops in **Larne, Ballygally, Glenarm,** and **Carnlough** (M-Sa 6-7 per day, Su 3 per day; off-season M-Sa 5-7 per day, Su 1 per day; £2.80-5.20) and sometimes continues to **Waterfoot, Cushendall,** and **Cushendun** (M-F 4 per day, Sa-Su 2 per day; off-season M-F 2 per day). Bus #150 runs between **Ballymena** and **Glenariff** (M-Sa 5 per day, £2.60), then to Waterfoot, Cushendall, and Cushendun (M-F 5 per day, Sa 3 per day; £4.30). The **Antrim Coaster** (a.k.a. #252) goes coastal from Belfast to **Coleraine** and stops at every town along the way (2 per day, £7.50). **Cycling** the glens is fabulous from Ballygally to Cushendun; beyond Cushendun, the hilly road makes even motorists groan.

GLENARIFF

Mirror, mirror, on the wall, who's the fairest Glen of all? Guarded from any would-be wicked stepmothers by the village of **Waterfoot,** beautiful, broad Glenariff is 9 mi. up the coast from Glenarm. The glen lies inside the large **Glenariff Forest Park,** 4 mi. south of Waterfoot on the Glenariff road (A43). The **bus** between Cushendun and Ballymena (#150) stops at the official park entrance (M-Sa 3-5 per day). If you're walking from Waterfoot, enter 1½ mi. downhill by taking the road that branches left toward the Manor Lodge Restaurant. The park's many trails range from ½ mi. to 5 mi. round-trips. The three-mile ⊠**Waterfall Trail,** marked by blue triangles, follows the fern-lined Glenariff River from the park entrance to the Manor Lodge. The entrance to the **Moyle Way,** a 17 mi. hike from Glenariff to Ballycastle, is directly across from the park entrance. All of the walks begin and end at the carpark, where you'll also find the **Glenariff Tea House ❶,** which has food *and* free trail maps. (☎ 2565 8769. Open Easter-Sept. daily 11am-6pm.) **Glenariff Forest Park Camping ❷,** 98 Glenariff Rd., is self-explanatory. (☎ 2175 8232. Tents £10, off-season £7.)

CUSHENDALL (BUN ABHANN DALLA)

Cushendall is nicknamed "the capital of the Glens," most likely because its village center consists of *four* shop-lined streets instead of just one. In addition to its commercial significance, Cushendall is also well-situated, less than 5 mi. from Glenaan, Glenariff, Glenballyeamon, Glencorp, and Glendun. Grab a bus to the picturesque seaside village of **Cushendun,** 5 mi. north of Cushendall on the A2, where the sights are concentrated. In 1954, the National Trust bought the entire miniscule village, a whitewashed and black-shuttered set of buildings lying by a vast beach and perforated by wonderful, murky **caves** carved into red sea cliffs. **Mary McBride's,** 2 Main St. (☎ 2176 1511), used to be the *Guinness Book of World Records*'s "smallest bar in Europe." The original bar is still there, but it has been expanded to create a lounge.

Ulsterbus (☎ 9033 3000) #162 runs from **Belfast** (£6.20) via **Larne** (£5.20), then north to **Cushendun** (July-Aug. M-F 4 per day, Sa-Su 2 per day; Sept.-June M-F 2 per day). Bus #252 stops everywhere, including Cushendun; #150 stops in Glenariff (see p. 710). **Ardclinis Activity Centre,** 11 High St. (☎ 2177 1340), **rents bikes** (£10 per day; deposit £50) and gives tips on hill- and gorge-walking and canoeing.

The **tourist information centre,** 25 Mill St., is near the bus stop at the Cushendun end of town. (☎ 2177 1180. Open July-Sept. M-F 10am-1pm and 2-5:30pm, Sa 10am-1pm and 2-4:30pm; Oct. to mid-Dec. and Feb.-June Tu-Sa 10am-1pm.) **Northern Bank** is at 5 Shore St. (☎ 2177 1243. Open M 9:30am-12:30pm and 1:30-5pm, Tu-F 10am-12:30pm and 1:30-3:30pm.) The **post office** is on Mill St. (☎ 2177 1201. Open M and W-F 9am-1pm and 2-5:30pm, Tu and Sa 9am-12:30pm.) **Post Code:** BT44.

⊠**Glendale ❷,** 46 Coast Rd., is friendly and spacious. (☎ 2177 1495. All rooms with bath. £17 per person.) **Ballyeamon Camping Barn (ACB) ❶,** 6 mi. south of Cushendall on B14, is far from town but close to Glenariff Forest Park and the Moyle Way. (☎ 2175 8451 or (077) 0344 0558. Book ahead and call for pickup. Blankets £2. Dorms £7.) **Spar Market,** 2 Coast Rd., past Bridge Rd., has plentiful fruits and veggies. (☎ 2177 1763. Open daily 7:30am-10pm.) **Arthur's ❶,** Shore St., serves fresh sandwiches. (☎ 2177 1627. Open daily 10am-5pm.) ⊠**Joe McCollam's (Johnny Joe's),** 23 Mill St. (☎ 2177 1876), features impromptu ballads, jigs, and limericks; guaranteed music on the weekends.

BALLYCASTLE

The sea-battered cliffs of the Causeway Coast, which runs from Ballycastle to Portrush, tower above white, wave-lapped beaches before giving way to the spectacular Giant's Causeway. Ballycastle, a bubbly seaside town that sees carloads of locals flock to its beaches, pubs, and discos in the summertime, is often the first stop for Causeway-bound tourists. The main street runs perpendicular to the waterfront, starting at the ocean as **Quay Rd.**, becoming **Ann St.**, and turning into **Castle St.** as it passes the **Diamond.** Most restaurants and shops are along Ann St. and Castle St. **Ulsterbus** stops at the end of Quay Rd., coming from **Belfast** (3hr., 6 per day) and **Cushendall** (50min., M-F 1 per day). The **Antrim Coaster** also stops here. **Cushleake B&B,** Quay Rd., **rents bikes.** (☎2076 3798. £6 per day.) The **tourist office,** 7 Mary St., has 24hr. computerized info outside. (☎2076 2024. Open July-Aug. M-F 9:30am-7pm, Sa 10am-6pm, Su 2-6pm; Sept.-June M-F 9:30am-5pm.) Other services include **First Trust** bank, Ann St. (☎2076 3326; open M-Tu and Th-F 9:30am-4:30pm, W 10am-4:30pm) and the **post office,** 3 Ann St. (☎2076 2519; open M-Tu and Th-F 9am-1pm and 2-5:30pm, W 9am-1pm, Sa 9am-12:30pm). **Post Code:** BT54 6AA.

Watch out for the **Ould Lammas Fair,** held the last Monday and Tuesday in August—B&Bs and hostels fill long in advance. The **Castle Hostel (IHH)** ❶, 62 Quay Rd., slightly out of town next to the Marine Hotel, offers a relaxed atmosphere. (☎2076 2337. Dorms £7; private rooms £8.50 per person.) **Ballycastle Backpackers (IHO)** ❶ is on North Rd. next to the Marine Hotel. (☎2076 3612 or (077) 7323 7890. Dorms £7.50.) **Fragrens** ❷, 34 Quay Rd., is one of Ballycastle's oldest houses. (☎2076 2168. £17-18 per person.) For groceries, try **SuperValu,** 54 Castle St., a 10min. walk from the hostels. (☎2076 2268. Open M-Sa 8am-10pm, Su 9am-10pm.) ▩**Flash-in-the-Pan** ❶, 74 Castle St., prepares disorientingly delicious chipper fare. (☎2076 2251. Open Su-Th 11am-midnight, F-Sa 11am-1am.) **Herald's** ❷, 22 Ann St., serves big-yet-cheap portions. (☎2076 9064. Internet access. Open daily 8am-9pm.) Tourists head for tiny, fire-warmed **House of McDonnell,** 71 Castle St. (☎2076 2975. F trad, Sa folk.) **Central Bar,** 12 Ann St., rollicks. (☎2076 3877. Su piano sing-alongs, W trad, Th and Sa karaoke.)

Just off the coast at Ballycastle, bumpy, boomerang-shaped **Rathlin Island** ("Fort of the Sea") offers the ultimate in escapism for 20,000 puffins, the odd golden eagle, 100 human inhabitants, and four daily ferry loads of tourists. Its windy surface supports few trees, but it's a paradise of orchids and purple heather. For a more complete presentation of the island's intertwined history and myths, visit the island's **Boat House Heritage Centre** at the opposite end of the harbor from the ferry. (☎2076 3951. Open May-Aug. daily 10am-4pm; other months by arrangement. Free.) The **lighthouse** is the best place from which to view birds, but it's accessible only with the warden's supervision (call ☎2076 3948 in advance). **Caledonian MacBrayne** (☎2076 2024) runs a ferry service from Ballycastle to the island. The small office at the Ballycastle pier, open before each departure, sells tickets. **Soerneog View Hostel** ❶ (SIR-nock; ☎2076 3954; 2-bed dorms £8) is less secluded than **Kinramer Camping Barn (ACB)** ❶, 4½ mi. from the harbor (☎2073 3948; sheets £1; dorms or camping beds £5). **McCuaig's Bar** is the single entertainment center and food source for the entire island. (☎2076 3974. Food served 9am-9pm.)

GIANT'S CAUSEWAY

Advertised as the eighth natural wonder of the world, the ▩**Giant's Causeway** is Northern Ireland's most popular attraction, so don't be surprised to find that 2000 other travelers have picked the same day as you to visit. Geologists believe that the unique rock formations found here were formed some 60 million years ago, when molten lava broke through the surface, cooled, and shrank at an unusually steady rate. Though locals have very different ideas, everyone agrees that the causeway is an awesome sight. Composed of over 40,000 perfectly symmetrical hexagonal basalt columns, the sight resembles a large descending staircase that leads out from the cliffs to the ocean's floor below. In addition to the Grand Causeway itself, several other formations, including **The Giant's Organ, The Wishing Chair,**

The Granny, The Camel, and The Giant's Boot, can also be viewed. Giant's Causeway Visitor Centre sits at the pedestrian entranceway to the Causeway from the carpark. (☎ 2073 1855. Centre open July-Aug. daily 10am-7pm; June 10am-6pm; Mar.-May and Sept.-Oct. 10am-5pm; Nov.-Feb. 10am-4:30pm.) Every 15min., it runs Causeway Coaster minibuses the ½ mi. to the columns (£1 return).

DERRY (DOIRE CHOLM CILLE)

Derry became a major commercial port under the Ulster Plantation of the 17th century. Under the English feudal system, the city became the outpost of London's authority, who renamed it Londonderry. (Phone books and other such bureaucratic traps use this official title, but many Northerners call the city Derry.) The past three centuries of Derry's history have given rise to the iconography used by both sides of the sectarian conflict. The city's troubled history spans from the siege of Derry in 1689, when the now-legendary Apprentice Boys closed the city gates on the advancing armies of the Catholic King James II, to the civil rights turmoil of the 1960s, when protests over religious discrimination against Catholics exploded into violence publicized worldwide. In 1972, the Troubles reached their pinnacle on Bloody Sunday, when British soldiers shot into a crowd of peaceful protesters. Hearings into the incident were recently reopened, and will be held in Derry's Guildhall over the next few years.

NORTHERN IRELAND

▣ TRANSPORTATION

Trains: Duke St., Waterside (☎ 7134 2228), on the east bank. Trains go to **Belfast** via **Antrim,** and stop at several towns in between (2½hr.; M-F 7 per day, Sa 6 per day, Su 4 per day; £7.80). Connections may be made from Coleraine to **Portrush.**

Buses: Most stop on Foyle St. between the walled city and the river. **Ulsterbus** (☎ 7126 2261): #212 to **Belfast** (1½-3hr.; M-Sa 15 per day, Su 6 per day; £8); #234 to **Coleraine** and **Portrush** (M-F 4 per day, Su 1 per day; £5.40); #274 to **Dublin** via **Omagh** (4-6 per day, £10); #273 to **Omagh** (8-13 per day, £5). **Lough Swilly** (☎ 7126 2017) heads to: **Buncrana** (35min.; M-Sa 10-12 per day, Su 4 per day; £3); **Letterkenny** (1hr.; M-F 10 per day, Sa 13 per day; £4); **Malin Head** (1½hr.; M, W, and F 1 per day, Sa 3 per day; £5). **Northwest Busways** (☎ (077) 82619 in the Republic) runs to **Malin Town** via **Carndonagh** (M-Sa 7 per day) and to **Buncrana** (M-Sa 9 per day).

Taxi: Derry Taxi Association (☎ 7126 0247). Also offers tours for around £20.

Bike Rental: Rent-A-Bike, 245 Lone Moor Rd. (☎ 7128 7128). Rents a range of accessories and offers pickup service. £9 per day, £35 per week; ID deposit.

◪ 🛈 ORIENTATION AND PRACTICAL INFORMATION

Derry straddles the **River Foyle,** just east of the border with Republican Co. Donegal. The **city center** and the **university area** both lie on the Foyle's western banks. The medieval **walled city,** now Derry's downtown, has a pedestrianized shopping district around **Waterloo St.** In the center of the old city lies the **Diamond,** from which radiate four main streets: **Shipquay St., Butcher St., Bishop St.,** and **Ferryquay.** The Catholic **Bogside** neighborhood, which became Free Derry in the 70s, is west of the city walls; most of the Protestant population lives on the Foyle's eastern bank. The train station can be reached from the center by way of the **Craigavon Bridge** or a free shuttle at the bus station.

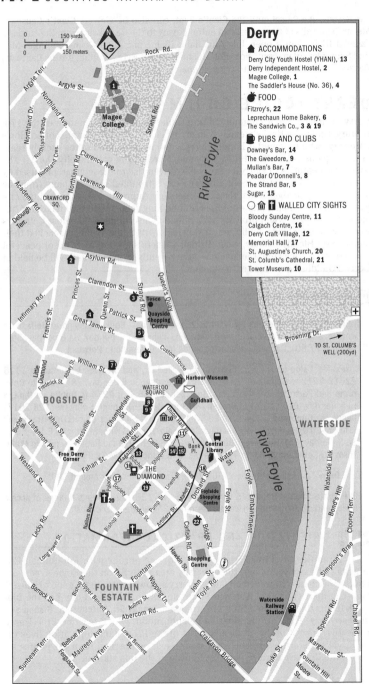

Derry

⌂ ACCOMMODATIONS
Derry City Youth Hostel (YHANI), **13**
Derry Independent Hostel, **2**
Magee College, **1**
The Saddler's House (No. 36), **4**

🍴 FOOD
Fitzroy's, **22**
Leprechaun Home Bakery, **6**
The Sandwich Co., **3 & 19**

🍺 PUBS AND CLUBS
Downey's Bar, **14**
The Gweedore, **9**
Mullan's Bar, **7**
Peadar O'Donnell's, **8**
The Strand Bar, **5**
Sugar, **15**

○ ⛪ 🛈 WALLED CITY SIGHTS
Bloody Sunday Centre, **11**
Calgach Centre, **16**
Derry Craft Village, **12**
Memorial Hall, **17**
St. Augustine's Church, **20**
St. Columb's Cathedral, **21**
Tower Museum, **10**

Tourist Information Centre: 44 Foyle St. (☎7126 7284), in the Derry Visitor and Convention Bureau. Ask for the *Derry Tourist Guide, Visitor's Guide,* and free city maps. 24hr. computerized info kiosk. Books accommodations throughout the North.

Bank: First Trust, 15-17 Shipquay St. (☎7136 3921). Open M and F 9:30am-4:30pm, Tu-Th 11:30am-4:30pm.

Launderette: Duds 'n Suds, 141 Strand Rd. (☎7126 6006). Wash £1.80, dry £2; students £1.25. Open M-F 8am-9pm, Sa 8am-6pm. Last wash 1½hr. before closing.

Emergency: ☎999; no coins required.

Police: Strand Rd. (☎7136 7337).

Hospital: Altnagelvin Hospital, Glenshane Rd. (☎7134 5171).

Internet Access: bean-there.com, 20 The Diamond (☎7128 1303). £2.50 per 30min. Open M-F 9am-7pm, Sa 10am-6pm, Su 2-6pm.

Post Office: 3 Custom House St. (☎7136 2563). Open M-F 8:30am-5:30pm, Sa 9am-12:30pm. **Post Code:** BT48. Unless addressed to 3 Custom House St., Poste Restante letters will go to the **Postal Sorting Office** (☎7136 2577), on the corner of Great James and Little James St.

ACCOMMODATIONS

Derry Independent Hostel (Steve's Backpackers), 4 Asylum Rd. (☎7137 7989 or 7137 0011). 7min. from the city center down Strand Rd. This relaxed hostel offers maps and advice and organizes trips to Giant's Causeway. Internet free for residents. Laundry £3. Dorms £9; doubles £24. ❶

The Saddler's House (No. 36), 36 Great James St. (☎7126 9691). Friendly, knowledgeable owners make their Victorian home your ultimate comfort zone. They also run **The Merchant's House,** 16 Queen St. Both £20 per person, with bath £25. ❸

Derry City Youth Hostel (YHANI), Magazine St. (☎7128 4100), off Butcher St. Large. Continental brekkie £1.50, Irish £2.50. Laundry £3.50. Check-out 10am. 10-bed dorms £9, with bath £10; 6-bed £10.50; 4-bed £12.50. B&B singles without bath £15; doubles with bath £35. ❷

Magee College (☎7137 5255), on the corner of Rock Rd. and Northland Rd. The housing office is on the ground floor of Woodburn House, a red-brick building just after the main building. Laundry free. Mandatory reservations M-F 9am-5pm. Available mid-June to Sept. Singles in 5-bedroom flats £14.10, students £11.75. ❷

FOOD

Excellent takeaways and cafes abound in Derry, but restaurants are pricey. **Tesco,** in the Quayside Shopping Centre, is a few minutes' walk from the walls along Strand Rd. (Open M-Th 9am-9pm, F 8:30am-9pm, Sa 8:30am-8pm, Su 1-6pm.) Stores with later hours are scattered around Strand Rd. and Williams St.

Fitzroy's, 2-4 Bridge St. (☎7126 6211), next to Bishop's Gate. Modern cafe culture and filling meals, from simple chicken breast to mango lamb. During the day most meals £4-6; dinners £7-12. Open M-Tu 9:30am-8pm, W-Sa 9:30am-10pm, Su noon-8pm. ❷

The Sandwich Co., The Diamond (☎7137 2500), and 61 Strand Rd. (☎7126 6771). Your choice of breads stuffed with a wide range of tasty fillings. Journey to the Strand location at lunch to avoid queues. Sandwiches £2-3. Both open M-F 8:30am-5pm. ❶

Spice, 162 Spencer Rd. (☎7134 4875), on the east bank. Cross Craigavon Bridge and continue as it turns into Spencer. Rumored to be the best food in Derry. Appetizers £3-4. Daily veggie specials £8. Open 12:30-2:30pm and 5:30-10pm. ❷

Leprechaun Home Bakery, 21-23 Strand Rd. (☎7136 3606). Eclairs, buns, cakes, and whatnot; sandwiches, salads, and meals (£3-4). Open M-Sa 9am-5:30pm. ❶

👁 SIGHTS

THE WALLS. Derry's city walls, 18 ft. high and 20 ft. thick, were erected between 1614 and 1619. They've never been breached, hence Derry's nickname: "the Maiden City." A walk along the top of this mile-long perimeter takes about 20min. The stone tower topping the southeast wall past New Gate was built to protect **St. Columb's Cathedral,** the symbolic focus of the city's Protestant defenders. Stuck in the center of the southwest wall, **Bishop's Gate** was remodeled in 1789 into an ornate triumphal gate in honor of William of Orange.

ST. COLUMB'S CATHEDRAL. Built between 1628 and 1633, this was the first purpose-built Protestant cathedral in Britain or Ireland (all the older ones were confiscated Catholic cathedrals). The original lead-coated wood spire was in disrepair at the time of the Great Siege, so the city's defenders removed its lead and smelted it into bullets and cannonballs. Like many Protestant churches in the North, St. Columb's is bedecked with war banners, including flags from the Crimean War, the World Wars, and the two yellow flags captured from the French at the Great Siege. A tiny, museum-like **chapter house** at the back of the church displays the original locks and relics from the 1689 siege. (Off Bishop St. ☎ 7126 7313. Open Easter.-Oct. M-Sa 9am-5pm, Nov.-Easter M-Sa 9am-1pm and 2-4pm.)

TOWER MUSEUM. Derry's top attraction utilizes engaging walk-through dioramas and audio-visual displays to relay Derry's intriguing history, from its days as a mere oak grove, through the siege of 1689, and onward to the Troubles. (Union Hall Pl. ☎ 7137 2411. Open July-Aug. M-Sa 10am-5pm, Su 2-5pm; Sept.-June Tu-Sa 10am-5pm. Last admission 4:30pm. £4.20, concessions £1.60.)

THE FOUNTAIN ESTATE. The Protestant Fountain Estate is reached from the walled city by exiting through the left side of Bishop's Gate; it's contained by Bishop St., Upper Bennett St., Abercorn St., and Hawkin St. This small area of 600 residents holds the most interesting Protestant murals.

THE BOGSIDE. This famous Catholic neighborhood is easily recognizable. A huge sign west of the city walls at the junction of Fahan St. and Rossville Sq. declares "You Are Now Entering Free Derry." It was originally painted in 1969 on the end of a row house; the houses of the block have since been knocked down, but this endwall remains, with a frequently repainted but never reworded message. The powerful mural is surrounded by other striking Nationalist artistic creations, and the spot is referred to as **Free Derry Corner.** Nearby, a stone monument commemorates the 14 protesters shot dead on Bloody Sunday.

🍺🍷 PUBS AND CLUBS

🏆 **Mullan's Bar,** 13 Little James St. (☎ 7126 5300), on the corner of William St. and Rossville St. An incredible pub with idiosyncratically lavish decor, from stained-glass ceilings and bronze lion statues to plasma flat-screen TVs. Hosts frequent and excellent jazz.

Peadar O'Donnell's, 53 Waterloo St. (☎ 7137 2318). Named for the Donegal Socialist who organized the Irish Transport and General Workers Union and took an active role in the Irish Civil War. The floor is ankle-deep in craic. Live bands nightly.

The Gweedore, 59-61 Waterloo St. (☎ 7126 3513). The back door has been connected to Peadar's since Famine times. Rock, bluegrass, and funk nightly.

The Strand Bar, 35-38 Strand Rd. (☎ 7126 0494). 4 decadent floors. W-Sa trad downstairs; nightly 70s-80s DJs on 2nd floor; M-Sa nightclub on 3rd floor (cover £2-5).

Downey's Bar, 33 Shipquay St. (☎ 7126 0820). Surreal decor attracts a young and colorful crowd. 20 purple pool tables and an open ceiling over the bar. Live bands nightly.

Sugar, 33 Shipquay St., behind Downey's. Downey's sweaty cousin and the newest nightclub in Derry. Big-name DJs drop in on weekends. Th 18+, F-Sa 21+. Cover £3-5.

REPUBLIC OF IRELAND (ÉIRE)

THE EURO. As of January 2002, the euro is the official currency of the Republic of Ireland. *Let's Go's* price diversity scheme is as follows:

SYMBOL	❶	❷	❸	❹	❺
ACCOMM.	Under €15	€15-24	€25-39	€40-54	€55 and up
FOOD	Under €5	€5-9	€10-14	€15-19	€20 and up

To Ireland, I.
    —William Shakespeare, *Macbeth*

Literary imaginations have immortalized Ireland's natural scenery since ancient times, and travelers who come with heads full of poetic imagery will not be disappointed: this largely agricultural and sparsely populated island still looks very much the same as it did when bards roamed the land. Windswept scenery wraps around the coast and mountain chains ripple the interior expanses of bogland. The landscape is punctuated with pockets of civilization, ranging in size from one-street villages to urbane cities. Dublin is a cosmopolitan center, radiating sophistication into its immediate surroundings. While some fear that international influence threatens their native culture, the survival of traditional music, dance, and storytelling proves otherwise. The Irish language lives on in small, secluded areas known as *gaeltachts*, as well as in national publications, road signs, and a growing body of modern literature. Today's Ireland promises her visitors an old-world welcome with just the right amount of urban edge.

It's useful to know that Ireland is traditionally divided into four provinces: **Leinster,** the east and southeast; **Munster,** the southwest; **Connacht,** the province west of the river Shannon; and **Ulster,** the north. Six of Ulster's nine counties make up Northern Ireland, part of the United Kingdom. "Ireland" can mean the whole island or the Republic, depending on who's listening. It's best to refer to "Northern Ireland" or "the North" and "the Republic." "Southern Ireland" is not a viable term.

For even more detailed coverage of the Emerald Isle, run—don't walk—to your nearest book emporium for a copy of the lovely *Let's Go: Ireland 2003.*

HIGHLIGHTS OF THE REPUBLIC OF IRELAND

DUBLIN Relax on the grounds of **Trinity College** (p. 739), windowshop on **Grafton St.** (p. 726), then head around the corner to **Temple Bar** for a night of tomfoolery (p. 738).

RING OF KERRY Run the peninsula's circuit (p. 776), taking in exquisite mountains, lakes, and forests in **Killarney National Park** (p. 777).

GALWAY Down pints of Guinness while enjoying the musical vigor and copious *craic* of the city's myriad pubs (p. 790).

COUNTY DONEGAL Brush up on your Gaelic in Ireland's largest *gaeltacht* (p. 808), and hike past Europe's highest sea cliffs at **Slieve League** (p. 806).

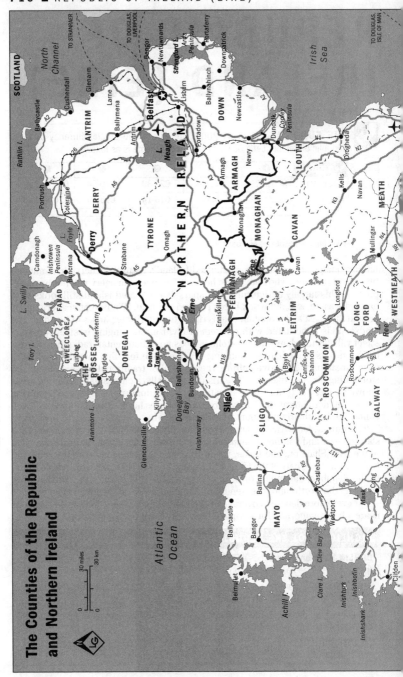

The Counties of the Republic and Northern Ireland

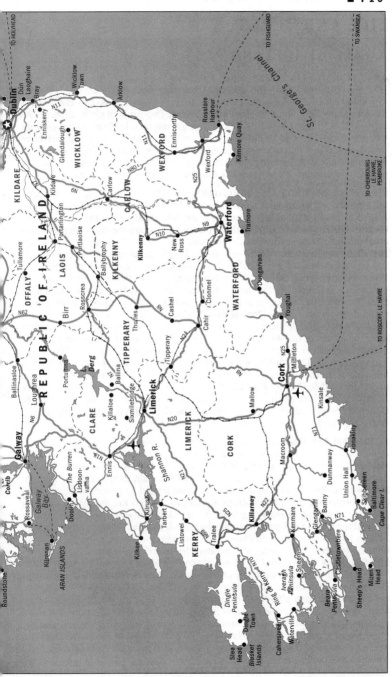

LIFE AND TIMES

A TALE OF IRELAND PAST

ANCIENT HISTORY. Our fragmented knowledge of ancient Irish culture comes from the scant remains of the stone structures left behind. Among these remains are **dolmens,** table-like arrangements of huge stones; **passage tombs** (like **Newgrange,** p. 756), and pint-sized **stone circles.** This original civilization, which arrived from Britain around 7000 BC, was soon replaced by **Celts.** Although some Celts may have arrived as unfashionably early as 2000 BC, their real migration started in 600 BC. This new group prospered, living in small farming communities with regional chieftains and provincial kings ruling territories called *túatha*. The pagan life was good—or so epics like the *Táin* would have us believe.

PIRATES AND VIKINGS AND CHRISTIANS, OH MY! Born in Scotland in the early 5th century and kidnapped by Irish pirates (*arr*), **St. Patrick** was enslaved and forced to tend pirate sheep (*baa…arr*) in Ireland. After finding Jesus, Paddy escaped back to Scotland, but at the command of a prophetic vision he performed an about-face and returned to the Emerald Isle. Other, later monks helped St. Patrick bring Christianity to the island—and at the same time, they recorded the indigenous system of writing they found on **ogham stones** and introduced the Viking-inspired **round tower** to the architectural lexicon. Between the 6th and 8th centuries, Continental barbarians took their pillaging a bit too far, and new hordes of asylum-seeking monks came to Ireland. Here they built **monastic cities,** illuminated manuscripts like the **Book of Kells,** and earned Ireland its reputation as the "land of saints and scholars." The monkish prosperity was later interrupted by **Viking** invasions of the 9th and 10th centuries. The hornéd ones raided most frequently along the southern coast and founded settlements at Limerick, Waterford, and Dublin. In 1002, High King **Brian Ború** set off a period of inter-*tuath* strife; after his death, chieftains sought the assistance of English Norman nobles to bring peace. Richard de Clare (a.k.a. **Strongbow**) arrived in 1169 and cut a bloody, Anglo-Norman swath through south Leinster. Strongbow then married **Aoife,** daughter of Ború's successor, affirmed his loyalty to King Henry II, and with characteristic generosity offered to govern Leinster on England's behalf.

FEUDALISM AND ITS DISCONTENTS. Thus the English came to Ireland and settled down for a nice, long occupation. There was constant bickering between Gaelic lords, who dominated agrarian Connacht and Ulster, and the English, whose strongholds included the **Pale,** a fortified domain around Dublin. The two sides were culturally similar, though the Crown fretted up a storm over potential cross-pollination; the 1366 **Statutes of Kilkenny** banned English colonists from speaking, dressing, or marrying Irish. Feudal skirmishes and economic decline plagued the island until the rise of the charismatic **Earls of Kildare,** who ruled from 1470 to 1534; they were so charismatic, in fact, that the fussy Crown passed more oppressive laws. Then Henry VIII created the Church of England, and the 1537 **Irish Supremacy Act** declared him head of the Protestant **Church of Ireland**—effectively making the island property of the Crown. **Thomas FitzGerald,** at odds with Henry, sponsored an uprising in Munster in 1579. Not to be outdone by Leinster, the Ulster Earl **Hugh O'Neill** led his own rebellion. The King of Spain promised naval assistance; his Armada arrived in Kinsale in 1601, but sat around polishing its blunderbusses while English armies demolished Irish forces. O'Neill and the other major Gaelic lords left Ireland in 1607 in the **Flight of the Earls.** While the world looked on in feigned astonishment, the English took control of the land and parceled it out to Protestants.

PLANTED PROTESTANTS AND THE ASCENDANCY. The English project of dispossessing Catholics of their land and replacing them with Protestants (mostly Scottish tenants and laborers, themselves displaced by the English but too polite to mention it) was known as the **Ulster Plantation.** In 1642, **Owen Roe O'Neill** returned from the Continent to lead the now-landless Irish in insurrection and formed the **Confederation of Kilkenny,** an uneasy alliance between the Church and Irish and English lords. The concurrent English Civil Wars (see p. 72) made a *really* big mess of things; **Oliver Cromwell's** victory rendered negotiations between King and Confederation something of a moot point. Once things were settled in England, the Lord Protector turned his attention to Ireland, and following standard procedure, destroyed anything he did not occupy. Catholics were massacred and towns razed as tracts of land were confiscated and doled out to soldiers and Protestant vagabonds. Native Irish could go **"to Hell or to Connacht,"** both desolate and infertile, one with a more tropical climate. By 1660, most Irish land was owned by Protestant immigrants. The Restoration settled things down a bit; Charles II passed the 1665 **Act of Explanation,** requiring Protestants to relinquish one-third of their land to the "innocent papists." But we all know how well that must have worked.

In 1688, Catholic **James II,** driven from England by Protestant **William of Orange** and his Glorious Revolution (see p. 72), came to Ireland to gather military support. James tried to take Derry in 1689, but a rascally and heroic band of **Apprentice Boys** closed the gates on him and started the 105-day **Siege of Derry.** William ended the war and sent his rival into exile on July 12, 1690, at the **Battle of the Boyne.** Many Northern Protestants still celebrate the victory each year on July 12 (called **Orange Day** in honor of King Billy). At the turn of the 18th century a set of **Penal Laws** brought further Irish oppression, banning (among other things) the practice of Catholicism. In Dublin and the Pale, the Anglo-Irish garden-partied, gossiped, and architectured their way toward a second London. The term **"Ascendancy"** was coined for them; it described a social class whose elitehood depended upon Anglicanism. **Trinity College** was their quintessential institution. Away from the Ascended nonsense, the Catholic merchant class grew in cities like Galway and Tralee; they were taught in secret **hedge schools** and practiced their religion furtively, using large, flat **Mass rocks** when they couldn't get their hands on altars.

REBELLION AND UNION. The *liberté*-fever inspired by the American and French revolutions was particularly strong among a secret group called the **United Irishmen.** The bloody **Rebellion of 1798** erupted with a furious band of peasants and priests, and any hopes England held of making Irish society less volatile by relaxing anti-Catholic laws were dashed by such misbehavior. With the 1801 **Act of Union,** the Crown abolished Irish "self-government" altogether. The Dublin Parliament died, and "The United Kingdom of Great Britain and Ireland" was born. The Church of Ireland entered into an unequal arranged marriage, changing her name to the "United Church of England and Ireland." Dublin's mad gaiety vanished, the Anglo-Irish gentry collapsed, and agrarian violence and poverty escalated. Union did, however, mean Irish representatives now held seats in the British Parliament. Using their newfound suffrage, Irish farmers elected **Daniel O'Connell** in 1829, forcing Westminster to repeal the anti-Catholic laws that would have barred him from taking his seat. "The Liberator" promptly forced Parliament to allot money for improving Irish living conditions. Unfortunately, O'Connell's crusade for the welfare of his people wasn't enough to protect them from a malicious little fungus.

THE FAMINE AND SOCIAL REFORM. The potato was the wundercrop of the rapidly growing Irish population, and their reliance on it had devastating effects when the heroic spud fell victim to fungal disease. During the years of the **Great Famine** (1847-51), an estimated two to three million people died and another million emigrated. After the Famine, the societal structure of surviving Irish peasants completely reorganized

REPUBLIC OF IRELAND

itself. The bottom layer of truly penniless farmers had been eliminated altogether. Depopulation continued, and **emigration** became an Irish way of life. English injustice fueled the formation of angry young Nationalist groups—in 1858, crusaders supporting a violent removal of the oppressors founded a secret society known as the **Fenians,** while the 1870s saw the creation of the **Land League,** which pushed for further reforms.

In 1870, MP **Isaac Butt** founded the **Irish Home Rule Party.** Home Ruler **Charles Stewart Parnell** was a charismatic Protestant aristocrat with a hatred for everything English. Though he survived implication in the **Phoenix Park murders,** he couldn't beat an 1890 adultery rap; the scandal split all of Ireland into Parnellites and anti-Parnellites. While squabbling politicians let their ideals fall to the wayside, civil society waxed ambitious. The fairer sex established the **Irish Women's Suffrage Federation** in 1911 and Marxist **James Connolly** led strikes in Belfast and Dublin. Meanwhile, various groups (like the **Gaelic Athletic Association** and the **Gaelic League**) tried to revive an essential, unpolluted "Gaelic" culture. Arthur Griffith began a tiny movement and little-read newspaper, both of which went by the name **Sinn Féin** ("Ourselves Alone"). Thousands of Northern Protestants opposing Home Rule organized a quasi-militia called the **Ulster Volunteer Force (UVF).** Nationalists led by Eoin MacNeill responded by creating the **Irish Volunteers.**

THE EASTER RISING, INDEPENDENCE, AND CIVIL WAR. Summer 1914: Irish Home Rule seemed imminent, and Ulster was ready to go up in flames. Instead, someone shot an archduke, and the world went up in flames. British Prime Minister Henry Asquith passed a **Home Rule Bill** in return for Irish bodies to fill out the British army; 670,000 Irishmen signed up to fight the Kaiser. Meanwhile, the Fenians and **Padraig Pearse** planned a nation-wide revolt for **Easter Sunday, 1916.** A crucial shipment of arms went astray, however, and the uprising fell through. The Pearse group rescheduled their rebellion for the following Monday, April 24; they seized Dublin's **General Post Office** and hunkered down for five days of brawling in the streets. The Crown retaliated—15 "ringleaders" were publicly executed. The Irish grew sympathetic to the rebels and increasingly anti-British. The Volunteers reorganized under Fenian bigwig **Michael Collins,** who brought them to Sinn Féin, and **Éamon de Valera** became the party president. In 1918, the British tried to introduce a draft in Ireland, and the Irish lost what little complacency they had left.

Extremist Irish Volunteers started calling themselves the **Irish Republican Army (IRA)** and became Sinn Féin's military might. Thus the British saw another **War for Independence.** In 1920, British Prime Minister **David Lloyd George** passed the **Government of Ireland Act,** which divided the island into Northern and Southern Ireland. Hurried negotiations then produced the **Anglo-Irish Treaty,** creating a 26-county Irish Free State but recognizing British rule over the northern counties. Everyone split on whether to accept the treaty. A nay-saying portion of the IRA occupied the Four Courts in Dublin and sparked two years of **civil war.** To skip over all the ugly details: the pro-treaty government won. Sinn Féin denied the legitimacy of the Free State government and expressed their disapproval by refusing to refer to the country by the official name of **Éire.**

IRELAND TODAY

THE ERA DE VALERA. Under the guidance of **Éamon de Valera,** the government ended armed resistance by Republican insurgents. In 1927, de Valera founded his own political party, **Fianna Fáil,** won the 1932 election, and held power for much of the next 20 years. In 1937, he and the voters approved the permanent Irish Constitution. It establishes the country's legislative structure, consisting of two chambers: the **Dáil** (DAHL) and the **Seanad** (SHA-nud). The Prime Minister is the **Taoiseach** (TEE-shuch), and the **President** is the ceremonial head of state. Ireland stayed officially neutral during WWII (known as **The Emergency**), though many Irish citizens identified with the Allies, and about 50,000 served in the British army. Then, in 1948, "the Republic of Ireland" was officially created, ending British Commonwealth membership altogether. The Crown, which didn't quite catch all that, recognized the Republic a year later and declared (harumph!) that the UK would maintain control over Ulster until the North consented to join the Republic.

RECENT EVENTS. In the 1960s, increased contact with the rest of the world accelerated economic growth, put the brakes on emigration, and fueled national confidence. Ireland entered the European Economic Community, now the **European Union (EU),** in 1973. In 1985, the **Anglo-Irish agreement** let Éire stick an official nose in Northern negotiations. The Irish broke progressive social and political ground in 1990 by choosing **Mary Robinson,** who happened to be of the female persuasion, to be their President. The small, leftist **Labour Party** also enjoyed enormous, unexpected success, paving the way for further social reform. In 1993, Taoiseach **Albert Reynolds** declared his top priority was to stop violence in Northern Ireland. A year later he announced a cease-fire agreement between Sinn Féin and the IRA. Fianna Fáil won the June 1997 general election, making **Bertie Ahern,** just a spring chicken at 45, the youngest Taoiseach in Irish history. Ahern joined the peace talks that produced the **Good Friday Agreement** in April of 1998. (For the recent status of the Agreement, see p. 696.) In the summer of 2001, the Irish populace defeated the **Nice Treaty,** which was the first step in the addition of 12 new nations to the EU. The referendum shocked Ireland's pro-Treaty government and caused quite a little stir on the Continent. In other EU-related news, the **euro** was formally introduced into Ireland on January 1, 2002 and the Irish pound (the punt) was given the boot.

CULTURE AND CUSTOMS

Although there's little reason to walk on pins and needles when interacting with the Irish, a notoriously friendly and warm people, an awareness of certain customs and practices will save you accidentally giving insult. If you avoid **jumping the queue** (patience is a virtue—stay in line and wait your turn), shirking your **responsibilities at the pub** (drinks among small groups are often bought in rounds—observe the golden rule), and making inane references to leprechauns or Lucky Charms, you should be fine. **Conversation** is an art in Ireland, and it's important to distinguish between casual and sensitive issues; abortion, divorce, gay marriage, and the Troubles up North, for instance, are not topics for the pub or the bus stop. Above all, be sensitive, mind your Ps and Qs, and **never, ever,** call an Irish person "British."

LANGUAGE AND LITERATURE

HISTORY OF THE IRISH LANGUAGE. The oldest vernacular literature and the largest collection of folklore in Europe are both Irish. The constitution declares Irish the national language of the Republic, yet there are only 60,000 individuals in exclusively Irish-speaking communities, or **gaeltacht** (GAYL-tacht). The most prominent *gaeltacht* are in Connemara, Co. Donegal, the Dingle Peninsula, and the Aran Islands; these geographically disparate communities are further divided by three almost mutually incomprehensible dialects: **Connemara, Donegal,** and the southern **Munster Irish.** The language reentered the lives of the privileged classes with the advent of the **Gaelic Revival.** In 1893, **Douglas Hyde** (who later became the first president of Éire) founded the **Gaelic League** in order to inspire enthusiasm for Irish. Today, Irish has grown in popularity among native English speakers.

REPUBLIC OF IRELAND

LEGENDS AND FOLKTALES. In early Irish society, what the **bards** sang about battles, valor, and lineage was the only record chieftains had by which to make decisions. Poetry and politics of the Druidic tradition were so intertwined that *fili*, trained poets, and *breitheamh*, judges, were often the same people. Poets living in chieftains' households invented the art of verse satire and composed "cycles" of tales narrating the lives of a set of heroes and villains. The most extensive is the **Ulster Cycle,** spinning the adventures of King Conchobar (Conor) of Ulster, his arch-enemy (and ex-wife) Queen Medbh of Connacht, and his nephew and champion **Cúchulainn** (KOO-hu-lin).

SWIFT, WILDE, AND SHAW. In long-colonized Dublin, **Jonathan Swift** (1667-1745) wrote some of the most marvelous satire in the English language. While he defended the Protestant Church of Ireland, Swift yet felt compelled to write about the sad condition of starving Irish Catholic peasants. In the mid-19th century, Dublin's talented young writers often moved on to London to make their names. **Oscar Wilde** (1856-1900) produced many sparklingly witty works, including *The Importance of Being Earnest* (1895). Playwright **George Bernard Shaw** (1856-1950), winner of the 1925 Nobel Prize, was also born in Dublin but moved to London in 1876.

YEATS AND THE REVIVAL. Toward the end of the 19th century, a vigorous and enduring effort known today as the **Irish Literary Revival** took over. The early poems of **William Butler Yeats** (1865-1939) create a dreamily rural Ireland of loss and legend. In 1923, Yeats became the first Irishman to win the Nobel Prize for Literature. In 1904, he and **Lady Gregory** founded the **Abbey Theatre** in Dublin (see p. 745), but conflict arose almost immediately: how exactly was this new body of "Irish" drama to be written? A sort of compromise was found in the work of **John Millington Synge**, whose experiences on the Aran Islands led him to write *The Playboy of the Western World* (1907), destroying pastoral myths of "classless" Irish peasantry. **Sean O'Casey's** plays, such as 1924's *Juno and the Paycock*, were well received by Dublin's middle class.

JOYCE, BECKETT AND RECENT AUTHORS. Ireland's most famous expatriate is **James Joyce** (1882-1941), godfather and patron saint of modernism. Joyce's most accessible writing is the collection of short stories titled *Dubliners* (1914), while his masterwork is generally agreed to be the ground-breaking mock-epic *Ulysses* (1922). Like Joyce, **Samuel Beckett** (1906-89) fled to Paris to pursue his writing career; unlike Joyce, he left most of vernacular Ireland behind. His novels, plays *(Waiting for Godot)*, and bleak prose poems convey a stark pessimism about language, society, and life. Beckett won the Nobel Prize in 1969, but did not accept it on the grounds that Joyce had never received it. After the 1940s, Irish poetry once again commanded widespread appreciation. **Patrick Kavanaugh** (1906-67) debunked a mythical Ireland, while **Paul Muldoon** adds quirk and confusion to humdrum existence. Notorious wit, playwright, poet, and terrorist **Brendan Behan** created semi-autobiographical works about delinquent life in plays like *The Quare Fellow* (1954). Mild-mannered schoolteacher **Roddy Doyle** won the 1994 Booker Prize for *Paddy Clarke Ha Ha Ha*. Ireland's most famous living poet is **Seamus Heaney,** who won the Nobel Prize for Literature in 1995.

MUSIC

Irish traditional music, or **trad,** is the centuries-old array of dances, melodies, and embellishments that has been passed down through generations of musicians. The tunes can be written down, but trad more often consists of improvisation. Best-selling trad studio artists include **Altan** and the **Chieftains,** but most traditional musicians play before smaller, more intimate audiences of locals. **Pub sessions** typically alternate between fast-paced instrumental music and folk songs.

In Ireland there is surprisingly little distinction between music types—a fine musician uses a variety of sources. The London-based **Pogues** fused rock and trad, and whipped out reels and jigs of drunken, punk-damaged revelry. **My Bloody Valentine** wove shimmering distortions to land themselves on the outskirts of grunge. Ireland's rock musicians have also set their sights on mainstream super-stardom; **U2** is Ireland's biggest rock export, and **Sinéad O'Connor** developed her style in Ireland long before she became a phenomenon in America. In recent years, **The Cranberries** and **Boyzone** have also achieved success abroad.

MEDIA AND SPORTS

The largest **newspapers** in the Republic are *The Irish Times* and *The Irish Independent. The Times* takes a liberal stance and is renowned for its excellent coverage of international affairs. *The Independent* is more internally focused and often maintains a chatty writing style. Many regional papers offer in-depth local news; the largest is *The Cork Examiner*. **British papers** are sold throughout Ireland. In 1961, the Republic's national radio service made its first television broadcast, naming itself **Radio Telefís Éireann (RTE)**. The government's most recent developments include the start of Irish-language radio and TV stations, called **Telifís na Gaelige**, aimed at promoting the use of Irish in modern media forms.

The Irish take enormous pride in their two native sports: Gaelic football and hurling. In 1884, the **Gaelic Athletic Association (GAA)** was founded to establish official rules and regulations for these and other ancient Irish recreations. **Gaelic football** is like a cross between football and rugby, though older than both. As fans like to say, if football is a game, then **hurling** is an art. This fast and dangerous-looking sport was first played in the 13th century, and is perhaps best imagined as a blend of lacrosse and field hockey. (The women's version of the game is called **camogie.**) **Football** (or soccer) enjoys nearly as fanatical a following, and the Irish are also fiercely devoted to the football clubs of England. Co. Kildare is well-known as a breeding ground for champion **racehorses.** On the byways of Ulster and in certain places in Cork, the strange, quasi-golf game of **road bowling** sees enthusiastic fans lining the twisty playing fields ("roads," that is).

FOOD AND DRINK

The basics of Irish cuisine are simple: specialties include *colcannon* (a potato dish), Guinness stew, and Irish stew. Loud and long will the Irish bards sing the praises of the man who first concocted **black pudding;** as one local butcher put it, it's "some pork, a good deal of blood, and grains and things—all wrapped up in a tube." **White pudding** uses milk instead of blood. Regional specialties include Cork's **crubeen** (tasty pigs' feet), Dublin's **coddle** (boiled sausages and bacon with potatoes), and Waterford's **blaa** (sausage rolls). Best of all culinary delights is **soda bread,** a heavy white loaf especially tasty when fried. Another indigenous bread is **barm brack,** a spicy mixture of dried fruits and molasses mixed to a lead-like density. **Seafood** can be a real bargain in smaller towns' **chippers.**

People of all ages and every social milieu head to **pubs** for conversation, food, drink, music, and **craic** (pronounced "crack"; "a good time"). Most pubs host evening trad sessions, and in rural areas there's a chance that a *seanachaí* (SHAN-ukh-ee; travelling storyteller) might drop in. Pubs are generally open Monday through Saturday from 10:30am to 11:30pm (11pm in winter) and Sunday from 12:30 to 11pm (closed 2-4pm). Many pubs, especially in Dublin, are now able to obtain late licenses; others have been granted special "early" permits allowing them to open at 7:30am (yee-haw!). **Beer** wins a landslide victory as the drink of choice, and **Guinness** inspires a reverence otherwise reserved for the Holy Trinity. Known variously as "the dark stuff," "the blonde in the black skirt," or simply "I'll have a pint, please," it's a rich, dark brew with a head thick enough to stand a match in. **Murphy's** is a similar, slightly creamier Cork-brewed stout. **Irish whiskey,** invented by clever monks, is sweeter than its Scottish counterpart; **Jameson** is popular everywhere. In the west, you may hear locals praise "mountain dew," a euphemism for **poitín** (put-CHEEN), an illegal methanol-based distillation (sometimes given to cows in labor) that ranges in strength from 115 to 140 proof.

COUNTY DUBLIN

DUBLIN   ☎01

In a country known for its rural sanctity and relaxed lifestyle, the international flavor and boundless energy of Dublin (Baile Átha Cliath) are made all the more visible. With the whole of Ireland changing at an almost disconcerting pace, the Dublin environs, with close to a third of the country's population, lead the charge. Fueled by international and rural emigration and the deep pockets of the EU, the city's cultural and economic growth has been all but unstoppable. But while Dublin may seem edgy by Irish standards, it's still as friendly a major city as you'll find. Not quite as cosmopolitan, but just as eclectic as New York or London, Ireland's capital is home to vibrant theater, music, and literary communities, and multiple generations of pubs learning to coexist peacefully. Though this may hardly look like the rustic "Emerald Isle" promoted on tourist brochures, its people still embody the charm and warmth that have made their country famous.

◨ INTERCITY TRANSPORTATION

Rail lines, bus lines (both state-run and private), and the national highway system radiate from Dublin. Because intercity transport is so Dublin-centric, you may find it more convenient to arrange your travel in other parts of the Republic while you're in the capital.

Airport: Dublin Airport (☎844 4900). **Dublin buses** #41, 41B, and 41C run from the airport to Eden Quay in the city center (every 20min., €1.50). The **Airlink shuttle** runs non-stop to Busáras Central Bus Station and O'Connell St. (☎844 4265; 20-25min., every 10min. 5:15am-11:30pm, €4.50), and to Heuston Station (50min., €4.50), but is hardly worth the markup from the #41.

Trains: Irish Rail Travel Centre, Iarnród Éireann (EER-ann-road AIR-ann), at 35 Lower Abbey St. (☎836 6222). Purchase tickets in advance at the Travel Centre, or at a station 20min. before departure. Open M-F 9am-5pm, Sa 9am-1pm. Trains to: **Belfast** (☎805 4277); **Cork** (☎805 4200); **Galway/Westport** (☎805 4222); **Killarney/Tralee** (☎805 4266); **Limerick** (☎805 4211); **Sligo** (☎805 4255); **Waterford** (☎805 4233); **Wexford/Rosslare** (☎805 4288). Bus #90 connects Connolly, Heuston, and Pearse Stations, as well as Busáras. Connolly and Pearse are also **DART** stations serving the north and south coasts (see below).

Connolly Station, Amiens St. (☎703 2358 or 703 2359), north of the Liffey, close to Busáras. Buses #20, 20A, and 90 head south of the river, and the DART runs to Tara Station on the south quay. Open M-Sa 7am-10pm, Su noon-9pm. Trains to: **Belfast** (2hr.; M-Sa 8 per day, Su 5 per day; €27); **Sligo** (3½hr., 3-4 per day, €19); **Wexford** via **Rosslare** (3hr., 3 per day, €14).

Heuston Station (☎ 703 2132, night ☎ 703 2131), south of Victoria Quay and west of the city center, a 25min. walk from Trinity College. Buses #26, 51, 90, and 79 run from Heuston to the city center. Open daily 6:30am-10:20pm. Trains to: **Cork** (3½hr.; M-Th and Sa 8 per day, F 11 per day, Su 6 per day; €43); **Galway** (2½hr.; 4-5 per day; €21, F and Su €28); **Kilkenny** (2hr.; M-Th and Sa 5 per day, F 1 per day, Su 4 per day; €15.80); **Limerick** (2½hr., 9 per day, €34); **Tralee** (4hr., 4-5 per day, €44); **Waterford** (2½hr., 3-4 per day, €16.50).

Pearse Station, Pearse St. and Westland Row (☎ 703 3634), just east of Trinity College. Open daily 6:30am-11:30pm. Receives southbound trains from Connolly Station.

Buses: Intercity buses to Dublin arrive at **Busáras Central Bus Station,** Store St. (☎ 836 6111), directly behind the Customs House and next to Connolly Station. Info at the **Dublin Bus Office,** 59 O'Connell St. (☎ 872 0000; www.dublinbus.ie). **Bus Éireann** (www.buseireann.ie) window open M-F 9am-5:30pm, Sa 9am-1pm. To: **Belfast** (3hr., 6-7 per day, €16.50); **Cork** (4½hr., 6 per day, €19); **Derry** (4¼hr., 4-5 per day, €16.50); **Donegal** (4¼hr., 5-6 per day, €13.50); **Galway** (3½hr., 13 per day, €13.30); **Kilkenny** (2hr., 6 per day, €9); **Killarney** (6hr., 5 per day, €19); **Limerick** (3½hr.; M-Sa 13 per day, Su 7 per day; €13.30); **Rosslare** (3hr.; M-Sa 10 per day, Su 7 per day; €12.70); **Sligo** (4hr., 4-5 per day, €12.10); **Waterford** (2¾hr., 5-7 per day, €8.85); **Wexford** (2¾hr., 7-10 per day, €10.10); **Westport** (5hr., 2-3 per day, €13). **PAMBO** (Private Association of Motor Bus Owners), 32 Lower Abbey St. (☎ 878 8422), can provide the names and numbers of the many private operators. Open M-F 10am-5pm.

Ferries: Bookings online (www.dublinport.ie/Ferries.html) or in the Irish Rail office (see above). **Irish Ferries** (☎ 638 3333 or (1890) 313 131; www.irishferries.com; 2-4 Merrion Row; open M-F 9am-5pm, Sa 9:15am-12:45pm) arrive from **Holyhead** at the **Dublin Port** (☎ 607 5665), from which buses #53 and 53A run every hr. to Busáras (€1); **Dublin Bus** also runs ferryport connection buses tailored to ferry schedules (€2.50-3.20). **Norse Merchant Ferries** docks at the Dublin port and goes to **Liverpool** (7½hr.; 1-2 per day; €25-40, with car €105-170); booking available only from **Gerry Feeney**, 19 Eden Quay (☎ 819 2999). The **Isle of Man Steam Packet Company** (UK ☎ (1800) 551 743) docks at Dublin Port and sends 1 boat per day to Man; rates from €50. **Stena Line** arrives from **Holyhead, Wales** at the **Dún Laoghaire** ferry terminal (☎ 204 7777); from there the **DART** shuttles passengers into central Dublin (€1.70).

▆ LOCAL TRANSPORTATION

The most important pamphlet for the bustling traveler is the free "Which Ticket Type Are You?" leaflet. Along with the *Map of Greater Dublin* and the Dublin Bus timetable, this handy guide will clue you in to every variety of special ticket and student discount available. **Travel passes**, called "Ramblers," were designed for people intending to move around a *lot;* each pass has a time limit that requires several trips a day to validate its price. **Travel Wide** passes offer daily or weekly unlimited rides (1 day €4.50, 1 week €16.50). A Dublin Bus week runs from Sunday to Saturday inclusive, so a weekly pass bought Friday will expire after only one day. Other tickets allow for both bus and suburban rail/DART travel. (**Short hop** daily €7.20, weekly €12.60, monthly €86.)

Buses: Dublin Bus, 59 O'Connell St. (☎ 873 4222). Open M 8:30am-5:30pm, Tu-F 9am-5:30pm, Sa 9am-1pm. Buses are cheap (€0.80-1.50) and run most frequently 8am-6pm (generally every 8-20min., off-peak hours every 30-45min.) Dublin Bus runs a **NiteLink** service to the suburbs (M and W 12:30am and 2am, Th-Sa every hr. from 12:30-3:30am; €3.80-5.70; passes not valid.). **Wheelchair-accessible** buses are limited: the only options are the **OmniLink** service, which cruises around Clontarf (#300, €0.65) and the #3 bus from Whitehall to Sandymount via O'Connell St.

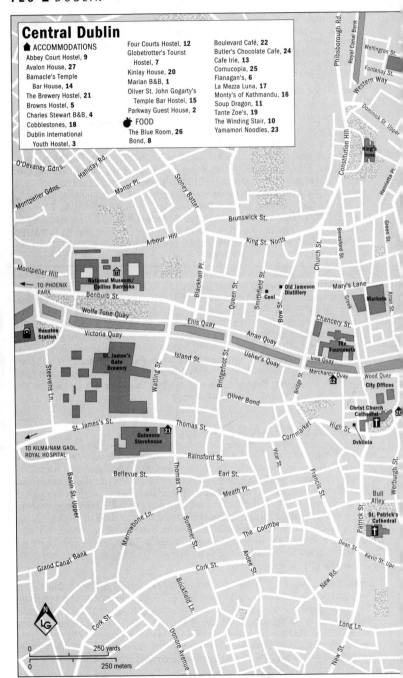

Central Dublin

ACCOMMODATIONS

Abbey Court Hostel, **9**
Avalon House, **27**
Barnacle's Temple
  Bar House, **14**
The Brewery Hostel, **21**
Browns Hostel, **5**
Charles Stewart B&B, **4**
Cobblestones, **18**
Dublin International
  Youth Hostel, **3**

Four Courts Hostel, **12**
Globetrotter's Tourist
  Hostel, **7**
Kinlay House, **20**
Marian B&B, **1**
Oliver St. John Gogarty's
  Temple Bar Hostel, **15**
Parkway Guest House, **2**

FOOD
The Blue Room, **26**
Bond, **8**

Boulevard Café, **22**
Butler's Chocolate Cafe, **24**
Cafe Irie, **13**
Cornucopia, **25**
Flanagan's, **6**
La Mezza Luna, **17**
Monty's of Kathmandu, **16**
Soup Dragon, **11**
Tante Zoe's, **19**
The Winding Stair, **10**
Yamamori Noodles, **23**

DART: From **Connolly, Pearse,** and **Tara St. Stations** in the city, the electric DART trains shoot south past **Bray** and north to **Howth.** Tickets are sold in the station and must be presented at the end of the trip. Trains every 10-15min. 6:30am-11:30pm. €0.75-1.40.

Suburban Rail: From **Connolly Station** trains run north- and southbound (stopping also at **Tara St.** and **Pearse Stations**), and west to **Mullingar.** From **Heuston Station** west to **Kildare.** Trains are frequent (roughly 30 per day except Su).

Taxis: Blue Cabs (☎ 676 1111), **ABC** (☎ 285 5444), and **City Group Taxi** (☎ 872 7272) have wheelchair-accessible taxis (call ahead). Another option is **National Radio Cabs,** 40 James St. (☎ 677 2222). All available 24hr. Alternatively, taxi stands are found outside Trinity College, on Lower Abbey St. at the bus station, and on Parnell St.

Bike Rental: Raleigh Rent-A-Bike, Kylemore Rd. (☎ 626 1333). Arranges 1-way bike rentals; €19 surcharge. **Cycle Ways,** 185-6 Parnell St. (☎ 873 4748). €20 per day, €80 per week. Deposit €80. Open M-W and F-Sa 10am-6pm, Th 10am-8pm.

Hitchhiking: Since Dublin is well served by bus and rail, there is no good reason to thumb it, and *Let's Go* does not recommend trying. Still, those who choose to hitch from Dublin usually take buses to the outskirts where the motorways begin.

■ ORIENTATION

In general, Dublin is refreshingly compact, though navigation is complicated by the ridiculous number of names a street adopts along its way; streets are usually labelled on the side of buildings at intersections and never on street-level signs. Buying a map with a street index is a smart idea. The most compact is *The Dublin Popout* (€4), which fits easily in a pocket and has excellent detail.

The **River Liffey** forms a natural boundary between Dublin's **North** and **South Sides,** the former claiming most of the hostels and the latter flaunting famous sights and fabulous restaurants. The streets running alongside the Liffey are called **quays** (KEYS); the name of the street changes each block as it reaches a new quay. If a street is split into "Upper" and "Lower," then the "Lower" is the part of the street farther east, closer to the Liffey. The core of Dublin is ringed by **North** and **South Circular Rd.,** which enjoy their own assortment of name changes. Most of the city's major sights are located within this area. **O'Connell St.** is the primary link between north and south Dublin. One block south of the river runs **Temple Bar** (a name which usually applies to the area as a whole). **Trinity College** is the nerve center of Dublin's cultural activity; the college touches the northern end of **Grafton St.** Grafton's southern end opens onto **St. Stephen's Green,** a sizable and famous public park. Merchants on the North Side hawk merchandise for cheaper prices than those in the more touristed South. **Henry St.** and **Mary St.** comprise a pedestrian shopping zone that intersects with O'Connell just after the **General Post Office,** two blocks from the Liffey. The North Side is reputed to be a rougher area, especially after dark. This reputation may not be wholly deserved, but tourists should avoid walking in unfamiliar areas on either side of the Liffey at night, especially when alone. It is wise to steer clear of **Phoenix Park** after dark.

■ PRACTICAL INFORMATION

TOURIST AND FINANCIAL SERVICES

Tourist Information: Main Office, Suffolk St. (☎(1850) 230 330 or 605 7700; UK ☎(0171) 493 3201; www.visitdublin.com). Near Trinity College, in a converted church. Books beds for €4. **American Express** maintains a branch office with **currency exchange** here (☎ 605 7709; open M-Sa 9am-5pm) and **Bus Éireann** has representatives, as does **Argus Rent a Car** (☎ 605 7701 or 490 4444; open M-F 9am-5pm, Sa 9am-1pm). Main Office open July-Aug. M-Sa 9am-8:30pm, Su 11am-5:30pm; Sept.-June M-Sa 9am-5:30pm. Reservation desks close 30min. earlier. **Northern Ireland Tourist Board:** 16 Nassau St. (☎ 679 1977). Books accommodations up North. Open M-F 9:15am-5:30pm, Sa 10am-5pm.

Community and Youth Information Centre: Sackville Pl. (☎878 6844), at Marlborough St., east of O'Connell St. Resources on outings, travel, hostels, sports, and referrals. **Work opportunities** listing board and free **Internet access** (call ahead). Open M-W 9:30am-1pm and 2-6pm, Th-Sa 9:30am-1pm and 2-5pm.

Budget Travel: usit NOW, 19-21 Aston Quay (☎602 1777), near O'Connell Bridge. The place for Irish travel discounts, especially for ISIC cardholders and people under 26. **Internet access** with ISIC card €1 per 15min., €2.50 per 45min. Open M-W and F 8:30am-6:30pm, Th 8:30am-8:30pm, Sa 9:30am-5pm.

Hosteling Organization: An Óige Head Office (Irish Youth Hostel Association/HI), 61 Mountjoy St. (☎830 5808; www.irelandyha.org), at Wellington St. Follow O'Connell St. north, ignoring its name changes. Mountjoy St. is on the left, 20min. from O'Connell Bridge. Book and pay for HI hostels here. Also sells bike and rail package tours. The *An Óige Handbook* lists all HI hostels in Ireland and Northern Ireland. Hugely beneficial membership card €15, under 18 €7.50. Open M-F 9:30am-5:30pm.

Financial Services: Bank of Ireland, AIB, and **TSB** branches with **bureaux de change** and **24hr. ATMs** cluster on Lower O'Connell St., Grafton St., and in the Suffolk and Dame St. areas. Most open M-F 10am-4pm. **American Express:** 41 Nassau St. (☎679 9000). Open M-F 9am-5pm. Branch inside the Suffolk St. tourist office (see above).

LOCAL SERVICES

Luggage Storage: Connolly Station. €2.50 per item. Open M-Sa 7:40am-9:20pm, Su 9:10am-9:45pm. **Heuston Station.** €2-5 per item. Open daily 6:30am-10:30pm. **Busáras.** €3 per item, lockers €4-9. Open M-Sa 8am-7:45pm, Su 10am-5:45pm.

Women's Resources: Women's Aid Helpline (☎(1800) 341 900) offers info on legal matters and support groups (10am-10pm). **Dublin Rape Crisis Centre** (24hr. hotline ☎(1800) 778 888). **Dublin Well Woman Centre,** Lower Liffey St. (☎872 8051), is a private health center for women. It also runs a **clinic** (☎668 3714) at 67 Pembroke Rd. **Cura,** 30 South Anne St. (☎505 3040; Dublin office ☎671 0598). Catholic-funded support for women with unplanned pregnancies. Open M and W 10:30am-6:30pm, Tu and Th 10:30am-8:30pm, F-Sa 10:30am-2:30pm.

Gay and Lesbian Resources: Gay Switchboard Dublin is a good resource for events and updates and sponsors a hotline (☎872 1055; Su-F 8-10pm, Sa 3:30-6pm). **National Gay and Lesbian Federation,** Hirschfield Centre, 10 Fownes St. (☎671 0939), Temple Bar, offers counseling on legal concerns. **Lesbians Organizing Together (LOT),** 5 Capel St. (☎872 7770). Drop-in resource center and library open Tu-Th 10am-5pm. **Outhouse,** 65 William St. (☎670 6377). Queer community resource center.

Laundrette: Laundry Shop, 191 Parnell St. (☎872 3541). Open M-F 8am-7pm, Sa 9am-6pm, Su 11am-5pm. **All-American Launderette,** 40 South Great Georges St. (☎677 2779). €7; full service €8. Open M-Sa 8:30am-7pm, Su 10am-6pm.

Work Opportunities: Helpful job listing board at the **Community and Youth Information Centre** (see above). **Working Ireland,** 26 Eustace St. (☎677 0300; www.workingireland.ie), is a multi-tasking agency that arranges short- and long-term job placement throughout Ireland. **The Job Shop,** 50 Grafton St. (☎672 7755) can also help.

EMERGENCY AND COMMUNICATIONS

Emergency: ☎999 or 112; no coins required.

Police *(Garda):* Dublin Metro Headquarters, Harcourt Terr. (☎666 9500); Store St. Station (☎666 8000); Fitzgibbon St. Station (☎666 8400); Pearse St. (☎666 9000). **Police Confidential Report Line:** ☎(1800) 666 111.

Counseling and Support: Tourist Victim Support, Harcourt Sq. (☎478 5295; 10am-5pm helpline ☎(1800) 661 771; www.victimsupport.ie). Open M-Sa 10am-6pm, Su noon-6pm. **Samaritans,** 112 Marlborough St. (☎(1850) 609 090 or 872 7700). **AIDS Helpline** (☎(1800) 459 459). Open daily 10am-5pm.

Pharmacy: O'Connell's, 56 Lower O'Connell St. (☎873 0427). Open M-Sa 7:30am-10pm and Su 10am-10pm. Other branches around the city, including 2 on Grafton St.

Hospital: St. James's Hospital, James St. (☎453 7941). Take bus #123. **Mater Misericordiae Hospital,** Eccles St. (☎830 1122), off Lower Dorset St. Buses #10, 11, 13, 16, 121, and 122. **Beaumont Hospital,** Beaumont Rd. (☎837 7755 or 809 3000). Buses #27B, 51A, 101, 103, and 300.

Internet Access: Several chains around, the best being **The Internet Exchange,** at 146 Parnell St. (☎670 3000) and Fownes St. in Temple Bar (☎635 1680). €4 per hr., €2.50 with €5 membership. Open daily 9am-10:30pm. **Global Internet Cafe,** 8 Lower O'Connell St. (☎878 0295), 1 block north of the Liffey. €6 per hr., students €5, €3 with €5 membership. Open M-F 8am-11pm, Sa 9am-11pm, Su 10am-11pm.

Post Office: General Post Office, O'Connell St. (☎705 7000). Poste Restante pickup at the **bureau de change** window. Open M-Sa 8am-8pm, Su 10am-6:30pm. Smaller post offices around the city open M-F 8:45am-6pm. **Post Code:** Dublin 1. Dublin is the only place in the Republic with post codes.

⌐ ACCOMMODATIONS AND CAMPING

Dublin has a handful of marvelous accommodations, but high demand for lodging keeps less-than-marvelous places open too. Reserve at least a week ahead, particularly for holiday or sporting weekends and during the peak summer season (June-Aug.). Phoenix Park may tempt the desperate, but camping there is a terrible idea, not to mention big-time illegal. If the accommodations below are full, consult Dublin Tourism's *Dublin Accommodation Guide* (€3.80).

HOSTELS

▨ **Abbey Court Hostel,** 29 Bachelor's Walk, O'Connell Bridge (☎878 0700). Great location in Temple Bar. Clean, smoke-free, and with bathrooms/showers in most rooms. Continental breakfast included. Internet access €1 per 15min. Full service laundry €8. 12-bed dorms €17-20; 6-bed €22-25; 4-bed €25-28. Doubles €76-88. ❷

▨ **Four Courts Hostel,** 15-17 Merchants Quay (☎672 5839). The non-central location of this 250-bed, first-rate mega-hostel is made up for by its extremely friendly staff and relaxing atmosphere. Clean rooms (most with showers), kitchen facilities, laundry (€5), carpark, and long-term stays available. Continental breakfast included. Internet access €1 per 10min. 16-bed dorms €15-16.50; 8-bed €17-19; 4- to 6-bed €20-21.50. Doubles €54-65; family room €25-26.50 per person. ❷

▨ **Avalon House (IHH),** 55 Aungier St. (☎475 0001; www.avalon-house.ie). Turn off Dame St. onto Great Georges St.; the hostel is a 10min. walk down on your right and just a stumble away from Temple Bar. Wheelchair-accessible and very secure. Continental breakfast included. Internet access. Storage cages €1 per day. Towels €2, deposit €8. Large dorms €15-20; 6-bed €20-30. Singles €30-37; doubles €56-70. ❷

Oliver St. John Gogarty's Temple Bar Hostel, 18-21 Anglesea St. (☎671 1822). The location is unbeatable if you're frolicking in Temple Bar. Drink and boogie with the ghosts of Joyce and Gogarty at the pub and disco next door. Internet access. Laundry €4. Dorms €13-23; doubles €46-56; triples €63-75. Oct.-May €2-4 less. ❷

Globetrotter's Tourist Hostel (IHH), 46-7 Lower Gardiner St. (☎ 873 5893; www.iol.ie/globetrotters). A dose of luxury for the weary. Beds are snug, but there's plenty of room to stow your stuff (plus free luggage storage). Full Irish breakfast included. Internet access. Towels €1. Dorms €19-21.50; singles €60-66.50; doubles €102-110. ❷

Browns Hostel, 89-90 Lower Gardiner St. (☎ 855 0034; www.brownshostelireland.com). Brand-new hostel attached to Browns Hotel (see below). Glistening yellow decor with TVs and A/C in every room. Breakfast included. Internet access. Lockers €1. Towels €1. 20-bed dorm €12.50-15; 10- to 14-bed €15-20; 4- to 6-bed €20-25. Discounts for longer stays. ❶

Kinlay House (IHH), 2-12 Lord Edward St. (☎ 679 6644). Slide down the oak banisters in the lofty entrance hall, snuggle into the soft couches in the TV room, or gaze at Christ Church Cathedral from your room window. Breakfast included. Internet access €1 per 15min. Lockers €2, deposit €5. Laundry €7. 15- to 24-bed dorms €15-17; 20-bed partitioned into 4-bed nooks €16-18; 4- to 6-bed €20-24, with bath €22-26. Singles €40-46; doubles €50-56, with bath €54-60. Nov.-May €2 less. ❷

The Brewery Hostel, 22-23 Thomas St. (☎ 453 8600). So close to the Guinness Brewery you can smell the hops, and only a 15min. walk from Temple Bar. Rooms are a bit snug, but the beds are good. Continental breakfast included. All rooms with bath. Carpark. Luggage storage. Awkward 1-key-per-room system. 10-bed dorms €16-22; 8-bed €18-24; 4-bed €19-28. Doubles €65-78. 1-bedroom apartment €75-100. ❷

Dublin International Youth Hostel (An Óige/HI), 61 Mountjoy St. (☎ 830 4555; www.irelandyha.org), in a converted convent. Don't forget to say grace during the free breakfast, served in the chapel. Carpark and buses to Temple Bar. Wheelchair-accessible. Towels €1. Laundry €5. Dorms €20; doubles €52-56; triples €75-81. ❷

Cobblestones, 29 Eustace St. (☎ 677 5614). A breath of fresh air from the more industrial hostels, right in the middle of Temple Bar. Friendly staff, bright rooms, and a kitchen with fridge and microwave. Breakfast included. Cheap Internet access. Dorms €18-21; doubles €48. Student and group discounts available. ❷

Litton Lane Hostel, 2-4 Litton Ln. (☎ 872 8389), off Bachelors Walk. A former studio for the likes of U2, Van Morrison, and Sinead O'Connor. Internet access €1 per 20min. Laundry €5. Key deposit €1. Check-in 3pm, check-out 10:30am. Dorms €16-25; doubles €70-80. 1-bedroom apartments €80-110; 2-bedroom €120-150. ❷

Barnacle's Temple Bar House, 19 Temple Ln. (☎ 671 6277). Right in the hopping (and noisy) heart of Dublin. All rooms ensuite; water pressure that will make you sing. Continental breakfast included. Laundry and luggage storage. 12-bed dorms €13-16.50; 10-bed €15.50-19; 6-bed €18-21.50; 4-bed €20.50-23. Doubles €62-74. ❶

B&BS AND HOTELS

B&Bs with a green shamrock sign out front are approved by Bord Fáilte; those without haven't been inspected but may be cheaper and better located—establishments with good locations often find that Bord Fáilte's advertising is unnecessary. On the North Side, B&Bs cluster along **Upper** and **Lower Gardiner St.**, on **Sheriff St.**, and near **Parnell Sq.** Exercise caution when walking through the inner-city area at night. There are also several accommodating B&Bs outside the city center.

▧ **Parkway Guest House**, 5 Gardiner Pl. (☎ 874 0469). Rooms are high-ceilinged and tidy, and the location is perfectly central. Run by a mother-and-son team. Full Irish breakfast. Singles €32; doubles €52-60, with bath €60-70. ❸

▧ **Mona's B&B**, 148 Clonliffe Rd. (☎ 837 6723), outside the city. Gorgeous house run for 37 years (and probably 37 more) by Ireland's most lovely proprietress. Homemade bread accompanies the Irish breakfast. Open May-Oct. Singles €35; doubles €66. ❸

▨ **Mrs. Bermingham,** 8 Dromard Terr. (☎668 3861), on Dromard Ave. Take the #2 or 3 bus. Disembark at the Tesco and make the next left. Down the street, the road forks— the left fork is Dromard Terr. 1 room has a lovely bay window over the garden. Soft beds with fluffy comforters. Open Feb.-Nov. Singles €28; doubles with bath €52. ❸

Marian B&B, 21 Upper Gardiner St. (☎874 4129). The McElroys provide lovely rooms at a better price than the neighborhood competition. Singles €30; doubles €54. ❸

Charles Stewart B&B, 5-6 Parnell Sq. E. (☎878 0350). Continue up O'Connell St. past Parnell St. and look to your right. More a hotel than a B&B. Renovations expected to be complete by 2003. Full Irish breakfast. Singles €50-63.50; doubles €76-89; triples €120; quads €140. Very small private room with shared bath facilities €31.75. ❹

The Kingfisher, 166 Parnell St. (☎872 8732). A combined B&B, restaurant, and Internet cafe. Offers clean, modern rooms, uncomplicated food (fish and chips €8), and a full Irish breakfast. TV/VCR in each room, kitchenettes in some. Cheap Internet access. Singles €60; doubles €110; triples €165. ❺

Mrs. Molly Ryan, 10 Distillery Rd. (☎837 4147), off Clonliffe Rd. On your left if you're coming from the city center, in a yellow house attached to #11. Small rooms, small prices, no breakfast. As honest as they come. Singles €15; doubles €30. ❷

Rita and Jim Casey, Villa Jude, 2 Church Ave. (☎668 4982), off Beach Rd. Bus #3 to the first stop on Tritonville Rd.; Church Ave. is back a few yards. Mr. Casey is the former mayor of Sandymount, and he and lovely Rita specialize in the royal treatment. Clean rooms, big breakfasts, and good company. Doubles €45. ❸

River House Hotel, 23-24 Eustace St. (☎670 7655; www.visunet.ie/riverhouse). A quiet establishment right in the middle of thumping Temple Bar. Modern rooms and a space-age pub. Delicious and filling full Irish breakfast included. Mar.-Oct. singles €90; doubles €135; triples €180. Nov.-Feb. singles €70; doubles €95; triples €115. ❺

Browns Hotel, 90 Lower Gardiner St. (☎855 0034; www.brownshotelireland.com). Elegant Georgian building with newly refurbished rooms and a professional, hospitable staff that aims to take care of all your needs. Full hot breakfast included. Connected to Browns Hostel (see above). Singles €65-75; doubles €70-100. ❺

CAMPING

Most campsites are far from the city center, but camping equipment is available in the heart of the city. **The Great Outdoors,** on Chatham St. off the top of Grafton St., has an excellent selection of tents, backpacks, and cookware. (☎679 4293. An Óige/HI 10% discount. Open M-W and F-Sa 9:30am-5:30pm, Th 9:30am-8pm.)

Camac Valley Tourist Caravan & Camping Park, Naas Rd., Clondalkin (☎464 0644), near Corkagh Park; take bus #69 (35min., €1.50). Food shop and kitchen facilities. Wheelchair-accessible. Dogs welcome. Laundry €4.50. €7 per person; €14 per 2 people with car; €17 with caravan; €15 with camper. Showers €1. ❶

Shankill Caravan and Camping Park (☎282 0011). The DART and buses #45 and 84 from Eden Quay run to Shankill, as does #45A from the Dún Laoghaire ferryport. €9 per tent plus €2 per adult, €1 per child. Showers €1. ❶

🅒 FOOD

Dublin's many **open-air markets** sell fixins fresh and cheap. Vendors hawk fruit, fresh strawberries, flowers, and fish from their pushcarts. The later in the week, the more lively the market. The cheapest **supermarkets** around Dublin are the **Dunnes Stores** chain, with full branches at St. Stephen's Green (☎478 0188; open M-W and F-Sa 8:30am-7pm, Th 8:30am-9pm, Su noon-6pm), and the ILAC Centre, off Henry St., on N. Earl St. off O'Connell. The **Runner Bean,** 4 Nassau St., vends whole foods, homemade breads, veggies, fruits, and nuts. (☎679 4833. Open M-F 7:30am-6pm, Sa 7:30am-3pm.) Health food is also available around the city at various branches of **Nature's Way;** the biggest is at the St. Stephen's Green shopping center. (☎478 0165. Open M-W and F-Sa 9am-6pm, Th 9am-8pm.)

🔳 **La Mezza Luna,** 1 Temple Ln. (☎671 2840), in Temple Bar. Refined and classy, minus the pretension. Celestial food with a giant a la carte dinner menu ranging from pasta and seafood to Asian noodles and tortilla wraps. Try the wok-fried chicken (€8.25). Open M-Th 8am-11pm, F-Sa 9:30am-11:30pm, Su 9:30am-10:30pm. ❷

🔳 **The Blue Room,** Copperinger Row (☎670 6982), near Grafton St. Wonderful, family-friendly pastel cafe. Sandwiches to die for (€6.35), sweets, and coffee. Known for their pesto and homemade cranberry sauce. Open M-F 10am-6:30pm. ❷

The Winding Stair Bookshop and Cafe, 40 Lower Ormond Quay (☎873 3292), near the Ha'penny Bridge. Relaxed cafe overlooking the river shares its lower level with a bookshop. Contemporary Irish writing, periodicals, and soothing music wind you down. Salads around €8; sandwiches €4. Open M-Sa 9:30am-6pm, Su 1-6pm. ❷

Cafe Irie, 11 Fownes St. (☎672 5090). Travel up Fownes St. from Temple; it's on the left above the clothing store Sé Sí Progressive. Small, hidden eatery with an impressive selection of lip-smackingly good sandwiches (€2-4). A little crunchy, a little jazzy, and a whole lotta good. Vegan-friendly. Open M-Sa 9am-8pm, Su noon-6pm. ❶

Cornucopia, 19 Wicklow St. (☎677 7583). If you can find the space, sit down for a rich meal (about €8.50) or snack (€2). This vegetarian horn o' plenty spills huge portions onto your plate. Open M-W and F-Sa 8:30am-8pm, Th 9am-9pm. ❷

Flanagan's, 61 Upper O'Connell St. (☎873 1388). "A well-regarded establishment whose tourist trade occasionally suffers from being too close to a McDonald's," writes Tom Clancy in *Patriot Games.* (Sorry, Tom—now there's a Burger King across the way too.) Entrees €8.50-13.50. There are cheaper eats (€8-10) and leopard-print seats at the pizza-pasta joint upstairs. Open daily noon-11pm. ❸

Monty's of Kathmandu, (☎670 4911), just off of Dame St. on the right. Nepalese food with decor to match. Entrees €13-18; try the Sekuwa Chatpate Chicken or the spicy Begum Bahar with the unorthodox mix of chicken and lamb (both €14). Open M-Sa noon-2:30pm and 6-11:30pm, Su 6-11:30pm. ❹

Boulevard Café, 27 Exchequer St. Walk inside to the outside of an Italian street. This funky little place has recreated an Italian boulevard within its walls. Flower pots line even the faux balconies. Good tapas (€5.70) and pasta (€8.25); dinner entrees €14-22. Cafe open daily 10am-6pm; restaurant open daily 6pm-midnight. ❸

Soup Dragon, 168 Capel St. (☎872 3277). A dozen different soups (€4.10-11.35) by kitchen wizards, as well as healthy juices, fruits, and breads. Open M-F 8am-5:30pm and Sa 11am-5pm. ❷

Tante Zoe's, 1 Crowe St. (☎679 4407), across from the back entrance of the Foggy Dew pub. New Orleans Creole food in an elegantly casual setting. Staff will help you get just the right spiciness. Entrees €16.50-19. Open daily noon-4pm and 6pm-midnight. ❹

Yamamori Noodles, 71-72 South Great Georges St. (☎475 5001 or 475 5002). Exceptional and reasonably priced Japanese cuisine. Cleaner than a hospital. Traditional black, red, and white decor. Entrees €12-14; tofu steak €12. Open M-W and Su 12:30-11pm, Th-Sa 12:30-11:30pm. ❸

Bond, Beresford Pl. (☎855 9249). Minimalist design accented by bright blue chairs. Young professionals power-lunch on a range of exquisitely prepared French cuisine. Choose a wine from downstairs and enjoy it with your meal. 8oz. fillet of beef served with Cajun-herbed and mozzarella potatoes (€22). Dress casual plus. Open for lunch daily noon-3pm; coffee 3-6pm; dinner M-W 6-9pm, Th-Sa 6-10pm. ❺

Butler's Chocolate Cafe, 24 Wicklow St. (☎671 0591). Sinning never felt so good. In this luxury sweet shop, lattes start at €2.20 and a Bailey's milkshake is just €2.90. Open M-W and F-Su 8am-6pm, Th 8am till late. ❶

Bendini & Shaw. Retro gourmet sandwich shop with locations around Dublin. Grab off the shelf for a quick bite on the run. Smoked salmon, avocado, and ham salad on a baguette just €3.80. Delivery available for orders over €15. Five branches: 4 St. Stephen's Green (☎671 8651); 20 Upper Baggot St. (☎660 0131); 1A Lower Pembroke St. (☎678 0800); 2A Upper Fownes St. (☎671 0800); 4 Lower Mayor St. (☎829 0275). All open M-F 7am-5pm, Sa 8am-6pm, Su 9am-5pm. ❷

⚑ PUBLIN

James Joyce proposed that a "good puzzle would be to cross Dublin without passing a pub." When a local radio station once offered £100 to the first person to solve the puzzle, the winner explained that you could take any route—you'd just have to stop in each one along the way. Dublin's watering holes come in all shapes, sizes, specialties, and subcultures. Ask around or check *In Dublin*, *Hot Press*, or *Event Guide* for music listings. Note that a growing number of places are blurring the distinction between pubs and clubs, with rooms or dance floors opening after certain hours. So pay attention, and hit two birds with one pint. The *Let's Go* **Dublin Pub Crawl** will help you discover the city. We recommend you begin your expedition at Trinity gates, stroll up Grafton St., teeter to Camden St., stumble to South Great Georges St., then triumphantly drag your soused and sorry self to Temple Bar. Start early—say, noon.

GRAFTON STREET AND TRINITY COLLEGE AREA

▨ The Long Stone, 10-11 Townsend St. (☎671 8102). Old books and handcarved banisters lend a rustic medieval feel. Lots of interesting rooms; the largest has a huge carving of a bearded man whose mouth serves as a fireplace. Carvery lunches 12:30-2:30pm. Open M-W noon-11:30pm, Th-F 10am-12:30am, Sa 3pm-12:30am, Su 4-11pm.

Sinnott's, South King St. (☎478 4698). A classy crowd of 20-somethings gathers in this spacious, wooden-raftered basement pub. Fancies itself a spot for writers, but let's be honest: it's for drinkers. Dance floor packed 'til 2am. Big screen TV is great for watching the big match. Open M-F 10:30am-2:30am, Sa noon-2:30am, Su 4pm-1am.

McDaid's, 3 Harry St. (☎679 4395), off Grafton St. across from Anne St. The center of Ireland's literary scene in the 50s. Book-covered walls and a gregarious crowd downstairs; during peak hours it's hotter than the devil's behind. Open M-W 10:30am-11:30pm, Th-Sa 11am-12:30am, Su 11am-11pm.

Davy Byrne's, 21 Duke St. (☎677 5217), off Grafton St. A lively, middle-aged crowd fills the pub in which Joyce set the "Cyclops" chapter of *Ulysses*. The images of the writer himself on the walls hint at more recent redecorating. Open M-W 11am-11:30pm, Th-Sa 11am-12:30am, Su 11am-11pm.

The International Bar, 23 Wicklow St. (☎677 9250), on the corner of South William St. A great place to meet kindred wandering spirits. Excellent improv comedy M, stand-up W and Th, jazz Tu and F, trad Su. W-F cover €8. Go early for a seat during the comedy shows. Open M-W 10:30am-11:30pm, Th-Sa 10:30am-12:30am, Su 12:30-11pm.

The Pavilion, Trinity College (☎608 1000). Head to the far right corner of campus from the main gate. Enjoy a summer cricket match over Guinness with Trinity heads. Open M-F noon-11pm. During term, join the students under the vaults of **The Buttery,** in a basement to the left as you enter campus. Open M-F 2-11pm.

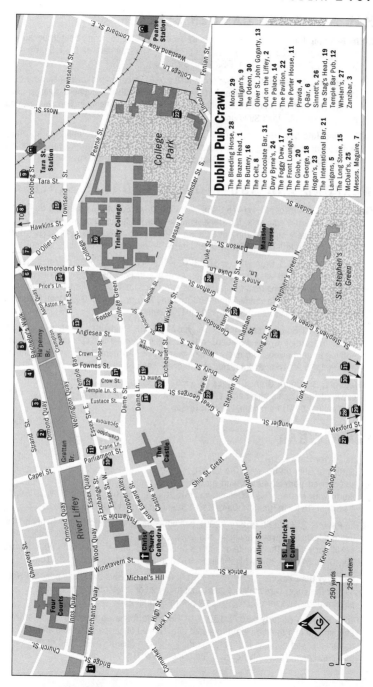

Dublin Pub Crawl

The Bleeding Horse, 28
The Brazen Head, 1
The Buttery, 16
The Celt, 8
The Chocolate Bar, 31
Davy Byrne's, 24
The Foggy Dew, 17
The Front Lounge, 10
The Globe, 20
The George, 18
Hogan's, 23
The International Bar, 21
Lanigans, 5
The Long Stone, 15
McDaid's, 25
Messrs. Maguire, 7
Mono, 29
Mulligan's, 9
The Odeon, 30
Oliver St. John Gogarty, 13
Out on the Liffey, 2
The Palace, 14
The Pavilion, 22
The Porter House, 11
Pravda, 4
Q-Bar, 6
Sinnott's, 26
The Stag's Head, 19
Temple Bar Pub, 12
Whelan's, 27
Zanzibar, 3

REPUBLIC OF IRELAND

HARCOURT AND CAMDEN STREETS

▨ **The Bleeding Horse,** 24 Upper Camden St. (☎475 2705). You can't beat it, because it ain't dead yet. All sorts of little nooks for private affairs. Late bar with DJ Th-Sa. Open M-W until 11:30pm, Th 2:30am, F-Sa 2am, Su 11pm.

The Odeon, Old Harcourt Train Station (☎478 2088). A columned facade and the 2nd-longest bar in Ireland (after the one at the Galway races). Everything here is gargantuan, though the upstairs is cozier. Come to be seen. Sa DJ. Other nights casino, lounge, and dance. Cover €9. Open Su-W until 12:30am, Th-F 2:30am, Sa 3am.

The Chocolate Bar, Harcourt St. (☎478 0225), in the Old Harcourt Train Station. Young clubbers drink here every night. Dress sharp. Arrive early on Th-Sa and you've got the golden ticket to escape the €10-20 cover at **The PoD** (see **Clublin,** p. 746).

WEXFORD AND SOUTH GREAT GEORGES STREET

▨ **Whelan's,** 25 Wexford St. (☎478 0766), continue down South Great Georges St. People in the know know Whelan's. The stage venue in back hosts big-name trad and rock, with live music every night starting at 9:30pm (doors open at 8pm). Cover €7-12. Open 12:30-2:30pm for lunch (€8-12). Open late W-Sa.

The Stag's Head, 1 Dame Ct. (☎679 3701). The beautiful Victorian pub has stained glass, mirrors, and yes, you guessed it, evidence of deer decapitation. The student crowd dons everything from t-shirts to tuxes and spills out into the alleys. Excellent grub; entrees €10. Food served M-F noon-3:30pm and 5-7pm, Sa 12:30-2:30pm. Bar open M-W 11:30am-11:30pm, Th-Sa 11:30am-12:30am.

The Globe, 11 South Great Georges St. (☎671 1220). Frequented by artsy-fartsy wannabes (according to one barkeep)—attracts those who like to get a little freaky, but nothing to get nervous and dye your hair over. Open M-W noon-11:30pm, Th-Sa noon-midnight, Su 2-11pm. **Rí Rá** nightclub attached (see **Clublin,** p. 746).

Hogan's, 35 South Great Georges St. (☎677 5904). Attracts an attractive, trendy crowd, despite its no-frills name and minimalist decor. Self-proclaimed "surly bar staff" (not really). Su DJ from 4pm. Late bar Th-Sa.

TEMPLE BAR

▨ **The Porter House,** 16-18 Parliament St. (☎679 8847). Way, way, way more than 99 bottles of beer on the wall. The largest selection of world beers in the country plus 8 self-brewed porters, stouts, and ales. Excellent sampler tray includes a sip of stout made with oysters (€9). Occasional trad, blues, and rock. Open M-W 10:30am-11:30pm, Th-F 10:30am-1:30am, Sa 10:30am-2am, Su 12:30-11pm.

▨ **The Palace,** 21 Fleet St. (☎677 9290), behind Aston Quay. This classic, neighborly pub has old-fashioned wood paneling and close quarters; head for the comfy seats in the sky-lit back room. The favorite of many a Dubliner and the only true Irish Pub in Temple Bar. Open M-W 10:30am-11:30pm, Th-Sa 10:30am-12:30am, Su 12:30-11pm.

The Foggy Dew, Fownes St. (☎677 9328). Like a friendly, mellow village pub, but twice as big. The Foggy Dew makes a great spot for a pint or 2 without the flash of other Temple Bar pubs. Live rock Su nights. Late bar Th-Sa until 2am.

Oliver St. John Gogarty (☎671 1822), at Fleet and Anglesea St. Lively and convivial atmosphere in a traditional but touristed pub. Named for Joyce's nemesis and onetime roommate, who appears in *Ulysses* as Buck Mulligan (see p. 749). Start or finish your pub crawl here. Trad daily from 2:30pm. Open daily 10:30am-2am.

Messrs. Maguire, Burgh Quay (☎670 5777). Hours of enjoyment for those who explore this classy watering hole under the spell of homemade microbrews. The Weiss stout is a spicy delight (€4.20). Late bar W-Sa. Trad Su-Tu 9:30-11:30pm. Open Su-Tu 10:30am-12:30am, W-Th 10:30am-1:30am, F 10:30am-2am, Sa 12:30pm-2am.

Q-Bar, Burgh Quay (☎677 7435), at the O'Connell bridge. Modernistic and funky, with chrome pillars and bright red, cushy airline chairs. Draws a young, hip crowd. The dance floor opens with pop and chart at about 10pm. Open 10:30am-late.

Temple Bar Pub, Temple Ln. South (☎672 5286). This sprawling bar is a worthwhile stop, and one of the very few wheelchair-accessible pubs. Outdoor beer garden is great on fine summer nights. Music M-Sa 4-6pm and 8pm-closing, Su all day.

THE BEST OF THE REST

▨ **The Brazen Head,** 20 North Bridge St. (☎679 5186), off Merchant's Quay. Dublin's oldest and one of its liveliest pubs, established in 1198 as the first stop after the bridge on the way into the city. The courtyard, with its beer barrel tables, is quite the pickup scene on summer nights. The United Irishmen once met here to plan their attacks on the British. Nightly Irish music. Late bar F-Sa until 1am.

▨ **The Celt,** 81-82 Talbot St. (☎878 8655). Step out of the city and into Olde Ireland. Small, but not cramped; comfortably worn and genuinely welcoming. Nightly trad. Open Su-W 10:30am-11:30pm, Th-Sa 10:30am-12:30am.

Zanzibar (☎878 7212), at the Ha'penny Bridge. Mix of Oriental/Arab decor and pop culture. Quite the hotspot. Get your heart in rhythm as you make your way through the fabulous high-ceilinged bar to the dance floor in back. DJ M-Th from 10pm, F-Sa from 9pm. Open M-Th 5pm-2:30am, F-Sa 4pm-2:30am, Su 4pm-1am.

Mulligan's, 8 Poolbeg St. (☎677 5582), behind Burgh Quay off Tara St. Upholds its reputation as one of the best pint-pourers in Dublin. A taste of the typical Irish pub: low-key and nothing fancy.

Lanigans, Clifton Court Hotel, Eden Quay (☎874 3535). Imagine a pub with Irish singers that attracts more Dubliners than tourists. Stop imagining and head to Lanigans. Half of it is quiet and dark throughout the day—the other half has live music nightly at 9pm. Irish dancing M-Th. Open M-W 10:30am-11:30pm, Th-Sa until 1am, Su until 11:30pm.

Pravda (☎874 0090), on the north side of the Ha'penny Bridge. The Russian late bar and Russian DJ action goes Russian Th-Sa. Actually, there's nothing Russian about the place, other than Cyrillic on the wall murals. Trendy, popular, gay-friendly, and crowded. Late bar F-Sa until 2:30am.

⊙ SIGHTS

TRINITY COLLEGE. Behind ancient walls sprawls Trinity's expanse of stone buildings, cobblestone walks, and green grounds. The British built Trinity in 1592 as a Protestant religious seminary that would "civilize the Irish and cure them of Popery." The college became part of the path members of the Anglo-Irish elite trod on their way to high positions. Until the 1960s, the Catholic church deemed it a cardinal sin to attend Trinity; once the church lifted the ban, the size of the student body more than tripled. (*Hard to miss—between Westmoreland and Grafton St., in the very center of South Dublin. The main entrance fronts the block-long traffic circle now called College Green. Pearse St. runs along the north edge of the college, Nassau St. to the south.* ☎608 1000. *Grounds always open. Free.*) Trinity's **Old Library** holds an invaluable collection of ancient manuscripts, including the duly renowned *Book of Kells*. Upstairs, the **Long Room** contains Ireland's oldest harp—the **Brian Ború Harp,** seen on Irish coins—and one of the few remaining **1916 proclamations** of the Republic of Ireland. (*The library is on the south side of Library Sq. Open June-Sept. M-Sa 9:30am-5pm, Su noon-4:30pm; Oct.-May M-Sa 9:30am-5pm, Su noon-4:30pm. €6, concessions €5.*)

REPUBLIC OF IRELAND

GRAFTON STREET. The few blocks south of College Green are off-limits to cars and ground zero for shopping tourists and residents alike. Grafton's **street performers** range from string octets to jive limboists. Upstairs at the Grafton St. branch of Bewley's and inside the coffee chain's former chocolate factory is the **Bewley's Museum.** Tea-tasting machines, corporate history, and a display on Bewley's Quaker heritage number among the marvels. *(Open daily 7:30am-11pm. Free.)*

LEINSTER HOUSE. The Duke of Leinster made his home on Kildare St. back in 1745, when most of the urban upper-crust lived north of the Liffey. By building his house so far south, where land was cheaper, he was able to afford an enormous front lawn. Now Leinster House provides chambers for the Irish parliament, or An tOireachtas (on tir-OCH-tas). When the Dáil is in session, visitors can view the proceedings by contacting the Captain of the Guard, who conducts tours. *(☎678 9911. Passport necessary. Tours leave from the adjacent National Gallery Sa on the hour.)*

ST. STEPHEN'S GREEN. This 22-acre park was a private estate until the Guinness clan bequeathed it to the city. Today, the grounds are teeming with public life: punks, couples, gardens, fountains, gazebos, strollers, swans, a waterfall, a statue of Henry Moore, and a partridge in a pear tree. During the summer, musical and theatrical productions are given near the old bandstand. *(Kildare, Dawson, and Grafton St. all lead to it. Open M-Sa 8am-dusk, Su 10am-dusk.)*

MERRION SQUARE. The Georgian buildings and elaborate doorways of Merrion Sq. and adjacent **Fitzwilliam St.** feed your architectural longings. After leaving 18 Fitzwilliam St., Yeats took up residence at 82 Merrion Sq. Farther south on **Harcourt St.,** playwright George Bernard Shaw and Dracula's creator, Bram Stoker, were neighbors at #61 and #16, respectively. At **#29 Lower Fitzwilliam St.,** you'll find a townhouse-turned-museum that demonstrates the lifestyle of the 18th-century Anglo-Irish elite. *(☎702 6165. Open Tu-Sa 10am-5pm, Su 2-5pm. A short audio-visual show leads to a 25min. tour of the house. €3.15, concessions €1.25.)*

NEWMAN HOUSE. This fully restored building was once the seat of **University College Dublin,** the Catholic answer to Trinity. *A Portrait of the Artist as a Young Man* chronicles Joyce's time here. The poet Gerard Manley Hopkins spent the last years of his life teaching classics at the college. The cursory tour is geared to the architectural and the literary. *(85-86 St. Stephen's Green South. ☎706 7422. Admission by guided tour. Open to individuals only June-Aug. Tu-F noon-5pm and Sa 2-5pm. Groups admitted throughout the year with advance booking. €4.)*

TEMPLE BAR. West of Trinity, between Dame St. and the Liffey, the Temple Bar neighborhood writhes with activity. In the early 1980s, the Irish transport authority intended to replace the neighborhood with a seven-acre transportation center. The artists and nomads who lived there started a typical artist-and-nomad brouhaha about being forced into homelessness. Temple Bar immediately grew into one of Europe's hottest spots for nightlife, forcing the artists and nomads into homelessness. (Ah, the sweet irony of life.) To steer the growth to ends more cultural than alcoholic, the government-sponsored **Temple Bar Properties** has spent over €40 million to build a whole flock of arts-related tourist attractions, with independent coattail-riders springing up as well.

DUBLIN CASTLE. Norman King John built the castle in 1204 on top of the Vikings' settlement; more recently, a series of structures from various eras has covered the site, culminating in an uninspired 20th-century office complex. Since 1938, every Irish president has been inaugurated here. Next door, the intricate inner dome of **Dublin City Hall** (designed as the Royal Exchange in 1779) shelters statues of national heroes. *(Dame St., at the intersection of Parliament and Castle St. ☎677 7129. State Apartments open M-F 10am-5pm, Sa-Su and holidays 2-5pm; closed during official functions. €4.50, concessions €3.50. Grounds free.)*

CHRIST CHURCH CATHEDRAL. Sitric Silkenbeard built a wooden church on this site around 1038; Strongbow rebuilt it in stone in 1169. Further additions were made in the following centuries. Stained glass sparkles above the raised crypts, one of which supposedly belongs to Mr. Strongbow and his favorite lutefisk. *(At the end of Dame St., uphill and across from the Castle. ☎ 677 8099. Open daily 9:45am-5:30pm except during services. Donation of €3 strongly encouraged.)*

ST. PATRICK'S CATHEDRAL. The body of this, Ireland's largest cathedral, dates to the 12th century, although much was remodeled in 1864. St. Patrick allegedly baptized converts in the park next door. Artifacts and relics from the Order of St. Patrick lie inside. **Jonathan Swift** spent his last years as Dean of St. Patrick's, and his crypt is above the south nave. *(From Christ Church, Nicholas St. runs south and down-hill, eventually becoming Patrick St. ☎ 475 4817. Open Mar.-Oct. daily 9am-6pm, Nov.-Feb. Sa 9am-5pm and Su 9am-3pm. €4, concessions free.)*

▓ GUINNESS STOREHOUSE. Discover how it brews its black magic and creates the world's best stout. The Storehouse offers a self-guided tour with multimedia eye-candy and hyper-technical fun. As your reward, ye shall conclude your pilgrimage on the top floor, overlooking 64 acres of Guinness and imbibing a free pint of dark and creamy goodness. *Sláinte. (St. James's Gate. From Christ Church Cathedral, follow High St. west through its name changes—Cornmarket, Thomas, and James. Take bus #51B or 78A from Aston Quay or #123 from O'Connell St. ☎ 408 4800. Open Oct.-Mar. 9:30am-5pm, Apr.-Sept. 9:30am-7pm. €12, students €8, seniors and children €5.30.)*

KILMAINHAM GAOL. A place of bondage and a symbol of freedom—almost all the rebels who fought in Ireland's struggle for independence between 1792 and 1921 spent time here. The jail's last occupant was **Éamon de Valera,** the future leader of Éire. Today, Kilmainham is a museum that traces the history of penal practices over the last two centuries. *(Inchicore Rd. Take bus #51 or 79 from Aston Quay, #51A from Lower Abbey St. ☎ 453 5984. Open Apr.-Sept. daily 9:30am-4:45pm, Oct.-Mar. M-F 9:30am-4pm and Su 10am-4:45pm. Tours every 35min. €4.40, students €1.90, seniors €3.10.)*

DUBLINESE Mastering the Dublin dialect has been a persistent challenge to writers and thespians of the 20th century. James Joyce, Brendan Behan, and Roddy Doyle are just a few ambitious scribes who have tried to capture the nuances of this gritty, witty city. The following is a short introduction to Dubliners' favorite phrases.

Names for Outsiders: The rivalry between Dubliners and their country cousins is fierce. For Dubliners, all counties outside their own blur into one indiscriminate wasteland populated with "culchies," "plonkers," "turf-gobblers," and "muck-savages."

In Times of Difficulty: Dublinese is expeditious in keeping others in line. Idiots are rebuked as "eejits" or "gobshites." Total exasperation calls for "shite and onions." When all is restored to order, "the job's oxo and the ship's name is Murphy."

Affectionate Nicknames for Civic Landmarks: Over the past couple of decades, the government has graced the city with several public artworks that personify the Irish spirit in the female form. Dubliners have responded with poetic rhetoric. Off Grafton St., the statue of the fetching fishmongress Molly Malone is commonly referred to as "the dish with the fish" and "the tart with the cart."

O'CONNELL STREET. Dublin's biggest shopping thoroughfare starts at the Liffey and leads to **Parnell Square.** At 150 ft., it was once the widest street in Europe. The central traffic islands contain monuments to Irish leaders: **O'Connell's statue** faces the Liffey and O'Connell Bridge; at the other end of the street, **Parnell's statue** points toward nearby Mooney's pub. A block up O'Connell St., where Cathedral St. intersects it on the right, the 1988 statue of a woman lounging in water is officially named the Spirit of the Liffey or **"Anna Livia,"** but has many pseudonyms. On Grafton St., a newer statue of **Molly Malone** has her own aliases (see **Dublinese,** above). One monument you won't see is **Nelson's Pillar,** which stood outside the General Post Office for 150 years. In 1966 the IRA commemorated the 50th anniversary of the Easter Rising by blowing the Admiral out of the water.

GENERAL POST OFFICE. Not just a fine place to send a letter, the Post Office was the nerve center of the 1916 Easter Rising (see p. 722). Padraig Pearse read the Proclamation of Irish Independence from its steps. When British troops closed in, mailbags became barricades. Outside, a number of bullet nicks are visible. *(O'Connell St. ☎ 705 7000. Open M-Sa 8am-8pm, Su 10am-6:30pm.)*

CUSTOM HOUSE. The city's greatest architectural triumph, the Custom House was designed in the 1780s by James Gandon, who gave up the chance to be St. Petersburg's state architect and settled in Dublin. Carved heads along the frieze represent the rivers of Ireland; Liffey is the only lady. *(East of O'Connell St. at Custom House Quay, where Gardiner St. meets the river. ☎ 878 7660. Visitors center open mid-Mar. to Nov. M-F 10am-5pm, Sa-Su 12:30-2pm; Dec. to mid-Mar. W-F 10am-5pm, Su 2-5pm. €1.50.)*

FOUR COURTS. On April 14, 1922, General Rory O'Connor seized the Four Courts on behalf of the anti-Treaty IRA; two months later, the Free State government of Griffith and Collins attacked the Four Courts garrison, starting the Irish Civil War (see p. 722). The building, another of Gandon's works, now houses Ireland's highest court. *(Inn's Quay, several quays west of the Custom House. ☎ 872 5555. Open M-F 9am-4:30pm. Free.)*

OLD JAMESON DISTILLERY. Learn how science, grain, and tradition come together to form liquid gold—whiskey, that is. A film recounts Ireland's spirit-ual rise, fall, and renaissance; the subsequent tour walks you through the actual creation of the drink. The experience ends with a glass of the Irish firewater of your choice; be quick to volunteer in the beginning and you'll get to sample a whole tray of different whiskeys. *(Bow St. From O'Connell St., turn onto Henry St. and continue straight as the street dwindles to Mary St., then Mary Ln., then May Ln.; the warehouse is on a cobblestone street on the left. ☎ 807 2355. Tours daily 9:30am-5:30pm. €7, concessions €4.)*

DUBLIN BREWING COMPANY. A new kid on the block trying to best the heavyweights, this small brewery runs fun, personal tours with plenty of hops to smell and beer to taste. You also get more beer for your money than at the *other* brewery. *(144-146 N. King St. From Old Jameson, go up to N. King St., turn left, and it's on the left. ☎ 872 8622. Tours every hr. noon-6pm, and by appointment. €9.)*

PHOENIX PARK. Europe's largest enclosed public park is most famous for the "Phoenix Park murders" of 1882. The Invincibles, a Republican splinter group, stabbed Lord Cavendish, Chief Secretary of Ireland, and his trusty Under-Secretary 200 yd. from the **Phoenix Column.** A Unionist journalist forged a series of letters linking Parnell to the murderers. The Column, capped with a phoenix rising from flames, is something of a pun—the park's name actually comes from the Irish *Fionn Uísce,* "clean water." The 1760 acres incorporate the **President's residence** (Áras an Uachtaraín), the US Ambassador's house, cricket pitches, polo grounds, and red deer. The park is peaceful during daylight hours but unsafe at night. *(Take bus #10 from O'Connell St. or #25 or 26 from Middle Abbey St. west along the river.)* The **Dublin Zoo,** one of the very oldest and Europe's largest, is in the park. It contains 700 critters and the **world's biggest egg.** *(Bus #10 from O'Connell St. ☎ 677 1425. Open M-Sa 9:30am-6:30pm, Su 10:30am-6:30pm. Last admission at 5pm. Closes earlier in winter. €10, students €7.70, children and seniors €6.30.)*

🏛 MUSEUMS AND GALLERIES

NATIONAL GALLERY. This collection of over 2400 canvases includes paintings by Vermeer, Rembrandt, and El Greco. Works by 19th-century Irish artists comprise a major part of the collection. The new **Millennium Wing** houses a 20th-century Irish Art exhibit, a Yeats archive, and a multimedia system exploring many of the museum's rooms in virtual reality. (Merrion Sq. West. ☎661 5133. Open M-Sa 9:30am-5:30pm, Th 10am-8:30pm, Su noon-5pm. Free guided tours Sept.-June Sa 3pm; Su 2, 3, 4pm. July-Aug. daily 3pm. Admission free. Concerts and art classes €6-20.)

🏛 **NATURAL HISTORY MUSEUM.** When taxidermists and entomologists die, St. Peter meets them here. Three creepy skeletons of giant (yes, huge) Irish deer greet visitors at the front, and the museum is stocked with many more beautiful and fascinating examples of classic taxidermy, all displayed in old Victorian cabinets. (Upper Merrion St. ☎677 7444. Open Tu-Sa 10am-5pm and Su 2-5pm. Free.)

NATIONAL MUSEUM OF ARCHAEOLOGY AND HISTORY. The largest of Dublin's museums has extraordinary artifacts spanning the last two millennia. One room gleams with the **Tara Brooch,** the **Ardagh Hoard,** and other Celtic goldwork. Another section is devoted to the Republic's founding years and shows off the bloody vest of nationalist hero **James Connolly.** (Kildare St., next to Leinster House. ☎677 7444. Open Tu-Sa 10am-5pm and Su 2-5pm. Free. Guided tours €1.50; call for times.)

COLLINS BARRACKS. The barracks are home to the **National Museum of Decorative Arts and History.** The most sophisticated of Dublin's three national museums, the barracks gleam with exhibits that range from the deeply traditional to the subversively multi-disciplinary. The Curator's Choice room displays a range of objects in light of their artistic importance, cultural context, and historical significance. (Benburb St., off Wolfe Tone Quay. Museum Link bus leaves from the adjacent Natural History and Archaeology museums once per hr. All-day pass €2.50; one-way €1. Or hop on bus #10 from O'Connell St.; #90 stops across the street from the museum. ☎677 7444. Open Tu-Sa 10am-5pm, Su 2-5pm. Museum free. Guided tours €1.30; call for times.)

NATIONAL LIBRARY. Its entrance room chronicles Irish history and exhibits many literary goodies. A genealogical research room can help visitors trace even the thinnest twiglets of their Irish family trees. The reading room is stunning, with an airy, domed ceiling. (Kildare St., next to Leinster House. ☎661 2523. Open M-W 10am-9pm, Th-F 10am-5pm, Sa 10am-1pm. Free. Academic reason required to obtain a library card and enter the reading room; just "being a student" is usually enough.)

IRISH JEWISH MUSEUM. The museum is a restored former synagogue that houses a large collection of artifacts, documents, and photographs chronicling the history of the Jewish community in Ireland since 1079 (five arrived and were sent packing). The most famous Dublin Jew covered is, predictably, Leopold Bloom of *Ulysses* fame. (3-4 Walworth Rd., off Victoria St. South Circular Rd. runs to Victoria St.; from there the museum is signposted. Any bus to South Circular Rd., including #16 and 20, will get you there. ☎490 1857. Open May-Sept. Tu, Th, Su 11am-3:30pm; Oct.-Apr. Su 10:30am-2:30pm. Groups may call to arrange an alternate visiting time.)

DUBLIN WRITERS MUSEUM. Read your way through placard after placard describing the city's rich literary heritage, or listen to it all on an audio tour. Manuscripts, rare editions, and memorabilia blend with caricatures, paintings, a great bookstore, and an incongruous Zen Garden. (18 Parnell Sq. North. ☎872 2077. Open June-Aug. M-F 10am-6pm, Sa 10am-5pm, Su 11am-5pm; Sept.-May M-Sa 10am-5pm. €5.50, concessions €5. Combined ticket with either Shaw birthplace or James Joyce Centre €8.)

JAMES JOYCE CULTURAL CENTRE. This museum features Joyceana ranging from portraits of the individuals who inspired his characters to more arcane fancies of the writer's nephew, who runs the place. Call for info on lectures, walking tours, and **Bloomsday** events. (35 N. Great Georges St. ☎ 878 8547. Open M-Sa 9:30am-5pm, Su 12:30-5pm; July-Aug. extra Su hours 11am-5pm. €4, concessions €3.)

SHAW BIRTHPLACE. This museum serves as both period piece and glimpse into the childhood of G.B. Shaw. Mrs. Shaw held recitals here, sparking little Georgie's interest in music; her Victorian garden inspired his fascination with landscape painting. (33 Synge St. Stroll down Camden, make a right on Harrington, and turn left onto Synge St. Convenient to buses #16, 19, or 122 from O'Connell St. ☎ 475 0854 or 872 2077. Open May-Sept. M-Sa 10am-5pm, Su 11am-5pm; no tours 1-2pm. Open for groups outside hours by request. €5.50, concessions €5, children €3; joint ticket with Dublin Writers Museum €7, with James Joyce and Writers Museums €9.)

HOT PRESS IRISH MUSIC HALL OF FAME. Dublin's anthem to its musical wonders has found itself a great location. A headset tour takes you through memorabilia-laden displays on the history of Irish music from bards to the studio, heaping lavish praise on such stars as Van Morrison, U2, and, uh, Boyzone. The concert venue **HQ** (see **Music,** below) is attached. (57 Middle Abbey St. ☎ 878 3345; www.irishmusichof.com. Open daily 10am-6pm. €7.60, concessions €5.)

GAELIC ATHLETIC ASSOCIATION MUSEUM. Those intrigued and/or mystified by the world of Irish athletics will appreciate this establishment at **Croke Park Stadium.** The GAA presents the rules, history, and heroes of its national sports, with the help of touchscreens and audiovisual displays. (☎ 855 8176. Museum open May-Sept. daily 9:30am-5pm; Oct.-Apr. Tu-Sa 10am-5pm, Su noon-5pm. Last admission 4:30pm. €5, concessions €3.50, children €3. Stadium tour plus museum €2-4 more.)

🎵 ENTERTAINMENT

Whether you fancy poetry or punk, Dublin is equipped to entertain you. The free weekly *Event Guide* is available at the tourist office, Temple Bar restaurants, and the Temple Bar Info Centre. The glossier *In Dublin* (€2.50) comes out every two weeks with feature articles and listings for music, theater, art exhibitions, comedy shows, clubs, museums, gay venues, and movie theaters. *Events of the Week*—a much smaller, free booklet—is jammed with ads, but also has good info buried in it. Click to www.visitdublin.com for hotspots updated daily.

MUSIC

Dublin's music scene attracts performers from all over the world. Trad is not only a tourist gimmick, but a vibrant and important element of Dublin's music world. Pubs see a lot of musical action, since they provide musicians with free beer and a venue. *Hot Press* (€1.90) has the most up-to-date listings, particularly for rock. Some pubs in the city center have trad sessions nightly, others nearly so: ◪**Whelan's, Oliver St. John Gogarty,** and **McDaid's** are always good bets (see **Publin,** p. 736). The best pub for trad is ◪**Cobblestones,** King St. North (☎ 872 1799), in Smithfield. No rock here, but live shows every night, a trad session in the basement, and real live spontaneity. Big-deal bands frequent the **Baggot Inn,** 143 Baggot St. (☎ 676 1430); U2 played here in the early 80s and some people are still talking about it.

   The Temple Bar Music Centre, Curved St. (☎ 670 9202), has events and concerts virtually every night. The **National Concert Hall,** Earlsfort Terr., provides a venue for classical concerts and performances, hosting nightly shows in July and August, and a summer lunchtime series on occasional Tuesdays and Fridays. (☎ 671 1533. Tickets €8-16, students half-price; summer lunchtime show €4-8.) Programs for the **National Symphony** and smaller local groups are available at classical music stores and the tourist office. The new **HQ** (☎ 878 3345), in the Irish Music Hall of Fame (see **Museums**, above), considers itself one of the nicest venues in Europe. Big acts play **Olympia**, 72 Dame St. (☎ 677 7744), and **Vicar St.**, 99 Vicar St., (☎ 454 6656), off Thomas St. The stars also perform for huge crowds at the **Tivoli Theatre**, 135-138 Francis St. (☎ 454 4472), and the musical monsters come to **Croke Park**, Clonliffe Rd. (☎ 836 3152), and the **R.D.S.** (☎ 668 0866), in Ballsbridge.

THEATER

There is no true "Theatre District" in Dublin—but smaller theater companies thrive off Dame St. and Temple Bar. Box office hours are usually for phone reservations; the window stays open until curtain on performance nights, generally 8pm. Dublin's most famous stage is the ◪**Abbey Theatre**, founded by Yeats and his collaborator Lady Gregory to promote the Irish cultural revival and modernist theater (a bit like promoting both corned beef and soy burgers). Today, the Abbey is Ireland's National Theatre. *(26 Lower Abbey St. ☎ 878 7222. Tickets €12-25; M-Th students €10; Sa matinees 2:30pm €10. Box office open M-Sa 10:30am-7pm.)* The **Peacock Theatre** is the Abbey's experimental downstairs stage. *(☎ 878 7222. Tickets €17, Sa matinee 2:45pm €13. Box office open M-Sa at 7:30pm.)*

CINEMA

Ireland's well-subsidized film industry reeled with the arrival of the **Irish Film Centre**, 6 Eustace St., in Temple Bar. The IFC mounts tributes and festivals, including a French film festival in October and a **gay and lesbian film festival** in early August. A variety of classic and European art house films appear throughout the year. You have to be a "member" to buy most tickets. (☎ 679 3477; www.fii.ie. Weekly membership €1.30; yearly membership €14, students €10. Membership must be purchased at least 15min. before start of show. €6.30, matinees €5. 18+.) **The Screen**, D'Olier St. (☎ 672 5500), also rolls artsy reels. First-run movie houses cluster on O'Connell St., the quays, and Middle Abbey St. The **Savoy**, O'Connell St. (☎ 874 6000), and **Virgin**, Parnell St. (☎ 872 8400), offer a wide selection of major releases. General movie tickets cost about €7.50 per person.

SPORTS AND RECREATION

Dubliners aren't as sports-crazed as their country cousins, but that's not saying much. Games are still serious business, especially since most tournament finals take place here. The season for **Gaelic football**

THE INSIDER'S CITY

N. Circular Rd.

Cloniffe Rd.

Jones Rd.

Drumcondra Rd.

N. Circular Rd.

Fitzgibbon St.

Gardener St. Upper

Summerhill

Croke Park

A DAY AT CROKE PARK

Before you can brag about having "done" Dublin, you have to first experience what it's like to be a spectator at a raucous Gaelic football match.

1 Spend Saturday night at **Parkway Guest House** (see p. 733) so you can get to the park early the next morning. Follow North St. to Gardner Pl.

2 Push and shove and bite and pinch—whatever it takes to get to the **ticket booth**, on Fitzgibbon St.

3 Run into the **GAA museum** inside the stadium to learn all you will need to know about the game.

4 Watch the game from the stadium's best seats at **Hill 16** or **Hogan's Stand**, where you'll find Dubliners sitting and drinking.

5 Celebrate the victory or mourn the loss with the rest of the locals at **Quinn's Pub** (42 Lower Drumcondra Rd; ☎ 830 4973).

6 Pass out on the **left side of the street** if your team lost, and on the **right side of the street** if they won: left-side street cleaning takes place Monday morning.

and **hurling** (see **Sports,** p. 725) runs from mid-February to November. Action-packed and often brutal, these contests will entertain any sports-lover. Games are played in **Croke Park** (Clonliffe Rd., a 15min. walk from Connolly station; buses #3, 11, 11A, 16, 16A, 51A, and 123; tickets €15-40) and on **Phibsborough Rd.** Tickets are theoretically available at the turnstiles, but they tend to sell out quickly. For more sports information, check the Friday papers or contact the **Gaelic Athletic Association** (☎836 3222; www.gaa.ie).

❦ FESTIVALS

BLOOMSDAY. Dublin returns to 1904 each year on June 16, the day of Leopold Bloom's 18hr. journey, which frames the narrative (or lack thereof) of Joyce's *Ulysses.* Festivities are held all week long, starting before the big day and (to a lesser extent) continuing after it. The **James Joyce Cultural Centre** (see p. 744) sponsors a reenactments and a Guinness breakfast. (☎873 1984.)

MUSIC FESTIVALS. The **Festival of Music in Great Irish Houses,** held during mid-June, organizes concerts of period music in 18th-century homes across the country (☎278 1528). The **Feis Ceoil** music festival goes trad in mid-March (☎676 7365). The **Guinness Blues Festival,** a three-day extravaganza in mid-July, gets bigger and broader each year (☎497 0381; www.guinnessbluesfest.com). Ask at the tourist office about *fleadhs* (FLAHS), day-long trad festivals that pop up periodically.

ST. PATRICK'S DAY. The half-week leading up to March 17 occasions a city-wide carnival of concerts, fireworks, street theater, and intoxicated madness, celebrating one of Ireland's lesser-known saints. (☎676 3205; www.paddyfest.ie.)

FILM AND THEATRE FESTIVALS. The **Dublin Film Festival** brings nearly two weeks of Irish and international movies with a panoply of seminars in tow. *(Early to mid-Mar.* ☎679 2937; www.iol.ie/dff.) The **Dublin Theatre Festival,** a premier cultural event held the first two weeks of October, screens about 20 works from Ireland and around the world. Tickets may be purchased all year at participating theaters, and, as the festival draws near, at the Festival Booking Office. *(47 Nassau St.* ☎677 8439. *Tickets €13-20, student discounts vary by venue.)*

☒ CLUBLIN

In Dublin's nightlife war, clubs currently have a slight edge over pub rock venues, though the pubs are fighting back with later hours. As a rule, clubs open at 10:30 or 11pm, but the action really heats up after the 11:30pm pub closings. Most clubs close between 1:30 and 3am, but a few have been known to last until daybreak. To get home after 11:30pm, when Dublin Bus stops running, dancing queens take the **NiteLink bus** (1 per hr. Th-Sa 12:30-3:30am, €3.30), which runs designated routes from the corner of Westmoreland and College St. to Dublin's suburbs. **Taxi** stands are located in front of Trinity, at the top of Grafton St. by St. Stephen's Green, and on Lower Abbey St. Be prepared to wait 30-45min. on weekend nights.

> **Rí-Rá,** 1 Exchequer St. (☎677 4835), in the back of the Globe (see **Publin,** p. 736). Generally good music that steers clear of pop and house extremes. 2 floors, several bars, more crannies than a crumpet, and really quite womb-like downstairs. Open daily 11pm-2am. Cover €7-10.

The PoD, 35 Harcourt St. (☎478 0225). Corner of Hatch St., in an old train station. Spanish-style decor meets hard-core dance music. The truly brave venture upstairs to **The Red Box** (☎478 0225), a separate, more intense club with a warehouse atmosphere, brain-crushing music, and an 8-deep crowd at the bar designed to winnow out the weak. Often hosts big-name DJs—cover charges skyrocket. Cover €10-20; Th ladies free before midnight; Th and Sa €7 with ISIC card. Open until 3am. Start the evening at the Chocolate Bar or The Odeon, which share the building (see **Publin,** p. 736).

The Shelter, Thomas St. (☎454 6656), at the Vicar St. theater where Cornmarket changes names. Near the Guinness Brewery. Funk, soul, and a little bit of Austin Powers sound mixed with people wearing multiple shades of gray, black, and brown. Live bands and DJs. Cover €9. Open Th-Sa.

Gaiety, South King St. (☎677 1717), just off Grafton St. This elegant theater shows its late-night wild side midnight-4am every F and Sa. 4 bar areas. Enjoy the best of all worlds with DJs and live music, salsa, jazz, swing, latin, and soul. Cover around €10.

Club M, Blooms Hotel, Anglesea St. (☎671 5622), in Temple Bar. Look for the big orange building. One of Dublin's largest clubs, attracting a crowd of all ages and styles, with multiple stairways and a few bars in the back. If at first you don't succeed, grind, grind again. Cover Su-Th €7, ladies free before midnight; F-Sa €12-15.

Club Aquarium (Fibber's), 80-82 Parnell St. (☎872 2575). No charts here; mostly indie. Houses Ireland's only metal club. Occasional goth nights. If the darkness, heat, or doom gets to be too much, head outside to the deck to finish things up. Weekend cover €7. Open Su-W until 2am, later Th-Sa.

Switch, 21-25 Eustace St. (☎670 7655). The only 18+ club in Temple Bar; a younger crowd flocks in. M gay night, F drum 'n' bass, Sa techno, Su funky groove, otherwise a lot of deep house. Cover Su-Th €7, F €10, Sa €13.

The Palace Niteclub, Camden St. (☎478 0808), in Camden de Luxe Hotel. A meat market mostly for younger 20-somethings. Pop faves blast under a barrel-vaulted ceiling. Upstairs for charts, downstairs for 70s-80s. Cover M-Th €5.50 with €2 drinks, Sa free until 10pm. Open M-Sa until 2:30am.

Mono, 26 Wexford St. (☎475 8555). Newly renovated 2-floor glittering pub/club. Bands play Th-Sa from 7-10:30pm (cover €5-15), then DJs come in for chill-out, jungle, and house downstairs. Cover €10 after 11pm. Open Th-Sa until 3am.

GAY AND LESBIAN NIGHTLIFE

🗹 **The George,** 89 South Great Georges St. (☎478 2983). This throbbing, purple man o' war is Dublin's first and most prominent gay bar. A mixed-age crowd gathers throughout the day to chat and sip. The attached nightclub opens W-Su until 2am. Frequent theme nights. Su night Drag Bingo is accompanied by so much entertainment that sometimes the bingo never happens. Look spiffy—no effort, no entry. Cover €8-10 after 10pm.

🗹 **The Front Lounge,** Parliament St. (☎670-4112). The velvet seats of this gay-friendly bar are popular with a very mixed, very trendy crowd. Open M and W noon-11:30pm, Tu and Sa noon-12:30am, F noon-1:30am, Su 4-11:30pm.

Out on the Liffey, 27 Upper Ormond Quay (☎872 2480). Ireland's 2nd gay bar; a play on the more traditional Inn on the Liffey a few doors down. Lots of dark nooks in which to chat and drink. The short hike from the city center ensures a local crowd most nights. Tu drag, W karaoke, F-Sa DJ. No cover. Late bar W-Th until 12:30am, F-Sa until 2am.

DUBLIN'S SUBURBS

Strung along the Irish Sea, Dublin's suburbs are a calm alternative to the voracious human tide swarming about the Liffey. The DART, suburban rail, and local buses make the area accessible for afternoon jaunts.

HOWTH (BINN EADAIR)   ☎ 01

The secret is out. Howth (rhymes with "both"), an affluent Eden dangling from the mainland, is becoming an increasingly popular destination. If the sun is shining, expect the place to be full of madding (and maddening) crowds. And who could blame them? Less than 10 mi. from the center of Dublin, Howth plays like a highlight reel of Ireland: rolling hills, pubs, fantastic sailing, and a castle.

A great way to experience Howth's heather and seabird nests is on the narrow, 3hr. **cliff walk** that rings the peninsula. At the harbor's end, **Puck's Rock** marks the spot where the devil fell when St. Nessan shook a Bible at him. (It was just that easy.) The nearby **lighthouse,** surrounded by tremendous cliffs, housed Salman Rushdie for a night during the height of the *fatwa*. To get to the trailhead from town, turn left at the DART station and follow Harbour Rd. around the coast. Several sights are clustered in the middle of the peninsula; go right as you exit the DART station and then left after ¼ mi. at the entrance to the Deer Park Hostel. Up that road lies the private **Howth Castle**, a charmingly awkward patchwork of materials, styles, and degrees of upkeep. Just offshore, **Ireland's Eye** once provided both religious sanctuary and strategic advantage for monks, whose former presence is visible in the ruins of **St. Nessan's Church** and one of the coast's many **Martello towers. Ireland's Eye Boat Trips** jet passengers across the water. Find them on the East Pier, toward the lighthouse. (☎831 4200 or (087) 267 8211. 15min.; every 30min. 11am-6pm, weather permitting; €8 return, students €4.)

The easiest way to reach Howth is by **DART:** just take a northbound train to the end of the line (30min., 6 per hr., €1.45), but pay attention at the Howth Junction, as the line splits to serve Malahide as well. **Buses** #31 and 31B to Howth leave from Dublin's Lower Abbey St. Turn left out of the DART station and walk toward the harbor on the aptly-named Harbour Rd. Most B&B proprietors will pick you up at the DART; otherwise it's quite a climb or a short bus ride to their hilly locations. **Gleann na Smól ❸** ("The Valley of the Thrush"), on the left at the end of Nashville Rd. off Thormanby Rd., is an affordable option close to the harbor. (☎832 2936. Singles €38; doubles €60.) **Highfield ❸,** on Thormanby Rd., is on the left a half-mile past the Church of Assumption. When the weather cooperates, a lovely view of the harbor complements tidy floral-themed bedrooms and a traditional, antique-laden dining room. (☎832 3936. All rooms with shower and TV. Singles €38.)

Maud's ❶, Harbour Rd., is a spunky cafe with sandwiches and ice cream. (☎839 5450. Ice cream €1-4.50. Open 10am-8pm.) The newest entrant in the best of Harbour St. is **Citrus ❹,** a Thai restaurant offering unique selections (chicken stir-fry with oyster sauce €15.95). Try to grab a table outside for people-watching. (☎832 0200. Open Tu-Su 5pm-late, also Sa-Su noon-4pm.) Climb Thormanby Rd. for drinks and an incredible view of North Howth at **The Summit** and its adjoining nightclub **K2.** (☎832 4615. Club open F-Su. Cover €3 before 11pm, €9 after.)

DÚN LAOGHAIRE   ☎ 01

As one of Co. Dublin's major ferry ports, Dún Laoghaire (dun-LEER-ee) is many tourists' first peek at Ireland. Fortunately, this is as good a place as any to begin your rambles along the coast. Couples stroll down the waterfront on summer evenings, and the whole town turns out for weekly sailboat races.

REPUBLIC OF IRELAND

🖅🔢 TRANSPORTATION AND PRACTICAL INFORMATION. You can reach Dún Laoghaire in a snap with the **DART** from Dublin (€1.40), or on southbound **buses** #7, 7A, 8, or (a longer, inland route) #46A from Eden Quay. If you're staying here but want to party downtown, the 7N **nightbus** departs for Dún Laoghaire from College St. in Dublin. (M-W 12:30 and 2am, Th-Sa every 20min. 12:30-4:30am.) From the ferryport, **Marine Rd.** climbs up to the center of town. **George's St.,** at the top of Marine Rd., holds most shops; many are right at the intersection in the **Dún Laoghaire Shopping Centre. Patrick St.,** the continuation of Marine Rd., is the place for cheap eateries. The **tourist office,** humming at the ferry terminal, will outfit you with maps. (Open M-Sa 10am-6pm.) Exchange money at the ferry terminal's **bureau de change** (open M-Sa 9am-4pm, Su 10am-4pm) or cash out at the **Bank of Ireland,** 101 Upper George's St. (☎ 280 0273; open M-F 10am-4pm, Th until 5pm). Free **Internet access** is available at the **Dun Laoghaire Youth Info Centre,** in the church on Marine Rd. (☎ 280 9363. Open M-F 9:30am-5pm, Sa 10am-4pm.)

🏠🛏 ACCOMMODATIONS, FOOD, AND PUBS. The best hostel within walking distance of town is 🖼**Belgrave Hall ❷** at 34 Belgrave Sq. From the Seapoint DART station, head left down the coast, then zigzag through the intersections: right on Belgrave Rd., left on Eaton Pl., right across from the blue and yellow doors, and left again across from Belgrave House. This top-tier hostel feels old but not run-down. (☎ 284 2106. Free parking. Continental breakfast included. Laundry €7. 10-bed dorm €20-25.) Dún Laoghaire is also prime ground for B&Bs. Fall off the DART or ferry and you'll find **Marleen ❸,** 9 Marine Rd. (☎ 280 2456. TV and tea facilities. Singles €35; doubles €60.) **Avondale ❸,** 3 Northumberland Ave., is around the corner from Dunnes Stores. A crimson carpet and a darling cocker spaniel (Oscar) lead guests to their big beds. (☎ 280 9628. Doubles €50.)

Tesco sells groceries in the Dún Laoghaire Shopping Centre. (☎ 280 0668. Open M-W and Sa 8:30am-7pm, Th-F 8:30am-9pm, Su 11am-6pm.) The best family restaurant in town is **Bits and Pizzas ❷,** 15 Patrick St. Go early or be prepared to wait. (☎ 284 2411. Pizzas and pasta €6-10; homemade ice cream €1.40. Open daily noon-midnight.) For vegetarian fare in a bohemian setting, look behind the blue door of **Old Cafe ❷,** 56 Lower George's St. (☎ 284 1024. Open M-Sa 9am-5pm.) **Farrell's ❸** can be found upstairs in the Dún Laoghaire Shopping Centre; the panoramic coastal view looks just fine through a pint glass. The pub also serves sandwiches, fish, burgers, and salads from €8-12. (☎ 284 6595. Open M-W 10:30am-11:30pm, Th-Sa 10:30am-12:30am, Su 12:30-11pm.) Next door to the Marina Hostel, the 🖼**Purty Kitchen** pub opens its loft to a nightclub with trad Tuesday and Thursday, and pop and jazz Friday through Sunday. (☎ 284 3576. Cover €10.)

🔳🎿 SIGHTS AND ACTIVITIES. To get to the 🖼**James Joyce Tower,** Dún Laoghaire's main attraction, take bus #8 from Burgh Quay in Dublin to Sandycove Ave. In September 1904, a young Joyce stayed here for six tense days as a guest of Oliver St. John Gogarty. Joyce later infamized his host in the first chapter of *Ulysses:* the novel opens in the tower on the "snotgreen" sea, with Buck Mulligan playing Gogarty. The tower's museum is a motherlode of Joycenalia, displaying his death mask, love letters to Nora, and many editions of *Ulysses.* (☎ 280 9265. Open Apr.-Oct. M-Sa 10am-1pm and 2-5pm, Su 2-6pm; Nov.-Mar. by appointment. €5.50, students €5.) At the base of the tower lies·another Joyce-blessed spot, the **forty foot men's bathing place,** where skinny-dipping goes on year-round.

The Dún Laoghaire **harbor** itself is a sight, full of car ferries, fishermen, and yachts cruising in and out of the marina. Frequent summer-evening **boat races** draw much of the town. The **Irish National Sailing School & Club,** on the West Pier, offers beginner weekend and week-long sailing courses. (☎ 284 4195; www.inss.ie. Prices from €172-190.) **Dublin Adventures** arranges canoeing and kayaking trips and rock climbing. (☎ 668 8047 or (087) 287 3287; www.adventure-activities-ire-land.com.) For indoor fun and dance, Dún Laoghaire's best *craic* can be had at the 🏴Comhaltas Ceoltoiri Éireann (COLE-tus KEE-ole-tori AIR-run), next door to the Belgrave Hall hostel. This is the headquarters of a huge international organization for Irish traditional music, and it houses bona fide, non-tourist-oriented trad sessions (seisiuns), as well as *céilí* dancing. (☎ 280 0295. July to mid-Aug. sessions M-Th at 9pm, with informal jam session after, €8-10. Year-round F night *céilí* €6.)

ULYSSES PUB PRIMER

So you meant to read *Ulysses* but were intimidated by its 700-odd pages, thousands of cryptic allusions, and general screwiness. Despite ranking in the estimations of many as the greatest book of the 20th century, very few people have read the Modernist masterwork in its entirety. *Let's Go: Britain and Ireland*, a somewhat more accessible text, is here for you: the factual fragments below should help you in even the most hoity-toity society.

The letter "s" both begins and ends the book. "S" stands for "Stephen" (Dedalus, one of the three main characters); "P" is for "Poldy" (nickname of Leopold Bloom, the second main character); and "M" for "Molly" (Poldy's wife, and the coolest of the three). Taken together, S-M-P stands for subject-middle-predicate, or logical sentence structure. The form (a syllogism) suggests a logical and narrative structure that readers can grasp, but which eludes the central characters.

By calling him "Poldy," Molly takes the "Leo," or lion, out of her husband, suggesting a theme of female domination, and yet the final words of the book, from her stream-of-consciousness monologue—"yes I said yes I will Yes" (remembering her response to Bloom's marriage proposal)—have drawn much critical attention as a moment of submission and affirmation. Another theory hinges on the final "Yes": in Molly's mind words are not capitalized, but on the page they are, thus granting supremacy to Joyce.

Ulysses uses 33,000 different words, 16,000 of which are used only once. William Shakespeare, in all his plays, only used 25,000. Joyce once said that he expected readers to devote nothing less than their entire lives to untangling his epic. For the less ambitious, this Primer should suffice.

BRAY (BRÍ CHUALAIN)   ☎ 01

Although officially located in Co. Wicklow, Bray functions as a suburb of Dublin: the DART and Dublin Bus trundle through the town regularly, bringing flocks of city folk to its beach. Polished but not pretentious, Bray's well-tended gardens and cotton candy-laden seafront manage to stimulate the demanding tourist without sacrificing its small-town charm. Along the beachfront, predictable arcade palaces cater to a crowd of Dublin beachgoers. The **National Sea Life Centre**, on the Strand, marks the dawning of the age of aquariums. (☎ 286 6939. Open daily 10am-5pm. €8, concessions €6, children €5.50.) Those un-thrilled by fenced-in fishies should head to the summit of **Bray Head,** high above the south end of the Strand and away from the neon lights. The trail begins after the short paved pedestrian walkway begins to curve up the hill. The hike is very steep and requires some climbing over rocks. Aim for the cross atop the hill and in about 30min. you'll be enjoying incredible views of the Wicklow Mountains and Bray Bay.

Bray is a 40min. **DART** ride from Dublin's Connolly Station (€3.30 return). **Buses** #45 and 84 arrive from Eden Quay. To reach **Main St.** from the DART station, take **Quinsborough Rd.** or **Florence Rd.,** which run perpendicular to the tracks. Bray's **tourist office** is the first stop south of Dublin for Wicklow info. The office is downhill on Main St. (☎ 286 7128. Open June-Sept. M-F 9am-5pm, Sa 10am-4pm; Oct.-May M-F 9:30am-4:30pm, Sa 10am-3pm. Closed M-F for lunch 1-2pm.) **B&Bs** line the Strand, but cheaper ones are on Meath St. closer to the town center. Anne and Pat

Duffy welcome guests to ◪**Moytura ❸,** Herbert Rd., on the right just before the fork with King Edward Rd. The Duffys offer superb homemade bread and chats on Irish history and literature. (☎282 9827. All rooms with bath. Singles €35; doubles €60.) The best meal in town is on the creative, veggie-friendly menu at ◪**Escape ❹,** Albert Ave., at the intersection with the Strand. (☎286 6755. Entrees €14. Open M-F 4-10:30pm, Sa 12:30-10:30pm, Su 12:30-8:30pm.) For cheaper lunches try Escape's sister cafe, **Escapade ❷** (☎204 2696); continue down Albert Ave., go under the bridge then left on Meath Rd., and it's on the left. **Clancy's** is a dark, olde-tyme pub with wooden plank tables. (☎204 0427. Trad Tu and Th.)

ENNISKERRY AND POWERSCOURT. The **Powerscourt Estate,** in nearby **Enniskerry,** and the tremendous **Powerscourt Waterfall,** a bit farther, both make for a convenient daytrip from Bray. Take an Alpine bus to the Powerscourt garden entrance or #185 to Enniskerry; #45 runs direct from Dublin. Built in the 1730s, the estate has become an architectural landmark. Outside, the terraced **gardens**—displaying everything from Italian opulence to Japanese elegance—justify the high admission. (☎204 6000. Open daily 9:30am-5:30pm. House and gardens €8, concessions €6.50; gardens only €6/€5.) The **falls** are 3½ mi. outside Enniskerry; take a bus from Enniskerry and follow the somewhat cryptic signs from town. The 398 ft. plunge makes Powerscourt Ireland's tallest permanent waterfall—a record challenged by the temporary falls on Hungry Hill in Co. Kerry. Although worth the visit in any season, the falls are by far most impressive in late spring and after heavy rains. A 40min. walk begins at their base and rambles through quiet, untended woods. (Open June-Aug. 9:30am-7pm; Sept.-May 10:30am to dusk. €2.50.)

EASTERN IRELAND

Woe betides the unfortunate soul whose exposure to eastern Ireland is limited to what he sees from inside a bus headed west from Dublin—the untouristed towns of the east hold many a marvel. Though the lush and mountainous, sparsely populated Co. Wicklow coast seems a world away from jet-setting Dublin, the county is actually right in the capital's backyard; its major sights are accessible by bus from the capital, though traveling here is best accomplished by bike or car.

WICKLOW (CILL MHANTÁIN)   ☎ 0404

Touted both for its seaside pleasures and as a gateway for aspiring Wicklow mountaineers, Wicklow Town has a wide selection of restaurants and plenty of accommodations within walking distance of its pubs. An eager traveler can exhaust the sightseeing potential in the town itself fairly swiftly, but there are many afternoons' worth of hiking and cycling in the hills.

🖃🛂 **TRANSPORTATION AND PRACTICAL INFORMATION. Trains** run to **Dublin Connolly Station** (1¼hr., 4-5 per day, €9.50) and to **Rosslare Harbour** via Wexford (2hr., 3 per day, €19). The station is a 15min. walk east of town on Church St. **Bus Éireann** leaves for Dublin from near the gaol at the other end of Main St. (1½hr., 6-9 per day, €6.20). A **guided driving tour** of Glendalough and the Wicklow mountains leaves daily at 10am and 2:15pm. (☎45152. 4hr. Call for prices.) **Wicklow Hire,** Abbey St., **rents bikes.** (☎68149. €13 per day, €39 per week. €40 deposit. Open M-Sa 8:30am-1pm and 2-5:30pm.) The **tourist office,** in Fitzwilliam Sq., provides free maps of town, and extensive information on the Wicklow Way. (☎69117. Open June-Sept. M-F 9am-6pm, Sa 9:30am-5:30pm; Oct.-May M-F 9:30am-5:30pm; closed

FROM THE ROAD

"UNSETTLED" WEATHER

One month into my Irish travels, I hadn't had a single day in which there was not at least a brief spell of rain. I had long since given up on checking the forecast: the weather in Ireland is terminally "unsettled," as the meteorologists euphemistically label the reliable mixture of rain and rain. I had nearly forgotten what my skin looked like, as my raincoat had become the quintessential fixture of my wardrobe. When my editors back in sweltering Boston asked if I had been renting bikes to get around I scoffed, "You do realize that you can't hold an umbrella and ride a bike at the same time?"

Nor did locals offer any solace, as the daily reminders that this was the worst summer they had seen in three, five, even 50 years did little to buoy my spirits. What I wanted to hear was that the clouds would somehow "run out" of rain, and that the remainder of my summer would be bone dry. No such luck; I instead was told that rainy Junes precede rainy Julys.

With this in mind, I was less than excited by the approach of the 4th of July, at home in America typically celebrated with cookouts, fireworks, and trips to the beach. My plan for the 4th did include a trip to the beach—Bundoran—but a beach in 50F° weather is somehow not quite the same. I was also scheduled to check out the somewhat nearby Errigal Mountain. Although I was tempted to go see *Spiderman* and dine at McDonald's, I decided I would climb Errigal, rain or shine.

for lunch 1-2pm.) An **AIB,** with its 24hr. **ATM,** is on your left as you approach the busiest section of Main St. (Open M 10am-5pm, Tu-F 10am-4pm.) The **Wicklow IT Access Centre,** on Main St. across from the AIB, has **Internet access.** (Open M-F 10am-1pm, 2-6pm, 7-10pm; Sa 10am-1pm and 2-6pm. €6 per hr.) From the town center, walk down Main St. toward Market Sq., and the **post office** is on your right. (☎67474. Open M-F 9am-5:30pm, Sa 9:30am-12:50pm and 2:10-5:30pm.)

🛏 **ACCOMMODATIONS AND CAMPING.** The lovely ◼**Wicklow Bay Hostel ❶** garners *Let's Go's* most enthusiastic recommendation. From Fitzwilliam Sq., walk toward the river, cross the bridge, and head left until you see a big, yellow building called "Marine House." You'll find good beds, clean rooms, amazing views, and an extraordinarily friendly, helpful atmosphere. (☎69213. Closed Jan. Dorms €12-14; private rooms €16 per person.) Travelers will be content in almost any of the B&Bs on Patrick Rd., uphill from Main St. and past the church. It takes a bit of energy to hike the 15min. to Helen Gorman's **Thomond House ❸,** on Upper Patrick Rd., but splendid panoramas and superbly comfortable rooms justify your efforts. (☎67940. Open Apr.-Oct. Singles €36; doubles €52.) Several campgrounds are scattered around the area. **Webster's Caravan and Camping Park ❶** at Silver Strand beach, 2½ mi. south of town on the coastal road, will let you pitch a tent. (☎67615. Open June-Aug. 1-person tent €6; 2-person €10. Showers €1.) In **Redcross,** 7 mi. down the N11, **River Valley ❶** lets you camp in the lap of luxury. (☎41647. Open Mar.-Sept. €4 per adult, €2 per child. Showers €1.)

🍴 **FOOD AND PUBS.** Greasy takeaways and fresh produce shops glare at each other across Main St. **Tesco,** out on the Dublin road, has a wide range of edibles. (☎69250. Open M-W and Sa 8:30am-8pm, Th-F 8:30am-10pm, Su 10am-6pm.) Expect nothing short of fine dining at ◼**The Bakery Cafe ❸.** Come before 7:30pm on weekdays and spoil yourself with three delectable courses (€21). The menu changes every month but maintains its vegetarian options. (☎66770. Su brunch €9. Open M-Sa 6-10pm, Su noon-4pm and 6-10pm.) **Casapepe ❸** serves up no-frills Italian fare: pizzas €8-9; pastas, poultry, and fish €13-18. (☎67075. Open daily noon-midnight.) **Philip Healy's ❷,** Fitzwilliam Sq., serves food all day and doubles as a lively nocturnal hotspot on weekends. (☎67380. Open Su-W noon-11:30pm, Th-Sa noon-12:30am.) The **Bridge Tavern,** Bridge St., reverberates with the sweet sounds of trad (nightly 10pm), local chatter, and clinking pints. (☎67718. Open M-W 10:30am-midnight, Th-Sa 11:30am-12:30am, Su 11:30am-11:30pm.)

◎ ❀ SIGHTS AND FESTIVALS. Wicklow's premier attraction is ◪**Wicklow's Historic Gaol.** The newly opened museum fills nearly 40 cells with audio clips, displays, and interactive activities relating to the gaol, its history, and the messy business of shipping convicts off to Australia. (☎61599. Tours every 10min. Open Apr.-Oct. daily 10am-6pm; last admission 5pm. €5.70, concessions €4.40, children €3.50.) A cliff trail provides smashing views en route to ◪**St. Bride's Head** (a.k.a. **Wicklow Head**), where St. Patrick landed on Travilahawk Strand in AD 432. Cut through the golf course from the **Black Castle** or head out the coastal road past the clubhouse and find the trailhead in the parking lot on the left. At Market Sq., Main St. becomes Summer Hill and then Dunbur Rd., from which beaches extend south to **Arklow.** From Wicklow, the closest strips of sand are **Silver Strand** and **Jack's Hole,** though most people head to larger ◪**Brittas Bay,** halfway to Arklow.

Beginning the last week of July, Wicklow hosts its annual **Regatta Festival,** the oldest such celebration in Ireland. At night, amicable pub rivalries foster singing competitions and general revelry. The **Wicklow Gaol Arts Festival** livens up mid-July nights with plays and concerts. (☎69117; www.wicklowartsweek.com. Tickets €10-15.) Contact the tourist office for more information.

WICKLOW MOUNTAINS

Over 2000 ft. high, carpeted in fragrant heather and rushing with sparkling water, the Wicklow summits provide a happy home to grazing sheep and scattered villages alike. This region epitomizes the romantic image of pristine rural Ireland.

GLENDALOUGH (GLEANN DÁ LOCH) ☎0404

In the 6th century, a vision instructed St. Kevin to give up his life of ascetic isolation and set up one humdinger of a monastery. He offset the workaday austerity of monastic life by choosing one of the most spectacular valleys in Ireland in which to found Glendalough (GLEN-da-lock; "glen of two lakes"). More recently, the valley has become known for ruins, excellent hikes, and swarms of tourists.

The amiable staff at the **Glendalough Visitors Centre** presents ample information on the valley's intriguing past. Your admission fee covers an exhibition, a tour of the ruins, and a 17min. audio-visual show on the history of Irish monasteries in general and St. Kevin's in particular. (☎45325. Open June-Aug. daily 9am-

Waking up to rain (surprise!) that morning, I decided to splurge a bit and take a taxi to Dunlewy. As I hiked through the village, the rain continued unabated, and as I set out for Errigal, with water beginning its ascent from my soaked-jean legs, I wasn't entirely sure I would resist calling the cab again if I ran across a pay phone. Luckily, I was afforded no such "wuss out" opportunities, and by the time I reached the foot of the mountain, my resolve to reach its pinnacle was strong. I knew that it probably wasn't entirely wise to climb a mountain by myself on a rainy day; *Let's Go* would certainly not recommend doing so. But with each step I took, pressing into the wet wind, I felt better and better, and there was no way that I was turning back before reaching the top.

Halfway up my umbrella busted entirely, having flipped inside out too many times. I laughed out loud as suspicious sheep eyed the wet and wild-haired madwoman I had become. No more would I fight or fear the rain, I loved it. And when I reached the summit and circled the cairn, my head literally in the clouds I had so often cursed, I had to marvel at the beauty of having that moment to myself, on top of the world.

—Abby Shafroth

6:30pm; Sept. to mid-Oct. 9:30am-6pm; mid-Oct. to mid-Mar. 9:30am-5pm; mid-Mar. to May 9:30am-6:30pm. Tours every 30min. in summer. €2.50, students €1.20.) The well-preserved ruins, which are free and always open, reflect only a small part of what the monastery looked like in its heyday. A tiny 3 ft. base supports the 100 ft. **round tower** of Glendalough, which is one of the best-preserved in all of Ireland. The **cathedral**, constructed in a combination of Romanesque architectural styles, was once the largest in the country. In its shadow stands **St. Kevin's Cross,** an unadorned high cross that was carved before the monks had tools to cut holes clean through the stone. (We're talking *old*.) The 11th-century **St. Kevin's Church,** whose stone roof remains intact, acquired the misnomer "St. Kevin's Kitchen" because of its chimney-like tower. The **Upper and Lower Lakes** are a rewarding digression from the monastic site. Cross the bridge at the far side of the monastery and head right on the paved path for 5min. to reach the serene Lower Lake. Twenty-five minutes later, the path hits a **National Park Information Office,** the best source for hiking information in the region (☎45425; open May-Aug. daily 10am-6pm, Apr. and Sept. Sa-Su 10am-6pm) and the magnificent Upper Lake, where Mel Gibson wed his ill-fated bride in the film *Braveheart*.

Little Glendalough sits on a tributary of R756, just where the **Glenealo River** pools into the Upper and Lower Lakes. Pilgrims come by car on R756, on foot along the Wicklow Way, or in buses run by **St. Kevin's Bus Service** (☎(01) 281 8119; departs from St. Stephen's Green in Dublin M-Sa 11:30am and 6pm, Su 11:30am and 7pm; €13 return) and **Bus Éireann** (☎(01) 836 6111; Apr.-Oct. daily 10:30am, return 5:45pm; €25, students €23.) Road signs will lead you to the Bord Failté **tourist office,** located in a small trailer across from the Glendalough Hotel. (☎45688. Open mid-June to Sept. M-Sa 10am-1pm and 2-6pm.) The **post office** is tucked into a row of B&Bs to the left of the Wicklow Heather restaurant (see below).

Cramped Dublin hostels can't possibly compete with the grandeur of ▓**The Glendalough Hostel (An Óige/HI)** ❷, a 5min. walk up the road past the Glendalough Visitors Centre. Prices are a bit high, but good beds, an in-house cafe, and the inspiring Wicklow Mountains backdrop make it by far the best option in the area. (☎45342. Bike rental and Internet both available. Wheelchair-accessible. Picnic lunch €4.50; full Irish breakfast €6.50; dinner €9.50. Dorms €19.50; doubles €43.) One mile up the road, the village of **Laragh** has food options and plenty of B&Bs. Tucked into the forest on the road up to St. Kevin's Church, **Pinewood Lodge** ❸ offers excellent rooms furnished with, appropriately, pinewood. (☎45437. All rooms with bath. Singles €36-40; doubles €52-60.) Laragh's **Wicklow Heather** ❸ is family- and vegetarian-friendly and is about the only place in the area open for breakfast. (☎45157. Breakfast €5-8; entrees €10-18; Su 3-course lunch €17.95. Open daily 8am-midnight.) **Lynham's** ❸ piles plates high with hot edibles; the Guinness beef stew (€11.50) is fabulous. (☎45345. Open daily 12:30-3:30pm and 5:30-9pm.) The attached **Lynham's Pub** lures travelers with siren-like cover bands and rock sessions every Wednesday, Thursday, and Saturday. (☎45345. Open daily until 11:30pm.)

▓ THE WICKLOW WAY

Ireland's oldest marked hiking trail (est. 1981) is also its most spectacular. Stretching from Marlay Park at the border of Dublin to Clonegal in Co. Carlow, the 76 mi. Wicklow Way meanders north to south through Ireland's largest highland expanse. As you weave over heathered summits and through steep glacial valleys, yellow arrows and signs help you stick to the Way's various footpaths, dirt tracks, and even paved roads. Civilization is rarely more than 2 mi. away, but appropriate **wilderness precautions** should still be taken: bring warm, windproof layers and raingear for the exposed hills, and, although the terrain never gets frighteningly rugged, sturdy footwear is a must. Most tourist offices in the county sell the *Wicklow Way Map Guide*, which is the best source of information on the trail and its sights (€6.35; you're not crazy, the map is oriented with north pointing down). Hiking 7-8hr. each day for six days will carry you from one end to the other, though there are plenty of attractive abbreviated routes. Numerous side trails make excellent day hikes; *Wicklow Way Walks* (€8) outlines several of these loops. An Óige publishes a pamphlet detailing 4-5hr. hostel-to-hostel walks (available at hostels in Wicklow and Dublin). For further information on the Way, contact the **National Park Information Office** (☎45425).

▐ **TRANSPORTATION. Dublin Bus** (☎(01) 873 4222) runs frequently to Marlay Park in **Rathfarnham** (#15A and 15B from Trinity College) and **Enniskerry** (#44 or 185 from Bray). **Bus Éireann** (☎(01) 836 6111) comes somewhat near the Way farther south, with infrequent service from Busáras in **Dublin** to Aughrim, Tinahely, Shillelagh, and Hackettstown. **St. Kevin's** runs two shuttles daily between **Dublin's** St. Stephen's Green West, **Roundwood**, and **Glendalough** (☎(01) 281 8119; €14 return). To combat trail erosion, **bikes** are allowed only on forest tracks and paved sections, but many off-Way roads are equally stunning.

▐ **ACCOMMODATIONS AND CAMPING.** The splendor of the Wicklow Way isn't exactly a well-kept secret—many accommodations take advantage of the endless stream of bodies trekking along. An Óige (☎(01) 830 4555) runs a cluster of hostels that lie close to the Way. The superior ▨**Glendalough Hostel (An Óige/HI)** ❷ is just a stone's throw from the Way, by the monastic ruins (☎(0404) 45342; dorms €19.50; doubles €43), while **Knockree (An Óige/HI)** ❶ is right on the Way. From Enniskerry, take the right fork of the road leading uphill from the village green and follow the signs to Knockree; the hostel is also just 2 mi. from Powerscourt Waterfall. (☎(01) 286 4036. Sheets €1.25. Lockout 10am-5pm. Dorms €11-12.) **Camping** is feasible along the Way but requires planning ahead. National parklands are fine for low-impact camping, but pitching a tent in state plantations is prohibited. A number of B&Bs offer camping and pickup if you call ahead; the *Wicklow Way Map Guide* lists about 20.

▐▨ **FOOD AND PUBS.** All hostels include self-catering facilities, but only Glendalough sells meals and boxed lunches; bring food along or expect to walk a few miles to a grocery store. Water can be replenished at the hostels and B&Bs along the Way; it is very important to drink plenty of fluid during the strenuous hike as many people fall ill from dehydration. Hikers may also want to keep their blood/alcohol content at an acceptable Irish standard; when you reach Glencullen or Enniskerry, be sure to make the climb to ▨**Johnnie Fox's,** Ireland's highest pub (1200 ft. above sea level). Here, Wicklow Way walkers drink and dine while enjoying the pub's excellent *craic*. The nightly trad and delicious food (entrees €9-18) make the journey worthwhile. (☎(01) 295 5647. Open M-Sa 10am-11:45pm and Su noon-11pm.)

BOYNE VALLEY   ☎041

The thinly populated Boyne Valley of Co. Meath hides Ireland's greatest archaeological treasures. Massive passage tombs like Newgrange create subtle bumps in the landscape that belie their cavernous underground chambers. These wonders are older than the Pyramids and at least as puzzling. The Celtic High Kings once ruled from atop the Hill of Tara, leaving a healthy dose of mysterious folklore in their wake. Every so often, farmers dig up artifacts from the Battle of the Boyne.

REPUBLIC OF IRELAND

BRÚ NA BÓINNE: NEWGRANGE, KNOWTH, DOWTH

Along the curves of the River Boyne, between Slane and Drogheda, sprawls Brú na Bóinne ("homestead of the Boyne"). The Boyne Valley may not have all the passage tombs in the world, just the biggest and best—there are 40 in this 2500-acre region, each with more than five millennia of history. Neolithic engineers constructed Newgrange, Dowth, and Knowth within walking distance of each other, likely with future lazy travelers in mind. The work was sluggish (it took 80 megamen ten days to move one kerbstone), and larger mounds took a half-century to build, back when a decent lifespan was just 30 years.

The most impressive of the three main sights, for archaeologists if not for visitors, is **Knowth** (rhymes with "mouth"). The enormous passage tomb, quite unusually, houses *two* burial chambers, back to back, with separate entrances east and west—possibly a nod to the Sun's movement across the horizon. Knowth's carvings are well preserved as prehistoric art goes, with unexplained spirals and etchings adorning the passage. Long-term excavations prevent the general public from entering, but the Visitors Centre **tour** (see below) offers a peek. **☒Newgrange** gives tourists the best glimpse at the structure and innards of a spectacular passage tomb. During a massive reconstruction in 1962, archaeologists discovered a roof box over the passage entrance. At dawn on the shortest day of the year (Dec. 21), 17 gilded minutes of sunlight shine through the roof box, reach straight to the back of the 60 ft. passageway, and irradiate the burial chamber. The tour provides a brilliant simulation of this experience, leaving visitors in awe. Those wishing to see the real event must sign up for a lottery, held every October. Ongoing excavations have kept **Dowth** (rhymes with "Knowth") closed to the public for several years. To gain admission, get a Ph.D. in archaeology.

Do not try to make your way directly to the sites—a guard minds the gate. Instead, head to the **☒Brú na Bóinne Visitors Centre,** located across from the tombs, near Donore on the south side of the River Boyne, and immediately book a tour. Remember to dress appropriately when visiting—most of the tour takes place outside and Neolithic tombs lack central heating. (☎988 0300. Open June to mid-Sept. 9am-7pm; May 9am-6:30pm; late Sept. 9am-6:30pm; Mar.-Apr. and Oct. 9:30am-5:30pm; Nov.-Feb. 9:30am-5pm. Admission to Visitors Centre only €2.50, seniors €1.90, students and children €1.20, families €6.30; Centre and Newgrange tour €5/€3.80/€2.50/€12.70; Centre and Knowth €3.80/€2.50/€1.50/€9.50; Centre, Newgrange, and Knowth €8.80/€6.30/€4.10/€22.20. Last tour 1½hr. before close. Last admission to center 45min. before close.) **Bus Éireann** (☎836 6111) shuttles to Brú na Bóinne from **Dublin** (1½hr.; M-Sa every 15min., Su every hr.; €12.70 return). Several **bus tours** from Dublin include admission to the sights (Bus Éireann Sa-Th, €24.20).

HILL OF TARA   ☎046

Home to 142 former Irish Kings, the largest collection of Celtic monuments in the world, and a sacred site for ancient Irish religion, Tara beckons visitors to its flourishing green expanse. From prehistoric times until the 10th century, Tara was the socio-politico-cultural heart of Ireland. Many secrets are buried under the 100 acres of grassy mounds, and the grounds are free and open to the public for casual perusal. Located at Tara is the sacred *Lia Fáil* ("Stone of Destiny"), an ancient phallus carved out of rock and used as a coronation stone; the rock was said to roar when the rightful king of Tara placed his hands upon it. The **Mound of Hostages,** the resident burial mound, dates to 2500 BC.

Tara is about 5 mi. east of Navan on the N3. Take any **local bus** from Dublin to **Navan** (1hr.; M-Sa 37 per day, Su 15 per day; €7) and ask the driver to let you off at the turnoff, which is on the left and marked by a small brown sign. Then you've got about a mile of uphill legwork to enjoy. The actual buildings—largely wattle, wood, and earth—have long been buried or destroyed; what you'll see are concentric rings of grassy dunes. They are always open for exploration; to make sense of them, hit the **visitors center** in the old church for an excellent guided tour (35min.; by request only; call ahead) and a slideshow on Tara's history. (☎25903. Center open mid-June to mid-Sept. daily 9:30am-6:30pm; May to mid-June and mid-Sept. to Oct. 10am-5pm. €1.90, seniors €1.20, students €0.70.)

SOUTHEAST IRELAND

A power base for the Vikings and then the Normans, this region has town and street names that ring of the Norse or Anglo-Saxon, rather than the Gaelic. The Southeast's most fruitful tourist attractions are its beaches, which draw native admirers to the coastline stretching from Kilmore Quay to tidy Ardmore. The medieval city of Kilkenny is packed with historic sights and convenient to many of the region's finest attractions; Cashel boasts a superbly preserved castle and cathedral complex perched on a giant rock. Wexford is a charismatic town, packed with historic sites and convenient to many of the region's finest attractions, while Waterford has resources, nightlife, and the grit of a real city.

KILKENNY (CILL CHAINNIGH)   ☎056

In a sense, Kilkenny is like a miniature version of Dublin—it has its own river, a renowned castle, excellent shopping, a tremendous selection of pubs, fantastic *craic*, and its own brewery. What it doesn't have are Dublin's headaches: the traffic is bearable, everything is walkable, it's impossible to get lost, and the hordes of tourists go to the castle and then disappear. A casual walk down Kilkenny's handsome streets reveals the city's attempt to recreate its 15th-century charm.

▐▀ TRANSPORTATION

Trains: Kilkenny MacDonagh Station, Dublin Rd. (☎22024). Open M-Sa 7am-8:15pm, Su 9am-1pm and 2:45-9pm. Always staffed, though the ticket window is open only at departure time. On the main **Dublin-Waterford** rail route (3-5 per day). Trains to: **Dublin** (2hr.); **Thomastown** (15min.); **Waterford** (45min.).

Buses: Kilkenny Station, Dublin Rd. (☎64933 or (051) 879 000), as well as a stop in the city center at **The Tea Shop.** Buses to: **Cork** (3hr., 2-3 per day, €15.20); **Dublin** (2hr., 5-6 per day, €9); **Galway** via Athlone or Clonmel (5hr.; M-Sa 5 per day, Su 3 per day; €19); **Limerick** via Clonmel (2½hr.; M-Sa 5 per day, Su 1 per day; €13.30); **Rosslare Harbour** via Waterford (2hr.; M-Sa 5-6 per day, Su 3 per day; €7). **Buggy's Coaches** (☎41264) run to **Ballyragget** (30min., M-Sa 2 per day) and **Castlecomer** (15min., M-Sa 2 per day, €1.30) with stops at the An Óige hostel (15min.) and Dunmore Cave (20min.). **J.J. Kavanagh's Rapid Express** (☎31106) has prices that beat Bus Éireann's (Dublin: M-Sa 4 per day, Su 2 per day; €5.70).

Taxis: All companies have a €5.10 minimum charge, plus an additional €1.50 per mi. after 3-4 mi. **O'Brien's Cabs** (☎61333); **Kevin Barry** (☎63017); **Kilkenny Cabs** (☎52000). **Castle Cabs** (☎61188) also **stores luggage** for €1.30 per day.

Bike Rental: J.J. Wall Cycle, 88 Maudlin St. (☎21236), is the only place in town to rent bikes. €12 per day, €65 per week. ID deposit. Open M-Sa 9am-6pm.

✈ 🛈 ORIENTATION AND PRACTICAL INFORMATION

From **MacDonagh Station**, turn left onto burgeoning **John St.** and go downhill to the intersection with **High St.** and **the Parade**, dominated by the castle on the left. Most activity occurs in the triangle formed by **High, Rose Inn,** and **Kieran St.**

Tourist Office: Rose Inn St. (☎51500), on the 2nd fl. of a 1525 pauper house. Free maps. Open M-Sa 9am-6pm, Su 11am-1pm and 2-5pm; "flexible" hours.

Banks: Bank of Ireland, Parliament St. (☎21155), has an **ATM**; the High St./Parade intersection has several more. All open M 10am-5pm, Tu-F 10am-4pm.

Laundry: The Laundry Basket (☎70355), top of James St. Full service wash and dry from €5. Dry-cleaning facilities. Open M-F 8:30am-7pm, Sa 9am-6pm.

Pharmacy: Several on High St. All open M-Sa 9am-6pm; Su rotation system.

Police (Garda): Dominic St. (☎22222).

Internet Access: Compustore (☎71200), in the High St. shopping center. €6 per hr. Open M-F 9:30am-6pm, Sa 10am-6pm. **Kilkenny e.centre,** Rose Inn St. (☎60093). Open M-Sa 10am-9pm, Su 11am-8pm.

Post Office: High St. (☎21891). Open M and W-Sa 9am-5:30pm, Tu 9:30am-5:30pm, Sa closed 1-2pm.

🏠 ACCOMMODATIONS AND CAMPING

🏰 **Foulksrath Castle (An Óige/HI),** Jenkinstown (☎67674; call ahead, leave a message 10am-5pm). On the N77 (Durrow Rd.), 8 mi. north of town, but well worth the hike. Turn right at signs for Connahy; the hostel is ¼ mi. down on the left. Buggy's Buses run from the Parade (20min.; M-Sa 2 per day, call hostel for times; €2). Housed in a 15th-century castle, this is literally royal accommodation. Grand views from the roof, a common room with a fireplace, and paintings by the wonderful and artistic warden make up for the less-than-great bathrooms. Dorms €12-14, under 16 €1 less. ❶

Kilkenny Tourist Hostel (IHH), 35 Parliament St. (☎63541). Fun, near all the popular pubs, and next to Smithwick's Brewery. Brightly colored rooms brim with activity: people bustle about in the kitchen, lounge on couches, and sip Guinness on the front steps. Kitchen with microwave. Laundry €5. Check-out 10am. 6- to 8-bed dorms €12-13; 4-bed €13.50-14.50. Doubles €31-33. ❶

Demsey's B&B, 26 James's St. (☎21954). A little old house by the Superquinn supermarket, off High St. Delightful proprietors rent out spacious, well-decorated, TV-blessed rooms. Parking €1 per night. Singles €28-30; doubles with bath €60-64. ❸

The Bailey, 13 Parliament St. (☎64337). Excellent rooms located above the Witness Box pub. Convenient, if a bit loud during music sessions below. €30 per person. ❸

The Kilford Arms Hotel, John St. (☎61018). New hotel between Ó'Faoláin's bar and the White Oak restaurant. Nice rooms, all with bath. Check out the Bengal tiger in the lobby. F-Sa singles €70; doubles €120. Su-Th €40/€70. ❺

Nore Valley Park (☎27229 or 27748). 7 mi. south of Kilkenny between Bennetsbridge and Stonyford. Take the New Ross road (R700) to Bennetsbridge; take the signposted right just before the bridge. A class act, with hot showers, TV room, and a play-area for the kiddies. Crazy golf course (€2), pedal go-carts (€1.50), picnic and BBQ areas. Wheelchair-accessible. Open Mar.-Oct. €5; 2-person tent €11. Laundry €5.70. ❶

Tree Grove Caravan and Camping Park (☎70302). 1 mi. past the castle on the New Ross road (R700). 2-person tent €12. Free showers. ❶

🍴 FOOD

Dunnes Supermarket, Kieran St., sells housewares and food. (☎ 61655. Open M-Tu and Sa 8:30am-7pm, W-F 8:30am-10pm, Su 10am-6pm.) Everything in Kilkenny's restaurants is great except the prices, which all hover somewhere in the lower stratosphere. Below are some reasonable options; otherwise, hit the pubs.

▨ Pordylo's, Butterslip Ln. (☎ 70660), between Kieran and High St. One of the best eateries on the island. Zesty dinners (€10-23) from across the globe, many of which love vegetarians. Reservations recommended. Open daily 6-11pm. ❹

La Creperie, 80 John St. Sweet and savory crepes and sandwiches, all for a great price (crepes €3.60-5.10, sandwiches €2.45-4.50). Open M-F 10am-7:30pm, Sa 10am-8:30pm, Su 11am-6:30pm. ❶

Langton's, 69 John St. (☎ 65123). The eccentric owner has earned a gaggle of awards for his ever-changing highbrow restaurant. Full lunch menu with an Irish twist (€8-11) served daily 12:30-3:30pm; sophisticated dinner (€19-23) 6-10:30pm. ❹

Ristorante Rinuccini, 1 the Parade (☎ 61575), opposite the castle. Couples enjoy authentic Italian delights and romantic music in this glittering first-rate establishment. Lunch (€8-11) served noon-2:30pm; dinner (€15-19) served 6-10:30pm. ❹

The Tea Shop, Patrick St. (☎ 70051). An excellent little cafe in the city center where you can grab tasty breakfasts (€6) or sip herbal teas (€1.40) before catching the bus outside. Open M-F 8am-6pm, Sa 8am-5:30pm. ❷

Italian Connection, 38 Parliament St. (☎ 64225). Decked out in mahogany and carnations, and but not too fancy-shmancy. Lunch specials (€7.50-8.25) served noon-3pm. Dinner €11.50-19. Open daily noon-11pm. ❸

🍺 PUBS

Kilkenny, "The Marble City," is also known as the "Oasis of Ireland"—its watering holes have a range of live music on most nights, especially in the summer.

▨ Ó'Faolaíns, John St. (☎ 61018). Throbbing new bar with 3 floors, a 25 ft. high ceiling, and a rebuilt Welsh church crafted into the walls. Late bar (W-Sa until 2:30am, Su-M until 2am) and dance club (cover €5-10) make for a great place to end the night.

Breathnach's Steak and Ale House, John St. (☎ 56737). Large, multi-floor pub with a few bars and a terrific grill (steaks €12.60-15.90).

Matt the Miller's, 1 John St. (☎ 61696), at the bridge. Huge, thronged, and magnetic. Pilgrims are sucked in and forced to dance to silly Europop or a bizarre trad/reggae mix. M rock music and late bar until 2am; cover €5. Th and Sa DJ; Tu and F bands.

Tynan's Bridge House Bar (☎ 21291), just around the corner from the tourist office, on the river. Double award-winning and the most original bar in Kilkenny. Extremely tiny, but terrific atmosphere.

Kyteler's Inn, Kieran St. (☎ 21064). The oldest pub in Kilkenny and the 1324 house of Alice Kyteler, Kilkenny's witch, whose husbands (all 4) had a knack for poisoning themselves on their 1st wedding anniversaries. The food and drink have since become safer. Trad fills the air twice a week. F-Su fiddle away the evening at **Nero's,** a nightclub that burns down the house. Cover €8-12. Open 11pm-2am.

The Witness Box, Parliament St. (☎ 64337), across the street from the Kilkenny Tourist Hostel and run by the owners of The Bailey B&B (see above). Lots of local flavor. Th-M live music, W trad.

The Pump House, 26 Parliament St. (☎63924). Remains a favorite among locals and hostelers. Loud, conveniently located, and packed. Ultra-hip upstairs enclave will make you wish you packed some Prada. M-Th summer trad, Su rock and blues.

Anna Conda, Parliament St. (☎71657), near Cleere's. Outstanding trad fills the pub from the low ceilings in front to the high rafters in back. New beer garden overlooks the ducks on the Suir. M and F-Sa music. No cover.

👁 SIGHTS

▨ KILKENNY CASTLE. Although Kilkenny city is a sight in itself, its 13th-century castle, on the Parade, is simply the bee's knees. The 50 yd. **Long Galley,** a spectacle reminiscent of a Viking ship, displays portraits of English bigwigs, giant tapestries, and a beautiful Italian double fireplace. The basement houses the **Butler Gallery** and its modern art exhibits. (☎21450. Castle and gallery open June-Sept. daily 9:30am-7pm; Oct.-Mar. 10:30am-12:45pm and 2-5pm; Apr.-May 10:30am-5pm. Castle access by guided tour only. €4.40, students €2.) Across the street, the internationally known **Kilkenny Design Centre** fills the castle's former stables with expensive Irish crafts. (☎22118. Open Apr.-Dec. M-Sa 9am-6pm, Su 10am-6pm; Jan.-Mar. M-Sa 9am-6pm.)

SMITHWICK'S BREWERY. Rumor has it that 14th-century monks, known to be a crafty bunch, once brewed a light ale in the **St. Francis Abbey** on Parliament St. Though the abbey is in ruins, the industry survives in the yard, at the **Smithwick's Brewery.** Each day 50 free tickets are given out at the security guard station; turn right after the Watergate Theatre and the gate is straight ahead. Collect your ticket and show up at 3pm outside the green doors on Parliament St. for a tour, followed by **two free pints** in the private pub below the factory. (☎21014. Tours July-Aug. M-F.)

WALKING TOUR. If you're interested in Kilkennalia, including the down-and-dirty on folkloric tradition, take a **Tynan Walking Tour.** Besides spinning some animated yarns, the tour is the only way to see the **old city gaol.** Tours depart from the tourist office. (☎65929 or (087) 265 1745; www.tynantours.com. 1hr. tours Mar.-Oct. M-Sa 6 per day, Su 4 per day; Nov.-Feb. Tu-Sa 3 per day. €5, concessions €4.50.)

🎵 🎭 ENTERTAINMENT AND ACTIVITIES

The tourist office provides a bi-monthly guide to the town's happenings; The Kilkenny People (€1.30) is a good newsstand source for arts and music listings. **The Watergate Theatre,** Parliament St., stages drama, dance, and opera. (☎61674. Tickets €10-20, student discounts available. Box office open M-F 10am-7pm, Sa 2-6pm, Su 1hr. before curtain.) Each August, Kilkenny holds its **Arts Festival,** with daily programs of theater, concerts, and readings by European and Irish artists. (☎52175. Tickets up to €15.25; concessions vary by venue.) The city's population increases by more than 10,000 when the **Cat Laughs,** a festival held the first weekend of June and featuring international comedy acts (☎63837). Activities in and around Kilkenny are plentiful, especially for outdoors enthusiasts. The **Kilkenny Anglers Club** (☎65220) can set you up for **fishing** on the Nore. If you'd prefer to paddle over the fish, call **Go with the Flow River Adventures** (☎(087) 252 9700) to **kayak** on the river Barrow. The **Kilkenny Golf Course** (☎65400), out Castlecomer Rd., is an 18-hole championship course open to non-members.

CASHEL (CAISEAL MUMHAN)   ☎ 062

The town of Cashel lies tucked between a series of mountain ranges on the N8, 12 mi. east of Tipperary town. Legend has it that the devil furiously hurled a rock from high above the plains when he discovered a church was being built in Cashel. The assault failed to thwart the plucky citizens, and today the town sprawls defiantly at the base of the 300 ft. Rock of Cashel.

🖃🔁 TRANSPORTATION AND PRACTICAL INFORMATION. All but one of Cashel's **buses** leave from the Bake House on Main St., across from the tourist office; the Dublin bus departs from Rafferty's Travel a few doors down. **Bus Éireann** (☎62121) serves: **Cork** (1½hr., 6 per day, €12); **Dublin** (3hr., 6 per day, €15); **Limerick** (1hr., 5 per day, €12). Cashel's **tourist office** splits rent with the Heritage Centre (see below) in City Hall on Main St. (☎61333. Open July-Aug. M-Sa 9:15am-6pm, Su on demand; Apr.-June and Sept. M-Sa 9:15am-6pm.) The **post office** rocks the Cashel on Main St. (☎61418. Open M-F 9am-1pm and 2-5:30pm, Sa 9am-1pm.)

🖃🔁 ACCOMMODATIONS, FOOD, AND PUBS. A 5min. walk from town on Dundrum Rd., and near the promiscuous ruins of Hore Abbey, lies the stunning **🖫O'Brien's Farm House Hostel ❶,** deserving of several gold stars for its incredible view of the Rock, cheerful rooms, and extremely courteous hosts. (☎61003. Full-service laundry €8-10. Dorms €13-15; doubles €40-45. **Camping** €6.) Just steps from the Rock, in a quiet residential neighborhood on Dominic St., you'll find a bargain at the quaint **Rockville House ❸.** (☎61760. Singles €38; shared rooms €25 per person.) While waiting for the bus, enjoy decadent sweets at **The Bake House ❶,** across from the tourist office. (☎61680. Open M-Sa 8am-7pm, Su 9am-6pm.) The superior pubmunch (€7) at **Ó'Suilleabáin ❷** (O'Sullivan's), Main St., makes it the local lunchtime haunt. (☎61858. Food served M-Sa noon-2:30pm.) Start the pub-crawling night at **Feehan's** (☎61929), where the atmosphere is timeless. If the stars are out, move to the multi-level beer garden at **Mikey Ryan's** (☎61431). Cross over Main St. for some singing and joke-telling at **Davern's** (☎61121; music M and W), and end the night down the street at **Dowling's,** where bartenders make it their only business to pour the best pint in town.

🗺 THE ROCK OF CASHEL. You'll notice it on the horizon from miles away—that huge limestone outcropping topped with medieval buildings is the **🖫Rock of Cashel,** sometimes called **St. Patrick's Rock.** Periodic guided tours are informative, if a bit dry; exploring the buildings while in earshot of the guide is a more attractive option. The 1495 burning of the **Cashel Cathedral** by the Earl of Kildare was a highlight of Cashel's illustrious history. When Henry VII demanded an explanation, Kildare replied, "I thought the Archbishop was in it." As any Brit worth his blue blood would, the King made him Lord Deputy. Next to the cathedral, a 90 ft. **round tower,** built just after 1101, is the oldest part of the Rock. The **museum** at the entrance to the castle complex preserves the 12th-century **St. Patrick's Cross.** (Rock open mid-June to mid-Sept. daily 9am-7:30pm; mid-Sept. to mid-Mar. 9:30am-4:30pm; mid-Mar. to mid-June 9:30am-5:30pm. Last admission 45min. before closing. €4.40.) Smart visitors head to the **Heritage Center,** on Main St., before heading Rockwards. (☎62511. Open May-Sept. daily 9:30am-5:30pm; Oct.-Apr. M-F 9:30am-5:30pm. Free.) The **🖫Brú Ború Heritage Centre,** below the Rock, hosts wonderful trad and dance. (☎61122. Mid-June to mid-Sept. Tu-Sa 9pm. €13, with dinner €35.)

WEXFORD (LOUGH GARMAN)   ☎053

Conquest after bloody conquest has left Wexford with an interesting tale to tell. Incessant fighting between Gaels, Vikings, and Normans gave birth to a labyrinth of narrow, snaggling streets. Park the car and pound the pavement to visit this huddled harbor town's main attractions—its quality pubs and restaurants.

🖃 TRANSPORTATION. Trains chug into **O'Hanranhan (North) Station,** Redmond Sq. (☎22522; info 7am-7:40pm), then hustle to Connolly Station in **Dublin** (2¾hr., 3 per day, €17) and to **Rosslare** (15min., 3 per day, €2.50). **Buses** stop at the train station. If the station office is closed, check the Station Cafe (☎24056) across the street for info. Buses run to **Dublin** (2¾hr., 8-10 per day, €10) and **Rosslare** (20min., 9-12 per day, €3.35); those to and from **Limerick** (4 per day, €16) connect with Irish Ferries and Stena-Sealink sailings. A list of **taxi** companies is posted in the train station. **Hayes Cycle Shop,** 108 South Main St., **rents bikes.** (☎22462. €20 per day, €75 per week. €75 or ID deposit. Open M-Sa 9am-6pm; bikes available by arrangement on Su.) **Hitchers** find that the odds of getting a ride are highest around noon or 5-7pm; savvy hitchers make a point of specifying either the Dublin road (N11) or the Waterford road (N25). *Let's Go* does not recommend hitchhiking.

■ ▮ **ORIENTATION AND PRACTICAL INFORMATION.** Most of the town's action takes place one block inland, along the twists and turns of **Main St.** A plaza called the **Bullring** is near the center of town, a few blocks from where North Main St. changes to South. Another plaza, **Redmond Square,** sits at the northern end of the quays near the train and bus station. The **tourist office** is on Crescent Quay. (☎23111. Open Apr.-Sept. M-Sa 9am-6pm; Nov.-Mar. M-F 9:30am-5:30pm) Banks with 24hr. **ATMs** include **AIB** (☎22444) and **Bank of Ireland** (☎21365; both open M 10am-5pm, Tu-F 10am-4pm). The **library** has free **Internet access;** call ahead to reserve a slot. (☎21637. Open Tu 1-5:30pm, W 10am-4:30pm and 6-8pm, Th-F 10am-5:30pm, Sa 10am-1pm.) **Megabytes,** located in the Franciscan Friary, has computers and coffee. (€5 per hr. Open M-Th 9am-9:30pm, F 9am-5:30pm, Sa 10am-2pm.) Find the **post office** on Anne St. (☎22587. Open M-Sa 9am-5:30pm.)

▮ **ACCOMMODATIONS AND CAMPING.** If you're planning to be in town during the opera festival, book as far in advance as possible; rooms are often reserved up to a year ahead. ▨**Kirwan House Hostel (IHH) ❶,** 3 Mary St., is a 200-year-old Georgian house right in the heart of town with some slants and creaks in its wooden floors, a BBQ-friendly patio out back, and loads of local info from the staff. (☎21208. Laundry available next door. Dorms €12-12.50; doubles €32; triples €48.) View the castle from your room at ▨**The Blue Door ❸,** 18 Lower George St. Look for the crisp white building with flower baskets and, you guessed it, a blue door; head downstairs for veggie-friendly meals. (☎21047. €30-40 per person.) On the eastern edge of town, **Ferrybank Caravan and Camping Park ❶** has clean sites with striking ocean views. (☎44378. Open Easter-Oct. 1-person tent €7.60; 2-person €10.20. Showers €1.30. Laundry €1.90.)

▮ ▨ **FOOD AND PUBS. Dunnes Store** on Redmond Sq. has everything from groceries to clothes to lampshades. (☎45688. Open M-Tu 9am-8pm, W 9am-9pm, Th-F 9am-10pm, Sa 9am-7pm, Su 10am-7pm.) Check out all those old Guinness ads at **The Sky and the Ground ❸,** 112 S. Main St. Scaled-down versions of the pricier fare served by the late-night restaurant upstairs (**Heavens Above ❹;** entrees €14-21) are available here until 6pm. Lunch is so good they occasionally sell out the entire menu. (☎21273. Main courses €9-10. Su-Th live music, typically trad.) **Gusto's ❶,** S. Main St., is to be relished. Its small, cafe-like appearance belies high-quality breakfasts (€3.20-5.10), sandwiches, and a slightly arty-sophisticate vibe. Panini (€4) are a warm treat. (☎24336. Open M-F 8:30am-5:30pm, Sa 8:30am-5pm.)

The two halves of **Mooney's Lounge,** Commercial Quay, by the bridge, comprise Wexford's hot late-night venue. One side opens up for a disco bar after 9:30pm while the other continues as a pub. (☎21128. All sorts of live music Th-Su. 18+. Occasional €7 cover. Open M-W until 11:30pm, Th-Su until 2:30am.) A classy crowd flocks to **The Centenary Stores,** Charlotte St. off Commercial Quay—a stylish pub and dance club situated in a former warehouse. Try the patio for those sunny afternoon pints. (☎24424. Excellent trad Su mornings and M and W nights. DJ spins techno and top-40 Th-Su 10:30pm-2am. Nightclub cover €8.) On the corner of Redmond Pl. facing the water, **The Ferryman,** 12 Monck St. is large and bright with ample skylights and faux torches. (☎23877. Carvery lunch served 12:30-3pm. Open M-W 10:30am-11:30pm, Th-Sa 10:30am-12:30am, Su 10:30am-11pm.)

⬛🗗 SIGHTS AND ENTERTAINMENT. The remains of the Norman **city walls** run the length of High St. **Westgate Tower,** near the intersection of Abbey St. and Slaney St., is the only one of the wall's original six gates that still stands. The tower gate now holds the **Westgate Heritage Centre,** where an excellent 30min. audio-visual show recounts the history of the town. The center is staffed by volunteers whose sporadic bouts of do-goody intentions make for erratic hours—contact the tourist office for more information. Next door, the peaceful ruins of **Selskar Abbey**—site of Henry II's extended penance for his role in Thomas à Beckett's murder—act as a flower-bed for glorious weeds. (Enter through the wicket gate by the Heritage Centre. Open M-F 10am-4pm. Free.) At the **Friary Church,** in the Franciscan Friary on School St. (☎22758), the peaceful fellows gadding about in brown robes are Franciscan monks of an order that has lived in town since 1230.

For detailed information on events throughout the county, pick up *The Wexford People* (€1.50) from any local newsstand or pub. The funky **Wexford Arts Centre,** Cornmarket, presents free visual arts and crafts exhibitions and performances of music, dance, and drama throughout the year. (☎23764. Tickets generally €9-10. Centre open M-Sa 9am-6pm.) The **Theatre Royal,** High St., produces shows throughout the year, culminating in the internationally acclaimed **Wexford Festival Opera,** held in late October and early November. (☎22400; box office ☎22144; www.wexfordopera.com. Box office open May-Sept. M-F 11am-1pm and 2-5pm; Oct.-Nov. M-F 9:30am-5:30pm.) Wexford's hilly countryside and beaches make for excellent horseback riding. **Shelmalier Riding Stables,** 4 mi. away at Forth Mountain, has riding for novices and experts (☎39251; booking essential). **Boat trips** from Wexford Harbour are another way to explore the area and are perfect for those seeking close-up pictures of the **seals** at Raven Point. (☎40564. 30min. tour €7.)

ROSSLARE HARBOUR (ROS LÁIR) ☎053

Rosslare, best viewed from the deck of a departing ship, is a decidedly pragmatic seaside village whose primary function is welcoming voyagers and bidding them *bon voyage* as they depart for France or Wales. **Trains** run from the ferryport to: **Dublin** (3hr., 3 per day, €14.50); **Limerick** (2½hr., 1-2 per day, €13.35) via Waterford (1¼hr., €8.25); **Wexford** (15min., 3 per day, €2.50). The rail office (☎33592) also houses the bus station (☎33595). Most **buses** stop by the Kilrane Church and the Catholic church and go to: **Dublin** (3hr., 10-12 per day, €12.70); **Galway** via Waterford (4 per day, €22); **Killarney** (M-Sa 5 per day, Su 3 per day; €20.50) via Cork (€17.10) and Waterford (€11.70); **Wexford** (20min., 13-17 per day, €4). **Stena Line** (☎61567; 24hr. info ☎61505) and **Irish Ferries** (☎33158) both serve the port. **Ferries** shove off for **Britain** (1 per day) and **France** (1 every other day). Trains and buses often connect with the ferries; **Irish Rail** (☎33114) and **Bus Éireann** (☎(051) 879 000) have desks in the terminal. If you need help at the ferry port, head to the **port authority desk** (☎33114). Exhausted passengers often take what they can get in town, but better B&Bs swamp N25 just outside of Rosslare. 🎏**Mrs. O'Leary's Farmhouse ❷,** off N25 in Kilrane, a 15min. drive from town, stands out from the rest of the rabble. Set on a glorious 100-acre farm right by the seaside, this well-kept home is a holiday unto itself. A grassy lane leads past dunes of wildflowers to a secluded beach. (☎33134. Call for pickup. €23 per person, with bath €25.50.)

IN RECENT NEWS

WHERE HAVE ALL THE HOSTELS GONE?

Recently, budget travelers have been arriving in the larger Irish cities only to find few hostels left that can take them in. Two main factors seem to be causing this trend: the first is the general down-turn in tourism over the past year, which has weakened the travel industry and closed businesses in Ireland and throughout Europe.

A second, more salient explanation accounts for why those hostels that do remain open no longer take in travelers: for the first time in modern history, Ireland is experiencing a population influx. Each year, thousands of refugees fleeing persecution in their native countries arrive in Ireland seeking political asylum. Unable to suitably house all of these immigrants, the government has turned to hostels to solve the housing crunch. Many hostels throughout the country are now being offered three- to four-year contracts in which they agree to only house refugees and asylum seekers; the owners are not allowed to take in tourists during that time. In return they are paid as though their hostel is full each night.

However, rumor has it that some hostel owners, particularly in the southeast, have become greedy, ignoring this important caveat and allowing unknowing tourists to stay despite the governmental restrictions. When booking accommodations in the area, be sure to check with the local tourist office to see which hostels can legally take you in.

WATERFORD (PORT LÁIRGE) ☎ 051

A skyline of huge metal silos and harbor cranes greet the visitor to Waterford. Fortunately, behind this industrial facade lies a city with ten centuries of fascinating history. The Vikings founded Vadrafjord around AD 914, making it the oldest city in Ireland. Traces of Viking influence persist in Waterford's streets, despite the massive freighters that have replaced the longships.

■ TRANSPORTATION. Trains (☎317 889 M-F 9am-6pm; 876 243 for 24hr. timetable) arrive at Plunkett Station (☎879 000; open M-Sa 8:15am-6pm), across the bridge from the Quay, and run to: **Dublin** (2½hr., M-F 5-6 per day, €17-21); **Kilkenny** (40min., 3–5 per day, €7); **Limerick** (2¼hr., M-Sa 2 per day, €14); **Rosslare** (1hr., M-Sa 2 per day, €8). The bus station is on the Quay, across the street from the tourist office. **Buses** run to: **Cork** (2½hr., 10-13 per day, €13.30); **Dublin** (2¾hr.; M-Sa 10-12 per day, Su 6 per day; €9); **Galway** (4¾hr., 5-6 per day, €17); **Kilkenny** (1hr., 1 per day, €7); **Limerick** (2½hr.; M-Th and Su 6 per day, F 7 per day; €13); **Rosslare** (1¼hr., 3-5 per day, €11.60). **Altitude**, 22 Ballybricken St., past the *Garda* station at the far side of the green, **rents bikes.** (☎870 356. €20 per day.) For **taxis,** either go to the cab stand on Broad St. or try **7 Cabs** (☎877 777), **Five-O Cabs** (☎850 000), or **Rapid Cabs** (☎858 585). Waterford's few **hitchers** place themselves on the main routes, away from the tangled city center; others take city buses out to the Crystal Factory before sticking out a thumb. *Let's Go* does not recommend hitchhiking.

■▪ ORIENTATION AND PRACTICAL INFORMATION. Modern Waterford sits on the ruins of the triangular Viking city. The hornéd ones must have had a knack for urban planning, because the area between **the Quay, Parnell St. (the Mall), and Barronstrand St. (Michael and Broad St.)** is still hopping, even without the sweet music of falsterpibes filling the air. The city's **tourist office** is on the Quay, across from the bus station. (☎875 823. Open July-Aug. M-Sa 9am-6pm and Su 11am-5pm; Sept.-Oct. and Apr.-June M-Sa 9am-6pm; Nov.-Mar. M-Sa 9am-5pm.) **Banks** with 24hr. **ATMs** line the streets; on the Quay, they're at **AIB** (☎874 824), by the clock tower, and **Bank of Ireland.** (☎872 074. Both open M 10am-5pm, Tu-F 10am-4pm.) The friendly people at the **Youth Information Centre,** 130 the Quay (☎877 328), will help with finding **short-term work.** Access the **Internet** here, too, or at **Voyager Internet Cafe,** 85 the Quay (☎843 843; €1.20 per

15min.; open M-Sa 10am-7pm). The largest of several letter-dispensaries (a.k.a. **post offices**) is on the Quay. (☎874 321. Open M and W-F 9am-5:30pm, Tu 9:30am-5:30pm, Sa 9am-1pm.)

⌂ ACCOMMODATIONS. All Waterford's hostels have gone the way of the dodo, and most B&Bs in the city center are nothing to write home about. **The Anchorage ❸**, 9 the Quay, offers upscale accommodations right on the Quay. Each room at this hotel-esque B&B has TV, phone, and tea/coffee-making facilities. (☎854 302. Singles €35-40; doubles €65-75.) Mrs. Ryan invites you into her charming home at the **Beechwood ❷**, 7 Cathedral Sq. From the Quay, go up Henrietta St.; the B&B is located on a quiet pedestrian street. (☎876 677. Doubles €42.) The amiable Ryders offer quiet, subdued rooms at simple prices to go with the biscuits and bottomless pots of tea at **Mayor's Walk House ❸**, 12 Mayor's Walk, a 15min. jaunt from the train station. (☎855 427. Open Feb.-Nov. Singles €25; doubles €44.)

❒ ▥ FOOD AND PUBS. Get cheap groceries at **Dunnes Stores** in the City Square Mall. (☎853 100. Open M-W 9am-7pm, Th-F 9am-9pm, Sa 9am-6pm, Su noon-6pm.) Eat as often as you can at ▧**Haricot's Wholefood Restaurant ❷**, 11 O'Connell St. The menu of healthy, innovative dishes and vegetarian-friendly meals is constantly changing and everything (including the *craic*) is made from scratch. (☎841 299. Entrees €8-10. Open M-F 9am-8pm, Sa 9am-6pm.) **Cafe Luna ❷**, 53 John St., is a late-night cafe serving pasta, salads, and sandwiches with a creative twist. (☎834 539. Homemade soup and half-sandwich for €4.15. Most entrees €5-7. Open M-W until midnight, Th-Su until 3:30am.) Eat delicious skewer-grilled dishes with your vino at **Goose's Barbecue and Wine House ❸**, 19 Henrietta St. This stone-wall, eclectically decorated establishment will make veg-heads happy. (☎858 426. Entrees €14-18. Open Tu-Sa 6-11pm.)

The Quays are flooded with pubs, and the corner of John and Parnell St. has its share as well. ▧**T&H Doolan's**, George's St., has been serving for a respectable 300 years, in an awe-inspiring building with low, low ceilings that have been standing for over 800. Ask about Sinead O'Connor, who crooned here during her college days. (☎841 504. Trad nightly 9:30pm.) After you peer into the working well and play some snooker (€6 per hr.) at ▧**Downes**, Thomas St., finish up your pint and get in a few games of squash (€5 per 40min.) on one of the two courts up the back steps. (☎874 118. Open Su-Th until 11:30pm, F-Sa until 1:30am.) A small, traditional pub, **The Woodman** (☎858 130) at Parnell and John St. shuts down at 12:30am on weekends, so click those heels and head to the adjoining **Ruby's Nightclub**, which throbs with chart hits until 2:30am. Get your pre-boogie buzz in the pub's front lounge before 10pm to evade the €7-8 cover.

◙ SIGHTS. What do fancy dinner sets, the Times Square Millennium Ball, and all major sporting trophies have in common? They were all handcrafted at the spectacular ▧**Waterford Crystal Factory**, 2 mi. from the city center on N25 (the Cork road). Watch master craftsmen transform molten goo into sparkling crystal or admire the finished products—and their astronomical prices—in the gallery. To get there, catch the City Imp outside Dunnes on Michael St. and request a stop at the factory (10-15min., every 15-20min., €1) or take city bus #1 (Kilbarry-Ballybeg, €1.10), leaving across from the Clock Tower every 30min. (☎373 311 or 332 500. 1hr. tours every 15min. €6; audiovisual shows on demand. Mar.-Oct. daily 8:30am-4pm; Nov.-Jan. M-F 9am-3:15pm. Gallery open Mar.-Dec. daily 8:30am-6pm; Jan. M-F 9am-5pm; Feb. daily 9am-5pm.)

To brush up on the 1000-year history of Waterford, head to **Waterford Treasures** at the Granary, connected to the tourist office. Named the 1999-2000 Ireland Museum of the Year, this €4.5 million project is well worth a visit. The actual artifacts, such as the town's written charters, make quite an impressive show. (☎304 500. Open June-Aug. M-F 9am-9pm, Su 10am-9am; May and Sept. M-F 9:30am-6pm; Oct.-Apr. M-F 10am-5pm. €6.) Hulking down at the end of the Quay, **Reginald's Tower** has guarded the city's entrance since the 12th century. Tiny models illustrate the contributions Vikings, Normans, and English kings have made to Waterford's growth. (☎873 501. Tours on demand. Open June-Sept. daily 9:30am-6:30pm; Oct.-May 10am-5pm. €1.90, seniors €1.20, students €0.70.) You can cover all of Waterford's sights in a day, but only if you're as swift as a Viking raider and as organized as a Norman invader. Buying the **City Pass** from **Waterford Tourism**, 1 Arundel St. (☎852 550), or at the Waterford Crystal Factory, Waterford Treasures, or Reginald's Tower, will get you into all three for €9.20.

🎭 🎪 **ENTERTAINMENT AND FESTIVAL.** The tourist office can provide an annual list of major events in town, and any local newspaper, including the free *Waterford Today*, has more specific entertainment listings. The seasonal **Waterford Show** at City Hall offers Irish music, stories, and dance. (☎358 397 or 875 788; after 5pm try ☎381 020. May-June and Sept. Tu, Th, and Sa 9pm. July-Aug. Tu-Th and Sa 9pm. Tickets €12.) The **Garter Lane Arts Centre**, 22a O'Connell St., supports all different forms of art inside its old Georgian brick. (☎855 038. Centre and box office open M-Sa 10am-6pm; performance nights until 9pm. Concerts €15; concessions €3-5 less.) Waterford's largest festival, the **Spraoi** (rhymes with "whee"), is held during the August bank holiday weekend, attracts bands from around the globe, and culminates in a sizeable parade. (☎841 808; www.spraoi.com.)

SOUTHWEST IRELAND

With a dramatic landscape ranging from lush lakes and mountains to stark, ocean-battered cliffs, Southwest Ireland is rich in storytellers and history-makers. The urban activity of Cork city and the area's frantic pace of rebuilding and growth contrast with the ancient rhythm of nearby rural villages.

CORK (AN CORCAIGH)   ☎021

In its capacity as Ireland's second-largest city, Cork (pop. 150,000) orchestrates most of the athletic, musical, and artistic activities in the Irish southwest. The river quays and pub-lined streets reveal architecture both grand and grimy, evidence of a history of ruin and reconstruction.

🚍 TRANSPORTATION

Airport: Cork Airport (☎431 3131), 5 mi. south of Cork on the Kinsale road. **Aer Lingus** (☎432 7155), **British Airways** (☎800 626 747), and **Ryanair** (☎(01) 609 7800) connect Cork to Dublin, Paris, and several English cities.

Trains: Kent Station, Lower Glanmire Rd. (☎450 6766; www.irishrail.ie), in the northeast part of town across the river from the city center. Open M-Sa 6:35am-8:30pm, Su 7:50am-8pm. Train connections to: **Dublin** (3hr.; M-Sa 7 per day, Su 5 per day; €44.40); **Killarney** (2hr.; M-Sa 7 per day, Su 4 per day; €17.70); **Limerick** (1½hr.; M-Sa 7 per day, Su 4 per day; €17.70).

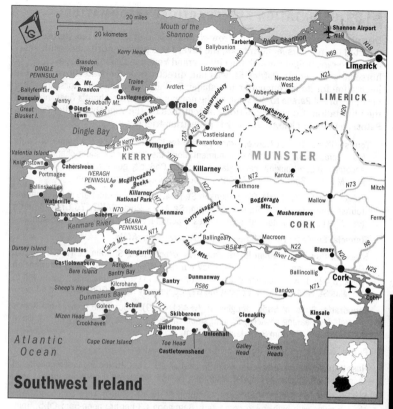

Southwest Ireland

Buses: Parnell Pl. (☎ 450 8188), 2 blocks east of Patrick's Bridge on Merchant's Quay. Inquiries desk open daily 9am-6pm. **Bus Éireann** goes to: **Dublin** (4½hr.; M-Sa 6 per day, Su 5 per day; €19); **Galway** (4hr.; M-Sa 7 per day, Su 4 per day; €15.80); **Killarney** (2hr.; M-Sa 13 per day, Su 10 per day; €11.80); **Limerick** (2hr., 14 per day, €12.10); **Rosslare Harbour** (4hr., 3 per day, €17.10); **Sligo** (7hr., 5 per day, €21.10); **Waterford** (2¼hr., M-Sa 13 per day, €13.30). **City buses** run M-Sa every 10-30min. 7:30am-11:15pm, with reduced service Su 10am-11:15pm. Fares from €0.95.

Ferries: Ringaskiddy Terminal (☎ 427 5061), 8 mi. south of the city. Call **Brittany Ferries** (☎ 437 8401) or **Swansea-Cork Ferries** (☎ 427 1166).

Bike Rental: The Bike Shop, 68 Shandon St. (☎ 430 4144). Rents bikes for €9 per day, €40 per week. The Raleigh Rent-a-Bike program at **Cycle Scene,** 396 Blarney St. (☎ 430 1183), allows you to return their bikes at the other Raleigh locations across Ireland. €15 per day, €80 per week. €100 or credit card deposit.

Hitching: Hitchhikers headed for West Cork and Co. Kerry walk down Western Rd. past the An Óige hostel and the dog track to the Crow's Nest Pub, or they take bus #8. Those hoping to thumb a ride to Dublin or Waterford may want to stand on the hill next to the train station on the Lower Glanmire Rd. *Let's Go* does not recommend hitchhiking.

✦ 🛈 ORIENTATION AND PRACTICAL INFORMATION

Downtown Cork is the tip of an arrow-shaped island in the **River Lee.** Before being diverted to create its modern moat, the River Lee's present north and south channels once ran straight through the city in grand Venetian fashion. The pavement of horseshoe-shaped **St. Patrick St.** was laid directly over the waterflow, thus the inspiration for its unconventional U-shape. St. Patrick St. ends its horseshoe and becomes **Grand Parade** to the west; to the north it crosses **Merchant's Quay,** home of the bus station. Downtown action concentrates on the vaguely parallel **Paul, St. Patrick,** and **Oliver Plunkett St.** Cork is pedestrian-friendly.

Tourist Office: Tourist House, Grand Parade (☎427 3251), near the corner of South Mall, across from the National Monument along the River Lee's south channel. Offers accommodation booking, car rental, and a free Cork city guide and map. Open June-Aug. M-F 9am-6pm, Sa 9am-5:30pm; Sept.-May M-Sa 9:15am-5:30pm.

Budget Travel Office: usit, Oliver Plunkett St. (☎427 0900), around the corner from the tourist office. Open M-F 9:30am-5:30pm, Sa 10am-2pm. **SAYIT,** 76 Grand Parade (☎427 9188), is similar with shorter lines. Open M-F 9am-5:30pm, Sa 10am-4pm.

Financial Services: Lots of **banks,** and most have 24hr. **ATMs.**

Bisexual, Gay, and Lesbian Information: The Other Place, S. Main St. (☎427 8470). Open Tu-Sa 10am-5:30pm. Hosts a gay bar (see **Nightlife,** below). **Gay Information Cork** (☎427 1087). Helpline W and F 7-9pm. **Lesbians Inc. (L.Inc.)** recently moved to Douglas St. (☎480 8600). Consult the *Gay Community News* (GCN) for event info.

Laundrette: Duds 'n' Suds, Douglas St. (☎431 4799), around the corner from Kelly's Hostel. Dry-cleaning services, TV, and small snack bar. Wash €2.50, dry €3.50. Open M-F 8am-9pm, Sa 8am-8pm; last wash 7pm.

Police *(Garda):* ☎452 2000.

Hospital: Mercy Hospital, Grenville Pl. (☎427 1971). €25 fee for emergency room access. **Cork Regional Hospital,** Wilton St. (☎454 6400), on the #8 bus route.

Internet Access: 🖳**Web Workhouse,** Winthrop St. (☎434 3090). Lofty converted warehouse hums with high-speed computers. 8am-noon €3 per hr.; noon-5pm €4-5; 5pm-3am €2.50; Su €2.50 per hr. all day. Open M-Th and Su 8am-3am, F and Sa 24hr. **Cork City Library** (☎427 7110). €1.30 per 30min. Open Tu-Sa 10am-1pm and 2-5pm.

Post Office: Oliver Plunkett St. (☎427 2000). Open M-Sa 9am-5:30pm.

🏠 ACCOMMODATIONS

Most of Cork's hostels are excellent, and popular, so call ahead. A few terrific B&Bs populate **Patrick's Hill;** the best ones congregate nearer **Glanmire Rd. Western Rd.,** leading out toward University College, is knee-deep in pricier B&Bs.

🖳 **Sheila's Budget Accommodation Centre (IHH),** 4 Belgrave Pl. (☎450 5562). Centrally located, with a big kitchen and summertime BBQs in a secluded backyard. All rooms ensuite and non-smoking. 24hr. reception desk doubles as a general store; breakfast €3.20. Sauna €2. Bike rental €12. Internet access €1 per 15min. Check-out 10:30am. Dorms €15-16; singles €30; doubles €40-50. ❷

🖳 **Clare D'Arcy B&B,** 7 Sidney Place, Wellington Rd. (☎450 4658; www.darcysguest-house.com). The most authentically luxurious guesthouse in Cork. Elegant Parisian-style interior: chandeliers, wide staircase, original paned glass windows. Freshly squeezed OJ and smoked salmon for breakfast. Doubles €80; shared rooms €35-45 per person. ❹

Kinlay House (IHH), (☎450 8966; www.kinlayhouse.ie), down the alley to the right of Shandon Church. The bright colors and warm atmosphere offset its large, motel-like layout. Renovations have brought wonderful family-sized rooms to the house. Continental breakfast included. Internet access €1 per 15min. Laundry €7. Free parking. 10- to 14-bed dorms €14. Singles €25-30; doubles €40-44. Family-sized rooms €70. ❷

Roman House, 3 St. John's Terr., Upper John St. (☎450 3606), in a muted red building with a black front door, across from Kinlay House. Colorfully decorated in decadence, Roman House is Cork's only B&B catering specifically to gay and lesbian travelers (though any and all are welcome). Bath, TV, oversized armchairs, and coffee-making facilities in every room. Vegetarian breakfast option. Singles €40; doubles €60. ❷

Cork International Hostel (An Óige/HI), 1-2 Redclyffe, Western Rd. (☎454 3289), a 15min. walk from the Grand Parade. Bus #8 stops across the street. Immaculate and spacious rooms with high ceilings in a stately brick Victorian townhouse. All rooms with bath. Continental breakfast €2.50. Internet €1 per 10min. Check-in 8am-midnight. 10-bed dorms €14; 4- to 6-bed €15. Doubles €41. Discounts for under 18. ❷

🍴 FOOD

The **English Market,** accessible from Grand Parade, Patrick St., and Oliver Plunkett St., sells a wide variety of meats, fish, cheeses, and fruits fresh from the farms and fisheries of West Cork. The **Tesco** on Paul St. is the biggest grocery store in town. (☎427 0791. Open M-W and Sa 8:30am-8pm, Th-F 8:30am-10pm.)

▨ Quay Co-op, 24 Sullivan's Quay (☎431 7660). Large townhouse-style windows enliven the vibrant colors and youthful intellectual buzz. A veg(etari)an's delight, and no chore for carnivores either. Excellent soups and desserts. Apricot and yogurt flan €2.50. Specials €6.50. Open M-Sa 9am-9pm. Store open M-Sa 9am-6:15pm. ❷

▨ Tribes, Tuckey St. (☎427 6070). Crunchy low-light college java shop with south islander theme and the only late-night coffee shop serving full cafe food until the wee hours. Global spectrum of coffee blends (€1.65). Hawaiian bagel sandwich €5.40; Bronx burger €5.40. Open M-W noon-1am, Th-Sa noon-4am. ❶

Ivory Tower, Princes St. (☎427 7939), upstairs in the old exchange building. Escapes pretension by a hair's breadth; dark wood paneling, gold tapestry cushions, and large bay windows. Start with the gnocchi with wild mushrooms and finish with the blood-orange sorbet. 5-course dinner €50. A la carte €23-30. Dinner only Tu-Su 6-10pm. ❺

THE LOCAL STORY

THE PERFECT PINT

Bartender Glenn, of a local pub, helps Let's Go resolve the most elusive question of all...

LG: Tell us the most important thing about pouring a pint.

BG: The most important thing is to have the keg as close to the tap as possible. The closer, the better.

LG: And why's that?

BG: Well, you don't want the Guinness sitting in a long tube while you wait to pour the next pint. You want to pull it straight out of the keg, without any muck getting in between.

LG: Does stopping to let the Guinness settle make a big difference?

BG: Well, you can top it straight off if you want, but you might get too big a head with that. You don't want too small or big a head, so if you stop ¾ of the way, you can adjust the pint until the head is perfect. A true Guinness lover will taste the difference.

LG: Because of the head?

BG: No, because of the gas. If you pull the Guinness straight from the tap and get a big head, it means you've gotten too much gas. It kills the taste. That's why you have to tilt the glass.

LG: Anything else to look for?

BG: Well what you don't want is a window-clean glass; you don't want a glass that you can see through when you're done. Good Guinness leaves a healthy film on the glass. If it doesn't, you didn't get a good Guinness.

LG: Well, Glenn, you sure make pouring pints sound like an art form.

BG: Oh aye, but only with Guinness—everything else you just chuck into a glass and hand out.

REPUBLIC OF IRELAND

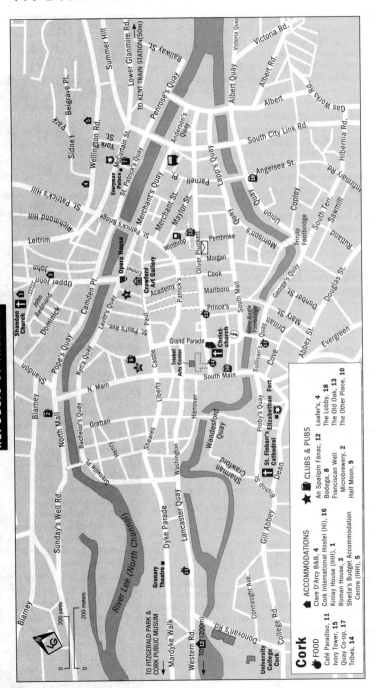

Cork

FOOD
Café Paradiso, **11**
Ivory Tower, **15**
Quay Co-op, **17**
Tribes, **14**

ACCOMMODATIONS
Clare D'Arcy B&B, **4**
Cork International Hostel (HI), **16**
Kinlay House (IHH), **1**
Roman House, **3**
Sheila's Budget Accommodation
Centre (IHH), **5**

CLUBS & PUBS
An Spailpín Fánac, **12**
Bodega, **8**
Franciscan Well
Microbrewery, **2**
Half Moon, **9**
Loafer's, **4**
The Lobby, **18**
The Old Oak, **13**
The Other Place, **10**

TO FITZGERALD PARK &
CORK PUBLIC MUSEUM

TO 12 (200m)

University
College
Cork

Café Paradiso, 16 Lancaster Quay (☎ 427 7939). Award-winning vegetarian meals bordering on gourmet. Cool-colored Mediterranean feel, and popular with the laid-back jet-setting crew. Lunch €9; dinner €9-18. Open Tu-Sa 12:30-3pm and 6:30-10:30pm. ❸

🏠 🍺 PUBS AND CLUBS

Cork's nightlife has the variety of music and atmosphere you'd expect to find in the Republic's second-largest city. To keep on top of the club scene, check out *List Cork*, a free biweekly schedule of music available at local stores.

The Lobby, 1 Union Quay (☎ 431 9307). Arguably the most famous venue in Cork; has given some of Ireland's biggest folk acts their first shining moments. 2 floors overlook the river. Live music nightly, from trad to acid jazz. Come early to the parlor-sized upstairs room for more popular acts. Occasional cover €2.50-6.35.

An Spailpín Fánac (on spal-PEEN FAW-nuhk), 28 South Main St. (☎ 427 7949), across from the Beamish Brewery. One of Cork's more popular pubs as well as one of its oldest (est. 1779). Intermingled crowd of visitors and locals come for the live trad offered most nights; storytelling last Tu of every month.

Half Moon, Academy Ln., on the left side of the opera house. Cork's most popular dance club. Wide open spaces and a young, hip crowd (minus the teeny-boppers). 18+. Tickets must be purchased in advance from the box office across the street. Cover €9.

Bodega, 46-49 Cornmarket St. (☎ 427 2878), off the northern end of Grand Parade and the western end of Paul St. Stone front, wood floors, and a stratospheric hall ceiling. An artsy-fartsy cafe by day, transforms at night into an upscale, classy club. Great wine selection and an intimate balcony. Dress sharp.

The Old Oak, Oliver Plunkett St. (☎ 427 6165), just across from the grand old General Post Office. Year after year it wins a "Best Traditional Pubs in Ireland" award, and with good reason. Packed and noisy; each section has its own particular vibe. Bar food served M-F noon-3pm. Bar closes F-Sa 1:45am.

Franciscan Well Microbrewery, 14b North Mall (☎ 421 0130), along the North Quay, just east of Sunday's Well Rd. Fantastic local brews; great Belgian selection. The home-brewed Blarney Blonde and Rebel Red come highly recommended. Backyard beer garden in summer. Packed venue for Oct. Belgian Beer Festival.

Loafer's, 26 Douglas St. (☎ 431 1612). This favorite gay and lesbian pub fills up nightly with all age groups. Live bands, lively conversation, the good life.

The Other Place (☎ 427 8470), in a lane off South Main St. Gay and lesbian disco rocks F and Sa 11:30pm-2am. Dance floor and a bar/cafe upstairs (opens earlier). Highly appreciated by Cork's gay population. Cover €5, free before 10pm.

👁 SIGHTS

All of Cork's sights can be reached on foot. For guidance, pick up *The Cork Area City Guide* at the tourist office (€1.90).

UNIVERSITY COLLEGE CORK (UCC). Built in 1845, UCC's campus is a collection of brooding Gothic buildings, manicured lawns, and sculpture-studded grounds, all of which make for a fine afternoon walk or a picnic along the River Lee. One of the newer buildings, **Boole Library,** celebrates number-wizard George Boole, mastermind of Boolean logic and model for Sherlock Holmes's arch-nemesis, Professor James Moriarty. *(Main gate on Western Rd. ☎ 490 3000.)*

■ **FITZGERALD PARK.** Rose gardens, playgrounds, and a permanent parking spot for the ice cream man are all found within the park. Also present are the befuddlingly esoteric exhibitions of the **Cork Public Museum,** which feature such varied goodies as 18th-century toothbrushes and the clothes of James Dwyer, Sheriff of Cork. *(From the front gate of UCC, follow the signposted walkway across the street. ☎ 427 0679. Museum open M-F 11am-1pm and 2:15-5pm, Su 3-5pm. M-Sa free; Su €1.50.)*

CORK CITY GAOL. If your time in town is tight, go directly to jail (do not pass Go, do not collect $200). This museum is a reconstruction of the city gaol as it was in the 1800s. Descriptions of Cork's social history accompany tidbits about miserable punishments, such as the "human treadmill" that was used to grind grain. *(Sunday's Well Rd. From Fitzgerald Park, cross the white footbridge at the western end of the park and turn right onto Sunday's Well Rd. ☎ 430 5022. Open Mar.-Oct. daily 9:30am-6pm; Nov.-Feb. 10am-5pm. Last admission 1hr. before closing. €5, concessions €4, families €14; includes audio tour.)*

ST. ANNE'S CHURCH. Commonly called **Shandon Church,** St. Anne's sandstone-and-limestone-striped steeple inspired the red and white "rebel" flag still flying throughout the county. Notoriously out of sync, the clocks gracing each side of the tower have been held responsible for many an Irishman's tardy arrival at work, and have earned the church its nickname, "the four-faced liar." *(Walk up Shandon St., take a right on unmarked Church St., and continue straight. ☎ 450 5906. Open June-Sept. M-Sa 9:30am-5:30pm. €4, concessions €3.50, families €12. Group rates available.)*

🎵 ENTERTAINMENT

Everyman Palace, McCurtain St., hosts the big-name musicals, plays, operas, and concerts. (☎ 450 1673. Box office open M-F 9am-6pm, Sa 10am-5:30pm, until 8pm on show nights. Tickets €10-23.) **The Opera House,** Emmet Pl., next to the river, presents an extensive program of dance and performance art. (☎ 427 0022. Open M-Sa 9am-5:30pm.) From June through September, **hurling** and **Gaelic football** take place every Sunday afternoon at 3pm. For additional details contact the Gaelic Athletic Association (☎ 439 5368; www.gaa.ie) or consult *The Cork Examiner;* buy tickets to games at the GAA stadium, **Pairc Uí Chaoimh** (park EE KWEEV). The massive **Mardyke Arena** holds three training gyms, a lap pool, basketball courts, and climbing walls. (☎ 490 4751. Day passes €10. Call ahead.) The **Cork Midsummer Festival** (☎ 427 0022) promises to enchant from mid-June through the beginning of July. Big-name musicians play for free in local pubs and hotels during the three-day **Guinness Cork Jazz Festival** (☎ 427 8979) in October.

🔳 DAYTRIP FROM CORK

BLARNEY CASTLE. In the middle of the idyllic countryside stands Ireland's tourism epicenter, **Blarney Castle,** resting place of the celebrated Blarney Stone. You might just find yourself bending over backwards to kiss that hunk o' rock in hopes of acquiring the legendary eloquence bestowed on the smoocher. *(Bus Éireann runs from Cork to Blarney (M-Sa 15-16 per day, Su 10 per day; €4.10 return). Arrive by 9:30am or wait for up to 3hr. Castle info ☎ 438 5252. Open May-Aug. M-Sa 9am-7pm, Su 9:30am-5:30pm; Sept. M-Sa 9am-6:30pm, Su 9:30am-sundown; Oct.-Apr. M-Sa 9am-6pm or sundown, Su 9:30am-5pm or sundown. Last admission 30min. before closing. €4.50, concessions €3, children €1.50.)*

WEST FROM CORK

From Cork city, you have two choices for your westward rambles—either an inland or coastal route. A coastal **bus** runs to **Skibbereen**, stopping in **Bandon** and **Clonakilty** (M-Sa 8 per day, Su 3 per day). An inland bus travels to **Bantry**, via Bandon and Dunmanway (M-Sa 6 per day, Su 4 per day). Located in relative isolation at the intersection of R586, R587, and R599, **Dunmanway** (Dún Mánmhaí) is a hidden treasure, one of the few Irish towns that truly prizes tradition over tourism. Of course, it doesn't hurt to have a fabulous hostel like the ⊠**Shiplake Mountain Hostel (IHH) ❶**, located in the hills 3 mi. from town. Shiplake's luckiest guests stay in three colorful gypsy caravans, equipped with heat, electricity, and breathtaking views. (☎(023) 45750; www.shiplakemountainhostel.com. Bike rental €9 per day. Breakfast €2.50-5; bag lunch €5; vegetarian entrees €7-10. Dorms €11; caravans €12.50-13.50 per person. **Camping** €6 per person.) Over the mountains to the northwest, quiet **Ballingeary** (Béal Áthán Ghaorthaídh) is the failing heart of one of western Cork's declining *gaeltachts*.

Every summer the population of upscale **Kinsale** (Cionn tSáile) temporarily quintuples with a flood of tourists. Visitors come to swim, fish, and eat at any of Kinsale's 12 famed and expensive restaurants. **Clonakilty** (Cloch na Coillte; "Clon"), home to Irish hero Michael Collins, lies between Bandon and Skibbereen on N71. The fishing village of **Union Hall** (Breantra) is home to the legendary ⊠**Maria's Schoolhouse Hostel (IHH) ❶** (☎(028) 33002; 3-course dinner with occasional musical accompaniment F-Sa €22; laundry €7; dorms €12; doubles €38-50) and the zany ⊠**Ceim Hill Museum**, 3 mi. outside town (☎(028) 36280; open daily 10am-7pm; €4). The biggest town in western Cork, **Skibbereen** (An Sciobairín; "Skib") is a convenient stop for travelers roaming the coastal wilds. The tiny fishing village of **Baltimore** (Baile Taigh Mór) has traded its pirates for tourists, who come to explore its aquatic offerings and stay in ⊠**Rolf's Hostel (IHH) ❶**, a 300-year-old complex of stone farmhouses just 10min. from the waterfront. (☎(028) 20289. Bike rental €12 per day. Laundry €5. Dorms €12-13; doubles €35; family rooms €47.) The coastal road continues past the sleepy town of **Schull**, and 15 mi. later, Ireland comes to an abrupt end at spectacular **Mizen Head**, whose cliffs rise 700 ft. above the waves. To get to the **Mizen Vision** museum and the nearby **lighthouse** you'll have to cross a suspension bridge only slightly less harrowing than the virtual shipwreck that waits inside. The small, windy viewing platform is the most southwesterly point in Ireland. Return to the newly opened **Visitor Centre**, to peruse exhibits or indulge in pricey items from the **cafe**. (☎(028) 35115. Open June-Sept. daily 10am-6pm; mid-Mar. to May and Oct. 10:30am-5pm; Nov. to mid-Mar. Sa-Su 11am-4pm. €4.50, students €3.50, under 12 €2.50, under 5 free.)

CAPE CLEAR ISLAND (OILEÁN CHLÉIRE) ☎028

The scenery of Cape Clear Island visible from the ferry landing is desolate and foreboding; the landscape of patchwork fields separated by low stone walls hasn't changed much since Spanish galleons stopped calling here hundreds of years ago. Along with windmills, lighthouses, a castle, and a bird observatory, Cape Clear has **Cléire Goats** (☎39126), some of the best-bred furry beasts in Ireland. For €1.50 you can test the owner's claim that his **goat's milk ice cream** is richer and more scrumptious than the generic bovine variety. Swallow a hefty dose of island lore in early September at Cape Clear's annual **International Storytelling Festival**, which features puppet workshops, music sessions, and a weekend's worth of memorable tales. (☎39157. €7 per event, €30 for all weekend.) Capt. Cierán O'Driscoll runs **whale- and dolphin-watching** excursions. (☎39172. €15 per person.)

Capt. Conchúr O'Driscoll (☎39135) runs **ferries** to and from **Baltimore** (2-6 per day; €11.50, children €5.50). For ferries direct to **Schull,** speak to Capt. Molloy. (☎28138. 45min. June 1 per day, July-Aug. 3 per day. €11.50 return.) Life here is leisurely and hours are approximate—for current opening hours and general island information head to the **information office** in the Pottery Shop, on the left just up from the pier. (☎39100. Open July-Aug. daily 11am-1pm and 3-6pm; June and Sept. 3-6pm.) There are **no banks or ATMs** on the island.

Cléire Lasmuigh (An Óige/HI) ❶, the Cape Clear Island Adventure Centre and Hostel, is a 10min. walk from the pier; follow the main road and keep left. The hostel is in a picturesque stone building with killer views of the harbor. (☎39198. Check-in strictly 3:30-8pm. Dorms €9-11.) Basic groceries are available at **An Siopa Beag** (☎39099), on the pier. The shop also has a small **coffee dock ❶** that peddles takeaway pizzas (June F-Sa 5-7pm, July-Aug. daily 6-8:30pm). Multi-generational **Ciarán Danny Mike's ❷** (☎39172) is Ireland's southernmost pub and restaurant. Ciarán (son), Danny (father), and Mike (grandfather) serve slurpalicious soups (€3) and tempting dinners (€8-15). Closer to the pier, **Cotter's Bar ❶** serves bar necessities: pub grub and Guinness. (☎39102. Open daily noon-9pm.) Without a resident *Garda* to regulate after-hours drinking, the Cape Clear fun often rolls on past 3am.

BANTRY (BEANNTRAI) ☎027

According to the big *Book of Invasions*, Ireland's first human inhabitants landed just 1 mi. from here. These days, the invasion racket has died down considerably, but Bantry still has plenty to plunder for the eager explorer. The town's main attraction is the incredibly elegant ▓**Bantry House and Gardens,** a Georgian manor with magnificently restored grounds dramatically overlooking the Bay. The long and shaded driveway to the house is a 10min. walk from town. If doomed missions and grandiose nobles don't pique your interest, you might take a cruise on one of the **sea trips** that drop you at **Whiddy Island,** where quiet beaches attract birds and their watchers. (☎51739. Departs July-Sept. daily at 2:30, 4, and 6pm; M, W, F also 9:30 and 11am. €7 return.) Bantry hosts the **West Cork Chamber Music Festival** during the last week of June and early July. Flex your fervor for seafood during the annual **Bantry Mussel Fair,** held the second weekend in May.

Buses stop outside Julie's Takeaway in Wolfe Tone Sq. Bus Éireann heads to **Cork** via Bandon (M-Sa 8 per day, Su 4 per day; €10) and to **Glengarriff** (2-3 per day, €3.25). From June to September, buses go twice a day to **Killarney** via Kenmare, to **Tralee,** and to **Skibbereen. Bike rental** is available from **The Bicycle Shop,** on Glengarriff Rd., Newtown, near the Independent Hostel. (☎52657. €12.15 per day, €50 per week. ID or credit card deposit. Open June-Aug. M-Sa 9:30am-6pm; Sept.-May M-Tu and Th-Sa 10am-5pm.) The **tourist office,** Wolfe Tone Sq., has maps and a **bureau de change.** (☎50229. Open July-Aug. daily 9am-6pm; Apr.-June and Sept.-Nov. M-Sa 9:30am-5:30pm.) **AIB,** Wolfe Tone Sq. (☎50008), has an **ATM,** as does the neighboring **Bank of Ireland** (51377; both open M 10am-5pm, Tu-F 10am-4pm). The **library,** at the top of Bridge St., provides **Internet access** to Co. Cork library cardholders; purchase a card for €2.50 at any participating branch. (☎50460. Open Tu-W and F-Sa 10am-1pm and 2:30-6pm, Th 10am-6pm.) The **post office** is at 2 William St. (☎50050. Open M-Sa 9am-5:30pm, Tu open 9:30am.)

Bantry Independent Hostel (IHH) ❶, on the former Bishop Lucey Pl. in Newtown, is the most comfortable and relaxed of Bantry's hostels. If you're coming in by bus on Glengarriff Rd., save yourself the 8min. walk and ask the driver to let you off at O'Mahoney's Quickpick Food Store. From there, walk up the hill across the road and take a right around the bend. (☎51050. Laundry €5. Open mid-Mar. to Oct. 6-bed dorms €10; doubles €24.) For delicious toasted sandwiches (€3-4) and a great choice of sweet treats, turn off New St. onto Main St. and follow your nose to

Floury Hands Cafe and Bakery ❶. (☎52590. Open M-Sa 8am-5:30pm.) **Anchor Bar,** New St. (☎50012), is usually the liveliest of Bantry's pubs, luring the locals with a pub disco atmosphere on weekends and live music on summer Thursdays.

Bantry is a good place to access **Sheep's Head** (Muintir Bhaire), an alternative for anyone eager to evade the company of camera-toters and the exhaust of tour buses. Walkers and cyclists take advantage of the peaceful roads and the well-plotted **Sheep's Head Way** (info available at the Bantry tourist office).

BEARA PENINSULA

Beara Peninsula's rugged and desolate landscape offers a haunting canvas for the lonely explorer. Fortunately, the mobs circling the Ring of Kerry usually skip the Beara altogether, but in doing so they miss out on some of the best views of the Iveragh from across the bay. The spectacular **Caha** and **Slieve Miskish Mountains** march down the center of the peninsula, separating the rocky south from the lush northern shore. The dearth of cars west of the quiet gateway **Glengarriff** makes **cycling** the 125 mi. of **Beara Way** a joy. Those who want to start fresh plant themselves at ■**Murphy's Village Hostel ❶,** located in the middle of Glengarriff on Main St., and don't leave until they've sampled Mrs. Murphy's banana chocolate-chip muffins. (☎63555. Internet €6.50 per hr. Laundry €6.50. Dorms €11; doubles €29.) The **Healy Pass,** running between **Adrigole** in the south and **Lauragh** in the north, offers stunning views of counties Cork and Kerry as it winds through some of the highest peaks in Ireland. The curvaceous pass is best explored by car; to enjoy the full effect of the breathtaking views you'll want to travel from south to north.

One of Ireland's largest fishing ports, the commercial hub of **Castletownbere** (Baile Chaisleain Bhearra) on the southern edge of the peninsula attracts rigs from as far away as Spain. Cyclists often speed through en route to villages farther west and north, and the town occasionally fills with nirvana-seekers heading to the nearby Buddhist center. Castletownbere's seat at the foot of hefty **Hungry Hill** (2245 ft.) makes it a fine launch pad for daytrips up the mountain. Beara's best scenery is on **Dursey Island,** reached by Ireland's only cable car. The 10min. aerial trip out is the most thrilling aspect of the island, whose enchanting tranquility and sweeping panoramas may inspire poetic musings but are unlikely to set your heart racing. The cable cars depart 5 mi. out from **Allihies,** off the Castletownbere road. (Runs M-Sa 9-10:30am, 2:30-4:30pm, and 7-7:30pm; Su hours vary. Return €4, children €1.) Castletownbere also sends ferries to **Bere Island,** via Murphy's Ferry Service (☎(027) 750 14l; 30min.; June-Aug. 8 per day; Sept.-May 4-5 per day; return €6) and Bere Island Ferry (☎(027) 75009; June 21-Sept. M-Sa 7 per day, Su 5 per day; return €4.) The island used to be a British naval base—military remnants are scattered across it—and the Irish Army now uses it for training. The spectacular ferry ride to the tiny fishing community on the island is alone worth the journey.

Bus Éireann offers year-round service from Castletownbere to **Cork** (3hr., 1-2 per day, €17.80) and a summer route to **Killarney** via Kenmare (M-Sa 2 per day, €11.20). **Rent bikes** at SuperValu. (☎70020. €10 per day. Open M-Sa 8am-9pm, Su 9am-9pm.) The molehill-sized Castletownbere **tourist office** is behind O'Donoghue's by the harbor (☎(027) 70054; open June-Sept. M-F 10am-5pm), and the **AIB** has the peninsula's **only ATM** (☎70015; open M 10am-5pm, Tu-F 10am-4pm). Six miles west on the Allihies road is ■**Garranes Farmhouse Hostel (IHH) ❶.** The sea views from this clifftop cottage are worth the trek, or the €9 cab, from Castletownbere. Sometimes the attached **Dzogchen Buddhist Centre** (☎73032) absorbs all the rooms, so phone ahead. (☎73147. Laundry €10. Dorms €10; singles €20; doubles €25-28.) Seafood lovers should head to **The Lobster Bar ❸,** the Square, for its homemade bread, potato salad, and seafood platters (€10-12) practically large enough for two. (☎70031. Main menu served June-Aug. only noon-9pm.)

RING OF KERRY

The term "Ring of Kerry" is generally used to describe the entire **Iveragh Peninsula**, but it more correctly refers to a particular set of roads: N71 from Kenmare to Killarney, R562 from Killarney to Killorglin, and the long loop of N70 west and back to Kenmare. If you don't fancy prepackaged private bus tours running out of Killarney, **Bus Éireann** offers a regular summer circuit through all the major towns on the Ring (☎ (064) 30011; mid-June to Aug., 2 per day). Buses travel around the Ring counterclockwise. Another bus runs year-round in the mornings, traveling clockwise from Waterville back to Killarney (1 per day). **Bikers** may find themselves jammed between coach and cliff on the narrow, bumpy roads, though traffic can often be avoided by doing the Ring clockwise. A new bike route, which avoids the main roads and affords better views, is signposted. Drivers must choose between lurching behind large tour buses and meeting them face-to-face on narrow roads.

KILLARNEY (CILL AIRNE)   ☎064

Only a short walk away from some of Ireland's most extraordinary scenery, Killarney manages to celebrate its tourist-based economy without offending those leprechaun-loathing travelers out there.

TRANSPORTATION. Kerry Airport (☎976 4644) is in **Farranfore**, halfway to Tralee on the N22. **Ryanair** (☎(01) 609 7800) flies to London Stansted (2 per day); **Aer Arann Express** (☎(1890) 462 726) goes to Dublin (4 per day). **Trains** come into **Killarney Station** (☎31067, recorded info (1890) 200 493, inquiries (1850) 366 222), off East Avenue Rd. near the intersection with Park Rd. Four trains per day run to: **Cork** (2hr., €17.80); **Dublin** (3½hr., €45); **Limerick** (3hr., €19.70). The **bus station** is on Park Rd. (☎30011). **Buses** go to: **Cork** (2hr., 10-14 per day, €12); **Dingle** (2hr.; M-Sa 7 per day, Su 4 per day; €11.60); **Dublin** (6hr., 5-6 per day, €19); **Galway** via Tarbert Ferry (6-7 per day, €17.10). Many buses leave from here on the **Ring of Kerry Circuit**. There is also a summer **Dingle/Slea Head** tour (June to mid-Sept. M-Sa 2 per day, €12.40). You'll find several places to **rent bikes** in Killarney, including **O'Sullivans**, Bishop's Ln., next to Neptune's Hostel. (☎31282. Free panniers, locks, and park maps. €12 per day, €70 per week. Open daily 8:30am-6:30pm.)

ORIENTATION AND PRACTICAL INFORMATION. Most of Killarney is packed into three crowded streets. **Main St.**, in the center of town, begins at the **Town Hall**, then becomes **High St. New St.** and **Plunkett St.** head in opposite directions from Main St. **East Avenue Rd.** connects the train station back to town hall, meeting the **Muckross road**, which leads to Muckross Estate and Kenmare. The **tourist office** on Beech St. is deservedly popular. (☎31633. Open July-Aug. M-Sa 9am-8pm, Su 10am-1pm and 2:15-6pm; June and Sept. M-Sa 9am-6pm, Su 10am-1pm and 2:15-6pm; Oct.-May M-Sa 9:15am-1pm and 2:15-5:30pm.) Other services include: **TSB**, next to Town Hall; **Internet access** at **Cafe Internet**, 18 New St. (☎36741; open June-Aug. M-Sa 9:30am-11pm, Su 11am-11:30pm; Sept.-May M-Sa 9:30am-10pm, Su 10am-10pm); and the **post office** on New St. (☎31051; open M and W-Sa 9am-5:30pm, Tu 9:30am-5:30pm).

ACCOMMODATIONS AND CAMPING. With every other house a B&B, it's easy enough to find cushy digs in Killarney. The best hostel in town is the immense and immaculate ■**Neptune's (IHH) ❶**. (☎35255. Tours: Dingle €17, Ring of Kerry €16.50, Gap of Dunloe €24. Internet access €2 per 30min. Wheelchair-accessible. Breakfast €2.50. Free luggage storage; €10 locker deposit.

Laundry €7. Curfew 3am. 8-bed dorms €11; 6-bed €11.50; 3- to 4-bed €12. Doubles €34. 10% ISIC discount.) **The Railway Hostel (IHH) ❶**, Park Rd., the first right toward town from the bus station, is a modern building with sunny, cutely named rooms. (☎35299. Internet access €1 per 8min. Curfew 3am. Dorms €11.50; singles €21; doubles €34.) **The Súgán (IHH) ❶**, Lewis Rd., is only 2min. from the bus or train station. Ship-like bunk rooms blur the distinction between intimacy and claustrophobia; exuberant staff and impromptu story-telling and music in the common room provide a happy escape. (☎33104. 4- to 8-bed dorms €12; singles €14.)

Outside town, you'll find ▨**Peacock Farms Hostel (IHH) ❶**, overlooking Lough Guitane and surrounded by wooded slopes. Take the Muckross road out of town, turn left just before the Muckross post office, then go 2 mi. and follow the signs up a steep hill; or call for a ride from the bus station. (☎33557. Free daily buses to town at 9am and 6:30pm. Wheelchair-accessible. Organic breakfast €3.50. Open Apr.-Oct. Dorms €10-12; doubles €28.) **Camping** is not allowed in the national park, but there are excellent campgrounds nearby. **Fleming's White Bridge Caravan and Camping Park ❶**, on the Ballycasheen road, is an award-sitting site offering laundry, a TV room, and modern showers. (☎31590. €4.50-5.50 per person.)

▢▨ **FOOD AND PUBS.** Food in Killarney is affordable at lunchtime, but prices skyrocket when the sun goes down. ▨**The Stonechat ❸** specializes in veggie meals, though chicken and fish dishes are also available. (☎34295. Lunch €5.35-7.60, dinner €10.20-13. Open M-Sa 11am-5pm and 6-10pm.) **Cyrano's ❷**, on the lower level of Innisfallen Centre, knows variety. Sate that silver tongue with dessert and a cappuccino. (☎35853. Lunch specials €7.40. Open M-Sa 9:30am-6pm.) **Little Sal's ❷**, New St., offers a variety of cheap but tasty meals, from burgers to lasagna. (☎36344. Sandwiches €3.25-4.95; meals from €7.95.)

Trad is a staple in Killarney's pubs on summer nights, but herds of tourists looking for the next great jig have made for a crowded, noisy drinking experience. Several nightclubs simmer from 10:30pm until 2:30 or 3am; most charge €6-8 cover but often offer discounts before 11pm. Patrons both foreign and domestic mingle in the upbeat, comfortable atmosphere of ▨**O'Connor's Traditional Pub**, 7 High St. (☎31115. Trad M and W-Th 9:30-11:30pm.) ▨**The Grand**, High St., is an extremely popular club. (☎31159. Arrive before 11pm and dodge the €5-8 cover.)

KILLARNEY NATIONAL PARK

Glaciers sliced up the Killarney region, scooping out a series of lakes and glens and scattering silk-smooth rocks and precarious boulders across the terrain before continuing their march toward the next defenseless landscape. As a result, Killarney National Park makes for preternaturally dazzling hiking, biking, and climbing. The park, stretched across 37 sq. mi. of prime Kerry real estate between Killarney to the northeast and Kenmare to the southwest, incorporates a string of forested mountains and the famous **Lakes of Killarney.** An indigenous but elusive herd of 850 red deer is reported to be at large in the glens that surround the lakes. The park's size demands a map; as luck would have it, maps and other printed materials are available at the Killarney tourist office or the **National Park Information Centre,** behind Muckross House. (☎31440. Open July-Sept. daily 9am-7pm.) The park's most popular destinations are **Ross Castle** and **Lough Leane, Muckross House** on **Middle Lake,** and the **Gap of Dunloe** just west of the park area and bordered in the southwest by **Macgillycuddy's Reeks,** Ireland's highest mountain range. Killarney National Park is also a perfect starting point for those rugged few who plan to walk the spectacular 134 mi. **Kerry Way.**

THE KERRY WAY

If you'd rather avoid the tour bus superhighway that is the Ring of Kerry road, you need not write off the Iveragh entirely; just a step from the N70, solitude and superior scenery reward walkers along the **Kerry Way.** This well-planned route traverses a wide variety of terrain, from rugged inland expanses to soaring coastal cliffs. Described as an "inner" ring of Kerry, the Way brings walkers above the road, to higher ground and better views. Its 135 mi. route follows a smorgasbord of paths—from pastures to old "butter roads" to ancient thoroughfares between early Christian settlements—and crosses the main road just often enough to make daytrips convenient from almost anywhere on the Ring. Look for the wooden posts marked with a yellow walking man and you won't be far off. Those who like their landscapes stark and a little rough around the edges will enjoy the dramatic stretch from **Kenmare** through **Killarney** and northwest to **Glenbeigh.** An especially inspiring stretch of the Way runs between **Waterville** and **Caherdaniel,** filled with views known to elicit a tear or two from even the gruffest pint-puller.

KILLORGLIN TO VALENTIA ISLAND   ☎066

Killorglin (Cill Orglan) lounges on the banks of the River Larne, 13 mi. west of Killarney and in the shadow of Iveragh's mountainous spine. Tourists tend to pass through on their merry way west to the showier scenery, but what the town lacks in sights it more than makes up for with its annual festival dedicated to he-goats—the ancient **Puck Fair** held in mid-August celebrates the crowning of a particularly virile specimen as King Puck. Be aware that the town's hostel and B&Bs often book up as early as a year in advance of the revelry. The bright and bountiful **Laune Valley Farm Hostel (IHH) ❶,** 1¼ mi. from town off the Tralee road, beds guests alongside its more permanent population of cows, chickens, dogs, and ducks. (☎976 1488. Wheelchair-accessible. Dorms €12-14; doubles €31-35.60. **Camping** €5 per person.) Tent up at **West's Caravan and Camping Park ❶,** 1 mi. east of town on the Killarney road in the shadow of **Carrantoohill,** Ireland's tallest peak. (☎976 1240. Fishing, table tennis, and tennis courts. Laundry €4. Open Easter to mid-Oct. 1-person tent €4.50; car, tent, and 2 adults €13.50. Showers €2.)

Although best known as the birthplace of patriot Daniel O'Connell, **Cahersiveen** (Cathair Saidbhin; CARS-veen) serves as a useful base for exploring nearby archaeological sites and for short trips to Valentia Island and the Skelligs. The **Sive Hostel (IHH) ❶,** 15 East End, Main St., has a welcoming and well-informed staff, comfortable beds, and a third-floor balcony. (☎ 947 2717. Sheets €0.65. Laundry €5.10. Dorms €10.50; doubles €25-32. **Camping** €5 per person.) The freshest seafood available can be found at ▧**QC's Chargrill Bar & Restaurant ❹**, Main St. (☎ 947 2244. Entrees €15-22. Food served 12:30-3pm and 6-9:30pm.)

A welcome escape for travelers sick of dodging tour buses and those that ride them, **Valentia Island's** (Dairbhre) removed location offers stunning views of the mountains on the mainland. A comically short **car ferry** departs every 8min. from **Reenard Point,** 3 mi. west of Cahersiveen, and drops passengers at **Knightstown,** the island's population center. (☎ 947 6141. May-Oct. M-Sa 8:15am-10pm, Su 9am-10pm; cars €7 return, pedestrians €2, cyclists €3.) The bridge connecting Valentia to the mainland starts at **Portmagee,** 10 mi. west of Caher-siveen. Valentia has a surprising variety of budget accommodations in and around Knightstown, including the lovely ▧**Coombe Bank House ❷**. (☎ 947 6111; call ahead. Continental breakfast €4. Free laundry. Dorms €16. B&B €25 per person, without breakfast €20.)

WATERVILLE TO CAHERDANIEL ☎ 066

Wedged between the quiet Lough Cussane and crashing Atlantic waves, **Water-ville's** (An Coireán) human traffic comes from the tour bus captives released for a seaside lunch before rumbling on to Sneem for sweater shopping. The meditative traveler is left to amble along the shore, which was once treasured by Charlie Chaplin for the liberating anonymity it granted him. **B&Bs** line the length of Main St. (prices run €25-32), but the only hostel in Waterville is **Peter's Place ❶**, on the southern end of town facing the water. Cheap rates and a candlelit sitting room make up for stiff mattresses and a small bathroom. (☎ 947 4608. Skellig trips €35. Dorms €10; doubles €12.50. **Camping** €5.)

About 8 mi. off the shore of the Iveragh Peninsula, the stunning **Skellig Rocks** rise abruptly from the sea. While the multitudes rush around the Ring of Kerry, a detour to the Skelligs rewards with an encounter unforgettable for bird-lovers and the ornithologically indifferent alike. As **Little Skellig** comes into view, the jagged rock pinnacles appear snow-capped; increased proximity reveals that they're actu-ally covered with 24,000 pairs of crooning gannets—the largest community in Europe. Boats dock at the larger **Skellig Michael.** Climb the vertigo-inducing 630 stone steps, past many more gannets and puffins, to reach an ancient **monastic set-tlement.** There is no toilet or shelter on the rock, and the trip is not recommended for young children, the elderly, or those who suffer from serious medical condi-tions. The fantastic and sometimes soggy **ferry voyage** takes about 1hr. (Apr.-Oct., usually departing 10am with 2hr. ashore, depending on conditions, point of depar-ture, and boat; €32-35). Joe Roddy and Sons (☎ 947 4268 or (087) 284 4460) and Sean Feehan (☎ 947 9182) depart from **Ballinskelligs;** Michael O'Sullivan (☎ 947 4255) and Mr. Casey (☎ 947 2437 or (087) 239 5470) leave from **Portmagee.** Seanie Murphy picks up from **Reenard** and **Portmagee** (☎ 947 6214 or (087) 236 2344). Phone ahead to confirm and reserve spaces.

There's little to attract the Ring's droves of travel coaches to **Caherdaniel.** However, the hamlet (that is, two pubs, a grocer, a restaurant, and a takeaway) does lie near **Derrynane National Park** and miles of beaches ringed by sparkling dunes. Guests have the run of the house at **The Travelers' Rest Hostel ❶.** A relaxed sitting room and small dorms make this hostel look and feel more like a B&B. (☎ 947 5175. Continental breakfast €4. Dorms €12; private rooms €15 per person.) Campers perch over the beach 1 mi. east of town at **Wave Crest Camping Park ❶.** (☎ 947 5188. Laundry €5. Shop open 8am-10pm. Site open mid-Mar. to Oct. and off season by arrangement. €5 per person. Showers €1.)

REPUBLIC OF IRELAND

KENMARE (NEIDIN) ☎ 064

A bridge between the Ring of Kerry and the Beara, Kenmare has adapted to a continuous stream of visitors. Everything you'd expect of a classic Irish town is here (yes, we're talking about colorful houses and misty mountain views and the like). Tourists fresh off the bus may dilute Kenmare's appeal, but pleasant surroundings overshadow the sweater stalls and postcard stands.

TRANSPORTATION AND PRACTICAL INFORMATION. Buses leave from Brennan's Pub on Main St. to **Killarney** (1hr.; M-Sa 2-3 per day, Su 2 per day) and **Sneem** (35min., June-Sept. M-Sa 2 per day). **Rent bikes** at **Finnegan's**, on the corner of Henry and Shelbourne St. (☎41083. €12 per day, €75 per week. Open June-Aug. M-Sa 9:30am-9pm; Sept.-May M-Sa 9:30am-6:30pm.) The **tourist office** is on the Square. (☎41233. Open July-Oct. M-Sa 9am-6pm, Su 10am-5pm; May-June M-Sa 9am-1pm and 2-5:30pm.) An **AIB** is at 9 Main St. (☎41010. Open M 10am-5pm, Tu-F 10am-4pm.) The **post office** has **Internet access** on the corner of Henry and Shelbourne St. (☎41490. €1 per 10min., cheaper 6-8pm. Open June-Sept. M-F 9am-5:30pm, Sa 9am-1pm; Oct.-May M-F 9am-1pm and 2-5:30pm, Sa 9am-1pm. Computers available June-Aug. 8am-8pm, Sept.-May 8am-6pm.)

ACCOMMODATIONS, FOOD, AND PUBS. Proprietress Maureen runs a tight ship at the excellent and immaculate **Fáilte Hostel (IHH) ❶**, on the corner of Henry and Shelbourne St. (☎42333. Curfew 1am. Open Apr.-Oct. Dorms €12; doubles €32-40; triples €42; quads €56.) **Keal Na Gower House B&B ❸**, a small B&B within earshot of a brook. (☎41202. €28-30 per person.) Three miles west of town on the Sneem road, the **Ring of Kerry Caravan and Camping Park ❶** overlooks mountains and a bay. (☎41648. Laundry €3.50. Open Apr.-Sept. 1-person tent €7, 2 people with car and tent €16.50. Showers €0.50.) **The Pantry**, Henry St., has a limited selection of healthy organic stuff. (☎42233. Open M-Sa 9:30am-6pm.) Italian award-winners (from €13) are served in an old stone townhouse at **An Leath Phingin ❹**, 35 Main St. (☎41559. Book ahead July-Aug. Open Mar.-Nov. M-Tu and Th-Su 6-9:30pm.) Kerchiefed belles serve up bakery and deli delights at **Jam ❶** (☎41591; open M-Sa 8am-5pm). Kenmare's pubs attract a hefty contingent of tourists, making live music common in summer. **O'Donnabháin's** (☎42106), Henry St., is a favorite of all ages. Wise visitors follow locals to **Moeran's Bar**, at the top of Main St. (☎41368. Nightly trad June-Sept.)

SIGHTS. There are plenty of good hikes in the country around Kenmare but few sights in the town itself. The ancient **stone circle**, a 2min. walk down Market St. from the Square, is the largest of its kind (55 ft. diameter) in southwest Ireland. (Always open. €1.50.) The stones are one stop on Kenmare's **tourist trail** (maps at the tourist office). **The Kenmare Lace and Design Centre**, upstairs next to the heritage center, has demonstrations of the famous Kenmare lace-making technique. (☎42636. Open Mar.-Sept. M-Sa 10am-1pm and 2-5:30pm. Free.)

DINGLE PENINSULA

For decades, the Dingle Peninsula was the Ring of Kerry's under-touristed second banana. Word has finally gotten out, and the tourist blitz encroaches on spectacular cliffs and sweeping beaches. While Dingle Town is well-connected to Killarney and Tralee, public transport on the peninsula is scarce. The Tralee bus station (☎712 3566) has detailed information. Dingle is best explored by **bike**—the entire western circuit is only a daytrip, while the mountainous northern regions make for more arduous excursions. Maps available in area tourist offices describe the **Dingle Way**, a 95 mi. walking trail that circles the peninsula.

Ventry (Ceann Trá) is home to the ⬛**Ballybeag Hostel ❷** (☎ (066) 915 9876; bike rental €7 per day; laundry €2; wheelchair-accessible; €20 per person), as well as the ⬛**Celtic and Prehistoric Museum** (☎ (066) 915 9931; open Mar. to mid-Nov. daily 10am-5pm, other months call ahead; €5, students €3.50, children €3). Glorious ⬛**Slea Head** (Ceann Sléibhe) presents to the world a face of jagged cliffs and a hemline of frothy waves, and offers soft grassy headlands perfect for afternoon napping.

Appearing like a mirage off the westernmost tip of Ireland, the ghostly ⬛**Blasket Islands** (Na Blascaodaí) occupy a special place in Irish cultural history and in the hearts of all who visit. Whether bathed in glorious sunlight or shrouded in impenetrable mist, the islands' magical beauty and aching sense of eternity explain the disproportionately prolific literary output of the final generation to reside there. **Blasket Island Ferries** bridge the gap between the Blaskets and Dunquin in about 20min. (☎ (066) 915 6422. Apr.-Oct. daily every 20min. 10:30am-6pm, weather permitting. €17.80 return, students €15.25.) If rough seas keep you from visiting the Blaskets, or even if they don't, check out the outstanding exhibits at the ⬛**Great Blasket Centre** in Slea Head, just outside of Dunquin on the road to Ballyferriter.(☎ 915 6444. Open July-Aug. daily 10am-7pm; Easter-June and Sept.-Nov. 10am-6pm. Last admission 45min. before closing. €3.10, students €1.20.)

Right across from the turnoff to the Blasket Centre is **Dunquin's** (Dún Chaoin) **An Óige Hostel (HI) ❶**. (☎ 915 6121. Continental breakfast €3. Sheets €1.30. Reception 9-10am and 5-10pm. Lockout 10am-5pm. May-Oct. 8- to 10-bed dorms €11.50-12.50; 4- to 6-bed €13-14; doubles €30-32. Jan.-Apr. and Nov.-Dec. €1.30-2.50 cheaper.) Back toward the pier, the ferry captain's home doubles as the delightful ⬛**Gleann Dearg B&B ❸**. (☎ 915 6188. Open Apr.-Oct. €25 per person.) Nearby **Kruger's ❸** is purportedly the westernmost pub in Europe. (☎ 915 6127. Mains €6.35-12.70. B&B €25 per person.)

DINGLE TOWN (AN DAIGEAN) ☎ 066

Although the *craic* is still home-grown, ever-expanding armies of tourists smother the docks and pubs of this bayside town. To be fair, Dingle does have fantastic hostels, a swingin' music scene, easy access to its namesake peninsula's more isolated hideaways, and one helluva dolphin.

⬛ TRANSPORTATION. **Buses** stop by the harbor, on the Ring Road behind the SuperValu. **Bus Éireann** runs to: **Ballyferriter** (M and Th 3 per day, €3.20); **Dunquin** (M and Th 4-5 per day, Tu-W and F-Sa 1-2 per day; €3.15); **Tralee** (1¼hr.; M-Sa 6 per day, Su 4 per day; €7.90). From June to September additional buses tour the south of the peninsula (M-Sa 2 per day). **Paddy's Bike Shop,** Dykegate St., rents quality bikes. (☎ 915 2311. €10 per day, students €8; €50 per week, €40. Panniers €2 per day. Open daily 9am-7pm.) For **taxi** service try **Cooleen Cabs** (☎ (087) 248 0008) or **Dingle Co-op Cabs** (☎ 915 1000).

⬛ ⬛ ORIENTATION AND PRACTICAL INFORMATION. The R559 heads east to Killarney and Tralee, and west (called **Slea Head Dr.**) to Ventry, Dunquin, and Slea Head. In downtown Dingle, **Strand St.** runs next to the harbor along the marina, while **Main St.** is its parallel counterpart uphill. **The Mall, Dykegate St.,** and **Green St.** connect the two, running perpendicular to the water. In the eastern part of town, a roundabout splits Strand St. into **The Tracks,** which continue along the water, **The Holy Ground,** which curves up to meet Dykegate St., and the **Tralee Road.**

Dingle's **tourist office,** Strand St., vies for the attention of scores of dolphin-crazed tourists. (☎ 915 1188. Open July-Aug. M-Sa 9am-7pm, Su 10am-5pm;

Sept.-Oct. and mid-Mar. to June M-Sa 9:30am-6pm, Su 9:30am-5pm.) An **AIB** (☎915 1400) and **Bank of Ireland** (☎915 1100) are on Main St. and both have multi-card tolerant **ATMs**. (Both open M 10am-5pm, Tu-F 10am-4pm.) Access the **Internet** at the **library** (☎915 1499; 50min. free per day; call to arrange a time; open Tu-Sa 10:30am-1:30pm and 2:30-5pm) or amidst the leather chairs at **Dingle Internet Cafe,** Main St. (☎915 2478; €2.60 per 20min., €6 per hr.; open May-Sept. M-Sa 10am-10pm, Su 2-6pm; Oct.-Apr. daily 10am-6pm). The **post office** is on Upper Main St. (☎915 1661. Open M-F 9am-5:30pm, Sa 9am-1pm.)

⌂ ACCOMMODATIONS. Most of Dingle's hostels are great, but only some are close to town. Accommodations in town and along Dykegate and Strand St. fill up fast—always call ahead. Smack in the middle of town and just a brief stagger from Dingle's finest pubs is the **Grapevine Hostel ❶,** Dykegate St., off Main St. The friendly folks here guide you through the cushy-chaired common room to close but comfy bunk rooms. (☎915 1434. 8-bed dorms €10.80-12; 4-bed €12-13.35.) Take Strand St. west out of town and continue straight through the roundabout for ¼ mi. to reach the **Rainbow Hostel ❶,** and its warm, cavernous kitchen. The "Rainbow-Mobile" makes trips to and from town every few hours. (☎915 1044. Bike rental €6 per day. Internet access €1 per 10min. Laundry €7. 5- to 12-bed dorms €12; private rooms €14 per person. **Camping** €6.50.) Look out onto Main St. or opt for creepy and gaze upon the old graveyard behind **Ashe's B&B ❸,** Lower Main St. The rooms are tastefully decorated with soft cream colors and antique bureaus. (☎915 0989. All rooms with bath and TV. €30 per person.)

◧▣ FOOD AND PUBS. Dingle is home to a wide range of eateries, from doughnut stands to gourmet seafood restaurants. **SuperValu,** the Holy Ground, stocks a SuperSelection of groceries and juicy tabloids. (☎915 1397. Open June-Aug. M-Sa 8am-10pm, Su 8am-9pm; Sept.-Apr. M-Sa 8am-9pm, Su 8am-7pm.) Brothers Kieran and Sean of **▨Murphy's Ice Cream ❶,** Strand St., deserve all the superlatives you'll exclaim. The ex-pat New Yorkers scoop Ireland's only truly homemade ice cream (from €2), whipping up inventive, slightly alcoholic creations. (☎915 2644. Open June-Sept. 10:30am-6pm and 7:30-10pm; mid-Mar. to May 10:30am-6pm.) Dine on homemade gourmet pizzas (€7.30-11.50) or *paella* amidst soft Italian music at **El Toro ❸,** Green St., the only Spanish and Italian specialist in town. Look out on the hills or admire the owner's knack for oil painting as your tastebuds enjoy his talent for cooking. (☎915 1820. Dinner daily 6-10pm.) Swish through a beaded curtain into the Bohemian wonderland that is **Cafe Po'oka ❷,** Main St. Feast on crepes (€3.50-7) or all-day breakfasts (€3.50-6.50), and listen to the cheerful staff croon along to everything from spicy Latin beats to funky down-home blues. (☎915 0773. Open 11am-6pm, or thereabouts.) The most popular pub in town, **▨An Droichead Beag** ("The Small Bridge"), Lower Main St. (☎915 1723), unleashes 401 sessions of trad a year—9:30pm every night and the odd afternoon as well.

◙▨ SIGHTS AND FESTIVALS. When **Fungi the Dolphin** was first spotted in Dingle Bay in 1983, the townspeople worried about the effect he would have on the bay's fish population. To say he is now welcome is an understatement, as he single-flipperedly brings in droves of tourists and plenty of cash to his exploiters. **Dolphin Trips** leave to see him from the pier between 10am and 7pm in the summer. (☎915 2626. 1hr. €10, children under 12 €5, free if Fungi gets the jitters and doesn't show.) Watching the antics from the shore east of town is a cheaper, squintier alternative. **Sciúird Archaeology Tours** will take you on a whirlwind bus tour of the area's ancient spots. (☎915 1606 or 915 1937. 3hr. 2 per day. €15. Book ahead.) The **Dingle Regatta** hauls in salty dogs on the third Sunday in August. In mid-August, try your luck at the **Dingle Races.** During early September, the **Dingle Music Festival** lures big-name trad groups and other performers from across the musical spectrum. (☎915 1983; www.iol.ie/~dingmus.)

TRALEE (TRÁ LÍ)　☎066

As the economic and residential capital of Kerry, Tralee (pop. 20,000) offers little appeal to the long-term visitor. Still, large storefronts line the city's main streets, and quality pubs serve up bar food and trad. Ireland's second-largest museum, detailing the history of Kerry, stands out, but no tourist development could possibly top the city's famed gardens. The annual **Rose of Tralee** is a centuries-old pageant that has Irish eyes glued to their TVs in August.

⬛ TRANSPORTATION. Trains (☎712 3522) tie Tralee to: **Cork** (2½hr., 3-4 per day, €22.90); **Dublin** (4hr., 3-4 per day, €45.10); **Galway** (5-6 hr., 3 per day, €45.10); **Killarney** (40min., 4 per day, €7.50); **Waterford** (4hr., M-Sa 1 per day, €16.50). **Buses** (☎712 3566) go to: **Cork** (2½hr.; M-Sa 14 per day, Su 10 per day; €12.70); **Dingle** (1¼hr.; July-Aug. M-Sa 8 per day, Su 5 per day; Sept.-June M-Sa 4 per day, Su 2 per day; €7.90); **Galway** (1¼hr.; July-Aug. M-Sa 8 per day, Su 5 per day; Sept.-June M-Sa 4 per day, Su 2 per day; €7.90); **Killarney** (40min.; June-Sept. 12-14 per day, Oct.-May 5-6 per day; €5.85); **Limerick** (2¼hr., 7-8 per day, €12.20); **Skibbereen** (3hr., June-Sept. 2 per day, €14.60). **Rent bikes** from **O'Halloran,** 83 Boherboy. (☎712 2820. €10 per day, €50 per week. Open M-Sa 9:30am-6pm.)

⬛ ORIENTATION AND PRACTICAL INFORMATION. Tralee's streets are hopelessly knotted; in-the-know travelers arm themselves with free maps from the tourist office. The main avenue is variously called the **Mall** (as it passes by the **Square**), **Castle St.,** and **Boherboy. Edward St.** connects this main thoroughfare to the train and bus stations. **Denny St.** runs south to the **tourist office,** in Ashe Memorial Hall. (☎712 1288. Open July-Aug. M-Sa 9am-7pm, Su 9am-6pm; May-June and Oct. M-Sa 9am-6pm; Nov.-Apr. M-F 9am-5pm.) **AIB,** Denny St. (☎712 1100), and **Bank of Ireland** (☎712 1177), a few doors down, have **ATMs** throughout town. (Both open M 10am-5pm, Tu-F 10am-4pm.) **Millennium Computer College,** Ivy Terr., offers **Internet access.** (☎712 0020. €1 per 10min. Open M-Sa 10am-6pm.) The **post office** is on Edward St. (☎712 1013. Open M and W-Sa 9am-5:30pm, Tu 9:30am-5:30pm.)

⬛ ACCOMMODATIONS, FOOD, AND PUBS. Rows of pleasant B&Bs line the area where Edward St. becomes Oakpark Rd.; others can be found along Princes Quay, close to the park. Tralee's hostels can barely contain the August festival-goers—reserve ahead. **Courthouse Lodge (IHH) ❶,** 5 Church St., is centrally located but buffered by a quiet street. (☎712 7199. All rooms with bath. Internet access €1 per 10min. Linens €1. Laundry €6. Dorms €14; doubles €32.) An ideal location with 14 rooms, **Seán Óg's ❸,** 41 Bridge St., is also home to a traditional pub downstairs. The B&B offers exceptionally friendly service and an easy crawl to bed after several pints. (☎712 8822. €25 per person.) **Woodlands Park Campground ❶,** Dan Spring Rd., is a national award-winner. (☎712 1235. Laundry €6. Open Apr.-Sept. 2-person tent €15. Showers €1.)

If they don't sell it at the massive **Tesco** in the Square, you probably shouldn't be eating it. (☎712 2788. Open M-W and Sa 8:30am-8pm, Th-F 8:30am-9pm, Su 10am-6pm.) Get quality homemade Irish food, fast, fresh, and cheap, at ▨**Pocott's ❷,** 3 Ashe St. (☎712 9500. Most entrees €6-8. Open July-Sept. M-Sa 9am-9:30pm, Su noon-7pm; Oct.-June M-Sa 9am-7pm, Su noon-7pm.) Head to **Mozart's ❸,** 4 Ashe St., for a medley of well-prepared delights—bagel sandwiches (€3.20) in the morning, stuffed baguettes (€3.80-5.10) in the afternoon, stir-fries and steaks (€8.25-16.50) in the evening. (☎712 7977. Open M-Th 9am-6:30pm, F-Sa 9am-9:30pm.) JP and Mike serve as your personal drinking consultants at ▨**Seán Óg's,** 41 Bridge St. (☎712 8822. Trad M-Th.) Across the street, **Abbey Inn** draws an edgy crowd with live rock most weekends. When U2 played here in the late 70s, the manager made them sweep the floors to pay for their drinks because he thought they were so bad. (☎712 3390. Th live music, M-W and F-Sa DJ. Open M-Sa until 2:30am, Su live band until 1am. Food 9am-9:30pm.)

◙ **SIGHTS.** Tralee is home to Ireland's second-largest museum, ▨**Kerry the Kingdom,** in Ashe Memorial Hall on Denny St. (☎712 7777. Free multilingual audioguides. Open mid-Mar. to Oct. daily 10am-6pm; Nov. noon-4:30pm. €8, students €6.50, children €5.) Across the way, another from the ranks of Ireland's "second largests"—**town park,** in this case—blooms each summer with the **Rose of Tralee.** Just down the Dingle road, true superlativity occurs at the **Blenneville Windmill and Visitors Centre,** the largest operating windmill in the British Isles. (☎712 1064. Open Apr.-Oct. daily 10am-6pm. €4, students €2.50.)

LIMERICK (LUIMNEACH)   ☎061

Despite a thriving trade in off-color poems, Limerick has long endured a bad reputation associated with its recent industrial developments. However, this is now a city on the rise. The Republic's third-largest metropolis boasts an intense arts scene, top-quality museums, and a well-preserved 12th-century cathedral.

◲ **TRANSPORTATION. Trains** (☎315 555) run to **Cork** (2½hr., 5-6 per day, €17.70); **Dublin** (2hr., 9-10 per day, €33.10); and **Waterford** (2hr.; summer M-Sa 2 per day, winter 1 per day; €22.80). Buses arrive and depart from **Colbert Station,** just off Parnell St. (☎313 333; 24hr. timetables ☎319 911.) **Bus Éireann** sends buses to **Cork** (2hr., 14 per day, €12.10); **Dublin** (3½hr., 13 per day, €13.30); **Galway** (2hr., 14 per day, €12.10); **Kilkenny** (1½hr., 2 per day, €13.30); **Killarney** (2½hr.; M-Sa 6 per day, Su 3 per day; €12.40); **Waterford** (2½hr., 6-7 per day, €13.30). A **local bus** network runs from the city center to the suburbs (M-Sa 2 per hr. 7:30am-11pm, Su 1 per hr. 10:30am-11pm; €0.95). **Top Cabs** (☎417 417) takes you to most places in the city for under €3.80 and to Shannon airport for about €25. **Emerald Alpine,** 1 Patrick St., **rents bikes.** (☎416 983. €20 per day, €70 per week. Deposit €50. Return to any participating Raleigh location. Open M-Sa 9:15am-5:30pm.)

◪▨ **ORIENTATION AND PRACTICAL INFORMATION.** Limerick's streets form a no-frills grid pattern, bounded by the **Shannon River** to the west and the **Abbey River** to the north. The city's most active area lies in the blocks around **O'Connell St.** (which becomes **Patrick St.,** then **Rutland St.** to the north, and **the Crescent** to the south). The city itself is easily navigable by foot, but the preponderance of one-way streets makes it a nightmare for drivers. The **tourist office** is in the space-age glass building on Arthurs Quay. From the station, follow Davis St. as it becomes Glentworth; turn right on O'Connell St., then left at Arthurs Quay Mall. (☎317 522; www.shannon-dev.ie Open July-Aug. M-F 9am-6:30pm, Sa-Su 9am-6pm; May-June and Sept.-Oct. M-Sa 9:30am-5:30pm; Nov.-Apr. M-F 9:30am-5:30pm, Sa 9:30am-1pm.) Many **banks** count their euros on O'Connell St. Just uphill, **Surfers Cafe,** 1 Upper William St., has **Internet access.** (☎440 122. €7.50 per hr., students €6.30.) The **post office** is on Lower Cecil St., just off O'Connell St. (☎315 777. Open M-Sa 9am-5:30pm, Tu open 9:30am.)

⌂ **ACCOMMODATIONS.** In the year of our Lord 2002, all of the hostels in Limerick passed away. We will mourn them, and remember them for their budget-saving prices, eclectic mix of characters, and slightly discolored pillowcases. In the meantime, we will search the area around O'Connell St. for other accommodations. One of the better **B&B** values found in the city is **Alexandra House ❸,** O'Connell St., several blocks south of the Daniel O'Connell statue. All rooms come with TV and tea-making facilities. (☎318 472. Full Irish breakfast. Singles €26; shared rooms €24-32 per person. Student discounts.) **Cherry Blossom Budget Accommodation ❶,** O'Connell St., next to Alexandra House, is Limerick's newest kid on the block; the energetic proprietress aims to fill the gap created when the city's hostels fled town. (☎318 472. Dorms €14-15; doubles €32-38.)

▐▌ 🖥 FOOD AND NIGHTLIFE. Inexpensive and top-notch cafes around Limerick's center offer refreshing alternatives to fast food and pub grub. Forage for groceries at **Tesco** in Arthurs Quay Mall. (☎ 412 399. Open M-W and Sa 8:30am-8pm, Th-F 8:30am-10pm, Su noon-6pm.) ▧**Dolans ❷,** 4 Dock Rd., is a friendly little pub that doubles as a spirited restaurant out back. Quoth John, a patron: "Best damn seafood chowder this side of the Atlantic." (☎ 314 483. Lunch around €5-9 all day.) Candlelit ▧**Sean Cara Restaurant ❹,** 3 Dock Rd., is adjacent to Dolans. The stone masonry walls, finished plank wood floors, excellent wine selection, and live harpist on weekends complete the intimate, elegant atmosphere. (Dinner 6-10pm.) Limerick's vegetarian headquarters is **The Green Onion ❸,** Rutland St. The interior of this converted library building, with its high molded ceilings, is bold and dramatic. After 6pm, dinner prices fly high (€13-20), but the "all-day" lunch (€7-9) menu offers simpler and cheaper options. (☎ 400 710. Open M-Sa noon-10pm.)

A wide range of musical options caters to the city's diverse pub crowd and its immense student population. It's worth a Shannon-side walk from the city center to hear the nightly trad played for rambunctious local patrons at **Dolan's,** Dock Rd. (☎ 314 483). The **Warehouse** nightclub is in the same building. Alternatively, join the classy crowd on the quay-side patio of the **Locke Bar and Restaurant,** Georges Quay (☎ 413 733). Or head inside where owner Richard Costello, a former member of Ireland's national rugby team, joins in trad sessions several nights a week. Limerick's insatiable army of students keeps dozens of nightclubs thumping from 11:30pm until 2am nightly. Cover charges can be steep (€6.35-10.20), but keep an eye out for promotions. **The Globe,** Cecil St., offers two floors of manic clubbery, with suggestive artwork and flashing video screens. (☎ 313 533. Cover €7.)

◙ SIGHTS. The fascinating ▧**Hunt Museum,** in the Custom House, houses Ireland's largest collection of art and artifacts outside Dublin's National Museum. Browse through drawers to find surprises like the world's smallest jade monkey. (☎ 312 833. Open M-Sa 10am-5pm, Su 2-5pm. €7, concessions €4.) The visitors center of **King John's Castle** has vivid exhibits and a video on the castle's gruesome past. Outside, the mangonel—used to catapult pestilent animal corpses into enemy castles—is a particularly convincing testament to perverse military tactics. (☎ 411 201. Open Mar.-Dec. daily 9:30am-5:30pm. Last admission 4:30pm. €6.50, concessions €5, families €16.) **Walking tours** cover either the northern, sight-filled King's Island region or the more downtrodden locations of Frank McCourt's memoirs. (☎ 318 106. Island tour daily 11am and 2:30pm; *Angela's Ashes* tour daily 2:30pm. Both depart from St. Mary's Action Centre, 44 Nicholas St. €5.50.)

WESTERN IRELAND

Ask the gentleman sitting next to you at the pub—he'll probably agree that the west is the "most Irish" part of Ireland. Western Ireland's gorgeous desolation and enclaves of traditional culture are now its biggest attractions. Though wretched for farming, the land from Connemara north to Ballina is a boon for hikers and cyclists. Galway, long a bustling seaport, is currently a haven for young ramblers. The Cliffs of Moher, the barren moonscape of the Burren, and a reputation as the center of the trad music scene attract travelers to Co. Clare.

DOOLIN (DUBH LINN)   ☎ 065

Something of a shrine to traditional Irish music, the little village of Doolin draws thousands of travelers to its pubs for *craic* that will go straight from your tappin' toes to your Guinness-soaked head. Most of Doolin's 200-odd residents run its accommodations and pubs; others split their time between farming and wondering how so many visitors end up in their small corner of the world. However, serious sessions at ⊠**McDermott's,** Upper Village, prove that Doolin's trad is more than a tourist trap. Local foot-traffic heads this way around 9:30pm nightly, and remains at a standstill 'til closing; a 9:20pm arrival may win you a seat. (☎707 4328. Grub until 9:30pm.) The busiest and most touristed of Doolin's three pubs is **O'Connor's** (☎707 4168), Lower Village, with drink and song nightly at 9:30pm all year. Like its brothers, **McGann's,** Upper Village, also hosts music nightly at 9:30pm in the summer. (☎707 4133. Music Th-Su at 9:30pm in the winter.)

Barbell-shaped Doolin is made up of two villages about 1 mi. apart. Close to the shore is **Lower Village,** connected to **Upper Village** by **Fisher St./Roadford. Buses** stop at the Doolin Hostel and Nagle's Camping Ground—purchase advance tickets at the hostel. Route #15 runs from **Kilkee** and from **Dublin** via Ennis and Limerick (2 per day); #50 comes from **Galway** (1½hr.) via other **Burren** destinations on its way to the **Cliffs of Moher,** 15min. away (summer M-Sa 5 per day, Su 2 per day; winter M-Sa 1 per day). The **Doolin Bike Store,** outside Aille River Hostel, **rents bikes.** (☎707 4260. €10 per day. Open daily 9am-8pm.) The nearest **ATM** is in Ennistymon, 5 mi. southeast. A traveling **bank** comes to the Doolin Hostel once a week (Th 10:30am). There may or may not be a **post office** in 2003, depending on whether someone chooses to run it; no one has stepped up since the previous postman died.

Tourists pack Doolin in the summer, so book early. Musicians often stop by ⊠**Aille River Hostel (HIH) ❶,** Main St., halfway between the villages, to warm up before gigs. The hostel offers a friendly, laid-back atmosphere in a gorgeous location: the Aille River gurgles around a tiny wildflower island out front and an unofficial beer garden sets up on the island just before hostelers head to the pubs. (☎707 4260. Internet access €6 per hr. for guests. Washer free, dryer €2. Dorms €11-11.50; private rooms €13.50 per person. **Camping** €6.) The rooms of the ⊠**Westwind B&B ❸,** Upper Village, are sunny and immaculate; the French toast is breakfast happiness. The owners give advice to spelunkers and other Burren explorers. (☎707 4227. €25 per person.)

Doolin's few restaurants are excellent but pricey; first prize (and perhaps a small fortune!) goes to the entrepreneur who opens an affordable restaurant in this four-hostel town. Until then, be grateful that all three pubs serve quality grub. **The Doolin Deli ❶,** Lower Village, is the only place to go for food under €8. It packs overstuffed sandwiches (€2.50), bakes scones (€0.90), and stocks groceries. (☎707 4633. Takeaway only. Open June-Sept. M-Sa 8:30am-9pm, Su 9:30am-9pm.) The "cafe" part of **The Doolin Cafe ❹,** Upper Village, refers to the casual atmosphere, not the excellent, upscale food. The early-bird special (5:30-7pm) is pricey, but still an outstanding value, with four gourmet courses for €22. (☎707 4795. Open for dinner daily 5:30-10pm, lunch Sa-Su noon-3pm.)

CLIFFS OF MOHER

The ⊠**Cliffs of Moher,** members of an elite group of Ireland's über-touristy attractions, draw more gawkers on a good July day than many counties see all year. The stunning view from the edge plunges 700 ft. straight down to the open sea. The majestic headland affords views of Loop Head, the Kerry Mountains, the Twelve Pins, and the Aran Islands. Adventurous visitors climb over the stone walls and trek along an officially closed clifftop path for more spectacular views and a greater intimacy, with potential falls. The seasonal **tourist office** houses a **bureau de change** and a **tea shop.** (☎(065) 708 1171. Open May-Sept. daily 9:30am-5:30pm.) To reach the cliffs, head 3 mi. south of Doolin on R478 or grab the Bus Éireann summer-only Galway-Cork **bus** (2-3 per day). **Liscannor Ferries** cruises from Liscannor and sails directly under the cliffs. (☎ (065) 708 6060. 1¾hr., 2-3 per day, €20.)

THE BURREN   ☎ 065

Entering the Burren's magical 100 sq. mi. landscape is like happening upon an enchanted fairyland. Lunar limestone stretches end in secluded coves, where dolphins rest after a long day of cavorting with the locals. Mediterranean, Alpine, and Arctic wildflowers announce their bright contours from cracks in mile-long rock planes, while 28 of Ireland's 33 species of butterfly flutter by. Geologists have no explanation for why such a variety of animalian and botanic species coexists in the area, except that it has something to do with the end of the Ice Age. The best way to see the Burren is to **walk** or **cycle,** but be warned that the dramatic landscape makes for exhausting climbs and thrilling descents. Tim Robinson's meticulous maps (€6.35) detail the **Burren Way,** a 26 mi. hiking trail from Liscannor to Ballyvaughan; *Burren Rambler* maps (€2.55) are also extremely detailed. **Bus** service in the Burren is some of the worst in the Republic. **Bus Éireann** (☎ (065) 682 4177) connects Galway to towns in and near the Burren a few times a day during the summer, but infrequently during the winter. **Buses** stop at: the Doolin Hostel in **Doolin,** Burke's Garage in **Lisdoonvarna** (Lios Dún Bhearna), Linnane's in **Ballyvaughan** (Baile Uí Bheacháin), and Winkle's in **Kinvara** (Cinn Mhara). Other year-round but infrequent buses run from Burren towns to **Ennis** (Inis). Based in **Lahinch** (Leacht Uí Chonchuir), Gerard Hartigan gives a **minibus tour** of the Burren and the Cliffs of Moher. Please take proper precautions—his enthusiasm is infectious. (☎ (086) 278 3937. 4½hr. €14.)

ARAN ISLANDS   ☎ 099

On the westernmost edge of Co. Galway, isolated from the mainland by 20 mi. of swelling Atlantic, lie the spectacular Aran Islands (Oileán Árann). The green fields of Inishmore, Inishmaan, and Inisheer are hatched with a maze of limestone walls—the result of centuries of farmers piling stones up to clear the fields for cultivation. The landscape is as moody as the Irish weather and tends to adopt its disposition, from placid blue calms to windy torments. Little is known of the earliest islanders, whose tremendous cliff-peering forts seem to have been constructed by the secret designs of the limestone itself. Early Christians flocked here seeking seclusion; the ruins of their churches and monasteries now litter the islands.

THE HIDDEN DEAL

AER ÁRRAN

Have you ever noticed how expensive it can be to travel to an island? Because islands' secluded yet inconvenient locations blatantly preclude all notions of driving, walking, or biking, enterprising ferry companies develop veritable monopolies on the island-transit business, and therefore charge whatever they please. The three ferries that travel to the islands charge between €19-35 round-trip—a high price for budget travelers to pay. At these prices, however, the €44 round-trip air journey offered by Aer Árran suddenly becomes a hidden deal. For only €9-24 more than the ferry, travelers can enjoy the luxury of flying to and from the magnificent isles. It's double the fun and takes just a fraction of the time, and it's especially attractive considering how unreliably the ferries run. Better yet, a combined flight/sail option (€37) satisfies those who can't decide on one mode of locomotion. (*Aer Árran* ☎(1890) 462 726; www.aerarran.ie. *Flights to all three islands leave from the small airport in Inverin, 19 mi. west of Galway, and can be booked over the phone or at the Galway tourist office. To Inishmore: 10min.; 8 per day; return €44, students €37. Shuttle bus to the Airport leaves from Kinlay House in Galway 1hr. before departure, €6.)*

◖ TRANSPORTATION

Three ferry companies (all with booths in the Galway tourist office) operate boats to the Aran Islands. **Island Ferries** (☎(091) 561 767 or 568 903), has main offices in the Galway tourist office and on Forster St., close to Eyre Sq. One ferry sails to **Inishmore** (Apr.-Oct. 3 per day, Nov.-Mar. 2 per day) and another to **Inishmaan** via **Inisheer** (2 per day); both depart from **Rossaveal,** several miles west of Galway (return €20, students €16.50). A bus runs from Galway's Kinlay House B&B to the ferryport (departs 1½hr. and 1hr. before sailings; €6, students €5). **Queen of Aran II** is the only ferry company based on the islands, but it only runs to Inishmore. (☎566 535 or 534 553. 4 departures daily. Return €19, students €12.) Queen of Aran boats also leave from Rossaveal, with a bus departing from Kinlay House (1¼hr. before sailings; €6, students €5). **O'Brien Shipping/Doolin Ferries** runs a somewhat daily service in the summer, and three times per week in the off season. (Doolin ☎(065) 707 4455; Galway ☎(091) 567 676. Galway to any island, return €20-25. Doolin to Inishmore return €32, Inishmaan €28, Inisheer €25. Unreliable inter-island trips €10.) The Island Ferries and Queen of Aran boats serving Inishmore are fairly reliable and leave daily. Traveling to or between the Islands can be difficult, to say the least—purchase all of your tickets before setting sail.

INISHMORE (INIS MÓR)

The archaeological sites of Inishmore, the largest and most touristed of the islands, include dozens of ruins and churches and the amazing Dún Aengus fort. Crowds spread from Kilronan Pier, at the island's center, and lose themselves amid countless species of wildflowers, 7000 mi. stone walls, and harrowing cliffs.

◖◗ **TRANSPORTATION AND PRACTICAL INFORMATION.** Roving **minibuses** cost about €10 per 2hr. **Aran Bicycle Hire** rents bikes. (☎61132. €10 per day. Deposit €10. Open daily 9am-5pm.) The Kilronan **tourist office** sells the *Inis Món Way* map (€1.90), holds bags (€1), and changes money. (☎61263. Open July-Sept. daily 10am-6:45pm; Oct. 10am-5pm; Nov.-Mar. 10am-4pm.) The **post office** is uphill from the pier. (☎61101. Open M-F 9am-1pm and 2-5pm, Sa 9am-1pm.)

◖◗ **ACCOMMODATIONS, FOOD, AND PUBS.** Many minibuses make stops at hostels and B&Bs that are farther away; ask at the tourist office for more information. ▨**Mainistir House (IHH) ❶,** 1 mi. from "town," attracts visitors to its magazine-filled sitting room, where big windows look out to the sea. (☎61169. Bike rental €10 per day. Laundry €6. Dorms €12; singles €20; private rooms €16 per person.) Joël prepares legendary ▨**dinners ❸,** far and away the best deal on the island. Fill up for days on magnificent, mostly vegetarian buffets. Eight-person tables are arranged to encourage conversation with fellow travelers or locals in search of epicurean bliss. (8pm; reserve ahead. €12.) The dorms at **Kilronan Hostel ❶,** adjacent to Tí Joe Mac's pub, are small, ensuite, and immaculate. (☎61255. Bike rental €10. Dorms €13.) **The Artist's Lodge ❶** is cozy and inviting, with an impressive video collection and crackling fire. Take the turnoff across from Joe Watty's pub on the main road, walk a bit, and look right. (☎61457. Dorms €10.)

The **Spar Market,** past the hostel in Kilronan, functions as an unofficial community center. (☎61203. Open summer M-Sa 9am-8pm, Su 10am-6pm.) If you can't get a seat at Mainistir House, try **Tigh Nan Phaid ❷,** in a thatched building at the turnoff to Dún Aengus, which specializes in home-cooked bread and home-smoked fish. (☎61330. Open daily 11am-5pm.) Locals and hostelers savor their pints at popular **Tí Joe Mac's,** overlooking the pier. (☎61248. Sessions W.) Despite its name, **The American Bar** (☎61130) is an Irish pub through and through.

◐ ⬚ SIGHTS AND ENTERTAINMENT. The time-frozen island, with its labyrinthine stone wall constructions, rewards wandering visitors who take the day to cycle or walk around its hilly contours. The **Inis Mór Way** is a mostly paved route that makes a great bike ride, circling past a majority of the island's sights. The tourist office's maps of the Way (€2) purportedly correspond to yellow arrows that mark the trails, but the markings are frustratingly infrequent and can vanish in fog; it's best to invest in a Robinson map for serious exploring or simply follow the crowds and hope for the best. If you only have a few hours, high-tail it to the island's most famous monument, the magnificent **Dún Aengus,** 4 mi. west of the pier at Kilronan. The fort's walls are 18 ft. thick and form a semicircle around the sheer drop of Inishmore's northwest corner. **Be very careful:** strong winds have been known to blow tourists off the cliffs. The **Black Fort** (Dún Dúchathair), a mile south of Kilronan over eerie terrain, is larger than Dún Aengus, a millennium older, and greatly underappreciated. Uphill from the pier in Kilronan, the new, expertly designed **Aran Islands Heritage Centre** beckons the inquisitive, providing a fascinating introduction to the islands' monuments, geography, history, and peoples. (☎61355. Open June-Aug. 10am-7pm; Apr.-May and Sept.-Oct. 11am-4pm. Exhibit and film €5; each €3.50, students €3.) Finish off your day on Inishmore with ◧**Ragus,** performed at the Halla Rónáin—an hour-long jaw-droppingly energetic display of traditional music, song, and dance that costs almost twice as much in Dublin. (Tickets available at the door or from the Aran Fisherman Restaurant, ☎61104. Shows at 2:45, 5, and 9pm. €13.)

INISHMAAN (INIS MEÁIN)

Seagulls circle the cliffs and goats chew their cud, but there's little human activity to observe in the limestone fields of Inishmaan. Despite recent dramatic changes on the other two islands, Inishmaan remains a fortress, quietly avoiding the hordes of barbarians invading from Doolin and Galway. Even residents of Inishmore report that stepping onto Inishmaan is like stepping 20 years into the past. The *Inishmaan Way* (€2) describes a 5 mi. walking route that passes all of the island's sights. The thatched cottage where John Synge wrote is 1 mi. down the main road. A bit farther is 7th-century **Dún Chonchúir** (Connor Fort), and at the western end of the road is **Synge's Chair,** where the writer came to reflect and compose. The landscape gets even more dramatic when the coastline comes into view. To the left of the pier, the ruins of 8th-century **Cill Cheannannach** church were a burial ground until the mid-20th century. Entering the **Knitwear Factory,** near the island's center, is uncannily like stepping into a Madison Ave. boutique. (☎73009. Open M-Sa 10am-5pm, Su 10am-4pm.) For **tourist information,** as well as the chance to buy a variety of local crafts, try the **Inishmaan Co-op** (☎73010. Open M-F 8:30am-5pm). **Mrs. Faherty's B&B ❸** is signposted from the pier and serves dinner. (☎73012. Open mid-Mar. to Nov. Dinner €12. Singles €30; doubles €50.) **Tigh Congaile ❸** is on the right side of the first steep hill from the pier. (☎73085. Singles €35; shared rooms €30 per person.) Its **restaurant ❸** perfects seafood. (Lunch under €6.80, dinner from €16. Open June-Sept. daily 10am-7pm.) **Padraic Faherty's** thatched pub is the center of life on the island and serves a small selection of grub until 6:30pm.

INISHEER (INIS OÍRR)

The Aran Islands have been described as "quietness without loneliness," but Inishmaan can get pretty damn lonely, and Inishmore isn't always quiet. Inisheer, the smallest isle, is the perfect compromise. On clear days of otherworldly peacefulness, daytripping visitors wonder if these few square miles hold the key to the pleasures of a simpler life. The **Inis Oírr Way** covers the island's major attractions on a 4 mi. path. The first stop is in town at **Cnoc Raithní,** a burial mound 2000 years older than Christianity. Walking along the shore leads to the overgrown graveyard of **St. Cavan's Church** (Teampall Chaomhain). Below the church, a pristine beach stretches back to the edge of town. Farther east along the water, a grassy track leads to majestic **An Loch Mór,** a 16-acre inland lake brimming with wildfowl. The ring fort **Dún Formna** is above the lake. Past the lake you'll find the **Plassy Wreck,** a sunken ship that washed up on Inisheer in 1960. The walk back to town leads past the remains of 14th-century **O'Brien Castle,** razed by Cromwell in 1652. On the west side, **Tobar Einne,** St. Enda's Holy Well, is believed to have curative powers. ▨**Ara's Eanna** ("House O'Culture") screens films, organizes art exhibits, and runs workshops and a cafe. (☎75150. Films €3, concerts €7. Gallery free. Open 10am-5pm.)

Rothair Inis Oírr rents bikes. (☎75033. €8 per day, €50 per week.) **Internet access** is at the **library** (☎75008. Open Tu, Th, and Sa 2:30-5pm), a beige building up the road from the pier and past the beach. The **Brú Hostel (IHH) ❶,** visible from the pier, is spacious and promises great views. (☎75024. Continental breakfast €4, Irish breakfast €6.50. Laundry €5. 4- to 6-bed dorms €12; private rooms €16 per person.) **The Mermaid's Garden ❸,** on the other side of the beach and signposted from the airstrip, rents out a lovely, big room and serves a wonderful selection of breakfasts. (☎75062. €25 per person; €60 per family.) The **Ionad Campála Campground ❶** stretches its tarps near the beach. (☎75008. Open July-Aug. €5 per tent, showers included.) **Tigh Ruairí,** an unmarked white pub-shop on the main road, has Inisheerie groceries. (☎75002. Shop open July-Aug. daily 9am-8pm; Sept.-June M-Sa 10am-6pm, Su 10:30am-2pm.) **Fisherman's Cottage ❷** serves organic, island-grown meals. (☎75053. Soup and bread €2.50, dinners €12.70. Open daily 11am-4pm and 7-9:30pm.) **Tigh Ned's** pub, next to the hostel, caters to a young set; the **Ostan Hotel's** pub (☎75020), just up from the pier, is dim and crowded.

GALWAY (GAILLIMH) ☎091

Welcome to the fastest-growing city in Europe. In the past few years, Co. Galway's reputation as Ireland's cultural capital has brought flocks of young Celtophiles to Galway city. Mix more than 13,000 local university students, a large population of twentysomething Europeans, and waves of international backpackers, and you have a college town on some serious *craic*.

▐ TRANSPORTATION

Trains: Eyre Sq. (☎561 444). Station open M-Sa 9am-6pm. Trains to **Dublin** (3hr., 4-5 per day, €21-30) via **Athlone** (€11-14); transfer at Athlone for all other lines.

Buses: Eyre Sq. (☎562 000). **Bus Éireann** heads to: **Belfast** (7hr., M-Su 2-3 per day, €27.50); the **Cliffs of Moher** (late May to mid-Sept. M-Sa 3-4 per day, Su 1-2 per day; €11.40) via **Ballyvaughan** (€7.80); **Cork** (4½hr., 13 per day, €15.80); **Donegal** (4hr., 4 per day, €15.20); **Dublin** (4hr., 14 per day, €12). Private coach companies specialize in Dublin-bound busery: **Citylink** (☎564 163) from Supermac's, Eyre Sq. (9 per day, last bus 5:45pm; €10); **Michael Nee** (☎51082) from Forester St. through Clifden to Cleggan, meeting the Inishbofin ferry (M-Sa 2-4 per day; €7.80, return €11.20); **P. Nestor** (☎797 144) leaves from the Forster St. carpark (5-7 per day, €10). **City buses** (☎562 000) leave from the top of Eyre Sq. (every 20min., €0.95) and head to every neighborhood. Commuter tickets €12 per week. Students €10.

Taxis: The biggest companies are **Big O Taxis,** 21 Upper Dominick St. (☎585 858), and **Cara Cabs,** Eyre Sq. (☎563 939).

Bike Rental: Europa Cycles, Hunter Buildings, Earls Island (☎563 355). €7 per day, €40 per week. Deposit €40. Open M-Sa 9am-6pm, Su 9am-noon and 4-6pm.

Hitchhiking: Dozens wait on the Dublin road (N6) scouting rides to Dublin, Limerick, or Kinvara. Most catch bus #2, 5, or 6 from Eyre Sq. to this main thumb-stop. University Rd. leads drivers to Connemara via N59. *Let's Go* does not recommend hitching.

ORIENTATION AND PRACTICAL INFORMATION

Bus or rail to Galway will deposit you at **Eyre Sq.**, a central block of lawn and monuments with the train and bus station uphill on its southeastern side. B&Bs huddle northeast of the square along **Prospect Hill;** commerceland spreads out in the other direction. West of the square, **Woodquay** has quiet(er) commercial and residential activity. **Station Rd.**, a block east of **Williamsgate St.**, leads into the pedestrian-only heart of Galway, where cafes and pubs *craic*kle with activity. Fewer tourists venture over the bridges into the more bohemian **left bank** of the Corrib, where great music and some of Galway's best pubs await untapped. The pubs along **the docks** in the southeast of the city are largely fishermen hangouts. When weather permits, guitar players and lusty paramours lie by the river along the **Long Walk.**

Tourist Office: Forster St. (☎537 700). Aran info. Bureau de change available. Open July-Aug. daily 9:30am-7:45pm; May-June and Sept. daily 9am-5:45pm; Oct.-Apr. M-F and Su 9am-5:45pm, Sa 9am-12:45pm.

Budget Travel: usit now, Mary St. (☎565 177). Open May-Sept. M-F 9:30am-5:30pm, Sa 10am-3pm; Oct.-Apr. M-F 9:30am-5:30pm, Sa 10am-1pm.

Finanical Services: Bank of Ireland, 19 Eyre Sq. (☎563 181). **AIB,** Lynch's Castle, Shop St. (☎567 041). Both have 24hr. **ATMs.** Open M-F 10am-4pm, Th until 5pm.

Work Opportunities: Contact **FAS** (☎534 400; www.fas.ie; open M-F 9am-5pm) or the **Galway Peoples' Resource Centre** (☎564 822 or 562 688; open M-F 9am-5pm).

Police *(Garda):* Mill St. (☎538 000).

Hospital: University College Hospital, Newcastle Rd. (☎524 222).

Internet Access: Celtel e.centre, Eyre Sq., is conveniently located. €4.80 per hr., 10% student discount. Open daily 8am-10pm.

Post Office: Eglinton St. (☎562 051). Open M-Sa 9am-5:30pm, Tu from 9:30am.

ACCOMMODATIONS AND CAMPING

In the last few years, the number of accommodating beds in Galway has tripled; it now approaches one thousand. Nevertheless, it's wise to call at least a day ahead.

HOSTELS AND CAMPING

Salmon Weir Hostel, 3 St. Vincent's Ave. (☎561 133). Not as impressively stacked or spacious as some of its brethren, but extremely homey, with a friendly, laid-back vibe. Free tea and coffee. Laundry €6. Curfew 3am. 12-bed dorms €9-10; 6-bed €13-14; 4-bed €14-15. Doubles €35. ❶

Sleepzone, Bóthar na mBán (☎566 999; www.sleepzone.ie), northwest of Eyre Sq. Big, beautiful, and fully loaded—huge kitchen, common room with flatscreen TV, carpark, Internet access (€4.50 per hr.), and a peaceful terrace. Wheelchair-accessible. Laundry €6. 8- to 10-bed dorms €16.50; 6-bed €18; 4-bed €20. Singles €40; doubles €54. Weekends €1.50-10 more; Nov.-Apr. €2-17 less. ❷

Kinlay House (IHH), Merchants Rd. (☎565 244), half a block off Eyre Sq. A surprisingly huge, well-located hostel with all manner of rooms and services. Discounts when you book with their other locations in Cork and Dublin. Bureau de change. Wheelchair-accessible. Small breakfast included. Laundry €7. 8-bed dorms €15; 4-bed €16, with bath €19. Singles €27; doubles €40, with bath €48. ❷

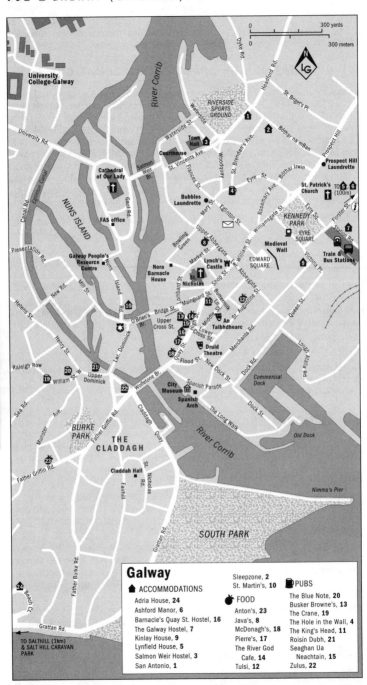

Galway

🏠 ACCOMMODATIONS

Adria House, **24**
Ashford Manor, **6**
Barnacle's Quay St. Hostel, **16**
The Galway Hostel, **7**
Kinlay House, **9**
Lynfield House, **5**
Salmon Weir Hostel, **3**
San Antonio, **1**

Sleepzone, **2**
St. Martin's, **10**

🍎 FOOD

Anton's, **23**
Java's, **8**
McDonagh's, **18**
Pierre's, **17**
The River God
    Cafe, **14**
Tulsi, **12**

🍺 PUBS

The Blue Note, **20**
Busker Browne's, **13**
The Crane, **19**
The Hole in the Wall, **4**
The King's Head, **11**
Roisín Dubh, **21**
Seaghan Ua
    Neachtain, **15**
Zulus, **22**

The Galway Hostel, Eyre Sq. (☎566 959), across from the station. Busy and hospitable. Light breakfast included. Internet access (€5 per hr.). 24hr. reception. Large dorms €15; 4-bed €19, with bath €22. Doubles €45-50. ❷

Barnacle's Quay Street Hostel (IHH), Quay St. (☎568 644). Bright, spacious rooms in the eye of the Quay St. storm. Über-convenient for post-pub crawl returns, but that same convenience can make front rooms quite noisy. Big dorms €15; 8-bed €16.50; 6-bed €19; 4-bed €20. Singles €50; private rooms €25 per person. Rates lower in winter. ❷

Salthill Caravan and Camping Park (☎523 972). Beautiful bay location, about ½ mi. west of Salthill, 1hr. along the shore from Galway. Open Apr.-Oct. €6 per person. ❶

B&BS

St. Martin's, 2 Nun's Island Rd. (☎568 286), on the west bank of the river at the end of O'Brien's Bridge. The gorgeous back garden spills into the river. Located near the city's best pubs; just across the river from the main commercial district. All rooms with bath. Singles €32; doubles €60. Large family room €25 per person. ❸

Adria House, 34 Beach Court (☎589 444; www.adriaguesthouse.com). On a quiet cul-de-sac off Grattan Rd., between the city center and Salthill. Home to a dynamic duo of owners. €20-55 per person, prices highest July-Aug. ❹

Lynfield House, 9 College Rd. (☎567 845), just past the tourist office. Only a few blocks from Eyre Sq. and the bus/train station. Another deluxe B&B run by the same family as Adria, with the same room configurations and fluctuating rates. ❹

Ashford Manor, 7 College Rd. (☎563 941), by Lynfield House. A classy, if pricey B&B, complete with TVs, phones, and hair dryers in every room. Ample parking. Big breakfast selection. €45-48 per person. ❹

San Antonio, 5 Headford Rd. (☎564 934), a few blocks north of Eyre Sq. Rooms with multiple single beds are backpacker-friendly, as are the owners. €20 per person. ❷

🍴 FOOD

The east bank has the greatest concentration of restaurants. **SuperValu,** in the Eyre Sq. mall, is a chef's playground. (☎567 833. Open M-W and Sa 9am-6:30pm, Th-F 9am-9pm, Su noon-6pm.) On Saturday mornings, an 🖼**open market** sets up cheap pastries, ethnic foods, and fresh fruit, as well as jewelry and artwork, in front of St. Nicholas Church on Market St. (Open 8am-5pm.)

🖼 **Anton's** (☎582 067). Just over the bridge near the Spanish Arch and a 3min. walk up Father Griffin Rd. Self-consciously hip eateries on the other side of the river could learn a lot from this hidden treasure, where the food does the talking. Scrambled eggs with smoked salmon €5. Open M-F 8am-6pm, Sa 10am-5pm. ❶

🖼 **Java's,** Abbeygate St. (☎567 400). Hip, dimly lit cafe. The New York-style bagels are excellent (€4.75), as are the brownies. As reliable as Irish rain—only closes early Christmas Eve. Open daily 10:30am-3am. ❶

🖼 **McDonagh's,** 22 Quay St. (☎565 001). Fish and chips madness—locals and tourists alike line up and salivate at this century-old institution. Takeaway fish fillet and chips €5.65. Open daily noon-midnight; takeaway M-Sa noon-midnight, Su 5-11pm. ❷

The River God Cafe, High St. (☎565 811). French and Asian flavors combine in subtle seafood curries and tofu dishes. Entrees €10-14. Open daily 5-10pm. ❸

Tulsi, Buttermilk Walk (☎564 831), between Middle and High St. This award-winning restaurant serves Ireland's best Indian food. Open daily noon-3pm and 6-10pm. ❷

Pierre's, 8 Quay St. (☎566 066). If you're going to break the bank, it ought to happen at this oasis of quiet amidst the din of Quay St. Save room for dessert—the raspberry mousse floating in a chocolate cup is divine. 3-course meal €21. Open 6-10:30pm. ❹

🔲 🔝 PUBS AND CLUBS

With approximately 650 pubs and 70,000 people, Galway maintains a healthily low person-to-pub ratio. Music is alive and well—whether alternative rock, live trip-hop, or some of the country's best trad. Very broadly speaking, **Quay St.** and **Eyre Sq.** pubs cater to tourists, while locals stick to the trad-oriented **Dominick St.** pubs. Between midnight and 12:30am, the pubs drain out and the tireless go dancing.

■ **Roisín Dubh** ("The Black Rose"), Dominick St. (☎586 540). Intimate, bookshelved front hides one of Galway's hottest music scenes. Largely rock and singer-songwriters, but folk and blues put in appearances, and sessions are quite frequent. Cover M-Tu €5-20.

■ **Zulus,** Dominick St. (☎581 204). Galway's first gay bar. Approximately 95% male, but all are welcome to join the fun at this friendly little place. Lively local banter and laughter ricochet off the walls until late into the night.

■ **The Blue Note,** William St. West (☎589 116). Where all the cool kids go. Twentysomething hipsters amass on lush couches, getting up to mingle or dance. Galway's best bet for turntable music, with top-notch guest DJs. Occasional indie films in the winter.

■ **The Crane,** 2 Sea Rd. (☎587 419), a bit beyond the Blue Note. A friendly, musical pub, known as *the* place to hear trad in Galway. 2 musicians quickly become 6, 6 become 10, 10 become 20. Trad every night and all day Su. Set dancing Tu.

■ **The King's Head,** High St. (☎566 630). Like visitors to the city itself, pubbers come here expecting to pass a single night, but fall in love and end up living here instead. Upstairs music varies. Su jazz brunch 1-3pm.

■ **The Hole in the Wall,** Eyre St. (☎565 593). This surprisingly large pub fills up with college-age singletons year-round. Flirtation spills into the small beer garden. Quality of music varies, but *craic* is a constant.

■ **Cuba,** on Prospect Hill, right past Eyre Sq. Far and away the best club. Upstairs provides a little more room, a little less flash, and wonderfully varied but danceable live music. Cover varies (€5-10).

Busker Browne's (☎563 377), between Cross St. and Kirwin's Ln. in an old nunnery. Get thee to this upscale, 20-something bar. If the first 2 floors leave you unimpressed, head to the fantastic 3rd floor ■ **Hall of the Tribes,** easily the most spectacular lounge in Galway. Su morning excellent live jazz downstairs.

Stranos, William St. West (☎588 219). A mixed lesbian and gay bar/club/meeting house with a pool room on the 3rd floor. Frequent theme nights; check out the *GCN* at Charlie Byrne's for current listings. DJs Th.

Seaghan Ua Neachtain (a.k.a. **Knockton's**), Quay St. (☎568 820). The oldest pub in Galway, dating back to 1894. Afternoon pint-sippers munch sandwiches and study the streams of pedestrians from street-corner tables. Nightly trad.

Skeffington Arms (☎563 173), across from Kennedy Park. "The Skeff" is a splendid, multi-storied hotel pub with 6 different bars to wander between. Suspended walkways overlook the rear. A well-touristed, multi-generational pub crawl unto itself. DJs F-Sa.

GPO, Eglinton St. (☎563 073). A student favorite during term; the inescapable yellow smiley faces try to convince summer clubbers that it should be theirs as well. Tu 70s night, W comedy club. Cover €6.

🎦 🎵 SIGHTS AND ENTERTAINMENT

Rededicated as John F. Kennedy Park, **Eyre Square** has a small collection of monuments around its grassy common stand. Across the river to the south of Dominick St., **Claddagh** was an Irish-speaking, thatched-cottage fishing village until the 1950s. Stone bungalows replaced the cottages, but a bit of the small-town appeal and atmosphere still persists. The famous Claddagh rings, traditionally used as wedding bands, are mass-produced today. The **Nora Barnacle House**, 8 Bowling Green, is the home of James Joyce's life-long companion. (☎ 564 743. Open mid-May to mid-Sept. W-F 10am-1pm and 2-5pm. Times vary; call ahead. Mid-Sept. to mid-May by appointment only. €2.50.) By the river, the **Long Walk** makes a pleasant stroll, bringing you to the **Spanish Arch.** If you're pressed for time, half- or full-day group **tours** may be the best way to see the sights of Galway, the Burren, and **Connemara** (see below). Hop-on/hop-off **buses** line up outside the tourist office (most €9, students €8) and cruise the city; **Bus Éireann** (☎ 562 000), **Healy Tours** (☎ 770 066), **Lally Tours** (☎ 562 905), and **O'Neachtain Tours** (☎ 553 188) depart for Connemara and the Burren from various points in the city (€20-25, students €15-20).

The free *Galway Advertiser* provides entertainment listings. For tickets to big events throughout Ireland, make your way to **Zhivago** on Shop St. (Ticket hotline ☎ 509 960. Open June-Sept. M-Sa 9am-9pm, Su 10am-6pm; Oct.-May M-W and Sa 9am-6pm, Th-F 9am-9pm, Su noon-6pm. €1.90 booking fee.) Festivals rotate through Galway all year long, with the greatest concentration during the summer months. Reservations for accommodations during these weeks are of the utmost importance. Ireland's biggest film festival—the **Galway Film Fleadh**—is a jumble of films, lectures, and workshops in early July. (☎ 569 777; www.galwayfilmfleadh.com.) For two crazed weeks in mid-July, the largest **arts festival** in Ireland reels in famous trad musicians, theater troupes, and filmmakers. (☎ 583 800; www.galwayartsfestival.ie.) The gates go up on the **Galway Races** at the end of July.

CONNEMARA (CONAMARA)

Connemara, a thinly populated region of northwest Co. Galway, extends a lacy net of inlets and islands into the Atlantic Ocean. The rough gang of inland mountains, desolate stretches of bog, and rocky offshore islands are among Ireland's most arresting and peculiar scenery. Driving west from Galway City, the relatively tame and developed coastal strip stretching to Rossaveal suddenly gives way to the pretty fishing villages of Roundstone and Kilkieran. Farther west, Clifden, Connemara's largest town, draws the largest crowds and offers the most tourist services. Ancient bogs spread between the coast and the rock-studded green slopes of the two major mountain ranges, the **Twelve Bens** and the **Maamturks.** Northeast of the Maamturks is Joyce Country, named for a long-settled Connemara clan. Ireland's largest *gaeltacht* is also located along the Connemara coastline, and Irish-language radio (Radio na Gaeltachta) broadcasts from Costelloe.

Cycling is a particularly rewarding way to absorb the region. The 60 mi. routes from Galway to Clifden (via Cong) and Galway to Letterfrack are popular despite fairly challenging dips and curves at their ends. The seaside route through Inverin and Roundstone to Galway is another option. **Hiking** through boglands and along coastal routes is also popular—the **Western Way** footpath offers dazzling views as it winds 31 mi. from Oughterard to Leenane through the Maamturks. **Buses** serve the main road from Galway to Westport, stopping in Clifden, Oughterard, Cong, and Leenane. N59 from Galway to Clifden is the main thoroughfare; R336, R340, and R341 make more elaborate coastal loops. **Hitchers** report that locals are likely to stop; *Let's Go* does not recommend taking advantage of such generosity.

CLIFDEN (AN CLOCHÁN)   ☎091

The town of Clifden is a cluster of touristically directed buildings resting between a small cliff and a pair of modest peaks. Socially, Clifden serves as a buffer between the built-up southern half of Co. Galway and pristine northern Connemara. During the off season (Sept.-May), the town is relatively quiet, but tourists flood in during the summer months.

▐▌ TRANSPORTATION AND PRACTICAL INFORMATION. Bus   Éireann (☎56200) pulls into the library on Market St. from **Galway** via Oughterard (2hr.; mid-June to Aug. M-Sa 6 per day, Su 2 per day; Sept.-May 1-3 per day; €9) and **Westport** via Leenane (1½hr., late June-Aug. M-Sa 1 per day). **Michael Nee** (☎51082) buses from the courthouse to **Cleggan** (mid-June to Aug. 3 per day, Sept.-May 3 per week; €6) and **Galway** (2hr., 2 per day, €11). **C&A Hackney** (☎21309 or (086) 859 3939) and **Joyce's** (☎21076 or 22082) run **taxis. Rent bikes** from **Mannion's**, Bridge St. (☎21160, after hours 21155. €9 per day, €60 per week. Deposit €20. Open M-Sa 9:30am-6:30pm, Su 10am-1pm and 5-7pm.) **Market St.** meets **Main St.** and **Church Hill** at **The Square.** The **tourist office,** Galway Rd., has info on all of Connemara. (☎21163. Open June M-Sa 10am-6pm; July-Aug. M-Sa 9am-6pm and Su noon-4pm; Sept.-Oct. M-Sa 10am-5pm; Mar.-May M-Sa 10am-5pm.) An **AIB bank** is in the Square. (☎21129. Open M-F 10am-12:30pm and 1:30-4pm, W until 5pm.) The **post office** is on Main St. (☎21156. Open M-F 9:30am-5:30pm, Sa 9:30am-1pm.)

▐▌ ACCOMMODATIONS, FOOD, AND PUBS. B&Bs litter the streets; the going rates are €25 per person and up. Reservations are necessary in July and August. **The Clifden Town Hostel (IHH) ❶,** Market St., has great facilities, spotless rooms, and a quiet atmosphere close to the pubs. Despite the modern decor, stone walls remind you that the house is 180 years old. (☎21076. Dorms €12-15; doubles €32-34; triples €32; quads €56-60.) The clean, roomy dorms of **Brookside Hostel ❶,** Hulk St., overlook fat sheep in the backyard. Head straight at the bottom of Market St. (☎21812. Laundry €6. Wheelchair accessible. Dorms €11.50; doubles €30.)

Clifden has a surprising variety of culinary options, ranging from family-run kitchens to pub fare, aspiring gourmet cooking to Chinese and fast food. **O'Connor's SuperValu,** Market St., provides supermarket standards. (Open M-F 9am-7pm, Su 10am-6pm.) **Cullen's Bistro & Coffee Shop ❸,** Market St., is a family establishment that cooks up hearty meals (thick Irish stew €12.50) and tempting homemade desserts. (☎21983. Open daily 11am-10pm.) **Walsh's ❶,** the Square, is a busy bakery with a large seating area and food for under €5. (☎21283. Open June-Sept. M-F 8:30am-6pm, Sa-Su 9am-6pm; Oct.-May M-Sa 8:30am-6pm.) Revelers sit on the floor when the chairs and pool table fill up at **Malarkey's** (☎21801), Church Hill, or join in the music at **Mannion's,** Market St. (☎21780).

◙ SIGHTS. The 10 mi. long **Sky Rd.** provides a lovely route for hiking, biking, or a scenic drive. The trail loops around west of town, paving the way to some dizzying heights. A mile down Sky Rd. stands what's left of **Clifden Castle,** once home to Clifden's founder, John D'Arcy. Farther out, a peek at the bay reveals the boggy spot near Ballyconneely where US pilots John Alcock and Arthur Brown landed the first nonstop transatlantic flight. One of the nicer ways to acquaint yourself with Connemara is to hike south to the **Alcock and Brown monument,** situated just off the Ballyconnelly road, 3 mi. past Salt Lake and Lough Fadda.

INISHBOFIN (INISH BÓ FINNE)
☎095

Inishbofin, the "island of the white cow," 7 mi. from the western tip of Connemara, has gently sloping hills (flat enough for pleasant cycling) scattered with rugged rocks, and near-deserted sandy beaches. Days on Inishbofin are best spent meandering through the island's four stone- and wildflower-strewn peninsulas. Most items of historical interest are on the southeast peninsula. **Knock Hill** affords spectacular views of the island. **Bishop's Rock,** a short distance off the mainland, becomes visible at low tide. The ragged northeast peninsula is fantastic for **bird watching:** gulls, cornets, shags, and a pair of peregrine falcons fish among the cliffs and coves. Inishbofin provides a perfect climate for vegetation hospitable to the **corncrake,** a bird that's near extinction everywhere except in Seamus Heaney's poems. Two pairs of these rare birds presently call Inishbofin home.

Ferries leave for Inishbofin from **Cleggan,** a tiny village with stunning beaches 10 mi. northwest of Clifden. Two **ferry companies** serve the island. Malachy King operates the *Island Discovery* and the *Galway Bay,* which comprise the larger, steadier, and faster of the two fleets. (☎44642. 45min.; July-Aug. 3 per day, Apr.-June and Sept.-Oct. 2 per day; return €15, children €7.50. Tickets available at the pier, in Clifden, or on the boat.) The *M.V. Dún Aengus/Queen of Aran* runs year-round. (☎45806. 45min.; July-Aug. 3 per day, Apr.-June and Sept.-Oct. 2 per day, Nov.-Apr. 1 per day; return €12.70. Tickets purchased most conveniently on the ferry.) Stock up at **Spar** before you go, especially if you're taking a later ferry. (☎44750. Open daily 9am-10pm.) **Bike rental** is available at the Inishbofin pier (☎45833) for €7 per day. To sort out your stay, call ahead or visit the **Community Resource Centre** (☎45909) to the left of the pier on the main road. The pleasant staff provides maps (€1.20-4.50), updated information on services, and **Internet access.**

Kieran Day's excellent ▨**Inishbofin Island Hostel (IHH) ❶** is a 15min. walk from the ferry landing; take a right at the pier and head up the hill. The hostel is the unmistakably yellow building. (☎45855. Sheets €1. Laundry €5. Dorms €10. **Camping** €5 per person.) The **Emerald Cottage ❷,** a 10min. walk west from the pier, welcomes guests with home-baked goodies. (☎45865. Singles €20; doubles €40.) Close to the pier, **Day's Pub** (☎45829) serves food from noon to 5pm. **Cloonan's Store** is behind the pub and sells picnic-applicable items year-round. (☎45829. Open M-Sa 11am-1pm and 3-5pm, Su noon-3pm.) The smaller, more sedate **Murray's Pub,** 15min. west of the pier, is great for conversation, slurred or otherwise.

CONNEMARA NATIONAL PARK
☎095

Connemara National Park occupies 8 sq. mi. of mountainous countryside and is home to a number of curiosities, including hare runs, orchids, and roseroot. The far-from-solid terrain is composed of bogs thinly covered by a screen of grass and flowers. Guides lead free walks (2-3hr.; July-Aug. M and F at 10:30am) and offer children's programs on Tuesdays and Thursdays. The ▨**Visitors Centre** and its adjoining museum team up with perversely funny anthropomorphic peat and moss creatures to teach visitors the differences between hollows, hummocks, and tussocks. Follow this with a dramatic 25min. slide show about the park, which elevates the battle against opportunistic rhododendrons to epic scope. (☎41054. Open June daily 10am-6:30pm; July-Aug. 9:30am-6:30pm; May and Sept. 10am-5:30pm. €2.50, students €1.25.) The **Snuffaunboy Nature** and **Ellis Wood Trails** are easy 20min. hikes teeming with wildflowers; the former features alpine views while the latter submerges walkers in an ancient forest. A guidebook mapping out 30min. walks (€0.60) is available at the Visitors Centre. For the more adventurous, trails lead from the back of the Ellis Wood Trail and 10min. along the **Bog Road** onto ▨**Diamond Hill,** a 2hr. hike that rewards climbers with views of bog, harbor, and forest, or, depending on the weather, impenetrable mist. (Diamond Hill was closed in 2002 for erosion control; call ahead to confirm opening.) Park visitors often base themselves in nearby **Letterfrack** at the ◪**Old Monastery Hostel** ❶ (a sharp right and up the hill from the crossroads), one of Ireland's finest. Owner Steve cooks buffet dinners in the vegetarian and (mostly) organic style during the summer (buffet €9, plate €7; call by 5pm); he also provides fresh scones and porridge for breakfast. (☎41132. Bike rental €9 per day. Laundry €5. 6- and 8-bed dorms €10; 4-bed €12. Doubles €15. **Camping** €6.)

WESTPORT (CATHAIR NA MART) ☎098

In lovely Westport, palm trees and steep hills lead to quaint, busy streets of brightly-colored pubs, cafes, and shops. Visitors would be well-advised to follow the river's lead and head to the Quay, then have a sunset pint and watch the wide, blue water become red, then blue again. Hustle back to Bridge St. for pure, unadulterated *craic*. Book your bed in advance or you might have some trouble; tourists flock to Westport like hungry seagulls to harbor feed.

🖼🚩 **TRANSPORTATION AND PRACTICAL INFORMATION. Trains** puff into **Altamont St. Station** (☎25253 or 25329) from **Dublin** via Athlone (2-3 per day, €21-23). **Buses** leave Mill St. on the Octagon for Achill, Ballina, Castlebar, and Galway. For a **taxi**, call **Brendan McGing** (☎25529). **Rent bikes** from **Sean Sammon**, James St. (☎25471. €8 per day. Open M-Sa 10am-6pm, Su by prior arrangement.) The tiny **Carrowbeg River** trickles through Westport's Mall. **Bridge St.** and **James St.**, the town's main drags, extend south. **Shop St.** connects the **Octagon,** at the end of James St., to the **Town Clock** at the end of Bridge St. **High St.** and **Mill St.** lead out from the town clock, the latter to **Altamont St.**, where the train station lies beyond a long stretch of B&Bs. The **tourist office** is on James St. (☎25711. Open July-Aug. M-Sa 9am-6:45pm, Su 10am-6pm; Apr.-June and Sept.-Oct. M-Sa 9am-5:45pm.) The **Bank of Ireland** is at North Mall. (☎25522. Open M-F 10am-4pm, Th until 5pm.) **Internet access?** Try **Dunning's Cyberpub**, the Octagon, and have a Guinness with your e-mail. (☎25161. €1.30 per 10min., €7.60 per hr. Open daily 9am-11:30pm.)

🖼🔲 **ACCOMMODATIONS, FOOD, AND PUBS. The** ◪**Granary Hostel** ❶, a 25min. walk from town, at the bend in Quay Rd, is flanked by a peaceful garden and conservatory. (☎25903. Open Apr.-Sept. Dorms €10.) Award-winning Irish breakfasts and hospitality have kept travelers coming back to ◪**Altamont House** ❸, Altamont St., for 36 years. (☎25226. €25 per person, with bath €27.) Peruse local art while waiting for a table at ◪**McCormack's** ❷, Bridge St. Locals praise the exemplary sandwiches and salads. (☎25619. Open M-Tu and Th-Sa 10am-5pm.) All the cool people (and apparently everyone else) go to ◪**Matt Molloy's**, Bridge St., owned by the flautist of the Chieftains. Officially, trad sessions occur nightly at 9:30pm; in reality, any time of the day is deemed appropriate. (☎26655. Open M-W 12:30-11:30pm, Th-Sa 12:30pm-12:30am, Su 12:30-11pm.) A run-down exterior hides the vibrant **Henehan's Bar,** Bridge St. (☎25561), and its beer garden. It has music in summer nightly and on winter weekends.

🔲🔳 **SIGHTS AND HIKING. Westport House's** current state of commercial exploitation must be a bitter pill to swallow for Lord Altamont, its elite inhabitant, but the **grounds** there are beautiful, free, and a 45min. stroll from town (from the Octagon, ascend the hill and bear right, then follow the signs to the Quay). More interesting is the **Clew Bay Heritage Centre** at the end of the Quay. A veritable garage sale of history, this charmingly crammed center brims with scraps of the past. The Centre also provides a **genealogical service.** (☎26852. Open July-Sept. M-F 10am-5pm, Su 2:30-5pm; Oct.-June M-F 10am-2pm. €3, students €1.50, children free.)

Conical **Croagh Patrick** rises 2510 ft. over Clew Bay. The summit has been revered as a holy site for thousands of years; it was considered most sacred to Lug, the Sun God and one-time ruler of the Túatha de Danann. After arriving here in AD 441, St. Patrick engaged in praying and fasting for the standard 40 days and 40 nights, argued with angels, and then banished snakes from Ireland. The barefoot pilgrimage to the summit originally ended on St. Patrick's feast day, March 17, but the death-by-thunderstorm (an act of god, no doubt) of 30 pilgrims in AD 1113 moved the holy trek to Lughnasa—**Lug's holy night** is on the last Sunday in July, when the weather is slightly more forgiving. Others climb the mountain just for the exhilaration and incredible views. The hike takes 4hr. roundtrip, but be fore-warned: the terrain can be quite steep, and the footing unsure. Well-shod climbers start their excursion from the 15th-century **Murrisk Abbey;** pilgrims and hikers also set out for Croagh Patrick along the Tóchar Phádraig, a path from **Ballintubber Abbey.** The new and useful **Croagh Patrick Information Centre** offers tours, showers, luggage storage, food, and directions to the summit.

ACHILL ISLAND (ACAILL OILÉAN) ☎098

Two decades ago, Achill (AK-ill) Island was Co. Mayo's most popular holiday des-tination. Its popularity has inexplicably dwindled, but Ireland's biggest little island remains one of its most beautiful and personable. Ringed by glorious beaches and cliffs, Achill's interior consists of a couple of mountains and more than a few bogs. The town of **Achill Sound,** the gateway to the island, has the most amenities of any nearby settlement, but **Keel** has more promising nightlife. **Dugort,** north of Keel, is less busy, but its hostel, pub, and restaurant provide services enough for any weary backpacker. To the West of Keel, the seaside resorts of **Pollagh** and **Dooagh** form a flat strip along Achill's longest beaches and serve as brief stopovers on the way to Achill's more westerly (and more potent) vistas at Keem Bay and Croag-haun Mountain. **Cycling** the Atlantic drive is a great way to see the island. The **Achill Seafood Festival** goes down the second week in July, and during the first two weeks of August, Achill hosts the **Scoil Acla** (☎45284), a festival of trad and art.

Buses run infrequently over the bridge linking Achill Sound, Dugort, Keel, and Dooagh to **Westport, Galway,** and **Cork** (June-Aug. M-Sa 5 per day, Sept.-May M-Sa 2 per day), and to **Sligo, Enniskillen,** and **Belfast** (June-Aug. 3 per day, Sept.-May 2 per day). If the buses are too infrequent, call for a **taxi.** (☎(087) 243 7686.) Hitchers report relative success during July and August, but cycling is more reliable and *Let's Go* doesn't recommend hitchhiking. The island's **tourist office** is beside the Esso station in Cashel, on the main road from Achill Sound to Keel. (☎(098) 47353. Open M-F 10am-5pm.) There is an **ATM** in Achill Sound but no bank on the island, though **currency exchange** is available at Achill Sound's post office.

Achill Sound's strategic location at the island's entrance accounts for its high concentration of shops and services, but practicality isn't the only reason to stop here. Come for the ATM and stay for the internationally famous stigmatic and faith healer who holds services at **Our Lady's House of Prayer,** about 20 yd. up the hill from the town's main church. (Open for services daily 9:30am-6pm.) The healer draws thousands to the attention-starved town each year, but local opinions remain polarized. About 6 mi. south of Achill Sound—turn left at the first cross-roads—two ruined buildings stand in close proximity. The ancient **Church of Kildav-net** was founded by St. Dympna after she fled to Achill to escape her father's incestuous intentions. Nearby, a lonely and crumbling 16th-century tower house with memories of better days calls itself the remains of **Kildavnet Castle,** once owned by Grace O'Malley, Ireland's favorite medieval pirate lass.

Achill Sound has a **SuperValu** (open M-Sa 9am-7pm), a **Bank of Ireland ATM,** a phar-macy (☎45248; open July-Aug. M-Sa 9:30am-6pm; Sept.-June M-Sa 9:30am-6pm), and a **post office** with a **bureau de change** (☎45141; open M-F 9:30am-12:30pm and 1:30-5:30pm). **Bike rental** is sometimes available at the **Achill Sound Hotel.** (☎45245. €9 per day, €40 per week. Deposit €50. Open daily 9am-9pm.) The **Wild Haven Hostel ❶,** a block past the church on the left, positively glows with polished wood floors and antique furniture. (☎45392. Sheets €1.30. Laundry €5.50. Dorms €13; private rooms €17-19 per person. **Camping** €5.) If that doesn't work out, try the **Railway Hostel ❶,** just before the bridge to town. Housed in a former rail station (the last train pulled out about 70 years ago) the hostel is bursting with recently renovated dorm-style rooms. (☎45187; Find the proprietors at the Mace supermarket in town. Laundry €3. Dorms €10; doubles €25.) Across the way, **Alice's Harbour Bar ❷** flaunts gorgeous views, a stonework homage to the deserted village, and a boat-shaped bar, as well as a brand-new disco that spins top-40 hits on summer weekends. (☎45138. Pub grub €5-8; served noon-8pm. Cover for disco €7.)

BALLINA (BÉAL AN ÁTHA)   ☎096

Ballina (bah-lin-AH) is a fisherman's mecca. Armies in olive-green waders invade the town each year during the salmon season (Feb.-Sept.). There is at least one non-ichthyological attraction, though: every Saturday night, almost everyone in a 50 mi. radius, from sheep farmers to students, descends on the town like a stampeding herd of lemmings. These weekly influxes ruffle the feathers of the humble hub, but leave it slightly hipper for the wear. **Gaughan's** (☎70096) has been pulling the best pint in town since 1936. No trad or TV here—just great grub, homemade snuff, and a welcome conversation with Pints O'Guinness. Jolly, musical drinkers raise **The Parting Glass,** Tolan St., over and over again. (☎72714. Trad weekly and live music most nights; call ahead for schedule.) **Murphy Bros.,** Clare St. (☎22702), pours pints for twenty-somethings amongst dark wood furnishings. Top 40-lovin' folks arrive in herds when **The Music Box,** Ballina's most popular nightclub, opens its doors. (Open W and F-Su 11:30pm-2:30am. Cover €7-9.) At **The Loft,** Pearse St., young and old mix like oil and water. (☎21881. Live music Tu-F and Su.)

Ballina's **train station** is on Station Rd. (☎71818). **Trains** arrive from Dublin (M-Su 3 per day, €20.90). The nearby **bus station** (☎71800; open M-Sa 7:30am-9:30pm) hosts **buses** from: Dublin via Mullingar (4hr., 6 per day, €12.10); Galway via Westport (2hr.; M-Sa 6 per day, Su 5 per day; €11.50); Sligo (2hr., M-Sa 3-4 per day, €9.75). The **tourist office** is on Cathedral Rd., on the river by St. Muredach's Cathedral. (☎70848. Open June-Aug. daily 10am-5:30pm; May and Sept. M-Sa 10am-1pm and 2-5:30pm.) A **Bank of Ireland** is on Pearse St. (☎21144. Open M and Th-F 10am-4pm, Tu 10am-5pm, W 10:30am-4pm.) **Moy Valley Resources** offers **Internet access** in the same building as the tourist office. (☎70905. Open M-Th 9am-1pm and 2-5:30pm, F 9am-1pm and 2-5pm. €8 per hr.)

Much to the budget traveler's chagrin, there are no hostels in Ballina, but B&Bs line the main approach roads into town, charging €27-35 per person. **Lismoyne House ❸,** Kevin Barry St., next to the bus station, has stately rooms with high ceilings and big bathtubs. (☎70582. €35 per person.) **Belleek Camping and Caravan Park ❶** is 2 mi. from Ballina toward Killala on the R314, behind the Belleek Woods. (☎71533. Open Mar.-Oct. 1-person tent €5; camper with 2 people €13. Laundry €4.) Aspiring gourmets can prepare for a feast at the **Quinnsworth** supermarket on Market Rd. (☎21056. Open M-W and Sa 8:30am-7pm, Th-F 8:30am-9pm, Su noon-6pm.) Takeaway is cheap and lard-soaked; fortunately, most Ballinalian restaurants are attached to pubs and serve similar menus in the pub at a cheaper price. **Cafolla's ❷,** just up from the upper bridge, is one of the town's two unique Irish diners, open late and serving everything from eggs and toast to curry burgers and tongue-tingling milkshakes. (☎21029. Open daily 10am-midnight.)

SLIGO (SLIGEACH) ☎071

A cozy town with the sophistication of a city, present-day Sligo often gets lost in a haze of Yeats nostalgia. The town's thriving nightlife is as diverse as any in Ireland, running the gamut from traditional bars to musical pubs to modern and trendy clubs. The Yeats Memorial Building and countless other landmarks remember the bygone days of the wordsmith.

◨ TRANSPORTATION

Trains: McDiarmada Station, Lord Edward St. (☎69888). Open M-Sa 7am-6:30pm, Su 20min. before each departure. Trains to **Dublin** via **Carrick-on-Shannon** and **Mullingar** (3hr., 4 per day, €19).

Buses: McDiarmada Station, Lord Edward St. (☎60066). Open M-F 9:15am-6pm, Sa 9:30am-5pm. Buses to: **Belfast** (4hr., 2-3 per day, €22); **Derry** (3hr., 4-7 per day, €13.30); **Donegal** (1hr., 3-7 per day, €9.75); **Dublin** (3-4hr., 4-5 per day, €12.40); **Galway** (2½hr., 4-6 per day, €11.40); **Westport** (2½hr., 1-4 per day, €12.70). Frequent **local buses** run to Strandhill and Rosses Point (return €3.80).

Taxis: Cab 55 (☎42333); **Finnegan's** (☎77777, 44444, or 41111). €5 for first 2½ mi.

Bike Rental: Flanagan's Cycles, Market Sq. (☎44477; after hours 62633). Rental and repairs. €15 per day, €60 per week. Deposit €50. Open M-Sa 9am-6pm.

✱🖈 ORIENTATION AND PRACTICAL INFORMATION

To reach the main drag from the station, take a left on **Lord Edward St.** and follow it straight onto **Wine St.,** then turn right on **O'Connell St.** at the post office. More shops, pubs, and eateries beckon from **Grattan St.,** a left turn off O'Connell St. To get to the river, continue down Wine St. and turn right just after the Yeats building onto idyllic **Rockwood Parade,** where plenty of swans and locals take their feed.

Tourist Office: Northwest Regional Office, Temple St. (☎61201), at Charles St. From the station, turn left along Lord Edward St. and follow the signs right to Adelaide St. and around the corner to Temple St. Provides info on the northwest. Open June-Aug. M-Sa 9am-7pm, Su 10am-6pm; Sept.-May M-F 9am-5pm.

Financial Services: AIB, the Mall (☎42157). 24hr. **ATM.** Open M-W, F 10am-4pm, Th 10am-5pm.

Laundrette: Pam's Laundrette, 9 Johnston Ct. (☎44861), off O'Connell St. Open M-Sa 9am-6pm.

THE BIG SPLURGE

MARKREE CASTLE

For those seeking the royal experience, enormous Markree Castle provides travelers with the opportunity to live out the grandeur of a regal life, at least for a night. The magnificent castle, as it stands today, dates from around 1802, though the land itself has been in Cooper family hands since it was bestowed on Edward Cooper some 350 years ago for his military service to Oliver Cromwell. The castle fell into disuse following WWII, and its future remained uncertain until Charles and Mary Cooper turned the former family home into a hotel in 1989. This elegant guesthouse now exists as the only Irish castle still owned by direct descendants of the original family.

Today, awestruck travelers ascend the red-carpeted grand staircase to view an enormous stained-glass window featuring the Cooper family tree. Gorgeous, spacious rooms are filled with antique furniture, and grand windows look out onto either the River Unsin or the beautiful parks and gardens that surround the castle. Breakfast is served in a gilded, chandeliered dining room that makes room service look like punishment. *(15 mi. southwest of Sligo on the N4. ☎67800; www.markreecastle.ie. Breakfast included. Set dinner €37.50. Horseback-riding from the castle's stables €17 per hr. May-Sept. singles €108; doubles €189.90; triples €227.90; Jan.-Apr. and Oct.-Dec. €98.50/€169.40/€206. Children under 12 in parents' room €19, under 4 free.)*

Police *(Garda):* Pearse Rd. (☎42031).

Internet Access: Cygo Internet Cafe, 19 O'Connell Street (☎40082). €6.50 per hr., students €5.25. Open M-Sa 10am-7pm.

Post Office: Wine St. (☎59266). Open M and W-Sa 9am-5:30pm, Tu 9:30am-5:30pm.

▸ ACCOMMODATIONS

There are plenty of high-quality hostels in Sligo, but they often fill up quickly, particularly in mid-August when summer school is in session.

▨ **Eden Hill Holiday Hostel (IHH),** off Pearse Rd. A 20min. trek from the bus station. Follow Pearse Rd. and turn right at the Marymount sign just before the Esso station; take another quick right after 1 block. Fully renovated and restored in 2001, this hostel reopened in 2002 to reveal its original Victorian look. Showers are only hot for a few hours each morning and evening. Laundry facilities. Dorms €11. ❶

The White House Hostel (IHH), Markievicz Rd. (☎45160). Take the first left off Wine St. after Hyde Bridge; reception is in the brown house. Wonderfully convenient to the heart of town, with a view of the water to boot. Key deposit €3. Dorms €10. ❶

Harbour House, Finisklin Rd. (☎71547). A 10min. walk from the bus station, away from town. A plain stone front hides a luxurious hostel with a classy TV lounge and additional TVs in some rooms. All rooms with bath. Limited kitchen hours. Dorms €16. June-Aug. private rooms €18 per person; Sept.-May €17. ❷

▸ FOOD

Little-known Yeats lyric: "For fresh fruits you can fondle/ for not too much dough/ head to O'Connell/ and go to **Tesco.**" (☎62788. Open M-Tu and Sa 8:30am-7pm, W-F 8:30am-9pm, Su 10am-6pm.) **Kate's Kitchen,** Castle St., offers sophisticated pâtés. (☎43022. Open M-Sa 9am-6:30pm.)

▨ **Bar Bazzara,** 34 Market St. (☎44749). An alternative spot to sip fantastic coffee concoctions. For the full experience, head to the cozy back room, where funky lanterns and board games predominate. Open M-Th 9:30am-6pm, F 9:30am-8pm, Sa 10am-8pm. ❶

Coach Lane, 1-2 Lord Edward St. (☎62417). Winner of the "Newcomer of the Year" award in 2000; it's easy to see why. A venturesome meal might start with a goat cheese purse (€6), followed by monkfish sauteed in Chardonnay (€23), ending in tiramisu ladyfingers (€5.50). Open nightly 5:30-10pm. ❹

Castro's, 10-11 Castle St. (☎48290). A painting of Fidel that graces the cheery walls of this little Cuban-Irish cafe proves that the owners have no hang-ups about dictatorship and communism. Spicy tortilla wraps (with salad, €6) are a welcome break from standard sandwich fare. Open M-Sa 9am-6pm. ❷

Fiddler's Creek, Rockwell Parade (☎41866). New and popular "pubstaurant." Dinners are pricey (veggie menu €11, meats €14-20), but a casual atmosphere prevails. Lunch noon-3pm; dinner 6-9:30pm. Pub 21+. Open daily noon-1am. ❹

▸ PUBS AND CLUBS

Over 70 pubs crowd Sligo's main streets, filling the town with live music during the summer. Events and venues are listed in *The Sligo Champion* (€1.27). Many pubs post signs restricting their clientele to 21+, but you're really only stuck if you're under 18—those without proof won't be given the time of day.

◙ **Shoot the Crows,** Grattan St. Owner Ronin holds court at this hippest of destinations for Sligo pint-seekers. No phone, so unnecessary ringing can't interrupt weekend revelry. Music Tu and Th 9:30pm.

◙ **McLaughlin's Bar,** 9 Market St. (☎44209). A true musician's pub, where all manner of song may break out in an evening, from trad sessions to folky or grungy acoustics. Open M-W 4-11:30pm, Th-Sa 4pm-12:30am, Su 7am-11pm.

McLynn's, Old Market St. (☎60743). Three generations in the making, with the fourth up and coming, McLynn's is an excellent spot for trad, with owner-cum-fiddler Donal leading the music Th-Su. Open M-W 4-11:30pm, Th-Sa 4pm-12:30am, Su 7-11pm.

The Clarence Hotel, Wine St. An alternative for those tired of MTV remixes. DJs stay ahead of the game with cutting-edge sounds in the club and international jazz in the front bar. Draws a faithful and appreciative crowd. Cover €4.50-8, with early birds catching discounts. Bar open Su-Th until 12:30am, F-Sa 'til late. Club Tu and Sa.

Equinox, Teeling St. (☎44721). Recent renovations have turned this into the place to be. Navigate through its dark bar rooms or retreat to the bathrooms to watch music videos on flatscreen TVs. (*Let's Go* is as bewildered as you are.) Open W-M 11pm-2:30am.

◎ SIGHTS

One of Sligo's W.B.-free sights is the well-preserved 13th-century **Sligo Abbey,** on Abbey St. (☎46406. Open Apr.-Oct. daily 10am-6pm; Nov.-Mar. call for weekend openings. Last admission 45min. before close. Tours on request. €1.90, concessions €0.70.) ◙**The Model Arts Centre and Niland Gallery,** on the Mall, holds an impressive collection of modern Irish art in an elegant, airy space. (☎41405. Open Tu-Sa 10am-5:30pm, June-Oct. also Su noon-5:30pm. Free.) The **Sligo County Museum** preserves small reminders of Yeats, including pictures of his funeral. (Open June-Sept. Tu-Sa 10:30am-12:30pm and 2:30-4:50pm; Oct.-May 10:30am-12:30pm. Free.) The Yeats Society displays info on their main man, in the **Yeats Memorial Building** on Hyde Bridge. (☎42693. Open daily 10am-4:30pm. Free.) The **Sligo Art Gallery,** in the same building, rotates contemporary Irish art with an exhibit on northwest Ireland in October. (☎45847. Open M-Sa 10am-5:30pm.)

▶ DAYTRIPS FROM SLIGO: YEATS, YEATS, YEATS

DRUMCLIFFE. Yeats composed the epitaph that was to be placed on his gravestone a year before his 1939 death in France. His wife didn't get around to carrying out his dying wish (to be buried in France, disinterred a year later, and buried next to Benbulben; see below) until nine years later, which is sort of creepy. The grave is in **Drumcliffe's** churchyard, 4 mi. northwest of Sligo, to the left of the church door. In response to another little-known Yeats lyric—"My final resting station/ should be near film animation"—the church also projects an informative animated feature on Drumcliffe's pre-Yeatsian significance as a 6th-century Christian site.

BENBULBEN. Farther north of Drumcliffe, **Benbulben Mountain,** rich in mythical associations, protrudes from the landscape like the keel of a foundered boat. St. Colmcille founded a monastery on the peak in AD 547, and it continued to be a major religious center until the 16th century. The 1729 ft. climb is inevitably windy, and the summit can be extremely gusty. If you can keep from being blown away, standing at the 5000 ft. drop at the mountain's edge can be a humbling and beautiful experience. Signs on the Drumcliffe road guide travelers to Benbulben; for detailed directions to the trails, ask at the Drumcliffe gas station.

NORTHWEST IRELAND

Northwest Ireland is comprised entirely by Co. Donegal (DUN-ee-gahl). Among Ireland's counties, Donegal is second to Cork in size and second to none in glorious wilderness. The landscape here offers a sharp contrast to that of Southern Ireland, replacing lush, smooth hillsides with jagged rock and bald, windy cliffs. Donegal's *gaeltacht* is a storehouse of genuine, unadulterated Irish tradition, left largely untouched by the Irish tourist machine; be assured that you'll encounter fewer camera-toting tourists here than anywhere else in the country.

DONEGAL (DÚN NA NGALL)   ☎073

A gateway for travelers heading to more isolated destinations to the north and northwest, the pub scene in this sometimes sleepy town ignites on the weekends. The town swells with tourism during July and August, but it manages to do so without losing its unique, lethargic charm—somehow this "fort of the foreigner" keeps a full-scale invasion at bay while providing splendid scenery and a smile.

⌐ TRANSPORTATION

Buses: Bus Éireann (☎21101; www.buseireann.ie) leaves for: **Derry** (M-Sa 6 per day, Su 3 per day; €10.30); **Dublin** (5-7 per day, €13.35); **Galway** (M-Sa 4 per day, Su 3 per day; €13.35); **Sligo** (3-7 per day, €9.80). **McGeehan's Coaches** (☎(075) 46150) go to **Dublin** and **Killybegs, Ardara, Glenties, Glencolmcille,** and **Dungloe** (3 per day). Both stop outside the Abbey Hotel on the Diamond; timetables are posted in the lobby.

Taxis: McCallister (☎(087) 277 1777) and **McBrearty Quinn's** (☎(087) 762 0670).

Bike Rental: The Bike Shop, Waterloo Pl. (☎22515), the first left off the Killybegs road from the Diamond. Bikes €10 per day, €60 per week Open M-Sa 10am-6pm.

■✱ 🛈 ORIENTATION AND PRACTICAL INFORMATION

The center of town is **the Diamond,** a triangle bordered by Donegal's main shopping streets. Three roads extend from the Diamond: the **Killybegs road, Main St.,** and **Quay St.** (the **Ballyshannon road**).

Tourist Office: Quay St. (☎21148; www.donegaltown.ie). With your back to the Abbey Hotel, turn right; the tourist office is just outside of the Diamond on the Ballyshannon/ Sligo road, next to the quay. There are **few tourist offices** in the county: stop here before heading north. Open July-Aug. M-Sa 9am-6pm, Su noon-4pm; Sept.-Oct. and Easter-June M-F 9am-5pm, Sa 10am-2pm.

Financial Services: AIB (☎21016), **Bank of Ireland** (☎21079), and **Ulster Bank** (☎21064); in the Diamond, with 24hr. **ATMs,** and open M-F 10am-4pm, Th until 5pm.

Laundrette: Dermó's Launderette & Dry Cleaning, Millcourt Suite 8, the Diamond (☎22255). Large wash and dry €13, shared load €10. Open M-Sa 9am-7pm.

Police *(Garda):* ☎21021.

Internet Access: The Blueberry Tea Room has a cyber-cafe on its 2nd floor (see **Food,** below). €3.50 per 30min. €6 per hr. Open M-Sa 9am-7pm.

Post Office: Tyrconnell St. (☎21007), past Donegal Castle and over the bridge. Open M-Sa 9am-5:30pm.

ACCOMMODATIONS AND CAMPING

Donegal Town has some of the most welcoming hostels in the country, and if you're looking for the full fry in the morning, the tourist office will provide you with a list of B&B options.

Donegal Town Independent Hostel (IHH/IHO), Killybegs Road (☎22805), a 10min. walk from town. Linda and her daughters greet you with a smile, and make home feel not so far away. Call for possible pickup. Popular with travelers in the know, so call ahead. Open June-Aug. Dorms €10.50; doubles €22. **Camping** €6 per person. ❶

Ball Hill Youth Hostel (An Óige/HI), Ball Hill (☎21174), 3 mi. from town. Go 1½ mi. out of town on the Killybegs road, turn left at the sign, and continue toward the sea. This fun-loving hostel offers a whole host of activities, including horseback riding, swimming, hiking, boating, and bonfires. Dorms €10.50. ❶

Atlantic Guest House, Main St. (☎21187). Unbeatable location. Despite being on a busy street, this 16-room guest house offers the privacy of a fancy hotel. Each room has plush carpets, TV, phone, and sink. Singles €30-35; doubles €45-60. ❸

FOOD

A good selection of cafes and takeaways occupy the Diamond and nearby streets. For groceries, head to the **SuperValu,** minutes from the Diamond down the Sligo road. (☎22977. Open M-W and Sa 9am-7pm, Th-F 9am-9pm, Su 10am-6pm.) **Simple Simon's,** the Diamond, sells fresh baked goods, local cheeses, and homeopathic remedies for the hippie in you. (☎22687. Open M-Sa 9:30am-6pm.)

The Blueberry Tea Room, Castle St. (☎22933), on the corner of the Diamond that leads to the Killybegs road. Justifiably popular, with sandwiches, daily specials, and all-day breakfast. Entrees around €6.50. Open M-Sa 9am-7pm. Cyber-cafe upstairs. ❷

Dom Breslin's Restaurant and Bar, Quay St. (☎22719). Specializes in steaks (€12-19) and seafood (€13-17). Lunch 12:30-4pm; dinner and a la carte from 4-9:30pm. Trad nightly July-Aug. and Sept.-June F-Sa. Nightclub open July-Aug. W and Sa. ❹

Donegal's Famous Chipper, Main St. (☎21428). The quintessential takeaway. Any guess as to what's on the menu? Around €4 for the day's catch, plus any kind of potatoes you want (as long as it's chips). Open M-Tu and Th-Su 4:30-11:30pm. ❶

PUBS

Donegal's pubs are well-equipped to deal with a town's worth of thirsty visitors. Weekends in the summer are busy and full of music, particularly in early July during the Summer Festival, when many pubs host touring acts.

The Schooner Bar and B&B, Upper Main St. (☎21671). A great mix of hostelers and locals gather for the best trad and contemporary sessions in town, which take place here on weekends from June-Aug. Sa nights summon trendy DJs.

The Olde Castle Bar and Restaurant, Castle St. (☎21062). Low-key; this is the place to have a soulful conversation with that lad or lass you've been eyeing. Bar food noon-3pm. Open June-Aug. M-Th until 11:30pm, F-Su 12:30am; Sept.-May until 11pm.

Charlie's Star Bar, Main St. (☎21158). Well-lit and spacious. Sip your Guinness around the huge horse-shoe shaped bar. Folks gather here for GAA games and ballads.

McGroarty's, the Diamond (☎21049). The biggest bar in town packs in a well-mannered crew of locals and tourists for blues and ballads on the weekend. Food M-F noon-4pm.

The Voyage Bar, the Diamond (☎ 21201). This pub keeps its patrons happy, but ask the jovial proprietor about its name and a tear glints in his eye: "Everyone has a voyage to make in life." Younger crowd. Rock music on weekends.

The Coach House, Upper Main St. (☎ 22855). Spontaneous sing-alongs are known to break out at any time of day in this wood-beamed local hangout. Downstairs, the **Cellar Bar** opens its doors nightly at 9:15pm for trad and ballads. Confident musicians and singers are encouraged to join in. Cover €2.

👁 SIGHTS

Six craftspeople open their workshops to the public in ◪**Donegal's craft village,** about 1 mi. south of town on the Sligo road. The innovative work of a potter, a jeweler, a painter, an ironsmith, and two sculptors make great gift alternatives to the legions of mass-produced leprechauns sold elsewhere. (☎ 22225. Open July-Aug. M-Sa 10am-6pm, Su noon-6pm; Sept.-June call ahead.) Once the seat of chieftains, Donegal was torn apart by Irish-English conflict in the 17th century. Evidence of this turmoil remains at **Donegal Castle,** the former residence of the O'Donnell clan and various English nobles. (Castle St. ☎ 22405. Open Mar.-Oct. daily 10am-5:15pm; Nov.-Feb. Sa-Su 10am-5:15pm. Guided tours on the hour. €3.80, seniors €2.50, students and children €1.50, families €9.50.) A new addition to Donegal Town's tourism machine, the **Waterbus** shuttle provides aquatic tours of Donegal Bay. Among the highlights are a colony of seals, a shoreside castle, and an oyster farm. (Ferry leaves from the quay next to the tourist office, depending on tides. Call ahead ☎ 23666. €10; concessions €5.) The most worthwhile of Donegallian sights actually lies a few miles outside of town at **Lough Eske** ("fish lake"), an idyllic pond set among a fringe of trees and ruins. The crumbling but majestic **Lough Eske Castle,** built in 1861, lies loughside, its slightly overgrown grounds and seriously decrepit buildings providing a gorgeous site for picnics and afternoon rambles. Follow the path around front to find a **Celtic high cross,** surrounded by breathtaking gardens that contain the burial site of the castle's former master. The hike to the lough and back takes about 2hr. Follow signs for "Harvey's Point" (marked from the Killybegs road). After about 3 mi., you'll come to half of a metal gate supported by a single stone pillar. Turn right at the gate and follow the path to the castle remains.

SLIEVE LEAGUE PENINSULA ☎073

Just west of Donegal Town, the Slieve League Peninsula's rocky cliffs jut imposingly out of the Atlantic. The cliffs and mountains of this sparsely-populated area harbor coastal hamlets, untouched beaches, and some of the most dramatic scenery in all of Ireland. R263 extends along the peninsula's southern coast, linking each charming village to the next. Backpackers and cyclists navigating the hilly terrain are advised to work their way westward, then northward, toward Glencolmcille. **Ardara** and **Glenties** make pleasant stops along the inland route back. Although most easily covered by **car,** the peninsula is a spectacular opportunity for **cycling** (though you can expect to walk your bike on frequent, serious hills). Despite recent improvements in service, **buses** to area hostels remain infrequent.

THE SLIEVE LEAGUE WAY

◪**Slieve League Mountain** lays claim to the hotly-contested title of the highest sea cliffs in Europe. The face of its sheer 2000 ft. drop is spectacular—on a clear day, a hike over the cliffs will move you to marvel at the infinite expanse of the Atlantic and the compact hamlets along the inland portion of the peninsula. To reach the mountain, turn left halfway down Carrick's Main St. and follow the signs for Teelin. A right turn at the Cúl A' Dúin pub will put you on the inland route to Slieve League. The more popular route involves hanging a left at the pub and following the coastal route to **Bunglass** (a 1½hr. walk from Carrick), where there's a carpark at the head of the cliff path. From here, the trail heads north and then west along the coast. One hour along the path from the carpark, the mountaintop narrows to 2 ft., becoming the infamous **One Man's Pass**. On one side, the cliffs drop 1800 ft. to the ocean below. No worries, though—the rocky floor on the other side is only 1000 ft. down. There are no railings here, and those prone to vertigo generally opt to lower their centers of gravity by slithering across the 33 yd. platform. The path continues along the cliffs all the way to **Rossarrell Point,** 6 mi. southeast of Glencolmcille. The entire hike from the Teelin carpark to Rossarrell Point takes about 4-6hr. **Never go to Slieve League in poor weather;** it's always a good idea to ask a local expert for advice and to tell someone when you expect to return. The Ordnance Survey Discovery Series #10 will help you navigate the trek.

GLENCOLMCILLE (GLEANN CHOLM CILLE)

Wedged between sea-cliffs at the northwestern tip of the Slieve League peninsula, ⬛**Glencolmcille** (Gleann Cholm Cille; glen-kaul-um-KEEL) is actually a parish—a collection of several tiny, Irish-speaking villages that have come to be regarded as a single entity. This sometime-pilgrimage site centers around the street-long village of **Cashel,** which lies just off R236 along the aptly-named Cashel St. Though few venture to the desolate, wind-battered cliffs that lie just beyond civilization, buses often roll in to Glencolmcille to see the **Folk Village Museum and Heritage Centre,** the town's attraction for non-hiking, non-Irish-speaking tourists. The museum is housed in thatch-roofed stone cottages, which date from 1700, 1850, and 1900; guided tours describe the furniture and tools from each of these eras in Irish history. (☎30017. Open Easter-Sept. M-Sa 10am-6pm, Su noon-6pm. Tours July-Aug. every 30min.; Apr.-June and Sept. every hr. Tour €2.50.) Today, the town is renowned for its handmade products, particularly sweaters, which are on sale at numerous "jumper shops" on the roads surrounding town. The **Foras Cultúir Uladh** (FOR-us KULT-er UH-lah; "The Ulster Cultural Institute") runs the **Oideas Gael institute** for the preservation of the Irish language and culture, and offers language classes. (☎30248. Open June-Aug. daily 9am-6pm; Sept.-May M-F 9am-5pm.)

Fine beaches and cliffs make for excellent hiking in all directions. When a sunny day happens to grace Donegal, a trip to the **Silver Strand** will be rewarded with stunning views of the gorgeous beach and surrounding rocky cliffs. An hour's walk north of town through land dotted with prehistoric ruins, **Glen Head** is easily identified by the Martello tower at its peak. A third, 3hr. walk from town begins at the Protestant church and climbs over a hill to the ruins of the ghostly "Famine village" of ⬛**Port,** in the valley on the other side, which has been empty since its last, hunger-stricken inhabitants emigrated. The road east from Glencolmcille to Ardara proceeds through the stunning **Glengesh Pass,** 900 ft. above sea level.

Bus Éireann (☎21101) leaves from the village corner to Donegal Town (July-Sept. M-Sa 3 per day, Su 1 per day; Oct.-June M-Sa 1 per day). **McGeehan's buses** leave from Biddy's Bar bound for **Carrick, Kilcar, Killybegs, Ardara, Glenties,** and **Letterkenny** (July-Sept. 2 per day; Oct.-June M-Th 1 per day, F-Su 2 per day). The **tourist office** is on Cashel St. (☎30116. Open July-Aug. M-Sa 10am-7:30pm, Su 11am-6pm; Apr.-June and Sept. to mid-Nov. M-Sa 10am-6pm, Su 11am-1:30pm.) The nearest **banks** and **ATMs** are in Killybegs and Ardara. The **post office** is east of the village center. (☎30001. Open M-F 9am-1pm and 2-5:30pm, Sa 9am-1pm.)

A trip to Donegal wouldn't be complete without a visit to Mary at the ⬛**Dooey Hostel (IHO) ❶.** To get there, turn left at the end of the village and follow the signs uphill for almost a mile. Simply put, don't miss this one—it's been the high-point of many a traveler's journey. (☎30130. Wheelchair-accessible. Dorms €9.50; doubles €21. **Camping** €5.50.) **Byrne and Sons Food Store,** Cashel St., supplies basic nutritive and printed matter. (☎30018. Open M-Sa 9am-10pm, Su 9am-1pm and 6-9pm.) **An Chistin** ❸ (AHN KEESHT-ahn; "the kitchen"), at the Foras Cultúir Uladh, is especially affordable for lunch. (☎30213. Entrees €6.50-15. Open May-Sept. daily 9am-9pm; Apr. and Oct. noon-9pm.) The pubs, which are usually a haven for locals, develop an affinity for visitors during July and August. The most famous of the bunch is 120-year-old **Biddy's,** at the mouth of Carrick Rd. and a favorite of the older crowd. (☎30016. Trad 3 times per week during the summer.)

THE NORTHWEST GAELTACHT ☎075

The four parishes in Co. Donegal's northwest corner comprise the largest *gaeltacht* in the Republic. Though the Rosses, Gweedore, Gartan, and Cloghaneely all maintain distinct identities, they are united by their intensely traditional culture, which has flourished in geographic isolation. There are few visitors to the area, and locals often feign incredulity about its appeal. Do not let them fool you—there will always be plenty to discover in the isolated north.

DUNLEWY, ERRIGAL MOUNTAIN, AND GLENVEAGH

R251 leads east through the village of **Dunlewy** (Dún Lúiche), past the conical **Errigal Mountain,** and on to **Glenveagh National Park.** Dunlewy, which straddles the border of Gweedore and Cloghaneely parishes, makes a great base for exploring the **Derryveagh Mountains.** Its hostels offer proximity to a pub and store and their own set of scenic trails, including the ascent to Errigal, a ramble through the **Poison Glen,** and the paths in the national park. The **Errigal Youth Hostel (An Óige/HI) ❶,** only 1 mi. from the foot of Errigal, is clean but basic—perfect for backpackers with their minds on the trail. (☎31180. Lockout 10am-5pm. Curfew 1am. June-Sept. dorms €11; bunked private rooms €14.50 per person. Oct.-May €9.50/€13.)

A few minutes up the road is a turnoff to **Dunlewy Lake** and the **Poison Glen.** Within the glen is the former manor of an English aristocrat and his abandoned church. If you continue along the paved road around a few curves, you'll reach an unmarked carpark that signals the beginning of the trail up the side of **Errigal Mountain** (at 2466 ft., Ireland's second-highest peak). Expect your scramble through loose scree and over a narrow ridge to take 2-3hr. Be sure to keep an eye on the clouds—if visibility drops, your trip down could be shortened by several hours.

East of Dunlewy on the R251, you'll find **Glenveagh National Park's** 37 sq. mi. of forest glens, bogs, and mountains. The park is often pretty deserted, so hold on to that map as you explore. Rangers lead **guided nature walks** and more strenuous **hill walks.** The **visitors center** has information about these as well as self-guided routes and a cafeteria-style **restaurant.** (☎ (074) 37090. Park and center open Mar.-Nov. daily 10am-5pm. Call ahead for info or to schedule a walk.)

BUNBEG, DERRYBEG, AND THE BLOODY FORELAND

Bunbeg Harbour, the smallest enclosed harbor in Ireland, lies on the R257 in an area great for cycling. Relics of British occupation line the harbor. Boats (☎32487 or (087) 293 4895) sail from Bunbeg (An Bun Beag) to **Tory Island** (Oileán Thoraigh) and **Gola Island,** a nearer, but not larger, land mass that has deserted beaches and beautiful views. The mile of R257 between Bunbeg and **Derrybeg** (Doirí Beaga) has not escaped the roaming hand of tourism; those who have grown tired of beautiful hikes and remote wilderness are sure to find relief in Derrybeg's suburban splendor. North of Derrybeg on R257, the **Bloody Foreland,** a short length of scarlet rock, juts out into the sea. At sunset on clear evenings, the foreland composes one of Ireland's most famous views. Farther west, the headland at **Meenlaragh** (Magheraroarty) offers miles of unspoiled beaches.

To reach Derrybeg by **bus,** try **Swilly's** (☎(074) 22863), whose Donegal-Derry service hits the town daily. Derrybeg's **AIB** has a **bureau de change.** (☎31193. Open M-F 10am-12:30pm and 1:30-4pm, Th until 5pm.) The **post office** (☎31165) is open weekdays 9am-1pm and 2-5:30pm. There are no budget accommodations in Bunbeg or Derrybeg; the best places to seek beds are Crolly, Dunlewey, and, for the truly adventurous, Tory Island. The **Bunbeg House** ❺ (☎31305), on the waterfront, offers a steep prix-fixe dinner (€30), as well as a **B&B** ❸ (€35 per person). At the west end of Derrybeg is **Teach Niocáin,** which is not only a **grocery** with a fantastic hot bar and sandwich shop, but also a **laundrette.** (☎31065. Laundry €6.35. Open daily 8am-10pm.) The irresistible ▨**Hudi Beag's** pub, at the west end of town, grounds Derrybeg's musical tradition. (☎31016. M trad.)

LETTERKENNY (LEITER CEANAINN)   ☎074

Letterkenny is the commercial center and transportation hub of the Donegal region. Though its traffic is a civil engineer's nightmare, the town is a surprisingly cosmopolitan breeze in an otherwise rustic atmosphere. Still, most tourists arrive only for travel connections.

▣ **TRANSPORTATION.** The almighty **Bus Depot** is on the eastern side of the roundabout at the junction of Port (Derry) Rd. and Pearse Rd., in front of the shopping center. **Bus Éireann** (☎21309) runs a "Hills of Donegal" tour, going to Dungloe, Glenveigh National Park, and Gweedore (M-Sa 1 per day, €16.50) and runs regular service to: **Derry** (30min.; M-Sa 6 per day, Su 3 per day; €6.35); **Dublin** (4½hr., 5-6 per day, €12.70); **Galway** (4¾hr., 4 per day, €15.25) via Donegal Town (50min., €6.35); **Sligo** (2hr.; M-Sa 5 per day, Su 4 per day; €11.50). Doherty's Travel (☎(075) 21105) sends buses to **Dungloe** and **Burtonport,** departing from Dunnes Stores daily at 5pm. **Feda O'Donnell Coaches** (☎(075) 48114 or (091) 761 656) go **Galway** (2-3 per day, €12.70) via Donegal Town (€6.35). Lough Swilly Buses (☎22863) head to: **Derry** (M-Sa 9 per day, €6); **Dungloe** (M-Sa 4 per day, €10); **Fanad Peninsula** (M-Sa 2 per day, €9); **Inishowen** (M-F 4 per day, Sa 3 per day) via Buncrana (€5.70). **McGeehan's** (☎(075) 46150) sends two buses per day to **Glencolmcille** (€11.50) and **Killybegs** (€8.90); **McGinley Coaches** (☎35201) sends just as many to **Dublin** (€14) and to **Gweedore** via Dunfanaghy. **Northwest Busways** (☎(077) 82619) buses cruise **Inishowen** (M-Sa 3-4 per day), making stops in Buncrana (€6), Carndonagh (€7), and Moville (€7). **Rent bikes** at **Church St. Cycles,** by the cathedral. (☎26204. €20 per day. €80 deposit. Open M-Sa 10am-6pm.)

▨ **PRACTICAL INFORMATION.** The **tourist office** is just off the rotary at the intersection of Port (Derry) Rd. and Blaney Rd.; ¾ mi. out of town past the bus station. (☎21160. Open July-Aug. M-Sa 9am-8pm, Su 10am-2pm; Sept.-June M-F 9am-5pm.) The **Chamber of Commerce Visitors Information Centre,** 40 Port Rd., is closer but has a smaller selection of info. (☎24866. Open M-F 9am-5pm.) An **AIB** (☎22877) is on Upper Main St., **Bank of Ireland** (☎22122) is on Lower Main St., and **Ulster Bank** (☎24016) is on just plain Main St. (all open M-F 10am-4pm, Th until 5pm; AIB and Bank of Ireland both have 24hr. **ATMs**). **Duds 'n' Suds,** Pearse Rd., offers laundry services. (☎28303. €8.50 per load. Open M-Sa 8am-7pm.) Access the **Internet** at **Cyberworld,** Main St., in the basement of the Four Lanterns takeaway (☎20440; €6.35 per hr., students €4.45; open M-Sa 10:30am-9:30pm) or at the **Letterkenny**

Central Library on Main St. (☎24950; open M, W, and F 10:30am-5:30pm; Tu and Th 10:30am-8pm; Su 10:30am-1pm; book ahead). The Letterkenny **post office** is halfway down Main St. (☎22287. Open M and W-Sa 9am-5:30pm, Tu 9:30am-5pm.)

⌂ ACCOMMODATIONS. In a sheltered glade up the hill from the An Grianán Theatre lies **The Port Hostel (IHO) ❶,** Orchard Crest, with easy access to the city center. In addition to ever-important bus schedules, the proprietress offers a variety of directed fun, including barbecues, pub crawls, and roadtrips to the beach and Glenveagh (€7.60). Some rooms have balconies. (☎25315. Laundry €4.45. Dorms €12; private rooms €13-16 per person.) **The Arch Hostel (IHO) ❶,** Upper Corkey, is 6 mi. out of town in Pluck. Take Port (Derry) Rd. from the roundabout near the bus station and continue straight. Turn right at the sign for Pluck and fork right at Seamus Doherty Auto Parts; the hostel is the unmarked farm to the right after the stone arch. Better yet, call from town for pickup. (☎57255. €10 per person.) **Covehill House B&B ❷,** just before The Port Hostel, offers all the amenities one could need for a pleasant stay. (☎21038. Doubles €46, with bath €52.)

◪▨ FOOD AND PUBS. Letterkenny is a culinary haven for budget travelers, with several quirky options for cheap meals with fresh ingredients. **Tesco,** in the Shopping Centre behind the bus station, has all you could ask for, including an **ATM.** (Open M-Tu and Sa 8:30am-7pm, W 8:30am-8pm, Th-F 8:30am-9pm, Su noon-6pm.) **Java ❶,** 3-4 Oliver Plunkett Rd., at the end of Main St. across from the library, offers full breakfasts, desserts, and sandwiches (€3-5) in an often-frantic but always-funky coffee shop. (☎29808. Takeaway available. Open M-F 8:30am-5:30pm, Sa until 6pm, Su 11am-5pm.) Takeaway from **India House ❸,** Port Rd., across from the Theatre, promises vegsters and meat-eaters alike a variety of flavors at moderate prices. (☎20470. Open Tu-Su 5:30-11pm.) At **The Brewery ❹,** Market Sq., enjoy better-than-average pub grub in the downstairs bar, or take a table for the a la carte dinner meal (€15-22.50) upstairs from 5:30-10:30pm. (☎27330. Carvery lunch M-F noon-3pm. Bar food M-F 3-7pm, Sa-Su noon-7pm.)

McGinley's, 25 Main St., has a hugely popular student bar in its chapel-like upstairs, while an older-but-still-hip crowd gathers on the Victorian ground floor. (☎21106. W-Su rock and blues.) **Globe Bar,** Main St., has a fuchsia facade and gaggles of hipsters within. Drink promotions (M-Th) lure the kids in, and DJs keep them there. Join the crowd on the dance floor, or establish your supremacy at the pool table. (☎22977. Live band Tu and Th, karaoke F.)

APPENDIX

CLIMATE

Avg Temp (lo/hi), Precipitation	January			April			July			October		
	°C	°F	mm	°C	°F	mm	°C	°F	mm	°C	°F	mm
London	2/6	36/43	77	6/13	43/55	56	14/22	57/72	59	8/14	46/57	70
Cardiff	2/7	36/45	108	5/13	41/55	65	12/20	54/68	89	8/14	46/57	109
Edinburgh	1/6	34/43	57	4/11	39/52	39	11/18	52/64	83	7/12	45/54	65
Dublin	1/8	34/46	67	4/13	39/55	45	11/20	52/68	70	6/14	43/57	70

2003 BANK HOLIDAYS

Government agencies, post offices, and banks are closed on the following days (hence the term "Bank Holiday"), and businesses—if not closed—may have shorter hours. Transportation in rural areas grinds to a halt, while traffic congestion can reach ridiculous levels. Sights, on the other hand, are more likely to be open, but can get crowded with holidaymakers.

DATE	HOLIDAY	AREAS
January 1	New Year's Day	UK and Republic of Ireland
March 17	St. Patrick's Day	Republic of Ireland and Northern Ireland
April 18	Good Friday	UK and Republic of Ireland
April 21	Easter Monday	UK and Republic of Ireland
May 5	May Day Bank Holiday	UK and Republic of Ireland
May 26	Spring Bank Holiday	UK
June 2	First Monday in June	Republic of Ireland
July 12	Battle of the Boyne (Orangeman's Day)	Northern Ireland
August 4	Summer Bank Holiday	Republic of Ireland and Scotland
August 25	Summer Bank Holiday	UK except Scotland
October 27	Halloween Weekend (last Monday in October)	Republic of Ireland
December 25	Christmas Day	UK and Republic of Ireland
December 26	Boxing Day/St. Stephen's Day	UK and Republic of Ireland

MEASUREMENTS

Britain and Ireland operate on the metric system, though Britain's conversion is as yet incomplete: while the weather report will give the temperature in Celsius, road signs still indicate distances in miles. Gallons in the US and those across the Atlantic are not identical: one US gallon equals 0.83 Imperial gallons. Pub aficionados will note that an Imperial pint (20 oz.) is larger than its US counterpart (16 ounces). The following is a list of Imperial units and their metric equivalents.

MEASUREMENT CONVERSIONS

1 inch (in.) = 25.4mm	1 millimetre (mm) = 0.039 in.
1 foot (ft.) = 0.30m	1 metre (m) = 3.28 ft. = 1.09 yd.

MEASUREMENT CONVERSIONS

1 yard (yd.) = 0.914m	1 kilometre (km) = 0.62 mi.
1 mile (mi.) = 1.61km	1 gram (g) = 0.035 oz.
1 ounce (oz.) = 28.35g	1 kilogram (kg) = 2.202 lb.
1 pound (lb.) = 0.454kg	1 millilitre (ml) = 0.034 fl. oz.
1 fluid ounce (fl. oz.) = 29.57ml	1 litre (L) = 0.264 gal.
1 UK gallon (gal.) = 4.546L	1 square mile (sq. mi.) = 2.59km²
1 acre (ac.) = 0.405ha	1 square kilometre (km²) = 0.386 sq. mi.

LANGUAGE

The varieties of world English can sometimes lead to bewilderment. The vocabulary of American English, in particular, diverges from British English to a considerable extent. Here's a list of British words travelers are most likely to encounter.

BRITISH ENGLISH	AMERICAN ENGLISH	BRITISH ENGLISH	AMERICAN ENGLISH
all over the shop	in disarray	boot	car trunk
aubergine	eggplant	boozer	pub
bap	a soft bun	braces	suspenders
barmy	insane, erratic	brilliant	awesome, cool
bed-sit, or bed sitter	studio apartment	cashpoint	ATM or cash machine
biro	ballpoint pen	caravan	trailer, mobile home
biscuit	a cookie or cracker	car park	parking lot
bobby	police officer	cheeky	mischievous
give a bollocking to	shout at	cheers, cheerio	thank you, goodbye
bonnet	car hood	chemist, chemist's	pharmacist, pharmacy
chips	french fries	mate	pal
chuffed	happy	mobile phone	cell phone
coach	intercity bus	motorway	highway
concession	discount on admission	naff	cheap, in poor taste
courgette	zucchini	petrol	gasoline
crisps	potato chips	phone box, call box	telephone booth
dear	expensive	take the piss	make fun
dicey, dodgy	problematic, sketchy	pissed	drunk
the dog's bollocks	the best	plaster	Band-Aid
dosh	money	prat	stupid person
dual carriageway	divided highway	props	pub regulars
dustbin	trash can	pudding	dessert
ensuite	with attached bathroom	pull	to seduce
fag	cigarette	public school	private school
fanny	vagina	punter	average person
first floor	second floor	quay	river bank
geezer	man	queue up, queue	line up
fortnight	two weeks	quid	pound (in money)
full stop	period (punctuation)	return ticket	round-trip ticket
gob	mouth	ring up	to phone
grotty	grungy	roundabout	rotary road interchange
half-six in the morning	6:30am	rubber	eraser

BRITISH ENGLISH	AMERICAN ENGLISH	BRITISH ENGLISH	AMERICAN ENGLISH
high street	main street	sack	to fire someone
hire	rental, to rent	self-catering	with kitchen facilities
holiday	vacation	self-drive	car rental
hoover	vacuum cleaner	serviette	napkin
ice-lolly	popsicle	a shag, to shag	sex, to have sex
interval	intermission	single carriageway	non-divided highway
"in" a street	"on" a street	single ticket	one-way ticket
jam	jelly	snogging	making out
jelly	Jell-O	sod it	forget it
jumper	sweater	sultana	a type of raisin
kip	sleep	sweet(s)	candy
kit	sports team uniform	swish	swanky
knackered	tired, worn out	tariff	cost
lavatory, "lav"	restroom	toilet	restroom
lay-by	roadside turnout	torch	flashlight
wanker	masturbator; see prat	tosser	term of abuse; see prat
way out	exit	trainers	sneakers
W.C. (water closet)	toilet, restroom	trunk call	long-distance phone call
legless	intoxicated	vest	undershirt
to let	to rent	waistcoat (weskit)	men's vest
lift	elevator	wellies	waterproof rubber boots
loo	restroom	yob	prole
lorry	truck	"zed"	the letter Z

BRITISH PRONUNCIATION

Berkeley	BARK-lee	Maryleborn	MAR-lee-bun
Berkshire	BARK-sher	Magdalen	MAUD-lin
Birmingham	BIRM-ing-um, not "ham"	Norwich	NOR-ich
Derby	DAR-bee	Salisbury	SAULS-bree
Dulwich	DULL-idge	Shrewsbury	SHROWS-bree
Edinburgh	ED-in-bur-ra	Southwark	SUTH-uk
Ely	EEL-ee	Thames	TEMS
Gloucester	GLOS-ter	Woolwich	WOOL-ich
Greenwich	GREN-ich	Worcester	WOO-ster
Hertfordshire	HART-ford-sher	gaol	JAIL
Grosvernor	grovnor	quay	KEY
Leicester	LES-ter	scones	SKONS

WELSH WORDS AND PHRASES

Consult **Language,** p. 462, for the basic rules of Welsh pronunciation. Listed below are a number of words and phrases you may encounter on the road.

WORD/PHRASE	PRONUNCIATION	MEANING
allan	ahl-LAN	exit
ar agor	ahr AG-or	open
ar gau	ahr GUY	closed

WORD/PHRASE	PRONUNCIATION	MEANING
bore da	boh-RA DAH	good morning, hello
cyhoeddus	cuh-HOY-this	public
diolch yn fawr	dee-OLCH uhn VOWR	thank you
dydd da	DEETH dah	good day
dynion	dihnion	men
Ga i peint o cwrw?	gah-EE pint oh coo-roo?	Can I have a pint of beer?
hwyl	huh-will	cheers
ia	eeah	yes (sort of—it's tricky)
iawn	eeown	well, fine
llwybr cyhoeddus	hlooee-BIR cuh-HOY-this	public footpath
merched	mehrch-ED	women
nage	nahgah	no (sort of—it's tricky)
nos da	nos dah	good night
noswaith dda	nos-WAYTHE tha	good evening
os gwelwch yn dda	ohs gwell—OOCH uhn tha	please
perygl	pehr-UHGL	danger
preifat	"private"	private
safle'r Bus	savlehr boos	bus stop
stryd Fawr	strihd vahor	High Street
Sut mae?	sit my? or shoo my?	How are you?

SCOTTISH GAELIC WORDS AND PHRASES

Consult **Language,** p. 542, for information on Scottish Gaelic. Listed below are a number of words and phrases you may encounter on the road.

WORD/PHRASE	PRONUNCIATION	MEANING
Ciamar a tha sibh?	KI-mer a HA shiv?	How are you?
Tha gu math	HA gu MA	I'm fine
Gle mhath	GLAY va	very well
Gabh mo leisgeul	GAV mo LESH-kul	excuse me
Tapadh leibh	TA-pa LEEV	thank you
De an t-ainm a th'oirbh?	JAY an TEN-im a HO-riv?	What's your name?
Tha mi ag iarraidh uisge-beatha.	HA mee ag EAR-ee OOSH-ka BAY-ha.	Give me whisky.
Slainte mhath	SLAN-che VA	cheers, good health
Is mise...	ISH MISH-uh	My name is...
Seo	SHAW	This is... (to introduce someone)
Madainn mhath	MA-ting VA	good morning
Latha ma	LA-huh MA	good day
Oidhche mhath	a-HOY-chuh VA	good night
Failte gu...	FAL-chuh goo	Welcome to...
taigh	TAI	house
ionad	EE-nud	place, visitor center
sraid	SRAHJ	street
rathad	RAH-hud	road
beinn	BEN	mountain

WORD/PHRASE	PRONUNCIATION	MEANING
gleann	GLAY-ahn (smushed together)	valley
coire	COH-ruh	corry
baile	BAL-eh	town
dubh	DOOV	black
ruadh	ROO-ah	red
buidhe	BOO-ye	yellow
allt	ALT	stream

SCOTS WORDS AND PHRASES

Consult **Language**, p. 542, for more info on Scots, a distinct dialect of English. Listed below are some of the many Scots words and phrases used in standard Scottish English:

WORD/PHRASE	PRONUNCIATION	MEANING
ben		mountain
the bonny		awesome, cool (Glasgow only)
brane	BRAY	slope, hill
braw		bright, strong, great
burn		stream
craic	CRACK	great fun, "it's a craic"
glen		valley
Haud yer weesht		shut up, be quiet
ken		to know
kirk		church
Sassenach	SAS-uh-nach	Lowlander
strath		broad valley
Teuchter	TYOOCH-ter	someone from north Scotland
tipple		a drink
Weegie	WEE-gee	Glaswegian
Yer gleachit!	YER GLEECh-it	You're falling apart!

IRISH WORDS AND PHRASES

The following bits of the Irish language are either used often in Irish English or are common in Irish place names. Spelling conventions almost never match English pronunciations: for example, "mh" sounds like "v," and "dh" sounds like "g."

WORD/PHRASE	PRONUNCIATION	MEANING
An Lár	on lahr	city center
Baile Átha Cliath	BAL-yah AW-hah CLE-ah	Dublin
bodhrán	BOUR-ohn	traditional drum
Bord Fáilte	bored FAHL-tshuh	Irish Tourist Board
Conas tá tú?	CUNN-us thaw too?	How are you?
céilí	KAY-lee	Irish dance
craic	krak	good cheer, good pub conversation
Dáil	DOY-il	House of Representatives
Dia dhuit	JEE-a dich	good day, hello
Dia's Muire dhuit	JEE-as MWUR-a dich	reply to "good day"
dún	doon	fort

WORD/PHRASE	PRONUNCIATION	MEANING
Éire	AIR-uh	Ireland; official name of the Republic of Ireland
fáilte	FAWLT-cha	welcome
fir	fear	men
fleadh	flah	a musical festival
gaeltacht	GAYL-tokt	a district where Irish is the everyday language
garda, Garda Síochána	GAR-da SHE-och-ANA	police
go raibh maith agat	guh roh moh UG-ut	thank you
inch, innis, ennis	inch, innis, ennis	island, river meadow
kil	kill	church, cell
knock	nok	hill
lei thras	LEH-hrass	toilets
lough	lohk	lake
mná	min-AW	women
mór	more	big, great
ní hea	nee hah	no (sort of—it's tricky)
oíche mhaith dhuit	EE-ha woh ditch	good night
Oifig an Phoist	UFF-ig un fwisht	Post Office
poitín	po-CHEEN	moonshine (semi-toxic homemade liquor)
rath	rath or rah	earthen fort
sea	shah	yes (sort of—it's tricky)
seanachaí	SHAN-ukh-ee	storyteller
Seanad	SHAN-ud	Senate
Sinn Féin	shin fayn	"Ourselves Alone"; the political wing of the IRA
sláinte	SLAWN-che	cheers, to your health
slán agat	slawn UG-ut	goodbye
sraid	shrawd	street
Tá mé i mo idirgalacht-ach bhithiúnach.	ta-MAY imah va-HOO-nock idder gah-lachtach	I am an inter-galactic space criminal.
Taoiseach	TEE-shukh	Prime Minister
trá	thraw	beach
uilleann	ILL-in	"elbow"; bagpipes played with the elbow

INDEX

INDEX